CW00677155

BIBLIOTHECA INDICA.

WORK No. 161.

TANTRAVĀRTTIKA.

ENGLISH TRANSLATION.

KUMĀRILA BHAṬṬA

TANTRAVĀRTTIKA

A COMMENTARY ON ŚABARA'S BHĀṢYA
ON THE PŪRVAMĪMĀṀSĀ SŪTRAS OF JAIMINI

TRANSLATED INTO ENGLISH BY

MAHĀMAHOPĀDHYĀYA GAṄGĀNĀTHA JHĀ, M.A., D. Litt

Principal, Sanskrit College, Benares,
Vice-Chancellor, University of Allahabad

VOLUME I

PILGRIMS BOOK PVT. LTD.
DELHI - 110033

THE TANTRAVĀRTTIKA
OF KUMĀRILA BHAṬṬA
Volume - I (Fascicles I–IX)

First Edition - 1924
Reprint - 1998

Published by
PILGRIMS BOOK PVT. LTD.
416, Express Tower, Azadpur Commercial Complex,
Delhi-110 033
Phone: 7132459 Fax: 91-11-7249674

Distributed by
PILGRIMS BOOK HOUSE
and
KAILASH BOOK DISTRIBUTORS
P.O. Box 3872, Kathmandu, Nepal
Fax: 977-1-424943
E-mail: info@pilgrims.wlink.com.np
E-mail: info@3d.wlink.com.np
Web Site: http://gfas.com/pilgrims

ISBN 81-7624-025-7

Produced by Printing Production Service Centre, Delhi-110009.

CONTENTS.

INTRODUCTION

The Introduction to a book like the Tantra-Vārtika is expected to contain (1) an account of the Author and (2) a brief account of the contents of the work. As regards (1), I have secured a contribution from my esteemed friend, Pandit Gopinath Kaviraj of the Sanskrit College, Benares, which is given below. As regards (2), I have nothing very much to add to what I have already said in my work on the Prābhākara School of Pūrva Mīmānsā. I have however come across certain criticisms upon this latter work, and I shall take the opportunity afforded by this Introduction to state how far, if at all, I am prepared to modify my earlier opinions in the light of the said criticisms.

Pandit Pashupatinath Shastri has just brought out his book on the 'Introduction to Pūrva Mīmānsā.' On page 10 of this book the learned writer demurs to my view that Kumārila has denied the creation of the world by God. He admits that "Kumārila has said that God does neither superintend nor is the cause of this creation, and that the creation or dissolution of the world is impossible." This is enough for my purposes; what was the motive that led Kumārila to deny all this belongs to a sphere of psychological research which is beyond the purview of my somewhat dull intellect.

As regards Prabhākara's view, Pandit Pashupatinath Shastri says : "If we accept this view (that the Upaniṣads are Arthavāda) the Vedanta darshana will be lost to the Prābhākaras . . . . The loss of such a system is not a trifling matter . . . . If it be admitted that one text is not Arthavāda, it can be no longer said that other texts of the same class are mere Arthavāda."

One is surprised at finding such an opinion coming from a professed student of Pūrva Mīmānsā, which teems with Adhikaranas among which, while some passages are regarded as Arthavāda, others "of the same class" are not regarded as such.

The writer admits here also that "the Prābhākaras have denied the creation of the world"; but here, as before, he proceeds to examine the motive underlying the denial.

In an important matter like this, writers like Kumārila and Prābhakara, having made a categorical denial, would certainly have supplemented it by an equally categorical affirmation of creation by God if they had held it to be true; and they would not have left their motive to be unravelled by a writer appearing more than 1,000 years later.

We know that Kumārila and Prabhākara were firm believers in the soul and therefore they have both devoted a section of their works to that subject. If they had been equally firm in their belief in a creator-God, they would certainly have devoted an important section of their work to that important subject also. This they have not done; and their negative view also with regard to the existence of a creator they have brought in only as a side issue. The learned Shāstri is at pains to show that these two writers are not atheistic, Nāstika. I may be permitted to point out that there is a confusion of thought on this question. In the domain of Sanskrit philosophical literature, the word 'Nāstika' is not generally synonymous with 'Atheist.' In fact the common definition of the Nāstika that we meet with is that he is one who decries, *i.e.,* does not believe in, the authority of the Vedas;—or in more philosophical works, as one who does not believe in the existence of a soul or a world other than the physical. If we take the word 'Nāstika' in these connotations, certainly neither Kumārila nor Prabhākara is a Nāstika, because both of them uphold the authority of the Vedas and believe in the existence of soul and of the other world. This disposes of the reference to the Nyāyaratnavalī, which has declared the Bhaṭṭa and the Prābhākara systems to be *Āstika.*

In Chapter II, the writer, towards the end, has drawn a distinction between words conveying their meaning and giving rise to valid cognitions. But in this he has apparently missed the whole point of the theory that every cognition is self-sufficient in its validity. If the word conveys a meaning, that is, if it brings about a cognition, that cognition must be valid *per se,* and for the sake of validity there need be no dependence upon anything else; so that if according to the author a word has to be dependent, for the sake of validity, upon other words, it comes to the same thing as to say that it does not convey any meaning at all.

As regards the cognition of the soul, if the cognisor is *Ahampratyayagamya,* it means that he is 'the object of the notion of *I*'; and I would certainly accept the verdict of the Shāstradīpikā rather than that of its very modern commentary.

What we have said above is applicable to the whole of Chapter III, which deals with the question of God specifically, the whole of which, if one may be permitted to say so, appears to have been the outcome of the extremely righteous temperament of the writer, which does not allow him to be reconciled to the view that such eminent writers as Kumārila and Prabhākara could deny the creatorship of God.

Further, we have understood Kumārila's position to be that a knowledge and recognition of the soul is essential for the purpose of the performance of one's duties, and in that sense it is essential in a way to final liberation. But it is not the direct cause of liberation, as has been held by other philosophers. Knowledge is certainly necessary; but only as an accessory. It is in this sense also that knowledge of the soul is subservient to Karma. The writer admits that knowledge alone is not enough to destroy all Karmas and hence lead to liberation. That is exactly the view that I hold as Kumārila's, and I fail to see where I have not paid attention to the context.

As regards Pandit Kuppuswami Shastri's remarks in the paper read by him at the Oriental Conference, I have nothing to say. Until we have actually discovered the works of the various Vṛttikāras, we must agree to differ on the subject; but I do feel inclined to accept the conclusions which the learned Pandit has drawn. But this question, as also the question of the relationship between Kumārila and Prabhākara must remain an open one, until the older *vṛttis* have been discovered and also until the work of Prabhākara himself has been thoroughly studied with the attention that it deserves; till then we must hold our soul in patience and welcome all contributions from such learned colleagues as Pandit Kuppuswami Shastri and Pandit Pashupatinath Shastri.

I cannot let this opportunity pass of acknowledging my obligations to (1) Mahāmahopādhyāya Pandit Chitradhara Mishra, with whom I read all the Mīmānsā that I know, (2) to my friend, Babu Govinda-dasa, of Benares, my life-long 'literary mentor,' and (3) to my patron, the late Maharaja Laksmishvara Singh Bahadur of Darbhanga to whose kindness and loving care I owe what I am, have, and am going to be in the world.

The work has taken long to be completed. This has been due to causes over which no one seems to have had control.

THE UNIVERSITY, ALLAHABAD, GANGĀNĀTHA JHA
April 11th, 1924

THE TANTRA-VĀRTIKA AND ITS AUTHOR
(By PAṆḌIT GOPINATH KAVIRAJ).

THE following pages embody a translation, made for the first time into English or for that matter into any language, of the famous Mīmānsā treatise, Tantra-Vārtika, by the great Kumārila Bhaṭṭa. The translation commenced in 1896, and after a laborious and sustained work carried on through over 25 years has now come to a close.

The Tantra-Vārtika, together with Çloka-Vārtika and Ṭuptīkā, represents a complete explanation by Kumārila of the Texts of Çabara's Bhāṣya. The Çloka-Vārtika, which is in verse and deals with the Tarkapāda of the first Chapter of Jamini Sūtra, was translated long ago by the translator of the present volume. and the translation appeared in the same series (Bib. Ind.). The Tantra-Vārtika deals with the rest of the 1st Chapter and with Chapters II–III. The Ṭuptīkā treats of the remaining chapters.

The Tantra-Vārtika is a very elaborate work and requires close study. Even in ancient times it was not always or everywhere that a master of these Vārtikas could be found. Not to speak of Mīmānsā, in which the place of this Vārtika is unique, even the other systems of Indian Philosophy cannot boast of several works of equal merit. The translation of a book like this, so full of technicalities and the minutæ of ritualistic details many of which are not easily intelligible, involves immense difficulty. It is hoped therefore that the publication of this translation, as coming from the pen of an encyclopædic scholar who is not only a master of all the schools of Indian Philosophy and of Sāhitya and Dharmaśāstra, but is the highest living authority in all matters connected with Mīmāmsā, will make more widely accessible a work which for its abstruseness has hitherto remained a sealed book to many. For it is an undeniable fact that even the so-called specialists in Mīmānsā hardly care, or are patient enough, to trudge through the pages of such a stupendous work.

Kumārila's place in Indian Thought.

The time does not seem to have yet arrived when we can correctly assign to Kumārila his proper place in the history of contemporary Indian thought. But it is certain that he was, like his successor Çaṅkarāchārya, the foremost protagonist of Vedic revival. The early Hindu revival which took place in the day of the Çuṅgas and Kāṇvas was characterised by an eager desire to re-establish the glory of the Vedic rituals. As it was Karma-Kāṇḍa against which the early Buddhism carried on its crusade, it was the same which raised its head when the dominant hand of the last great Maurya Emperor was laid low in death. The performance of Açvamedha was only a symbolical event. The same thing recurred under the Guptas, after Buddhism had once more emerged in the days Kaniṣka and his immediate successors. But there was this difference, viz. that though Hinduism reappeared in a new form, Buddhism was not still on its way to decline. Far from it. The Gupta and Harsha periods form really, from the strictly intellectual standpoint, the most brilliant epoch in the development of Indian Philosophy. The two religions flourished side by side. The accounts of Fa Hien, Hiouen Tsang and Itsing furnish no evidence of mutual animosity or bitterness or struggle of one party to gain ascendance over the other. But the most remarkable feature of the age was that, apart from Çaiva, Vaiṣṇava and Tāntrika renaissance, of which no reasonable doubt exists, there appeared a re-awakening of interest in the complexity of Vedic ritualism. The composition of a work like the Tantra-Vārtika would be an anomaly—nay, an absurdity —in an age in which, by reason of absence of ritualistic practices, the technical details so elaborately set forth in the work would lose their significance.

It is interesting to observe that this is exactly the period when Buddhism began to decline. And it is generally believed that Kumārila, the protagonist of Vedic ritualism, was one of the most potent forces actively employed in bringing about this decline.

Kumārila and Buddhism.

There were many internal causes which led to the disintegration of Buddhist Church. The corruption of the Church was one such factor. The abuse of Tantric practices ended in moral degeneration; and there was an absolute lack of any element of check or restraint upon the free play of the passions. All this tended to the overthrow of the dignity of Buddhism. The story of persecution is however exaggerated. Even assuming that the Buddhists were persecuted by Mihir Gula and the Hunas in Kashmir, by Çaçāñka Narendra, and by others, these are hardly worth mention, being so few and far between. The belief that Kumārila instigated Sudhanvan to root out Buddhism at the point of the sword is not historically correct,[1] though Kumārila's tirades against the Buddhists are numerous, and in many cases they are well founded. In the Çaṅkara Digvijaya of Mādhava (7. 90) Kumārila is reported to have said that the Buddhist teachers with their own following used to propitiate kings and through them to persuade people to accept Buddhism and discard Vedic faith. This sort of invidious procedure was certainly such as was likely to bring down contempt upon its followers, and it actually set aflame an independent spirit like that of Kumārila with righteous indignation. The statement of the Digvijaya (7. 90) is not unworthy of credence, for we know that Buddhism had always been a religion of royal patronage. It had no stamina to grow from within under its own auspices. Aśoka, Kaniṣka and others extended patronage towards it and gave it a push forward, on which it became popular and universal; but as soon as such patronage and the missionary activities which it implied were withdrawn it shrank back within narrow limits and its progress was at once arrested. The entire history of this faith bears a similar nature.

In Kumārila's time the Buddhist University of Nālandā was still in a flourishing condition, and there was a large number of Buddhist thinkers all over the country. Hindu philosophical thought was mercilessly attacked in all quarters. In Nyāya Uddyotakara who had already recovered his Science, especially Vātsyāyana's work, from the attack of Dignāga, was himself made the victim of bitter assaults. Probably Dharmakīrti was one of these assailants. It was left to Vāchaspati in a subsequent century to reclaim Uddyotakara. The Vedic culture was also eclipsed by the Buddhists. And we find in Kumārila's Vārtikas, more particularly in the Çloka-Vārtika, a vehement criticism of the Buddhist Philosophy. To one who has carefully

[1] It is not believed by historians; cf. Eliot, Rādhākṛṣṇa, Carpenter, etc. The struggle between Buddhism and Hinduism was a war of the pen and not of the sword.

studied the Tantrā-Vārtika and the Çloka-Vārtika, it will be evident that Kumārila was very fully acquainted with the various Buddhist systems.

Kumārila's Conversion.

There is a tradition recorded in Tibetan works, e.g. Chos-byun by Tarānātha and Dpag-bsam-ljon-bzan (ed. by Sarat Chandra Das), that there was a controversy between Kumārila Bhaṭṭa and the Buddhist philosopher Dharmakīrti. It is said that Dharmakīrti, desiring acquaintance with the secrets of the Hindu Philosophy and hearing that Kumārila Bhaṭṭa was the greatest exponent of the Tīrthika system, disguised himself as a slave and entered into Kumārila's service. Satisfied with his work Kumārila expounded to him the secret doctrines. Thereupon Dharmakīrti left off his employment and invited all Brahmanic philosophers to an open controversy with him. It is said that the debate lasted several months, and that many Brahmans who were defeated were converted to Buddhism. Kumārila, with a large following, then entered the lists. It was arranged that whoever was defeated should adopt the doctrines of the winner. The debate took place and Kumārila with his followers was defeated and converted to Buddhism.[1]

In the Çankara Digvijaya of Mādhava we find however a different account. Reading the two accounts together we feel convinced that Dharmakīrti in disguise studied with Kumārila who gave out his secrets to him in confidence. But Kumārila was not then as fully conversant with Buddhist Philosophy as Dharmakīriti had become with Hinduism, and the result was that Kumārila was defeated in debate. This defeat of Kumārila is recorded in the Tibetan tradition and is supported by the evidence of Mādhava :

अवादिषं वेदविघातदक्षै-
स्तन्नाशकं जेतुमबुध्यमानः ।
तदीयसिद्धान्तरहस्यवार्धी-
न्निषेध्यबोधाद्धि निषेध्यबाधः ॥

Kumārila confesses here plainly that being ignorant of the secrets of the Buddhist Thought he was not able to defeat his Buddhist opponents in debate. Tradition also has it that Kumārila, by birth a

[1] S. C. Vidyābhuṣaṇa, "History of Indian Logic" (1923), pp. 304–5.

Brahmana, had been a Buddhist monk but that he abjured it and adopted Hinduism (Eliot, Hinduism and Buddhism, II, pp. 110, 207).

It is said that Kumārila wept once on hearing the Veda refuted. The Buddhists suspected him, seeing the tears. They threw him down from the roof of a high building, on which Kumārila exclaimed: "IF Çrutis are authoritative then I shall live." For the hesitant expression (viz. "if") and for hearing the Çāstras in disguise (व्याजेन), one eye of Kumārila was destroyed. Kumārila says that the teacher of a single letter is to be worshipped as a Guru, while his teacher was omniscient (सर्वज्ञ) and yet he denied him—an unpardonable fault.

Kumārila's Last Scene.

We owe it to the Çankara Digvijaya that Kumārila committed suicide by entering the flames in order to expiate (अपाकरिष्णुः) his sins. He says that his sins were twofold, viz. (1) that, though he accepted discipleship under a Buddhist teacher he set himself subsequently against him and his doctrines. This was an unpardonable sin (गुरोरुन्मथनप्रसक्तं महत्तरं दोषमपाकरिष्णुः). (2) The other fault consisted in denial of the Godhead.

It is said that Çaṅkara, who had already prepared his Bhāṣyas, met Kumārila on his death-bed on the pyre, when his body was already half-burnt. Çaṅkara asked Kumārila to prepare a Vārtika on his Bhāṣya and on Kumārila's refusal to comply with his request on the ground of there being no time for it, he offered to revive him by means of his Supreme Yogic power, if the latter only consented to it. But Kumārila did not like the idea.

Contrast with Çaṅkara *re* Buddhism.

It is a well-known fact that both Kumārila and Çaṅkara comprise in themselves the best intellectual fruits of the anti-Buddhist reaction which was already set afoot in the Gupta revival of the earlier centuries. In this respect both of them occupy a footing of equality. But from a careful comparison of the contents of Çaṅkara's Bhāṣyas and of Kumārila's Vārtikas the conclusion seems irresistible that Kumārila's knowledge of Buddhist Philosophy was more profound and more accurate, though Çaṅkara is better known as having been more deeply influenced by Buddhism. The nickname प्रच्छन्नबौद्ध, which was applied to Çaṅkara by the Vaiṣṇavas (and by Vijñāna Bhikṣu) and in certain Purāṇas, was not unfounded. But it seems, as Prof. Yamakami has brilliantly shown in his 'Systems of Buddhist Thought' that

Çaṅkara's knowledge of Buddhist Philosophy was naturally superficial, in as much as he had no access to the secrets of its teachings.

Kumārila's Native Place.

There are no certain data for determining the birth-place of Bhaṭṭa Kumārila. Tārānāth says that he was a native of Southern India. But it is also believed that he was a Brahman of Bihar who abjured Buddhism for Hinduism.[1] The tradition associating Kumārila with Northern India receives some support from the statement of Ānandagiri in his Śaṅkara Vijaya (Calcutta Edition, p. 235) that Kumārila came from the North (उदक्देशात् [2]) and persecuted the Buddhists and Jains in the South.

Kumārila's Family Life.

We know nothing about Kumārila's family life. The Tibetan works assert that Kumārila was a family man. He was in possession of a large number of rice fields, and 500 male and 500 female slaves, and he was liberally patronised by his King. Ānandagiri's statement[3] that Maṇḍana was Kumārila's sister's husband (भगिनीभर्त्ता) is not probably correct. Mādhavāchārya however observes that Maṇḍana was Kumārila's pupil.

Kumarila's Religious Belief.

It is hardly possible to make a definite pronouncement on the religious convictions of Kumārila. Whatever the position of Pūrva Mīmānsā might have been in this respect, Kumārila was very probably not an atheist in the ordinary sense of the term. The introductory verse of the Śloka-Vārtika runs thus :

विशुद्धज्ञानदेहाय त्रिवेदीदिव्यचक्षुषे ।
श्रेयः प्राप्तिनिमित्ताय नमः सोमार्द्धधारिणे ॥

This refers evidently to a personal God, viz. Çiva. The commentator Pārthasārathi himself says that this is a stuti addressed to "Viçveçvara Mahādeva"[4]; but the verse lends itself, as the scholiast observes,

---

[1] Eliot, Sir Charles, *Hinduism and Buddhism*, Vol. II, pp. 110, 207.

[2] The term उदक्देश is vague. It may loosely stand for any part of Northern India from Kashmir to Magadha and Bengal, though generally the term is used for Kashmir and the Punjab. Magadha and Bengal are usually reckoned among the eastern countries.

[3] Çaṅkara Vijaya (Bib. Ind. Edn., pp. 236–37).

[4] "विश्वेश्वरं महादेवं स्तुतिपूर्वं नमस्यति ।" Eliot also records the tradition (*Hindu-*

to an interpretation, though a strained one, in favour of *Sacrifice*. Kumārila observes that the Mīmānsā was reduced to the position of the *lokāyata* system (by Bhartṛmitra and others as Pārthasārathi notes) and he takes the credit of having tried to recover it into the *Āstikapatha*.

That Kumārila believed in the Unity of Paramātmā and in the multiplicity of Jīvas, and in the essential identity of the two, we gather from the exposition of his system in the Sarvasiddhāntasaṅgraha. It is plainly stated that Ātmā is One as well as many (भिन्नाभिन्नात्मकस्त्वात्मा)—One as the Supreme Self and many as the individual selves (जीवरूपेण भिन्नोऽपि त्वभिन्नः पररूपतः). The Supreme Self, which alone is enternal, is one and is present in every individual ('असत् स्याज् जीवरूपेण सद्रूपः पररूपतः' and 'परमात्मा त्वनुस्यूतश्चिज्जीवेऽपि बुध्यताम्'). This is exactly the teaching of Vedānta. And the Çloka-Vārtika itself is clear on the point, viz. where it is stated that the theory of the Self is to be studied in detail in the Vedānta,[1] thereby implying that in this respect the teachings of the two systems are the same. Kumārila's belief in the Unity of the Supreme Self, considered as impersonal, is thus established. As to whether he had any faith in a personal God, of which there seems to be an indication in the first verse of the Çloka-Vārtika, opinion differs. But I am inclined to think that he was at heart a believer. Vāsudeva Dīkṣita in his *Kutūhalavṛtti* (Vol. I, p. 47) also holds the same opinion regarding Kumārila's belief in God.[2] But God as creator of the Universe he has expressly denied in the Çloka-Vārtika.

Kumārila's Date.

Although the chronology of Indian History is as a rule the most uncertain and vexed section of Indian Studies, we are not on such uncertain ground in regard to the date of the author of Tantra-Vārtika; but it must be confessed

ism and Buddhism, Vol. II, p. 207) that Kumārila was a worshipper of Śiva. This need not militate against the popular belief that he was an incarnation of Kārtīkeya (cf. Çaṅkara's *Sarvasiddhāntasaṅgraha*).

[1] इत्याह नास्तिक्यनिराकरिष्णुरात्मास्तितां भाष्यकृदत्र युक्त्या ।
दृढत्वमेतद्विषयश्च बोधः प्रयाति वेदान्तनिषेवणेन ॥

Çloka-Vārtika, Chowkhamba Sanskrit Series, pp. 727–728.

[2] The Çaṅkara Digvijaya plainly says that Kumārila confessed before his death that he had been throughout his life a believer in God.

that even here there are not lacking difficulties and that our conclusion can only be more or less of the nature of approximation.

The Tibetan Lama Tāra Nātha, in his History of Indian Buddhism, speaks of our author as Gzhon-un-rol-pa, which literally rendered is equivalent to "Kumāralīla." There is evidently no doubt that by this name is meant the author of the Mīmānsā Vārtika. Tārā Nātha describes him as a contemporary of Srong-tsan-Gampo, who ruled in Tibet in the 7th Century (627–650) A.D.

It follows from the tradition referred to above about Kumārila's conversion that his date synchronises with that of Dharmakīrti. We know that Dharmakīrti was the disciple of Dharmapāla, who had been the head of the University of Nālandā and the contemporary of Bhartṛhari, the author of Vākyapadīya. Dharmapāla was prior to 635 A.D. when Hiuen Tsang visited Nālandā. Dharmakīrti may therefore be assigned to a period after 635 A.D.[1] But he became already famous before 650 A.D. when Srong-tsan-Gampo died. And this supposition is confirmed by the fact that Itsing, who visited India in 671–695 A.D., refers to Dharmakīrti among scholars of late years.[2] It is even likely that during the period when Itsing was travelling through India Dharmakīrti was living.

It is of interest to note that Itsing does not mention the name of Kumārila. But this need not mean that Kumārila lived after Itsing. It seems that Itsing did not care to notice Kumārila simply because the latter became a staunch anti-Buddhist. This being so, the silence of Itsing does not militate against the contemporaneity of the two scholars.

Bhavabhūti, who calls himself Kumārila's pupil, lived in the court

---

[1] Cf. Vidyābhūṣaṇa, *loc. cit.* Dr. Kern holds (*Manual of Indian Buddhism*, p. 130) that Dharmakīrti lived between the stay of Hiouen Tsang, who does not refer to him, and that of Itsing, who speaks of him as a recent celebrity, i.e. about the last quarter of the 7th Century.

[2] Max Müller (*India: what can it teach us*, pp. 305, 408) was misled by Śivarāma's statement in his Commentary on a passage in the Vāsavadattā (viz. (बौद्धसङ्गतिमिवालङ्कारभूषिताम्) to hold that Subandhu referred to Dharmakīrti's work. See Kern, *Manual of Indian Buddhism*, p. 130, note 11; Lévi, 'La Date de Candrogomim' in *Bulletin de l'École d'Extreme Orient*, 1903, p. 18; Gray, Introduction to Vāsavadattā (Columbia University Publication), p. 8; Thomas, Introduction to his edition of *Kavivachanasamuccaya*, pp. 47–43.

of Yaçovarmā of Kanauj who flourished about 730 A.D. Assuming that Bhavabhūti was then a man of advanced age, say 50, and that he held his studentship under Kumārila in his early years, it stands to reason that Kumārila may have lived into the beginning of the 8th Century. Probably he survived Dharmakirti, with whom his controversy may be assigned to the end of the 7th Century. Dharmakīrti was probably an older contemporary of Kumārila, though he read with the latter in disguise, as tradition has it. Kumārila also read with a Buddhist teacher later on, but the name of this teacher is not known.

The date of Çaṅkarāchārya is still a question of dispute. But it is probable that the tradition regarding the interview of Çaṅkara with Kumārila is historically unfounded. The tradition is preserved by both Ānandagiri and Mādhavāchārya, the former making Prayāga the place of interview and the latter Rudrapur in Southern India. In his Vārtika on Çaṅkara's Upadeça Çāhasrī, Sureçvara speaks of a verse as borrowed by Çaṅkara from Dharmakīrti. Kumārila was a contemporary of Dharmakīrti and consequently Çaṅkara must have succeded Kumārila. MM. H. P. Shastri is of opinion that Kumārila preceded Çaṅkara by two generations (Introduction to his edition of *Six Buddhist Nyāya Tracts*), which is not impossible. But the tradition regarding Maṇḍana *versus* Sureśvara, as being once a disciple of Kumārila [1] and then of Çaṅkara, cannot be brushed aside easily. For the two names refer to an identical person.

It seems that Çaṅkara was living in the middle or third quarter of the 8th Century. The acceptance of 788 A.D. as the date of Çaṅkara's birth would make it difficult to explain how Maṇḍana, who must be dated in the early years of the 8th Century, should have been also a pupil of Çaṅkara whose intellectual activities on that supposition must be assigned to the beginning of the 9th Century. And the date of Vāchaspati being 898 Saṃvat [2] or 841 A.D., it is likely that

[1] Both Ānandagiri and Mādhava say that Māṇḍana was Kumārila's principal pupil. As to whether he is to be identified with Bhavabhūti and Bhaṭṭa Umbeka it is hard to say anything correctly in the present stage of our knowledge. See Introduction to Maṇḍana's *Bhāvanāviveka*, Sarasvatī Bhavana Texts, No. 6, published from the Government Sanskrit Library, Benares.

[2] This must refer to the Saṃvat Era, for otherwise the interval between Udayana and Vāchas ati becomes practically nil.

Çaṅkara preceded him by two or three generations or say about a century.

Kumārila and Prabhākara.

Opinion seems to be divided about the chronological relation between Kumārila and Prabhākara. The traditional view is what is recorded in the "Prabhākara School of Pūrva Mīmānsā," which represents Prabhākara as the pupil of Kumārila. This has of course the sanction of Sarvasiddāntasaṅgraha, attributed to the great Çaṅkarāchārya,[1] and of Mādhava's Çaṅkaradigvijaya (7. 77).

But it has been shown in the 'Prabhākara Mīmānsā' that considerations of style, etc., would not justify the acceptance of the traditional view as historically sound. And the probability is that Prabhākara was older than Kumārila.

Dr. Keith, who likewise rejects the current view in regard to the synchronism of the two authors and their mutual relation, assigns Prabhākara to 600–650 A.D. This is of course on the assumption that Çālikānātha was the pupil of Prabhākara and that he lived before Kumārila. I am afraid both these assumptions are erroneous. That Çālikānātha is of the same school as Prabhākara is undoubted, but there is no proof to show that he was Prabhākara's direct pupil. The statement in Nītipatha, Section 2 of the Prakaraṇapañchika, viz.,

अथासंस्पर्शिताशङ्का यथा शब्दस्य वार्यते ।
प्रभाकरगुरोः शिष्यैस्तथा यत्नो विधीयते ॥ (Benares Edition, p. 13)—

need not imply immediate succession.[2] On the other hand it is very likely, as it has been shown in the Introduction to Varadarāja's Com-

---

[1] It is difficult to say exactly whether this Çaṅkara is the same as the famous author of the Çārīraka Bhāṣya. That the two were believed to be identical as early as the time of Madhusūdana Sarasvatī (1500–1600 A.D.), whose pupil commented on the Sarvasiddhāntasaṅgraha, is no real proof of their identity.

[2] By way of illustration we may point out that Kāmandaka, who lived about 300 A.D., calls Kauṭilya (400 B.C.) his own guru, though there is an interval of no less than 700 years between the dates of the two authors. The second chapter of Kāmandaka's Nītisāra deals with the classification of vidyās after the manner of the *Vidyāsamuddeça* section in Kauṭilya's Arthaśāstra. The fourth view, therein summed up, is that of Kauṭilya himself as set forth in the Arthaçastra. Kāmandaka says: विद्यास्तस्र एवैता इति नो गुरुदर्शनम् (verse 6, p. 27, Trivandrum Edition). The commentator Çaṅkarārya notes in the Jayamangalā: शास्त्रकारस्य कौटिल्यो गुरुः ।

mentary (Bodhanī) on the Nyāyakusumāñjali,[1] that Çālikānātha was a native of Bengal and belonged to the 10th Century A.D., and was presumably an older contemporary of Udayanāchārya. He could not therefore have preceded Kumārila. This date of Çālikā will be quite consistent with the fact of his having quoted from Kumārila's Çloka-Vārtika and referred to Maṇḍana Miçra's Vidhiviveka. But though Çālika is not prior to Kumārila, Prabhākara's date, as given by Dr. Keith, is by no means affected, for Çālikā was not the immediate successor of Prabhākara.

Pandit S. Kuppuswami Shastri has recently contributed an interesting paper on this vexed question (appearing in the Proceedings of the Second Oriental Conference, held at Calcutta, pp. 407–412), in which he has sought to defend the traditional view regarding the relation of the two Mīmānsā scholars. But I am afraid his argument is not convincing. Vāchaspati Miśra speaks in his Nyāyakaṇikā of an ancient school of Prabhākara as distinguished from the modern. Vāchaspati's time being the middle of the 9th Century A. D., we must allow a sufficiently long interval to have already lapsed before Prabhākara's immediate followers could have been rightly denominated as belonging to the "Ancient School."

There is evidently no reference to Kumārila in the expression वार्त्तिककार in the extract quoted from the Bṛihatī. This Vārtikakāra must have been a predecessor of Kumārila. There existed at least one Vārtika on the Mīmānsā Sutras before the days of Kumārila, and there is an explicit reference to this in the following passage in the Tantra-Vārtika : "सूत्रेष्वेव हि तत् सर्वं यद् वृत्तौ यच्च वार्त्तिके ।
सूत्रं योनिरिहार्थानां सर्वं सूत्रे प्रतिष्ठितम् ॥"
इति ये वदन्ति तान् प्रत्युच्यते (Tantra-Vārtika, Benares Edition, p. 606).

On the age of Kāmandaka Prof. C. Formici contributed a paper to the 12th International Oriental Congress at Rome (=Alcuni Osservazioni Sull' epoca del Kāmandakīya Nītisāra, Bologna, 1899), wherein he tried to show that Kāmandaka was a contemporary of Varāhamihira or even earlier For Jacobi's views, see his "Zur Frühgeschichte der indischen Philosophie," p. 742. Dr. Frederick ascribed him to a date earlier than 400 A.D. Cf. Sarkar, The Positive Background of Hindu Sociology, p. 8.

[1] Introduction (pp. vii–ix) to the 'Kusumāñjalibodhanī,' edited by G. N. Kaviraj (*Sarasvatī Bhavana Texts* Series, No. 4, Benares).

There is no reason to preclude the supposition that Prabhākara had in view this particular Vārtika work or another of its kind.

Kumarila's Linguistic Knowledge

Kumārila makes a distinction between the language of the Āryas and that of the Mlechchhas in the Tantra-Vārtika. Any language other than that of the Aryans was put under the category of Mlechchha. This was quite in keeping with the earlier tradition as preserved in Manu Saṃhitā, Vātsyāyana Bhāṣya on Nyāya and Patañjali's Mahābhāṣya. Kumārila observed that Veda could not be read in the presence of the Mlechchhas and that the Aryans had no talk with the Mlechchhas (T. Vārt, p. 156). The habitat of the Mlechchhas was the country outside Āryāvarta, so that the Deccan was naturally regarded as a Mlechchhadeça. From this point of view even the South Indian languages, in fact any non-Sanskrit language, would be ranked as Mlechchha, and Kumārila expressly says so. His reference to द्राविडादिभाषा is really meant for the Tamil language. He mentions the following Tamil words:

(1) चोर्=Tamil coru (boiled rice).
(2) नडेर्= ,, naḍai (path).
(3) पाम्प्= ,, pāmpu (snake).
(4) ब्राल्= ,, āḷ (person).
(5) वैर्= ,, vāyiru (belly).[1]

From this attitude towards the Dravidian language as Mlechchha Dr. Burnell inferred that in Kumārila's time Brahmin civilisation had not much penetrated Southern India and there were very few Brahmins settled in the South. This conclusion gains some support from Hiouen Tsang's report that the people of Southern India (about 700 A.D.) were mostly Nirgranthas, with a few Buddhists, and there were no Brahmins. Kumārila's reference to Tamil loosely as आन्ध्रद्राविड is a further evidence in favour of general ignorance of the Aryans about the South. Whatever this might mean, it is difficult to agree with Dr. Burnell in his view of the spread of Brahminical civilisation in the South. For we know that Agastya was one of earliest Aryas to have gone to the

[1] All these words are such as end in consonants, and they are converted into Sanskrit, according to the genius of the latter, by addition of a vowel to the end. Mr. Kane (J.B.B.R.A.S., 1921–22, p. 96, foot-note 3) thinks that the words belong to Malayali language.

South. The whole of the Ramayana represents the story of Aryan immigration into the South in the pre-Buddhistic ages.

Kumārila then refers to the Pārasī, Barbara, Yavana, Raumaka and other languages. The first and third terms are evidently meant for Iranian and Greek. Romaka is usually identified with Roman, i.e., Latin. But this is doubtful. Very often in ancient times the word रोम[1] meant Constantinople, and *not Rome*. In that case the language referred to would be some early form of Turkish. The Barbara language is according to Dr. Burnell either (1) Bod-pa, i.e. Tibetan, or (2) Mramma, i.e. Burmese. The Sanskrit word बर्बर is generally traced to the Greek *Báboras* (see Fick, Indo-germanisches Wörterbuch). In the Bṛihat Saṃhitā (5.42, 14.18) the Barbara people have been assigned to the South-West.

Kumārila knew Lāṭabhāṣā. When he affirms that in no other language than the Lāṭa can द्वार be changed into वारः (नापि द्वारशब्दस्य स्थाने लाट भाषातो ऽन्यच वारशब्दो दृश्यते), he must be referring to the provincial dialect of the Lāṭa country (Guzerat) in his day, and not to any Prakrit language as described in the Grammars.[2] And on p. 989 of the Vārtika Kumārila speaks of the Lāṭa people too.

He was acquainted with grammatical Prakrits also. He says that the sacred writings of the Buddhists and Jains abound in Prākrit.

It is usually believed that the Pali literature went out of general use after the Council of Kaniṣka, and that in the Gupta and post-Gupta periods there were very few people in India who knew its contents at first hand. It may be of some historical interest to note—and it was a credit to Kumārila—that Kumārila apparently read, as late as 700 A.D., even the original Buddhist works in Pali. The passage in the Tantra-Vārtika, p. 171,[3] represents a well-known Buddhist Theory,

---

1 We have such expressions as पश्चिमे केतुमालाख्ये रोमकाख्या महापुरी। But it is vague. The word occurs in the Bṛih. Saṃ. (16.6). Kern equates it with 'Roman'. Alberuni says (Vol. I, p. 303) that Roma and Yamakoṭi are removed from each other by half a circle (according to Hindu Geography).

2 For it is well-known that in Mahārāṣṭrī and Apabhranśa we can have वार for द्वार (see Chaṇḍa, 3.7; Hemachandra, 1.79, 2.79.112; etc.). In the Ardhamāgadhī too द्वारवती is changed into बारवई (according to Nāyadammakahā and Nirayāvaliyāo).

3 मम विद्दि भिक्खवे कम्मवच इमौ सवे। तथा भक्खित्ते लोडम्मि उवे अत्थि कारयं

viz. that all *Saṃskṛtadharmas*, i.e. products, proceed from causes, but that their destruction (विनाश) is without any cause. The authorities are cited by Poussin in J.R.A.S., 1902, p. 371.

His Literary Works.

Kumārila is well known for his famous Commentary on the Mīmānsā Bhāṣya of Çabara Svāmi. This commentary consists of three parts :—

(1) Çloka-Vārtika, in 3099 verses of Anuṣṭup metre. It extends to the first pada (तर्कपाद) of the first Chapter.

(2) Tantra-Vārtika (in prose). It extends from the second pada of Chapter I to the end of Chapter III.

(3) Ṭup-ṭīkā (in the form of brief notes in prose), extending from the 4th Chapter to the end of Chapter XII.

The Tantra-Chūḍāmaṇi of Kṛiṣṇa Deva observes[1] that Kumārila was the author of two more commentaries, known as *Bṛihaṭ-ṭīkā* and *Madhyama-ṭīkā*, on the Çabara Bhāṣya. It remarks that Tantra-Vārtika, otherwise called Tantra-Tīka, is only a summary of the Bṛihaṭ-ṭika. It is interesting to note that Someśvara refers to this Bṛihat Commentary.

Apart from these, which are well-known, it is believed that Kumārila also wrote a Commentary on Mānava Kalpa Sūtra. A facsimile of this MS. (No. 17 in the Library of His Majesty's Home Government of India) was printed in 1867 by Th. Goldstücker.

On the Çivamahimnastotra there is a Commentary, which records the tradition attributing the authorship of the Stotra to Kumārila (see Descriptive Catalogue of Government Oriental Library, Mysore, No. 11120). This, were it correct, would be consistent with the benedictory verse in the Çloka-Vārtika. But it is likely that the tradition is unfounded.[2]

पडणे णत्थि कारणम् । अणुभवे कारणं इमे संकडाधम्मा संभवन्ति सकारणा अकारणा विणसन्ति अणुप्पत्तिकारणम् । This is the reading of the Text as published in the Benares Sanskrit Series. For different and in some cases better readings of a few words in the above extract, see I.R.A., 1902, p. 371.

[1] See Hall, *Bibliography*.

[2] It is written in Somadeva's *Yasastilakachampu*, dated 959 A.D. (Kāvya Mālā, Part II, p. 255) that Grahila was its author. See Indian Antiquary, 1917, July, p. 164.

COMMENTARIES ON TANTRAVĀRTIKA.

The following Commentaries are known to exist on the Tantravārtika :—

(1) *Nyāyasudhā* (or Sarvopahariṇī or Rāṇaka). By Bhaṭṭa Someśvara, son of Bhaṭṭa Mādhava, called Trikāṇḍimīmānsāmaṇḍana. (Pub. Chaukhambhā S.S., Benares.)

(2) *Tautātitamatatilaka.* By Bhaṭṭa Bhavadeva *alias* Bāla Balabhi Bhujaṅga (Ind. Off. Cat., p. 690).

(3) *Commentary.* By Pārthasārathi Miśra. This is referred to by Kṛṣṇadeva in his Tantrachūḍāmaṇi, but it is not known whether it is meant for a distinct commentary or only for the author's Nyāyaratnamālā.

(4) *Nyāyapārāyaṇa.* By Gaṅgādhara Miśra. A manuscript of this work, Chapter 3, exists in the Govt. Sanskrit Library, Benares.

(5) *Commentary.* By Kamalākara Bhaṭṭa, son of Ramakṛṣṇa Bhaṭṭa and grandson of Nārayaṇa Bhaṭṭa.

(6) *Subodhinī.* By Annam Bhaṭṭa, son of Tirumatārya of Rāghava Somayaji family. This commentary is said to have been prepared on the model of Nyāyasudhā.

(7) *Mitākṣarā.* By Gopāla Bhaṭṭa.

(8) *Ajitā* (or Tantraṭikānibandhana). By Paritoṣa Miśra. Manuscripts of this exist in the Govt. Oriental MSS. Library. Madras.

Besides the above, there was probably another commentary on the Tantravārtika by Bhaṭṭa Umbeka, as observed by Kṛṣṇadeva. The author of the Çāstradīpikā (2.1.1) refers to Maṇḍana as a commentator on the Tantravārtika. And there is reason to believe, as Mādhavāchārya says in the Çaṅkara Digvijaya, that Umbeka was only another name of Maṇḍana Miçra. As Umbeka is already known to have written a commentary on the Çlokavārtika, Kṛṣṇadeva's statement about his authorship of a commentary on the Tantravārtika seems to gain in weight.

TANTRAVĀRTTIKA.

ANALYTICAL LIST OF CONTENTS.

ADHYĀYA I.

PĀDA II.

PĀDA III.

Adhikaraṇa (5).

Adhikaraṇa (6).

Page

PĀDA IV.

ADHYĀYA II.

PĀDA I.

PĀDA II.

PĀDA III.

ADHYĀYA III.

PĀDA I.

PĀDA II.

PĀDA IV.

PĀDA VI.

19

20

PĀDA VIII.

END.

AN ENGLISH TRANSLATION

OF THE

TANTRA-VĀRTIKA

OF

KUMĀRILA BHATTA.

ADHYĀYA I.

PĀDA II.

Treating of the Arthavāda.

ADHIKARAṆA (1).

(*On the authority of the Arthavāda passages.*)

Aphorism **(1): "The purpose of the Veda lying in the laying down of actions, those (*parts of it*) which do not serve that purpose are useless; and in these is the Veda non-eternal."**

The authority of the Veda with regard to *Dharma* having been established all round, the Aphorisms now proceed to explain the uses of Injunctions, *Arthavādas* and *Mantras* (the three parts of the Veda).

The foregoing *Pāda* (dealt with in the *Çlokavārtika*) has established the authority of the Veda *in general;* and the author now proceeds to deal with the authority of the various portions of the Veda, taken separately. Or, it may be, that having ascertained the authoritative character of the

[Pāda I has been dealt with by the author in his *Çlokavārtika*, which has been translated for this Series—Nos. 965 *et seq.*]

Veda, the author now proceeds to explain the usefulness, with regard to Dharma, of the whole of the Veda, consisting of *Vidhis* (Injunctions), *Arthavādas* (valedictory passages), *Mantras* and Names, each of these being considered separately with reference to its own specific uses.

Now then, on this point we have the following PŪRVAPAKSHA[1]:—

"Having begun with the declaration that 'the nature of *Dharma* "lies in a purpose having the Veda for its sole authority,' it has been "shown that the means of knowing that *Dharma* is the Injunction; "and the final conclusion arrived at (in the foregoing Pāda) was that the "objects of Injunctions were laid down for the purpose of Actions. This "clearly shows that the said authority belongs only to the Injunctions and "the Prohibitions (contained in the Veda). Consequently *Dharma* or "*Adharma* cannot be pointed out by any words other than these (In- "junctions and Prohibitions).

"It has also been explained that words serve no other purpose save "that of expressing that which has not been known before. Therefore it "may be that due authority belongs to the passages included in the Injunc- "tions and the Prohibitions, which serve to point out the Results, the "Means and the Methods of the various Actions; but as regards the pas- "sages other than these, *viz.:* those that fall in the category of the "Arthavāda, or the Mantra or the Name,—such *f.i.*, as '*S'orodīt*,' '*Īshē*, "&c.,' and the like,—though they may be independent of all human "authorship, and may be duly expressive, yet they cannot have any author- "ity in the matter of *Dharma* and *Adharma*; for the simple reason that they "do not serve any purpose with regard to these; specially as when taken in "their direct significations, these passages do not point out anything (with "regard to *Dharma* or *Adharma*); and as such their uselessness with "regard to them is quite patent.

"If, by means of some indirect method of implication, the usefulness of "these be sought to be established, even then, there being no standard for "definitely fixing (these significations), it would never be possible to get at "any definite conclusions with regard to *Dharma* and *Adharma* (by means "of such passages). It is only that sentence which has been duly compre- "hended (in a definite sense) that can be twisted about to afford other "meanings, by means of elliptical and other modifications; consequently the "sentence being only in the form '*S'orodīt*' ('He wept'), it may be taken to "have two (contrary) implications: (1) since a great man wept, *we ought to* "*weep*; and (2) since even great men are subject to such disorders, *we ought* "*to try our best to avoid them.* And thus inasmuch as we are unable to decide "as to whether the passage is to be taken as an Injunction or as a Prohibi- "tion (of weeping), it cannot in any way help us to definitely ascertain

[1] The view of the opponent.

"the character of *weeping*,—as to whether it is *Dharma* or *Adharma*. On "the other hand, it is quite clear that *weeping* is opposed to direct scriptural "injunctions (which lay down the necessity of auspicious actions, while "*weeping* is distinctly inauspicious). Then, again, the passage in question is "also clearly opposed to direct Sense-perception (inasmuch as it speaks of "the tears being silver, while as a matter of everyday perception, we find "the tears to be liquid and quickly evaporating). It may be urged that they "serve to describe a certain state of things; but though they may be quite "true in this, the description does not serve any useful purpose; and as "such the uselessness of such passages (with regard to *Dharma*) remains "unchanged.

"Similarly such passages as 'the smoke alone of the fire during "the day, &c.,' are untrue, even in their direct significations, as we shall "point out later on.

"As for the fact of these *Arthavāda* passages being taken in connection "with other direct Injunctions, this only serves to spoil their own natural "forms; and for such interpretation, too, there is no authority. Taken by "themselves (*i.e.*, even apart from any Injunctions) these passage are "capable of giving some sense; and so long as they do point out something "definitely, the mere fact of their being useless (with regard to *Dharma* "and *Adharma*) cannot justify our saddling upon them other implications, "which may serve certain purposes (with regard to *Dharma*), but which "are not capable of being cognised directly (by means of the said passages). "For when we come across a piece of stone, the mere fact of its being "useless cannot justify the assumption that we have seen a mass of gold. "It is a rule with all means of right notion that they point to facts that "are directly amenable to themselves—be they either useful or useless; "and it is in accordance with this that they are held to lead to such results "as the acceptance of that which is useful, the avoidance of that which is "harmful, and the neglect of that which is useless. [This diversity would "not be possible if they always pointed to useful things] when acceptance "would be the only result. And again, it is only after the means of right "notion has appeared (and pointed out its object), that we can ascertain "its usefulness or uselessness; and certainly this ascertainment does not "constitute the source of that means. Consequently, the usefulness or the "uselessness of a thing must be ascertained with reference to itself, as "soon as it comes to be cognised; and there is no such rule as that only "useful things should be cognised. Even in a case where the means of "knowledge (the Eye for instance) is absolutely at the person's command, "such a rule is not possible; how, then, can it be applied to the case of such "things as are only cognisable by means of the Veda, which is eternal, and "has not been composed by an author? Nor has it been ascertained that "the Veda points out only useful things; in fact, this is what we are considering now—what the Veda has got to say with regard to such and such a thing; and having ascertained this we shall be able to act up to its direct declarations; consequently we cannot, at this stage of the enquiry, raise any extraneous questions with regard to the Veda—such, for instance, as does the Veda speak of useless things?—If so, what is the use of studying it and retaining it in memory? Because in the matter of the Veda, all men are mere interpreters; and as such they are all dependent upon it; and it is only after the Veda has been duly studied, that there arises an occasion for examining its contents; no one can ever commence such examination, without having previously fully studied the Veda. And when, subsequently, he does come to examine of his previous study does not help him in arriving at any conclusions, if he has studied the Veda, without comprehending its meaning; as we have shown in the foregoing *Pāda*.

"For these reasons, the instance of the passages dealing with the *Agnihotra*, whose uselessness is denied on the ground of their use being distinctly perceptible, cannot lead to the conclusion that the passages in question (*Arthavādas*) also have their use. Because for such investigations we can do nothing better than duly comprehend what is directly laid down. People undergo all the trouble of assuming (through a far-fetched connection with an indirect Injunction) that the passages in question imply either *glorification* or *villification* [1]; but these do dot fall within the three factors of the *Bhāvanā* (denoted by the Injunction), and as such cannot be accepted (as in any way connected with the Injunction); because what is not included in the *Bhāvanā* does not serve as the basis for either Injunction or Prohibition; and that which is not thus related to these is far from constituting a desirable end of man.

"Then, again, if such passages were assumed to signify *glorification* or *villification*, there would be a mutual interdependence; inasmuch as it is only as consisting of such *glorification* or *villification*, that these passages can be taken along with direct Injunctions; and this connection with direct Injunctions also depends upon the implication of the latent *glorification* or *villification*. None of these two are ordinarily recognised as being the real basis of another; and hence nothing definite can be ascer-

1 If by these you mean the fact of the particular action leading to desirable or undesirable results, or that of its being enjoined or prohibited, then, inasmuch as these are expressed by other means, they cannot be said to constitute the use of the *Arthavāda* passages. There is no other purpose that can be served by these in connection with Injunctions: nor can these latter be said to be indicated by the *Arthavāda* passages. And hence they could serve some purpose if they fell within the *Bhāvana*; but this they do not do.

"tained (in the matter of such interdependence). For these reasons we "conclude that inasmuch as these passages stand apart (from the Injunc- "tions) it is far more reasonable to regard them as absolutely useless.

"Says the *Bhāshya* : '*This is an attack upon only a part of the whole "sentence.*' Though the *Arthavāda* is distinct from the direct signification "of the Injunction, yet it is spoken of, by the *Bhāshya*, as being a part of "the (Injunctive) sentence, in accordance with the orthodox *Mīmānsā* tenet "(that the *Arthavāda* is to be taken along with the Injunction). This is not "in accord with the view of the Objector, who treats of the *Arthavāda* as a "sentence entirely distinct (from the Injunction). Or the words of the *Bhā-"shya* may be taken to mean that the attack is only upon a few of the sen-"tences (of the Veda, *viz.*, the *Arthavāda* passages). As for those that are "accompanied by direct Injunctions, there is no question (as to their useful-"ness or authority); and as for those that, containing injunctive words, and "thereby capable of expressing direct injunctions, even without the *Artha-"vāda* passages, subsequently come to be related to these latter, and thereby "become mixed up with the relation of the *glorification* and the *glorified*,— "the authenticity of such passages is questioned only so far as their connec-"tion with the Arthavādic signification is concerned, and not with regard "to their usefulness to man, based upon their injunctive character.

"Such passages, however, as only describe certain present events, and "are incapable of any injunctive signification, without the help of the "*Arthavāda*,—*e.g.*, 'one who uses a *Sruva* of the *Khadira* wood, offers, as "it were, the very essence of the Vedas',—have been attacked (in the Sutra), "by means of a questioning of the authority of a part of them (namely, the "*Arthavāda*)."

***Aphorism* (2) : "Also because of the contradiction of the scriptures and directly perceived facts."**

"Whether the *theft* and the *lie* exist or not, in the *mind* and the *speech* "respectively, the declaration of such facts (in the Vedic sentences '*stēnam "manah*,' '*anṛtavādinī vāk*') with reference to *Dharma*,[1] cannot have any "authority, even with regard to their own direct denotations. If an elliptical "construction be put upon the sentences,—they being taken to mean that "inasmuch as the *mind* and *speech* are the principal factors in the body, the "said conduct of these ought to be imitated by the other sense-organs,—then "we have a contradiction of the scriptures.

"It may be urged that these sentences serve to point out the alternative

1 Because the mind can never steal, and speech can never tell a lie, the two sentences fail even in their direct significations. Even if they be held to be explanatory of certain unseen events, then, too, serving no useful purpose in regard to an action, they can have no authority.

"course of conduct (to that which is laid down in such sentences as 'never "commit a theft,' 'never tell a lie') inasmuch as the *theft* and *lying* are "enjoined (by the sentences in question), and are also prohibited (by other "sentences). But this theory is not tenable, on account of there being a "difference in the processes of the said Injunction and Prohibition, inas-"much as the former has got to be assumed by means of an elliptical con-"struction, &c., while the latter is distinctly laid down (by a direct prohibi-"tive Injunction).

"*Objection*[1]: 'But even though a Direct Injunction be weak in itself, "yet it becomes equal in strength to the Prohibition that owes its very "existence to the former, as will be shown later on, under the first aphorism "of the eighth *Pāda* of the Tenth *Adhāya*.'

"*Reply*: True; in a case where the action prohibited is such as can be "performed only in obedience to a certain Injunction contained in the Veda, "there may be such dependence (of the Prohibition upon the Injunction). "But in a case (like the one cited) where we have the Prohibition of an "action that is performed, under the goad of passion (for wealth f.i.), the "Prohibition asserts itself independently of any Injunctions; and as such "it becomes stronger in its operation, as we shall explain in the Pāda "above referred to, in the second aphorism, following the one quoted above.

"*Stealing* and *Lying* are performed independently of any Vedic texts "enjoining these actions; and as such the Prohibition of these is indepen-"dent of all Injunctions; and this prohibition cannot but set aside any "Injunctions that might be *assumed*. For this reason we conclude that the "*Arthavāda* passage in question is absolutely useless.

"We now proceed to prove the uselessness of *Arthavāda* passages, as "shown by their own meanings and implications.

"It is a fact of common experience, that during the day as well as during "the night, we perceive, in the fire, both smoke and flame; and we cannot "say either that it is purely smoke, or that it is only flame (while this is "what is done by the *Arthavāda* passage 'Smoke alone is perceived during "the day'). Nor is it possible to ascertain definitely that during the day "the flame of the fire enters into the Sun, while during the night, the Sun "enters into the flame (in support of which the former *Arthavāda* passage "seems to have been brought forward); because the fact that has been "adduced in support of such mutual transferences of the Sun and the Fire, "has not yet been fully established as true.

"Or, again, the 'non-ascertainment' (spoken of in the *Bhāshya*) may

[1] Though the Prohibition may refer to a particular case, yet without a general Injunction, no such Prohibition can be possible; and thus both being equally indispensable, we cannot but accept both as equally reasonable alternatives; such is the sense of the objection.

"mean that it is not possible for us to assume this passage to have been "said in praise of the fact of the sun shining only during the day and fire "shining only at night; because this latter statement is not true.

"Or, the 'non-ascertainment' may mean that it is not possible to de- "finitely specify that the *mantra* '*Sūryo jyotih, &c.*,' is to be employed in "the morning, and '*Agnirjyotih, &c.*,' in the evening.

"Or, lastly, it may mean that we are not able to ascertain that the "whole of the Veda is an authority for *Dharma*.

"The *Bhāshya* has first of all cited an instance of the contradiction of "scriptures (in the shape of the assertion of *stealing* and *lying* with refe- "rence to *mind* and *speech*); and then it has cited two instances (the seeing "of *smoke* alone during the day, and the mutual transference of the Sun "and Fire) of the contradiction of direct perception; and again it has ad- "duced an instance ('We know not whether we are Brāhmaṇas or non- "Brāhmaṇas') of the contradiction of scriptures. And the reason for so "many similar examples being cited, as also for the want of proper sequence "in their citing, lies in the fact of the *Bhāshya* having in view the sense "and the order of the subsequent *Sutras*, that embody the final position of "the *Siddhānta*, and which meet each of the arguments now adduced in the "*Pūrvapaksha*.

"The passage 'We know not, &c.,' is meant to be taken along with the "Injunction of the appointing of the *Ārshēya priest*. But inasmuch as the "passage does not signify either this action (of appointing) or anything "related to it, it cannot be accepted as having any authority bearing upon "that Action. For certainly, no ignorance, doubt or misconception, with "regard to Brāhmaṇahood could be of any use in the Sacrifice. Nor can "we admit that as a glorification which is contradictory to direct Percep- "tion. Nor, again, can the passage have any authority, so long as it only "speaks of mere ignorance of Brāhmaṇahood.

"It may be asked how this declaration of ignorance contradicts a fact "of direct Perception, when, as a matter of fact, among a certain number "of men resembling one another, the fact of one or many of them being a "Brāhmaṇa can be ascertained only by means of scriptures. But in reality "this is not a subject for scriptures; because the class *Brāhmaṇa* is as much "an object of ordinary perception as the class *tree*.

"*Question:* 'How can the class *Brāhmaṇa* be known by ordinary "men?'

"*Answer:* It is known by direct Sense-perception.

"*Question:* 'But, then, how is it that even when the person is before "our eyes, if we do not know the details of his parentage, &c., we are "unable to ascertain whether he is a Brāhmaṇa or not, until someone tells "us of it?'

"*Answer :* Well, the reason for this lies in the absence of proper faculties in us for perceiving the Brāhmaṇahood; exactly in the same way as we are unable to recognise a certain object as the 'tree' until the meaning of the word has been explained to us.

"The following arguments might be urged against us: 'The cases of the Brāhmaṇa and that of the Tree are not quite identical; because even before the explanation of the word *tree*, the particular class denoted by the word has ever been recognised as differentiated from other classes, and inhering in all individual trees,—these latter appearing in the shape of a certain object with leaves, branches, &c.; while in the case of the class *Brāhmaṇa* such is not the case (because there are no perceptible marks that could differentiate the Brāhmaṇa from other men), and, again, in the case of the Brāhmaṇa, even when one has fully comprehended the meaning of the word, he is unable, in the absence of other means, to ascertain the fact of a particular person being a Brāhmaṇa. For instance, neither the wearing of the sacred thread, nor the study of the Veda, can be the means of such ascertainment; because these two features are common to all the three higher castes; as for the work of teaching (which is laid down for the Brāhmaṇas exclusively), inasmuch as such Kshatriyas and Vaiçyas as have transgressed the limitations to their duties, are also found to be engaged in that work, this can serve only as a very doubtful index. In fact, all these can belong to Çūdras also,—such of them as are not mindful of their own specified duties and transgress the limitations laid down in the scriptures. Consequently none of these can serve as a sure index of Brāhmaṇahood. And if one were to accept a man as a Brāhmaṇa, without proper consideration, such a person would, as reasonably purchase a piece of shell, thinking it to be silver?'

"These arguments, however, do not touch our position. The dissimilarity of the case of the class *tree* cannot affect our conclusion with regard to the perception of the class *Brāhmaṇa;* specially as it has already been explained (in the section on *Ākṛiti*, in the *Çlokavārtika*) that there are different methods for the cognition of different classes. (Consequently the fact of the process of cognising the class *Brāhmaṇa* not being exactly similar to that of the cognition of the class *tree*, cannot in any way invalidate our perception of the former).

"Thus, then, just as, in accordance with the exigencies of each individual case of the cognition of a class, we admit of various causes, in the shape of, (1) the sense of vision; (2) the remembrance of a word that has its denotation extending over many individuals; (3) proximity to the greatness of a certain individual; (4) the perception of a particular form, and so forth,—exactly in the same manner, we could assume the remembrance of the caste of the progenitor (as the cause of the cognition "of the class *Brāhmaṇa*, with reference to any individual Brāhmaṇa). "This relation of the progeny and the progenitor is directly perceptible "only with reference to the mother; while that with regard to others, it "will have to be cognised either by means of Inference, or upon the "Verbal Testimony of a trustworthy person.

"Nor is it necessary that the cause of sensuous perception should "always be such as has itself been perceived by means of the senses; "because we find the Eye, and the other organs of sense, often serving as "the means of perceiving such objects—as have never been cognised "before; and we have also proved (in the chapter on *Sense-perception*—"*Çlokavārtika*)—that we often have a perception in accordance with the "contact of the Senses, which is mixed up with an intervening element of "memory; and it has also been shown that if a certain thing does not "happen to be perceived on the spur of the moment, it can never be "perceived even if a concentrated effort be made to bear upon it.

"The *Bhāshya* itself says that on account of there being chances of the "mother having misbehaved, it would be extremely difficult to ascertain "the relationship of the child (with the father of a particular caste). "But this difficulty cannot deprive the cognition (of the class *Brāhmaṇa*) "of the character of Sense-perception; for certainly, if we have to climb "up to the top of a mountain in order to see an object, the character of "Sense-perception is not denied to the perception of that object. Then again, "because we may have found a certain woman to have misbehaved, that "cannot enable us to assume the same misbehaviour in the case of all women; "because such an assumption, being directly contradictory to all ordinary "experience, could never be valid; as we find that women of respectable "families always try their very best to save their character (and with "success). And it is for the sake of making their respective castes duly "and authoritatively recognised, that the Brāhmaṇas and Kings have in-"troduced the system of writing up and preserving their genealogical trees, "which serve to preserve and perpetuate the names of their forefathers. "And as these records distinctly point out the particular excellences "and defects of each family, it is always in accordance with these that; "we find people being attached to, or repulsed from, particular families.

"Nor is it necessary that the misbehaving of a woman ....
".. should produce a child of a mixed caste;
"..
"..
".. It is "quite possible that such misbehaviour might subject the woman to "unpleasant experiences hereafter; but it can in no way make the child a "bastard.

"Nor, again, is it necessary that the misbehaviour should be with a "man of different caste; and a child produced by one of the same caste as "the mother cannot be said to be of a mixed caste.

"It is also laid down in the *Smrtis* that even the bastard regains the "original purity of the caste of his either parent, by a continuous excel-"lence, or otherwise, of conduct and relationships, when he reaches the "fifth or the seventh generation downwards (*i.e.*, if the conduct and rela-"tionship of each descendant remains good, the caste of the family "reverts to the caste that is the higher of the two parents, and *vice versâ*). "And in this matter, the only factor for which we cannot have any author-"ity than that of the scriptures, is that of the specific number of genera-"tions being five or seven; the rest is all based upon facts of ordinary "experience.

"Thus then, just as in the case of some birds, though both the male "and the female are exactly similar, yet we can easily distinguish the sex "of each by certain characteristic marks,—so, in the same manner, we "can recognise the class *Brāhmaṇa*, by means of direct Sense-perception, "as aided by a remembrance of certain facts directly perceived (in times "gone by) and handed down to us by an unbroken line of tradition.

"For these reasons, the assertion 'we know not whether we are Brāh-"maṇas, &c.,' must be admitted to be contradictory to direct perception.

"This contradiction remains just the same even with regard to such "people as have their Brāhmaṇahood based upon their own individual "good conduct (as in the case of Viçwāmitra); though as a matter of "fact, there is no authority for differentiating castes by individual con-"duct. Because certain special rules of conduct are laid down as per-"taining to the Brāhmaṇas that already exist; and so if the strict following "of such rules were the cause of Brāhmaṇahood, there would be a mutua-"interdependence—the rules being based upon Brāhmaṇahood, and Brāh-"maṇahood being based upon the following of the rules. And further, "one and the same man would be a Brāhmaṇa when performing a good "deed, and a Çūdra when doing a bad one; and thus there would be no "fixity of the castes. Similarly when a man would be found to be per-"forming an action that would give pain to a person, as well as afford him "relief (as in the case of surgical operations), the person would come to "be considered a Çūdra and a Brāhmaṇa at one and the same time, which "would be an absurdity.

"The upshot of all these arguments is this: Brāhmaṇahood is not an "aggregate of Pennance, &c.; nor is it a certain purification brought "about by these; nor is it a caste manifested by these; what it really is, "is a caste signified by the cognition of the caste of the parents; and as "such, it is cognisable directly by Sense-perception.

"Thus, then, the differentiation of the castes being accomplished in "the manner shown above, such declarations as 'by doing such a deed for "a month the Brāhmana becomes a Çūdra,' and the like must be taken "either as decrying the particular action, or as pointing to the fact of the "person being no longer entitled to the specific duties laid down for the "three higher castes.

"And as before, the direct perception of the caste cannot be accepted "to have, for an optional alternative, its non-cognition, which latter can "only be held to be based upon the authority of a Vedic Injunction *assumed* "(for the sake of the particular *Arthavāda* in question). But no such "Injunction can be possible in the present case; even though it were "quite possible in the former case of *stealing* and *lying*, which are *actions* "(and as such capable of forming the object of optional Injunctions); "because the *caste* is a concrete object; and as such, being of one uniform "character, can never form the subject of any optional alternatives.

"As for the passage—'who knows what exists or not in the other "world,'— as we have already shown above, no Ignorance, Doubt or Delu-"sion can be of any use with regard to *Dharma*; and as such, passages "like this cannot but be admitted to be useless; and even intrinsically, the "declaration is useless, because (it is false; as) that which is herein said "to be incapable of being known, is actually known to such persons as are "assured of the authoritative character of the Veda, and are well posted "up in all branches of the three Vedas.

"Then as regards the possibility of the passage laying down an optional "alternative, this cannot be; as we have shown above, with regard to the "former passage ('we know not whether we are Brâhmaṇas,' etc.)

***Sūtra* (3). "Also because of the absence of results."**

"With reference to the *Gargatrrātra-Brāhmana*, it is said—'The face "of one who knows this brightens up;' and again, 'a horse is born for him.' "Now, if, at the time of knowing the particular Brāhmana and Mantra the "*brightness of the face* and the *birth of the horse* already exist, then a mere "mention of these cannot serve any purpose with regard to *Dharma*. On "the other hand, if these do not exist at the time, the passages become false "even intrinsically by themselves (as declaring what does not exist). If "the passages be held not to refer to the present state of things, (but to lay "down certain results that would follow at some future time),—then they "become contradicted by the fact of our never perceiving the occurrence of "any such results.

"And as all learning is meant to capacitate the agent for the perform-"ance of sacrifices,—these, being complete in themselves, exactly like the "bathing of the sacrificer at the sacred places, cannot be accepted as the

"*Injunctions of Results*, as will be shown in the first *Adhikarana* of the "third *Pāda* of the Fourth *Adhyāya*.

"It may be urged that as the matter will be fully dealt with in that "place, the question should not have been repeated here; but then, there "is a difference; as what is proved in that *Adhikarana* is that the "passages in question are no Injunctions of Results, but mere *Arthavādas*; "while what we are declaring now is that the *Arthavāda* passages in "question are absolutely useless (and as such there is no repetition).

"Nor can these passages be taken as mere glorifications; because as a rule "false statements cannot be accepted as constituting (proper) glorification.

Sūtra (4). "Because of the uselessness of others."

"The aforesaid arguments suffice to prove the intrinsic uselessness of "such passages as—'By means of the *Pūrṇāhuti* one attains all that he "desires,' '*He who* performs the *Paçubandha* conquers all worlds,' 'He who "performs the *Açwamēdha*, as well as one who knows this, passes beyond "death,' etc., etc.

"The present *Sūtra*, however, admits, for the sake of argument, that "these are real Injunctions of Results; and then proceeds to point out "other discrepancies with regard to them: As a matter of fact, none of the "passages quoted can be the Injunction of Results; because (1) the "*Pūrnāhuti* is only a particular step towards the due consecration of the "Fire; (2) the *Paçubandha* sacrifice only helps in the due performance of "the *Jyotishtoma*; and (3) the knowledge of the *Açwamedha* sacrifice only "serves to prepare the sacrificer for the action. But we grant for the "sake of argument, that these are Injunctions of Results; even then we find "that they lead us to believe other actions (laid down in the Veda) to be "useless. In the case of a number of actions, which, though leading to "the same results, are yet performed independently of one another, it is "open to us to perform anyone of them; and none of them need be "rejected as entirely useless. The cases of the *Pūrnāhuti* and the *Paçu-"bandha*, however, are different. Because without the *Pūrnāhuti*, the *Agni-"hotra* cannot be completed; and similarly, without the *Paçubandha*, the "*Jyotishtoma* cannot be complete; and as the specified results will have "been accomplished by these smaller actions, as explained under XI, i. 43, "there would be no need of performing the other elaborate actions (of the "*Agnihotra* and the *Jyotishtma*); and as such, the Injunctions of these "latter would become entirely useless.

"To this effect, the *Bhāshya* cites the instance of *one going in search "of honey*, etc. The person may go on to the mountain in search of "honey, by a path other than the one whereby he could find the honey "in the way itself; but he cannot go along, if he happens to pass by this "latter road and finds the honey in the way without going all the way "to the mountain. Thus then, in order to establish the authority and "usefulness of *many direct* Injunctions, it is certainly advisable to accept "the uselessness of the Injunctions that have been *assumed* (on the strength "of the *Arthavāda* passages in question).

"Nor can these Injunctions be said to lay down new actions for those "who would desire better results, than those obtained by means of the "former actions; because no difference between the two is mentioned. "And when the direct assertion of the Veda is the same in both cases, we "cannot assume any exceptional results to follow from any particular "actions, specially when we are unable to perceive any such results. And "we have already said that the declarations being found to be false, can-"not be accepted as glorifications.

***Sūtra* (5). "Because of the negativing of that which is not "capable of being negatived."**

"In the feda we find the sentences—'Fire is not to be laid on the "earth,' 'it is not to be laid in the sky,' 'it is not be laid in Heaven'; and "each of these contain a negation of that which is not capable of negation. "That it is to say, as for the Sky and Heaven, no laying of fire in these "is possible; and as such, any negation of these is wholly irrelevant. Nor "can these be taken as exceptions, because (the laying in Heaven and "in the Sky never being possible) these could not rightly be held to be the "objects of exception; because the *laying* is *always* found to be done "on the Earth, which is neither Sky nor Heaven.

"If the two sentences be said to be a mere description of the natural "state of things; then they cannot be held to serve any useful purpose with "regard to the performance of sacrifices. And as for the first sentence—"'not on the Earth'—any negativing or excepting of the laying on Earth "is not possible, without setting aside the Injunction of the *laying* itself; "and this setting aside would render a direct Injunction wholly futile. "Even if the two sentences be taken as laying down optional alternatives, "then, too, there would be a partial setting aside (in one case) of the "direct Injunction. Specially as the Veda itself lays down many alter-"natives with regard to the laying of fire, as done with a view to different "results; and as such it is not right to accept Prohibitions for the mere "pointing out of optional alternatives.

"And then, this Prohibition, too, would be extremely weak [that is to "say, it cannot be said that even in the absence of any particular desires, "the Prohibition would serve the purpose of pointing out optional alter-"natives; because, in the absence of any desires, there can be no perform-"ance of such actions as have been laid down simply for the fulfilment of "certain definite ends, and as such no prohibition of these is necessary (or "possible); and if the Prohibition be taken as pointing out mere qualifi-"cations,—then as such, being only an assumed factor, with regard "to the sacrifice, it would be too weak to rightly point out any optional "alternatives].

"When the prohibition is taken with regard to the Earth, then "(as no such prohibition of the Earth as the place of *laying* could be "possible, unless there were a likelihood of the action of the *laying* "being performed) it would be necessary to assume an Injunction of this "*laying*; (and then as all the places where the fire could be laid,— "the Earth, the Sky and Heaven,—are negatived, by the sentence under "consideration, such negation would lead us to the assumption of an "Injunction wholly prohibiting the aforesaid *laying*); and this is what "is meant by the '*self-contradiction*' mentioned in the Bhāshya.

"The said prohibition would also contradict other direct Injunctions "—such, for instance, as '*the Fire should be laid* after the golden plate "has been put in,' and 'the Fire is laid upon bricks' (both of which dis-"tinctly mention the Earth as the place on which the Fire is to be laid).

"Nor is it posible for the sentences to be taken as only meant to attract "people, to a certain course of action, and not as a regular injunction.

Sūtra (6). "Because of the mention of non-eternal (objects)."

"In the case of such passages as—'Babara Pravāhani desired' and "the like—, from among all possible significations, the words 'Babara "Pravāhani,' &c., cannot be taken as pointing to anything else (either "anything in connection with sacrifices, or a glorification) except "*Babara, the son of Pravāhana;* and (as such a person cannot be said to be "eternal) this comes to be a mention (in the Veda) of a transitory object.

"The mention of such objects, when brought forward and urged against "the authority of the Veda as a whole, can be explained in some way or "other (as has been done above, in I—i—21). But when we make use of "our discretion in the matter of authoritativeness, and accept, on the ground "of some reasonings, the absolutely authoritative character of only the *Vidhi* "(Injunction) portion of the Veda,—exactly as among all verbal De-"clarations, the Veda alone is held to be absolutely authoritative—then, "in that case, just as we deny the authority of the other portions of the "Veda, so too we could deny that of such portions of it as make mention "of transitory objects, on the ground of such mention itself; and there "would be nothing to prevent us from doing so.

"Therefore, in the case of such passages, all that we can do is to take "no notice of their significations, and to assume particular results to "follow from the mere repetition of these. Or, it may be more reasonable "to admit of the fact of such texts being read up only for being rejected; "just as we accept the *Arthavāda* passages as only meant to be disregarded.

"It may be asked—'Why cannot these passages be used as *Mantras* "in the Actions, in connection wherewith they happen to be read?'

"They cannot be so used, simply because they (not pointing to any "actions) cannot possibly be taken along with any action. As for *Mantras*, they too are employed at sacrifices, not only because they happen "to be mentioned in the Veda, but because their words distinctly point "out their connection with those sacrifices. In the passage in question, "however, there is no such implication.

"Or, lastly, we may take these passages as meant to be accepted in "their mere verbal forms (without any heed being paid to their significations), exactly as has been done in the *Pūrvapaksha* relating to the "Mantras (Vide *below*, Sūtras 31-39).

"The word '*anitya*,' in the Sūtra, refers to *living beings*, and not to "*that which is useless* (as in I—ii—1)."

In reply to the above *Pūrvapaksha*, we have the following:—

SIDDHĀNTA—*the Orthodox Mīmāṅsā view.*

***Sūtra* (7). But they are taken along with the injunctive passages; and as such could be (authoritative) as eulogising the particular Injunctions.**

[The *Bhāshya* cites the passage—'*Vāyurvai kshēpishthā dēvatā*'—as an instance of *Arthavāda*; and on this, the *Vārtika* starts with the question].— "It was proper for the *Bhāshya* to put forward its own view with reference to the same *Arthavāda* passages that have been cited in the *Pūrvapaksha*; for what special reason then, does he bring forward a different passage?"

In reply to this, some people assert that as the bearing of all *Arthavāda* passages is the same, it does not make any difference, whether this or that passage be cited in the *Pūrvapaksha* or the *Siddhānta*.

But though this may be the case, yet the citing of a new example always implies an ulterior motive (in the mind of the author); and this motive we proceed to explain: As regards the passages cited in the *Pūrvapaksha*, even their literal significations are open to doubt; and consequently to begin with them would entail the additional initial effort of proving them to be true; and inasmuch as this initial effort would be of no consequence, and as such not very desirable, the *Bhāshya* has cited a passage, which, in its literal signification, is universally recognised to be true; whereby it becomes easier to explain, that such passages are glorifications, to be taken along with the Injunctive passages, and as such come to help in the knowledge of *Dharma.* And to facilitate the matter still further, the author of the *Bhāshya* proceeds to show the use of *Arthavādas* as glorifications, by means of a passage which is instantly recognised as one to be taken along with (and forming part of) a direct Injunction.

But before proceeding further, we have to explain the following difficulty: "Why is it that the natural form of the Veda is perverted, with "a view to establish a forced syntactical connection? Or (if it be declared "that we have recourse to this in order to establish a direct relationship "of the Veda to human ends) how is it that the Veda is said to be for the "sake of man's ends? It might be urged that these assumptions are made, "because such is found to be a fact, in the case of ordinary human assertions. "But, then, the case of these latter is entirely different; as what they speak "of is cognisable by other ordinary means of cognition; and, on the strength "of these latter, such far-fetched assumptions are admissible; whereas in "the case of a Vedic passage, treating as it does of supersensuous things, "even if the slightest change be made in its original form, it becomes a "creation of the human mind (and thereby loses the very basis of its "authority). Even in the case of human assertions, when the subject "spoken of is not amenable to the other means of cognition, save verbal "Testimony, we do not have any changes in the form of the assertion."

To this, some people make the following reply: It will be proved in the next *Sūtra* that the whole of the Veda is meant to serve some useful purpose for man. And certainly, if it did not serve some useful purpose, the intelligent people of old would not have made such efforts to preserve it and hand it down in an unbroken tradition. Though it is just possible that a single man may have erred in his estimate of the usefulness of the Veda; yet there is no reason for saying so, with regard to the extremely intelligent enquirers that have gone before us. And for this reason, it is only right that we should even break up the natural form of the Veda, in order to make it serviceable to man.

This explanation, however, does not appear to be quite satisfactory; because, if such be the case, then the authoritativeness of the Veda would depend upon man. If we were to assume even such meanings as are not signified by the actual words of the Veda, and if the usefulness of the Veda to man were to rest on the sole authority of the efforts made to present it, then the authority of the Veda would become dependent upon our own efforts. If the preserving of the Veda by another be held to be the cause, then, too, that other person would base his authority upon the efforts of another man, and so on and on, we might go backwards, referring it to the efforts of other people; and this would be like a description of colour handed down among blind men; and there would be no fixity for the authority of the Veda. Specially in the case of each man, the idea that we would have would be that 'this man knows it thus,' and not that 'such is its meaning.' Consequently then, though, in the case of particular students, we might infer the fact of their knowing the Veda to be useful to them, yet, as there can be no secure foundation for this notion, the authority of the Veda cannot rest solely upon that fact. Therefore it must be admitted that until the Veda itself does not directly declare itself to be serviceable to man, it cannot be accepted as authoritative.

But we can explain the difficulty in the following manner: As for the whole of the Veda, its study is directly enjoined in the sentence '*Svādhyāyo'dhyētavyaḥ.*' ("The Veda should be duly studied),"—the sense of which is that *we should accomplish something by means of the study of the Veda.* And as for what is to be accomplished,—though the 'study' itself presents itself as the object, yet, inasmuch as an Injunction, which has the power of persuading people to action cannot but have for its object something that is of use to the man, the mere 'study' ceases to be accepted as the *object to be accomplished,* and becomes mixed up with the *instrument* or means of the said accomplishment; because this instrumental character is quite compatible with its nature, and is the most proximate (the sense of the Injunction thus being that the desirable object is to be accomplished *by means of the study*).

What next appears to be the object to be accomplished is *the getting up of the mere letters* of the Veda, in accordance with the maxim that anything 'that is capable of being accomplished is the object.' But this, too, in itself, can be of no direct use to man. However, this *getting up of the letters* points to *the knowledge of the words,* which in its turn points to the *knowledge of the meanings of these words,* which last points to *the knowledge of the meaning of the sentences* composed of those words; and this leads to the *acting* (in accordance with the injunctions contained in these sentences), which *acting* finally leads to the attainment of such desirable results as Heaven and the like. And it is only here that the *object* to be accomplished being duly ascertained, all the information required (in connection with the injunction "the Veda should be studied") becomes fully supplied. And thus in the case of all Injunctions, there is no resting until we get at some purpose of man (to be accomplished by means of the action therein enjoined).

But it is by no means absolutely necessary that, whenever we meet with an Injunction, we must assume such results as Heaven and the like (to follow from the action enjoined); because when we find that a certain action is actually capable of bringing about the accomplishment of a certain result, we conclude this latter to be its effect. And hence, whenever we find an action directly capable of bringing about a certain result, even after the lapse of a certain period of time and space, we cannot rightly assume any other result; because the soundness of the Vedic Injunction is established also by means of such results as follow after the lapse of time (and not only by those that follow immediately after the Action); and as such there is no Apparent Inconsistency (in the Injunction) that could lead us to the assumption of other results.

In those cases, however, in which we do not find any particular desirable results following, either directly or indirectly (from the Action),—as, for instance, the action of the libation reaching the Fire, and being burnt to ashes,—we give up the idea of the necessity of the desirable element in the result, and assume a transcendental result to follow from the action itself.

In all cases, however, we have to bear in mind the following: In the case of a certain action (the *threshing* of the corn, for instance) that is laid down in the Veda, and stands in need of a result, if we find, following from it, a series of actions, not of the nature of a result,—and then, in the middle we find laid down something (in the shape of the making of the cake) that would help the sacrifice, or one (the *offering* itself) that would accomplish a desirable result,—we conclude these latterly enjoined actions to be the means of the two latter results; and the original Injunction (of the *threshing* of the corn) is accepted as merely helping in these latter actions (and not having its efficiency reaching up to the final accomplishment of the agent's desires).

As for the other actions (of *pounding*, &c., of the corn) that are laid down by a subsequent Injunction, these are to be taken as helping in the previously enjoined action (of *threshing*, specially as they are its necessary concomitants) in the accomplishment of the cake (which could not be made unless the corn were pounded after the *thereshing*),—exactly like the burning of the fuel (which is a necessary concomitant of the sacrifice). And these actions of *pounding*, &c., are not held to be the direct means of accomplishing either the *threshing* or the *cake*, because they are not found to have been laid down before, with any reference to the relationship of means and consequences. That is to say, if we had any assertion, prior to the Injunction of *threshing*, of the *pounding* of the corn being a means of accomplishing the *cake*, then alone could the latter be held to be the direct means of the making of the *cake;* but, as it is, we find the *threshing* laid down first of all, and the *pounding*, &c., are only mentioned afterwards (merely as concomitants of that *threshing*). Hence we are led to conclude that it is the *threshing* that is the real means of the accomplishment of the *cake*, and that the *pounding*, &c., are to be taken only as helping the *threshing* in that accomplishment.

In such cases, however, in which nothing that forms part of the series is laid down in the middle, it is the directly enjoined action alone which is to be taken as the means of accomplishing the final result, through all the various actions that are laid down in connection with it.

Thus, then, all the Injunctive passages that lay down the means of accomplishing the directly mentioned, or the assumed, ends of man are included—even up to the ascertaining of such causal relationships—in the Injunction that "the Veda should be studied." (That is to say, in this case the study is held to be for the purpose of the ascertaining of the said relationships, exactly as the *threshing* is held to be the means of accomplishing the cake; and the intermediate actions of getting up the words of the Veda help in the final result, exactly as the *pounding*, &c., do in the making of the cake).

As for the result accruing from the ascertaining of the meaning of Vedic texts, such result has been pointed out by other texts (such as: "That Action alone has a strong influence which is performed with a full knowledge, faith, &c."); and as such the former Injunction of Vedic study is not made to extend so far (as to the pointing out of its result).

And as for the other Injunctions that are found in the same connection, they are also to be taken as serving, by means of the getting up of the verbal text, &c., to help towards the fulfilment of the single result, in the shape of the comprehension of the meanings of Vedic sentences; and they cannot be taken as, in any way, directly helping the performance of any sacrifices. Because the performance of sacrifices depends, for its procedure, only upon such means as bring about supersensuous results; and as such, they can have no connection with the mere getting up of the Verbal text, which serves only a visible purpose; and as such the action of such getting up is accepted only as helping towards the fulfilment of the final result (of comprehending the meaning of those texts).

Thus, then, we find that the subsidiary sentences or Injunctions (of getting up the Vedic text) are similar to the principal sentence or Injunction (of the due comprehending of the meaning of the Veda) (in so much as both are equally related to the human purpose mediately, through an intervening agency), though the subsidiary Injunctions themselves are one degree further removed. (As for instance, the Injunction of the comprehending of the meaning of the Veda gives a knowledge of the sacrifices, which fulfil the desirable end of man, there being, in the case, only one intervening agency; in the case of the subsidiary Injunctions, on the other hand, we find that they lay down the getting up of the verbal text, which brings about a cognition of the meaning of these texts, which point out the sacrifices that fulfil the desirable ends of man, there being, in this case, two intervening agencies).

In the same manner, the passages speaking of the *washing*, &c. (of the

Vrīhi), having their sole purpose in the purification of the corn, are found to be very distantly related to the principal sacrifice, through the intervening agencies of the Rice, the Flour, the Cake, and the *Dvyavadāna* Offering, &c.

Similarly, we may explain the connection (with the principal sacrifice) of such secondary passages as are not found in the same context, and as such help the sacrifice only indirectly, as well as those that are of direct use. And the only peculiarity with the relationship of these is that the Principal Action is connected only with what these passages signify, and has nothing to do with the mere words, as the passages are not in the same context.

The passages speaking of the 'laying of the fire' and such other actions, have their sole use in the preparation of the sacrificial fire, which forms a part of the principal sacrifice leading to certain definite results; and as such come to have all their relationships fulfilled by means of the remote Result (of the Principal Sacrifice).

In the same manner the Upanishads have their existence justified by their explaining the real nature of the person that performs the sacrifices.

And as for the Mantra and the Names, we shall explain their uses, in their respective places (at the end of this Pāda and in the fourth Pāda).

Thus, then, it is established that all parts of the Veda are included in the *Bhāvana* (which is denoted by the direct Vedic Injunctions).

It has been argued above that the *Arthavāda* passages not being included in any of the three factors of the *Bhāvana*, they cannot be recognised (as parts of the Vedic Injunctions). On this point, we offer the following explanation: It is true that the *Arthavāda* is not so recognised apart, by itself; but it is actually included (in the factors of the *Bhāvana*).

"How"?

In the following manner: In the case of the sentences which contain Injunctive words, there are two kinds of *Bhāvanā* that are always comprehended—one consisting of the words, and another of their significations. Those of the latter class do not stand in need of the *Arthavāda* passages; but these passages are certainly included in those of the former kind (*i.e.*, the Verbal *Bhāvanā*).

The Verbal *Bhāvana* operates in the following manner: The Injunction of the study of the Veda serves the purpose of employing all other Injunctions, as also the 'self' ('*Swa*') mentioned in the word "*swādhyāya*"; and this employing or urging is in the form—"should think of accomplishing." And in this the Injunctive Word is the nominative of the *prompting*, and the Person is its objective.

Hence when the question arises—'What is to be accomplished (by the Injunctive passage)'?—the answer, that presents itself is—"The activity of the Person.' If, however, the peculiar character of the said Injunction were taken to signify the action of Injunction itself—in the form, 'should prompt,'—then the Person himself would become the objective (the meaning being that *the Person should be prompted* or urged to activity). Though, on account of the inanimate character of the Injunctive, such actions of *prompting* or *urging* are not possible, yet, as the Person himself being the object prompted cannot be its nominative, we conclude the power of prompting to belong to the Injunctive, through the Intelligence of the Person himself. For if some such assumption were not made, then the Injunctive could never be called 'the prompter.'

Secondly, when the question arises—'By what is it to be accomplished'?—we have for the reply—'By means of a knowledge of the Injunctions, as guided by a previous experience of certain relationships (of particular actions with certain definite results).'

And lastly, to the question—'How is the prompting to be accomplished'?—we have the answer—'Through a knowledge of the excellent character (of the particular Action).'

The explanation of all this is very simple. People with any degree of intelligence, when proceeding to do a certain action do not engage themselves in it, until they have ascertained that it is really good and well worth the doing. It is in this work of attraction that the potency of the Injunction fails; but in this it is helped by the cognition of the excellence of the Action enjoined (as described in the *Arthavāda* passages). And as for the result of the Action, which is always in the shape of something desired by man, the Agent is known to be naturally attached to it; and as such that does not stand in need of any description of its excellence, by the Veda. But as for the *means* (of attaining the Result), and the *method*, the excellence of these has to be be pointed out, to the person who has not engaged himself in the Action; and this can be done only by means of the *Arthavāda* passages; and it is in this that lies the use of these passags.

Now then, when the question arises—'By what means shall I obtain a knowledge of the said excellence'?—the answer may, in the first place, be presented by the mention of the particular Result, which leads to the conviction that inasmuch as the Action brings prosperity, *it is good* and well worth doing; or (2) the excellence of the Action may be pointed out by the fact of its being enjoined in the Veda, which is free from all discrepancies; or (3) it may be recognised by means of the fact of its being connected with excellent Deities, Materials, and Methods.

As for the word that expresses the Result, as it has a distinct purpose to serve, in the shape of the pointing out of the Result, it cannot be dragged to any other use (such as the indicating of the excellence of

Actions); and also because the desire to learn its excellence arises only *after* one has become acquainted with its Injunction, in which, too, the word mentioning the Result is always put first; and as such, this word cannot be accepted as supplying an answer to the above question; it can only be held to indicate such excellence, &c., indirectly; but such indirect indication cannot be rightly had recourse to while there is a possibility of a direct expression of the same fact; and, lastly, a double function at one and the same time would involve a self-contradiction. For these reasons the words mentioning the Result cannot be taken to point out the said excellence.

And we shall explain under the *Parṇamayi-Adhikaraṇa*, how,—when a certain text (f.i. the text, 'He whose *Juhū* is made of leaves does not hear evil of himself'), has a totally different purpose (the praising of the particular *Juhū*) to perform,—even if it be found to indicate a certain means to an end (in this case, the *Juhū* of leaves as leading to a particular Result)—no authoritative significance can be attached to such indication. For these reasons, the word mentioning the result cannot be rightly accepted as pointing out the excellence of the Action; because if that word were so accepted, then no significance would be attached to the Result mentioned; exactly as in the case of the text cited, where the expression, 'He hears not evil of himself,' is explained not as pointing to a result, but only as praising a certain object.

For this reason, in the case in question, as the words mentioning the Result have this distinct purpose to serve, even though they indicate the excellence of the Action, yet no significance can be attached to this idea of the excellence thus obtained. And, as a general rule, we know that whatever happens to be indicated or implied by a text, does not come to be recognised as the purpose or chief end of that text. As for instance, when it is said 'the former man runs,' though this implies the existence of the 'latter man,' yet this latter is not accepted as connected with the action that is spoken of with regard to the former. In the same manner, though the excellence of the Action and the consequent attraction of the agent to it are indicated by the word mentioning the Result; yet, as this has other functions of its own, it cannot be accepted as having anything to do with the pointing out of the excellence. Because such indication could be accepted only on the ground of Apparent Inconsistency; but we know that it is only when all other means of knowledge have failed that Apparent Inconsistency can be had recourse to; and this failure of the other means of knowledge, too, can rightly justify a man to seek the aid of Apparent Inconsistency, with any degree of correctness, only ofter he should have tried his very best to seek for aid from those other means. Hence, if we failed to obtain an idea of the excellence, either by direct teaching or by supplementary declarations, then alone could we assume a double potency or signification for the Injunction itself; just as when we have no *Sruva* at hand, we pour the libations into the fire by means of the spoon. But in case this idea of excellence were obtainable by any other means, however remote, then it would be absolutely necessary to follow up this means; for until this means is duly found to afford the requisite notion of excellence, the needs of the Injunction remain unsatisfied.

Similarly in the case of such passages as—" *Vāyurvai kshēpishthā-dēvatā* (" Vāyu is the swiftest deity ") and the like,—we believe them to have been laid down with reference to the accomplishment of certain purposes of men, on the ground of their forming a part of the Veda, a full study whereof has been enjoined for men. But inasmuch as a mere *Arthavāda* by itself is not capable of being directly related to the Injunction (as not having the forces of the Injunctive affix, &c.), so long as it is not recognised as leading to the accomplishment of the purposes of man, it can only be taken in the literal meaning afforded by the words (composing the passage), which consists merely in a description of a certain state of things as they exist; and as thus far it is not found to serve any useful purpose, it remains deficient on an important point.

That, however, which is implied by such description—namely, the excellence of the sacrifice offered to Vāyu indicated by the fact that, the effect being similar to the cause, the sacrifice offered to a swift Deity always accomplishes its result quickly,—is clearly needed by the Injunction found in close proximity to it; and as such the passage in question comes to be recognised as helping in the accomplishment of the man's purpose; and hence it is accepted as forming an integral part of the Veda, whose study has been laid down as necessary.

And this mutual dependence of the *Arthavāda* and the comprehension of *excellence* is based upon their mutual requirements; exactly as in the case of two charioteers, if the horse of one dies, while the other's chariot itself is burnt, the horse of this latter is yoked to the former chariot and the needs of both become supplied.

Thus, then, when such close relationship between the two is possible, though the Injunctive and the *Arthavāda* passages actually stand in need of the Declaration of Excellence and Injunction respectively, yet inasmuch as this Declaration of Excellence and Injunction are expressed by the *Arthavāda* and the Injunctive passages respectively, we cannot reasonably assert that Excellence is expressed by the Injunctive, and the Injunction by the *Arthavāda* passage. And as the words of the *Arthavāda* passage cannot do anything else except the declaring of Excellence, we conclude, from the very fact of both the *Arthavāda* and the Injunctive passages appearing in the Veda, that they express two distinct things (*viz.*, Excellence and Injunction, respectively) (*i.e.*, the fact of both appearing in the text of the Veda leads us to some such conclusion as that 'it is only the performance of such an Action as is enjoined by the Injunctive passages, and rendered attractive or pointed out as excellent by the *Arthavāda* passages, that can accomplish the desired results to the fullest extent').

In the same manner, we can explain the deprecatory (*Arthavāda*) passages also, as serving the purpose of creating an aversion (in the mind of the agent), which is a factor necessary for all Prohibitions; because, unless the knowing person comes to have an aversion to a certain course of action, he does not desist from it; and this aversion is brought about by the cognition of the non-excellent, or evil character of the action; and inasmuch as this idea of the evil character cannot be duly brought about by the negative expressions in the Prohibitive passages themselves, which serve to lay down the mere negation, along with its result and procedure,—and not either the excellence or non-excellence of the action,—a clue of knowledge of its non-excellence cannot be obtained by any other means save by the deprecatory *Arthavāda* passages, which, too, have no other purpose to serve.

Thus it is that the *Arthavāda* comes to be taken along with (*i.e.*, as forming a part of) the Injunction; specially as it is always found that it is only the continuations of the Injunctive and Prohibitive passages, respectively, that become the means of ascertaining the praise or the deprecation of the action concerned.

Nor is the character of Praise or of Deprecation altogether exclusive; because we often find a praise expressed in the form of a deprecation, and *vice versâ*; as will also be declared later on that—"a deprecatory passage is added not with a view to deprecate that which is evil, but to indirectly praise that which is good and has been laid down as to be performed." As, for example, in connection with the *Traiyambaka* Cake we read (in the 10th Adhyāya): "If one performs the *Abhighāraṇa*, he throws his cattle into Rudra's mouth, while if one does not perform it, he does not throw them into His mouth"; and in this case, though it is the non-performance of the *Abhighārana* that is praised, yet it has not been accepted as the right course of action; whereas, though its performance is deprecated, yet it has to be accepted as the proper course laid down as to be performed, on the ground of its being subsequently directly enjoined.

In a case where it is not quite clear whether Praise or Deprecation is really meant, a definite conclusion can be arrived at on this point by referring to the context; as, for instance, we shall find later on the sentence —"We know not whether the Asuras are praised or censured,"—which is said on the occasion of the declaration (referred to in the 9th Adhyāya)—

"If one sings the *Ṛk*, the Asuras come along, &c." It is doubtful whether this is to be taken as praising the action, in that it subjugates even the Asuras to the will of the sacrificer; or it is a deprecation of the action, in that it attracts such undesirable companions as the Asuras; and on this point, inasmuch as towards the end it is the *singing of the Sāma* that is enjoined, we conclude the passage to be a deprecation of the singing of the *Ṛk* verses.

In the case of all *Arthavāda* passages there are certain words that express either praise or deprecation; and it is as taken along with these words that other passages (such as 'He wept' and the like, which do not express either the one or the other) come, indirectly, to indicate such praise or deprecation. Even in a case where we have no such words, we can admit of Indication, or, even of Indicative-Indication, on the ground of the (otherwise) Apparent Inconsistency. (That is to say, in the case of the sentence 'the water is calm,' we have no word expressive of either Praise or Deprecation; yet we find, close to it, the sentence 'He draws the fire either by means of the *Vētasa* branch, or by the *Vakā*'; and on the ground of its proximity to this latter Injunction, we take the former passage to indirectly indicate the praise of the *Vētasa* and the *Vakā*, which are laid down in the latter passage. Here we have pure Indication, while if we take the passage to be a praise of the *drawing of fire*, then it will be a case of Indicative-Indication). Specially as Injunctions and Prohibitions are always accompanied by Praise and Deprecation, respectively: whenever we find the one, we can always infer the other, and thereby complete the full sentence.

The above explanations apply also to the passages occurring in the *Mahābhārata*, and *Purāṇas*, &c., as with regard to these, we have the express injunction—"One should recite these before persons of the four castes," which shows that they are the means of accomplishing certain desirable ends; and when we proceed to seek for this desirable end, we do not accept the mere recitation of the words as bringing about any result; and find that the true result lies in a full comprehension of the causes of *Dharma*, *Artha*, *Kāma* and *Moksha*, as also of their contraries, *Adharma*, *Anartha*, *Duhkha* and *Saṅsāra*,—for the purpose of acquiring those of the former set, and avoiding those of the latter.

And in certain portions of these works,—as in the chapters on '*Dāna*' '*Rājadharma*' and '*Mokshadharma*' of the *Çānti-Parva* of the *Mahābhārata* —we meet even with direct Injunctions; while in others there are *Arthavādas*—in the two forms of '*Parakṛta*' (those that describe certain actions as having been done by other good men) and '*Purākalpa*' (those describing certain actions as having been done by good men in bygone ages).

As for the other portions, those containing descriptions of events and stories,—if we accept these in their literal sense, then, with reference to these at least, the Injunction of reciting them would become useless (as no purpose could be served by these mere descriptions); hence we take these to indirectly imply the *praise* or *deprecation* (of certain courses of action). And as these descriptions have been inserted with the sole purpose of such *praise* or *deprecation*, they need not be necessarily taken as absolutely correct with regard to facts.

Guided as they were by their study of the Veda, Vālmiki, Vyāsa, and others composed their works on the same lines as the Veda (and hence it is that we find in the works of these men, as in the Veda, many apparently useless stories, &c.); and as those for whom these works were intended were persons of varying degrees of intelligence and diverse tastes, it was only proper for them to insert every kind of matter in their works (so that they might be of use to all men). Hence it is that in certain parts we find pure Injunctions, while in others the Injunctions are mixed up with *Arthavādas*; and among these latter, too, some have only brief *Arthavādas*, while others have extensive ones; the sole motive for this diverse procedure lying in the making of the work attractive to all men.

Some of these Injunctions (in the *Mahābhārata, &c.*), are based directly upon the Veda; while others are based upon considerations of ordinary pleasure and pain, as experienced in the world. Similarly, among the *Arthavādas*, too, some are those that appear in the Veda, some are based upon ordinary experience, while there are some that are purely imaginary, like ordinary poetry. But all of these have an authoritativeness based upon the fact of their *praising* (the enjoined Actions).

As for those portions of the Purānas, however, which are not capable of being taken along with any Injunction, some of them are such as give pleasure in the mere listening to them,—such are the descriptions of the *Gandhamādana*, &c.; and some, as for instance, the descriptions of wars, &c., serve to encourage the brave as well as the coward, and thereby serve a distinctly useful purpose for the Kings of men. In those cases, however, where none of these is possible,—such, for instance, as the hymns to deities, which we do not find capable of bringing about any perceptible results,—we assume an unseen result.

(*Here ends the explanation of the main Siddhānta.*)

Says the *Bhāshya: Though such passages as 'Vāyurvai kshēpishthā dēvatā', and the like, are not related directly to any actions, yet inasmuch as they can be taken along with an Injunction, they are accepted as authoritative.*

Some people explain this passage in the following manner: "From "the assertion of the *Bhāshya—Why should there be a praise? Because* "*without praise, how could people be attracted to, and perform, such actions'?*—it seems that the *Arthavāda* serves to bring about the performance of an action by means of praises, or the avoiding of other "actions by means of deprecations; and as it is these very facts—*performance* and *avoidance*—that are expressed by the Injunctions, we "conclude that both (*Arthavāda* and Injunction) serve the same purpose. "And inasmuch as those that have the same purpose to fulfil cannot be taken "together,—hence in the case of such Injunctive affixes as are without any "*Arthavādas*, or such *Arthavādas* as are without Injunctive affixes,—we can "take them with reference to their own particular subjects exclusively; "and thereby accept them as *Persuading* or *Dissuading* from particular "courses of actions. In those cases, however, where we have a mixture "of both, as only one of them would suffice for the fulfilment of their common "purpose, it becomes necessary to reject one; and under the circumstances, "it is always necessary to show preference to that which is more extensive; and hence, in accordance with the maxim—that 'one should "renounce a single person for the sake of the whole family'—we come "to reject the Injunctive affix (in favour of the much more extensive "*Arthavāda*); and not being of any use with regard to its main purpose, "the only purpose that the Injunctive affix can serve is to amplify that "Injunction (of actions) which is indicated by the Persuasion contained "in the *Arthavāda* that has the sole purpose of aiding it (by such persuasion).

"And as an instance of such amplification by the Injunctive affix, "we have the passage—'*satrādudavasāya pṛshthaçamanīyēna yajēran*'— "where the Injunctive affix in '*yajéran*' has been explained as only "amplifying the *performance* pointed out by the past participle affix in "'*Udavasāya*.'

"Thus, then, in the passage in question—'*Vāyavyam Çvētamālabhēta* "*bhūtikāmah, Vāyurvai kshēpishthā dēvatā*'—when the Injunctive affix has "been set aside, all that is meant by it is the *seizing and killing of the Çvēta* "*consecrated to Vāya*; and it is this *seizing* that is spoken of (in the *Bhāshya*) as '*Vidhyuddeçā*' (the subject of the Injunction). And as an action "can be praised only after its connection with a desirable result has been "established, it is *the sentence ending with the clause* '*bhūtikāmah*' that is "taken as referred to by the word '*Vidhyuddeça*.'

"We interpret the *Bhāshya* in the above manner, as meaning the setting aside of the Injunctive affix, because if the *Bhāshya* had meant that the "*persuasion* is accomplished by means of the Injunctive affix, then it should "not have put in the word '*Uddēça*' (but should have simply said '*Vidhēya*').

"In reality, however, it is not possible for the *Arthavāda* to be taken "along with the Injunctive affix, as pointed out in the *Sūtra*; and it is this "impossibility that is spoken of in the *Bhāshya*—'The sentence cannot be "construed as that one desirous of prosperity *should seize.'*

"The assertion of the *Bhāshya*—*because prosperity follows from it*—" points out the relationship of the *praise* and the *praised*, that has been accept-"ed (in reference to the passage in question) in preference to that of the "*Injunctive* and the *Enjoined*, which has been rejected. Thus alone can the "fact of the bringing about of prosperity be construed with the passage "(that is to say, when the fact of the *seizing* bringing about prosperity has "been laid down, the question naturally arises—how is it that it brings "about prosperity ?—and in answer to this we have the following *Arthavāda*, "which serves to point out the reason for the said potency).

"The *Bhāshya* says—*these two facts are entirely different ;* and the *facts* "referred to are the two relationships (of the *Praise* and the *Praised*, and "that of the *Injunctive* and the *Enjoined*), (and the sense of the *Bhāshya* "is that if we admitted both these relationships in the passage in question, "as they are entirely different from one another, we would have a syntactical "split: consequently we must reject the relation of the *Injunctive and the* "*Enjoined*, and admit only that of the *Praise* and the *Praised*).

"Says the *Bhāshya*—*If we are asked, for what purpose we have the* "*Praise* —......; and the sense of the question is that when you have set "aside the Injunctive affix (the action cannot be enjoined, and) what "would be the use of praising that which is not enjoined ? Or, the ques-"tioner may have in his mind the argument that, inasmuch as the *persuasion* "that you hold to be the purpose of the Praise can be accomplished by "means of the Injunctive affix itself, there is no need for the Praise.

"And the Teacher (*i.e.*, the author of the *Bhāshya*),—bearing in mind "the fact, that even when the Injunctive affix has been set aside, our pur-"poses are served by the *Arthavāda* alone, and that when both are possible "preference is to be given to the *Arthavāda*,—says: *How else, could it be* "*attractive ?*

"The questioner, however, puts forward his position more clearly : "'When the purpose of pointing out the performability of the Action has "been already served by the Injunctive affix, there could be no need for the "Praise.'

"The *Bhāshya* replies: *Not so ;* because in all cases where there is a "long (involved) sentence, the smaller sentences composing it have no "authority or significance of their own (that is to say, the meaning of the "latter cannot have any preference over, or stop the functioning of, the "longer sentence), exactly as when a higher number (*twenty*, f.i.) is "spoken of, no importance is attached to the lower numbers (*eight, ten* "*twelve, &c.*) It is only when the smaller sentences are uttered by them-"selves that they have any authority or significance ; because, in that "case, they do not stand in need of anything else; as, for instance, the "small sentence—'The cloth exists.' But the mere fact of this small "sentence serving all necessary purposes when it is used by itself cannot "justify the conclusion that 'in all cases (even where this sentence is used "as the part of a longer sentence) all that is wanted will be accomplished by "this small sentence alone.' For a sentence is accepted to be complete only "when it is not accompanied by such expressions as are significant (of a sense "more extensive than that afforded by itself); and when there happens "to be such an expression, people who think over it intelligently find that "there is something wanting in it over and above the said expression. But "when this something is not perceived, the feeling of want (or deficiency) ceases (and we conclude that there is nothing more really wanting). Hence it is only where this something more is actually perceived "that we construe the additional expression along with the former sentence; "while when it is not perceived, even though the expression may be "there all the same, we do not take it along with the original sentence; "and it is only in such cases that the smaller sentence can have any "significance apart from the longer one,—and not in the former case, "where it can have no significance of its own.

"It is with all this in view that the *Bhāshya* says; *When there are no "valedictory expressions, the necessary persuasion is accomplished by the Injunctive affix itself; but when there is a valedictory sentence it is by means "of that that the persuasion is fulfilled.*

"*Objection:* 'What you say is quite right, as regards such cases in "which the purposes of the longer sentence and the shorter are different; "as for instance, in the case of *The cloth* (*exists*) and *is red.* In the case "in question however, the purpose of the two sentences (the Injunction "and the Praise) being the same, is it right that the longer sentence should "be used to set aside the shorter one? This is what is meant by the "*Bhāshya* passage—*That longer sentence which subverts the injunctive potency "of the shorter sentence may well be got rid of, the persuasion being accomplished by the Injunctive expression itself.*'

"To this the *Bhāshya* replies: *It is true that the persuasion will be "accomplished by the Injunctive expression, even without the valedictory sentence; but as a matter of fact this latter does exist,* etc. The sense of this "is that the above objection should have been addressed to the author of "the Veda (if there were such a one)—namely, that, when it was possible "for him to express the persuasion by the shorter Injunctive sentence, why "should he have had recourse to the longer Valedictory one. But as there "is no such author, any such objection would be entirely out of "place.

"In any case, the objection cannot have much force; for the using of a "longer sentence for expressing that which could have been equally well ex-"pressed by a shorter one, would, at the worst, be only like going to a village "by a circuitous route (literally by the way round the pastures around the "village); and it could not be said to fail in its object, which would be "attained all the same, though with greater effort and fatigue. It is often "that we meet with such roundabout methods of expression; as, for in-"stance, though the single letter *kha* would be enough to signify Space, "we often make use of longer words, such as '*Ākāça*' and the like; and "certainly, we are not taken to task for doing so. In the same manner, in "the case in question, though the persuasion could be accomplished by "means of the Injunctive affix alone, yet the Veda has made use of the "Valedictory sentence for the purpose.

"There is yet another explanation that may be given: exactly as even "though there are many means of performing a sacrifice, yet it is only "when it is done in the way pointed out by the *Mantra*, that it brings about "the best results,—so, in the same manner, though the Injunctive persua-"sion could be got at by other means (such as the Injunctive affix, &c.), "yet it is only when it is expressed through the agency of the Valedictory "passage, that the Action in question can lead to the best results.

"Another objection is raised in the *Bhāshya*; '*Even though the vale-"dictory expressions exist, yet as the preceding sentence is in the form of an In-"junction, this Injunctive form cannot be disregarded.*'

"The sense of this objection is this: 'What you say is all right, as re-"gards cases where the roundabout method is adopted before the shorter one "is known; but in the case in question, such is not the case; as the shorter "and simpler method, that of the Injunctive affix, which is also the more "efficient, is already used before the other is introduced; hence exactly as "in the instance you have cited, when one has used the word '*Kha*,' he does "not, at that very time, make use of the longer word '*Ākāca*,' so also in "the present case, when the necessary persuasion has been accomplished by "means of the Injunctive affix, there is no need of having recourse to the "valedictory expressions. It may be urged that in that case, these vale-"dictory expressions would become absolutely useless. But what of that? "Let them be useless.'

"The reply to this is that we have already proved above the useful-"ness of these valedictory expressions; as a matter of fact, they can never "be absolutely useless; as we have already shown that when the purpose "of persuasion is capable of being served by both (the Injunctive affix and "the valedictory words), inasmuch as the latter is perceptibly capable of "being construed with the former, we accept its utility (on that score) in "preference to that of the former.

"The *Bhāshya* puts forward another objection: '*The persuasive Injunc-*

"*tion may be comprehended by means of the Injunctive sentence independently* "*of the valedictory words.*'

"An opponent objects to this objection being raised over again, it "being already included in the former objection. But there is a difference "between the two: the former was brought forward with a view to the "total rejection of the valedictory words; whereas the sense of this second "objection is this: 'Though the compound sentence, as a whole, may be "taken as signifying Praise, yet it cannot be denied that the first part of "it signifies a distinct Injunction; and if the expressive potency of the In- "junctive be once set aside, there being no means of reviving it, it would "come to be absolutely incapable of any significance.'

"And to this objection we make the following reply: It is true that "the first sentence has an injunctive potency: but this potency can very "well be discarded; specially as the fact of its being discarded in one place "cannot deprive it of its expressiveness in all cases; and conversely, the "fact of its having manifested itself in one place does not necessitate its "manifestation in every other place. As a matter of fact, in the case in "question, when the valedictory expressions signify something entirely "different, then the potency of the previous Injunctive is fully operative; "whereas when the former expression manifests a potency of its own, "which sets aside that of the latter, this latter entirely disappears, lest "there be a syntactical split. It is this probable syntactical split, already "noticed before, that is again pointed out by means of the present ques- "tion and answer (in the *Bhāshya*). Hence we conclude that, inasmuch "the purpose served by both (the Injunctive and the Valedictory expres- "sions) is exactly the same, the necessary persuasion should be taken as "fulfilled by means of the Praise expressed by the latter.

"Says the *Bhāshya: Stutiçabdāh stuvantah kriyām prarocayamānā* "*anushthātrnāmupakarishyanti kriyāyāh* (*i.e.*, the valedictory expressions in "praising the Act, tend to make it attractive, and thereby help the actions "of the agents).

"In regard to this, a grammatical difficulty is raised: The word "*anushthātr* should have had the Dative affix (in accordance with Pānini's "*Sūtra* I—iv—33), as it denotes the persons for whom the actions are made "attractive. It cannot be rightly urged that the said *Sūtra* mentions the "particular root *ruci*, while in the sentence in question we have an entirely "different root *roci*. Because, whether the root be *ruci* or *roci*, the sense of "*attractiveness* remains the same, and that is the only condition laid down "in the *Sūtra* (for the application of the Dative). Nor can it be argued "that the Genitive affix is due to the fact of the relationship expressed "being general, and not any special relation (such as that of the Dative). "Because this cannot be rightly asserted, when we actually have a "particular relation (that of being attractive) distinctly mentioned. Consequently we must construe *prarocayamānā* with *kriyāyāh;* and as for the persons to whom these Actions are made attractive, the context naturally points to the *performers.* Or, *Anushtatṛnām* may be taken with *upakarishyanti* (the meaning being that *they help the performers*), the word *kriyāyāh,* in this case, being taken as the Ablative—the meaning being that the valedictory expressions serve to make the action attractive, much more strongly than is done by the Injunctive expression (the word *kriyā* being taken in the sense of Injunction). Or lastly, the word *kriyāyāh* in the Genitive may be taken to mean *for the sake of the Action.*

"In the sentence *kancidartham stuvanti,* &c. (in the Bhāshya) the word '*stuvanti,*' is to be taken as a present participle (Plural, Neuter); and the meaning is that *while eulogising a certain object,—viz.:* the object meant to be laid down, or something related to it—*they lay down* the Action or something else related to it; and this *laying down* is by means of the Praise; hence the authoritative character of the *Arthavāda* passages can be established, only by discarding the Injunctive affixes."

The above interpretation of the *Bhāshya* is not accepted (by the orthodox *Mīmānsaka;* and that for the following reasons): When the Injunctive affix is discarded, there is nothing to express the Injunction of the action; and as such there would be nothing that would be in need of the Praise. For there is, in this case, no desire, on our part, to learn the method of the Verbal *Bhāvanā.*

Though it is possible to assume a desire to learn the *why* and *wherefore* of the *Bhāvanā,* yet this, too, could only be with reference to the method of the Injunction; because the Praise is only meant to help the Injunction;—the only difference of this *why* of the Verbal *Bhāvanā* from the method of the Injunction lying in the fact of its being expressed in different words. Then, again, even this want is possible for the person only after he has been *enjoined* or prompted to do an Act, and not when the Action is merely mentioned (by name). For certainly, when the mere action, the *seizing of the Çvēta consecrated to Vāyu,* is mentioned, so long as it is not asserted whether this *seizing* should be done or not, there is no desire to know whether the Action is praiseworthy or otherwise. And when the idea of such praiseworthiness is not desired, the *Arthavāda* passages themselves literally only describing certain facts, would not imply any such excellence, &c.

And as for the denotation of the verbal root itself, there is no chance of any person having any relations with it, or having any desires with regard to it; because all these desires, &c., belong to the *Bhāvanā*. And as this *Bhāvanā* will have been set aside by the discarding of the Injunctive affix, what would be there that could be in want of anything?

Hence when all the three factors will have been set aside (along with the Injunctive word), we could have no ideas, either of Prosperity as the *result*, or the Sacrifice as the *means*, or anything else as the *method*. Under these circumstances, even if the excellence of the Action should happen to be expressed by the *Arthavāda*,—unless this declaration of excellence be capable of being taken as an answer to the query as to why the Action should be performed,—the mere recognition of the fact of a certain Action being good,—unless this fact is recognised as a reason for its performability,—could not give us any idea of the performability of the Action. Even if, somehow or other, a notion of performability (*Kartavyatā*) were got at, the meaning got at would be '*praçastah kartavyah*' (*i.e.*, the Action *should be made praiseworthy*); exactly as we have the expression '*Patah kartavyah*' (the Cloth should be made).

And so long as a direct Injunction of the Action is not assumed, all such notions would be absolutely useless. And certainly to reject a direct Injunctive expression, and then to assume such Injunction indirectly, through the *Arthavāda*, would be a very objectionable method to follow. Then, too, inasmuch as the necessary Injunction is already directly expressed by the Injunctive expression, there can be no reasonable ground for making any indirect assumptions of it. The Injunction could be indirectly got at by means of the *Arthavāda*, only if it had not been expressed by other more direct means; and as, in the present instance, it is clearly pointed out by the direct Injunctive expression, there is no such inconsistency (to avoid which we should assume an Injunction by indirect means).

So, too, if the *Arthavāda*, by itself, did not serve a distinctly useful purpose in the persuasion,—as in the case of mere descriptions of events,—then it could be discarded. But we have already shown above that it does serve a useful purpose in the persuasion, and as such it is not discarded; and hence if the necessary persuasion could be accomplished by other means, then there would have been no need of the *Arthavāda*. But, as a matter of fact, the persuasion, finding no other means of its accomplishment, seeks the help of the *Arthavāda* itself.

And in all matters relating to the Veda, the assumption of words is based upon the sole ground of the apparent inconsistency of certain well-recognised facts; and from this assumption of words follows the necessary accomplishment of the objects. Hence the persuasion could only lead to the assumption of the Injunctive word, and not to that of actual Injunction. But on the occasion of such assumption of the Injunctive word, the direct appearance of such a word, in the shape of '*ālabhēta* (*should seize*) would bar the way to the inference of any other expressions; exactly as in the case of the passages dealing with the '*Aindra*' and the '*Vāyvya*,' as soon as the injunctive sentence—'*Somēna yajēta*' (should sacrifice with the Soma)—presents itself, no other sacrifice is assumed.

Then, again, it is only when two sentences express the same meaning that there can be either a rejection of the one by the other; or they may be taken as optional alternatives. But in the case of the Injunctive word and the *Arthavāda*, we find an absolute difference between their meanings, the former dealing with that which is to be helped (by the praise), and the latter with that which helps (*i.e.*, the Praise); and as such we cannot but take them jointly, construing them together into a single complex sentence.

If there were a setting aside of the Injunctive affix, then there would be no trace left of the fact of the action being for one's own sake or for that of others,—a fact that is pointed out by the number, &c., of the nominative agent (which in the present case is expressible only by means of the Injunctive affix).

It may be argued that what we set aside is only the factor of *injunction*, and not the ideas of the *number*, &c. (denoted by the Affix). But this is not possible; because if the affix be retained for the purpose of denoting the number, &c., it could never fail to denote the Injunction also. And what has been once denoted and duly cognised can be rejected only in two ways: (1) either on account of its being not in contact with the Injunction,—as in the case of the 'oneness' of the vessel (*Vide*. III-i-12 *et seq*,)—, or (2) on account of its being a mere explanatory description—as in the case of the *Homa* done for the sake of one who wants the sense-organs. The Injunction, however, cannot itself be said to be not-Injunction (hence the first condition is not applicable to the present case); nor can it be taken to be a mere explanatory description; because till the Injunctive expression is uttered, that which it enjoins has not been enjoined or pointed out by any other means. As the fact that is pointed out by the passage in question, is not in the form that—'the seizing of the *Çvēta* dedicated to Vāyu, which should be done, is good or praiseworthy,'—but in that—'it should be done, because it is good or praiseworthy.'

In the example of the *Udavasānīya* that has been cited above, the participial affix '*ktvā*,' while indicating the mere *Action*, independently of any notions of Injunction or Prohibition, has clearly pointed out (*literally*, attained the position of) the Injunction; and as such it cannot serve as a proper example. For if it did not point to the Injunction, then the denotation of the verb itself would fall into the place of the *object to be accomplished*; and as such it would become absolutely useless.

Thus we find that the *Arthavāda* can be said to be taken along with the Injunction, without in any way subverting the *Sutra.*

Hence has the *Bhāshya* declared: *The real indicator of the Injunction extends up to the expression 'desiring prosperity'* (in the sentence '*vāyavyam çvētamālabhēta bhūtikāmah*'), which shows that the Injunction itself is included in it; for if the *Bhāshya* did not mean the Injunction to be so included, it would have declared the *meaning of the verbal root* only to be the indicator of the Injunction; but the mere fact of the meaning of the verbal root embodying an action is not enough to justify us in holding it to be the indicator of Injunction. Consequently, we conclude that it is the Injunctive Affix alone, which, as signifying the Injunction, is held to be the indicator of Injunction. As it is not possible for the *Arthavāda* to be taken along with that which is pointed out by the Injunction (which is a particular Action), the *Bhāshya* has added the word "*Uddēça*" to the *Sūtra* (the expression '*Vidhyuddēça*' meaning the *indicator of Injunction*, which, being in the form of the Injunctive affix, can be taken along with the *Arthavāda*). The addition of the clause extending up to the word '*desiring prosperity*' is made with the purpose of affording an occasion for the Praise, after the Action has been comprehended as bringing about a particular desirable result.

Objection: "Under the circumstances, in a case where the verb is in the present tense (f.i. '*Dadhnā juhoti*'), there being no desire to seek after any other thing, the *Arthavāda* passage could not be taken along with it."

Reply: Though it is so, yet no other means of cognition being applicable, the *Arthavāda* comes to be connected with the Injunction, which is assumed [to be pointed out, either (1) by the instructions of method (contained in the Brāhmaṇa passage in connection with the sentence "*Dadhnā juhoti,*" or (2) by the fifth verbal mood (*Lēt*), or (3) by the Apparent Inconsistency of the Present Tense, which remains inexplicable without the assumption of the said Injunction].

Even in a case where we assume an Injunction, on the sole strength of the *Arthavāda* passage, our only refuge lies in the Apparent Inconsistency (or Inexplicability of the Praise contained in the *Arthavāda*). And so long as we have these resources at our command, it is not right to have recourse to the uselessly elaborate processes (detailed above, by the Opponent).

It has been urged above that if this interpretation be accepted, there would be a syntactical split on account of the sentence being made to express two distinct relationships. But we have sailed clear of this objection by putting the sense of the passage in this form: *One should seize the Çvēta, on account of* such *seizing being good or praiseworthy.* This does not give rise to any syntactical split, because that which is enjoined stands in need of Praise (for the sake of persuasion) ; and as such, there being no necessity for having recourse to any breaking up of the sentences, the two factors (*viz.*: the Injunction and the Praise) can very well be taken together. Then, again, if the delineation of such distinct relationships were to be marked down as causing a syntactical split, then the pointing out of such factors as the Means, the Result, and the Method (as is done by all Injunctive passages) would also have to be rejected as giving rise to such a split.

It is in connection with these facts that we should take the *Bhāshya* passage : *This relationship is not what is meant to be expressed.* That is to say, the former half of the passage by itself is not meant to be taken as expressing the Injunction with all its accessories ; because in that case, the Injunction having been duly accomplished by the former half, it is only indirectly, through this Injunction, that the Persuasion, meant by the latter half, could be accomplished ; and this process being much too complicated, a syntactical split would be inevitable.

The question (in the *Bhāshya*)—"*What is the use of the Praise?*"—is put with a view to the fact of the necessary persuasion having been accomplished by means of the former (Injunctive passage.

And the reply that is given—*How else could there be a persuasion?*—is based upon the fact of the Injunction being helped (in its potency) by the Persuasion expressed in the subsequent *Arthavāda.*

The sentence in the *Bhāshya* beginning with *nanu prāyapi* explains what has gone before.

The passage *na hi*, &c, means that it is only when there is no direct Praise that the Injunctive passage can be assumed to have the double signification (of the Injunction as well as the Praise) ; and this assumption is not allowable when the Praise can be expressed by another sentence. In that case, if the *Arthavāda* be neglected, the Injunction of the action to be performed by one desirous of prosperity would remain incomplete.

The clause *yathā patah* has already been explained above.

The passage--*Vidhiçabdēna tadā prarocanā*—serves to point out the manifold purposes served by the Injunction and the Praise.

The meaning of the objection—"*nanvēvamapi, &c.*"—is that, "when the Injunction itself is capable of persuading, why should it require an *Arthavāda* passage to do this?"

The reply to this is given by the sentence—*satyam*, &c. That is to say, it is only when there is no valedictory sentence,—and not when there is such a direct sentence,—that the purpose of the Praise can be held to be served by the Injunctive sentence itself. This purpose is none other than Praising; and it cannot be said to be served exclusively by the *Arthavāda* alone; because the object praised being pointed out by the Injunctive sentence, and no praise being possible without the object that is praised, the Injunctive sentence must also be accepted as serving the purpose of Praising. But it is only when there is no *Arthavāda* passage that we have recourse to the highly complicated process of attributing the signification of both (Injunction and Praise) to the Injunctive sentence exclusively.

The sentence—'*nanu satsvapi, &c.*,' is to be explained as before.

Then we have the sentence—*ato'smādvidhēh*, &c.; and the meaning of this is that we comprehend the Praise not from the Injunctive sentence itself, but from such sources as the Genitive case-ending, the supplementary sentences (in the shape of the *Arthavāda*), and the like.

Then there is another objection—" *nanu nirapēkshādapi,* " &c.; and the sense of this objection is this: " When in certain cases, even in the absence of any mention of the method of the particular Action enjoined, the Injunction is accepted to have the capability of urging men to that action, wherefore should it stand in need of anything else (that may be sought to be expressed by the *Arthavāda*)? And hence, as a matter of fact, even when such *Arthavāda* passages actually exist, it is best to disregard or reject them."

The Author of the *Bhāshya* replies to this objection in a jocular style: This may be the case where we have the Injunctive expression appearing alone, by itself, independently of all else; because in that case, there would be no contradiction. But this is not possible in the case in question; because in this case, the Injunction is expressed by certain words that stand in need of other factors (as Praise and the like). Any single sentence can be accepted as laying down or expressing only one relationship of a certain thing; hence if we make the Injunction indicate the two factors (of Injunction and Praise), then there would be an inevitable syntactical split.

The sentence—*esha hi guṇo*, &c.—shows the persuasive force of the *Arthavāda*, as eulogising the factors pointed out by the Injunctive sentence.

For these reasons, we conclude that the *Arthavāda* passages have a distinct purpose to serve, as helping the Injunctions, by being taken along with these latter.

***Sūtra* (8). The connection of long-established tradition also is equal.**

With a view to justify the word '*ca*,' the *Bhāshya* has introduced the *Sūtra* with the objection: "*The Arthavādas may be accepted as entirely useless.*"

And the reply is that this cannot be; because the aforesaid reasonings have shown that they serve a distinctly useful purpose.

Or, the passage supplying the reply may be interpreted as—*This cannot be* (*tanna*), because of the usefulness having been shown in this (aforesaid) manner (*evamarthāvagamāt*), and *also because the connection of tradition, &c., &c.*,—the *Sūtra* being thus construed along with the reply to the assumed objection.

There are certain rules and regulations (*Dharmas*) laid down with regard to the study of the Veda; and these have the sole purpose of keeping up the traditional system; because the regulations are distinctly laid down in the *Smṛtis*, as calculated to preserve such a system; and, secondly, because the said regulations can have nothing to do with such other human ends, as the attaining of Heaven, and the like; nor have we any authority for postulating a different purpose for these regulations, and for rejecting the fact of the proper accomplishment of the traditional course of study, which in itself is admitted to be distinctly useful, and is most closely connected with the said regulations. In connection with the traditional system of study, the strict observance of these regulations serves the distinctly useful and much-needed purpose of removing obstacles from the way of such studies; and we admit the fact of these regulations serving the purpose of removing the obstacles, on the ground of these having been laid down with this avowed purpose; specially as any other use that may be assumed could not, in any way, help in the process of study. For if the attainment of Heaven be assumed to be the purpose served by the said regulations, then these would come to be the means of accomplishing a direct purpose of the agent (and would have nothing to do with the proper completion of Vedic study).

It may be assumed that it is only when the Veda is studied in accordance with the said regulations that the sacrifices can bring about their proper results (and as such the Regulations serve the purpose of helping in the proper accomplishment of the results of sacrifices). But, in that case, the Regulations would have only an indirect use, helping something (the sacrifice) very remote from itself. For these reasons, we cannot but conclude these Regulations to serve the extremely useful purpose of helping a man in the proper accomplishment of his study of the Vedic texts (by the removal of obstacles).

Then, again, we do not want the obstacles to be removed from the way of a thing that is absolutely useless. Because obstacles to such useless things are always desirable; so as there may be no useless trouble in accomplishing that which does not serve any useful purpose (but, on the other hand, hinders it.)

Thus we find that inasmuch as the *Arthavāda* passages are treated, by students, with as much respect and attention as the Injunctive passages which are apparently useful, we must accept the former also to be equally useful. And as the said Regulations are based upon the Veda (and these are observed equally with regard to the Injunctive and the *Arthavāda* passages), this equal regard must be regarded as authorised by the Veda itself. And this regard could not be possible, unless the *Arthavāda* passages actually served a useful purpose; and thus, we arrive at the general fact of the *Arthavāda* being distinctly useful. And then, in accordance with the reasoning embodied in *Sūtra* I—iv—30, finding these passages to be capable of signifying Praise, we come to the conclusion that they serve the useful purpose of *praising* (that which has been enjoined in the Injunctive passages).

It is with a view to all this that we read in the *Bhāshya: The remembrance is quite strong.*

Or, this passage may be taken as pointing to the fact that the usefulness of the *Arthavāda* passage can be inferred from the fact of all men keeping up a firm hold (or remembrance) of the text of the whole Veda, which could not have been possible unless all men had been fully convinced of the usefulness of the whole of it (the Injunctions, the *Arthavādas*, the *Mantras*, &c., all included). The fact, too, of people having this firm conviction of its usefulness is implied by certain sentences; and as such it cannot be said to be (based upon mere Inferential assumption, and as such) wanting in true authoritativeness. If it were not so, and people considered certain portions of the Veda to be useless, they would neglect such portions, and study only certain portions of it—either the Injunctive passages alone, or the *Arthavādas* alone. And in that case, there could not be a *firm remembrance* of the portions thus neglected. But, as a matter of fact, we find that people have a firm remembrance (of the *Arthavāda* passages, as much as that of the Injunctive passages); and hence we cannot reject these as useless interpolations. And from this too, we cannot but admit them to be distinctly useful.

The *Sūtra* may also be interpreted in another manner: The Vedic text—"The Veda should be studied"—of which the sole purpose is the establishing of a long tradition (of study), and which has been chiefly instrumental in bringing about the eternal tradition of Vedic study,—refers *equally* to the *Arthavāda* and the Injunctive passages; inasmuch as both of these equally constitute the Veda; and hence, in accordance with the arguments propounded above, there being no chance for their usefulness apart from the accomplishment of certain purposes of man, the *Arthavāda* passages must be accepted as capable of expressing *Praise*, and thereby serving the useful purpose of *praising* (an Action which has been laid down as bringing about a certain desirable result, and thereby persuading the man to its performance).

***Sūtra* (9). The aforesaid objections are not applicable; because there would be a contradiction only if these pointed out an action; but as it is they do not point to an action; and hence there is no incongruity.**

With this *Sūtra* begins the refutation of the objections urged (in the *Pūrvapaksha Sūtras*) against the authority of the *Arthavāda* passages.

The objections that have been urged above—viz.: *the contradiction of the Scriptures and facts of ordinary perception, &c.*—against the assumption of Injunctions in connection with *Arthavādas*,—we do not find to be applicable to our theory.

Or the *Sūtra*—when '*aprāptām*' is read as '*aprāptam*'—may mean that we do not find the above explanation of Praise to be open to the said objections.

And the reason given is that if the sentences (*Arthavādas*)—that speak of the 'weeping,' 'cutting out of the fat,' 'misconception of the quarters,' 'theft,' 'untruthfulness,' &c.—were taken as laying down certain Actions to be performed, then alone could there be a contradiction (of Scriptures or of ordinary facts of perception). But, as a matter of fact, we do not take these sentences in their literal sense; nor do we supply into them words from without, in order to make them signify a direct Injunction; all that we hold them to signify is *Praise* only; and certainly, there can be no contradiction in this; and hence there can be no incongruity in our theory.

Or, the expression (in the *Sūtra*)—*Çabdārthastu*—may be taken to mean that the *Arthavāda* passage *serves the purpose of helping the Injunctive words;* and as such, not being connected with the performance of any action that may be mentioned in itself, it does not come to be put into practice; and as such it cannot be incongruous.

There are three different readings of the *Sūtra:* (1) *Aprāptāncānupapattim,*—in this case the words '*we find*' have got to be supplied; the meaning being—*we find the said objection to be not applicable, &c.* (2) *Aprāptancānuppattim,*—in this case we have to supply the words 'our explanation'; the meaning being—*our explanation is not open to the said objection.* (3) *Aprāptā cānupapattih,*—the meaning in this case being—*The objection is found to be inapplicable to our theory,*—the words 'found in our theory' being supplied from without.

***Sūtra* (10). It is indirect description.**

[This *Sūtra* meets the objections urged in *Sūtra* (1).]

A question is now raised: "The *Arthavāda* may be taken along with the Injunction, when both of them refer to the same subject; but how can they be said to be so related, when their subjects are totally different"?

The reply to this is that there can be an indirect relationship between the two. As for instance, when a certain object connected with a certain Action is praised, that praise indirectly applies to the other relatives of the same Action also; or, when a certain object has got to be praised, we praise the source from which it proceeds. And as both in the Veda and in ordinary parlance, the praise of one object is found to be applicable to another object related to it, this indirect method of praising a thing is often resorted to. And as such, the fact of the subject-matter of the *Arthavāda* and the Injunction being different cannot in any way affect our aforesaid conclusions.

The signification of such Praises will be exemplified and explained later on;—*e.g.*, when the *water* is praised as *calm*, it is indirectly taken to signify the fact that anything connected with, or proceeding from water, being a source of calmness or peace, would remove the troubles of the sacrificer.

The present *Sūtra* by itself directly meets the cases of the three *Arthavādas:* (1) 'He wept, and from his tears silver was produced'; (2) 'Prajāpati cut out his own fat' and 'The gods having ascertained it to be a sacrifice to the gods knew not the quarters.' And the following *Sūtras* too will be taken as bringing forward arguments in support of the conclusions arrived at under this *Sūtra.*

As for the means of ascertaining the fact of the *Arthavādas* under question having secondary or indirect significations, only a few of them will be explained now; the rest will be explained in detail under *Sūtra* I—iv—23.

In the case of the *Arthavāda*—"He wept, &c."—each factor of the *Arthavāda* is to be taken along with each factor of the Injunction, because of their mutual requirements. That is to say, the word 'He' ('*sah*') refers to the subject spoken of; because this word always denotes the subject treated of.

Or, the expression '*tatpratyayāt*' (in the *Bhāshya*) may be taken as pointing out the fact of the pronoun '*tat*' being well-known to refer to the subject in hand; and hence whenever the word "*Sah*" is used, it immediately points to its base '*Tat*,' and thence to the subject spoken of. Hence the construction of the aforesaid *Arthavāda* passage should be thus explained: "That which followed as his tears is the 'Silver.'" And all this is said in support of the subsequent deprecation and prohibition (of the giving of silver); and hence after the Prohibitory Passage (that silver should not be given), it is only natural that we should have the Deprecatory Passage under question.

The *Bhāshya* cites the said deprecatory passage: 'One who gives silver at the *Varhi*-sacrifice, falls into some trouble (that makes tears flow in his family) before the year closes.' The reason why this trouble befalls the giver of silver is next explained: The *effect* always being similar to the *Cause*, if one makes a gift of silver, which is a product of weeping, it is

6

only natural that it should bring about an effect similar to itself, in the shape of some tear-producing (heartrending) calamity; and from all this it follows that silver should not be given.

And thus we find that the *Arthavāda*—"He wept, &c."—serves, a distinctly useful purpose, being, through the said Deprecation, supplementary to the Prohibition of the giving of silver.

This Indirect Assertion too is based upon words,—the fact of *weeping* (*Rodana*) having been inferred from the mere verbal sound of the word '*Rudra.*' And the silver comes to be deprecated on account of the mere assumption that if drops of tears, could be solidified, in as much as they are white, they would be like silver (and as such this metal being similar to tears, should not be given); or, silver may have been spoken as produced by *weeping*, on account of the fact of an expenditure of wealth (of which silver always forms the principal portion) bringing tears to the eyes of persons related to the spendthrift.

And thus we find that in some way or other a due comprehension of the Deprecation invariably helps us in getting at the real Prohibition; and as such it does not matter, if the *Arthavāda* is unable to point out the Prohibition directly.

The same process of construction is also applied to the passage speaking of Prajāpati having cut out his fat. This passage is taken as praising a good action, thus: 'A good action is performed even at such personal discomfort as the cutting out of one's own fat,—what then can be said with regard to the spending of one's external possessions over a good action'? For instance, even in ordinary parlance, we find people eulogising the extremely charitable, as that 'he gives a way even his very eye-balls.'

It is true that the passage in itself describes a certain event; but no Vedic passage has any authority in its mere descriptive form; there is always an element of truth in the Praise that is signified by it; and hence the passage having been recognised as true, in reference to this Praise, which is found to serve a distinctly useful purpose, it does not stand in need of having its signification transferred to a *mere description*, which, even if true, could be of no use (in regard to *Dharma*).

Or again, the *Arthavādas* may be taken as parts of the Verbal *Bhāvanā* (of an Injunction); and even then, their sole use would lie in the giving rise, in the mind, to the idea of engaging in a certain action ('may I do this'); and in this, the literal signification of the passages (as consisting of mere descriptions) could have no use (the aforesaid idea being accomplished by the mere recognition of the excellence of the Action, independently of any descriptions of persons or things). (And in such cases as 'He wept, and from his tears silver was produced,' the literal meaning is apparently contrary to all sense-perception, and as such totally inadmissible). But in the case of such passages as point to the fact of Heaven being attained by means of the performance of a certain sacrifice, it is a well established fact, that there is no contradiction (of any facts of ordinary perception).

Nor can it be urged that there can be no proper Praise or Deprecation indicated by such descriptions as are apparently false. Because the implied Praise or Deprecation is always distinctly comprehended (even when the description is false). As a matter of fact, it is only in the case of real descriptions of facts that we find people saying—"What is the use of inferring from it a Praise or a Deprecation, the Description itself is quite true, and admissible?" It is in the case of the false descriptions—where that which is generally known to be bad is described as good, or *vice versâ*, —that people reason thus: "(1) Inasmuch as this sentence describes as *good* that which is generally known as *bad*, it is clear that it persuades me to have recourse to it; and (2) inasmuch as it describes as *bad* that which is generally believed to be *good*, it distinctly dissuades me from it"; and having reasoned thus, they engage in the eulogised course of Action, which he finds himself unable to abandon.

Then again, it is admitted on all hands that the Veda is absolutely authoritative; and it is also a well-recognised fact that the knowledge of the excellence or non-excellence of an Action known to the man is of help in his (*i.e.*, is utilised by him in) engaging in it or avoiding it; and in the case of the *Arthavāda* passages, we find that such knowledge is brought about by the Veda itself; and hence we are led to the conclusion that we must regulate our actions accordingly.

Even in the ordinary world, we find that there are certain actions, which, though bringing about other results, are held by trustworthy persons to impart to the performer an excellent Memory (or Intelligence); and when seeking to persuade a person to do that act, they point out to him the Action as leading to many other desirable results, such as wealth, good luck, &c., even though this may not be quite true. And having performed the Action, as urged by such descriptions, the man actually obtains the real result (Excellence of Memory). Though the person prompted knows full well that all the results that are described to him do not really follow from the Action, and are described to him in accordance with his own inclinations, yet being convinced of the impossibility of trustworthy persons prompting him to absolutely useless (or harmful) Actions, he concludes that though all the results described may not follow, yet something desirable is sure to follow from the Action; and accordingly he engages himself in it.

In the same manner, in the case of the Veda, though the real result may have been spoken of in the Injunctive passage itself, yet the *Arthavāda*, even though describing only imaginary results, may serve the purpose of making the enjoined Action more attractive to the Agent; and as such it does not matter whether the results described in it are false or real; specially as its sole use lies in the persuading of the Agent to do the Action (enjoined), which is accomplished equally well (even when the Results described are only false). And even though the results described in the *Arthavāda* are recognised to be false, yet the learned people do not abandon the Action praised by it; because they are fully cognisant of the fact that the result that will surely follow is the one mentioned in the Injunctive passage (and this is quite desirable by itself).

For these reasons we conclude that the fact of the description being false does not in any way affect the question. For instance, when a man mistaking a piece of shell for silver, picks it up, and if in picking up the shell, he comes across a piece of real silver, he is not said to have been wholly deceived (as to the silver). And as in this case, we have the shell as the real substratum of the notion of silver, so some such real substratum of truth can always be found (in the case of the false descriptions contained in the *Arthavāda*), through the similarity of Verbal sounds.

That is to say, in the case of the *Arthavāda*—"*Prajāpati cut out his own fat and offered it into the Fire, and there appeared the aja* (*unborn one* or *goat*), *by making use of which people obtain cattle*,"—the word '*Prajāpati*' may be taken as denoting the Elements, as these *support* ('pānti') *the creation* or *living beings* ('prajāh'); '*Vapā*' ('fat') = the innermost essence of these Elements—as Rain and the like; and this was offered into the '*Fire*' which = (1) the fire of Lightning (into which Rain was offered), (2) the fire in the body (into which Air was offered, as the Air moves within the body, exactly as the offering does in the fire), and (3) the ordinary fire (into which its rays are offered, as it is into the fire that the rays become extinguished); thence came 'the *unborn*,' by which are meant the *seeds*, &c., which are generally believed to be eternally continuous; and having got there, men obtain cattle; because all animals are only different modifications of the various grains. And this interpretation will supply the substratum of truth in the said *Arthavāda* passage.

But though this interpretation makes the passage appear as a truthful description, yet it entirely loses its eulogistic character; and hence we proceed to explain the passage in such a way as to represent it as truthful, and at the same time, accomplishing its appointed purpose of *Praising*.

On the strength of the *Mantras*, *Arthavādas*, *Purāṇas*, and *Itihāsas*, we accept the fact of there being a Creation and a Dissolution of the Universe. Hence we deduce the following meaning from the said passage: 'At the beginning of the Creation, Prajāpati—who is spoken of as the *Lord of Creation*, on account of His former righteous deeds—finding no other animal at hand, changed himself, by mere will-force, into the form of an animal, and then cut out the fat out of his own body, &c., &c.; and before the offering, &c., were quite finished, a hornless animal (*aja*=goat) rose from sacrificial fire.' This description indicates the fact of the particular sacrifice being so quickly efficacious as to bring about its result immediately after (or even before) its completion; and that it was for this reason that Prājapati took such a lot of trouble over its performance. And in this, the descriptive element (as well as the Praise) is quite true. Nor does the description of this particular event make the Veda necessarily non-eternal; because like the signs of each succeeding season, it is possible for the same action to be repeated at each beginning of the Creation.

Similarly too, in the case of the passage—"*Dēvā vai dēvayajanam, &c.*" —the word "*Dēvāh*" = those who *shine* with cleverness in actions, *viz.*, the Sacrificial Priests; and these Priests, having comprehended the *Dēvayajana*, and finding the actions in connection with the *Soma* to be entirely different to what they had been used to, during the performance of the *Darça* and the *Pūrṇamāsa*, become bewildered as to the course of action to be adopted; and as such they are spoken of as 'not knowing the East from the West, &c.' Thus it is that even in ordinary every-day life, when a man is bewildered as to the course of action to be adopted by him, he says: 'The quarters (East, West, &c.), appear to me confused.' And it is as helping to remove this bewilderment that the *Aditi* sacrifice is praised (by means of the said *Arthavāda* passage); and the bewilderment is removed on account of there being an interval of time for ascertaining the real character of the subject (on which the man is bewildered). That is to say, during the time that the man is going through the performance of the well-practised primary actions in connection with the '*Prāyaṇīya*,' he gets time to recollect his wits about the Actions that are to come next (about which there is generally a confusion in the minds of the performers). Otherwise (if the said actions were not performed), and there were no interim between the two Primary Actions, the agent would not have time to concentrate his mind upon what he would have to do next. And as this interim is afforded by the '*Aditi*' sacrifice, it is this that is praised as helping to remove the confusion in the Agent's mind.

Sūtra (11). (The indirect signification is) based upon form, and upon the character of the greater part.

[This *Sūtra* meets the first two objections urged in *Sūtra* (2).]

(The meaning of the *Sūtra* is that the mind is spoken of as 'thief,' in the *Arthavāda* passage, on account of its "form"; *i.e.*, just as the *thief* has his *form* or body concealed, &c., so has the *mind* also; and thus the name of "thief" is applied to the mind only indirectly or figuratively. So also speech is spoken of as '*liar*,' on the ground of the speech of people, for the greater part, consisting of lies only; and hence the character of the *speaker* is figuratively attributed to the *speech* itself).

In ordinary life, whenever something has got to be done, what the person does is to form a determination in his *mind*, and then to express it in *words or speech*, and then to do it; and as such even though the Mind and the Speech are very closely related to the Action to be performed, yet they are spoken of as of much less significance than gold, because they have the character of the *thief* and the *liar* respectively. (The said *Arthavāda* appearing in the wake of the Injunction that *one is to keep some gold in his hand*). If the signification of the passage rested merely in the said Deprecation (of Mind and Speech), it could only point to a Prohibition; and it is only when signifying the Praise (of gold) that it can be taken along with the said Injunction; specially as it is only the supporting of the Injunction that is found to serve a visible purpose; as will be explained later on, under *Sūtra* X—viii—7.

Sūtra (12). Because of the greatness of distance.

[This *Sūtra* meets the third objection urged in *Sūtra* (2).]

The *Arthavāda*—'During the day the smoke only is perceived'—occurs in support of the declaration that 'During the day, the Fire goes away to the Sun.' And as to the question—why should this declaration be made?—, we reply that it is with a view to eulogise the Injunction with regard to the *mantra* recited at the *Agnihotra—viz:* "*Sūryo jyotirjyotih sūryah swāhā* is to be employed at the morning offering, and *Agnirjyotirjyotiragnih swāhā* in the evening offering," where we have *mantras* having their implications intermixed with one another.

Question: "How can these implications of the said *mantras* be said to be intermixed, when we find them referring to two distinct deities, Agni and Sūrya?"

To this question, some people make the following reply: "The word '*Jyotih*' in the *mantra* '*Agnirjyotih, &c.*,' signifies the *Sūrya*, while in the other *mantra* it signifies *Agni;* and as such the significations of the two *mantras* become intermixed."

But this explanation is not quite satisfactory; because the word "*Jyotih*" signifies *Light in general;* and as such can be taken as qualifying both the *Agni* and the *Sūrya;* specially if the word were synonymous with any one of these two, it could not be used with reference to the other. That is to say, in a case where any two words are synonymous, if one of them is used, another is not used along with it; so that if the word '*Jyotih*' were synonymous with '*Sūrya*,' it could not be used in the *mantra* of the morning offering—"*Sūryojyotih, &c.*"; while if it were synonymous with "*Agni*," it could not be used in that of the evening offering.

Hence we conclude that the *mantras* have been wrongly cited. The proper *mantras* to cite here are: "(1) *Agnirjyotirjyotih sūryah swāhā*, (2) *Sūryo jyotirjyotiragnih swāhā*" (the former being enjoined as the *mantra* to be employed in the evening libation, and the latter in the morning one). And it is this Injunction that can be taken as eulogised by the *Arthavāda* in question; because the Injunction serves to set aside, in this case, the general rule that the *mantra* is to be employed in accordance with the implications of the words composing it; and as such the Injunction being one of intermixed implications, it comes to be supported by the said Praise. And the reason for this intermixture is laid down as that, 'during the day, *Agni* (Fire) enters into the *Sūrya* (the Sun), while during the night the Sun enters into the Fire'; and hence it follows that the offerings are not to be made only to the deities pointed out in the *mantras*.

In this explanation too, the former *mantras* (cited in the *Bhāshya*) serve as examples of the Injunction that is set aside by the latter Injunction; and the latter *mantras* quoted by us, to which the praise of the *Arthavāda* refers, were not quoted by the *Bhāshya*, because they are pointed out by the mention of the fact of "the implications being intermixed" (which could not refer to the *mantras* quoted).

Or, it may be that the *Arthavāda* in question occurs between the two sets of *mantras* (the one set quoted in the *Bhāshya*, and laying down the libations to be offered to the Deities mentioned in the *mantras*, and the other set quoted by us, where the implications of the two *mantras* are mixed up in the Injunction). For the latter Injunction we may have some other Praise; the Praise in question referring to the former (which lays down the morning libation to be offered to the Sun, and the evening one to *Agni*); and this praise may be explained thus: *Inasmuch as during the day the Fire enters into the Sun, the Sun is the only light; and similarly as at night the Sun enters into the Fire, Fire is the only light;* and as such it is necessary that the morning libation should always be offered to *Sūrya* and the evening one always to *Agni*.

Question: "But how is it that the passage speaks of the *smoke alone*, &c.?"

Answer: The explanation of this lies in the fact, that during the day, when we look at the Fire burning *at a great distance*, we see *the smoke only*; while at night we distinctly perceive the *light* (and not the smoke); and as such this statement of a well-known fact serves as a sort of basis for the aforesaid Praise.

***Sūtra* (13). Through the failings of women, the son is often found to belong to the man.**

[This *Sūtra* meets the fourth objection urged in *Sūtra* (2).]

It is laid down that,—"during the recounting of the *Pravaras* (the particular *Ṛshis* among one's ancestors) the sacrificer should say—*Dēvāh pitarah, &c.*" ; as a praise of this recounting of the *Pravaras*, we have the declaration that even a non-Brāhmaṇa becomes a Brāhmaṇa by this recounting.

Against this some people raise the following question : "In the case of those whose Brāhmanical character is well-known, the acquisition of the said Brahmanahood would be useless (and as such the recounting of the *Pravaras* cannot be necessary for well-recognised Brāhmaṇas)."

It is in anticipation of this question that we have the declaration—"We know not whether we are Brāhmaṇas or non-Brāhmaṇas." The mention of the *known* as the 'unknown' implies that *it is hard to be known ;* because that which cannot be known easily is as good as *unknown ;* and certainly, the fact of any person being a Brāhmaṇa is extremely difficult to ascertain, on account of the *failings of the woman.*

But even in the case of the woman's failings, if the son always belonged to the mother or to her master, the caste of these two being always well-known, there would be no difficulty in ascertaining the caste of the son ; the caste of the Parents also being ascertained by that of the grand-parents, and so on and on, the caste of all the ancestors from the very beginning of time, could be easily ascertained. But we find such declarations in the *Smṛtis* as—"The mother is only a leathern bag, the son belongs to the father" ; and as in the case of the woman having been led astray, it is not easily ascertained who the actual "father" is,—and it being quite possible for him to belong to a caste other than that of the woman,—the offspring, in this case, would be one of an uncertain, or even a mixed caste. In the Veda too, we read—"one should carefully guard this thread (of caste),"—which shows that the caste is liable to be lost ; and as such this passage could be explicable only if the caste of the offspring be accepted to be regulated by that of the *man.* Because if the caste were not liable to such changes, it would remain intact, even when not guarded ; and as such there would be no use of the Vedic Injunction just quoted.

Thus we find that there is an occasion, or use, for the said Praise (of the recounting of one's *Pravaras*) ; the meaning of the Praise being that a recounting of the *Pravaras* or Ancestors of universally recognised Brāhmanahood shows that the person so recounting is a descendant of such great Brāhmaṇas ; and thereby he himself comes to be recognised as a true Brahmaṇa.

Sūtra (14). There is a desire for present comfort.

[This *Sūtra* meets the fifth objection urged in *Sūtra* (2).]

That which appears at the present time is spoken of as "*ākālika*" ; and certainly that which does not take much time to appear is what is desired by all men. And hence in the making of the sacrificial House, the *making of windows* is particularly eulogised; because the windows serve the immediately useful purpose of allowing an easy exit for the smoke, and thereby remove one great cause of discomfort to the persons connected with the performance of the sacrifice. Whereas the final Result—Heaven, &c.—that would follow from the sacrifice, can appear only after the lapse of some time.

And hence the meaning of the *Arthavāda*—"who knows whether there is a Heaven, &c."—is that, *who knows now whether the great result will follow from the sacrifice?*—because, the means of knowing that the result will come lies in the scriptures; while we know from direct sense-perception that the letting out of smoke brings immediate relief; and hence it is in comparison with this latter fact, that the fact of the sacrifice leading to Heaven has been spoken as "unknown" (or doubtful),—a process which only tends to eulogise the *making of windows*.

The form "*ākālika*" (signifying that which has its beginning and end at the same time) is in accordance with Pāṇini's *Sūtra* "*ākālikadadyantavacanē*" [V—i—114].

Some people read "*Akālika*"; and in that case the word means *that which does not take time in its appearance*. The word "*kāla*"=remoteness of time: "*kālika*"=that which appears at a remote point of time (*kāla* + *thañ*); and hence that which is not so is "*akālika*."

Sūtra (15). It is a praising of the knowledge.

[This *Sūtra* meets the objections urged in *Sūtra* (3).]

The *Arthavādas*—"His face shines," and "His children become wealthy"—appearing in connection with the passages enjoining *study*, they cannot be taken as laying down the results of an Action; they must be taken simply as descriptions of the ordinarily perceived facts of *the face becoming beautiful* and the *person obtaining horses*.

For the beauty of the face, there is not only one standard. Such peculiarities as the symmetry of form, the general pleasing properties, and the peculiar loveliness of sheen, pertain to the faces of woman; while in the case of learned persons, it is when they are found to be making excellent declarations, in keeping with good form and reason, that their face is said to be "beautiful." And hence, in this case, the word "shines or becomes beautiful" need not be taken in an indirect sense, the direct meaning being quite compatible with the fact of the passage being *a praise of the learned person*.

And as for the declaration that "his children become weathly,"—the *wealth* referred to may be the wealth of Brahmic glory; and though in this case the word would be taken in a figurative sense, yet that could not militate against the fact of the passage being taken as *a praise of the learned.*

Sūtra (16). The mention of 'all' refers only to that which the agent is entitled to.

[The *Sūtra* meets the objections urged in *Sūtra* (4)].

The *Arthavāda*—that by the *Pūrṇāhuti one obtains all that he desires*—referring to a particular action in connection with the preparation of the fire, it cannot be taken as laying down certain results. But it can be taken as a praise of the *Pūrṇāhuti*,—the substratum of truth in this Praise being found in the fact of the character of the *consequence* being attributed to the *means;* that is to say, the meaning of the sentence—" He obtains all that he desires "—is that *he obtains the fire in all its forms, these being the general means of the performance of all actions bringing about all desirable results.*

And the *Sūtra* may be explained in the following manner: Inasmuch as the person has duly laid the Fire, he is entitled to the performance of all actions, which are the means of obtaining all that is desired; and it is with a view to eulogise this fact of his being entitled to the performance of all actions, that the passage in question has figuratively used the word 'all' with reference to the *actual obtaining* (of the results that would follow from all the actions, to the performance of all of which the person offering the *Pūrṇāhuti* becomes entitled).

The following objection may here be raised: "There are certain "results, such as the reaching of the *Ākāça* and the obtaining of celestial "damsels, which are absolute impossibilities; and these would also be "included in the category of 'all that is desired.' But certainly, for these, "it is not possible to be described as actually coming about, even figura-"tively, through the means, in the shape of any action laid down in the "Veda. (That is to say, in the case of the results that are laid down as "following from certain sacrifices enjoined by the Veda, it is possible to "explain the word 'all' referring to them, as referring to the Actions "bringing about these results, to which the person becomes entitled; on the "other hand, in the case of the said impossible results, which are also "included in 'all,' we cannot take the word 'all' as referring to the Actions "bringing about these results, &c., &c.; for the simple reason that there "are no Actions laid down as bringing about the said results)."

There being a great deal of truth in this objection, we offer another explanation of the *Sūtra:* In ordinary parlance we often come across such assertions as—"all the rice has been cooked"; and in this case we do not mean *all the rice* in the world, but only that which had been set apart for being cooked for a special purpose. In the same manner, when the Veda says: "one who offers the *Pūrṇāhuti*, obtains *all that he desires*," all that is meant is that the person becomes capable of obtaining all the results that follow from the Actions that are performed in connection with (consecrated) Fire. And as such there can be nothing incongruous in the said *Arthavāda.*

***Sūtra* (17). The result being accomplished by means of Actions, there would be a difference in the results in accordance with the measure, or extent of the Actions, as in the ordinary world.**

The assertion made in the *Sūtra* would be of use in the consideration of such sacrifices as the *Agnihotra* and the like, all of which lead to the same result, in the shape of the attainment of Heaven. All effects being similar to the cause, all the results that would follow from the mere *Pūrṇāhuti*, would be in small measures. And hence for one who would want to obtain the results in great measures, the Veda lays down other Actions—such as the *Agnihotra* and the like; and hence the Injunctions of the Actions cannot be said to be useless.

Against this the following objection is raised: "In the ordinary world "we actually perceive the results of such actions, as the *cultivating of fields*, "&c., to be in keeping with the causes; while in the case of the *Pūrṇāhuti*, "the matter resting altogether upon the authority of the scriptures, inas-"much as no distinct result is specially mentioned (as following from it), on "what basis can we make the said specific assumptions with regard to its "results? For as a matter of fact, there is no difference between the "Heaven as attained by means of the *Agnihotra*, and that reached by "the *Jyotishtoma;* nor in such a transcendental matter, can we have any "functioning of Inference; (and as such we cannot admit of any difference "between the result as obtained by means of the *Pūrṇāhuti* and the same "as acquired by means of certain other sacrifices)."

To this we make the following reply: The specification that we have assumed is based upon the strength of the Injunction itself. That is to say, if the result obtained by means of the simpler Action were exactly equal to that obtained by the more elaborate Action, then, in that case, the desired result having been obtained by means of the former, no person would ever be inclined to the more elaborate and difficult one; as says the proverb —'If one can find the honey in his own house, why should he go to the distant mountain for it?' And hence the Injunction (of the elaborate Action) would lose all its efficiency (which only lies in urging people to Action). But as a matter of fact, the efficiency of the Injunction can never be set aside; and as such the very Injunction of the elaborate Action points to the fact of its results being greater than that of the simpler Action,—as is explained under the *Sūtra* I—iv—30. Consequently as the assumption of the particular result of the *Viçvajit* sacrifice is accepted as authoritative, so also is the differentiation of the measure or quality of the result (following from the *Pūrṇāhuti* as differing from the same as obtained by means of other Actions).

And when of two actions, one is greater than the other, even though no difference in their results is directly mentioned, yet there must always be a differentiation of the extent of the results, based upon their respective positions. That is to say, in a case where the subsidiaries are mentioned in the same order as the Primary, that which is mentioned first is performed with the first Primary, and so on; and exactly in the same manner, in the case of Actions, when the smaller Action is performed, the result that appears in its connection is always of the same character (*i.e.*, small); and so on with the great Action, it is only a great result that appears; and thus we find the results differentiated on the ground of their respective positions.

We also meet with direct scriptural declarations that support such differentiation. For instance, with reference to the *Cāturmāsga Homa*, we have the following *Arthavāda* with regard to its result: "When one performs the *Agnihotra*, he obtains a result ten times that of the household sacrifice, in a single night . . . . By the due performance of the smaller *Agnihotra* for ten years, the person obtains the result equal to that of a single performance of the *Darça—Pūrṇamāsa*"; and this clearly shows that the smallness or greatness of the Action makes the result also small or great respectively.

Sūtra (18). What has been said above applies to the last two (_Sūtras_ of the _Pūrvapaksha_).

Just as the deprecation of Speech and Mind have been shown to signify the praise of gold, so also the prohibition of the *laying of the Fire on the bare ground* would, in accordance with the *Sūtra* X—viii—7, mean the praise of the placing of a plate of gold on the ground, and not a mere prohibition. And the prohibition of the *laying in the sky* or in the *Heaven* may be taken as the statement of a bare fact, laid down with a view to support the prohibition of the *bare ground.* The meaning of the passage would thus be that—'just as the laying of the fire is known to be impossible in the Sky or in Heaven, so also is it on the bare ground without a plate of gold,'—this being the praise of the use of the golden plate.

As for the mention of non-eternal things in the Veda, this has already been explained under *Sūtra* I—i—31.

The use of this discussion lies in the consideration of the *Rātrisatra* sacrifice, in connection with which the *Pūrvapaksha* is that the result of this sacrifice is the attainment of Heaven, while the orthodox view (*Siddhānta*) is that its real result is that which is mentioned in the *Arthavāda* passage relating to it.

ADHIKARAṆA (2).

[*Treating of the Arthavāda passages that have the form of Injunctions.*]

***Sūtra* (19). "It would be an Injunction, as laying down something not known before; because a mere description would be useless."**

Those *Arthavādas* that contained mere descriptions of facts having been explained above, we now proceed to consider those that appear in the form of Injunctions.

And with regard to these, the following are the grounds of doubt: In the former *Adhikaraṇa* it has been shown that as the *Arthavādas* serve no purpose directly by themselves, they have to be taken in the indirect sense of Praise. But in that case, even the Praise would be as good as useless. As for the factor of Injunction, however, it cannot be got at from any other source; while it has been already shown above that Persuasion (which is the avowed object of *Arthavādas*) can be got at through the indications of the Injunctions themselves. And again, in all cases, the Injunction is the primary, and the Praise the secondary, factor; consequently, when a certain assertion can be taken as related to the primary factor, it must be taken as such (and not as related to the secondary); and it is only when the indication of the Injunction has been fully accomplished that there can be any use for the *Arthavāda*. And it is while the Injunction is being comprehended, that all the factors of the *Bhāvanā* present themselves; specially so the factor of the Result, as it is the first and the most important factor (in the *Bhāvanā*, and as such the first to be comprehended, in the indication of the Injunction). It is with a view to these facts that the *Pūrvapaksha* in the *Sūtra* speaks of its *laying down something not known before;* and hence it is in comparison with this that it declares the mere expression of Praise to be useless.

At the very outset, of the discussion, however, the following objection is raised against the *Adhikaraṇa* as a whole: "We have a consideration of "such Injunctions and *Arthavādas* of Results, later on, under the *Sūtras* "IV—ii—1 *et seq;* and as such it is not proper to introduce the same dis- "cussion, in this place."

1. To this, some people make the following reply: 'As the discussion that is repeated in the Fourth *Adhyāya* is introduced here for the first time, the above objection should be raised with reference to that *Adhyāya* and not to this.'

This may be true enough; but if by postponing the discussion till the Fourth *Adhyāya*, we can procure a better reply to the objections against *Arthavādas*, it is only right that we should seek for it there. Inasmuch as, however, it was equally reasonable for that same reply to have been given on the present occasion, there could not be much harm in its being put forward here.

2. Others reply to the said objection as follows: It is only the denial of the fact of the passage cited being an Injunction of Result that is explained in the Fourth *Adhyāya*, whereas in the present *Adhikaraṇa*, it is the character of the *Arthavāda* that is denied (in the *Pūrvapaksha*); because the clause—*it would be an Arthavāda* (in the *Sūtra* IV—iii—1)—must be taken as denying the fact of its being an Injunction.

But this explanation is not right; because those *Arthavāda* passages, that would be denied (in the Fourth *Adhyāya*) the character of Injunctions, and would thereby become open to the charge of uselessness, have already been shown, in the foregoing *Adhikaraṇa*, to serve the distinctly useful purpose of *praising;* as has been shown with regard to the sentence—"His face becomes beautiful, &c."

3. Some people meet the aforesaid objection thus: It is only right that sentences like '*Vāyu* is the eftest deity' should be taken as Praise; but the case of such sentences as the one cited in the present instance is different; and though the present *Adhikaraṇa* serves to make it a mere Praise, denying it the character of an Injunction,—yet there is something left to be done; and it is this: just as the character of Injunction is denied to the said passage, so also can the character of Praise be denied to it, as the case of the present passage is not similar to that of the former passage; and hence it is absolutely necessary that we should accept it as an Injunction, so that any dissimilarity to passages appearing at a different time would not affect its position; and it is this latter point that is very rightly raised in the Fourth *Adhyāya*.

But even this explanation is not quite satisfactory; because even though the collective argument, that there is a clear disagreement with the Veda, may be a new one, and as such, in this much, there may be no repetition, yet the bodies of the *Adhikaraṇas* remain the same. As for the 'disagreement' (or dissimilarity), too, there is none of these that has not been met and explained under *Sūtra* I—ii—10; and hence these very arguments could be brought forward again, whenever any such disagreement would be put forward against any *Arthavāda* passage.

4. With a view to all this, some people offer the following explanation: The present *Adhikaraṇa*, in its *Pūrvapaksha*, speaks of "Injunctions" in general, without any specifications; while in the Fourth *Adhyāya*, we have the expression "Declaration of the Result" ('*Phalaçrutiḥ*'); and hence the passages considered in the present *Adhikaraṇa* are such of the *Arthavādas* as have the form of the Injunction of *all* such factors as the Substance, Property, Action and the like; while those treated of in the Fourth *Adhyāya* are only those that have the form of the Injunction of the *Result* only. For instance, *Sūtras* 23 and 24 of this *Pāda*, are found to refer to such instances as—"The Horse has its origin in the water, and the Cane also has its origin in the water," and the like (which treat of the mere forms, &c., of Substances); and if the present *Adhikaraṇa* also referred only to such *Arthavādas* as have the form of an Injunction of Result, the citing of the said passage would be entirely irrelevant.

But though it may be so, yet in that case the subject matter of the *Adhikaraṇa* in the Fourth *Adhyāya* would be only a particular phase of that of the present *Adhikaraṇa*; and so would be included in it; and as such, the repetition would remain unexplained. Consequently some people disregard the examples cited in the *Bhāshya* and set about citing other instances, with the restriction that under the present *Adhikaraṇa* they cite only those *Arthavādas* that have the forms of the Injunctions of the Substance, &c., while under that in the Fourth *Adhyāya* they cite those that have the form of the Injunction of Results.

But upon this, we have to make the following observations: Is it absolutely necessary to have two *Adhikaraṇas* that we should put this restriction upon the examples to be cited? Then again, as a matter of fact, a mere difference in the examples cited does not make the *Adhikaraṇas* necessarily distinct; because in that case, there would be no repetition in a case where certain discussions, having been carried on with regard to the sacrificial post as made of the *Khadira* wood, should be repeated again with the sole difference that in the latter case the post as made of the *Udumbara* wood would be cited as the instance. As a matter of fact, the subject matter of *Adhikaraṇas* being, not any particular examples, but certain rules (and arguments in support of the rules), it is only when there is a difference in the *rules* treated of in the two *Adhikaraṇas* that these can be accepted as distinct. And as for the *Arthavādas* having the form of the Injunctions of Substances, all of these too are not considered under the present *Adhikaraṇa*,—some of these being considered under *Sūtra* I—iv—23, some under *Sūtras* III—iv—1, *et seq*; some in the shape of '*Parakṛta*' and '*Purākalpa*' under *Adhyāya* VI, some under IX—ii—29, and others, having the form of the Injunctions of the *Jartila* and the *Gavīdhuk*, in *Adhyāya* X. And hence what we should say in reply to the aforesaid objection is that such repetition is not very objectionable.

Or, we may justify the two *Adhikaraṇas* on the following four grounds :—

1. One and the same rule has one part of it discussed under the present *Adhikaraṇa*, and another part in that of *Adhyāya* IV.

2. The subject-matter of the the two *Adhikaraṇas* may also be explained to be entirely different. What is done under the present *Adhikaraṇa* is that all *Arthavāda* passages having the form of Injunctions are shown to be *Arthavādas*, and not real Injunctions. While under the *Adhikaraṇa* in *Adhyāya* IV, the purport of the *Pūrvapaksha* is this : "When an Injunction has "been pointed out by the *Arthavāda*, it stands in need of a certain result "(for the sake of which it would lay down an Action) ; even though the "result that appears in the *Arthavāda* is mentioned with another osten-"sible purpose (that of Praising), yet this result is found to be related to "it more closely than any other declarations of the procedure of sacrifices ; "and when such relationship has been once ascertained, a specification "of the relationship becomes a compartively easy matter. Otherwise we "would have to assume the Relationship itself as well as its specific form ; "and hence we conclude that just as the Injunction of the *Rātrisatra* "sacrifice is one that enjoins the particular result—the obtaining of *fame*,—"so too, the passage speaking of the '*Juhū* made up of leaves' cannot but "be taken as an Injunction of the particular result—*the not hearing of any* "*evil report with reference to one's self.*" And the *Siddhānta* arrived at is that when it is possible for the passage to be taken in the light of another purpose (*i.e.*, of Praising), it is not right to attribute to it two purposes (that of *enjoining the Result*, and *Praising*) ; and as such the passage in question must be taken as a pure *Arthavāda*.

The same process may be employed in differentating the present *Adhikaraṇa* from those dealing with *Nivita*, *&c.* (III—iv—1 *et seq*). Or, these latter may be taken as consisting of some considerations and argumentations with reference to certain supposed objections and questions based upon the *Pūrvapaksha* of the *Audumbara-Adhikaraṇa* (the present one) ; as in these a question is raised as to whether the *Arthavāda*, that is accepted to be an Injunction, refers to the Agent or to the Sacrifice ; and then the conclusion arrived at is that it is a pure *Arthavāda*. So also in the case of the *Adhikaraṇas* on *Parakṛti and Purākalpa* (as explained in *Adhyāya* VI), a fresh question is raised as to whether the Action, (the eating of *māsha f.i.*) that is mentioned in the Veda as having been done by a great man of old, is to be done only by the descendants of that great man, or by all men (and it is this extra question that is treated of in the *Adhikaraṇa* in *Adhyāya* VI). The discussions with regard to "*Ūha*" and "*Bādha*," as contained in *Adhyāyas* IX and X, are also of a similar character (*i.e.*, dealing with extra questions). And as for the *Sūtra* I.—iv—23, it merely points out the several grounds for accepting a Word in its secondary or indirect signification. And as such in none of these do we find any useless repetition.

3. Or, the difference between this *Adhikaraṇa* and that in *Adhyāya* IV may be explained on the ground that the present *Adhikaraṇa* treats of only such passages as have the form of the Injunctions of Results, in which the factor that expresses the *Praise* is distinct from that which mentions the *Result;* as for instance, the passage cited in the *Bhāshya*. The sentence, 'The *udumbara* is powerful and so also are the animals,' which signifies *Praise*, is distinct from the sentence 'For the increase of power' (appearing at the close of the passage) which points out the *Result* (that follows when the sacrificial post is made of the *Udumbara* wood); while in the Fourth *Adhyāya*, the discussion is with reference to those cases, in which the same sentence may be taken either as *Praise* or as a mention of the *Result.*

4. Or, lastly, the difference between the two *Adhikaraṇas* may be explained thus: The first *Sūtra* of the *Adhikaraṇa* in the Fourth *Adhyāya* [IV—iii—1] lays down the fact of the passage *being for another's purpose* (*parārthatvāt*) as the reason for the conclusion arrived at; and as it is only a well-known reason that can be brought forward in all discussions, the passages that can serve as instances for this *Adhikaraṇa* are only those that are well-known to be *for another's purpose*,—*e.g.*, the passage "one whose *Juhū* is made entirely of leaves, &c." In this case it is necessary that the fact of *being made of leaves* should be distinctly mentioned with reference to the *Juhū;* as the former is incapable by itself of having any independent relation with the result. It is a general rule that whenever a certain property (or qualification) is laid down, with special reference to a particular result, it stands in need of a proper receptacle (or substratum) for itself; we cannot get hold of any such receptacle, apart from the context (in which the said passage occurs). And hence, if the passage—"one whose *Juhū* is made of leaves never hears any evil spoken of himself"—be taken to imply the injunction—that *one should think of obtaining the said result by means of the particular property of leafiness*,—the question naturally arises: *wherein is this property to exist* (as the mere abstract property by itself can be of no use)? What is the object (which, having the property of *leafiness*, would accomplish the said result)? It cannot be the *Juhū;* (1) because that would lead to a split in the sentence; (2) and until the Action has been found (in which the *Juhū* is to be used) the *Juhū* itself is not an accomplished (fully comprehended) object (and as such cannot be taken as bringing about any results); nor is there any authority (in the sentence itself) for connecting the *Juhū* with any action.

And thus (not having all the necessary factors fulfilled, if we accept the aforesaid construction or explanation of the sentence) we are forced to have recourse to another explanation (or construction). We find that the said sentence occurs in the same context as the sentence—"one pours the libations by means of the *Juhū*"; and when we come across this sentence, it becomes necessary for us to know the kind of the *Juhū* that is to be employed; but the sentence itself does not afford us any information on this head; and this want of information is found to continue until the mention of the fact of its *being made of leaves*; and as until this information is obtained, the use of the former sentence ("Pours libations by means of the *Juhū*") is not fully comprehended, the latter sentence (declaring the fact of the *Juhū* being made of leaves) comes to be recognised as subsidiary to the former (declaring the fact of the libations being poured by means of the *Juhū* made of leaves). Thus then, all the information that is wanted in connection with the *Juhū* having been obtained in this very sentence, there is no reason for the assumption of a result. And as such it is only proper that the sentence should be taken as an *Arthavāda*. (Such is the upshot of the *Adhikaraṇa* in Adh. IV).

In the present *Adhikaraṇa*, on the other hand, we have for our example, the declaration of the fact of the sacrificial post being made of the *Udumbara* wood, which is met with in the context treating of the animal to be sacrificed at the subsidiary sacrifice; and the fact of this declaration *being for another's purpose* is not fully recognised; and as such this could not form the subject of the *Adhikaraṇa* in the Fourth *Adhyāya*. Specially because, in the present case, unless the *post* has been already recognised (from other sources), it is not possible to have any declaration of its character; and the recognition of the *post* is accepted as fulfilled by means of the sentence treating of the Primary Sacrifice, which speaks of the post as made of the *Khadira* wood; and as such all the information (even that of kind or material), that is wanted with regard to the *post*, having been obtained by means of this passage itself, there is no use for any injunction of another material (the *Udumbara* wood) for it; and consequently the sentence (speaking of the post as being made of the *Udumbara* wood) is taken (by the *Pūrvapaksha*) as only an injunction of the Result (*attainment of power*). As for the information with regard to the substratum of the property of *being made of Udumbara wood*, this too is supplied by the mention of the "post," in the sentence enjoining the Primary Sacrifice; and as such this too does not affect the former conclusion. Thus then, we find that, prior to the ascertainment of the sentence being for another's purpose, it is absolutely necessary to connect the action therein spoken of with a certain definite result,—this connection being ascertained by means of other arguments (than those based upon the fact of a sentence being for another's purpose, as done in Adh. IV).

And as such the introduction of this present *Adhikaraṇa* becomes necessary.

There is yet another theory with regard to these two *Adhikaraṇas:* Both the sentences—the one dealing with the fact of the post being made of the *Udumbara* wood, as well as that speaking of the *Juhū* being made of leaves—can serve as examples, in both *Adhikaraṇas* (the present as well as the one in Adh. IV). And inasmuch as two different factors of the *Bhāvanā* are treated of in the two *Adhikaraṇas,* they cannot be said to be mere repetitions of one another. Both of them are equally capable of being connected with certain means and consequences, only when they are put forward in their full efficiency, and not otherwise. And in the *Adhikaraṇa* in Adh. IV, the discussion is based solely upon the factor of "consequences," and that of the "means" is either purposely disregarded or taken for granted; and the discussion then turns mainly upon the following question:—Is the *Result* capable of being rightly pointed out by means of words that speak of it as being accomplished at the present time, without any mention of the word "*Kāma*"? While in the present *Adhikaraṇa* the discussion is with regard to the factor of the "means," that of the "consequences" being either disregarded or taken for granted; and the discussion turns upon the following question:—In the absence of any Injunctive affix, is it possible for certain Substances, Properties or Actions to be laid down as the means of obtaining definite results? Whatever may be pointed out in a certain form, it stands in need of the cognition of a certain definite co-relative, and comes to be related with such a one, as expressed by another word. And hence when a certain sentence has been recognised as pointing out the Consequences, the rest is taken to indicate the Means; and *vice versâ;* thus both factors being ascertained in their true forms. Consequently, the factor of the "Means" that is considered under the present *Adhikaraṇa,* comes to be connected with the factor of the "Consequence"; and it is this connection as here indicated that is accepted, in Adh. IV, as a well-established fact, and serves as the reason for the conclusion there arrived at. Conversely, the indication of the factor of the "Means," that we have in Adh. IV, is here accepted as a well-established fact, and is only slightly touched upon. And thus the two *Adhikaraṇas* are not mere repetitions.

Objection: "But in that case, the present would be a discussion with regard to the indication of the Injunction,—and as such could not have any connection with the *Adhikaraṇa* on *Arthavāda.*"

Reply: This does not affect the case; because the signification of the Injunction is got at through the *Arthavāda.* That is to say, if the Action spoken of were, in the very first instance, comprehended as being *enjoined,* then the passage could not have the character of the *Arthavāda;* but as it is, it is only through the Praise (as signified by the passage) that we comprehend the Action as being enjoined; and as such the character of the *Arthavāda* is not denied to the passage.

The sense of the *PŪRVAPAKSHA* embodied in the *Sūtra* is this: "That which is declared in close proximity to the Result, cannot but be re-"cognised as the Means, even though it is not expressly laid down as such; "because on hearing of the Result, our only desire is to know the Means. "And hence, just as in the case of the mention of the Result, we at once "comprehend the Sacrifice to be the means, on account of the expression "'*Yāgeña*' ('by means of sacrifice') directly presenting itself to our mind; "so in the same manner, the mention of the Result, in the case of the "passage in question, would at once bring to our mind, the expression "'*Audumbarēna*' ('by means of the post made of the *Udumbara* wood'). "For, what could a direct Injunction do? It could only prompt the agent "to action. And as this prompting is done by the mere mention of the "Result, what would be the use of a distinct direct Injunction? Or, the "passage may be taken as merely pointing out the connection of a certain "Result with that which has been enjoined in a passage laying down the "procedure of a certain Action. Or, the Injunction may be taken as "expressed by the fifth Mood, *Lēt*. And it has also been already explained "that the Injunction may, in certain cases, form only a part of the "*Arthavāda*.

"Hence we conclude that the Dative ending in '*Avarudhyai*' denotes "*purpose;* and as such the Result is pointed out (by means of this affix) "even more clearly than it would have been by the word '*kāma*' itself; "and hence it is with reference to this Result that the passage enjoins the "*post* to be made of the *Udumbara* wood. (It is in this way alone that the "passage can be interpreted as an Injunction). It can never be an Injunc-"tion *of the Result;* because it is shown under II—i—1 *et seq* that there can "never be an Injunction of the Result. As for the sentence—'The *Udum-*"*bara* is power'—it is a distinct Praise of the particular wood; and there "is nothing incongruous in this. Consequently, inasmuch as it is possible for "the passage as a whole to be taken primarily, or directly, as an Injunction, "it is not right to take it in its indirect sense—making it indicative of "mere Praise."

Sūtra (20). "*Obj:* 'As in ordinary parlance, so here also.'

"Against the above we may have the following arguments: 'In ordi-"nary experience, we find that people never make use of the slightest expres-

"sion, without some purpose. As for instance, in ordinary parlance we "meet with such assertions as: *This cow should be brought, it gives a "large quantity of milk, &c., &c.* And here the former sentence—*The cow "should be brought*—laying down something to be done, the latter sentence "is taken as a praise of the cow, which lends more force to the former "direction, and thereby prompts the person concerned to speedy action. And "the mention of the fact of the cow giving much milk is never taken as "the injunction of any transcendental result; as it is a directly perceptible "fact in itself; and hence it cannot but be taken as the praise of the cow. "The same reasoning can be employed in the case of Vedic passages also. "And as for having recourse to indirect indication, as no direct assertion "is possible, there can be no objection to it.'

***Sūtra* (21). "*Reply:* Not so; because it is known beforehand."**

"To the last *Sūtra*, we make the following reply: The instance that "you cite does not apply to the present case. Because a Praise depends "upon certain conceptions derived from other means of knowledge; and as "the operation of such other means is possible with regard to the facts of "ordinary experience, we can accept such ordinary assertions in the sense "of *Praise*. In the Veda, on the other hand, as we have descriptions of facts "not otherwise known, people would have no faith in them; as even in "ordinary parlance, people do not believe a person who describes what is "absolutely unknown.

"Says the *Bhāshya*: *Pūrvavacanādiva;* and this may mean that "people do not have any confidence in descriptions of unknown facts, "exactly as they have none in the Injunctions of facts already known; or "it may be taken as a simile of contraries, the meaning in that case "being that in the descriptions of unknown facts people do not have the "confidence that they have in those of well-known facts.

"And then again, the mere mention of the fact of the cow giving much "milk does not serve to persuade the person; it is only when he "actually *sees* the cow giving much milk, that he is persuaded to take it.

"In the Veda too, finding the *Arthavāda* to be false, the person would "begin to suspect the authenticity of the Injunction connected with it; "and as such, he would not undertake the Action. And one, who would "neglect the Injunction and seek for the *Arthavāda*, would be taken as an "unbeliever of Injunctions. And if one has no confidence in Injunctions, "wherefore should he have any in the concomitant *Arthavāda?*

"Then again, in the Veda, we find a disagreement from the actual facts "of experience; as for instance, the passage in question praises the action "as fulfilling a *reservation of power* at the present time; while no such "reservation is perceptible; and thus this declaration of the Veda would "be exactly similar (in falsity) to the description of a cow as giving much "milk, when as a matter of fact it gave no milk at all.

"As a matter of fact, the *Udumbara* is not found to have the character "of (strength-giving) food, which, for this reason, cannot rightly serve as "the Predicate of the Minor Premiss; nor is it found to be invariably con- "comitant with the appearance of power; and hence it cannot serve as the "middle term (the subject of the Major Premiss). *That whatever is food* "*is also sacrificial post* is a fact recognised, neither in the Veda nor in "ordinary experience; and as such the assertion is entirely absurd.

"And thus, as by making it signify mere *praise*, we find it to be "incompatible (with facts of ordinary experience), it is much more "reasonable to take it as an Injunction than as a Praise, which stands in "need of the corroboration of experience."

In reply to the above we have the following:—

SIDDHĀNTA.

***Sūtra* (22). The fact of its being indirectly implied by the sentence has alreay been explained.**

The sentence—'the *Udumbara* is strength'—is to be taken together with the clause—'for the increase of strength'; because it embodies a justification of this latter; and it is not a distinct Praise apart by itself. Because the mere assertion of the *Udumbara being food* does not serve to point out the fact of its being something excellently desirable for man; while there is no doubt that the assertion—'for the increase of strength'——serves to make the particular action specially attractive to him; and hence it is only right that the other sentence—'*Udumbara* is food'—should be taken as justifying and supporting the said attraction (or persuasion). Therefore the whole passage may be taken either as pointing out a definite result as following from the Action in question, or as persuading the agent to that course of Action.

And even if there were an Injunctive word, a passage like the one in question could not but be taken as an *Arthavāda;* and it is all the more so, when the verb in the passage is only in the Present Tense, which has the sole purpose of accomplishing the Injunction. And when we find the context distinctly pointing to a definite purpose in the shape of the effect that it has towards the fulfilment of the sacrifice,—what could be our reason for assuming a separate *result,* for the expression of which we have no direct word? Nor can it be urged that, that which is indicated by the Context is always set aside by that indicated by the Sentence itself. Because in the case in question there is no contradiction of the one by the other. That is to say, it is only when two contradictory facts are indicated both by the Context and the Sentence, with reference to one and the same object, that there can be any rejection of the one by the other. But in the passage in question, we have the Context pointing to the injunction of the *post* being made of the *Udumbara* wood; and this Injunction takes within itself the persuasion expressed by the sentence 'the *Udumbara* is strength'; and certainly, there can be no contradiction of the Context, which, in this case, is found to indicate the Injunction of the *Udumbara*, as qualified by the said persuasion. Thus then, there being nothing to indicate any Injunction of the Result, there is no possibility of the Context being set aside; and as such we cannot very well disregard the signification of the said Context.

(Even if the whole passage be taken as laying down a Result) the persuasion, which is held to be indirectly implied by the sentence, could never be accepted as being assumed through the implications of the Injunction itself. Because in other cases it might be possible for the Injunction to imply a persuasion; but in the case in question, the Injunction itself is extremely weak (not being mentioned by any directly expressive Injunctive affix, &c.); and as such, what could it do with the persuasion?

Then again, that which has once been made to serve the purpose of *praising* (a certain action) can never rightly be accepted as having any action towards the pointing out of any results, like the acquiring of fame (said to follow from the *Juhū* of leaves). In the case of the *Rātrisatra*, we have recourse to a highly complicated assumption, because there is no other way out of the difficulty; while in the case in question, we have already shown that a particular purpose (served by the Action in question) is distinctly pointed out by the Context.

The particular species (*Udumbara*) is, by its very nature, known as a part of the more extensive class 'Wood'; and it can never be taken as pointing to any Result. The word 'post' (*Yūpa*) also denotes the piece of wood as affected by the sacrificial performance; and as such it can be taken as only indicating the post as it presents itself. And thus all the words being found to serve totally extraneous purposes, the sentence (containing them) cannot but be taken as an *Arthavāda*.

It has been urged above that, inasmuch as no other wood—*Khadira*, *&c.*,—would be available, the 'post' does not stand in need of any mention of the special class of wood (the *Udumbara*). But this is not quite correct, because just as in the case of the *Çyēna* sacrifice, the distinct mention of *Reed* as the special kind of grass to be employed sets aside the possibility of the use of any other grass—*Kuça* and the like,—the use of which is indicated by the fact of their being employed in other sacrifices; so, in the same manner, in the case in question, the distinct mention of '*Udumbara*' would serve to set aside all other woods. Nor is there any means by which this setting aside could be avoided; specially as it is admitted, even when the making of the post of the *Udumbara* wood is taken as bringing about a definite result.

The only difference, however, between us is this: In your case, the *making of the post of the Udumbara wood* being an action *for the sake of the agent* (as bringing about a particular result), while the *Khadira*, &c., are for the sake of the sacrifice (which is helped by the post), the former would set aside the latter only indirectly, by the mere chance of their being related to the object (the post); whereas according to us, both being for the sake of the sacrifice itself, there would be a direct co-subjectivity between them, which makes the setting aside, of the one by the other, more natural.

And when a certain definite kind of wood has been laid down with a view to a certain result,—just as the *curd* is laid down as the material to be offered, with a view to obtain for the sacrificer efficient sense-organs,—there is no idea of the substratum of the Class (and for this also we cannot admit of any such results following). That is to say, it is the 'Animal sacrifice' that is the primary action concerned; but this is found incapable (of any relationship with the *Udumbara* wood); while the 'tethering of the animal,' is found to be capable of such relationship, through the post (to which the animal is tethered); but this 'tethering' together with the *post*, does not form the primary action. Nor can the relationship, being found useless with regard to the primary, be transferred to its subsidiaries; because it is only that which is laid down as helping the Primary that is held to be helpful to the subsidiaries; which is not the case here; as in the present case, we have a certain property (the *Udumbara-ness* of the post) forming part of the Primary, which stands in need of a substratum for itself; and though it has the Primary (Animal-sacrifice) in close proximity to it, yet, as this is not found capable of serving as the required substratum, we cannot but construe the Injunction in an altogether different manner; and we can never rightly transfer the property downwards (to the subsidiaries).

Nor is the sentence itself found capable of affording the required substrate; because if it be construed in a manner supplying this substratum, this would involve a syntactical split; because in that case the sentence would be declaring two relationships: (1) the relationship of the Property with the particular Result, and (2) that of the Property with its Substratum. And further, in that case, the property of 'being made of *Udumbara* wood' would have to be taken, in two different forms, at one time (*i.e.*, in the sentence 'The making of the post of *Udumbara* wood brings about such and such a result') as the Subject, and at the other (*i.e.*, in the sentence 'the post should be made of *Udumbara* wood') as the Predicate. Even if it be taken as the Predicate in both cases, then too, while being taken along with the *result*, it will have to be disjoined from the *post;* whereas when taken in connection with the *post*, it will have to be separated from the *result* (and thus too there would be a syntactical split).

As for the independent-spirited person who would take up the performance of certain actions, without any Injunctions, we can have nothing to say to him. The fact of any action bringing about a result desired by man is not recognised until an Injunction to this effect is met with; because prior to this, the sentence is wholly taken up by the laying down of the object to be accomplished, which, in this case, is the making of the post of the *Udumbara* wood.

It has been asserted that the connection of the Result would be laid down by the passage that would contain the necessary directions for the Action. But such a passage can have no reference to any result desired by man; as will be shown under the *Sūtra* '*asamyuktam prakaraṇāt*' [III—iii—11]. For if it does happen to be laid down by such a passage, it comes to be an action for the sake of the Action itself (and not for that of man).

As for the 'fifth *Lakāra*' (*Lēt*), as its form is similar to that of the Present Tense, its signification always remains doubtful; (and as such the verb in the passage cannot be taken as the Injunctive *Lēt*).

For these reasons, we conclude that the result, in the passage in question, is described only with a view to persuade the person to a certain course of action; specially because the verb describing it is found in the Present Tense; and also because we shall prove in the fourth *Adhyāya*, that, any passage, not distinctly containing the expression 'with the desire for such and such a result,' cannot be taken as actually laying down the real result of an Action. And as for the passages like the one in question being always taken as mere Praise, it is no use enquiring as to the truth or otherwise of the means spoken of in them; because they are meant to serve the sole purpose of bringing about a certain cognition; and also because they are in keeping with the descriptions of certain qualifications. But even if they must be taken as real *means*, they may be taken to be the means of fulfilling the pleasure or satisfaction of the persons concerned.

***Sūtra* (23). In some cases, such Injunctions would be useless; hence they must be taken as expressing Praise; and the same may be said with regard to all other passages similar to these.**

If the passages in question were Injunctions, then all the *Arthavāda* passages quoted before would also be Injunctions of Materials, Accessories or Actions; for instance, the sentence '*Vāyu* is the eftest deity' would mean that *one should make Vāyu the eftest deity ;* and the sentence 'The horse has its origin in water' would mean that *one should make the horse have its origin in water ;* and similarly we would have such injunctions as—'One should make the *Vētasa* or the *Avaka*, originate in water,' 'the water should be made peaceful,' 'the *Udumbara* should be made strong,' and so forth.

And though some of the *Arthavāda* passages are capable of being taken as Injunctions of Actions, yet the passages that we have been dealing with in the present *Pāda* can never be taken as such; because some of the descriptions—such as those of *Vāyu*, *Vētasa* and the like—are mere statements of facts in nature (and these cannot be made or brought about by man); and the *Udumbara*, &c., too, cannot be brought about by man, however much he might try (and hence there can never be any Injunctions for making these).

The *Bhāshya* proceeds to show what sort of *praise* the passage—('the horse proceeding from the water,' &c.)—expresses: *The connection of the horse with the water, which is pacifying, brings peace to the master of the sacrifice.*

The irrelevancy of this passage of the *Bhāshya* in the present connection has been explained away by some commentators by the flat denial of this sentence forming part of the *Bhāshya* text.

The irrelevancy referred to is this: The passage does not mention any connection of the pacifying character with either the Horse or the *Avaka*, the *Vētasa* alone being mentioned; while this latter does not appear in the above explanation of the Praise.

The true explanation of this, however, is the following: The *Avaka*, &c., have been cited as instances, only on account of their similarity to the *Vētasa;* and the said explanation does not assert any relationship between the *Horse* and the *Avaka ;* all that it does is to declare these to be related to the *water;* and as this fact alone does not indicate any Praise, there is a need of another *Arthavāda* passage; and this is pointed out, in the sentence—'the water is peaceful'; and it is this latter sentence that, having lost the character of an Injunction, expresses the excellent character of the *water*; and certain things, ordinarily well known to be connected with water (f.i., the *Vētasa*), come to be praised by this praise of the water only; while others (f.i., the Horse), come to be praised, through the declaration of their relationship with the water; and the meaning of the praise thus comes to be that—'being related to the water which is known to be peaceful, the Horse also comes to be known as quiet; and hence the sacrifice, connected with this Horse, pacifies or removes all the troubles of the Master of the sacrifice; which shows that the sacrifice is an excellent one.' In the same manner, the sacrifice that is offered to a swift Deity, brings about its results quickly; and if the sacrificial post is made of foodstuffs, the sacrificer obtains plenty of foodstuffs. Such being the explanations of the passages in question, we can say the same with regard to all other passages that may be found to be similar to these.

***Sūtra* (24). When a certain expression can be rightly taken in its own context, it is not right to transfer it elsewhere; specially as such an Injunction would have no use with regard to that particular sacrifice.**

The taking of such passages as Injunctions is also open to the following objection: In the case of the sentence—'That which is burnt becomes the property of the *Rākshasas*' (a sentence found in connection with the *Darça-Pūrṇamasa*)—if we take it exactly as it is, then it can only be taken as enjoining another Deity (the *Rākshasa*) for the cake that is burnt; and this would necessitate the removal (or transfer) of the Deity mentioned in the original Injunction (of the sacrifice).

[If the word '*Apakarsha*' be taken as *that which removes*, then the meaning would be that 'the newly enjoined Deity would remove the one mentioned in the original Injunction.']

This setting aside could be possible, on the ground of its being for a definite purpose,—as we have in the case of the *Abhyuditēshti*—, but only if there were no other way of explaining the sentence. When, however, it can be taken in a different manner, no such setting aside can be allowable.

Fighting shy of this argument some people might have recourse to a transposed construction of the sentence,—explaining it as 'that which is to be offered to the *Rākshasas* should be burnt'; but as the '*Rākshasa*' is not mentioned as a Deity in the present context, the *burning* of the cake will have to be transferred to another context, where the *Rākshasa* may have been laid down as the Deity; and this would militate against the direct declarations of that context. Nor is such contradiction of the context allowable, when there are means of avoiding it. Hence we must take the passage as an *Arthavāda*, which does not necessitate any such transference or removal.

***Sūtra* (25). If these be taken as Injunctions, there would be a syntactical split.**

In the passages in question, if, on account of the praise contained in the passages, the verb in the Present Tense were to be taken as being in the *Lēt* (the Vedic Injunctive), then, by the same fact, we would have to assume a particular result to follow from the Action laid down; and this would bring about a split of the sentence [for instance, the construction would be—(1) The post of the *Udumbara wood is excellent*, and (2) *this should be made for the obtaining of power*]. Hence we conclude that we cannot but take these passages as *Arthavādas*.

ADHIKARAṆA (3).

[*Treating of such Arthavāda passages as appear to contain reasons for the performance of certain actions*].

Sūtra (26). "They must be taken as putting forward reasons, because of usefulness and possibility."

As instances, we can have all the passages that appear—on account of the use of such words as '*hi*' and the like—to contain reasons, though as a matter of fact they do not contain them—(for instance, the passage 'Çūrpēna juhoti, *tēna hi annan kriyatē*).'

Some people object to this *Adhikaraṇa*; they argue thus:

"If the character of the reason be said to be *enjoined* by the passage, "then these come in the same category as those dealt with in the foregoing "*Adhikaraṇa*; if not, then the *character of the reason* that is spoken of here "must be taken in connection with the relationship of the *Çūrpa-homa*; and "as no such relationship can exist unless it is duly enjoined, for what could "the *reason* be brought forward? If however, the passage be taken only "as describing a fact in nature, then this would be in the same category as "the sentence speaking of *Vāyu* as the 'eftest deity.' Thus then, in "any case, there appears no reason for introducing the present discussion."

To this we make the following reply: As a matter of fact the passage in question does not lay down the fact of the latter sentence containing a reason for what has gone before; nor is it the mere description of a fact in nature: what it really does is only to assert by Apparent Inconsistency, a certain fact, which serves to set aside a certain doubt with regard to the performability of an Action which has been laid down (in the previous sentence) simply as a well-established duty to be performed; specially as all Reasoning pre-supposes a certain well-established fact (which, in this case, is the performability of the *Çūrpa-homa*). And some people hold that this statement of the Reason also serves the purposes of an *Arthavāda*, showing, as it does, why a person should perform it. Even when the sentence is taken as a pure *Arthavāda*, it contains within itself a statement of the Reason also; and hence the Injunction comes to be taken as referring to the *Homa* by the *Çūrpa* and all other articles whereby food is prepared (such as the *Darvī* and the like); and as such the latter sentence might be taken as bringing forward a Reason (as held by the *Pūrvapaksha*) as well as containing an *Arthavāda* (as held by the *Siddhānta*).

On the main question then, we have the following :—

PŪRVAPAKSHA.

"Says the Bhāshya: *The fact of the Cūrpa being a means of preparing the "food is brought forward as a Reason for performing the Homa with the Çūrpa.* "And though what is directly enjoined is the relationship (of the *Homa* "with the *Çūrpa*), yet the Reason that is brought forward for this *relation-"ship* could also refer to the *Homa*.

"An objection is raised in the *Bhāshya*: '*A case (like that of the* "*Çūrpa* and the *food*), *where the relation of cause and effect is not generally* "*recognised, cannot be rightly said to have been brought forward as a Reason*.'

"Some people explain this by pointing to the premiss that all Inference "must be one of cause and effect, as the *Bhāshya* declares later on in "connection with the sentence—'One should offer a *Homa* of curd for the "sake of one who wants to acquire a sense-organ.'

"But this is not correct; because even in cases where there is no relation "of cause and effect, as in the case of the asterisms of *Krttikā* and *Rohiṇī*, "following one another, we find that a perception of the former acts as "a reason (or means) for the cognition of the latter.

(1) "Therefore we must take the *Bhāshya* to mean only the relation-"ship of the *comprehended* and *the means of comprehension*, by the mention "of '*the relation of cause and effect*.' It may, however, be urged that— "'even the relationship of the *comprehended* and *the means of comprehension* "being cognisable only by means of an Inference, it could not be asserted "with reference to a fact not universally recognised.' True; but there "being another relationship prior to the general recognition of the fact, "all that is meant by the bringing forward of the said relationship of "*the comprehended* and *the means of comprehension* is simply to point out "the particular relationship upon which all further Inferences are based.

(2) "Or, the *Bhāshya* may be taken as referring to the *potentiality* "of things, the meaning of the objection in the *Bhāshya* being that we "admit the character of true Reason only in cases where, at the time of "comprehending an invariable concomitance between the two things con-"cerned, we actually perceive in them a *potentiality* consisting of that "causal relationship which consists of the relationship of the *comprehended* "and the *means of comprehension*.

(3) "Or again, the *Bhāshya* may be taken as only referring to the "specific instance cited,—the sense of the objection being that an invariable "concomitance between any two things, can be based upon many relations, "such as those of cause and effect, master and servant, or on mere association, and the like; and as none of the others are possible in the case of "the fact of the *Çūrpa* as the means of preparing food being asserted as the "reason for performing the particular *Homa*, we must accept it to be based "on the causal relation only; and inasmuch as such causal relationship "is not generally found to exist between them, the assertion that the latter "sentence puts forth a Reason for the *Homa* is untenable.

"In reply to the above objection, the *Bhāshya* says—*True it is, &c.* "And the meaning of this is this: It is true that in the ordinary course of "business, before a person puts forward a certain Reason, he always seeks "to base it upon a well-recognised relationship; but in the case of the Veda, "on account of the Apparent Inconsistency of the *mention of a Reason*, as "expressed by the use of such words as '*hi*' (*because*), and the like, we "assume the existence of another sentence expressing the relationship "(upon which the aforesaid causal relation could be based),—such a sentence, in the case in question, being that 'whatever is the means of "preparing food should be used in the offering of the *Homa*'; and in the "light of this sentence, the Reason (brought forward in the sentence 'because the food is prepared by its means') becomes quite relevant.

"The *Bhāshya* puts the question—*what special purpose would be served*, "*i.e.*, if the Reason should become relevant? The reply given is that the "use lies in the fact that it is only then that the *Homa* could be offered by "means of all things that are used in the preparation of food.

"The *Bhāshya* puts another question—'*why*'? And this question may "be taken as put by the *Siddhanti*; or it may mean—'How can the *Darvī* "&c., be the means of preparing the food'? The reply given is that—we "actually find these *of use* in the preparation of food; and it is this *usefulness* "alone that is mentioned in the *Sūtra* (by the word '*arthavattva*'). The "*Bhāshya* also adds—*we can prepare* the food by means of these also; and "this is what is meant by the word '*upapatti*' ('possibility') in the "*Sūtra*.

"Against this explanation an objection is raised—'It seems that, in "this way, the words (*arthavattva* and *upapatti*) are synonymous (and as "such both should not have been used).'

"But the mention of both words may be explained as pointing to "the capability of the same fact being expressed in two different ways: the "sense being that that which is *of some use* in an Action may, in a way, be "also spoken of as its *means*. Or, the word '*arthavattva*' may be taken as "pointing to that which is expressed by the instrumental case-ending; and "inasmuch as it is the fact of the food being prepared, *at the present time*, by "means of the *Çūrpa*, &c., that has been brought forward as the Reason "(which is not found to be applicable to the *Homa*, which is not found to "prepare any food at the time), the word '*upapatti*' may be taken as "pointing to the *possibility* of the food being prepared by means of the "*Homa*; and this is what is meant by the *Bhāshya*—'*the food can be pre-* "*pared by means of that also.*'

"Another objection is raised in the *Bhāshya*: 'The passage in question "distinctly says that the food *is prepared* by means of it; why then, should "you say *it can be prepared*'?

"The reply given to this is that it is absolutely impossible to speak "of the Present Tense (because the *Çūrpa* is not found to prepare the food "actually *at the time that the Homa is being offered*).

"Or, the *Bhāshya* may be taken as replying to a self-raised objection; "the sense in that case, would be this: If the passage be taken as "refering, not to the *Çūrpa*, but to the *Darvī*, &c., on the ground of these "latter not being the means of preparing the food *at the present time*,— "then, the same might be said with regard to the *Çūrpa* also; and the "passage would cease to be any Praise at all; hence just as the *Siddhānti* "would make the passage out to be a Praise, exactly in the same man- "ner could we also explain it as only laying down a reason for the "*Homa*.

"The *Bhāshya* sentence following this is '*Hētau ca Çrutiḥ*,' &c.; and "as this is quite irrelevant as it is, we must take it along with the closing "sentences of the *Bhāshya*.

"Says the *Bhāshya*—*there can be only an indirect indication of Praise*; "and this means that the sentence in question indicates the excellence of "the *Homa*, indirectly, through the fact of its bringing about a universally "desirable result in the shape of food.

"And in this case, the sentence—'*Çūrpēna hi annan kriyatē*'—is to "be taken as only describing a fact of nature, the general *preparation of* "*food* with reference to the particular object, *Çūrpa*.

"Or, the *Sūtra* may be construed in the following manner: If we take "the sentence as laying down a Reason, we have an '*arthavattva*'—*i.e.*, it "serves a much more useful purpose than if it were a mere *Arthavāda*;— "and even though the relationship between the *Çūrpa* and the *preparation* "*of food* is not quite recognised, yet we have its '*upapatti*' (proof "or possibility) based upon the assumed Vedic sentence referred to "above.

"For these reasons, we conclude that the sentence in question must be "taken as laying down a Reason *for the performance of the Homa by means* "*of the Çūrpa*."

In reply to the above we have the following:—

SIDDHANTA.

***Sūtra* (27). It is a Praise; because of its being preceded by verbal authority; while there is no Injunction of another.**

The Instrumental case-ending in the word '*Çūrpēṇa*' directly points to the performance of the *Homa* as to be done by the *Çūrpa;* and as such having the direct support of the Veda, it cannot be urged,—either as a mere acceptable alternative, or as an optional alternative, or as a companion alternative,—that the *Homa* is to be performed with the *Darvī*, &c., the instrumentality whereof is only pointed out by Inference. Because the *Homa* having all its requirements fulfilled by the *Çūrpa*, does not stand in need of any other thing; and as there is no direct Vedic text laying down the instrumentality of the *Darvī*, &c., the mere recognition of the instrumentality of the *Çūrpa* (as pointed out in the Vedic text) shuts the way of the inference of any Vedic texts (in support of the instrumentality of the *Darvī*, &c.) This is what is meant by the expression—*There is no Injunction of another*,—(*i.e.*, of the *Darvī*, &c.)

As for the pointing out of a reason (for the performance of the *Homa* in a certain way), this becomes accomplished by the Praise itself; and as such by taking the sentence as pointing out such a Reason only, we only court the necessity of having to assume unheard of instances.

Then again, the direct assertion of the *Çūrpa* (as the instrument to be employed) falling within the scope of the Injunction, being found to be distinct, and not having any other purpose to serve, it cannot be altogether neglected. Hence, there are only two ways of taking the expression—*because it prepares the food*:—(1) this expression having no direct connection with the Injunction 'this should be done,' we can take it as indirectly indicating the fact of the *Çūrpa* possessing an excellent quality; or (2) it may be taken as directly expressing this latter fact. Any way, the expression by itself is incapable of being taken as laying down a Reason in support of the Injunction; and hence it comes to be taken as mentioning the reason for the excellence which stands in need of the support of a Reason that happens to be mixed up with the force of the Injunction, and of which the object of the Injunction stands in need. The meaning of the said expression thus comes to be: *The Çūrpa is an excellent instrument, because it prepares the food.* Both of these explanations are capable of being supported by well-recognised instances, and as such do not necessitate the Inference of any unheard of Vedic texts. Because it is a universally recognised fact that, (1) that which is excellent deserves to be done, and (2) that, that which is a means of preparing the food is excellent.

The sentence—'*there is no Injunction of another*' may be explained in another way: According to you, all that is a means of preparing the food, will be the objects of Injunction; but *Darvī*, &c., are not the means of preparing the food; because it is the action, of *cooking* f.i., that is known to be the direct means of the preparation of the food. This introduces the next *Sūtra.*

***Sūtra* (28). *Obj.:* "Any praise of that which is useless is not allowable."**

Some people might argue—"If *cooking*, &c., are the means of preparing the food, the *Çūrpa* cannot be recognised as the means of its preparation; and as such there can be no such praise of it, as explained above." To this we make the following *reply*:—

***Sūtra* (29). *Reply:* But there is a use for it; inasmuch as it forms part of the Injunction; as even in the ordinary world.**

According to us, there is a distinct use which forms the object of the praise,—this use consisting in the fact of the *Çūrpa* being the means of the preparation of food. Inasmuch as it forms part of another sentence, the mention of such instrumentality is found only to serve the purpose of another (*i.e.*, the Injunction), and thereby has only a secondary position; and as such, it must be taken as thereby describing a certain fact, with reference to another object that forms the object of the Injunction. Such description again can be only of a fact that is well known; and consequently we find the very words (of the Vedic text) distinctly pointing to the conclusion that the sentence describes only such useful instrumentality of the *Çūrpa* as has been met with in ordinary experience; (and as such the instrumentality of the *Çūrpa* cannot be denied).

This also explains the use of the present tense (in '*Kriyatē*'); but even though the present tense has been used, yet it is an admitted fact that, whether something *is to be done* (in the future) or *has already been done* (in the past), whenever we have got to describe, or praise, such an object, we speak of it as *being done* ('*Kriyatē*'). As to why the present tense has been used in a Praise,—all that we can say is that it is due to the fact that men, as a rule, are more attracted to the present than either to the past or to the future; and as a matter of fact, it is only by recalling the fact of the effects, that a certain action brings about at the time that it is performed, that people are attracted to it, even at other times; consequently with a view to praising the *Çūrpa*, we have the sentence 'it *prepares* the food.'

Or, we may take the sentence as praising the *Çūrpa*, after having transferred the *present character* of the capability of preparing the food to the *preparation* itself (which would justify the use of the present tense in '*Kriyatē*'); because people are attracted more to what is actually manifested than to any latent capabilities; and as such the Praise could be duly effective only when describing a fact as actually manifested in the *present*, and not when merely pointing out a *capability*.

On the other hand, in your theory, inasmuch as you hold the sentence to contain the Injunction (of a Reason), there would be a distinct harm done by the non-comprehension of the *instrumentality* of the preparation of food and the *present* character, (with direct reference to the *Çūrpa*).

"Why so"?

Well, because, there can be an Injunction of only that which has not been got at by any other means; and hence in the case of an Injunction, the acceptance of anything apart from what is directly expressed by it is not allowable. This is what is meant by the *Bhāshya*:—*In the Injunction, there is no need of the meaning of any other words*, because it is only in the case of indirect indication, that there is a need of the help of the meanings of other words. And it would be necessary to assume the word in the present tense ('*Kriyatē*') to indicate the meaning of a word in the past ('*Akāri*'), and in the future ('*Kārishyatē*'), or that of a word denoting the *present character of the Capability* (such as '*Çakyatē*'); and it is only when the word '*Kriyatē*' could be taken in accordance with these assumptions, that the Instrumental case ending in '*Çūrpēna*' could be taken as denoting *direct instrumentality*. As a matter of fact, however, instances of such assumptions have never been met with; and as such they cannot be allowable.

If, again, the words be taken in their direct signification, then, it would not be possible for the Veda to enjoin anything as capable of being brought forward, while it would be pointing out either the present time or the chief Instrument. That is to say, the *Homa* is not capable of being performed either by the *Çūrpa, &c.*, while these are actually being employed in the preparation of the food, or by the *cooking* which is held to be the chief Instrument (or means) of the preparation of food. Therefore, in both cases, the theory is absolutely untenable.

According to our theory, on the other hand, inasmuch as the sentence in question is taken only as explanatory of the foregoing, the words can be taken in their indirect significations. For instance, in ordinary parlance, we find such an expression as *Balavān Dēvadattah*, where though the affix '*Matup*' (in *Balavān*) has been laid down to be in the sense of *Excess*, yet we do not find it clearly expressed as to in comparison with whom Dēvadatta is strong; and the direct signification of the word '*balavān*' would be that he is the strongest among all living beings; but this is not possible because, as a matter of fact, there are many stronger animals, such as the Lion, &c.; hence we take the word to signify the presence of a strength greater only than that of those animals that are known to be weaker than Dēvadatta. Exactly in the same manner, we can speak of the *Çūrpa* as the 'chief instrument' (in the preparation of the food), in comparison to such objects as the plough and the like, which have a much more remote instrumentality in that preparation.

It may be argued that—"in that case such comparative signification of the word would come to be its chief denotation; and it is for this reason that the word '*balavān*,' used with reference to Dēvadatta, is not admitted to have any indirect signification."

This is true enough, when the word '*balavān*' is used with reference to Dēvadatta, in comparison with *weaker persons* in general; but when the word is found to be incapable of referring to certain weak persons in particular, it would directly give rise to an idea of Dēvadatta being stronger than even those who possess greater strength; and in that case, if we take the word to point to the fact of Dēvadatta being stronger than those weaker than him, then this would be taking it in an indirect sense. In the same manner, when the fact of being the means of the preparation of food is taken to be brought forth as descriptive of the *Çūrpa*, which forms an object of the Injunction,—then (1) such description may be taken in its direct signification—that the *Çūrpa* is the more important means (or Instrument) in the preparation of the food, than the *remoter instruments* in general; or (2) it may be taken in its indirect signification, inasmuch as no such remoter Instrument is mentioned; and the meaning would be that the *Çūrpa* is the one principal instrument in the preparation of food (which is not true).

In accordance with your theory, on the other hand, the sentence being an Injunction, and as such laying down something not got at by other means, the fact of the *Çūrpa being the principal Instrument*, as also its *present character*, would have to be taken as mentioned with reference to the Action in question; and as such there would be no ground for any *Comparison* or *Secondary* (*indirect*) *character;* and hence there would be a greater difficulty in the interpretation of the sentence. And thus there is no equality between the two theories.

***Sūtra* (30). If it were a Reason, it would be restricted (to the Çūrpa only); because of the specification. If it be urged that through singularity (the Darvī, &c., would also be taken as referred to),—then, in that case, there would be an indecisiveness of the Injunctions.**

This *Sūtra* admits, for the sake of argument, the position of the opponent. Even if the sentence were an Injunction of the Reason that

Injunction could not be taken as referring to the *Darvī*, &c. Because it is distinctly with reference to the *Çūrpa* that the sentence lays down the Reason, in the shape of its being an instrument in the preparation of food. And specially as such instrumentality is not recognised in ordinary experience, the only resource that we have, for taking the injunction to refer to the *Darvī*, &c., also, is to assume a Vedic text bringing forward an instance in support of the sentence in question. But for assuming such a text, the only ground that we can have is the apparent inconsistency of another direct Vedic text (the sentence in question); and as a matter of fact, this apparent inconsistency cannot justify the assumption of anything more than what is absolutely necessary for the consistency of the Vedic text in question.

Then again, the connection of the *Çūrpa* with the *Homa* having been laid down, the mention of the properties of any other things would be no reason for such relationship; and hence it would be necessary to mention a certain quality of the *Çūrpa* alone,—*viz.*, its instrumentality in the preparation of the food; and on account of the proximity of the description of the quality to a mention of the *Çūrpa*, we conclude that the description refers to the *Çūrpa* alone.

Even in ordinary parlance, we always find that when a certain property is mentioned in connection with a certain object, the quality is cognised, first of all, only as belonging to that object (as for instance in the argument 'Fire, because smoke'; the smoke which is the Reason is cognised at first, as residing in the particular mountain only); and it is only when the corroborative instance comes to be cited ('Whatever has smoke is fiery, as the culinary hearth') that we come to recognise the fact that it is the *smoky substance* in general that is meant; as otherwise, with the particular case alone, there could be no unified collective idea of the *presence of fire* (that is to say, unless we have an idea that *wherever there is smoke there is fire*, we cannot deduce the *presence of fire* from the *presence of smoke*).

In the Veda, the Reason is not cognised as appertaining to what has to be proved by it, either in its genuine or specific form; the particular sort of relationship has always got to be assumed in accordance with Apparent Inconsistency. And in the case in question, we find, (1) that a definite *particular* object (*the Çūrpa*) is distinctly mentioned, (2) any generic instrumentality is not ordinarily recognised, and (3) there is no reason for rejecting what is directly mentioned: and hence all the Apparent Inconsistency that there can be in the case is limited to the particular case (of the *Çūrpa* being employed in the *Homa* and its being the instrument for preparing food); and as such it can justify the assumption of only that text which would show an instance corroborating that particular case only; because it would be, in the absence of this particular instance only, that the mention of the Reason (with regard to the *Çūrpa*) would remain inconsistent. On the other hand, if we omit to assume the fact of the *Homa* being connected with such other implements as the *Darvī* and the like, there is nothing, either directly perceived or mentioned in the Veda, that would remain inconsistent (for want of such an assumption). Therefore the only instance that we could assume would be in some such form as—'whichever *Çūrpa* is found to be instrumental in the preparation of food, is also used in the offering of the *Homa*.'

The inference of such a text would be what is technically known as the '*Viçēshadṛshta*' Inference. For instance, even in ordinary experience, if the smoke that is perceived is recognised as proceeding from a particular grass, the fire that is inferred is also that proceeding from the burning of that grass, and not Fire *in general;* and again though the root '*gam*' is generally recognised as denoting *to go;* yet when perceived, in the word '*gō*' (cow) f.i., after the word has been found to denote the particular animal with dewlaps, &c., it comes to be recognised as pointing to the 'going' *of the cow* only, and not to that of *all moving things.* Exactly in the same manner, inasmuch as the Reason—the Instrumentality in the preparation of food —has been mentioned in distinct connection with the '*Çūrpa*,' it cannot be regarded as pertaining to any other things.

Thus then, the meaning of the sentence would be this: 'Whichever *Çūrpa* is found capable of preparing the food should be used in the offering of the *Homa*'; and any other objects, the *Darvī*, &c., cannot be included in this. For instance, when a strongly blown fire is mentioned as the Reason for burning, it points to the fact that, if not strongly blown, the Fire would not burn, and not that the conch-shell, when strongly blown, would burn.

Thus alone could any definite interpretation be arrived at.

If however the 'Instrumentality in the preparation of food, as mentioned with reference to the *Çūrpa*,' be taken as pointing to its concomitant —*viz.*, the great genus ("Instrument in the preparation of food")—, then, whatever is perceived in the world could, in some way or other, be spoken of as an 'instrument in the preparation of food'; and as such, there being an indecisiveness (as to the Instrument really meant), the sentence could be taken as referring to all the objects connected with the *Homa;* and hence the expression 'instrumental in the preparation of food' would be absolutely useless.

For these reasons, we conclude that the sentence cannot be rightly taken as laying down a Reason; and as such we must take it as containing a Praise (of the *Çūrpa* as the one thing to be used in the offering of the *Homa*).

ADHIKARAṆA (4).

[*Treating of the Mantras.*]

***Sūtra* (31). "Because the Scriptures lay down directions (for the use of mantras, they cannot be meant to convey any meanings)." (A).**

Finding the word '*Anartha*' mentioned in the *Pūrvapaksha* in connection with the *mantras*, some people put forward the question of this *Adhikaraṇa* as—'Have the *mantras* any meaning, or are they absolutely meaningless'?

But this is not quite the correct form of the question considered here. Because all words are distinctly found to convey some sort of a meaning; and as such there can never be any question as to their having a meaning; for instance, Fire being found to actually burn certain things, we do not proceed to consider whether or not it is capable of burning. As a matter of fact, in all cases, the potentialities of words are inferred from the effects that they actually bring about; and in the case of *mantras*, we find that as soon as they are pronounced, they convey a certain definite meaning. Nor are the *Pūrvapakshas* on this point capable of being answered by the single *Sūtra* I—ii—40.

For these reasons, considering the above question inappropriate, the *Bhāshya* lays down the question in the following form: "Are the *mantras* meant to convey a meaning, or are they not so meant"?

It may be argued that for the aforesaid reasons, even this question cannot be a fit object for discussion. But this is not true; because even the sentences that have a definite meaning, we find to be of two kinds (some being pronounced for the purpose of conveying some meaning, while others are pronounced only for the sake of the verbal expression). And as a matter of fact, though the utterance of the sentence, and the conveying of its meaning, always go hand in hand, yet it is possible that the desire of the speaker may lie in only one of these; and in this there is some sort of a difference between the two; for instance, when a person desires to express a certain fact, the utterance of the sentence comes as a matter of course; whereas when he desires only to express the mere verbal forms of sentences, the expression of the meaning comes about only by the way (through the exigencies of the force of concomitant circumstances); as we find in the case of *Japa*, and the repetition of *mantras* for the curing of poisons. And hence there is an occasion for discussion on this point.

Objection: "But what connection has this question got with the "treatment of the means of knowing *Dharma*"?

Reply: We have already considered the *Pūrvapaksha* that the Veda having the sole purpose of pointing out the Actions to be performed, that which is not found to serve such a purpose must be concluded to be useless and untrustworthy; and hence the question of the authority of the *mantras* in the matter of *Dharma* being only a phase of this previous *Pūrvapaksha*, the answer that we have given on the former occasion would apply to this case also; and as such there can be no need for bringing up the question of the authority of the *mantras*. Specially as we all know that when even such apparently incoherent sentences as—'He wept and from that was silver produced'—are capable of being somehow or other made out to be an authority with regard to *Dharma*, there can be no doubt with regard to the authority of the *mantras*. And hence all that we have got to consider now is the question of the particular uses of the *mantras*.

That the *mantras* are neither Injunctions nor mere Valedictory sentences will be shown by the Author himself later on, when it will be pointed out that they cannot be Injunctions, because they have not the form of an Injunction; and that they cannot be Valedictory sentences, because there can be no Praise of that which is laid down elsewhere. Then the only use that is left lies in the employment of the *words* of the *mantras*; and hence it is only natural to consider the question as to their being used for the purpose of conveying some meaning, or for that of giving evpression to the mere words. In the case of the *Sāmas* too, though they have no meanings, yet we can have a doubt as to whether they are pronounced merely for the sake of being pronounced, or for the sake of giving expression to the letters composing them.

A question might here be asked—"How could the *Pūrvapaksha* account for the use of such *mantras* as are not connected with any direct direction in the Veda (and are used only in accordance with their own meanings)"?

To this, some people make the following reply: "It is with a view to stop the use of such *mantras* that the *Pūrvapakshi* proceeds to establish the fact of the speaker having no desire to convey any meaning by the use of *mantras*, because he knows that no one ever uses *mantras* that have no meanings. Thus it is that the sentence in the *Bhāshya—do the mantras help by the mere utterance*—which savours of being the declaration of a well-established fact—ceases to be absolutely incoherent. And the evil motive lurking in the mind of the *Pūrvapakshi* is somewhat like this: 'If the *Siddhānti* should declare that the *mantras* help by mere utterance, then I shall be able to show to him that such *mantras* can never be used.' And the *Pūrvapakshi*, in the *Bhāshya*, in pointing out the use of the *mantra* '*Varhirdevasadandāmi*,' is found to be denying the fact of the *mantra* being used on the occasion of the *chopping of grass*; and what he means by this is to strike at the very usefulness of the *mantra*."

Or, it may be that the *Pūrvapaksha* accepts the fact of the *mantras* being actually used, as being in accordance with the theory of persons knowing all about sacrifices; and hence not discussing this, it takes up another discussion. And as for the question—'How is it that the theory of persons knowing the details of sacrifices has been left aside, and its correctness or incorrectness has not been tested'?—, the reason why this point has been disregarded is this: That the *mantras* are actually used is a fact firmly established by the mere fact of their being accepted as such by all the best men of the three higher castes,—exactly like the works on *Smṛti*; this fact cannot be set aside; and hence it is the very source or basis of this fact that we proceed to consider. And if the *Pūrvapaksha* theory turns out to be the correct one, then, there being no other authority for the said fact, we shall seek for it in the Inference of Vedic texts laying down the use of the *mantra* in question; while in accordance with the *Siddhānta* theory the Indicative Power and the *Context* of the *mantra* itself would serve as the required authority.

Or, the *PŪRVAPAKSHA* (A) may be expounded in the following manner. "That the *mantras* serve a distinctly useful purpose of man is pointed "out by the very Injunction of the study of the Veda; and hence whatever "is found to be in contact with the *Darça-Pūrṇamāsa* and other sacrifices, "either through *syntactical order* or through *Context*, is accepted as serving a "useful purpose; such for instance are the sentences dealing with the "*Prayājas*, as also the forms of the *mantras*. Of these the former are found "to serve a purpose, by a distinct pointing out of what they directly signify "(*viz.*, the performance of certain minor sacrifices); and hence though they "have certain verbal forms of themselves, they do not serve any purpose, "through these verbal forms. As for the *mantras*, however, they are found "to be expressing meanings, that are not of any use in the sacrifices; and "as such we can have no need of these, so far as their meaning is con- "cerned; as for the purposes of Praise, Injunction, and Remembrance, "these are found to be fulfilled by other means; and hence we cannot "but conclude that the only purpose that the *mantras* can serve is in the "use of their mere verbal forms, as is also pointed out by the passages "that lay down their uses. As for the Injunction of the study of the "Veda, this too, having its purposes fulfilled by the more proximate "verbal text of the *mantras*, cannot extend to the more distant deno- "tation (or meaning) of these *mantras*. In the case of the passages "dealing with the *Prayājas*, &c., also, though our first impression is that "of these also, it is the verbal text only that is to be employed,—yet, such "use is concluded to be improper, when it is found that they express certain "facts, that are distinctly useful in the actual performance of the sacrifices. "No such facts, however, are found to be expressed by the *mantras*. Then "again, it is only when the verbal text is not found to be of any use that we "conclude the purpose of a sentence to be in what it signifies; in the case "of the *mantras*, however, we find that it is their verbal texts that serve "distinctly useful purposes. And even if the meaning of a sentence be "held to be more important than its verbal form, it is only to the *word* "that a person has to be directed first of all; because the meaning is "expressed *after* the word has been used. And hence we conclude that "it is the mere verbal form of the *mantra* that is of use (in the per- "formance of sacrifices). And it is in view of these facts that we have to "take the following *Pūrvapaksha Sūtras*.

"In consideration of the order of the *Siddhānta Sūtras*, we should "change the order of the examples cited, from the '*Abhryādāna*' down- "wards. The *Bhāshya*, however, has not paid any heed to the order of the "examples, because it was thought that the discussion would be equally "clear, wherever the examples might be cited, and hence he begins with "the *mantra*—'*Uruprathā, Uruprathasva*,' &c.

"Says the *Bhāshya*: *Just as one who has eyes, &c.* And the meaning "of this is that though a person who has his eyes intact, yet having his "vision blurred by some cause or other, when he is found being led by "another person, the irresistable conclusion is that he does not see with his "eyes; and exactly, in the same manner, when a person comes across the "text of a *mantra*, though his first impression is that it has a certain mean- "ing, yet, as soon as he finds another sentence laying down its uses, he "naturally concludes that the *mantra*, itself, has not the capability of "indicating its own use; and this distinctly shows that the meaning of the "*mantra* is to be disregarded altogether; for if any importance were attach- "ed to the meaning, the use of the *mantra* would be indicated by the *mantra* "itself, through such a meaning.

"An objection is raised in the *Bhāshya*: '*The mantra may have the* "*character of an Arthavāda*,—that is to say, as a Praise of the Injunction of "the *mantra* inferred from the exigencies of its indicative Force and Context.'

"The reply given in the *Bhāshya* is that *it is not so*; because *Arthavādas* "have been shown to serve the purpose of Praising only when taken along "with Injunctions; in a case however where the Injunction, whether direct "or inferred, appears apart from the passage in question, there being no "Praise found in proximity to the Injunction itself, the necessary persua-"sion is accepted as being acomplished by its own force; and as such, there "being no need for any other persuasive agency, no remote Praise can serve "any useful purpose with regard to that Injunction.

"Similarly, too, in the case of the *Abhryādāna mantras*, their very form "points to the fact of their being employed at the action in question; and "as such the subsequent direction that 'one is to hold by all the four' is "useless. Even if this direction served the purpose of indicating the "number 'four' (which is not indicated by the *mantras* themselves), the "number thus indicated would be that which appertains to the *mantras*, and "not to the *Action*; because the property of one thing cannot be transferred "to another. The number too, not being an *Action*, could not be taken to be "laid down as an auxiliary to the Action.

"Thus then, the construction of the sentence would be somewhat in "this form: 'These that are four in number, by means of these, one should "hold the *Abhryas*'; but these were four, even before the declaration; "hence the assertion would be absolutely useless. And further the number "not being auxiliary to the principal Action, and there being no collective "word, the potentiality in question would have to be accepted as appertain-"ing to each of the four *Abhryas*; and as such there would be nothing to "set aside the contingency of these being taken as four optional alterna-"tives.

"In accordance with our theory, however, the peculiar transcendental "result being only capable of being indicated by the repetition, there "would be no means of ascertaining its existence, before all the four had "been held; and as such, it is only proper that these four should be taken "collectively.

"In the case of the sentence—*Imāmagṛbhnam, &c., ityaçvābhidhānī-"mādattē*,—as for the holding of the reins of the Horse and the Ass, "it is distinctly indicated by the exigencies of the circumstances; and "as such there can be no injunction for the holding of these. And as "for the *mantra* too, its use is indicated by its very form; and as such "the direction *ityāçvābhidhānīmādattē* cannot be of much use.

"An objection is raised in the *Bhāshya*—'*The direction would serve "the purpose of rejecting the holding of the reins of the ass.*'

"And the reply given is—'*na çaknoti parisankhyātum, parisancakshāṇo "hi*, &c., &c. That is to say, in the word '*parisaṅkhyā*,' the prefix '*pari*' "signifying *rejection*, the word must be taken as denoting the *idea* of such "rejection or exclusion; and this *idea* could refer either to the *holding of the "reins of the ass*, or *to the using of the mantra at such holding*; and both these "alternatives are open to three objections, *viz:* (1) if the direction be taken "as an Injunction, then the *said idea of the rejection* would be that 'such and "such reins are *not held*'; and in this the Injunction would be abandoning "its own original meaning or purpose (of laying down the *holding* of certain "reins); (2) it would be necessary to bring in the meaning of another "sentence—that *the reins of the ass are not to be held* (which is not signified "by the sentence in question); (3) we would have to set aside the "employment of the *mantra* at the holding of the ass' reins, though such "employment is indicated by the form of the *mantra* itself. When how-"ever, the direction is taken as indicating a certain transcendental result, "(as we hold) it could be taken along with anything we please, being ex-"actly like a blind man. In the sentence '*ityaçvābhidhānīmādattē*, if there "were a certain definite relationship between the word '*iti*' and the "word '*açwābhidhānīm*,' then it could be taken as indicating the re-"jection (of the holding of the ass' reins). As a matter of fact, however, "there is no such relationship; because all case-nouns having the pur-"pose of accomplishing the work of the Verb, there can be no mutual "relationship among themselves; and for this very reason, the sentence "too would be connected with the Verb only; and this is only one; and the "exigencies of the context and the particular transcendental result apper-"tain equally to both *holdings* (those of the reins of the horse and the "ass); and hence there can be no *Parisankhyā* or exclusion.

"The *Bhāshya* sums up the whole discussion thus:—*Thus we conclude* "*that the mantra, 'Varhirdēvasadandāmi,' cannot be taken as pointing* "*to the fact of the mantra being employed in the chopping of grass.* And "we find that the Principal Direction (laying down the procedure of "the sacrifice) itself distinctly points out all *mantras* to be employed at the "Principal sacrifice; and as such having no use apart from the perform-"ance of this sacrifice, they could never have any connection with the "subsidiary Actions. Nor would there be any chance of the *mantras* being "repeated in the wrong place; because the occasion of their use is "fixed by the order of the context in which they occur; and hence there "could be no chance of people ignoring the conditions of the sacrifices, and "repeating at once the whole of the *Anuvāka* or *Adhyāya* (of the Veda "dealing with the sacrifices).

***Sūtra* (32). (B) "Also, because of the fixed order of the sentences."**

"In the case of the *mantra*—'*Agnirmūrdhā, &c.*,'—the sense that would "be got from this form of the sentence would be exactly the same as that "obtained, if the sentence were read as—'*Mūrdhāgnih, &c.*'; and as such, "any restriction or fixity of the order of the words would be useless (if any "meaning were desired to be conveyed by the *mantra*). If, however, we take "the *mantras* as being repeated only with a view to a certain transcendental "result, following from a repetition of the words in a fixed order,—then "there would be no ground for believing the same result to follow if the "order of the words were changed; and as such the restriction of the order, "in this case, would serve a distinctly useful purpose. If it be urged that "there is a certain transcendental result that follows from the cognition of "the meanings of each of the words in the particular order in which they "occur in the *mantra*,—then (we reply that) such a result would be accom-"plished by the mere repetition of the text of the *mantra;* because the "particular order of the cognition of the meanings of the words depends "upon such repetition only.

"In a case where the restriction is found to serve a visible pur-"pose,—for instance, the restrictions of roots, affixes and compounds, that "we meet with in connection with such words as '*Indrāgnī*,' '*Nīlotpalam*,' "'*Rājapurushah*,' '*Citraguh*,' '*Nishkauçāmbih*,' and the like—it is only "proper that we should have one; as, otherwise, the words would either be-"come incorrect, or signify something totally different, or become absolutely "meaningless. The sequence of the words in the aforesaid compounds is "in accordance with such rules as that—'in a *Dvandva* compound the word "that begins with a vowel and ends with the letters of the *at pratyāhāra* "should be placed first' (*Pānini* II—ii—33), and the like; and hence the "compound '*agnīndrau*' would be grammatically incorrect; and the "compound '*Purusharājah*' would have a meaning different from that of "'*Rājapurushah*'; while the word '*Kauçāmbinih*' would be absolutely "meaningless. If we meet with the word '*Agnīndrau*' in the Veda, we "should explain the anomaly as being a peculiarity of the Veda, or formed "in consideration of the fact of *Agni* being taken as the more important "deity of the two; when, however, both of them are considered to be "of equal importance, '*Indrāgnī*' would be the only correct form.

"It may be urged that—'in the case in question also, any change in "the order of the words would make the sentence lose the character of a "*mantra*.' But this would be the case only if no meaning were desired to "be conveyed by the *mantra;* while (if the meaning were desired to be "conveyed, then) inasmuch as a change in the order of the words would "not make any difference in the meaning of the *mantra,* we do not know "on what ground it could be said to lose its true character.

"(1) And thus the present *Sūtra* could be taken as pointing to the fact "of the character of the *mantra* being established with regard to a certain "sentence, on the ground of the *order of the words being fixed.* (2) Or, it "may be taken as laying down the fact of a *mantra* being used at a sacri-"fice in accordance with the *rules* laid down in a particular context, as a "reason for holding that no meaning is desired to be conveyed by the "*mantra ;* because if any significance were attached to the meaning of the "*mantra*, there would be no such differentiation, in the case of the same "*mantra*, as that, 'this belongs to one sacrifice and that to another.' (3) "Or, it may be taken to mean that, inasmuch as the denotative power of all "sentences—whether occurring in *mantras* or in ordinary parlance—is "the same, any such restriction as that a certain sentence is a *mantra* "cannot but have a certain transcendental result in view. (4) Or, the "reason propounded in the *Sūtra* may be taken as that, inasmuch as the "Deity could be thought of by such means as *contemplation* and the like, "the fact of there being a restriction that it should be done by means of "the *mantra* only, shows that this restriction is in view of a certain trans-"cendental result; because as far as the visible results are concerned, there "appears to be no difference between the *mantra* and such other means as "*contemplation* and the like.

***Sūtra* (33). (C) "Because of the directions pertaining to the learned."**

"We find that there is an Injunction.—'One should move about, "pronouncing *agnīd agnīd*'; and in connection with this it is urged that, "in accordance with the law arrived at in an *Adhikaraṇa* of *Adhyāya* III, "(*Vide*, III—viii—18) that *an ignorant Priest is not in keeping with the* "*injunctions of the Veda*, it becomes necessary for the Priest to know the "meaning of such words as '*agnīd*' and the like, before he begins the "sacrifice itself; and as such the direction accompanying these words could "not be taken as pointing out the meaning of these words because (as for "one who does not know the meaning, he is not entitled to the position of "the Priest; while as for the learned priest) the pointing out of the meaning "would be a useless repetition; and hence we conclude that the direction "must have been put forth only with a view to a transcendental result.

"Nor can it be urged that the *mantra* serves the purpose of reminding "the Priest (of the meaning of the words); because such remembrance is "found to be accomplished by means of the expert character of the Priest, "obtained from a thorough study of the *Brāhmaṇas*. And as for the means "of manifesting this expert character, we could accept either the completion "of the previous action, or the duly studied *Brāhmana* itself, to be this "means; and hence the *mantras* could serve no useful purpose in connec-"tion with this manifestation.

"Even the particular *Sanskāra* (or Capability), that is held to be "brought about by means of the *mantras*, could be none other than a certain "transcendental result; and hence this theory comes within the *Pūrva-"paksha* itself.

"Then again, even when a meaning of the *mantra* is accepted, it is "not found capable of serving any visible purpose; so in this case also, "it becomes necessary to assume, in the end, a transcendental result. "Why then should not we assume such a one, in the very beginning, "holding it to follow from the mere utterance of the *mantra*"?

Sutra (34). (D) "Because they speak of things that do not exist."

"We find a certain *mantra* speaking of 'four horns'; and certainly "we do not perceive any such thing, in any way connected either with "the Primary or the Subsidiary Sacrifices. Even though it might be "taken as figuratively describing certain things in connection with the "sacrifice, yet as no such thing as the 'four horns' is found to be any "object of the performance (of the sacrifice), there can be no use of "reminding one of such a thing. Specially as it is not quite clear when "and where the *mantra* in question is to be employed. While on the "other hand, it is quite clear, from the text of the *mantra* itself, and the "order of its words, that it has got to be repeated; and hence the "theory of the *Pūrvapaksha* becomes duly established.

"The *mantras*—'*Mā mā hinsīh*' ('Do not kill, &c., &c.'), being laid down "with reference to the altar, where the offering-material is kept, cannot "be admitted to be uttered with any desire to convey a meaning; because "such requests can never be proffered to an inanimate object (like the "altar); as it is absolutely impossible for the altar to 'kill,' it is simply "absurd to request it 'not to kill.'"

Sutra (35). (E) "Because they are addressed to insensate things."

"We meet with such *mantras* as—'*Oshadhē trāyasva*' (Protect us, "O plant!), '*Orṇota grāvāṇah*' (*Listen, O ye stones!*), which are ad- "dressed with the purpose of attracting attention to the action in "hand; but no such attraction of insensate things is possible; nor can the "direction prompt men either to the *protection* of the animal, or to "the listening to the Morning Hymn; and hence if any significance is "attached to the meaning of these *mantras*, they are found to be absolutely "useless."

Sutra (36). (F) "Because there are contradictions in the signification."

"In the case of the *mantra*—'*Aditirdyauraditirantariksham*'—we find "that the same object is spoken of both as 'Heaven' and 'Sky'; so also in "the *mantra*—'*Eko rudrō na dvitīyo' vatasthē,......asaṅkhyātāh sahasrāṇi yē* "*rudrāh*, &c., &c.,' we find the same Rudra mentioned both as *one* and as "*many*; and these are clear cases of self-contradiction.

"Then again, how could Aditi, a Deity, be either the Heaven or the "Sky? Nor can these discrepancies be explained away as mere Praise; "because it is only such Praises as are connected with certain Injunctions "that are accepted to have any use; and as for the Praise contained in "the *mantra*, it cannot serve any useful purpose; and as such we can "attach no importance to it."

Sūtra (37). (G) "Because there is no teaching of the meaning, as there is of the text of the mantras."

"It is a universally admitted fact that the Veda is studied for the sake "of the performance of sacrifices; and as such only that part of it has "to be learnt by people, which is found to serve a useful purpose in "such performance. And as a matter of fact, we find that all revered "teachers learned in the Veda put forth their efforts towards the teaching, "to the students, of the mere Verbal Text of the *mantras*, and not to-"wards that of its meaning, though it is always in close proximity to the "text. And from this also we conclude that the *mantras* help in the "performance of the sacrifice, by their mere recital.

Sūtra (38). (H) "Because their meaning is unintelligible."

"In the case of certain *mantras*, we find that the meaning of some "words cannot be made out; while in others we find whole sentences "unintelligible. Nor can the meaning of the *mantras* help the sacrifice by "its mere existence, if it happens to be lost sight of at the time of the "performance of the sacrifice. Hence we conclude that it is by its mere "reciting, which can always be done, that the *mantra* can help the "performance."

Sūtra (39). (I) "Because they speak of transient things."

"In accordance with the theory that the *mantra* is always used with "a view to the conveying of a certain meaning,—the *mantra* can only "point to that meaning, which belongs to it; and we find that some *mantras* "are capable of signifying only non-eternal (perishable) things; for in-"stance—'What do your cows do in the *Kīkata* country'? This *mantra* is "known to have been seen (propounded) by Viçwāmitra, as is distinctly "pointed out by a well-established tradition current among the students of "the Veda; at a certain time, he asked Indra for a gift of riches in "order to enable him to perform a certain sacrifice; and he is represented as "asking Indra; 'Lord of the Three worlds, what are your cows doing in the "*Kīkata* country'?—the sense of the question being this—'the people of "that country are atheists, and regarding all sacrifices to be useless, they do "not perform any; and as such they do not milk the cows for the preparation of the *Soma;* nor do they warm the atmosphere (by the sacrificial "smoke); and not warming the atmosphere they do not help in the bringing of rain; therefore please carry the wealth that at present belongs to "Pramaganda, the king of the *Kīkata*, to my country, the *Naicāçākha;* "[The 'bha' for 'ha' in '*ābhara*' is a Vedic anomaly; or the word "'*ābhara*' may be taken as equivalent to '*Vibhrihi*'=*fatten up for us*]; and "so, 'O Maghavan, fulfil this work of mine.' [the long 'yā' in '*sandhayā*' is "a Vedic anomaly.]

"If this meaning were desired to be conveyed by the *mantra* in "question, then this being distinctly found to be speaking of many transient objects, the Veda (containing this *mantra*) would come to have a "beginning, as composed by a human author; and this would wholly shake "its authoritative character.

"Nor can the *mantra* be said to have another meaning; as it is not "found to express any other.

"For these reasons, we conclude that in the case of *mantras*, we "should attach no significance to the presence or absence of their meaning, "and must accept them as helping the performance of sacrifices, by the "mere recitation."

SIDDHANTA.

***Sūtra* (40). But there is no difference in the signification of sentences (in the Veda from those in ordinary parlance).**

The repetition of the *mantra* ending in the mere comprehension of its verbal text cannot, by this alone, be recognised as in any way forming part of the sacrifice; specially as the mere letters of the *mantra*, like the materials used, not forming part of the Procedure of the sacrifice, cannot be held to be comprehended by means of the Context.

Similarly, the cognition of the meanings of the component *words* also are wholly taken up by the indication of the meaning of the sentence (composed by them); and as such, this too cannot be said to be comprehended by means of the Context.

The only element then, that is left unutilised is the meaning of the sentence: and as such, it is this alone that can be regarded as pervading throughout the Context; and being of the nature of an action, it supplies an integral factor in the declaration of the method of the action; and thereby it attains the character of the *Procedure*, inasmuch as it serves to remind us of that which has to be performed.

And in this case, there is no ground for assuming any transcendental result (as following from mere recitation). Because the only ground for such an assumption is the Apparent Inconsistency of something laid down in the Veda; and when this latter is duly justified on the ground of the *mantra* having a distinct meaning, there can be no ground for assuming any transcendental result to follow from it. Even when there might be an occasion for such an assumption, the transcendental result could be taken as following from a comprehension of the meaning of the sentence constituting the *mantra*, and not from the sentence itself, independently of its distinctly useful meaning.

With regard to the visible and transcendental results of anything that has to be employed, we must bring forward evidences; and in the case in question we find that the fact of the *mantra* having a visible use is borne out by the *Indicative Power* (*Linga*) of the *mantra* itself; whereas the fact of its having only a transcendental result can, at best, be supported by the *Context* alone.

Then again, as a matter of fact, no amount of Context can rightly lay down the employment of a certain thing accomplishing that which it is absolutely incapable of accomplishing; and hence the long and short of the whole thing is that we should employ the *mantra* in the fulfilment of that which is capable of accomplishing. And as for the fact of the *mantra* bringing about any transcendental results, we have no evidences of it, either in the Veda, or in ordinary experience. Consequently, the Context also would point only to a visible result for the *mantra*, thereby becoming quite reconciled with the *Indicative Power* of the *mantra* itself.

Thus then, the usage of persons learned in the sacrifices becoming supported (by the *mantra* itself) there is no need of taking all the trouble of assuming any other grounds (for the usage). And hence it is only natural to conclude that it is the meaning of the *mantra* that is the chief factor (being of use at the sacrifice).

An objection is raised: "*It is not so:* because the mere fact of a "certain visible result having been accomplished, cannot justify the con- "clusion that that is the sole use of the *mantra;* specially as, if the *mantra* "does not bring about any result in itself desirable by man, the Injunc- "tion of the study of the whole of the Veda would become useless. Nor "can it be held to be necessary to assume the usefulness of the meaning of "the *mantra*, on account of the facts urged in *Sūtras* 33, 34, and 35; and "when we cannot avoid the assumption of a transcendental result, in the "end, we must assume it to follow immediately from there repetition; for "there is no reason for postponing it; specially as the necessity of repeat- "ing the *mantra* is acknowledged by both of us; and it is this fact "that gives rise to the assumption of the transcendental result in question."

To this, we make the following reply: *In the performance of sacrifices, the only useful purpose that the mantra can serve lies in the indicating of something auxiliary to the sacrifice.* Though such auxiliaries are not capable of being used like the ordinary things of the world, yet the mere indication of the forms of these would help the performers of the sacrifice. Therefore we conclude that it is only those parts of the *mantra*—as the words of address, &c., in the Vocative—that do not serve the purpose of indicating such auxiliaries, that can be said to be uttered, without any desire on the part of the speaker, to convey a definite meaning; and this mere fact cannot justify us in rejecting the significance of the whole *mantra;* specially as there is nothing in the world that is always of one and the same form and character.

For these reasons, inasmuch as a theory must be in keeping with well-recognised facts, we must conclude that such *mantras* as—'*Varhirdēvasadandāmi*'—are always used with a desire to convey a definite meaning.

As for the sentence '*tāncaturbhirādattē* (Vide *Bhāshya* on *Sūtra* 31) we offer the following explanation:—

Sūtra (41). The repetition is for purposes of qualification.

Though the *mantras* are already got at by means of their own denotative power, yet the sentence in question, which lays down that '*the four mantras are to be repeated at the time of holding the reins,*' may be taken as laying down the number *four.* And hence, in accordance with the reasonings brought forward in connection with the passage—'he purchases the *Soma* with an one year old cow, &c.,'—the qualifications tend to limit one another; and hence, if no collective potentiality be admitted, there could not be an Injunction of the *holding of the reins with the mantras numbering four;* consequently it is clear that this Injunction is a direct result of the collective potentiality of the qualifications.

Or, it may be that long before we proceed to assume, with reference to each particular *mantra*, a distinct Vedic direction, as indicated by the *indicative power* of the *mantras* themselves,—the direct declaration in the shape of the sentence ('he holds it with the four *mantras*') will have enjoined the *mantras* as qualified by the number *four;* and as such enjoining something not got at by other means, the sentence comes to be a pure Injunction.

As for the pointing out of the *mantras* themselves, these could be pointed out by their own *indicative power*, even without the direction; and as such the sentence in question could be of very little use in that connection; consequently we take the direction to have the sole purpose of pointing out the number *four*, which is not got at by any other means.

Sutra (42). There is an exclusion.

So long as the purpose of the laying down of the *mantra* has not been duly realised, and the treatment of the subject-matter remains deficient in certain points, whatever assumptions we might make, for the accomplishment of these purposes, must be accepted as having the support of the Veda; while when all deficiencies have been supplied, if we make the slightest assumption, it cannot but be absolutely without any authority. And we shall show later on that Indicative Power, Context, &c., have no authority of their own, unless they point to a direct Vedic text.

It is with all this in view that the *Bhāshya* says—*It is only when there is a sentence that the Indicative Power of Words can serve to point out the use of the mantra.* That is to say, it is only when the Context enables to ascertain whether the *mantra* is to be employed in the offering of the sacrifice or in the holding of the reins, that the addition of the clause 'the reins of the horse' can serve to restrict it.

Says the *Bhāshya : The construction of the Vedic direction is not that 'with the mantra one should hold,' but that 'he should hold the reins of the horse'*; and this refers to the relationship of the verb,—no relationship with the noun being possible,—and not to mere relationship in general; and thus we conclude that the *mantra* is laid down as to be used, not in all *holding*, but in the *holding of the horse's reins.*

Or, it may be that what the sentence does is to bring forward the subsequent relationship of the noun in the Accusative case; because this is all that is necessary for the particular result aimed at (that is to say, the relationship is that of the particular Noun, and is perceived after the Injunction of the *holding with the mantra* of the reins of the horse).

In any case the objections urged under *Sūtra* I—ii—31 do not apply to our theory, if we accept the explanation thus put forward. If the direction contained in the Veda expressed exactly what is denoted by the *mantra*, then alone could we be subject to reproach.

It may be urged that—'in that case this comes to be an Injunction of something not otherwise got at; and as such it should not be spoken of as an *Exclusion*.' But inasmuch as we speak of it in accordance with what it actually comes to be, the objection cannot affect us. Because in all cases, except where we have the word '*Parisaṅkhyā*' (Exclusion) itself, or the word '*Ēva*,' the Veda does not exactly mean that it is a real *Parisaṅkhyā* (Exclusion) or *Niyama* (Restriction). Hence in the case in question it is an Injunction that is spoken of as '*Parisaṅkhyā*,' on account of the peculiar character of what it finally leads to.

Question: "What then would be the difference among Injunction, Restriction and Exclusion"?

4

Reply : An Injunction is of that which lays down something not got at by any other means; we have a Restriction where the thing in question is already got at partially; and we have an Exclusion where the thing is found to exist in two contrary positions.

And thus we find that it is the Injunction itself, which, by certain qualifications, comes to adopt these three forms.

For instance, (1) in a case where we find that the act in question has never been got at, nor is there any chance of getting at it by any other means but by the sentence in question, we cannot but admit it to be a pure order; and this is what is known as 'Injunction' proper; *e.g.*, '*Vrīhīn prokshati.*'

(2) In a case where it is found that apart from the sentence in question, the act is partially got at by other means, then the Injunction that merely supplies the part that is wanting, serves as a restriction, and as such is known as '*Niyama*' (Restriction); *e.g.*, '*Vrīhīn avahanti*,' where we find that the *threshing* of the corn being pointed out by the mere fact of its serving the purpose of preparing the rice, the mere *threshing* cannot be held to be the sole object of the Injunction, which must be taken as supplying the element that is wanting (not being got at by any other means); because unless this additional something were pointed out by the Injunction, the mere preparing of the rice being capable of being accomplished by other means also, these other means would also come to be the objects of Injunction. When however, the missing element is supplied by the Injunction, then the preparation of the rice comes to be only implied by the sentence secondarily, and not expressed by it directly.

Nor can the Restrictive Injunction be taken merely as rejecting the other alternative (of preparing the rice by other means); because in that case it would be only a *Parisaṅkhyā.* And the restricting of the means of the preparing of rice to *threshing* only is more proximate (to the sentence) than the setting aside of another alternative. So long as there was an idea of the rice being capable of being prepared by both means, there was no such restriction as that it should be done by *threshing* only; and hence when this restriction has been accomplished by the Injunction, all other alternative methods fall off by themselves. And further, the Injunction is not found to have been laid down after we had cognised all the methods of preparing rice; and as such none of these could be set aside by the Injunction; for it is only that which has been cognised to be applicable that can be set aside; in fact, it was prior to any such recognition that the person was prompted to an action; and in the prompting, the potentiality of the thing in question to point to many methods having been restricted, only one of these has been pointed out by the sentence in question; and as for the setting aside of the other methods, this is cognised only as a necessary consequence of the former restriction; and hence the sentence is not named in accordance with this *setting aside* (or *Exclusion*).

(3) In a case where, prior to the direction contained in the sentence in question, both methods have been already cognised as applicable to the case in question,—and where there is a chance of both being employed,—we have a rejection of one of them in favour of another; and this is a case of *Parisaṅkhyā* (Exclusion); *e.g.*, the sentence already in consideration ('*Açvābhidhānīm, &c.*'), and also in the case of the fifth alternative of the *Gṛhamēdhīya* sacrifice.

But in the case in question, the sentence does not appear actually after both actions have been pointed out, because we have not assumed any Vedic direction for the holding of the reins of the ass; hence all that we mean is that if we had not the sentence '*ityaçvābhidhānīm, &c.*,' then, the *mantra* could be employed in the holding of the reins of the ass also. Specially as in the case of all direct assertions of the Veda, we do not take them as serving the sole purpose of barring the way of all assumed sentences; (that is to say, if it were so, then the sole use of the sentence in question would be in this *barring*, and it could not be taken as setting aside the application of the *mantra* to the holding of the reins of the ass); because what would be the use of having a sentence for a purpose (the barring of the way of assumed sentences) that could be served by other means? Hence for the sake of the Vedic sentence in question, we assume its purpose to lie in the setting aside of the application of the *mantra* to the holding of the ass' reins.

Thus then, taking for granted, for the sake of argument, the opposite contention, we offer the following explanation: If we had not the sentence in question, what would be the nature of the action performed? The *mantra* would come to be employed in the holding of the reins of the horse, and also in that of the reins of the ass. When however the use of the *mantra* is distinctly restricted by the sentence in question, all that we want to know being duly pointed out, no room is left for the assuming of Vedic texts laying down the common application of the *mantra* (to the reins of the horse as well as of the ass); and hence it comes to be definitely ascertained that the *mantra* is to be employed in the holding of the reins of the horse only; and thus there being no repetition, the sentence in question is found to serve a distinctly useful purpose.

Sūtra (43). Or, it may be an Arthavāda.

In the case of the sentence—"With the *mantra* 'O, magnificent one, become greatly magnified,' he enlarges the cake,"—followed, at a certain distance, by the sentence, 'by this the master of the sacrifice himself becomes magnified,'—though the latter, being in a different place, cannot be taken as eulogising the former injunction of the *mantra*, yet inasmuch as it is the magnifying or enlarging of the cake that forms the object of the Injunction, the whole sentence could be useful, only if it helped in persuading the agent to such enlarging; and it is in support of such persuasion that we have the latter sentence.

Objection: "As the cake itself could not be prepared without an enlargement (of the lump of flour), any Injunction of such enlargement would be absolutely useless."

Reply: This is not necessarily the case; for if the dough happens to be rather loose, it would be advisable to enlarge it by the addition of more flour; and hence what the Injunction does is to lay down that the flour should be kneaded in such a way as to leave it capable of being increased (by the addition of more flour). And thus too, it becomes clear that the enlarging is to be done by the *Adhvaryu* priest; because the *mantra* in question, when repeated, comes to be known as '*Ādhvaryava mantra*,' and thereby restricts itself to a particular agent. As for that which is implied by the *mantra* itself, inasmuch as that could not form the basis of any name (of the *mantra*), it could not by itself definitely point to any particular agent. Hence even though the meaning of the *mantra* could be wholly got at from itself, yet we must comprehend its meaning by means of one subsequent sentence.

Thus then we find that the praising of the enlargement serves a distinctly useful purpose.

Objection: "In that case the praise of the enlargement being accomplished by means of the sentence—'verily it magnifies the master of the sacrifice himself,'—the mention of the *mantra* would be absolutely useless."

Reply: Not so; because the valedictory sentence has been added with the sole view of praising the *mantra* alone; and the whole thing comes to this: The enlargement should be done; the *mantra* serves as a means of this enlargement; and to the *mantra* are also added the words '*uru tē yajnapatih prathatām*' (May your master of the sacrifice also become magnified!). And in that case, the sentence, 'Verily the master of the sacrifice himself becomes magnified,' comes to point out a sacrificial accessory (in the shape of a few words to be added to the *mantra*).

The *Bhāshya* puts the question: '*Is this then the sole purpose of the sentence*' ('*Yajnapatimava, &c.*')?—and answers it in the negative; because, as a matter of fact it serves the purpose of praising, in accordance with the rule laid down in the *Sūtra* IV—iii—1. And though in the case in question, on account of the *mantra* being laid down as an Instrument (in the enlarging of the cake) we assume the fact of the master of the sacrifice being magnified to be the result following from the said enlargement, yet that which is described in the *Brāhmaṇa* cannot but be regarded as a Praise. Specially as the *mantra* also, having its use pointed out by the indicative power of its own words, cannot, by itself, point to a Result. Anything, of which the use is pointed out by the Instrumental case-ending, cannot but be taken as bringing about a particular result, as otherwise any employment of it would be wholly inexplicable (apparently inconsistent). Whereas a text whose existence is inferred from the indicative power of certain words in the *mantra* stands in need of the mention of an Action, and as such comes to be recognised as to be used merely in the pointing out of the Action. Consequently, even a *mantra* that is so inferred should be taken as a Praise, consisting of the description of the principal result (following from the action in question).

The *Bhāshya* raises the question: 'How is it that the sentence in question uses the word *prathayati*, when there is no real *prathana* (increase)'?

To this question an objection is raised: "To which *prathana* does this "question refer?—(1) to the *prathana* of the cake that forms the object "of the Injunction, or (2) to the *prathana* of the master of the sacrifice, "mentioned in the *Arthavāda?* In both cases, the question is not "quite proper; because, (1) as for the *prathana* of the cake, inasmuch "as it is directly enjoined, there can be no question with regard to it; "and secondly, the question could not be taken as referring to the "*prathana* of the cake; because the reply that the *Bhāshya* gives to "the question is that—'the existence of the *prathana* is pointed out by "the *mantra* itself'; while as a matter of fact, we find that the *prathana* "of the cake is not so pointed out,—it being an entity in itself; and as "such the reply would be altogether irrelevant. (2) If again the question "be taken as referring to the *prathana* in the *Arthavāda*—the question being "just like the question with regard to the *Arthavāda* ('He wept')—'How "when there is no actual *weeping*, &c., &c.'?—in that case too, the reply that "is given would be totally incoherent; because the *mantra* being employed "by the *Adhvaryu* priest in the *prathana* of the cake, the *prathana* is dis-"tinctly found to be connected with the cake, and not with the master of "the sacrifice. Therefore the passage containing the question cannot be "accepted as a part of the *Bhāshya* and must be regarded as an inter-"polation."

But as a matter of fact whichsoever of the two alternatives be accepted, there is no incoherence in the question. (1) Granted that the *prathana* questioned about is that of the cake; we find that the procedure adopted by some sacrificers is that they employ the *mantra* in describing the cake, *after it has been enlarged;* and it is one of these sacrificers that puts the question from his own standpoint—'how is it that one enlarges the cake with the *mantra*, before the enlargement has been accomplished'? And the answer that is given half admits the contention,—it being, that 'on account of its being pointed out by the *mantra*': that is to say, inasmuch as the enlargement, being an already accomplished fact, could not be performed with the *mantra*, all that the *mantra* does is to describe it as an accomplished fact.

Or, it may be that in the case of all objects, the operations of the *Prompter* are always preceded by those of the *Prompted*; and the same must be the case with words also. So in the case in question, the enlargement has been said to be enjoined, for the sake of the accomplishment of the object of the Praise.

"On this, the following question is raised: "No such Injunction is "possible; because there can be no object of Injunction in this case. If "we had any cognition of the action of the Prompter, then alone could "it refer to an Injunction; but as a matter of fact no action of the "Prompted being mentioned, no action of the Prompter can be cognised; "and hence, as unless the expression '*should sacrifice*' has been pronounc-"ed, we do not make use of the words, 'he *sacrifices*,' so in the case in "question, so long as the (prompting) words 'should enlarge' have not "been uttered, we cannot say 'he enlarges'; nor have we any Injunction—"either in the form that 'the cake should be enlarged,' or that 'the "*mantra* should be employed in its enlargement'; and in the absence of "such an Injunction, the declaration 'enlarges' must be regarded as an "absurdity."

It is this declaration that is justified in the reply given in the *Bhāshya*: 'on account of its being pointed out by the *mantra*.' That is to say, the Injunction is contained in the *Brāhmaṇa* words 'he enlarges,' which contain the opening words of the *mantra*, that express the action of the *prompted* (man).

Says the *Bhāshya*—'He who utters the words *be enlarged* enlarges the cake'; and this simply shows that all that the *Adhvaryu* priest does is to fulfil the making of the cake.

Though another reply that was possible was that the word can very easily accomplish the functions of the Prompter, even without making any mention of the action of the Prompted, whose activity is taken for granted,—yet the *Bhāshya* has spoken of the fact of the priority of the mention of this latter, because of the richness of the materials for replying that it had at its command.

(2). Or, the question may be taken as referring to the enlargement *of the master of the sacrifice*,—the sense of the question being that 'all Praise having some sort of a basis, either in fact, or in mere words, what sort of a basis has the Praise in question got'? And the reply given is that the Praise is based upon what is described in the *mantra*.

The assertion that 'the *Adhvaryu* priest addresses the *mantra* to the cake' does not refer to the actual enlargement of the cake; but what it means is simply that the priest addresses the cake—'May the master of your sacrifice become magnificent.' The particle '*iti*' after '*prathasva*' too is used in the sense of *etcetera*, and not as pointing to the mere word '*prathasva*.' The sentence—'He who says *become magnificent*,' &c., means that 'He who says *may your sacrificer* be enlarged'; the meaning of the sentence thus comes to be that—'one who says *may the sacrificer become magnificent* thereby actully makes him magnificent';—this meaning being got at by means of indirect (or figurative) indication.

Or, the word '*prathayati*' may be explained in its direct original sense of 'speaks of the enlargement'; and thus it is upon this mention of *enlargement* that the Praise may be said to be based.

Sūtra (44). The Assumption is not incompatible.

It has been urged (under *Sūtra* 32) that the utterance of the *mantra* can have only a transcendental result. And for one who holds this view, it would be necessary to assume an altogether different transcendental result, that would follow from the particular order of the words in the *mantra*; and inasmuch as we could also assume such a result to follow from the particular signification of the *mantra*, there can be no incongruity in this assumption.

The same reasoning applies to the argument based (in the same *Sūtra*) upon the fact of only certain sentences being recognised as *mantra* (as apart from other sentences having the same meaning). That is to say, even though there are other means of expressing the same meaning, it is only the particular form of a sentence that is recognised as a *mantra*. Yet the leaving off of the other means, (and the employment of the particular *mantra*) could be assumed to bring about a definite transcendental result. And hence it is established that the *mantras* are meant to convey a certain meaning.

Sūtra (45). In reference to the directions (relating to the mantras), there can be no objection based upon the reproach attaching to the action (of signification); because it serves the purpose of purification.

It has been urged under *Sūtra* 33 that, in the case of the sentence—'*Agnīd agnīd viharēt*'—there can be no significance of the *mantra*, because in that case it would express only what is expressed in the direction, which would be absurd; and that for this reason, the action of signification (with regard to the *mantra*) cannot be admisible.

But this objection is not applicable; because the direction in question serves the purposes of purification. That is to say, though the signification of the *mantra* is duly comprehended at the time that it is studied, yet, inasmuch as the idea obtained at that time is not capable of continuing in the man's mind, till the time when he is going to perform a certain sacrifice, it becomes necessary for him to recall what has been learnt before; and what the direction does is to point out that the *mantra* alone is to be employed as the means for recalling that idea.

Or, we may explain the clause '*sanskāryatvāt*' in the following manner: If the comprehension of the *mantra* had remained permanent, there would be no room for any directions; in the case in question however, it is only a slight impression of the former comprehension that remains in the mind; and as such there is an occasion for a full manifestation of this impression, by means of the idea produced by the said direction; and hence the *mantra* cannot be regarded as meaningless.

Sūtra (46). The significant mantra is an Arthavāda.

The sentence 'four horns, &c.,' serves, through a Metaphor, to eulogise the sacrifice; and as such serves the purpose of encouraging the sacrificer at the time of the performance.

The *mantra* is employed in regard to the Butter, of the *Hotṛ* priest, in connection with the *Vishuvat Homa;* and inasmuch as (1) this *Homa* is related to Agni, and (2) the Day has the Sun for its Deity—it is Agni that is praised in the shape of the Sun.

Thus then the "four horns" refer to the four parts of the Day; the "three feet" to the three seasons, Winter, Summer, and the Rains; "two heads"=the two half-yearly periods; "seven hands" is meant as a praise for the seven horses of the Sun; "thrice bound" refers to the three offering-times (morning, midday, and evening); "Bull (*vṛshabha*)" serves to eulogise the Sun as the cause of rain (*vṛshti*); "cries (*roravīti*)" refers to thunder; and the Sun, being known to all the world is spoken of as "the Great God, who entered into all living beings"; and the meaning of this is that in serving the purpose of encouraging men He entered into their hearts.

In this way then, the *mantra* is found to serve the purpose of recalling certain means of accomplishing a certain *Dharma.*

Sūtra (47). On account of the expression being figurative, there would be no contradiction.

It has been urged under *Sūtra* 36, that in such *mantras* as 'Aditi is Heaven,' we find a certain contradiction of facts. But the fact is that the sentence does not actually mean that Aditi is Heaven itself; all that is meant by it is the mention of Aditi; and the attribution of several properties to this Aditi is with a view to the praise of that deity; and the relationship of the two may be explained through figurative interpretation; just as in the case of the *Adhikaraṇa* on '*Audumbara*.' (Adh. I, Pāda iii).

***Sūtra* (48). The fact of (the learning of the meaning of mantras) not being mentioned in the sentence laying down the study of the Veda is due to the fact of (such knowledge) not having any connection (with the actual performance of sacrifices).**

Though the idea combated in this *Sūtra* has not been brought forward in the *Pūrvapaksha*, yet, inasmuch as it is quite possible that it may be brought forward, the *Sūtra* offers an explanation of it. If, at the time of the study of the Veda, the mention of the meaning were of any use, then it would certainly have been mentioned in the Injunction; but as a matter of fact, such is not the case; as it bears no connection with the actual performance of sacrifices. And as for the getting up of the meanings (in the same way as the text is got up), this is not enjoined, because, the ascertaining of the meaning of a *mantra*, being like the ordinary acts of washing, &c., is a much easier affair than the getting up of the *mantra* itself.

***Sūtra* (49). Moreover, there is an ignorance of really existing (meanings).**

It has been urged under *Sūtra* 38, that the meaning of some *mantras* cannot be made out. But this is scarcely true; because as a matter of fact, there is always a certain meaning present; and it is only when there is a certain discrepancy in the understanding of the man that he fails to comprehend it.

The means of getting at the meanings of *mantras* are the following: (1) The use of the *mantra*, (2) the Context, (3) the particular hymn in which it occurs; (4) the Deity to whom it refers, (5) the *Ṛshi* who propounded it, (6) such explanatory works as *Nigama*, *Nirukta*, *Vyākaraṇa*, and the like. And the only reason why all these are kept up is that they help us in getting at the true meanings of *mantras*.

And just as in the case of Grammar, as it always refers to well known words, such agencies as those of 'delesion,' 'modification,' &c., are brought in only as means to an end (the explanation of already existing forms of words); and yet ignorant people think that Grammar creates new words by these means;—so in the same manner, in the case in question, in the matter of the comprehension of the meaning of eternal sentences (composing the *mantras*), the mention of the names of the *Ṛshis* who propounded them,—though appearing to deprive the *mantra* of its eternal character—only serves as the means of getting at their real meanings.

Then again, (1) we find that, while explaining a certain sentence, people often adopt the plan of speaking of the words as intelligent beings, and then attributing to them certain functions of signification,—as when they say 'this word *says* this while that word *says* something else' and so forth; (2) and also when explaining a discussion, the two opponents are only assumed for the sake of a clear exposition of the two sides of the question; exactly of the same kind is the assumption that a certain *mantra* was propounded by such and such a *Ṛshi*.

Or, it may be that the *mantras* were actually *uttered* by these *Ṛshis*; but that does not mean either that they were *composed* by them, or that they were not known to other people and were brought out by them; but the fact is that, just as even now-a-days when a man wishes to say something, in order to strengthen his assertion, he quotes some old saying or verse instead of expressing the same idea in his own words,—so in the same manner, in the case in question, *Bhṛgu* and other *Ṛshis* learned in the Vedas and having their minds fully saturated with Vedic sayings, quoted certain significant *mantras*, with a view to express their own thoughts, in their ordinary parlance, instead of framing their own sentences; and it is owing to this that at present we come to take the *mantras* as inseparable from such meanings (as were expressed secondhand by these *mantras*); and it is thus that they come to be connected with non-eternal facts, &c.; and the recalling of the name of the *Ṛshi* is only with a view to show that the idea expressed is supported by authority.

In connection with this, people relate a story to the effect that a certain *Ṛshi*, Bhūtānça by name, in order to conquer old age and death, addressed the Hynns '*Sṛnyēva, &c.*,' to the Açwins; and as towards the close of the Hymn, we find the words '*Bhūtānço Çwinōh Kāmamaprā*,' this shows that the Hymn was addressed by the *Ṛshi* Bhūtānça to the Açwins. And as for the words themselves, "*Sṛnī*" = those that are driven by the *Sṛnī* or the goad,—*viz.*: elephants; the broad 'ā' (in Srīnyā) is a Vedic form of the dual; '*jarbharī*' = having all the right parts of the body engaged in striking; '*turpharī*' = killing; '*naitāshan*' = fighting; or '*turphari naītāshan*' = striking and killing like fighting soldiers; '*parpharīkā*' = brilliant ones; '*udanyatih*' = the *cātaka* birds born during the rains; '*jēmanau*' = having plenty of water (*jēmana*, which has the possessive force); and the sense is that, just as these birds are intoxicated on obtaining water, so in the same manner, these are '*madērā*' = intoxicated; and may these two make one '*jarāyu marāyu*;' *i.e.*, free from old age and death. Thus the purport of the whole sentence comes to be this: 'The Açwins—who strike at their enemies and kill them, as if they were two elephants urged by the goad,—and though thus striking, they shine with beneficence; and being intoxicated with wine, just as the *cātaka* birds are with water,—may these Açwins free me from old age and death!'

The Hymn beginning with '*Amyak sātah*' proceeded from the *Ṛshi*

Agastya; and he addressed it to Indra, with a view to obtain the wealth of immortality; hence it is that in the following verse, we find the assertion—'May you, Indra, give us that wealth.' And it is in the light of this sentence that the *verse* in question should be taken. The verse, then, is found in the Hymn addressed to the Maruts, recited on the second day of the *Chandomat*; and the word '*amyak*'=companion, being formed from the indeclinable '*amā*,' (the same that is found in the word '*amātya*'); hence '*amyaksā*'=*amā* (*saha*) *ancati*, i.e., that which lives together; '*Ṛshti*' =a weapon thrown by the hand; '*asmē*'=for us; '*sanēmi*'=ancient; '*abhram*'=water, the Maruts; '*junanti*'=sprinkle; '*agniçcit*' brings forward a simile; '*atasē*'=dry grass; '*çuçukvān*'=burnt; and 'just as the water gets at the island, so do you get at the foodstuffs.' When taking the sentence as a whole, the first word is to be taken with the third, and the second with the fourth; and the pronoun '*sa*' implies a corresponding '*yat*,' in the third foot of the verse; the meaning being that 'that which appears like Fire among dry grass, such a weapon of yours, your constant companion, extremely dear to you, has become ours, through your kindness; and those that sprinkle water in the form of rain, and hold all foodstuffs, as the water holds the island, these, being your dear friends, have become ours; and thus having become like us please impart to us your immortality.'

The Hymn '*Ekayā*, &c., is also addressed to Indra, the meaning being—by a single effort, *i.e.*, all at once, Indra drank, the '*sarānsi*'=the vessels filled with *Soma*; '*Kānukā*'=desirous, the word being a Vedic modification of the word '*Kāmuka*,' while the broad '*ā*' indicates the particular case-termination; or the word '*Kānukā*' may be taken as synonymous with '*Kāntakāni*,' &c., that have been mentioned in the *Nirukta* as synonymous with it.

Thus then in the case of all *mantras*, it being found to be quite possible for learned people to get at their meanings even though they may not be generally known, yet there is nothing incongruous in the acceptance of these meanings in the Veda. And as such the fact of *mantras* having certain definite meanings cannot be denied.

Sūtra (50). The presence of the mention of transient things has already been explained.

That is, under the *Sūtra* I—i—31. The Master of the Sacrifices is always the petitioner, and Indra the person appealed to; and as for the word '*Kīkata*,' though it is the name of a country, yet this country is not transient; or the word may be taken as synonymous with '*Krpaṇāh*' (*Misers*) that exist among all people. "*Pramaganda*" is the name of the usurer; because such a one gives away in the hopes of getting back more in return (which is signified by the parts of the word '*pramaganda*'). "*Nīcāçāk-*

kah"=the impotent man; and the wealth that belongs to him is "*Naiçāçākha*"; and 'as this wealth is of use in sacrifices, while they themselves do not perform any, therefore please make over all that wealth to me.' The rest is clear enough.

Sūtra (51). The teaching through expressive power shows that the mantra has the same meaning.

In the sentence '*Agnēyyāgnimupatishthatē*,' the fact of the word '*Āgnēyī*' pointing out Agni to be its Deity, through the indicative power of the word, distinctly shows that the *mantra* itself is capable of pointing to Agni. That is to say, the nominal affix in '*āgnēyi*' is one that is possible only when the compound means 'that whereof the Deity is Agni;' and again it is a well recognised fact that that object (or Deity) which is directly pointed out by the *mantra*, is its own Deity; and the fact of the *mantra* belonging to any particular Deity cannot be established by the mere mention of the name of that Deity, in the *mantra;* for instance in a *mantra* that is well known to belong to a single Deity, even though the names of many Deities may be present, yet that does not make the *mantra* pertain to these deities. And we cannot ascertain which Deity is directly expressed by the *mantra*, unless this latter be admitted to have a certain signification; and hence also the *mantras* cannot be absolutely meaningless.

Sūtra (52). So also is the *Ūha*.

As for an instance of *ūha*, in the case of the sentence 'the Mother grows not,'—as the growing of the *age* and *fatness*, &c., of the body of the mother is an apparent fact, it cannot be rightly denied; and hence, in accordance with the rule laid down under *Sūtra* III—i—18, it is concluded that the denial of growth refers to the *Word.* But in case of the word, there can be no such growth as *fattening*, &c.; consequently the word 'growth' is taken in the general sense of '*more material;*' and accordingly the denial is concluded to be that of the Dual and Plural numbers of the word. And such a denial is possible only when the sentence in question has a meaning, which points to the possibility of the mother, &c., of all animals being taken up, as also to the cognition of the presence of the 'growth' of other words.

Though in the case of the Mother, Father, &c., these words being relative terms, and thereby pointing to their relatives, the difference among them would be established by the difference among their respective relatives themselves, and as such there can be no *ūha* in this case;—yet, inasmuch as it is a well recognised fact that there can be no *ūha* in a case which is amenable to a definite law, while there is an *ūha* in cases not amenable to any law, it is clear that in the case in question, a certain meaning must have been desired to be conveyed by the sentence. For otherwise, all the particular transcendental results would follow from the same word without its being in any way modified.

So also the sentence—'*tvam hi agnē prathamō manotā*, &c.,' shows that though the animal may be dedicated to another Deity, the *Manotā* hymn to be employed must be that which is sacred to Agni; and this meaning of the sentence would be possible only when the hymns sacred to other Deities —Vāyu for instance—could be pointed out by *Ūha*.

So also in the sentences '*usrāṇām mēshāṇām*, &c.,' the mention of the various animals—which are really pointed out by *Ūha* only—could not but have been with a desire to convey a definite meaning. Otherwise, there would be two distinct transcendental results—one following from the rejection of the original word, and another from the assumption of another.

***Sūtra* (53). So also are the Injunctive words.**

In the Brahmanas we find certain Injunctions, which very often make mention of the parts of certain *mantras* by means of synonymous words; and this also shows that the *mantras* express a definite meaning. For if they had no meanings, such Injunctions would be absolutely meaningless.

For these reasons it must be admitted that the *mantras* are always used with a desire to convey a definite meaning.

Thus ends the Second *Pāda* of *Adhyāya* I.

PĀDA III.

TREATING OF THE SMṚTIS.

—o—

ADHIKARAṆA (1).

Authority of the Smṛtis.

***Sūtra* (1). "Dharma being based upon the Veda, all that is not Veda is to be disregarded."**

We have already established the usefulness, with regard to *Dharma*, of the Veda, consisting of *Vidhis* (direct Injunctions) *Arthavādas* (valedicts passages), and *mantras*. We now proceed to consider the case of the *Smṛtis*, of whose meaning and limits we are fully cognisant, as composed by such human authors as Manu and the rest,—and also the case of established *Usages*, not so compiled. And as there can be no discussion without a concrete example, we take up the *Smṛtis* relating to the "*Ashtakā*," which is mentioned in the works of Manu and others; and upon this we proceed with the consideration of their authoritativeness or otherwise (with regard to *Dharma*).

Note.—The propriety of introducing this discussion here is explained in various ways: (1) We can form no idea of the authority of the Veda, until we have fully understood it in all its bearings; and as it is only by the help of the *Smṛtis* and established *Usage* that it can be so understood, it is only right that the nature of these should be investigated. (2) Finding *Smṛtis* and *Usage* to serve as authorities for *Dharma*, we might take exception to the conclusion arrived at, under Sūtra 2, Pāda I, that the Veda is the sole authority for *Dharma;* and in order to guard against this, it is to be shown that these are also based upon the Veda from which alone they derive their authority. (3) The subject-matter of this Philosophy has been declared to be the "Investigation of the nature of *Dharma;*" and after the authority for *Dharma*, in the shape of the Veda has been fully dealt with, it is only right that the nature of its other authorities should be considered.

The consideration of the *Smṛtis* precedes that of the "*Nāmadhēya*" (which is a portion of the Veda) because the latter do not in any way affect the former, though the former do at times help in the full comprehension of the latter.

The reasons for doubt as to the authoritativeness or otherwise of these are thus explained: Inasmuch as these *Smṛtis* are dependent (upon human authors), we conclude that their authority is not self-sufficient; and as for the absolute falsity (or untrustworthiness), this is set aside by the firmness (of popular acceptance and trust in them). To explain—The *Smṛtis* of Manu and others are dependent upon their memory; and memory depends for its authority upon the truthfulness of its source; consequently the authority of not a single *Smṛti* can be held to be self-sufficient, like that of the Veda. And inasmuch as we find them accepted, as authoritative, by an unbroken line of respectable people learned in the Vedas, we cannot conclude them to be absolutely false either. And hence, it is only natural, that there should be a doubt on the point.

On this question then, we have the following:—

PŪRVAPAKSHA.

"The authority of the *Smṛtis* cannot be accepted; because it is only "the cognition of some previous cognition that is called *Smṛti* or Remem-"brance; and hence we can never consider it true, in the absence of such "previous cognition.

"To explain further: As a matter of ordinary experience, we find "that all remembrances appear with reference to objects that have been "previously cognised by Sense-perception, or some other means of cogni-"tion, and being always similar to this previous cognition, strengthen "the idea of the object cognised. Now, we have already proved (in the "*Tarkapāda*) that Sense-perception and the other means of right notion "do not apply to the notion of the capability of such actions as the "*Ashtakā* and the like, to bring about superphysical results, like "Heaven, &c.

"As for Verbal Authority too, though we find such authority (in "the Veda) for the *Agnihotra*, &c., we cannot find any texts in support of "the *Ashtakā*; and as for the assumption of a Verbal Authority, inasmuch "as the object is not cognised by Sense-perception, such an assump-"tion would be a remote (and a far more complicated) operation than "the assumption of a *Dharma*, without any such authority. To explain "further: Sense-perception is the only means of knowing such texts; and "if even when not so known, such an authority be assumed,—it would be "far more reasonable to assume a *Dharma*, without any authority at all.

"Nor can Inference help us in the assumption of a Direct Vedic In-"junction for the *Ashtakā*; because Remembrance is not invariably con-"comitant with such Direct Injunction; nor do we know of anything else "that (being so concomitant) could lead to the Inference thereof. Just "as there is no inferential mark to prove the existence of *Dharma* (as has

" been explained in the *Tarkapāda*, Ch. on *Inference*), so, for the same rea- " sons, we cannot have an Inference leading us to any Vedic texts with re- " gard to the *Ashtakā*.

" Nor can we get at such Vedic texts by means of Verbal Authority— " either eternal or produced; because we can have no confidence in any " newly produced Verbal Assertion; and as for an eternal assertion, no " such is possible (with regard to the *Smṛti*, which is itself not eternal). " Though such texts, being amenable to Auditory perception, may be " capable of having their existence supported by human assertions, yet, " inasmuch as human assertions are found to abound in deception, we can- " not have any confidence in them; and as such cannot admit of the texts, " on the sole authority of these. Even at the present day, we find many " people declaring certain facts to be supported by the Scriptures, though " as a matter of fact, there is no such support.

" Consequently people who have often been put into trouble by deceit- " ful people naturally have grave doubts as to whether Manu actually " found a Vedic text laying down the *Ashtakā*, &c., and hence declared his " *Smṛti* to be based upon the Veda, or that without having found any such " text, he only made the declaration, in order to inspire confidence in his " assertions. And the mere fact of there being such a suspicion sets " aside the authoritative character of the *Smṛtis*.

" And as for the Veda itself, this being eternal, can never set about " pointing out a basis for the *Smṛtis*, that have a beginning in time. " The *mantra*, &c., themselves can never serve as such bases; because these " are devoid of any direct Injunction; nor can they point to any other " reasonable basis, because they have other functions to perform.

" Nor do we find a total accord amongst the many compilers of the " *Smṛtis*, themselves; and hence on the mere strength of human assertions, " we cannot accept the *Smṛtis* to be based upon previously cognised Vedic " texts.

" Nor do we know what sort of Vedic text these authors really came " across; we find that by the *Arthavāda* and other such supplementary texts, " many people have been led astray (*e.g.*, the author of the *Kalpasūtras*, *Vide* " Adh. III). That is to say, if we were absolutely certain that Manu had " actually found Vedic texts in the proper form of Direct Injunctions, then " the said assumption would have been possible; but as a matter of fact, " even at the present day we find many people being led astray, by the " *Arthavāda* passages, which have entirely different significations (but are " mistaken as being Direct Injunctions).

" And hence we have our suspicions with regard to Manu and others " also.

" And as for the fact of the authority of these being based upon texts "contained in such portions of the Veda as have been lost to us, such on "assumption would be like a case meant to be supported by the evidence "of a person that is dead; and if such an assumption were accepted, people "would be assuming such an authority for anything that they liked.

"For these reasons we conclude that Vedic support for the *Ashtakā* is "not cognisable by Verbal Authority.

"As for Analogy, it can have no application in the case of an object "that has never been perceived, and an object similar to which has never "been recognised; and as such, it cannot be the means of cognising a Vedic "support for the *Ashtakā*.

"Though Apparent Inconsistency might be held to give an idea of such "Vedic support, yet such Inconsistency could be equally urged in support "of the untrustworthy character of the *Smṛtis*; inasmuch as mistakes "are not impossible. If the *Smṛtis* (Remembrances) were not possible "without an assumption of the Veda, then alone could they be accepted as "having a right basis (through Apparent Inconsistency); but as a matter "of fact, Remembrance is often found to be based upon (such untrust-"worthy sources as) Dreams, &c.; hence finding the ground of the said In-"consistency not absolutely true, either Apparent Inconsistency or Inference "cannot be rightly brought forward (as giving rise to an idea of Vedic "support for the *Smṛtis*).

"Thus then such Vedic texts being found to be amenable to Negation "only (*i.e.*, being found to be non-existing), though there may be other "sources or supports (for the *Smṛtis*), yet inasmuch as we do not find any "such support as we should like to have, we conclude them to be absolutely "baseless (and devoid of authority).

"Says the *Bhāshya* (in opposition to the above arguments): '*Those* "*who know a certain action to be fit for being done, how could they declare it* "*to be incapable of being done?* And the meaning of this is that those who "know a certain action as fit to be done in a certain manner, and as leading "to a particular result,—or (simply) those who know the action as capable "of being performed,—knowing this, how could they, only for deluding us "say that it ought not to be done? Though it may be urged that one who "declares it as fit to be done may be different from one who declares it to "be unfit,—yet, how is this difference possible? For, in any case, we have "a due comprehension of the *Smṛti*, only when we know that the pro-"pounder knew and remembered it thus (the two factors belonging to "one and the same person). Or, the passage in the *Bhāshya* may be "(better) explained thus: If Manu and others, knew a certain action (f.i., "the *Ashtakā*) as not fit for being performed, how could they declare it to be "fit for being performed, and thereby lead astray the people of the present "day, who have done them no harm?'

"Says the *Bhāshya* (in reply to this intermediate objection): *Because* "*of the impossibility of remembrance.* The notion (*of Ashtakā*) that the "people later than Manu have cannot be said to be a *Remembrance*, because "they have never cognised it before; so, in the case of Manu also, if any "means of recognising it previously were possible, then there could be a "*remembrance* of it; and not otherwise (but we have already shown that "none of the recognised means of right notion is applicable to the case; "and hence we conclude that no *remembrance* was possible even for Manu).

"[Says the *Bhāshya*, in answer to the question—'Knowing it to "be unfit for being done, how could Manu delude people by declaring the "*Ashtakā* as fit to be performed?']—*A barren woman may declare that* "*a certain thing was done by her grandson; and then subsequently recalling* "*the fact that she had no daughter, she could never believe her former assertion* "*to be true;* and to this an objection is raised: 'How is it that the *Bhā-* "*shya* has left off the *Son* or the *Daughter*, and cited the *Grandson* as an "example?' The reason for this is the similarity of positions. That is "to say, Manu stands in the place of the *Father*, his previous cognition "stands in the place of the *Son* or the *Daughter*, and his remembrance "stands in the position of the *Grandson;* hence (the sense of the Instance "is that) just as the woman having thought of the absence of the Daugh- "ter, concludes her remembrance of her grandchild to be a mistake,—so, "in the same manner, Manu could conclude his remembrance (of the "performability of the *Ashtakā*) to be a mistake, when he would find that "it could never be cognisable by Sense-perception or any other means "of right notion (and as such there could be no incongruity in the fact of "his having, under a misconception, laid down the *Ashtakā*).'

"Says the *Bhāshya* (in answer to the above arguments): '*Just as there* "*being an unbroken remembrance with regard to the Veda* (it is considered "authoritative, so could the same ground be urged in favour of the *Smṛtis*).' "[And though this argument refers to the *Verbal text* of the *Smṛtis*, yet "the opponent takes it as applying to an unbroken remembrance of their "*subject-matter*, and proceeds to reiterate the fact of there being no basis "for them]:

"The case of the Veda is entirely different (from that of the *Smṛtis*); it "is amenable to direct Sense-perception; and hence having by its means "cognised its existence in another person, exactly as one would cognise the "existence of the *jar* at a certain place, people learn it from him, "and then remember it: and others cognising it as thus remembered, "get it up in their turn, and give it to others, who go on doing the same; "and so the process has gone on eternally; and as the remembrance "of every individual is preceded by a rightful cognition of it, there is "no want of proper basis in this case. All that is solely dependent upon

" the usage of experienced people, is the fact that the texts thus learnt and " remembered are named *Veda;* but even prior to the recognition of the " name, people directly perceive it to be something entirely different in " character from other things, and (in the case of a particular Veda as " being learnt by a particular student) different from the other Vedas, " in the form of the *Ṛgveda* (for instance) as consisting of *mantras* and " *Brāhmaṇas* different from all other things. The names of all these are " eternal; and by means of these, whenever, subsequently, they come to be " cognised, they are cognised by direct Sense-perception, as we have " already proved.

" In the case of the *Ashtakā,* on the other hand, even when it is " *seen* as being performed by another person, and this performance " is cognised by Direct Sense-perception), there is no such basis for " any idea of its having a causal potentiality (in leading the performer " to Heaven), like the action of the potter (which is actually *seen* to " result in the ready made *jar*). If it be the mere *form* of the *Ashtakā* " that was remembered by Manu, then other people would also have re- " membered it, on having seen it with their eyes, like the ordinary action " of *cooking,* as being performed by others. But it is the causal potentiality " of the *Ashtakā* towards leading the agent to Heaven, that is said to be " remembered (and is laid down as such) by Manu ; but no such capability " (of proceeding to Heaven) is seen to appear in another person (by " the performance of the *Ashtakā*) ; and as such we conclude the traditional " assertion of such causal potentiality of the *Ashtakā* to be like the " description of a certain colour handed down by one blind person " to another.

" Such a rude simile has been brought forward, because people are " impudent enough to attribute Veda-like eternality to all such asser- " tions, on the ground of an assumed eternality of usage. Though as a " matter of fact, in the Veda, we have an eternality of faithfulness and " authoritativeness; while, in the case in question, we have an eternality of " falsity and inauthoritativeness. Specially because (in the case of the " description handed down by the blind man) the person that had the idea " in the first instance did not himself see the colour; and no authority " can attach to that which is not cognised by one's own self independently. " Exactly similar is the case with the remembrance of the *Ashtakā.* " That is to say, we do not find any Vedic Injunction on which it is " based; nor can any such Injunction be *inferred,* when it has not had " any of its relations cognised (by Sense-perception). If the *Smṛtis* " had been invariably propounded, on the basis of certain Vedic Injunctions " that had been found (by the Authors), then such Injunctions would " also have been handed down to us,—exactly as the subject-matter is said "to be (by means of the *Smṛtis*)—being pointed out as the source "from which Manu and others got their compilations.

"It may be urged that the people of old were fully satisfied with re-"membering the sense, and having thus neglected the original text, this "became lost through negligence. But this is not right; because it is not "possible that people should forget that upon which rests the authority "of the sense; as the remembrance of the sense has no self-sufficient "authority (like the Veda). All men are cognisant of the fact, that in "such cases, nothing can be accepted as authoritative, until its source is "found in the Veda; how, then, could they forget it so completely?

"Then again, how is it that Manu and others did not make the "same efforts to hand down the original Vedic Injunctions, as they did "in propounding their own compilations? If even those Authors only "knew the sense, and had not found the original Veda, then we could "put the above question to their predecessors; and thus the tradition "being found, at each step, to be without a basis (in the Veda), you would "not become free from the charge of your *Smṛtis* being absolutely baseless.

"If it be assumed that they have a basis in the portions of the Veda, "that have become lost, then the authority of the *Smṛtis* of the *Bauddhas* "could also be established, by means of a similar assumption. And people "would be utilising the authority of such assumed Vedic texts now lost, "in support of anything they might wish to assert.

"If on the other hand, the *Ashtakā* had its authority in the Veda "as we have it, then other people could also find it, just as Manu may be "said to have done; and it would, in that case, be a more proper course "to learn such facts directly from the Veda; and as such, the compilation "of the *Smṛtis* would be absolutely useless (if all that is said in the "*Smṛtis* were to be found by us in the Veda itself).

"Nor do we exactly know the nature of the Vedic passage that Manu "found as his authority (for the *Ashtakā*),—whether it was in the form of "a direct Injunction (and as such possessed of inherent absolute autho-"rity), or in that of a mere *Arthavāda* (and as such of doubtful authority). "And, as a matter of fact, we find that, in the dark, however much a "person may try with his hand, he can never distinguish *white* or *black* "(which could be done by the eye alone; and in the same manner the "fact of the *Ashtakā* being enjoined in the Veda cannot be accepted un-"less we actually find the Vedic Injunction in support of it). Nor can we "be convinced of its being based upon the Veda, by the declarations of "Manu himself (as that 'the whole Veda is the source of *Dharma*' and so "forth); because it is just possible that he never found any Vedic texts, "and made these declarations, simply with a view to delude the people.

"For these reasons, we conclude that the *Smṛtis* are not authoritative."

SIDDHANTA.

Sūtra (2). But on account of the agent being the same, the fact could be established by reasoning (Anumāna).

As a matter of fact, we find that the *Smṛtis* have been compiled by Manu and others in a correct manner, unlike the compilations of the (*Bauddhas*), and also that the fourteen Sciences (*Purāna*, &c.), similarly compiled, give very correct explanations of their respective subjects. Consequently, inasmuch as these Authors themselves are not to be met with now (and what they say is well said and as such cannot be without some sound basis), it becomes necessary to assume a certain unseen basis for their cognitions.

And in this connection, only five assumptions are possible :—(1) that they were totally mistaken; (2) that what they assert is based upon their personal observation and experience; (3) that they learnt it from other persons; (4) that they have wilfully made wrong statements, with a view to delude the people; and (5) the last and the most simple and reasonable one, that their assertions are based upon Direct Vedic Injunctions.

This last is the most reasonable assumption, as it is this alone that is in keeping with actual facts (*viz.:* the authoritative character of the assertions of Manu). That is to say, when it becomes necessary to make assumptions of the unseen, we must try, as far as possible, to make only such assumptions as are not contrary to directly perceptible facts, and do not, in their turn, necessitate the assumption of other unseen facts.

Now, then (1) if we assume the fact of Manu being totally mistaken in the assertions he has made, this assumption would be contrary to the directly perceptible fact of his works being excellent compilations (and containing many correct and excellent teachings, &c.); and it would also tend to set aside the universally accepted authoritative character of his assertions; and this assumption would also necessitate many other gratuitous assumptions,—namely: (*a*) that the people of his own days accepted and followed the mistake propounded by Manu; (*b*) the means adopted by Manu, in order to prove to others that it is not a mistake, and so forth.

(2) In the case of the assumption that the assertions are based upon the compiler's own personal observation,—(*a*) in the first place, we have to assume this observation itself; (*b*) then we should have to assume an extraordinary faculty in the compiler, contrary to all that we know of among the people of the present day (by means of which they could directly perceive such superphysical entities as *Dharma* and the rest); and the possibility of any such extraordinary faculty, we have already set aside, in course of the refutation of the omniscience (of Buddha, *vide Çlokavārtika Sūtra* 2, *Kārikās* 134 *et seq.*)

(3) As for the assumption that these assertions are based upon those of

other persons, this has already been set aside (in the preceding *Sūtra*), as resembling a description of colour handed down by blind men; nor does any such baseless tradition ever attain any authority.

(4) Similarly in the case of the assumption that Manu has purposely sought to delude people, we have to assume, in the first place, this fact of his purposely deluding people; secondly, we have to assume his motive in thus seeking to delude people; thirdly, the fact of people having fallen into the mistake; fourthly, the fact of the continuation of the mistake up to the present time, and so forth, we shall have to make endless assumptions. Then again, this assumption would mean the denying of the authority of the firm conviction (of the teaching, of Manu being true); and this would be a contradiction of a directly perceptible fact.

(5) Therefore it must be admitted that, instead of these, it is far more reasonable to assume a direct Vedic Injunction (upon which the assertions of Manu are based). In this case, we have to assume only one unseen fact (the existence of such an Injunction in the Veda); and it is only with this assumption that all other facts of the acceptance of the *Smṛtis* by the great and the learned become reconciled.

And in the case of Manu, it is quite possible that there should be Vedic Injunctions that served as the source of his conceptions. It is this that is meant by the *Bhāshya* passage,—*For this reason, it becomes possible for the three higher castes, to be connected with the Veda.* In the case of the *Mleccha*, and others of that class, for whom there is no possibility of any contact with the Veda, when we meet with the assertions of these with regard to supersensuous objects, and we set about investigating the source of these, there is no chance of the Veda ever being found to be their source; and as such we are obliged to seek for their source in one of the aforesaid four sources of misconceptions; and thereby conclude the assertions to be absolutely untrustworthy. In the case (of the Brahmāna, &c.), where there is every possibility of the Veda supplying the source sought after, all other sources being thereby set aside, there is no chance of the assertions being baseless; and as such we cannot but admit the source of these to lie in the Veda itself.

Then, there is the question—"How is it that this Vedic Injunction (of the *Ashtakā*) is not found?"

To this, some people make the following reply: 'Such Vedic Injunctions are always to be inferred; they are never directly mentioned; exactly like those injunctions that are assumed on the strength of the implication of certain *mantras* (*e.g.*, the *mantra* "I cut the grass, the seat of the gods" is accepted as pointing to the assumed injunction that *this mantra should be recited* at the cutting of the grass). Though it may be questioned how an injunction that is never uttered can ever be recognised as the requisite basis,—yet that cannot affect our position; because, the fact of such Injunction being the source is established by an unbroken *remembrance*, which is as unbroken as the handing down of the Vedic text itself. (That is to say Manu also knew of the *Ashtakā* as having been laid down by previous teachers; and as this continued tradition is not otherwise explicable, it is quite reasonable for us to assume an original Vedic Injunction). Just as in the case of the text of the Veda, it is accepted as existing in its original form, only on the ground of its having been handed down by an unbroken line of teachers,—so too in the case in question, we can establish an unbroken line of such Vedic Injunctions, as are inferred through the (Apparent Inconsistency of the) declaration of the remembrance of the *Ashtakā* (*i.e.*, by all teachers of the old times, one after the other).

But this explanation is not quite satisfactory; because the tradition has already been spoken of as resembling the description of colour handed down by blind men. As for the Vedic Injunction that is never uttered, as this can never be cognisable by any means of right notion, it is scarcely possible to prove its existence; and thereby the *Smṛti* comes to resemble the grand-child of the barren woman (as urged under the last *Sūtra*). As for the assumption of Vedic Injunctions on the strength of the implications of the *mantras*, these latter are eternal, and as such there is nothing contradictory in their having the eternal potentiality of pointing to the existence of Vedic Injunctions; whereas in the case of the *Smṛtis*, they themselves stand in need of the basic Vedic Injunction, and as such cannot rightly be made the means of inferring non-uttered injunctions).

For these reasons, it would be far more reasonable to assume the *Smṛtis* to have their source in the Injunctions contained in such portions of the Veda as have been lost; nor is such disappearance of the Veda impossible, as even now we find the Veda losing much of itself, either through the negligence or laziness of the students, or through the gradual disappearance of people versed in it. It cannot be urged that any and every theory could declare itself to be based upon such authority; because such lost Vedic texts can be assumed only on the ground that without such texts, the firm conviction and remembrance of highly respectable people of the three higher castes remain inexplicable.

Or, we may hold that the *Smṛtis* are based upon texts contained in the very portions of the Veda that are available now-a-days. If it be questioned—how is it that they are not found?—we make the following reply: (1) Because of the various branches of the Veda being scattered; (2) because of the negligence of the people learning it; and (3) because of the texts being contained in diverse sections of the Veda;—we fail to actually lay our hands upon those texts that form the basis of the *Smṛtis*.

There has been a further question—" Why then were these Vedic texts themselves not collected together " ?

And the reply to this is that this was not done, for fearing of destroying the natural order of the text of the Veda. It is only a fixed order of the verbal text of the Veda the study of which has been enjoined. And as for the rules of conduct dealt with in the *Smṛtis*, these are scattered about here and there, in various branches, chapters and sections of the Veda. And of these (as appearing in the Veda), some actions are laid down with direct reference to human agents, while some are such as are laid down in connection with the various sacrifices, but are, for some reason or other, explained as referring to the human agent also; as for example, we have such prohibitive injunctions as "One should not talk to his wife if she be, &c.," " One should not threaten a Brāhmana." (These occur in the section on the " *Darça-Pūrnamāsa* sacrifice; and as in connection with this sacrifice, it has already been laid down once before that if the sacrificer's wife happen to be in a certain condition, she is not to be present at the sacrifice, the prohibition of any conversation with her becomes absolutely irrelevant, if taken as applying to the sacrifice; and for this reason it is explained as a general rule of conduct, to be observed in ordinary intercourse. The same is the case with the *threatening of the Brāhmana*).

And if Manu went about extracting only such texts (as bear upon the general conduct of men), and teaching these separately, then as the natural order of the Veda would be disturbed, he would be directly going against the injunction of the study of the text of the Veda. And on the strength of this example set by Manu, people might leave off the *Arthavāda* portions (as useless) and read only the *Vidhi* portions of the Veda, or only such portions of it as would be of help in the performance of the sacrifices; and thereby the Veda itself would gradually disappear.

Then again, Manu himself could not necessarily have studied all the branches of all the Vedas (and as such he could not always lay his hands upon all Vedic texts). What he must have done was to try and find out the texts from various students of the different branches, and then to have kept in mind the meaning of these texts, which he must have embodied in his compilation.

Nor can it be reasonably urged (as has been done in the *Pūrvapaksha*) that, 'we do not quite know whether the texts on which Manu based his rule were in the form of a Direct Injunction, or only in that of *Arthavādas*'; because just as the firmness of the conviction in the *Smṛti* precludes the fact of its being based upon a misconception, so would it also preclude the chance of its being based upon an *Arthavāda* passage. For without doubt Manu was capable of distinguishing a Direct Injunction from an *Arthavāda*. And inasmuch as we find the *Smṛti* itself to have the form of Direct Injunction, it could only point to a homogenous Vedic Text, which therefore must be admitted to be of the form of Direct Injunction; and there can be no grounds for holding the *Smṛti* to have a heterogenous source in an *Arthavāda*.

And further, the authors of the *Smṛtis* themselves have completely bound themselves by such declarations as—"The whole of the Veda is the root of *Dharma*," "all of it is mentioned in the Veda," and so forth; and certainly these assertions could not have been blindly accepted by the people of their own days (without their having fully examined the truthfulness of these assertions, which could have been accepted only after the people had found the base of all that is laid down in the *Smṛtis*, in direct Vedic Injunctions). Hence we conclude that the *Smṛtis* have their authority through the Veda itself.

[1] Some people seek to establish by Inference, the self-sufficient authority of the *Smṛtis*, or the fact of their being based upon the Veda, by means of the premiss—"because the agent is the same." But their argument becomes *too wide*, when we refer to such actions as are performed by the same people under the influence of some temporary impulse (which actions too would come to be equally authorised); and further, if the *Smṛtis* be held to be proved "self-authoritative," then such an argument would be directly contradicted by the apparent fact of many *Smṛti* Injunctions having their source in Direct Vedic Injunctions that are easily accessible. For these reasons, we must admit Apparent Inconsistency alone, as has been mentioned in the Sūtras, as establishing the fact of the *Smṛtis* having their source in the Veda; as there are no insuperable objections to this; and "Apparent Inconsistency" can also be called "*Anumāna*," inasmuch as it gives rise to cognition, *after* or *in the wake of*—'*anu*'—Sense-perception (*māna*).

Says the *Bhāshya*—*Asyā ēva Smṛterdradhimnah kāranam anumāsyāmahē*; and this may be explained as—'we shall infer the source (of the

[1] The Author has based his arguments in favour of the fact of the *Smṛtis* being based upon the Veda, on the Apparent Inconsistency of the facts therein treated of being remembered by an unbroken line of respectable people; and he has explained the expression "because of the agent being the same" (of the Sūtra) as only pointing to the possibility (in the case of the *Smṛtis* of the three higher castes) of their being based upon Direct Vedic Injunctions. He now sets about refuting the view of some commentators who explain the Sūtra in the sense of a direct Inferential Argument, seeking to prove, by means of the premiss, the fact of the *Smṛti* either being self-authoritative, or having its source in the Veda; this argument being expanded into the following form: "The *Smṛtis* are authoritative,—because the persons that perform the acts laid down in them are the same as those that perform those laid down in the Veda,—just as the Veda (is authoritative)," and so forth.

Smṛti in the Veda) *from the firmness* (of its conviction and remembrance)'; or as—'we shall infer the source *of this firmness* (of its conviction) (to lie in the Veda).'

Says the *Bhāshya—Even in this life men are not found to directly perceive such facts* (as the *Ashtakā*, &c.) And the sense of this is that inasmuch as the course of our existence is separated from another by a process of death that destroys all previous impressions, we can never be said to carry (in our present existence) any ideas, gained from direct perception, of certain courses of action leading to certain superphysical results (and as such the *Smṛtis* of Manu, &c., cannot be said to have their source in any direct perception of their Authors).

The Bhāshya says—*Because of the fact of the performer of the acts laid down in the Smṛtis being the same as that of those enjoined in the Veda, it is possible that the three higher classes should have found the (requisite) Vedic texts;* and this is said only in order to show that it is possible for a Direct Vedic Injunction to be the source of that contained in the *Smṛti.*

Says the *Bhāshya—It is possible that they* (the Vedic texts) *may have been forgotten.* Even at the present day, we find people forgetting the texts, and the texts becoming lost. Even when the requisite texts had existed in other branches of the Veda, it is possible that (at the time that the *Smṛti* was being compiled) it may have been forgotten in which particular branch the particular text was to be found (and this may have been the reason why Manu did not mention the corroborative texts); though he only carefully cherished the fact of his assertion being authoritative as based upon the Veda; and as for the direct recognition of such basic text, he did not consider it of much use, and so let it drop off.

The *Bhāshya* says that such rules of conduct (laid down in the *Smṛtis*) as are laid down to be observed, as occasion for each presents itself—such rules, for instance, as 'the Teacher is to be respectfully attended upon,' 'old men are to be reverenced,' and so forth—have their authority based upon their perceptible uses.

But this is not quite right; because the standpoint upon which we have started is that the *Smṛtis* are an authority in matters relating to *Dharma;* and as such it is not quite reasonable to assert their authority to be based upon ordinary perceptible purposes, and thereby make the duties therein laid down, similar to such ordinary acts as the *tilling* of the ground and the like (which have only a visible use). We have not taken upon ourselves the task of establishing the authority of all actions; as it is only the desire to know the nature of *Dharma* that is our sole purpose. If such actions, as the *attending upon the Teacher* and the like had only visible results, they would be like the ordinary actions of the world, *tilling the ground, &c.;* and as such they could not have any authority bearing upon *Dharma;* and would be entirely irrelevant in the present connection.

It may be said that these have been mentioned as unauthoritative acts (and not as authoritative and as such bearing upon *Dharma*). But this is not possible; because in that case they should have been brought forward under the *fourth* aphorism "*Hētudarçanācca*" (I—iii—4) (where the unauthoritative portions of the *Smṛti* are pointed out); and in that case, the citing of the example—"Hence when the good one goes forward, the bad one follows him"—would be entirely irrelevant and useless (as this is a Vedic passage, and as such cannot rightly be cited as an instance in support of an unauthoritative injunction of the *Smṛti*).

Nor again can the injunction 'the teacher should be attended upon' be said to have the visible end of propitiating the Teacher *who* (as the *Bhāshya* says), *thus propitiated, would teach well, and explain satisfactorily all the knotty points of the scriptures;* because there is no such hard and fast rule as that without obeying the teacher the scriptures cannot be learnt; as we do find the Teacher being induced to teach, by means of requests and remonstrances. And in this lies the use of the restrictive Injunction (that "it is by means of *attendance* alone that the Teacher should be approached and made to teach"). And as for the fact of the visible use, in the case of all actions (Vedic as well as worldly) we can always point out in the way that the *Bhāshya* has done, some visible purpose or other, in the shape of acquiring a King's assistance, protection of one's self, acquiring of some form of pleasure and the like. As even in the case of such actions as the "threshing" of the corn, and the *Kārīrī* sacrifice (which are laid down in the Veda), the fact of their having visible purposes does not make them devoid of Vedic authority.

Thus then, even though the aforesaid *Smṛti* Injunctions serve visible purposes, yet it is quite possible that they may have a basis in the Veda; as for instance, the invisible result that is to follow from the restriction of the specified courses of action (as being the only one advised, out of many others leading to the same result) cannot have any other authority (save the Veda, which is the only true authority for superphysical facts).

For these reasons, the *attending upon the Teacher, &c.*, being of the nature of a "*naimittika*" Injunction (*i.e.*, the Injunction of a course of action to be followed on a certain occasion), a non-performance of it would constitute a sin, which would be avoided by the performance of the said action (this is one transcendental result); and the visible result will be (as pointed out in the *Bhāshya*) that the Teacher being pleased with the pupil would teach him well; and the effect of the restrictive Injunction (of this particular means of acquiring learning) would be in the shape of an invisible potency that would enable him to finish his course of studies without any obstacles. And it is only when we accept this *attendance upon the Teacher* to have both visible and invisible results, that the discussion—as to whether such attendance is to be performed only once or over and over again, as propounded in *Sūtra* 30, of the second Pāda of Adhyaya VI—can be possible. [The conclusion arrived at, in the *Adhikarana* referred to is that, inasmuch as such attendance has both visible and invisible results, it is to be performed over and over again]; and if the action had only a visible result, there could be no question or doubt as to whether it should be repeated or not; as in that case it would be like the action of drinking water; and as in the case of this latter, people raise no questions, but conclude that the drinking is to be repeated whenever one feels thirsty; so too in the case of the action of *attendance*, people would conclude that as it has only a visible result, we may repeat it whenever we may want the particular visible result; (and as such there could be no doubt on the point, and hence no ground for the aforesaid discussion).

Then the assertion of the *Bhāshya*—that *these have their authoritativeness based upon the fact of their bringing about perceptible results*—must be taken as laying another strong point home to the opponent,—the sense of the argument being this:—you may succeed perhaps in shaking the authority of such *Smṛti* Injunctions as have been laid down as leading to transcendental results; but how can the said Injunctions, that are actually found to bring about the results that are mentioned, be said to be unauthoritative and false? Though we do not assume any particular Vedic texts with regard to the establishing of Assembly Rooms and the founding of water-drinking stations, yet all such philanthropic deeds become included in the Vedic text that enjoins the doing of good to others as a duty; and it is from this general Vedic Injunction that such actions derive their authority.

(As for the Vedic texts in support of the particular *Smṛti* Injunctions enumerated in the *Bhāshya* we have the following):—(1) In connection with the fetching of the *Ishtakā*, it is laid down in the Veda that in the cart the horse is to be yoked in front of the ass; and it is added "when the good one goes along, the bad one follows him," which indicates the necessity of the lower (disciple) following (and hence obeying) the greater (Teacher). (2) It is said in praise of a certain deity—"you are a boon to others, just like the water-drinking station in the desert"; and this praise of the particular institution points to the advisability of founding such stations for the good of others. (3) It is laid down in the *Smṛtis* that one should have his *Çikhā* (lock of hair on the head) done up in a definite way, in order to serve as a mark for the particular class of *Ṛshīs* from whom he is descended. And in this case, the restrictive Injunction as to this particular method to be followed must have a transcendental result; and hence the authority of this Injunction cannot be held to rest upon the said visible result alone; for certainly, there are many other means by which the particular class of *Ṛshīs* could be indicated. Consequently, the real purport of the Injunction must be something else. And it is this: in order to regulate the number of "*avattas*" (offerings) at sacrifices (which is in accordance with the *Gotra* of each priest), it is absolutely necessary that the name of the *Gotra* should be distinctly marked; and in this Vedic fact would lie the foundation of the *Smṛti* Injunction of arranging the *Çikhā* in a definite way; and as for the restriction of this particular means, as we cannot find out any other reason, we are obliged to assume that this particular method would produce a certain effect upon the man himself. And thus all *Smṛtis* having distinct purposes to serve, their authoritativeness becomes fully established.

Among the *Smṛtis* themselves, such portions as are related to *Dharma* or Deliverance have their origin directly in the Veda; while those that have pleasure, &c., in view, are based upon the ordinary experience of the world. This rule also holds good respecting the exhortations contained in the Itihāsas and Purānas.

As for stories met with in these, they serve the purposes of the *Arthavāda*, as explained above. The description of the various parts of the Earth (contained in the Purānas) serve the purpose of pointing out and distinguishing the places fitted for the performance of *Dharma* and *Adharma*, and also for the proper experiencing of the effects of such performances; and these are based, partly upon the Veda, and partly upon the common experience of the world. The histories of the various families (recounted in the Purānas) serve the purpose of differentiating the people of different castes, and are based upon Direct Perception and Memory. The descriptions of the various measures of space and periods of time, serve the purpose of regulating the ordinary practices of the world, as also the sciences of Astronomy and Astrology; these are based upon direct perception, as also upon inferences deduced from various mathematical theories. The descriptions of the state of things to be in the future (as recounted in the Purānas) serve the purpose of pointing out the nature of the various periods of eternally-revolving time, and also the variegated character of the results of righteous and unrighteous conduct; and these have their origin in the Veda itself.

Among the Auxiliary Sciences too, there are certain portions that treat of things that are of use in sacrifices, and these have their origin in the Veda, while other parts treat of such as are useful only in the serving of some visible worldly purpose; and these have their basis upon ordinary experience.

(1) In the *Çikshā*, the differentiations of the organs of pronuncia-

tion of letters, their accents and time, &c., have their perceptible uses; while the assertion, that if a sacrifice is performed with a full knowledge of these details, there follows a particular result—*e.g.* "If the *mantra* be recited without correct accents or pronunciation, it kills the sacrificer"—is based upon the Veda.

(2) In the case of the *Kalpasūtras*, we have explanations of the real purport of the Injunctions deducible from the rules that are found scattered in the various branches of the Veda, intermixed with *Arthavāda*, &c.; and as such these explanations have their origin in these latter. In these we also meet with certain rules of conduct to be followed by the priests; and these are based upon considerations of their convenience; and as such have their origin in ordinary experience.

(3) In the case of *Vyākaraṇa*, the knowledge of correct and incorrect forms of words has a perceptible use, exactly like a knowledge of the differences among trees; and as such, it is based upon direct Sense-perception; and the assertion—that the use of correct words fully accomplishes the result of the action performed, while that of incorrect words creates obstacles in its fruition,—has its origin in the Veda.

[(4) The case of *Nirukta* is similar to that of *Vyākarana*, as it also serves the purpose of regulating the sense in which a word can be correctly employed, and hence this has not been mentioned separately].

(5) As for the science of *Chanda*, the correct differentiation of the *Gāyatri* and other metres, is found to be of perceptible use in the Veda as well as in ordinary experience; and as such it is based upon direct perception, while the assertion—that a certain result follows from a sacrifice when performed with a full knowledge of the metre of the *mantra* employed—is founded upon the Veda; as for instance, we find the following declaration in the Veda—"One who, at his own sacrifice, or at the sacrifice of others, makes use of a *mantra* or a *Brāhmaṇa* of which he does not know the *Ṛshi*, the metre and the deity, &c., &c."—which mentions a distinctly undesirable result as following from such conduct.

(6) In the case of the Science of *Jyautisha*, the knowledge of the dates and asterisms, —as computed by means of the various periods of time as divided into regularly revolving cycles, and by a knowledge of the revolutions of the sun and the moon,—is based upon inferences deduced from such mathematical theories as have been handed down from times immemorial. In this science we also meet with the declaration that certain good and evil results, as following from previous good and bad deeds, are indicated by the good or bad position of the planets at the time of one's birth; and it also lays down certain expiatory rites to be performed with a view to ameliorate the planetary conditions; and through these rites, the science comes to have its origin in the Veda.

The above remarks apply also to the sciences of Palmistry, Architecture, &c. ; with regard to these two, however, we may assume such direct Injunctions as that "when one comes across such signs in a man's body, or such marks in the houses, he should take these signs to mean such and such a thing," &c., &c.

As for *Mīmānsā*, it is based upon the Veda, upon ordinary experience, and also upon Direct Perception and Inference, &c., based upon these; and it has been reared up by an unbroken line of scientific teachers; no single person could ever have been able to compile such vast collections of arguments.

The same may be said also of the science of Reasoning. The meaning of Vedic passages is expressed by means of the meanings of words; but in ordinary usage, the denotation of words is found to be mixed up with the several factors of Class (Property, Action, and Name); and these can be directly discriminated, never by themselves, but only by means of Sense-perception and the rest, as distinguished by their respective characteristics, and as put forward by their learned expounders. The Veda itself being scattered over many branches can be rightly ascertained and made to serve its purpose only by these means of right notion; consequently, all these should be properly learnt by the help of the science of Reasoning. This has been declared by Manu also, who says: "Sense-perception, Inference, and Verbal Authority, as based upon various scriptures,—these three should be well learnt by one who desires a (knowledge of) pure *Dharma*"; and again—"He who approaches *Dharma* by means of Reasoning, he alone, and none else, understands it"; and all these point to the necessity of the science of Reasoning. For the most part, now-a-days, people are much more prone to unrighteousness; and thereby having their intuition blurred by ignorance, they take to evil paths. Consequently (with a view to set these people right), what the science of Reasoning,—as based upon experience, *Arthavāda*, the Veda, (direct Injunctions) and the Upanishads,—does is to point out the trend of the misconception and also of the correct conclusion (with regard to a certain point),—then to lay down the arguments in support of both,—and lastly, to arrive at the correct conclusion, after having fully considered the comparative strength of the arguments adduced from both sides. If it were not for such systematic argumentations, various arguments would be appearing to people at random, and would be giving rise to all sorts of misconceptions, through sheer ignorance (of the various phases of the question). And (if the correct conclusion were not properly shown, deduced from the proved premisses, and if only the arguments from both sides had been put down) people would be employing their own mistaken judgments in the choosing of the arguments, and in rejecting some and accepting others, without reference to any definite standard.

16

And as for the dogmatically persistent acceptance and expounding of such entities as *eternality* and *non-eternality*, *oneness* and *separateness*, *generality*, *speciality*, *distinction*, and so forth, these are due to the fact of the impossibility of any definite conclusion being arrived at, unless a certain position is at first dogmatically taken up as the expounder's own. As all the peculiarities of any object are not capable of being comprehended all at once, the expounder cannot but dogmatically take up each of them separately, in order to bring about a correct discrimination of the various denotations of words as they happen to apply to one or the other of the various factors (of the Class, the Property, the Action, or the Name). Otherwise such people as have not comprehended the arguments in favour of one or the other of the aforesaid factors of Generality, Speciality, and the like, could not, by mere personal observation, ascertain any definite factor of an object, as denoted by a particular word.

The *glorifications* and the *villifications* too, as contained in the *Arthavāda* passages, come to be taken as forming parts of specific injunctions and prohibitions, only by means of absolute acceptance of the *eternality* or *non-eternality*, the *oneness* or *separateness*, of the various objects; and consequently, if it were not for the variegated character of objects as dogmatically propounded (at first), these glorifications, &c., would become absolutely baseless. (And for these reasons, the nature of all objects must be fully considered, and as a correct conclusion cannot be arrived at unless each individual theorist puts forth his own arguments in the strongest language possible, each separate system of philosophy has its use).

As for the various theories with regard to the fact of the world originating from a contact of Primordial Matter and the Soul, or from a God, or from an atom, and to that of its being continually created and dissolved,—these have all their origin in the ideas given rise to by the *mantra* and the *Arthavāda*, and point out the fact of the *gross* being a modification of, and proceeding from, the *subtile*; and the use of all this lies in the recognition of the relation of cause and effect, between the sacrifice and its results, the attaining of heaven and the like.

The acceptance of creation and dissolution has its use in the proper differentiation of the scopes of Destiny and Personal Effort (and the pointing out of the fact of Destiny being stronger than Effort); as in all cases (f.i. in the case of creation, though there is no Effort) the action is brought about by the sheer force of Destiny (as also in the case of Dissolution, though the efforts of all beings are pointed towards the continuation of the world yet), there is a cessation of the creative process simply because the Destiny of Creation has ceased to operate.

And as for the theories of Idealism, momentary character of the things, denial of the self, &c.—all of which have their origin in the Upanishads,—they have been propounded, only with a view to dissuade people from cultivating an excessive affection for the things of the world.

Thus then, all the *Smṛtis*, as well as all Auxiliary Sciences, have been proved to be authoritative. In the case of such results as are to follow at a distant point of time, no personal experience can be found to serve as its basis; and consequently in all such cases we infer the basis to lie in the Veda itself. While in the cases of directly perceptible results, as in the case of the curing of scorpion-bites by means of incantations, we actually observe it to be true in the case of other people, and thence come to the conclusion that the science of such treatment cannot but be true and authoritative. This discrimination (of the basis lying in the Veda or in ordinary experience) can always be successfully made.

ADHIKARAṆA (2).

The greatest authority rests in direct Vedic declarations.

***Sūtra* (3). When there is a contradiction between the *Smṛti* and the *Çruti*, the former is to be disregarded; it is only when there is no such contradiction that we have an assumption of the Vedic text.**

The authoritativeness of the *Smṛti* has been established in a general way; and as such authoritativeness belong to all sorts of *Smṛtis*, the author now proceeds to lay down exceptions to the general authoritativeness established before, with special reference to the case of such *Smṛtis* as are found to be directly contradictory to universally-accepted Vedic texts.

Whenever there is any such contradiction, the authority of the *Smṛtis* is to be totally disregarded; as it is only when there is no such contradiction that we have an inference of a Vedic text in support of the particular *Smṛti* injunction. The contradiction meant here is that of Vedic declarations, when such declarations do not lend any countenance to (on the other hand directly lay down the contrary of) the declarations in the *Smṛti*.

The present *Adhikaraṇa* (of the *Bhāshya*) cites such instances of the *Smṛti* as are directly contradictory to direct Vedic Injunctions, and then having considered all the arguments bearing upon the point at issue, comes to the above conclusion.

The *Doubt*, that gives rise to the *Adhikaraṇa*, is expressed in this form: Is such contradictory *Smṛti* also to be accepted as an authority with regard to *Dharma*, or is it an exception to the authoritativeness of *Smṛtis* in general?

The reasons for such doubt are thus explained: The *Smṛti* contradicting the Veda, being capable of having this contradiction explained in some way or other, and the authority of the Vedic Injunction assumed as the basis of this *Smṛti* (in accordance with the last *Adhikaraṇa*) having an authority equal to the direct Vedic Injunction that the *Smṛti* is found to contradict, there naturally arises the question,—Is such a *Smṛti* to be accepted as authoritative?

or is it to be totally disregarded, on account of such contradiction, not allowing of the application of any one of the two aforesaid reasons to the case of such *Smṛtis?* When two notions are found to present two contradictory ideas with regard to one and the same object, they are said to contradict one another; and the question, as to which of the two is to be accepted to the preclusion of another, is decided according to their comparative strength (or authority). (1) Under such circumstances, when we come to suspect a certain *Smṛti* injunction of being contradictory to a direct Vedic Injunction, it is just possible that the suspected contradiction could be explained and set aside, by showing that the two do not exactly refer to the same subject; or even when they do treat of the same subject, as there would be no contradiction, if one could be explained as a General Injunction, and the other as the prohibition of a particular phase of it, the two texts could be accepted side by side; specially as in another case (where the particular prohibition would not be applicable), both of them could be found to be equally applicable, and as such they could both be accepted as optional alternatives, both equally authoritative; and thus there would be no absolute contradiction between the two texts. And secondly, the idea brought about by the Vedic text assumed in support of the particular *Smṛti* text being Vedic in its character, as that produced by a direct Vedic Injunction, and thereby both being equally strong in their authority, both the texts could be accepted as equally authoritative. And consequently, with reference to the particular subject, the authority of the *Smṛti* could not be absolutely disregarded. (2) On the other hand, when we find that however much we may try, we are unable either to explain the contradictory texts as referring to two distinct subjects, or to accept both of them side by side, as referring to the general and particular aspects of the same subject, or to admit of both as equally authoritative optional alternatives,—we cannot but conclude that the two texts contradict one another entirely. And as for the Vedic text that is assumed or inferred, and that which is directly laid down in the Veda, there is a vast difference in the authority of the two, as much as there is between ordinary Sense-perception and Inference. Consequently, then, there being no chance of both being accepted side by side, we cannot but totally disregard the authority of the *Smṛti*, in contradistinction to the direct Vedic Injunction which has been shown to possess a much higher authority. [These are the two ways of looking at the contradiction; and both having a show of reasonableness about them, they naturally give rise to a doubt in the mind of the student, and thus give occasion for the present *Adhikaraṇa.*] On this question then, we have the following :—

PŪRVAPAKSHA.

" The conclusion that presents itself at first is in this form : ' Even when " there is a contradiction, the authority of the *Smṛti* cannot be denied; " because if the *Smṛti* be once held to be unauthoritative, it would be a sad en- " croachment upon the limits laid down before (*i.e.*, there would be no per- " manency in the notion of the authoritativeness of *Smṛtis*). In matters " relating to the performance of *Dharma*, we are always able to assert the " unfeigned authority of such *Smṛtis* as have been found to be based upon " Direct Vedic Injunctions ; and with regard to these all suspicions of their " origin lying in Deception or Illusion have been set aside. If we once " began to doubt the authority of the *Smṛtis*, upon such grounds as the " *Contradiction of Vedic Injunctions, the presence of such reasons for action as* " *avarice and the like* (as shown in the next *Sūtra*), *mutual contradictions* " *among the Smṛtis themselves*, and other such like arguments,—then, how " could we ever be able to ascertain whether or not any particular *Smṛti* " is contradicted by any Injunction contained in the Veda ; specially as the " Vedas have an endless number of rescensions differing from one another " in whole chapters, and whose authority is of a variegated character,—being " based upon Injunctions by Direct Assertions as well as by Indirect Impli- " cations, and also upon Indirect Transference of relations by means " of significant names, &c. ? Consequently people having their suspicions " once aroused could not come to have any confidence in any *Smṛti* Injunc- " tion; and this want of confidence would deprive the *Smṛti* of even the " slightest shade of authority. For if the *Smṛti* even once happens to " lose hold of its basis in the Veda, and comes to be attributed to its " source in the realms of illusion, &c., even Indra himself could not step " in to save it (from total submergence in illusion ; and as such the efforts " made in the last *Adhikaraṇa* to prove that the *Smṛti* is not altogether " based upon Illusion would become useless). When the *Smṛti* is once " decided to have its origin in one source (that of the Veda), then it is " only right that we should set aside the possibility of any other origin " for it (in the shape of Illusion and the like), in order to remove all doubts " as to its authoritative character (and as such in our case the effort to " prove that the *Smṛti* is not based upon Illusion, &c., becomes useful) ; but " this cannot be so, when there is no permanent fixity to the idea that the " *Smṛti* has its sole basis in the Veda (in which case all the efforts of the " last *Adhikaraṇa* become absolutely useless).

" And further, if there were no contradictions among the Vedic texts " themselves, then alone could the contradiction of the Veda by the *Smṛti* " justify us in seeking for the source of the latter elsewhere (in the realms " of Illusion, &c.) But as a matter of fact, we often find the Vedic texts "themselves laying down contradictory courses of actions, such for in-"stance as the Injunctions—(1) *Pours the libation before the Sun has risen,* "and (2) '*Pours the libation when the Sun has risen*'; '*Holds the Shoḍaçi* "*vessels at the Atirātra,* and *does not hold the Shoḍaçi vessels at the Atirātra,*' "and so forth,—where it is absolutely impossible to follow both the courses "laid down.

"Under the circumstances, if by chance, a few *Smṛti* Injunctions, "based upon certain texts of other Rescensions of the Veda, be found to "lay down certain facts in opposition to those laid down by the particu-"lar Rescension that one may have himself studied,—this mere fact of "their support not being found in what we ourselves may have read, "cannot justify us, who base our conduct upon the whole of the Veda "in all its several branches, to absolutely deny the existence of such "corroborative Vedic texts as are distinctly pointed out, by these very "*Smṛti*, Injunctions, as having been found and duly studied by other "persons of bygone ages (Manu, for instance); specially as all Vedic texts "are equally authoritative for all men, as we shall show under the *Sūtra.*— "*The Veda is not addressed to any one person* (II—iv—18); and also because "the *Smṛti* is as good a means of ascertaining the Vedic texts, as a study "of the Veda itself.

"Therefore, just as you accept the authority of even such Vedic texts "as are mutually contradictory, in the same manner, you should also "accept the authority of the Vedic and *Smṛti* texts, that may be found to "contradict one another.

"Then again, from what you say, it would seem that when there is "no contradiction of the Veda, the *Smṛti* has its foundation in the Veda; "while, when there is a contradiction, it has its foundation elsewhere (in "Illusion, &c.); and certainly this would be a very half-hearted theory. "[*Ardhavaiçasa* literally means *half-killing*].

"Secondly, with a deal of effort it has been proved above (in the last "*Adhikaraṇa*) that the *Smṛti* has no foundation in anything else (save the "Veda); and to revive the question again, on the mere presence of a "seeming contradiction, is an excess that cannot be very well allowed.

"For these reasons, we must conclude that the *Smṛti* is always based "upon the Veda. For if even the slightest chance of other sources (as "that of Illusion and the like) be introduced, all hope for any authority "of the *Smṛti* might well be given up.

"Then again with regard to the *Smṛti*, in certain cases you would be "denying the possibility of any such basis as those of Illusion and the like "(with a view to establish their authority, as has been done in the previous "*Adhikaraṇa*); while in other cases you would be admitting the possibility "of such bases (in order to deny their authoritative character); and such "a suicidal process (of reasoning) not being allowable, the denial (of "the authority of even such *Smṛtis* as contradict the Veda) cannot be "considered right. Therefore, whether the *Smṛtis* be authoritative or "not, this authoritativeness or its contrary must be accepted as absolute-"ly undisputed; and there can be no half and half authority and absence "of authority (exactly as one and the same woman cannot be half young "and half old).

"And certainly the authors who compiled the *Smṛtis* must have been "cognisant of the fact of certain declarations therein contained being con-"tradictory to the direct assertions of the Veda; and this clearly leads to "the conclusion that they must have braved this contradiction, only on "the strength of certain other Vedic texts, on which they based their "declarations.

"If the mere fact of perceptible worldly motives being found for the "actions laid down in the *Smṛtis* were to make them unauthoritative, "then, inasmuch as there is always a likelihood of some such motive "being found, in connection with all that is laid down in the Veda, all "the scriptures would have to be considered equally unauthoritative. For "instance, such grounds of the alleged unauthoritativeness of the *Smṛtis*, "as the presence of the motives of affection, aversion, vanity, recklessness, "delusion, laziness, avarice, and the like, are capable of being attributed "to all actions (Vedic as well as non-Vedic). So long as our own minds "are pure and devoid of all wickedness, we can always admit the *Smṛtis* "to have a sound basis (in the Veda); and it is only when our own "minds become tainted that we begin to suspect their authoritative "character.

"What performance of *Dharma* is there, in which some sort of a "perceptible motive cannot be found, and which cannot be found to be "contradictory to some other Direct Vedic Assertions? (The chances of "contradiction are equally present in all Injunctions, whether the action "laid down be found to have a perceptible motive or not). And then "again, the terribly ignorant Atheists have no other business except find-"ing some sort of a worldly motive for all actions,—even those that are "not due to any apparent perceptible worldly motive. Even the actions "laid down in the Veda are made by them to be due to certain "worldly motives; and on the slightest grounds they explain one Vedic "Injunction to be contradictory to other Vedic texts. And under the "circumstances, if the *Mīmānsakas* once give an opportunity to the "Atheists (and encourage them by borrowing their arguments, in dealing "with the *Smṛti* texts that contradict the Veda), thus encouraged, the "Atheists would not leave the authority of any path of *Dharma* safe. "Because these Atheists do not trouble their objectives until these latter "themselves give them an opportunity of attack. And when they have "once been given an opportunity, by such persons as borrow their imag- "inary attacks upon the authority of the scriptures, who (*i.e.*, which "scripture) can hope to escape alive, if once fallen in the way of their "(argumentative) path? For these reasons, it is not right for the *Mimān-* "*sakas* to help the accomplishment of the purposes of the Atheists, who are "bent upon the destruction of all *Dharma*.

"You have (in the foregoing *Adhikaraṇa*) accepted the authority of "*Purānas*, *Smṛtis*, *Çrutis*, and *Usage*, at first by mere faith; and then you have "proved, by means of arguments, that the authority of these, as pointed "out in the scriptures, is quite sound; you should stick to this conclu- "sion by all means, and not slacken your faith midway; because such "slackening would lead to the destruction of the whole fabric (of the "authoritativeness of *Smṛtis* as proved in the foregoing *Adhikaraṇa*); "exactly like a cart, whose fastenings have become loosened. When a man "has accepted a certain theory, he should carry it through, fearlessly; "otherwise he would lose it all, through fear, to the wicked intrusions of "such opponents as are always prone to attack timid people.

"Then again, if the Veda itself were not found to lay down certain "actions, that have worldly motives, and some that are contradictory to "other Vedic texts,—then alone could these two facts be rightly turned "to account to prove that the *Smṛtis* that lay down such actions can have "no foundation in the Veda. As a matter of fact, however, we find the "Veda laying down thousands of such actions as *Threshing*, *Pounding*, and "the like, which have only visible results; and then what is the harm "if such results are also found to apply in the case of actions laid down "by the *Smṛtis*? There are also other actions laid down in the Veda, "which have only visible results (and which can be attributed to motives "of avarice, &c.), such as, the giving of the gifts to the priests, and the "sacrificer's action with regard to the *Tanūnaptra* butter. Under the "circumstances, if these actions be said to be not based upon the authority "of the Veda (because of their having visible results), then, in that case "alone could the *Smṛtis* laying down similar actions be also denied the "support of the Veda. And when we actually find many such actions "laid down in the Veda itself, how can the mere fact of the action "having visible results be accepted as proving the non-Vedic origin of "the *Smṛtis* enjoining them?

"For these reasons it is rightly incumbent on the *Mīmānsaka* to carry "through the theory of the *Smṛtis* being based upon the Veda, that was "arrived at before (in the foregoing *Adhikaraṇa*): and why should he "flinch now? We conclude, then, that even though the *Smṛtis* are found "to lay down actions with visible results, and also those that are contrary "to direct Vedic Injunctions, yet no sound arguments can rightly be "brought forward to shake their authoritativeness. Specially as it was "an unqualified authoritativeness of all scriptures that was established "in the foregoing *Adhikaraṇa*, it must be allowed to remain intact, even if "they be found to be contradictory to direct Vedic Assertions."

SIDDHANTA.

To the above arguments, we make the following reply: All authority of the *Smṛti* becomes inadmissible, when it is found to be contradictory (to Vedic Assertions); and it is only when there is no such contradiction that the Veda affords an inferred basis for the authority of the *Smṛti*. Those *Smṛti* passages that we find to be in direct contradiction to the Veda must have their origin in Ignorance, &c., and can never be admitted to have any foundation in the Veda itself.

In the case of the *Smṛti* we do not admit of a self-sufficient authority; and as for its authority being based upon the Veda, this is found to be contrary to the perceptible fact (of its being contradictory to the Veda). We can assume a Vedic passage (in support of a *Smṛti*) only so long as we do not find a direct Vedic text bearing upon the same subject; and when such a text is found (and found to be contradictory to the assertion of the *Smṛti*), then we can never allow of an assumption of any other Vedic texts in support of this latter; for certainly, when we actually see the elephant passing before us, we do not seek to infer its existence by means of its footprints. And *Smṛtis* are the means of leading us to the inference of Vedic texts, exactly as the footprints lead to the inference of the elephant; consequently when this efficiency of the *Smṛti* is found to be contrary to a direct Vedic text, its efficiency (to lead to the assumption of a Vedic text) is set aside exactly as in the case of the elephant. And *Smṛtis* based upon such inferential assumptions can flourish only so long as their basis is not cut off by directly perceptible texts to the contrary. And when their basis has been so cut off, they have not a much longer span of existence left to them; and die off exactly like the branches of a tree that has been uprooted.

A direct self-sufficient authority is not possible for the *Smṛtis* themselves, by which they could be independent of extraneous support; and as for this support, we do not find any (in the case of such *Smṛtis* as are contary to Vedic Texts). Nor can there be an inference of a Vedic text that is opposed to a direct Vedic text already extant; because, when all that people want to know with regard to a certain matter is known by means of the direct text already available, there can be no necessity for an inference of assumed texts.

If with regard to a certain matter, the *Smṛti* text dealt with a phase of the subject other than that treated of in the Vedic Text (contradicting it), then to a certain extent, its authority could have a chance of being admitted (with reference to that particular phase). But when the subject mentioned in the *Smṛti* has already been dealt with, either in the same or in a contrary manner, by the Veda, then, with regard to that object, the *Smṛti* cannot be admitted to have any authority. Because in the case of any two means of cognition operating contrary ways, with regard to a common objective, the one that has a quicker action accomplishes its object sooner, and leaves no chance for the accomplishment of the slower. And even if the latter is only one degree slower than the former, it is bound to lose in the long run, because its opponent will have reached the goal long before it. On the other hand, in a case where there is no swift opponent tending to deprive it of its objective, the weaker process might take its own time, and there is no chance of its being interrupted.

Nor is there any such unflinching command as that which has once been found to be authoritative must always be accepted as authoritative. (And even though in certain cases the *Smṛti* has been found to have an authority that can force us to admit its authority even in cases where it is contradicted by the Veda yet) it is a general rule that whenever a certain thing is going to be brought forth, it comes to be accomplished only if it is not interrupted in its accomplishment by something that is contradictory to it. Whereas that, which has its very foundation cut off while it is not fully brought forth, or which has its very source cut off, can never attain an accomplished condition. (And this is the case with the authority of the *Smṛtis* in question). But even though it is not accomplished, when interrupted by a stronger opponent, yet it does not follow from this that it would not be accomplished, even in the absence of such opposition. (Hence though the *Smṛti* that is contradictory to the Veda may not have real authority, yet that does not affect the authority of other *Smṛtis* that are quite compatible with the Veda). Conversely, even though a thing may be accomplished in the absence of opposing forces, yet from this it does not follow that it will be accomplished, even when there are strong forces opposing its accomplishment. (Hence though the *Smṛtis* compatible with the Veda may be authoritative, yet that does not establish the authoritativeness of those that are contrary to it). Because, in all cases where we have a general rule and an exception, all cases cannot be covered by the general rule itself ; on the other hand, while the exception sets aside the general rule, in a particular case, it does not follow that the general rule would be thus set aside in all cases. What is proper in such cases is to carefully differentiate the cases where the general rule and the exception may be severally applicable, and then accordingly, ascertain where the one will set aside the other; which cannot be ascertained by means of a vague general perception. For one, who would base his actions upon such general perceptions, would succeed in allaying his thirst by the waters of the mirage (because in this case also he has a general perception of water); conversely, having found his idea of water to have been an illusion in the case of the mirage, he would not perform his ablutions, even in a tank, fearing lest he be deceived in this case also. As a matter of fact however (in the case of the mirage) the notion of water is accepted as true, only so long as one has not acquired the knowledge that *it is not water, but only a mirage.*

In the same manner, then, Inference is accepted as true, only so long as its objective is not found to be covered by a Sense-perception contrary to it. Thus then, the authority of the *Smṛti* can be accepted to be based upon inferred (assumed) Vedic Texts, only so long as the subject of that *Smṛti* is not found to be covered by a direct Vedic Text contradictory to it. From these reasons, if we conclude that in certain cases the *Smṛtis* are authoritative, while in some cases they have no authority, we cannot be said to be open to the charge of "half-heartedness." Because just as the notion of *water* is found to be true, in the case of the perception of real water, while untrue in that of the mirage, in the same manner we can, as reasonably, accept the *Smṛti* to be authoritative when it is found to be in keeping with the Veda, while reject it as having no authority, when found to be contradictory to direct Vedic Texts. And it cannot be rightly urged that either all *Smṛtis* should be accepted as authoritative, or, if its authority be denied in one case, the whole of it should be considered unauthoritative.

Thus then, we conclude that the *Smṛtis* that are contradictory to the Veda, have no authority, because any assumption of Vedic Texts in their support being precluded by direct Vedic Texts, they cannot but have their origin elsewhere (in Illusion, Ignorance, &c.)

Question: "Why cannot such *Smṛtis* be accepted as laying down optional alternatives to those laid down in the Texts that they are found to contradict?"

Answer: All alternative options are open to eightfold objections (explained below); and as such, it is not very desirable to accept them. And further if (by the acceptance of such option) a partial unauthoritativeness of the *Smṛti* be accepted, it becomes very easy for us to deny its authority completely (on the strength of the well-established authority of the Vedic Texts that it is found to contradict). Even in those cases where both alternatives are equally strong, there is an eightfold discrepancy attaching to the option; and it is accepted, only under the pressure of necessity, when there is no other way out of it. How then can it be accepted in the present case, where the authority of one alternative is one step further removed from that of the other, and is got at by means of external aids? That is to say, before the particular *Smṛti* would succeed in acquiring its authority (secondhand, from the assumed Vedic Text), it would be set aside by the Direct Vedic Texts, that are self-authoritative (and as such not depending upon any extraneous authority).

Thus then, in matters relating to *Dharma*, the *Smṛti* not being accepted to be self-sufficient in its authority, it cannot be admitted as pointing out an alternative to the Veda, which could be done only if both were equally strong in their authority. And having its authority dependent upon extraneous aids, the *Smṛti* can never attain any authority, when it is just checked by Direct Vedic Assertion; and as such, it can never raise its head again.

The acceptance of option, even in a case when both the alternatives are equally authoritative, cannot be accepted until we assume the partial unauthoritativeness of both of them. And the assumption of such (partial) unauthoritativeness of that which is decidedly self-sufficient in its authority (*i.e.*, the Veda) would be open to two objections: (1) it would set aside the eternally apparent and universally recognised authority of the Veda, and would thereby run counter to a well-ascertained idea; (2) such unauthoritativeness could be cognised only by means of Negation; but (in accepting the alternative theory) we would be denying the really existing authority (of the Veda), in the absence of any such Negation (*i.e.*, any assertion denying the authority of the Veda); this would be the second objection, based upon the fact of your making a contradictory statement with regard to Authority (that is to say, you assert that *Authority is non-authoritative*). Even though in the first instance (*i.e.*, in the acceptance of one alternative), you may, for some reason or other, accept the responsibility of the above two objections, yet when you would proceed to accept the other alternative, you would render yourself open to two other objections: (1) You had asserted (in the former instance) that the Authority (of the Veda) is cognisable by Negation (that is to say, *non est*); and now (when you are accepting the authority of the Veda as the second alternative), you would set aside this assertion of yours, and thereby make yourself liable to the first charge of self-contradiction; and (2) secondly, in the first instance, you had denied the self-evident authority (of the Veda); and now you would be reasserting this authority, and thus render yourself liable to another charge of self-contradiction. Thus then, in the case of a single sentence, we have shown the acceptance of Option to be open to four objections; and the same would be found to be the case with regard to any other sentence.

But with all this an option has been accepted in the case of the two sentences laying down the *Vrīhi* and the *Yava* as the grain to be used at sacrifices; because in that case, there is no help; as if one proceeds to act according to the Injunction of the *Vrīhi*, he is drawn away from it by the Injunction of the *Yava;* and *vice versâ;* and thus being drawn from two sides, by these two texts, as if by two celestial women (equally attractive), not finding any difference in the strength or authority of any one of them, and not finding any means of reconciling them, with reference to any one object, the person would naturally conclude that being mutually contradictory, both the texts are unauthoritative (partially), and in this case the unauthoritativeness of that which (being a part of the Veda) is fully capable of all authority, is accepted, because there is no help in the matter: if there were any way out of it, such an assumption could never be allowed.

In the case in question, on the other hand, we can never deny the authority of one alternative (the Veda); and the unauthoritative character of the other alternative (the *Smṛti*) alone, cannot establish the unauthoritativeness of both. Even in ordinary worldly affairs, we find that when a man falls in a position where he must lose either one thing or many things, when there is a chance of all being lost, he gladly renounces half the number (and keeps the other half) (so in the case in question, when we are given the option of either denying the authority, at least partially, of both the Veda and the *Smṛti*, or accepting the authority of the Veda and the *Smṛti* in keeping with it, and denying that of the contradictory *Smṛti*,—we cannot but gladly choose the latter alternative as decidedly the wiser and the more reasonable of the two).

And when both are rejected, then we have a destruction of the authority of both; which is also the case if the sacrificer offers at his sacrifice, mixed offerings of *Yava* and *Vrīhi;* because no such mixed offering has been laid down anywhere. The Injunction of the *Yava*, as well as that of *Vrīhi*, is a restrictive one; and each of these implies the incapability of any other substance being used at the sacrifice. And the *Vrīhi* is pointed out as being independently by itself, the article to be used at the sacrifice; so is also the *Yava;* and as such we can never get at any Injunction of the mixture of both. If the *Vrīhi* alone, or the *Yava* alone, were found unable to accomplish the desired sacrifice, and if, for that reason a mixture of the two were used, these facts would set aside the authority of both the Injunctions (of *Yava* as well as of *Vrīhi*). Thus then, we find that this idea of employing their mixture is equal in all respects to the suspicion (that none of the two is able to accomplish the desired sacrifice); and as such this would also lead to the complete denial of the authority of both; and it would be far better to attribute unauthoritativeness to each of them by turns. This leaves the character of both extremely uncertain; but no such uncertainty is allowable where a certainty is capable of being arrived at. And in every case we can carry on our business only by means of such objects as have been duly ascertained to be of one definite nature.

Consequently, that which is authoritative, must always remain authoritative, while that which has no authority cannot be held ever to have any authority. If the same thing be considered authoritative at one time and unauthoritative at other times, we can place no confidence in such a thing. And all this anomaly faces us directly, in the case of the alternative Injunctions of the *Vrīhi* and the *Yava*, where there is no way out of the difficulty. Specially as in this case there is nothing to justify us in adhering to any one of the two, exclusively, which one we shall accept as authoritative, while denying the authority of the other.

On the other hand, in the case of the Direct Vedic Text and a contradictory *Smṛti* Text, we have two means at our command, by which we can definitely decide to accept the Vedic Text as absolutely authoritative and totally reject the *Smṛti* as having no authority at all.

I. In the first place, to the Veda and the *Smṛti* belong authoritativeness and unauthoritativeness, respectively, naturally by themselves; consequently, their respective unauthoritativeness and authoritativeness can be due only to extraneous influences. A property that is natural to a thing can be denied or set aside, only if we can find a strong reason for such denial; and in the present case an idea proceeding from a *Smṛti* text can never have strength enough for setting aside or negativing that which proceeds from a direct Vedic assertion; while, on the other hand again, the idea proceeding from the Vedic assertion is admitted to be of superior strength, and as such is acknowledged to be capable of negativing that which is due to the *Smṛti*.

This comparative strength and weakness, as the ground for effective negativing, we have already explained in detail while treating of Sense-perception and Inference; and the comparative strength of Direct Assertion and Indirect Implication is also explained in III—iii—1, where it is shown that that which is nearer to its objective than the other is always to be accepted as the stronger of the two; and if we apply the same standard to the case of the *Smṛti* and *Çruti* texts, we find that the *Çruti* authoritatively points out its objective, long before the *Smṛti* succeeds, in establishing its own authority (by means of an assumed Vedic Text).

(It might be argued that the *Smṛti* also would in due time come to indicate its own objective, contrary to the Veda, and as such it could be accepted as laying down an optional alternative to the course laid down in the foregoing Vedic Text; but this is not possible; because both the texts refer to the same object, and) it is not possible for the same object to have contradictory properties. And then too, when the objective has been already taken up by one that moves faster (in the present case, the Vedic Text), there is nothing left for the slower one (the *Smṛti*); for instance, an object that has been taken away by horses can never be got at by asses. And it is always found to be the case that long before the *Smṛti* succeeds in pointing (for its authority) to an assumed Vedic Text in support of its own assertion with regard to a certain object, a contrary idea of the object has already been arrived at by other means (*i.e.*, by means of the directly perceptible Vedic Text), which is much swifter in its operation, not being hampered by the necessity of seeking elsewhere for its authority.

It is only so long as the person has not quite ascertained what is to be done, that the operation of such means of the cognition (of Duty) can last; when this has been duly ascertained, there is no more necessity of any means of cognising it. If the Vedic and the *Smṛti* texts were to point to their objective simultaneously, at one and the same time, then there would be no ground for difference in them (whereby we could accept one to be stronger than the other); and in that case both could be accepted to be (optional alternatives) of equal authority.

Or (the difference between the operations of the two texts may be thus explained): We find the Vedic Text pointing out its objective directly; and if at this very point of time the *Smṛti* could also succeed in pointing out the assumed Vedic Text (that would serve as its authority),—then, in that case, somehow or other, we could accept them to be of equal strength, as regards their being the means of cognition; because while the former would be acting as the means of cognising its particular objective, the latter would also be operating towards the bringing about of a cognition of the assumed Vedic Text; even though this latter would still be further removed from the real objective, yet as it would have been found to give rise to some cognition, it could have been accepted to be a means of right notion; and as it would have been found to be functioning simultaneously with the Vedic Text, we could have accepted both to be of equal strength. But as a matter of fact, even when we find the *Smṛti* providing an idea of its objective, while it looks about for a corroborative Vedic Text, without which it is not sufficiently established (in authority), it becomes set aside by a (contrary) directly perceptible Vedic Text, which is ever well-established in its self-sufficient authority. A *Smṛti* that would not need a corroborative basis (in the Veda) would fall off from its position of *Smṛti* (Remembrance, which is held to be that of a Vedic Text to the same effect); and as it stands in need of such basis, while it is without such basis, it is always set aside by a (contrary) Vedic Text.

This is the first method whereby we reject the authority of the contradictory *Smṛti*, before it has been allowed to attain the position of an optional alternative.

II. To explain the other method: we grant for the sake of argument that both the Veda and the *Smṛti* are of equal strength, and that they are to be accepted as laying down optional alternatives. Even then as in this case also, the *Smṛti* would be accepted to be partially unauthoritative, it would be completely set aside.

That is to say, even if we admit the contradictory *Smṛti* as laying down an optional alternative (to the Vedic Injunction), when we would be accepting the alternative laid down in the Veda, we would be admitting the authority of the Veda; and then, we could not but admit the *Smṛti* in question to be unauthoritative; and this unauthoritativeness could not be said to be an entirely foreign property imposed upon it, as it is admitted to be in the case of the Veda; because the sole authority of the *Smṛti* lies in the fact of its being based upon the Veda; and as such when we are admitting it to be unauthoritative, all that we are doing is to declare the fact of its not having any basis in the Veda. And as soon as the absence of such Vedic support has been duly ascertained, we are forced to seek for its origin elsewhere (in the realms of Delusion and the other causes, that have been refuted in the foregoing *Adhikaraṇa*); and it is fully admitted on all hands, that it has been compiled by human authors (Manu and others); and for these reasons, we cannot accept its want of origin or basis to be (like that of the Veda) due to its eternal character; and (as it is found to have no basis in the Veda) we cannot but conclude that it has source in the realms of Deception, Illusion, Ignorance, &c. And if we assume, for the *Smṛti*, any basis other than the Veda, this very basis entirely destroys its authoritative character.

In the case of the Injunctions of the *Yava* and the *Vrīhi*, on the other hand, at the time that we accept the latter alternative and use the *Vrīhi* at the sacrifice, we *impose* upon the former Injunction, an unauthoritativeness which is altogether foreign to it (as being a Vedic Text, it is self-sufficient in its inherent authority); and in the same manner, at the time that we accept the other alternative and make use of the *Yava*, the extraneous unauthoritativeness that had been imposed upon it is set aside by its own inherent authoritative character; specially is such the case because of both the texts being equal in their authority, both equally forming part of the same Veda, and there being no difference between the two, with regard to the proximity or otherwise of their respective objectives.

In the case of the *Smṛti*, on the other hand, when its authority having no basis in the Veda has been once lost in the pools of Illusion, Ignorance, &c., there can be no chance of its being picked up again. Because with regard to the same *Smṛti* text, it is not possible that it should have its basis in an assumed Vedic Text, at the time that we do not accept the alternative laid down in the Direct Vedic Text; and that it should have its basis in Illusion, &c., at the time that we accept the said Vedic alternative (because one and the same thing cannot have one kind of origin at one time, and a totally contrary origin at another).

The following arguments are urged (in support of accepting the aforesaid *option*) : "All that you say would be quite correct, if the person "accepting the option always found the Vedic Text before coming across "the alternative *Smṛti* text ; and then if, after having acted in accordance "with the former, he sought to follow the course laid down by the latter, "then alone could the authority of the *Smṛti* be said to be totally destroyed. "But this is not possible, in a case where it is the *Smṛti* text that is found "and followed first.

"That is to say, in the case where a man has come across the *Smṛti* "text alone, he at once infers that it has a basis in a certain Vedic Text; "and when he has once got a definite idea of such a Vedic Text (in support "of the *Smṛti*), even if a certain direct Vedic assertion to the contrary "present itself subsequently, this latter cannot set aside the authority of "the former inferred Vedic Text. Because when the ass (though slow) "has once reached its objective, the horse reaching it afterwards, cannot "deprive the ass of what it has already got.

"There is no such law as that where a *Smṛti* text is contradictory to a "Vedic Text, it is the former that is always cognised first. Because when "many people are conducting a number of enquiries, the various texts "present themselves to them in various orders; and no significance is "attached to the order of their appearance, in the determining of the "comparative authoritativeness of the texts. For certainly, when a man "is reading the Veda, if he finds the Injunction of *Vrīhi* in the first chapter, "and that of the *Yava* in the second, this does not make the authority of "the latter at all less than that of the former (as you also hold these two "to be possessed of equal authority).

"We also find that the authors of the *Kalpasūtras*, in making a com-"pilation of the Injunctions contained in their own particular Veda with "those contained in other Vedas, always treat the latter Injunctions (when "any of them is found to be contrary to one of the former) as laying "down another alternative course of action. (And as one's own Veda is "studied before any other is taken up, if that which is cognised first were "to be always accepted as the most authoritative, then the Injunctions con-"tained in one's own Veda would always be taken as setting aside those "contained in the other Vedas; and as such the *Kalpasūtras* could not "treat them as equally authoritative and laying down optional alternatives). "Such joint compilation of all the Vedas is also what is favoured by Jaimini "himself; as he also holds that that which is comprehended beforehand "would set aside all subsequent Injunctions.

"Consequently, we should attach no significance to the order in which "the texts appear; what we have to do is to follow the law laid down "under *Sūtra* II—iv—18:—*The Veda is not laid with special reference to* "*any one person;* and hence those men,—whose ideas (of duty) are "dependant upon all the various branches of the Vedas, those that are "directly perceived as well as those that are only remembered, all being "equally authoritative, in that they are equally eternal,—when inves-"tigating the significations of the various texts, should attribute to the "weakness of their own perceptive faculties, the fact of one text being "perceived after the other, and should accept all of them to be equally "authoritative; just as even though the letters and words composing a "sentence are cognised one after the other, yet they are all taken to be "equally important factors in the comprehension of the sentence. And thus, "like the instructions received from one's Father and Mother (those of the "Mother always preceding those of the Father and yet both being accepted "as equally binding), they should, without the least doubt, accept all the "texts to be equally authoritative and binding.

"Otherwise if the mere fact of appearing beforehand were to be taken "as a sure mark of superior authority, and that appearing afterwards were "taken as a mark of unauthoritativeness, what intelligent man could ever "arrive at a decisive conclusion on the point of the authoritativeness or "otherwise of different texts? (As there is no certainty that that which "appears first at one time would do the same at all times).

"And again, if the mere fact of its appearing subsequently were made "the ground for relegating the *Smṛti* to the realms of illusion, then even "in a case where the *Smṛti* is not contradicted by the Vedic Text, it could "not be accepted to be authoritative (as in this case also the *Smṛti* would "be appearing after the Vedic Text).

"For these reasons, we must conclude, either that all *Smṛtis* are based "upon the Veda (and as such equally authoritative), or that all of them "are the products of illusion; and there can be no admixture of their "origin (that is, it is not right to accept some of them to be based upon "the Veda, and others to be based upon Illusion.")

To all this, we make the following reply: Though in a case where we come across a certain *Smṛti* text, if we do not meet with a direct Vedic Text to the contrary, we can safely infer a Vedic Text in support of that *Smṛti*, free from all hinderances for the time being. But if at some future time, we come across a direct Vedic Text to the contrary, we cannot but at once set aside the former *Smṛti* (as unauthoritative); and thus all chance of its having any basis in the Veda having been set aside, we would be forced to the conclusion that it must have its origin in some sort of an illusion, &c. And thus after we have found the Vedic text to the contrary, we are naturally led to think that the idea that we have had from the *Smṛti* is false; and from this we are forced to admit that this idea must have been false, even at the time that we had met with the *Smṛti* for the first time. Even in ordinary experience, we find that a man who is unable to distinguish the false coin from a true one, uses the latter as the real coin; but from this it does not follow that he will continue to use and accept the false coin for the true, even after he has become capable of recognising its false character; and his subsequent discrimination leads him to the conclusion that his notions with regard to the false coin are false, not only at the time when he is able to distinguish it from the true one, but that it has always been false, even at the time when he accepted it as true. (In the same manner, when we do find a Vedic Text, we conclude the *Smṛti* to be false, not only now, but always, even when we first met it, and had not found the Vedic Text contradicting it). As the idea afforded by the *Smṛti* now (when we have founded the Vedic Text to the contrary) is just the same as that afforded by it before, this former idea too becomes set aside (when we find the contrary Vedic Text); for if the former idea were not false, the latter, being identical with it, could never be false.

Objection: "Even when we have found the contrary Vedic Text, we must conclude that it contradicts, not the *Smṛti*, but the Vedic text that had been assumed as the basis for that *Smṛti* (and thus the contradiction being between two Vedic texts, these being equally authoritative, you cannot but admit of the theory of *Option*)."

Reply: But this cannot be; because at the time of the performance of each individual action, there is an investigation into the character of its authority. For if one always depended upon the conclusion that he may have arrived at in one case, then the man, who has discarded the *Vrīhi* and accepted the alternative of *Yava*, at any one sacrifice, would always, throughout his life, use the *Yava* alone, and never use the *Vrīhi;* and it would never be possible for both of them to be used by every man, as optional alternatives. Consequently, then, when a man happens to consider the authority of a particular action, which he is going to perform for the first time, and he finds that he has not yet directly come across any such Vedic Text as he had assumed, in support of the *Smṛti* text, on whose strength he had performed the action for the first time, he is again led by the *Smṛti* text itself to argue that inasmuch as the *Smṛti* has been compiled by a person who is known to be an orthodox performer of all Vedic actions, it must have its origin in the Veda; and thus he again sets about inferring the existence of such a Vedic Text; but now, if at the very outset, he be met by a direct Vedic Text to the contrary, he would find that the undoubted self-authoritativeness of this text could not be otherwise possible, and is forced to admit that the contrary *Smṛti* text must be unauthoritative; and the final conclusion that he arrives at is that the origin of the particular *Smṛti* text lies, not in any Vedic Text (as inferred before), but elsewhere (in the realms of Illusion, &c.); and by this he is not led to impose an unauthoritativeness upon the Vedic Text that was assumed to be the basis for the *Smṛti;* because the unauthoritativeness of this is directly perceptible by the mere fact of its not being found anywhere (in the Veda; and as such there is no need of any such imposition). (And thus we find that the direct Vedic Text contradicts, and points to the unauthoritativeness of, not the assumed Vedic Text, but the *Smṛti* text that was sought to be based upon that assumption; and thus there is a contradiction, not of one Vedic Text by another Vedic Text, but that of a *Smṛti* text by a Vedic one).

You have argued above that, as there is no such fixed rule as that the Vedic Text must always be cognised, prior to the *Smṛti*, or *vice versâ*, there could be no fixed idea as to the authoritative character of the one or the other, if their authoritativeness or the contrary were to be ascertained solely by their prior or subsequent cognition. But this *non-fixity* applies to your theory also: and as such, it should not be urged against my theory alone. In a case where we directly find a Vedic Text contradicting the *Smṛti* text, and have no opportunity for assuming a Vedic Text in support of this latter, it is naturally concluded to have its origin elsewhere (in Illusion, &c.); and as such is completely set aside. And in a case where the contrary direct Vedic Text is found at some other time, even then, the contradiction and the consequent rejection of the *Smṛti* is duly ascertained at that distant time; and this rejection of authority for ever afterwards, attaches to the *Smṛti,* which cannot clear itself of such unauthoritativeness.

As for those that cognise the *Smṛti* text before the contrary Vedic Text, though they themselves may not be cognisant of the contrary Vedic Text and the consequent rejection of the *Smṛti*, yet, inasmuch as the authority of such a *Smṛti* text has been set aside elsewhere by a previous recognition, by other people, of the Vedic Text contradicting it, the *Smṛti* can never free itself from this unauthoritativeness, attaching to it permanently. And even in ordinary experience, we find that the contradiction of the cognition of other people is by no means a very slight means of ascertaining one's own cognition to be false; as for instance, when (by some disorder of the eye) we see the moon as duplicate, or when we are mistaken in our notions as regards the various directions, we conclude our own ideas to be false, only when we find them to be contrary to those of other people.

Objection: "In the case of the Vedic Injunctions of the *Yava* and the *Vrīhi* also, when one would decide to use the *Yava*, his conclusion would be contrary to that of another person who has decided to make use of the *Vrīhi* and thereby the former conclusion would have to be accepted as wrong."

Reply: But in that case, both the Injunctions are equally of direct Vedic origin; and as such the authoritativeness or otherwise is only like the rising or sinking (of an object) (*i.e.*, though the authority ever continues, yet when it rises up, we accept its authoritativeness, and we make use of one Injunction; and when it sinks down, its authority is only hidden from view, and that of the other Injunction having come up, we accept this latter and act up to it); and as such both of them being equal in the eyes of all men, we are unable to find any other ground of difference (between the two).

(If it were a rule with all people that they always cognised a *Smṛti* text before cognising any Vedic one, then it might have been possible for the former to have led to the inference of a corroborative Vedic Text and base its authority upon it; but) as a matter of fact, such people, as always cognise a *Smṛti* text beforehand, are not to be found, in any number, the unauthoritativeness pointed out by the contrary Vedic Text cannot leave its hold upon the *Smṛti.*

Further, in the case of *Smṛtis*, there is an inherent ground of unauthoritativeness (in that they have never any authority of their own, but only one borrowed from the Veda); and the falsity attaching to them upon this ground alone renders them unable to set aside any direct Vedic Text. All that you can do is to impose upon the Veda an unauthoritativeness, which is absolutely foreign to its very effulgent self-authoritative character; and as this unauthoritativeness is actually found in the *Smṛti* (contrary to the Veda), wherefore should you go about assuming it in the Veda (where there is no room for it)? When you find a Vedic Text and a *Smṛti* text contradicting each other, it is absolutely necessary that you should reject the authority of one of them; and as you would proceed to *assume* the unauthoritativeness of the Vedic Text (your action in this resembling that of the covering up of a really existing thing with a piece of cloth in order to deceive yourself into the belief that it does not exist), the inherent unauthoritativeness of the *Smṛti* would present itself before you, and would set aside, once for all, all your doubts as to which of the two is to be rejected; and would leave you no ground for assuming the absolutely unreal unauthoritativeness of the Vedic Text.

Even in the case of such *Smṛti* texts as are not contradicted by a direct Vedic Text, the fact of their being based upon the Veda is by no means always quite certain. Though this fact can be got at by means of Inference, yet it can also be negatived by other similar means of cognition.

Thus then, we find that the case of the *Smṛti* text contradicting the Vedic Text is not identical with that which is not found to be so contradictory; because of the causes of the two being different (that of the former being actually decided to be Illusion, &c., while that of the latter is only the particular cognition of the Author of the *Smṛti*); and as for the origin of these texts, it can be ascertained, only in accordance with the bearing of their contradictories (*i.e.*, the *Smṛti* that has a Vedic Text for its contradictory is decided to have its origin in Illusion, &c., while that which has not such a formidable contradictory is believed to have some authority). And thus we have proved that the charge of "half-heartedness" cannot be laid at our door.

Exactly as in the case of Direct Assertion, Indirect Implication, &c., (explained under *Sutra* III—iii—14), their comparative strength or weakness is ascertained, according as the one that follows is found to be contradictory to, or supported by, that which precedes it,—in the same manner we could also ascertain the authoritativeness or otherwise of the various *Smṛti* texts, according as they are found to be contradicted or supported by Vedic Texts; and there can be no admixture of the two; nor can all *Smṛti* texts (those contrary to the Veda and those not contrary to it) be said to be of the same class.

[Another instance of contradiction of the Veda by *Smṛti*, that is cited in the *Bhāshya*, is that the *Smṛti* lays down that the whole of the sacrificial post is to be covered over; while the Veda enjoins that the sacrificer should sing a certain hymn while touching the post]. And here, though the *covering over of the post* is laid down in the *Kalpasūtra*, which is of a class different from the ordinary *Dharmaçāstra Smṛtis*, and which has been compiled with the avowed object of collecting together the precepts actually found in the Veda,—yet, we shall prove later on that the difference between the *Kalpasūtra* and the ordinary *Smṛti* is very slight; and also as both of them are equally the works of human authors, the *Bhāshya* has cited the *Kalpasūtra* in the same category as the ordinary *Smṛti*.

[The next instance cited is that in the *Smṛtis* it is declared that as soon as the sacrificer has purchased the *Soma*, the priests can dine at his place; while the Veda declares that they can dine at his place only when he has completed the *Agnīshomīya-sansthā*]. And here, though the former passage is found in the Atharva-Veda,—yet (1) as we find that this particular Veda does not in any way help any sacrificial actions that are performed in connection with the sacred fire,—(2) as we find this particular declaration contradicted by the said declaration which is found in the three Vedas that are related to such sacrificial actions,—(3) and as the point at issue is in reference to such a sacrificial action,—we follow the law laid down in the *Sūtra* III—vi—9, where it is distinctly declared that authority which is directly related to the point at issue is stronger than that which is not so related; and from this law we conclude the said declaration of the Atharva-Veda to be weaker in its authority than the other declaration; and for this reason, it has been cited in the *Bhāshya*, in the same category as the ordinary *Smṛtis*.

[Another instance of the contradiction is, that the *Smṛtis* lay down that the Brāhmana is to remain a student for forty-eight years; while the Veda lays down the performance of the *Agnihotra* (and hence of marriage) by one whose hairs are not yet grey and who has got a son.] And here, though the period indicated by the absence of *greyness in the hair* is most indefinite, and it may be that he may not have got a son till then, yet we accept the particular period to be 'youth,' as pointed out by such *Smṛtis* as—"one should seek after *Dharma* while he is still young,"—or as extending, at the very utmost, to 'middle age'; while if one were to remain a student for forty-eight years, these forty-eight years added to the four or six years before the *Upanayana*, would bring the life of the religious student up to the fifty-second or fifty-fourth year of his age or even more than that (if the *Upanayana* be delayed to the 10th or 12th year); and this would certainly be getting beyond the 'middle age'; (and as up to this time he could not marry, the person could not perform the *Agnihotra*) the contradiction between the two Injunctions becomes quite patent.

In connection with the contradiction that has been pointed out with regard to the *covering of the post*, it may be argued that even when the post has been covered, it is quite possible for it to be touched (and as such there is no contradiction). But how can you deny this contradiction? Because *Touching* is the *feeling of an object* by means of the tactile sense; and when the post is covered by a piece of cloth, there can be no such feeling of it; because if the cloth is touched, that would not be the touching of the post; because the touches of these two differ in points of their *genus*, *individuality*, &c. If by the touching of an object connected with another object, the latter were also touched, then the touching of the Earth would also be the touching of the post (and as the sacrificer is always touching the earth, any Injunction of the touching of the post would be entirely irrelevant).

An objection is raised: "Firstly, we do not think the Earth to be the Post, while we have a distinct notion of the *post*, even in a post that has been covered by the cloth; and as such there is a difference between the case in dispute and the instance you have cited. And *secondly*, even when the *Cāndāla* happens to touch the cloth that we are wearing, we can become pure only by undergoing the same processes of bath, &c., as those that are laid down for one who is touched by him directly."

Reply: True it is that we have got to bathe in the case you mention; but that is owing to our contact with the cloth, that has been defiled by the direct touch of the *Cāndāla*. We are led to this conclusion by the fact that, even when a piece of cloth that we are not wearing is touched by the

Cāndāla, if we happen to touch this cloth, we have got to bathe, &c., exactly as if we ourselves had been touched.

Another question is raised: "How is it that you have brought forward a sort of defilement—that of ourselves by touching the cloth that has been touched by the *Cāndāla*—which is not mentioned in the codes of morality? If such defilement were real, how is it that you do not accept such defilement in the case of metals, wood, &c.; when these having been touched by the *Cāndāla*, happen to be touched by us? Certainly, no reasons appear to help us here."

To this we make the following reply: With regard to wood, grass, &c., it is distinctly laid down that they are purified by the air itself; while there is no purification of the cloth, except by washing. It may be urged that this purification has been laid down as necessary only when the cloth happens to be besmeared with unclean matter. But we do not find the word "besmeared" in the text of the *Smṛti*, where it is simply said, that "*an unclean cloth* is to be washed"; and certainly the cloth that has been touched by the *Cāndāla* cannot but be accepted as "unclean"; and as such, it can be purified only by being washed in water.

Obj.: "It is only for the man himself that the *Smṛtis* have enjoined certain expiatory rites as to be performed when he happens to be touched by a *Cāndāla*; and hence it would seem that such *uncleanness* attached to the man alone; and not to any other substance, like the cow or the horse. And when we come to consider whether the cloth, like the cow, is not made unclean, by the touch of the *Cāndāla*, or it is rendered unclean, like the man,—we naturally conclude that it is, like the cow, not made unclean by the touch."

Reply: But we find the *Smṛti* laying down that a man when thus touched is to dip into the water, with all his clothes on; and from this we infer that the clothes are also rendered unclean, and its case is not like that of the cow, &c. And then again, when we happen to touch the *Cāndāla*, with our hand (and there being no direct contact of the *Cāndāla* with the cloth), even for this case, the *Smṛti* lays down that we should bathe with all our clothes on; and from this also it is clear that the cloth is rendered unclean even by its contact with the human body which has been touched by the *Cāndāla*; and consequently it is not unreasonable to declare it unclean when it has been touched by the *Cāndāla* directly. As for the cow, horse &c., even when they happen to be touched by the *Cāndāla*, the *Smṛti* Injunctions do not make it necessary for them to be washed; and as such we do not accept the fact of these animals being defiled by such contact; and as such the case of the cloth cannot be taken as identical with that of these animals.

For these reasons, in the case in question, the *touching of the cloth* cannot be regarded as identical with the touching of the *post* (covered by it)

If the Injunction be explained as laying down the necessity of the priest singing the hymn, while touched by the *post*,—then too, it would be necessary for his body to be in direct touch with the skin of the post. And even if the Injunction, be taken to mean only that he should *rest* upon the post, then too the necessity of direct contact remains just the same; and as such, even this *resting* would not be possible if the post were completely covered up. For, in that case, the priest would sing while resting upon the *cloth* (and not upon the post); because even though the cloth itself, would be resting upon the post, yet it could serve as the rest or support of the priest. For these reasons, we conclude that there is a direct contradiction between the *Smṛti* Injunction of the covering of the whole post, and the Vedic one of touching it; and as such it is only right that we should clearly discern which is to be given the preference.

Says the *Bhāshya* (in support of the option theory): "*But wherefore are not these two Injunctions not accepted as laying down optional alternatives?*" And this must be taken as basing the authority of the *Smṛti* Injunction upon an assumed Vedic Injunction inferred to form part of a different Branch of the Veda; because, as it is, the *Smṛti* by itself has no injunctive power, and is not equal in its own authority to the contrary Vedic Injunction.

The *Bhāshya* says (in reply to the above question): *This cannot be: because we accept two statements as optional alternatives, only when we do not perceive one of them to be a distinctly mistaken one.* And as we have shown above, one of the two Injunctions must be held to be a mistaken one; and in this the mistake cannot but be laid at the door of the *Smṛti.*

The compound "*Vyāmohavijnānam*" may be explained either as a *Genitive-Tatpurusha*—the meaning in that case being 'the ascertainment of another cognition'—or as a *Karmadhāraya*, the meaning being 'the mistaken character of the cognition itself.'

Says the *Bhāshya*: *One who would accept the theory of option in the present case would be accepting the authority of the Vedic Text, when he would touch the post; and as this authority is that of a direct Vedic Text, if it is once accepted, it can never be reasonably taken as having only a partial application.* And this is to be taken as proving the fact that, inasmuch as all chance of the *Smṛti* text being based upon the Veda is cut off, it cannot but be held to have its root in Illusion. And if such character of the *Smṛti* once admits of the authority of its contradictory Vedic Text, the authority of this latter can never be suspected to be partial; because the Veda can never be reasonably open to an imposition of falsity; it is with this view that the *Bhāshya* says *it can never have a partial application.* And as for the *Smṛti* text laying down the covering up of the whole post, as it is always shrouded in the cloud of unauthoritativeness, and is never capable of being cleared from it, this *Smṛti* is also said in the *Bhāshya* to be *never partial* (in its unauthoritativeness).

Or, if we accept the reading (in the *Bhāshya*) "*Pākshikanca*" (instead of "*Apākshikanca*"), the meaning would be that even in accordance with the option-theory, at the time that we would accept the alternative laid down by the Veda, there would be no chance of the assumption of a Vedic Text in support of the contrary *Smṛti* Injunction; and as such, we would be obliged to conclude the *Smṛti* text to be based upon ignorance, &c.; and hence it could never clear itself from this taint of falsity, and so it could never be accepted as authoritative.

As for the Vedic Text, on the other hand, when it has once got the slightest occasion for asserting its authority, it can never be set aside as false, because its opponent (the contrary *Smṛti* Text) is very much weaker than itself (and as such can never set aside the authority of the Veda). It is with this in view that the *Bhāshya* says: *That which serves as the basis of the authority of the Vedic Text, at the time that its injunction is accepted as the desired alternative, &c.*, &c.

It cannot be reasonably urged that the reading of the Vedic Text (that is found to contradict a *Smṛti* Text) is wrong; inasmuch as it appears quite possible for the *Smṛti* itself to have its origin in such faulty sources as a wrong comprehension of the Vedic Text, or illusory dream-like cognitions.

The *Bhāshya* says: *Thus then, it cannot be assumed that the idea has been wrongly transferred to the Veda.* And by 'idea' here is meant the idea of its authoritative character; and by the negation of the expression *wrongly transferred to the Veda*, what is meant is the denial of the fact of assuming the partial unauthoritativeness of the Veda by the assumption of the fact of its consisting of mistaken statements. Or, it may mean that the idea brought about by the *Smṛti* having previously (at the time when the Vedic alternative is accepted) found to be a mistaken one, it can never attain even to partial authoritativeness; and thus the passage may also serve to point out the fact of the *Smṛti* text being contradicted by the Vedic one, specially on account of the former having its origin in Illusion &c.

Says the *Bhāshya*: *Because the origin of the Smṛti is the same in both cases.* That is to say, inasmuch as the *Smṛti* has been set aside by a very much stronger opponent, in the shape of the Veda, all possibility of the assumption of a corroborative Vedic text is closed for ever; and as such the *Smṛti* can never attain to any sort of authoritativeness.

Says the *Bhāshya*: *Api ca itarētarāçraye anyatahparicchēdāt*; and in this sentence the expression "*itarētarāçraya*" means *mutual contradiction*, as explained below. In a case where two means of cognitions are found to contradict each other, exactly like the syllogistic Middle Term which is concomitant both with the Major Term and its contradictory, the point at issue can be decided only by a third means of cognition.

The *Bhāshya* here has used the expression "*pramāṇāyam smṛtau*" and the *Vārtika* raises a grammatical difficulty: "If the word *pramāṇa* be taken as equivalent to the word *jnāna* (neuter),—or, even if it be explained as *that which is cognised* (made up with the nominal affix *lyut*),—we should have had the form *pramāṇē smṛtau*, exactly as we have *Vēdah pramāṇam*; if, however, it be explained as *that by which something is cognised* (made up with an Instrumental affix), it should have to be used in the same gender and person as the word it qualifies (the word "*Smṛti*"); and as such a final '*i*' will have to be added to the word, according to Pānini's *Sūtra* IV—i—15; and the word having thus been transformed into *pramāṇī*, the above clause should have been *pramāṇyām smṛtau.*"

Finding the *Bhāshya* to be grammatically inconsistent in both ways, with a view to defend the expression in the *Bhāshya*, we should have recourse to the following arguments: The *Smṛti* can be rightly spoken of as *pramāṇā*,—this latter word meaning *that which attains its authority* in a corroborative Vedic text, the word being formed by adding the affix *Kvip* to the root '*ay*' (*to go* or *to reach*) (the meaning of the expression being '*when the Smṛti attains an authority based upon a corroborative Vedic text*'). (The formation of the word "*Pramāṇa*" being thus grammatically explained, *Pramāṇa* + *ay* + *Kvip*, the *ya* of the root being deleted, on account of its being followed by the *Ka* in *Kvip*, which is included in the *pratyahāra* '*bal*,' in accordance with Pānini's *Sūtra* VI—i—66; and as for the letters of the '*Kvip*' affix itself, it disappears entirely, the '*K*' being deleted according to I—iii—8 the '*v*' by VI—i—67, the '*i*' according to I—iii—2, and '*p*' according to I—iii—3). Though the affix *Kvip* will be the first to be deleted, on the ground of its deletion being necessary in all cases, and thereby the '*ya*' of the root will not have a following *ka*, yet we will have the deletion of the *ya* of the root, through the potency of the letter '*k*' of the affix which leaves this potency behind, (even when the affix is deleted), in accordance with the *Sūtra* I—i—62. Nor can it be urged that there could be no such deletion, based upon the peculiarities of any letter; because the *Sūtra* VI—i—66 distinctly lays down the deletion of the letters '*v*' and '*y*' when followed by the letters included in the '*bal*' *pratyāhāra* (this '*bal*' being not a *letter*, but an *affix*). Or, we may divide the *Sūtra* VI—i—67, into two parts "*vēh*" and "*apṛktasya,*" and thus the first part would mean that the letters '*v*' and '*y*' when followed by '*vi*' are deleted; and in accordance with this, the '*y*' of the root '*ay*' becomes deleted, on account of its being followed by the '*vi*' in '*kvip*' (the '*k*' always disappearing

as soon as the affix is brought in). And thus the ' y ' having been deleted, all that remains is *Pramāṇa* + *a* and then the feminine sign of ' $ā$ '
being added, in accordance with the *Sūtra* IV—i—4, we have the form
pramāṇa + *a* + *ā*, and the second ' *a* ' blending with the final ' $ā$,' we have
pramāṇa + *ā*, according to the *Sūtra* VI—i—101, which also tends to the ' $ā$ '
being blended with the preceding ' *a* ', and we get the word ' *Pramāṇā*.'

The *Vārtika* next proceeds to explain that the expression " *itarētarāçraya* " of the *Bhāshya*, can also be taken in the ordinary sense of ' mutual
interdependence.' We find that the authoritativeness of the *Smṛti* text is
based upon the unauthoritativeness of the contrary Vedic Text; and the
unauthoritativeness of the Vedic Text is inferred from the authoritativeness of the *Smṛti* Text. Similarly, on the other hand, the unauthoritativeness of the *Smṛti* is inferred on the strength of the authoritativeness
of the Veda; and the authoritativeness of the Vedic Text is ascertained
from the unauthoritativeness of the *Smṛti* Text. And thûs, for one who
would accept the two texts to be optional alternatives, there could be no
escape from the two " *itarētarāçrayas* " explained above; whereas for one
who totally rejects the authority of the *Smṛti* Text (contrary to the Veda),
there is only one kind of " *itarētarāçraya*," (that of mutual interdependence, just explained, and it is not open to the *contradiction* that has been
shown to attach to the Option Theory).

And as in the case of the mutual contradiction of two means of cognition, the matter in question can be ascertained by a third means; so it
becomes necessary, in the present case, to point out the third means; and
this means has been pointed out by the *Bhāshya* (in the shape of a reason
for accepting one text and rejecting the other): *The authority of the touching of the post is a permanent entity* (in the shape of the Veda), *while that
of the Smṛti Text* (laying down the covering up of the post) *has got to be
assumed.* And here we find that this third means is not one that is altogether unconnected with the two objects of discussion (*i.e.*, the two texts).
And the two texts we had found to be open to the discrepancy of " *itarētarāçraya* "; consequently, inasmuch as we do not find the discrepancy in the
third reason pointed out, we are enabled, by its help, to come to a definite
satisfactory conclusion. The Veda being self-sufficient in its authority, the
authoritativeness of the Vedic Text has an unimpeded permanence; whereas the authoritativeness of the *Smṛti* being dependent upon the assumption
of a corroborative Vedic Text, its authority has still got to be assumed.

Thus we find that the authoritativeness of the *Smṛti* depends upon
the rejection of the authority of a direct Vedic Assertion; while the
authority of this Vedic Text is rejected on the sole ground of the authoritative character of the *Smṛti* Text (which it contradicts); and this mutual
interdependence cannot by any means be avoided.

As a matter of fact, however, no amount of assumed unauthoritativeness can touch the Veda; and so long as this unauthoritativeness has not been established, there is no chance for the authoritativeness of the *Smṛti.* For one, who is ambitious enough to think of acquiring glory by suppressing one who is stronger than himself, cannot but be quickly annihilated, exactly as the foot-soldier is destroyed by the elephant. And consequently, in the very action of the assumption of the authoritative character of the *Smṛti*, its upholder becomes vanquished (by the superior strength of the Veda).

On the other hand, when we proceed to consider the aforesaid 'mutual interdependence,' as applying to the acceptance of the superior authority of the Vedic Text, we find that here, it is through the authoritativeness of the contrary *Smṛti* Text that the Vedic Text attains to an *undisputed* authority; and consequently, when we proceed to seek for the ground for rejecting the authority of the *Smṛti*, we find that from the very beginning, the *Smṛti* by itself (without the support of the Veda) is ever unauthoritative; and thus (before it has succeeded in pointing to an assumed Vedic Text as its authority) even a single moment having been found by the contrary Vedic Text, this latter fully asserts its own authority during that time (and leaves no opportunity for the assumption of any texts). That is to say, when we have just found the *Smṛti* Text, and have not yet got at its corroborative Vedic Text, we conclude, at least for the time, the *Smṛti* Text to be without any authority; and by this mere fact the authority of the contrary Vedic Text having been established, its authority remains for ever unmolested; and this conclusion is got at by a means other than the two texts themselves.

Thus then, we find that in one case, (*i.e.*, when we have the Vedic Text alone), the authoritative character of that Text is ascertained through its inherent self-sufficient authority; while in the other case (*i.e.*, when we have come across a contradictory *Smṛti* Text, the authoritativeness of the Vedic Text is ascertained from the (aforesaid) momentary unauthoritativeness of the *Smṛti.* And when the Vedic Text has once asserted its authority, at the first moment, basing it upon a certain basis (of the temporary unauthoritativeness of the *Smṛti* Text),—it gets a firm footing in its complete form long before the next moment (of the assumption of a text corroborative of the *Smṛti*) has fully appeared.

The *Bhāshya* explains this, in one way, in the passage—*As the basis of the Smṛti has still got to be assumed, its authority cannot be ascertained;* specially so long as its corroborative Vedic Text has not been found,—on account of there being no grounds for assuming it. The other way of explaining the same thing is that when once the Vedic Text has obtained an authoritative footing, it cannot but be kept up until finally its authority becomes beyond all cavil and dispute.

In the cases of an acknowledged option—such as those of *Vrihi* and *Yava*, and the *Bṛhatsāma* and the *Rathantarasāma*,—we accept the option, because there is no way out of it; specially as the injunctions being found in the Veda, there is no difference in their force, as there is in the case of two men, one standing on a step higher than the other (*i.e.*, none of the two stand in need of the intervention of the authority of any assumed texts); and as such, both being of equal strength, we can have no reasonable preference for either the one or the other; and hence in such cases, we must admit of option, as explained before.

Thus we conclude that no authority attaches to such *Smṛti* texts, as are contradictory to direct Assertions of the Veda.

End of Adhikaraṇa (2).

ADHIKARAṆA (3).

[*Treating of the unauthoritative character of such Smṛti Texts as have their origin in ordinarily perceived worldly objects*].

Sutra 4. (Also because we find reasons).

For the following reason too, the *Smṛtis* in question cannot be accepted as authoritative; because we find them to be due to other causes. Nor is it possible to assume the existence of corroborative Vedic Texts either by preference or by Apparent Inconsistency, on the ground of the authors of the *Smṛtis* being such persons as were the performers of the actions laid down in the Veda. Because this reason is found to be too wide (and as such not invariably pointing to an authoritative text). For when the capability of the *Smṛti* to point to a corroborative text has been destroyed by the contrary Vedic Text, we can have no inference of any such text; and then, when we proceed to look for the source of the *Smṛti* elsewhere, we find its sources, sometimes in Illusion, sometimes in Avarice, and sometimes in perversions of arguments,—any or all of these being incapable of being denied as a sufficient cause of such freaks of imagination (as we meet with in the *Smṛtis*). These sources can belong only to such *Smṛtis* as have been maimed by a contrary Vedic Text, and not to the Vedic Text itself; because a contradiction of the Veda always sets aside the *Smṛti*, and never *vice versâ*. It may be argued that—"Just as we are unable to find a basis for the *Smṛti* in any Vedic Text, in the same way, we may be unable to find its basis anywhere else (in Illusion, etc.)." In view of this question, the *Bhāshya* adds—*It is more reasonable* (and more in keeping with facts) to assume its basis in Illusion, etc., than in the Veda; because when we can find any perceptible basis (in Illusion, etc.), we can have no ground for an unseen one (in the Veda).

[The above explanation makes the *Sūtra* a part of the preceding *Adhikaraṇa*]. *It may also be taken as an independent Adhikaraṇa*, says the *Bhāshya*.

Whenever an alternative interpretation is suggested, there can be only one of the following two reasons: (1) either that the former explanation is not quite satisfactory, or (2) that the second explanation brings out certain facts not got at by means of the former.

And in the present case, the unsatisfactory character of the former interpretation consists in the fact that when the unauthoritative character of the contrary *Smṛti* Text has been already established on the exceptionally strong ground of its being contradicted by Vedic Texts, it is not much use bringing forward further arguments in support of the same conclusion. On the other hand, when we take the *Sūtra* as a distinct *Adhikaraṇa* by itself, we find it affording an argument, which, independently of the former arguments (detailed in the preceding *Adhikaraṇa*), is capable of setting aside the authority of the *Smṛti* texts; and for this reason we explain it as constituting an *Adhikaraṇa* by itself.

In the case of such *Smṛti* texts, as are not directly contradicted by the Vēda, and yet are incapable of any authoritativeness, we find other reasons for asserting this unauthoritativeness; and there is no possibility of such texts being set aside by any means (other than those pointed out by this *Sūtra*). For instance, the *Smṛti* lays down—"The *Adhvaryu* priest takes the cloth worn at the *Vaisarjana Homa*"; and it is in accordance with this that the priest takes away the cloth in which the Soma is brought, and also that worn by the Sacrificer during the performance of the *Vaisarjana Homa;* and though this Injunction is not found in any of the metrical texts of Manu, &c., yet it is inferred on the strength of such being the practice of the priests. Similarly we have a *Smṛti* injunction laying down the giving away of the "*yūpahasti*," by which the cloth enclosing the sacrificial post is meant; and this acceptance of the cloth by the priest is also based upon an Injunction, which is itself based upon the fact of such being the recognised practice of priests.

In the case of these *Smṛtis* too, though it would seem that, inasmuch as the performers of such deeds are the performers of Vedic sacrifices, these injunctions must have a basis in the Veda, yet no assumption of such Vedic texts is possible; because they may be explained as being due to *avarice*, &c. The priests know that the sacrificer is bound to them as it were, on account of the necessity of his finishing the sacrifice that he has commenced, and also that he would be free from their clutches as soon as it is finished; and consequently, while he is still busy with the sacrifice, they beg from him various things, basing their petitions upon various claims, and also upon imaginary texts laying down and eulogising the gifts asked for, whereby they seek to convince him of the sacred character of their petitions; and in this they behave exactly like the slaves at the harvest, who prefer several requests to their master, basing their requests upon long established claims of sorts. And the Sacrificer too finds the texts that the priests bring forward to be similar to the well-known Vedic texts laying down other gifts; and thereby being convinced of the necessity of the gifts asked for by them gives them the things they ask for; and consequently the *Smṛti* texts may be those very imaginary texts, whose tradition has been kept up by a line of selfish priests; and while we have this suspicion, no assumption of a Vedic text in support of such texts is possible. And as shown above, it is far more reasonable to conclude them to be due to avarice, &c.; and so the suspicion becomes a certainty. And it may be pointed out that this fact has already been hinted by the *Bhāshya*, by the expression "*Tulyakāraṇatvāt*" (*i.e.*, the fact of avarice being the source applies to the case of the *Vaisarjana* cloth, as also to the *covering* of the post).

But with reference to the two foregoing *Adhikaraṇas*, the following points are worth consideration :—

The fact of the *Smṛtis* being based upon the Veda having been fully established, even if, perchance, a certain *Smṛti* text be found to be contradicted by a certain Vedic text, how can we attribute it to such other causes (as Illusion and the rest)?

It is a well-known fact that Vedic texts are scattered over various branches of the Veda, known to different persons; and that they do not occur in the Veda in the order in which they are used at the performance of sacrifices; and consequently, it is only right that, with a view to protect intact the context of the whole Veda, the authors of *Smṛtis*, when laying down the performance of certain actions, should not quote the Vedic texts themselves; but simply point to them, by means of expressing the same sense in their own words, and then collect them as such in one place; and in so doing the words used by these authors serve to indicate the words of the Vedic texts (which are themselves not available), exactly in the same manner as certain distinctions of tone, accent, &c. (serve to indicate the different meanings of words, &c.) And as, when a student goes to a teacher with a book in his hand, when the teacher points out a certain text as forming part of the work, even though it be not found (in the particular book carried by the student) he accepts the text as true; in the same manner, the words of the authors of the *Kalpasūtras*, occupying with us the same position as the words of the teacher, simply point to the existence of Vedic texts in keeping with themselves; and as it is only in this pointing out that their function ceases, they cannot be rejected as unauthoritative, on the ground of their proceeding from a human source; exactly as though proceeding from them, yet the distinctions of tones, accents, &c., are not rejected as altogether unauthoritative.

Then again, that the Vedas are in such and such a form can be pointed out by such men as either read or *remember* them; and no difference is made whether the one or the other means is employed. As at the time that the person is not actually repeating the Veda, even those who have read it all up, retain the Veda either by the impressions left by them, or by his memory (and in the case of *Remembrance* also, the text is retained by memory). Thus then those Vedic texts, whose sense is remembered and reproduced (by the authors of the *Kalpasūtras*), and as such clearly pointed out as really existing in the Veda, are equal in authority to those texts that are directly found in the Veda as one may have learnt it; and as such, on what grounds could they be rejected? If a single *Smṛti* work could be found to be, through and through, against the Veda, then alone could we reject that work, and employ the others (in our practice). (But no such *Smṛti* work is found). As a matter of fact, all the *Smṛtis* that we know of,—such for instance, as those treating of the *Upanayana, &c.*,—are found to be based upon direct Vedic texts, of the several rescensions, the *Katha*, the *Maitrāyāni*, and the rest; and if by chance any single sentence in such *Smṛti*, be found to be not in keeping with Vedic texts, we dare not conclude, on the strength of that solitary instance, that that particular *Smṛti* text must have its origin elsewhere (in the realms of Illusion, &c.) And when such a *Smṛti* text is rejected by some person, over-fond of logical reasoning, if he is soon made acquainted with a Vedic text, of a different *Çākhā*, corroborating that very *Smṛti*, how sorry would the countenance become, of this clever logician? And (as the *Smṛti* text would be found to be contradicted by one Vedic text and corroborated by the other) there could be no certainty as to whether its authority is to be rejected or accepted.

As for the *Smṛti* text enjoining the *covering up of the whole post*, which has been cited as an instance of a text contradictory to the Vedic text laying down *the touching* of the post,—this *Smṛti* text is entirely corroborated by direct Vedic texts; as has been clearly shown by Jaimini himself in his work the "*Chandogyānupada*," as also while dealing with the subject of the "*Audumbari yūpa*" as laid down by direct Vedic texts of the *Çākatāyani* Brāhmaṇa,—where it is pointed out that the people belonging to the *Çākatāyani* Rescenion, should, in covering the post, have the "*thread-ends*" at the top; which distinctly shows the necessity of its being *covered by cloth*, as is also pointed out by the following text: "the cloth is praised, the cloth is prosperity, the cloth is peace;" and in connection with this, Jaimini has (in the aforesaid work) also explained the covering of the *Audumbarī* post by a piece of cloth as being based upon direct Vedic texts. And thus being based upon Vedic texts, how can it serve as the instance of a text to be rejected as unauthoritative? On the other hand, it is only proper to accept it as laying down an optional alternative to the Vedic text; as both have been found to be equally strong in their authority.

As a matter of fact, however, there would have been a possibility of its being totally rejected, only if there were a real contradiction; but in the present case, there is no contradiction at all; for mere *covering* cannot be contradicted by the text that enjoins its *touching*. Because if the post were covered up, leaving a few inches uncovered, could not the *touching* be very well done? That the *whole* of the post should be covered is not laid down in the *Kalpasūtra;* and as a matter of fact too, nobody covers it near the root of its ears. Even if the particle '*pari*' (in the *Sūtra*) were taken to imply the covering of the *whole post,* then too the *Sūtra* would have its purpose fulfilled even if the post were left uncovered in the small place (near its ear).

It has been said that this *covering* of the whole of the post can only have originated in the greed (of the priest for the cloth); but the greed would have been better satisfied by covering the lower and the upper parts by two pieces, exactly as two are used by females for the lower and upper coverings (which would give the priest two instead of only one piece); and then again, the priest should have laid down that it should be a splendid silk cloth; and not that it should be one only, and that too without any qualifications. That the injunctions of the various coverings are not due to any greed on the part of the priest is amply proved by the injunction that the post is to be covered by *Kuça* grass; and it is after the post has been covered by the *Kuça* grass that it is covered by the cloth. And certainly in the case of the text laying down the covering by *Kuça,* no such cause (as that of greed and the like) can be found; and in the case of the cloth-covering also, we cannot find any such cause for the restriction that the cloth should have its thread-ends pointing upwards.

As for the text that lays down the propriety of eating at the place of the Sacrificer when he has pruchased the *Soma,* it is a text from the *Atharva Veda;* and certainly there can be no reason for asserting its unauthoritativeness. Even though this particular text of the *Atharva Veda* does not serve any purpose in connection with sacrifices, yet what is there to set aside its authority with regard to other matters? The performance of *Çānti* (pacification of evil influences), *Pushti* (actions meant to bring prosperity) and *Abhicāra* (killing of enemies, &c.), are all laid down in the *Atharva Veda,* as to be performed for the sake of the same person (that performs the sacrifices), and by the very same priest; and thus we find that the *Atharva Veda* serves the purpose of explaining its own particular province of Actions, exactly in the same way as the other three Vedas do with regard to their respective subjects (of the performance of the various sacrifices, &c.) (And as such there is no reason why the authority of the

Atharva Veda should be rejected in favour of that of the other three Vedas). And again, the Injunction of eating (at the place of the Sacrificer who has purchased the Soma) does not refer to any part of the sacrifice; exactly as the actions of *Çānti*, &c., do not form part of any; therefore both (the *Eating* and the *Çānti*) referring simply to a desirable purpose of man, the authority of the Injunction of the said *Eating* cannot be reasonably rejected (*i.e.*, as the *Eating* is not a part of the sacrifice, the authority of the *Atharva Veda* cannot be doubted with regard to it).

(The *Eating* does not form part of any sacrifice because) it has been laid down, not with any special reference either to the sacrificer or to the priests, but with regard to all men in general. There are certain other texts that prohibit a man to eat at the place of one who has been initiated for a sacrifice; and we find two texts that allow him to eat at the sacrificer's place; but each of the texts defines different limits of time,—one of them allowing of the eating only when the sacrificer has finished the "*Agnīshoma-sañsthā*," and the other pointing out the "purchasing of the Soma" as the time after which one could eat at his place; and (there is no contradiction between the two texts, as) they can be taken as laying down alternative restrictions; exactly as there are alternatives laid down with regard to the cessation of the various "Periods of Impurity"—(where we do not reject any one alternative in favour of another).

An objection is raised: "The distinction that is made in the periods "of 'impurity' is due to considerations of the impediments to the performance of sacrifices; and for this reason the various limits of impurity "are not equally authoritative; and as such they cannot be accepted as "alternatives. One who could become purified, or capable of feeding others, "in a shorter time,—why should he wait for the lapse of the longer time? "Thus then, if the Brāhmaṇa could become pure after the lapse of either "one or three days, how could the impurity ever continue for ten days? "Because by 'purity' is meant the disappearance of sin, or the capability "of performing sacrifices; and how could these properties be held to be "both existent and non-existent, before the lapse of ten days? In the same "manner, in the case of the food given by the initiated sacrificer, we can "never know it to be both pure and impure, before the *Agnīshomasañsthā* "has been finished.

"It may be argued that—'The limit of the impurity in the case "of each person may be acknowledged to be that which he and his forefathers have been accepting from before, exactly as whether the "*Agnihotra* offerings are to be made before or after sunrise, is decided by "what the man himself or his forefathers may have been doing (and as we "accept the two times to be optional, so too we can also hold the limits of "purity to be optional).'

"But this cannot be; because in the case of the two times of "the *Agnihotra*, both are equally authoritative; and hence an option "is allowable; nor, in this case, is any contradiction of any previous "text (as there is in the case of the food, the mention of its purity "being contradictory to that of its impurity, before the finishing of the "*Agnīshoma*). Because the mention of the advisability of making the "offering before sunrise does not make that of making it after sunrise alto-"gether useless. And further in this case, the two alternatives do not "differ in the least, in the amount of trouble and expense that each in-"volves. While, on the other hand, in the case in question, if the purity "that is accomplished in a shorter time, be postponed till a much longer "time,—this action would in the first place be in direct contradiction to "such express injunctions (of Manu), as that *one should not extend the period* "*of impurity*; secondly, the acceptance of the longer period involves a much "greater trouble; and as such no one could accept it; and as no one would "accept it, the declaration of this longer period would become absolutely "useless. Therefore until we can find out some reason or object for the two "declarations, we cannot admit them as optional; and such object, or reason, "for the lessening of the number of impure days, we have found to lie in the "considerations of the impediments to the proper performance of sacrifices, "(*i.e.*, as the greater number of the days of impurity would keep the per-"son away from sacrifices for a longer time, the period is shortened); and "in this case there is no extension of the period of impurity; and "as for shorter periods of impurity, we find these limited to—(1) four "days, (2) three days, and (3) one day—in the case, respectively, of the "deaths of the child, (1) that has cut its teeth, (2) that after whom "another child has been born, and (3) that which has not had its tonsure; "and in these cases too, there is no extension of the period of impurity. "Says Gautama (laying down reasons for the lessening of the period of "impurity): *It is done, for the sake of the proper transaction of business, in* "*the case of the Kshatriya, and for the performance of sacrifices, in the case of* "*the Brāhamaṇa.*

"Or, it may be that the injunction of not extending the period "of impurity may have its application in a case where another cause "of impurity comes about within ten days from the first cause, in "which case the lapse of these ten days purifies the man from the "impurities due to both events. The meaning of the said injunction "would, thus, come to be that one should not extend the period of im-"purity, even if a cause for further impurity comes about; because the "period of the former impurity would apply to the latter also; and hence "it is that when the ten-day period of impurity due to a certain cause has "begun, and has not come to an end, before another event happens in the

" *interim*, the former includes this latter; because the number of days " limited to *ten* spreads over all these ten days completely, and as such it " is only proper that it should have its sway over any other event that " may happen within its limits, and thereby limit the period of impurity " due to this latter. Purity and Impurity being imperceptible entities are " accepted, just as they are declared to be in Vedic texts (and as such we " cannot always find a reason for the continuance or cessation of the " periods of impurity due to various causes).

" In the case of the *eating* (at the place of the initiated sacrificer), " however, we do not find any cause or object for any limit; and hence " the longer limit would always be rejected in favour of the shorter. " Consequently it is absolutely necessary to find out an object for " the laying down of the two limits. It may be urged that—' in the " case of the said *eating* also, when it is impossible to wait for the " longer limit, or when the sacrificer happens to offer the food (which is " not considered right to refuse), then (under these two contingencies) " his food may be taken, even after he has only finished the purchase of the " Soma. The *Dharmaçāstras* have often laid down certain secondary " causes of action, to be followed, in times of trouble, when it is impossible " to follow the course primarily laid down; and in the same manner, it " may be held that when one is on the point of death by starvation, he " can partake of the food given by the initiated sacrificer, even if this latter " may only have purchased the Soma at that time.' Well, this is only " another way of declaring the injunction of the shorter limit to be un- " authoritative; because, in the event of starvation, Viçvāmitra even ate " of the thigh of a dead dog (which does not mean that the eating of the " dog is allowable."

To all this, we make the following reply: In one case (as in the case of the eating of the dog) a certain evil deed is unavoidably done, which is not expressly permitted; and in another (as in the case of eating at the place of the sacrificer when he has purchased the Soma) that which is done as unavoidable, is also expressly permitted; and certainly, this contitutes a deal of difference. It cannot be denied that there is a difference between the general permission (that in troublous times men can, under pressure of circumstances, do prohibited deeds), and a specific permission (that such and such an act is to be done); because there is no sin attaching to this latter act, while to the former, there is a slight taint of it. Manu also has laid down the following, with regard to the course of action permissible in times of trouble: 'The sins committed during such calamitous times will be purified when such times have ceased; and the person, who has lowered himself by the performance of a slightly evil or a gravely heinous deed, can purify himself, when (on favourable times having arrived) he is able to do so, by the performance of deeds of righteousness.' And the first act of righteousness that will have to be performed would be in the shape of an expiatory rite; and when the man will have purified himself by its means, then alone will he be entitled to the performance of such other acts, as will bring to him particular desirable results, (*i.e.*, the various sacrifices).

Thus then, it must be admitted that the injunction, that permits the eating at the place of one who has purchased the Soma, is meant to imply that, in a case where there is no other means of saving one's self from starvation, if he eats at his place, he does not, by that, commit a sinful act. And in this connection, it may also be pointed out, that in a case where one is able to abide by the primary injunction, if he has recourse to the secondary alternative, he does not obtain the proper results,—as has been explained in the case of sacrifices. Thus then, inasmuch as the acceptance of the simple alternative, without sufficient grounds for the renouncing of the chief injunction, has been condemned as useless (and not permissible), it must be concluded that when it is possible for the man to obtain food elsewhere, he should not, for mere worldly reasons, partake of food at the place of the sacrificer, (if he has only purchased the Soma, and not finished the *Agnīshoma-Sansthāk*).

Or, we may explain the case in the following manner: The two courses of action referring to different points of time, and thereby not being capable of being taken as equally authoritative alternatives, we must explain away their seeming contradiction, by finding different purposes (or significations) for them. (And this is done in the following manner): So long as the initiated sacrificer has not purchased the cow, any partaking of his food is never allowable; and when he has purchased the Soma (one might eat at his place, but), if one desist from such eating even then (and wait until the finishing of the *Sansthā*), he would be imposing upon himself a certain penance, which is by no means compulsory (though leading to excellent results), exactly as the not partaking of any food at the *Çrāddha* ceremonies, or of giving up the eating of meat,—which, as penances, are good and bring about very good results, though they are by no means compulsory; as neither the eating at *Çrāddhas*, nor the partaking of meat, is absolutely prohibited. Because what is absolutely prohibited is the eating at a place where a *Çrāddha* is performed, within the ten days of impurity, as also (according to some authors) the eating at the Anniversary- *Çrāddhas*; and there is no prohibition of eating at all functions that are performed in honour of the Forefathers; and hence we understand that if one desists from eating at all such functions, he is performing a particular penance, which leads him to Heaven. In the same manner, the eating of meat is absolutely prohibited on the sixth, eighth, fourteenth, and fifteenth (and the thirtieth) days of the month; and from this it follows that the householder can eat it on the other days, if he so wish it; and hence if one desists from its eating, he acquires a peculiarly excellent merit; as has been expressly laid down (by Manu): 'There is no harm in eating meat, or in drinking wine, &c.; such is the general inclination of men; but cessation from these leads to excellent results.'

The opponent may argue thus: "In the case of the eating of food at "a place where a *Çrāddha* is being performed, we find that there are in "reality two distinct sentences; and as such we can interpret it as two "sentences; in the case in question, on the other hand, there is a single "sentence prohibiting the eating of any food at the house of one who has "been initiated for a sacrifice; and as such, how can the single sentence "express two (unconnected) facts, as that one should not eat before the "person has purchased the Soma, and also that if one does not eat at his "place before he has finished the *Agnīshomīya-Saṅsthā*, he will be obtaining "excellent results?"

To this, we reply as follows: The latter may also be taken as two sentences, as laying down distinct limits; the former general prohibition of *eating* ends with the purchase of the Soma; and we do not connect the second limit with this general prohibition; because this latter is one only (and as such cannot reasonably be connected with two limits). And then from the fact of there being a second permission (that one can eat at the place when the *Saṅsthā* has been finished), we infer that there must be some other prohibition of the *eating* referring to the time intervening between the purchasing of the Soma and the finishing of the *Saṅsthā* (and that the latter injunction sets aside the inferred prohibition). Otherwise (if there were no such intermediate prohibition, why should that, which has been already permitted (by the sentence that permits the *eating after the Soma* has been purchased), be permitted again (by the sentence permitting the *eating after the Saṅsthā has been finished*)?

For instance, when the sacrifical priest has got his permission at the very beginning, what would be the use of according him another permission for the performance of the *Nirvāpa?* At the time that the priest is appointed, the sacrificer already accords him the permission to do everything in connection with the sacrifice; and hence the word '*prasava*' in the *Mantra* employed at the *Nirvāpa* is not taken as indicating another permission by the sacrificer. In the same manner, the permission of *eating* accorded by the passage that lays down the purchase of Soma as the limit would be needlessly repeated in the permission accorded by that which lays down the finishing of the *Saṅsthā* as the limit; and in order to avoid this, we must admit, either that the *desisting from eating* between the two mentioned limits is a particular penance bringing about excellent results,—or that the latter passage permits the *eating* which has been prohibited by another (inferred) passage which operates between the time included between the two limits. And as the permitting of that which has been prohibited gives rise to the notion of an *option*, such a process is open to the eightfold discrepancies (of an Option, as explained above).

For these reasons, we conclude that the permission is only of that which had been set aside as an exception (by the inferred intermediate prohibition). That is to say, this intermediate passage (whose existence we have inferred) serves to lay down, for those who may be desirous of certain excellent results, an observance, in the shape of the *not-eating* of the food of the initiated person (even after he has purchased the Soma); because before such a passage, the second permission would be meaningless; specially as it cannot be accepted as a distinct Injunction; as in that case we would have to assume an invisible Transcendental Result (to follow from the act of eating after the *Saṅsthā* has been finished). Thus then, the purpose and the object of the two passages (laying down the two limits of abstaining from the food of the sacrificer) being entirely different, they cannot be said to contradict each other.

As for the *Smṛti* text that enjoins the life of the religious student for forty-eight years, this has been mentioned, in the *Smṛtis* also, only as an alternative course; or, it may be explained as referring to conditions of life other than that of the prospective householder; and as such there is no contradiction by this of the said Vedic text. Manu speaks of the person "having studied the three, two or even one Veda, in due order"; and from this it is clear that the three alternatives are laid down, either in consideration of the diverse capabilities of different students, or as referring to different conditions of life. Gautama has also declared that—"with a view to the studying of *one* Veda, the man should remain a student for twelve years"; and this is the first alternative, laid down for those desirous of soon entering into the householder's state. And as the second alternative, he lays down the necessity of leading the student's life, extending to twelve years for each Veda,—thus making up a sum total of forty-eight years.

And in connection with these alternatives, we can make the following distinction: The longer period has been laid down for those that are either blind, or lame, or otherwise incapable of entering upon the duties of the householder. For such people, there is either life-long studentship, or a life of Renunciation; and as such, they can very well accept the longer course of study, which is thus laid down for them, to prepare them, from the very beginning, for their religious life. Because it is only right that the *Upakurvāṇaka* student (who is incapable of affording any help to others, in the shape of wife or children), should spend the greater part of his life in long-continued study; as that would endow him with great knowledge; and as such having all his sins destroyed by means of pious deeds (of worship, *Japa* and the like), and thereby becoming duly purified by means of pure study, he would reach the desirable goal, even if he succeeds in fulfilling only a few of the ordinary duties of life. Dvaipāyana and others have also declared thus—"The Brāhmaṇa having all his duties accomplished by means of pure study, may or may not do any other actions; and he is called a '*Maitra-Brāhmana.*'".

Then again, we find it declared that the daily performance of such actions as the study and explanations of the three Vedas and the various *Sūtras*, &c.—which go under the name of '*Brahmayajna*'—bring about certain results, in the shape of Heaven and the like; and if these were taken to apply to such persons also as are capable of, and entitled to, the performances of the various sacrifices, then the Injunctions of these elaborate sacrifices (as leading to such results as Heaven and the like) would become absolutely useless; and consequently we take them as referring to the life-long Student and the Renunciate, who are entitled only to such actions as *Japa* and Meditation; and as the results following from such actions become greater by a greater knowledge of the Veda, the *Smṛtis* lay down twelve years as the time to be employed in the study of each Veda.

Or, it may be that if a student turns out to be exceptionally clever, and quickly reads up all the four Vedas, not neglecting, within the same time, a full comprehension of the meaning of the Veda, he can certainly take his stand upon the Injunction—that the life of the religious student should last only so long as the Vedas have not been studied—and can accordingly enter into the state of the householder directly (*i.e.*, even before he has completed the twelve years); and in the case of this person, the particular Injunction has set aside both the injunctions that lay down, respectively, twelve and forty-eight years as the extent of studentship. Consequently then, (inasmuch as these are only various alternatives laid down in accordance with the exigencies of particular circumstances) none of them can be cited as an instance of the contradiction of a Vedic text.

Thus then, we do not find any *Smṛti* text contradicting the Veda; the contradiction that we do meet with is only between two Vedic texts; but this also is capable of being explained in some way or the other. (I) Consequently, the *Sūtra* (the third) must be taken to signify only the advisability of a certain course to be adopted at the time of action (where it is always desirable to accept the alternative laid down in the Veda); (II) or, if it be absolutely necessary to take it as laying down the rejection of the *Smṛti* this "*Smṛti*" must be taken to refer to the *Smṛtis* compiled by people outside (the pale of Vedic religion). To explain—

I. With a view to offer a salutary advice to the people, what Jaimini says in the *Sūtra* is that, in a case where we find the Vedic text laying down one action, and the *Smṛti* laying down another,—and thus there being an apparent contradiction between the two, on that point—it is desirable that, in practice, we should adopt the course laid down in the Veda. (Nor can it be argued that even this would be an indirect rejection of the authority of the particular *Smṛti* text; because) even in the case of the alternative Injunctions of the *Vrihi* and the *Yava*, both of which appear in the Veda, if some person continues to employ only one of the two (the *Yava* alone, f.i.) at his sacrifices, throughout his life, he does not, by that, become open to the charge of having rejected the authority of the alternative Injunction (of the *Vrihi*). In the same manner, even when the *Smṛti* is found to be possessed of an authority equal to that of the Veda, if one adopts the course laid down in the Veda, there is no harm done to the *Smṛti*. Thus then, all that is meant is that in cases where the *Smṛti* texts have only expressed,' in other words, the sense of certain Vedic texts, without taking the trouble of directly quoting such texts,—they make their authority dependent upon the inference of the Vedic texts on which they base themselves; the Vedic text, on the other hand, is self-sufficient in its authority which does not depend upon anything else; and as such this latter becomes more capable of confidence, which makes people have greater faith in these, and adopt the course laid down by them, in preference to that laid down by the *Smṛti* text.

Thus then, the *Sūtra* (the third) should also be explained thus: *When there is a contradiction between the ideas expressed by the Vedic text and the Smṛti, that which is independent of all else*—(or if we read "*anapēkshyam*," that which has not the need of resting upon anything else)—*should be accepted as authoritative*, the word 'authoritative' being supplied from the preceding *Sūtra;* and this is laid down with a view to the course that is advisable to be adopted under the circumstances.

Thus, we find that we cannot reasonably accept the absolute rejection of the *Smṛti* text, when there is every chance of our finding it to be based upon an independent Vedic text, to be found in another rescension of the Veda. Nor will the adoption of the course laid down in the *Smṛti* render the person open to the charge of having neglected the action laid down by a direct Vedic text; because at the time that we actually find, in another branch of the Veda, the Vedic text in support of the *Smṛti*, both courses of action would become equally authoritative, and as such capable of being both accepted as optional alternatives.

On this, it may be argued that—"as in the case of the contradiction of the *Smṛti* by the Vedic text, we only accept the former to be less trust worthy than the latter only (and as such not to be given the preference);

so, in the same manner, when we find a course of action, laid down in another branch of the Veda opposed to that laid down in our own Veda, the former would be capable of rejection (in favour of the latter, which is more trustworthy for us)."

It would certainly be so rejected, so long as it is only known by hearsay; when, however, we actually come across it in the Veda, it does not in any way differ from the text met with in our own Veda. Thus, we conclude that the *Sūtra* points out this peculiar relation between the *Smṛti* and Vedic texts, that the former is not altogether set aside by the latter, nor is it equal to it in its authority.

II. Or, the *Sūtras* (third and fourth) may be taken as pointing out the fact of the unacceptability of the subsequent *Smṛti* compilations on the ground of their being opposed to the Veda, and on account of their origin being found in the perceptible causes of Avarice, &c. These *Smṛtis* that are not honoured by those who know the Vedas, are: (1) The compilations of certain texts relating to *Dharma* and *Adharma*, by *Çākya*, and the propounders of the systems of *Sāṅkhya*, *Yoga*, *Pancarātra*, *Pāçupata* and the like, all of which have in them a certain mixture of the Veda, and are hidden under a thin cloak of righteousness, treating of the various means of gaining popularity, wealth, respect and fame, and based upon the strength of certain visible results, quite unconnected with the Veda, and upon arguments seemingly based upon Sense-perception, Inference, Analogy and Apparent Inconsistency; (2) those that lay down certain instructions, with regard to the gaining of a living, but are slightly mixed with a Vedic touch, through the mention of such Vedic teachings as those of not-killing, truthfulness, self-control, charity, mercy and the like, and as treating of certain *Mantrās* and recipes for the treatment of poisons, subjugation of the wills of other persons (hypnotism), mysteriously sending away of other people, &c., the efficacy whereof are based upon their success in a few solitary instances; and (3) the extremely foreign compilations that lay down absolutely repugnant practices fit for Mlecchas, such as the eating together of many persons, and the like.

This rejection of the authority of such compilations has not been spoken of in any other *Adhikaraṇa* (and as such it cannot be said to be a useless repetition here); nor is it altogether unnecessary to explain the reasons for their rejection; because the aforesaid compilations have a wide circulation; and as such it is absolutely necessary to explicitly deny their authority, exactly as it is necessary to denounce the use of such current incorrect forms of words, as "*Gāvī*" (for "*Gauh*") and the like. If we altogether disregard such compilations, and do not strongly deny their authoritative character, then people might be led to think that their authoritativeness is too strong to be set aside, and thence they would come to regard them as equal in authority (to the Veda and the *Smṛtis* compiled in accordance with it); or, it may be that people might be more easily attracted to those *Smṛtis*, either on account of the apparent beauty of the actions laid down by them, or on that of the comparative ease with which these actions are performed, or on being misled by their reasonings, or under the influence of the evil times we are living in; and thence men would become misled and deluded on all points relating to the various sacrifices and sacrificial slaughters, &c.; which would ultimately be entirely renounced; or finding them to be the compilations of *Brāhmaṇas* and *Kshatriyas*, like Manu and others, even the intelligent and the well-meaning would be led to infer them to be based upon the authority of the Veda, like the works of Manu, &c.; and as such they would come to accept them, as laying optional alternatives to the courses of action laid down in the Vedas and the Vedic *Smṛtis*. Consequently, even in a case where the declarations of these *Smṛtis* would be found to be contradictory to one of Manu, people might adopt the course laid down in them (as they would consider both courses to be equally authoritative alternatives).

Until all that is wholly contradictory to the Vedic religion has not been duly rejected and set aside, we can have no purity of *Dharma* (which will continue to be mixed up with false semblances of it). Because as for the authority afforded by the acceptance by great men, and by the fact of their being handed down by one's forefathers,—the upholders of these anti-Vedic *Smṛtis* also bring these forward in support of their own *Smṛtis*, which, they urge, is accepted by great men of other countries. And the only reason, that limits one's choice of different courses of action, lies in his own faith; because each man is naturally inclined to follow in the path trodden by his own forefathers (and as such authority could be equally brought forward by the other party, there would be no means of dissuading him from it, until we actually explained why only certain *Smṛtis* are to be accepted as authoritative).

In connection with the compilations of Manu, &c, some people have held that they (at least in the portions that are not found to be supported by any Vedic texts) are based upon the Vedic texts that have become lost; but against these people, the *Bauddha* can very easily assert the fact of their *Smṛtis* also being based upon similar texts. For, how could any limit be put upon the assumption of such lost texts? And then, any action that may have been accepted by some people for a certain time,—if found to be incompatible with the Vedic texts—might be assumed to be based upon lost texts; and as such would come to appear as of equal authority with the Veda. And it is with all this in view that the *Sūtra* has expressly declared that *when there is a contradiction, that which contradicts the Veda is to be totally rejected.*

As for the fact of these compilations being dependent upon human agency, their upholders have also accepted it by their admission of the fact of their being compiled by particular personages; and those that have listened to their teachings, infer the same from their theory that all words are non-eternal (which sets aside the possibility of any compilations being eternal). And as for the support of Vedic authority, inasmuch as they consider their own compilations to be equal to the Veda in their authority, they either cannot bear to think of seeking for its support, or feel too ashamed to seek it; and hence they absolutely disown any such origin, exactly like ungrateful children who are eventually inclined towards their parents, and hence disown their real parentage.

There is yet another point (of difference between the *Smṛtis* of Manu and those of the *Bauddhas*): In the case of Manu, we find only one text, by the way, which is found to be contrary to the Veda; whereas in the case of the *Smṛtis* of the *Bauddhas*, barring a few stray declarations of such virtues as self-control, charity and the like, all that they have to say is contrary, not only to the Veda, but to the approved conclusions of all the fourteen subsidiary sciences; and these latter are also compiled by irreligious men like Buddha, whose practices were all opposed to the injunctions laid down in the Veda, and were taught to the deluded men of the lowest caste, outside the pale of Vedic religion; and as such, they can never even be thought of as based upon the Veda.

Then again, we find that the *Bauddha* teachings were given by one who was a born Kshatriya; and as such, he transgressed the duties of his own class, in taking upon himself the works of *teaching* and *receiving presents* (which are the monopoly of the Brāhmaṇas); and hence how can we believe that true *Dharma* or Duty would be taught by one who has transgressed his own *Dharma*? It has been well said: 'One who is found to be doing deeds opposed to a prosperous hereafter, should be shunned from a distance; because how can one who deceives himself offer any salutary advice to others?' Such transgression of *Dharma* by Buddha is clearly mentioned in the *Alankārabuddhi* (a *Bauddha* work), where Buddha is represented as saying—"May all the pain proceeding from the sins due to the Iron Age, rest in me, and leave humanity at large absolutely free!" And in connection with this, his followers eulogise his virtues in the following strains: "For the sake of the well-being of humanity, He transgressed his own duties of the Kshatriya, and having taken up the duties of the Brāhmaṇa, he taught, even to the people outside the pale of Vedic religion, such truths relating to *Dharma*, as were not taught by the Brāhmaṇas who were unable to transgress the prohibition (of such teachings being imparted to outsiders); and thus prompted by his mercy to others, he even went to the length of transgressing his own *Dharma!*" And we actually find His followers behaving in a manner entirely at variance with the teachings of the Veda.

Thus then, inasmuch as we find the authors of these *Smṛtis*, as well as their disciples and followers, behaving contrary to the direct teachings of the Veda, we cannot but deny the authority of the *Smṛtis* themselves. Because, as has been shown above, they are professedly opposed to the Veda, and hence they have no capacity for leading us to assume Vedic texts in their support.

As for the loss of certain rescensions of the Veda, no such complete loss would be possible, because the Veda has been proved to be eternal. Nor are the *Bauddha Smṛtis* found to have any other perceptible basis. In the case of the *Smṛti* (Manu) texts relating to the *Upanayana*, &c., we find them in keeping with the texts of other branches of the Veda; but no such support is possible for such actions (laid down in *Bauddha Smṛtis*) as the bowing to the *Caitya*, giving of gifts to *Cūdras* and the like. And as for assuming any other authoritative basis, we have already proved it to be impossible.

On the other hand, we find that they are largely due to Avarice and other such visible causes, in the presence of which, there can be no inference of any other origin. And as a matter of fact, in the course of their teaching of *Dharma*, Buddha and others themselves never make any assertions that are not supported by arguments based upon actual experience. Nor do they, like Gautama and other Vedic Teachers, assert their teachings to be based upon the Veda; on the other hand, they put forward many such arguments, as are very far removed from true *Dharma*.

It is these persons that should not be respected even by words; and they have been denounced (in the *Manusmṛti*) as "Heretics, Sinners and Sceptics." And it is the compilations of these people that Manu and others have declared to be fit only for being avoided: "Those *Smṛtis* that are opposed to the Veda, as also those that have evil tendencies, all these are absolutely useless; and have their basis in dark Ignorance." And thus it is established that in matters relating to *Dharma*, such *Smṛtis* as are outside the pale of the Veda should be totally rejected as absolutely devoid of authority.

End of the third Adhikarana.

ADHIKARANA (4).

[*The superior authority of the declaration of the Substance*].

***Sūtra* (5). If it be urged that, when there is no disturbance of the Vedic Injunction, the Smṛti text cannot be held to be contradicted by it,—**

(This *Sūtra* only serves as a means of introducing the next *Sūtra*, which embodies the real *Pūrvapaksha* of the *Adhikaraṇa.*)

As regards the *Smṛtis* dealing with the actions relating to the purposes of man, we have explained above (in accordance with the *Bhāshya*) how they are to be accepted as authoritative, or rejected as unauthoritative, according as they are found to be supported, or contradicted, by the Veda. And under the present *Adhikaraṇa*, we proceed to consider those *Smṛti* texts that deal with the actions in connection with sacrifices—such for instance as the *Smṛti* texts laying down the *changing of the sacred thread*, the *rinsing of the mouth*, the *use of the right hand alone* and the like, to be done during the performance of the sacrifices, laid down in the Veda, and with regard to these we shall only consider whether they are contradictory or not to the Veda; and when this has been settled, the authoritativeness or its contrary will be inferred from the preceding *Adhikaraṇa*.

[The instances cited here by the *Bhāshya*, are the *Smṛti* texts that lay down the *changing of one's sacred thread* as soon as it breaks, the *rinsing of the mouth* whenever one sneezes; and the contradiction that is suspected is that if the sacrificer should stop in the middle of the performance of the sacrifice, in order to change his thread, then there would be a break in the continuity of the sacrificial routine, which would involve a transgression of the Vedic Injunction. Another instance is that of the *Smṛti* text laying down that everything in connection with sacrifices should be done by the right hand alone; and if one were to adhere to this strictly he may not be able to finish all that has to be done quickly, and within the specified time,—which would involve a transgression of the Vedic Injunction].

In the case of these texts, the only standard by which we should judge whether they are contrary or not to the Veda, would be the ascertaining whether the acceptance of the *Smṛti* Injunction would, or would not, in any way interfere with the proper accomplishment of the actions laid down in the Veda. That is to say, if we find that the *changing of the sacred thread,* as happening in the middle of the sacrificial functions, is either not allowed, or distinctly prohibited, by the Vedic texts laying down the action and its procedure, then we conclude that there is a contradiction; if, however, we find that such actions enter into the very constitution of the sacrifice, helping its accomplishment, like any other ordinary actions mentioned in the same context, and are supported by certain Vedic texts, assumed in accordance with the *Smṛtis,* and do not in any way interfere with anything that has been laid down by the Vedic texts in connection with the sacrifice,—then we conclude that there is no contradiction.

There is yet another way of putting forward the difficulty or doubt that has given rise to the *Adhikaraṇa*: the question being—when there is a contradiction between the *Smṛti* text and the Vedic text, it is doubtful which is to be accepted as the more authoritative, when it is found that the former deals directly with a certain definite entity (in the shape of an Action); while the latter (at least that part of it which is found to be interfered with by the *Smṛti*) is found to treat of secondary qualifications; because there is a difference in the acceptance of the comparative strength of one or the other, when both texts are dealt with merely as the means of cognitions, from that which is accepted when they are compared with reference to what they speak of. That is to say, we have already decided as to which of the two is to be accepted as of greater authority, when the *Smṛti* and the Vedic texts are found to contradict each other; but when it happens that the contradiction is between a qualification or property on one side, and a definite entity or substance on the other, then it is to the latter that preference is shown; as will be explained under *Sūtra* XII-ii-25. For instance, in the case in question, the *Smṛti* texts do not in any way tend to set aside or reject any definite action laid down in the Veda; as for the order or time in which the actions are to be performed (which alone is found to be interfered with by the *Smṛti* texts), these are always acknowledged to be the qualifications of the main substance of the Action. Thus then, if in this also, we depend upon the comparative strength of the *Smṛti* and the Veda generally considered as authoritative (means of knowledge), then, even though the Order, &c., of the Actions, being the qualifications, are weaker than the *rinsing of the mouth,* &c., which, as distinct Actions, are the stronger,—yet, inasmuch as the former are laid down by the Veda, which by itself is possessed of a stronger authoritativeness than that of the *Smṛti,* the latter Actions will necessarily have to be set aside by considerations of the Order, &c., of the performance of the sacrifice. If, however, we accept the comparative strength as between the subject-matter of the two texts, then, inasmuch as the definite actions of *rinsing*, &c., will always be stronger than the *Order*, *&c.*, which are mere qualifications of Actions, even though the former are laid down by the *Smṛti*, which by itself is weaker in authority than the Veda,—yet being definite Actions, they will set aside the qualifications of the *Order*, &c., which, as qualifications, are in themselves the weaker of the two.

The question being thus stated, the answer that suggests itself is that these *Smṛti* texts, that lay down certain actions in connection with the Vedic sacrifices, are not contradictory to the Veda; because the performance of the actions laid down by them does not interfere with the performance of the Vedic sacrifice. Because, in the cases of the six means of ascertaining the meaning of Vedic Injunctions—namely, *Direct Assertion*, *Indirect Implication*, *Context*, *Syntactical Connection*, *Position* and *Name*,—among which there is a difference in the authority of each of them,—even when that which is pointed out by the strongest of these has been accepted as the principal course, all that is indicated by the others are not totally discarded, but accepted as helping, in their secondary or subordinate character, the Primary Action; and as such come to be taken along with the procedure, &c. of the Action as laid down in certain scattered passages; in the same manner, (just as in the case of the above six) also when the seventh means of knowledge, in the shape of the *Smṛti*, or a long-established usage, happens to lay down certain actions, these may be accepted, as helping the Final Result, by being taken along with the Procedure of the Primary Vedic Action; even as certain actions laid down by the *Smṛti* (the *Ashtakā* for instance) are accepted as the direct means to a final Result. That is to say, as no limit has been fixed to the help that may be accorded to the accomplishment of the Final Result, by means of various methods and processes,—whatever method or process may be pointed out by whatever means of knowledge or authority, as helping in the accomplishment of that Result, it is accepted to be subsidiary to the Primary Action. Thus then, *the rinsing of the mouth*, &c., may, in accordance with this argument, be rightly accepted as subsidiary to the Primary Sacrifice; (and as such there need be no contradiction).

On this we have the following PŪRVAPAKSHA:

***Sūtra* (6). "This cannot be; because the limit is fixed by the Scriptures."**

"That is to say, as the limit of all set Vedic Actions is distinctly fixed "by the Veda itself, any addition of new Actions will mean an exceeding of "its proper bounds; and who can transgress with impunity a limit that has "been fixed by the Veda?

"The limit of Actions is fixed by the Scriptures in three ways: (1) "by laying down a definite order in which the various actions are to be "performed; (2) by distinctly laying down the extreme limits of the Action "itself; and (3) by laying down the necessity of finishing the Action "quickly (within a certain limited period of time). And this Scriptural "limit will certainly be transgressed (by the intrusion of such actions as "the *rinsing of the mouth* and the like). Because the Time, Limit and "the Order of the Primary Action, having been definitely laid down by "means of the two sets of the six-fold means of ascertaining the details of "Vedic Actions (*viz.*, Direct Assertion, Indirect Implication, Syntactial Con-"nection, Context, Position and Name forming one set, and Direct Decla-"ration, Meaning, Context, Position, Principal Action and its Procedure "forming the other),—if any such actions as are laid down either by the "*Smṛtis*, or by long-established usage, were to be inserted in the middle of "a Vedic sacrifice, these would certainly lead to the transgression of the "aforesaid *Order*, &c.

"It is distinctly laid down in the Vedic text that points out the "method of performing sacrifices, that no actions in connection with the "Principal Sacrifice are to be separated from it, in point of time. But "if, in the middle of the performance of such a Principal Action, we were "to intrude certain actions laid down either by the *Smṛti* or by usage, or "if we were to stick to the *Smṛti* injunction of using the right hand alone "and thereby causing unnecessary delay in the main sacrifice, there would "certainly be a disturbance of the aforesaid proximity of the original "subsidiary actions with the Main Action; and the delay would cause the "transgression of the laws that lay down the morning or the mid-day as the "proper time for all Vedic Actions. The order of Actions is ascertained "by means of Direct Declaration, Meaning, Context, Position, Principal "Action, and the Procedure of the Action itself (as explained in the Fourth "*Adhyāya*); and this Order, as affecting the Vedic Actions, having the "limits of their acceptance and authority duly recognised, would certainly "be disturbed by the intrusion of the *rinsing of the mouth* after sneezing.

"The same may be said with reference to the *Smṛti* Injunction of "putting on a fresh sacred thread, if, through continued bodily work, it "happen to slip off the body.

"And again, the intervening performance of the actions laid down in "the *Smṛti*, has no fixed order laid down by the Veda; and for the order "and the limit of the Vedic Sacrifice, we do not admit of any authority "save the Veda itself. Therefore, in order to get together all the subsidi-"ary actions in connection with the main sacrifice, without neglecting the "least amongst them, it is absolutely necessary for the priests to ascertain "the limits of the various Minor Actions constituting the Main Sacrifice, "recognised by means of Direct Assertion, Implication, &c. Consequently, "if he happens to perform, in the middle, an action laid down by the "*Smṛti*,—which was not known before as one to be performed, and which "has cropped up only subsequently,—then, there would certainly be a trans-"gression of the Order, &c., that has been ascertained before; and thereby "he would be unable to ascertain exactly what he has done and what he has "left undone (of the Main Sacrifice); and thus, being extremely suspicious "of the incomplete character of his sacrifice, he would fail to achieve the "confidence of having duly accomplished it; and thereby the potency of "the Final Result having been extremely weakened, the fruit of the "action accruing to him would come to be much lessened in quality, as "well as in quantity. But the potency of the Final Result has been duly "pointed out by the Injunction as taken along with the *Arthavāda* passage; "and as such it can never bear a single jot of abatement; consequently it "necessarily rejects the *Smṛti* texts laying down such intrusions.

"(Or, the *Sūtra* may be interpreted in a different manner). As the "limits and number of the subsidiary sciences of the Veda have been defi-"nitely restricted to the Teachings and Commentaries in connection with "it, which are fixed within certain limits, there is no room for any other "science (as the *Smṛti*) being admitted as another subsidiary to it. In "connection with any Vedic sacrifice, all the actions that are laid down are "understood as to be performed simultaneously; and as such the priests go "through all the actions with a hurry (in order to preserve the simulta-"neity as far as possible); but as an absolute simultaneity is an impossi-"bility, the Vedic text that lays down the procedure permits only such "delay (and consequent separation of the various actions), as is absolutely "necessary, between the end of one action and the beginning of another. "Hence, if one were to make an unnecessary delay, even when he were able "to avoid it, then such transgression could never be allowed to pass with "impunity, by the direct Vedic assertion of the particular Procedure. "Thus then, we conclude that as the said *Smṛtis* disturb the three-fold "Order of the Vedic Actions, the performance of such actions as the *rinsing* "*of the mouth*, &c., (in the course of sacrifices) cannot but be rejected as "contradictory to the Veda."

SIDDHĀNTA:

***Sūtra* (7). But when we do not find any cause for (the enjoining of) such actions, we conclude them to be of use (at the sacrifice).**

Or, this *Sutra* may be taken to extend up to "*tēshvadarçanādvirodhasya*" (*because we do not perceive any contradiction in them*), which the *Bhāshya* has transferred to the next *Sūtra;* specially as the next *Sūtra* already contains the word '*Vipratipatti*,' which signifies the (*absence of*) *contradiction*, it would be useless to add the aforesaid clause to it; while, on the other hand, in the present *Sūtra*, it is absolutely necessary to deny the *contradiction* which has been urged in the *Pūrvapaksha*. Even if the clause had some use in the next *Sūtra*, we could take it with both *Sūtras* by means of transference, just as the single eye of the crow is transferred from one socket to the other.

(The *Sūtra* is thus explained). Inasmuch as we do not find any visible cause for such actions as the *rinsing of the mouth* and the like, we cannot hold them to be in any way contradictory to the order of actions laid down in the Veda. When we find a certain *Smṛti* text to be debarred by its contradiction of the Veda, from all chance of having any basis in this latter,—and then, if we could find out some other visible cause (as Greed, &c.,) which could be pointed out as possibly being the origin of the particular text,—then, in that case, a very slight effort (of argumentation) would lead us to ascertain its absolute unauthoritativeness. But in a case where no such visible cause is perceptible (or even assumable), we cannot but admit that, inasmuch as it is not found to have its origin in any such cause (as Greed, &c.), the *Smṛti* text cannot but have its basis in the Veda.

In the case of the *Smṛti* texts laying down such actions as the *rinsing of the mouth*, &c., we cannot attribute them to any such cause as Desire Greed, Anger, Aversion, Shame, &c., the possibility of which would have barred all their chance of having their origin in the Veda. Thus then, not finding the origin of the *Smṛti* text anywhere else, we admit of its origin lying in the Veda; and as such even if it is found to contradict any particular Vedic text, it does not, on that account, lose all its authority. As for the *Limit*, the *Order* and the *Time* that have been specified for each sacrifice, by particular Vedic texts, inasmuch as these are the qualifications of the Action, they are unable to set aside the authority of the *Smṛti* texts, which lay down the Actions themselves, which are stronger than the former *Limit, &c.*, which should have been the stronger, on account of their being mentioned in Vedic texts (if they were not the qualifications of Actions, and as such of lesser importance than the Actions themselves).

It may be argued that—"inasmuch as it is the comparative strength of the Veda and the *Smṛti*, considered solely as the means of knowledge, that is considered beforehand, it would seem that the conclusion arrived at by this *consideration* has a decided preference over that arrived at by the subsequent consideration of the comparative authoritativeness of their subject-matter. (That is to say, when it has been concluded beforehand that the Veda has an authority greater than that of the *Smṛti*, we must not give up this conclusion even if the Veda text be found to deal with qualifications, and the *Smṛti*, with Actions)."

In reply to this we add—There is no inherent contradiction between the Veda and the *Smṛti,* taken by themselves; nor is their strength compared with regard to themselves solely as two means of knowledge; all these considerations, as well as all the contradiction that there may be, is only with regard to the matter that they may severally deal with. That is to say, it is only when we find the matter dealt with by them, to be contradictory to each other, that we conclude that there is a contradiction between the two means of knowledge themselves. Therefore, as a matter of fact, the comparative authoritativeness of their subject-matter is ascertained at the very moment that they are found to be contradictory to each other. And (when considering this comparative authoritativeness of their subject-matter), when we have once definitely ascertained the fact of the qualifications of Actions being of lesser importance than the Actions themselves,—even if these qualifications happen to be supported by Vedic texts (as in the case in question),—they do not regain their authority (in preference to that of the Actions); and conversely, when we have once ascertained the fact of the Actions being of greater importance than the qualifications, even if these actions happen to be based upon the weaker authority of the *Smṛti,* they do not lose their authority (in preference to that of the qualifications). Because it is only that which is absolutely and always without any authority, that can be totally set aside; in all other cases, authoritativeness and unauthoritativeness are always correlative.

Thus then, when the authority of a certain *Smṛti* text has been ascertained on the ground of the superior authority of its subject-matter, this authority cannot be set aside by any considerations of the comparative authoritativeness of the *Smṛti* and the Veda, considered by themselves, as two means of knowledge, independently of their subject-matter. But, on the other hand, though the subject-matter of the Vedic text be found to be of lesser authority, yet that does not totally set aside the authority of the Vedic text itself; because the *Smṛti* losing all its strength in imparting a greater importance to its subject-matter, it can never be able to reject the text as well; specially as in opposition to the Vedic text, it is enough concession to the *Smṛti* that it is not itself completely rejected; and as for the setting aside of any Vedic text, the greatest of *Smṛtis* can never do that.

As a matter of fact, however, two Actions can be said to contradict each other only when they are based upon equal authorities, and are laid down as to be performed at one and the same time; in the case in question, however, we find none of these two conditions of contradiction; and hence we conclude that there is no real contradiction. Because the considerations of Time, Limit and Order always come at the end of all the Actions (the Primary as well as the Secondary); while the Actions, even though based upon a lesser authority, have their turn long before them. Because it is only when the Actions have been performed that we stop to consider the *Order* in which they are performed ; and the Order that has been directly perceived with regard to the Actions that have already appeared,—by what could this ascertained Order be set aside ? Specially as being the qualification of the Actions, and as such appearing after these, the Order is held to be of secondary importance in the performance of the Actions.

As for the *Limit*, that has been definitely laid down with regard to the Vedic Actions, it is never found to be laid down directly by any Vedic text; it is only indirectly implied by the necessity of not forgetting any the smallest action that forms part of the sacrifice; and as this Limit is always perceptible by itself, it is always accepted as subsequently including the Actions that may have been performed (during the sacrifice) in accordance with the *Smṛti* texts (and as such the performance of these latter need not necessarily be a contradiction of the order of the Vedic Action). That is to say, the Limit of an Action is not defined by any means of knowledge ; hence we could accept the unflinching authority of the declaration of a certain Limit, only if it was found that, apart from this declaration of the Limit, there were no other means of avoiding the missing of any Actions during the performance of the sacrifice. But even when such is actually found to be the case, it often happens that at certain sacrifices, even before we have come to the end of the Limit directly laid down by the Vedic Injunction, we admit the more extensive limits of Actions that are pointed out (as subsidiaries to the main Action) by the various means of Direct Assertion, Implication, Context &c. ; and when we admit the limits laid down by these latter, there is no reason why those pointed out by *Smṛti* texts and well-established usage should not be equally accepted. (And the admission of the Actions laid down in the *Smṛtis* being quite in keeping with the character of the Vedic sacrifices, these *Smṛtis* cannot be said to be in any way contradictory to the limits laid down for the Vedic Actions).

Time too is only a secondary element in the performance of sacrifices ; and as such comes to be considered only at the end of all the Actions ; consequently, the limitations of Time that are laid down will always include that taken up by the performance of the Actions laid down in the *Smṛti* texts as well. Because the Time that is laid down is that with regard to the performance of the main Action, *together with all its subsidiaries.*—whether these be laid down in the Veda or in the *Smṛti* ; and because it is with reference to such Principal Actions as have many subsidiaries, that it has been laid down, that it is not proper to separate them from (any of) their subsidiaries.

For these reasons, we conclude that inasmuch as the time that is specified is with reference to the finishing of all the Actions—from whatever source their injunction may have emanated in connection with the main Action,—it cannot be said to be contradicted by the performance of any of the subsidiary Actions therein included; and it is this *non-perception of any contradiction of these*—Order, Time and Limit—that is meant by the clause "*tēshvadarçanādvirodhasya*"; or this clause may be explained as referring to *the non-perception of any contradiction in the performance of these,—Rinsing of the mouth &c.*

Then again, such purificatory actions as the *Rinsing of the mouth*, as also the *wearing of the sacred thread*, are not independent Actions by themselves; they are only subsidiary actions meant to help in the proper accomplishment of the main Action; and as such, their perform nce cannot be taken as an interference in the Principal Action. That which can interfere in the course of one Action must always be an independent Action which is equal in authority to the former Action, and is not in any way subsidiary to it; and there can be no interference by an Action that is of a subsidiary character, and always serves to bring about the proper accomplishment of the main Actions. For instance, after having prepared the *bundle of the Kuça grass*, the Action that is laid down in the Vedas as to be performed next is the *preparation of the Sacrifical Altar*; but if, after the former action has been finished, the priest happens to sneeze, and he performs the consequent *rinsing of the mouth*, he is said to be engaged in the *preparing of the Altar*; and the reason is that if he prepared the Altar, without rinsing the mouth after sneezing, there would be a certain impurity in it, and its preparation would not be properly accomplished; and as the rinsing of the mouth would only serve to remove this impurity and to make the Altar perfect, it could not be said to have interfered with the *preparing of the Altar* (and thus the Order of the Vedic Actions). It is with a view to this that the *Bhāshya* has said—*such Actions as the rinsing, &c., do not become the interfering agents in the performance of the Vedic Action.* For, if this assertion were made without the acceptance of the fact of these Actions being subsidiary to the Main Action, it would evince a sad lack of philosophic insight.

Thus then, such actions as the Rinsing of the Mouth &c. being found to be forming parts of the main Action itself, they cannot be said to be contradictory to the texts that lay down the Order, Limit and Time of the performance,—all these coming to be considered only after the Action with all its subsidiaries has been duly accomplished.

[*The above is an exposition of the Adhikaraṇa, in accordance with the interpretation of the Bhāshya. And as this is not in keeping with the Author's own view of the last two Adhikaraṇas, he proceeds to take the three foregoing Sūtras in a different sense.*]

It is not quite correct to cite the *wearing of the sacred thread* as an action contrary to the Vedic Sacrifice. Because it is directly mentioned by the Veda, in connection with the *Darça-Purnamāsa* Sacrifice, that the wearing of the thread is a mark of godliness, which lays down its wearing as a necessary accompaniment of the sacrifice. The wearing of the thread has also been laid down as a general rule, in the *Kstha* Rescension (of the *Yajurveda*), where it is laid down, not with reference to any particular sacrifice, but as a necessary accompaniment of all sacrifices, as well as Vedic studies; says the text in question: "It was by means of the *Prasṛta* Sacrifice that the gods subdued the *Asuras*; and it was because the *Asuras* did not employ the *Prasṛta* Sacrifice that they were subdued by the gods; a *Prasṛta* sacrifice is that which is performed by a sacrificer with the sacred thread; and an *Aprasṛta* Sacrifice is that which is done without the thread; if the Brāhmaṇa reads with the sacred thread on, he is performing a sacrifice by that act; therefore one must always wear the sacred thread when reading, sacrificing, or helping at the sacrifices of others; as it is thus that the *Prasṛta* character of the sacrifice is duly accomplished."

Similarly with regard to the Injunction of the *rinsing of the mouth*, we meet with the following text, which lays down such rinsing: "Having his sacred thread hanging from the left shoulder, on the right side, the sacrificer should wash his hands, and thrice rinse his mouth, wiping it twice, and touching, once, his forehead, eyes, ears, and breast; as by that, the *Atharvāngirasās*, the *Brāhmaṇas*, the *Itihāsas*, the *Purānas*, the *Kalpas*, the *Gāthās*, and the *Nārāçansis*, all become delighted in him; he should then spread the grass, put his hands between the knees, and then sitting down with his face to the East, he should begin to read the Veda." And though this passage occurs in connection with the *Brahmayajna* (the daily duties of the Brāhmaṇa), yet it distinctly points out the necessity of the *rinsing of the mouth* whenever the Veda has to be recited; and as such it comes to be recognised as a necessary accompaniment of all Vedic utterance; and as all sacrifices are accompanied by the recitation of Vedic *mantras*, we conclude the *rinsing* to be a necessary accompaniment of the sacrifice itself. Secondly the Vedic text, that "the mouth does not become impure by the tasting of the Soma," prohibiting the rinsing of the mouth after one has drunk the Soma, distinctly points out the necessity of the rinsing at all other times (whenever any impurity attaches to the mouth).

As for the *Smṛti* Injunction that 'one should perform all actions by the right hand alone,' it is an accepted general rule that it is the right hand alone that is to be always used at the sacrifices, except in the few cases where it is distinctly laid down that the left hand is to be used, and in which the right hand is not used at all; and there is no doubt as to the use of the right hand in all other cases. And we meet with the passage—"As the right hand, so is also the sacrifice to the gods"—which occurs in connection with the Injunction that the sacrificial altar is to be made sloping either to the East or to the North; and the said simile could be possible only if the using of the right hand were as necessary for the correct performance of the sacrifices, as the fact of the sacrifices themselves being offered to the gods.

And thus we find that none of the three *Smṛti* texts, cited by the text, should have been brought forward as contradicting Vedic Injunctions.

For these reasons, we conclude that the present is not to be taken as a distinct *Adhikarana*, and that the three *Sūtras* may be interpreted as bringing forward and refuting certain objections against the preceding *Adhikaraṇas*.

The Fifth *Sūtra* may be interpreted as follows: "That which does "not contradict any Vedic Injunction, and which is not unpleasing to good "men, such a declaration of the Buddha, &c.—as for instance, the injunc-"tions of the founding of resting places and public gardens, of dispassion, "meditation, practice, non-slaughter, truthfulness, charity, and the like—"can be accepted as authoritative, without any fear of contradicting the "Veda."

If this be urged by the opponent, then—*we deny this; because of the number of authoritative Scriptures being limited.* (*Sūtra* 6).

That is to say, the number of authoritative Scriptures has been limited to the 'fourteen or eighteen' sciences, which alone are acknowledged by all good men to have any authority with regard to *Dharma;* and these fourteen sciences include the Vedas with its *Angas* and *Upāngas*, the eighteen *Dharmasamhitās* and *Purānas*, the *Çikshā*, and the *Dandanīti*. And we do not find the works of Buddha and others included among these. And even if we find in them certain facts in keeping with the said Scriptures, yet, as this might be only a pretence for doing something else (deluding people into Atheistic paths), we cannot accept it as having any binding authority with regard to *Dharma*. Just as if a Pandit, when presenting the method of performing a certain expiatory rite as laid down by Manu, were to quote corroborative verses either composed by himself or by others, then (even though the subject-matter would be all right, in keeping with the laws of Manu, yet, no person with any true regard for *Dharma*, would go to him for the prescription.

And it is a fact ascertained once for all, that in matters relating to *Dharma*, we accept as authoritative, the assertions only of those persons whose names, which as *words* are eternal, are mentioned in the Vedas as of the propounders of *Dharma*,—persons who are found to be expounding the *Dharma*, in each succeeding Manvantaric cycle. As for instance, we find the passage in the Veda that, "the *Ṛk* verses of which Manu is the Ṛshi are the *Sāmidhēni*;" and in continuation of this, it is declared "whatever Manu said was the very medicine of medicines;" and what is meant by this is that the expiatory rites that Manu laid down are as effective in destroying sin, as medicine is in removing the disease.

Nor can the mention of the name of Manu in the Veda be said to be a mere similarity of sound (and not as the mention of the name of any person) [as has been held under Sūtra I—i—31]; because it is quite possible for a name to be mentioned in the Veda, even though it is eternal; because just as in each sacrifice there is a priest (who is mentioned by name in the Veda), so also in each *Manvantara* there is a Manu; as it is declared by Manu himself that in each *Manvantara*, there is a different *Smṛti*. And we know as a matter of fact, that there have been fourteen Manus, in all the cycles, that have gone by. Thus then there is every possibility of there being a compilation by Manu in each cycle. And as such the continuous succession of Manus being unbroken (and as such as good as eternal), there is nothing incongruous in the person being mentioned by name in the eternal Veda, which, in speaking of his declarations, does not necessarily become non-eternal; just as in each sacrifice there being sixteen priests (and this has always been the case, since time immemorial), the Veda does not become non-eternal, by laying down the duties of these priests. To this effect, it has been said—just as in each succeeding season, we find the marks of the same season in the past appearing; so in the same manner, the entities that have existed in one cycle, are found to appear in another cycle. Thus it is that though the *Itihāsas* and the *Purānas* are known to be composed by human authors, yet we find them mentioned, as sciences, in the Veda, which is itself without beginning. As we read in the (*Chāndogya*) Upanishad (Nārada saying to Sanatkumāra). "Sir, I shall study the *Ṛgveda*, the *Yajurveda*, the *Sāmaveda*, and the fourth *Atharvaveda*, and also the fifth, *Itihāsas and Purānas*."

Thus then, we conclude that in matters relating to *Dharma*, we accept as authoritative, the declarations of only such persons as are mentioned in the Vedic *mantras* and *Arthavādas*, as being the authors of the propounded sciences, such authors being mentioned by names which remain fixed, among all the endless changes of cycles and *Manvantaras*.

(And in this we have the indirect support of the Veda also; as for instance) we find in the Veda, that after having laid down the expiatory rites to be performed, on the failure of such sacrificial accessories as are laid down in the Ṛgveda, it is added: 'If there be a failure of something that is unknown,'—and then another rite is laid down; and this latter 'failure' must be taken as that of something that has been laid down, as necessary, in the works of these Vedic authors; because all that is laid down in the Veda, is known directly from the Veda itself, and as such, could not have been spoken of as "unknown;" and if we did not accept the authoritativeness of such *Smṛti* works as are said to be based upon the Veda, but whose original Vedic texts have not been found,—then nothing that is of unknown authority could be possibly done at any sacrifice (as it is only that which is known as duly authorised that is performed at sacrifices); and then there could have been no use of laying down an expiatory rite for the failure of the "unknown."

From these considerations, we conclude that *Dharma* brings about its due results, only when it is understood with the help of those scriptures that are recognised to be not incapable of having their basis in the Veda. On the other hand, just as we do not admit that knowledge of *Dharma* to be true, which is obtained from an improper study of the Veda, or as learnt merely from the written book (without the help of a qualified teacher), or as learnt by the *Çūdra*,—so in the same manner, in the case of such Authors as are known to have a conduct against the teachings of the Veda, even when some of their declarations are found to be in keeping with the teachings of the Veda, we do not accept them as the valid means of knowing *Dharma*. And we also find it distinctly mentioned in the *Purānas* that during the Iron Age, Çākya and others would disorganise the whole fabric of *Dharma*. Under the circumstances how can we listen to anything that they may have to say? And just as the powdered alum sprinkled on melting gold, disappears in the gold, so even the few Vedic truths that we find in their works are so mixed up with the rest, that they lose themselves in these, and so become equally unacceptable to us. That is to say, the few Vedic truths that are in them are found in the very midst of such misrepresentations of *Dharma*, as are based by them upon such arguments as—'the Analogy based upon Similarity of Actions' (*i.e.*, as the sacrifice causes pain to the animal, it must result in pain to the sacrificer), 'Inference from generals,' (*i.e.*, the Vedic slaughter is as sinful as ordinary slaughter), and 'Apparent Inconsistency,' (*i.e.*, as pain is the only result of sin, the experiencing of much pain destroys a large amount of sin); and as such they are as milk put in the skin of the dog; and hence they are useless and incapable of commanding our confidence. Consequently, so long as even such truths are found only in the works of the *Bauddhas*, and not in any of the above-enumerated Vedic Sciences, they remain unacceptable to us. And when they come to be found in any parts of these Sciences themselves, then, as we get at a full knowledge of the truths by means of these very Sciences, the works of Çākya and others remain useless for us.

Therefore, we conclude that all that is apart from the Vedic Sciences enumerated above, we do not accept as having any authority in matters relating to *Dharma;* and as such, they are to be totally rejected.

Then, we have the *Seventh Sūtra*, which means that, *those actions with regard to which we cannot find any perceptible cause, and are yet found to be performed, must be recognised as Dharma.* And this *Sūtra* is to be taken as forming an *Adhikaraṇa* by itself, treating of the authoritative character of the practice of good men, of which we are going to cite a few instances, which will be shown to be the means of the accomplishment of the three ends of man (*i.e.*, all except Final Deliverance).

Among good men also, we find some behaving contrary to the Law, just like the Doctors leading unhealthy lives; and as such their practice fails to command our full confidence; and yet the fact of the act being done by a wise man would point to the fact of its being in accordance with a certain Vedic text; and thus, there being a doubt with regard to the authoritative character of such practice, the *Pūrvapakshī* would bring forward, against it, all the arguments urged by him under the first *Sūtra* of this *Pāda*, or, in some cases, those under the third *Sūtra.*

The Pūrvapaksha.

"Even in the practice of good men, we often find a transgression of "*Dharma*, and also certain extremely bold excessess as in the cases of Prajāpati, Indra, Vaçishtha, Viçvāmitra, Yudhishthira, Kṛshna Dvaipāyana, Bhīshma, Dhṛtarāshtra, Vāsudēva, Arjuna and others, as also of "many good men of our own days.

"For instance, (1) we find Prajāpati falling in an incestuous love "with his own daughter, Ushā; (2) Indra, as also Nahūsha in his place, "is said to have committed adultery; (3) Vaçishtha, when stricken down "with grief on the death of his hundred sons, is said to have contemplated "a terrible excess, in the shape of suicide; (4) Viçvāmitra helped a *Candala* (Tṛshanku) to perform a sacrifice; (5) Purūravas thought of committing suicide, when Urvaçī left him; (6) Kṛshna Dvaipāyana, who "was under the vow of lifelong celibacy, brought forth children from the "wives of his younger brother, Vicitravīrya; (7) Bhīshma led a life contrary to all caste-regulations; and did an irregularity in performing sacrifices, even though he was unmarried; (8) Dhṛtarāshtra, though blind "(and as such not entitled to the performance of any sacrifice), performed "many sacrifices, and that too with the wealth amassed by his brother "Pāndu (to which he had no rightful claim); (9) Yudhishthira married a "wife that had been won by his younger brother (Arjuna), and told a "base lie with the sole motive of causing the death of his own Brāh-"mana-Preceptor; (10) Vāsudēva and Arjuna are said to have been drunk "to excess.

"Among the people of modern days we find the Brāhmaṇa women of "the countries of Ahicchatra and Mathura to be addicted to drinking; the "people of the North carry on the business of giving, and accepting in gift, "buying and selling, lions, horses, mules, asses, camels and the animals with "two rows of teeth; and they are also used to eating in the sâme dish with "their wives, children and friends; the people of the South marry the daugh-"ters of their maternal uncles, and partake of food while sitting upon "chairs; while among the people of the North, as well as of the South, there "are many such instances of gross transgression, as the partaking of the "food left by one's friends or relations, taking of beetles touched by people "of all castes, the non-washing of the mouth after meals, the wearing of "clothes brought directly from the back of the washerman's ass, the keeping "in society of people committing the greatest crimes, with the sole exception "of killing a Brāhmaṇa; and we also find endless minute transgressions of "the *Dharma* appertaining to each man's family or caste.

"Then again, the practices of the good people of different countries "are mutually contradictory; and many of these practices have their origin "in such visible causes as those of greed and the like. And certainly "people can have no confidence in such diverse practices, as having any "authority relating to *Dharma.*

"And further, you think those people as *good* whose conduct is good; "and you hold that conduct to be *good* which consists in the acts of these "people; and thus there being an interdependence, none of the two "can be definitely ascertained.

"It may be urged that 'Manu and others have also spoken of the "practices of good men as an authority for *Dharma;*' but then, they have "also mentioned the agent's own *inner satisfaction* as having an autho-"rity; and certainly there can be no fixity to this (satisfaction); be-"cause, as a matter of fact, we find that different people have differ-"ent causes for inner satisfaction, on account of the diversities in their "habits and dispositions,—some people being satisfied by the performance "of good deeds, some by that of bad ones, while others, by that of such "Actions as are neither good nor bad. As an instance of people feeling sat-"isfied in the doing of evil, we have Çākya, the Buddha, who was quite "pleased with himself at finding faults and arguments against the Veda and "the *Brāhmaṇas.* And again, we find that the *Brāhmaṇas* are satisfied by "the performance of sacrifices at which animals are slaughtered; while "the very same actions give pain to the *Bauddhas,* who have a great aversion "to them. Similarly too, certain *Brāhmaṇas* are quite satisfied at eating "the food given by the *Çudra;* the people of the South are happy when they "get a chance of marrying the daughter of their maternal uncle; while other "people are averse to such acts, considering them to be most sinful.

"And just as the fact of the agent's satisfaction being a highly fickle "standard leads us to put a different interpretation to Manu's declaration of "such satisfaction being an authority for *Dharma,*—so, in the same manner, "we regard the declaration of the authoritativeness of the practice of good "men as to be interpreted in some such different manner. And again, the "authors of the *Smṛtis* (Manu and others), in laying down the authori-"tative character of the Practice of good men, without having found a "basis for these in the Veda, do not show themselves to a very great advan-"tage; hence the declarations of such authoritative character must be "held to have some other meaning.

"Then again, all good men, to become good, should frame their con-"duct according to the injunctions of the *Smṛtis;* otherwise, by acting "by themselves, independently of these, they would become decidedly *bad,* "and not *good.* Because, for the practices of good people we find no basis "in the Veda; but if there were any such authority in the Veda, such prac-"tices would have been laid down in the *Smṛtis* (and not left to rest upon "the sole authority of the conduct of good men.) And thus, there being "no basis for the practices of good men, these are to be rejected (as having "no authority in matters relating to *Dharma*)."

The Siddhānta.

To the above we make the following reply: ***But as we do not find any causes, these, as actually in practice, should be accepted*** (*Sūtra 7*).

That is to say, when we find that certain actions are performed by good men, and we cannot attribute them to any such perceptible motives as Greed and the like, they should be accepted as *Dharma.* Such actions as are performed either for the maintenance of the body, or for one's mere pleasure, or for some material gain,—are not considered, by good people, as '*Dharma.*' It is only those actions, that are held by the good people to be *Dharma,* and are performed as such, that are accepted as *Dharma;* because the persons that perform these are the same as those that perform the sacrifices enjoined in the Veda.

To the latter class belong the following actions: Charities, *Japa, Homa,* the offering of the oblations to the Fathers, such celebrations as those of the *Çakradhvaja* and other such like festivities in connection with various temples, the keeping of the married girls upon certain strict observances during the four days after marriage, Illuminations, the giving away, on the first day of the month, of sweetcakes and other uncooked foods, the various festivities held on the 7th and the last days of Māgha and the first day of *Phālguna*, as also those held in honour of the advent of spring-time; and the authority for all this cannot lie anywhere else except in the Scriptures. And the Authors of the *Smṛtis*—in declaring the authoritative character of 'the practices of good men' and 'the usages of particular countries and castes, in keeping with Scripural teachings,'—admit of the general authoritative character of such of these as are not contrary to the teachings of the Veda. (And the aforesaid festivities have the support of the *Smṛtis* and the Vedas); inasmuch as in the chapter on 'Holidays,' is found (in the *Smṛtis*) the following—"Festivities should be held after breakfast;" and this serves as the authority for all festivities in any town or country. In the Veda too, we have the passage in connection with the *Mahāvrata*—"The *Hotṛ* priest gets upon the swing and sings;" and in continuation of this, we read—"when people are holding a feast, they get upon the swing;" and this mention of the "feast" serves as an authority for the aforesaid festivities.

It has been urged above that, inasmuch as *Dharma* and *Adharma* are treated of, with any degree of authority, only by the fourteen Sciences enumerated above, the Practice of good men not being included in these, it cannot be admitted to have any authority. But this objection has already been set aside by the fact of the possibility of the inference of Vedic texts in support of the said practices.

Nor can it be held that the asssertion of the *Smṛti* that—"the practices of good men have an authority in connection with *Dharma*"—is without any foundation in the Veda; because when we find pretty lengthy declarations of the *Smṛtis* to be supported by the Veda, by the very slighest references to them, it is no wonder that we cannot lay our hands upon the Vedic texts (though they really exist) corroborative of such brief assertions as the one declaring the authoritative character of the said Practices. And it is quite possible for us to infer Vedic texts exactly like those in the *Smṛtis*. And the inference may be in this form: The Scriptural text, that declares the otherwise unknown results of actions performed by good men, has also its use (in the pointing out of the authoritative character of such actions),—exactly as the milking of the cow, &c. We do not hold that alone to be authorised by the scriptures, which is described therein in its detailed form; specially as all authorities take up only one of the many phases of the object they treat of; hence though the external forms of the Practices are cognised by Sense-perception, exactly like the preparing of the curd, the milking of the cow and the like, yet the fact of their bringing about particular results (in the shape of Heaven, &c.) cannot be got at by any other means save the scriptures. For the matter of that, even in the case of sacrifices, a perception of their external forms does not stand in need of any Scripural authority. It is only the fact of their leading to certain definite results that, being not perceptible by the senses, stands in need of such authority.

Nor can there be any inter-dependence (as urged in the *Pūrvapaksha*); because it is not always necessary that the good men, in all that they do, should always recall the scriptural authority for their actions; the fact is that from times immemorial we have always found the practices of good men to be in keeping with the scriptures; and hence people coming to recognise the authoritative character of such practices (and not always taking the trouble, to seek the further authority of the scriptures), take up these practices as the basis; and from that they deduce certain actions as leading to Heaven, &c.; and as such they lose sight of the fact of such actions being only occasional, and gradually come to recognise them as necessary. The "good men" whose practices are meant here are only those that inhabit the country called "*Āryāvarta*" (the tract bounded by the Ocean on the East and the West, the Himalaya on the North, and the Vindhya on the South); and this limit, we may infer to be based upon Vedic passages, that speak of the 'disappearance of the Sārasvatī' and the 'drippings from the Plaksha tree' (the former expression really referring to the place where the '*Sārasvata Satra*' was commenced, and the latter where it was completed; but capable of being taken as implying the tract round Kuruksēhtra, in the planes of which the Sarasvatī river is said to have disappeared).

The following objection may be brought forward: "The goodness of "a man depending upon the fact of his acting in accordance with the "teachings of the scriptures, the mention of his practices, in the scrip- "tures, as *good*, would involve a mutual inter-dependence."

But these people are called 'good,' not because of their good conduct, but, simply because they are always found to be acting in accordance with scriptural injunctions. People come to be recognised as 'good,' by always acting in accordance with the direct teachings of the Veda; and when they have thus acquired the title of 'good,' even if they happen to do something else, in accordance with a fixed tradition, (even though the direct Vedic texts on the point may not be available), such actions are believed to be the means of attaining to Heaven, and to have the character of *Dharma*. And as for the 'mutual inter-dependence' urged above, even in the case of the Veda, we read "If one who is *learned in the Veda*, learned in the sciences, eloquent, *fully knowing the Veda*, should read, &c., &c.," where we find the "knowers of the Veda" mentioned in the Veda; but inasmuch as there is an eternal relationship between the Veda and the words it uses and the subject-matter it deals with,—and as such the precedence of one or the other is as impossible to be ascertained as in the case of the mutual relationship between Day and Night,—such mutual inter-dependence is not held to be faulty. And as for the *Smṛti* texts, laying down the actions already supported by the practice of good men (they cannot be said to be useless on the ground of all necessary authority for such actions being found in the said practices as supported by direct or assumed Vedic texts); because it may be held that having come across the particular practice, or even the Vedic text in support of it, the *Smṛti* may have expressed its own acquiescence in it.

It has been urged above that, inasmuch as we find such practices based upon perceptible motives of greed, &c., they cannot have any basis in the Veda. But such perceptible motives being also found in the case of the Actions laid down directly in the Veda,—this fact alone cannot justify us in rejecting the fact of the practices having a basis in the Veda. That is to say, we find the injunctions of many actions in which there is always some touch of a perceptible motive; and hence the presence of such motives in the practices of good men cannot debar them from having a basis in the Veda.

However, there are certain actions, which are also common among the Mlecchas, for the performance of which there is no fixed rule or time—such things as are the means of physical-pleasures; as for instance, agriculture, commerce, foods and drinks, soft beds, comfortable houses, pleasure-gardens, painting, singing, dancing, perfumes, and the like; but nobody ever thinks of these as *Dharma;* and hence the nature of these cannot rightly lead us to reject the authority of all practices of good men (that have any visible causes); nor can the fact of some such actions being accepted as *Dharma* establish the Dharmic character of all of them. Even among people who are similar to the Mlecchas, we find the prevalence of such actions as the worshiping of the gods and *Brāhmaṇas*; and certainly we accept these to be *Dharma*, because they also appear in the practice of good men. Among ordinary people, certain practices are distinctly specified as *good*, while there are other actions, which are common to all living beings (such as those of *eating* and the like, which help to keep the body), and which, as such, are performed by the good men also. But among all practices, those alone that are current among the good people only are called *Dharma*, and not all the Actions that are common to all living beings (and as such among the good also).

From this it also follows that in the case of men, whose minds have been fully impressed with the idea that only such Actions as are laid down in the Veda are *Dharma*, their inner satisfaction is an authority in distinguishing *Dharma*. And it is not possible for such people, as have their minds purified by a fill of knowledge of the Veda and its meaning, and whose intention always functions in accordance with the path of duty laid down in the Veda,—to have any ideas contrary to the Veda; and with a view to this, it has been said—"whatever the man learned in the Veda utters, it becomes Vedic"—*i.e.*, having its source in the impressions left by the Veda, it becomes as authoritative as the Veda itself. Just as in the case of salt mines, and in that of Meru the land of bright gold, whatever is produced in them, becomes salt and gold (respectively),—so also in the case of the inner satisfaction of one who knows the Veda (which imparts Vedic authority to all that it touches). This idea has also been expressed by many learned people, and has been also poetically put thus: "Whenever any doubtful point presents itself to good men, they are helped by their own minds, which always help them to come to the correct conclusion." (*Çakuntalā*, Act I). And as a matter of fact, for those whose minds are pervaded by the ideas imbibed from a long continued study of the Veda, it is not possible to have an inner satisfaction, in anything else save the doing of that which is *Dharma*; and hence that Action, which when performed gives them inward satisfaction, is accepted as *Dharma*.

Or, we may accept the fact of the inner satisfaction of good men being a means of knowing *Dharma*, on mere verbal testimony (of Manu and others); and just as, even though many persons may perform any single pious act, yet a contemplation of these persons brings about excellent results to ordinary people (as it is laid down that whenever an evil thought enters one's mind he should think of a pious person),—in the same manner, even though many actions may be connected with the inner satisfaction of the good man, yet they are accepted as being conducive to excellent results. And we may employ the same reasoning to the case of the practices of good men (which are laid down as authoritative, in the text "the practices of good men also, &c., &c."). Just as (1) in the case of one who has been favoured by some deities with a boon to the effect that anything he would utter would counteract the most virulent poison, when he utters some such thing, and it is found to effect a cure, people cherish that utterance of his, to serve them in curing similar cases of poisoning (in this case the mere fact of the words being uttered by the favoured person, imparts to them the potency),—(2) in the science of snakes, it is laid down that whatever herb the mongoose happens to hold by its teeth, it becomes a potent cure for all poisons—(in this case the mere touch of the animal's teeth imparts the potency to the herb),—(3) whatever place a pious man happens to inhabit, that place (by his mere contact) attains a sanctity that purifies all other people coming to it,—exactly in the same manner, the practices and the inner satisfaction of such people as have their minds saturated with *Dharma*, themselves become the means of *Dharma;* and as such they are to be accepted, by people seeking after a knowledge of *Dharma*, as laid down in the Veda itself.

The *Pūrvapaksha* has brought forward certain specific instances of the admittedly evil doings of eminently recognised good men: for instance, that Prajāpati made advances to his own daughter, that Indra had an intercourse with Ahalyā; and so forth; and from these instances of gross transgressions of the Law by recognised good men, it has come to the conclusion that the mere practice of good men cannot be accepted as an authority for *Dharma.*

In the first place, the passages (in the Purāṇas and Vedas) that are interpreted on these lines, may be only a fortuitous coincidence of words and expressions (the texts never having actually meant what they seem to mean now); or, *secondly*, the prohibition of such actions may be held to pertain to men only, and not to superhuman beings; or, thirdly, the actions may be justified on the ground of the persons concerned being very powerful and super-human beings, and as such not subject to the same limitations (of conduct) as the weaklier human beings; or, fourthly, we can explain the said texts in such a way as to deprive them of all repulsive significations.

E.g. (1) The word "*Prajāpati*" means 'one who protects all creatures;' as such it can be taken as a name of the Sun; and it is an ordinary fact that towards morning the sun reaches the early Dawn, ('*Ushā*'); and as the early Dawn is brought about by the approach of the Sun, it is called his "daughter;" and it is the fact of the Sun letting his rays fall in (or on) the Dawn that has been figuratively spoken of as the intercourse of a man with a woman.

(2) The word "*Indra*"—proceeding from the root '*Idi*' which signifies *great glory*—would signify *one possessed of a resplendent glory*; and as such it is taken as another name of the Sun; and he is the '*jāra*'—*destroyer* (*jarati-nāçayati*)—of '*Ahalyā*'—(*ahani līyatē*) *that which disappears during the day, i.e.*, Night; as it is only when the Sun rises that the darkness of night is destroyed; and it is in this sense that we should take the sentence—"*Indro' halyāyā jārah,*"—which cannot be taken in its ordinary sense, of an illicit connection with a woman.

(3) As for *Nahusha*, it is true that when he reached the position of Indra, he made advances towards Çacī, Indra's wife; but through this unlawful act, he fell from his place and was born as a big snake; and this clearly shows that it was a sinful act that he had done; and as for Çacī, as

she proved very constant in her devotion to her own husband, her greatness and effulgence become enhanced to a tremendous extent, which shows that such faithfulness is an act of *Dharma*.

(4) In the case of Vaçishtha, it is clear that his action was due to excessive grief, and hence nobody accepts it as *Dharma*. It is only that Action which the good men know to be *Dharma*, and perform it as such, hat is to be accepted as *Dharma*; while those Actions that, even when performed by good men, are clearly found to be due to an undue influence of desire, anger, greed, delusion, grief and the like,—are to be classified as '*Dharma*' or '*Adharma*,' according as they happen to be enjoined or prohibited in the scriptures (without any consideration for the fact of their being performed by good men).

(5) Hence, in the case of Viçvāmitra also, as he had reached a very high degree of penance, even though he did, in certain cases transgress the law under the influence of passion or anger,—yet we can allow such transgressions to pass unnoticed, in accordance with the maxim that 'for a strong man everything is equally healthy' (*i.e.*, for a pious man all actions are equally lawful); or, we may absolve him from all blame, on the ground that he would destroy all such sins by means of excessive penances, and the performances of proper expiatory rites, which would leave him as pure as ever. But for people of lesser penances, such transgressions would be as irretrievably harmful, as the eating of the (poisonous) leaves of the *Mahāvata* for the elephant.

(6) As for Dvaipāyana, he, under his mother's orders, got children from the wife of his brother (related to him through his mother), in accordance with the scriptural injunction: "A woman without a husband, if desirous of progeny, may, if ordered by her superior, have recourse to her husband's younger brother;" and even if a transgression, it disappears in the light of his great penances, prior to, as well as after, the committing of the deed. If there be another person with an equal degree of Brahmic glory, he might do such deeds with impunity.

(7) Rāma and Bhishma, both considering the wife to be only necessary in the performance of the sacrifice they had undertaken, did not take to a wife—the former on account of his great love for his first wife Sītā, and the latter because of his great reverence for his father to whom he had promised that he would never marry; and as both were free from the debt they owed their fathers—the one by his direct offspring, and the other by the children of his mother,—there was no impediment to their sacrifices being duly accomplished. Then again, Rāma kept by him, at the sacrifice, a golden image of Sītā, because for the sake of reputation (he could not have kept Sītā in person), and for the sake of showing that he was not cruel to the memory of Sītā (he did not take another wife to him-

self). And as for Bhíshma,—the text of Manu laying down that if among many uterine brothers, even one gets children, all the rest become endowed with offspring, through these very children,—having been freed from the debt he owed his fathers, by the birth of the sons of his brother, Vicitravīrya,—he may have taken to a wife for the mere fulfilment of the sacrificial conditions; and this we may infer from the Apparent Inconsistency of such an irregularity in the conduct of a blameless person like Bhīshma, who, [*Mahābhārata*—Anuçāsana Parva, 84] when offering his libations at Gayā, did not place the offering in the hands of his father (who had appeared to him in person), in consideration of the scriptural texts that lays down the offering of the libations on the ground—(one who was so scrupulous in following the scriptural teachings) how could he, alone, without a wife, have dared to perform sacrifices?)

(8) As for Dhṛtarāshtra, we find it related in the *Āçcarya Parva* that, through Vyāsa's favour, he got his sight for looking upon his sons; and from this we can infer that through the same agency he was able to see when the sacrifice was being performed (and hence at that time he was not blind). We are told of the Maharshi being capable of wonderful curses and blessings; hence, just as we know of Dhṛtarāshtra to have been born blind in accordance with a curse pronounced by Vyāsa; so we can infer, from the apparent inconsistency of a blind person engaging in sacrifices, that during the performance he got his vision through a blessing of Vyāsa. Or, in the passages that describe Dhṛtarāshtra as performing *yajnas*, the word 'Yājna' may be taken to mean 'charity, gifts,' as the root '*yaji*' is equally expressive of *sacrifice* and *giving*. And we find Charity laid down as leading to results similar to those of sacrifices; hence the giving of charities may have been figuratively spoken of as the "performance of sacrifices."

(9) The unlawful intercourse of the five Pāndavas with a common wife has been very well explained by Vyāsa himself: "Draupadī appeared, in the full bloom of youth, out of the sacrificial altar; and as such she is Lakshmī (the goddess of wealth) herself; consequently, she does not become tainted by her intercourse with many owners." To the same effect, we have also the following: "The Brahmarshi pointed out her wonderfully beautiful form to be superhuman; inasmuch as the great-souled beautiful one (Draupadī) became younger day by day." All this tends to show that she was not an ordinary human being; and hence she has been spoken of as "superhuman" (and as such her actions are not to be judged by the ordinary standard of human proprieties). It is for the very same reason that Kṛshna himself promised to Karṇa that Draupadī would go to him on the sixth day (after having been with the five Pāndavas for five days). If it were not on account of the superhuman character of the

woman, how could such an authoritative person as Kṛshna himself have promised such a transgression.

Another explanation is that there were five distinct Draupadīs; but as they were all alike, they have been spoken of as one; this conclusion being led to by the apparent inconsistency of such a transgression appearing in the conduct of such blameless characters as Yudhishthira and his brothers.

Or, it may be that she was the wife of Arjuna alone (by whom she was actually won); and yet she is spoken of as being the wife of all of them, simply with a view to show, by a hyperbolical representation, that there was not the slightest point of disagreement among the five brothers. Her superhuman character is further pointed out by the fact that when being dragged to the assembly of kings, at the gambling, though she was not actually in her courses, yet, on the spur of the moment, she made herself look exactly as if she were so, simply with a view to show the action of Dhṛtarāshtra in the worst possible light. And her character of Lakshmī, too, is fully recognised, only when she is considered as the wife of Arjuna alone (who is Nara, the counterpart of Nārayaṇa). Then again, she has been spoken of, as the common wife of all the five brothers, simply with a view to show that there was such a close friendship among them that even such an exclusive possession as the wife may be spoken of as belonging to all of them, and as such there was no mutual distrust among them, and so much the less chance of any differences arising.

Thus then, when all these apparent transgressions are found to be capable of various rational explanations, and when, as a matter of fact, all good men are actually found to avoid all that has its source in passion and greed, &c., it is not right to question the righteousness of the Practice of Good Men.

(10) Thus too, as regards the action of Yudhishthira in telling a lie to compass the death of Droṇa, some authors have laid down that expiatory rites can be performed even when the evil is done purposely; and as the rites laid down for the particular transgression, are the performance of an *Açwamēdha* sacrifice, Yudhishthira did perform this sacrifice, and thereby distinctly showed that what he had done was sinful; and as such it cannot be accepted as the "Practice of good men."

(11) Then remains the case of Kṛshna and Arjuna being drunk with wine, and having married the daughters of their respective maternal uncles, both being instances of direct transgressions of the law. But it is only the wine distilled from grains, which is called '*Surā*,' that is prohibited for the three higher castes; says the *Smṛti*: "*Surā* is the impure essence of the grains and it is evil that is spoken of as *impure*;

hence the Brāhmana, the Kshatriya and the Vaiçya should never drink *Surā*." As for the particular wines "*Madhu*" (wine distilled from certain fruits, as grapes and the like), and the '*Sīdhu*' (that distilled from molasses), these are not prohibited for the Kshatriya and the Vaiçya; as "*all* intoxicating drinks" have been prohibited for the Brāhmana alone. Though there is a passage that declares—"all the three kinds of wine, the *Gaudī* (that distilled from molasses) *Paishthi* (that distilled from grains) and *Mādhvī* (distilled from fruits), being the same, they should not be drunk by the *Brahmavādis*,"—yet here the word "*Brahmavādi*" should be taken as denoting the Brāhmanas only; as the word literally means 'one who is capable of teaching Brahma,' or 'whose duty it is to teach Brahma', or 'whose excellence lies in such teaching'; and as the root '*Vada*' is synonymous with '*Brū*' such duties are distinctly restricted to the Brāhmana alone, by such texts as—"from among the three higher castes, the Brāhmana alone should teach.". And it has also been pointed out in connection with the villificatory Arthavāda, that are taken along with the prohibition of wines in general, that the Brāhmana, deluded under the influence of wine, might do many such things as should not be done, which shows that *wine* in general is prohibited for the Brāhmana only. Hence we take the passage—"All the three kinds of wine, &c.," to mean that just as the one, *Surā* distilled from grains, is not drinkable by the three higher castes, so are all the three undrinkable by the Brāhmana. Otherwise, if the simple prohibition of *wine* in general were meant, then the words '*Yathaiva, &c.*,' and '*Brahmavādibhih*' would be totally redundant. The mention of "the three castes" we shall supply from out of another verse. For this reason, the fact of Kṛshna and Arjuna—both Kshatriyas—being intoxicated with '*Madhu*' (grape wine) is in no way a transgression of the law.

And, as a matter of fact, we have Vedic texts that distinctly show (1) that the prohibition of wine is for others (*i.e.*, Brāhmanas), and also (2) that it is distinctly permissible (in the case of others): For instance, (1) "That which was impure came out afterwards; wine is that impurity, this became attached to the Kshatriya; hence it is that superiors, daughters-in-law, and the father-in-law drink the wine and go on talking; evil indeed is impurity; hence the Brāhmana should not drink the wine; lest he be attached to evil"; and (2) "The Kshatriya should say to the Brāhmana—'the drinking of wine does no harm to him who knows this'"; and this latter is with reference to the '*Madhu*' and the '*Sīdhu*' (and not the '*Surā*' which is in no case allowed to anyone else but the Cūdra).

As for Kṛshna and Arjuna, having married their maternal cousins, such relationships of brothers and cousins come to be mentioned, even where there is no blood relationship (and hence it may be that Kṛshna and Arjuna are spoken of as cousins simply because of their close friendship). Though Subhadrā is spoken of as 'Kṛshna's sister,' yet, we know that only three persons—Baladēva, Kṛshna, and Ēkanañçā—have been spoken of as uterine brothers and sisters; and hence we conclude that Subhadrā must have been a distant cousin of Kṛshna's, as is clear from the fact of her being married to Arjuna, who could be said to have transgressed the law, only if he had married a child of Vasudeva's (who was his maternal uncle); and certainly he committed no transgression in marrying one who was only a distant relation of Vasudeva. And how could such a great Law-giver as Kṛshna, who is always cited as an example of righteous conduct, allow of an incestuous marriage, when he was fully alive to his position of a Law-giver, as is clearly shown by his own declarations: *viz.*: "O Pārtha, all men follow my path," "Whatever the great one does, the others follow; that which he authorises, people act up to it."

The above arguments will serve to explain the marriage of Kṛshna himself with Rukminī (who is said to have been his cousin).

As instances of transgressions, in modern times, of the laws laid down in the *Smṛtis*, the *Pūrvapakṣha* has cited the drinking of wine among the Brāhmana women of the countries of Ahicchatra and Mathurā, and the marriage with maternal cousins, current amongst the people of the South.

In explanation of this, some people assert that as the *Smṛti* and the Practice of good men are both independent of each other, being equally based upon the Veda, both of them are of equal authority, and as such whenever we find them contradicting each other, we can accept both as laying down equally authoritative alternatives; and as such the transgressions need not be rejected as transgressions of *Smṛti* laws, and as such sinful.

But this explanation cannot be accepted as correct, in view of the statement of the comparative strength of the various authorities of *Dharma* (where it will be distinctly shown that the *Smṛti* has a greater authority than the Practice of good men).

Others again offer the following explanation: All Laws are laid down with special reference to certain definite parts of the country; as Āpastamba has distinctly pointed out that certain actions are not allowed in one part of the country, and they are quite permissible in another. And hence we conclude that the said practices would not be sinful only for those whose forefathers have been used to them: as has been declared by Manu also: "The path by which one's father and forefathers have gone on, by that path of the good should one proceed; as by such procedure alone does he not become attached to sin." And, as a matter of fact, we find that those people, whose forefathers have not accepted the aforesaid practices which have been prohibited in other *Smṛtis*, still avoid them; and if by chance they do become addicted to it, they are cast out by their own people.

But this explanation too will not serve our purpose; because Gautama has declared that "all practices contrary to the Scriptures are unauthoritative." It may be argued that as a matter of course, when we find the practices to be contrary to the Veda, we do not accept them as authoritative; and the term 'Scriptures' does not apply to the *Smṛtis*. But this is not correct; because the term 'Scripture' is applicable to *Smṛti* works also. In connection with "*Smārta Dharma*" Çankha and Likhita have declared "*Āmnāyah smṛtidhārakah*," which clearly shows that the works of Manu and others—called '*Āmnāya*' (Scriptures)—which were composed by them on the strength of their own remembrances of Vedic texts—have been laid down for the sake of the students of these works, for the purpose of ascertaining a definite basis for the said compilations in such rememberances. Hence, it is absolutely impossible for us to accept the authoritative character of such practices as are contrary to the laws laid down by Manu and others. As for the declaration of Āpastamba, quoted above, it has been completely refuted by Baudhāyana, who has cited many instances of practices contrary to the *Smṛtis*. And further, as we find all such practices originating from visible causes, such as passion and the like, we can never accept the fact of there being a Vedic basis, either for such unlawful practices, or for the above quoted declarations of Āpastamba.

It may be asked—"What is the text that prohibits the drinking of wine for Brāhmana women?" Well, we have the text—"For this reason, the Brāhmana and the Kshatriya, and also the Kshatriyā, should not drink wine."

Against this, it may be urged that the word "Brāhmana" being in the masculine gender, the said text cannot be taken as prohibiting it for women; and as such the practice of the women of Mathura cannot be held to be contrary to the *Smṛti* text quoted.

But, in that case, even in the case of the prohibition—"A Brāhmana should not be killed," it may be the killing of the man alone that can be said to be prohibited; and in the same manner, a significance may be attached to the singular number in 'Brāhmana'; and thence a man would only once desist from killing *one* Brāhmana; and he would conclude that he has obeyed the law fully, in that one desisting, and thenceforward he might go on killing Brāhmanas with impunity. Or, in the prohibition in question too, we find the word "Brāhmana" in the singular; and so the law would have been fully obeyed by any single Brāhmana desisting from wine; and thenceforth, we would have the same contingency as before in the case of the prohibition of killing (*i.e.*, the other Brāhmanas would go on drinking with impunity).

The other party retorts: "As for the significance of the singular "number, as this may be applicable either to each individual Brāhmana, "or to the single Brāhmana-class (considered as one composite whole), "there would be no harm in accepting it. That is to say, even if the pro-"hibition of the *killing*, as well as of the *drinking*, refer to each individual "Brāhmana that may happen to become a fit object of such prohibition,— "as the mention of this singularity would be a mere repetition, it could not "qualify either the *action* (of *killing* or *drinking*) or the *prohibition*—(and "as such the singular number could not be held to have any significance); "specially if the singularity is distinctly found to refer to the *Brāhmana-"class*, (as this class is always universally recognised to be *one*), any "mention of its singularity would all the more be a mere repitition (and as "such in any case no significance can be attached to the singular number; "though there are no such objections to the admitting of the significance "of the masculine gender). [Then, as for the argument that if the mas-"culine gender be significant, in the case of the word 'Brāhmana' as "occurring in the prohibition, 'the Brāhmana should not drink wine,' the "same may be said in the case of the prohibition 'the Brāhmana should "not be killed'] there is a deal of difference between the two cases; as in "the prohibition of *killing*, ('*Brāhmano na hantavyah*') the 'Brāhmana' "being the real objective, appears in the form of the subject (on account "of the passive affix *tavya*); and as such no significance is attached to the "masculine gender in this case; exactly as in the case of the sentence "'one desirous of heaven should offer sacrifices,' no significance is at-"tached to the masculine gender in '*svargakāmah*,' simply on the ground "of its being the subject; while in the case of the prohibition of *drinking*, "though the Brāhmana, as the person warned off from sin, has the "character of the subject, yet considered as the agent of the *drinking*, "he becomes a part of the predicate, by means of the Nominative and "the Instrumental affixes (the real construction of the prohibition being "'*Brāhmanēna-surāpānam pāpajanakam*'); and as such in this case, it be-"comes absolutely necessary to attach a significance to the masculine "gender; exactly as in the case of the 'measuring of the sacrificial post' by "the sacrificer, as the sacrificer is mentioned as the predicate, his gender "is taken into consideration.

"To further explain (how no significance can be attached to the mas-"culine gender in the word 'Brāhmana,' in the sentence 'the Brāhmana "should not be killed'): The meaning of the sentence is that '*one who is* "*a Brāhmana* should not be killed'; and when this construction has been "once comprehended, (the prohibition has been fully understood and) no "other gender, &c., can be predicated, either of the Brāhmana, or of the "prohibition; (because that would lead to a split of the original sentence), "which would have to be construed somewhat like this: 'one who is a "Brāhmana should not be killed, and that Brāhmana should be a male'; "which is not in any case allowable. That is to say, the Injunction in "question serves to lay down a prohibition; and as no prohibition of mere "*killing* (without an object) is possible, we take it to mean the prohibition "of the *killing* as qualified by (*i.e.*, as pertaining to) the *Brāhmana-class*; "and its operation ceasing with this, if it be called into requisition again, "with a view to the injunction of any such peculiarities as the gender and "the like, with reference either to the *Brāhmana*, or to the *Killing*, or to "the *Prohibition*,—then it would be necessary to repeat the Injunctive "affix (which has once enjoined the *non-killing*, and which is now called "upon to lay down the gender, &c.); and as such, this would lead to the "split of the sentence. Even for those who hold Injunction and Prohibi-"tion to be two distinct facts signified by Vedic sentences, the Nega-"tive ('not' in the prohibition 'the Brāhmana should not be killed'), "having its own denotation helped by that of the Injunctive affix, comes "to have an additional meaning (in the shape of *prohibition*), and serves the "purpose of prohibiting that (*killing*) which has been signified by the In-"junctive affix in ('*hantavyah*'), with special reference to the Brāhmana-"class; because, as explained before, no prohibition of mere *killing* in the "abstract would be possible; and it cannot be again called into requisition "to prohibit any such further peculiarities, as those of gender and the "like, in connection with, either the Brāhmana, or the Killing, or the In-"junction; consequently, though a particular gender is mentioned in the "sentence, yet, as it does not serve any useful purpose, no significance can "be attached to it. The construction of the said passage may be amplified "in the following manner: 'That the Brāhmana should be killed through "anger &c., is not.' But according to those who accept the Injunction to "be the only signification of the Veda (and explain the Prohibition as "only a negative Injunction), the sentence may be amplified thus: 'The "killing of the Brāhmana should not be done,' or 'He who is a Brāh-"mana, him one should not kill,'—the passage being thus explained, "either as the prohibition of the *killing* as pertaining to the Brāhmana, "or as the prohibition of a *killing* which has its object distinctly pointed "out as the Brāhmana. In any case, we cannot escape from accepting "the Brāhmana as the Subject; and as pertaining to the Subject, either "the Gender or the Number can have no significance.

"On the other hand, in the case of the prohibitions—'the Brāhmana "should not drink the wine, ' and ' the wine should not be drunk by the "teachers of Brahma '—, the 'Brahmana' has not the character, of either "the 'cause,' or 'place,' or 'time' or 'result,' or 'the object of purification,'—which are the only five possible forms of that which is already "known (*i.e.*, Subject); and in the former sentence, the Brāhmana has "the full character of the qualification of the nominative, and as such, "is capable of being defined by the singular number which is predicated "of it by the verbal affix ('in *pibēt*'); and in the latter sentence as the "Instrumental ending distinctly points to the subordinate (or predicative) character of the Brāhmana, he cannot but be admitted to be "specified by the masculine gender. And in accordance with this, even "the former sentence should be taken as the prohibition of *drinking*, for "the Brāhmana, as qualified by the Masculine gender."

"And thus, as the drinking of wine is not found to have been prohibited, for Brāhmana women, the drinking of wine by the women of the "countries of Ahicchatra and Mathura cannot be said to be a transgression of the law."

SIDDHĀNTA.

This is not so; because even in the case of the prohibition of drinking, no significance can be attached to the gender, because the Brāhmana is the subject, here also, exactly as in the case of the prohibition of Brāhman-killing. As a matter of fact, the mere fact of a certain thing being yet to be known is not the only ground for attaching a significance to the qualifications of the gender, &c., because Predicability is the one important ground for such significance; as that which is described—*i.e.*, the Subject of a proposition—is described just as it is found to exist; and in connection with that, nothing more than what is necessarily required by the Predicate can be said to be predicated.

Hence, if we had any such injunction as that 'the Brahmana should drink wine' prior to the appearance of the Prohibition, then alone could there be any chance for the subordinate and predicative character belonging to the Brāhmana, which could justify our attaching a significance to everything (that is both the masculine gender and the singular number). But, as a matter of fact, we know that the only agent that prompts the Brāhmana to the drinking of wine is Passion or Delusion, &c.; and so there is no possibility of there being any such Injunction (of the drinking of wine). And as for an Injunction being deduced from the prohibitive text itself (as urged above), no such deduction is possible, as all chance for it is barred by the fact of the sentence ending in a direct prohibition. Therefore, whether the said prohibition be construed as—'That the Brāhmana should drink wine is not,'—or as 'He who is a Brāhmana should not drink wine,'—it being taken either as the prohibition of drinking as pertaining to wine, or as the Injunction of a prohibition,—in any case, inasmuch as he is the object that is helped by being warned off from the drinking, the *Brāhmana* cannot be held to be *predicated* either of the *drinking* or of the *prohibition* (and as such no significance can be attached to the gender, &c.)

Even in ordinary experience, we find that there is a chance of both the male and the female (Brāhmana) being addicted to drink; and hence in the sentence prohibiting the drinking, the mention of the Brahmana must be taken as pertaining to both sexes (because as the Subject of the sentence, it must be taken exactly as it is found in ordinary experience). And it cannot be construed as 'The Brāhmana that should drink'—'and he be a male'; because such connection of the gender cannot be established without the operation of Predication (which is absent in this case). (That is to say, when the 'Brahmana' has once been spoken of as the Subject, it is not possible to make it the Predicate without a Predicative word). (But such Predication is not found in the present case). (Because the whole sentence cannot be taken as serving the sole purpose of predicating the relation of the gender; as the Injunction, or the Predication, does not proceed any further than the prohibition of drinking). Hence, we conclude that in both cases (*i.e.*, in the case of the prohibition, 'The Brāhmana should not be killed,' as also in that 'The Brāhmana should not drink wine') we cannot attach any significance to the gender or the number (of the word 'Brāhmana').

It may be argued that—"if such be the case, then the killing of the Brāhmana woman would be as sinful as that of the male Brāhmana; and as such, how is it that the full expiatory rite, necessary on the killing of a Brāhmana, has been restricted (in the case of the female Brāhmana) to the *Ātrēyi* woman only (which shows that the killing of other Brāhmana females is not equally sinful)?"

To this we make the following reply: Who is there that denies the equal sinfulness of the killing of the female Brāhmana? As for the expiatory rites being different, this is due to the fact of the one being a female and the other a male (but this does not show that there is any difference in the sinfulness of the two slaughters); and certainly the comparative slightness of the expiatory rite does not remove the character of 'Brahmana-slaughter' from the killing of the female Brāhmana; because under certain circumstances the expiatory rite that has been laid down as necessary for one who has killed even a male Brāhmana, is also comparatively slight; and this fact would also come to imply the lesser sinfulness of this killing (which is absurd). Therefore, because the expiatory rite laid down for one who kills a female Brāhmana is comparatively slight, from that we cannot doubt the fact of the killing of the woman being sinful and prohibited.

In the case of the drinking of wine, however, we do not meet with any distinction in the expiatory rites that are laid down; and as such all chance of there being any support for such drinking by women having been lost, we conclude that the said practice of the Brāhmana women of the two countries, is a direct transgression of the laws laid down in the *Smṛtis*.

It has been argued above that on the strength of a declaration of Āpastamba, we can accept the two as optional alternatives; but as this drinking of wine by the Brāhmana has been prohibited by the Veda itself—"Therefore, the Brāhmana should not drink wine"—the mere equality of two contradictory *Smṛtis* cannot justify us in accepting an option in the matter; and hence we cannot admit the authoritativeness of such practices.

(*The Adhikarana differently construed*).

With a view to establish the authoritative character of the Practices of good men, we can construe both these *Sūtras* as laying down this same *Adhikarana*. And this further consideration is based upon the instances of the practices of the good people inhabiting the part of the world known as '*Āryāvarta*' which has been defined as that country where the black antelope is found to roam and graze. The question is—That which the Āryas (gentlemen of the said country) are found to perform, as *Dharma*, is that authoritative or not? And the ground of doubt is that on account of these persons being the same as the performers of Vedic sacrifices, we conclude their practices to be authoritative; while inasmuch as we do not find such practices duly coded and compiled, there is a chance that they may be unauthoritative.

It may be argued that the Authors of the *Smṛtis* themselves have declared the authoritativeness of such practices, in such texts as,—"the remembrance and the conduct of people knowing the Veda," "the practices of good men," "the practice that obtains in a country," and so forth—and as such the authority of the practices is implied in that of the *Smṛtis*.

But this will not do; as the opponent might very rightly argue thus: "Inasmuch as we do not find such practices to have any origin (in the "Veda) and as we find them to be due to other motives of greed and the "like, we cannot accept them as authoritative; because even of *Smṛti* texts, "we admit the authority of only such of them as are found to have any basis "in the various branches of the Veda; but on the sole authority of the pre- "valence of certain practices, we cannot infer the existence of corroborative

Smṛti texts, and at the same time, that the Vedic texts in support of these "latter. Because the Authors of the *Smṛtis* must have seen these practices "exactly as we see them; and hence the *Smṛtis* cannot point out any Vedic "basis for them. Specially because, if these Authors knew of the Vedic texts "in support of the practices, they should have included them among the other "acts laid down in their works. And hence, inasmuch as we do not find "them laying them down in their works in the same manner as they have "done the other acts for which they had supports in the Veda,—and as they "declared them to be authoritative, simply on account of the confidence "that they had in the good men of their day,—we can by no means "ascertain such practices to have any basis in the Veda."

Consequently there is certainly an occasion for due consideration. The foregoing two *Adhikaraṇas* have laid down the conclusion that the Practices of good men are authoritative, because the people among whom these are prevalent are the same as the performers of Vedic sacrifices, and also because we do not find them to be contrary to the Veda or the *Smṛti*. As a matter of fact, we do not find any practices of good men to be contrary to any *Smṛti* or Vedic texts; and as such, from the fact of the persons concerned being the same in both cases, they are accepted to be authoritative; and in support of this we have the declarations of the Authors of *Smṛtis*, who could not have lent their support to anything which they did not actually know to be based upon the Veda.

Against this conclusion, however, we have the following:—

PŪRVAPAKSHA.

"*Inasmuch as the scriptures are limited in their scope* (*Sūtra* 6), the "practices of good men, devoid of Vedic support, cannot have any author- "ity, with regard to the ascertaining of *Dharma* or *Adharma*. The scope "of the scriptures has been limited to matters relating to *Dharma* and "*Adharma*: and the scriptures have been limited to the number *fourteen*, as "made up of the Veda and its subsidiary sciences, none of which includes "any such thing as the Practices of good men; nor can such Practice be "said to form a scripture by itself; nor can the *Perception* or the *Perform-* "*ance* of such Practices be said to form a scripture; because the former "depends upon other persons; and as for the latter it is the subject-matter "dealt with by the scriptures, and cannot itself be the scripture. And as "for the *Smṛti* text supporting the authoritative character of the Prac- "tices, it has already been shown that it has no basis in the Veda.

"And if we proceed to consider the question, as to whether these "Practices have one basis or many,—we find that neither of the two is "possible to be inferred. Because for such Practices as are found to be "different in different countries, and among different communities and fami-

" lies, it is not possible to be based upon any single Vedic text; nor is there " any such Vedic text as would include all such practices; as it is absolutely " impossible for them to be spoken of either as distinct individuals, or as " forming a class by themselves, which are the only two possible denotations " of words. And if one were to assume a Vedic text for each of these Prac- " tices, he would be composing a Veda by himself; as it is not possible for " any single sentence to speak of, and give rise to, an indefinite number " of practices; nor can it be said that, it was the finding of such a sentence " in the Veda that led the authors of the *Smṛtis* to declare the authoritative- " ness of the practices; because in that case these would come to have as " great an authority as the other *Smṛti* texts that lay down other duties " (on the basis of the Veda). And again, the *Smṛti* text that would be " composed after the perception of the Practice, cannot serve as its basis: " as that would disturb all the rules that regulate the relations of the sup- " porter and the supported, and the comparative strength of the various " authorities. (Because in that case the Practice would serve as the origin " and basis of the *Smṛti* text).

" Hence, inasmuch as it is only amongst a limited number of scrip- " tures that the basis for any action can be assumed, as we do not find " any basis for many of the said Practices among the scriptures, we con- " clude them to be absolutely baseless. Nor is it possible for us to assume a " a Vedic text similar to the *Smṛti* that could also be assumed as corro- " borative of the practices; because in that case, the Veda would come to " have its origin in these practices; which would turn all ideas of the com- " parative strength of the various authorities upside down. That is to say, " the Vedic text assumed would be in some such form as—'The Practices " of good men are authoritative;' but this would imply the existence of the " practices, prior to the Vedic text; and as that which follows cannot serve " as the basis for that which has existed before it, such an assumed text " cannot be held to be the basis of the practices which therefore remain as " baseless as before.

" Or, the *Sūtra* (6th) may be taken in the following manner: *the scope " of the scriptures is limited* to a definite number of subjects; and as the " number of the practices is indefinite, they cannot have the character of " the scripture.

" Or, it may mean that the subject-matter of the scripture is " *limited* to such facts only as are not cognisable by any other means. " While in the case of the practices, we find many such visible motives as " Greed and the like; and hence we cannot admit them to have any author- " ity in the scriptures. Hence we conclude that inasmuch as the practices " are subsidiary to considerations of material pleasures, they cannot " have the character of *Dharma*. We find in the case of the Vaiçyas,

"Servants, and Doctors, and other people in the towns, that their practices "are based upon motives of material pleasures; and hence we conclude "the same to be the case with all human practices.

"For these reasons, we conclude that the Veda and the *Smṛtis* are "the only authorities in matters relating to *Dharma*; and as for the conduct "and practices and inner satisfaction of men, they are just the same as "drinking bouts and jokes (current among ordinary people)."

[*Sūtra* 7 would embody the *Siddhānta* in reply to this *Pūrvapaksha.*]

Or, the three *Sūtras* (5, 6, and 7) may be taken as dealing with this same *Adhikaraṇa*; and in this case, the practices current among the good people of *Āryāvarta* may be cited as instances; and with regard to these, a question may be raised as to their authoritativeness or otherwise. And (the *Pūrvapaksha* being supplied from without, on the same lines as shown above), all the *three Sūtras* may be taken as putting forward the *Siddhānta* only, which would run thus:

That which is taught ('*Çishta*') in the Veda and the *Smṛtis*—if this is not contradicted by the practice of good men, such practice can be accepted, as an authority for *Dharma*; but whenever there is the least contradiction of the said teachings, then, as there would be a contradiction among the authorities, the Practice can never be admitted to have any authority in matters relating to *Dharma*.

ADHIKARAṆA (5).

[*A word is always to be taken in the sense that is attributed to it in the scriptures*].

A.—The Adhikaraṇa explained in accordance with the Bhāshya.

***Sūtra* (8). "The contest would be equal."**

The clause—"because we do not find any contradiction amongst them"—may be taken as the opening of this *Sūtra*.

When we find even good men using a word in two different meanings the following doubt arises in the mind of the listener: Inasmuch as a single word is used by good men in different senses, often contradicting one another, which one shall we accept as being the real meaning of the word? For instance, the word '*yava*' (barley-corn) '*Varāha*,' (Boar), and '*Vētasa*' (Cane), are, in other countries, used in the sense of '*priyangu*' (Long pepper), '*Vāyasa*' (Crow), and '*Jamboo*' (Blackberry), respectively. Hence there arises a doubt as to the real significations of these words, in the minds of those who have not thought out the difficulty, and who base all their ideas only upon what they actually perceive.

And on this point, we have the following—

PŪRVAPAKSHA.

"There should be no doubt at all on this point; because the usages of "all men are equally authoritative. In the case of every word, in whatever "sense it happens to be used in a country, for that country the expressive-"ness of the word rests in that sense alone; and this local denotation of "the word is authoritative for all men of all countries; specially as the "following arguments necessitate such universal authority:

"The word cannot be said to have that sense for a few men only; "nor can it be said not to have that sense for any men; the only difference "that is possible is on the point of such sense being known or not known; "and it is only this difference that can be perceived, in connection with "several men of various countries. Consequently, even if a certain sense "of a word, be not known to certain men, they should accept it unhesitatingly; as it is as authoritative as the meaning that is known to "them.

"The reality, or the authority, of the denotations of words do not "depend upon either the greater or lesser number of persons using them "in different senses; as in the case of such words (which are held to have "many meanings even by the same people) as '*aksha*' '*pala*' and the "like: though only very few people use the word '*Aksha*' in the sense "of the *terminalia belerica*, yet this meaning of it is admitted as freely as "that of the '*axle* of the cart.' Similarly, too, it has been declared that "the root '*çava*' is used in the sense of *moving* among the Kambojas; while "the Āryas use it to signify *modification* or *putrefaction*, as when they "speak of the *dead body* as a '*çava*;' and there are many verbs and nouns "that are found to be used in different senses in different countries. "Hence we conclude that the contest between (or the authority of) all the "significations is equal.

"So also in a case where a certain fact in connection with the subsidiary "sacrifices is mentioned by a word that appears in the same form (though "perhaps in a different sense) in connection with the primary sacrifice,—we "accept the Subsidiary to have been performed exactly as the Primary, "and thereby quite in keeping with the Injunction that the Subsidiary is "to be performed like the Primary. It is with special reference to such a "case only that the clause—'because we do not find any contradiction "among them'—can be admitted (as a part of the *Sūtra*); because it is "only in such cases that the diversity can be said to be non-contradictory; "in all other cases, there being no possibility of a co-existence of diversity "and non-contradiction.

"Thus then the different usages being equally authoritative, we must "accept them to be optional alternatives."

To all this, we make the following reply:

SIDDHĀNTA.

***Sūtra* (9). That which is supported by the scriptures (is the more authoritative), because that (the scripture) is the source of authority.**

The sense that appears in the scriptures is the more authoritative; because the scriptures are the only source of authority; as for the sense accepted in ordinary parlance, such signification can be accepted as secondary. Whenever there is a difference of opinion, the ordinary people of the world are not accepted as the decisive authority, but it is always that which has the support of the scriptures that is accepted as the most authoritative; because as for acceptance in ordinary parlance, all are equally accepted; while the latter has the additional authority of the scriptures, which makes it the most authoritative of all.

Or, the *Sūtra* may be explained thus: *the sense in which the word is used by those persons that take their stand upon the scriptures, is to be accepted as the most authoritative; because it is more trustworthy than any other sense.*

It is a peculiarity with the people taking their stand upon the scriptures, that if there is even a slight discrepancy in what they assert, the whole purpose of the scriptures becomes defeated (that is to say, in the course of a sacrifice, if there is the slightest mistake in the pronunciation, &c., of *mantras*, the sacrifice becomes faulty, and fails to bring about the proper results); whereas in the case of ordinary usage, even if there be slight discrepancies, there is no such contingency. The doctors of medicine, when considering their own science of medicine, ascertain the meanings of the words "*Yava*" and the like (as they occur in particular contexts), in accordance with the taste, nutritious properties and digestibility of the particular article, that may be meant there; and the sacrificial priests proceed to ascertain their meanings, with reference to the proper performance of *Dharma*. Therefore in the case of a work on medicine, a word should be accepted to have that sense (primarily) which has been given to it, from times immemorial, by the doctors of that science and so also in the case of sacrifices, only that sense is to be accepted which has been admitted by people learned in the sacrifices.

And when it is thus possible to definitely ascertain the meaning of a word, we cannot accept it to be of an uncertain signification; nor can we admit of an option in the matter; because all options are open to eight objections (as shown above).

As a matter of fact, whenever we find a word invariably used in the Veda, in the same sense, this definite ascertainment of its signification leads us to a similar conclusion, in the case of ordinary parlance also. As for instance, in the case of the word '*Yava*,' the Veda has laid down the injunction—'the post of the *Udumbara* wood is to be washed with the water mixed with *Yava*;' and in connection with this passage, it is declared—'when all other plants are drooping, these continue to flourish luxuriantly'. (This passage we meet with in various rescensions of the Veda; the Bhāshya has cited that which occurs in connection with the *Varunapraghāsa* sacrifice; but as a discussion, as to which passage is really meant, would serve no purpose, we may accept it as quoted by the *Bhāshya*). As a matter of ordinary experience, we find that in the month of *Phālguna* (February-March) the leaves of all the trees fall off, and it is only the barley-corn that flourishes most luxuriantly. On the other hand, the '*Priyangu*' (long-pepper) ripening during the Autumn, disappears entirely long before *Phālguna*, and flourishes during the rains, when no other plants are found to be drooping, as all of them are in luxuriant foliage during the rains (hence we cannot accept the Long-pepper to be that which 'flourishes luxuriantly when all other plants are drooping'). (Hence we cannot but accept the word '*Yava*' to mean *barley-corn*).

In the same manner, the significations of the words '*Vētasa*' and '*Varāha*' are also ascertained from the sense in which they are used in the scriptures.

(*Here ends the Explanation of the Adhikaraṇa according to the Bhāshya*).

[*Arguments against the above interpretation of the Adkiharaṇa.*]

In all the three words cited, the significations that have been sought to be supported by scriptural texts, are such as are already accepted to be the most authoritative, even on the authority of ordinary usage; and as such they cannot serve as examples of words having their significations defined by the authority of the scriptures. For in no country is the word '*Yava*' used in the sense of *long-pepper*, nor the words '*Vētasa*' and '*Varāha*' in those of *blackberry* and *crow* respectively. Why then should we assume such usages and thereby create a difficulty for ourselves uselessly?

Inasmuch as under the *Sūtra* I—iv—29, it will be shown that in all doubtful cases, a definite conclusion is arrived at, by the help of subsequent passages; and hence, the above instances coming under the same category, there is no need of considering them over again on this occasion. It is true that under the said *Sūtra*, no notice is taken of the denotations of the words, the consideration referring solely to the *object* to be used (*i.e.*, the point there to be considered is not what the word "*akta*" *anointed* means, but that what is the material with which the gravels are to be anointed); and in the case as treated of there, the conclusion arrived at is only applicable to the particular time and place, and not everywhere (*i.e.*, it does not conclude that wherever there is to be an *anointing*, it is always to be done by *butter*, but only that in the particular instance, only butter should be used); while on the present occasion, what we are considering is the general denotation of the word ('*yava*'); and as such the conclusion that we arrive at is universally binding; and from these facts it may be argued that there is no repetition. Yet with all this, the process of reasoning employed in the two cases is the same; and exactly as under the said *Sūtra*, the *butter* is concluded to be the object that is to be employed, on the strength of the subsequent passages; so in the same manner, in the present case also, it is by the aid of the subsequent passage that we arrive at a definite conclusion with regard to the significations of the words '*yava*' and the like.

And again, under the *Sūtra* I—iv—23 we shall show that there are various causes of secondary (or indirect) signification, such as *similarity* and the like; and hence even if the word '*Vētasa*' be not admitted to be directly denotative of the *blackberry*, the similarity of the two would enable it to be used (indirectly) in that sense; (and as such, such signification being only indirect, it could not have the preference over the natural signification); and hence no purpose is served by the citation of such words as the instances to be considered.

For these reasons, we should base our consideration of the present *Adhikaraṇa* upon other examples.

[*B. The Adhikaraṇa as explained by the Vārtika.*]

When there happens to be a difference in the usages of the *Arya* and the *Mlēccha*, there arises a doubt as to whether both are equally authoritative, or one is more authoritative than the other. And on this we have the following

PŪRVAPAKSHA.

"For all people that have to do only with perceptible things, the "*contest would be equal;* as it is only in the case of invisible (or super-physi-"cal) things that the *Aryas* can have any superior authority;—in the case "of visible things, the authority of the *Ārya* and the *Mlēccha* is equally "strong.

"Because all words are used with the sole purpose of expressing "certain things; and certainly the things that are thus talked of are those "that are met with, and are of use, in ordinary experience. Hence, in a "case where we find exactly the same word being used in an entirely dif-"ferent sense, among the *Mlēcchas*, we conclude the expressiveness "of the word to be eternal; exactly as we have the notion of eternality "with regard to the expressiveness of words used by the *Āryas;* as the "reasons for accepting the eternality of the relations between the word and "its meaning are equally applicable in the two cases of the *Ārya* and the "*Mlēccha.* As among the *Mlēcchas* too, we cannot trace the beginnings of "the usages of words; and hence we can perceive no difference between "two equally beginningless expressive potentialities of words. For instance, "even among the *Mlēcchas*, the perception of smoke leads to the conclusion "of the existence of fire; and hence (as we find their position correct in the "case of one means of knowledge) we conclude that the sense in which a "word is used by them is really one that is expressed by it. Consequently "then, in the case of the word '*pīlu*,' as denoting *a particular tree* (according to the *Āryas*) and the *elephant* (according to the *Mlēcchas*), the "contest between them (for authority) would be equal."

SIDDHĀNTA.

In reply to the above, we have the *Sūtra* (9), which can be explained exactly as it has been done above.

And further, the notion of real expressiveness that we have with regard to the words used by the *Mlēcchas* is as erroneous as the notion that we have with regard to those words that, though pronounced wrongly on account of ignorance, inability, &c., are yet perchance found to resemble another correct word. That is to say, exactly as we have corruptions of the verbal forms of words, so also we have those of meanings,—these latter being due to such causes as the indirect (secondary) significations of words, or the inability of the person to discern the right meaning. And these corruptions can be discerned only by those people that take their stand upon the scriptures, and are seeking after the virtue that is attainable only by the correct performance of duties as correctly comprehended from the Veda; exactly as a false coin can be picked out only by those who are experts in the art. And certainly, when there is an opposition between the cognitions of the learned and the ignorant, the former is always the stronger of the two; specially as it is very easy for us to get at reasons and facts upsetting the ideas of the ignorant.

Hence we conclude that, inasmuch as the inhabitants of *Āryāvarta* take their stand upon the scriptures, their ideas alone can have any authority in the matter of such significations of words as appertain to *Dharma* and its accessories. And even among these people themselves we should accept that sense in which the word is used by one who is more learned and more conversant with the scriptures, in preference to those sanctioned by the usage of people less learned in them.

[*C. The Adhikaraṇa interpreted differently.*]

We may take the *Adhikaraṇa* as dealing with the contradictions between *Smṛtis* and *Usage.* And on this point, we have the following

PŪRVAPAKSHA.

"Inasmuch as both have their origin equally in the Veda, *the contest* "*between them would be equal.* Because, just as the authority of the *Smṛtis* "is based upon the fact of their being based upon the Veda, so too is that "of Usage; and as such we can perceive no difference between the two, in the "point of authority. Or, we may go a step further: Usage is stronger in "its authority than *Smṛti;* because its results (in the shape of actions) "are directly perceptible, as leading to equally visible results; and certainly, "that authority (or means of knowledge) which is dissociated from its "result, becomes greatly weakened. The Vedic text, that would be the "basis of Usage, is perceived directly in the result; and hence, while "having found a *Smṛti* text, we would be still looking after a Vedic text "to serve as its basis, the Usage, having obtained its footing long ere this, "will have asserted itself; and certainly when a thing has once asserted "itself, how can it be ousted? Therefore, we must admit either that the "Usage is more authoritative than *Smṛti*, or that both are equal in "authority."

SIDDHĀNTA.

But the *Smṛti* is held to be more authoritative, because of its being based directly upon the scriptures; and certainly the support of the Veda is not equal in the two cases. Because the *Smṛti* has been compiled, in a proper manner, by trustworthy persons; and this fact directly leads to an unimpeded inference of its teachings being based upon the Veda. Whereas in the case of Usage, the Usage leads to the assumption of a corroborative *Smṛti*, which in its turn leads to that of a Vedic text in support of it; thus in this case the support of the Veda being one degree further removed, its authority becomes weakened. And certainly there is no single Vedic text that sanctions the authority of all Usages at once; and at best the Vedic texts, supporting the Usages, are various and scattered all over the Veda; and as such they cannot be got hold of without the aid of the *Smṛtis;* specially as such Vedic texts are not found grouped together in a single *Adhyāya*; but they are scattered among various chapters, and can be got at only here and there, and that too, with great difficulty.

For instance,—(1) In connection with the preparation of the sacrificial fire, we read—"The sacrificer places the cake on both sides of himself, and hence it is that people carry the food with both hands, and then eat it;" and here, though the passage itself gives reasons for the particular action, yet the fact cited as reason is not very well known; and hence this only leads to the inference of a direct Injunction, in accordance with the argument that 'things are enjoined by Vedic sentences.' Nor can it be urged that the passage being merely explanatory of a certain useful method—like the passage "as human children having lived in the womb for ten months come to be born in the eleventh, so do the mules, &c., &c." ; and as such it cannot point to an Injunction, because the method described is not necessarily calculated to fulfil any purpose. Nor can it be said to be explanatory of a well-established natural fact—as in the case of the passage "hence people in old age are supported by their children" (because the said method of eating is not generally recognised as a well-established natural fact). Hence though the passage has an entirely different meaning, yet the special ratiocinative style adopted serves to indirectly point to an Injunction of the particular method of eating.

(2) The same process of reasoning is followed in the case of the passage—"because the food is kept on the right side, therefore it is only by the rigth hand that one eats," (which though referring to a particular action at sacrifices, is made to point to an Injunction of the said method of eating).

(3) Similarly, too, in the passage—"the person initiated for the sacrifice should apply the collyrium to the right eye first, because men ordinarily are found to apply it to that eye first," (which though referring to the sacrifice, is yet made to point to an Injunction whereby women are enjoined to apply the collyrium to the right eye first).

(4) So also with reference to the passage—"two strings were applied to each post, hence it is that a man takes many wives, though a woman does not take more than one husband"— which we find in the section on '*Yūpaikādaçinī*'—(which is made to point to the injunction of one man taking many wives, and the prohibition of one woman taking many husbands).

(5) In the same manner, in the chapter on *Darçapūrnamāsa*, passing over the Injunction dealing with the *Agnīshomīya*, we read a passage descriptive of the fact of the third part of Indra's sin, consequent upon his having killed a Brāhmana in the person of Tvashṭṛ's son (Vṛtra), having been relegated to women in their courses; and this description is made the means of pointing to the injunction of certain observances for the woman in her courses, a fact which has nothing to do with the main subject, the *Agnīshomīya*—these observances being *sleeping upon the ground, not bathing, desisting from meat-eating, unguents, collyrium, spinning, washing of the teeth, pairing of the nails, thread-twining*, and so forth, all of which are to be kept up for three days.

Thus then, we find that the Vedic texts, that can be chosen out as lending support to Usages, are so scattered and difficult to get at, that any collection of them in any single place is impossible, without the help of the *Smṛtis;* and hence between the Usage and the Vedic text, we have to admit of an intervening agency of the *Smṛti*. Consequently, long before the Usage succeeds in pointing to its corroborative Vedic text through the *Smṛtis*, the (contrary) *Smṛti* gets at its own corroborative Vedic text, and succeeds in pointing out the *Dharma* (long before the contrary Usage has had time to assert its third-hand authority).

[*D. Another interpretation of the Adhikaraṇa.*]

Such words as '*trivṛt*,' '*caru*' and '*açvabāla*' are found, in ordinary parlance, to express meanings entirely at variance with those accepted in the Veda, and by people taking their stand upon the Veda. And the question arises, whether, as all authorities are equally strong in the matter of the significations of words, the contest between the two authorities is equal, or the Vedic use has the greater authority. And on this question, we have the following

PŪRVAPAKSHA.

"In ordinary parlance, the word '*trivṛt*' is found to mean *threefold*, "as in the expressions '*trivṛt rajjuh*,' '*trivṛt granthih*'; while in the Veda it "is used in the sense of '*ninefold*'; as we find that after having mentioned "the '*trivṛt Vahishpavamāna*,' the Veda speaks of it as consisting of the "threefoldness of the triad of Ṛk verses, thus making the *nine Stotriya* "*Ṛk verses*, the word '*trivṛt*' thus being found to denote *nine*.

"Similarly in ordinary parlance, the word '*caru*' is found to be ex-"pressive of the *saucer*, while in the Veda it is found to denote the '*rice*.' "That is to say, people who are engaged in the performance of sacrifices are "always found to use the word '*caru*' in the sense of *cooked rice*, which is "still hot, and from which the gruel has not been thrown out. In "the Veda, too, we find that, having spoken of the '*Prāyaṇīya Caru* as "belonging to Āditi,' it goes on to lay down that 'Aditi is to be appeased by "the offering of cooked rice,' which clearly shows that the word '*caru*' "is used in the sense of *cooked rice*.

"So, too, in the case of the expression '*açvabāla-prastarah*,' it would, "in ordinary parlance, be explained as 'the bedding made up of horse-"hair'; whereas from the Vedic passages following the expression, it is "clear that the word '*açvabāla*' is used in the sense of *reed*. The passage "in question is that which describes the event that the sacrifice took the "shape of the horse, and flying away from the gods, fell into the water, "and when the gods took hold of the tail, the horse freed itself from their "grasp and then disappeared; and the hairs of the tail that were left in the "hands of the gods being thrown on the ground became what is now known "as the *reed*; and hence as the reed is so very pure (being a part of the "body of the sacrifice itself), the bedding is to be made of this material. "In the same manner, in the expression '*aikshavīyam vidhṛti*,' the word "'*aikshavīyam*' would ordinarily be taken to mean 'made of sugar-cane, " while in the Veda, it means the *roots of the reed.*

"In all these cases, inasmuch as the significations are different, " and as both are equally well comprehended, the two meanings of the " words must be accepted to be optional alternatives. Though it may be " urged that in matters relating to *Dharma*, the comprehension based upon " the Veda has always a greater authority than that based upon ordinary " parlance, yet no such superior authority is really possible; because in " the matter of the significations of words, the Veda does not in any way " differ from the other sources of verbal knowledge; for it is only in " matters transcending the senses, that the Veda is held to have a superior " authority. Consequently we conclude that the comprehension from both " sources would be equally authoritative.

"Or, inasmuch as ordinary parlance always precedes a reading of the " Veda, it must be held to have an authority superior to that of the Veda. " That is to say, we fully comprehend the sense of all ordinary expressions " independently of the Veda; whereas we can never comprehend any " Vedic expression without finding in it words similar to those that we " have met with in ordinary parlance. Hence among Vedic uses of words " we can accept only those that are not contrary to ordinary usage; " because when they transgress the limits of such parlance, they are never " properly comprehended.

"The clause—'because we do not perceive any contradiction among " them'—refers to the absence of contradiction among the words employed " in ordinary usage. As for the passage quoted above—'the sacrifice " became the horse, &c.'—in support of the Vedic sense, it is an *Arthavāda*; " and as such, cannot be admitted as a means of arriving at the real mean- " ings of words; firstly, because all *Arthavādas* have an entirely different " purpose; and as such they can at best have only an indirect secondary " bearing upon the matter in question; *secondly*, because all *Arthavādas* " have their sole purpose in the accomplishment of the attractiveness of a " certain course of action; as we find in the case of such of them as—'the " post is the sun,' 'the sacrificer is stone,' 'the *Āhavanīya* fire is the " Heaven,' and so forth; and *thirdly*, because they have no action in the " matter of the creation and explanation of the expressiveness of words and " meanings. For, if the meanings of words were to be accepted according " to the *Arthavāda* ('the sacrificer is stone' for instance), there would be " a direct contradiction of the Injunction (as whenever an action will be " enjoined as to be performed by the 'Sacrificer,' we would represent the " action as done by a piece of stone). Hence the clause—'because we do " not perceive any contradiction, &c.'—may be taken to mean that, in- " asmuch as we do not find the aforesaid contradiction of the Injunction, at "the actual performance of the sacrifice (*i.e.*, as we do not find a piece of "stone substituted in place of the sacrificer) we conclude that *Arthavādas* "cannot be accepted as regulating the significations of words.

"On the point at issue, our position is supported by such authors as "Manu and others, who speak of the 'cotton sacred thread of the Brāh-"maṇa being *threefold* (*trivṛt*), with a threefold (*trivṛt*) knot.'

"Hence we conclude that if not stronger, the ordinary Usage cannot "be denied to be equal in authority to the Veda."

SIDDHĀNTA.

To all this we make the following reply: That signification of the word which is based upon the scriptures is decidedly the more authoritative; because the knowledge of *Dharma*, which consists of certain means and consequences, is gained by means of the scriptures alone. Even the signification of words that is based upon the *Arthavāda* is stronger in authority than ordinary usage; because the particular *Arthavāda* (describing the fact of the sacrifice having become a horse, &c., &c.), has no other purpose save that of explaining the particular meaning of the word '*açvabālah*.' If a certain signification is once adopted in the Veda, whether it be secondary or primary, it is only that which can be accepted as the means of accomplishing *Dharma*.

As for the word '*trivṛt*' when it has been used in the Veda in the sense of the *nine Stotriya Ṛk* verses, who can set aside this meaning, even if he were to be born a hundred times? Hence whenever we meet with the expression '*trivṛt Agnishtoma*,' we must accept the word in the sense inparted to it by the Veda. Similarly, though the word '*stoma*,'—in such ordinary expressions as '*Brāhmaṇastoma*'—is found to signify a *group*, yet in the case of such words as '*stoma*,' '*trivṛt*,' and the like, we cannot but reject their ordinary significations; because (1) we find the Veda making such declarations, as 'the *stoma* is *trivṛt*, (threefold),' 'the *stoma* is fifteenfold'; (2) the persons versed in sacrifices have laid down that *stoma* is the measure or limit of the prayer; and (3) we find the grammarians laying down the rule that the affix 'da' is added to the word '*stoma*,' simply for the sake of its connection with the words 'fifteen' and the like (which distinctly shows that the word '*stoma*' is to be taken as denoting the threefold or fifteenfold measure of the Prayer).

As for the declaration of Manu that has been cited in the *Pūrvapaksha*, as the assertions of human beings depend upon those significations that are founded upon ordinary usage, as also upon those adopted in the Veda, it is not to be wondered at that Manu has used a word in the ordinary popular sense. Or, even in that passage the word '*trivṛt*' may be taken in the sense of 'ninefold'; specially because, as a matter of fact, each thread of the sacred thread is actually made up of nine-fold threads. The same may also be said in the case of the '*trivṛt*' character of the string (which may be held to be ninefold). Or, we may have recourse to the reasoning that, inasmuch as when the word '*trivṛt*' has been found to be used in the sense of 'nine' with reference to the *Stotrīyā* verses, it can be used only in such cases where there is a possibility of the number *nine*; in cases where the object referred to has a different number, we can admit the Vedic signification to be secondary, and the popular signification to be the primary one; and in such cases, inasmuch as the popular signification is the primary one, we should accept this in preference to the Vedic sense,—a point that we shall explain in detail in the following *Sūtra* (the 10th).

In the same manner, the word '*caru*' having its unreasonable multifarious expressiveness barred, it comes to be restricted to a single meaning; and this single meaning is necessarily accepted to be 'cooked rice,' which is sanctioned by the Veda as well as by the usage of persons versed in the sacrificial science.

As for the words '*āçvabālah*' and '*aikshavī*,' inasmuch as their significations of 'reed' and 'the root of the reed' respectively, belong to the words conventionally taken as independent wholes (apart from any idea of their component parts), and are sanctioned by the usage of the Veda, they cannot but be admitted to have an authority greater than that of the ordinary popular meanings, which are based upon the significations of the component parts of the words (which are admitted by all to be weaker than the significations that are based upon convention through and through). And from this, too, we conclude the signification sanctioned by the Veda to have a greater authority than that of popular signification.

In the case of the '*Çyēna*' *sacrifice* which has been compared to the *Çyēna bird*, though the word '*Çyēna*' in this connection cannot but be held to have been accepted as the name of the sacrifice, only by secondary or indirect signification, yet it is this secondary signification (of the name of the sacrifice) that is accepted, in such passages as 'the other procedures are exactly like those of the *Çyēna*'; where the word '*Çyēna*' is taken to mean the *Çyēna sacrifice*, though it is the secondary figurative meaning; simply because as sanctioned by the scriptures, it cannot but be accepted as of greater authority, in matters relating to *Dharma*.

Even though the signification is an indirect and secondary one, yet it is the more authoritative; because as sanctioned by the Veda, it cannot by any means be set aside. A meaning that is accepted by the Veda can never be set aside by anyone, no matter whether it be the secondary or the indirect one, or got at by a splitting of the sentence.

Nor can the *Adhikaraṇa*, as thus explained, be said to be a mere repetition of what is going to be explained under the *Sūtra* I—iv—29; because in the case treated of here, there is no *doubt* with regard to any of the two significations considered. That is to say, just as there is no doubt with regard to the popular signification being correct with regard to its own objects, so too there is none with regard to the Vedic signification; and hence there is every likelihood of the latter being set aside by the former (whereas the *Sūtra* I—iv—29 deals with cases of doubtful significations of words).

For these reasons, we conclude that it is the signification based upon the scriptures that has the superior authority; and it does not resemble stray popular usages, which are scattered far apart, and often mixed (with mistakes and inaccuracies).

ADHIKARAṆA (6).

[*Treating of the authority of words as used by the Mlēcchas.*]

Sūtra (10). *(The word used by the Mleccha)* should be recognised as sanctioned by the Veda, because there is no contradiction of any authority.

There are certain words (used even in the Veda) that are not in use among the people of *Āryāvarta:* (1) And we now proceed to consider whether or not we should accept the meaning that is given to them by the *Mlēcchas.* (2) The second point for consideration is whether greater authority is to be attached to the meaning that may be got out of the etymological or grammatical roots and bases of these words, or to that which is sanctioned by usage among the *Mlēcchas.* Even though the authority of the supporters of the latter is distinctly weaker, yet it appears to be more authoritative; because of the fact of the conventional meaning of the word as a whole being admittedly more authoritative (than that which is got at grammatically or etymologically). And we have now got to consider the point as to, between the weakness of the supporters and the inherent strength of the word itself, which should carry the greater weight. (3) The third point that will have to be considered, in connection with this, is whether greater authority attaches to the meaning got at through the etymological and grammatical basis of the word, as being the one sanctioned by the scriptures, or is it the less authoritative, as being due to the breaking up of the component parts of the word.

Thus then, there being many doubtful points on the subject, we have the following—

PŪRVAPAKSHA.

"The meaning got from the etymological and grammatical bases has "a greater authority; because even though this would be a newly assumed "meaning, yet, as being based upon (grammatical) scriptures, it cannot but "be held to have a greater authority. For certainly, it is better to accept "the authority of that which has a proper basis, even though it be one

" that has got to be newly assumed, than that of one which, though well-" established, is faulty in its origin.

" How could words occurring in the Veda be taken in the sense that " is recognised only among the Mlēcchas ? Specially when the very sight " of a Mlēccha, makes us stop our recitation of the Veda. Nor is it allow-" able for the people of Āryāvarta to have a conversation or consultation " with the Mlēccha; and hence how could we ever come to know the " sense in which any word may be current among them ?

" Thus then, not knowing any usage sanctioning a particular mean-" ing of a word, the person (that would depend upon the usage of the " Mlēcchas) would have to seek after such usage among all Mlēccha coun-" tries; and there would be nothing left to be done by the commentaries " (upon the Veda). And then, too, the countries inhabited by the Mlēcchas " being innumerable, how could one succeed in getting at all their usages ? " And if any such usage were not found with regard to any particular " word, the signification of that word would always remain doubtful; and " certainly it would scarcely be possible for us to ascertain the endless " usages of the innumerable countries of the Mlēcchas.

" And (not finding such usage with regard to any word) if we were to " deduce a meaning from the roots of the word, by the help of the commen-" taries and grammars, this would come to be set aside and rejected, if after " two or three days, a contrary usage of the Mlēcchas happened to be found " out.

" On the other hand, if we totally reject the authority of the usages of " the Mlēcchas, then it would be quite practicable to hunt up usages (with " regard to the signification of a word) in Āryāvarta itself; and this " being a single country limited within reasonable bounds, the existence or " non-existence of a usage, would be easily found out in a short time; and " thereby the commentaries, &c., also would come to have their use in the " pointing out of meanings (with regard to which we could not find any " usage). Thus then, for the sake of the usefulness of these commentaries, " &c., it becomes a necessity to reject the authority of the usages of the " Mlēcchas.

" And again, inasmuch as the Mlēcchas are found to have no regard " for *Dharma*, it is just possible that they may have distorted the meanings " of words, exactly as they are found to have distorted the forms of words, " because we do not find a single *sanskṛta* (or correct) word in use among " them.

" Though there are a few words in use among them that appear like " *sanskṛta* words, yet these are found to be used in senses other than " those recognised by us; and as even these are used without the neces-" sary affixes, &c., they are not properly expressive; and as such they "can never be held to have any real denotation. Even when an Ārya "attempts to find traces of his own (*saṇskṛta*) words among those of the "Mlēcchas, he can only find them by grouping together the letters of two "different words (*e.g.*, in '*a custom*,' they find the *saṇskṛta* word '*ēka*'); and "sometimes he finds therein his own words, either a little too short, or one "too long.

"As for example, in the Drāvida language, though all words are used "as ending in the consonant, yet the Āryas are found to assume in them "the affixes, &c., that can be appended only to words ending in vowels, "and thence make the words give a sense, in accordance with their own "(*saṇskṛta*), language For instance, when the Dravidas call 'rice,' "'*cor*,' the Ārya reads in it his own word '*cora*' (thief), and comprehends "the meaning accordingly. And when the Dravidas call the *road* '*atar*,' "he reads it as '*atarah*,' and declares that as the road is difficult to cross, "it is really '*atara*' (uncrossable). Similarly they call the snake '*pāp*,' "and he takes it as '*pāpa*' (evil), and argues that the snake is really an "*evil* animal. So, too, in the case of the word '*māl*' which they use in "the sense of the *woman*, the word is taken as '*mālā*.' The word "'*vair*,' used by them in the sense of the *stomach*, is taken as '*vaira*' "(enemy); and the use is justified on the ground of the hungry man "being capable of doing many sinful deeds, which proves that the *stomach* "is an *enemy* of the man.

"Thus then, when the Ārya stands in need of such groundless assump- "tions, even in the case of the words current among the Dravidas (who "inhabit a part of Āryāvarta itself),—how could we ever reasonably "deduce *saṇskṛta* words from those current among such distant peoples "as the *Parsis*, the *Barbaras* (Barbarians), the *Yavanas* (Greeks), the *Rau*- "*makas* (Romans), and the like.

"Hence we conclude that those words of the Mlēcchas that are accept- "ed (or used) by the Āryas can never be fully trusted in the ascertain- "ment of words or their meanings. While those meanings, that are got "from the etymological or grammatical bases of the words—'*pika*,' "'*nēma*,' and the like—, can be the only true ones."

SIDDHANTA.

To all this, we make the following reply: Even among the Mlēcchas, if we find the word used by them to be exactly the one found in the Veda, we cannot but accept the sense that is imparted to it by them (in cases where the word is entirely foreign to our own vocabulary). As for the distorted forms of words, however, that are current in various dialects, as there have been many modifications, we cannot easily discern the real from the unreal. But when we find a certain word, '*pika*' for instance, used in the Veda and its subsidiary sciences, and then subsequently we find exactly the same word current among the Mlēcchas used by them as having a certain definite signification,—we can accept the word to have the same meaning in the Veda also; specially as such signification is not contrary to any other authority.

That is to say, in the case of such words as] "*pika*," "*nēma*," and the like, when met with in the Veda, in connection with certain sacrifices, when the matter is duly pondered over, if a person happens to be conversant with the two languages, he finds that the words are used in a certain sense among the Mlēcchas; and from this he can reasonably take them in the same sense in the Veda also; specially when such interpretation is not against the authority of the Veda with regard to *Dharma*.

(*The 2nd interpretation of the Sūtra*). And again, the action of man being dependent upon his comprehension of the relation between the meanings and the words (used in the Injunction addressed to him), it is quite reasonable for him, with a view to the correct comprehension of the sentence, to have recourse to any usage that he may come across. Hence in the case of the words '*pika*,' &c., the sense, in which we find them used by the Mlēcchas, not being against any authorities, must be admitted to be pointed out by the Veda itself.

(*The 3rd intepretation of the Sūtra*). The word '*coditam*' (laid down, pointed out) may be taken with '*pramānēna*,' *i.e.*, '*vēdēna*,' (by the authority of the Veda); and the meaning then would be that, inasmuch as such usage of the Mlēccha is pointed out by the Veda, it can very well be accepted, specially as it is not against the Āryas, who actually stand in need of some such usage (for the proper understanding of certain Vedic texts).

Just as when such words as '*loma*' (hair) are used in the Veda, the priests themselves do not quite understand what the word exactly denotes; and they ascertain its exact meaning only by referring to such people (always of the lowest classes) as are always engaged in killing animals (whose authority is accepted on the point as unimpeachable). In the same manner, it is laid down in the Veda, that at the '*Nishādēshti*,' it is only a false coin that can be given as the final gift; and the point, as to whether or not any particular coin is false, is decided on the sole authority of persons (always of very low character) who carry on a business in such coins. Exactly in the same manner, when we find such words as '*pika*,' '*nēma*,' '*tāmarasa*,' used in the Veda, and find that we cannot ascertain their meaning either from the Veda itself or from the usages of the Āryas, we can certainly accept the meanings imparted to them by the Mlēcchas. Specially as such acceptance would be quite in keeping with our own authority; as it would not be contrary to our theory that the eternal significations of eternal words can be ascertained by means of the usages of men (and certainly the Mlēcchas are also men).

It has been argued above that the scripture being stronger in its authority the usage of the Mlēccha cannot be accepted. But this is scarcely correct; because when there is no contradiction, there is no harm in accepting the weaker; that alone is to be totally rejected which, on the very face of it, is distinctly untrue, and incapable of any support, exactly like the perception of the mirage and the like. And that (Usage of the Mlēccha),—which is rejected as unauthoritative on the sole ground of its being contrary to the stronger authority (of the Veda or of Ārya usage),—cannot but be accepted as authoritative, when there is no such contradiction. And certainly we can find no contradiction in the case of the words '*pika*,' &c., with regard to which we know of no other usage (among the Āryas) that could be contradicted.

It is for this very reason that in the case of the meaning of Vedic sentences, we can assert the superior authority of only such usages of the learned Āryas as are bearing upon the words and objects in question. That is to say, it is only when there is a usage among the Āryas, that we accept it as of superior authority; and the assertion of such authority in the absence of the usage itself would be exactly like a description of the strength of the son of a barren woman. For instance, in the case of the *Smṛti* passages dealing with the *Ashtakā*, &c., which relate to things transcendental, and have their origin in the Veda,—as also in the case of the words 'cow,' &c., and their meanings,—it is true that the Āryas are more trustworthy and more competent. But in the case of the words '*pika*' and the like, all that the Ārya usage does, is to point out that they are *words expressive of certain meanings*, without hinting anything as to what these meanings are; and it is here that the operation of the Ārya usage ceases; consequently, then, we ascertain these meanings from the usages of the Mlēcchas,—these usages too, like the words, being such as pertain to the relations of words and meanings, based upon a beginningless use of the words for the purpose of the accomplishment of the comprehension of visible objects. And in this there is no contradiction of any higher authority; on the other hand, a distinctly useful purpose (in the shape of the understanding of the Vedic text) is served.

As for the commentaries, &c., we do not find them pointing out any other meanings of the words in question, which would serve our purpose (of understanding the Veda), and thereby enable us to reject the usages of others (*viz.*, the Mlēcchas). And there can be no doubt that a usage that is already well-established is more authoritative than that which is newly assumed; and hence, so long as we have the former, there can be no room for the latter.

As for the comparative strength of the upholders of different usages (*viz.*, the Mlēcchas and the Āryas), the superior authority of the latter has been laid down only in matters relating to *Dharma* directly; as for the ordinary worldly things, such as agriculture and the like, all usages are equally authoritative. Consequently, in matters relating to menial service, house-building, and the like, we can freely admit the superior authority of the Mlēcchas.

In matters relating to the correct forms of words, however, we find that the Mlēcchas are not very expert, and as such likely to be gradually losing the correct forms; and hence now no longer able to discern the correct from the incorrect. But if a certain word happens to retain its original correct form, even in their usage, this use of theirs would be as eternally traditional as any words in Ārya usage; and as such how could he set them aside? Specially in the cases of such words as '*patrorna*' (a silken or jute fabric), '*vāravāṇa*' (armour) and the like, as these articles are produced only in the Mlēccha countries, if they did not point out what they meant, how could we comprehend the words?

Hence, we conclude that the usage of the Mlēccha cannot be held to be of an inferior authority.

As for the Nirukta and other commentaries, &c., they operate only in connection with well-established facts and things, and that, too, only by means of such established things and facts: and they cannot function towards such objects as are not established (or known). That is to say, all that the Niruktas do, is to explain the words that are already in use among the people; and these too are explained only as pertaining to certain actions denoted by the roots, &c., that constitute the words. And all that Grammar does is to point out the correct forms of only such words as have their significations fully known; and it is only once in a way that the meaning of a word is pointed out. And as such, these two (the Nirukta and Grammar) cannot serve to set aside an usage, even though weaker, when dealing with subjects other than their own specified ones (explained above).

In the case of a word, where we fail to find any usage, however much we search for it, we would be forced to have recourse to an assumption of its meaning, by means of the etymological explanations afforded by the Nirukta, &c. Though such assumptions would be confused and in diverse forms, and as such giving rise to many doubts, yet when there are no other means at our disposal, we cannot but have recourse to them.

Nor can it be urged that, inasmuch as the Nirukta, &c., would not help in pointing out the meanings of words, they would be useless. Because they have their use in helping in the proper accomplishment of sacrifices, which is possible only by means of a knowledge of the Veda with all its subsidiary sciences. For instance, we read in the Mahābhārata: "Being *great* and relating to the family of Bharata, this work is called the 'Mahābhārata'; and one who knows this signification of the word, becomes freed from all sins."

And (1) inasmuch as the accomplishment of such results as Heaven and the like are brought about by means of only such actions as are performed with a full knowledge of them, derived from the Veda as aided by its six subsidiary sciences, the Nirukta and the like;—and (2) as even though the forms of the words themselves are known, yet the real transcendental results do not follow, until one has duly comprehended the sentence with the help of a due cognition of the meanings of words, as pointed out by the component roots, &c., which are explained in the Nirukta,—we conclude that even with regard to the comprehension of such words ('*pika*,' &c.), as are used among the Mlēcchas only, the Nirukta, &c., are not without their use (which lies in the helping towards the proper accomplishment of the transcendental results).

ADHIKARAṆA (7).

THERE IS NO INDEPENDENT AUTHORITATIVENESS IN THE KALPASŪTRAS.

***Sutra (11).* If it be urged that "they constitute the science of rituals."—**

With reference to the *Kalpasūtras*, we proceed to consider the following points :—

(A) Whether, like the Veda, the *Kalpasūtras* are self-sufficient in their authority, or are they, like the *Mantras* and the *Brāhmanas*, a part of the Veda itself? (This inquiry is necessary, because) the case of these *Sūtras* is not identical with the *Smṛti*, inasmuch as they are mere compilations of what is directly laid down in the Veda.

Question: What are *Kalpas?* And what are the *Sūtras?*

The answer is that the *Kalpas* are those treatises that point out the methods of sacrifices, in the form of well-established regulations; and the *Kalpasūtras* are those that serve to point them out. They are called '*Kalpas*' because of their *laying down* (*kalpanāt*) of the sacrificial procedure, and thereby helping in the accomplishment of sacrifices; and the *Sūtras* are so called, because of their *pointing out* (*sūcanāt*) the said procedure. Inasmuch as, with regard to each sacrifice, the *Kalpas* themselves lay down the rules of procedure, they appear in the form of the bare statement of facts (without any explanations or embellishments), as we find to be actually the case, in the works compiled by Baudhāyana, Varāha, Maçaka and others. While the *Sūtras* serve to explain the technical uses of words, and thereby to differentiate between general rules and exceptions; and they contain arguments and instances (in support of what they lay down); hence it is only that which fulfils these conditions that can be called a '*Sūtra*'; such are the works compiled by Āçvalāyana, Vaijavāpi, Drāhyāyani, Lātīya, and Kātyāyana.

[A] And there is a great difference between the status of the *Kalpasūtras* and that of the ordinary *Smrtis;* because, while the former lay down the rules of sacrificial procedure exactly as are pointed out in the Vedic texts that are directly available, the latter are compilations based presumpably upon such Vedic texts as have become lost, and whose existence can at best be only inferred; and for this reason the authority of the *Kālpasūtras* could not be made dependent entirely upon the arguments that have been brought forward in a previous *Adhikaraṇa* in support of the authority of the *Smṛtis.*

Firstly, because in that *Adhikaraṇa*, the *Pūrvapaksha*, as contained in the first *Sūtra* of this Pāda, bases its arguments upon the fact of the *Smṛtis* not being based upon the Veda; and this could not be urged against the *Kalpasūtras*; because texts in support of these are directly available in the Veda; and for this reason they cannot be said to be devoid of Vedic authority. And *secondly*, because the *Pūrvapaksha* cannot declare these *Sūtras* to be absolutely false, as it does in the case of the *Smṛtis.* In the *Adhikaraṇa* on *Smriti*, the *Pūrvapaksha* having urged the unauthoritative character of the *Smṛtis* on the ground of their having no basis in the Veda, the *Siddhānta* has established their authority as being based upon assumed Vedic texts (*see above*). And the *Kalpasūtras* have not been included there advisedly; because the arguments of that *Pūrvapaksha* are not applicable to them (as they cannot be said to be '*açabda*,' 'non-Vedic').

Then again, in the present *Adhikaraṇa* also, we are not going to prove the authoritativeness of these *Sūtras*, (because there can be no doubt as to that); all that we proceed to prove is the fact that they have no authority of their own, as apart from that of the Veda.

[B] Or, we may admit that the former *Adhikaraṇa* also refers to the *Kalpasūtras*; and the present one applies to the *Smṛtis* also; because these latter too have no independent authority of their own. (The former *Adhikaraṇa* may be taken to have established the authoritative character of the *Smṛtis*, as also of the *Kalpasūtras*, and the present proving the fact of none of these two having an authority apart from the Veda).

Now then, if the *Smṛtis* be admitted to have any authority in matters relating to *Dharma*, then they would either become the Veda itself, or be equal to the Veda in authority; and as such they could be said to have an authority of their own, independently of inferred corroborative Vedic texts.

[C]. Or, by the word '*prayogaçāstra*' we can take the subsidiary sciences of (*Çikshā*, &c). And these may be considered equal to the Veda; specially as the *Smṛtis* have spoken of them as being the Veda: "The name *Veda* is applied to the *Mantra* and the *Brāhmana*, and some people apply it to all the six subsidiary sciences," where it is clearly stated that the subsidiary sciences are also called the 'Veda.' And hence, the conviction might very well arise, that these also are the Veda, having an independent authority of their own. And for these reasons, it becomes absolutely necessary to consider the matter from a different standpoint.

[D]. Or, the *Adhikaraṇa* may be taken altogether differently, as dealing with the scriptures of the *Bauddhas.* The character of the *Smṛti* having been denied to them (in a previous *Adhikaraṇa*), they may be taken as similar to the various recensions of the Veda; and this notion has got to be set aside. The *Bauddhas* are found to declare thus: "The scriptures of the Bauddha being taken either as composed in accordance with facts, or as not being a product (of human agency) at all, there can be no doubt as to the eternal character of the *Dharma* as delineated in them." Thus, then, if these Bauddha scriptures come to be as eternal as the Veda, then even those *Dharmas* (Duties) that are laid down in them would be such as *have the Veda for their sole authority* (which has been laid down as the sole characteristic of our idea of *Dharma*, which is quite contrary to that of the Bauddhas). And thus one (the Bauddha scripture) who was not allowed by the armed wardens of *Smṛti* to enter into the village (of *Dharma*) would now enter it by the open highway (of the Veda).

Thus, then, all the above four questions being capable of being dealt with together, the inquiry that is carried on with special reference to the *Kalpasūtras* would apply to all others; and it is for this reason that the Bhāshya has cited the *Kalpasūtras* only.

On the question of the status of the *Kalpasūtras*, we have the following—

PURVAPAKSHA.

[A]. *Kalpasūtras.*

"There is no doubt that the *Kalpasūtras* constitute the science of "Rituals, and as such the character of the Veda can never be denied to them. "Or, they may be taken as entirely independent of the Veda, having an "authority of their own, as the Veda itself has sanctioned their authority "in matters relating to *Dharma.* Or, they may be taken as the Veda itself, "on the ground of there being many points of agreement between them "and the Veda.

"It may be argued that, on account of their having been composed by "human authors, they can be admitted neither to be the Veda itself, nor "to be equal to the Veda in authority. But we can prove the fact of their "being independent of human agency, exactly as we have done with regard "to the Veda; the names of '*Maçaka*' and the rest (as pertaining to the "*Kalpasūtras*) may be explained on the same grounds as the names "'*Kāthaka*,' &c., as pertaining to the Veda. That is to say, just as the "Vedic texts repeated by Katha having come to be known by the name of "'Kāthaka,' the application of the name does not debar us from proving "the eternality of these texts; in the same manner, we could also hold the "eternality of the *Kalpasūtras* that have only been repeated by *Maçaka* and "others. Or, just as in the case of the different *Sāmas*, even though each "of them is called after a distinct Ṛshi, that does not serve to deprive them "of their eternality; so, in the same manner, the fact of the *Kalpasūtras* "being called after certain persons cannot deprive them of theirs.

"Because, even in the case of the *Kalpasūtras*, we do not find any men- "tion of authors that are not Ṛshis; and as for the authorship of Ṛshis, "it is a fact common to these *Sūtras* and the Veda. For instance, we read "with regard to the *mantra* called *Çaiçava*: 'It is called *Çaiçava*, because "Angiras was a child, and yet an author among the composers of the "*mantra*'—where it is clear that the word 'composer' or 'author' means "'*one who used*' (Angiras having brought the particular *mantra* into use). "In the same manner, the word 'author' as applied to the compilers of "the *Kalpasūtras* may be taken as signifying '*one who uses*.'

"In connection with the injunction of the daily duties of the "Brāhmaṇa, we read (in the Veda):—'knowing this, the Brāhmaṇa should "read the Veda'; and then proceeding to lay down the details of this "study, the passage continues—'he should read the Ṛk, the Yajush, "the Sāma, the Brāhmaṇas, the Itihāsas and Purāṇas, the *Kalpas*'; and as "this passage distinctly lays down the *Kalpas* as to be read every day like "the Veda, it is clear that they too are *Ārsha* (a name applied to Vedic "*mantras*); specially as it is absolutely impossible for any works of ordi- "nary men to be mentioned in an eternal (Vedic) injunction as accomplish- "ing a certain *Dharma* by means of its study.

"Then again, (1) because some of the Brāhmaṇas too—those of the "*Aruṇa* and the *Parāçara* Çākhās—are in the form of *Kalpas*; (2) because "persons learned in the sacrifices accept these Brāhmaṇas to have exactly "the same authority as the *Kalpas* belonging to the *Çākhās* other than "their own; and (3) because a few *mantras* that are mentioned in the "*Kalpas* are actually employed at sacrifices, exactly like the *mantras* of the "other Çākhās,—we cannot but accept the *Kalpas* to be equal to the Veda "in authority.

"Then, again, the word '*ārshēya*' is accepted as synonymous with "'eternal;' and all the *Kalpās* are known as '*ārshēya*;' (and this also points "to their eternal character).

"The authors of the *Kalpasūtras* too—such as Lāti and Drāhyāyaṇi— "while dealing with the authority of the *Kalpas*, have declared that "the *Māçaka Kalpa* is found to lay down that which is directly percep- "tible; and as such being an *ārsha*, it does not stand in need of the "assumption of corroborative texts; this shows that they have "admitted the authority of the *Ārsha Kalpa* to be superior to the "injunctions contained in the Brāhmaṇas. Kātyāyana also, in the section "dealing with the *Lakshaṇasūtra*, has declared, in the closing sentences "of the section on the hymns laid down in the Brāhmaṇas as to "be sung at the sacrifices,—'we will not act according to the "injunctions of the Brāhmaṇas as apart from the *Kalpas*, as we will, in "accordance with those contained in the *Māçaka Kalpa*.' So, too, in connec- "tion with the *Prāyaṇīya Sāma* sung at the *Agnishtoma*, it is laid down "in the *Pancaviṇça-Brāhmaṇa* that there is an option between the "*Yajnāyajnīya* and the *Jarābodhīya Sāmas*; hence either the one or the "other may be sung; but under the *Sūtra* '*Jarāsāt*,' Katyāyana has laid "down that the *Jarābodhīya Sāma* is to be sung as the third from the "*Gāyatra Sāma*, as occurring among the seven *Sāmas* that constitute the "*Ārbhava* Hymn (and have nothing to do with the *Prāyaṇiya*). In connec- "tion with the *Ārbhava* Hymn, the *Sāma* that appears next after the "*Gāyatra*, has been named by him '*Sam*;' and next after this he men- "tions the *Jarābodhīya* referred to by him by quoting a part of the first "word of this *Sāma*; while by means of the word '*dhē*,' which is the "name of the *Agnishtoma Sāma* in connection with the *Jyotishtoma*, it has "been shown that it is the *Yajnāyajnīya* alone that is held to be the "*Sāma* belonging to the *Agnishtoma*. And certainly, if Kātyāyana would "have considered the Brāhmaṇa to be superior to the *Kalpa*, he should "unhesitatingly have accepted the option that is distinctly laid down "in the Brāhmaṇa.

"And certainly the rule, that has been laid down by such a person "as Kātyāyana, who is known to have been learned in many Vedas, can "never be declared to be illogical, by people like ourselves (who have not "studied a single Veda fully). Even the Veda itself has declared the "unimpeachable authority of the declarations of great teachers; and certainly "the authors of the Subsidiary Sciences were all 'great teachers.'

"Again, just as all rescensions of the Veda are admitted to be equal "in their authority, on the ground of their agreeing with one another,— "in the same manner, and on the same ground, we could accept the *Kalpa*- "*sūtras* to be equal to the Veda, in authority.

" Even the assertions of untrustworthy persons are accepted as " true, when found to be corroborated by other means of knowledge; how, " then, can it be denied in the case of the assertions of persons universally " held to be truthful ? specially when the assertions of such persons, are " found to be in keeping with those in the Veda, and thereby ascertained " to be true,—who can reasonably declare otherwise ?

" And again, as a matter of fact, we find the persons learned in " sacrifices to be performing sacrifices by the help of the *Kalpas*, even " without (any knowledge of) the Veda; while with the help of the *Mantra* " and *Brāhmaṇa* portions of the Veda, without that of the *Kalpas*, they " are never able to perform any.

" The authority of long-established tradition, too, is equal in the two " cases of the *Mantra* and the *Kalpa*, as is shown by the details laid " down in connection with the injunction of Vedic study,—the sentence " above quoted containing the name of the *Kalpas*, together with those " of the *Mantra*, the *Brāhmaṇa* and the rest. And the agents of tradition " (*i.e.*, the genteel people of our own day), as also the students of the " Veda, are found to be making as great efforts to learn the *Kalpasūtras*, " as they do in that of the *Mantra and the Brāhmaṇa.*

" As the uses of the different portions of the Veda keep on continu-" ously revolving, like the moving of a pulley, no Veda is held to be " complete in all its parts, without the *Kalpasūtras.*

" Hence, we conclude that this science of Rituals, the *Kalpasūtras, &c.*, " must be either the Veda itself, or equal to the Veda in authority.

[B and C]. *Kalpasūtras and Smṛtis.*

" The above arguments would also prove that the character of " the Veda belongs to the ordinary *Smṛtis*, as also to the six Subsidiary " Sciences; or these too, like the *Kalpasūtras*, may be held to be equal " to it in authority. How can any person knowing the Veda deny the " character of *the science* or *Scripture Method* to such *Smṛtis* as have al-" ways been known as *Dharmaçāstra* (scripture of *Dharma*) ? Specially as " the Vedas, its six Subsidiary Sciences, and the Dharmaçāstras, are all " counted together, by persons knowing the Veda, as constituting the " Fourteen Sciences.

" And further, just as we find *Mantras* pointing to the actions laid " down in the *Brāhmaṇas*, so also we find *Mantras* pointing to those laid " down in the Dharmaçāstras—such as the *Ashtakā* and the like. In the " same manner, such penances,—as the performance of the *Avakirinī* " sacrifice, the *Kṛcchra*, the *Cāndrāyana* and the like,—being distinctly " pointed out by Vedic *Mantras*, how can they be said to be contrary to " the Veda ? Then again, the description in the *Mantras* of the young

"Brāhmaṇa boy as being without his *Çikha*, which speaks of the absence "of his *Çikhā* as a well-established fact, cannot but be taken as authorising "the *tonsure* of the Brāhmaṇa, which is clearly enjoined in the *Smṛtis*; and as "such how could this *tonsure* ceremony be said to be contrary to the Veda?

"Thus then, why should we seek to assume Vedic texts in support "of the *Smṛti* injunctions, when these latter themselves can be accepted "either as Veda itself, or equal to it in authority. If we have to assume a "Vedic text, the fact of the injunction being based upon the Veda would "make it necessary for us to accept the injunction as eternal; and cer-"tainly it is much better to assert its eternality, just as it is found in the "*Smṛti*, without calling in the intermediate aid of the Vedic text. And "certainly, the *Smṛti*-injunctions being themselves well-established facts, "it is far easier to admit them to be eternal in themselves; or they may "be accepted to be Veda itself, on the ground of their dealing with the "the same subjects as the Veda.

"Consequently then, inasmuch as we do not find any beginning of "these *Smṛtis*, even during thousands of years, we cannot admit them to "be non-eternal, but based upon an eternal basis. Because, as a "matter of fact, it is far more reasonable to assume that the texts as we "find them in the *Smṛtis* are the very same that we assume to be present "in the Veda (and this does away with the assumption of a different text "for each *Smṛti*-injunction).

"And it stands to reason that, while laying down their teachings for the "sake of students learned in the Veda, Manu and others could not but "have brought forward the direct texts of the Vedas themselves. Conse-"quently, it would appear that these authors, in their compilations, have "only brought together the Vedic texts themselves. For in the presence of "the Vedic texts (whose existence all parties admit), who could accept their "counterparts (as put together in the *Smṛtis*)?

"Then again, inasmuch as we do not find any counterparts of the "*Dharmaçāstras* composed, even till now, we cannot admit the composition "of any counterparts of the Vedas. It may be argued that Manu and others "did not bring together the Vedic texts themselves, for, in so doing, they "would have disturbed the continuity of the verbal text of the Veda; but "by arguing on these lines, we would have to admit that they did not "compose the *Smṛtis*. Because when they did not dare to quote the Vedic "texts in parts,—how could they have ever thought of writing a work, "to replace the Veda itself?

"It is a fact admitted on all hands that the actions laid down in the "Veda can bring about their proper results, only when they are learnt "from the Veda itself; and not from those that are learnt from other works "of human authors; as these would be similar to the actions inferred from

" false semblances of the Vedic *mantras.* And it is evident that Manu and " others did not compose any counterparts of the *Mantras*, simply be" cause they were sure of the fact of the incapability of such counterpart " *Mantras* to bring about proper results; and on the same grounds, it must " be held that they could not have composed the counterparts of the *Brāh*" *maṇas* either; as they knew it equally well that Actions that are not " laid down in the Veda do not bring about proper results.

" Nor can it be held that the *Smṛtis* are the orderly collections of " Vedic texts scattered in different portions of the various Vedas (and as " such, they would be the products of human agency). Because the *Smṛtis* " are distinctly recognised as independent works of a certain form. That " is to say, it is far more reasonable to hold that there is a distinct Veda in " the exact form of the *Smṛtis* themselves, than to assume that they have " their basis in assumed Vedic texts.

" Thus then, it is clear that the fact of the *Smṛtis* constituting the " *Scripture of Action* (*Prayoga-çāstra*) cannot but be admitted, if they are to be " accepted as having any authority with regard to *Dharma*. For when it " has been already ascertained that *Dharma is that which has the Veda for* " *its sole authority*, anything that is not Veda, even if it be a *Brāhmaṇa*, " cannot be accepted as having any authority regarding *Dharma*.

" Thus then, it must be admitted, either that these *Smṛtis* have no use " with regard to *Dharma*, or that they are so many Vedas; there can be " no intermediate course. It cannot be rightly held that they point out " the *Dharma*, and yet have to point to Vedic texts for their authority. " Because their authority extends only so far as the significations of their " words allow. (That is to say, in that case, the whole force of the *Smṛti* will " have been taken up in pointing to the Vedic text, and they will be ab" solutely incapable of any action with regard to *Dharma*). Specially as, " if we make the words of the *Smṛtis*, renounce that (direct mention of " *Dharma*) which they distinctly signify, and point to that (corroborative " Vedic text) which is not signified by them, (on the ground of the incon" sistency of the directly signified meaning),—then (we ask), inasmuch as " this latter assumed Vedic text is also made to signify the same (mention " of *Dharma*) that had been previously signified by the *Smṛti* text, how " can there be said to be an inconsistency in this latter (which could be " set aside by the said assumption)? (for if the mention of the particular " *Dharma* is inconsistent, it is as much so when signified by the *Smṛtis*, as " when expressed by an assumed Vedic text). Hence, we conclude that in " the matter of that *Dharma* which is directly mentioned by the *Smṛti* " text itself, this text cannot but have an authority of its own, indepen" dently of any intercession of the Veda.

[D]. *Bauddha Scriptures.*

"The fact of the works of Buddha and others being *Smṛtis* having "been set aside (in a previous *Adhikaraṇa*), we proceed to show that "they have the character of the *Scripture of Action* (*Prayogaçāstra*), and "as such are so many Vedas.

"We can prove the eternality of the Bauddha scriptures by means "of the same arguments that have been brought forward to prove the "eternality of the Veda. As in the Vedas, so in these scriptures also, "their authority is self-sufficient, because of their being perfectly ex- "pressive (and comprehensible) assertions; as we have no doubts as "to their meanings; nor have we any mistaken ideas about them. And "being, like the Vedas, without a human author, they are free from "all discrepancies consequent upon such origin; because, as in the "Vedas, so in these scriptures also, the possibility of a human author is "absolutely denied. As for the name '*Buddha's Assertion*,' as applied to "these scriptures, it only shows that they were *explained* (and not com- "posed) by Buddha, or that it was Buddha who saw (or found out) these "scriptures; exactly as the names *Kāthaka*, *Āngirasa* and the like are "applied to certain recensions of the Veda. In short, whatever arguments "may be brought forward to establish the authority of the Veda, can all "be used in proving that of the Bauddha scriptures. Consequently, just "as the character of the *Scripture of Action* belongs to the Veda, so too "can it be quite reasonably asserted by the Mimānsaka to belong to the "Bauddha scriptures."

SIDDHĀNTA.

To all this, we make the following reply:

***Sutra* (12). Not so; because of the want of proper regularity.**

(It is *Purvapaksha* [D] that is taken up first) What has been said above appears to be distinctly irregular (in its argumentation).

As a matter of fact, with regard to any subject, people can have only one correct idea; as for other mistaken notions with regard to it, even though they do not appear in the man's own mind, yet if they happen to be borrowed from another person, they cannot but be faulty (and incompatible with the former conviction). At the time that one is having a discussion with another person, it often happens that fresh arguments cross up in the disputant's mind, being occasioned at that very time, by the reasonings urged by his opponent. Hence it so happens that though the person may be fully cognisant of his own standpoint, yet he is tempted to bring forward counter-arguments to those urged by his opponent, even though in so doing, they retain a mere semblance of his own theory.

Thus it is that the Çākyas, Vaibhāsikas and other Buddhistic sects, being afraid of the arguments put forward by the Mīmāṅsaka, lose their heads completely, and make the astounding declaration that their scripture also is eternal. They have such a hatred for the Veda, that they can never allow it any precedence over their own scriptures; and desiring to base upon this fact of non-precedence of the Veda, the truthfulness of such assertions of theirs as are contrary to those of the Veda, they declare even those of their assertions as speak of 'non-slaughter,' &c., to be independent of the Veda, taking their stand upon pure reasoning. But in that case, their scriptures, being as they are composed by human authors, come to be taken as unauthoritative in regard to transcendental matters; and (in order to save themselves from this predicament) they are taken in and led astray (from their own path) by the semblances of the arguments that have been brought forward (by the Mīmāṅsaka) to establish the eternality of the Veda.

Even an ordinary Mīmāṅsaka having proved the fact of human assertions having no authority with regard to transcendental matters, the Bauddhas find themselves unable to set aside the well-established and unimpeachable authoritative character of the Veda, from which all chance of discrepancies had been set aside by the single fact of its being independent of human agency; and thus finding no cogent arguments to bring forward against the Mīmāṅsaka, they lose their heart by having to fall back upon the device of repeating the arguments of the opponent; and having no reasons of their own to bring forward, they say—"Our scriptures are eternal"—forgetting in this all their own former declarations, and only apishly imitating the assertion of his opponent; and this action of theirs is exactly like that of an ignorant bridegroom, who was asked by his father-in-law what his *gotra* was; but not knowing what it was he said—"My *gotra* is the same as yours" (not knowing that this would make his marriage impossible).

And when taunted by the Mīmāṅsaka on the point of this argument belonging to the Mīmāṇsaka, and not to the Bauddhas, they turn round and say—"It is our argument, stolen by the Mīmāṇsaka." And certainly, if one were to shamelessly continue to bring forward such meaningless arguments, thereby seeking to deceive other people, he could never lose his point!

But by asserting the eternality of their scriptures, in imitation of the Veda, the Bauddhas give up their well-known theory of the momentary character of all things. The Buddha has laid down the momentary character of all things that are brought into existence; such a text of the Bauddhas being—"*All saṅskāras (impressions) are momentary;* and how can impermanent things have any action? barring the two non-entities (Destruc-

30

tion and Void) *all that is cognisable is a product and is momentary.*" They have the following text also:—"Inasmuch as, in accordance with a rule of the Intellect, a word can be related to a certain definite object, *there can be no eternal manifestation of the object by the word;* because (whether the manifestation be held to be brought about by a modification of the sense-organ, or by that of the object) in both cases such a manifestation would be highly objectionable,"—which clearly shows that the Bauddhas have always held the non-eternal character of the relations of words to their meanings; and under the circumstances, the declaration of the eternality of the scriptures, in contradiction to the aforesaid theory of non-eternality, would only make a laughing stock of the Bauddha.

For certainly, if the weaver took up only the threads, and threw away the shuttle, when proceeding to weave a cloth, he would be striking with his fist at the sky. So then, the eternality of words,—which is the staple wood on which the whole fabric of the eternality of scriptures stands—having been apparently burnt (denied, at least by the Bauddha) by means of the fire of fallacious arguments, it becomes impossible for the Bauddha to rear up the fabric anew (in regard to his own scriptures). As for the *eternality of usage* (of words) (which the Bauddha admits), it is synonymous with the *eternality of actions* (of words); and when the very relations of words and their meanings are declared to be transient, how can any usage based upon these (relations) be said to be eternal? because upon what could the usage rest (in the absence of the relations)? Consequently, those who do not admit the eternality of word, its meaning and the relation between the two, can never reasonably hold the usage, which would have no legs to stand upon, to be eternal. Because when the word, &c., will have disappeared, upon what could the usage rest?

Hence the assertion—"This *Dharma*-scripture of the Bauddha is eternal"—comes to be absolutely meaningless. Specially as that which is momentarily disappearing can never be pointed out or spoken of as 'this'; and hence it becomes all the more impossible for it to be spoken of as '*eternal.*'

(1) Thus, then, there being no chance for the eternality of the scriptures of those who hold the words to be transient, and it being impossible for human assertions, treating of transcendental subjects, to be accepted as "Scriptures of Action,"—the authority of the Bauddha scriptures (in regard to *Dharma*) is denied, on the ground of "*asanniyama*"—the meaning of this expression in this case being 'the *niyama*, or *acceptance*, of *assattva* or *transient character* (of all objects in general, and of words in particular).'

(2) Or, the scriptures of the Bauddha, the Jaina and others, being full of incorrect words, they cannot be accepted as "scriptures," "because *of assanniyama*"—the meaning in this case being, 'because they are composed

of incorrect words and expressions.' Being full of vernacular words of the Māgadhi and other languages, they are found to be very bad compositions. For instance, we meet in them with such expressions as—*mama vihibhikkhavē kammavacca isīsavē, ukkhittē lodammi uvvē atthi kāraṇam padaṇē ṇatthi kāraṇam aṇubhavē kāranam ime sakkadā dharmā sambhavanti sakāraṇā akāraṇā viṇasanti, aṇupyatti kāraṇam*, and so forth.

Thus, then, the words themselves being unreal, how could the objects denoted by them be accepted as real? And when we actually find the words to have deteriorated forms, how can we accept them as eternal?

Though in the case of the Veda too, we have such fallacious arguments as—'the Veda is non-eternal, because it is a collection of words and sentences, like the Mahābharata, &c.'—yet these can produce an idea of the transitoriness of the Veda, only so long as the actual form of the Veda has not been perceived. No sooner are the forms of the Ṛk, &c., perceived than the aforesaid conception of their transitoriness disappears entirely.

Even when we know the mere beginnings of the Veda, we can never intelligently believe them to have been composed by human authors. In the ordinary world, we find that people, following the bent of ordinary experience, compose works of poetry, &c., in connection with the facts of ordinary life only by means of words that are in keeping with ordinary experience. And who could ever have composed the Ṛgveda, consisting as it does of words which have almost never been met with in ordinary usage, and which have definitely regulated accents, spreading over sixty-four *Prapāthakas?* How could the first verse of the Ṛgveda—"I adore Agni, the foremost priest of the sacrifice, the glorious Deity, the Inviter, the receptacle of Jewels"—ever be the assertion of a man? Where could he have found such a metrical method of expression, by the help of which he would compose the verse? What, too, would be his motive for composing it? Where has Agni been seen to be a 'priest,' that one could describe him as such? Where, too, has anyone met with the word '*ilē*' in the sense in which it is used in the passage? Where again, has it been found that Agni is the 'Deity' of the sacrifice? Because the Deity of each sacrifice is defined by Vedic injunctions alone. There is no such material class as 'Deity'—(a 'Deity' is only the name of one to whom offerings are made,—and this could not be perceived by the ordinary means of worldly perception). Nor does any man know the fact of Agni, being either an "Inviter" of the gods, or a "receptacle of jewels"; and certainly it is not possible to eulogise those properties that one knows nothing of. Hence we conclude that such assertions could be made only by the Veda as independent of everything else.

Similarly in the case of the first *mantra* of the Yajurveda: "O

Grass, &c."—, how could such an assertion be made by a human being? How, too, could people know of this *mantra* being of use in the chopping of the twigs? Similarly, too, how could the *mantra* "*Urjē*, &c.," be known by any man, capable of understanding things before he does an act, to be of use in the washing of the twigs? What man again could lay down that the *mantra* '*Vāyavah stha*' is to be used in the separating of each calf from its mother (at the time of milking it). That is to say, that the word '*vāyu*' in the plural indicates each of the calves as separated from its mother could never have been thought of by any human being, given to thinking over things.

So, too, in the case of the first mantra of the Sāmaveda, such forms (in singing) as—"*O gnā ī*," &c.—could never have been composed by a human being; as there appears to be no visible purpose for singing it in this form. That is to say, how could any intelligent person transform the fully expressive words of the verse—"*Agnē āyāhi*, *&c.*"—into the form '*O gnā*,' &c., which is never met with in ordinary parlance, and which is incapable of any grammatical construction? So also, how could any intelligent person, unless he had lost his head, transform the correct 'i' in '*Vītayē*,' the '*ta*' into '*tō*,' and the '*yē*' into '*āya*'?

Thus, then, we conclude, that the form of the Veda itself establishes the fact of its being independent of human agency. There are only a very few passages in the Veda, that resemble ordinary sentences; but in these too the learned detect certain Vedic peculiarities.

Hence, whenever the teachers, or the students, or other persons near them come to ponder over the words and sentences of the Veda, and their significations, they at once recognise the fact of its being independent of human agency, which is clearly indicated by the Veda itself. And since this is not enough to convince the logicians outside the Vedic pale, all that the Mimaṅsakā has done is to bring out such arguments from the Veda itself, as go to prove the independence of the Veda of all human agency; and thus the Mīmaṅsakā has (by this unbelief of the Bauddha) only obtained the glorious name (of having proved the independence of the Veda, which is really established by the Veda itself).

On the other hand, in the case of the Bauddha scriptures, even though we come across, here and there, with words that appear to have been correctly used in their original forms; yet, even in these cases we often find such uses as those of '*prajnapti*' (in the sense of *jānāti*), '*vijnāpti*' (=*vijānati*), '*paçyata*' (instead of *driçyatā*) and so forth; and hence it is very rarely that we find any purely correct uses of words. When such is the case with words that appear to be correct, what can be said of those that are found to be used in forms that are more deteriorated than even the deteriorated vernaculars? For instance, in the case of the word '*bhikkhavē*' quoted above, even in the Prākṛta, we have often found the letter *ē* at the end of Accusative Plural, but never in the Nominative or in the Vocative; in place of the word '*saṅskṛtā*' all that the Prākṛta is found to do is to duplicate the 'K,' delete the nasal 'ṅ,' and change the 'ṛ' into 'a'; and it does not add a 'da' sound, as is found to be done in the word '*sakkaḍā*' quoted above which is thus found to have completely destroyed the unimpeachable form of the word '*saṅskṛtā*.'

Thus, then, we conclude that on account of their being composed of incorrect words and expressions, the scripture of the Bauddha, &c., can never be held to be either a Veda, or an eternal scripture.

(3). Grammar supplies the only means of ascertaining the eternal and primitive forms of words. And while we find the Veda full of grammatically correct words, we do not find the Bauddha scriptures to be so; and thus there being no strict observance of the grammatical forms of words in these latter, they cannot be accepted as scriptures. In this case, the expression '*asanniyamāt*' would mean 'because of there being no strict observance of grammatical rules.'

(4). Or, the expression '*asanniyamāt*' may be taken as referring to the absence of any permanence in the Bauddha works, which did not exist (prior to their composition by Buddha), as is clearly proved by the Buddha himself, who seeks to establish the transitoriness of all things, on the ground of the momentary character of all that exists.

(5). Or, the expression '*asanniyamāt*' may be explained as '*asatām niyamāt*,' which would mean that, inasmuch as these works invariably lay down such evil and false doctrines as the momentary character of things, the world being a mere void, there being be no self, and so forth—or inasmuch as they seek to establish their conclusion by false reasonings,—no authority can belong to those declarations of *Dharma* that proceed from the same persons as have laid down the aforesaid doctrines.

Nor can these scriptures be held to be eternal, because there is a clean remembrance of their authors (Buddha, and others). And hence in matters relating to *Dharma*, which is amenable only to an eternal scripture (as proved under *Sūtra* I—i—2), we cannot admit of the independent authority of the Bauddha scriptures.

(The *Pūrvapakshas* [B] and [C] and [A] are next taken up.)

In the case of all the Subsidiary Sciences and the *Smṛtis* too, inasmuch as we have a distinct knowledge with regard to their authors, they cannot be accepted as independent scriptures (in regard to *Dharma*). (As urged under *Pūrvapakshas*, B and C.)

The same arguments also serve to set aside the independent authority of the *Kalpasūtras* (as urged in *Pūrvapaksha* A; because of these too we know the authors, which fact is enough to prove that they had no existence before they were composed by these authors (and as such they cannot be held to be eternal). The arguments that have been brought forward in support of the eternality of the Veda, are not applicable to the case of the *Kalpasūtras*, because of people having firm convictions with regard to their having been composed by human authors. That is to say, just as the teachers and students know of the existence of the *Kalpasūtras* and other *Smṛti* works, exactly in the same way are they also cognisant of their authors, Āçvalāyana, Baudhāyana, Āpastamba, Kātyayana, and others.

From this it is clear that they had no existence prior to their being composed by these authors ; and, for this reason, how can they be accepted as *Scriptures of Action*, either as a distinct Veda, or as similar to the Veda ?

(6). We do not base the fact of the *Kalpasūtras* having been composed by authors on the mere ground of their being called by the names of certain persons ; and hence our arguments cannot be met by the replies advanced under the Sūtra I—i—30 (" The name is due to their having been explained by certain persons "). The fact is that the idea of these authors is brought about by means of an endless traditional conviction; and this is only supported by the said names as applied to the *Kalpasūtra*, &c. In the case of the names " *Kāthaka* " and the rest, as applied to the Veda, the names themselves can be held to be eternal, as based upon the fact of the eternal Rescensions of the Veda having been explained by such eternal personalities as Katha and others ; but no such explanation is possible with regard to the names " *Māçaka*," &c., as applied to the *Kalpasūtras*, for the simple reason that these *Sūtras* are never recognised as eternal ; because the words,—" *Māçaka*," " *Baudhāyana*," and " *Āpastamba* " —distinctly point to individual non-eternal (created or born) personalities; and as such, they cannot serve as the basis for an explanation of these names belonging to eternal books. Hence the *Sūtra* may be explained as— ' because the names '*Māçaka*,' &c., distinctly indicate the fact of *previously non-existing* (*asatām*) books having been composed (*niyamāt*) in the form of the *Kalpasūtras*, &c., these cannot be accepted as Scriptures of Action.

(7). It may also be explained as—' because in the *Kalpasūtras*, there are no such rules and regulations as there are in the Veda, they cannot be accepted as scriptures.' [' *asanniyamāt* ' = on account of the non-existence of *niyamas*.]

(8). Another explanation of the *Sūtra* is this—' The *Kalpasūtras* cannot be accepted as scriptures, *because there are no restrictions of time*, &c.,

with regard to them, as there are with regard to the Veda,'—as is distinctly mentioned in the *Sūtra* 'The Subsidiary Sciences may be studied whenever one likes.'

The *Bhāshya* has explained the *Sūtra* as referring to the absence of accentuation in the *Kalpasūtras*. But this would apply also to the case of the *mantras* that are quoted *in extenso* in the *Kalpas;* as also to the *Chāndogya Brāhmaṇas* laid down in the *Gṛhya-Sūtras* ; which would also come to be denied true scriptural character and authority. Because the eight Brāhmaṇas with their esoteric explanations, that are studied by the *Chāndogas*, have got no definite accentuation; and this absence of accentuation would make them lose their Vedic character.

Consequently we must take the *Sūtra* to refer to the absence, in the *Kalpasūtras*, of the self-evident eternality and independence of human agency (that have been pointed out with regard to the Veda); for though the Veda has a definite accentuation, yet this is not all that it has got (in contradistinction to other so-called scriptures).

Sūtra (13). Also because of the absence of explanatory passages.

The fact of the Veda having explanatory passages also serves to point to the same fact (of the Veda being independent of human agency). Inasmuch as, in the Veda we find many such explanatory passages, as are not possible in ordinary parlance, we conclude, from this, that the Veda is not the product of human intelligence. For what intelligent human being could be capable of composing such *Arthavāda* passages, as—"Bṛhaspati sang for the gods," "Indra killed Vṛtra," "Prajāpati cut out his own fat," "Cows performed this sacrifice, hence they have their horns growing after ten months," and so forth. Specially because, even as we find the *Arthavādas* in the eternal Veda itself, it becomes extremely difficult to connect them with Injunctions ; and then, if a human author were to compose such apparently incongruous passages to be taught to his students, he would come to be marked as a fool.

As a matter of fact, however, in the *Kalpasūtras*, we find nothing like such explanatory passages, which could lead us to conclude them to be independent of human agency.

And further, the fact of these *Kalpasūtras*, &c., being devoid of anything like direct Injunctions, distinctly establishes the descriptive character of these (that is, since they do not contain any direct Injunctions, they must be taken as mere descriptions or explanations); and it also shows that they are not capable of laying down anything new (in the shape of Injunctions on *Dharma*). In the case of the Veda we find that verbs in the present tense, when rendered attractive by means of *Arthavāda* passages, become endowed with injunctive force. While in the *Kalpa-sūtras*, there are no *Arthavādas* (and as such there is no chance for the verbs in them, which are invariably in the present tense, to have any injunctive force). (Nor can it be held that these verbs are in the fifth mood, *Lēt*, which has an injunctive signification, and not in the *Lat*, (Present) the forms of both being the same; because) the fifth *mood* (*Lēt*) has been distinctly laid down, as to be used in the Veda only; and as the *Kalpa-sūtras* are neither *Mantras* nor *Brāhmanas* (which two alone constitute the Veda), it is not possible for them to contain any verbs in that mood.

Though the declaration that 'according to some people all the six Subsidiary Sciences are Vedas' would make the *Kalpasūtras* known as 'Veda,' yet like the Mīmāṅsā, they cannot attain to the position of Veda proper (metrical); because the regulations of Veda proper (metrical) apply only to the *Mantra* and the *Brāhmana* portions of the Veda. That is to say, in accordance with the *Sūtra* of Kātyāyana—"the Injunction, the Enjoined, and the Argumentative Science of Mīmāṅsā, all constitute the Veda"—though the name "Veda" becomes applicable to the Mīmāṇsā, which consists of a compilation of all the arguments connected with the Veda, yet, it does not become affected by the rules and regulations relative to Veda proper; and hence the *Kalpasūtras* too, being exactly in the same position, cannot be accepted as forming a *Scripture of Action*, which is only another name for *Injunction*.

It has been urged above that as the *Kalpasūtras* have been enumerated by the Veda, among the subjects to be studied in course of the *Brahmayajna*, they must be held to be eternal; but this premiss becomes too wide; inasmuch as the *Itihāsas* and the *Purāṇas* are also similarly enumerated. That is to say, the said Vedic text has mentioned the *Kalpas* together with *Itihāsas* and *Purāṇas;* which shows that even the products of human agency (such as the *Itihāsas* and *Purāṇas* are universally admitted to be) are included among the sciences (to be studied in course of the *Brahmayajua*).

(There is yet another explanation of the mention of the name of *Kalpa* in the Veda). There must have been other *Kalpasūtras* before our present *Kalpasūtras* were composed (that is to say, since the very beginning of time, there must have always been some sort of a *Kalpasūtra*, in each *Kalpa*, exactly as in each *Kalpa*, there has been a *Smṛti*) ; because, in the absence of such *Sūtras*, any thorough orderly comprehension of the methods prescribed in the extensive Vedas is absolutely impossible; whence it follows that ever since there has been a Veda, there has been a performance of sacrifices, and ever since then, there never has been a total absence of any of the Subsidiary Sciences (and it may be this endless series of *Kalpas* that has been mentioned in the Veda); as there is nothing against holding this series to be eternal; though any particular *Kalpasūtra* cannot be admitted to be independent of human agency.

And as for the word "*Kalpa*," it signifies nothing more than an *explanation of the meaning of the Veda;* and as a name significant of this, the '*Kalpa*' can very well be held to be eternal; and it is as such that it has been enjoined as forming part of the daily Recitation (of the Brāhmaṇa); but all that is meant by this Injunction is that the Brāhmaṇa should make it a point every day to recall to his mind (and go over) the procedure of the various sacrifices (laid down in the Veda); and though there can be no doubt as to this procedure being eternal, that does not necessarily mark the books dealing with this procedure (*viz.*, the books on *Kalpasūtras*) as eternal.

As for the points of agreement between the Veda and the *Kalpasūtras*, such agreement is quite explicable on the ground of the latter following (or being based upon) the former; and hence as they only follow what has been laid down in the Veda, the *Kalpasūtras* cannot be said to have any independent authority of their own.

Further, no students have ever regarded the Subsidiary Sciences as Veda; as for the declaration—"*according to some*, all the six sciences are Veda"—, it by no means expresses the generally accepted theory.

And again, as a matter of fact, whenever any two declarations are found to agree with one another, it is always concluded that one of them is explanatory of (and subsequent to) the other; and finding such agreement between the *Brāhmaṇas* and the *Kalpasūtras*, we instinctively conclude that inasmuch as the former is replete with direct Injunctions, it cannot be held to be explanatory of the latter; and hence we are forced to the conclusion that it is the *Kalpasūtras* that are explanatory of, and subsequent to, the *Brāhmaṇas*.

Nor can the case of the authoritativeness of the *Kalpasūtras* be held to be analogous to that of the different recensions of the Veda; because of the same persons being the students of the Veda as well as of its *Kalpa*. In the case of the different recensions of the Veda, the students of each are distinct from one another (and hence the Injunctive authority of all of them is admissible); whereas in the case of the *Kalpa*, as each *Kalpa* only explains the meaning dealt with in detail in the particular Veda to which it belongs, and as such the students of both of these being the same, the former can never be admitted to have an injunctive authority (apart from the Veda which supplies all necessary authority).

Then again, we find that the authors of the *Kalpas* explain certain facts in accordance with the reasonings supplied by the *Brāhmaṇas;* and as such, the *Kalpas* can never be held to be equal to the *Brāhmaṇas*, in authority.

We also find that the passage in the *Brāhmaṇa* has a signification entirely different from what is assigned to it by the explanatory *Kalpa*; and hence too, we cannot admit the *Kalpa* to be independent of the *Brāhmaṇas*. Hence, though it is possible that certain similarities of subjects and expressions between the *Brāhmaṇas* and the *Kalpas* may give rise to the misconception that the *Kalpas* are also independent *Brāhmaṇas* by themselves, yet the above arguments instantly remove such misconceptions.

It has been urged above that the Veda itself speaks of the independent authority of the assertions of the great Teachers (among whom the authors of the *Kalpasūtras* are included). But there too, the word '*Ācārya*' in the Vedic text is only a chance coincidence of sound (that is to say, the world '*ācārya*' in the text does not mean 'teacher' but the 'Veda' itself, the word being explained 'as that which improves (*ācinoti*) the intellect'). Or, it may be taken as laying down the absolutely trustworthy authority of the Teacher, with special reference to the students whom he should be teaching the text and the meaning of the Veda. Manu has thus explained the meaning of the word "*ācārya*": "One, who having initiated his disciple, teaches him the Veda, with all the subsidiary sciences and esoteric explanations, is called the *ācārya*"; and in order that at the time of such teaching of the Veda, the disciples should have an implicit confidence in the words of the Teacher, the Veda has declared the authoritative character of the assertions of the Teacher; and this declaration of the Veda does not refer to the authors of the *Kalpasūtras*.

***Sūtra* (14). Because of the action being laid down for all cases; and because of the proximity of scriptural authority.**

All assertions of human beings are not accepted to be true; because, as a matter of fact, their assertions are generally found to be false. As has been declared elsewhere: "Hence it is that speech speaks of both, truth and untruth, because it has been pierced with evil." Such falsity of the assertions of the *Kalpasūtras* is distinctly pointed out by the Veda itself; specially as we meet with many assertions that are contrary to one another (and to the Veda). This is what is meant to be pointed out by the first half of the *sūtra*; the latter half meaning that the contrary scriptural passages being in close proximity, the disagreement (or contradiction) is easily perceptible.

The example of such disagreement that has been cited in the *Vrtti*, that with reference to the "*Sthālīpāka*" of the sacrifice on the 15th day of the month, has been disregarded; because in that case the declaration of the *Gṛhyasūtra* in connection with this *sthālīpāka* has been attributed to the *Kalpasūtra* which treats of the *Darça-Pūrṇamāsa*; and as such it seems as if the *Vṛtti* had purposely, with a view to entirely suppress the authority of the *Kalpasūtra*, fastened a foreign assertion on to it. We have a declaration of the *Gṛhyasūtra* to the following effect: "In the *Akshata Homa*, until the evening offering has been made the morning offering should not be given up; nor should the evening offering be abandoned until the morning offering has been made"; and just as this passage is not taken as referring to the *Agnihotra*,—so too, the following passage of the *Kalpasūtra* cannot be taken as referring to the *Darçapūrṇamāsa*: "Until the offering of the last day of the month has been made, that of the fifteenth day should not be abandoned; nor should the offering of the thirtieth day be abandoned until that of the fifteenth day has been made." And as such, there being no real contradiction of the *Kalpasūtra* by the Veda (in this case), we must cite another example (for instance, the *Kalpasūtra* says—"The *Paryagni* is made of all the sacrificial materials," which lays down *the making of the Paryagni with reference to all the materials*; while we have the *Brāhmaṇa* text which lays down the *Paryagni* as *to be made out of the puroḍāça* only; and there can be no doubt that there is a distinct disagreement between the two).

ADHIKARAṆA (8).

[*The Holākādhikaraṇa—treating of the fact of the Vedic text assumed in support of a usage having universal application and authority.*]

***Sūtra* (15). "Inferences being restricted in their application, usages can have only a limited authority."**

With reference to certain popular local customs, the present discussion is started; the question being as to whether these customs have an authority limited within certain areas, or they have a universal application. In this connection, we have got to consider all the Injunctions and Prohibitions that are marked by the acceptance or avoidance by certain people, taking each of these one by one.

There are certain customs that are followed by the Eastern people, though avoided by the exceptionally good amongst them; and we proceed to consider whether these customs have been laid down for those people alone, or for all men. In the same manner, there are certain customs that are peculiar to the Southerners, some to the Westerners, and others to the Northerners; and we have got to take into consideration each of these.

The first two *sūtras* of this Adhikaraṇa (*viz*: the 15th and 16th *sūtras*) can also be taken as referring to the question as to the locally limited or universal authority of such works as the *sūtras* of Gautama, the *Gṛhyasūtras* and the like. That is to say, we find that, barring the *Purāṇas*, the *Smṛti of Manu*, and the *Itihāsas*, all other *Smṛti* works—such as those of Gautama, Vaçishtha, Çaṅkha, Likhita, Hārīta, Āpastamba, Baudhāyana and others—as also the works on *Gṛhya*—are each studied exclusively by only certain sections of the Brāhmaṇas, and each of them has its relation restricted to only a definite Veda, exactly like the *Prātiçākhyas.* For instance, the *sūtras* of Gautama and Gobhila are accepted by the Chandoga (Sāmavedī) Brāhmaṇa only; those of Vaçishtha by the Ṛgveds; those of Caṅkha and Likhita by the Vājasnēyīs; and those of Āpastamba and Baudhāyana by the Kṛshna—Yajurvedis. Thus then, the fact of such limited acceptance of these *sutras* affords matter for reflection; the question being—is each of these *sūtras* authoritative only for the particular sect by which it is accepted? Or, are they all equally authoritative for all people? And on this, we have the following:—

PŪRVAPAKSHA.

"Inasmuch as we find the *sūtras* being studied only by the parti-"cular sects of the Brāhmaṇas, we conclude that their authority is also "limited to these Brāhmaṇas alone; specially as the authority of the *sūtras* "is based upon certain assumed texts, which as the objects of inference, "can be believed to have an existence only where the inferential indicative "'the *Smṛti*,' exists; that is to say, the *Smṛti sūtras* being found to be "current only among certain limited sects, the Vedic texts pointed to by "these cannot have their existence outside this pale. Hence, whether it "be an Injunctive or a Prohibitive Vedic text, its existence cannot be in-"ferred outside those limits.

"That is to say, the compilations of the *sūtras*, or the usages can "lead to the inference of Prohibitive or Injunctive texts (in support of "themselves), only with reference to those persons among whom they "themselves are current, and not among other people. For example, the per-"ception of smoke in one house cannot lead to the inference of the existence "of fire in another house; nor can this latter be inferred by people who "have not seen the smoke (hence the authortative Vedic text corroborating a "Usage can have no authority for those among whom the usage is not cur-"rent).

"Thus then, the Injunction of *Agnihotra* can refer to only those per-"sons for whom the *Upanayana* and the *Ādhāna* have been laid down. And "exactly as certain duties and rules of conduct are restricted to certain "definite families and castes, so too the duties and the rules of conduct "obtaining in a certain country would have their authority restricted "to that country alone.

"If the Prohibitions and Injunctions had a universal application, "Usages (which are all based upon such Injunctions &c.) would also come "to have a universal authority, there being no reason for limiting the "scope of their authority. And then the Usage, based upon the texts that "have universal application, would be followed by the capable men of all "countries, exactly like the Injunction of the *Agnihotra*.

"As a matter of fact, however, we find the usages being followed "only by limited classes of people; and hence we conclude that the Vedic "texts authorising such usages must also refer to these limited communities "only. Because the only reason for assuming the Vedic texts is to

" substantiate the otherwise inexplicable usages current amongst the people; " and hence such texts could not have any application to those people " among whom the particular usages themselves are not current. And as " in the case of usages, so also in that of the *Gṛhyasūtra* &c., the assumed " corroborative Vedic texts can have no relation to those people among " whom the *Gṛhyas* are not current. And hence we conclude that these " Usages and *Gṛhyasūtras* &c., have only limited applications.

" It has been shown under *sūtra* I—ii—30, that, if the fact of the grains " having been prepared by means of the *çūrpa* be taken as the reason for " making the offering by means of it, then the instance that has been " cited would also apply to that alone; hence the meaning would be that " inasmuch as the *çūrpa* is the means of preparing the grain, the offer- " ing is poured by means of it; and there cannot, in such a case, arise any " question as to the offering being poured by means of the *darvī* or the " *pithara* &c.

" And, in the same manner, as we find all usages to have only a limited " local currency, we cannot but conclude that the corroborative Vedic texts " inferred in support of such usages, can have only a local application. " Thus then, all inferences being restricted within certain definite limits " of place, time &c., the Vedic text that is inferred cannot but be admitted " as having an authority only within those limits."

SIDDHĀNTA.

***Sūtra* (16). But the duty must be universal, because of the universal character of the Injunctions.**

In this *sūtra* we have the reply to the above *Pūrvapaksha*:

On account of the universal charactar of the Injunctions the *Dharma-çāstra*, &c., must be taken as applying to all persons capable (of performing the duties laid down.)

Having come across certain *Smṛtis* and *Usages*, when we proceed to infer the Vedic texts in support of these, the inference that we can have must be of such causes as are similar to the effects (the *Smṛtis* &c.),—according to the law that the effect always follows in the wake of its cause. And consequently the positive injunction, technically called '*Bhāvanā*,' that is inferred, must be that which lays down certain definite actions, sacrifices, charities, offerings, fastings and penances &c.—expressed by means of verb roots,—as leading to specific results, like Heaven and the like, by means of certain specified processes; and in the case of certain actions of the body, the sense-organs and the mind, that are shunned by certain people, the inference is that of a prohibitive text, pointing out the prohibited action as leading to undesirable results in the shape of Hell and the like.

And thus we find that in both cases, the injunctions or the prohibitions distinctly refer to all persons that have the capability of doing the acts enjoined or prohibited; and as such, none of these, Usages or *Smṛtis*, can ever be taken as having a limited application, as referring to any particular place, time or persons.

Specially because as a matter of fact, we know that with regard to each action, the character of the agent is ascertained, only in three ways: (1) by capability (for instance in the case of the *Agnihotra*, we ascertain that anyone who has the capability of performing it, should perform it); (2) non-prohibition (as in the case of certain actions that are done with a special object in view, we ascertain that all men can perform the actions, except those for whom it is distinctly prohibited); and (3) by special qualifying words (as for instance, in the case of the *Rājasūya* sacrifice, it is distinctly laid down that it is only the "*Rājā*" (*Kshatriya*) that can perform it.

And in the case in question, we find that the capability (of doing the acts) laid down in the *Smṛtis* &c., belongs to the people of all castes and conditions, inhabiting the whole country of the Āryāvarta, except the blind, the deaf, the mad and the dumb, who are precluded from such actions. The capability too, of doing the prohibited acts, we find existing in the two, three or four castes (*i.e.*, certain actions that are prohibited for the Brāhmaṇa may be allowable for the other castes, and so on); and where we find the avoidance of the action much more extensive, we conclude the capability of its performance to reside in the Mleccha (who are believed to be capable of all actions howsoever abhorrent).

In a case, however, where we infer a Vedic text, in support of a certain usage, we do not find, in this text, any qualifying expressions, limiting its application to any particular countries or persons. Nor can we infer any texts that could prohibit the said usages, with reference to the people other than those among whom it is prevalent.

In certain cases it does happen that, though the capability of performing the action, belongs to all men, yet the action is distinctly restricted to certain definite classes of men by means of restrictive qualifying words; as for instance the *Rājasūya* is laid down as to be performed by the Rājā (Kshatriya), the *Vaiçyastoma* by the Vaiçya; and so on.

But in the cases in question, it is not possible for us to infer the existence of one or many qualifying words (in the Vedic text), that would in any way specify the persons among whom the authorised usage may be prevalent. Because all denote either the *Class* or the *Individual* while in the case in question, any such restrictive words that we would infer could not specify either the *Class* or the *Individual*.

Because the restrictive words could be only such as "the *Easterners* (should perform the *Holāka*)"; but as a matter of fact there can be no such definite class as "the Easterners," which would exclude all the people of the other parts of the country, and include all of the Eastern part; and as such we could have no such specification as that "the *Holāka* is to be performed *by the Easterners* alone." As for the classes, "Man," "Brāhmaṇa" and the like, that are found to include the Easterners, they equally include the *men* and the Brāhmaṇas of all parts of the country; and as such could not serve to specify the text as referring only to those people (the Easterners) among whom the particular custom might be prevalent.

As for the words denoting individuals—*i.e.*, the proper names,—they refer to one person only, like "Dēvadatta" and the like; and the presence of such words could not point out the custom as referring to any number of persons. Nor is it possible to have anyone name for all the people of the Eastern country, because it is absolutely impossible for us to have any conception, either individually or collectively, for all the endless varieties of people inhabiting the Eastern part of the country. This also shows that words cannot signify individual persons, as endowed with certain particular properties and actions and as belonging to a particular class. Because there are no individual properties, actions or classes, that could be capable of pointing to particular individual persons, as inhabiting particular parts of the country; as each individual is found to be specified, separately (by means of the properties belonging to each singly by himself).

Nor do words denote anything other than classes and individuals, and hence there is nothing upon which we could base the specification of the persons for whom the custom may be authoritative.

It is with a view to this that the *Bhāshya* has declared that we cannot reasonably admit the qualifying word—that may be inferred to restrict the application of the Injunction that by its very nature refers to all capable persons—to be denotative either of the Class or the Individual.

That is to say, such customs as those of the *Holāka* and the rest, cannot be said to belong either to a particular *Class*, or to a particular individual. Nor is it possible for us to have any *name* that would apply only to those people among whom the custom is prevalent.

Some people read the *Bhāshya* passage as—"*That qualifying expression can only denote the Class and not the Individual.*" And what they mean is this: Under *sūtra* VI—i—8, it is shown that the expression "*svargakāmah*," (one desiring Heaven), though expressing the meaning that is signified by its component parts, is yet made to signify the *whole class of human beings* that desire Heaven, irrespective of the gender and number in the word "*svargakāmah*" (which is in the Masculine Singular); on the ground that, as the expression occupies the position of the nominative no significance can be attached to its gender &c., and hence the injunction—"one desiring Heaven should perform sacrifices"—is made applicable to all human beings in general. In the same manner, in the case in question, because all local Customs and Observances, point to their being applicable to all persons that desire the particular results following from those actions, and are capable of performing them,—therefore it must be admitted that all men in general are entitled to the performance of such actions.

There are other commentators however, who, in connection with the present passage of the *Bhāshya*, proceed to consider the signification of verbs; and as such having found fault with this last reading, accept the former reading, (that we have explained above); and being led astray by the direct mention of the word "*vidhāna*" in the *sūtra*, and being unable to perceive any difference between the *Vidhi* and the *Bhāvanā*, fight shy of having to differentiate the forms of these two; and consequently upsetting the conclusion arrived at in the *Bhāvārthādhikaraṇa* (II-i-1-4), favour us with the following explanation :—

"The *Bhāvana* (signified by the Injunctive affix, &c.,) is incapable of being specified by its properties, by means of any other words (save the Injunctive affix, &c.)." And if some one, desiring to learn the real meaning of the verbal affix asks them—what is this "*Bhāva* or *Bhāvanā*"? —all that they can say is that it is nothing more than the expression '*kuryāt*' (*should do*) itself; because they hold it to be inexpressible by any other word, they can only speak of it by means of the Injunctive affix; but any use of the affix by itself being impossible, they have recourse to the next best method of uttering the affix in connection with the root '*kṛ*' (to do), which is a common substitute for all verbal roots. [Though the conclusion arrived at in the *Sūtra* II-i-1 is that, the *Bhāvanā* is *denoted* by the Injunctive affix, and is not the Injunctive affix itself]. And then they proceed thus: "All that is expressed by the word is either in the form of a *Class* or an *Individual*; but we find the verb to have passed beyond the Class and the Individual; and hence we are forced to the conclusion that the signification of the verb is inexpressible." [Though the *Bhāvārthādhikaraṇa* distinctly points out that the signification of the verb lies either in the Accusative or in the Instrumental.] (They proceed) "it is this very fact that is mentioned in the *Bhāshya* passage in question: *It* (the verb) *cannot be held to denote either the Class*

32

or the Individual; the word 'it' being taken as referring to the word '*vidhāna*' (in the *sūtra*), which is thus declared to be incapable of expressing either the Class or the Individual. For when one says 'should do', the man has the conception 'I do'; and as such the *Vidhi*, or the *Bhāvanā* (as appearing in the word '*kuryāt*') cannot be said to be either a Class or an Individual."

But all this is altogether irrelevant and groundless; and is due to a mere chance similarity of words, which, though having quite a different meaning, have been twisted by the commentators, into a signification entirely at variance with the *Bhāshya*, with the sole purpose of displaying their ingenuity; exactly as the text—"the bull with four horns, &c.,"—has been twisted (by Patanjali) into a reference to the science of grammar (*vide* above, the section on *mantra*).

The present passage of the *Bhāshya* occurs in connection with the treatment of the fact of local customs having a universal authority. And hence it can be reasonably taken along with the *sūtra*, only if it be explained, as we have explained it, as denying the possibility of any restrictive qualifications in the Vedic texts (assumed in support of customs and usages). But if this explanation is renounced, and the passage is taken as pointing out the inexpressibility of the *Bhāvanā* (which we hold to be denoted by the verbal affixes), on the ground of its being neither a Class nor an Individual, then the passage would become well worth rejecting, on account of declaring what is entirely irrelevant, useless and unreasonable in the present connection. For in that case the passage could be construed with the rest of the *sūtra*, only in the following manner: "Because the verb cannot denote either the Class or the Individual, therefore the action enjoined by it has an universal application!" And certainly this would be a truly astounding declaration! For all that it would mean is that, "if the Injunctive affix, &c., could denote the *Bhāvanā* or the *Vidhi* either as the Class or the Individual, then such customs as the *Holāka*, and the like, would have only a limited authority; but because as a matter of fact the meaning of the said affix, &c., is distinct from either the Class or the Individual, and as such, altogether inexpressible, therefore that which is signified by the said verb must have a universal authority!" And certainly this would serve as a first-rate example of irrelevancy.

And having at first declared the *Bhāvanā* to be inexpressible, they speak of (express) it by means of certain synonyms of their own creation (such as '*Bhāva*'); and thus they contradict their own former declaration. That is to say, with a view to show their own vollubility, they have spoken of the absolutely impossible synonymous character of such words as '*vidhi*

(Injunction), '*upadēça*' (advice), '*kartavyatā*' (duty), and *bhāvanā* (the thinking of a certain result as proceeding from a certain action) ; and by this they have certainly succeeded in proving the inexpressible character of the *Bhāvanā*! !

Even if the verbal affix denoted either the efficiency of the agent, or the substratum of his efficiency (the Accusative),—then too, having, as in the case of the expression "the Brāhmaṇa sacrifices," its specifications based upon the qualifying words (as "Brāhmaṇa"), the fact of its signifying the Class or the Individual would depend solely upon such qualifications ; and as such any consideration of the question of the verbal affix itself signifying or not signifying the Class or the Individual, could not in any way help us in ascertaining the scope of the authority of local customs and *Smṛtis* ; and under the circumstances, any consideration of the signification of the affix would become all the more useless, when it actually signifies only the *Vidhi* or the *Bhāvanā*, independently of any denotation of the agent.

And again, if the mere fact of the verbal affix not signifying either the Class or the Individual were made the sole ground of the universality of an Injunction, then, even in the case of such Injunctions—as "The Rājā should perform the *Rājasūya*," "The Vaiçya should perform the *Vaiçyastoma*" and the like,—the verbal affix being as inexpressive of the Class or the Individual, as in any other Injunction, these too would have to be accepted as applying to *all men* !

If it be urged that—"in these cases, though the affix is truly inexpressive, yet the qualifying words, '*Rājā*' &c., serve to restrict their application,"—then, in that case, it becomes clear that one who holds these customs &c. to have only a local authority, should argue that there are such qualifying words (in the Vedic texts assumed in support of the customs, &c., ; while one who holds them to have a universal authority, should argue that no such qualifying words are possible. And this is exactly what we have done, having rejected the possibility of such qualifying words on the ground that any indication (by such words) of either a Class or an Individual, in accordance with particular customs, is absolutely impossible ; and as such the Injunctions (assumed) cannot but be taken as referring to *all men* as a class, which is implied by the force of the Injunction.

And it is only as referring to the rejection of the possibility of any such qualifying words that the next two, *eighteenth* and *nineteenth*, *sūtras* can have any connection in the present context.

And hence, the Injunctions being always found to have a universal application, we must conclude all local customs, as well as the

Gṛhyasūtras, &c., that are prevalent only among certain sects, to have a universal authority.

***Sūtra* (17). The restrictions (in other cases) would be based upon direct perception.**

It has been urged in the *Pūrvapaksha*, that the customs should be held to have a limited authority: as are the usages and duties that are restricted within the limits of certain families or sects, so, in the same manner we could infer Vedic texts (in support of the customs) having similar restrictions.

But this is not possible; because in the cases cited—(*viz*: those of certain special sects of Brāhmaṇas having three locks, others having one &c., &c.)—because we actually find (see with our eyes) restricted usages, we can admit of such restrictive qualifications as the *class* ('Brāhmaṇa') *property*, etc., and which are all expressible by means of single words; exactly as we find in ordinary experience that the number of quartering the sacrificial Cake differs in the case of different Brāhmaṇas; and then finding that there are directly perceptible Vedic texts that specify these numbers for each particular sect, (in the same manner, actually finding the number of hair locks differing in different classes of Brāhmaṇas, we may infer from that very fact, on the ground of analogy with the quartering of the Cake, that there are Vedic texts restricting the number of locks also). That is to say, in the case of the quartering of the Cake, we actually find that for those that belong to the family of Bhṛgu, Vaçishtha, Çunaka, Atri, Budhnyaçva, Kaṇva, Sañkṛti, and the Kshatriyas, recourse to the second *prayāja* called the "*Nārāçañsa*," while for others that which is called "*Tanūnapāt*," is laid down; and thus finding this to be invariably the case, we are led by these very perceptible facts to the direct Injunctions of these restrictions in the Veda itself. And the same process holds good in the case of the usages, &c., that are actually found to belong to only certain particular families and sects—such as one sect having one lock of hair, while others have three and so on,—all of which point to direct Vedic texts in support of this. Whereas in the case of the *Holāka*, &c., this method is not applicable (as they are not actually found to be keeping strictly within any definite bounds); and as such, there is a world of difference between the example and the fact sought to be supported by it.

***Sūtra* (18). Also because there are no distinguishing marks of any specific agent.**

It has already been shown that it is not possible for the text (assumed in support of a Custom) to have any qualifying words that would denote either the Class or the Individual (to whom it is restricted) ; and we now proceed to show that it is also impossible for it to contain any such qualifications as that '*one who has red eyes* (should observe the custom).'

The opponent declares : "Though there may not be any restrictive "qualifying words in general, that could denote the Class or the Indivi- "dual,—yet it is quite possible for the text to contain words that would "point out the form, complexion and other qualifications of the person fol- "lowing the Custom,—exactly as the Injunction of the *laying of fire* lays "down such qualifications as 'having a son,' 'with black hair,' and "so forth,—which would restrict the authority of the Custom."

And in reply to this, we have the following: There being no distinguishing marks, any specification of a particular agent is not possible. It is only by means of constant or exclusive distinguishing marks that any particular agent can be positively singled out; while in the case of such qualifications or distinguishing marks, as the *having of red eyes*, &c., that could be pointed out as belonging to the Southerners, we find that these marks are also common to other people, who do not observe the particular custom (of the Southerners) ; and conversely, we find the Custom being observed by people not possessing the said features (*f.i.*: those of the Southerners whose eyes are not red). Hence the authority of the Custom cannot be restricted by means of any such distinguishing characteristics of agents.

The *Bhāshya* has taken the word '*nityasya*' (in the *sūtra*) as qualifying the word "*liṅga*"; but in that case the compound "*liṅgābhāva*" would be inexpressive (or impossible) ; inasmuch as the word '*liṅga*' being the subordinate member in the compound would (in that case, be *dependent* (*i.e.*, connected with, or qualified by, something—*viz.*, '*nityatā*'—which is expressed by a word—'*nitya*'—that does not form a member of the Compound).

It might be urged in reply, that the word '*liṅga*' being ever dependent (upon that which possesses the *Liṅga* or mark), it would always imply the other co-relative of its ; and thereby not losing its efficiency, the Compound would be quite possible ; exactly as we have in the case of the expression—"*Dēvadattasya gurukulam.*"

But this is not possible ; because the present case is not similar to that of this last expression ; because the relations in the two cases are totally different ; the word '*liṅga*' does not always stand in need of (*i.e.*, has not its denotation dependent upon) *constant* ('*nitya*') ; while the word '*Guru*' (teacher) has its denotation ever dependent upon that of 'Devadatta' (the disciple). That is to say the word '*guru*' can have its denotation only as with reference to the disciple (*i.e.*, the Guru is always recognised as the Guru of some disciple, and there can be no idea of the Guru, which is not accompanied by that of the disciple); and hence in the case of the expression—"*Dēvadattasya gurukulam*"—the word '*guru*' has its denotation included in its permanent relationship to the disciple 'Dēvadatta'; and as such this dependance (of a word not in the compound) does not necessarily vitiate the compound. In the case of "*liṅga*" and "*nityasya*," on the other hand, the word "*liṅga*" has its denotation dependent only upon a *Liṅgi*, that which possesses the *Liṅga*; and certainly the word '*nityasya*' cannot be said to be in any way synonymous with this *Liṅgī*; and as such the permanent relationship of the *Liṅgi* and the *Liṅga* cannot justify the compound "*nityasya liṅgābhāvāt*."

Though it is true that the word "*liṅga*" is used only where there is a relation of the Indicator and the Indicated, (and this relation is eternal) yet the denotation of that word does not depend entirely upon 'eternality', as that of the word 'Father' depends upon that of the word 'Son,' or that of the word 'Teacher,' on that of the word 'Disciple.'

And further, it is the word "*liṅgi*" itself which, having its denotation fixed by those of its component parts, depends upon the word "*liṅga*"; and the word "*liṅga*" does not stand in need of anything besides the verbal root from which it is formed. And inasmuch as the word "*liṅga*" denotes *that by which something is marked or indicated*, there is a distinct dependence upon the relationship of the *action of indicating*; and as such, though it is not spoken of as *related to anything*, yet it is not independent of the Object, the Instrument, &c., of the Action; and on this ground, we could justify the efficiency of such compounds as "*liṅgino liṅgadarçanam*," specially because the denotation of the word "*liṅgi*" depends upon that of the word "*liṅga.*" In the case of the word "*nityasya*," however, it is only after the denotation of the word "*liṅga*" has been duly accomplished, that the word "*nityasya*" comes to be related to it as expressing, by means of the Genitive, one of its properties; and hereby the need of this relationship not being supplied (by the word "*liṅga*" itself), the compound, '*nityasya liṅgābhāvāt*' remains absolutely inefficient or inexpressive.

For these reasons, the word "*nityasya*" must be taken as qualifying either the *agent*, as distinguished by certain definite distinguishing features, or the *authoritative application* of the text assumed in support of the Custom; the meaning of the *sūtra* being that, inasmuch as there can be no exclusive distinguishing marks, that could single out any particular agent, or point out the limits of the authority of the text assumed (in support of the Custom),—it cannot be held that such customs as the *Holāka* and the rest have a limited authority as based upon certain assumed Vedic texts containing certain words that point out the distinguishing characteristics (marking out the particular agent &c., &c., &c.).

Sūtra (19) The name is based upon a connection with place.

This *sūtra* refers to such qualifying words as the names 'Easterner' and the like, which the Custom is found to follow in its entirety.

Says the opponent: "All local customs are observed by men, speci-"fied by such names as 'Easterners,' 'Southerners,' and the like; and they "are never found to be prevalent among people that are without such "names; consequently the Vedic texts that are assumed in support of "such customs cannot but contain these distinguishing names; and as "such they must more reasonably be accepted as having only a limited "authority."

To this we make the following reply: Because such names are applied to the agent on the sole ground of his connection with certain places, we conclude that the Vedic Injunction assumed in support of the Customs, must contain words that denote the qualifications of place. Then, as for the place, as qualified by a certain quarter (East or West, &c.) or in the shape of the quarters East &c., themselves—there can be no one particular country in the world that can be exclusively and invariably known as the *East* (the inhabitant of which would always exclusively be known as the *Easterners*, &c.) (and even if there be such a fixed place) as a matter of fact the Custom in question (*f.i.*, the *Holāka*) is not found to be limited exclusively and invariably within those limits; as we find that it is observed by many people residing outside the limits of the place called the 'East'; while many people residing therein are found not to observe it.

Thus then, for such names, there being no basis other than the place, the Customs, supported by Vedic texts as qualified by the particular places (indicated by the names) could not have their prevalence dependent upon any other cause than the relationships of these places. But as a matter of fact, we do not find the prevalence of these Customs regulated by these, either positively or negatively; as we find that the *Holāka* is observed by certain people not inhabiting the Eastern country, and also that it is not observed by some men of that country; and hence we conclude that there can be no assumption of Vedic Injunctions qualified by specifications of place by means of certain names pointing to certain places.

The opponent finding in the above argument a (fancied) support to his own theory, springs forward with the following:—

Sūtra (20) "As the Custom could not be found to be

prevalent in other countries (the names cannot be held to be based upon the specifications of place)."

"If you have succeeded in refuting the fact of the names being based "upon specifications of place, we can easily point out another basis for "them. For certainly, if the names were based upon the specifications of "place, then the Customs could not be found to be prevalent among other "countries; therefore we must find for them another basis in the shape of "*Class*, &c.

"Or, we may accept the names by themselves, as independent of any "causes; even then, they could serve to qualify the Injunctions (or the "Agents). For, all that we have got to do is to find a basis for the Cus- "tom; and this basis being found in the Vedic Injunction as qualified by "by such *Names*, we do not stand in need of any further enquiry into the "basis of these Names. That is to say, the restriction of the authorita- "tive application of the Custom having been accomplished by means of "the Names, independently of any basis for themselves, there is no reason "for assuming the fact of their being based upon specifications of place, "specially when such specification has been found to be distinctly faulty."

To this, we make the following reply:—

***Sūtra* (21) The names would be literally significant, like the word 'Māthura.'**

The specifications of place are made on various grounds—as those of *habitation*, *birth*, or *departure*. That is to say, the name "Easterner" cannot be applied to any man, except upon one or other of the following grounds: (1) either he must be an inhabitant of the Eastern country or (2) he must have been born in that country, or (3) he must have come from that country; and so forth. And thus we find that such Names are never independent of some sort of a connection with a place.

And we have already shown that the prevalence of the Custom is not always in accordance with these names; since we find many inhabitants of that (Eastern) country not observing the Custom (*Holāka*); while, on the other hand, certain inhabitants of another country, whose fathers or grandfathers had originally migrated from the Eastern country, are still found to be keeping up the Custom. And hence we conclude that the Names could not serve to restrict the authority of the Injunctions (supporting the local Customs).

The *Bhāshya* has explained the word "*Māthura*" as also denoting *one who has started for Mathurā*; but the affix, that is present in the word can be possible, only if the word be taken to mean 'a *messenger* going to Mathurā' in accordance with Panini's *sūtra*: iv-iii-85; or, if applied to all men that may be going to Mathurā, the word cannot but be held to be used as such by untrustworthy (ignorant) men; as the affix could not be possible in the case of *all persons going to Mathurā* being meant.

Having thus found it absolutely impossible to infer an Injunction with qualifications specifying the agent, the Opponent proceeds to the theory that the Injunction assumed must refer to the special places, as constituting a part of the Custom itself.:

***Sūtra* (22) "The specification of place may be a property of the Action itself, like the sloping &c."**

"In connection with certain sacrifices the Veda has declared that the "altar should be sloping towards the East and to the North, or to the "East only; and just as these specifications of place are laid down as "parts and parcel of the sacrifices themselves (as it is only when per-"formed upon such an altar that the sacrifices can bring about their proper "results); so, in the same manner, the specifications of the *Eastern* coun-"try may be taken as laid down by the assumed Injunction, as forming a "constituent part of the Custom itself (*i.e.*, the *Holāka* can bring about its "proper results only when performed in the Eastern country)."

To this we make the following reply:

***Sūtra* (23) But this too is similar to the qualification of the Agent.**

Just as the qualification of the Agent has been shown (in *sūtra* 18) to be inconstant (inexclusive); so also would be the qualification of place; because there is no strict fixity either of the "Eastern Country," or of "the country with black soil" (which are the two qualifications of place that have been cited in the *Bhāshya*). That is to say, the country (*f.i.*, India) which is "Eastern" according to some people (of Afghanistan), is "Southern" according to others (the Thibetans); and similarly there is no single country that could be exclusively spoken of as the "Northern" or the "Western." And as for the presence of "black soil," it is found in many countries, and as such could not serve to distinguish any particular country among these.

For these reasons, we conclude that the Injunctions of the *Holāka*, &c., cannot be qualified by any specifications of place &c., with reference to the men (inhabiting these places); because, as a matter of fact, we find that many people actually inhabiting "a country with black soil" do not observe the Custom; while it is duly observed by people inhabiting other countries (with red soil); and hence any specifications of place cannot be accepted as regulating or restricting the authority of the Injunctions assumed in support of such Customs, &c.

ADHIKARANA (9).

[*Treating of the necessity of using the correct forms of Words*].

PŪRVAPAKSHA.

Sūtra (24) "The Science of Grammar not having the character of Scripture, there could be no restriction to the usage of words."

"In a case where a single word is found to be used variously with "entirely different meanings—*e.g.*, in the case of the word '*yava*' which is "used in the sense of the *barley corn* and also in that of *long-pepper*,— it "has been shown above (*Adhi.* 5) that both meanings cannot be held to be "optional alternatives, because of all options being tainted by eight discrepancies; also that the same word cannot be accepted as having different meanings; as that would necessitate the unreasonable assumption of "various potencies in the same word; consequently, the only method that "was found to be reasonable, was the taking of only one meaning as the "primary denotation of the word, all others being relegated to the secondary position; and then again, it has been shown that we accept that meaning of the word as authoritative which is supported by scriptural usage, "and as such, reject those that have their sole support in ordinary usage.

"But in a case where the single object, *Cow*, is found to be spoken "of by means of many words—such as '*go*' (the Sanskrit word), and '*gāvī*' "(and such other vernacular corruptions),—it is quite reasonable to accept "the expressive potency of all these words, as they are found to be used "by old and experienced men; and there being no contradiction of the "scriptural forms of words by the vernacular forms, and the Scriptures "being in the form of sentences, their full functioning is always *preceded* "by that of the words (constituting the sentences); and as such the scripture can never reasonably have anything to do with the pointing out of "certain words as *correct* or *incorrect* (*sādhu* or *asādhu*); because in that "case there would be a mutual interdependence (between the Words and "the Scripture). That is to say, because the Action of the Scriptures "depends upon the ordinarily accepted significations of words, no words in "ordinary use can ever be differentiated by them as *correct* or *incorrect*.

"In the case of *Sentences*, as appearing in the Veda or in the *Smṛtis*, "or as giving expression to certain usages, we accept the one that pre- "cedes to have a greater authority than that which follows; because we "perceive a distinct contradiction among them. In the case in question, "however, this is not possible (*i.e.*, the science of grammar pointing out "the correctness or incorrectness of words cannot be accepted to be more "authoritative than ordinary usage); because in this case, the order is "reversed; that is to say, the correctness or incorrectness of words can "be acertained only by means of ordinary usage; specially as *correctness* "and *incorrectness* are universally recognised as identical with *expressive-* "*ness* and *inexpressiveness*, respectively (*i.e.*, the word that expresses some "meaning is accepted as correct, and that which is meaningless as incorrect; "and whether a certain word expresses a meaning or not can be ascertained "only by ordinary usage).

"It is only an indistinct sound, or single letters, or a conglomeration "of letters without any reference to their signification,—as for instance, "the letters of the alphabet repeated by the boy,— that can be said to be "*incorrect* (*asādhu*). That is to say, the sound made by the beating of a "drum, the single letters '*ga*,' &c., pronounced either singly by themselves "or together with all of the same class (*i.e.*, *ka*, *kha*, *ga*,*gha* and *ñ*),— "all these do not express any meanings; and as such are *incorrect*. And "in this case, it is only from ordinary usage that we ascertain the fact of "these sounds expressing no meanings, and hence being *incorrect*. On the "other hand, the vernacular words, '*gāvī*' and the like are found to be cap- "able of denoting the *Cow*, just as well as the Sanskrit word '*go*'; in fact "they are quicker than the Sanskrit word in their action of denoting the "object, as they are used more commonly than the Sanskrit word. And "hence though all these words are denotative of the single object "'*Cow*,' yet, inasmuch as they are quite capable of expressing their "meaning, they cannot but be recognised as correct; exactly as the words "'*hasta*,' '*kara*,' '*pāṇi*,'—all signifying the *hand*—are all accepted to be "correct.

"Thus then, if the words '*gāvī*,' &c., be declared to be incorrect on the "ground of their *inexpressiveness* (which has been shown to be the only "reason for *incorrectness*), then such declaration, being in direct opposition "to a well-recognised fact of ordinary experience (that the words in ques- "tion do actually denote the *cow*), cannot be accepted (as true).

"If the *Correctness* or *Incorrectness* of words be said to depend on cer- "tain unseen transcendental facts, then, inasmuch as such *correctness*, &c.,

"are not found to be laid down in the Veda itself, they could not be accept-"ed on the strength of any other means of knowledge. (1) As for Sense-"perception, the letters of all words, Sanskrit as well as Vernacular, are "equally perceived to be pure letter-sounds; and we do not perceive, "by the senses, the correctness or incorrectness, of these letters, taken "either singly or in groups. (2) Nor can these be ascertained by means of "Inference; because as they are not amenable to Sense-perception, it is not "possible ever to perceive any invariable concomitance of these with any-"thing. (3) As all human assertions are based upon Sense-perception and "Inference, and Correctness, &c., have been shown to be not amenable to "these, they cannot be held to be capable of being ascertained by means of "such assertions. (That is, we cannot accept a word to be correct or in-"correct because a man pronounces it to be so). While as for Vedic "assertions, we have already shown (in the *Arthavāda* section) that when "they contain only descriptions of certain things or their properties, with-"out any connection with Injunctions or Prohibitions, they have no author-"ity. (That is, we do not accept the authority of a Vedic sentence that "would merely describe a certain word to be correct). And the *correctness* "*or incorrectness* of words not having the character of an *Action*, it can "never form the object of an Injunction or a Prohibition.

"It may be argued that, as *correctness* and *incorrectness* appear as *In-"struments* in the *Bhāvanā* of *Denotation* (*i.e.*, as we recognise the fact that "true denotation can be realised only by means of such and such words, "and that true denotation cannot be realised by means of such and such "words), they can form the objects of Injunctions and Prohibitions. But "this is not possible; because it is absolutely impossible to assume end-"less Injunctive and Prohibitive texts, referring to each individual word. "And then, too, when as a matter of fact, we have never come across any "authoritative list enumerating all the correct words, how is it possible "for us to have any idea of the Vedic texts authorising the use of each of "these words? And as for the incorrect forms of words, their number is "even greater than that of the correct ones; and as such it is absolutely "impossible for the use of each of these to be prohibited singly, like the "prohibition of the eating of *kalanja* (the flesh of an animal killed by a "poisoned arrow). In the case of such objects as the *Vrihi* and the "*Kalanja*, we have distinct notions of the extent of the denotations of "these words, as restricted within certain well-defined limits of *Class* or "*Property*, &c.; and as such they are found to form the objects of Injunction "and Prohibition respectively. While so far as the words '*go*' and '*gāvī*,' "are concerned, they cannot form the objects of Injunction and Prohibition, "either as a definite Class or an Individual. Because *correctness* or *incorrect-*

" *ness* is never perceived in the shape of a *genus*, either of objects or of proper-
" ties, pervading over all individuals (*i.e.*, all correct or incorrect forms of
" words are never perceived together as included in any *class* or as having
" any property in common); and as such we cannot assume only two texts,
" one a general Injunction ('all correct forms should be used'), and another
" a general Prohibition ('no incorrect forms should be used') (the former re-
" ferring to *all correct forms* and the latter to *all incorrect ones*). Because
" all words—be they correct or incorrect—are equally included in the
" general class 'Word,' and there are no two intermediate secondary classes
" that could refer to the two (the correct and the incorrect word) separate-
" ly. And hence if each individual word were to be enjoined or prohibited
" then we would have to assume as many Injunctive and Prohibitive texts
" as there are words; and thereby the number of Vedic texts, assumed in
" support of the various *Smṛtis* and the endless number of words, would
" be more than the whole universe could contain. And as a matter of fact
" it is not possible for even a millionth part of these to be directly declared,
" and the text that is not directly declared cannot serve as the basis of
" any *Smṛti*; because we have already shown above that the *Smṛtis* cannot
" be said to be based upon such Vedic texts as can only be inferred (and
" not capable of being ever directly perceived).

" Nor is it possible for the Injunctions and Prohibitions to be based
" upon the *expressiveness* or *inexpressiveness* of words; because all words
" —correct or incorrect—are equally expressive. Hence we can have no
" such injunction as that 'one should use only expressive words'; because
" such use is an established fact (there being no inexpressive words used)
" (and as such it could not stand in need of an Injunction, which always
" lays down something that is not got at by other means). Nor is it pos-
" sible for us to have any such prohibition as that 'No inexpressive words
" should be used'; because as there never is such a use, its prohibition
" would be useless and impossible. For we cannot have such Injunctions and
" Prohibitions as—'one should drink water,' 'one should not drink fire'—
" (because the former is unnecessary, and the latter impossible).

" In the case of the *Smṛtis* relating to the science of Grammar, it is
" necessary that we should assume a Vedic text enjoining the use of
" correct words, or one prohibiting the use of all incorrect words, or one
" that combines the said Injunction and Prohibition. But writers upon
" Grammar have preferably had recourse to the first alternative—bas-
" ing their Science upon the Vedic text enjoining the use of correct
" words. If the science of grammar were based upon the Prohibition of
" the use of incorrect words, then,—inasmuch as these incorrect forms
" are indefinitely innumerable, it would be absolutely impossible to have

" any definite idea of the science ; and hence the writers have based it upon " the Injunction of the use of correct words, which naturally (through Apparent Inconsistency) implies the prohibition of the use of incorrect words ; " just as in the case of the *Smṛti* injunction—' Only five of the five-nailed " animals are fit for eating, '—it implies the prohibition of the eating of all " other five-nailed animals. In the case of the Injunction of the use of " the correct words, these words have got to be remembered. In both " cases, the one (Prohibition or Injunction) implies the other also ; and as " such the Injunction of the use of correct words also serves to give us an " idea of the impropriety of the use of incorrect words.

" Thus then, in the case of the Science of Grammar, whichever of the " three alternatives is employed, it becomes possible to include all cases " within a definite compass ; and as such there may be some sort of definiteness ; whereas it is absolutely impossible to have any definite idea of the " Injunction and Prohibition with regard to each individual word ; because " it is not possible for us to read up an endless number of sentences. And " it was with reference to this impossibility that the *Bhāshya* has declared, " in the section on *Holāka* : ' the word cannot be said to be expressive of " either the Class or the Individual.' And thus there being no basis for the " Science of Grammar, in any Vedic texts, it must be concluded to be a " misconceived *Smṛti*.

" And again, a fact that is already established by other means can " never be the object of a scriptural Injunction or Prohibition ; and the " *word* and its *use* in a definite sense are such as are already accomplished " (or ascertained) by means of ordinary experience.

" It may be argued that, even though the word is already known, from " ordinary experience, to have a definite meaning, yet the scriptures may " point it out, for the sake of *Dharma* (as it is only that which is laid " down in the scriptures that can be of any use in matters relating to " *Dharma*) ; and as such the the science of the usage of words (*i.e.*, grammar) cannot but be accepted to have the character of a scripture.

" But this is not possible ; because in the case in question there is no " object of *restriction* (*Niyama*). That is to say, it is only one whose application is uncertain that is restricted in its application by the scriptures ; " while the word has its application or use always certain ; and as such it " can never be an object of restriction. And one that has no application " at all (*e.g.*, the incorrect word) can never be the object with regard to " which anything else (the correct word) can be restricted. (That is to " say, that which is used cannot be said to be differentiated from that " which has never had an application). And certainly the words ' *gāvī* ' " &c. can be said to be such as have no application at all ; in fact, we "accept them to be actually used (or applicable to usage). Hence in both "cases, there is no possibility of Restriction.

"And again, what sort of a restriction would you assume: (1) either "that one should utter only correct words, or (2) that one should always "utter the correct words? If the (1), then it would not be a restriction "(or differentiation) from the incorrect words, because there is no chance "of these being used (as by 'incorrect words' we only mean 'words with-"out a meaning,' and these cannot be anywhere used). And if the (2), "then the man who is silent would be incurring a grievous sin (as infring-"ing the injunction of the continuous utterance of correct words).

"If the correct and the incorrect words were capable of being used "with regard to one and the same object, then alone could there be an oc-"casion for restricting the use to the correct word (and rejecting the in-"correct one); but according to you the incorrect word being absolutely "meaningless can never be capable of being used anywhere: and as such "any restriction of the correct word could not serve the purpose of pro-"hibiting the use of such an incorrect word (because it is naturally pre-"cluded from usage on account of its meaninglessness).

"The restriction may be said to serve the purpose of setting aside such "forms of words, as happen to be used, either through the natural incapa-"city of the talker (to pronounce the correct word) or through his igno-"rance. But this is not correct; because, as a matter of ordinary experience "we find that if one is habituated, either through ignorance or incapacity, "to the use of an incorrect word, no amount of scriptures can dissuade "him from its use.

"If it be urged that, 'we do find incorrect words being used for the "purpose of expressing certain meanings (and as such it cannot be argued "that there is no chance for an incorrect word being used),'—we make "the following reply: as for such expressiveness, we often find people "having recourse to certain gestures and squints of the eye, &c., for the "purpose of expressing certain meanings; but we do not find any restric-"tions that would prohibit the use of such gestures, &c. Nor again can "restrictions be said to serve the purpose of negativing the contrary; as this "purpose is served by *Parisaṅkhya* (or Negation); nor can the case in "question be said to be an object of *Parisaṅkhyā*; because there is no "simultaneity in the case (the incorrect word not being used simultaneously "with the correct one).

"Nor can the use of the correct word be said to bring about a trans-"cendental result; because when the necessary explanation is found in the "facts of ordinary experience, it is not right to have recourse to the trans-"cendental. That is to say, there is no Apparent Inconsistency in the case

" that could justify the bringing in of the transcendental element. As for " the declarations of certain transcendental results following from a correct " use of words, the sole purpose of these is to persuade other people to such " usage ; and as such they can be taken as mere *Arthavāda*.

"And when there is no transcendental result, we cannot assume the " correct use of words to bring about an *Apūrva* (an unique agency that " would bring about certain results in the hereafter).

"Nor can we ascertain the substratum of this agency of the *Apūrva* that " would be brought about by the said Restriction (of the usage to correct " words) ; because such a substratum could be found only among the fol- " lowing: (1) the Word; (2) its meaning; (3) the Person addressed ; (4) " the cognition (of the word and its meaning) ; (5) the speaker ; and (6) " the utterance. But none of these is possible; because, (1) as for the " Word, as it is distinctly uttered for the sake of another person, any " *Apūrva* residing in it could be of no use (to the speaker himself). (2) " As for the meaning, though as being the object of denotation, it is the " primary factor in the case, yet it is found to be a part of the Word, even " in ordinary parlance, where there is nothing transcendental, in the shape " of an *Apūrva ;* and as such the *Apūrva* cannot in any way help the meaning. " (3) As for the Person addressed, there can be no mention of such a per- " son in the Restrictive Injunction (which would be in the form 'one should " use only the correct forms of words') ; and any *Apūrva* brought about by this " Injunction cannot in any way affect the Person addressed. (4) As for " the cognitions (of the word and its meaning), these last only for a mo- " ment ; and as such cannot serve as the receptacle of the *Apūrva*, " which continues for a long time. (5) As for the Speaker, he occupies " only a subordinate position in the utterance of the correct word (*i.e.*, in " the said Injunction, the primary factor is the *correct Word*, and the " *Speaker* has only a secondary position) ; and as such he cannot be said " to be in any way affected by the *Apūrva* brought about by the Restrictive " Injunction ; specially as in this Injunction there is no word that could " assign the primary importance to the Speaker, as there is in the case of " the Injunction '*one desiring heaven* should perform sacrifices' (where the " clause italicised serves to attribute the primary importance to the " Agent) ; nor do we find the genitive signifying any relationship of the " Speaker, which could impart a primary importance to him. In the case " of such injunctions, as that 'one should take his food, facing the East,' " and so forth, the *Apūrva* that is brought about by facing the particular " quarter is believed to affect the Agent, through the action of *eating*, which " serves a direct visible purpose of the Agent himself (the appeasing of " hunger) ; in the case of utterance, on the other hand, the action (of " *utterance*) is not found to serve any visible purpose for the Speaker ; and "as such its conditions cannot be held to be analogous to those of the "aforesaid *eating*. (6) Lastly, as for the *utterance* itself, as it is extremely "transient, it is absolutely incapable, like Cognitions, to be affected by the "*Apūrva*.

"Thus, then, the works relating to the Usage of Words (*i.e.*, the works "on Grammar), not having a basis in the Veda, they cannot be held to "serve the purpose of laying down rules helping the accomplishment of "*Dharma* (either directly or through the medium of an *Apūrva*); nor can "they be accepted to be Scriptures by themselves (independently of the "authority of the Veda).

"And it is with a view to this fact that we have the *Sūtras* I—iii—11. "12.

"Nor again can the works on Grammar be said to have the same position "as the Veda, and as such a self-sufficient authority. On the contrary, as "their very existence is due to human agency, they can have no authority "at all. Because in the case of all human assertions, what we conclude "from such an assertion, is only that *this person knows the matter thus*, and "not that *such is the real state of things*. And hence as all that the works "on Grammar do is to give expression to the view of the speaker, they can "never rightly help in differentiating the really correct or incorrect forms "of words.

"Nor do we find any other *Smṛti* treating of the subject (of Gram-"mar); and as such, the matter resting upon the sole authority of gram-"matical works, the assumption of corroborative Vedic texts is not quite so "easy as in the case of the *Smṛtis* treating of *Upanaya*..., &c. (which are "treated of in many *Smṛti* works). That is to say, the works of Manu, "Vaçishtha, Gautama and others, mostly treat of the same subjects, and as "such the authority of these being strengthened by the absence of any "contradiction among themselves, it becomes a comparatively easy matter "to assume corroborative Vedic texts.

"The works on Grammar, however, do not treat of the same subjects "as the said works of Manu and others. And as for the various writers "upon Grammar itself, there are endless contradictions among the asser-"tions of the *Sūtra* (Pāṇini), the *Bhāshya* (Patanjali), and the *Vārtika* "(Kātyāyana); how then can one ascertain what the truth is?

"And again, Pāṇini has not mentioned any purpose of the Science of "Grammar. And it still remains to be explained how he forgot to explain "the purpose, in such an extensive work. It is a general rule that when-"ever a work begins to be written, its aim is always definitely stated, in "order to encourage the student in the study of the work; and as a "matter of fact we actually find the aim definitely stated, even in the "case of works whose aim is apparent from the very beginning; as also "in those for the getting up of which much effort is not required; as for "instance, 'we are going to explain *Dhārma*,' 'we are going to explain "the sacrifices,' and so forth. While, even though the Science of Gram- "mar is extremely difficult, yet the Author when composing the *Sūtras*, has "not stated either *Dharma* (Duty) or *Artha* (Wealth), or *Kāma* (Pleasure), "or *Moksha* (Deliverance) to be the aim of the science. And certainly it "was not proper for him to disregard the most important factor (in the "treatment of a subject). Nor can it be held that the aim was too well- "recognised to require a distinct mention; because it was so well-recog- "nised, that even till now there is no unanimity among Grammarians on "the point!

"(Nor is it possible for *Dharma* to be held to be the aim of the Science "of Grammar, because) *Dharma* too is described to consist in such actions "of sacrifice, &c., as bring about certain definite results; and we do not "find any such Actions laid down in grammatical works. It is true that "writers on Grammar have held that the knowledge of the Science of "Grammar, or the using of words in accordance with the rules therein "laid down, constitutes a *Dharma*; but this too is not as it should be, in "the case of scriptural works. That is to say, the purpose or scope of a "scripture is always of a well-defined form; while in the case of Gram- "mar, we find that there is no certainty upon the point. As for instance, "Patanjali has declared that the knowledge of Grammar constitutes "*Dharma*; and Kātyāyana, fearing that such a conclusion would make the "knowledge of incorrect forms of words also *Dharma* (as the knowledge "of Grammar includes that of correct as well as incorrect forms), de- "clared that *Dharma* consisted in the using of words in accordance with "Grammar; and then again Patanjali reiterates his own theory that it "consists of the Knowledge of Grammar. And certainly, when there is "such a diversity of opinion on the point, we cannot ascertain exactly what "the *Dharma* is (that would be accomplished by the Science of Grammar).

"It is a well-recognised fact that of two correlated things, if one is "held to have the character of *Dharma*, the other being only subsidiary "to it, cannot itself be recognised as *Dharma*. And hence (of the two "correlated things, the Knowledge of Grammar and the Using of Words "in accordance with grammatical rules) if the knowledge be accepted as "having the character of *Dharma*, then the *usage* (of words) which is a "well-established fact of ordinary parlance, being accomplished by means "of the said *knowledge*,—even though it (the Usage) is found to accord "a distinct help, it cannot be recognised as having any direct use; just "as the water that is left in curd after the solid particles have been "removed is not accepted to have any direct use of its own.. Con- "versely, if the usage of words according to grammatical rules be taken "as constituting *Dharma*, then the Knowledge of the Science having all its "purpose fulfilled in the helping of the Usage, there is no desire on our "part to seek for any other use for it; and hence even if we meet with "any Vedic texts speaking of results (as following from the Knowledge of "Grammar), we must take them as mere *Arthavādas*, in accordance with "the arguments laid down under *Sūtra* IV—iii—i. And we have already "explained (under *Sūtra* I—ii—4) that when two things treat of the same "subject, if one of them be recognised to be the means of accomplishing "a certain result, the other is not cognised as accomplishing the same re-"sult; as for instance, in the sentence—"one who performs the *Açva-"mēdha* sacrifice, and also one who knows this passes beyond all sorrow, "&c.'—if the knowledge of the sacrifice be recognised as really bringing "about the said result, why could any person engage in the elaborate "sacrifice itself?

"And again, as the Science of Grammar itself has had a beginning in "time, we can never admit the character of *Dharma* to belong either to its "*knowledge* or to a *usage* according to it. Nor do we find any Vedic texts "standing in need of Grammar. It is only when the knowledge is "afforded by the eternal Veda that any action in keeping therewith can "be accepted as bringing about a transcendental result. The know-"ledge of Grammar, however, depends solely upon the works of human "authors; and as such the mention, in grammatical works, of transitory "things &c. cannot be explained away by means of the arguments that we "have employed with regard to the mention of such things in the Mantras "and Arthavādas of the eternal Veda; and as such, they cannot be held "to be treating of the same subjects as the Veda.

"Nor is Grammar itself ever recognised as eternal; because such "eternality is set aside by the mere fact of our being fully cognisant of "its propounders. If the eternality of Grammar were to be assumed on "the ground of the eternality of the usage of words in accordance with its "rules,—then too, the Science of Grammar being found to have been pro-"pounded by many authors, it can never be admitted to have any basis in "the Veda; in accordance with the law contained in the *Sūtra* I—i—29 "(and hence not being eternal, it cannot be the means of accomplishing "*Dharma*).

"Nor is there any such (eternal) *class* as '*Vyākaraṇatva*'; specially as "all collections of sentences (that make the works on Grammar) being "non-eternal (as composed by human authors), where could the eternal "*class* subsist?

"It may here be urged that, 'the works on Grammar consisting of *rules* "(*lakshaṇas*) and the *subject of the rules* (*i.e.*, the words treated of and "explained under the rules), though the former are the works of human

" authors and as such non-eternal, yet the latter being eternal, the existence " of (eternal) Vedic injunctions (in support of these) is quite possible.'

" But this cannot be; because the words being innumerable and entirely different (from one another), unless there is a rule or assertion " embracing all of them, it is not possible for them to be spoken of in " any Injunctions, as we have shown above, (that in the absence of an all-" embracing assertion, we would require an endless number of Injunctions. " And as the rules are non-eternal, there can be no Injunctions treating of " them).

" *Objection*: 'But we find the eternality of Grammar indicated by the " Veda itself when we read—*tasmādēsha vyākṛtā vāgudyate* (then comes " forth a *vyākṛta* sentence)?'

" But it is not so; because all Vedic sentences being *vyākṛta* (sancti-" fied or clarified) by a traditional course of study, the sentence quoted " refers to these same Vedic sentences that are uttered at sacrifices or " during the study of Veda. That is to say, the Vedic sentence,—hav-" ing its form definitely ascertained by means of the regulations with re-" gard to its consonants, vowels and accents, as handed down from teacher " to the disciple, in the course of an eternal tradition,—is spoken of as " '*vyākṛta* (clarified), in contradistinction to all ordinary sentences, " which are not so sanctified. And certainly there is a *Dharma* in the " knowledge of such Vedic sentences, as composing the Mantras and the " Brāhmanas, as also in the performance of actions in accordance with In-" junctions laid down in these.

" The Grammarians quote the following passage from the Veda, in " support of the theory that Grammar in itself affords the means of ac-" complishing Dharma: 'A single word correctly known, duly used, in " accordance with scriptures, becomes a means of fulfilling all desires in " Heaven and on Earth.' But this also is in praise of Vedic study itself. " In continuation of the Injunction that 'one should read the Veda every-" day,' we have an obligatory rule which lays down the necessity of the " daily reading up of even a single *Ṛk*, *Yajush* or *Sāma*; and in reference " to this, we have the praise above quoted, which means that in a case one is " unable to read up even a single complete *Mantra*, if he manages to utter " a single word as found in the scripture, that single word becomes a " means of fulfilling all his desires; the expression '*Çāstrānvita*' thus mean-" ing *that which is found in the Veda*; '*correctly used*'=uttered or studied " in full accordance with the regulations of study—such as Initiation, " living with the tutor, attending upon him, with the sacred *Kuça* in " hand, and so forth.

" Another passage that they bring forward is—'Hence the Brāhmana " should not behave like the *Mleccha*, *i.e.*, he should not talk incorrectly, "because an incorrect word verily is *Mleccha.*' But this passage only "lays down the prohibition of distorting the traditional readings of the "Veda. It is only the ordinary expression of the word that can be un-"derstood as '*apaçabda*' (incorrect word), as it would be at variance with "Vedic modes of expression; and that which is at variance only with ordinary "every-day expressions can never be known as '*apaçabda.*' Because even "such words as '*gāvī*' &c., (which the orthodox Grammarian would call "an *apaçabda*) are perceptible by the *ear*; and as such they cannot but "be accepted as denotable by the *word* '*Çabda,*' as comprehended under "the *idea* of '*Çabda,*' and as included in the *class* '*Çabda.*' If it is abso-"lutely necessary to apply the word '*apaçabda,*' to expressions at variance "with ordinary expressions,—then, we cannot apply it to the languages of "the Barbara and other countries not included within the sacred limits of "Āryāvarta defined as the country included between the Himālaya and "the Vindhya mountains, where the black deer roam about; because "with regard to the languages of such foreign countries, we have the "prohibition, 'One should not teach the *language of the Mlecchas,*' and the "above-quoted passag e speaks of '*Mleccha word*' as synonymous with '*apaç-"abda*;' therefore we must apply the word '*apaçabda*' to the words cur-"rent in foreign languages (which are at variance with those current in "Āryāvarta). And as all practices and usages of these foreign countries "are prohibited for the Ārya, it is only natural that they should avoid "their language also. And further we can never apply the word 'Mlec-"chic' to any such words and expressions as '*gāvī*' &c., that are current in "Āryāvarta, because the Āryāvarta can never be spoken of as 'Mleccha'; "and hence these words can never be spoken of as '*apaçabda*'; specially "as an analogous word we have '*apavṛta*' (contrary conduct); and this "is found to be applied only to such conduct as is not permitted in "Āryāvarta.

"Another passage quoted by the Grammarian is—'If one who has "taken to the Agnihotra happen to utter an *apaçabda*, in expiation of "this, he should perform the *Sārasvatī* sacrifice.' But this only lays down "an expiatory rite that is to be performed if the person happen either to *tell "a lie*, or to *distort a Vedic reading*, or to *pronounce a word of some foreign "language*; and it does not refer to the use of words that may not be "sanctioned by the comparatively modern rules of Grammar. Because if "the use of words at variance with those sanctioned by these rules were "so very sinful, how could all Agnihotris deviate from this rightful path "(and we actually find them making use of such words as '*gāvī*' and the "like)? Or, how could they escape from being cried down as vulgar? As "a rule, we find that in the case of persons who have their minds always "engaged in the performance of *Dharma*, it is only once in a away that they "can be found slightly infringing any rules (of conduct or of speech). And as "a matter of fact, we do not find the using of such words as '*gāvī*,' and the "like marked down as an 'infringement'; nor do we find people having "any doubts or aversion to their use, as they have to the eating of *Kalanja* "(flesh of an animal killed by a poisoned arrow). And even if we take the "cases of a thousand Agnihotris, we do not find anyone of them to be "using only such words as are sanctioned by the modern rules of Grammar.

"Even among the authors of the *Kalpas*, the *Sūtras*, works on *Smṛti*, "*Mīmānsā* and the *Gṛhyas*, many excellent writers are found to be "making use of words at variance with the rules of Grammar. For "instance, in the *Kalpa* of Maçaka, we meet with such sentences as "'*Samānamitaram* Jyotishtomēna,' which is in imitation of the rule "'*Samānamitarat çyēnēna*,' and which has the ungrammatical form "'*itaram*,' in the place of, '*itarat*.' In the *sūtras*, we read—'Sadasi "*stuuīran*,' where 'stuvīran' is in the *Ātmanepada* which is a highly un-"grammatical form; as the result of the action of *hymning* does not per-"tain to the *person hymning*, and as such the proper form would have "been the *Parasmaipada*, as in '*yajanti* yājakāh.' So too we find Āçvā-"lāyana saying—'*pratyasitvā prāyaçcittam* &c.,' where the word '*pratya-*"*sitvā*' being a compound, the correct past participial affix to use would "have been '*lyap*' (and not '*ktvā*'); and again, we find him saying "'ājyēnākshiṇī *ajya*,' where there being no compound in '*ajya*,' '*lyap*' "was not the right affix to use. Nārada says in his *Çikshā*—'*pratyūshē* "brahma cintayēt,' where the word '*pratyūshē*' (instead of '*pratyūshasi*') "is as ungrammatical as the words '*gāvī*' and the like. We find Manu him-"self saying—'jnātārah santi *mētyuktvā*,' where the correct form would "have been '*mē ityuktvā*,' and still he has disregarded the rules of Gram-"mar on the point and has merged the 'i' of 'īti' into the 'ē' of 'mē.' "In the Mīmānsā, we have the *sūtra* '*gavyasya* ca tadādishu,' (viii-i-18) "where the word '*gavya*,' applicable, according to approved grammatical "rules, to *something proceeding from the body of the cow*, has been applied in "the *sūtra* to the '*Gavāmayana*' sacrifice. Then again, we have the *sūtra* "'*dyāvostathēti* cēt,' where the word '*dyāvoh*' is wrongly used for '*dyāvā-*"*pṛthivyōh*.' So also we find the author of the *Gṛhyas* speaking of *mūr-*"'*dhanyabhijighrāṇam*' instead of '*mūrdhanyabhighrāṇam*.' Through-"out the *Nirukta*, we find many words used against all rules of grammar; "such, for instance, as the assertion 'brāhmanō *bravaṇāt*,' which occurs dur-"ing the interpretation of the word 'brāhmaṇa' as occurring in the *mantra* "'*Samvatsaram çāçāyānā*' &c., where the word 'brāhmaṇa' is explained "as apylying to one who is *capable of speaking or explaining*; and here the "proper form to use would have been 'brāhmano *vacanāt*' and not '*brava-*"*ṇāt*;' because in such cases the root 'brū' is transformed into 'vaci,' "according the *sūtra* '*bruvō vacih*' (Pānini II—iv—53). And as for Purānas "and Itihāsas, there is no end of such ungrammatical words in them, as "for instance, '*ubhābhya*' which is applied by tamers of elephants, "Royal Princes and others, to such elephants as are *capable of striking with* "*both tusks simultaneously*; and this is not in keeping with any rules of "grammar. Even in the Veda, we find many forms that are not in accord-"ance either with general grammatical rules, or with those rules that have "been framed with special reference to Vedic usage.

"Nor can these anomalies in the Veda be said to be in accordance with "such grammatical rules as lay down exceptions with reference to the "Veda—as for instance, 'the rules with reference to the terminations &c., "are not always observed in the Veda,' or that 'in the Veda there are "many anomalies,' and so forth. Because there are certain instances "where even these exceptions do not serve to justify the uses. E. g., "'madhyē *āpasya*,' where the change of '*apām*' into '*āpasya*' is in no way "justifiable; so also in 'nīcīna*vāram*,' where instead of the word '*dvāra*' "we have '*vāra*' which is found nowhere else except in the *Lāta* "language.

"From these considerations we conclude that there is no use of hav-"ing any rules with regard to the uses of words as are laid down in gram-"matical works, for the simple reason that no such rules can take in all "the words that are used.

"And further, even those who occupy the utmost pinnacle of gramma-"tical knowledge, are actually found to be making use of such ungrammatical "forms of words as '*gāvī*' and the like. For instance, in the *Sūtra* (Pāni-"ni), the *Vārtika* (of Kātyayana) and the *Bhāshya* (of Pātanjali), we "come across many corrupt forms of words. And certainly those sitting "on the horse, could never forget of the horse's existence, if they had the "slightest intelligence.

"For instance, we have the *sūtra* '*Janikartuh prakṛtih*' (Pānini—I-iv-"30), where we find two grammatical mistakes; the word '*Jani*' signifies "*the root* '*jan*' (to produce), and certainly the *sūtra* does not lay down "the Ablative termination for the *producer* (*kartā*) *of the root*; and the "word '*Jani*' never being capable of signifying 'that which is produced,' "'*Janikartṛ*' can never mean the 'producer,' (which is what was really "meant); and hence we conclude that the word '*Janikartṛ*' is as in-"correct in the sense of 'producer,' as the word '*açva*' in the sense of "'poor.' (2) The second mistake is that the compound '*Janikartuh*' itself is "absolutely ungrammatical, being a direct infringement of the *sūtra* (Pani-"ni II-ii-15) that lays down that there can be no compounding with the "nominatives ending in the affixes *tṛc* and *aka*; as here we have the com-"pounding of the word '*kartṛ*' (*kṛ* and *tṛc*); so also in the *sūtra*

" *prayojako* hetuçca,' (Panini I-iv-55) where we have the compounding of " the word '*proyojaka*' which ends in '*aka*.'

" So also in the *Vārtika* (of Katyāyana), we meet with the sentence, " 'dambhērhalgrahaṇasya *jātivācakatvāt* siddham,' where the compound " '*jātivāçaka*' is an infringement of the *sūtra* II-ii-15 (the word '*vācaka*' " ending in '*aka*'). And again, we read—'*ānyabhāvyantu* kālaçabdāvya- " vāyāt,' and here, in the first place, the compound in '*ānyabhāvya*' itself " is not easily explicable; and even when we are able to explain the com- " pound, the name 'compound' would preclude the name 'adjective'; and " as such we would have the affix '*shyañ*' used in a word which is not " an Adjective; and this would be an infringement of the *sūtra* of Panini " V-i-124 (and then too the affix would be absolutely useless, as it would " not change the meaning of the original word).

" In the Bhāshya (of Patanjali) too, we find the expression '*aviravi-* " *kanyāyēna*,' which is a *Tatpurusha* compound containing within itself a " *Dvandva* compound (*aviçca avikaçca = aviravakau, aviravikayoh nyāyena =* " *aviravikanyāyeña*); and here, it was absolutely necessary to delete in the " former compound the nominative termination in the first '*avih*,' in accor- " dance with the *sūtra* of Panini II-iv-71; but this has not been done in " the expression cited (the correct form of which should have been '*avya-* " *vikanyāyēna*'). And again, we read—*anyathākṛtvā* cōditam *anyathā-* " *kṛtva* paribārah'; where we find that the affix '*ṇamul*' has not been " used even though its use is distinctly laid down by Pānini in *sūtra* " III-iv-27.

" Nor can the use of the above expressions be justified on the ground " of their being '*nipātas*' (grammatical forms assumed to be correct) and " as such quite correct. We can apply the mechanism of the '*nipāta*' " only to those words that are not found to be subject to any other rules. " For those however that come directly under certain rules, their use is " entirely barred by such rules (if the use is against them). Because " we have already shown above that when there is contradiction between " *usage* and *Smṛti*, the latter always sets aside the former. And in the " instance cited above, we find the expressions *Janikartuh*,' &c., to be " directly against certain distinct rules. A word is said to be correct on " the ground of its being a *nipāta*, only when it is not found to be against " any direct Rule; because in that case, there being no *Smṛti* (*i.e.*, Rule) " applying to the word, the mere fact of its being *used* is made the ground " of *assuming* a rule relating to the parts of the word; and thereby the " word may be justified.

" Some people might argue that the rules (laid down by Pānini) are " not applicable to the language of the rules (the *sūtras*) themselves; be- " cause it is impossible for anything to have an action upon itself, and "because that which is the '*lakshaṇa*' (the means of pointing out) cannot "itself be the '*lakshya*' (the object pointed out).

"But we cannot admit of any such arguments; because the word "appearing in one *sūtra* can very well form the object of, and be amenable "to, the definitions (and rules) contained in another *sūtra*, exactly as one "word is always capable of being pointed out by another word. (And this "would not be a case of anything having an action upon itself).

"And as a matter of fact, we find the Mahābhāshya itself applying "one rule or *sūtra* (of Pānini) to another *sūtra*; as, for instance, we read "under *sūtra* I-i-1—'why have we not here the *K* instead of the final *C*?' "this question distinctly showing that *sūtra* I-i-1 is meant to be amenable "to *sūtra* VIII-ii-30; and again under *sūtra* II-i-1, we read—'*koyam çab-* "*dah*' &c., which goes on to explain the word in question in accordance "with another *sūtra*. And as a matter of fact, if *sūtras* were not applicable "to *sūtras*, whole works of grammar would form a mass of mistakes. And "any half-and-half application of the rules would make the work entirely "untrustworthy.

"Some people might argue thus: 'The rule that one should use only "correct words is laid down with special reference to the words used dur- "ing the performance of a sacrifice, and not to those used in the *sūtras* or "in their commentaries.'

"But this is not right; (1) because the using of correct words is "spoken of as 'bringing about all desirable results *in this world* as well as "in heaven'; and (2) because otherwise the mention of 'one who has "taken to the fire' (Agnihotri) would be absolutely redundant in the "Vedic text which lays down that if such a person utters an incorrect "word he should perform the *Sārasvatī* sacrifice, because the person enga- "ged in a sacrifice is always 'one who has prepared the fire'; and hence if "the using of correct words were necessary for him only, it would not be "necessary to mention such a person in the above text laying down the "*Sārasvatī* sacrifice.

"In the chapter on *Jyotishtoma*, we read—'*tasmād brāhmaṇairna* "*mlēcchitavai*' (said with reference to the Vājasnēyis); and though this "occurs with special reference to the performance of a sacrifice, yet in this "case, the word '*mlēcchitavai*' means the distorting of the readings of the "Veda established by tradition, or the using of the language of the *Mlēc-* "*chas*, as we have already shown above. (And hence this text can have no "bearing upon the point at issue).

"Then again in the *Mahābhāshya*, we find that, having put the question "—'which are the words here treated of?' the author replies—'the "words *Vedic* as well as *worldly*,' where *the words used in the Veda* are re- "presented as something absolutely different from *those in ordinary use*.

"But as a matter of fact, we find almost all the words in the Veda to be "the same that are met with in ordinary usage; and as such only a very "slight differentiation, if any, was needed. And hence an assertion like "the above—expressing as it does an absolute difference between them— "cannot be justified.

"Again, the *Mahābhāshya* has cited the words '*gauh*,' '*gāvah*,' &c., "as being *those met with in ordinary usage*; but this is not quite right; be- "cause all these words are found in the Veda also; and have been borrow- "ed from the Veda itself. It is only such words as are spoken of in the "*sūtras* as being used in '*ordinary usage only*,' that should have been cited "(as the examples of *words in ordinary usage*). In the same manner, as "examples of '*Vedic words*,' the *Mahābhāshya* has cited—'*Çanno dēvīrabhish-* "*tayē &c. &c.*;' but this too is not correct; because the words contained in "these—'*Çam* &c.'—are also met with in ordinary usage; and the parti- "cular order in which they occur in the particular sentence cannot justify "us in speaking of them as exclusively '*Vedic*.' Nor does Grammar treat "of sentences. And hence it is only such purely Vedic forms as '*grbh-* "*ṇāmi*,' '*datvāyātha*' and the like, that should have been cited here; and "not '*Canno dēvī &c.*' But such purely Vedic forms could not be com- "patible with another declaration of the *Mahābhāshya*—that '*the meanings* "*of words are known from ordinary usage*' (because the purely Vedic forms "can never have their meanings ascertained by ordinary usage).

"And on the other hand, if Grammar treated of only such words "as are met with in ordinary usage, it could refer to only such words as "'*gāvī*' and the like; as it is only these that are exclusively 'worldly,' "never being met with in the Veda. And as for the words '*gauh*' and "the like, they can certainly be said to have been borrowed, in ordinary "usage, from the Veda itself. As says Manu: 'Each of the various "works on *Smṛti* &c., were composed out of the Veda itself.' And as a "matter of fact, even nowadays we find that persons learned in the "Vedas, make use of whole sentences from the Veda, even in giving ex- "pression to thoughts relating to every-day life; and in that case, it is by "no means impossible for single words to have been borrowed from the "Veda.

"Then again, the words contained exclusively in the Veda, having their "forms indelibly fixed by the well-regulated traditional system of the "getting up of each individual word therein contained, do not stand in "need of any rules or definitions (for the pointing out of the correct "forms of words), specially as for these there can be no better, or more "authoritative, means of comprehending than the Teacher himself. "And in fact Pānini himself has declared the rules and definitions to be "dependent upon the Veda, which clearly shows that these rules can have "very little use, with reference to the purely Vedic forms of words. "Because the laying down of any rules with regard to Vedic words would "be as useless as the laying down of rules for agriculture &c., which are "matters of ordinary every-day experience.

"The *Mahābhāshya* has pointed out various uses of the Science of "Grammar, chief among which are (1) *Rakshā*, (2) *Ūha*, (3) *Āgama*, (4) "*Laghu*, and (5) *Āsandēha*; but none of these is tenable; because all these "are accomplished by means other than Grammar, which is found to be "of very slight, if any, use in them.

"(1) As for '*Rakshā*' or the *preserving* of the Veda, the greatest "means of this protection consists in the relationship of the Teacher and the "pupil; because it is a well-known fact that the form and order of the "vedic sentences which have got nothing to do with grammar, have been "kept intact only on account of the fact of their being continually studied; "and the slightest disarrangement in the *order* has been said to be a very "serious offence; (which is not pointed out by Grammar, according to which "any difference in the order of the sentence is not a matter of any conse- "quence). And with regard to this, it has been said—'That by means "of which the object in question is *fully* comprehended is accepted as its "*lakshaṇa* or definition; and that which leaves off even the hundredth "part of the object, can be accepted to be of very little use in the matter.' "That is to say, the traditional system of teaching the Veda is found to "have ever been the means of keeping intact, *everything* in connection "with it; while Grammar deals with the single factor of *words*, and leaves "off all the more important ones, of the sentence, its order &c.; and as "such Grammar cannot be held to be of much use, in matters relating to "the Veda, specially in the *preserving* (*Rakshā*) of it.

"We also find that even in what is known as the *Sāma Vēda*, there are "certain rules and definitions; and it is these that are proper and useful, "helping the accomplishment of all things (in connection with the *Sāma*); "while, on the other hand, the Grammar has got very little use with re- "gard to what should be done. That is to say, in the *Aucchikya* section "of the *Sāmavidhāna*, we find all the parts of the *Sāma* defined in accor- "dance with a definite order; and this helps us to all the information that "we want with regard to the form of the *Sāma*; and these definitions "serve the further purpose of dividing the *Sāma* into its five parts of the "*Prastāva* &c., specially at the time that we are passing from one verse to "another. While as regards the Grammar, as its sole use lies in the defi- "ning of certain forms of *words* only, it can have but very little use in the "keeping of the Vedas, which are collections of various combinations "of words and sentences, and which can never have their words newly "created or formed. For a person who could keep up the words and sen- "tences, and the various combinations of these, as contained in the Veda, "by the help of the rules &c., detailed in the Veda itself,—he could cer- "tainly successfully keep up, by the same means, the idea of the roots and "affixes &c., (and for this small matter of roots &c., there can be no use "of a different branch of study in the shape of Grammar).

"And again, if the persons learned in the Veda would believe in the "fact of the Veda being kept up by means of the Grammar, whenever "they would have any doubts on any point relating to the Veda, they "would proceed to the Grammarian to have them removed. But (as a "matter of fact the means of keeping up the Veda being contained in the "Veda itself, why should the Vaidika seek the help of the Grammarian; "because) when a person has a vessel full of water hanging by his own "side, wherefore should he seek after other sources of water for washing "his hands? And even in ordinary life we find that when a man wants "to know something, he betakes himself to persons that are recognised to "be authorities on the subject in question. For instance, the *Āyurvēda* be- "ing the science most needed in regard to medication, it is from the "doctors of that science that people learn all about the nature and the "medicines of diseases.

"In the same manner, whenever in the mind of the Vedic student "there arise doubts or misconceptions with regard to the words and sen- "tences of the Veda, the only persons that afford any help in clearing "away the difficulties, are the more advanced among his own fellow- "students of the Veda, and not the grammarians. Hence, as a matter of "fact, we find that the whole of the Veda is kept up by means of these "students themselves; and even when there are actual mistakes in the "accents and the letters, the Vaidika student never condescends to seek "the help of the teachers of other sciences (which they consider to be far "beneath their own science of the Veda). And hence, the teachers of the "Veda, who are exceptionally devoted to the good of their disciples and "always anxious to help them in their difficulties, are the only persons "that help in keeping up the Veda; and hence it is this traditional system "of teaching alone that can be admitted to be the means of the Veda being "kept intact.

"And thus we find that the Science of Grammar cannot be said to be "studied for the purpose of *preserving* the Veda.

"And as for ordinary parlance too, all that is necessary, in the way "of talking and writing—even of poetical works and the rest—is actually "found to be accomplished, even without any Grammar, by the help of the "languages themselves.

"Even though found to serve no useful purpose in ordinary talk-" ing &c., the Science of Grammar may be held to have its use in the composi-" tion of Sanskrit poetry, exactly as the rules and regulations contained in" the several Prākṛta Grammar &c., have their use in that of Prākṛta" poetry and drama &c.,—yet (we could explain the *sūtra* as that) the" Science of Grammar not affording the rules and regulations with re-" regard to the composition of poetry, and such compositions being capable" of being accomplished by means of the mere languages themselves, the" said grammar could not rightly be accepted as laying down any proper" rules for the usage of words. Even in the matter of the ornaments of" Poetry, grammar is not found to be of much use; on the contrary, it is" only on account of the restrictions of grammar that authors are often" obliged to use distinctly unmelodious and unrythmical words and ex-" pressions.

"Then again, the mere fact of a certain word being grammatically" correct, cannot justify us to use it, if it happens to be one that is not ac-" cepted in ordinary usage; and as for the words that are already estab-" lished in ordinary usage, any rules or definitions would be absolutely use-" less.

"And thus we find that even in ordinary parlance, Grammar cannot" serve the purpose of keeping up any words or expressions &c.

"(2) As for *Ūha* (Conjecture or supplying of ellipses), the Science of" Grammar can serve no useful purpose in this conjecture or supplying of" words; because this purpose is distinctly found to be served by other" means, exactly like the differentiation of that which can be thus supplied" from that which cannot (which differentiation is done by the science of" *Mīmānsā* itself).

"For instance, the Mantras that are employed in the Primary sacri-" fice,—on such grounds as (1) the fact of their having a direct bearing" upon it, (2) that of their serving a certain visible purpose with regard" to it, (3) that of their forming an integral part of the sacrifice itself,—" in these five cases, there can be no conjectural modifications made in the" Mantras, when they come to be employed at the corresponding subsidiary" sacrifices. While in cases other than those thus specified, the Mantras" undergo conjectural modifications, according to the special purposes that" present themselves.

"And when one can obtain all these informations from other sources," independently of the Science of Grammar, how could he fail to get at the" proper words to give expression to these? At all times, the Veda is the" only Model or Receptacle (of words and expressions); and as such," people could very easily get all the words that they want from the Veda" itself (and there would be no use of Grammar in this). And again, "when we find such words as '*gāvī*' and the like being actually used with "reference to certain definite objects, how could this well-established "usage be ever set aside?

"As regards the words signifying the names of deities, we have the "law laid down under *sūtra* X-iv-23, which shows that they are employed "in the sacrifices in the very form that is pointed out by the parts of the "same or other sentences, in accordance with the procedure laid down in "the original Injunction, without the slightest reference to any considera-"tions of the correctness or otherwise of one or the other of the various "synonyms of words. And on this point we have certain Sciences, like "the *Kalpasūtras* and the *Mīmānsā*, which serve to point out the use of "the said names in regard to *Dharma*.

"As for the words that signify the substances and their properties "&c., these have their complete forms pointed out by the objects lying near "the person concerned, and as such come to be used in connection with "the sacrifice; and hence there being no chance for the use of any words "not so pointed out, even though there may be certain words (denotative "of substances and properties) that are used with reference to an object "meant to supply the deficiencies in the Mantras concerned,—yet their "use cannot be regulated by the Science of Grammar, as this is not found "to have any bearing upon such usage. The use of Mantras in the Primary "sacrifice is in accordance with certain scriptural Injunctions, (contained "in the Veda), while in the subsidiaries, their use is regulated by the "exigencies of the circumstances and objects concerned; and this does not "necessarily consist of only such forms of words as are in keeping with "grammatical rules.

"As for the rules of Grammar itself, they cannot have any basis in the "Veda; and as they are the products of the human brain, they cannot have "an injunctive force; and as they are found to have their own authority "shaken by the additions and alterations, deletions and contradictions, "contained in the *sūtras* themselves,—to contain in themselves endless "discrepancies in the modifications of roots and affixes that are gratuitous-"ly laid down (in grammatical works),—and to depend upon such known "human agencies as those of Pānini and others,—they can never be ac-"cepted as scriptures bearing upon the eternal use of words during the "performances of the eternal sacrifices.

"Thus then, those persons who are experts in the knowledge of the "sacrifices and their accessories, having all their necessary conjectural "modifications accomplished by means of the usage of words in the Veda "and in ordinary parlance,—what would be the use of Grammar (in re-"gard to such Conjectures)?

"And it is with a view to this well-known incapability of the Science "of Grammar to accomplish any such conjectural modifications (in the "Mantras) that the Commentators (on the *Kalpasūtras*) have declared "as follows: 'The subsidiaries (*Purānātyā, &c.*), the names of relations "('*mother*,' &c.), the organs of sense (the Sun as the *Eye*)—these do not "undergo any conjectural modifications; as we find in the case of the "*Adhrigu Mantra* (*Dēvyāh çamitārah, &c.*)' (this shows certain cases where "such modifications are possible, and certainly these cannot in any way be "affected by the rules of Grammar).

(3) "The third use of Grammar that the *Māhābhāshya* speaks of is "*Āgama* or Scripture; but in that case, wherefore has not the study of the "Veda been described as the result of sacrifices? That is to say, the scrip-"ture is known to be the origin of all that has to be done in the way of "sacrifices, and not as their purpose (and hence to assert the scripture to "be the purpose served by the rules of Grammar would be as reasonable "as to declare the study of the Veda to be the result of the sacrifices laid "down in it).

"If it be urged that what the *Mahābhāshya* means is that the use of "Grammar is that which is pointed out as such, in the scriptures;—even "this could not hold water; because we do not find any such use mentioned "in the scriptures; and also because the text that is brought forward in "support of the study of Grammar distinctly mentions the fact of such "study not serving any purpose. That is to say, the Vedic text in ques-"tion is—'the Veda with all its six subsidiary sciences is to be studied "without a view to any result'; and this distinctly shows that the study "of grammar has no use. As for scriptures, we do not admit of any such, "apart from the Vedic texts themselves; and certainly, how could the *eternal* "Veda contain any injunctions with regard to the study of the rules of "grammar, which have had a beginning in time?

"Thus then, we see that the only Injunction that we actually have in "the Çatapatha Brāhmaṇa is that 'the Veda should be studied,' which "lays down the study of the Veda alone; and this is the only Injunction "that could be found in the Veda; as this is the only one that refers to an "eternal subject of study. And as for the Injunction of the study of gram-"mar or any other of the subsidiary sciences, we do not find any such in "any branch of the Veda. And again that (grammar) which consists of "things (rules) that have had a beginning in time, cannot be said to have "the character of the Veda, or to have a self-sufficient authority; as both "these facts are dependent upon *eternality*.

"And as a matter of fact, Grammar has got no claims to be count-"ed among the 'subsidiary sciences' of the Veda; because it does not serve any "necessary purpose with regard to the Veda; nor does it form an integral "part of it. That is to say, none of the six means of interpretation—

" Direct Assertion, Indirect Implication, Context, Syntactical Connection " Position or Name—points to Grammar as serving any useful purpose " with regard to the Veda; and as for being an integral part of the Veda " how could that which has had a beginning in time form part of that which " is eternal?

" For these reasons, we must explain the expression 'the Veda with " its six subsidiary sciences' as referring to its constituent parts, in the " following manner: The 'six subsidiaries' referred to must be taken to " be the six means of interpretation—Direct Assertion &c.; as it is only " when interpreted through these that the Veda becomes capable of rightly " pointing out *Dharma*.

" An objection is here raised: 'If the subsidiaries referred be taken " as those contained in the Veda itself (*i.e.*, Direct Assertion, &c.), and not " as anything outside it (as Grammar, Nirukta, &c.), then in that case the " qualification *with the six subsidiaries* would be absolutely meaningless. " Specially as we can have a qualification, only when such a one is possi- " ble, and when a qualification is actually needed for the purpose of set- " ting aside certain incongruities (or contradictions); and certainly as there " is no incongruity in the Veda with regard Direct Assertion &c., what " could be specified by a qualification of these subsidiaries? [That is to " say, Grammar not being invariably concomitant with the Veda, a " qualification is needed in order to make it an object of study together " with the Veda; while Direct Assertion, &c., are always contained in the " Veda; and hence any qualification of these would be absolutely mean- " ingless].'

" *Reply*: Our firm conviction is that one who studies the Veda, " with a full knowledge of these—Direct Assertion, &c.,—and a due differ- " entiation of these, by means of the causes, forms and results (of actions),— " he alone fulfils in full the conditions of the said Injunction (that one " should study the 'Veda with its six subsidiaries').

" Or, we might take the expression *should study* in the sense of *should* " *understand or know*; and in that case the said Injunction would mean " that *one should know the Veda as consisting of Direct Assertion, &c.* Or, we " could take the expression '*Vedodhyēyah*' as '*vedah dhēyah*' (and not as " '*vedah adhyēyah*'), the meaning of the Injunction being that one should " contemplate on or ponder over the Veda, which has all its meanings mani- " fested by means of Direct Assertion, &c.

" Thus we find that the said Injunction lays down the pondering over " the meaning of the Veda, in the way shown in the Mīmānsā *sūtras*; and " it can never be taken as laying down the study of Grammar.

" Then again, as a matter of fact, we have certain grammatical facts " in the Veda itself; and the said Injunction of the study of the six "subsidiaries may be taken as referring to the Grammar that is contained "in the Veda. As for instance, the Veda points out the reason why the "curd is called 'dadhi,' and so forth; and in this way we have in the Vedic "Arthavadās, many grammatical and etymological explanations of words. "And the said Injunction may be taken as laying down the study of the "Injunctive portions of the Veda, together with the Arthavādas that contain such explanations.

"Or again, there are certain *Prātiçākhyas* in relation to each branch "of the Veda, which are studied with as much regard as the Veda itself; "and as these are actually found to be of use in matters relating to the "Veda, they can certainly be taken as the 'Subsidiaries' of the Veda. "That is to say, those that are actually found to have a certain use (or "operation) in regard to the Veda, cannot but be accepted, by that fact "alone, as its subsidiaries; but this cannot be said with regard to the works "of Pānini and the rest, which only here and there treat of Vedic sentences; and that too, only with a view to cloak it in Vedic authority.

"If it be urged that the grammars of Panini and others could be accepted "as 'scriptures' relating to Actions, just like the *Prātiçakhyas*,—we cannot "but deny it; because the grammars of Panini and the rest do not at all "treat of the form of the Veda itself; that is to say, all that these grammars do is to lay down certain purified forms of words, without any "reference to the form of the Veda. While the *Prātiçākhyas* deal with "accent, conjunction of letters, hiatus, explanations, precedence and sequence, &c., all of which are directly connected with the study of the text "of the Veda itself. And as such this fact distinctly points to the fact of "the *Prātiçākhyas*, and not the grammars of Pānini, &c., being the real "'subsidiary' of the Veda.

"Nor again is the declaration of *Scripture* (as being the purpose of "the grammars) quite compatible with what has been asserted before in "the *Mahābhāshya*. Because the *Scripture* that is here meant is the mere "getting up of the verbal text; while the *Mahābhāshya* has, on a former "occasion, asserted the *teaching of words* to be the purpose of the Scripture "(and as no such teaching can be possible without a knowledge of the "meaning of the Veda, the mere getting up of the verbal text cannot be "accepted to be of any use in such teaching).

"And further, the said Injunction distincly lays down the study of the "Veda with its six subsidiaries, which does not bring any worldly results "to the students; and hence the assertion of the *Mahābhāshya* that 'the "knowledge of Grammar constitutes a Dharma,' or that of the *Vārtika* that "'the using of words in accordance with grammatical rules brings prosperity,' cannot but be rejected as being directly contradictory to the aforesaid Vedic Injunction.

(4) "Another use of Grammar that the *Mahābhāshya* speaks of is that "it tends to simplify (make '*laghu*') the process of differentiating the correct "from the incorrect forms of words. But this is only proper, being the only "resource left to him, when all other uses have been shown to be untenable; "and this is true enough!

"Or, it may be that the 'simplification' spoken of really means 'com- "plication,' by the process of 'contrary expression' (*i.e.*, ironical method), "exactly as the word 'coward' is applied to a really brave man! "That is to say, all that grammatical works are found to do is to point "out the forms of words that already exist and are known in the ordinary "world, after having gone through endless complicated processes, such as "the laying down of most difficult verbal root forms, and queer *unādi* and "other affixes, mixed up with an endless number of extraordinary nomen- "clatures and postulates, dealing with gratuitous arguments and counter- "arguments. And yet with all this, there are only a few students who "can rightly apply these elaborate processes to words other than those "that are actually cited as examples. And thus we find that the process "employed is terribly complicated; and then to speak of it as 'simplify- "ing' cannot but be taken as mere empty praise (ironical).

"Some people have declared that the real character of words cannot "be known without Grammar. But it would have been as reasonable for "them to say the same thing with regard to the perception of Colour, "Taste, Odour and Touch! Certainly, in regard to matters perceptible by "the senses, how could any person, knowing the real nature of the scriptures "and ordinary experience, declare them to be capable of being compre- "hended by means of the scriptures? Hence we must read the said declara- "tion thus—'the real nature of words is not known without the sense "of audition'; because on this point there is no difference of opinion; as "we actually find that there is no perception of words by the deaf, &c.

(5) "The fifth use of Grammar that the *Mahābhāshya* has spoken of is "that it helps to remove all doubts with regard to the meanings of Vedic "passages ('*Asandēha.*') But this also is not correct; because grammar does "not in any way help us to ascertain the meanings of words or sentences. "For as a matter of fact, we find that many doubts with regard to the "meanings of words are set aside by the observation of the usage of ex- "perienced and learned people; and the few that are still left are cleared "by the help of commentaries, etymological explanations, *Kalpasūtras*, and "the persons versed in matters relating to the Veda; because all these "latter deal with the meanings (of words and sentences). On the other "hand, Grammar takes no notice of the meanings of words, dealing with "merely verbal forms; and as such it cannot in any way help us in ascer- "taining the meanings of Vedic passages.

"For instance, in the case of a certain noun, grammar points it out "as being made up of certain roots and affixes, and as such connected with "a certain action (denoted by the verbal root), while, as a matter of fact, "we find that when the noun is actually used, there is not the slightest "idea of the said action: *e.g.*, the word '*Go*' is explained as made up of "the root *gam* (*to go*) and the affix *dō*; and these would make the word "'*gō*' applicable to all that *moves* (or goes). But as a matter of fact we "find the word used with reference to a particular *class* (of animals); "and certainly the explanation of a word must be in keeping with "its generally recognised signification (and not an arbitrary one). In "the same manner, we have the words, '*kuçala*' and '*udāra*' which, as "grammatically explained, would mean, *the chopper of grass*, and *one whose* "*wife is good* (respectively); but as a matter of fact we do not find these "words used in the sense fastened to them by the arbitrary grammatical "rule. And so also, though the words '*açvakarna*' and '*ajakarana*' are "grammatically explained as compounds (thereby being made to mean "the *ear of the horse* and the *ear of the goat* respectively),—yet in ordin-"ary usage, they are used in the sense of certain *herbs*, which have no con-"nection with the signification of the several constituent parts of "the words; exactly like the word '*vṛksha*' which grammatically "would mean *that which is being cut*, while ordinarily, it is used in the "sense of the *tree*. So too in the case of the word '*Rājanya*,' though "grammatically it is made up of the word '*Rāja*' with a patronymic affix "(and thereby it would mean the *king's son*), yet the generally recognis-"ed meaning is entirely different from the said etymological one.

"Then again, we find certain grammatical rules to be directly against "the Veda itself; and certainly, even if we accept these, they cannot be "accepted as subsidiary to the Veda. For instance, grammar points out "the word '*kālēya*' to be made up of '*kali*' and '*dhak*,' and the word "'*Vāmadēvya*' of '*Vāmadēva*' and '*dya*'; and thus according to this, these "names as applied to the *Sāmas*, would mean the *Sāmas seen by Kali* and "*Vāmadēva* respectively, whereas in the Veda we find these names of the "Sāma explained differently: 'because plenty of riches flow forth from "it, the Sāma came to be known as *Vāmadēvya*' and 'because the Sāma "*removed* all impediments, therefore it came to be known as *Kālēya*.' "And these Vedic explanations cannot but set aside the interpretation "supplied by grammar. In the same manner, we find in the *Kalpasūtra*, "such expressions as '*Kṛshnaçam vāsah*, '*Kṛshnavalakshē ajinē*, used in the "sense of *the cloth or skin that has black threads*; and such meanings can never "be got at even by the help of a hundred grammars; all these being capable "of being learnt only from an uninterrupted tradition of the teachers and "students of the Veda; and so also are words like '*yūpa*' and the rest, "which are explained in accordance with the sequence and precedence "of Vedic passages.

"And as in the case of these words we actually find their meanings "duly ascertained, independently of grammar, we conclude that even in "the case of such words as '*sthūlapṛshatī*' and the like (where the signi-"fication of the word depends upon the nature of the compound, which "can be learnt only by means of the *accent* as regulated by grammatical "rules), we can safely have recourse to the commentators themselves (for "the ascertaining of the actual meaning of the said words). And as such "there can be no use of Grammar on this point.

"Then again, with regard to the true meanings of sentences, thousands "of doubts arise in our minds; and Grammar is not found to be able to "express even a single phase of the question (to say nothing of being "able to set aside the doubt completely and point out the true conclusion).

"If the use of Grammar lay in the removal of all doubts with regard "to the meaning of Vedic passages, then it would certainly have helped "to slove questions like the following: (1) Are the Arthavāda passages "capable of expressing independent meanings of their own, or are they "only supplementary to the Injunctive passages? (2) Is the mention of "the fact of the *Udumbara* wood being 'power' to be taken as pointing out "a result that would follow if the sacrificial post were made of that wood, "or it only serves to eulogise the particular wood? (3) Whether a certain "passage mentioning a reason is to be taken as an Injunction or an Artha-"vada? (4) Whether the use of a certain *Mantra* brings about a seen or "an unseen result? (5) Whether it is only one or all the vessels that one "has got to wash? &c., &c. If it be urged that—'these questions being "treated of by the Mīmānsā are not taken up by grammar,'—then, "inasmuch as we find many such words as '*sthūlapṛshat*' and the like "having their meanings duly ascertained in the *Kalpasūtras*, with regard "to such words, it becomes all the more improbable for grammar to serve "any useful purpose.

"And again, whenever there are any doubts as to the meaning of the "grammatical rules themselves, the true meaning is ascertained through "the explanations contained in the commentaries; and certainly, there is "nothing to debar such explanatory commentaries appearing with refer-"ence to the doubtful words occurring in the Veda (and as such there "would be nothing left to be done by grammar). And inasmuch as "there is a postulate that explanatory commentaries serve the purpose "of bringing about specific ideas,—just as the fact of there being certain "doubts with regard to a certain grammatical rule does not deprive it of "its character of a 'rule'; so too the mere fact of there being doubts "with regard to a Vedic passage cannot deprive it of its *Vedic* character.

" And until one knows the actual meanings of certain words, he can never " explain any Vedic passage by the mere help of Grammar; and as such " this latter cannot be said to be the means of ascertaining the meaning " of the passage. And the explanatory commentaries to the Veda " being as eternally continuous as the Veda itself, such words as " '*sthūlapṛshat*' and the rest are found to be explained, without the help of " Grammar.

" [Nor can the accents as treated of in Grammar be said to help in " the ascertaining of the meanings of words]. No words in ordinary " usage being found to be accentuated, we conclude that accents are some- " thing entirely beyond the pale of usage; and as such they cannot be uti- " lised in ascertaining the meanings of Vedic passages. As a matter of fact " the ascertaining of the real meanings of words is always accomplished " by means of the usage of experienced people. And as we meet with no " differentiation of accents,—as that *the last word of the compound is acute* " and so forth,--in the usages of these people, any specialities of accents " can never be accepted to have an effect upon the significations of " words. And if the cognition of the meanings of sentences depended upon " the specialities of accents, there would be no cognition of the meanings " of those Vedic passages, whose accentuation has not been ascertained. " But as a matter of fact, as we find the meanings of such passages duly " ascertained by means of Context, &c., (independently of the Accents), " the denotativeness of those meanings cannot be said to belong to the Ac- " cents. And hence we conclude that the accentuation of the Vedic texts " can have only an unseen (transcendental) result; specially as it is only " found in connection with the reciting of Mantras at the sacrifices in- " cluded under the ordinary *Brahmayajna* (Daily sacrifices or Duties of the " Brāhmaṇa).

" And hence even the grammatical rules that refer to Accents may be " said to serve some sort of a purpose with regard to such transcendental " matters; but never with regard to the words in ordinary usage; because " Accentuation is found to have absolutely no use in ordinary parlance. " And as a matter of fact, the Accentuation, as laid down in Grammar, is " never found to help us in ascertaining the real meanings (of words or " sentences); specially because what we find in grammatical works, " is only a teaching of the verbal forms of words, and not of their " meanings.

" Thus then, we conclude that Grammar cannot be said to be necessa- " rily studied as serving the purpose of removing doubts with regard " to the meanings of Vedic passages; specially as it is not found to treat " of such Accentuation or uses of words, &c., as could be of any use in the " ascertaining of the meaning (of words or sentences).

"After having laid special stress upon the five aforesaid uses of "Grammar, the *Mahābhāshya* proceeds to enumerate 'many other uses' of "it; but of these some are such as cannot be spoken of as 'uses'; a few "are such as have the mere semblance of a 'use'; while some are entirely "groundless. And again when the usefulness of the science has not been "established by means of the five, that were spoken of as the '*primary* "uses,' that it will be proved by that of the secondary uses, is a hope too "sanguine to be realised; and the attempt has all the resemblance of a "drowning man catching at a straw.

(1) "The *Mahābhāshya* quotes the Vedic text—'The Asuras ut-"tered the (incorrect words) *helayah*, and hence they were defeated ... "... the utterance of an incorrect word is behaving like a *Mleccha*'; and "from this concludes that the use of Grammar lies in protecting us from "being a Mleccha. But what the real meaning of the word 'Mleccha' "is we have explained above (as referring to the distorting of the textual "readings of the Veda).

(2) "The second use spoken of by the *Mahābhāshya* is that it protects "us from the misfortunes that befall those uttering incorrect words, as "evinced by the text—'a word pronounced incorrectly, either as to its "accents or letters, becomes a thunderbolt killing the sacrificer, as for in-"stance the word *indraçatru* (which was addressed to Vṛtra, as the *killer* "*of Indra*, a Genitive Tatpurusha, but as the accent that was used was that of "the Bahuvrīhi compound, Vṛtra became *one whose killer was Indra*).' But "here the *Mahābhāshya* has substituted in this text the word 'word' for "'Mantra,' which is the reading known to many men; and this substitution "of a different reading only shows an undue degree of partiality to his own "theories. And as for the misfortunes of sinfulness befalling the sacri-"ficer who employs incorrect *Mantras*, it is a fact that no one denies; speci-"ally as we have many texts,—f.i. 'the sentence that is killed (spoilt) by "the priest, kills the sacrificer himself'—that clearly point to the fact of "the discrepancies in the use of *Mantras* by the Priests bringing about evil "results to the sacrificer. And it is because the text refers to the mistakes "of *Mantra* that it has cited the use of a *Mantra*—'*indraçatro vardhasva*' "—as an example.

(3) "The *Mahābhsāhya* cites a passage from the *Nirukta*:—'That "which is pronounced simply verbally, without a knowledge of its meaning, "is not effective, being like dry fuel being placed where there is no fire to "burn it;' and from this it concludes that the study of Grammar is neces-"sary, inasmuch as it helps us to know the meaning of *Mantras*, thereby "saving us from the predicament spoken of. But the text here quoted "we have explained in course of the explanation of the word *atha* in *sūtra* "I—i—1, as authorising a postponement of the Final Bath, after the mere

"getting up of the text of the Veda; and we have there shown that if we did "not postpone the Bath, we would be making the Veda, which has a pur- "pose to serve, absolutely without a use; as the purpose that the Veda is "found to serve is the pointing out of *Duty* (and this could not be pointed "out to the person that finishes his study with the mere getting up of the "text and pays no attention to the meaning); and hence the meaning of "the text quoted is that 'the Veda that is not explained, not expressing "any meaning, becomes totally ineffective'; and this is quite true; "though in this, there can be no use for Grammar; because it is a well-"recognised fact that the Science of Grammar has no bearing upon any "thing relating to *Action* (or sacrifices). Nor can it be asserted that gram-"mar is a scripture relating to *words*; because we have shown above that "there is no basis in the Veda for the rules of grammar that treat of "words; and as such, these rules cannot be accepted as rightly regulating "the use of words either. Thus then, inasmuch as the meaning of the "*Mantras* and the *Brahmaṇas* that one has studied can be ascertained only "by the help of the *Kalpasūtras*, the *Niruktas* and the *Mīmānsā*, the use "pointed out by the *Mahābhāshya* should be attributed to these, and not "to Grammar (which is not found to afford any help in the ascertaining of "the meanings of any passages of the Veda).

(4) "The next passage that is quoted by the *Mahābhāshya* is—'an expert "in the knowledge of the relations of sentences, who makes use of the "correct forms of words, obtains victory in the next world; while by the use "of incorrect words he becomes tainted (with sin)'; and from this it con-"cludes that the use of Grammar lies in this leading to victory in the "next world (as it is by the help of Grammar alone that we can differ-"entiate the correct from the incorrect forms of words). But this passage "also refers to the fact of the use of the correct forms of *Mantras* "and *Brāhmaṇas* bringing about excellent results; exactly as the use of "the incorrect forms of these—*i.e.*, not as they appear in the Veda—"taints the person with sin; and as such, we take the passage to be "supplementary to another Vedic text—'If the sacrifice fails in regard "to the verses recited, &c, &c.'—, which speaks of similar results follow-"ing from the distorting of the reading of the Veda, during its *reading*, "teaching, sacrificing, either directly or indirectly. Hence we take the "expression—'one who is expert in the knowledge of the relations of "words'—to mean the person who is fully cognisant with all relationships "of words as established in the ordinary usages of the word; and as such, "with reference to the *Brāhmaṇas*, the expression would mean one who "has ascertained the true forms of sentences, by means of a proper "differentiation of the Subject from the Predicate, the Primary from the "Secondary, and so forth; while with reference to the *Mantras*, we take it

"to mean the person who is fully acquainted with the real character of "the *Mantras*, differentiating the enjoined from the unenjoined, as also "one that expresses its own meaning from that which expresses that of "another, and so forth? For these reasons we cannot take the expression "to mean the *Grammarian*; because Grammar is found to have no bearing upon the aforesaid facts (in connection with *Mantras* and *Brāhmanas*).

(5) "The fifth text quoted by the *Mahābhāshya* is—'when the person "saluting another is ignorant of the fact of the last vowel of a name being "acute, the person saluted should response as to a woman'; and from this "it concludes that if we wish to avoid the treatment accorded to women, "we should learn Grammar, which is the only means of learning the "acuteness, &c., of vowels. But the fact of a vowel being acute is well-"known through ordinary usage; and as such the condition laid down by "Manu in the passage quoted being fulfilled by ordinary usage itself, any "science dealing with these conditions of acuteness, &c., cannot be admitted to the position of a scripture relating to the performance of actions. "Nor does the above passage serve to point out either the fact of the "differentiation of the correct from the incorrect forms of words being "necessarily due to a knowledge of the roots and affixes as dealt with in "grammatical works; or to that of such knowledge being of any use in "the said differentiation.

(6) "The sixth passage cited is the Injunction—'The Prayājas are to "be performed with due attention to the grammatical terminations'—"which is taken as laying down the necessity of learning Grammar (which "is the only means of knowing the terminations.) But in the first place "a knowledge of the terminations here spoken of is very easily acquired "by means of the direct teachings of persons versed in sacrifices; secondly, "all the seven terminations are found to be enumerated in the *Shaḍaha* "section of the *Chāndogya-Brāhmaṇa;* and lastly, we find all these terminations duly pointed out in the Mantras themselves—as in 'Agni (nominative) killed the Vṛttras,' 'we address Agni (in the accusative) the "killer of Vṛttra,' and 'the fire is lighted by the fire (Instrumental),' and "so forth; and all this shows that even without the grammatical works, "we can have a due knowledge of the said terminations, by merely paying "due attention to the words having the terminations (as they are met with "in ordinary usage); and thus thereby the said *Prayāja* being duly performed, Grammar cannot be held to be a scripture bearing upon its due "performance.

(7) "Another passage quoted is—'one who knows the science of "speech, as consisting of words, accents and letters, he alone is capable of "rightly performing the duties of a sacrificial priest'; and this is taken to

" point out the necessity of grammatical study. But as a matter of fact, " this passage only speaks of the person *who has duly learnt the Veda*.

(8) " The eighth passage quoted is—' there are four kinds of " words; and it is only those Brāhmanas that know them that are said to " be *learned*; of these three are not pronounced by ordinary people, who " speak out the fourth only'; and the 'four kinds' are explained by the " *Mahābhāshya* as referring to Nouns, Verbs, Prefixes and Nipātas; and " as a knowledge of these cannot be acquired except by the help of Gram- " mar, the passage is taken to lay down the necessity of grammatical " study. But in dealing with the 'four kinds of words' as mentioned in " this passage, the Niruktas have,—in accordance with their own maxim " that 'all words are to be explained in accordance with the similarities " of the letters therein contained,'—spoken of many quartets, such as— " (*a*) the *Praṇava* together with the three *Vyāhṛtis*, (*b*) the four Vedas, " (*c*) the four kinds of speech, *Parā*, *Pçyantī*, *Madhyamā* and *Vaikharī*; " and certainly in regard to none of these can Grammar serve any useful " purpose. Even if the quartet referred to be taken as that consisting of " Nouns, Verbs, Prefixes, and Nipātas, even then, inasmuch as all these are " learnt from ordinary usage itself, a knowledge of these could not stand " in need of grammatical study. But in reality, this cannot be taken as " the quartet referred to; as in that case, the sentence—' it is the fourth kind " alone that men make use of'—would be absolutely inexplicable, as men " are actually found to make use of all the four kinds (Nouns, &c.). There- " fore the *Mantra* quoted cannot but have the following meaning, which " is the only one that is in keeping with the context (of the Mantra): " The expression '*Vākparimitāpadāni*=the four means of right notion,— " Sense-Perception, Inference, Analogy and Apparent Inconsistency,—by " which alone is speech (*Vāk*) cognised (*padyatē bodhyatē*); thus then " people *do not actually utter those three kinds of speech*, or sentence which " are cognisable by means of the last three of the said means of right " notion,—*viz*: (*a*) Inference, (*b*) Analogy, and (*c*) Apparent Inconsistency,— " which originate respectively, (*a*) in the mention of the first word of the " sentence in an Injunction (as, for instance, we have the Injunction " '*Ishētvēti* çākhām chinatti,' where the mention of the first two words " of the Mantra leads us to infer the whole of the Mantra, which does not " stand in need of being wholly quoted in the Injunction), (*b*) in the " similarity of the Subsidiaries to the Primary sacrifice (as for instance " we have the Injunction '*prakṛtivadvikṛtih kartavyā*' which, through " Analogy, leads us to the conclusion that the Mantras used at the Subsi- " diaries are the same that are used at the Primary,—the Analogy thus " obviating the necessity of quoting all the Mantras in connection " with the Injunction of the subsidiaries), (*c*) and in the apparent

"explicability of a perceptible fact (as in the case of the *Viçvajit* sacrifice, "the fact of its actually being performed leads us to conclude that it "brings about a real result in the shape of Heaven; and as such, the "Mantras of the *Jyotishtoma* are employed at its performance); while that "part of the speech, which is cognisable by means of direct (Auditory) "Sense-perception alone, and not by the aforesaid three means of right "notion, is the only one that *men*—students of the Veda—*pronounce*—*i.e.*, "speak out directly or lay down completely. Out of the six means of "right notion, generally accepted, two have been totally removed from "doing anything with regard to the cognition of speech; one of these is "Negation, which refers only to non-existing objects; and as such cannot "help in the cognition of speech; another is Verbal Testimony; and this "in itself consists of speech only; and as such being a receptacle of that "(speech) *which has to be cognised*, it could not be accepted as the recep-"tacle of *that which brings about the cognition*. Or, it may be that, that "which is amenable to Verbal Testimony is that which is directly ex-"pressed in words; and as such this being included in Auditory Sense-"perception, is not mentioned separately.

(9) "Another passage quoted is—'The bull having four horns, three "feet, two heads, &c.......is the great God that makes a sound, and enters "all mortal beings'; and the 'bull' here spoken of is interpreted by the "*Mahābhāshya* as Grammar itself, the 'four feet' being taken as the "above mentioned four kinds of words (Nouns, &c.), the 'three feet' as "the three senses, the 'two heads' as the two shapes of words, the radical "and the modified, and so on; and in order that we may be like this great "God, it is necessary, says the *Mahābhāshya*, that we should study Gram-"mar. But this Mantra is spoken of with reference to the butter used "by the Priest at the *Vishuvat* sacrifice; and what its real meaning is we "have already explained in the *Adhikaraṇa* (of the 2nd *pāda* of this "Adhyāya) dealing with *Mantras* (under the *Sūtra* I—ii—46). And in "this, there can be no use of Grammar. The interpretation of 'four "horns' as the four kinds of words, &c., &c., has got no connection with "the performance of Actions; and as such these interpretations (of a "passage occurring in connection with the performance of certain sacri-"fices) can only be explained as put forth by the author of the *Mahā-"bhāshya*, with the sole purpose of showing off his cleverness acquired "from a long-continued course of grammatical study!

(10) "The *Mahābhashya* has cited the *Mantra*—'*Utatvah paçyan*, &c.' "which is taken as the praise of one knowing the science of words, and as "such, laying down the necessity of studying Grammar. But in reality "the passage is in praise of one who knows the true meanings of words, "as pointed out by ordinary usage, the Niruktas, the Kalpasūtras and the

"tenets of the Mīmānsā; and as such it cannot be taken as in any way "praising a study of Grammar.

(11) "There is yet another passage quoted which speaks of the "science of words having a purifying tendency 'like the sieve'; and this "the *Mahābhāshya* has taken to mean that it is the study of Grammar "that purifies all usage of words. But as a matter of fact the passage is "in praise of a due knowledge of the meaning of the Vedic text, purified "by a long course of uninterrupted study.

(12) "The passage—'If the Aginhotri happens to use an incorrect "word he should perform an expiatory rite'—has been taken by the "*Mahābhāshya* to signify the necessity of grammatical study. But the "real signification of this passage we have explained above.

(13) "In connection with the naming of a child, the *Kalpasūtras* lay "down that the name should begin with a certain kind of letter, and that "it should contain only two or four letters, and should be one made up "of a verbal, and never, a nominal affix, &c., &c.; and the *Mahābhāshya* "urges that these detailed instructions could never be followed unless one "studied and knew the rules, &c., laid down in grammatical works; as with-"out these, one could not know what a verbal affix was. But, as a matter "of fact, these expressions—'having a verbal affix' and the like,—could "not but have been borrowed by writers on Grammar from the vocabulary of "the day, which must have had a prior existence (and as such even now "we can very easily learn what they mean even without the help of a "grammar); as for the number of letters in a name, it is a fact of ordinary "perception accompanied by memory (and as such not dependent upon "any grammatical rules, &c.); as for the characters of the letters, &c., "these can be learnt from the explanations contained in the *Çikshās* and "the *Prātiçākhyas*. And we actually find people learned in the Vedas "very easily coming to a conclusion with regard to the naming of a "child. And hence we cannot admit Grammar to be a scripture govern-"ing the usage of words.

(14) "There is a *Mantra* addressed to Varuṇa, who is described as "having seven rivers, &c.; and the *Mahābhāshya* takes the *Mantra* as ad-"dressed to the science of grammar, explaining the 'seven' rivers as the "*seven case-terminations*, &c., and from this it argues that it is necessary "to study Grammar, for the purpose of learning what is meant by these "'terminations,' &c. But as a matter of fact all that grammar does is only "to attribute the name 'terminations' (*Vibhaktis*) to certain letters, &c.; "but even this name it may have only borrowed from ordinary usage; while "so far as the words made up of these terminations are concerned, they "are found by themselves both in the Veda and in ordinary parlance; and "there can be no necessity of learning grammar on this score. Then

"again, even if it be absolutely necessary to explain the words 'seven "rivers' figuratively, as meaning something other than actual rivers,— "then, too, there are many septenaries in connection with sacrifices, that "could be taken to be indicated by the said words; for instance, there are "seven persons, including the priests and the master of the sacrifices; "seven sentences pronounced by the Hotṛ priest; seven sentences "from the Sāma and its parts; and so forth. And all these being matters "dealt within the historical and sacrificial portions (of the Veda), there can "be no need of grammatical study on the score of these."

"You seem to hold that it is only the words grammatically purified "that are correct; and now it is for you to explain what it is that is puri- "fied, and in what manner. That is to say, if grammar be held to help "in the purification of words, it is not very easy to ascertain what it is that "is purified; and also whether the *purification* is in the shape of produc- "tion, or acquisition, or modification, or fructification into an *Apūrva*, or "the bringing about of a fresh potency.

"In the first place it is not possible for any individual of the class "'*Çabdatva*' or of the class '*Varṇatva*' to be the object purified; "because this would apply to all words and letters, and as such there "could be no restriction (of the correct or the incorrect). And if the "class '*Çabdatva*' were held to be the object purified, then any ordinary "sound (that of the beating of the drum for instance) would also come to "be spoken of as '*correct.*' And if the class '*Varṇatva*' were held to be that "object, then the letters contained in the words, '*gāvī*,' &c., being 'letters' "(as much as those in '*gauh*'), the case of these would be exactly similar "to that of the words '*gauh*' and the like.

"The same argument holds also respecting the *purification* as belonging "to the individual *letters*; and when the letter 'ga' has once been purified, "as occurring in the word '*gō*,' it being the same in the word '*gāvī*' also, this "latter word could not but be accepted as correct. And thus all indivi- "dual letters having been purified, no word could ever be rightly held "to be incorrect. And as for the purification applying to the collection "of letters, this cannot be possible, as no two letters being heard simulta- "neously, there can never be any 'conglomeration' of these.

"Those again, who hold all individual letters to be undergoing "momentary destruction, can never have any purification of letters; as "each letter being destroyed no sooner than produced, there would be "nothing left to be purified; and hence even though the letter be an "entity, it can have no existence at the time of the purification, it having "disappeared, even at the time that we may be thinking of purifying it. And "if it could be purified, no one would be able to perceive it in its purified "form; and hence this purification of the letter would be exactly like that "of the flour that may be said to be purified by being offered into the fire! "That is to say, in the case of the sentence, 'offers the flour,' the flour offered "into the fire having been burnt up by the fire, and as such becoming in-"capable of being seen or used again, if the Accusative ending in '*saktūn*' "be made the ground of accepting the view that the flour is *purified* by "the fire, then, in that case, every factor of the Injunction ('offers the "flour')—namely, the Flour, the Offering, the *Bhāvanā* and the Injunction "itself—would be absolutely meaningless; and for this very reason we "hold that there is no purification of the flour in the offering. Exactly "in the same manner, there would be a meaninglessness of all things "concerned, if we admitted of a purification of the momentarily disappear-"ing individual letters.

"And the declaration of 'uncertainty' in the Bhāshya,—as whether "the word be eternal or transient, the definition (of grammar) is equally "applicable—only shows, on the part of the author, that he has either "been purposely fighting shy of the above arguments, or simply trying to "hoodwink his disciples; and as such we cannot accept it. Specially as "it is only in regard to an object that is removed from us that there can "be any uncertainty; for who is there that has any uncertainty as to "whether fire is hot or cold?

"If however the word be held to be transient, then, the only puri-"fication (*saṅskāra*) that could belong to it would be *production;* and as "such it becomes all the more impossible for Grammar to be a scripture "dealing with the usage of words. That is to say, the grammarian, holding "all correct words to be produced by the rules of Grammar, himself rejects "all possibility of Grammar either having a basis in the eternal Veda, or "being a part of it (because that which is admitted to be transient can "never be a part of that which is eternal).

"If the Veda itself be said to have been composed by means of the "words *produced* by Grammar, then the Veda would also come to be as "unauthoritative as Grammar itself. And again, if the word be held to be "*produced* (and as such momentary), it would have no existence apart "from the moment of its production; and as such, there could be no "purification of it; nor could such a word be of any use.

"For these reasons, you cannot but give up the uncertain attitude that "you had taken up with regard to the eternality of a word; and hence, if "you hold the 'purification' to belong to the eternal word, then, (1) being "eternal, it could have no purification in the form of *modification*. "(2) And as for the purification in the shape of *Acquisition* (or perception), "this is found to be accomplished by means of the sense of audition, "without any action of Grammar. (Hence Gammar cannot be accepted "as the means of such purification). (3) As for a purification in the "shape of being made able to bring about a transcendental result, we "cannot admit of any such, in the absence of any Vedic Injunction on the "point; and specially as words being found to fulfil a perceptible end (that "of expressing certain meanings), they can have nothing to do with anything "beyond the senses; for instance, the corn that is meant to fulfil the "perceptible end of satisfying the hunger of a man can have no connection "with any transcendental result following from its 'washing' (which is ap-"plicable only to the corn used at sacrifices). Nor do we find the gramma-"tical rules to be laid down in connection with the performance of sacri-"fices; and as such they cannot be held to bring about the purification of "words, serving to accomplish a certain *Apūrva* (or unseen Potentiality or "Agency). Nor is it possible for us to have a grammatical Injunction, "similar to that of the *threshing* (of the corn); because how could an eter-"nal Injunction speak of a process (that of grammar) that is a pure pro-"duct of the human brain? And for the same reason, there cannot be any "Injunction of the grammatical processes, even apart from the perfor-"mance of sacrifices; and even if this were possible, such an Injunction "could not serve any purpose with regard to the performance of sacrifices.

"And again, if the word were to be purified for the sake of the sacri-"fice only,—like the *Sruva* and other sacrifical implements,—then any "such word could never serve the purpose of expressing or describing the "sacrifice itself (in any Injunction); as the purification would not affect "the ordinary usage of the word (and it is this usage alone that can "make the sacrifice comprehended as being laid down by a Vedic Injunction).

"And as there is a difference between the words as occurring in the "Veda and in ordinary parlance, no grammatical processes could ever affect "the sacrifice pointed out by the word (in the Veda).

"And further, the word having its existence in *Ākāça*, in what way "could it be 'purified'? For being eternal and incorporeal, it is "as incapable of purification as the all-pervading character of *Ākāça* "itself.

"Then, if grammar be held to serve the sole purpose of purifying the "letters of the alphabet, this would be accomplished by means of the four-"teen *Pratyāhāra-sūtras* (A–I–U–Ṇ, &c.) only (which lay down the alpha-"bets); and there would be no use of the rest of Pāṇini's *sūtras*, &c., &c.

"As for the conglomeration of words, these can have no existence by them-"selves (apart from the constituent letters); and as such, no 'purification' "can be said to belong to them; and as a matter of fact, we find that even "though a number of bricks are piled together in a kiln, so as to form a "single block, the action of fire in the baking affects each individual brick "separately (so too even if the purification be held to belong to the word as "a whole, it could only be accomplished through the purification of each of "the constituent letters).

"Nor is it possible for a word to be built up by means of the com- "ponent letters into a single composite mass; and as such, there can be no "purification of the word as such; this we have already shown before "(under *Tarkapāda* in the *Çlokavārtika*, in the section on 'words'). And "as for such theories as those of *Sphota*, the *class* '*Goçabdatva*,' and the "*class* '*gatva*,' &c., all these have been rejected by the explanation that "we have given above (under *Sūtra* I—i—5) of the words '*gauh*' and the "like.

"Nor is it possible for a collection of all the letters of the alphabet to "undergo any process of purification; because any such collection not hav- "ing any meaning, it cannot be used to any useful end. And if groups "of three of four letters in each individual word be held to be purified, "then it would only be the particular member that would be purified; and "this purfication would apply to the incorrect words as well as to the cor- "rect ones.

"The particular sequence of letters (*ga*, *ū*, &c.) may be held to be "the object of purification; but such a sequence residing only in the hear- "ing or the pronunciation of the word, cannot be accepted as a property "of the word itself (and as such the purification of the sequence could not "affect the word); and moreover, inasmuch as there is a certain sequence "in the words '*gāvī*,' &c., also (a purification of the sequence would be "applicable to these as well as to the Sanskrit words). And if you hold "the hearing and pronouncing of words to be the object of purification, "this cannot be; because it is impossible for an *action* (*pronouncing*, for "instance) to be accomplished by means of another action (purification), "as we shall show later on, under *Sūtra* III—i—19.

"Nor can the various *places* of utterance—the palate, &c.,—be held to "be purified by means of grammar; because these are found to be purified "by the rules and regulations laid down by the doctors of medicine!

"If again, the Mind, or the Man himself, be held to be the object of "purification, then it would be absolutely meaningless to speak of grammar as "the 'Science of Words.' Because a science is that which teaches some- "thing that is capable of being taught; and as words are incapable of be- "ing taught, any science of these would be absolutely useless.

"As for the *Sphota* of a word, it is absolutely impossible for it to "undergo any purification; because in the *Sphota*, there is a total absence "of the roots and affixes (that form the subject-matter of grammar).

"As for the *Sphota* of sentences, which some people hold to be devoid "of all component parts, a declaration of the purification of the nouns and "verbs as forming these sentences would be exactly like speaking of the "horns of a hare! If it be urged that we can speak of the purification of "the nouns, &c., as extracted out of the syntactical *Sphota*, then it could be "as reasonable to speak of the purification of the horn as extracted out of the "hare! If you hold the extraction of the part of the sentence to be accom-"plished through the similarity of the part of other things, then, why can-"not the extraction of the hare's horns be equally accomplished through the "similarity of the horns of the ass? As for similarity too, we have spoken "of a certain sort of similarity existing between the parts of the body of the "*gavaya* and that of the Cow; but in this case we actually perceived a "similarity between real parts; and do you employ the same arguments "to the present case, where the parts spoken of are only imaginary? "The fallacy of this we shall show in detail under the *Vākyādhikarana* "(in *Adhyāya* II). And hence the assumption of *extraction* too is by no "means admissible.

"Then again, if grammar were to explain words that have no real exis-"tence, but are only conjecturally extracted (from the syntactical *Sphota*), "then this very fact would make it as unauthoritative and untrustworthy "as any ordinary tricks of jugglery.

"Thus then, as far as the words are concered, they can never be the "objects of teaching; and hence with regard to these, Grammar cannot be "said to be a *science;* and as for *sentences*, Grammar is not found to teach "anything with regard to them (dealing as it does with the formation of "words only).

The *Mahābhāshya* has distinctly spoken of *purification* as belonging to "words as used with reference to certain meanings; while as a matter "of fact, we find that it is only sentences that are found to be so used; and "never the words, which by themselves (apart from the sentence) have no "significance (and yet Grammar is found to be dealing with words alone "which is hardly compatible with the former declaration).

"In grammatical works (for instance, in the *Vākyapadīya*) we meet "with such declarations as—'as in the compound *Brāhmanakambala*, there "is no significance in the word *brāhmanah*, so also would the word *dēva-"dattah* have no significance in the sentence *dēvadattah pacati*; and thus the "word by itself being found to be incapable of being used with any "significance, it would have been proper for Grammar to treat of sentences; "but as a matter of fact this has not been done: we find the later commen-"tators making as contradictory statements as the authors of the *Sūtras*, "the *Bhāshya* and the *Vārtika*; and this goes to show directly that the "science of Grammar has been propounded by absolutely untrustworthy "persons.

"Thus then, the science of Grammar being found to consist mostly "of random declarations contradicting one another, to be devoid of any "basis in the Veda, and to be absolutely without any use, it cannot be "accepted as in any way regulating the usage of words.

"Then again, apart from the study of the Veda itself, and also the "usage of the Veda in the performance of sacrifices, there can be no "regulation (by means of grammar) even in the case of the words of "ordinary parlance. And hence we should make use of all words; they "are all equally correct.

"And on this point, we have the following arguments:

"(1) The words '*gāvī*,' '*gōṇī*,' &c., are equally expressive of the *cow*,— "because they are used in that sense by experienced people—exactly like "the words '*gauh*,' '*usrā*,' and the like.

"(2) All these are correct words; because they are found to denote a "certain object—(like the words, '*gauh*,' &c.)

"(3) They are not corruptions,—because they are comprehensible "by the ear—like the words ('*gauh*,' &c.) instanced before.

"(4) They are all eternal;—because we cannot trace their usage "to any beginning in time, specially as, just as in the case of the word "'*gauh*,' so in that of these also, we can always find one speaker prece- "ding the other *ad infinitum*.

"(5) Those that utter only grammatically correct words cannot, by "that, attain to any transcendental result; because they are all found to "accomplish the visible purpose of expressing a meaning; just as the per- "ception of smoke leads to the cognition of fire (and not to any transcen- "dental result).

"(6) The grammatically correct words cannot bring about trans- "cendental results, because they are not the subjects of perpetual Injunc- "tions, exactly like the words of Buddha.

"(7) Grammar cannot be held to be a scripture; because it has not "the form of the Veda; exactly like the explanations of the formations of "Vernacular words.

"(8) The authority of Grammar cannot be held to rest upon the "fact of its having its basis in the Veda; because it is not found to deal "with the subjects that are treated of in the Veda;—exactly like "dramatical works, &c.

"(9) Grammar cannot be a part of the Veda; because it is not found "to serve any purpose of the Veda; exactly like an ordinary story, &c.

"(10) Grammar cannot be held to serve any useful purpose of the "Veda; because the Veda is found to express a meaning, even without the "help of Grammar.

"(11) Nor can Grammar be held to be a necessary appendage to the "use of words; because it is capable of being propounded only when "the usage already exists. And that which is such cannot be a necessary "appendage is found in the case of the inference of the eye. That is to "say, the perception of colour being accomplished, independently of "the perception of the eye, even though the impossibility of the former "perception in the absence of the eye distinctly points to the inference "of the existence of the eye, yet this latter inference is not admitted to be "a necessary appendage of that perception; exactly in the same manner, "inasmuch as Grammar is found to have been composed long after the "usage (of words)—both Vedic and ordinary—has been an accomplished "fact, it cannot be admitted as a necessary appendage of such usage.

"For the above reasons, we conclude that the word '*gauḥ*,' *gāvī*' "'*goṇī*,' &c., being synonymous, like the words '*taru*,' '*bṛksha*,' &c., are "all found to be used in ordinary parlance; and that such usage of these "is not prohibited by any scriptures."

—o—

To all this we make the following reply:—

SIDDHĀNTA.

***Sūtra* (25). Its accomplishment being due to an effort, there is a chance of discrepancies in the word.**

(1) The words '*gāvī*' &c., have been declared to be eternal on the sole ground of the Apparent Inconsistency of the fact of their being used in ordinary parlance and affording definite meanings. But we proceed to show the doubtful character of this Apparent Inconsistency, by proving that the said usage and expressiveness are explicable otherwise (than by accepting the words to be eternal). When a word is found to be never used, except in its expressive character, then alone can the expressiveness of the word be admitted to be proved by the facts of its usage and expressiveness.

At present we content ourselves by merely making the conclusion of the *Pūrvapaksha* open to doubt; because when this has been accomplished the task of establishing our own theory becomes comparatively easy. That is to say, when a certain conclusion to the contrary has been laid out in an exceptionally strong manner, if one proceeds to immediately point out the true theory, it involves a very hard work; and hence with a view to lighten this burden, the present *sūtra* proceeds only to weaken the contrary view by throwing it open to doubt.

(2) Or, the words '*gāvī*' &c., having been declared to be eternal on the ground of their being accepted in well-established usage, the present *sūtra* may be taken as throwing such eternality open to doubt, by showing that there is likelihood of there being discrepancies in such usage.

That is to say, if it were always the case that the word pronounced by one man is exactly like that which he has heard from others, then alone could long-established usage justify the conclusion that, as in the case of the words '*go*' &c., there has been no time at which the words '*gāvī*' &c., have not been in use; and this conclusion would justify us in accepting these latter to be eternal. But as a matter of fact, we often find the pronounciation of words to be due to certain discrepancies (or mistakes); and as such the continuity of the usage being doubtful, it cannot warrant any conclusion as to the eternality of all words.

The expression 'accomplishment being due to an effort' means that *because the word is manifested by means of an effort in accordance with arguments detailed above* (in the section on the '*Eternality of Words*,' *Çlokavārtika*). (This is added because the Mimānsaka holding the word to be eternal cannot admit of its being *produced* by any effort).

(3) Some people read the *sūtra* as '*aprayatnanishpattēh*' &c.; and they explain it thus: In the case of a man for whom the word is manifested by means of an effort complete in all respects, all words being pronounced in accordance with a long-established tradition, they would all be equally authoritative; but it is often found that words are manifested by means of incomplete or faulty efforts; and in these cases, it is highly probable that the word that is pronounced may be at variance with the established usage; and hence all words cannot necessarily be held to be equally authoritative.

(4) Or, it may mean that the completion of the effort to manifest (or pronounce) a word is found to be tainted with certain discrepancies, even in the case of clever people with all their organs of speech intact; what then can be said of the words pronounced by ignorant persons, having deficient organs of speech, &c.? And the discrepancy that is found in the effort to pronounce the word, cannot but affect the word that is manifested (or uttered) by that effort.

Thus then, we conclude that those that are pronounced by a faultless effort are correct; while those whose utterance is due to certain discrepancies in the effort, are incorrect; and there is nothing that can be said against this criterion.

As a matter of fact, even in ordinary parlance, we find that, that which is not destroyed is called 'good,' and that which is destroyed is pronounced 'bad'; and such being the case, the existence of the correct forms of words, as also that of their corruptions, becomes possible by the same means. (That is to say, the word whose usage is found to be eternal may be pronounced to be correct, while that of which the use is not found to be so may be held to be a mere corruption).

(5) Or again, by 'correct' we may mean 'true,' 'incorrect' meaning 'untrue'; by this the subject of the correctness or incorrectness of words

would have a useful bearing upon a consideration of *Dharma* or *Adharma*. Truth being enjoined and untruth being prohibited, we can easily make these the means of ascertaning *Dharma* and *Adharma*; and certainly it cannot be doubted that these matters are really the subjects capable of being treated of in a scripture. As for truth too, just as we have a truth of matter, so also we have a truth of words; and a verbal untruth is to be avoided as much as an untruth of fact.

Thus then, the differentiation of the correct from the incorrect words being as useful (with regard to *Dharma*) as that of the food that should be eaten from that which should not be eaten, we cannot deny the fact of Grammar being a scripture dealing with the usage of words; and as such the reasoning propounded in the foregoing *sūtra* falls to the ground.

(6) Or, the *sūtra* may be taken as offering a reply to the following argument urged above—"Inasmuch as it is only the word that is correct (*i.e.*, expressive) that is always used, while that which is incorrect (*i.e.*, inexpressive) is never used, there can be no regulations with regard to their usage." And the sense of the reply is this:

Inasmuch as there is a chance of discrepancies (in the pronouncing of words), there is always a probability of both contingencies—*i.e.*, it may not be the correct word that is always used, and it may be the incorrect word that is used. That is to say, if a correct word, on being used once, were never to disappear, it could be said to be always used in that correct form; and thereby there being no possibility of the use of its corruption, any regulations with regard to it would be useless. But as a matter of fact, there always being certain discrepancies in the effort to pronounce the word, the chances of the use of both the correct word and its corruptions are very nearly equal; and as such the science that lays down the rules with regard to the use of the correct word cannot be said to be absolutely useless. As a matter of fact, we often find that through the inherent incapacity or carelessness of the man pronouncing it, a word is often distorted, being pronounced with a letter too short or too many, or in a different form altogether; and yet, though uttered in these corrupted forms, it is found to express the same thing that is expressed by the correct word. But as these corruptions are distinctly found to be due to a discrepancy in the pronouncer, they cannot be accepted as synonyms of the original correct word, and as independent words by themselves expressing the same meaning.

And again, even in the case of the names 'Dēvadatta' and the like, with regard to which there can be no doubts, we find young boys distorting them into the words '*tatta*' and the like; and this instance leads us to think that the corruptions '*gāvī*,' &c., are also due to certain discrepancies in the persons seeking to pronounce the word '*gauh*' (exactly as the boy wishing to pronounce the word 'Dēvadatta,' but being incapable of rightly pronouncing it, utters it as '*Tatta*'). That is to say, we actually find the object *Dēvadatta* being duly expressed by the corrupted form '*Tatta*' as pronounced by the child, or by the grown-up man imitating the child; and as such how can we accept a word ('*gāvī*' f.i.) to be really expressive of a certain object, on the mere ground of its being used and expressing a definite object?

Then again, even in the case of the corrupt forms '*gāvī*' and the like, that have become current in ordinary usage, we often find these also being corrupted into these forms, (and yet succeeding in denoting the cow). There are only a few such (corrupt) words, like '*gāvi*' and the like, that have been in usage for a very long time; and as such it is possible that people might come to think of them as correct words. But as a matter of fact we find these words also being distorted by ignorant people into new corruptions, like '*glāvī*,' &c.; and yet even in this corrupted form, the word is actually found to denote the *cow* (as well as the word '*gāvī*' or '*gauh*'); and thus as we find even these admittedly incorrect corruptions to be used and denoting a certain object, the mere fact of a word being used and expressing a meaning cannot rightly be accepted as sufficient reason for holding it to be correct.

Thus then, the argument propounded by you becomes open to the objection, that being doubtful in itself it cannot prove what you wish to prove by it. Just as a word, being pronounced otherwise than in its real form, falls from its true expressiveness, so does an argument, becoming doubtful, fall off from the position of correct reasoning!

Thus then, we conclude that even if a word is found to be current in ordinary usage, it is necessary that we should consider whether or not it is really and correctly expressive (of the sense in which it is used). And this is what is sought to be ascertained by means of the following *sūtras*.

Though the theory of the opponent has been rent asunder, yet our own theory is far from being thoroughly established; and hence we proceed with the next *sūtra*.

***Sūtra* (26). It is not quite reasonable to have many (synonymous) words.**

We proceed to show why it is not reasonable. There is a certain fixed denotative relation between the expressed meaning and the expressive word (that is to say, they are so related that the meaning is cognised when the word exists, and it is not cognised when the word does not exist); and hence if there were many words expressing the same meaning there would be no such relationship between the meaning and any of the words.

That is to say, it is only when the word and its meaning are very closely related to each other, that the one necessarily implies the other, and as such there is a fixed mutual relationship ; and hence if either of these—either the word or the meaning—were to be diverse, there would be a diversity in the said relationship, which would thus lose all its fixity.

And further, it is only by means of Apparent Inconsistency that we infer the potentialities of all things; and the expression of a meaning being quite explicable through the potentiality of a single word, there can be no ground for assuming any others. That is to say, when we find that the cognition of the meaning cannot be explained in any other way, we infer an unperceived potentiality in a certain word, on the sole ground of the Apparent Inexplicability of the Cognition of the meaning. And when this potentiality is once assumed as belonging to a certain word, if it were sought to be attributed to its corruptions also, how could any such word be assumed to have the potentiality, in the absence of the aforesaid "inexplicability" or inconsistency?

Further, a name is given to a thing, simply for the purpose of talking of it in ordinary parlance; and as this usage can be accomplished by means of one only, the assumption of other names is absolutely useless.

Then again, if many words be held to be alternatively expressive of the same meaning, then this would be open to all the eight objections that have been urged (above) against all alternative courses. When a certain object is known by a certain definite name, whenever any other name happens to be pronounced, it brings about the idea of another object ; all this we shall explain under the *sūtra* II—ii—22.

As for such universally recognised synonyms, as '*hasta*,' '*kara*,' &c., we accept all these many words to be expressive of the same object, because all of these being equally authorised by the *smṛtis*, there can be no other way out of it. While so long as we are able to depend upon the potentiality of a single word, we explain the denotation of the meaning by other words (corruptions) to be due to Analogy and Inference. (That is, when a person who is unable to pronounce the word '*go*' pronounces the word '*gāvī*,' we at once perceive, by means of Analogy, the similarity of the latter with the former ; then we infer the utterance of the word '*gāvī*' to be due to the desire on the part of the speaker to pronounce the word '*go;*' and thence we conclude the word '*gāvī*'—to have the same meaning as the word '*go*'). Thus then, we conclude that in the matter of the consideration of the form, relationship and the meanings of words, there can be a fixity of these only when the potentiality is attributed to a single word, and never when it is referred to many. As a matter of fact the corrupted forms of words become capable of expressing a meaning, only by manifesting the potentiality of the original word, through their similarity with it; this the Bhāshya will explain in detail under the *sūtra* I—iii—28.

Thus then, it must be admitted that when many words are found to be used with reference to the same meaning, it is only one that can be really related to that meaning; all the rest are due a certain incapacity in the speaker (to pronounce the correct word), and are capable of denoting the meaning, only through the intervention of the original word, which is indicated by them (through their similarity with it).

—o—

It is often urged that when many words are found to be equally current in usage and capable of expressing their meanings, it is impossible to ascertain which one of these is the real original word. And in view of this assertion, we have the following *sūtra*.

***Sūtra* (27). That (expressiveness) could be ascertained by means of the particular instances of close application (or learning).**

At the very outset, there arise the questions—what is the '*learning*'? what the 'particular instances'? how too could the expressiveness of words be ascertained by means of such instances? And we proceed to explain all these points.

'Learning' proceeds from listening to and carefully studying the various generic definitions or rules; while the 'particular instances' refer to an application of these rules to particular cases.

The number of words being endless, it is not possible for us to read up all of them; and hence for the indicating of all individual correct words, the only means that we have at our command is the laying down of certain general definitions or rules that would include all the individual cases concerned.

Hence it follows that, without the help of Grammar, neither the Veda nor ordinary parlance could ever enable us to get at an idea of all the correct words. And unless all the correct words have been known, we cannot arrive at any notion of those not included among these; and as such no Apparent Inconsistency could lead us to any knowledge of the incorrect words. And it is only when the general definition of 'correct words' has been duly obtained, that a word being found to be used in a form not in keeping with the said definition, we would at once conclude it to be of the opposite kind; and it is then alone that Apparent Inconsistency could help us in arriving at an idea of the incorrect words. And thus we find that Grammar is of use to us in the ascertainment of both correct and incorrect words; and hence it is that the *sūtra* speaks of the 'learning' of Grammar as the means of ascertaining the true expressiveness of words.

In the foregoing *sūtra*, it has been urged that as the grammatical rule cannot have its basis in the rule itself, it must have it in usage, and thus the rule would be based upon usage, and the usage upon the rule,—there being an inadmissible mutual interdependence. But this interdependence can be explained away by bearing in mind the fact that, in the first place by an observation of ordinary usage people become cognisant of the fact of certain words denoting certain meanings, though they may not have yet quite ascertained the true expressiveness of the words ; and it is these words that go to compose the rules of Grammar, which help to establish the correctness of certain other words; and then these latter are made the means of finally establishing the correctness (and the true expressiveness) of the former (words composing the rules).

There could be an irremediable interdependence, only if, without the help of Grammar the words were not expressive, or if their expressiveness were not cognised. But as a matter of fact, the fact of the word being expressive (of a certain meaning) having been known beforehand, when it is found that such correct words are often mixed up in usage with their corruptions, then it becomes the turn of the grammatical rule to step in and help us to distinguish the correct word from its corruptions. And thus we find that while Grammar helps us to realise the expressiveness of the correct words only, ordinary usage is the means of ascertaining that of these as well as their corruptions; and as such the two being found to be treating of two distinct subjects, the Science of Grammar cannot be said to be a needless repetition.

[The Vartika omits *sūtra* 28 and also *sūtra* 29, the sense of which has already been explained above].

An objection is raised—"As the Veda contains only correct words (we could ascertain from the Veda which words are correct), the propounding of the Science of Grammar is absolutely redundant." And to this we make the following reply:

[1]Not so; because it does not treat of all.

In the Veda, as also in ordinary usage, we find only a few of the correct words; and even as regards these who could ever get at any idea of all the words contained in the endless branches of the Veda, and used in ordinary parlance? That is to say, just as it is absolutely impossible for us to get up all the individual words used in ordinary parlance, so too is it impossible even to *hear* all the words contained in the various branches of the Veda,—to say nothing of getting these up. For who

1 In the Vārtika this has been printed as a *sūtra* ; but neither the Bhāshya, nor the Nyāyamālā-vistāra, has any such *sūtra*; hence the *sūtra*—numbering has been omitted, though the type of the *sūtra* has been retained.

could ever read up all the innumerable words that are referred to by the general rules treating of an endless number of roots and affixes ?

Thus then we find that, though there are grammatical explanations of the words contained in the Injunctive sentences that point out the fact of the use and knowledge of correct words bringing about certain transcendental results, both in connection with sacrifices and with the human agent, yet this cannot be said to involve an inadmissible interdependence, on the ground of the grammatical rules themselves being based upon a previous conception of the meanings of those words. Because if it were a recognised necessity that the Science of Grammar must always operate, after one has come across certain restrictive Injunctions with reference to sacrifices and human agents—as for instance, 'the Brāhmana should not pronounce an incorrect word at a sacrifice,' 'a single word duly learnt and rightly used brings about all desirable results both here and hereafter,' 'hence a grammatically correct speech rises,' and so forth,—then alone could our assertion be open to the charge of interdependence; for in that case alone could the Vedic Injunction be dependent upon the words explained grammatically, and Grammar itself would be dependent upon the said Injunctions. But, as a matter of fact, (1) we cannot think of any point of time, totally devoid of some work or other, dealing with the grammatical rules treating of the different kinds of roots and affixes; (2) we actually find the Vedic injunctions supplying the requisite basis for all the six factors of Grammar—*viz*: (*a*) the explanation of the grammatical formation of words, (*b*) the correct words, (*c*) the injunction of using the words thus explained, (*d*) the actual use of such words, (*e*) the prohibition of the use of the words not so explicable, and (*f*) the actual avoidance of the use of such words; and as such we come to recognise all these as having had no beginning in time; exactly like the Injunctions laying down the forms and uses of such things as the bundle of *Kuça* grass, the sacrificial altar, the sacrificial post, the sacrificial fire, the Priest, the milking of the cow, &c., &c.; and as such we never perceive any sequence or precedence between the Injunctions and the Rules of Grammar; and hence it is only the fact of the use of correct words bringing about transcendental results that can be said to be dependent solely upon the scriptures. And hence we find no discrepancy in the Rules dealing with the use of words, which have always (eternally) been found capable of grammatical explanation.

The *Pūrvapaksha* has also urged the following objection: "The *correct*-"*ness* and *incorrectness* of words being nothing else but their *expressive*-"*ness* and *non-expressiveness* (respectively), and the ascertaining of the "expressiveness or inexpressiveness of a word depending solely upon the "fact of the word being, or not being used in ordinary parlance to express "a definite meaning, the assertion that the words '*gāvi*' &c., are not "expressive would be a direct contradiction of a fact of ordinary experience; "and hence we conclude that among all the words current in ordinary usage, "none is incorrect, except those that proceed from the beating of the drum, "the mere repetition of the alphabetical letters, those that are pronounced "a letter too short, or too long, and those that are purposely distorted (as it "is only these that are found in ordinary parlance, to give no sense at all)."

And to this, we make the following reply: As a matter of fact we find the ordinary man incapable of discriminating the expressive from the inexpressive word; and it is the rules of Grammar alone that can help one to this discrimination. And as for the contradiction of a fact of ordinary usage, this cannot be objectionable; because we have already proved above that the *Smṛti* (in this case that of Grammar) has a stronger authority than any *usage*.

It is conjointly by means of Grammar and ordinary usage that the true expressive word is ascertained; and hence ordinary usage by itself is accepted as the means of knowing the expressiveness of words only so long as it is not found to be amenable to a certain grammatical rule. On the other hand, when the two are found to point in opposite directions, then we can have, as the *Pūrvapaksha*, all the arguments urged under *Sūtra* I—iii—8; and then, as the final *Siddhānta*, we will have the conclusions arrived at under *Sūtra* I—iii—9; which would prove the superior authority of the conclusion pointed out by Grammar; as also of the person learned in Grammar: all this we have already shown above.

Those who would seek to prove, by mere arguments, the fact of the words '*gāvī*' and the like being incapable of expressing a meaning, would be contradicting a fact of ordinary experience; but the fact of these words being contrary to the (Grammatical) *smṛti* is quite patent; exactly like the non-Brahmanical character of one who is actually a Brāhmana. That is to say, just as in the case of certain men, resembling one another in bodily form, ordinary perception can only afford a confused idea of their respective castes; and it is only by means of the remembrance of their parents that the castes can be rightly ascertained; so also in the case in question, ordinary usage being found to point promiscuously to the expressive character of all sorts of words (correct and incorrect), it is only by means of the remembrance (*smṛti*) of grammatical rules that we can rightly discriminate the correct word; and in this there is no contradiction of ordinary experience.

And just as one who, seeing a number of men resembling in bodily shape would declare all of them promiscuously to be of the same caste, would be making an assertion contrary to the *smṛti*; so too, one who would declare all words in ordinary usage to be equally expressive, would be contradicting the grammatical *smṛti.* And, exactly like the differentiation of castes, the distinction of correct and incorrect words, being at first established by the *smṛti*, subsequently comes to be a matter of ordinary perception, for all clever people.

There are certain facts pointed out by the *smṛti*—such as the fact of a certain result proceeding from a certain action—the time of whose appearance is not fixed; and hence not knowing when they could be actually realised, these cannot be said to be amenable to direct sense-perception; and as such we cannot but base these upon the sole authority of the Scriptures (*smṛti*). While in the case of words, though, in the first instance, the discrimination is arrived at by the help of *smṛti*, yet immediately afterwards, we find the previously ascertained correct word to be directly amenable to Sense-perception, specially for the person who is well-practised in the art; exactly as we find in the case of music, where though the discrimination of the various tones, &c., are ascertained by means of the definitions laid down in the musical *smṛtis*, yet subsequently they come to be perceived directly by the trained ear of the musician. And if to such a person, one were to say that all words are equally expressive (and correct) he would be making an assertion that would be set aside by a fact of Sense-perception, exactly as if one were to assert that all men are of the same caste (or that all musical tones are alike).

And thus what is against all evidential authority is the assertion that even incorrect words are truly expressive, and not the assertion that true expressiveness belongs only to those words that are authorised by the grammatical *smṛtis*.

And from this it follows that a knowledge of the correctness and incorrectness of words is also possible as the means of accomplishing Dharma and Adharma, in accordance with the Injunctions (of the use of correct words) and Prohibitions (of the use of incorrect words) that lay down certain transcendental results following from such uses.

The *Pūrvapaksha* has urged that "the correctness of words is not perceptible by the Senses (nor amenable to any other means of right notion)."

To this we make the following reply: (1) The correctness of words is actually perceptible by the Senses; (2) there is also a certain mark (that accomplishes the inference of their correctness); (3) the correctness is also pointed out by the scriptures; and (4-6) we also find an unmixed use of correct words.

(1) All the letters, (*a*) that are not either half-uttered, or wrongly uttered, or distorted, (*b*) which are pronounced in due accordance with the restrictions of the length or shortness of the vowel sounds, (*c*) and which are found to exist in the proper order of sequence, are all, like the various

accents, amenable to auditory perception, which also comprehends those expressive words that are in keeping with the grammatical *smṛtis*; and thus it cannot be denied that the correctness of words is perceptible by the Senses.

(2) Soon after the aforesaid auditory perception, we come across such specific distinguishing marks (of correct words) as the deletions, additions and alterations of the roots and affixes, in accordance with the rules laid down in the grammatical *smṛtis;* and these marks, together with the actual expressiveness of the words as used in ordinary parlance, lead to the inference of the correctness of such words.

(3) The two kinds of scriptures—the *Vedas* and the *Smṛtis*—are often found to serve the purpose of pointing out the means of the accomplishment of certain results in connection with Heaven, the ordinary world, and sacrifices, as also of showing the virtuous or the sinful character of actions; and as such the correctness of words can also be a subject dealt with by them; because one who makes use of uncorrupt forms of words accomplishes certain useful results, both indirectly in the performance of sacrifices, and (directly) in leading the person to Heaven; and during the performance of a sacrifice, if one happens to pronounce an incorrect word, the performance becomes as faulty as if he had committed a sin in the shape of telling a lie; as is declared elsewhere—'one who knows the relationships of speech becomes tainted with sin by the utterance of incorrect words.' These two subjects—sinfulness and virtuousness—are not amenable to any other means of right notion but the Verbal Authority of the scriptures.

Nor is it necessary to assume as many Injunctions and Prohibitions as there are words, because all of them are included in the single Injunction and Prohibition—that 'one who is desirous to accomplish the sacrifice and its result in the shape of Heaven should make use of only the correct words, and avoid that of all incorrect ones.'.

Nor is there any such law as that the scriptures should always treat of Injunctions and Prohibitions only, and never of the existing state of things; because we meet with many such declarations as—"this self is imperishable," &c., &c.—which describe the existing state of things (without any tinge of Injunction or Prohibition); and yet they are not found to be incapable of expressing the true state of things. Nor do they cease to be scriptures by the mere description of such things. But even if there be such a rule as that scriptures must consist only of Injunctions and Prohibitions, then too, we could have such an Injunction as that 'one should make use of such and such correct words,' or that—'if one desiring to obtain the results mentioned in other scriptural passages should wish to make use of uncorrupted forms of words, he should always employ such and such words, with such and such vowels and consonants, neither more nor less than what is absolutely correct;' and as it is possible to have such Injunctions and Prohibitions, the correctness of words can very well be regarded as amenable to the verbal authority of the scriptures.

(4) Even from the Analogy of such instances as the experienced man pronouncing the correct word 'Dēvadatta' and the child pronouncing the same word as 'Taṭṭa,' we can deduce the fact that words can have both correct and incorrect forms. And so also on finding certain uncorrupt Vedic words to be in keeping with the rules of Grammar, we deduce from Analogy the correctness of similar uncorrupted forms of words that occur in ordinary parlance.

(5) So too, the correctness of a word is cognisable, in the first instance, by means of the Apparent Inconsistency of the expressiveness of the word as found to be denoting a certain meaning in ordinary parlance; and secondly, the correctness could also be ascertained by another Apparent Inconsistency—namely that of the word being entirely free from all corruptions due to such causes as carelessness, idleness, a disorder in the organs of speech and the like.

(6) The corrupt forms of words are said to be correct, on the ground of their similarity with the correct words; but we ascertain the negation of such correctness, from the mere absence (or Negation) of the conditions of correctness laid down in grammatical rules.

Thus then, the correctness and the incorrectness of words being found to be amenable to all the six means of right notion, who would be bold enough to assert that none of them is applicable to the case; and that as such there can be no means of ascertaining the correctness of words?

Though we find ignorant people making use of both correct and incorrect forms of words, yet the learned would be always ready to discriminate between the two, just as they always distinguish the Brāhmaṇa from the non-Brāhmana. For just as those that are expert in the matter of jewelry, &c., can easily differentiate the real gem from the pieces of glass and other things that may be mixed up with it, so would the learned distinguish the correct from the incorrect forms of words. And just as for the testing of gems we have certain directions for knowing the real from the unreal; so too, for the knowing of the correct from the incorrect word, we have the rules laid down in the works on Grammar.

Even if the tradition of Grammar extended only from man to man, this could not be rejected as a mere case of one blind person following another blind person, because we perceive, in actual usage, the correctness pointed out by the Grammar; and also because we find it dealing with the discrimination (of words) which cannot be got at by any other means. In the case of grammatical study, the transcendental part of it is established by means of the Injunctions and Prohibitions (of the use of correct and incorrect words) contained in the Veda. And as for the knowledge of the uncorrupt forms of words, the using of which is said to accomplish the said transcendental result, it being immediate in its effects, can be very easily obtained by the help of the long-standing rules and regulations of Grammar, which are found to be in keeping with the usages of the Veda and all respectable people; and as such the fact of Grammar having been propounded by human agency cannot affect its authority adversely.

It has been argued above that "the using of correct words being found to serve a visible purpose, such usage would come about always by its very nature; and as such there can be no need of any Injunction with regard to it; as it is an admitted fact that an Injunction has its use only in laying down something not otherwise cognisable."

But we shall reply to this under the *sūtra—The Injunction serves the purpose of restricting* (the usage to the correct words only) (IV—ii—24).

Another argument brought forward in the *Pūrvapaksha* is that "the corrupt forms of words being absolutely inexpressive, they could never be used; and as such there being nothing to be set aside, the Injunction cannot be said to be a *restrictive* one (that is to say, if both correct and incorrect words were capable of being used, then alone could there be a restriction of usage to the correct words alone; but as a matter of fact the incorrect words are naturally incapable of being used)."

And to this we make the following reply: Though generally it is true that there can be no Restriction or Exclusion without something that could be set aside, yet why could not we have a Restrictive Injunction that would lay down something to be always adhered to, (and not as an alternative, which is the case in ordinary restriction)? That is to say, when one has got to say something, it is just possible that though he may at times express himself in correct words, yet at times he might either make use of corruptions, or mere silent gestures of the eye; and hence it is only right that we should have an Injunction that would lay down the necessity of using the correct words, for those that wish well of themselves; and hence by adhering to such usage a man would be creating an excellent *Apūrva* (Potentiality) for himself.

Even though it be absolutely necessary to have something to be set aside by a Restrictive Injunction, yet we can have, in the case in question, a setting aside of those words, that slightly resemble the correct words, and as such being found to denote the correct meaning indirectly through the correct words, come to be accepted on account of their long-continued currency, as really expressive; because the use of such words is not impossible. (That is to say, it is only the words having no resemblance with any correct words that have been said to be totally inexpressive; and hence it is the usage of these alone that can be said to be impossible; but in the case of such words as '*gāvī*', this word is actually found to point, by similarity, to the word '*go*,' and through this, to denote the cow; and a long-standing usage of such words is often found to lead to these slightly corrupt words to be accepted as really expressive; and as it is likely that people might be making use of such words, the Injunction serves the purpose of laying down that one should always use the correct words, and not the said corrupt ones).

Or, the incorrect words being nothing totally distinct (from the correct ones, of which alone they are the corrupted forms), the possibility of the employment of these cannot be of the same (alternative) kind as that of various materials, &c., in the performance of a single action; and as such, words cannot be the fit objects for being set aside by the said Restrictive Injunction. But the real fact is that while the person is actually thinking of using the correct word, he may, through carelessness, come to corrupt it (in pronouncing it wrongly); and what the said Injunction does is to lay down that one should never distort or corrupt the words he uses. And there are many examples of such Restrictive Injunctions; for instance, the passage,—'that cake which is burnt becomes fit for the Rākshasa,'—which in deprecating the burnt cake, points to the Injunction that one should so cook the cake as not to overburn it. So too, we have a deprecation of the use of incorrect words in the sentence—'a word used incorrectly either as to accent ...... kills the person;' and we have a prohibition of such use in the sentence—'The Brāhmana should not behave like a *Mleccha* in uttering incorrect words, because an incorrect word is a *Mleccha*' (where the word '*Mleccha*' indicating a confused sound or speech serves to point to the fact of an incorrect word being a corruption due to carelessness, and as such incapable of rightly fulfilling the duty of the word in the shape of expressing the meaning); and both these (deprecation and prohibition) go to show that the Injunction—'hence it is a duly purified speech that goes forth,'—serves to limit all rightful usage to the uncorrupted forms of words.

An objection is here raised: "Such discrepancies in the (pronunciation, "&c. of words) as are due to an inherent incapacity in the speaker, or to "carelessness (inevitable under certain circumstances) can never be "avoided; and as such these can never be rightly made the objects of "prohibition."

To this we make the following reply: The sense of the prohibition, is that one should not be careless in the use of words, and that he should try his best to obtain mastery over them; otherwise no regard could be shown to that prohibition. And again, if there were no such prohibition of carelessness, the persons, desirous of uttering words in forms that would be easy of pronunciation, would purposely distort the real forms of words, even though they were quite capable of pronouncing the correct word (though not with the same ease). And if a certain person incapable of pronouncing the real form would pronounce the corrupt one, other people, though knowing it to be the corrupt form, would yet, in flattering imitation of the former person, persist in pronouncing it in the same form; if such pronunciation were not distinctly forbidden. And it often happens that when conversing with persons, knowing only the corrupt form of a language, and quite incapable of using the correct one, even capable persons make use of the same corrupt forms. And thus there being many causes leading to the use of corrupt forms of words, it is only right that we should have a Restrictive Injunction that should make us avoid such corrupt usage (and take to the correct one).

Another argument of the *Pūrvapaksha* is that, "inasmuch as we find words fulfilling the visible purpose of the denoting of a certain meaning, Grammar cannot be held to be a scripture dealing with such usages as would lead to a transcendental result."

And to this we make the following reply: Even though there is a visible result, yet we hold a transcendental result to follow from the Restriction; and this transcendental result belongs either to the sacrifice or to the Agent, according as it happens to be in conjunction with, or disjoined from, one or the other (vide *Sūtra* IV—iii—5). It is only such conjunction and disjunction that make the same (result) to be both; and this, in the present instance, is ascertained in the following manner: the result that is mentioned in a sacrificial context is accepted as belonging to the sacrifice; while that which is described apart from any sacrifices, is held to belong to the Agent. (That is to say, in the case in question, as the prohibition that 'the Brāhmaṇa should not utter an incorrect word' is found in a context that treats of the performance of a sacrifice, it points to the fact of the utterance of an incorrect word spoiling the sacrifice; and thence it follows that the Restrictive Injunction that 'one should use only correct words' has its chief bearing upon the performance of sacrifices; while the passage that speaks of the correct use of a single word fulfilling all one's desires both here and hereafter is not found in connection with any sacrifices; and hence it follows from this that the use of correct words leads the Agent to heaven; and this makes the said Injunction refer to the personal Agent.) And again in the case of a passage whose main result belongs to the sacrifice, if there be a mention of certain results accruing to the Agent, who is something other than the sacrifice,—this very fact imparts to such mention the character of an *Arthavāda* (vide *Sūtra* IV—iii—1); whereas in the case of a passage describing certain results as belonging to the Agent (when the passage is not found in connection with any sacrifice) the result, being described as such, cannot but be accepted as really following from the action in question (*viz.*, the using of correct words)—as has been held by the revered Ātrēya (vide *Sūtra* IV—iii—18) That is to say, the *Apūrva* bearing upon the sacrifice, not having the means of its accomplishment fully known, is capable of containing within itself all the transcendental results in connection with it; and as such it withdraws within itself the *Apūrva* following from the Restriction (of usage to correct words), and then relegates the mention of the accruing of certain results to the human Agent to the realms of *Arthavāda*. Whereas in the case of the Restriction being for the sake of the Agent, it becomes absolutely necessary to assume a purpose for such Restriction; and as for the comprehension of meaning, this is often found to be obtained even by means of the corruptions of words as also through certain silent gestures; and hence the Restriction by itself, having all its wants fulfilled as shown above, is not capable of setting up the *Apūrva* or transcendental result; and as such it becomes absolutely necessary to accept as the true result (of following the Restriction), the *attainment of all desirable things both here and in heaven*, which is mentioned in the corresponding *Arthavāda* passage.

Another question put by the *Pūrvapaksha* is—"Where does this transcendental result of the Restriction reside?" And to this we make the following reply: That result which has its end in the sacrifice itself resides in the subsidiaries that go to make up the sacrifice, while that which is not mentioned with reference to any subsidiary character, resides in the person that performs the sacrifice. That is to say, in accordance with the reasonings brought forward in *Sūtra* III—iv—15, the transcendental result following from the restriction of all usage to correct words tends to impart a certain purity to the sacrificer, who (as the agent) is the means of accomplishing the transcendental result indicated by the word 'Brāhmana' (in the injunction, 'the *Brāhmana* should not use incorrect words') which appears in the context of the *Jyōtishtoma* sacrifice; and then in accordance with the conclusion arrived at under *Sūtra* III—viii—4, the *Apūrva* (or transcendental result) comes to be recognised as residing in the Person, in order to render him fit for acquiring the main result (of the sacrifice). And in the case of the passage ('one word correctly pronounced, &c.') which refers to the Person only, the result following from such correct use, is held to reside in the person knowing and using the correct word, exactly as the result of the main sacrifice is found to reside in the Person; because the mention of 'correct speaking' and 'correct knowing' directly point to such a *speaker* and *knower*, who is also universally recognised as the main receptacle of the results following from these actions (of *speaking* and *knowing*).

Though in the passage—'No incorrect words should be used *by the Brāh-*

maṇa'—the Instrumental ending in the word '*brāhmaṇēna*,' 'by the Brāhmaṇa,' indicates the secondary character of the speaker (and as such he may not be accepted as the receptacle of the main result), yet, inasmuch as it is the speaker that is affected by the purification (due to the correct use of words), the primary position may be assigned to him; exactly as in the case of the 'Remnant of the *Prayaja* butter.' That is to say, in the case of the passage 'Mixes the sacrificial material with the remnant of the *Prayāja*,' though the word 'remnant' has the Instrumental ending, yet inasmuch as it has to serve a useful purpose, it is accepted to be the chief object of the purificatior; exactly the same is the case with the word 'Brāhmaṇa' in the passage in question.

Or it may be that, the Instrumental ending in the word 'by the Brāhmana' points to the 'performer of the sacrifice'; and his primary character is got at from without, through the mention of the word '*kāmadhuk*' (*obtaining of all desirable results*,—which appears in another passage). And the Instrumental ending in '*Brāhmaṇēna*' may not be taken as referring to the 'person using the incorrect word'; and the construction of the passage may be thus explained: 'No incorrect words should be used *by the Brāhmaṇa who is performing the sacrifice.*' And it is a well-known fact that that which has a secondary position in the sacrifice, attains the primary position, in reference to the purification (as following from the sacrifice); and in the case in question the using of correct words does not affect the sacrifice indirectly through an *Apūrva*, but directly by imparting a certain purity to the Person performing the sacrifice. And the fact of the sacrifice being thus affected is indicated by the context, as also by the Instrumental ending (in the word '*Brāhmaṇēna*'); and it is this very fact that enables us to accept the purification, &c., as subsidiary (to the Person, who thus comes to be recognised to have the primary position).

Even when the said Restrictive Injunction refers to a Person, apart from any sacrifices, the word '*kāmadhuk*' expressing the fulfilment of the desirable and useful purpose of Man,—it distinctly indicates the primary position of the Person.

Though, as a matter of fact, the utterance of a correct word is not for the sake of the speaker or the sacrificer (but for that of one to whom it is addressed),—yet it is the Restriction and Prohibition referring to such use that can be accepted as being for the sake of the speaker and the sacrifice. For certainly, it is not necessary that the Restriction and Prohibition in connection with a certain action must be for the sake of the same person, for whose sake the action itself is performed. For instance, though such actions as 'intercourse with women' and 'eating of meat' are found to be performed for the sake of the person, yet the prohibition of these acts is accepted, through the peculiarities of the context, as referring to the sacrifice. And again, though the sacrificial post made of the *khadira* wood is apparently found to serve a useful purpose in the performance of the sacrifice, yet from the peculiarity of the passage limiting the material of the *post* to the one particular kind of wood, we come to recognise it as imparting strength to the *person* (performing the sacrifice.) And so also through the 'feeding of the guest,' when the action of 'eating' belongs to the guest, the peculiar transcendental result following from it is found to accrue to the person feeding him. In the same manner, even though the word is uttered for the sake of another person, yet the Restriction and Prohibition pertaining to it, when seeking for a receptacle of their result, distinctly point to the person speaking, as he is found to be in closest touch (with the word.)

Thus then, the fact of the Science of Grammar being based upon the Veda having been fully established, it is extremely unfair to deny the fact of its being a scripture dealing with the usage of words.

The character of Scripture has been denied to the Science of Grammar, on the ground of its having been propounded by human authors; but this is as much against a universally acknowledged fact as to assert that the 'Moon is not the moon.' That is to say, if the word '*Çāstra*' (Scripture) is to be taken in its ordinary conventional signification, then it must include all the 'fourteen sciences'; and as Grammar is included among these, the character of '*Çāstra*' cannot be rightly denied to it. If, however, the word '*Çāstra*' be taken in its literal sense—*that which teaches*—, then, as we actually find Grammar *teaching* us the correct forms of words, or the Roots and Affixes as making up these words, and also teaching the students all these words, &c., the application of the word '*Çāstra*' to it cannot in any case be doubted.

Thus then, the fact of Grammar being a *Çāstra* being universally acknowledged, if one were to deny it on the strength of certain arguments, he could as reasonably seek to deny the name to the Veda also, on the ground of its being eternal, and thus similar to the *Ākāça* (which is not a *Çāstra*)! That is to say, you seek to deny the character of *Çāstra* to Grammar, simply on the ground of its being similar to certain other works of human authors (Drama and the like which are not *Çāstras*); and then, on the ground of the Veda resembling, in its eternality, such things as *Ākāça*, Time, Place, Self and Atom (none of which are *Çāstra*), you could deny the character of *Çāstra* to the Veda also! And certainly, if one who had learnt the refined language of the city were to address harsh words to his parents in the country, who could check him? For when a child is found to misbehave towards others, his parents check him; but who could check the child who would be insulting to his own parents? In the same manner, one who is found to be making incoherent assertions with regard to subjects apart from the Veda, is checked by the Veda itself; but when he proceeds to deprive the Veda itself of one of its essential parts (the Grammar), by what could he be checked? And when a person becoming angry with another cuts off his limbs, one whose limbs are thus cut off lives only for a very short time. Hence it is only when one wishes to destroy the Veda, that he begins by striking at its parts (the subsidiary sciences); and then continuing in the same path, he cuts off the main source itself.

But as a matter of fact we have found that the authoritative character of the Veda and the *Smṛtis* has been firmly established by means of various reasonings (detailed above),—how then could any one dare to deny the authority and the scriptural character of the subsidiary sciences (parts of the Veda)?

It has been urged by the *Pūrvapaksha* that "all the *Smṛtis* are found to resemble one another; while that of Grammar is entirely different from all of them; and as such Grammar cannot be accepted to be one of the *Smṛtis*."

And to this we make the following reply: We find a great resemblance among the *Dharmasūtras*, because all of them treat of the duties of the various castes and conditions of life; and as such there cannot be any very great dissimilarity among them; while the subject of Grammar is entirely different, treating as it does of the rules and regulations that go to prove the correctness of a word; and as such a work on Grammar could have resemblance with other works on Grammar itself, and not with the *Dharmasūtras*. And as for the character of *Smṛti*, it belongs equally to the *Dharmasūtras* and the 'subsidiary sciences' of the Veda (among which Grammar is one.)

Even though the 'subsidiary sciences' were not called '*Smṛtis*,' yet we could not deny the fact of their being so many scriptures and having a decidedly authoritative character; because Manu has declared an equal authority to belong to the following: "the Purānas, the Science of Duty as laid down by Manu, the Veda with all its Subsidiaries, and the Science of Medicine."

In regard to *Smṛtis*, we have shown above, under *Sūtra* I—iii—2, that they must be admitted to be authoritative, because their authors are the very same persons who are found to perform the sacrifices laid down in the Veda; and this reasoning is equally applicable to the Subsidiary Sciences of the Veda. And we have just shown above, that as bringing about visible as well as transcendental results, the authority of the Subsidiary Sciences of the Veda is cognisable by all the six means of right notion; and as such their authority can never be denied.

When one of the Subsidiary Sciences has been found to be based upon the Veda, then it may come to be accepted as forming a sound basis for other works of human authors. And in regard to that work of the human author of which a basis is not found, if it be asserted that it has no basis at all, such an assertion would be as acceptable as the description of a colour by one who is born blind. While in the case in question we find that the work has its basis upon a *Smṛti* that is based upon the Veda; and as such it has a decided authority, though removed by one degree.

Another objection in the *Pūrvapaksha* is that, "inasmuch as we find many contradictions among the *Sūtras* (of Pāṇini), the *Vārtika* (of Katyāyana) and the *Bhāshya* (of Patanjali), we cannot accept the authority of Grammar."

And to this we make the following reply: The presence of contradictions cannot be accepted as shaking the authority of the *Smṛtis*, inasmuch as we find many contradictions in the Vedas themselves. In fact if the *Smṛtis*, that are based upon contradictory passages of the Veda, were to be without any contradictions, then alone would they be untrustworthy; as in that case they would not be in keeping with the character of their basic texts. Because it is only when the character of the *Smṛti* is in exact keeping with that of its basic Vedic text, and not otherwise, that it can be accepted as authoritative. And hence the presence of contradictions in the *Smṛtis* cannot be held to affect their authority; specially as whenever there are two contradictory texts, they can both be accepted as optional alternatives; and none of them can be said to be absolutely false (or unauthoritative). But as a matter of fact there is no contradiction among the *Smṛtis* on the subject of Dharma (that is to say, all of them agree on the point of the use of correct words accomplishing a Dharma); and as all the contradictions that we perceive is in the matter of details, the presence of these cannot be considered a fault, as they treat of entirely different subjects.

As for the attacks upon the *Sūtras*, as with reference to there being useless repetitions, that are made by the *Vārtika*, &c., these cannot be urged as shaking the authority of the *Sūtras*; because such attacks are always followed by explanations in defence of the *Sūtra*, the authority of which thus becomes doubly strengthened. And as for these attacks themselves, they cannot be accepted as contrary authorities, because they have no basis in the Veda, and as such cannot be accepted as affecting the authority of the *Sūtras* which are based upon the Veda. And as for the additions and alterations (proposed in the *Vārtika* and the *Bhāshya*) these are all based upon other grammatical *Smṛtis;* and certainly the addition of more matter does not shake the authority of the briefer work. For instance, though the statement of the duties of the Adhvaryu priest is very brief in the *Vājasanēyi* Sanhita, and that in the *Caraka* Sanhita is much more detailed, yet this fact does not shake the authority of the former brief statement. Hence the presence of such additions cannot be taken as faulty.

As for the reproach that the author of the grammatical *Sūtras* has not mentioned the purpose or motive of his work;—such an omission does not merit a reproach; because the purpose of grammar is fully known from all *Vedas* and *Smṛtis;* and at the close of the grammatical work itself, its purpose becomes self-evident. And again, it is a fact universally known that the telling of truth leads one to Heaven, and helps to accomplish the sacrifices. And we all know that 'truth' is of two kinds—the truth of matter, and the truth of words. And just as the assertion of a true state of things brings future happiness to the person, so also does the utterance of the true word; and conversely, just as the perversion of the true state of things is sinful, so also is the perversion of the true word. And we have already shown that a knowledge of the true (or correct) word is obtained from a careful study of grammar (which is thus found to be indirectly serving the purposes of leading the man to Heaven and accomplishing the various sacrifices). And thus, the author of the *Sūtra* did not mention the purpose of his work, simply because it was found to be too well-known to need such mention—this purpose being the explanation of all words. Nor is there any difference of opinion on the point of the purpose of Grammar. And as to whether this purpose is rightful or not (upon which there is a diversity of opinion), it is a different matter altogether.

The author of the *Vārtika* has, however, distinctly pointed out the use of Grammar to lie in the laying down of certain restrictions, which help in the fulfilling of *Dharma;* and of such restrictions, one is based directly upon the Veda itself, while the other is based upon Grammar. That is to say, Grammar serves the purpose of laying down two restrictions—(1) that one should use only the correct forms of words—the knowledge and the using of such words leading the person to Heaven and helping to accomplish the sacrifices; and this is known from the Veda itself; and as such, not depending upon any other authority, this restriction must be accepted as laid down by the Veda itself; (2) that such and such words are correct—which is pointed out by Grammar alone; as without Grammar, the correct words could not be rightly distinguished from the incorrect ones. Thus then, we find that the methods of Grammar, being a part of the Vedic *Dharma* that consists of the use of the duly discriminated correct forms of words, serves the purpose of pointing out such correct forms as are rightly expressive.

Katyayāna has said—'If the knowledge of the correct word be said to constitute a *Dharma*, then, as such knowledge would also indirectly involve that of the incorrect word, it would be mixed with an *Adharma*'; and having thus pointed out the chance of *Adharma* in this theory, he comes to the conclusion that it is the actual *using* of the correct forms of words, in accordance with grammatical rules, that constitutes *Dharma*, and brings happiness to the agent. And though the *Mahābhāshya* has again resumed the former rejected theory, in the sentence—'Or the knowledge of the correct word may be said to constitute *Dharma*,' yet this has been added only with a view to show that the argument urged against this theory is not quite irrefutable; and hence this resumption is not with a view to casting any aspersion upon the *Vārtika*, but simply as a gratuitous prolonging of the discussion.

As a matter of fact, however, the mention of the result as following from a knowledge of the correct word cannot be accepted as literally correct, but only as an *Arthavāda*, which latter character is distinctly pointed out by the fact of the *knowledge* being auxiliary to something else, as is shown by the fact of this something else becoming absolutely useless (if the said auxiliary be accepted as actually accomplishing the mentioned result). As for instance, in the case of the passage—"One who performs the *Açvamēdha*, and one who knows it becomes freed from the sin of Brāhmana—slaughter,"—if the mere knowledge of the sacrifice were to actually accomplish the said result, who would be foolish enough to undertake the performance of the expensive and troublesome sacrifice itself? and as such the Injunction of the sacrifice would become absolutely useless. In the same manner, if the mere knowledge of the correct word were to accomplish the *Dharma*, who would ever undertake the trouble of pronouncing the word, and thereby tiring out his organs of speech? Hence we conclude that, as in the case of the *Açvamēdha* sacrifice, so in that of words also, it is the use (of the correct word duly discriminated) that constitutes *Dharma* (and not the mere knowledge of it). And the *Mahābhāshya* speaks of the *knowledge* as constituting *Dharma*, in accordance with the rule of speaking of the cause (knowledge) as the effect (the use following from such knowledge)—just as the rice that is offered in the sacrifice that brings rain is spoken of as the 'rain,' itself; and this declaration of the *Bhāshya* has been made with a view to show that the arguments (in the *Vārtika*) based upon the mixture of *Adharma* are not quite irrefutable; and it is not added with a view to show that the result really follows from the knowledge itself. Specially as according to the conclusions arrived at under the *Sutra* IV—iii—1, the knowledge of the word having its sole end in purifying the word used by the man, it cannot have anything to do with any other result. In all cases knowledge is always found to be a means of purifying, and as such auxiliary to something else; with the sole exception of the knowledge of Self.

As for the knowledge of Self; both by Conjunction and Disjunction it is found to help the sacrifice as well as the Person; because unless one knows his self (to be something other than the body that perishes) he would never undertake the sacrifices whose results are said to accrue to the man in another birth. And then again, such passages as—"the Self free from all evil...is to be sought after, &c.," "one should worship the Self"—lay down the knowledge of Self as accomplished by a process accompanied by due reflection, &c; and then from such knowledge, we find that there accrues to the agents both kinds of result—Happiness as well as final Deliverance, as is shown by the following passages:—"He obtains all worlds and all desires, passes beyond all sorrow, &c., &c.,"—which speaks of all the eight perfections of Yoga accruing to the person knowing the self; and the passage—"passing his life thus he, after death, reaches the regions of Brahma, and from there he never returns"—which points to the attainment of the Supreme Self (Final Deliverance) also as following from a due knowledge of the Self. And inasmuch as these passages do not occur in connection with any sacrifices, while they are directly related to the Self, the results mentioned in these cannot be said to be mere *Arthavādas;* as they are not like the passages mentioning certain results as following from the making of the sacrificial post of the *Khadira* wood, and so forth, which are found along with passages dealing with certain sacrifices (and being auxiliary to the sacrifices, the making of the *post*, &c., cannot be accepted as having independent results of their own).

Nor can it be rightly urged that, because the Self is laid down as the object of knowledge, it cannot have any connection with actions. Because the duties, necessary as well as occasional, relating to the various castes and conditions of life, have got to be performed, for the double purpose of destroying the evil effects of former sins, and the removal of all chance of the appearance of the sin that would follow from the non-performance of the necessary duties. And inasmuch as these duties on the one hand, and the knowledge of Self on the other, have distinct purposes to fulfil, and proceed on two entirely different lines, they cannot be said either to reject each other, or to be accepted as optional alternatives, or to form parts of one another. The knowledge of words, on the other hand, is always auxiliary to its usage, and always precedes it; and as such it cannot have any result apart from that which follows from such usage; and hence we conclude that the said results follow only from the using of the properly discriminated correct forms of words.

Another objection urged in the *Pūrvapaksha* is that, "the correct use of words following upon a knowledge of Grammar having a beginning in time, the mention of any results following from it, can never form the object of an eternal (Vedic) Injunction." But the continuity of Grammar is as eternal as that of the making of the sacrificial post, &c., (and though, as in the case of the post, the individual use of a correct word may have a beginning in time, yet such usage has ever continued from time immemorial); and as such the objection does not affect the question. And the eternality of Grammar is also pointed out by the Vedic passage—"the speech grammatically purified is used." Nor can it be urged that the 'purification' here spoken of is that accomplished by a long-established usage. Because in that case the addition of the word 'used' would be a useless repetition. We find Manu also declaring, while enumerating the holiest of Brāhmaṇas: "One who grammatically explains a sentence, and he who investigates the nature of sacrifices, &c.," and this distinctly shows that "he who explains grammatically" is something different from the person who has studied the Veda and also from one who investigates the nature of sacrifices; and as such the said passage cannot but be taken as pointing to a knowledge of Grammar (as an independent condition of *holiness*); and this distinctly shows that Grammar is eternal.

End of the Vyākaraṇādhikaraṇa.

ADHIKARAṆA (10)

[(*A*) *Treating of the fact of the words used and objects described in the Veda being the same as those in ordinary parlance—as part of* (*B*) *the exposition of the fact of the denotation of a word consisting in Class or Form*].

(A)

***Sūtra* (30). On account of non-differentiation there is sameness of the object; as otherwise there would be no Injunction of performance.**

From among the four kinds of words—Nouns, Verbs, Prefixes and *Nipātas*,—we take the case of the Nouns; and from among Nouns, signifying the Class, Property, Action, Substance, Names and Pronouns, we take into consideration only those that denote the Class; and from these again, we single out the word 'Cow' as a typical instance. And with regard to this we proceed to consider whether the word denotes the *Class* or the *Individual*.

But leaving this point aside for a time, to be taken up later, we proceed, with a view to ascertain the character of the means (word) and consequences (signification of Vedic Injunctions), to consider the question as to whether the words used in the Veda, and the meanings signified by them, are the same as those in ordinary parlance, or different?

An objection is here raised: "What would be the use of proving that the words used in the Veda are the same as those in ordinary parlance, that this should be taken up first of all?"

To this we make the following reply: The use of this discussion will be found to appertain to the Vedic words; while the means of such discussion and ascertainment is found in the ordinary parlance of the people of the present day; and as such it becomes necessary to prove the two to be the same. That is to say, if the words used in the Veda and the sense in which they are there used, be the same as those in ordinary parlance, then alone could it be possible for us to ascertain whether any particular object is denotable by a certain Vedic word or not; and this can be done only by conducting the discussion—as to a word signifying the Class or the

Individual—in accordance with the various usages current among the experienced men of the present day. While any ascertainment, as to whether a word really denotes the Class or the Individual, would not serve any useful purpose in ordinary parlance. Because in ordinary parlance, a word being used with reference to various intermixed significations, brings about the idea of only some of these significations; and thus the purpose of the speaker having been duly fulfilled even by the signification that only forms a part of the undifferentiated denotation of the word,—and thereby the purpose for which the word was used having been fulfilled either by the Class or by the Individual,—what would be the use of discriminating (as to whether the word really denotes the Class or the Individual)?

It may however be argued that—"as in the case of the Veda, so in ordinary parlance also, such discrimination would serve the purpose of rejecting or accepting the generic or the specific denotation of a word." But as a matter of fact, we find, in ordinary parlance, that (in the case of such assertions as 'give the curd to the Brāhmaṇas, but the *takra* to Kauṇdinya') the giving of the curd, &c., (as the generic alternative) or of the *takra* (as the exception) is pointed out by the exigencies of the circumstances; and this obviates all necessity of considering as to whether a certain word is to be taken in its direct denotation or indirect indication. And thus we find that any such enquiry is absolutely useless with regard to ordinary parlance; but it would serve a distinctly useful purpose with regard to the Veda, where we have no other means of ascertaining the meanings of words (as in this case we have no usage of the Elders to guide us).

Thus then, if the words used in the Veda were different from those in ordinary parlance, then we should never have any occasion to consider the question as to the word denoting the Class or the Individual, for the sake of ascertaining what is expressed and what is not expressed (by a word in the Veda). Whereas if they be identical, then the significations of words, acertained by means of the words used in ordinary parlance, would serve a distinctly useful purpose in the Veda, even though it could be of no use in ordinary parlance itself.

Thus then, we find that it is only when the words used in the Veda are the same as those in ordinary parlance, that there can be an occasion for the *Akṛtyadhikaraṇa* (the discussion as to the Class being the denotation of a word); whereas there could be no occasion for it if the two classes of words were entirely different.

And hence we now proceed to lay down the arguments in favour of the theory that the words used in the Veda are different from those in ordinary parlance—which constitutes the

PŬRVAPAKSHA——OF (A)

"As a matter of fact, we find that that there are many differences "between the Veda and ordinary parlance; for instance, (1) in the Veda "we have certain restrictions of accentuation, while there is none in ordi-"nary parlance; (2) the deletions, additions and modifications of the roots "and affixes as found in the Veda are entirely different from those in ordi-"nary language; (3) with regard to the Veda, the time for its study is "limited, while there is no such limitation with regard to ordinary parlance; "(4) the Veda is to be explained only to one who has been duly initiated, "while there is no such restriction with regard to the teaching of ordinary "language; (5) the Veda is taught to the three higher castes only, while "ordinary language is common to all the four castes; (6) the study of the Veda brings about certain (transcendental) results, while that of ordinary "language does not; (7) the Veda can be learnt from a traditional line of "Teachers duly propitiated by proper attendance and service, while ordinary "language may be learnt in any way one pleases. And for these reasons "we conclude that just as the sentences of the Veda, and the matter des-"cribed by them, are totally different from those in ordinary parlance, so "also are the words used in the Veda, and the objects denoted by them, "totally different from those in ordinary parlance. And then, inasmuch "as it is only the ordinary language that is found to be of use in daily "life, while that of the Veda is absolutely useless, we cannot admit *Dharma* "to be that *which is pointed out by the Veda*.

"That is to say, the word in the Veda is held to be different from that "in ordinary parlance, because the latter is not affected by the peculiarities "of accentuation; and because the Vedic word can be studied only in "certain specified days, while that of ordinary language can be studied "whenever one likes; and also because we actually find certain words—"as 'Agni,' *f.i.*, in the sentence '*Agnirvrttrāṇi janghanat*'—having a "formation and a meaning entirely different from that in ordinary par-"lance; and the Vedic passage—'the cows of the gods walk on their "back'—is to be explained in the same way as the passage—'the cake that is "burnt becomes fit for *Rākshasas.*' [That is to say, in the passage '*uttānā* "*vai dēvagavā vahanti*,' the word '*gavā*' alone can never form the subject "of the proposition; as for the '*dēvagavāh*' '*cows of the gods*,' these are as "impossible as the *walking upon one's back;* and as for explaining some-"how or other the possibility of such *cows of the gods*, it is as explicable "as the fact of their *walking on their backs;* hence as the fact of being "mentioned in the beginning of the sentence points to the 'moving on "backs' as being the subject of the proposition, the fact predicated of such "walking must be the 'denotation of the word *go*'; and this construction "of the sentence rejects that which makes 'the cows of the gods' the "subject, and 'walking on the backs' the predicate, which would be the re-"lationship as expressed by such a sentence in ordinary parlance]. And all "Vedic words being different (from those in ordinary usage), the meaning of "no Vedic words could be ascertained by the help of other words preceding "and following it [*i.e.*, if only a few of the Vedic words were different "from those in ordinary usage, then the meaning of these latter being fully "known, these could help us to ascertain the meaning of the Vedic words "occurring among them; and thus the meaning of Vedic words being "ascertainable by means of the Veda itself, even if they were totally "different from the words in ordinary usage, we could have an oppor-"tunity for considering whether these words denote the Class or the Indi-"vidual. But as a matter of fact all Vedic words are different from those "in ordinary usage; and hence it is not possible.]

"Thus then, inasmuch as we find that the words of the Veda differ "from those of ordinary parlance, on the point of—(1) the former being "capable of being studied in a certain definite method specially laid down, "and the latter having no such method specified for it, and (2) the former "having its words and sentences irrevocably fixed, while the latter are ever "changeable, and (3) and the names and forms of the one being entirely "different from those of the other,—we conclude that all the words used in "the Veda, and the objects denoted by them, are entirely different from "those in ordinary parlance."

On this, we have the following:—

SIDDHANTA (A).

We cannot but admit the two classes of words to be identical; because otherwise, there could be no Injunction of the performance of any action. And if it be urged that "such Injunction being a result in itself, any non-accomplishment of this would not matter much,"—we reply, that we shall prove its impossibility on the ground of 'non-differentiation.' That is to say, if there be a difference, the words in the Veda would be entirely strange to an ordinary person; and as such any Vedic sentence would be absolutely meaningless to him; and there would be a complete absence of all such Injunctions as tend to prompt people to the performance of certain actions.

Or, the reasoning expressed in the clause '*prayogacodanābhāvāt*' (in the *sūtra*) may be explained as that it is only when the two classes of words are identical, that there can be any Injunctions of the performance of actions. The *sūtra* speaks of the identity of the objects expressed ('*arthaikatva*') (though that of words is also meant), because the object is the more important factor of the two; or the word '*artha*' may be taken in the sense of 'thing;' and this would apply to the word as well as to the object spoken of. That is to say, though the identity meant to be expressed is both of the words and the objects spoken of, yet the *sūtra* mentions the word '*artha*' alone; because this would naturally imply that of the 'word' also; or the word '*artha*' may be taken as signifying 'things' in general; and this would include both the words and the objects spoken of.

With a view to the fact that the arguments expressed in the clause '*prayogacodanābhāvāt*'—in whichever of the two ways it may be explained—would serve our purpose only when we would be having a discussion with an opponent who also believes in the Veda, and it would fail when addressed to others;—the Bhāshya raises the question—"The Injunction of performance spoken of is one of the uses of words; and it is a proof that you have to give."

And to this we offer the following reply: *Because of non-differentiation.* That is to say, in proof of the said identity, we have the following non-differentiations:—(1) The word '*go*' found in the Veda is recognised as non-different from that met with in ordinary usage; (2) the object expressed by the word '*go*' as used in the Veda is found to be non-different from that expressed by it in ordinary usage; (3) all the difference that we do perceive is only in regard to sentences, and none with regard to words and letters; (4) the pronunciation and the degrees of effort employed in the utterance of Vedic words are perceived to be non-different from those in that of words in ordinary parlance; and (5) the rules laid down by grammarians are not found to be different in the case of Vedic words and in that of the words in ordinary usage.

That is to say, inasmuch as we actually recognise the words used in the Veda to be the same as those used in ordinary parlance, we cannot but accept them to be identical. And it follows from this that the objects spoken of also being expressed by the same words must be accepted to be the same in both cases.

And though in certain Vedic passages—as in the passage 'the cows of the gods walk on their backs'—a well-recognised word is found to point to something altogether strange (i.e., *walking on the back*, which we do not perceive in the ordinary cow); yet even in this case, there being nothing incongruous in taking the word 'cow' to mean the same thing that it does in ordinary parlance, the word expressing the strange thing may be explained as simply showing a difference in the quality of the object denoted. (But this does not necessitate any difference in the object itself) as for instance, a cow that is abnormally dwarf is still known as a *cow;* and a man with a flat nose, or with his ears covered, is not denied the name of 'Man.' Exactly in the same manner, the denotation of the *cow* being the same in both cases, if there be a difference in the qualifications described, this cannot make any difference in the object itself; specially as the word ('cow') does not denote any individual cow (whose character could be affected by qualifications). And again (for the same reason) the cows that are spoken of in the above passage as belonging to the gods (and having the peculiarity of walking on their backs) need not always be those meant by the word 'cow' throughout the Veda; specially as we often find the Vedic passages laying down the gifts of cows at sacrifices, using the word 'cow' in the sense of the ordinary cow of the world.

In the same manner, though the trees on the Mēru Mountain (the residence of the gods) have their leaves of gold, yet the word 'tree' cannot be said to signify, in the region of the gods, anything other than the ordinary *tree.* So too, though what is *butter* for us be *honey* for the gods, yet the meaning of the words do not become different, specially as what we know as 'butter' is what is transformed, by certain modifications of taste and potencies, into the 'honey' of the gods. And as a matter of fact all Vedic words being equally strange to the ordinary man (according to theory of the *Pūrvapaksha*), not a single word of the said passage could be comprehended; and as such the expression 'walking on the back' being itself uncomprehended, it could not point to the 'cow' spoken of in the passage as being (on account of such *walking*) something other than the ordinary cow.

For these reasons, we conclude that the 'cows' spoken of as belonging to the gods and 'walking on their backs' must be the same that are known as such in the ordinary world, though belonging to the gods. Or, the passage may refer to the fact that it is the ordinary cows of the Earth that are referred to in the passage, as appearing to walk on their backs, owing to the revolutions of the Earth together with all the three worlds, as described in the Purāṇas. That is to say, just as we see the gods above us, so too, when in the course of revolution the Earth reaches a point above the abode of the gods, they see the things on the Earth as above them; and hence it is only natural that to them the cows walking on the Earth should appear to be walking on their backs.

Hence we conclude that the words used in the Veda, as also the objects denoted by them, are the same as those in ordinary parlance.

We now proceed to consider the question—

(B).

Does a word denote the Class or the Individual ?

And on this point, though the Bhāshya puts forth only two alternatives, yet the commentators thereupon could spin out innumerable alternatives; through individual restriction, alternation, acceptance of both separately, as well as together, the acceptance of their relationship, or collection, or that of the one qualified by the other. These alternatives again could be spun out into many others by mutual intermixture; as also by being blended with notions of gender, case, number, &c., taken singly or all together; and thereby the alternatives become innumerable.

For instance, at first we have the following eight alternatives as to the denotation of a word: Does it signify—(1) the Class only, or (2) the Individual only, or (3) either the Individual or the Class optionally, (4) both the Class and the Individual, or (5) the relationship of both, or (6) the two taken together, or (7) the Individual as qualified by the Class, or (8) the Class as specified by the Individual. Then again, does it signify —the Relationship qualified by the Class alone, or by the Individual alone, or by the Individual or the Class optionally, or by both taken together, or by the Individual as specified by the Class, or by the Class as specified by the Individual, or by these as specified by one another, or by both? Again, does the word signify the collection of both as qualified by the Class alone, &c., &c., as before? So also, does it signify the Relationship as qualified by the Class alone, &c., &c., &c.? Again, does the word signify the Class as qualified by the relationship, or by the collection, or by both the relationship and the collection optionally or by these as taken together? So also is it the Class alone or the Individual alone as qualified by these, either one by one, or by both taken together; or the Individual and the Class, one by one, or both together? Or is it the Individual as qualified by the Relationship as specified by the Class; or is it the Class as qualified by the Relationship specified by the Individual, or these one by one, or both taken together? So also in the case of the Collection of these two. So again, is it the Class alone as qualified by the Individual specified by the Relationship, or is it the Individual as qualified by the Class specified by the Class? Or, is it the Individual and the Class one by one, or taken together? And we will have the same alternatives with regard to the Collation of the two. Again, is it the Individual as qualified by the Relationship specified by the Class, or the Class as qualified by the Relationship specified by the Individual; or these two taken either separately or together? So also by making the Relationship specified by the Collation of these two. Again, is it the Individual as qualified by the Class specified by the Relationship, or the Class as qualified by the Individual specified by the Rela tionship; and so forth. So also we could have other alternatives by taking the specification of these by their Collation. In the same manner, does the word signify the Class or the Gender, the Class or the Case, the Class or the Number? And with each of these alternatives, we could have all those that have been ennunciated above; so also with the various combinations of the Gender, Case and Number.

Then again, we could have many alternatives as to the denotation of the word lying in the form of the word or in that of the Class, &c.; and thus would have all the aforesaid alternatives.

Though all these alternatives have not been pointed out by the *Bhāshya*, yet they are all as perceptible to the intellect, as the Distinctions of Class, Substance and Property. In all cases a slight difference is always perceptible by means of the sense-organs and the distinguishing mark (Inferential) of each of these; and Verbal testimony too points out the slightest differences among various objects. Thus then, beginning from the word, the Cognition that proceeds in a man has its flowers in the denotations of words, and fruits in the meanings of sentences.

Among all these alternatives, that of the Class being the object of denotation is on one side, and all the others are on the other,—all these latter being based upon the theory of the Individual being the object denoted by the word. And hence, when it has been proved that the Individual is not denoted by the word, all the other alternatives become rejected by it; and it is for this reason that the Bhāshya has not spoken of these, apart from the Individualistic theory. But this non-mention does not show that these alternatives do not exist, or that they are absolutely useless; in fact, when explained in all their details, they serve the purpose of expanding the intellect of the student. And hence, though we have shown out all the alternatives in detail, yet it is with reference to the two —Class and Individual—only that we proceed to consider which of them is directly denoted and which is indirectly implied.

And in order to justify the very introduction of the discussion, the Bhāshya proceeds to put a question and then explain what these (the Class and the Individual) really are.

Objection: "The *Ākṛti* that you proceed to consider now has already been dealt with in the *Tarkapāda* (See *Çloka-vārtika*, Trans. pp. 281-95); what then is the use of any question and answer with regard to the same thing?"

Reply: True it is that we have already described '*Ākṛti*' as being cognisable by sense-perception. But we proceed to explain that what is meant by '*Ākṛti*' is, not the *shape* or *form*, but the *Class*. This is what the Bhāshya means by declaring it to be *the commonality of Substances, Properties and Actions*.

The classes of these substances too are relative in their extension, one being included in another and so on. As for instance, the class 'Thing' is the highest that we can think of; and in this are included, in the order of lesser extension, the classes, 'Substance,' 'Air,' 'Fire,' 'Water,' 'Self.' Under 'Substance' again, we have in the same order, 'Earth,' 'Jar,' &c., ending with the individual jars. Under the class 'Tree,' we have the classes '*Çinçapā*' and the rest; under 'Body,' we have 'Cow,' 'Horse,' 'Elephant,' 'Man,' &c.; and then the classes '*Karka*,' &c., are expressive of the properties of horses; as under 'Elephant,' we have the various species '*Bhadra*,' '*Madra*,' &c. Under 'Man,' we have '*Brāhmana*,' '*Kaundinya*,' '*Katha*,' &c. And just under the class 'Substance' we have the above, so too under 'Property' and 'Action,' we have 'White,' &c., and the individual actions of 'Sacrifice,' 'Homa,' and such other endless actions as are differentiated by means of various verbal roots, as also by distinct Injunctions, Numbers, and Names and Properties, &c.,—as is held by other teachers of the Science. Or, all actions may be included in the one class of 'Action,' the only difference consisting in the distinctions of place, time, &c., as has been taught by Jaimini himself under the *sūtra-Rūpaçabdāvibhāgāt*.

Thus then, it is proved that *Ākṛti* is *Commonality*, and not the *shape* of things; specially as, if it meant the latter, how could it ever belong to such immaterial objects as the Self and the like? That is to say, such material objects as the *jar* and the like, may be found to have certain shapes, but in the case of such objects as Light, Water, Air and *Ākaçā*, all the shape that is perceived is that which belongs to the Earthy element in them, and not to them by themselves. While in the case of such purely immaterial objects as the Self, Space, Time and Mind, as also in that of 'Action' and 'Property,' there can never be any shape at all. Whereas Commonality or Class is found to apply to all things in the world. Hence we conclude that what is meant by the word '*Akṛti*' in the present Adhikaraṇa, is 'Class,' and not any material form or shape. Specially as the material shape of objects is destructible and varies in each individual, no such shape could ever be said to constitute the *Commonality* of objects. Even if the class 'shape' itself be said to be meant by '*Ākṛti*,' then such a class being equally applicable to the cow and the horse, &c., there would be a hopeless overlapping of classes. Because in that case there would be no such sub-class of shape as would form the denotation of the word 'cow' and pervade over all individual cows, excluding all other animals, like the horse, &c.; and when looking for such a differentiating factor, we cannot find any other except the *Class*; and thus it becomes established that '*Class*' is the only commonality of objects.

Thus then, inasmuch as the instances of '*Ākṛti*, cited in the *Tarkapāda*, being the various ornaments '*svastika*' and the like, it would seem that it was the material shape of objects that was meant, as held by the followers of Gautama; and it is with a view to remove this misconception that the Bhāshya has explained the real meaning by means of questions and answers. Therefore we conclude that prior to the perception of individual Substances, Properties and Actions, what is perceived of them, is all that is meant by the word '*Akṛti*'; this is indicated by the word '*mātra*' in the Bhāshya.

Says the Bhāshya : *Asādhāraṇaviçēshā vyaktih.* And some people explain this as defining the *Individual* to be the specific (*asādhāraṇāh*) peculiarities (*viçēshāh*).

But this is not correct; because the Individual is something entirely different from the peculiarities. Because what are held to be such 'peculiarities' are the '*khanda*' (presence of defective limbs) '*munda*' (absence of horns) and the like; but these are found to exist in various individuals of the same class, and in those of other classes; and so also are the peculiarities of the 'grey colour' and the like, which are found to apply to the progeny of a cow of the said colour. That is to say, the properties of the *Khanda*, &c., are found to exist in many individuals, of the same as well as different classes; *e.g.*, there are such cows, buffaloes and *gavayas*, &c.; and similarly too, one animal may be just as grey as the other; and the name '*Çāvalēya*' would also apply to the progeny of the *Çavala* (grey) cow; and thus the name '*Çāvalēya*,' whether it be based upon the presence of a particular colour, or a mere conventional name, is applicable to many individuals; and hence 'grey' (colour) cannot rightly be said to be a *specific* (*asādhāraṇa*) peculiarity (though as a matter of fact we always recognise the *grey cow* as an *individual*; and hence the peculiarities cannot be said to be the Individuals). And secondly, in this explanation of the Bhāshya passage, the plural number in '*Viçeshā*' would not be quite compatible with the singular in '*Vyaktih.*'

For these reasons we must explain the Bhāshya passage as defining the *Individual* to be *that which possesses certain specific peculiarities of character.*

Against this explanation of the compound as *Bahuvrīhi* it may be urged that, "as shown above the peculiarities *khanda*, &c., are found to be common to many individuals, and as for any such peculiarities as would belong to particular individuals only, no such are possible."

But to this, we make the following reply: we do not mean that each Individual is to have any property peculiar to itself exclusively; all that we mean is that certain characteristics, two or three together, are always recognised as being conjointly peculiar to a certain object, even when each of them singly may be found to belong to other objects as well. That is to say, even though certain properties may have been found to exist separately in many objects, yet taken together they are found only in a certain individual; and such an Individual may be said to be specifically characterised by these peculiarities (collectively). And as a matter of fact we find that certain properties that have been perceived in a certain object are never found to exist, exactly in the same proportions, in any other object; and the particular combination of properties that, never having been perceived elsewhere, is perceived in any object, comes to be recognised as its specific peculiarity. And thus, though there be an endless number of individuals, yet that does not make it necessary to assume an endless number of specific characteristics. Thus then, the necessary specifying peculiarity always being found, by only slight modifications, among a definite number of properties, all lesser (less extensive) classes also come to be recognised as individuals under the higher (more extensive) ones. And it is only the particular combinations of properties that come to be known by the name of '*Visçēha*' (Specific Peculiarity).

The difference between the Individual and the Specific Peculiarities will be distinctly pointed out by the Bhāshya itself later on, in the passage: 'That which is the object of the commonality, and *the receptacle of specific peculiarities* is the Individual.'

With regard to the denotation of words, some people (notably the author of the *Vākyapadīya*, and other grammatical writers) hold the following view: "The class 'cow' itself is the specific peculiarity (of the "individual cow); and as it is not possible for such a specific property "to be expressed by a word whose denotation is always generic, what is "really expressed by the word ('cow') is the *summmum genus*, known as "'Being' or 'Thing' or 'Entity,' as specified by the form of the word "('cow') and the specific peculiarity of 'cowness'; that is to say, it is "the 'being of the cow' that is expressed by the word 'cow'; specially as "the true explanation of what is really signified by words is that all "words denote their 'being'; and in this all of them resemble the words "'*Apūrva*' '*Dēvatā*' and '*Svarga*' (which denote only the *being or existence* of such supposed objects, which have no objective reality)."

But this view is not correct; as it makes no difference among the various classes themselves; and we can never admit that the word 'cow' denotes any such 'being' in general. The expressive potency of a word is always perceived, through Apparent Inconsistency, to be restricted to a certain definite object. And even such words as 'Substance,' 'Property,' and 'Action,' which are expressive of classes immediately under the *summum genus* of 'Being,' will be found to have their denotations hopelessly mixed up, if they be all accepted as denoting the class 'Being' only; what then, would be the case with the words that are expressive of other minor classes?

And again, those who hold all words to signify 'Being,' cannot define whether they denote pure *Being* by itself, or as qualified by something else; because none of these two alternatives is admissible.

For if it be pure 'Being' that is denoted by the word, then all the words in the world would be synonymous; and any use of the verb 'is' would be an inadmissible repetition ; and any such assertion as 'the cow is not' would be a hopeless self-contradiction ; as it is absolutely impossible ever to cognise that 'Being is not.' Even with regard to special times and places, the existence of 'Being' can never be denied ; because being eternal and all-pervading, it must exist at all times and in all places.

Nor does ordinary usage warrant the assertion that the denotation of all words is conventionally fixed in 'Being' alone. And for these reasons it is not right to assert that 'Being' is the conventionally fixed commonality of such things as 'Substance' and the like.

The word '*sattā*' (Being) is formed from the word '*Asti*' (is) as twice modified by means of two nominal affixes—(1) that which is *sat*, and (2) the character of *sat is sattā* ; and this is found to be applicable to all things at all periods of their existence, beginning from their production, and throughout all the various modifications that they undergo, to the point of time immediately preceding their destruction. And hence if this *summum genus* of 'Being' were the denotation (of all words), then it would have been more reasonable for the *Vākyapadīya* to assert 'things' to be the denotation of all things, than 'existence or being? Nor have the words '*sat*' and '*sattā*' any other meaning than that which is signified by their root (*to be*) ; and hence they being exactly like the word '*bhavat*' (the Present participle form of the root '*bhū*' *to be*), the word '*sattā*' must mean '*sadbhāva*,' *existence ;* and it cannot be gratuitously assumed, according to the *Vaiçēshikas*, to signify a Class consisting of the idea that we have of the existence of Substance, Property and Action.

Thus then, it has been shown that the word '*sattā*' is formed out of the indeclinable form '*asti*,' which is synonymous with 'thing,' and similar in character to the word '*bhavat*.' The word ('*asti*'), from out of which we have the forms '*astitva*' and '*astitā*' (Being), is that which denotes 'thing ;' and it has all the appearance of a verb ; though in reality it is not a verb ; because if it were a verb, it could not be a noun ; and as such no such nominal affixes as 'tva' or 'tvā' could ever be applied to it. And it is because it is not a verb that we have such compounds as '*astikshīrā*' in which the word '*asti*' (an Indeclinable) means 'existing.' The expression '*astikshīrā gauh*' cannot be said to contain a verbal compound ; and hence we must accept the compound as *Bahuvrīhi*,' consisting of an Indeclinable (*asti*) which is capable of taking declentional terminations, and the noun '*kshīra*,' the meaning being 'that (cow) which has (plenty of) milk' ; thus alone can the expression give any sense.

It is for this reason that having found (in the said compound, f.i.)

the word '*asti*' used in the sense of 'thing,' and also finding the word '*sat*' to be closely connected with it, and then applying to it the reflexive affix '*tal*,' as in the word '*devatā*' (*deva* and *tal*),—but disregarding all notion of the nominative of the verb 'to be,'—the Logicians come to accept the word '*sat*' and '*sattā*' to signify merely what is denoted by the root 'to be'; and it is from this that they come to the conclusion that the word '*sat*' signifies the *summum genus* 'Being' (*sattā*.) But inasmuch as this view is not authorised by the scriptures, it has been rejected by all Grammarians and Mīmānsakas; even though it has come to be so commonly believed in as to make the aforesaid 'Being' appear to be denotable by even such words as 'cow' and the like.

As a matter of fact, however, though the genus 'thing' is indicated by all words, yet it cannot be said to form part of its denotation; as for 'Being,' however, it points to an entirely different property; and as such how can it ever be accepted as forming the denotation of all words? In the case of the word 'thing,' though the genus that it signifies inheres in an altogether different *class* and *individual*, yet it is indirectly indicated by such objects as the cow and the like.

The denotation (by all words) of pure *Being* by itself having thus been found to be inadmissible, it becomes all the more unreasonable to assert the denotation of the word 'cow' to consist in the genus 'Being' as qualified by the *cow* (*i.e.*, the *being of the cow*). That is to say, this theory would be open to all the objections that we shall urge against the theory of the denotation of words consisting of the Individual as qualified by the Class, or of the Class as specified by the Individual. Specially as the qualifying factor would always be cognised beforehand.

That is to say, if the word 'cow' be held to express the *being of the cow*, then, we ask—does the word signify 'Being' as qualified (1) by the *class* 'Cow,' or (2) by the *individual* cows? (1) If the former, then, as in that case, the real denotation of the word 'Cow,' (as also 'Being') having been accomplished in the qualifying adjunct (*Class* 'cow') itself (which is always cognised beforehand), what would be the use of the denotation of 'Being' after that? That is to say, without a previous expression of the qualifying adjunct, it is always impossible to have any notion of the qualified; and then, the qualifying adjunct being closely related to the qualified, the previous cognition of the qualifying adjunct (the *class* 'Cow') could not but have indicated the genus 'Being' also; and as such we would not have any Apparent Inconsistency (of the idea of 'Being' entering into the conception of the *class* 'Cow') that could justify us in assuming this (notion of 'Being') to form part of the direct denotation of the word 'Cow.' (2) If, however, the word 'Cow' be held to denote the genus 'Being' as qualified by the *individual* cows,—

this too would be open to the same objections; and there would be the further objection of such a theory necessitating the assumption of the denotation of endless 'Beings' as preceded by that of an equally endless number of Individual cows by an endless number of words, by means of an endless potentiality of words bearing certain transitory relations (with the said endless Individuals, &c); and all this would make it as objectionable as the theory that the word denotes the *Individual.*

It has been asserted in the above quotation from the *Vākyapadīya*, that—"the case of these words is said to be similar to those of the word '*Apūrva*' '*Dēvatā*' and '*Svarga.*'" To this we make the following reply: It is a well-ascertained fact that the words '*Apūrva*,' &c., do not signify the genus 'Being'; in fact they too are actually found to denote certain specific individuals, as is proved by the Apparent Inconsistency (of the ideas of particular things brought about by these words). Some of these words are recognised as signifying certain particular individuals, either through the Apparent Inconsistency of what is directly heard, or through supplementary explanations, or through other sentences; and through this specific denotation of theirs, they also indicate, as the necessary concomitant of these, the genus 'Being'; which, thus, cannot be accepted as forming part of their direct denotation. Hence we conclude that, inasmuch as no object can avoid being concomitant with 'Being,' the idea of this latter is due to an indirect indication by these words.

We actually find the words '*Apūrva*,' &c., having a meaning distinctly apart from the genus 'Being'; as for instance, '*Apūrva*'=a certain potentiality of the Action; '*Dēvatā*'=Indra and others; and '*Svarga*'= unalloyed pleasure. To explain further, all objects in the world are cognised, through Apparent Inconsistency, to have distinct potentialities of their own; and hence we also admit of the existence of a potentiality, born of the performance of sacrifices, capable of bringing to the Agent a certain result at some future time; and to this potency, we give the name of '*Apūrva*,' so called because it had no existence prior to the performance of the sacrifice, from which it follows; and thus the name applying to the potency in its very literal sense. So also the word '*Dēvatā*' signifies those that *shine*, in the shape of the Sun, the Moon and the Stars, and those that are *eulogised* by all *Mantras* as constantly moving, in the shape of Vāyu and others; and thus this word also having its denotation duly ascertained as resting in certain individuals, it cannot be accepted as denoting the genus 'Being.' So also the word '*Svarga*' is found to signify either the *starry regions*, or the regions situated on the summit of Mount Meru, as described in the Arthavada passages of the Veda, and in various Purāṇas and Itihāsas; *e.g.*, we read in the Veda—"those men of pious deed who proceed to heaven, attain the regions of the star," and "they conquer those bright regions of the pious." As it may be taken to mean the summit of Mount Meru, as described in Purāṇas and Itihāsas. Or again, it may be taken as signifying pure pleasure, duly differentiated by means of negative and affirmative concomitances, which is experienced during a thousand years, and which is capable of being experienced in some other region, as is distinctly proved by the Apparent Inconsistency of the fact of such pleasure being free from all taint of such sources of pain, as hunger, thirst and the like; (all the pleasure in this world being always found to be mixed with more or less of pain). Though any such pleasure has never been experienced in this world, yet we can form an idea of it by abstracting it from the mixed experiences that we have; and thus the word '*Svarga*' directly denoting such pleasure, can only indirectly indicate the genus 'Being' which cannot be admitted to form part of its direct denotation.

Thus then, we find the denotations of the words '*Apūrva*,' &c., to be exactly similar to those of the words 'cow' and the like; and it is only when such denotations have been directly pointed out by the words, that they are capable of indirectly indicating the genus 'Being.' And hence we cannot admit the word 'Cow' to denote the 'being' of the cow.

Then, all the doubt that there is is with regard to the question of the denotation of the word consisting in the *Class* or in the *Individual*; and the present discussion is with regard to this question.

The Bhāshya says—"Wherefore should there be any doubt?" This is an objection to the discussion, emanating from one who, finding all business referring to the individual objects, holds the denotation of the word to consist in the Individual.

But to this objection we reply that from seeing all business referring to the individuals, we conclude the denotation of the word to be in the Individual; and yet on a consideration of the true expressiveness of the word, the denotation is not found to be apart from the Class; and hence there being a disagreement between the conclusions with regard to the true denotation of the word, as pointed out by the denotability of the object and by the conduct of ordinary business, it certainly becomes a matter for consideration, as to which of these two conclusions is the correct one.

And on this question, we have the following:—

PŪRVAPAKSHA (B).

"Inasmuch as we could have no Injunctions of Actions (if words "signified Classes), it is the Individual alone that can be denoted by a "word. Both the Individual and the Class cannot be said to be denoted by "it; because we have already shown above that a word can reasonably "have only one signification; and also because the Class is always cognis-"ed along with the Individual. Since all words that are laid down as "with reference to a certain purpose have the sole end of expressing "certain meanings, therefore their true denotation must always be as-"certained in accordance with what they are actually found to signify; "and hence the meanings of all words should be ascertained in such a "way as to render them capable of forming fit auxiliaries to the mean-"ings of the sentences in which they occur (and in sentences words "cannot but denote individual objects). Thus then, if the word '*Vrīhi*' "signified the Class (in the sentence 'washes the Vrihi'), what would be "the object washed? (for certainly no washing of the Class would be "possible). And in the sentence '*Somēna yajēta*,' if the word '*soma*' "denoted the Class, what would be the material offered at the sacrifice? "For certainly no offering of the Class is ever possible. And further, "the Class being incorporeal and eternal, there could never be any "'threshing' of it; and as such, any Injunction or Prohibition of such "'threshing' would not be possible.

"That is to say, we meet with such sentences as—'threshes the corn,' "'kills the animal,' 'presses the soma-juice,' 'purifies the soma,' 'one "should perform sacrifices with *soma*, animals, corns, &c., &c.'; and in all "these, the objects that are spoken of as being purified or employed for the "fulfilment of certain purposes, cannot but be those that are perishable "and corporeal; consequently we could have no such Injunctions of "actions, if the words 'corn' and the rest were significant of Classes; "while all these become possible if Individuals be held to be denoted by "them; and the cognition of the significations of words having their "chief use in the bringing about of the activity of human agents which is "brought about by Injunctions, we must always accept the significations "of all words to be such as are capable of properly fitting in the meanings "of sentences that appear as Injunctions. So also, in the case of Prohibi-"tions, such as 'the Brāhmana should not be killed' and the like, these "also depend upon a previous conception of the performability of such "actions (as are now prohibited); and it is only with regard to a certain "individual Brāhmana, that there could be any notion of the performabili-"ty of slaughter, which could never refer to the Class ('Brāhmana'); "and hence if the word 'Brāhmana' signified the Class, there being no "previous conception of the slaughter, any prohibition of it would be "absolutely useless. Hence, we can admit of only such significations of "words as would make it possible for us to have the Injunctions of "Actions; and we can never admit of any signification for mere transcen-"dental results.

"It may be argued that in the case of Injunctions that refer to

"Individuals we could accept the words to denote Individuals; while in "those referring to Classes, these could be accepted to be denoted by the "words.' But this would not be quite right; because we have already proved "by arguments that a word can have only one meaning; otherwise (if many "significations of words were accepted) such a process would necessitate "the most unreasonable assumptions of indefinite relationships, endless, "invisible, expressive potencies, and would be open to all the eight objec- "tions that have been shown to appertain to all options; and moreover "such assumptions would be absolutely uncalled for; as a comprehension "of the word could be accomplished by means of any *one* of the various "assumed significations.

"It may be asked—how then have we an idea of the Class? To this, "the *sūtra* replies: *Because of non-disjunction.* That is to say, inas- "much as the Class is always cognised along with the Individual, when- "ever the Individual happens to be denoted by a word, it indicates (its "concomitant) the Class also. It is with a view to this that it is said in the "*Tadbhūtādhikaraṇa*: (I—i—34) that when a certain meaning of a word "has been accepted, it is not possible to reject it; and hence any other "meaning that it may be found to have must be held to be indirectly "indicated by it.

"If it were a Class that was denoted by the word, it would belong "equally to all the Individuals included therein, and it could never be "rightly ascertained, which one of these was actually meant in any particu- "lar instance; whereas when it is an Individual that is denoted by the word "it can point to one Class only (of which it is a unit); and as such, in "this case the notion of the Class would be obtained by means of the in- "direct indication of the same word that directly denotes the Individual "(whereas in the former case we would have to postulate a certain unheard "of faculty in the word by which it could bring about the notion of the "Individual, while directly denoting the Class). For these reasons, we "conclude that it is the Individual that constitutes the denotation of a "word.

"As for the other innumerable alternatives spoken of above, none of "these can be rightly accepted, as we have notions of all these along with "that of the Individual (which alone can be accepted as denoted by the "word).

***Sūtra* (31): "Also because words would not denote a substance".** (if its denotation consisted of the Class, there would be no co-ordination with Adjectives).

[The *sūtra* has been translated in accordance with the interpretation of the *Vārtika*, which is at variance with that of the *Bhāshya*.]

The Sūtra explained according to the Bhāshya.

"And further, because of the impossibility of there being any word "expressive of the property (of substances), we must accept the Indivi-"dual to be denoted by the word; because there could be co-ordination "between the word signifying a Class and that which signifies a property. "For instance, if the word 'Cow' denoted the Class 'Cow,' in the case of "all such assertions as—'the *white cow*' 'purchases the Soma with a "*one-year old reddish cow with yellowish eyes*,' '*six cows* should be given,' "'one should offer the gift of a *single cow*,' and the like—the Nouns "denoting Classes, and the adjectives denoting particular properties, "there could be no co-ordination between the two; *i.e.*, the adjective "'white,' 'reddish,' &c., could not qualify the *class* 'cow.' Nor is there "any relationship possible between these, which would justify our using "such expressions as 'the white of the cow'; and hence it is all the more "impossible for them to be regarded as co-extensive (inhering in a single "substratum). For certainly, it is not the *Class* 'cow' that is either white "or red, or six in number; it is the *individual* cow that is always re-"cognised as having these properties; and hence we must hold the "Individual to be denoted by the word.

[The explanation of the *sūtra* in accordance with the view of the *Vārtika* itself is as follows :—]

"According to us, the word denoting the Individual, there would be a "co-ordination with adjectives; while according to the Class-theory, "there being no denotation of any individual substances by the word, "there would be as great a divergence between the noun and its qualify-"ing Adjective as between the Cow and the Horse. Whether the word "be accepted to denote the Individual as specified by the Class and a "certain property, or the Individual alone by itself, there would always "be a co-ordination, if our view of the case is accepted. And what is "referred to by the word 'Dravya' (substance) in the *sūtra* is the *Indivi-"dual cow as qualified* by the quality of 'whiteness'; and it is the im-"probability of the denotation of any such common substance that is pointed "out by the negative particle (in the compound '*Adravyaçabdatvāt*).'

"The way in which the Bhāshya has taken the *sūtra* has necessita-"ted the acceptance of an indirect signification of the word '*dravya*,' which "is made to indicate *that which is contained in the dravya—viz.*, Property,—"as also the acceptance of the negative particle forming part of a com-"pound, of which it is not in a position to form a part (inasmuch as it "is dependent for its full significance upon a certain word signifying "'existence' which is not contained in the compound). The meaning thus "got at from the *sūtra* would be that *in accordance with the Class-theory*, "*there could be no word expressive of the properties of an object.* But we "have rejected this interpretation, because it is too far-fetched, and "necessitates our having recourse to the secondary signification (of the "word '*dravya*') pointed out by something (the expression 'does not "exist,' which is supplied from without and is) not contained in the com-"pound itself.

"But the interpretation of the Bhāshya could be justified in a "way by construing its words in the following manner:—The word that "signifies that (the Property) which inheres, in the substance, is what is "spoken of as '*Adravyaçabda*,' a word signifying something apart from "the substance; and inasmuch as the Class is without any properties, "such a word can never be rightly used in any sentence, along with the "word signifying a substance (which according to the Class-theory, can "be nothing else but the Class); that is to say, there can be no such "sentence as—'the Class cow is white.' But even this far-fetched ex-"planation is open to the objection of the impossibility of co-extensive-"ness, which in this case, is found to pertain to the Individual-theory "also; and hence this interpretation being found faulty, we must accept "the one we have explained above."

[The *Vārtika* omits *sūtra* 32; and takes up the Bhāshya on *sūtra* 33], with which begins the

SIDDHĀNTA.

Sūtra (33): ***It is the Class*** **(that is signified by the word);** ***because it serves the purpose of Actions.***

[In explaining this *sūtra*, the *Bhāshya* says—*if the word 'Çyēna' signified the Class, we could not have the sentence 'one should make the altar like the Çyēna bird.'* And the *Vārtika* takes exception to this].

The *sūtra* does not show that the passage quoted means that it is the *Class* 'Çyēna' that is built with the bricks; nor could such an assertion be admissible; because [the Class by itself being eternal, could be said to be built only with reference to the individuals contained in it; but even in certain cases as in those of Self, &c., individuals are found to be ever existent, and as such not requiring any building; and even in the case of non-eternal (created) substances, though they are brought about in accordance with the character of their originative causes, yet they are always found to be inhering in their respective Classes; and hence] it is highly improbable for the Class 'Çyēna' to be built up with the bricks, which are incapable of making up even the individual *Çyēnas*, which are actually found to be made up of certain veins, arteries, tendons and muscles, &c. And hence, whichever of the two theories be accepted, the meaning of the said Injunction must be accepted to be, that the altar that is made should have the shape of the Çyēna bird, just as a lump of flour-paste is made into the shape of a lion. And this can be done only in accordance with the shape that belongs to the whole class 'Çyēna,' in contradistinction to those borne by other classes of animals,—and not with the shape or specific character of any individual Cyēna bird, in contradistinction to that of another individual bird of the same class. And as for the similarity of the mere individual (*i.e.*, mere *individuality* in general), it is a purely abstract property, and being entirely independent of all notions of either the genus or the species, it would be common to all substances alike; and hence it cannot be accepted as constituting the denotation of any word. And if the similarity (of the altar) were made according to the shape of a certain individual Çyēna, then, in that case, the altar could not be accepted as similar to the Çyena by another person, who may not have seen that particular individual Çyena; and hence the Injunction could not have served its purpose for this latter person. Hence we conclude that the building of the Çyēna-altar could never be properly accomplished if the word '*Çyēna*' were accepted as denoting an individual Çyēna.

[The *Bhāshya* has raised an objection.—"*But the altar could be built with the individual Çyēna birds as its material,*" and the reply that is given is that] In the compound '*Çyēnacita*,' the word '*Çyēna*' cannot be taken as the principal instrument. That is to say, the compound cannot be grammaticaly explained as 'that which is built *with the Çyēna*'; because the *sūtra* '*Karmaṇyagnyākhyāyām*' (*Pānini* III—ii—92) lays down the possibility of the particular affix that is found in the compound only under certain conditions, the chief of which is that the previous word should be in the Accusative; and hence the word '*Çyēna*' cannot but be taken as the objective, the meaning of the Injunction being that 'one should prepare the *Çyēna* by the building'; but as it is absolutely impossibbe for the actual Çyéna bird to be built, we take it to mean that *the altar should be built of a shape similar to that of the Çyēna bird.*

(Vide *Bhāshya*, Page 81, para. 3) (1) Inasmuch as it is absolutely impossible for any words to point to the *specific indiriduality* (*svalakshaṇa*) of any particular Individual of a Class,—(2) as being incapable of thus being pointed out, even if the word were to denote such a *specific individuality*, it could be that belonging to any of the various Individuals,—(3) as if the word denoted an Individuality in general, this would result in an option with regard to the acceptance of any one Individual from among the innumerable Individuals concerned (the word cannot be accepted to denote any specific individuality); and even though it is true that the denotation of the Individual would naturally lead to that of the *Class*, yet it being a well-recognised fact that it is only the generic character of the *contained* (*i.e.*, the individual cows) that points to the *container* (the Class 'cow') the Class could be pointed out only by the individuals themselves, and not by any specific Individualities (which latter therefore cannot be admitted to form the denotations of words). And as for the theory of the denotation of the Individuals themselves, it is open to many objections; for instance, (1) in that case no relationship (of the expresser and the expressed) could ever be expressed in words (because of the impossibility of laying down as many such descriptions as there are Individuals); (2) there would always be a vagueness in the use of the words (that is to say, the word 'cow' could not be accepted by any individual person to denote any other Cow than the one with reference to which he might have learnt the word); (3) there would never be any idea of cows in general; (4) and lastly, there would be the necessity of postulating a distinct expressive potentiality (for the word 'cow' with reference to each individual cow that may crop up), thereby necessitating the assumption of endless potentialities. And for these reasons, the exact denotation of a word being totally unascertainable, there would always be a doubt with regard to it; and that which is doubtful cannot be accepted as expressed by the word; and thus the word would become absolutely devoid of any object to be denoted.

The same arguments serve to set aside the two theories—(1) that it is the Individual, as apart from the Class, that is denoted by the word, and (2) it is the Class, independently of the individuals, that is denoted by it. And as for the (3) theory of the denotation of the Class as specified by the Individuals, it cannot be accepted; because this would involve a previous cognition of the Individual; as without such previous conception of the qualification, we can never have any idea of the qualified. And as for the denotation resting in (4) the Relationship of the Class and the Individual, or (5) in a mixture of the two,—there can be no conception of these (Relationship and Mixture) independently by themselves, specially as by themselves they are capable of being taken with regard to all the objects in the world (and not restricted to the Class and the Individual); and hence they must be accepted as qualifying the objects *related* and *mixed;* and thus these theories would necessitate the assumption of a triple potency in the word [(1) one for the Individual, (2) one for the Class, and (3) one for the Relationship or the Mixture]; but even in this (1) the assumption of any expressive potency with regard to the Individual would be open to all the objections urged above against the Individual-theory. (2) As for the Admixture, there can be no such Admixture of the Class with the Individual, because each of them has a distinct purpose to serve, and because one of them is subservient to the other. (3) And on account of the Class and the Individual not being two entirely distinct objects, between them, there can be no *relationship* or *admixture;* as these are properties of two entirely distinct objects. Nor can the word be said to denote a particular Individual as qualified by the Class, because as a matter of fact, no word is ever found to bring about the idea of any definite Individual. Nor can the word be said to denote the *mere Individual* (in general); because as a matter of fact, whenever a word is pronounced, that which it expresses is not, in the first instance, cognised as anything apart from the Class. And for the matter of that the word '*Mātra*' (*mere*) that you have added, signifies nothing more than *generality* (or commonality); and hence such an assertion too would only point to the Class as being the object of denotation.

All things in the world having various forms, their potencies too are always ascertained in accordance with these forms; and from this also we find the expressive potentiality of the word 'cow' to be based upon the form of the Class 'cow,' as is distinctly indicated by both affirmative and negative concomitance. And as for the next higher but partially co-extensive Class 'animal,' and the next lower Class 'grey cow' (ideas of which are found to appear concurrently with the class 'cow,' when the word happens to be pronounced with reference to an individual cow), these are indicated by the same Class 'cow,' through the facts of its being *contained* in the former and itself *containing* the latter.

And as for the objection that the Class ('Corn' for instance) being incorporeal, it could not be *washed* or *threshed* (as laid down in Vedic Injunctions),—the Class is not altogether distinct from the Individual; and as such the said objections are not quite applicable. As a matter of fact, what is denoted by the word is the *Class* itself; while in the case of any Actions spoken of with reference to any object, what is denoted is the Class as impressed by (or contained in) the Individual; and hence the actions of *washing*, &c., cannot be altogether impossible. As for *cutting* also (in the case of the Injunction of the cutting of the sacrificial animal), the action is quite possible on account of the Class being nothing absolutely distinct from the Individual; as a matter of fact when certain limbs of an animal have been cut off and its skin, &c., removed, it is not recognised as any particular animal; and hence the idea of *cutting* must be admitted to be applicable to the *generic character* of the animal (and not to any particular individual concerned).

It may be urged here that "the Class being impressed by the Individual, it would be transitory." But we actually accept such transient character, at least so far as the factor of the particular Individual is concerned; but inasmuch as, even when this particular Individual has been destroyed, there are always many other Individuals left extant, wherein the Class inheres equally well, the Class itself can never be found to be non-existent, and as such we cannot admit it to be absolutely non-eternal, and it is for this reason that it is spoken of as both eternal (in the pure form of the Class) and non-eternal (as contained in a particular Individual).

If the Class were something totally different from the Individual, it could never form the subject of any Injunction with regard to Dharma; because the Class 'Animal' being incorporeal could never form such a subject. And as for the substance qualified by the Class 'animal,' inasmuch as this substance itself could not be cognised without the Class 'substance' (in which the class 'Animal' also inheres), the substance must be accepted as indicated (by the Class 'Animal'), because both are found to inhere in a single substratum (the Class 'Substance'), and also because the class 'Substance' contains within itself the Class 'Animal.' But even then, the Class 'substance' also being incorporeal, the aforesaid objection continues to be effective. If again the Class 'Substance' be taken to indicate its substratum, this would be mere *substance* in general (and certainly this could be of no use in any sacrifice). And as for any particular cases of the Class 'Animal,' or of the Class 'Substance,' these, being less extensive than the Classes themselves, could not be said to be indicated by them. And that which is not cognised can never be connected with an Injunction; and that with regard to which there are doubts cannot be held to be duly cognised. Nor is it proper to perform a *Dharma* with regard to something else, when its performance is found to be impossible with regard to that in connection with which it has been laid down; and hence the *Dharma* that would be laid down in connection with the 'Class,' cannot be rightly performed in connection with particular Individuals. And as for these particular Individuals also, when they would be expressed in words, it could only be in the form of Classes; and as such the objections based upon the incorporeality of these would remain effective. And as regards the specific Individualities of objects, it has been already shown that no business is carried on with reference to these. Hence we conclude that (if the Class be held to be something totally different from the Individuals), we could never make out the real subject of the Injunctions of *Dharma* (sacrifices). And even the ideas of *co-extensiveness* (that we have with regard to the *cow* and *whiteness*, in the sentence 'the Cow is white') will, in that case, have to be explained, as obtained indirectly by means of Indication (of the Individual cow by the Class 'Cow' denoted by the word), while it is an universally recognised fact that an idea of such co-extensiveness is got at by direct denotation.

The Bhāshya, however, in the passage—"it is a self-perceptible fact that when a word is uttered, an Individual is cognised"—has admitted a difference (between the Individual and the Class), and has then spoken of the cognition of the Individual, only as the substratum of the Class (denoted by the word); because a particular Individual by itself is never cognised (by means of a word). And even the relation of the container and the contained (that is hinted at in the Bhāshya as subsisting between the Class and the Individual) is only an indirect (or assumed) one. And here too the pointing by the general (Class) to the particular (Individuals) should not be taken as a case of Indication; because it is only a case of mere hinting (or pointing).

Or, the clause in the Bhāshya—"by the word or by the Class"—may be taken as referring to the cognition of the Individual; the conclusion arrived at, by means of affirmative and negative concomitance being, that the cognition of the Individual is brought about by the Class. For instance, (1) when one has cognised the class 'Fire' (in the mountain), through the perception of Smoke, his desire to learn the character of the individual fire—in the shape of its brightness or dulness—is also fulfilled (which shows that the cognition of the Class 'Fire' has brought about by affirmative concomitance, the cognition of the Individual Fire); and (2) when through some '*disorder of the mind*'—*i.e.*, foolishness or dulness—one fails to recognise the denotation of the Class by a word, and cognises only the Individual, with reference to which a certain assertion of relations is made, to be expressed by the word, such a person, having had no idea of the Class, has no idea of any other Individual save the one directly described; (and this shows by negative concomitance, that without a cognition of the Class there is no cognition of the Individual). Or another way of explaining the same fact is that, though we cognise the Class by itself to be denoted by the word, yet we do not, in the same manner, cognise the Individual, unless we have previously recognised the Class.

A question is here raised—"what then is the difference between '*gotva*' (the Class 'Cow') and the word '*gō*' (Cow) (since both are equally held to denote the Class 'Cow')?"

The difference between the two is that in the case of one—viz., *the Class 'Cow'*—there is a slight difference (from the Individual); as, for instance, we find the individual (cow) belonging to the Class 'Cow,' being clearly spoken of as '*gotvavān*' (belonging to the Class 'Cow,') which distinctly shows that there is some distinction between the Individual 'Cow' and the Class 'Cow.' And as the expression '*gotvavān*' (belonging to the Class 'Cow') points to the Class also, the declaration of its describing the Individual is not open to the objections that have been urged against the theory of the Individual constituting the denotation of a word; specially as the word is found to be expressive of every one of the Individuals (as constituting the Class denoted). And in any particular case (as in 'one should sacrifice with corns') the only doubt that one has is with regard to the *number* (or quantity) of the object to be employed; and as for the object itself, there is a most definite cognition (of corns) (by means of the word).

The Bhāshya has cited "the words 'Cow,' &c.," with a view to all Nouns and Verbs.

The special purpose that is served by the above discussion is that the generic and the particular word referring to the same object, there would be no rejection of the general rule by the exception, in accordance with the view of the *Pūrvapaksha* (while according to the *Siddhāntā* such a rejection is duly accomplished).

———o———

[The Vārtika now proceeds to put forth another exposition of the above

ADHIKARAṆAS (A) and (B).]

Words like '*gauh*,' &c., having been shown to be correct, we now proceed to consider in which denoted object the operations of these words lie. Though the words are divided into four kinds—Nouns, Verbs, Prefixes and *Nipātas*—yet it is only the first two that are taken into consideration; because it is only with regard to the denotation of these—and not to that of Prefixes and *Nipātas*—that certain doubts are found to arise in our minds; specially as Prefixes and *Nipātas* do not by themselves serve to denote any objects; they only serve to illumine the meanings of Nouns and Verbs, which are the only really expressive words; and hence it is these latter only that are taken into consideration. Though certain *Nipātas*—as '***Pāçcātya***,' '*Anuyātya*' and the like—are found to be denotative of certain definite objects, yet there are no doubts as to the particular objects denoted by them. The *Nipātas* would have been taken up for consideration on the present occasion, only if they were found to bring about the cognitions of two objects; and so long as they are not found to give rise to any cognitions of 'Classes' (as also of Individuals), they cannot form the objects of the present discussion.

I. *Objection*: "Even Verbs cannot rightly form the subjects of the "present discussion; because the denotation of verbs will be dealt with "in detail, in the beginning of the Second Adhyāya; where we have a "detailed consideration of the question—'what is *Bhāva*?' (*Bhāva* = to be, "being the general name given to the denotation of verbs); and as "the true denotation of verbs has to be duly ascertained in detail, in that "place, it is not right to take it up on the present occasion."

To this we make the following reply: (1) What we have to deal with in the second Adhyāya, is the 'Bhāva,' which is the name given to the denotations of the *Affixes*: while what we are going to consider now is the denotation of the roots themselves. (2) Or, even though the denotation of the Affixes have to be ascertained there, we may now consider whether that deno ation consists of the Class or the Individual. (3) The fact of the roots '*yaji*' and the like denoting the *sacrifice*, &c., that will be put forward by the Bhāshya in the Second Adhyāya, is only by way of an explanation of what is duly ascertained in the present Adhikaraṇa. (4) Or, even with regard to the denotations of the roots '*yajī*,' &c., it is only proper that we should consider whether the denotations of these appearing in verbs, consist of the Class or of the Individual. (5) In reality, however, the question that has to be dealt with in the Second Adhyāya is as to whether the transcendental result (of the sacrifice) proceeds from what is signified by the verbs (in the Injunctions, 'should sacrifice,' &c.) or from the materials, &c., (*Soma* and the like) therein spoken of? And whatever else is to be explained there is only by way of supplementing the said question.

Thus then, it is with regard to the truly expressive Verbs and Nouns, that we proceed to consider whether they denote Classes or Individuals. A doubt on this point has arisen in our minds, on account of the usage of words, and their comprehension by the people pointing equally to both (Class and Individual), and also on account of grammatical works (notably the *Mahābhyāshya*) lending countenance to both the theories.

II. *Objection:* "Before proceeding any further, it must be explained, "what connection this discussion has, either with the subject-matter of "the Adhyāya (which treats of the means of knowing Dharma), or with "that of the present Pāda, which is dealing with the basic authority of "the *Smṛtis.*"

Reply: The present discussion is an offshoot of the treatment of the authority of grammatical *Smṛtis*, by means of which the correctness of a word having been ascertained, it is only natural to pass on to the consideration of the meaning of this word.

"But it is before the form of the word is ascertained that its meaning "should be ascertained; because until the meaning is known the correct-"ness of the word cannot be ascertained."

Even though the meaning of a word has not been thoroughly ascertained, as to whether it is in the form of the Class or the Individual, its correctness can be very well ascertained; and hence we now proceed to consider the nature of the meaning. It is only until the word has been known to have some meaning that its correctness cannot be ascertained; and certainly an ascertainment of the correctness of a word does not depend upon our duly ascertaining as to whether its meaning is in the form of a Class or an Individual.

Or, it may be that the authoritative character of all grammatical

Smṛtis having been laid down in a previous Adhikaraṇa, it is with regard to this universality of their authority that the present Adhikaraṇa raises a question, and comes to the conclusion that the grammatical *Smṛti* which speaks of the Individual as forming the denotation of a word, cannot be accepted as correct, because such an assertion being impossible, can have no authoritative basis (in the Veda); and hence on this point even a grammatical *Smṛti* cannot be accepted as authoritative. In this manner, the present Adhikaraṇa would be laying down an exception to the authority of *Smṛtis;* and thus it would be quite in connection with the subject-matter of the Adhyāya and the Pāda, as also with the foregoing discussion.

III. *Objection:* "Even if the word be admitted to be denotative of "the Class, all Injunctions and Prohibitions would refer only to the "*Individuals* signified by the words (contained in them); and as such what "is the use of the present discussion?"

Reply: Though it is true that there is no difference among people, in the interpretation of the Prohibitions and the Injunctions contained in the Veda (which are always taken with reference to Individuals), yet a discussion like the present would serve a useful purpose in ordinary parlance, where it is said: "give the curd to the *Brāhmanas*, but *takra* to *Kaundinya';* where if words were admitted to be denotative of Individuals, the word 'Brāhmaṇa' could be accepted as denoting the Individual Brāhmaṇa Kaundinya, who would thus come to be given both the curd and the *takra*; while when the word 'Brāhmaṇa' is accepted as denotative of the *Class* only, it could point to *Kaundinya* only by indirect indication, which would be set aside in favour of the direct denotation of the word '*Kaundinya*' itself (and Kaundinya would, in this case, receive the *takra* only, which was meant by the person issuing the instruction).

As a matter of fact, however, in the Veda too, in the case of the passages enjoining the washing of the *Corn*, there is a certain difference (in the true denotation of the word '*vrīhi*') as also in the case of the passage that lays down the offering of '*Dadhi.*' For instance, if the word 'corn' ('*vrīhi*') be accepted to be denotative of any individual corn, the washing would come to apply to even an ordinary corn (not to be used at the sacrifice); because the *washing* is restricted to the sacrificial corn only by means of the *order of proximity* of the word 'Corn' with the 'Sacrifice'; whereas it is found to be applicable to the ordinary corn, by the direct denotation of the word 'Corn'; and certainly Direct Denotation must always set aside any order of Proximity. On the other hand, if the word 'Corn' be admitted to be denotative of the Class only, then in that case, the case of the sacrificial corn alone being the object of washing would be much stronger than that of any ordinary corn; because, while the latter is pointed out only indirectly by the direct denotation of the Class 'Corn' which includes the ordinary corn also, the latter is pointed out both by the said order of Proximity and the Direct Denotation of the Class 'Corn,' which is found to inhere, in its entirety, in the sacrificial corn also. So also in the case of the offering of *Dadhi*, the word '*Dadhi*' could refer to the sacrificial *Dadhi* as well as to any ordinary *Dadhi*; and it is only when the word is held to be denotative of the Class, that the offering spoken of directly by the word '*Juhoti*' would come to refer to the sacrificial *Dadhi* only. These arguments could be applied to many other instances of Vedic Injunctions and Prohibitions. And hence we conclude that the present discussion being found to serve many useful purposes, we must take it up for due consideration.

IV. *Objection:* "All that is considered here having already been dealt "with, in the *Tarkapāda* (*Çlokavartika*—chap. on '*Ākṛti*'), it is scarcely "proper to start the same question over again."

Reply: (1) In the *Tarkapāda* all that has been done is merely to lay down the proposition that it is the Class that is denoted by words; and the present Adhikaraṇa serves to bring forward the arguments in support of that proposition. And even the Bhāshya has said (towards the close of the section *Ākriti* in the *Tarkapāda*) that the reasons in support of the proposition will be explained "later on" (and this can only be taken as referring to the present Adhikaraṇa). (2) Or it may be that in the *Tarkapāda* it is only the existence of Class that has been established; while in the present Adhikaraṇa, we seek to establish the fact of its being denoted by the word; and though its denotation has been spoken of on the previous occasion, yet on that occasion, it was only taken as granted and not duly discussed (which is done in the present Adhikaraṇa), (3) Or even if the previous section may have explained the fact of words being denotative of the Class, with a view to prove the existence of such a thing as *Class*,—yet the question, as to whether the Individual is denoted by a word or not, has not been considered there; and the present Adhikaraṇa may be taken as serving the distinctly useful purpose of proving that Individuals are not denoted by words.

———o———

And with a view to introduce the said discussion, we begin with the consideration of

ADHIKARAṆA (A)—

which deals with the question, as to the words found in the Veda, and the objects denoted by them, being the same as those in ordinary parlance, or different from them? It is only if the words in the Veda and the objects denoted by them are the same as those in ordinary parlance, that there can be any discussion as to the denotation of a word; because if they be different, there would be no doubt as to the true denotation of words (which would be found in the Veda to signify Individuals) ; and there would be no occasion for the discussion that follows; specially as all business is carried on with regard to concrete objects, there would be no use wasting time over the pure denotations of words; hence the present discussion cannot be held to be propounded for the sake of the ordinary business of the world. It is only in the case of the Veda, that the words and the objects denoted by them being recognised to be the same (as those in ordinary parlance), our cognition of the meanings of words could help us to differentiate what is directly denoted by them, and what is only indirectly indicated. For if the words in the Veda were totally different from those in ordinary parlance, then, whenever we would come across a Vedic passage, we would not be cognisant of their forms or signification; and these being totally unknown, there could be no doubt in our minds, with regard to the denotation of these words. Therefore for the sake of ascertaining the nature of the meaning that is cognised, it is necessary, in the first instance, to establish the fact of the words in the Veda and the objects denoted by them being the same as those in ordinary parlance.

Objection: "This identity of the word has been already clearly established under *Sūtra* I—i—20, where it has been shown that the word being "always recognised to be the same, the mere fact of its being pronounced "at different times does not constitute a difference in the word itself; "and thus it is found that there can be no other reason for the said identity, "except such recognition of the word; all other arguments that may be "brought forward in support of this identity would be only auxiliary to "the aforesaid Recognition. And hence no further discussion on the "point is necessary."

Reply: (1) What has been established under *Sūtra* I—i—20 is that in all ordinary human utterances, the word 'Cow' is always the same; and hence it is only proper that we should now establish the fact of all Vedic words being identical with those in ordinary parlance. (2) It has not been explained there why the fact of words in the Veda being spoken of of as 'Vedic,' in contradistinction to those in ordinary parlance which are described as 'worldly,' cannot be taken as pointing to a difference between them; and it is this that we proceed to consider now. (3) Even though the identity of the word may have been established under the said *sūtra*, yet the present Adhikaraṇa cannot be said to be a mere repetition; because what is considered here is whether the denotations (of the word 'Cow' as found in the Veda and as used in ordinary parlance) are identical. And it is only when the identity of the denotation has been established, that there can arise a question as to whether the Class or the Individual is denoted by the word, which question can have nothing to do with the identity of the word (and hence the present discussion is absolutely necessary as preliminary to the main point of the Adhikaraṇa).

And on this subject, there arises a doubt in our mind; because the fact of the words used in the Veda being spoken of as 'Vedic' in contradistinction to the 'worldly' words, points to the fact of there being a difference between the two classes of words; while as a matter of fact the words in the Veda are always recognised to be the same as those in ordinary parlance.

An on this point, we have the following—

PŪRVAPAKSHA.

"The words used in the Veda, and the objects denoted by them, "are different from those in ordinary parlance; (1) because we perceive "an actual difference in their names, in the Nouns used in them, in the "grammatical rules applying to them, in accentuation and pronunciation, and "in deletions and modifications of letters and syllables; (2) because we "find even the ordinarily known words used in the Veda, together with "such words as '*svaru*' '*yūpa*' and the like, which are distinctly different "from any words in ordinary usage; (3) because certain points of time "are laid down as unfit for the studying of Vedic words; (4) because "the Çūdra and the woman are forbidden to utter Vedic words; and (5) "because we find such words as '*Açvabāla*' and the like signifying "distinctly different objects (in the Veda and in ordinary parlance),—in the "Veda it being used in the sense of 'reed,' while in ordinary usage it "means 'the horse's hair'?

"The Bhāshya has also cited the word 'Agni' as having in the Veda—in the passage 'Agni killed the Vṛttras'—a meaning (*vṛttra-"killer*) different from that in ordinary parlance. But this is not right; "because a difference in the action does not alter the actor (*i.e.*, though "Agni may be said to have killed the Vṛttras, yet that does not necessarily make Agni something other than the Agni that *burns*). Specially "as the fact of Agni being the 'Vṛttra-killer' is expressed (not by the "word 'Agni' itself, but) by the meaning of the words contained in the "sentence (quoted above); and how can that which is not expressed by "a word be said to be denoted by the word 'Agni'? And then too "there is no means of ascertaining whether Agni really killed Vṛttra "or not; and as such how can the mention of an unreal action make us "believe the Agni to be different (from the ordinary Agni)? And further, "the object expressed by the word '*Vṛttra*,' as well as the verb ('*Janghanat*') being quite unknown in ordinary parlance, how can the passage in "question make us cognise the character of 'Agni' as belonging to the "'killer (of Vṛttra)'? Nor can the passage be taken as laying down a "new signification of the word 'Agni' (as that which killed the Vṛttras "is denoted by the word 'Agni'); because it is in the form of a pure "Arthavāda in praise of Agni; and also because the passage cannot be "taken as describing a real action of Agni, as will be explained by the "Bhāshya under the *Devatādhikaraṇa* of the Ninth Adhyāya.

"For these reasons, the words that should be quoted as showing a "difference between the meanings of words in the Veda and in ordinary "parlance, are '*Trvrit*,' &c., which (in the Veda) means *ninefold* (while in "ordinary usage it means *threefold*).

"In connection with the above-mentioned passage—'*Agnir-vṛttrāṇi* "*janghanat*'—the Bhāshya has said that this points to 'another form of "the word *Agni*'; but this is scarcely correct; as a difference in the "property or action of the object denoted does not make any difference in "the form of the word itself.

"Therefore the difference between the forms of Vedic and ordinary "words must be held to be based upon the differences of accentuation, &c., "as explained above, and not upon any differences in their significations. "And thus we find that there is a distinct difference between the word "used in the Veda and the objects signified by them on the one hand and "those used and expressed in ordinary parlance on the other."

---o---

In reply to the above, we have the following:—

SIDDHANTA (A).

The words used in the Veda and their meanings are the same as those in ordinary parlance. (1) Because if it were not so, the whole of the Veda would become absolutely unauthoritative; as its authority would be fully shaken by the fact of its meaning being unknown; and this non-recognition of the meaning of Vedic passages would lead to the contingencies that there would be no such Vedic actions as the *Agnihotra* and the like, and there could be no Vedic Injunctions; because the Injunctive affixes in the Veda could not signify Injunction (because they have this signification in ordinary parlance). Nor does the Veda lay down the use of words in any sense other than the ordinarily known ones; because it has been shown above that the relationship (between words and their meanings) is not fixed by scriptures; (and hence there would be no means of ascertaining what any word means in the Veda, if the ordinary meaning were not accepted).

(2) (*a*) The form of a word as used in the Veda is distinctly found over and over again to be non-different from the same as used in ordinary

parlance (as is pointed out by the clause '*Avibhāgāt*' in the *sūtrā*). Or (*b*) the 'non-difference' (*Avibhāga*) spoken of may be taken as pointing out the fact that whenever the word 'Cow' is uttered, we have always the same cognition of the class 'Cow' (whether the word be found in the Veda or in ordinary usage). Or (*c*) it may be taken as pointing to the non-difference of the rules of pronunciation, &c., as appertaining to the Veda and to ordinary parlance.

(3) In no way can the word, as found in the Veda, and its meaning be held to be different from those in ordinary parlance; because it is only when they are accepted to be identical that the fact commonly recognised by all sacrificers is not contradicted. (As all persons that perform the sacrifices laid down in the Veda accept the words that they meet with in Vedic passages to have the same meaning that they have in ordinary parlance).

(4) The Mīmānsā supplies the only means of ascertaining the true meanings of the words in the Veda; and in Mīmānsā we do not find the fact of the words in the Veda being called 'Vedic' in contradistinction to 'worldly' accepted as pointing to any actual difference between the words themselves.

Thus then, the words being actually recognised to be the same in both cases, the only difference in their forms that can be perceived, as also the fact of one being named 'Vedic' and the other 'worldly,' must be accepted as due to the differences in accentuation, &c. And as there is no question as to the *accentuation* in the Veda being different (the point at issue being the difference in the *word*), what is the use of bringing forward this difference on the present occasion?

(1) Then as for the words '*svaru*,' '*yūpa*' and the like, peculiar to the Veda, the mere fact of a few such words in the Veda being different from any words in ordinary usage, cannot prove all words in it to be so different; specially as such difference is actually denied by the directly perceptible recognition of the words being the same in both cases. (2) As for the fact of only certain times being laid down as fit for the study of Vedic words, and that of its utterance being prohibited for the *Çūdra*, these, as laid down directly in Vedic sentences, are properties appertaining to the *utterance* of Vedic words, as are also the methods of accentuation; and none of these can point to any difference in the *words* themselves. (3) As for the difference in the meanings of such words as '*Açvabāla*' and the like (as found in the Veda and in ordinary usage) there are only a few of such differences, distinctly laid down in certain passages of the Veda; and the difference of these cannot justify any assertion of such difference in the case of all other words, whose meanings are accepted as known ordinarily (and for whom no different meanings are

laid down in the Veda itself). (4) In the case of the passage—'the cows of the gods walk upon their backs' (which has been quoted as pointing to the fact of the meaning of the word 'Cow' being different from the ordinary cow)—it is not found to lay down the fact of the character of the *cow* to belong to certain animals walking on their backs; and hence inasmuch as any such animals are absolutely impossible, and the meaning of the word 'Cow' is not cognised as anything different from the ordinary, and as the passage itself is found to be supplementary to another Injunction, it cannot but be taken as a mere *Arthavāda*.

Thus then, in no way do we perceive any difference between the two classes of words; and hence we conclude that the words and their meanings that have been explained before, in connection with ordinary usage, must be accepted to be the same in the Veda also.

ADHIKARAṆA (B).

And now, we proceed to take up the question, to which the above discussion leads us,—namely, does the denotation of a word consist of the Class, or of the Individual, or of both?

There are various alternatives on this point; and in order to remove all misconceptions with regard to it, we again proceed to show them. Whenever the word 'Cow' is uttered, it is found to give rise to the ideas of seven things: the Class, the Individual, their Relationship, the Aggregate of these, a particular Gender, Case, Number, and the Word itself. In this manner there are eight alternatives with regard to each of these two. For instance, is it the Class that is denoted by the word, or the Individual, or both, or each of them alternately, or both together, or the Class qualified by the Individual, or the Individual qualified by the Class? In the same manner we would have as many alternatives, between the Class and the Relationship, the Class and the Aggregate, the Class and the Case, the Class and the Number, the Gender and the Class, and so forth; also with regard to each of them as taken all along with all others,—thereby we come to have alternatives six times eight (or forty-eight) in number; and yet many other combinations being possible, the number of alternatives becomes endless.

In the *Pūrvapaksha*, the Bhāshya has mentioned only four of these alternatives: Does the word signify—(1) the Class by itself, or (2) the Individual by itself, or (3) the Individual qualified by the Class, or (4) the Class qualified by the Individual? And these should be taken as including all the other alternatives; and as all these are set aside by means of the same arguments, they have not been all pointed out in detail. And hence at first we take up for consideration only two of the alternatives—Does the word denote the Class or the Individual?

The ground of doubt on this point has been explained by the Bhāshya thus: *sāmānyapratyayādvyaktau ca kriyāsambhavāt* (because the cognition is that of the Class, while the action that is laid down can pertain to the Individual). But this is not quite correct; because the Individual is often found to be cognised; and hence it is not quite correct to speak of the Class as being the *cognised* in all cases. For if the Individual were never cognised (by means of the word), there could be no question as to whether it is denoted by the word or not. Nor can the fact of the action appertaining to the Individual serve as a reason for accepting it to be denoted by the word.

Hence we must accept the ground of doubt to be as we have explained before, namely that, inasmuch as both *Usage* and *Cognition* are found to apply commonly to the Class and the Individual, and as grammatical works are found to lend special support to the Individual-theory, there naturally arises a doubt as to which is to be accepted as the real denotation of the word.

Or, the Bhāshya may be construed in the following manner: when a word is uttered, (1) there is a '*Sāmānyapratyaya*,' i.e., *common recognition* of the Class as well as the Individual; and (2) it is *in the Individual* ('*vyaktau*,') as also *in the Class* (this being indicated by the particle '*ca*') that Actions—such as *fetching, touching, building of the altar in the shape of the Çyēna,* and the like—are found to be capable of appertaining (hence there naturally arises a doubt as to the real denotation of the word). Or, the meaning of the Bhāshya may be explained thus: '*Sāmānyapratyayāt*'=because we have a cognition of the Class (*Sāmānya*) as also of the Individual; and '*Kriyāsambhavāt*' is to be taken in the same way as before.

The Bhāshya next starts the question—*What is the Class, and what is the Individual?*

Some people object to this question: "Why should this question be started over again, when the character of the Class has already been explained in the *Tarkapāda?*"

This objection does not affect the case. Because (1) the question may be taken as put by one who has not quite understood the nature of the Class as explained before. Or, (2) there being a doubt as to the true signification of the word, on account of its bringing about a cognition of both the Individual and the Class, the question may be taken as making an enquiry as to which portion of the Cognition (produced by the word) consists of the Individual, and which of the Class? Or (3) the question may be taken as put ironically—the meaning being this: when as a matter of fact, we do not perceive anything other than the bodies of the Individual cows, grey and the like, wherefore should there be any distinction made between the Class and the Individual? Or, (4) all discussion being for the sake of some business, even though the Class be denoted by the word, inasmuch as all actions are found to appertain to the Individual (and as such all purposes being served by accepting the Individual to be denoted by the word), there can be no use of any discussion as to what is the denotation of the word. But as the *sūtra* is actually found to be taking great pains in the consideration of the question, it appears that there does exist some such thing as *Class*, apart from the Individuals; (and hence it is only natural that we should consider the question as to what is this *Class* and what the Individual).

In reply to the above question, the Bhāshya says: *Dravyaguṇakarmaṇām sāmānyamātram jātiḥ*—(*Class is the commonality of Substances, Properties and Actions*).

A mere explanation of the form of the Class serves to satisfy those persons that had put the question either from ignorance, or from doubt; while for one who had put it out of spite, we offer the following explanation: Though the Class is not perceived as anything totally different from the Individual, yet at the time that we perceive certain individual cows, the grey one and the like, we have an idea of a certain character that is common to all the various individuals perceived, as has been shown in the *Tarkapāda;* and it is this *commonality* that constitutes the Class, and that which is other than this (*i.e.*, that which is peculiar to each cow) is the Individual.

This explanation of 'Class' in the Bhāshya does not serve either to assert the existence of the Class, or to bring forward proofs for its existence; it only serves to distinguish the Class from the Individual. It is with a view to this that we have the word '*mātra*' (mere); for if mere distinction from the Individual were not meant, this word would have been superfluous.

If the question be taken as asking what is the Class that is meant to be something apart from the Individuals, then the answer may be taken as pointing out that the Class that we mean is the mere commonality of individual Substances, Properties and Actions, and not anything totally different from the Individuals.

(1) And what is meant by this 'commonality' may be taken as the *summum genus* 'Being,' which s common to all Substances, Properties

and Actions, this including all the lower genera therein contained; (2) or the word 'commonality' may be taken separately with each of these (Substances, Properties and Actions), the Classes meant being the three classes of 'Substance,' 'Property' and 'Action'; as there is no business pertaining to the *summum genus* 'Being'; (3) or, on account of the word '*mātra*,' the Classes meant may be all the Classes known in the world—from the *summum genus* 'Being' down to the smallest Class in existence.

The Individual is explained by the Bhāshya as—'*asādhāraṇaviçēshā vyaktiḥ*'; and in this the compound '*asādhāraṇaviçēshāḥ*' must be taken as *Bahuvrīhi*,—the meaning of the Bhāshya being that *that which has a specific peculiarity is the Individual.* And it cannot mean that the *Individual* consists of *the specific peculiarities themselves* (the said compound being explained as *Karmadhāraya*); because in a subsequent chapter, the Bhāshya distinctly speaks of the *Individual* as the *receptacle* of (and as such something different from) *the peculiarities;* and also because we have certain *Smṛti* texts that point out the Individual to be different from the peculiarities.

Hence we conclude that it is only right to start the question as to whether the word denotes the Class or the Individual.

And on this point we have the following—

PŪRVAPAKSHA (B).

"We conclude that it is only the Individual that is denoted by the "word; (1) because it is only when the word signifies the Individual, "that we can have any *Injunction of such actions* (*Sūtra* 30) as *killing, washing, cutting* and so forth, which would be absolutely impossible if words "signified the Class; (2) because it is only then that we can have even "ordinary directions in the world, such as—'Dēvadatta, drive the cows,' "and the like; (3) because only in that case could we have the various "Numbers and Cases of Nouns; that is to say, if the Individual were "denoted by the word, then alone could we have such expressions as "*Vṛkshau, Vṛkshābhyām*, &c., where we have the Dual number, and the Instrumental Case, in addition to the Noun; as for the Class, it is only one, "and as such no Number, dual or plural, could pertain to it; nor (being immaterial) can it have any Cases belonging to it; and hence if the *Class* "were accepted to form the denotation, such expressions as '*Vṛkshau*,' and "'*Vṛkshābhyām*' would be absolutely impossible; (4) and hence if the "direct denotation of a word consisted of the Class, it would be necessary "in the case of each sentence, to accept an indirect Indication (of the "word) pointing to the Individual; and hence all Vedic passages would "come to be taken in their indirect significations only; on the other hand, "if the word be accepted to denote the Individual, in all sentences, there "would be a direct co-extensiveness—exactly as in the expression "'Dēvadatta is a man' (and there would be no necessity of having "recourse to any indirect signification); while in the Class-theory, it "would be necessary even in such simple instances to have recourse to "indirect Indication; and hence too, the Individual would come to be "acknowledged to be denoted by the word; (5) when we meet with such "Vedic Injunctions as—'one should kill the animal,' we proceed to "carry on the subsequent business with the Tongue, Heart, &c., of the "*individual* animal that is killed; and not with the whole Class 'animal'; "(6) and again, all actions stand in need of certain substances; and "hence if the words in an Injunction were accepted to be denotative of "the Individual, then alone could the Injunction be found to lay down "something that is needed, not otherwise; (7) the Individual being a "definite entity (acknowledged by all of us), that alone, and not the "Class, can be rightly accepted as being denoted by a word. And "for all these reasons, we conclude that it is the Individual that is denoted "by the word.

"Some people might ask—'Why should we not accept both the "Individual and the Class to be denoted by the word? That would be "quite in keeping with usage and comprehension.' This cannot be; "because this would involve the assumption of a manifold potency in the "word, which is not allowable; specially as the comprehension of the one "(the Class) can very well be explained as being due to the intimate "relationship that it bears to the other (the Individual); and hence we "must accept the Individual to be denoted by the word.

"It may be asked—'How then do you explain the idea of *com-"monality* that we have?' We can explain this as brought about by its "relationship to the Individuals.

"It may be argued that—'when we actually find that an action is "otherwise impossible, then alone can this Apparent Inconsistency justify "our accepting the Individual to be denoted by the word; whereas in "all other cases, inasmuch as it is the Class that is cognised first, we "must hold the word to be denotative of the Class.' This cannot be; "because this too would necessitate the assumption of manifold poten-"cies in each word; and as, in that case, the denotation being always "uncertain, the true meaning of an Injunction would always remain "doubtful.

"Some people argue thus: 'One who holds an Individual to be "denoted by the word, can have no ground for applying that word to any "other Individual.' But there is no such real difficulty; as there is "always such a ground available, in the shape of the fact of the one "Individual belonging to the same Class as the other.

"There is a difficulty in the Bhāshya here. Having started the "question—'*how then do we have an idea of commonality*'?—the Bhāshya "replies—'*the Class would serve as the mark*'? But the reply is quite "irrelevant; because what was wanted to be known was the reason for "the *idea of commonality*, while what the reply points out is the ground "for applying the same word to many Individuals! Therefore we must "take the Bhāshya here to be elliptical, explaining it thus: Question (1) "—'*How then do we have an idea of commonality?* Answer—'*Through the "relationship it bears to the Individuals.*' Question (2)—'*But how is the "same word applicable to another Individual?*' Answer—'*Through the Class "which serves as the mark* (common to all of them).' Or, we may explain "the Bhāshya in the following manner: Being asked—'How then do we "have an idea of commonality?'—the *Pūrvapakshi*, finding himself un-"able to absolutely deny the said idea of commonality, seeks refuge in "the theory that the word denotes the *Individual qualified by the Class*, "—the meaning of the word '*cihna*' being *qualification*, and the passage "'*ākṛtiçcihnabhūtā bhavishyati*,' meaning that *the Class* (commonality) "*could be recognised as the qualification of the Individual.*

"Thus then, even the idea of commonality cannot be urged against "the Individualistic theory. And we conclude that the denotation of a "word consists of the Individual, either by itself, or as qualified by the "Class.

"And it is only then that we can accept the number 'six'—in the "sentence 'six cows'—to belong to the cows (*Sūtra* 31).

"And also in the case of the Injunction that,—if the animal kept for "a sacrifice happens to be lost, we should obtain another of the same "colour—unless we accept the word 'animal' to denote the individual "animal, the word 'another' could not point to another *animal*; nor "would it be possible to speak of this another as being 'of the same "colour.' Because if the whole Class 'Animal' were denoted by the "word 'Animal'; the one animal would be as much an animal as the "other; and hence even if another animal had to be fetched, it would "not be *another* (but the same Animal); nor can the Class be said to "be 'of the same colour' (as the former animal). And hence we con-"clude that it is the Individual that is denoted by the word."

To all this we make the following reply :—

SIDDHANTA (B).

(as explained in the Bhāshya.)

It can never be that the Individual is denoted by the word; as it is the Class that is denoted by it; because we meet with such passages as—'*Çyēnacitam cinvīta*,' where the two meanings that could be possible are—(1) 'one should build up a particular *Çyēna* bird,' or (2) 'he should build the Class *Çyēna*.'

But as for the Individual Çyēna bird, any number of bricks could not build up any such bird; specially as we cannot build up a bird even with the arteries and tendons taken out of a dead bird; and thus the mention of 'bricks' precludes all possibility of the making of a live bird; and we would also have to assume a certain purpose for the building of a bird out of brick and mortar; in which case we would have the further disadvantage of having to take the word '*cinvīta*' in a figurative sense (*i.e.*, of *preparing*, instead of making); and lastly, such an intepretation would involve a breach of the grammatical law '*Karmaṇyagnyākhyāyam*' (Pāṇini III—ii—12) explained above. And hence the passage cannot be taken to mean that *one should make, by the building, a Çyēna bird.*

In the same manner, (1) it is equally impossible to build up the *Class* 'Çyēna' with bricks and mortar, as it is created by God alone; (2) such an interpretation would necessitate the assumption of some purpose for this making of the Class; (3) and also the taking of the word '*cinvīta*' in a sense not its own; and (4) this would also involve a breach of the grammatical rule quoted above. Hence the passage cannot be taken even to mean that one should make the *Class* 'Çyēna.'

Thus then, the only resource left to us is to take the passage to mean that *by the building* (*collection of bricks*) *one should make an altar of the shape of the Çyēnā bird.* In this case it is impossible for the altar to be made similar to any particular Çyēna bird; and we cannot make it similar to all the individual birds; specially as it is absolutely impossible to ascertain the similitude of such birds as have not yet been born, or of those that are yet to be born; and it is only possible to make an altar having a shape that is common to the whole *Class* 'Çyēna.' Hence we conclude that the Class alone can be held to be denoted by the word.

An objection is here raised: "Why cannot the passage be taken to mean that *one should build up the altar with the bodies of dead Çyēna birds*, the compound '*Çyēnacitam*' being taken as '*Çyēnnaiçcitam*' (the Instrumental *Tatpurusha*)"?

To this question, the Bhāshya replies that the word '*Çyēna*' is the objective (and not the Instrument). But this is not correct. In the passage itself the word '*Çyēna*' has no independent signification of its own; nor is it found to have the Accusative termination to itself, as this termination appears after the whole compound '*Çyēnacita*'; and as such it cannot be taken as signifying the objective. Therefore we must make use of the aforesaid grammatical *sūtra* in denying the fact of the word '*Çyēna*' having an Instrumental signification. The *sūtra* means that 'the *kvip* affix is added to the root *ci* when it is preceded by an *objective noun*, specially when the root *ci* signifies the *altar of sacrificial fire*'; and as the root '*ci*' by itself cannot signify the *altar*, it is only the root ending in the *kvip* affix—as is possible only in such compounds as '*Çyēnacita*' (where the noun '*Çyēna*' must be the objective, in order to make the particular affix *kvip* possible, in accordance with the above-quoted *sūtra*) —that can be taken to mean the *altar*; and the word '*Çyēna*' cannot be held to have any independent meaning of itself (apart from the compound). And hence we must conclude that the word '*Çyēna*' cannot be taken to be in the Instrumental Case. Even if the Instrumental Case were admitted, (1) there would be no rule by which we could have a compound, under the circumstances; (2) over and above this, we would have to assume the Instrumental case-ending, which does not exist; (3) by assuming the (bodies of the) *Çyēna* birds to be the materials for making the altar, it would involve an abandonning of the *bricks*, which have been distinctly laid down as the material to be employed in the building; and (4) there would be a needless sinful slaughter of so many *Çyēna* birds, when there are other means of accomplishing the same thing. Thus then, it being impossible for the word '*Çyēna*' to be taken in the Instrumental Case, we must take the passage to mean that *one should build the altar similar in shape to the Çyēna bird*. And as such an interpretation would be possible only if the word ('*Çyēna*') denoted the Class—as we have shown above— we must admit the Class to be denoted by the word.

Objection: "It is not so; the possibility of the single action of the "making of the altar cannot be accepted as sufficient reason for accept-"ing the Class to be the denotation of a word; specially as we have "already shown that there are many actions—like *killing*, *washing*, &c., "which would be possible, only if the Individual were accepted to be denoted "by the word. And as the passages laying down actions like these latter "are very many, while you have got only one passage in support of your "theory, it is far more reasonable to hold the word to denote the Indi-"vidual. If it be urged that—'even in accordance with the Class-"theory, in the case of the Injunctions of such actions as *washing* and the "like, we can have the Individual pointed out by indirect Indication,'— "we reply that it is far more reasonable to accept the Individual theory, "and have recourse to indirect Indication in the single passage treating of "the *Çyēna* (while you have got to have recourse to it in the case of "many passages); and it is certainly far more reasonable to have recourse "to an indirect signification in one case than in many. And as for the "Instrumental *Tatpurusha* (in '*Çyēnacita*') we can accept it, as being "absolutely necessary. For these reasons (it being possible to take the "passage to mean that one should make the altar of the bodies of *Çyēna* "birds),—and because it is only when the word is accepted as denoting the "Individual, that there can be different numbers and cases in connection "with Nouns,—we must conclude that a word always denotes the Indi-"vidual."

In view of these objections we proceed to offer another exposition of of the *Siddhānta.*

It is the Class that is denoted by the word. Why? (1) Because it is the Class or Commonality that is cognised before (the Individual); (2) because a word is not found to give rise to a mixed conception; and (3) because when the order 'bring the cow' is given, the person ordered brings any cow that he likes.

To explain these arguments—(1) when the word "Cow" is uttered, before we have an idea of any Individuals, it is the Commonality that we have an idea of; and when the form of this Commonality has been duly comprehended, then alone are the Individuals cognised. Thus then, inasmuch as for the cognition of the Class there is no other means (save the word), while the cognition of the Individuals is actually brought about by the cognition of the Class, we conclude that the word denotes the Class.

(2) If the Individuals were denoted by the word, then, inasmuch as the individual cows are found to have various characters—such as the variegated colour, absence of horns, &c.,—the idea brought about by the word would be a mixed one (partaking of all these characters), while as a matter of fact we find the word giving rise to a single uniform conception (of the Commonality); and thus too we conclude that it is the Class that is denoted by the word.

(3) When a person is ordered to 'bring the cow,' if no particular cow happens to be specially pointed out, either by the character of the work in hand or by the other concurrent circumstances, the person ordered is found to bring in any common cow, and not any particularly specified cow, or all the cows in the world. If, however, the individual cow were denoted by the word, then the mention of the word 'Cow' would have pointed to all the individual cows in the world, which would have to be

brought in by the person ordered; or he could bring in only that one particular cow which would be denoted by the word. But as a matter of fact we find that he brings in any common cow, with the only restriction that it should possess the *common character* of the 'Cow.' And hence too we conclude that the Class is denoted by the word.

If, however, the Individual be held to be denoted by the word, there could be only the following three alternatives: (1) That all Individuals should be denoted independently by themselves; (2) or that the conglomeration of all Individuals as qualified by a particular Individual should be denoted; (3) or that only one particular Individual be denoted.

(1) Now, it is not possible for all Individuals to be denoted; (*a*) because that would necessitate the assumption of manifold denotative potencies in the word; (*b*) because (the Individuals being transient) the relationship between the word and its denotation would become transient; (*c*) because, the conception of all the Individuals being absolutely impossible, the full relationship of the word with its denotation would never be comprehended, and as such, there could be no usage of the word or any business carried on (such as the following of one another's directions, &c.); as referring to many Individuals, the word 'Cow' would be always used in the Plural, like the word 'eight'; and as such it would never be possible to apply to it either the Dual or the Singular number; (*e*) as the white colour cannot exist in all the Individual cows denoted by the word 'Cow,' there could be no co-extensiveness (of the qualification and the qualified) in the expression 'white cow'; and (*f*) because in the case of the Vedic Injunction 'one should sacrifice with the animal,' as it would be impossible to perform a sacrifice with *all individual animals*, such Injunctions, and thence the Veda, would lose all authority.

(2) Similarly too, it is not possible to admit the Conglomeration of the Individuals to be denoted by the word; (*a*) because in this case also all the Individuals will have to be denoted, as forming the Conglomeration, and hence this theory too would be open to all the aforesaid six objections; (*b*) because such a theory would necessitate the assumption of a Conglomeration apart from the Individuals; (*c*) as no usage is found to appertain to any such Conglomeration, the denotation of words would be absolutely useless (as the sole use of denotations lies in the accomplishment of usage); (*d*) the Units forming the Conglomeration being all destructible, the Conglomeration would also be destructible; and hence the relationship of the word with its denotation would become transient; (*e*) the Conglomeration being one only, there would be no Plural or Dual Number in Nouns; (*f*) nor would there be any co-extensiveness between the qualification and the qualified, in the expression 'white cow'; because the Conglomeration of all cows cannot be said to be white; (*g*) the

Conglomeration being shapeless, no sacrifices could be performed with it; and that would shake the authority of all Vedic Injunctions.

(3) If a single Individual be held to be denoted by the word, then too,—(*a*) there would be a non-eternality of the relationship (of the word and its denotation); (*b*) as it could not be ascertained which one particular Individual is denoted, no business would be possible; (*c*) there could be no idea of Commonality; (*d*) Nouns could never have the Plural or the Dual number; (*e*) no use of the word 'Cow' could be possible, prior to the birth, and after the death, of the particular cow denoted; (*f*) the word 'Cow' giving rise to an idea of the 'Cow' in general, there can be no particular reason for asserting that it is only this particular cow, and not that, which is denoted by the word.

We now proceed to explain the text of the Bhāshya:

If any particular cow were denoted, the word could never give us an idea of any other cow; and as such it could never be used with reference to any other cow save the one held to be denoted; because at any other time, the particular cow denoted by the word on the former occasion would not be existing at the subsequent time, the one present at this time being totally different from the former. Specially as the Individual is said to be free from all generic and specific properties; and apart from such properties, there is nothing in the Individual, by which it could be referred to (by any word).

Question: "Just as one Individual is free from such generic and "specific properties, so would also the second be free from them; and "hence, just as the word is found to apply to the one Individual free from "such properties, in the same manner would it also be applicable to the "other Individual, which is equally free from them. If this other Indi-"vidual had the form of either the *genus* or the *species*, then alone would 'it be different in character from the former Individual; and in that case "alone would the word be found inapplicable to it. As a matter of fact, "however, both of them are found to be equally free from such forms; "and as such the word would be equally applicable to both of them."

Answer: If the application of the word to one Individual, as also to the other, be based upon the fact of their being free from generic and specific properties, then this freedom itself would constitute their *Commonality*; and as such your explanation would be a tacit admission of our theory; and it seems you are only opposed to the use of the word "Class."

Says the *Pūrvapakshi*: "We do not mean that the word applies to one "Individual, as also to another, on account of their freedom from generic "and specific properties; all that we mean is that the Individual is "cognised in the form of a *negation of all things that differ from it either "in its generic or specific form.* And in that case, how can our declaration "be said to be tantamount to the admission of the denotation of a com- "monality? Because an Individual is the substratum of the generic "and specific properties, it cannot be these properties themselves. And "hence what we hold is that just as the word is found applicable to one "Individual, which is different from generic and specific properties, so, "in the same manner would it be applicable to another Individual also."

The *Siddhānti* replies: If the word be applicable to Individuals on account of these latter being free from generic and specific properties, then in that case, the word comes to be denotative of a Commonality. And if there be no commonality, then one word cannot apply to two Individuals; because if a word were applicable to one Individual, without this latter having the commonality that belongs to another Individual denoted by the word, then the word 'Cow' would be applicable to an individual horse also! And certainly this would be a too extensive use of the word!

Says the *Pūrvapakshī*:—"It is not so; the application of all words "being independent of all *commonality*, their usage would be regulated by "actual usage; and as such there could be no such absurd usage of "words as you have pointed out."

The *Siddhānti*: If mere usage be held to regulate the application of words, then the word 'Cow' never yet having been been used with reference to the particular cow born to-day, this could not be spoken of as a 'Cow.' Thus then, if the application of words is regulated by usage, it becomes too limited; otherwise it becomes too extensive as shown above. Following this line of argument, the Bhāshya says that the common notion of the *Cow* would not apply to different Individuals—as that 'this is a cow' and 'that is a cow,' and so forth; but this is not quite relevant to what just precedes it; hence this argument of the Bhāshya must be taken along with (and in support of) the proposition that, 'if the word denoted a particular Individual it could never be applied to any other Individual.'

Says the *Pūrvapakshī*: "But the application of words could be re- "gulated by the denotative potencies of the words themselves; a word "applying, and being used with reference to that Individual which it may "be capable of denoting; while if in regard to any Individual it had "no such potency, it would not apply to it. And hence the word 'cow' "being capable of denoting the *Individual Cows* only, it is with reference "to these only that the word 'cow' could be used."

But this too cannot regulate the application of words; because the potentiality of a word cannot be ascertained before it has been used; and the cognition of the potentiality of a word would depend upon its usage; and as such being itself non-existent at the using of the word, how could the cognition of the potentiality of the word regulate the application (and the usage) of the word? And further, even though the person addressed could ascertain the potentiality of the word from its use, how could the speaker himself know that the word 'cow' is applicable to the individual *cow*, and not to the individual *horse?* And he would be as liable to using the word 'cow' with reference to the *horse* as to the *cow*.

The *Pūrvapakshī*: "Why could we not have the application regulated by the Class,—the word 'cow' applying to all individuals, that "would be found to be qualified by the *class* 'cow' (or generic character "of the cow); while it would not apply to those not so qualified; and "thus it would not apply to the *horse* (which is not found to be qualified "by the generic character of the *cow*); and in this manner, the application "of all words would be very easily regulated."

True; such a regulation would be possible; but you have come to our way of thinking. Because unless the word 'Cow' denotes the qualification, —the generic character of the *cow*,—how can the application of the word be restricted to the individual *cow* only? And if this generic character be held to be previously denoted, it would be an admission of the denotability of the Class by the word.

The *Pūrvapakshī* now brings forward another argument: "It is true "that the *class* is denoted; but the fact is that it appears as the qualification of the *individual*, occupying only a secondary position; while the "individual forms the primary element in the denotation of a word. "None of us are very anxious to assert that both (the Class and the Individual) are not expressed by the word. The fact is that some of us hold "one thing (the Individual) to be the primary and other (the Class) the "secondary denotation of the word; and hence has it been declared that "'the individual constitutes the primary denotation of the word.' Thus it "is that the regulation of the applications of a word, the cognitions of "both the Class and the Individual, the possibility of such actions as "*killing*, *washing*, &c.,—all become explicable."

To this, the other party makes the following reply: This is not possible; because if the Class be admitted to have been previously denoted by the word, the whole force of the word will have been taken up in this denotation, and it cannot be said to denote the Individual; nor is it proper to admit the word to have more than one denotation, when the cognition of the Individual is capable of being otherwise got at, through its connection with the Class (a cognition whereof is always found to point to that of the Individual); because it is only by means of the Apparent Inconsistency (of the fact of the cognition of something being brought about by a word) that we admit a potentiality, in that word, of expressing that thing; but in the case of the cognition of the Individual, we find that it is got at by other means; and as such the Apparent Inconsistency having disappeared, there can be no ground for postulating a potentiality, in the word, of denoting the Individual. Nor are words always found to denote only one particular Class; as we actually find words like '*Aksha*' denoting more than one Class (as it has many meanings). Invariable concomitance too, both negative and positive, is found to point to the fact of a word not denoting the Individual; for instance, even when the word has not been uttered, the person who has known the Class ('Cow') at once recognises the Individual; while even when the word has been pronounced, if the person addressed has never known the Class, he is found incapable of having any idea of the Individual. Hence we conclude that it is the Class that is denoted by the word.

The *Pūrvapakshī* puts forward another theory: "Why cannot we admit the denotation of the word to consist in *the Class as qualified by the Individual?*"

The propounding of this theory may be explained in various ways: (1) It may have been propounded as a combination of the two extreme theories; and as such, in keeping with both *usage* and *cognition*. (2) Or, it may be that it has been put forward with the indirect motive of establishing the Individualistic theory, the chain of reasoning, in the mind of the propounder, being somewhat like this: "The Siddhānti might, by my putting forward this theory, be lulled into the belief that in this his opponent admits the denotability of the Class; and hence, with a view to explain the possibility of such actions as *washing*, &c., he might come to admit of the denotability of the Individual also, though only as a qualification; and thus having made him admit the denotability of the Individual as qualifying the Class, it would become easy for me to lead him on to my main position, that it is the Individual, and not the Class, that is denoted by the word."

But the *Siddhāntī* fully understands the trick, and replies accordingly: If that be the case, the word would not be applicable to the Class as qualified by another Individual. That is to say, if the word be held to denote the Class as qualified by a particular Individual, then this theory too would be open to all the objections that have been urged above against the purely Individualistic theory—namely, the necessity of assuming manifold potencies in a word, &c., &c., and the impossibility of the word applying to another Individual; because in the case of each Individual the qualification (of the Class) would be different. Hence we conclude that the Class is denoted by the word.

Objection: "But the Class is always recognised as the secondary ele-"ment in the denotation of a word; and hence the primary denotation "must consist in something else."

It is not so; because it is the Class alone that is denoted by the word; as for its being the primary or the secondary factor in the denotation, if such character be dependent upon the wish of the speaker as to what he may desire to express by the word, we have nothing to say against it; but this cannot shake off the fact of the Class forming the true denotation of the word. And actually at the time that it is denoted by the word, it is not cognised as the secondary factor; and consequently the mere fact of its being meant to be the secondary factor cannot affect our position.

Objection: "On account of the arguments urged in the *Pūrvapaksha*, "we cannot but accept the Individual to be denoted by the word. If it "be urged that—'in that case the word could not be applicable to other "Individuals,'—(we reply) the Class would serve as the distinguishing "mark (even though itself not denoted by the word). For instance, when "two men have passed through a village, one of them asks—'which was "the house of Dēvadatta?'—the other replies: 'the house that had "many crows over it was Dēvadatta's'; and in this case we find that "though the *existence of the crows* is not denoted by the word 'Dēva-"datta's house,' yet it serves as a distinguishing mark whereby the man "knows the actual house called 'Dēvadatta's house'; in the same manner, "though the Class is not actually denoted by the word 'Cow,' yet it will "serve as the distinguishing mark whereby we would know the actual "Individual called 'Cow.'

"The Bhāshya has cited the word '*Danḍī*' (the man with the stick); "the sense being that just as the *Danḍa* is not actually denoted by the "word '*Danḍī*' though it serves as the distinguishing mark of the person "called '*Danḍī*,' in the same manner could the Class serve as the dis-"tinguishing mark of the Individual denoted.

"Against this example of the Bhāshya, the following objections are "raised: (1) 'In the word *Danḍī* its base *Danḍa* is actually found to "denote the *Danḍa*; how then can it be asserted that the word *Danḍī* does "not denote the *Danḍa*? (2) The fact that is under consideration is that "of the Class serving as the distinguishing mark; while the example that "has been cited is one of qualification'!

"But none of these objections affect the main position—(1) What is "meant by the assertion of the *Danḍa* not being denoted is that it is "not denoted by the affix (*ini*), in the word '*Daṇḍī*'; the sense thus being "that, just as in the case of the word '*Daṇḍī*,' though the *Daṇḍa* is not "actually denoted by the affix, and yet it is found to point to a *person* "*qualified by the possession of the Daṇḍa*, in the same manner in the case in "question, though the Class is not denoted, yet the word would denote the "Individual as qualified by the Class. (2) As for the objection that the "matter in question being the fact of the Class serving as the *distinguishing mark*, it was not proper for the Bhāshya to cite an instance of *qualification*,—this is not a proper objection; because the *distinguishing mark* "too is only a *qualification* after all. Or, it may be that the example cited "bears a similarity to the main question, in various phases of it— "such as some may be similar to it on the point of *non-denotability* (as in the "case of the word '*Dandī*), while some may be so only on the pont of "its serving as a distinguishing mark (as in the case of 'Dēvadatta's house'), "and thus there is nothing wrong in the example cited by the Bhāshya.

"And in this theory there can be neither a too narrow, nor a too "wide, application of the word (as urged above) against the purely Individualistic theory."

But all this is not quite to the point. It is true that the *house of Dēvadatta*, and the *man with the stick* are denoted (by the words 'Dēvadatta's house,' and '*Daṇḍī*'); but the *presence of the crows* serves as the distinguishing mark of the house, only when it is actually seen by the eyes; and so also the *possession of the stick* is recognised as the distinguishing mark of the *Dandī*, only by means of this latter word; while in the case in question, the class 'Cow' is not before us; and as such, not being in any way cognised, it could not serve as the distinguishing mark (unless it were admitted to be denoted by the word itself); and so long as the *qualification* (Class) has not been cognised, there can be no idea of the qualified (Individual). Nor is any portion of the word 'Cow' found to denote the Class 'Cow,' as the word 'Daṇḍa,' forming part of the word 'Daṇḍī,' is found to denote the *stick*; and as such we cannot admit that the first portion of the word 'Cow' denotes the Class (the qualification) while the second portion signifies the Individual (as qualified by it) [just as in the word '*Daṇḍī*,' the first part '*Daṇḍa*' signifies the qualifying *stick*, while the second part, the affix, denotes the person qualified by the stick]. Thus then, if the Class be held to be denoted by the word 'Cow,' it is this alone that can be accepted as constituting the true denotation of the word. And (if not, then) that which is not cognised not being capable of serving as the distinguishing mark, the contingency of the too wide an application of the word remains unexplained. In the case of the word '*Daṇḍī*,' the case is a little different; as the word cannot be used with reference to the *stick* only; and as such it cannot but be admitted to be denotative of the *person qualified* (by the possession of the stick); whereas the word 'Cow' cannot be said to be incapable of being used with reference to the Class 'Cow,' and as such, necessarily pointing to the Individual as qualified (by the Class). Because in the case of such expressions as '*Çyēnacita*' and the like, we actually find the word '*Çyēna*' used with reference to the Class. And also from invariable concomitance, both negative and positive, we conclude that the word denotes the Class: for instance, in the passage speak- of the '*Çyēnacita*,' we actually find the word '*Çyēna*' used with reference to the Class; and we never find any instance of a word being used with reference to the Individual independently of the Class.

The above arguments also serve to reject all the other alternative theories that have been put forward with regard to the denotation of a word. And thus we conclude that the Word denotes the Class.

The Pūrvapaksha arguments—*viz.*, of the impossibility of the Injunctions of such actions as *killing*, *washing*, &c.—that have been summed up under—

***Sūtra* (34). "There would be no Actions, and the Injunctions would refer to something else, and not to Substances"—**

Are set aside by the following—

***Sūtra* (35). The performance of the actions is for the sake of a transcendental result; and there is no disjunction.**

All actions of *washing*, *killing*, &c., being performed for the sake of certain transcendental results, their performance must be taken as part of the means of the accomplishment of such results; and the means of fulfilling the transcendental results are the Substances, and not the Class; as the former are pointed out by the sacrifices by themselves for their own accomplishment, while the latter is incapable of accomplishing any sacrifices. Consequently the denotation of the Class must be accepted, for the sake of the pointing out of the exact Substance, and not for the sake of the Class itself—(1) because a cognition of the Class by itself is not what is sought after; (2) because in that case a denotation of the Class alone would have only a transcendental result; and (3) because, being incorporeal, it is not found capable of helping the sacrifice in any way. Even in a case when the Class as signified by a basic noun is recognised as the means of performing a sacrifice (as in '*Somēna yajēta*'), it is recognised only as pointing to a definite Substance, and not to itself independently, as by itself it is of no particular use in the performance of the sacrifice. Thus then, the denotation of the Class pointing to a definite Substance, and the Substance being quite capable of being related to the actions of *killing*, *washing*, &c., as also to Genders, Numbers and Cases,—there is nothing that can be urged against our theory.

It is with a view to this that the *Sūtra* says—*there is no disjunction.* That is to say, (1) even in accordance with the Class-theory, there is no disjunction of the actions of *washing, &c.*, from the Substances; or (2) the denotation of the Class serving the purpose of pointing to a definite Substance, there is no disjunction of the performance of the actions mentioned above; or (3) there being no absolute difference between the Class and the Individual, the Substance is pointed out, at times in the form of the Individual, and at others, in that of the Class, in accordance with the wish of the speaker; and as such words being found to denote both forms of things, even when the Individual is denoted (by the word), it does not necessitate any multiplicity in the performance of the action; or (4) the Class not being totally different from the Individual, the sacrifices performed with reference to the Individual may be accepted as performed with reference to the Class also, and *vice versa;* and thus in no case is it necessary to make any difference in the performance of Actions (or Sacrifices); or (5) both the Class and the Individual serve the purpose of accomplishing a sacrifice; with reference to whichsoever of these two, the sacrifice may be performed, both of them come to be recognised as useful; and as such there is no disjunction (of the Actions) from the Substance.

Thus then, even in accordance with the Class-theory, such Actions as *killing*, *washing*, &c., being quite possible, we conclude that it is the Class that constitutes the denotation of the word.

Thus ends the Third—Smṛti—Pāda of the First Adhyāya.

ADHYĀYA I.

PĀDA IV.

Treating of the Names of Sacrifices.

ADHIKARAṆA (1).

(Divided into two Adhikaranas in the Vārtika : A.—that such words as 'udbhid, &c., also help in the knowledge of Dharma; and B.—that such words are names of sacrifies.)

Question: The authority of the Veda together with the *Smṛtis* having been established, the present was the time for considering the meanings of Vedā passages (which also are the means of knowing Dharma); wherefore and in what connection, then, should the Bhāshya before having furnished the consideration of the means of knowing Dharma, have taken up the consideration of the Names of sacrifices?

Some people offer the following explanation: "The question "dealt with is—do the words '*udbhid*' and the like, point out the "*materials* (to be used at sacrifices) or the *names* (of sacrifices)? (Thus "the question dealing directly with the *means of knowing Dharma.*")

But this is not quite correct; because in this manner all books could be explained as the *means of knowing;* because all Sentences may be explained as dealing with the question—does this sentence point out this fact or that?

Some people (notably the author of the Bhāshya himself) take the *Sūtra* (1) as the *Pūrvapaksha* and *Sūtra* (2) as the *Siddhānta* of the same *Adhikaraṇa;* but it is necessary for these people to point out what there is in *Sūtra* (1) that is not in keeping with the *Siddhānta* (that it should be taken as the *Pūrvapaksha*). For certainly the assertion of the fact of the words like '*udbhid*' being included in 'that which serves the purpose of fulfilling an action' is by no means unacceptable to the *Siddhāntī*. Hence we explain these two *Sūtras* as embodying the *Siddhānta* of the two *Adhikaraṇas*

(A. & B.), the *Pūrvapaksha* of both being supplied from without. [Our explanation dealing with the consideration of the authoritative character and usefulness of certain words with regard to *Dharma* makes the *Sūtras* connected with the main subject of the Adhyāya.]

ADHIKARAṆA (A).

With regard to words like '*udbhid*' (as occurring in such passages as '*udbhidā yajēta paçukāmah*'), we have a doubt as to whether they have any use in matters relating to *Dharma*, or not.

And on this point, we have the following

PŪRVAPAKSHA (A).

" These words have no use with regard to Dharma, because they have " no connection with the performance of actions, while the Veda deals with " such performance alone; as has been declared elsewhere also: 'Only " three parts of the Veda (viz., *Vidhi*, *Arthavāda* and *Mantra*) have an " authority with regard to Dharma; and the words in question being " different from all these three, they can serve no useful purpose with " regard to Dharma; and as such they are absolutely useless.' (1) These " words cannot be said to be included in *Vidhi;* because they do not signify " either the *Means* or the *Result* or the *Method* of any sacrifices; (2) " they are different from *Arthavāda*, because they do not signify any *Praise;* " (3) they cannot be said to serve the purpose of a *Mantra;* because they " do not indicate any accessories (Material, Deity, &c.) of sacrifices. And " apart from these three there is no other use of the Veda; and hence " the words in question cannot have any authority (with regard to " Dharma)."

In reply to the above, we have the following

SIDDHĀNTA (A).

***Sūtra* (1). It has already been explained that the Veda helps in the performance of sacrifices; and hence the whole of it should be accepted as serving that purpose.**

That is to say, the *whole* of the Veda being divided into the aforesaid three parts, and the authoritative characters of the three parts having been proved by means of the arguments urged above (in *Pādas* II *and* III), the authoritative character of words like '*udbhid*' cannot be denied, on the ground of their being different from the three parts (because the three parts take in the whole of the Veda, and the words in question are found in the Veda).

ADHIKARAṆA (B).

It having been shown by the foregoing *Adhikaraṇa* that the words in question have the same use as one of the three parts of the Veda, we proceed to consider which one of these uses are fulfilled by them.

Now then, (1) they cannot serve the purpose of the *Arthavāda;* because they are not found in connection with any other sentence. It may be asked—'How can they be denied to be supplementary to a sentence, when they are actually found in a sentence, exactly like the assertion—'*Vāyu is the eftest deity*?' But it is not so; that which is supplementary to something that is enjoined, is what is known as *'Arthavāda'*; while the words in question do not appear apart from the Injunction itself ('*yajēta*'); therefore they cannot be said to be supplementary to any Sentence; and we have already proved under the *Audumbarādhikaraṇa* that that which is capable of being taken along with an Injunction cannot be taken as mere Praise. Nor have we ever found any Praise expressed by a single word; neither do we comprehend any Praise as expressed by the word '*Udbhid*.' Though the word could be taken as Praise, inasmuch it is capable of being explained as 'that by which trees, &c., are cut properly,'—yet such an interpretation would be set aside by the most rational fact of the '*udbhid*' being an Instrument (in the performance of a sacrifice), as is pointed out by the Instrumental ending in the word '*udbhidā*'; for if mere Praise were meant, the noun would have had only the Nominative ending, as we have in the word '*Vāyuh*' in the acknowledged Arthavāda—'*Vāyurvai kshēpishthā dēvatā*.'

(2) Nor can the word '*udbhid*' be taken as a *Mantra*; because it is not recognised as one; and also because the students of the Veda do not remember any such *Mantra*. And being a single word it cannot be said to stand in need of something else (which it would indicate exactly as the *Mantra* indicates the Materials and Deities of sacrifices); and as it is recognised as the 'Instrument,' it cannot be said to bring about an idea of anything else (in the shape of the Material or the Deity). Nor do we find the word itself denoting anything that would form the material part of a Sacrifice; and no sentence that actually indicates anything not forming a material part of the Sacrifice, can be accepted as auxiliary to the sacrifice. If we set about assuming a material to be indicated by the *Mantra* (in the shape of the word '*Udbhid*'), it would be a most unwarrantable complication of matters. Nor do we find any Vedic text, like the *Sūktavāka* (which

lays down the fact of certain *Mantras* being employed at certain sacrifices) laying down the employment of this word as a *Mantra;* so that the aforesaid assumption of the material too is not possible. Nor again is the word itself capable of being employed as a *Mantra;* so that we cannot even assume any Injunctions of its employment, as we do in the case of the *Mantra* '*Ishē tvā*' and the rest. And lastly, it is evident that the word forms part of the Brāhmaṇa passage '*udbhidā yajēta*'; and as such, it cannot be taken as a *Mantra*.

Thus then, it being clear that the word forms part of the subject of the Injunction itself, we proceed to consider the question as to whether the word constitutes the Injunction of a Material, or it is only the name of a Sacrifice.

And on this point, we have the following

PŪRVAPAKSHA (B).

"It is the material (*axe*) that is enjoined by the word '*udbhidā*'; (1) "because the universally recognised fact is mostly authoritative; (2) be-"cause a distinctly useful purpose is served; and (3) because this inter-"pretation is much more capable of prompting men to the performance of "the particular action, than any other. (*a*) That is to say, it is an uni-"versally recognised fact that the noun '*udbhid*' literally signifies a "*cutting instrument* (the Axe); nor is the word '*udbhidā*' known to signify "anything else; and the meaning of a word that is not recognised in or-"dinary parlance cannot be got at from the Veda; because the relation-"ship of a word (to its denotation) is not fixed by the scriptures (but by "ordinary parlance). As for the Instrumental ending, it signifies mere "*Instrumentality*, and it is only a potent substance, or the potency re-"siding in the substance, that is known to be capable of serving as the "Instrument of an Action. And it is only when the Injunction is found "to serve a distinctly useful purpose that it can prompt people to the "particular course of action; that is to say, it is only those persons that "recognise the word '*udbhid*' to be an Injunction (of the material) that "can engage themselves in the particular action mentioned; for if such "an engagement could come about even without the recognition of the "fact of the Injunction serving a useful purpose, it would be as good as "the engagement that is not preceded by any distinctly-uttered Injunc-"tion.

"(*b*) Or, the word '*udbhidā*' may be taken as the Injunction of a "material; because of the universally recognised meaning of the word; "the '*arthavattva*' of the word may be explained as the 'fact of its hav-"ing a meaning'; the sense of the argument in this case being that in a

" *name* the literal significance of the word is not always recognised (while " it is recognised in the case of the word '*udbhid*,' which, therefore, can-" not be a *name*).

" (*c*) Or, the fact of the word '*udbhid*' having a significance only when " taken apart from the 'sacrifice,' may be employed as an argument " against its being taken as a Name; specially as the word '*udbhid*' serves " a purpose totally different from that served by the root *yaji* (= to sacri-" fice, in the word '*yajēta*'); and thus alone is it possible for the person " to be prompted to the particular action.

" It may be urged that, 'even a name while qualifying or specifying " the sacrifice, would serve to prompt the person to the particular course " of action.'

" But this is not possible; why? Because the Class 'sacrifice' not being " a fit object of Injunction, the root '*yaji*' itself points to the Individual " sacrifice; and if the name ('*udbhid*') be held to denote the *Class* 'sacri-" fice,' then it ceases to be a name! That is to say, when the root itself is " found to indicate the Individual sacrifice, on account of the Class (which " is directly denoted by it) not being capable of being enjoined, then what " is left to be done by the name? While if the name '*udbhid*' be held to " denote the Individual sacrifice, then a generic name not being desirable " for a particular sacrifice, the word would be altogether irrelevant; and " we shall explain later on that the object specified (*i.e.*, the sacrifice) " being itself a well-established entity, the name could not be accepted as " enjoining it. Even though at times it may be possible for words like " '*udbhid*' to have a specific (and not a generic) denotation, yet even " such specific denotation being invariably accompanied by the generic " element, it can have no connection with the root '*yaji*.'

" And further, the Injunction itself becomes much simpler, if the word " '*udbhidā*' is taken as laying down the material; because in that case, it " would be merely refering to the sacrifice enjoined elsewhere [that is " to say, the meaning of the Injunction would only mean that *one should " perform the sacrifice with the axe*, the Injunction enjoining only the mate-" rial, its work being thereby much more lightened than if it had to en-" join the *sacrifice* also].

" Against this it might be urged that, 'in that case the force of the " Injunction having been exhausted in the laying down of the material, " the sacrifice itself would remain unenjoined; and then, as there would be " no sacrifice laid down, there would be nothing at which the enjoined " material would be employed, and hence the Injunction of the material " would be absolutely useless.'

" In view of this objection, it is said—*prakṛtau jyotishtomē*—*i.e.*, the " sacrifice is enjoined along with the *jyotishtoma*, of which it is an auxiliary

"It may, however, be urged that—'if all names be taken as laying "down the materials to be used at the sacrifices, even the word '*Jyotish-* "*toma*' in the Injunction '*Jyotishtomēna yajēta*' would only point out a "material to be employed; and the sacrifice would remain as unenjoined "as ever.' But, as a matter of fact, there is no other way out of this "difficulty than to admit one of these sentences ('*Jyotishtomēna yajēta*' "and '*udbhidā yajēta*') to enjoin the sacrifice (and not the material); be- "cause in the absence of an Injunction of Action, any laying down of "materials is impossible; hence we admit the word '*Jyotishtoma*' alone to "be the name of a sacrifice (and not the Injunction of a material). Or, we "may take the sentence '*Jyotishtomēna yajēta*' to be the Injunction of "a *sacrific performed with the particular material pointed out;* while the "other words may be taken as Injunctions of materials only.

"It may be urged that—'in that case the Injuctions of all the "various subsidiaries of the *Jyotishtoma,* viz., the *Ēkāha,* the *Ahīna,* &c.— "being mere injunctions of so many materials, these sacrifices themselves "would not be different from the *Jyotishtoma* itself; and thus there being "no subsidiary sacrifices, the *Jyotishtoma* could not be the primary (*Prak-* "*ṛti*) of any sacrifices; and hence it could not be spoken of as such.'

"Some people reply to this that the assertion of the *Jyotishtoma* as "the primary sacrifice is in accordance with the view of the *Siddhānti* "(who holds all such words to be names).

"But we can explain the sentence '*Prakṛtau Jyotishtomē*' in a differ- "ent way altogether. *Prakṛti* is that a consideration of which has been in- "troduced; hence the sentence would mean that the sacrifice, at which the "*udbhid* would be used as a material, is enjoined in connection with the "*Jyotishtoma,* (as the passage '*udbhidā yajēta*' is found in the same con- "text as the *Jyotishtoma* sacrifice).

"Or, the *Jyotishtoma* could be spoken of as the 'Primary' (*Prakṛti*), "in comparision with the various sacrifices recognised as distinct sacri- "fices (apart from the *Jyotishtoma*),—being pointed out by the sen- "tences '*Athaisha Jyotih,*' &c., which being devoid of any Instrumental "terminations are unconnected with any verbs, and as such, are not cap- "able of being taken as Injunctions of materials.

"Another objection is raised: 'As for the *Jyotishtoma* sacrifice, its "original Injunction itself lays down the *Soma* and the *Jyotishtoma* as "materials to be employed at it, the Injunction of any other material for "it is not right.'

"But the materials like '*udbhid*' being laid down in view of the ob- "taining of certain definite desirable results, these would set aside all "other materials that may have been laid down in the original Injunction. "It is an admitted fact that the materials laid down in the original

"Injunction can be utilised only at the necessary Actions (*i.e.*, the Actions "that are performed as mere *duties* and not with a view to the obtaining "of any desirable results). Or, it may be that though the original Injunc-"tion has laid down the *Jyotishtoma* as to be performed with certain defi-"nite materials, yet the subsequent Injunctions (like '*udbhidā yajēta*,') "could be taken as laying down other materials for the same sacrifice, the "injunction of the sacrifice itself, without the material, being borrowed "from the original Injunction; and thus the material laid down by the "subsequent Injunction would be in no way different from that laid down "in the original one. Otherwise we would be, as the Bhāshya thinks, "obliged to accept both materials as optional alternatives."

SIDDHANTA (B).

***Sūtra* (2). That (*word*) must be a name, which at first appears new; because it cannot lay down (the material).**

We proceed to explain the words of the *Sūtra:* When a word—like "*udbhid*'—is such that, when first heard, it 'appears new'—*i.e.*, is not cognised as signifying anything definite,—then, if it be come across, first of all, in a Vedic Injunction, it must be taken as a *name*, on account of its co-extensiveness (with the sacrifice enjoined). Or, the clause '*utpattāvapūrvam*' may mean that inasmuch the word '*udbhid*' would point out a definite sacrifice (not otherwise got at) it would not be useless. Or, it may be explained thus: The question being—'whose name would the word be?'—, the *Sūtra* replies—'the name belongs to that sacrifice, the performance of which would accomplish a particular transcendental result.'

"Now, what is the reason for holding the word to be a *Name?* Says the *Sūtra* '*Avidhāykatvāt*'—'Because it cannot lay down (the material).

To explain—If the word laid down the material, the material could be laid down—(1) either with reference to the Result (the meaning of the Injunction being 'one should think of obtaining cattle by means of the *udbhid* axe); or (2) with regard to the sacrifice (the meaning being 'one should accomplish the sacrifice by means of the axe'); or (3) with reference to both taken together (the meaning being 'one should obtain the cattle by means of the sacrifice with the axe for its material.') But none of these is possible.

(1) If the Material were laid down with reference to the Result, then—(*a*) the Injunctive affix (in '*yajēta*') would lay down the relationship of words other than in which it happens to be (that is to say, the Injunction would refer to the causal relationship of the material *udbhid*, with the Result, *obtaining of cattle*, without having anything to do with

the sacrifice itself); (*b*) we would have to assume a direct relationship between the two words '*udbhidā*' and '*paçukāmah*,' which are mentioned (in the text) far apart from one another; (*c*) the verbal root '*yaji*' having nothing to do with the Injunction, the sole purpose of its use would lie in that it makes the use of the affix possible; (*d*) we would have to reject the *Soma*, which has been laid down in the original Injunction as the material to be used at the sacrifice; and (*e*) we would have the absurdity of the sacrifice being performed with a material (remnants of) which could not be eaten.

(2) If the material were laid down with reference to the Sacrifice, then—(*a*) the mention of the Result would be absolutely useless; nor could the Result be taken as qualifying the *Jyotishtoma* sacrifice, because this sacrifice has been spoken of as bringing about all desirable results; and as such, its qualification by any one result would result in a syntactical split; and the objections (*a*) (*c*) (*d*) and (*e*), pointed out above, would also apply to this theory, as also the contingency of the *axe* being accepted as an optional alternative to *Soma*.

(3) Similarly too, if the material be taken to be laid down as qualifying the sacrifice, then, (*a*) all the words in the sentence would have to renounce their own direct significations (as none of them has such a qualified mixed signification); (*b*) we would have to assume various denotative potentialities of the Injunction (as there could be no signification of the qualified without a distinct signification of the qualification); (*c*) we would have to resort to the indirect *possessive indication*, in the case of the word '*udbhidā*' (which would have to be taken as indicating '*udbhidvatā*' = *by that by which has the udbhid for its material*; (*d*) it would be necessary for us to reject the intimate relationship of co-extensiveness (between the 'sacrifice' and the '*udbhid*') which is distinctly pointed out by the fact of the former being signified by a verbal root with an Injunctive affix (which has also an Instrumental force), while the latter has in itself an Instrumental termination; and (*e*) lastly, the sacrifice would be performed with a material that could not be eaten.

For these reasons the word '*udbhidā*' cannot be taken as laying down the material for a sacrifice; and this is what is pointed out by the Bhāshya: (If it were the Injunction of a material) *the sentence would directly denote the udbhid and indirectly indicate that in which it would be employed as the material.* The Bhāshya may also be read as—*Vakshyanti lakshayēt* (the meaning being the same).

Having thus explained the implications of the noun '*udbhid*,' the Bhāshya proceeds to show that the same facts are also pointed out by the Instrumental affix (in '*udbhidā*'): *One should accomplish by means of the sacrifice, &c.* That is to say, whether the passage be taken as an independent

Injunction by itself or as supplementary to another Injunction, the *Sacrifice* is recognised to be the *Instrument* (of the accomplishment of a certain result); and hence the word ('*udbhidā*') also with an Instrumental, ending, occurring in close proximity to the words signifying *the sacrifice* cannot but be taken as denoting the Instrument.

The Bhāshya says—'*From the Noun which denotes the karaṇa*'—(Instrument), &c. &c.; and against this, it may be argued that—," in all cases the case-significations being held to belong to the Terminations (as is distinctly laid down in such passages as 'by means of the third case-termination which signifies *Instrumentality*, &c.'), how can the Noun be spoken of as expressing the *karaṇa* (or Instrument)?"

But this does not affect the position of the Bhāshya; (1) because what is meant by the passage in question is that the Noun signifies the *Substratum of the Instrumentality.* (2) Or, the assertion may be said to be based upon the fact of the Noun having a signification similar to that of the word '*karaṇa*' [that is to say the Noun '*udbhid,*' means 'that by which is shot forth (the particular result),' and this is similar to the signification of the word '*karaṇa*' which means 'that by which something is done.'] Specially as the word made up of the *kṛt* affix '*kvip*' (*viz.*, the word '*karaṇa,*' as also the word '*udbhid*') signifies a certain substance endowed with a definite case-potentiality, and not the potentiality alone, apart from the substance; and it is for this reason that we find the word '*karaṇa*' taking other case-terminations also—as '*karaṇāya*') with the Dative); '*karaṇam*' (with the Accusative) and the like; for if no substance were signified by the word ('*karaṇa,*') then the only case-termination applicable to it would be that which is indicated by the affix '*kvip*' (and this would be the Instrumental only); and the substance (that would be signified by the word '*karaṇa*') would not be capable of any other case-potentiality; because one potentiality cannot have another potentiality. Thus then, all words with the *kṛt* affix being found to be significant of certain substances with definite potencies, it is only proper to speak of the Noun ('*udbhid*') as signifying the '*karaṇa.*'

The upshot of all this is this: In the passage ('*udbhidā yajēta paçukāmah*') the Noun, that signifies what is recognised to be the Instrument, must take the Instrumental case-termination; and it is the *Sacrifice* and not the material, that is recognised to be the Instrument (or means) of obtaining the particular result, as we shall explain later on; and hence it is only when the word '*udbhid*' denotes the sacrifice, that it can have the Instrumental case-ending, and be capable of being properly taken along with (the word 'sacrifice' in) the sentence; whereas if it has any other meaning, it woud be altogether irrelevant (and unconnected with any portion of the sentence.)

Objection: "The fact of the word '*udbhid*' signifying a *substance* "being cognised by means of direct sense-perception, exactly as in the "case of such words as '*vrīhi*,' '*soma*' and the like, wherefore is "it sought to be set aside by the inference of the fact of its signify-"ing the Instrument? That is to say, in the case of such sentences as "'*somēna yajēta*,' even though the sacrifice is recognised as the *means* (of "obtaining a particular result), and the word '*somēna*' has the Instru-"mental case-ending,—yet this is not taken alone (as co-extensive) with the "sacrifice (the Soma being taken as the material); and there is nothing "very incongruous in this; we could have exactly the same thing in the "case in question also. [And, says the Bhāshya, though this would "involve the necessity of having recourse to possessive indication in the "case of the word '*udbhidā*' which would have to be taken as signifying "by *that which has the udbhid for its material,* yet there would be no "harm in having recourse to such Indication; because this is an ordinary "process of interpretation, while the assumption of something absolutely "unknown, for instance the fact of '*udbhid*' being the name of a parti-"cular sacrifice would be a most unwarrantable liberty taken by the "*Siddhānti*] (The Bhāshya uses the word '*hatha*,' which means the "green scum found on the surface of water, which, when removed by the "hand, closes in again, and cannot be kept away; and on the present occa-"sion, it is figuratively used in the sense of an *unwarrantable liberty*)."

To this objection, we make the following reply:—A word, whose signification is unknown, when occurring along with words of well-known meanings, has its meaning ascertained by means of these latter; whereas a word, the meaning of which is well-known, is never separated from this meaning. That is to say, such words as '*Vrīhi*,' '*Soma*' and the like have their meanings so very well-known, that they can never be taken apart from these meanings; and hence in such passages as '*somēna yajēta*,' as they cannot be taken along with (as co-extensive with) the sacrifice, we are obliged to take them as laying down the materials to be employed at the sacrifices. On the other hand, in the case of such words as '*udbhid*,' and the like, the only meaning that is recognised is that which is derived from the meanings of the parts composing the word (*ut* + *bhid* + *kvip*); and as such the word is as capable of being taken as signifying the *sacrifice* (*udbhidyatē paçu-prāptih yēna*, that which brings about the obtaining of cattle) as the *material* (*udbhidyatē chēdyatē anēna*, that by which tree, &c., are cut); and hence we do not find Direct Sense-perception lending any support to either; as there can be nothing very objectionable in having recourse to Inference, for ascertaining the true meaning of the word. And, as a matter of fact, for the ascertaining of the true meaning of all words, the one most important means is the well-known relation of co-extensiveness; and it is by this very means that the principal *Instrumentality*, having obtained its chief substratum in the sacrifice, becomes capable of drawing the Noun ('*udbhid*') also to its own purpose.

And further, if the word '*udbhidā*' be taken as pointing out the name of the sacrifice, all that has got to be done by the word is to signify a concurrent Instrumentality in connection with the sacrifice (which is directly recognised as the Instrument); and the task of the Injunction becomes much lightened; while if the word be taken as laying down a material for the sacrifice, even the Number and the Case of the word will have to be accepted as objects of the Injunction. That is to say, in accordance with your theory, it would be necessary to assume a distinct potentiality of the Injunction with regard to the special termination (in '*udbhida*').

Thus then, we conclude that the various parts composing the word '*udbhid*' are quite well-known as pointing to the sacrifice. Nor can it be urged that, inasmuch as the *Jyotishtoma*, &c., are also capable of *bringing forth* their results, the name '*udbhid*' would belong to them also; because the particles composing the word (as occurring in the sentence in question) can refer to only that sacrifice, a co-extensiveness with which is pointed out in the sentence; and as a matter of fact (this co-extensiveness is perceived only with reference to the particular sacrifice that brings about the *acquisition of cattle*, and) we do not find the word '*udbhid*' ever mentioned along with the *Jyotishtoma*, &c. (and as such its co-extensiveness with these can never be recognised). Or, it is only by means of the Apparent Inconsistency (of the expressed co-extensiveness) that the *bringing about* (*udbhēdana*) can be recognised as referring to a particular result only; and as there is no such Apparent Inconsistency in the case of the *Jyotishtoma*, &c., the name '*udbhid*' can never be attributed to them.

We have in the *Sūtra*, the word '*avidhāyakatvāt*'; and in explaining this, the Bhāshya says: *It will not enjoin* (or lay down), &c. And the sense of this is that we do not take the passage in question as actually *laying down* the name '*Udbhid*' as belonging to the particular sacrifice, as we have Pānini's *Sūtra* I–i–1, directly laying down that the name '*Vṛddhi*' belongs to *Āt* and *Aic*; (nor have we any necessity of taking the passage thus), because this fact is pointed out by the directly expressed co-extensiveness (of the *Udbhid* with the sacrifice) and the well-known meaning afforded by the component parts of the word '*Udbhid*.' But all that the Bhāshya means is that the passage does not mean that 'one should obtain cattle by means of the sacrifice, and this sacrifice is named *Udbhid*' (because that that would involve a syntactical split); but at the same time, it cannot be denied that the passage distinctly points to the fact of the name belonging to the sacrifice (as the only meaning that the passage can have is that 'one should obtain cattle by means of the *Udbhid*-sacrifice'); because it is thus alone that the passage could point to a particular sacrifice.

Though in the present case (the *Udbhid* and the Sacrifice not having the same case-ending) there is no direct co-ordination between the *name* and the *named*, yet the relationship between them cannot be any other than that of the *qualification* (name) and the *qualified* (named); because all that the name does is to point to a certain object as distinguished by its own verbal form. [That is to say, it is only when the co-ordination is between what are signified by the words that it is necessary for these to have the same case-ending; whereas in the case of the Name, it is by its mere verbal form that it specifies an object; and as such it does not stand in need of the co-ordination obtained from the fact of the two words having the same case-ending]. It may be urged that—"in that case you would have a denotation (by the word '*Udbhida*') of the *verbal form* of the word (which is not quite compatible with your tenets)." But, as a matter of fact, the verbal form of the word ('*Udbhid*') being cognised by direct Auditory Perception, it is only that which is specified by that form that can be accepted to be denoted by the word. And as for the law that *there can be no idea of the qualified until there has been an idea of the qualification*,—all that this law lays down is that the *qualification* should be *cognised* (before there is any cognition of the *qualified*), and not that it should be *expressed by a word*—(and in the case in question we have a previous cognition of the qualifying form of the word by means of Sense-perception, and it is not necessary for it to be actually expressed by the word). Nor does this involve the imposition of the *form* of the word (upon the sacrifice). [That is to say, it cannot be urged that the qualifying Name always bringing about an idea connected with its verbal form, this form would be imposed upon the object named]; because all that a word does, by differentiating its object from all other objects, is to draw out (and present to us) certain objects that already exist in the world (and as such any mention of these objects by these words cannot be said to impose the form of the word upon the object); as we have already explained under "Sense-perception" (in the *Çlokavārtika*).

And again, it is only by such names as '*Udbhid*' and the like, that the subsidiary sacrifices can be differentiated from their Primary; otherwise, in the sentence '*Udbhidā yajēta, &c.*,' if the sacrifice were not specified by the name (*Udbhid*), then the sentence would come to be taken only as pointing out certain other Materials and Results in connection with the Primary sacrifice itself, and not as laying down any distinct sacrifice.

Or, the relation of the *qualification* and the *qualified* (between the name '*Udbhid*' and the particular sacrifice) may be accepted as based upon the fact of all names really *expressing* some qualification of the Actions just as the words 'Red,' 'one-year old,' &c., express certain qualities of the cow; nor, in that case, can the mention of the *sacrifice* itself (by the word *yajēta*) be said to be redundant (on the ground of the name itself pointing to a *particular sacrifice*); because without the mention of the *sacrifice* by the root '*yaji*' there would be nothing to show that '*Udbhid*' was the name *of a particular sacrifice*; and it is through the mutual proximity (of the *name* with the 'sacrifice') that we get at the facts that *the name belongs to a sacrifice*, and that *the sacrifice meant is that which is specified by the name*, and not all sacrifices in general, or the Primary sacrifice of the *Jyotishtoma*; and thus the mention of both (the *name* and the 'sacrifice') is distinctly useful.

And as the Injunction is that of the *sacrifices as specified by the name* '*Udbhid*, both of these are matters actually laid down by the Injunction; and hence it cannot be said to be a mere supplementary explanation (of another injunction). And thus we find that the fact of '*Udbhid*' being the name of a sacrifice is not contrary to the fact of the passage being an Injunction (though it is contrary to the fact of its being an Injunction of a particular material). And thus it is apparent that the assertion of the *Pūrvapaksha*—that the word '*Udbhid*' forms part of the Injunction of a material,—as also the assertion (of a scion of the *Siddhānti*), that the *Name* is something apart from the three portions of the Veda, the *Vidhi*, the *Mantra* and the *Arthavāda*,—are equally wrong.

Nor can it be urged that, if the word '*Udbhidā*' be taken as pointing out the name of a sacrifice, it could be of no use in prompting men to the performance of any particular action. Because we actually find such names serving distinctly useful purposes in various periods of the performance of an action. For instance, during the appointment of the *Ṛtvik* priest, the Master of the sacrifice says, 'I have got to perform such and such a sacrifice,' where the mention of the mere name of the sacrificer is a very much simpler process of pointing it out than any description of the details of the sacrifice itself; so also when one is about begin the *Darça-Pūrṇamāsa*, the Master makes such declarations as—'May such and such a result follow from the performance of the *Darça* and the *Pūrṇamāsa*' (when the name is mentioned in connection with the accessories of the sacrifice), and again 'desiring Heaven I perform the *Darça* and the *Pūrṇamāsa* (where the names are mentioned in connection with the Result); and none of these would be possible if there were no such names of sacrifices as the '*Darça*' and the '*Pūrṇamāsa*,' &c.

Thus then, we conclude that such words as '*Udbhid*' and the like are the *names* of particular sacrifices.

ADHIKARAṆA (2).

[*Treating of the fact of such words as 'Citrā' and the like being names of sacrifices*].

***Sūtra* (3). That wherein accessories are laid down must be related to a Primary Sacrifice.**

We now proceed to consider those words that have a meaning fixed by convention, and not one that is signified by its component parts; such words, for instance, as '*Vrīhi*' and the like, which denote particular Classes and Properties. The case of these words cannot be said to be included in the foregoing *Adhikaraṇa*, because the meaning of these words which is directly expressed by the words themselves, cannot be neglected for the sake of an *Instrumentality* that is only inferred. [That is to say, in the case of the word '*Udbhid*,' in the sentence '*Udbhidā yajēta*,' we reject its literal meaning, on account of the Instrumentality of the *Udbhid* in the bringing about of the Result in question; in the case of the word '*Citrā*,' however, in the sentence '*Citrayā' yajēta*,' inasmuch as the meaning is directly denoted as fixed by convention, no amount of inferred Instrumentality can make us reject that meaning.]

Objection: "The Bhāshya should have cited such instances as the "passages (1) '*ājyaih stuvatē*,' (2) '*Pṛshthaih stuvatē*,' '*bahīshpavamānēna* "*stuvatē*,' which are all original Injunctive sentences (and not such secondary sentences as '*pancadaçājyāni*,' &c.). Because it is only when the "fact of a word being a *name*, or laying down an *accessory detail* of the "sacrifice, has been ascertained in connection with original sentences, "that it is accepted in all ordinary usage; and as such it is only such "sentences that should have been cited as instances."

All this may be true; but the *Sūtra* itself had not such original sentences in view, because it distinctly mentions '*that wherein an accessory is laid down*,' which shows that it had only the secondary sentences in view.

"But why should the *Sūtra* have neglected to cite the original sentences?"

Because there would be no difference in the main result of the discussion, whichsoever sentence be cited as an example. Or, it may be that secondary sentences have been purposely chosen, because it is only in the case of these that we have a *syntactical split*, which is the principal reason for rejecting the *Pūrvapaksha* theory. Or, it may be that in the case of the original sentences, whichever of the two theories be accepted (*i.e.*, whether the words '*ājya*,' &c., be taken as *names* or as pointing to accessory details) there is a certain factor that remains wanting; and as such there is no means to ascertain definitely which one of the two theories is to be accepted; and hence this ascertainment being got at only by other means, these sentences could not have served as the appropriate examples.

That is to say, the word '*ājya*' signifying *butter* cannot be recognised as a name of certain hymns; and what is mentioned in the passage is that 'one hymns by those that are *ājya*;' and here what are those that are named '*ajya*,' and how they are denoted by the word, cannot be ascertained by the original sentence itself, without some help from without; and further, it is necessary to explain the reason why in the original sentences, the words '*ājya*,' &c., abandon their conventional meanings, and become the names of the *hymns*, &c. And thus we find that the 'Name theory' stands in need of some extraneous help. In accordance with the other theory also (in which case the sentence would mean 'one hymns by the butter'), it is absolutely impossible for the *butter* to be an Instrument of *hymning;* and hence it would be necessary to take the word '*ājya*' as indirectly indicating the Mantra related to that word; and in that case we shall require another sentence laying down such relationship (of the word '*ājya*' with a particular *Mantra;* that is, we shall require a declaration that the word '*ājya*' means the 'Mantra that contains the word'); because if the original sentence itself be made to give this meaning, it would be necessary to have recourse to Possessive Indication. These objections cease to apply if the word '*ājya*' in the sentence in question, be taken only as pointing out a meaning or relationship laid down elsewhere; and thus in this case also the fact of certain *Mantras* being related to the '*ājya*' has got to be ascertained from other sources.

Thus then, we find that in the case of both theories, there is a certain element wanting that has to be supplied from extraneous sources; and hence the sentence comes to signify only the *hymning*, the sense of the word '*ājya*,' &c., being ascertained by other means.

As for the word '*pavamāna*,' some people hold that the word has a meaning ('sanctifier') that is pointed out by its component parts; and as such this has not been cited, on account of its being included in the foregoing *Adhikaraṇa.* While others treat of the case thus: The *stotra* cannot be taken as the nominative of the 'sanctifying,' as the *sacrifice* (in the previous *Adhikaraṇa*) has been taken as that of 'bringing forth;' because it is the *Soma* that is the real *sanctifying* agent. And the component parts of the word '*pavamāna*' not being found to be capable of directly pointing to any *Action*, the word will have to be taken as pointing to *an Action in which we use a mantra that has a sanctifying meaning;* and this would involve an indirect *Indication per Indication;* and this process is undoubtedly more complicated than simple *Possessive Indication;* and as such the case of this sentence also is met by the 'syntactical split' (that is to be shown in the *Siddhānta*); and hence this too is a fitting example.

In the *Pūrvapaksha* of this discussion also, the arguments based upon the universally recognised signification of the words, &c., &c., are just the same as those that have been detailed in the *Pūrvapaksha* of the foregoing *Adhikaraṇa.*

And inasmuch as the *Siddhānta* speaks of the word '*Citrā*' having been taken (in the *Pūrvapaksha*) as pointing to an *accessory of the sacrifice,* having the *Citra* (variegated) colour, we infer that the *Pūrvapaksha* takes the sentence '*Citrayā yajēta*' as the Injunction of an accessory of the *Agnīshomīya sacrifice.*

And in support of this, they advance the following arguments:—

PŪRVAPAKSHA.

"The *variegated colour* and the *feminine* character are naturally applicable to animals only; and as such the sentence in question cannot "but be taken as subsidiary to the *Daiksha* (Agnīshomīya) sacrifice, which "is the root or Primary of all sacrifices performed with animals. That is "to say, the differentiation into Feminine, Masculine, &c., apart from "animals, is based upon a mere likeness of words, while in the case "of animals, it is based upon real facts of nature. The Principal sacrifice, "however, (in whose context we have the sentence '*Citrayā yajēta*') having Curds, &c., for its material, cannot be accepted as having anything "to do with the two characteristics of *variegated colour* and *female character* "denoted by the word '*Citrayā*'; and hence we extract these two "characteristics out of their place, and take them as related to sacrifice in "general; but on account of the fact of such characteristics belonging "only to animals, they naturally tend mostly towards a sacrifice of animals; "and thence, in accordance with the rule laid down in *Sūtra* III—"vi—2, they become related to the *Agnīshomīya* sacrifice, which is the most "Primary of all such sacrifices. And though the connection of such an "animal (of a variegated colour and a female) would be in opposition to "the character of the animal for the *Agnīshomiya* sacrifice, that is pointed "out in the original Injunction of that sacrifice as the black and the red "male deer,—yet any one of these characters could be taken as rejecting "the other; or they may both be accepted as optional alternatives, as has "already been shown in a foregoing *Pūrvapaksha.*

"Or, we may bring forward here the arguments that have been shown "under the *Sūtras* III—vi—9 *et seq.* [That is to say, under these *Sūtras* "it has been shown that the number *seventeen* being found to be mentioned "in connection with the *Sāmidhēnis* only, the connection of this number with any particular sacrifice cannot be definitely ascertained; while "the relationship of the particular sacrifice with the number *fifteen* is "definitely ascertained; and hence it is only proper that the relationship "of the number *seventeen* should be set aside by that of the number *fifteen*; "in the case of the *variegated colour* and the *feminine character*, however, "inasmuch as these are found to be mentioned in connection with a sacrifice, their connection with a particular sacrifice of the *Agnīshomīya* is as "reasonable as that of the *black deer*, &c., because both of these are equally "connected with *animals*, and the rule laid down under the *Sūtra* III—vi—2 is equally applicable to both; and in the *Pūrvapaksha* of the "*Adhikaraṇa* beginning with III—vi—9, it has been argued that, inasmuch "as both the numbers *fifteen* and *seventeen* are equally related to the *Sāmidhēnī*, both are to be accepted as optional alternatives; and in the same "manner, in the case in question, the two different kinds of animals are to "be alternatively employed at the *Agnīshomīya* sacrifice]. And the "sense of all this is that, as there would be no syntactical split, there "would be an injunction of many things mentioned by a single word, "as is distinctly pointed out by the fact of the animal as qualified by the "*variegated colour* and the *feminine character* being expressed by the "single case-termination (the Instrumental). And as for the word "'*paçukāmah*,' it may be explained as forming part of the acquiring of the "cattle for the sacrifice, and as such it would be taken as only describing "an already existing fact, and not as pointing out the Result to be "obtained from the sacrifice; and certainly no animal-sacrifice can be "performed by one who does not want to obtain an animal (for the purposes of sacrifice.)

"Says the Bhāshya: *The sentence 'citrayā yajēta paçukāmah' is descriptive of the sacrifice, as it is already well-known.* The meaning of this "is that the Injunctive potentiality having, in all cases, been found to "have transferred itself to another word in the sentence, which is directly "connected with the verbal affix, the root itself cannot but be taken as "merely describing a well-established fact. That is to say, whenever we "proceed to seek for something else that would be enjoined by the verbal "root, we are faced by the contingency of having to assume innumerable "potentialities; and hence there at once arises in our minds a desire to "take it as only describing an ordinary fact; and hence in such cases we "cannot admit of the presence of an Injunction, unless we are obliged to "do it (on account of the impossibility of its being taken as descriptive of "an ordinary fact). In the case of the sentence in question, however, "we know of a particular sacrifice, the *Agnīshomīya*, being connected, "through the animal sacrificed, with the *variegated colour* and the *feminine*

" *character;* and as such there can be no difficulty in taking it as merely " describing this relationship.

" Says the Bhāshya: *If the result be held to follow from the material " itself, the root ' yaji ' becomes redundant.* And on this there arises the ques- " tion—' How is it that the *Pūrvapaksha* is represented as objecting to its " own theory of the sentence being the Injunction of a material?'

" Some people meet this difficulty by the assertion that the sen- " tence that should have formed part of the *Siddhānta*, has been " inserted here by mistake. While others offer the explanation that by " attributing the result to the material, it would become the principal " factor in the Injunction, and thereby losing its secondary (or auxiliary " character), the sentence could not be spoken of as an *Injunction of an " Accessory detail.*

" But none of these explanations is quite satisfactory. Because in " any case, the assertion that the word forms the Injunction of an acces- " sory detail is always opposed to the view that it supplies the name of a " particular sacrifice; and even when the Result is held to follow from the " accessory material thus enjoined, the fact of such injunction being " opposed to the fact of the word being a *name* remains unaffected. And " the Bhāshya itself declares later on: *It is only when this Adhikaraṇa " exists that we can have any discussion as to whether the word is the Injunc- " tion of an accessory material, or a name.* Even when the Result is attri- " buted to the particular material enjoined, there being no absolute co- " extensiveness of the material with the sacrifice, it would come to be ac- " cepted as the injunction of an accessory material.

" Therefore, we must explain the Bhāshya passage in the light of the " following facts:

" On the point at issue, there appear to be three distinct theories: " (1) The word enjoins an accessory detail, as leading to a particular " result; (2) it enjoins the accessory detail with reference to the sacri- " fice; and (3) it forms the name of a particular sacrifice. And any one of " these has got to refute the other two. Therefore one who takes his " stand upon the *Pūrvapaksha* is represented in the Bhāshya passage under " question, to refute the weakest of his two opponents (*i.e.*, the theory that " the word enjoins a material as leading to a particular result) on the " ground that in that case the root '*yaji*' will come to have a meaning " altogether irrelevant to the main subject.

" For these reasons, we conclude that the word '*citrayā*' lays down the " material for a sacrifice, just as the word '*vrīhibhih*' in the sentence '*vrīhi- " bhiryajēta.*' And though the 'sacrifice' is represented as the *means* " (of acquiring the Result), yet its *instrumentality* pointed out by the origi- " nal sentence laying down the sacrifice serves also to indicate the fact "of the sacrifice itself being an *object* to be accomplished (by means of the "'*Citrā*' material); and thus we find that it is this objective character of "the sacrifice with reference to which the particular material is enjoined; "and as such there is no need of having recourse to any Possessive Indica-"tion (the sentence being construed as—'one should think of obtaining "cattle by means of the sacrifice performed with the *Citrā* material'). Or, "it may be that the person who holds the word '*Citrā*' to lay down a "material, accepts the fact of the material being with reference to the "sacrifice, which fact cannot be dispensed with; while the theory that the "word lays down a material as leading to a particular result is open to all "the objections urged in the foregoing *Adhikaraṇa*.

"Similarly too, in the case of the sentence—'*pancadaçājyāni*'—we must "presume the existence of some such word as '*asti*' or '*bhavati*,' &c., the "sentence thus mentioning the *existence* of the *fifteen ājyas;* and it is to be "taken as an Injunction, because of its being a statement of the procedure "(of a sacrifice).

"*Objection:*—'Such words as *pancadaçāni* and *saptadaçāni* do not denote "merely the particular numbers, because in accordance with *Pāṇini*, the "affix 'da' (in these words) has the sense of '*stoma*' (or collection of Ṛk "verses); and this *Stoma* too does not signify anything other than the "particular number of Ṛk verses in the Hymn.'

"*Reply:*—This does not affect the case; because the *Stoma* being "only a measure of the Eulogy, as limiting the Hymn which is the means "of the Eulogy, whether the limitation be done by means of certain Ṛk "verses, or by means of Butter, the number as the limiting agent is "always called '*Stoma*' on account of its being a measure of the Eulogy. "[That is to say, the Ṛk verses being the means of the Eulogy, and the "number *fifteen* or *seventeen* serving to limit these verses, the Eulogy "itself comes to be limited by the number, which thus comes to be known "as the '*Stoma*;' and like the Ṛk verses the Butter (*Ajya*) also serves to "give rise to the Eulogy, and thus becomes one of its means; and as such "there is nothing wrong in the presence of the affix 'da' in the word "'*pançadaçāni*.'

"Nor is there any need of the Possessive Indication. Because it is only "when the sentence is found intact (in the Veda), that in assuming any "facts more or less than what is distinctly expressed by the sentence itself "we incur the improper responsibility of having recourse to Indirect Indica-"tions, Syntactical Split and the like; while there is no such danger when "the sentence itself is an inferred or assumed one. That is to say, in the case "of the sentence—'*pancadaçānyājyāni*,' the word '*ājya*' being found to "have no connection with the sentence as it stands, we must have recourse "to the assumption of the Injunction of a Procedure of Action, that would "have some sort of connection with what is met with in the original sen-"tence, the apparent inconsistency of which is the sole ground for the "assumption of this new sentence; and this new sentence may be as-"sumed as having a word that would directly denote what is sought to be "got at indirectly by means of Possessive Indication (*i.e.*, the sentence "assumed being somewhat in the form that 'the Hymn is to be helped "by means of the *Ājyas seventeen in number*.')

"Against this we may have the following objection: 'The *Ājya* be-"ing a substance, it cannot form part of a *procedure* which consists of "something *to be* done; and as such it could not be pointed out by the "Context, which only stands in need of a mention of the *Procedure*.'

"But in the case in question, we have a distinct action, in the "shape of 'existence;' and as such there is no occasion for the said ob-"jection. It being always necessary for the subsidiaries to exist in the "same place as the Primary, the *Ājya* must always exist in close proximity "to the Hymn. And hence, just as in the case of the sentence—'having "laid the fire, he proceeds with the hymn'—the fire helps the hymning by "its mere presence, so too, in the case of the sentence in question (the "*Ājya* or the Butter would help the Hymning by its mere presence or "existence). And as such, our theory not being open to any objection, we "conclude that the words in question lay down the accessory details of the "sacrifices."

SIDDHANTA.

To the above arguments, we make the following reply: *Must be related to a primary sacrifice* (*sūtra*). That is to say, the mention of many things can be possible only when there is an Injunction of a Principal Action. In the case in question it is held that the accessory is laid down in connection with a well-known Action. But there is no mutual relationship among the accessories themselves. And hence if any one of the accessories were laid down, it could not indicate any other accessory; and thus there being no Apparent Inconsistency in the matter, we would have to assume an endless number of direct Vedic Injunctions of the various accessories; and this would necessitate the frequent repetition of the Injunctive Affix, which would inevitably lead to a syntactical split, as has been well declared—Though the *Bhāvanā* indirectly implies the Injunction of many things, yet the Injunction of a qualification does not refer to any other qualification.

And thus we find that even though the two qualifications (of *variegated colour* and *female* character) are denoted by the same word (*Çitrā*), yet we have just the same necessity of having recourse to the greatly complicated process of assuming more than one Injunctive Potentiality (in the word).

And as a matter of fact, inasmuch as the original Injunction of the particular sacrifice has laid down a particular material, there can be no effective potentiality (in the Injunction of any other material). And it is a well-known fact that we can have the description of an Action just as it is pointed out in its original Injunction; and hence, when it has once connected itself with a particular material (f.i. the Black Deer) it can never have anything to do with any other material that is incompatible with the former. That is to say, in the description of a certain action, if it be absolutely necessary to describe its material, all its wants being found to be supplied (by that which is mentioned in the original Injunction), there can be no Injunction of any other material; specially as any such Injunction would be based upon the fact of the Action being wanting on that point.

Nor can it be urged that from out of the original Injunction of the *Agnīshomīya*, we could take out the sacrifice itself (apart from the materials therein mentioned); and then have its materials laid down by means of the sentence—'*Citrayā yajēta.*' Because in the first place the Action is always connected with the accessories mentioned in its own original Injunction; and hence any accessories mentioned in other sentences can never get at it apart from such natural accessories. In the case of the alternative materials—*Vrīhi and Yava*—mentioned in connection with the sacrifice, as the two Injunctions function independently of each other, they are both equally authoritative, and as such the two are accepted to be optional alternatives. In the case in question, however, it is only the original Injunction that would independently by itself lay down the accessory of the action; which could not be done by this other sentence, which only describes the sacrifice as laid down in the original Injunction; specially as there could be no description of that which has not already been laid down.

And further, on account of the mention of the *desire for cattle* (in the sentence in question, inasmuch as this involves the acceptance of the denotation of a word other than the Injunctive ("*yajēta*") we have an inevitable syntactical split. That is to say, though the Result is not enjoined, yet, (1) the sacrifice is enjoined, for the sake of the Result; and (2) the material *Citrā* is laid down for the sake of the sacrifice, thus there being a most complicated syntactical split. And there would be a further objection, that at one and the same time there would be an Injunction of the sacrifice with reference to the Result and a description of it with reference to the material.

Nor can the word "*paçukāmah*" be taken as only describing the already well-known fact of the presence of such a desire, as part of the desire for the acquiring of cattle for the purposes of the sacrifice. Because all that is desirable for man is desired for itself; and as for the fact of persons engaging in actions for the means and auxiliaries of that desirable object, this is not due to any desire for such auxiliaries (the desire being only for the main object, the auxiliaries being sought after only as means to that end, and not as desirable in themselves). That is to say, when proceeding to perform a sacrifice, one does not entertain any strong desire for the acquiring of the animal that would be required in the performance of the sacrifice; because even without any such desire, he proceeds to possess himself of the animal, because without that, he finds that it is impossible for him to obtain the particular result that he desires (which can be obtained only by means of a sacrifice performed with the animal). And thus, even though there may be a certain degree of desirability in the animal, it could be spoken of as desirable *indirectly* only. Therefore, it is only that which is found to be desired directly, in its direct denotation, that we recognise as the Result, which is mentioned in connection with the word '*kāma*' (Desire). We shall explain this in detail later on under the *Sūtra* VI—i—2.

The result of the *Agnīshomīya* sacrifice too, being a part of the sacrifice, cannot quite definitely be ascertained, whether it is this or any other; and as such there cannot be any description of it. [That is to say, it cannot be urged that the word '*paçukāmah*' may be taken as only describing the particular result in the shape of the acquiring of cattle, which is pointed out to be a result of the *Agnīshomīya* sacrifice by the fact of this sacrifice bringing about *all* desirable results; because in that case any description would be impossible, as a description of a secondarily indicated fact is absolutely useless; and if the word be taken as mentioning a particular qualification of the *Agnīshomīya* as pointed out by the fact of its bringing about *all* desirable results, there would be a syntactical split; and then we can recall all the reasonings brought forward in connection with the word '*udbhid*']. And this would lead to another anomaly, *viz.*—though the sentence occurs in connection with the *Prājāpatya* sacrifice, yet the result coming to be taken along with the *Agnīshomīya*, there would be a direct rejection of the context.

On the other hand, if the word '*Citrayā*' be taken as the name of a sacrifice, the sentence would only lay down a relationship between the sacrifice and a particular result; and there would be no room for any of the aforesaid objections.

In the case of the expression '*pancadaçājyāni*,' the particular material (*Butter*), as also the number (*Fifteen*), not being found to be in any way connected with the Hymns, any one of these might be taken as being enjoined (by the sentence) with regard to another which might be taken as described by it. In any case, the *material* is not cognised (in the sentence) as pertaining to any other Action; and if the sentence were to be taken as laying down a particular number with reference to the Butter employed in other Actions,—in that case (the sentence affording no idea of the Action), the Injunction would form part of the Material, and not of any Action (which fact would make the Injunction absolutely useless); and this would also lead to the rejection of the main Context (of the sentence). That it is not possible for the sentence to be taken as an Injunction of the *Material as qualified by the particular number*, we shall show later on under the *Sūtra* IV—i—11. As a matter of fact too, that which does not qualify a verb (Action) can never form the object of an Injunction; because the Injunctive word has no direct relationship with nouns; and in the sentence in question, we do not find any verb which would be the object of Injunction, and would, as such, point to many accessories (Materials, &c.). Nor is it possible for these (*fifteen butters*) to form the object of the sentence that lays down the recitation of the Hymns; because they have not the character of an Action (or Verb). As has been well said: 'The principal Action (or Verb) cannot take in any accessories or Materials as constituting its procedure, unless there is an intermediate action, assumed in accordance with the sentence.'

Nor can they be said to belong to the verb 'to be;' and it is a universal rule that any particular thing can operate elsewhere only when it has acquired its own existence in one place; and as for mere *existence* (denoted by the verb 'to be'), its business ends with the pointing out of the fact of an object being an entity; and as such the action of *being* can never be one that could be an object to be accomplished; nor does it stand in need of any other Action that could be taken as the object to be accomplished; and as such, there being no room for any help by the said *number* and *material*, these cannot be taken as forming part of the procedure of the action *to be*. Though in the case of the sentence—'*Rathantaram bhavati*, &c.' we admit of the fact of the Context pointing to such actions as those of *being*, &c., that are held to be enjoined by these sentences,—yet this is due to a cognition of the relationship (of the *Rathantaram*, &c.) with certain intermediate actions that are indirectly indicated. Nor is the existence of Butter, &c., such as is not fully established in the world; and as such their *existence* can never be taken as the object of a *Bhāvanā* (such as 'one should think of establishing the existence of Butter,' &c., &c.).

It may be urged that—'there may be a *Bhāvanā* of placing the Butter, &c., in proximity to the Hymn (which proximity is not an established fact).' But this too is not possible; because no such proximity forms the object of any Injunction. In the case of the sentence—'having laid the fire,' &c.,—the proximity of the fire (to the Hymning) is distinctly enjoined by the sentence itself; when this action (of the laying of fire) being apart from the action of mere *existing* (of the fire), is capable of being taken as constituting a part of the procedure. In accordance with the *Siddhānta* theory the sentence being found to serve a distinctly useful purpose, there is no apparent Inconsistency that would necessitate the assumption of any sentence laying down the relationship of the *Ājya* with the Hymn.

If the expression '*pancadaçānyājyāni*' were to lay down the number *fifteen* with reference to the Butter laid down in the sentence—'*ājyaih stuvatē*,'—then, as shown in the foregoing *Adhikaraṇa*, there would be a necessity of having recourse to Possessive Indication; and it is with a view to this that the *Bhāshya* says—*That the Hymns and the Ājya could be laid down by the word only by means of Indication.* And further, the Butter being a substance always liable to exist in one mass, the number *fifteen* could not apply to it directly; and hence it would be necessary to assume certain measures (or weights of it)—such as the *Pala* and the rest, which are not mentioned in the sentence itself.

From all this, it appears that though originally the word '*Ajya*' may not appear to have the character of a *name*, and there is no place for it in a sentence laying down the material of a sacrifice,—yet it is clear that there could be an Injunction of the number *fifteen*, only when the word '*Ājya*' is taken as the name (of certain Hymns), and not otherwise.

The Bhāshya has taken the word '*Ājya*' as a *name;* because that is the only way in which the expression '*pancadaçānyājyāni*'—which is subsidiary to the sentence '*ājyaih stuvatē*'—can be explained; and the reasons why this interpretation has been accepted are—(1) because in this manner alone can the two words '*pancadaçāni*' and '*ājyāni*' be construed together; and (2) because of the meanings of the component parts of the word, as pointed out in the Veda, both by way of explanatory sentences, and by that of *Arthavādas*.

That is to say, the explanation of the name '*Ājya*,' as belonging to the Hymns, is supplied by the Veda itself: 'As the gods went to battle with these, they are *Ajya*;' that is to say, because the gods, according to the advice of Prajāpati, went to battle, after having recited these Hymns, therefore they came to be known as '*Ājya*,' as fitting the gods for battle (*āji*). In the same manner, because the *Rathantara*, &c., were produced when the surface (*pṛshtha*) of the water was touched by *Vāyu*, therefore these *Sāmas* came to be known as '*Pṛshtha*.' Thus the explanation of these two names are found to be supplied by certain *Arthavāda* passages of the *Veda* itself. And as the *Vāmadēvya* and other Sāmas are the source of the *Rathantara*, &c., the name *Pṛshtha* belongs to them also.

Says the *Bhāshya*: "*Why should not we take the sentence as laying down, with reference to the Hymns, the Ājyas qualified by the number fifteen?"* This question should be taken as preceded by the sentence—"inasmuch as a single sentence cannot give us two distinct meanings." And the reply to this question given in the Bhāshya is: Because *there is no word expressive of such qualified Ājya*; and this refers to the non-mention of any principal verb in the sentence.

The Bhāshya, however, retorts: "*But the two words—'pancadaçāni' and 'ājyāni'—would supply the qualified denotation*"—, and this refers to the fact of these two words being connected with the verb 'to be.' The reply to this is that these two words too cannot serve to lay down the qualified *ājya*; because it is only the principal verb that draws all the qualifications together; and as for the verb 'to be,' which signifies mere *existence*, its function ends with each individual qualification itself, and as such it cannot help in drawing together the various factors of the sentence. And thus there can be no material relationship among the qualifications (through the verb 'to be') the only meaning capable of being got out of the sentence being that—*whichever things are fifteen* in number—and *whatever number* of *Ājyas there may be* (which are only two distinct unconnected assertions).

And hence we conclude that the two words cannot afford the necessary Injunction; nor can they be taken as descriptive of certain things (in connection with the Hymns): because no such thing as the *ājya* is generally known to belong to the Hymns; and as such any description of it would be absolutely useless.

For these reasons we conclude that the word in question must be a name; in that case one factor could be taken as being enjoined in connection with another which is only mentioned in the sentence as an established fact. That the word is an *injunctive* one has been often repeated; but all that is meant by this is that it serves to point out that which is the object of an Injunction; because a word that is a name has no injunctive force.

The mention of the number *fifteen* serving as a measure of the Ṛk verses which are the chief means of the Hymning, it directly comes to have the character of the *stoma*, through its limiting of the Hymn itself; and as such the affix '*da*' in the word '*pancadaçāni*' becomes easily explained.

ADHIKARAṆA (3).

[*Treating of the fact of such words as* 'Agnihotra' *and the like being the names of sacrifices.*]

Sūtra (4). There are other sentences mentioning the accessories.

Objection: "All names are of two kinds—*conventional* and *literal*; and as the names of both these kinds having been dealt with in the foregoing two *Adhikaraṇas* what is left there that we proceed to consider now?"

Reply: with regard to the literal *names*, it has been said above that they must be taken as names, because otherwise, it becomes necessary to have recourse to Possessive Indication; and hence the present *Adhikaraṇa* is taken up, in connection with such literal names as are capable of being taken as laying down the accessories of sacrifices, without having recourse to Possessive Indication. Similarly too, in the next *Adhikaraṇa* we shall treat of such conventional names as are capable of being taken as laying down the accessories of sacrifices, without leading to any syntactical split.

And on this point, we have the following—

PURVAPAKSHA.

"In the case of the word "*Agnihotra*" the *Siddhānti* also explains the "compound as 'that wherein the offering is made to Agni,' and the sense "of no other compound being cognised we can very easily take the "compound as a *Bahuvrīhi*, containing within itself a possessive implica-"tion (the compound being explained as 'that Deity Fire *to whom* the "offering is made'), and thereby the word can very easily be taken as "laying down an accessory—Deity—of the particular sacrifice. And in "support of this interpretation, we could bring forward all the arguments "that have been shown in the *Pūrvapaksha* of *Adhikaraṇa* (1). And "though it is true that the Deity Fire is distinctly mentioned in connec-"tion with the Evening Libation (of the *Agnihotra*), yet we could take "the word 'Agnihotra' either as laying down the Deity for the Morning "Libation apart from the Evening Libation, or as laying it down in "connection with *Homa* in general, and as such with particular reference "to the *Darvi-Homa*, &c., which have no Deities mentioned with them-"selves; specially as such is the force of the word '*juhoti*' in the sentence "speaking of the various *Homas*.

"In the same manner, an '*āghāra*' is 'that which is poured out;'

"and as such the word '*āghāra*' denotes all objects capable of being "poured out, such as Butter, Milk and the like. And in the sentence "'*āghāramāghārayati*' we find the word '*aghāram*' in the Accusative; "and as such pointing out the aforesaid Butter, &c., undergoing a certain "preparation by being poured out; and as there can be no such preparation without a definite purpose, we naturally seek for such a purpose. "And then, all that is meant by the substances being 'poured out' is that "they are rendered capable of being poured out, and not that they are all "poured out, because the function of the word '*āghāra*' rests only in "the mere signification of the word, and not in the actual carrying of it "into practice; and hence there is a desire to know what is to be done "with the substance of which (by way of testing) a portion has been "poured out. Even in ordinary experience, we find that when a certain "substance is going to be drunk, people make it undergo a process of "purification by being poured out. Thus then, the prepared or purified "substance, being exactly like the extracted juice of the *Putika* (a substitute for *Soma*) or the *Phalacamasa* prepared for food, stands in need "of an Action (that would be performed with it); and as such it connects "itself with the Primary sacrifices of the *Darça-Pūrṇamāsa.* But from "among these, there are some, such as the *Agnēya*, &c., that have their "own particular materials distinctly laid down; and hence it is only the "*Upāñçu* sacrifice that stands in need of the mention of a material; and "as such, the liquid material duly prepared, comes to be taken in connection with this *Upāñçu* sacrifice. As has been well said: 'A substance, which has been mentioned in connection with a certain process of purification,—though not related to the Principal sacrifices—"comes to be taken along with other sacrifices mentioned in the "same context; for otherwise, it would be incapable of any purification.'

"Or, it may be that it is the denotation of the affix only (that is to say, "the mere factor 'does' which is denoted by the 'tip' affix in '*āghārayati*') "that constitutes the *Bhāvanā* of the *Upāñçu* sacrifice—which alone "stands in need of the mention of a material—, with reference to which "the substance *āghāra* having been laid down by the sentence (in question), the meaning of the Verbal root (in '*āghāra*') comes to be taken as "mentioned only as the object of the aforesaid active affix. Or, it may be "that by the mere fact of the '*Dhrauvājya*' having been found to be mentioned, points to the *liquid* character of the material; and hence the "sentence comes to be taken as the injunction of all that is capable of "being poured out,—for instance, such liquids as Milk, Butter and the "like.

"And thus all that we want being accomplished by the direct

"denotation of the verbal root itself, what is the use of taking the word "'*āghāra*' as a name? Nor do we ever find any merely purificatory action "to have particular names.

"Says the *Bhāshya*: '*It is by direct assertion that the accessory material* "*is enjoined*;' and the meaning of this is that the direct mention of the "Accusative ending in the word '*āghāram*' points to the fact of the "*āghāra* being an object to be prepared or purified; and from this we are "led to the conclusion that such a substance duly prepared, cannot but be "the material of a particular sacrifice."

SIDDHANTA.

To the above, we make the following reply:—

Inasmuch as in the case in question, we find another sentence laying down the accessories of the sacrifice, any pointing out of it by the word in question would be absolutely useless; and hence we cannot but take it to be a name.

Against this the following argument may be urged: "If one took the "word '*Agnihotra*' to lay down a Deity for the Evening Homa, and "'*Āghāra*' to lay down a material for the *Upānçu* (for which the acces- "sories are distinctly mentioned), then alone could the laying down of the "accessory by the word '*Agnihotra*' or '*Aghāra*' be said to be use- "less, on account of the material being directly enjoined in the sentence "dealing with the Evening Libation, &c. As a matter of fact, however, "we take the word '*Agnihotra*' as laying down the Deity for a sacrifice "which has no Deity mentioned in connection with it, and the word "'*Āghāra*' as laying down the material for the *Upāncu* sacrifice, for which "no other material has been mentioned; and as such how can the other "sentences be said to have laid down the Deity and the Material (held to "be laid down by the words '*Agnihotra*' and '*Aghāra*')?"

To this we make the following reply: If the word '*Āgnīhotrā*' were an Injunction, it would stand in need of an object for itself; and the question would be whether this object would be included in the subject of the context, or would there be reasons for transferring it elsewhere? The relationship of *Agni* with the *hotra* (or *Homa*) having been established by other means (such as the Indication of the Mantra '*Agnirjyotirjyotih, &c.*'), and in accordance with this people being found to take up the performance of the *Agnihotra*,—the word '*Agnihotra*' distinctly comes to be merely descriptive (of a sacrifice laid down elsewhere). It is a general rule that all accessories are laid down in connection with that which is denoted by the Verbal root in the sentence; and Description too is never found to belong to any other action save that which forms the subject of the Context. And hence in the case in question, if the word '*Agnihotra*' be taken as laying down the accessory Deity in connection with the *Homa* that forms the subject of the Context, then such an accessory could not but be accepted as having been pointed out by another direct assertion of the Veda—that speaking of the Evening Libation of the Agnihotra (inasmuch as it is the *Agnihotra* as a whole that forms the subject of the Context, and this latter sentence distinctly mentions Agni as its Deity); and hence the word '*Agnihotra*' cannot be taken as enjoining the Deity, because such a Deity has already been pointed out elsewhere.

And further, in the case in question, there can be no description of that which is signified by the verbal root; because it cannot be spoken of as that 'this forms the subject of the Context' or that 'it does not.' Consequently the sentence '*agnihotram juhoti*' must be taken as laying down a particular action or *Homa* (named '*Agnihotra*'). As for the accessories of this Action, they are laid down in the passages dealing with the 'Evening' Libation, and that containing the word *ūrdhva*;' hence any such action as the *pure Agnihotra*, (*i.e.* without any, Deity, &c.) not being found to be directly mentioned in the Veda, it cannot be taken as the subject of the Context. Nor can the word be taken as being descriptive of that which is not in close proximity to it, because there are many intervening obstacles; and as such it is as incapable of entering our minds as any stray action, like the *Kaundapāyina Homa*.

If it be held that, 'the word might be taken as enjoining the *Homa* as qualified by the Deity *Agni*,'—then, we reply that this could be possible only if the accessories were not laid down by other sentences; as a matter of fact, however, we actually find them laid down by other sentences (and hence we cannot accept the explanation suggested).

Nor do we find any grammatical rule that could justify our explaining the word '*Agnihotra*' as a *Dative-Tatpurusha* (='the Homa *for the sake of Agni*'); and unless we have this we cannot take the word as laying down the Deity; and as for any ordinary relationship between Agni and the Homa, this could be pointed out by the Compound, taken as the *Genitive—Tatpurusha* (='the Homa *of Agni*') but this could not make the word an Injunction of the Deity.

When, however, the sentence '*Agnihotram juhoti*' is interpreted as—'that Homa wherein the offering is made to Agni comes to be known as the *Agnihotra*,'—the word '*Agnihotra*' being taken as a name, descriptive of a certain action, whose Deity has been mentioned in another sentence,—though the genitive in '*agnēh*' would signify a mere relationship in general, yet it could satisfy the conditions laid down for the Dative compound; because the word '*hotra*' being explained as *that which is offered* (*yat hūyatē tadhotram*), it becomes impossible for the word '*Agnihotram*' to be taken with '*juhoti*' unless we explain the compound as a Bahuvrīhi, pointing to something else (*agneh hotram agnihotram, yasmin karmaṇi agnihotram tacca agnihotram,* 'that action in which the *hotra* or the material offered belongs to Agni'); and in this manner the word '*Agnihotra*' could be taken in the first instance, as the *Genitive-Tatpurusha* (the *Homa of Agni*) having the force of the Dative; just as in the case of the compound '*Açvaghāsa*,' we know that the grass is *for the sake of* the horse, yet as the one is not the material cause of another (which is a necessary condition for a Dative-*Tatpurusha*), the compound cannot be spoken of as a Dative-*Tatpurusha;* and hence we declare the compound to be a Genitive-*Tatpurusha* having the sense of the Dative.

Nor can the word be taken as laying down the Deity Fire for the Morning Libation alone; as in that case, the *Homa*, as indicated by the *Bahuvrīhi* compound ('*Agnihotra*') having been already got at, it would be only its accessories,—in the shape of the material and the Deity, as denoted by two distinct words '*hotra*' and '*agni*' respectively,—whose relationship will have to be taken as being enjoined by the affix in the word '*juthoti.*' And again, though the Deity (Fire) is known (from the sentence mentioning the Evening Libation) only in connection with one part of the *Agnihotra*, yet this cannot remove the fact of the word '*Agnihotra*' being a name descriptive of the facts already got at from the other sentence (dealing with its various parts).

As for the word '*āghāra*,' it is with a very great difficulty that we can establish its relationship to the *Upānçu* sacrifice.

And though the meaning of the verbal root (*juhoti*, &c.) can be taken only in the character of the Instrument, yet the words '*Agnihotram*' and '*Āghāram*' (in the Accusative) could be taken along with that factor of the Action which is yet to be accomplished. [That is to say, there can be no instrumentality apart from the activity of the agent; and hence the Instrumental character of that which is denoted by the verbal root would always indicate an action of the agent; and this could not be possible without something to be accomplished by that action; and hence the meaning of the root would also contain an element of this something to be accomplished, which must be in the objective case, and as such quite capable of being taken along with such other objectives as '*Agnihotram*' or '*āghāram.*']

And again, the word '*āghāra*' is not very easily recognised as being the name of any particular material; nor again is a material ever found to be laid down by means of a word with the Accusative ending (as it is always enjoined by means of one in the Instrumental case); and hence these words, being recognised as descriptive of the sacrifice, cannot be taken as laying down other materials for it.

ADHIKARAṆA (4).

[*Treating of the fact of such words as 'Çyēna' and the like being the names of sacrifices.*]

Sutra (5). It points to the Action.

As passages treated of in the present *Adhikaraṇa*, we can take the sentences cited in the Bhāshya, and others also, but not the sentence '*athaisha jyotiḥ, &c.*'; because in this latter the word not having the Instrumental ending, it could never be taken as laying down an Accessory. When however these very words appear with the Instrumental ending, in other sentences, then they do become included in the present discussion. Or, even these may be accepted as forming the basis of the present discussion; inasmuch as though having the Nominative ending, yet the word '*jyotiḥ*' may be taken as merely mentioning a particular material; and it would be quite possible for another sentence laying down an action to be performed with this material.

PŪRVAPAKSHA.

"The word '*Çyēnēna*,' in the sentence '*Çyēnēnābhicaran yajēta*,' "must be taken as laying down the material for sacrifice; and in support "of this we could bring forward all the arguments shown in the *Pūrva*-"*paksha* of *Adhikaraṇa* (1). Nor do we find the component parts of the "word '*Çyēna*' pointing to any sacrifice. The only way of making it "refer to a sacrifice would be by making '*Çyēna*' = *Çyenavat* (*that which* "*is like the Çyēna*); and certainly this would be an extremely round-about "way of taking the word. And it is far more reasonable to have recourse "to Possessive Indication, explaining '*Çyēnēna*' as '*Çyēnavatā yagēna* "(the sacrifice which has the *Çyēna* or the Kite for its material). Nor is it "necessary to assume the existence of the possessive affix *matup* and then "eliminate it; because the *Çyēna* being distinctly recognised (through the "Instrumental case-ending) as the *means* (of obtaining the particular "result), it naturally points to its invariable concomitant, the Action "which is accomplished by its means. (That is, the word '*Çyēnēna* "itself would point to the sacrifice performed with the *Çyēna* as the "material)·

"And again, as for the *posssesive* implication, it would be cognised at "the time of the comprehending of the sentence, on account of the fact of "the words occurring in a single sentence. The implication of *similarity* "however would be cognised at the time of comprehending the word itself; "and as such this cannot be admitted to be much weaker than the former. "That is to say, if the word '*Çyēna*' be taken as laying down the *Kite* as "the material of a sacrifice, the word '*Cyēna*,' in subsequently indicating "the *sacrifice at which the Kite is used as the material*, does not entirely "give up its own signification; while when the word itself is pronounced "it only points to its own signification—the *Kite*—as the material to be "used. On the other hand, when the word '*Çyēna*' is taken as pointing to "*a sacrifice similar to the Kite*, in this no trace of the original signification of "the word is found to be pointing to something else similar (to the kites); "and thus this theory would involve the contingency of rejecting the "direct denotation of the word."

SIDDHĀNTA.

To all this, we make the following reply: That which is enjoined is always found to be eulogised by means of its similarity with a different thing; and it is never found to be eulogised by the pointing out of any similarity with itself. And in the case of the sentence in question, we meet with such eulogistic passages as—" just as the Kite springs upon its prey and kills it, so does the performer of this sacrifice fall upon his enemies," where we find the Praise based upon a similarity; and it is certain that the Praise must belong to that which has been enjoined (in the sentence '*Çyēnēnābhicaran*, &c.') If then, the word, '*Çyēna*' in this Injunctive sentence be taken as enjoining the *Kite* as the material for the sacrifice, then it would be the *Kite* that would be the object of the Praise in the above passage; but it is not proper to speak of it as being similar to itself.

It may be urged here that—" we do find certain instances where the "pointing out of absolute identity constitutes a great praise, inasmuch "as it shows that there is nothing equal to the object sought to be praised, "*e.g.*, we have such praises as—'the battle between Rāma and Rāvaṇa was "like the battle between Rāma and Rāvaṇa.'"

This is true enough; but in ordinary parlance we find that even such praises are based upon an assumed diversity of time, place, &c., (between that which is described and that which is cited in the simile). But in the case in question, we find that the word can be taken in such a way as to leave a difference between the object praised and the object cited, in the simile: and hence in this case we can have no ground for assuming any difference (of the Kite from itself). That is to say, if we take the word '*Çyēna*' as the name of a sacrifice, there is no difficulty in having the '*Çyēna*'-*Sacrifice* described (and praised) as being similar to the '*Çyēna*' *Bird.* Otherwise it would be necessary to have recourse to the indication of the possessive implication, as also that of an implication of similarity (the word '*Çyēna*' being made to indicate the '*Çyēnavat*' sacrifice, and then we would have to assume a similarity of the *Çyēna* bird with itself); and your theory would have to take recourse to another complication, of having to assume a difference of the Kite from itself (in order to explain the simile contained in the eulogistic passage). Nor is it possible for you to take the word '*Çyēna*' as pointing to the material of the sacrifice, and then to transfer the Praise (which really belongs to the sacrifice) to the material connected with it; because the Injunction of the sacrifice itself (by the sentence '*Çyēnēnābhicaran yajēta*') has not been set aside. That is to say, it is only the praise of something not enjoined that is transferred to something else; while, in the case in question, we find the sacrifice itself to be directly enjoined, and as such quite capable of being taken along with the Praise; and hence we cannot accept the material (Kite) to be either enjoined (by the sentence '*Çyēna*,' &c.) or praised (by the eulogistic passage quoted). And your theory of the transference of the Praise would involve another complication of making the sacrifice indicate the material.

And on account of the word '*Çyēnēna*' occurring along with the word '*yajēta*,' the former is as directly denotative of the *Sacrifice* as that of the *Material* (Bird). While you have recourse to Indication in the Injunction itself, I accept it only in the descriptive detail.

And as for the elimination of the possessive affix, such an elimination is possible only when the word expresses a *property* and not when it expresses a substance (like the Bird.) Vide *Vārtika* on *Pāṇini* I—iv—19—'*gunavacanēbhyah*,' &c. As for the implication of similarity, on the other hand, it is due to a distinct word, '*iva*,' which, being a word by itself, can appear of itself after any word (and there can be no such restriction as in the case of the Possessive affix *Matup*). And again, the Possessive Indication will have to be assumed while the *similarity* is a well-established fact, as pointed out by the simile in the eulogistic passage.

And in this connection also, we can bring forward, against the present *Pūrvapaksha*, all the objections that have been urged against the *Pūrvapakshas* of the foregoing *Adhikaraṇas*:—*viz*: The necessity of the Verb abandoning its own meaning and taking up that of another, the extreme remoteness of the meaning of the affix, and so forth.

ADHIKARAṆA (5)

[*Treating of the fact of such words as 'Vājapēya' and the like being names of sacrifices.*]

PŪRVAPAKSHA.

***Sūtra* (6). In the case of names, inasmuch as there is a distinct mention of Accessories, there would be an Injunction of these.**

"That which is denoted by the verb could be taken, by the system of "*Simultaneous Relationship* (Tantra), as an *Instrument* with reference to the "*Result*, and as the *Objective* with reference to the *Accessory* (Material); and "there would be no incongruity in this. For instance, in the case of the "sentence—'*udbhidā yajēta paçukāmah*'—the full signification would be "that 'the sacrifice should be accomplished by means of the *udbhid* mate-"rial, and the acquisition of cattle should be accomplished by means of "the sacrifice;' and thus the operation of both Injunctions going hand "in hand simultaneously (and thus there being no syntactical split), "the full construction of the sentence is got at, without having recourse "to Possessive Indication.

"In the same manner we could also explain the relationship of the "word '*ājya*' with the number (fifteen) of the Hymns, by the same method "of *Simultaneous Relationship*.

"Hence we conclude that in all cases of such words as you take to "be *names*, inasmuch as there is a distinct recognition of the mention of "*Materials* or other *Accessories*, based upon the universally accepted "meanings of words,—we can very well take them to constitute the In-"junctions (of such materials, &c.); and there is no reason for taking "them as *Names*.

"The present discussion thus bears upon perhaps all such words as "are taken to be *names*; but the *Bhāshyā* cites the particular sentence—"'*Vājapēyena svārājyākāmo yajēta*' only, with a view that the true meaning "of this sentence may also be arrived at. As a matter of fact, however, "the discussion may be taken as applying to all such sentences (as contain "the names of sacrifices); as it has well been declared: 'The Instrument "(of obtaining the *result*) having been laid down (in the shape of the "*sacrifice*) by means of the word *yajēta*' (inasmuch as the unaccomplished "sacrifice cannot operate as the Instrument) the sacrifice itself comes to "be recognised as an *objective* (something to be accomplished); and it "is for the sake of this *objective* that the accessory (*Vājapēya*) is laid down "as the Instrument; and thus there is no need for a Possessive Indication."

SIDDHANTA.

***Sūtra* (7). The two actions becoming the same, this cannot be.**

At first, with particular reference to the case of the *Vājapēya*, we offer the following reply:

The word '*Vājapēya*' would mean a certain preparation of *flour*, *sugar*, &c., and thus the sacrifice at which such a mixture of grain would be employed as the material, would, by this similarity of material, become an '*Aishtika*' sacrifice (which is a name given to all sacrifices with grains, '*Saumika*' being the name of all that are performed with the juices of creepers, and '*Paçu*' referring to all at which the flesh of animals is offered.) [And thereby the Principal Primary of all *Aishtikas* being the *Darça-Purṇamāsa*, it is the procedure of this sacrifice that would have to be followed in the sacrifice in question; whereas as a matter of fact, the procedure followed at it is that of the *Jyotishtoma*, which is the Principal Primary of all *Saumikas*.] And hence we conclude that the word 'Vājapeya' in the sentence in question cannot be taken as laying down the material for the sacrifice.

***Sūtra* (8). A single word would have an extraneous signification.**

We can have a *Simultaneous Relationship* only in a case where an object, in one and the same form, is found to be equally helpful (to both the factors with which its Simultaneous Relationship is desired). In a case however where the help accorded to the two factors is not equal, it becomes necessary to repeat the word (denotating the object so related) (and there can be no simultaneity in its Relationship).

There are two ways of having the Simultaneous Relationship,—either by taking each word or sentence by itself, or by taking them collectively, according as what is signified by the verb occupies the secondary or the primary position (in the sentence).

Thus then, in the case in question, if the material *Vājapēya* be held to be enjoined as a *means* or Instrument with reference to the sacrifice, then the Result (Sovereignty of Heaven) cannot be taken as the Instrument, because in that case, there would be no result for the sacrifice. Because in all cases the Result is such as is borne in mind (as something to be accomplished by means of the sacrifice); and hence, in the case in question, if the

Sovereignty of Heaven be taken as the Instrument for the accomplishment of the sacrifice, then it would be a mere accessory detail of the sacrifice itself (and as such could not be *something to be accomplished*).

As for the *Sacrifice* also, it can be taken as an Instrument, only for the accomplishment of the Result, and not for that of the Material; because if the Sacrifice were taken as the means of purifying or preparing the material, this would not be compatible with the Instrumental case-ending (in '*Vājapēyēna*') (because that which is spoken of as something to be purified, has always the Accusative ending). Nor do we find any use for the particular material thus purified by the sacrifice; and as such we cannot very well accept this interpretation.

In the same manner, it can be shown that the Sacrifice and the Result cannot be taken as the instrument for the accomplishment of the material.

Nor can both the Sacrifice and the Material be taken as Instruments in the accomplishment of the Result; because all that is necessary having been accomplished by only one of them, there could be no Injunction of the other (which would be comparatively useless). This we shall explain in detail later on (in *Adhyāyā II*) where the Bhāshya declares—'In a case where the transcendental result is accomplished by one sacrifice, anything else must be taken as having its use only in the help that it accords to the former sacrifice.'

Nor can we admit of the *Sacrifice, as specified by the particular material*, to be the object enjoined by the sentence in question; because that would necessitate our having recourse to Possessive Indication.

Thus then, the only construction that would apply to the sentence in question (if the 'Vājapeyā' be taken as laying down the material) would be this: "one should accomplish the *Result* by means of the *sacrifice*, and the *Sacrifice* by means of the *Material* vājapēya." Thus then, with reference to the *Result*, the *sacrifice* would be comprehended as—(*a*) the *Instrument*, (*b*) the *Object of Injunction* and (*c*) the *Secondary Element* (being only the means to an end); and at the same time, with reference to the *Material* the same *sacrifice* would be recognised as having the contrary characters of—(*a*) the *object in contemplation* (sought to be accomplished, (*b*) the *object described* (in contradistinction to that *enjoined*), and (*c*) the Primary factor (being the result sought to be accomplished). And as such there can be no *Simultaneous Relationship* (which thus necessitates the attribution of the aforesaid two sets of contradictory characters). Because if we admit of the one set of characters mentioned above, the other set (being its contradictory) cannot be accepted; while if both be accepted, a syntactical split would be the inevitable result. Because wherever we have to attribute to the sacrifice, the characters of the *object in contemplation*, as well as those of the *Instrument*, &c., it always becomes necessary to assume two distinct sentences (as one and the same sentence cannot express two contradictory properties).

The Objector is made to urge (in the Bhāshya): "*But in the present* "*case also, we actually find two separate sentences*—(1) '*one desiring the sover-* "*eignty of Heaven should perform the sacrifice,*' and (2) '*one should perform* "*the sacrifice with the Vājapēya material.*'" And all that is done in this is to put forth more explicitly the aforesaid *Simultaneous Relationship* of the Sacrifice.

The reply given in the *Bhāshya* is: *We find in the sentence only four words* ('*Vājapēyēna svārājyā-kamo yajēta*') [and not *five*, as shown in the construction]; and the sense of this is that, inasmuch as the relation that the *sacrifice* bears to the two (the *Material* and the *Result*) is not equal, there can be no such Simultaneous Relationship.

The idea, however, by which the Objector has been led away is that the form of the word '*yajēta*' is the same in the two sentences, and as such there can be no harm in taking it in common with the two sentences. And this is what the Bhāshya denies, on the ground that in the interpretation of a word, its denotation is the more significant factor; and as such the difference in the denotations of the word '*yajēta*,' as it appears in the two sentences, cannot but make us take the word itself to be different in the two sentences (as in one it denotes the object in contemplation, while in the other it denotes the object enjoined).

The Objector is made to retort (in the *Bhāshya*): "*It has been said that in case the word* '*Vājapēya*' *be taken as laying down the material for the sacrifice, the sacrifice becomes an object described; but by what would it be described, &c., &c.*" What is meant by all this is that there is no real difference (between the word '*yajēta*' as used in one sentence and as used in the other).

But, even in the case of an Injunction of the material, it is only a verb that can be taken as having the Injunctive character; and hence, the word '*Vājapēya*' not being a verb, it cannot be accepted to be Injunctive (of the material).

Says the *Bhāshya*: *If we admit of an Injunction in both cases, &c.* And the sense of this is that, if the *sacrifice* be held to be enjoined with reference to the *Result* and the *Material*, then,—even if we do not take into account the fact of the sacrifice having a secondary character,—the mere fact of the verb having only a secondary character would make each of the two sentences complete in itself (independently of the other); and as such there would be no connection between the two sentences, [and hence the *Vājapēya* could not be recognised as the material to be employed in that sacrifice which is performed with the purpose of obtaining the sovereignty of Heaven].

It may be urged that, the *Vājapēya* would be recognised as the material to be employed in the particular sacrifice, by the fact of the two sentences occurring in the same Context, just as in the case of the sentence, '*Vrīhibhiryajēta*'; though there is nothing in the sentence itself to show that the *Vrīhi* is the material to be employed in the *Darça-Purṇamāsa*, yet the fact of the sentence occurring in the context of that sacrifice distinctly points to the *Vrīhi* as a material to be employed in it.

But this cannot be; because the sentence in question is taken to be an injunction of the sacrifice only (while in the case of the sentence '*Vrīhibhiryajēta*,' the Context leads us to a definite conclusion, because in this, there is a transcendental result in question; while there is no such result in the case of the Injunction of the Sacrifice as the means of accomplishing the Material; and as such the Context cannot be of any help in the matter).

Thus then, we find that if the method of Simultaneous Relationship is accepted, then it is only independently of each other that the Material and the Result are found to be related to the Sacrifice; specially as if the Sacrifice be taken as related to the one as qualified by the other, a Syntactical split is the inevitable result.

And hence before the full context of all that is connected with the particular Result, in the shape of the sovereignty of Heaven, has been completed,—if the word '*Vājapēyēna*' be taken as laying down a material, such a material being connected with *sacrifices in general*, it would come to be recognised as related, either to all sacrifices, or to the Sacrifices bringing about certain transcendental results. The case of the sentence, '*Vrīhibhiryajēta*,' is different; because in that case, the context has been fully completed by means of the sentences dealing with the *Darça-Pūrṇamāsa* Sacrifices; and then, if the material *Vrīhi* is laid down, it is at once recognised as belonging to the *Darça-Pūrṇamāsa.* And this not being the case with the sentence under consideration, there can be no similarity between the two cases.

Thus then, we conclude that the word '*Vājapēya*' being found to be distinctly co-extensive with the *Sacrifice performed by persons desiring the sovereignty of Heaven*, we cannot neglect this co-extensiveness; and as such, the word cannot but be the *name* of the particular sacrifice.

ADHIKARAṆA (6).

[Treating of the fact of such words as 'Agnēya' and the like not being the names of Sacrifices.]

***Sūtra* (9). If they were not laid down by another sentence, the Sacrifice as well as its Accessories would be enjoined by the word; because of their being mixed up in the Injunctive word.**

The character and the function of *Names* having been explained, we proceed to consider certain exceptions to them.

It may be asked why the case of the *Darvi-Homa* also is not taken up for consideration on the present occasion. But the fact is that this Homa has also been dealt with under *Sūtra* I—iv—4. And, as a matter of fact, on the present occasion we are treating only of the words treating of the objects of Injunction, whereas in the 8th Adhyāya we shall treat of the words contained in Arthavāda passages, such for instance as—'If one should perform only one sacrifice, he should perform the '*Darvi-Homa.*' Or, it may be that when the fact of the word '*Darvi-Homa*' being the name of a sacrifice has been established, it is only its peculiarities that are considered in the 8th Adhyāya; while on the present occasion we consider only the general characteristics of names. And as for the question of the word '*Darvi-Homa*' laying down an Accessory Material, it has been brought in under the 8th Adhyāya, only by way of an objection to the theory propounded there, introduced only in the course of the discussion; because the main object of the 8th Adhyāya is the consideration of Apūrva.

Now then, which are the passages laying down the action of which the word 'Agnēyā' (as contained in the sentence '*āgnēyāshtākapālō bhavati*') could be the name?

The answer to this constitutes the

PŪRVAPAKSHA.

"The Sentence '*ashtākapālō bhavati*' expresses a *Bhāvanā*, with a certain order of sequence, pointed out by the material only; and for the sake "of such *Bhāvanās*, in the same order as themselves, we find certain *Mantras* "—the couplets of the *Yājyā* and the *Anuvākyā*, &c.—dedicated to such "deities as *Agni* and the rest; and these *Mantras*, coming to be employed "in the order of the *Bhāvanās*, distinctly point, through their own expres- "sive Power, to the Deities belonging to each of these *Bhāvanās*; as other- "wise, these *Mantras* could not be of any use in the sacrifices; as the only "useful purpose that the *Mantras* can serve in a sacrifice, is the pointing "out either of the process of the Action, or of such accessories connected "with it, as the Deity or the Material; and in the case in question "we find that the *Mantras* do not point out any Action or Material; "and if the *Agni*, &c., that are mentioned in them do not be recognised "as having any connection with the Sacrifices, the *Mantras* themselves "could not be accepted as having anything to do with the Sacrifices; "therefore on account of the fact of the *Mantras* forming parts of the "Sacrifice being well recognised, we cannot but conclude that Agni and "the rest, that are pointed out by the *Mantras*, must have some connection "with the sacrifices; and inasmuch as these form the chief objects pointed "out by the *Mantras*, *Agni* and the rest come to be recognised as Deities; "and as on this score the sacrifices do not differ from the *Mantras*, the same "Deities come to be known as the Deities of the sacrifices. And again, the "*Purodāça* or Cake spoken of as '*Ashtākapāla*' is of the nature of a *Havi* "(material to be offered to a Deity); and as such by its very nature it "appears to be something to be employed in the sacrifice; and as such by "its very character of an 'offering' it stands in need of the mention "of the Deity to whom it would be offered; and this want is supplied by "the *Mantras*. Thus then we find that the sacrifices having their *materials* "*and Deities* distinctly laid down in the sentence '*Ashtākāpālo bhavati*,' the "word '*Agnēyā*' must be taken as the *name* of these sacrifices, on account "of the reasons shown under *Sūtra* I—iv—4.

"Or, the *ashtākapāla*' having the character of an *offering* (because the "word signifies the cakes as *purified* in the eight vessels, and that which "is purified cannot but be meant as an *offering* to the gods),—we have an "Injunction for cutting them into two pieces, and then there is another "Injunction for spreading them and pouring them out, with a view to "purifying them, which process finally makes the cakes divided into four "pieces each; and then we have the Injunction 'offers the quartered "cake,' which points to the fact of the *Homa* also being four in number; "and thus the four Deities *Agni*, &c., also, as pointed out by the *mantras*, "coming to be recognised as the Deities of the *Homas*, the word '*Āgnēya*' "cannot but be taken as a *Name*. This explanation saves us from the "anomaly of accepting an Injunction of many objects (which is inevitable "when the word is not taken as a *Name*)."

SIDDHĀNTA.

To all this we make the following reply: When the sacrifices are not laid down by any other word, then these sacrifices as well as their accessories must be taken as enjoined by the word in question, because they are not separate from it.

The sacrifice cannot be taken as enjoined, by the mere mention of a certain relationship between a certain Material, a Deity and the *preparation of these* (as shown in the *Pūrvapaksha*). Why? Because the Material (*Cake*) by itself cannot have anything to do with the *Mantras* (the *Yōjyā*, &c.) (because it is only after the material has been recognised as one to be offered at a sacrifice that there arises a desire to learn with what *Mantra* the offering is to be made). Nor do we recognise the Material as having any connection with the words denoting something else (for instance, the words of the *Mantras* pointing out particular Deities). That is to say, the mere declaration '*ashtākapālo bhavati*' does not lay down any action of the human agent, during the performance of which the *Mantras* could be required as reminding the agent of certain details of the action. Nor is the mere *being of the cake* an action to be performed by the human agent, because each action has a definite agent (and the agent of this *being* is the Cake itself). And as the Material already exists, there can be no *making* of it by the agent, and as such even this cannot be taken as standing in need of the *Mantra* which would remind the Agent of it. As for the *Mantras* themselves—'*agnirmūrdhā*, &c.'—they do not express either the Material or its action; and as such, even through this there could not be any relationship between the *Mantras*, and the *Material;* specially as the *Material* has no connection with the words of the Mantra, that denote Agni and the rest.

And again, the *Cake* could not be recognised as having the character either of the *Sacrifice* or of an *offering* (*Havi*); and as such it could not stand in need of the mention of a Deity to whom it would be offered; and hence too, the *Mantras* could not have any connection with the *Material* (cake). That is to say, if the *Sacrifice* were recognised first of all, then alone could there be a desire to know the Deity to whom the sacrifice would be offered; and then alone could the *Mantras*, pointing out the Deities, have any connection with the *Material*; as a matter of fact, however, no Sacrifice is denoted by the word '*bhavati*' in the sentence '*ashtākapālo bhavati.*' And until its connection with the Sacrifice has been fully comprehended, the Cake cannot be recognised to have the character of an *offering* or *Havi*; because the word '*Havi*' is a relative term, (depending for its full connotation upon an idea of that to which the offering is to be made), and it is not an absolute term, denoting the natural form of any object by itself. Because we find that the same material, Milk, &c., which, when offered at sacrifices, is called by the name of '*Havi*' (offering), is not so called, when not in connection with a sacrifice.

The same arguments apply to the theory of the word '*āgnēya*' being a name, based upon the mention of the offering of the quartered 'Cake' (see above).

In the case of such words as '*āghāra*' and the like, the '*āghāraṇa*' (or pouring out) is an *action*; and as such by itself it stands in need of a *Mantra*; and this *Mantra*, thus pointed out, and having its use laid down by a distinct direction in the Veda, it is only right that we should accept it as pointing out a Deity.

And again, there are only three ways of pointing out the Deity of a sacrifice:—*viz*: (1) by means of a *nominal affix*, (2) by means of the *Dative case-ending*; and (3) by means of certain expressive words in the *Mantra*; and among these the one that follows is always weaker in authority than that which precedes it. And in the case in question, when we find the Deity being distinctly pointed out by the *nominal affix* in the word '*āgnēya*' (which is the most authoritative way of mentioning the Deity), why should we have recourse to the least authoritative method, holding the Deity to be pointed out by the words in the *Mantras* (the *Yājyā*, &c.)? specially as it is only an Apparent Inconsistency that can justify our having recourse to this method of arriving at the Deity; but when we find the Deity actually pointed out by the nominal affix, and there is no inconsistency, any recourse to it is most unjustifiable.

Thus then, we conclude that the relationship between the *Material* (Cake) and the *Deity* (Agni) is pointed out by the word '*āgnēya*,' and the *sacrifice* comes to be enjoined by means of the word '*bhavati*,' as aided by this word and certain Arthavāda passages (eulogising the offering of the cake as prepared in the eight vessels); and then it is that, there being a further desire to learn the details of the sacrifice, the Veda lays down the *Mantras* (the *Yājyā*, &c.) in a certain order of sequence. And thus we find that we cannot but accept the Injunction to lay down many things (the Deity, the Sacrifice, the *Mantra*, &c.).

The word '*Vidhānarthē*' in the *Sūtra* has been explained in the *Bhāshya* as *in the word with the nominal affix*; and the sense of this is that *the word with the nominal affix* is capable of serving the purposes of an Injunction.

All the following factors appear mixed up in (not separate form) this word '*āgnēya*': (1) the Deity is mentioned by the original basic noun '*Agni*;' (2) the material offered to that Deity is expressed by the nominal affix '*dhak*;' (3) the relationship of the Material and the Deity also is pointed out by the implication of the same affix; (4) the word '*ashtākapāla*' being in the same form, and hence co-extensive with the word '*āgnēya*,' it comes to be recognised, together with all its attendant qualifications (that is, the Cakes as prepared in the eight vessels), as qualifying, and thus included in, the denotation of the word '*āgnēya*,' (5) the fact of the *Material* being *āgnēya* (belonging to Agni) cannot be accomplished, unless it is made so by a human agent (offering it to Agni); and hence the word '*āgnēya*' indicates the *Bhāvanā* (action of the agent) also; and (6) lastly there could be no such *Bhāvanā*—*i.e.*, the material could not be made *āgnēyā*—without the performance of a Sacrifice; and hence the word '*āgnēyā*' must be taken as indicating also a particular Action of the Agent in the shape of the sacrifice.

Thus then, the chief Injunction being contained in the word with the Nominal affix, and all other attendant accessories also being indicated by it, there is no occasion for any syntactical split.

And as an Injunction of the Accusative Noun (*yāgam*) as denoted by the verbal root ('*yajēta*') is always preceded by an Injunction of the *Bhāvanā*, even though the *Bhāvanā* may not be directly mentioned, yet it is always accepted to be enjoined, as qualified by the 'sacrifice;' and all the other qualifications are indicated by Apparent Inconsistency (of the Injunction of the *qualified Bhāvanā*, which could not be possible without an injunction of the *qualifications*). It is this *Bhāvanā* that is meant by the word '*Sambandha*' in the *Bhāshya* (in the sentence—*sambandho hi vidhīyamāno na çakyatē sambandhināvavidhāya vihita iti vaktum*); because it is this *Bhāvanā* that contains within itself all the factors of the relationship in question; specially as it is not possible for any mere relationship of the Material and the Deity to be enjoined; because this relationship does not contain within itself any element of Action.

The word '*avibhāgāt*' means—'inasmuch as the word implies all the factors (enumerated above)'; and the qualifying sentence '*if they are not laid down by any other word*' points to the fact of Apparent Inconsistency being the only ground of accepting the Injunction of the various factors of the relationship.

ADHIKARAṆA (7).

[*Treating of the fact of such words as 'Varhih' and the like being expressive of a genus.*]

Sūtra (10). The words '_Varhih_' and '_Ājya_' being found to be applied even to such articles (grass and butter) as have not undergone any purificatory process, they cannot be taken to be expressive of such purified materials only.

In connection with Names, we proceed to consider, in the next three *Adhikaraṇas*, the significations of the names of Materials.

Though the *Sūtra* mentions only the two words '*Varhih*' and '*Ājya*,' yet the Bhāshya adds the word '*Purodāça*' also; because the case of all these words is exactly similar.

PŪRVAPAKSHA.

"According to the *Sūtra* I—iii—9, it is clear that these words are used, "by sacrificers, with reference to the purified materials only; and as there is "nothing incongruous in accepting the same fact in all cases, we conclude "that the words in question have their significations based upon the puri-"fication of the materials. Specially, as a matter of fact, we find that in "ordinary parlance, people do not make use of such words as '*purodāça*' "and the like; and hence just as the word '*yūpa*' is applied only to a post "that has undergone a certain process of preparation and purification, so "the words in question also express only such materials as have been pre-"pared and purified in a particular manner."

SIDDHĀNTA.

But it is not so; because when a word is found, even in one place, to be expressive of the *Class*, there being no reason for rejecting this denotation, we cannot assume any other signification of it (in the shape of *purified materials, &c*).

That is to say, it is a well-recognised fact that the words in the Veda are the same as those in ordinary parlance; and their significations too are the same in both; and hence the Veda being dependent upon the meanings of words as known among ordinary people, when a certain word has once been found to be denotative of the *Class*, there can be no ground for assuming any other expressive potency in the word. And further, as the Class '*Varhi*' (grass) is present in the purified grass also, we can have no reason for denying the fact of the *Class* being denoted by the word, even when it occurs in the Veda.

And further, even before the grass has undergone the process of *cutting*, &c., the Veda lays down the Injunction of such cutting (such as 'the grass should be cut'); and in this it is clear that the word 'grass' is used in the ordinary sense of the *Class* (because there could be no *cutting* of that which has already been cut).

Thus we find that the word 'grass' is never used apart from the *class*, while it is found to be used (in ordinary parlance) apart from any idea of the special processes of purification, &c.; because no purifications are laid down in connection with ordinary parlance, no words in ordinary parlance could be accepted as expressing any *purified material.*

Nor can the case of the word 'grass' be said to be similar to that of the word '*yūpa*'; because the denotation of the former is otherwise explicable; and in the case of the latter, we accept it to be expressive of the *prepared post*, because the word is not known to express anything in ordinary parlance.

That is to say, at the time that we come across the Injunction of the cutting of the wood for the post, or of the fastening of the animal to the post,—if we had any idea of any meaning of the word 'post,' as known in ordinary parlance, then we could never have any necessity of subverting the natural order of words—in the Injunction 'the post should be cut'—and construing it as—'that which is cut is the post' (in which case the *post* which is the subject in the original sentence is made the predicate, and *vice versa*). The case of the words 'grass,' &c., however, is different (their signification being fully recognised in ordinary parlance).

ADHIKARAṆA (8).

[*Treating of the fact of the word 'prokshaṇī' being taken in its literal signification.*]

***Sūtra* (11): In the case of such words as 'prokshaṇī' and the like, there is a distinct compatibility of the literal meaning.**

PŪRVAPAKSHA.

"The conventional meaning of a word being based upon the direct "mention of the word, it cannot but be accepted as more authoritative "than the literal meaning which is based upon the signification of its "individual component parts, whose functioning is like that of *Syntax* "(which is always weaker in its authority than *Direct Assertion*). That "is to say, in the case of the conventional meanings of words, people "cognise these directly by means of the letters of the word (as pronoun-"ced); whereas in the case of the literal meaning, it cannot but be more "or less indirect, inasmuch as it rests in the signification of the individual "component parts of the word."

SIDDHĀNTA.

All this may be quite true; but we must admit the component parts themselves to have individual expressive potencies of their own; as otherwise there could be no literal meaning of the word. And hence it is only where there is no literal meaning (compatible with the sentence) that a certain signification being found to have been assigned to the word by convention,—we are obliged to accept this latter meaning; there being no other way (of making the word compatible with the sentence in which it occurs).

That is to say, it is only when the conventional meaning has been fully established that it sets aside the literal meaning; and, as a matter of fact, it is accepted to be fully established, only by some other means of knowledge, when the word is found to be used in a sense totally different from the previously recognised literal one; as for instance, when the word '*açvakarṇa*' is used as the name of a tree, which has no connection with *horse's ear.* In this case, the word is found to be used in a sentence where it cannot have the meaning that is expressed by it literally; and hence from the Apparent Inconsistency of its such usage, we are obliged to assume (conventionally) another expressive potency for it. And thus it is only in such cases as that of the word '*açvakarna*,' that, though both significations are possible, yet there being no recognition of the literal meaning, the significations of the component parts of the word come to be set aside, and the comprehension of the mere Verbal form of the word brings about the comprehension of the conventional meaning (of the word as a whole), which thus, in this case, becomes more authoritative than the literal meaning.

In the case of the word '*prokshaṇī*' however, the word is made up of —*pra* (= excellently) + *sic* (= to besprinkle or wash) + *lyut* (= Instrumental), the literal meaning of the word thus being '*that by which washing is excellently done*;' and certainly this is quite as applicable to *water* (which is held to be the conventional meaning of the word as a whole), as any explanatory sentence; and thus there being no ground (in the shape of any Apparent Inconsistency for assuming any other conventional expressive potency of the word) it can have no conventional signification.

For instance, in the case of the word '*Açvakarṇa*' itself, if somehow or other, the 'ears of a horse' were found to exist in the particular tree denoted by the word, no one would ever assume an invisible conventional potency for the word as a whole.

Thus then we conclude that the word '*prokshaṇī*' cannot have its signification conventionally restricted to the *water* alone; and as such it must be taken as denoting all liquids in general.

[Says the Bhāshya—*The use of this Adhīkaraṇa lies in the fact that Butter also becomes a 'washing material'; and if the word be taken as referring to a purified material, then the direction would be in the form 'prokshaṇīrāsādaya.'*] And it is to this form of the direction that an objection is raised: "Even though the word may refer to a purified material, yet, from the "particular gender, &c., of the word '*prokshaṇīh*' it is clear that it refers "to the *water* (*āpah*); and hence the presence of the feminine sign '*ī*' "would set aside the possibility of Butter being brought in."

The reply to this is that—if prior to the addition of the feminine sign '*ī*,' the word had been recognised to be significant of the purified material, then (in accordance with the conventional meaning of the word), the feminine affix '*ī*' would come to be recognised as being due to the particular gender of the substratum (of the property signified by the word); and as such all substances of any other gender (such as '*ghṛta*' and the like) would come to be set aside; and the use too of the word in the direction in question being unique, even at the time of the purification of the materials, the word would remain in the same position — with a feminine ending; and as such its use being exactly like that of the word 'Vēdi,' the word could not be recognised to be denotative of any other thing; and in that case the feminine ending '*ī*' would be quite significant. When, however, the word is held to have a literal meaning, even before the addition of the feminine ending, the literal meaning of the word is recognised to be the same (*washing material*); and hence when the particular washing material meant is the Butter, the feminine ending is not added, the noun by itself is simply used (the direction being simply '*prokshaṇamāsādaya*'). And though in a case when Injunctions refer to the verbal form of a word, no changes in it are allowable, yet there can be no such restriction of words in the case in question; because the direction refers to materials, and not to their names; and hence it is by no means possible that the word '*prokshaṇī*,' (in the said direction) being incapable of being changed into '*prokshaṇa*,' the word to be used must be '*ghṛta*' only, as in the case of the words that have their significations conventionally fixed to the *class* (of objects).

ADHIKARAṆA (9).

[*Treating of the fact of the word 'Nirmanthya' being taken in its literal sense.*]

***Sūtra* (12): So also in the case of the word 'nirmanthya.'**

In the case of the word '*Nirmanthya*' (=the fire produced by friction) also, we can (as before) raise questions as to its signifying the *class* or a *purified fire*, and then we should set aside these names and finally prove that it must be taken in its literal signification.

[The *Bhashya* says that *in the sentence 'nirmanthyēna ishṭakāh pacanti' the word 'nirmanthya' means the 'fire that is produced by friction on the very spot;*' and it is against this that we have the following]

PŪRVAPAKSHA.

"The word '*Nirmanthya*' signifying only 'the fire produced by friction,' and as such having its sole purpose in the setting aside of the employing of such fires as are produced, either from electric sparks or by striking, or from the solar gem, &c.,—why should it be taken to mean the *fire produced on the spot?* In ordinary parlance—as for instance in the case of the sentence '*Nāvanītēna bhuṅktē*' cited in the Bhāshya—the signification of words being based upon the purposes that they serve, even though the word '*Nāvanītēna*' itself does not necessarily denote the fact of the *fresh-boiled* butter being meant, yet by the fact of the word 'ghṛta' alone being generally used in the sense of the ordinary butter, the special use of the word '*Navanītēna*' may be taken as indicating the *freshly-boiled* butter; because all *butter* being boiled out of *cream* (*nāvanītēna*), the repetition of the word '*nāvanītēna*' can be taken to signify the fact of the *freshly-boiled* butter being meant to be eaten. The case of the word '*Nirmanthya*,' however, is different. Because in this case the only authority is that of the words of the Veda (in this case, the word '*Nirmanthya*' itself); and this word having its sole use in the

" setting aside of the fire produced by other processes, it cannot indicate " anything as to whether the fire produced by friction meant here should " be one produced on the spot, or at any time; and as such how can it be " taken to signify the fire produced by friction *on the spot?* For certainly, " this *immediateness* does not form part of the literal signification of the " word, which rests only in the fact of the fire being produced by the " particular process of friction. Therefore the declaration of the Bhāshya " is not right."

SIDDHĀNTA.

But the above arguments do not affect our position; because the presence of the *Fire* itself being indicated by the word '*pāka*' (cooking) itself, the addition of the word '*Nirmanthya*' must be taken as with the sole view to lay down the particular qualification of the Fire that is meant; and this qualification (of being *produced by friction*) forming part of the aforesaid *cooking* could not but be brought about at the very place where the cooking is to be done.

That is to say, in the sentence—'the red-turbaned priests move about'—the presence of the priests themselves having been pointed out by other texts, the sentence is taken only as laying down the fact of their having *red turbans;* exactly in the same manner, in the case in question, the action of producing the fire by friction must be taken as a qualification (of the Fire) laid down as part of the *cooking;* and it is a well-known fact, which will be explained later on, that the subsidiary actions should be performed, at the same place and time, and by the same person, as the Primary Action; and hence the cooking spoken of in the sentence in question could not but be done by the Fire produced by friction, at the time of the Cooking, in the same place, and by the same person (that does the *cooking*); and this is all that is meant by the Bhāshya passage to which exception has been taken (in the *Pūrvapaksha*).

ADHIKARAṆA (10).

[*Treating of the fact of words like* 'Vaiçvadēva' *being names of sacrifices.*]

***Sūtra* (13): "In the case of the word '*Vaicvadeva*' there is an option."**

The case of the word '*Vaiçvadēva*' in the sentence '*Vaiçvadēvēna yajēta,*' does not come in any of the foregoing Adhikaraṇas; for (1) the Accessory-Deity in this case being mentioned by means of the nominal affix, the acceptance of such an Injunction does not necessitate the assumption of a possessive indication; (2) nor are there many objects of the Injunction, and as such there can be no syntactical split; (3) nor is there any other Injunction of the Deities of the whole *Cāturmāsya* sacrifice; (4) nor is the nominal affix inexplicit in this case, as is the compound in the word '*Agnihotra*;' specially as in all cases, the Deity is laid down by means of such nominal affixes; (5) nor does the word '*Vaiçvadēva*' point to any particular sacrifice, like the word '*Çyēna*' (pointing to the *Çyēna* sacrifice); (6) there being no mention of any result, in this case, there could be no diversity in the form of the root '*yaji,*' as has been found in the case of the word '*Vājapēya.*' And thus the present case not being included in any of those treated of above, we take up its consideration now.

Nor can this enquiry be said to have been interrupted by the consideration of the meaning of the words '*Vārhi,*' &c.; because in all these cases, it is only the names (of sacrifices and materials) that form the objects of enquiry. Or, it may be that in the case of such words as '*Nirmanthya*' and the like, it has been found that the names that have literal meanings signify something not got at before; and as such are found to serve the purpose of Injunctions; and the question very naturally follows—whether or not the same may be said of the word '*Vaiçvadēva*' also.

The *Pūrvapaksha* says 'there is an option;' but this is only an explanation of what follows if the word is taken as laying down an Accessory (*i.e.*, in that case, inasmuch as there are other Deities laid down by other passages, there would be an option among the Deities to whom the sacrifice in question could be offered).

In connection with the word, the following question is raised: 'If it is the Injunction of an Accessory, then the sacrifice itself cannot be enjoined; nor could the word refer to the sacrifice enjoined by a sentence, far removed from it; and hence the word cannot be taken as laying down a Deity for the Āgnēya sacrifice, which forms the subject-matter of the particular context; because any such Injunction of a new Deity is barred by the fact of the Deity of these sacrifices having been laid down in their own original Injunctions.'

And on this we have the following

PŪRVAPAKSHA.

"There could be an option in making the offering to the *Viçvēdēvas*, "or to the Deity pointed out in the original Injunction. And neither the "*Sūtra* nor the *Bhāshya* has yet shown that that which is mentioned in "the original Injunction is more authoritative than anything laid down "subsequently; and hence there is nothing to prevent us from accepting "all the Deities as equally authoritatively mentioned.

"And further, no useful purpose could be served by making the word "'*Vaiçvadēva*' refer (as a name) to all the sacrifices (that constitute the "*Cāturmāsya* sacrifice). Nor are the *Vaiçvēdēvas* known (prior to the sen-"tence in question) to belong either to one of these sacrifices or to all of "them taken collectively (and as such the word could not be taken as "referring to these sacrifices).

"That is to say, if the word did not lay down the Accessory-Deity, "the whole of the sentence in question would be useless. Because the "sacrifices in question, either singly or collectively, are not known to be "related to the *Viçvēdēvas;* and they could not be spoken of by the "name '*Vaiçvadēva;*' nor does the verbal root '*yaji*' (in the sentence "'*Vaiçvadēvēna yajēta*') signify the *Āmikshā* sacrifice only (which has been "distinctly pointed out as belonging to the *Viçvēdēvas*); nor again is the "word '*Vaiçvadēva*' held (even by the Siddhānti) to apply to the *Amikshā* "sacrifice only; hence we must take the word as laying down the "Acccessory-Deity for the seven sacrifices (which, with the *Amikshā*, form "the eight sacrifices of the *Cāturmāsya*).

"Against this the following might be urged: 'In that case, the same "'word *Vaiçvadēva* would be an Injunction with reference to the seven "sacrifices, and a mere Description, with reference to the *Amikshā;* and "this would involve a self-contradiction.'

"But it is not so; because although all the eight sacrifices form the "subject-matter of the context, yet the function of an Injunction can rest "only in that whereto that which is enjoined is not already known to be-"long; and hence there could be no self-contradiction in the matter."

SIDDHĀNTA.

***Sūtra* (14). But it is not so; because of the Context, and because of there being a direct Injunction; specially as the Context does not apply to the material.**

To the above *Pūrvapaksha*, we make the following reply: The word cannot be an Injunction of the Accessory-Deity for the sacrifices in question; because their Deity having been already mentioned, there is no room for any other Deity; nor can there be an option in the matter, because the authoritative character of the two Injunctions is unequal.

Agni, &c., have been laid down, by means of the Direct Denotation (Çruti) of the nominal affix (in the word '*āgnēya*,' &c.), as the Deities for the *Ashtākapāla*, &c.; while the fact of the *Vaiçvēdēvas* being their Deity is held to be pointed out by the syntactical order (of the sentence '*Vaiçvadēvena yajēta*') [and certainly Direct Assertion is more authoritative than any indications of the syntax]. It may be urged that in the former case also that which signifies the fact of Agni being the Deity of the *Ashtākapāla* is also a *sentence* (the syntactical connection between the words '*agnēya*' and '*ashtākapāla*'). But it is not so, because the relationship of the material (*Ashtākapāla*) with the Deity (*Agni*) having been established by the nominal affix (in '*āgnēya*'), all that the *sentence* does is to point out the fact of '*agnēya*' qualifying the '*ashtākapāla*.'

It might be urged that the same may be said to be the case with the word '*Vaiçvadēva*' also (as this also establishes the relationship of the material with the *Viçvēdēvas*). But that is not possible; because in this case the process would be a highly complicated and round-about one; as we shall have to assume the (word to signify) the relationship (of the Deity *Viçvēdēvas*) with a material that will have to be taken as indirectly *indicated* by the 'sacrifice' denoted by the word '*yajēta*'; for certainly the word '*Vaiçvadēvena*' is not found to be expressive of any material, either that which belongs to the sacrifices treated of, or any other; all then that we can say is that the co-extensiveness of the word '*Vaiçvadēvena*' with the denotation of the word '*yajēta*' points to the construction

54

that 'by means of the *Vaiçvadēva* sacrifice, &c., &c.'; and that as there could be no sacrifice without a material, the only material that could be made to reach the *Viçvēdēvas* (by means of this sentence alone) would be that which is indicated by the (apparent inconsistency of the sacrifice. But the sentence only pointing to the relationship of the sacrifice with the Deity, this relationship of the material could only be assumed by means of the exigencies of the Context; and such an assumption could be only in this form: 'when offering the *Āgnēya* sacrifice, one should offer it as the *Vaiçvadēva* sacrifice (*i.e.*, sacrifice of which the *Viçvēdēvas* are the Deities) and none other?

In the case of the Injunction of the *Āgnēya* sacrifice, however, there is no need for having recourse to any indirect indication, or for calling in the help of the Context; and this fact constitutes a great difference in the authoritative character of the two Injunctions.

Says the *sūtra—na hi prakaraṇandravyasya* (the Context does not apply to the material). This may mean—(1) either that *when the sentence lays down the relationship of the material with Agni, there is no need for calling in the help of the Context*; (2) or that *the Context of the material has not been accepted by the sentence* '*Vaiçvadēvena*, &c.' (*i.e.*, it does not make any mention of the material).

The Bhāshya explains this sentence (*na hi prakaraṇandravyasya*) as that *the Context cannot set aside the thing that is directly laid down*; and in this the Bhāshya evidently takes the word '*dravya*' as *thing* (and not as the *material* for a sacrifice), the sense of the Bhāshya being that *such a thing as Agni, which has been 'directly laid down' as the Deity, cannot ~~be set~~ aside by any considerations of the Context.* Or, in the Bhāshya sentence, the word '*Çrutasya*' (directly laid down) may not be taken as qualifying the word '*dravyasya*,'—the sense of the Bhāshya passage in that case being that, *Agni, which has been 'directly laid down' as the Deity 'in connection with the particular material,' cannot be set aside by the Context.*

[Thus then, it has been shown that the word cannot be taken as laying down a Deity for the sacrifices that form the subject-matter dealt with]. Nor can the 'sacrifice' denoted by the word '*yajēta*' in the sentence in question be taken, either as pointing out a Deity in reference to another sacrifice mentioned somewhere else (such as the *Upānçu* sacrifice for which no particular Deity has been laid down), or as laying down an altogether fresh *sacrifice together with its particular Deity.*

As for the pointing out of the whole set of sacrifices (constituting the *Cāturmāsya*) by the word '*Vaiçvadēva*' (taken as a name of all these taken collectively), this serves a distinct useful purpose (and is not absolutely useless as urged by the *Pūrvapaksha*); inasmuch as it serves to bring together the various sacrifices scattered here and there; and without the fact of all these sacrifices being pointed out collectively by the name '*Vaiçvadēva*' there could be no such Injunctions as—'*Vasantē Vaiçvadēvēna,*' '*prācīnapravaṇē Vaiçvadēvēna,*' and the like—which refer to all the eight materials laid down as being offered at the various sacrifices of the *Cāturmāsya*. Therefore we conclude that although the *Viçvedēvas* are actually mentioned in connection with only one of these materials (*viz.*, the *Āmikshā*), yet all the others could also be referred to by the word '*Vaiçvadēva,*'—exactly as in a group of ten or fifteen men, even though all of them may not have umbrellas, yet even if some of them happen to have it, it is said of them that 'the people with umbrellas are going'; and hence the word '*Vaiçvadēva*' can very well be taken as the name of all the *Cāturmāsya* sacrifices taken collectively.

Sūtra (15). There is no mutual relationship of significations.

The word '*Vaiçvadēva*' cannot be taken as laying down the Deity for the sacrifices of which the '*Vaiçvadēva*' is one; because in that case the same word '*Vaiçvadēva*' would be taken, once (in connection with the *Āmikshā* sacrifice) as only pointing to a well-established fact, and at the same time as an Injunction (of the Deity, with reference to the other seven sacrifices); and certainly this is highly improper.

Or, we may explain the *Sūtra* in the following manner: It has been urged in the Pūrvapaksha that, like the word '*Nirmanthya,*' the word '*Vaiçvadēva*' also, though a *name*, could also be taken as laying down the Deity; and in reply to this we assert that such mutual concomitance of the signification of the *name* and the *Injunction of an Accessory* is not possible; (*i.e.*, the same word can not be taken as both); and as for the word '*Nirmanthya*' we take it only as laying down an Accessory (fire).

Sūtra (16). Because the Accessories have a secondary importance (*lit.*, are for the sake of others).

This *Sūtra* may be taken as a part of the previous *Sūtra*, the two together being explained in the following manner: *If all the materials be offered together, there could not be thirty offerings in all; and this would constitute a sin* (*Sūtra* 15)—*because the material offered is an accessory* (*Sūtra* 16); and as such the material being of secondary importance, a mere difference in these materials (as *āmikshā*, *vājina* and the other materials offered at the *Cāturmāsya* sacrifices) could not justify a repetition of the action of offering; because (if the word '*Vaiçvadēva*' be taken as laying down a common Deity for all these sacrifices) the Deity of all the offerings being one and the same, it would certainly be a very much simpler process to make a single offering (of all the materials); and thus there being a possibility of making a single offering of all the materials, no repetition of the action of offering can be allowable. Specially as all the sacrifices have the same Deity, there would be nothing incongruous in this joint offering of all the materials. And this would go directly against the Vedic declaration that 'thirty offerings are to be offered (at the *Cāturmāsya* sacrifices),'—the thirty offerings consisting (according to some), of the nine *Prayājas, the* the nine *Anuyājas*, the two *Āghāras*, the two *Ājyabhāgas*, and the eight *Principal offerings*,—while some people leave off the two *Āghāras*, and count instead, the *Svishtakṛt* and the *Vājina* offerings. In any case the eight *Principal offerings* are always found to be offered separately (and not conjointly, as would be necessary if the word in question were taken as laying down the Deity).

ADHIKARAṆA (11).

[*Treating of the fact of the mention of the number 'eight,' in connection with the* Vaiçvānara, *being an* Arthavāda.]

***Sūtra* (17). "Those words that express something already known before, cannot serve the purposes of an Injunction. The aforesaid is also applicable to the sentence in question."**

The consideration of the question as to whether certain words are names of sacrifices or Injunctions of Accessories having been finished, we now proceed to consider whether certain words can be taken as Injunctions of Accessories. Or, it may be that, in the sentence in question—'*vaiçvānaram dvādaçakapālam nirvapēt......yadashtākapālo bhavati gāyatryaivainam brahmavarcasēna punāti*'—the *ashtākapāla* (the cake prepared in the eight cups) as included in the '*dvādaçakapāla*' (the cake prepared in the twelve cups), is co-extensive with the *Vaiçvānara*; and as such the number 'eight' having already been laid down by the mention of the number 'twelve,' the word '*Ashtākapāla*' might be taken as a mere *name*; whereas on the ground of the ordinarily accepted signification of the word, and on account of the number not having been laid down elsewhere, it may be shown that the word lays down an Accessory; and hence what we propose to do in the present *Adhikaraṇa* is to reject both these theories and show that the mention of the '*Ashtākapāla*' is a mere *Arthavāda*.

Some people explain the *Pūrvapaksha* contained in the *Sūtra*, in the following manner: "Those words whose meanings are already known can " be utilised only by being taken as Injunctions; while those whose meanings " are not known should be taken as names, as shown under the *Sūtra* " I—iv—2; and hence the mention of the number 'eight' must be taken " as laying down an Accessory. [In this case the reading of the *Sūtra* " would be '*pūrvavanto vidhānārthāh*,' and not "*pūrvavanto' vidhānārthāh.*]"

But this interpretation of the *Pūrvapaksha* is not correct; because the mere fact of the signification of a word being unknown cannot make it a *name*; on the other hand, just as the fact of a word being altogether new and having its ordinary signification unknown proves that it cannot be taken as laying down the Accessory of a sacrifice,—exactly in the same manner, it is all the more impossible for it to be taken as the name of any Vedic sacrifice; and hence such a word cannot be taken as a *name* either; because it is a well-recognised fact that it is only when the ordinary signification of a word is well-known that it can be taken as a Name, on the ground of its being mentioned along with a certain sacrifice.

Therefore we must accept the interpretation of the *Sūtra*, as given in the Bhāshya; and in accordance with this, the *Sūtra* embodies the following—

PŪRVAPAKSHA.

"When a word expresses a meaning that is already known, then it "is either a *name* or an *Arthavāda*; in the case in question however, as "the word signifies something not known before (it cannot but be taken "as laying down an accessory, a particular number of the cakes); and as "such there would be an option as to the number, exactly as there was "in the case of the word '*Vaiçvadēva*.'

"That is to say, if the number 'eight' be somehow or other, already "known to belong to the *cakes* employed at the *Vaiçvānara* sacrifice, then, "in accordance with this well-known fact, the word '*Ashtākapāla* would "be taken either as a *name* or as an *Arthavāda*; as a matter of fact, however, "we do not find the number 'eight' mentioned anywhere else, in con- "nection with the *Vaiçvānara* sacrifice; as the only number that is men- "tioned is 'twelve.'

"And as a matter of fact, though the smaller number 'eight' is "included in the greater number 'twelve,' yet when the word used is "twelve,' it does not signify the fact of the number 'eight' specifying "the object; and as such this latter number cannot be taken as qualifying "the object in question.

"That is to say, a *number* does not operate by its mere presence; "but the only operation that it has is through the specification of the "*numbered* object; and hence, when the cups have been specified by the "number 'twelve,' any other number, 'eight,' f. i., cannot be taken as "specifying them; and hence (as far as any usefulness is concerned) "these latter are as good as non-existent. Even though their existence "may, in some way or other, be admitted, yet all that the mention of the "number would mean would be that 'there are eight,' and not that 'there "are eight cups in which the cakes are prepared. And further, the "nominal affix in the word '*ashtākapāla*' is one which is possible only "when the material signified is a duly prepared and purified one (according to Pāṇini's *Sūtra* '*sanskṛtam bhakshāh*' IV—ii—16); and "the compound too is one based upon the peculiar character of the "nominal affix (according to Pāṇini's *Sūtra* '*taddhitārthottarapada, &c., &c.*' "II—i—51); and these too are possible only when the factors of the word "have the requisite capability; this requisite capability again is possible, "only when they are independent of all extraneous help. Consequently, "in the case in question, if the number *eight* be dependent upon the number *twelve*, we could not have the word '*ashtākapāla*' (as in that case "neither the particular nominal affix nor the compound would be possible); "and hence the word '*ashtākapāla*' cannot be accepted to be significant of "the *Dvādaçakapāla*. And hence, the word '*ashtākapāla*' not being found "to be descriptive of even the form of the *Dvādaçakapāla*, any Praise of "this latter by that word would be wholly irrelevant; specially as the number '*eight*' would not afford any more help in the sacrifice than the number *twelve;* because both are *numbers* (and *numbers* by themselves cannot "be of any use in sacrifices); although, however, a praise of the number "*eight* might mean a praise of the number *twelve* also, yet, any praise "of the *eight cups* could not belong to the *twelve cups;* because the nouns "and the adjectives in the two cases are totally different. And the number 'twelve' has a distinct praise of itself in the Vedic sentence— "*jagatyaivāsmin*, &c.' (and as such it does not stand in need of any other "praise).

"For these reasons, we conclude that the word '*ashtākapāla*' must "be taken as laying down the number 'eight' as an optional alternative "to the number 'twelve.'

"And inasmuch as all the sentences in question are found to end in "a single original Injunction *of the Vaiçvānara sacrifice as qualified by* "*many optional alternatives with regard to the number of cups to be employed* "(in the preparation of the cakes to be offered), there can be no difference "of authority among the various sentences (forming this original Injunc- "tion).

"The *Sūtra* adds—*the aforesaid is also applicable to the sentence in* "*question;* and the word 'aforesaid' refers to that which has been said "before, in the *Pūrvapaksha* with regard to the word '*Vaiçvadēva*'; and "the *Sūtra* means that all the arguments therein urged apply to the "sentence dealt with in the present *Adhikaraṇa;* while the Refutations "of these arguments (as shown under the Siddhānta in connection with "the word '*Vaiçvadēva*') do not apply to the present case. And hence we "cannot but take the words '*ashtākapāla*,' &c., as laying down the acces-"sories of sacrifices (in the shape of the particular numbers of cups to be "used)."

SIDDHANTA.

***Sūtra* (18). If the word in question be taken as laying down Accessories, these accessories, not belonging to the sacrifice, would be absolutely useless in the performance of any; because they can have no use with regard to it.**

The Accessory could not be laid down, either with reference to the sacrifice treated of in the Context, or to any other sacrifice; nor could there be an injunction of the material qualified in a certain manner.

That is to say—(1) The sacrifice in question having the number put down at *twelve*, any other numbers, as *eight*, *etc.*, could not be laid down with regard to it. (2) Nor could these numbers be laid down with regard to any other sacrifice, because there is no mention of any such in the sentence. (3) Nor could the sentence '*ashtākapālo bhavati*' itself lay down an altogether new sacrifice, qualified by the number *eight*, because the sentence does not point to any relationship of the material with a particular Deity. (4) The same reasons would also show that the sentence could not be taken (in any of the aforesaid three ways) as laying down the number of the cakes. (5) In the same manner, it can also be shown that the sentence could not be taken as laying down the Cake *as prepared in the eight cups*; because as for the sacrifice in question, when it has once had its material laid down as *the cake prepared in twelve cups*, it can never be made to take up any other cake (that prepared in eight cups for instance); and as for any other sacrifice, so long as it is not distinctly pointed out by a word peculiar to itself, no cake could be laid down for it; nor could there be an injunction of the cakes themselves, independently of any sacrifice; because in this manner, it would not be related to any result or the means of accomplishing it; and as such of what use could the Cake be? Nor is it possible for the *material* to be laid down; because it is not of the nature of an Action; and for this very reason, it is not possible for us to assume a Result, as in the case of the *Viçvajit* sacrifice.

Nor can the word '*Vaiçvānara*' of the preceding sentence be taken along with the following sentence, for the purpose of connecting this latter with a *sacrifice*. Because there is a diversity in the case-endings; and inasmuch as even without such a construction being accepted, there is no incosistency or uselessness of any words (we cannot assume a co-ordination between words with different case-terminations).

To explain:—It might be urged that the relationship of the word '*Vaiçvānara*' being transferred to the following sentence, this latter sentence ('*ashtākapālo bhavati*') could be taken as laying down the relationship of the Deity with such materials as the cakes prepared in the eight cups, and thus this would point to a sacrifice other than the *Vaiçvānara* itself (and there would be nothing incoherent in the number *eight* being laid down with regard to it). But this is not possible; because the word '*Vaiçvānaram*' being in the Accusative, could not be taken along with '*ashtakapālah*', which is in the Nominative. Nor could we change the case-terminations (through the exigencies of construction); because the sentence is quite capable of another construction. If without such construing of the Accusative with the Nominative and the changing of the endings, the word '*ashtākapāla*' were meaningless, then we could do anything to make it give some sense; but when we find the word quite capable of being taken as a Praise, it cannot be said to be meaningless (and hence there can be no ground for any anomalous construction being adopted). If the word be taken as a Praise, then it could be taken as being descriptive of the *Vaiçvānara* sacrifice; and in the case of a description the difference in the case-endings does not matter at all.

For these reasons we cannot take the word as laying down the Cake.

Nor are the Cakes prepared in eight cups found to have any separate existence of their own in the Cakes prepared in twelve cups; because the only difference that we find in the two lies in the number *eight;* and we have already shown that this number *eight* cannot be taken as being laid down either in connection with the sacrifice or with the Cake.

Nor is it possible for you to take the number *eight* along with the '*Dvādaçakapāla*'; because the objects enjoined by the two, as well as their purposes, are totally different; and certainly those that are so very diverse from each other cannot be said to be mutually dependent (*vide* conditions for taking one sentence along with another as explained under *Sūtra* II-i-46). If, however, the two could be taken together, all the sentences collectively would lay down a single *Bhāvanā* qualified by the qualifications mentioned in all the sentences; and as such there could be no room for any option in the matter (as held by the *Pūrvapaksha*).

And as for the numbers *eight*, etc., inasmuch as they are mere properties, each of the sentences cannot be taken as complete in itself and pointing out the performance of distinct Actions.

Nor is a collocation (or congregation) of different numbers possible (in any one place); because the appearance of any one number makes the existence of all other numbers impossible. And as for the congregation of many numbers, without the appearance of any new number,—in that case the numbers *eight*, &c., being already included in the number *twelve*, the former numbers would be got at by the injunction of the latter only; and as such any mention of them cannot but be taken in the light of a mere *description* (which cannot be very palatable to the *Pūrvapakshi*).

Hence it becomes necessary for you to admit that each of the sentences in question lays down a distinct number independently of those laid down in another. And in that case, with regard to the *Vaiçvānara* sacrifice (which is the only one mentioned in the sentence), the number *twelve* would be laid down in its own originative sentence, while the other numbers could be related to it only on account of the fact of the sentences (laying down these numbers) being found in the same Context; and as such (Context being weaker in its authority than Direct Syntactical Relation), the relationship of these latter numbers with the *Vaiçvānara* sacrifice would be impossible in face of that of the number 'twelve.' And hence the *Vaiçvānara* sacrifice having its particular number fixed at 'twelve,' could not stand in need of any other number, 'eight,' &c.

And further, no relationship of the number 'eight' with any sacrifice being possible, through the *Vaiçvānara* sacrifice, which has its number distinctly laid down as 'twelve,' it becomes necessary to assert its relationship with a sacrifice, independently of the *Vaiçvānara*; but the number 'eight,' apart from the Cake, is not capable of any relationship with a sacrifice; and when taken along with the *Cakes* it cannot attain to any relationship with the *Vaiçvānara* sacrifice; specially as the fact of its being related to the Cake by direct *Syntactical Relation* would naturally set aside any chance of its relationship to the *Vaiçvānara* sacrifice —which relationship would be based on the mere fact of the two occuring in the same *Context*;—and as such it could never belong to the *Vaiçvānara* sacrifice.

And thus not being a qualification of the *Vaiçvānara* sacrifice (*atadguṇāh*), and being related to the Cake only (apart from any sacrifice), the numbers 'eight,' &c., would be absolutely useless, in the performance of any sacrifice ('*prayōgē syuranarthakāh*') *because they can have no use with regard to the Cake* ('*na hi tampratyarthavattāsti*'). Or, this last sentence may be explained in the following manner: As to why these numbers are not related to the *Vaiçvānara* sacrifice, we reply—*because they can have no use in a sacrifice whose particular number 'twelve' has been already laid down.*

***Sūtras* (19-20): If it be urged that, 'the mention (of the numbers 'eight,' &c.) could not be supplementary (to any Injunction)'—then, inasmuch as these are not excluded from the Injunctive word they could be taken as serving the purpose of Praising.**

That is to say, inasmuch as in the absence of an Injunction of the numbers 'eight,' &c., any praise of them (as contained in the sentences '*Yadashtākapālo bhavati gāyatryaivainam brahmavarcasēna punāti,*' &c.) would be entirely irrelevant,—we must take these sentences as praising the number 'twelve' through its *parts* (*i.e.*, the numbers contained within it). For, as a matter of fact, that alone can be praised which is recognised as enjoined; in the case in question, it is the number 'twelve' that is enjoined; and hence we must take the eulogistic sentences as, in some way or other, praising this number. And as the number 'eight' happens to be mentioned in close proximity to it, we can very rightly take it as only pointing out a part; of the number 'twelve;' and it is a recognised fact that a praise of the part reverts to the whole. Thus then, the eulogy contained in the sentence may be expanded out in the following manner: 'The *Dvādaçakapāla* (*i.e.*, the cake prepared in the twelve cups) is such a grand thing, that when it is prepared, it accomplishes the *ashtākapāla*, &c., also; and these latter are so very effective as to bring about Brahmic glory, &c., and hence the *Dvādaçakapāla* also must be very excellently effective.'

It has been urged in the *Pūrvapaksha* that, "inasmuch as there is already a sentence in praise of the *Dvāadaçakapāla*, no other sentence could be taken as praising it." But this is not quite correct, because there can be no limit to a praise; and hence all that may be found to be mentioned in connection with an Injunction can very rightly be taken as pointing to the object of the Injunction. In all cases we find Praises in words, few or many; and as to whether any particular praise is useful or not depends upon the character of the person addressed; as for some people the mere fact of an action being enjoined is enough to prompt him to that action; and in the case of such a person all Praise of the action would be redundant; and hence, as shown above, the Praises must be taken as being laid down for the sake of those who are not so readily obedient to an Injunction. In the same manner it is quite possible that though a slight praise would suffice for persuading one man, another man would require a more elaborate praise, before he is persuaded to the performance of an action; and hence an elaborate praise cannot be rejected as useless.

Sutra (21): Obj.: "It might be the instigator."

["*Says the Bhāshya: why could not the Brahmic glory be taken as the* "*Kāraṇa of the number 'eight'? the sentence meaning that one who is desir-* "*ous of Brahmic glory should take to the Ashtākapāla*"?]

"And here the word '*Kāraṇa*' cannot be taken in the ordinary sense of "the *cause* or '*progenitor*'; because it is the number *eight* itself that is such a "cause of the various results, purification, &c.; we must therefore take it in "the sense of 'instigator'; these results being the instigators of the actions."

"It has been urged above that—'any Injunction or Praise of the "number *eight* would be absolutely useless, as the number pertaining to "the only sacrifice in question has already been laid down as *twelve*.' But, "as a matter of fact, there can be no such uselessness. Because the "mention of the number *twelve* is with reference to the sacrifice when "performed as a necessary duty (without any particular result in view); "when, however, a person desires such results as Brahmic glory and the "like, then for such a person, the text lays down the number '*twelve*,' "which, in this case, makes room for the particularly desired number "'*eight*.' (1) Because that which is performed with a view to a certain "desirable result, being closely connected with man's true purpose, always "sets aside that which is performed as a mere duty; and (2) because the "latter duty is laid down as a general rule, while the former is a special "case (and a special case always sets aside the general).

"That is to say, all efforts of man tend towards the accomplishment of "a desirable purpose; and hence that which is more closely related to it, "cannot but have a prior claim on the man's attention. In the case in "question, the number '*twelve*' is far remote from any desirable purpose "of man; because it serves to specify the cups required for the preparing "of the material to be employed at a sacrifice that would be performed for "the accomplishment of a desirable end; as for the number *eight*, this is "laid down as bringing about a desirable result, in the shape of Brahmic "glory, directly through the sacrifice itself; and thus being more closely "related to the desirable end, the number 'eight' must be accepted as "the more authoritative; and as such a mention of this cannot be said "to be absolutely useless.

"An objection might be raised here: 'You accept the obtaining of "Brahmic glory to be a definite result; but in the absence of any Praise, "how could you obtain a direct Injunction for words (*like bhavati*) that "are expressive of the *present* state of things?'

"And to this, some people make the following reply: We can arrive "at a direct Injunction in the way shown in the *Pūrvapaksha* of the *Adhi-* "*karaṇa* on '*Audumbara*' (*Sūtras* I—ii—19-25).

"But this is not quite correct; because the arguments therein pro- "pounded have already been refuted in the *Siddhānta* of the same *Adhī-* "*karaṇa.* Hence we offer the following explanation: The real result is "mentioned in the sentence—'*pūta ēva sa tējasvī, &c.*'; and the sentence— "'*gayatryaivainam brahmavarcasēna, &c.*, containing a Praise points to its "counterpart Injunction; and it is for this reason that each of the actions "mentioned, together with the Praises, in the sentences—'*yadashtākapālo* "*bhavati,*' '*yannavakāpālo bhavati,*' &c., &c.,—are connected respectively "with each of the results mentioned in the sentence '*sa pūta ēva sa tējas-* "*yvannādo, &c.*'"

***Sūtra* (22). *Reply:* On account of uselessness they cannot be instigators; because the instigator is of the agent; hence they must be taken as signifying mere Praise.**

If distinct results be assumed to follow from each of the accessories (that is if each of the numbers, *eight*, &c., be held to bring about a distinct result), then it would be necessary to have as many (Injunctive) Sentences as there are results mentioned; while in the case in question, it is clear that the whole thing refers to a single Injunction; inasmuch as it is distinctly perceptible that, from beginning to end, all that is mentioned, is in direct connection with the same subject.

That is to say, the context begins with 'A son being born one should perform the *Dvādaçakapāla*,' &c., &c., (*putrē jātē dvādaçakapālam*, &c., &c.'); and then having described the '*ashtākapāla*,' &c., it winds up with the declarations—'This *dvādaçakapala* that is accomplished' ('*yaddvādaçakapālo bhavati*'), and 'one on whose birth this sacrifice is performed becomes pure, endowed with glory, &c., &c.,' ('*yasmin jātē ētām ishtim nirvapē' pūta eva sa tējasvyannādo, &c., &c.*')—all of which refers to the same sacrifice that was mentioned in the opening sentence of the Context. And for this reason, the mention of the '*ashtākapāla*,' &c., cannot in any way be separated from that sacrifice. And, as a matter of fact, we find that they cannot be taken along with that sacrifice, unless they are taken to be mere Praises. And thus we find that, unless they are taken to be Praises, they can, as they are situated, serve no other purpose.

And the results '*purity*,' &c., could serve as *instigators*, only if they were related to the agent performing the sacrifice; as a matter of fact, however, they are found to be related merely to the *Vaiçvānara* sacrifice; and hence—*i.e.*, inasmuch as no other use is possible—they must be taken as serving the purposes of *Praising*. [That is to say, if we had such an Injunction as that 'for one who desires purity the number of cups should be eight,'—then the desired result, being found to be related to the performer of the sacrifice, could serve as his *instigator* or prompter; as a matter of fact, however, from the context it is clear that the results mentioned are related to the *Vaiçvānara* sacrifice only; and as such the mention of the results cannot but be taken as to be added in praise of the *Vaiçvānara* sacrifice itself].

And further, inasmuch as the results—*purity*, &c.,—are mentioned in the sentence '*pūta ēva sa*,' &c., where the Pronoun '*sa*' (he) distinctly refers to 'one on whose birth the Vaiçvānara sacrifice is performed;' and hence these results could not be connected with anything that has been mentioned before (such as the *Ashtākapāla*, &c.). Nor is the mention of the results entirely irrelevant, in connection with the *Vaiçvānara* sacrifice;

and hence there can be no ground for transferring their relationship from this to the *Ashtākapāla*, &c. [And inasmuch as all the results *purity*, *glory*, &c., are found to be mentioned as all appearing *together* in the son on whose birth the *Vaiçvānara* sacrifice is performed.] It is not possible for these results—*purity*, *&c.*,—to be taken as following, one by one, from the numbers *eight*, *nine*, &c., (of the cups) respectively; specially as each of these numbers has got a definite result of its own—such as Brahmic glory, and the like—mentioned along with itself. And so far as these differentiated results—Brahmic glory, &c.,—are concerned, you also admit of their mention being a mere Praise (see above). And hence the result, that is pointed out by the sentences—'*pūta ēva sa*, &c., (he becomes purified, &c.,)'—must be taken as pertaining to the sacrifice (*Vaiçvānara*), and not to the numbers *eight*, &c. (And though they may be taken as results following from the *Vaiçvānara* sacrifice, yet) in the first instance, a mention of these must be taken to be in praise of the sacrifice; specially as the expression 'having such and such a desire' does not appear in the sentences, they have not the form of the Injunctions of Results. And it is only when the results '*purity*,' &c., are taken as mentioned only in praise of the sacrifice, that the sentences '*yadāshtakapālo bhavati*,' &c., could be explained as serving the purpose of supporting the facts mentioned in the Praise (otherwise these sentences would be absolutely useless). And hence we conclude that the words '*Ashtākapāla*,' &c., cannot be taken as laying down the accessory of a sacrifice (in the shape of the *number* of the cups to be employed in the preparation of the cakes to be offered at it).

ADHIKARAṆAS (12—17).

Sūtras (23—28): The fulfilment of the signification (23)—Origin (24)—Similarity of shape (25)—Praise (26)—Large number (27)—the Inherence of signs (28),—(which form the bases of secondary or indirect signification)—are based upon qualities.

While treating of *Arthavādas*, we did not explain the fact of these being helped by figurative descriptions; nor did we explain the bases of such descriptions; and this is what we proceed to do now.

Objection: "But such cases of figurative descriptions have already been described under *Sūtras* I—ii—1, 12 *et seq.*"

Reply: It is true that they have been described there; but they have not been described *as defining such figurative Descriptions;* as a matter of fact, what has been shown there is only that the definitions here laid down apply to the cases considered there. While what we are going to explain here is the definition or characteristic of all secondary significations of words.

Objection: "Besides those enumerated here, Gautama and others "have spoken of many other bases of secondary signification—such for "instance, as *concomitance*, *similarity of position* and the like; and we find "examples of such bases in ordinary assertions also; as we often meet "with such expressions as—'Bring in the *lances*' (for the lancers), 'the "*elevated sheds* cry out' (for the persons occupying the sheds), 'the king "was conquered by a thousand *horses*' (for the riders); and it is neces-"sary for the *Sūtra* to mention all these."

Some people reply to this by the assertion that all these are included in the 'similarity of signs' (*Sūtra* 28); because the signification of the *lancer* by the word 'lance' is of the same nature as that of *persons without umbrellas* by the word '*Chatri*' when they are accompanied by some persons *with umbrellas*.

Or, we may meet the above objection by pointing out that it is of secondary (*Gauṇī*) signification that we are considering the bases, and not of Indication (*Lakshaṇā*).

"Is there, then, any difference between Indication and Secondary Signification?"

Certainly, there is; because when a word signifies something, not entirely disconnected from that which is the directly expressed meaning, then we have what is called *Indication;* whereas when the word signifies something (even though it be in no way connected with the expressed meaning), through the similarity of the qualities indicated (by the expressed meaning of the word), then this signification is called 'Gauṇa' or *Secondary.*

Thus then, just as the word, directly expressing the Class, indicates the Individual which is always present in the Class, in the same manner, it is by mere Indication, that the words 'lance,' 'elevated shed' and 'horse' signify the persons connected with them. (And it is not this sort of signification that we are dealing with). What we are dealing with is the case of such sentences as 'The Student is Fire,' where we are not cognisant of any sort of invariable concomitance of the *Student* with the *Fire;* what we are cognisant of in this sentence is that, (1) the word 'Fire' denotes the Class 'Fire'; (2) this Class indicates the qualities of Fire, such as the peculiar colour, brightness, &c.; and (3) the presence of these qualities in the student gives rise, through similarity, to the idea of his being Fire itself. And it is this sort of signification that we find in the case of such sentences as '*yajamānah prastarah,*' &c.; and hence the *Sūtra* has mentioned only the bases of such signification (and not those of Indication).

ADHIKARAṆA (12).

[In the case of the sentence 'yajamānah prastārah' (the grass-bedding is the master of the sacrifice), it is with a view to eulogising the bedding that it is spoken of as the 'master of the sacrifice.']

On this point there are three distinct theories: (1) Both the words being in a form that makes them co-ordinate, one may be taken as the *name* of the other; (2) there being no signs of any of them being a name, and any assumption of such signs involving the assumption of many potentialities in the same word, the word '*prastara*' may be taken as indicating the purposes served by it; and hence with a view to make the sentence serve a distinctly useful purpose, we can take it as laying down the accessory of the sacrifice—*viz.*, that the master of the sacrifice is to be utilised as the *grass-bedding*; or (3) that the sentence being incapable of affording this meaning, we must take it as *praising* the bedding (*prastara*).

THE PŪRVAPAKSHA

as propounded by the upholder of the theory that the sentence is the Injunction of an Accessory—is this:

"The mere fact of the '*yajamāna*' and the '*prastara*' being mention-"ed together cannot point to any *praise* of the one by the other; specially "as it is not possible, even in praising, to use one word in the sense of "another; nor do we find any ground for the application of the word "'*yajamāna*' to the *prastara*, or *vice versa*; and then, for such application "of the word we cannot find any other cause except the indication, by the "word '*prastara*,' of its uses, or *vice versa*; just as we find in the case of "the sentence 'the *Hotṛ* priest is the *Adhvaryu*.' But, in accordance with "the reasonings explained under *Sūtra* XII—ii—23, it is clear that in the "sentence in question, the word '*yajamāna*' is to be taken in its own direct "signification; while the word '*prastara*' is to be taken as indicating such "of its uses as the affording of a place for keeping the *Sruk*, &c.; and hence "the sentence must be taken as laying down an Accessory for the sacrifice "(as that 'the *yajamāna* is to be utilised as the '*prastara*')."

SIDDHĀNTA.

To this we make the following reply: None of the two words can be taken as indicating its uses; because the uses of one being incompatible with the other, there could be no such Injunction (of Accessories). For instance, it is laid down that—'Like the *Ēkakapāla*, the *prastara* is thrown into the fire, with the *Sūktavāka mantra*'; and certainly, if the Master of the sacrifice were to be thus thrown into the fire (in being utilised as the *prastara*), the whole performance of the sacrifice would come to a dead-lock!

For these reasons, we must take the two sentences—'*Yajamanāh, prastarah*' and '*Yajamāna ēkakapālah*' as eulogising the *prastarah* and the *ēkakapālah*,—the former for the sake of justifying its being kept to the north of the Fire, and the latter in justification of the direction for its being offered completely; because these directions are laid down along with the sentences themselves.

Question: "(1) But how can one word be used in the sense of another; and (2) what could be the form of the Praise?"

Reply: At a sacrifice, the Master is the most important personage; and the *prastara* too is such an important object, that it should be placed above the grass (this would be the form of the Praise expressed by the sentence '*Yajamānah prastarah*'); and the sense of that signified by the sentence '*yajamāna ēkakapālah*' is that—the *Āhavanīya* Fire having been eulogised as Heaven, inasmuch as it is the whole of the Master that is carried to the Heavenly regions, the whole of the *ēkakapāla* should be offered into the Heavenly Fire. And these significations of the words are based upon the qualities (possessed by the objects denoted by them).

The Bhāshya puts the question: "*How can a word, not expressive of qualities, denote qualities?*" And this question is based upon the misconception that the words are directly expressive of the qualities; however, what we actually hold is that all the significations of a word are somehow or other connected with its direct denotation; and hence so long as we can keep on the track of the original denotation, we can have no ground for assuming any other denotative potentiality in the word. And in such cases as of the sentence 'Devadatta is a lion,' we can very reasonably make the figurative signification of the word 'lion' based upon its original denotation; as the word 'lion' denotes the *class* 'lion,' this indicates such qualities as those of courage and the like, and the presence of these qualities in Devadatta gives rise to the idea that he is a lion. And when this interpretation is found possible, there can be no reason for assuming the word 'lion' to have another direct signification; (1) as this would make the true signification of this word always doubtful; (2) as such all usage of the word would be jeopardised; (3) and we would be rejecting a well-known meaning, and assuming one never heard of.

Another theory on this subject is this: "All such words as 'lion' "and the like, are directly denotative of the whole aggregate of the "particular Class, its Qualities and its Actions; and as the whole of this "is not applicable to Dēvadatta, some of the qualities and actions denoted "being found in him, the word is applied to him indirectly."

But with regard to this theory we make the following observations:

(1) If the word denoted such an aggregate, it could never directly denote any one part of this aggregate ; as for instance, the word 'hundred' does not directly denote the number 'fifty' ; while, as a matter of fact, we find the word 'lion' being used, when the only idea in the mind is that of the *Class* wholly devoid of the idea of any Actions or Qualities. And the Class, 'lion' is distinctly recognised to be directly denoted by the word, and the word is not recognised as being applied to it only indirectly, as to Dēvadatta, &c., (and this would be inevitable if the word were denotative of the whole aggregate). (2) And further, such a theory would be directly against the conclusion arrived at under the *Adhikaraṇa* on 'Class'—*viz., that the word denotes the Class.* (3) The number of Actions and Qualities being endless, any relationship of the word with each of these would never be comprehended. (4) Even in the case of a single Individual (to say nothing of the whole Class), we find that, at different periods of his life—infancy, youth and old age—his actions and qualities are different ; and certainly no such indefinite actions, &c., could be held to be denoted by any word ; for the simple reason that the word can have no relationship with them. (5) Nor could the fact of certain qualities and actions being possessed in common by certain individuals justify the assumption of these belonging to a certain '*Class*;' because there are many qualities and actions that may be common among various Classes.

Thus then, we must conclude that it is only the Class 'Lion' that could differentiate the lions from all other animals ; and it could not rightly serve as such a differentiator, if it were not denoted by the word 'lion' ; and if the class be admitted to be denoted by the word, then it cannot be accepted as denoting anything else. That is to say, unless the Class 'lion' be denoted by the word 'lion' it would be itself uncognised ; and as such it could not serve to differentiate the qualities and actions (possessed by lions) ; and if it be admitted to be denoted, then the idea of the Class being enough to give us an idea of all Actions and Qualities, there would be no need of assuming any other denotative potency (of the word 'lion,' with reference to these Actions, &c.). And for these reasons, we conclude that if the words were significant of an aggregate of such qualities, actions, &c., they could not, even indirectly, be any one portion of this aggregate.

Some people hold the following theory: "A word is *gauṇa* (*i.e.*, "secondarily applied to an object) when the character of that which "is denoted by the word is imposed upon that object. The sense of "this theory is that a word 'lion' being strictly denotative of a "particular *class* cannot be applied to another object (Dēvadatta), merely "through the presence therein of certain actions and qualities belonging "to that which is denoted by that word. And unless the word 'lion' be "applicable to Dēvadatta, we could not have any such sentence as that "'Dēvadatta is a lion,' which expresses a distinct co-extensiveness "between the lion and Dēvadatta; and the only explanation of the way in "which the word could be applicable to Dēvadatta, lies in the fact that "at times, a certain word imposes the nature of its own denotations upon "another object; and thereby making this latter object denotable by "itself, becomes applicable to it. That is to say, the actions and qualities "of Dēvadatta being found to be similar to those of the lion, the complete "nature of the lion is imposed upon him; and he comes to be recognised "as identical with the lion; and as such the word 'lion,' when applied to "him, does not signify anything other than the lion, which forms its own "original denotation. But this does not mean that Dēvadatta is denoted "by the word 'lion' directly; because, after all, the character of the lion "is only *imposed* upon him; and it is only when the denotation is directly "of the word itself, and there is no *imposition*, that it can be called a "*direct* denotation. And hence our theory is not open to any objection."

In regard to this theory, we make the following remarks: This cannot be, because any such *imposition* is absolutely impossible; for all objects having unique (unmixed) characters of their own, the character of one object could not be imposed upon another, for the purposes of denotation, by any persons not labouring under a gross delusion.

For instance,—(1) when a person, under a delusion, imposes the character of *Water* upon the *Mirage*, and speaks of it as 'water,' then in that case both the speaker and the person addressed comprehend the word 'water' in its direct denotation (though under the spell of the delusion); and in this case the delusory denotation is none other than the direct one (and there is no imposition);—(2) In a case where the speaker knows the *Mirage* to be a *Mirage* and not *Water*, and still he speaks of it as 'water,' with a view to delude the person addressed, who does not know that it is not water, then in the case of the former, inasmuch as he knows that it is not mirage, there can be no imposition of the character of *Water* upon the mirage; while in the case of the latter, what he comprehends under the delusion is, for him, the *Water* itself; and as such, even in his case there is no indirect application of the word 'water,' and hence there can be no Imposition in this case either;—(3) In a case where none of the two is under a delusion (both knowing the *Mirage* to be something other than *Water*), the comprehension that they have is one of mere *similarity* (and no Identity), and hence in this case too there can be no Imposition.

So also in the case of the sentence 'Dēvadatta is a lion,' both the speaker and the person addressed are fully cognisant of the difference between the *man* and the *lion*; and hence none of them can have the power to *impose* the character or identity of the one upon the other. That is to say, just as in the case of the different kinds of taste—Bitter, Sweet, etc.,—that are known to be different from one another, it never happens that any two of them being recognised to be identical, the character of the one is imposed upon the other; exactly in the same manner, among similar objects also, inasmuch as they are always recognised to be different from another, there could be *no imposition;* and certainly in the case of words, there is no cognition that is of any use in its usage, save that of its meaning.

And further, inasmuch as no word is ever used, unless there is a basis for its usage, how could there be any idea, by itself, independently of the object. (That is to say the class 'Lion' is the only basis for the use of the word 'lion;' and this class does not pertain to Dēvadatta; hence in regard to Dēvadatta how could one have any idea of the *lion?* Any such idea would be absolutely baseless. And hence no amount of imposition by the speaker, even if it were possible, could make the word 'lion' applicable to Dēvadatta). And that apart from the object, there is no Idea independently pertaining to itself, we have already shown in the chapter on '*Çūnyavāda*' (*vide* Çloka-vārtika *in loco*).

And again, in the case of all words, the first denotation that they recall to the mind is one that has been known before; and hence just as the word 'lion' would be pronounced, its direct denotation (the lion) would be directly comprehended (as this is the only meaning that is known from beforehand): and then, where could there be any room for Imposition?

That is to say, in all cases, the differentiation of significations into *direct* and *indirect* serves a useful purpose, only in the help that it affords the person addressed to ascertain the true signification of the word (in any sentence) (and it does not suit any purpose of the speaker). And as soon as the word 'lion' has been uttered, the persons addressed directly comprehend it, as not having its denotation imposed upon any other object; and then it is that, finding this direct denotation to be incompatible with its avowed coextensiveness with Dēvadatta, they conclude to take the word 'lion' in its indirect or figurative sense. And in this it is clear that the persons addressed comprehend this figurative meaning only through similarity, without having themselves imposed the character of the lion upon Dēvadatta.

And when we proceed to consider whether this comprehension proceeds from the *word,* or from its *denotation,* it becomes clear, through negative and positive concomitance, as also through the conclusion arrived at in the *Adhikaraṇa* on 'Class,' that it proceeds from the denotation. Because even when the word 'lion' has not been uttered, if we happen to have an idea in our mind of the animal, we at once recognise its similarity in Dēvadatta (if we find him possessed of exceptional courage, etc.); while, on the other hand, if we have no idea of the animal, even if the word 'lion' be uttered, we could have no idea of the similarity (of Dēvadatta to the lion.)

And when, as a matter of fact, there is no *Imposition* in the minds of the persons addressed, it follows that there could be none in that of the speaker; and hence when a man utters the sentence—'Dēvadatta is a lion'—the idea that the persons addressed have is, not that 'he has imposed the character of the lion upon Dēvadatta;' but the working of their minds may be explained as being somewhat to this effect: "What he means by the word *lion* here is an aggregate of certain properties and actions that are concomitant with the class *lion;* it is for the sake of brevity that he does not mention these properties, etc., by all the words that express them individually; specially as there is no single word expressive of all these; and hence in order to give an idea of all these properties, he uses the word 'lion,' because the properties he wishes to express are concomitant with the class *lion* (which is denoted by the word 'lion'); specially as all usage among men is carried on according to the already existing significations of words; and hence no usage can produce new significations of them."

And again, if the indirect or figurative signification of a word be held to be due to the aforesaid *imposition* by the speaker, then, inasmuch as there is no author of the Veda, we could not have any such signification in the case of the words of the Veda.

For these reasons, we conclude that the expression *Gauṇa* (or Secondary, Indirect, or Figurative) *Signification* must be defined as that which is based upon the fact of the existence of certain properties (*guṇa*) (in common between the two objects, Lion and Devadatta); and there can be no other definition.

Objection: "(1) If such be the case, then there could be no such "figurative assertion as that 'this is a *sky-flower*'; because there are no pro- "perties that are concomitant with the *sky-flower*; and (2) without an "Imposition, how could the Bauddha bring forward any arguments "against the Sānkhya theory of Pradhāna being the origin of the creation? "For unless he admits the existence of such a thing as *Pradhāna*, any "denial of it would be absolutely useless; and if he admits of it, such "denial would be a self-contradiction; and the denial could be possible "only by taking the character of the *cause of the world* to be imposed upon "the *Pradhāna.*"

To this we make the folowing reply: As a matter of fact it is to your own theory that the above objections are applicable. Because how can the character of the *sky-flower*, being itself a non-entity, be imposed upon that which does not exist (whose existence is sought to be denied by the assertion 'this is a sky-flower')? Because it is only that which is known to have an existence, and to be possessed of certain properties, with regard to which there can be any question as to whether it is imposed or not imposed.

In the case of such assertions as—'the self is a sky-flower,' 'this theory of yours is a sky-flower,'—where else have you perceived the class *sky-flower*,' which, like the class '*Lion*,' could be imposed (upon the self, &c.), as the class *Lion* is imposed? Hence you must admit that it is the mere form of the sky-flower itself that could constitute the Imposition. And a cognition of this cannot be said to be indirect (or figurative); because the word, 'sky-flower' has no other signification, which could be held to be the principal or direct meaning; specially as the form of the sky-flower, being cognised at first by means of the word, cannot be denied the character of the principal or direct meaning.

It may be asked—'How can a non-entity form the object of direct denotation?' But the same question would also apply to the case of the sky-flower being the object of an indirect signification.

[Nor can the fact of the sky-flower being an object of indirect denotation be held to be based upon the aforesaid Imposition, because] as a matter of fact, that alone can be said to be the indirect meaning, upon which something else is imposed, and not that which is imposed upon another; and in the case in question we find that it is the sky-flower that is imposed (upon the Self, &c.), and as there is no other object (the self being denied by the speaker), it would be imposed upon itself!

To the above the following objection might be raised: "It is the form of such entities as the *jar* and the like that is imposed upon the sky-flower, and as such the fact of its forming the indirect signification cannot be said to be merely an assumption."

But this is not quite true; because in the case of the sky-flower, we have no idea of any positive entity (such as the form of the *jar*, &c.). For as a matter of fact, the meaning of the word 'sky-flower,' that is comprehended on the first occasion of the perception of the relationship (between the two words forming the compound), must also be the one comprehended subsequently. Nor have any such objects as *Hare's horns* ('sky-flower,' &c.) ever before been recognised in the form of positive entities; nor are the sky-flower, &c., ever perceived to have any connection with the comprehension of any other positive entity; and though a distinct relationship is cognised to exist between the significations of the two words ('sky' and 'flower') forming the compound, yet these two significations are not indirect or secondary ones, because they are distinctly recognised as the direct denotations of the words.

Objection: "How then can there be such an assertion as that 'the "hare's horn does not exist,'—if the hare's horn has never before been "perceived as a positive entity? And if it has ever been perceived as a "positive entity, how could there be an absolute negation of it? For just "see—it is only when an object has been found to exist in one place, that "its existence is denied in another; and at one and the same place, no "object is ever recognised as both existing and non-existing. It may be "urged that—'it is for this same reason (that is, for the same reason that "makes the recognition of both the existence and non-existence of an object "in a single place contradictory) that we hold the form of the positive "entity to be imposed upon it.' But this cannot be; because that which is "imposed stands equally in need of having its existence recognised some-"where else (before it can be imposed). Nor can the existence of one "thing bring about the imposition of another; because there can be no "connection between the two. It may be asked—'How is it, then, that the "existence of the barren desert leads to the imposition of the form of "water (in the mirage)?' But the example does not fit in with the case in "question; because the existence of the water has been perceived else-"where. How then, we ask, can there be such an assertion as that 'the "hare's horn does not exist'?"

(1) The first explanation of the sentence given by some people is that the non-existence of the hare's horn having been recognised by the mere utterance of the word itself, all that the expression 'does not exist' does is to describe it once again. (2) Or, the words 'does not exist' point to all kinds of 'negation,' and the words 'Hare's horn' serves to specify this negation (as the most absolute one); and the 'hare's horn' is not specified by the expression 'does not exist'; because the general negation (expressed by the expression 'does not exist') is not incompatible with the particular (absolute) negation (expressed by the word 'hare's horn') [though the particular negation is not absolutely compatible with the general negation]. (3) Or, it may be that when a person has comprehended the meanings of the two words forming the compound, and has also got at the comprehension of the relationship between these two, as indicated by the compound—which is just like the compound '*Rājapurushah*' (the King's man),—if it so happen that he has never known the hare to have no horns,—the sentence 'the hare's horn does not exist' may serve the purpose of pointing out to such a person the fact of there being no connection (between the meanings of the two words forming the compound). (4) Or, it may be that, apart from the compound, the sentence may be taken as pointing out the Hare as the receptacle, and then referring to the horn as perceived in the Cow, &c.,—the expression 'does not exist' denying (without any imposition) the fact of there being any connection between the *horn* (as perceived in the cow) and the *hare*; and then the expression 'hare's horn' serves the purpose of pointing out the same absence of the connection that has been previously comprehended by means of the same word.

(5) Or, lastly, it may be that the apparent contradiction in the assertion may be explained on the ground of the object referred to by the sentence being taken, without any kind of imposition, to be the peculiar flat surface on the hare's head, which has not become hardened and lengthened by the gradually accumulating layers of flesh (like a horn) (and as such it is only a positive entity that is referred to by the sentence) (*like a horn*). As it has been well said that the action that is pointed out by such negations as 'he does not go,' &c., is the same that is expressed in a positive form by the expression 'he says.'

Thus then, words like 'hare's horn,' having in the above-mentioned manner got at their direct denotation, come to be applied indirectly (or figuratively) to any other object which appears in a form other than the generally recognised one. For you, however, the word having no direct signification of its own, any chance of its figurative use is very remote; specially because if the original meaning itself of the word be an indirect one, there can be no further indirect application of it to any other meaning (or object). Because in the sentence 'the student is Fire,' the word 'Fire,' applying to the student only indirectly (or figuratively), cannot apply indirectly to any other object (through the student). This will be explained later on, under the *Sūtra* VI—iii—32.

As for such negations as those of the *Pradhāna* of the Sāṅkhyas and the like, these too cannot be said to be based upon any Imposition; because they may be explained in the following manner: The sentence—'there is no *Pradhāna*' only points out that there is no *Pradhāna*, apart from such causes of the Universe, as the Atoms, Bodies, &c. That is to say, the word '*Pradhāna*' pertains to the Cause of the Universe; and it is such a Pradhāna that is denied by the Bauddha and others, on the ground that there can be no such cause apart from such causes as Atoms (as held by the Naiyāyika), or a series of 'Bodies,' and the like (as held by the Jaina); that is to say, the word '*Pradhāna*' denotes nothing other than these atoms, &c.' Therefore the secondary signification of these words also are based upon their own direct meanings; and as such there can be no incongruity in our theory as regards such relations.

For these reasons, in the case of the sentence '*Yajamānah prastarah*' the *yajamāna*, having been cognised, indicates *the character of fulfilling one's own purpose*; and the *prastara* and the *ēkakapāla* too are found, indirectly, to serve the purposes of the *yajamāna*; and as such being indirectly indicated by the word '*yajamāna*,' through their actions, they come to be taken as praised by means of that word (as shown above).

These explanations also apply to the case of the similarities of *origin*, &c. as shown below.

ADHIKARAṆA (13).

[*In the passage—' āgnirbrāhmaṇah, the word ' āgni ' is meant to be in praise of the Brāhmaṇa, &c., through the similarity of Origin* (*Sūtra* 24).]

The Bhāshya has cited as an instance under this head, the sentence '*āgnēyo brāhmaṇah,*' where the word '*āgnēya*' is said to be in praise of the Brāhmaṇa. But the word '*āgnēya*'—signifying as it does 'one whose Deity is Agni'—is applicable to the Brāhmaṇa directly, and there need not be an indirect signification in this case; because there is no doubt that the Brāhmana has some sort of relationship with Agni; and this is all that is signified by the nominal affix in the word. It is not necessary that it is only an offering that can be related to a Deity; because the offerer of the sacrifice also has some relationship with the Deity; and as such this can very well be spoken of as belonging to him; as the Bhāshya itself says later on: 'The Deity belongs to the sacrificing person also.' And hence this word cannot serve as the proper example in the present connection.

Therefore we must cite as instances such assertions as 'The Brāhmana is Agni;' where the word directly signifying the Fire, indirectly points to the Brāhmana, through the quality of being born from Prajapati's mouth (which is common to Agni and to the Brāhmana).

By the word '*jāti*' here is meant '*janma*' or origin; and though in reality there is no such thing (as the origin or birth of Fire) yet inasmuch as the fact of Agni and Brāhmaṇa having been produced out of Prajapati's mouth has been described in an *Arthavāda* passage, it can serve as the basis for the figurative expression used in the sentence in question.

ADHIKARAṆA (14).

[*In the sentence 'yajamano yūpah' and in 'ādityō yūpah,' the yupa is praised by the words 'yajamāna' and 'āditya' through the similarty of shape* (*Sūtra* 25).]

Objection: "*Sārūpya* or similarity is the basis of all figurative expressions; why then should it be cited as the basis of a particular expression?"

Reply: True it is so; but the 'Sārūpya' or *similarity* meant here is that of *shape*, which is perceptible to the eye. For instance, the *uprightness* and the *brightness* due to the painting, belonging to the sacrificial post (*yūpa*) are visible to the eye, and it is through these properties that it is eulogised by means of the words 'yajamāna' and 'āditya' (the master of the sacrifice and the sun being both upright and bright). Because the sentence in question cannot be taken as laying down the fact of the *yajamāna* being utilised as the sacrificial post; because in that case the *yajamāna* being stuck up in the ground (like the post) and having the animal tethered to him, could not perform the duties of the *yajamāna*; and this would be a most absurd incongruity. As for the Sun, it is absolutely impossible for him to be employed as the post. Even if a certain person, atheistically inclined, would make a wooden image of the Sun (and then employ this image as the post) then too the word 'Sun' would apply to such an image only indirectly; and in that case rather than admit of an indirect signification in an Injuuction, it would be far more reasonable to accept it in an *Arthavāda*.

ADHIKARAṆA (15).

[*In the sentence 'apaçavo vā anyē goçvēbhyah, paçavo goaçvāh'—the word 'apaçu' is an indirect praise of the Cow and the Horse, through mere Praise* (*Sūtra* 26).]

Objection: "It has been shown above that all figurative expressions are based upon *praise;* why then should it be brought in as the basis of a particular figurative expression?"

Reply: True; but in all other cases Praise is the result of the figurative expression, while in the sentence in question it forms its basis, just like the similarity of shape, &c.

"But how can it be so?"

The word '*paçu*' having signified the excellence of the cow and the Horse, the negative compound 'apaçu' indicates the absence of that excellence in all other animals.

As a matter of fact, however, it is not that the form of the '*paçu*' (animal) does not belong to the buffalo, &c.; because any such assertion would be contradicting a fact of ordinary sense-perception; nor can the assertion '*apaçavo vā anyē goçvēbhyah*' (all others besides the cow and the horse are non-animals) be taken as the mere denial of the true functions of the animal, in the buffalo, &c., because such animal-functions have been described in many Vedic passages, as belonging to these also.

Nor can it be held that these sentences could be taken as optional alternatives to the sentence that denied their animal functions. Because there is a distinct difference in the authoritative character of the two declarations; as in the case of the declaration of the functions belonging to the buffalo, &c., the Injunctions already exist; whereas in the case of the other declaration, the Injunction will have to be assumed. And when the use of the word 'non-animal' can be very easily explained as being in praise of the Cow and the Horse, there is no pressing need for assuming any such Injunction; specially as in both cases the abandoning of the direct signification is equally necessary (in the case of the Praise '*paçu*' = excellent, while in the other case, it = performing the functions of the animal); and further, in the case of such an assumption, the sentence '*paçavo goçvāh*' would be a useless repetition. Nor is it quite possible to deny the existence (in the buffalo) of the actions and properties inhering in the class 'animal' (by the word '*apaçu*'); nor too can this word be taken as denying the existence of such properties as are peculiar to the Cow and to the Horse; because in that case too, the assertion would not be of much use;

because this fact is pointed out by the word '*anyē*' in the sentence (and hence the use of '*apaçu*' would be wholly redundant). And it is absolutely necessary that the negative prefix in '*apaçu*' should have a function only when that which is to be negatived (*viz.*, the character of the animal) has been duly comprehended by means of the word after it ('*paçu*'); because there can be no negation, when there is nothing to be negatived.

Nor can there be any use for any other meaning of the word '*apaçu*' than mere *excellence*; and from its connection with the word, 'Cow' and 'Horse,' it is clear that it signifies excellence; although it is also capable of signifying *non-excellence* (of other animals), yet as the context does not stand in need of any mention of *non-excellence*, it must be taken (even if referred to other animals) as *denying the excellence;* but as any such mere denial does not serve a useful purpose, the word must be taken to indicate, through this denial, the superior excellence of others (*viz.*, the Cow and the Horse).

The full signification of the sentence therefore comes to be this: There is no other excellence in other animals, in comparison with the Cow and the Horse; and hence the indirect denial of excellence contained in the word '*apaçu*,' is due to the praise of the Cow and the Horse. And (though it is the denial of the excellence of other animals that is thus found to lead to the praise of the Cow and the Horse, and as such this Praise cannot be said to be the means of the said denial, yet) we speak of the Praise as preceding the denial, because there can be no other reason for the latter. In any other case, however, whenever the *praise* would be found to appear after the *denial*, it would not be spoken of as its *means*.

ADHIKARAṆA (16).

[*In the sentence 'Srshtīrupadadhāti,' the name 'Srshti' is applied to all the Mantras in question on the ground of the word being found in a great number of them* (*Sūtra* 27).]

If on the strength of the verb '*upadadhāti*' we accept the sentence to be an Injunction,—then the great difficulty would be that there are no *bricks*, that, either in *class* or in the properties possessed, are differentiated from other bricks, by the same '*Srshti*'; because any bricks, that may be put into the altar with these *Mantras*, may be called '*Srshti.*' And if the sentence be taken as an Injunction (*i.e.*, if the *Mantras* containing the word '*Srshti*' were enjoined with reference to the *putting up* of the bricks) in general, then the whole process of the *putting up* would be pervaded over by these *Mantras*, and as such there would be absolutely no use for those *Mantras*, which, though not laid down by means of any direct Injunction, are yet employed in the putting up of the bricks, in accordance with their uses pointed out by the expressive power of certain words contained in them and by the context in which they occur. For this reason, inasmuch as all these *Mantras* are found to be applicable to the *putting up*, as pointed out by the contexts in which they occur, the word '*Srshti*' must be taken as pointing to only a few of the *Mantras* to be so employed; and through the peculiar signification of the word '*Srshti*' (as that in which this word is present) the word in the sentence in question must be taken as employed with a view to eulogise all the *Mantras* used at the putting up of the bricks.

To this, some people make the following objection: "The *putting up* "of the bricks being included in the *collecting* of them laid down elsewhere, "and the *Mantras* to be employed in it being duly pointed out by the con-"text, as also by the expressive power of certain words contained in the *Man-"tras* themselves, it could have nothing to do with any *Arthavāda*, appear-"ing apart from itself; because the compatibility of the Arthavāda lies in "the fact of its forming one sentence (or being taken along) with the In-"junction, as we have already shown under *Sūtra* I—ii—42. Nor do we "find any other accessory mentioned, to which the sentence in question "could refer. And thus then, the sentence comes to serve the only purpose "of rejecting (other bricks) (*i.e.*, the meaning of the sentence comes to be "that we should make use of no bricks other than those that are put up "with the particular *Mantras*); and hence the uselessness of the sentence "continues as before; and it is necessary to point out its use."

To this, some people make the following reply: It is the *putting up* that is enjoined by the sentence; and the *Mantra* is referred to only with a view to show the great importance of the *putting up*,—the purport of the sentence being that the *putting up* is so very excellent that it is done with such important *Mantras.* It cannot be urged that this *putting up* is employed in the *collecting* (of the bricks); because mere *collecting* would be accompanied by the mere piling together of the bricks (whereas *putting up* means the arranging of them in a particular order, in making the sacrificial altar). Nor could the *putting up* be said to be of the bricks *collected* together; because, inasmuch as the *putting up* is laid down with reference to the bricks, its injunction would have to be repeated with regard to each individual brick of the collection. And further, even though the *putting up* may be pointed out by the mention of *collecting*, yet it would be necessary to mention it where it has been mentioned, in order to show that the name of '*Ādhvaryava*' belongs to the action; which would show that the *putting up* of all the bricks is to be done by a single person, the *Adhvaryu* priest. While if the *putting up* were left to be inferred from the mention of the *collecting*, there would be no such fixity as to its performer. Nor could all the *Mantras* be employed in the said *putting up*; as some of them do not have any such particular use expressed by any words in themselves; and these could be employed in the *holding* of the bricks also.

Then again, the bricks, directly mentioned in the *Brāhmaṇas*, being utilised in the middle altar (as will be shown later on), and the nature of these bricks being incapable of being ascertained without being connected with the *Mantras* whereby the *putting up* is performed, it becomes necessary, even for the accomplishment of the middle altar, to connect the *Mantras* with the *putting up*. Such being the case, those *Mantras* that appear in the chapter on *Aupānuvākya*, not being capable of any relationship (with any action) without explicit directions, the sentence in question cannot be said to be useless.

Nor is it absolutely necessary that the *Sūtra* should be taken as asserting the character of an *Arthavāda* (to belong to the sentence in question); as all that the *Sūtra* does is to show that, inasmuch as the word '*Sṛshti*' happens to occur in a greater number of the *Mantras* in question, the name is applied to all of them. And hence we cannot very well take the sentence to be an Injunction of the *Sṛshtis* as the materials to be employed.

The Bhāshya, however, only points out that the sentence could not be taken as an Injunction without taking certain words in the figurative sense (which is not allowable in an Injunction), and that for this reason, it must be taken as a descriptive *Arthavāda.* And what this means is that, though the *Mantras* in question are spoken of as one collective whole, as in the sentence 'he hymns by a single hymn,'—yet the distinguishing word '*Sṛshti*' is found only among a few of them, such as the *Anuvākya*, &c.; and hence if the word '*Sṛshti*' were applied to *all* the *Mantras*, it would be abandoning its direct signification, and accepting an indirect one (which is not allowable in an Injunction); and while indirectly indicating the *Mantras* (not containing the word) it would also denote those that do contain it; and this would be a very complicated process. If, however, it is taken as a mere *descriptive eulogy* of the *putting up*, any recourse to indirect or figurative expression cannot be considered undesirable.

ADHIKARAṆA (17).

[*The case of the word prāṇabhṛtah' in the sentence 'prāṇabhrita upadadhāti' is the same as that of the word 'Sṛshti' described above; the only difference being that in this case, this distinguishing word is found in fewer Mantras* (*Sūtra* 28).]

The Objection and the Reply, in the case of the word '*prāṇabhṛtah*' are the same as those in the case of the word '*Sṛshti*'; and the only reason why this is treated of separately is that in this case the word, though found in fewer *Mantras*, is applied to many of them. And as before, so in this case also, the original denotation is not wholly abandoned; and as such this process of indirect Indication is admitted, as it is often found that when the whole is mentioned, it brings about an idea of the part also.

[That is to say, the Indirect signification of a word being defined as one that is based upon the relationship of certain properties indicated by the direct denotation, though, in the cases in question words like '*Sṛshti*' are found to be used figuratively (indirectly), yet, inasmuch as such a word is unable to indicate any properties not connected with itself,—such, for instance, as a *multitude*,—and the multitude extending over all its constituents—even if one of these constituents is left out, the whole multitude becomes left out; and hence the word must be taken as pointing out the taking in of all the constituents. When, however, the figurative expression is differentiated from Indication on the ground of the former altogether neglecting the original meaning while the latter retains a trace of it, the signification of the word '*Sṛshti*' would be of the form of Indication. Thus then], the Çloka quoted should be construed thus: In a case where the word neglects all relationship of its original denotation, and points only to the form of a property of that which is denoted by it directly,—in the case of such a word the only comprehension that it brings about is that of the form of the object defined, and not of the *definer* also (because this forms only the means of the comprehension of the former). While in the case of the words '*Sṛshti*' and the like, the *Sṛshti* (directly denoted by the word) being abandoned by the multitude or collection of *Mantras* indicated by that word, on the ground of some of them containing that word,—inasmuch as the name does not extend over *all the Mantras*, the mere mention of the defining word not giving an idea of the whole *Multitude*,—it necessarily takes within itself an idea of the defining word '*Sṛshti*' also; and hence in this case the cognition of both the defining word and the defined is purely verbal.

ADHIKARAṆA (18).

[*Treating of the fact of all doubts being removed by subsequent passages.*]

Sūtra **(28): In all doubtful cases, a definite conclusion is arrived at by the help of subsequent passages.**

The Injunction and the Eulogy are always held to pertain to the same object; and hence if there is any doubt with regard to one of these, the real fact is ascertained by the help of the other (*e.g.*, in the case of the Injunction 'the pebbles should be wetted,' there arises a doubt as to the material with which the *wetting* is to be done; and this is set aside by the concluding 'sentence (Butter only is glory').

Question: "What could be the ground for any such doubt? Some people "hold that the ground lies in the fact of the Injunction refering to the object "Butter in its generic form. But this is not quite a correct answer; because "in that case the Injunction would bring about a definite idea with regard "to the generic forms, (and there could be no doubt). It may be asked— "'how can there be any idea of the generic forms of objects, without any "specifications?' But to this we reply that such an idea would be exactly "like what we have in the case of Butter; that is to say, in the case of Butter "also, there may be a doubt as to whether it is fresh or stale, produced out "of the milk of the cow, or from that of the buffalo; and just as in this "case, without any specification, we have have an idea of Butter in general, "and there is no doubt in our minds, so exactly in the same manner,—in "the sentence—'the pebbles should be wetted......Butter is glory itself'— "all doubts with regard to the word 'butter' ceases, by taking it to denote all "viscous liquids that can be utilised in the wetting of the pebbles.

"With a view to these arguments others hold that the doubt arises on "account of the mention, in the subsequent *Arthavāda* of a particular "material in the shape of Butter. But even this is not quite correct; be-'cause such a specification would be all the more a reason for arriving at a "definite conclusion; for instance, there is no doubt in our minds, on hear-"ing the sentence, 'bring the cow, the white one.'"

But this Analogy does not quite apply to the case in question; because if the specification were contained in the Injunction itself (as it is in the instance you have cited) then there could be no doubt in the mind of any person; but if, in the instance you have cited, the specification were contained in a subsequent *Arthavāda* passage (as there is in the case in question), the chance of doubt would be as great in this as in the sentence in question.

That is to say, if the sentence were in the form—"the pebbles should be wetted by butter"—then there would be no room for any doubt; on the other hand, if the sentence you have cited were in the form of the sentence in question—as "bring the cow......the white one is excellent,"—then there would certainly be a ground for doubt; and then this would also form a fit object of the present discussion. Hence, inasmuch as in the case of the sentence in question, the generic object is mentioned in one place, while the specific one is mentioned in another, this cannot but give rise to a doubt.

On account of this doubt, some people hold that the Injunctive sentence is something quite apart from the *Arthavāda* sentence; and in support of this they bring forward the following arguments:—

"If both of them formed a single sentence, it would end with the "pointing out of the specific object (Butter); and as such the sentence as a "whole bringing about the idea of this particular object, there would be no "room for any doubt. If, however, they are taken as two distinct sentences, "then one being found to point out the generic object (any liquid), "while the other speaks of a specific object.(Butter), it is only natural that "there should be a doubt. Though it has been explained above that the "*Arthavāda* forms a single sentence with the Injunction,—yet this only "refers to the subsequent relationship of the two, which is just like the relationship of the Primary sentence with the Subsidiary sentences; for "instance, it is only after the sentences have only ended with the signification of their own meanings, that they are joined together into one (complete) sentence, in accordance with their respective primary or subsidiary "character."

But this theory does not appear quite reasonable, because those individual collections of words, which serve to signify things that are of use in the performance of certain actions, can very rightly be taken as separate sentences. As for the *Arthavāda* passage, however, we find that before it has been coupled with an Injunction, it remains absolutely useless; and hence it cannot be admitted to be joined to the Injunction, before it has signified its own meaning. If the two were totally independent of each other, there could he no doubt at all; as one would rest in the signification of the generic, as the other in that of the specific object; and whichever thing is mentioned in any sentence it is comprehended without any doubt, by means of that sentence.

It may be urged that—"the Injunction resting in the generic object "could be subsequently specified, exactly like a *Mantra*, which is at first "comprehended in its general bearing, and then subsequently comes to be "recognised in its specific bearings (on particular sacrifices)." But in that case the subject would become included in the *Adhikaraṇa* treating of

Mantras, and its mention on the present occasion would be a useless repetition.

Thus then, it is only when they are taken as forming the two parts of a single sentence, that the beginning of the sentence being found to refer to the generic object, and the end to the specific object, there would be an apparent contradiction; but it is a recognised fact that the two must refer to the same object; and hence the question very naturally arises as to the signification of which part of the sentence is to be modified in accordance with that of the other.

The Bhāshya puts the question—'Which is the more reasonable?" And the sense of this is that the direct signification is the more reasonable, and not the indirect Indication.

And the doubt being thus established, we have the following—

PŪRVAPAKSHA.

"Inasmuch as *Arthavādas* are subsidiary to the Injunction, and are "merely descriptive, it is in them that we can have figurative expressions; "the Injunction, on the other hand, being the principal factor, we can have "none in it; specially as at the time that the Injunction appears, there has ap-"peared no *Arthavāda*, on account of the contradiction of which any word in "the Injunction could be taken figuratively.

"That is to say, that which is enjoined is praised; and *vice versa*; and "the Injunction, referring to something that has not been got at before, "cannot be separated from the direct denotation of its words. If the "sentence had begun with the *Arthavāda*—*i.e.*, if we had it in the form "'Butter verily is glory,...the pebbles should be wetted'—then in considera-"tion of the priority of the comprehension of the meaning of the *Arthavāda* "we might perhaps make the signification of the Injunction subservient to "it; but as a matter of fact the sentence begins with the Injunction—'the "pebbles should be wetted';—and hence the generic object having been pre-"viously signified by the Injunction, if the *Arthavāda* be found to be unable to "apply to it, it would be absolutely useless; and as such the *Arthavāda* can "never be independent of the Injunction. While, as for the object of the "Injunction, it is quite capable of independent existence; and as such it "can never be made subservient to the *Artkavāda*; whereas the *Arthavāda* "cannot but be subservient to the Injunction. And further, the specific "object (Butter) can always indicate its concomitant generic object (li-"quid in general), but the *generic* not being always accompanied by any par-"ticular specific object, it could never indicate this latter. And hence we "conclude that the word 'butter' in the *Arthavāda* signifies all oily liquids "in general.

"And again, the Injunction speaking of the general object, could apply "to the Butter, only with the help of the *Arthavāda*; whereas it would refer to all oily substances in general, without any help of the *Arthavāda* "(and hence it is the latter view that is the more reasonable of the two). "As for instance, even when the *Soma* is held up with the Mantra sacred to "Rudra, it is not offered to Rudra alone; because the Soma for other Deities "is capable of being held without a *Mantra;* in the same manner, the "Injunction could point to oil, fat and other such substances, without the "help of the *Arthavāda*. And again, with regard to that fact with reference "to which we find a Praise, the Injunction loses all its persuasive power; "whereas in that which is not praised, its persuasive faculty remains "unimpeded.

"For these reasons, we conclude that the word 'Butter' in the *Arthavāda* "must be taken as signifying all oily substances."

SIDDHANTA.

To all this we make the following reply: The functioning of the Injunction is not complete until it has been made attractive (by means of the *Arthavāda*); hence finding the praise applied to the Butter, we infer the Injunction also to apply to the same. Though it is true that at the outset the Injunction refers to even such substances as oil, fat and the like, yet on account of the Praise, it is concluded that it refers to the Butter alone, and not to oil and fat, which two therefore are not to be used in the wetting of the pebbles. Because with reference to oil and fat the persuasive power of the Injunction will have to be assumed, while with reference to the Butter, that power is already present (in the *Arthavāda*). And while this persuasive power already exists, if we were to assume another, syntactical split would be the inevitable result; and while accepting the persuasion to rest in the Butter, if we were to assume another persuasion with regard to oil and fat, the Injunction would have two different forms, and there would be a split of the sentence. And hence we conclude that Oil, Fat, &c., cannot even form the objects of the Injunction.

Even though the word in the Injunction be a generic one, that would make no difference; because any wetting by a generic *entity* being impossible, there is a need of the mention of a particular entity; and as the only such entity that is mentioned is the Butter, spoken of in the concluding sentence, we naturally infer the generic word in the Injunction to refer to it. And even if the Butter form the generic signification of the word in question, there would be nothing incongruous in the rejecting of oil, &c.,—none of which are expressed by any word—through the direct denotation of the word. All that this does is to remove the doubt; and in this it does not contradict the evidence of any means of right notion.

Then again, in the case in question it is the mere action of *wetting* that is enjoined, and not the Material (with which the wetting is to be done). And the Action could indicate any and every material, if there were no Vedic passage pointing to any one particular material. In the case in question, however, we find a distinct *Arthavāda* in connection with Butter; and hence when the generic form of the Injunction makes it necessary for us to assume a definite particular material, which is not mentioned in the Injunction itself,—there can be no ground for assuming any other save that which is eulogised in the *Arthavāda*; and hence we conclude the Injunction to mean that the pebbles are to be wetted with butter. And though there might be certain delusive notions of Oil, Fat, &c., yet inasmuch as there is no basis for these, no harm is done in rejecting them altogether.

And further, if we accepted the Injunction to refer to oil, &c., there would be a threefold Indication: *viz.* (1) the Action would indicate the Material, (2) the Material in general would indicate the particular Material, and (3) the word 'Butter' would indicate the generic entity.

Hence we conclude that it is the using of the Butter only that is supported by evidence.

Other commentators have cited certain *Mantras* also as objects included under the present *Adhikaraṇa.* But in that case, the *Mantras* having been treated of here, what would be left for being considered in the closing *Adhikaraṇa* of the sixth Adhyāya.

ADHIKARAṆA (19).

[*The indefinite is defined by the help of the peculiar potentialities of the Injunction.*]

S̄utra (30): Or, it is by means of the potency; since this forms a part (of the word).

In a doubtful case, where there is no subsequent sentence to help us, the real fact is ascertained by means of that potency which forms part of the Injunction.

For instance, in the case of bowing before a god with a view to propitiating him, the word '*añjali*' denotes the two hands joined together flatly, palm to palm; whereas in such sentences as 'one should not drink water with the *añjali*,' the same word denotes the two hands joined together in such a way as to appear like an elongated cup. And then, coming across the Injunction of *Saktuhoma*, wherein the flour is laid down as to be offered by the '*añjali*,' there is a doubt as to the way in which the two hands should be joined together; and there being no subsequent sentence helping to clear the doubt, we conclude the word to signify the cup-like shape, because no other shape could serve the purpose of making the offering.

Objection: "Such being the case, according to this rule, inasmuch as " we have a subsequent sentence in the form 'one should do what he can,' " it would seem that even the blind are entitled to the performance " of sacrifices, though apparently not to the looking into the butter, &c."

Reply: This could not be, because there is no doubt in the matter; what we have said above is only with a view to the removal of doubts; and there is no doubt with regard to any persons being entitled to sacrifices; specially as the subsequent sentence referred to is in the form—'one should perform the sacrifice *with all its accessories* in the best way he can;' and we actually find that there are many performers of these complete sacrifices, in the person of people with eyes intact; and hence there is no *Apparent Inconsistency* in the Injunction of the Action (which could serve as a ground for assuming the blind to be entitled to its performance). It is only in the case of the Injunctions of those actions that are laid down as to be performed throughout one's life, that after a person has once begun it, if he happen to become blind, he must continue it; and the leaving off of those details which his new conditions will have made impossible, would not vitiate the performance of the sacrifice as a whole;

and this we shall readily admit. Hence it follows that so long as the Injunction has not reached its true position, whatever is assumed (with a view to accomplish it) has a Vedic authority; after however the Injunction has been fully established, if anything happens to be assumed, it would have no authority, as originating from a human agent. Specially as the purposes of the subsequent sentence are served, in this case, by the peculiar potency (of the Injunction itself).

It is with a view to this that it has been said—just as the text of the *Smṛtis* is a means of the comprehension of their meaning, so also is their peculiar potency (or expressiveness). And it is for this reason that the details that are signified by such potencies are not mentioned directly if the Veda, which makes direct mention of only a thousandth part of it.

Having entered into the impregnable Fortress of Dharma,—which has many inlets to it in the shape of *Mantras*, Injunctions and *Arthavādas*, wherein the *Smṛtis* take the place of weapons, and which is protected on all sides by the various branches of the Veda,—the author now proceeds to consider the whole subject of the meaning of Vedic texts.

End of the Fourth Pāda *of the First Adhyāya.*

Here Ends Adhyāya I.

ADHYAYA II.

Pāda I.

The Introductory *Vārtika*.

In the opening passage, the Bhāshya points out the connection between the two Adhyāyas—First and Second.

"But at the very outset, we meet with the sentence—'In the First "Adhyāya, the *definition of Pramānas* has been given.' This is not "quite correct; because as a matter of fact, the author of the "*Sūtra* has not given any definition of *Pramānas*. For that is called "a *definition* which serves to differentiate a certain object from others "similar to it; and we find that the *Sūtras* have not been any such "definition of Sense-perception and the other *Pramānas*. Then again, "Inference and the rest have not even been mentioned in the *Sūtras*; "as for Sense-perception, that too has been mentioned in the *Sūtra*, only "as not being a means of knowing *Dharma;* and not as something to be defined. "Even Verbal Authority has not, in the First Adhyāya, been defined as a "*Pramāṇa;* in fact it is only in the present *Adhikaraṇa*, that it is going "to be defined as such. Though it is true that the author of the *Vṛtti* "has supplied us with the definitions of all the *Pramāṇas*, yet this fact "cannot justify us in speaking of such definition as forming the 'sub-"ject-matter of the First Adhyāya'; for the simple reason that those de-"finitions do not form the subject of the *Sūtras*. How too, could it be "possible for the *Sūtras* to lose all their force in regard to a subject "totally different from their own subject-matter?

"Secondly, the author of the *Vṛtti* too has spoken of the six "*Pramāṇas*, only as not forming the real objects of enquiry (on the ground "of their well-known character); and as such, even on the strength of "the Vṛtti, a definition of the six Pramāṇas cannot be spoken of as the "subject-matter of the Adhyāya. That is to say, the Vṛtti having spoken "of them only as not forming the objects of enquiry, any definition of "these cannot rightly be spoken of as forming the real subject-matter "of the Adhyāya."

In view of these reasons, the *Bhāshya* should be taken in reference to what has gone in the First Adhyāya. Thus then, the expression '*Pramāṇa-lakshaṇam*' (Definition of *Pramāṇas*) must be taken as = '*codanālakshaṇam*' (Definition of *Codanā*); as the treatment of Injunctions, &c., as occurring in the First Adhyāya, only serves the purpose of establishing the authority of *Codanā*.

That is to say, the whole of the First *Pāda* of the First *Adhyāya* forms part of the Second Sūtra, wherein *Dharma* has been spoken of as having the *Codanā* for its *lakshaṇa* (means of knowing). The word '*lakshaṇa* having its significance thus pointed out, the word '*Pramāṇa*' occurring (in the Bhāshya) along with it, must be taken as 'that which is known,'—*viz.*, *Dharma*; for though the word '*Pramāṇa*' (taken in the sense '*pramīyatē yat*') would refer *to all that is known*, yet in the present instance, it cannot but be taken as referring particularly to *Dharma*; as this is what forms the subject-matter of the enquiry.

Or, the word 'pramāṇa' might also be taken in the sense of the *means* (of knowing); then too, it is the '*lakshaṇa*' of this that has been described in the First Adhyāya. Though it is true that the First Adhyāya does not contain the definitions of all the *means of knowing*, yet, inasmuch as it has defined the *means of knowing Dharma* as '*Codanā*,' the Bhāshya speaks of it as having supplied the definition of *Pramāṇa*. For it is not necessary that in order to be a definition of *Pramāṇa*, it should speak of *Pramāṇas* in all their bearings; because the number of the particular forms of *Pramāṇas* being endless, there could be no definition of *Pramāṇas* at all. And as a matter of fact, the particular form of *Pramāṇa* meant is distinctly mentioned in *Sūtra* I–i–5, which points to a particular scripture (to the exclusion of all others).

Or, the Bhāshya may be taken as summing up the subject-matter of the First Adhyāya, in view of the fact that the Adhyāya contains a full *definition* of the particular *Pramāṇa* that was laid down as the object of enquiry—*viz.*, *Codanā*. Hence, even though the *sūtra* has not pointed out the forms of Injunctions, *Mantras or Arthavadas*, yet it has fully established the fact of all these serving useful purposes in connection with *Dharma*, with regard to which, therefore, they may be rightly accepted as *Pramāṇa*; and it was only for want of a proper opportunity that the specific forms of these have not been pointed out in detail.

Then (in the subsequent *Pādas*, it has been shown that) the character of *Pramāṇa*, as belonging to the *Smṛtis* depends upon the fact of these having their basis in the Veda; that of *Names* depends upon the fact of their being included in *Codanā* itself; while that of Supplementary Explanations and Indirect Implication, depends upon the fact of these serving the useful purpose of settling doubtful points. And thus there is nothing incongruous in speaking of the whole Adhyāya as treating of the *lakshaṇa* of *Pramāṇas*.

Then, says the Bhāshya—*This fact should not be lost sight of*; that is to say, it is only when one bears in mind the fact of the *Veda* being the *Pramāṇa* for *Dharma*, that he can bear the discussions with regard to the difference, &c., among sacrifices, such as those introduced in *Sūtra* II—ii—2; otherwise one would always hold that the Veda is absolutely useless.

[The *Bhāshya* says: *We next proceed to consider the Pramāṇas and the*

Subsidiaries, &c., &c., and on this an objection is raised] "As a matter of "fact we find that the consideration of the Primary and Subsidiary "character of actions is contained in Adhyāyas III & IV; why then "should this be spoken of in connection with the present Adhyāya?"

To this some people offer the explanation that the present Adhyāya treats of the Primary and Subsidiary characters, as subsisting between Substances and Actions; while the subsequent Adhyāyas treat of that subsisting between Action and Action; and as such there is no repetition.

But this explanation is not quite correct; because in the Fourth Adhyāya, under *Sūtra* IV—iii—1, we find all of these—Substances, &c.,—distinctly mentioned. Consequently, to the above objection, we make the following reply: What is explained in the present *Adhyāya* is that one Action is known to be different from another on account of the two being mentioned by different words; and it is in the wake of this difference that we have an explanation of the difference among the *Apūrvas* (resulting from the Actions); and lastly, it is for the purpose of ascertaining which is the Action that brings about the *Apūrva*, that we have the consideration of the fact of Actions having the character of the Primary or the Subsidiary.

That is to say, (1) the difference among Actions is the natural (direct) subject-matter of the *Adhyāya*; and the mention of the non-difference among certain actions is only a denial of the aforesaid difference. (2) And with a view to establish the difference and non-difference of Actions, we have an explanation of the difference and non-difference of their *Apūrvas*. (3) Thus then, so far, it would seem that for each distinct Action there is a distinct *Apūrva*; and here comes in the use of the consideration—as contained in Adhikaraṇa III—of the Primary and Subsidiary character of Actions, which serves to set aside the former misconception with regard to *Apūrvas* (inasmuch as it shows that it is only the Primary Action that has a distinct *Apūrva* of its own). For instance, even in the case of the sentences '*Vrīhīn prokshati*' and '*Vrīhīn avahanti*,' though the words '*avahantī*' and '*prokshotī*' are different, and as such though the true Actions are distinctly cognised to be different, yet inasmuch as these Actions are found to have their sole end in the visible effects (of the preparation of rice and its cleaning), we conclude that they cannot bring about any *Apūrva* (transcendental result). As for the *Apūrva* that is held to follow from the restriction of the method of preparing the rice, to *threshing* alone, it does not result from an *Action*, and as such is of no consequence in the present context. Hence we find that it is only when certain Actions have a distinctly primary character with reference to the substance, &c., that they are cognised as leading to distinct *Apūrvas*, and as such being totally distinct Actions. And it is for the due differentiation of such primary and subsidiary character, that the *Sūtra* (in Adhyāyas III & IV) will supply us with full explanations of such character; and it is an exception to these explanations that are delineated in the two *Adhikaraṇas* contained in *Sūtras* II—i—9, and II—i—13.

Thus then, the two characters of Verbs having been pointed out, a third has to be shown in the shape of 'Denotativeness'; and in connection with this, we have a consideration of the character of *Mantras*; and then follow the definition, &c., of these; and thus these definitions, &c., treated of to the very end of the *Pāda*, are indirectly connected with the main subject. Then, having spoken of the difference among Actions, as based upon the *difference of words*, and *repetition* (of Injunctions), the *Sūtra* will point out, under the Adhikaraṇa on '*Paurṇamāsya*' (II—ii—3 *et seq.*), an exception to the fact of 'Repetitions' being a ground of difference; because in the particular case in question the frequent repetitions are taken only as explanatory to the whole Context. Then as an exception to this exception, we have the *Adhikaraṇas* in *Sūtras* II—ii—9 to 20. Then the *Sūtra* proceeds to point out the difference among Actions as based upon differences of *Number*, *Name* and *Properties*; and the treatment of the difference of properties goes on till the commencement of the treatment of the differences of *Context*; and this continues till the beginning of the *Adhikaraṇa* treating of the differences of the *Branches* or Rescensions of the Vedas. And herein is also contained a denial of any other ground of difference among Actions, save the six, treated of above.

Thus then, the whole subject-matter of the Adhyāya on Differences is taken up in the setting aside of objections to the fact of the differences of Actions being based upon the difference of Name, Repetition, difference of Properties, and difference of Context. And it is necessary to explain this fact in detail; because such ascertainment of difference is absolutely necessary in the due knowledge of the relationship of subserviency between Actions; and as for other facts, the present is no opportunity for any mention of these.

Thus alone can the connection of the Adhyāya be shown. Because (1) the relationship between the Primary and the Subsidiary, &c., is dependent upon a due ascertainment of differences among Actions; (2) it is only when the Action has been duly cognised that there can be any question as to a person being entitled to its performance; and (3) it is only when the Injunctions have been duly comprehended that there can be a transference of the properties of one Action to another.

That is to say, until the Means of knowledge has been duly defined, there can be no consideration of the meaning of the Veda; and as such no discussion as to the *marks of differences among Actions* (treated of in Adh. II) can be introduced; and inasmuch as it is only in the case of Actions that have been found to be different, that there can be any idea either of *relationship of the Primary and the Subsidiary* (Adh. III), or of their usefulness or otherwise (Adh. IV), or of the *order* of their performance (Adh. V),—none of these discussions could be raised, until we had thoroughly considered the marks of differences among Actions; so too, it is only when the character of the Action has been fully cognised that there can be any consideration of the question as to whether a certain person is entitled to its performance or not (Adh. VI); and thus we find that this last question stands in need of all the five foregoing *Adhyāyas*. In the same manner, the Adhyayas VII—XII, treating as they do of the *Transference* of Properties, presuppose a full knowledge of all Injunctions; and as such the whole of this latter half of the *sūtras* is found to be dependent upon the whole of the former half.

And thus it is clear that after the consideration of the Pramāṇa, next comes that of the marks of difference, a treatment of which is therefore begun in Adh. II.

Says the Bhāshya: *Shaḍvidhah karmabhēdah, çabdāntaram*, &c., &c But inasmuch as those that are enumerated are not *differences of Action* (*karmabhēda*), (1) this word should be taken as meaning the 'grounds of such difference.' Though in accordance with the order observed in the forthcoming *Sūtras*, '*nāmadhēya*' should have been mentioned just after '*sañjñā*,' yet, on account of the fact of its being of the least importance, it is mentioned last. (2) Or the word '*iti*' may be taken as indicating the reason, the construction of the sentence being—'*shaḍvidhah karmabheda iti;*' *i.e.*, the difference of Actions is of six kinds, *as due to the following causes.* (3) Or, the word '*bhēda*' may be taken in the Instrumental sense ('*bhidyatē' nēna*) and thereby signifying the *means of differentiation of Actions*, the word '*karmabhedāh*' could be directly taken along with '*çabdāntaram*,' &c. That '*Sañjñā*' and '*Çabdāntara*,' and '*Saṅkhya*' and '*Guṇa*,' are not repetitions, we shall explain later on.

Each of these six treating of altogether different objects, there can be no question as to their comparative authoritativeness, as there is among 'Direct Assertion,' 'Indirect Implication,' &c. Therefore it is the explanation of Difference alone that forms the main subject of the present Adhyāya; all other discussions are only meant to be either Introductory or Supplementary; as that discussion which helps the accomplishment of the main discussion is said to be 'Introductory;' while those that follow from the main discussion are known as 'Supplementary.'

For instance, this following Adhikaraṇa will be introductory to the main discussion of the Adhyaya, because it treats of the difference among *Apūrvas*, which establishes that among the Actions.

ADHIKARAṆA (1).

The question to be treated of in this Adhikaraṇa thus comes to be this—*which is the word (in an Injunction) which, being related to the result, would point out the difference or non-difference among Apūrvas?*

If the sentence or its meaning were one complete whole by itself (in the shape of *Sphota*), there would be no relevancy to the question (raised in the Bhāshya) —*does each word signify Dharma?* It is for this reason that the Bhāshya has added—*In a sentence words have significations.*

But against this question, there is yet another objection: "*Dharma* "has been declared to be capable of being known by means of the *Codanā* "alone; then inasmuch as the *Codanā* is always in the form of a sentence, "how can there be any question as to *Dharma* being signified by each of the "words? That is to say, if *Dharma* were directly denotable by words, "then alone could there be any question as to whether or not it is signified by "each word. As a matter of fact, however, *Dharma* (as constituting the "meaning of the sentence) is only indirectly indicatable; and as such "there is no room for any such question as put in the Bhāshya."

To this the following reply is given: On account of its relationship to the Result, *Dharma* cannot but be recognised as denoted by the word; and hence it is only natural that there should be an enquiry as to whether it is denoted by any one word or by all the words (in the Injunctive sentence).

And then again, what is considered here is, not whether what is known as 'Dharma' is denoted by each of the words, but whether that which is denoted by each of the words comes to be *Dharma*, when cognised in the shape of the denotation of the Sentence, comprehended after its connection with the Result has been perceived; or that it is the meaning of a single word that, when aided by those of the other words, comes to be recognised as *Dharma*. It is only in accordance with this last alternative that all the words in the sentence can be found to be signifying the fact of a single Action being *Dharma*; specially as the character of *Dharma* is held to belong to that alone which is the direct means to the accomplishment of the Result. There is no single thing which is denoted by all the words; and as such all the words cannot be accepted to be denotative of the *Dharma*. It is only that word which is found to be related to the word signifying the Result, that is taken to be expressive of *Dharma*, the direct means of the particular *Apūrva* (bringing about that Result).

ADHIKARAṆA (A).

[*The Apūrva follows from that which is directly connected with the result.*]

Thus then, the question resolves itself into this form—Are all the words connected with the Result, or only one of them? And on this, we have the following

PŪRVAPAKSHA (A).

"Each one of the words is connected with the Result; because, inas-"much as a uniform relationship is possible only with the principal factor "in a sentence,—and as it is the Result that is the principal factor,—each "one of the words must be taken as uniformly related to it. If we could "perceive any difference among the words, whereby we could ascertain "that one of them, and not the rest, is related to the Result, then we "could accept the theory that only one word is so related; so long, how-"ever, as we are not cognisant of any such difference, we cannot but "admit all the words to be related to it. If only one word were held to "be connected with the Result, and all other words to be connected with "that word, then, in accordance with the *Vājapēyādhikaraṇa* (Sūtras V—ii "—1 *et. seq.*), that which would be denoted by that one word would, with "reference to the Result, have the threefold position of the Predicate, the "Injunction and the Subsidiary; while with reference to the other (namely "the material of the sacrifice) it would have the contrary threefold "character of the Subject, the Description and the Primary; and this "contrariety of character would lead to a split of the sentence. On the "other hand, when all the words are taken as Predicates with reference to "the Result, then there is an uniformity of character, which makes a "simultaneous relationship of the words possible. And as a rule, every-"thing comes to be connected with the principal factor, whenever this is "possible,—and hence the denotations of all the words, being related to the "Result, must be admitted to be *Dharma*. And as to whether each of the "*Dharmas* thus signified fulfils the full Result, as in the case of com-"munistic sacrifices (where the complete Result accrues to each sacrificer), "or all of them conjointly accomplish it,—and as to whether they are to "be employed as optional alternatives or all conjointly—, on these matters "we can accept any theory that we choose. But as a matter of fact, the "most reasonable theory is that each of them fulfils the Result in its "entirety; because the Result being an immense one, it cannot be men-"tioned by a single word, and because each of them is distinctly cognised "as being capable by itself of accomplishing the Result. Or, in accord-"ance with the conclusion arrived at under *Sūtras* III—i—12 *et. seq.*, the "whole thing being mentioned by the single sentence, the Result may be "held to be accomplished by all the *Dharmas* taken collectively. Or "again, the Result being fulfilled by a single *Dharma* it cannot have any-"thing to do with any others; and as such, the *Dharmas* must be taken "as optional alternatives."

SIDDHĀNTA (A).

To all this we make the following reply: The *Apūrva* is held to follow only from that which is directly connected with the Result; and as this is accomplished by the relationship of the denotation of a single word, there can be no ground for postulating the relationship of any others.

That is to say, if the sole purpose of the sentence rested solely in the relationship of the Result, then, it might have been possible for the denotations of all the words to be connected with it. As a matter of fact, however, the mere relationship of the Result not being enough for establishing the full character of Dharma, it becomes necessary to assume an intermediate *Apūrva.* And the only ground for such an assumption is the Apparent Inconsistency of the mention of the Result, &c. Hence when this inconsistency of the sentence has been removed by the assumption of the *Apūrva*, there is no ground for the assumption of any other unseen agency. And even he who would assume many *Apūrvas* must assume one *Apūrva;* and no sooner has this one *Apūrva* been assumed than the aforesaid Inconsistency disappears, and leaves no ground for the assumption of any other *Apūrva.* For these reasons, there can be only one thing that can be related to the Result; and it is from this one thing that the *Apūrva* proceeds; while all else only helps the action leading to the Result. Nor is there any contradiction (in the fact of the Action being signified by the single word of the Verb, while the Instrumental ending is found in the word signifying the material); because the contradiction can be explained away on the ground of the word in the Instrumental being taken as the *name* of the particular Action (*i.e.*, the sentence '*Çyēnēna yajēta*' may be taken as 'one should perform the sacrifice called *Çyēna*'); or when no other explanation is possible, the contradiction can be explained by having recourse to possessive indication; *e. g.*, the sentence '*daçāpavitrēṇa graham sammārshti*' is taken as 'one should purify the cup by a washing with the *daçāpavitra*.' Or, the meaning of the verb may be taken as referring to its Instrument, through the factor of the Result indicated indirectly.

ADHIKARAṆA (B).

[*The Apūrva is pointed out either by the Noun or by the Verb.*]

Now there arises the question—the denotation of which one of the words should be connected with the Result? And the

PŪRVAPAKSHA (B)

is that, "as the assumption of unseen agencies is obviated by connecting the Result with any one of the words, there can be no fixed rule as to any one of these being so connected."

SIDDHĀNTA (B).

And to this we make the following reply: That which is connected with the Result is the *Principal* factor; while that which is related to the Principal factor is the *Subsidiary;* and hence the character of both the Primary and the Subsidiary cannot belong to one and the same thing. That is to say, in a single sentence, one and the same word cannot, at one time, be the Principal, on account of its direct relationship to the Result, and at another time, the Subsidiary, on account of its being an aid to that which is directly related to the Result; because the character of the Principal and the Subsidiary is not variable.

For these reasons, the *Apūrva* must be always admitted to be pointed out either by the Verb or by the Noun.

ADHIKARAṆA (C).

[*Bhāvārthādhikaraṇa.—All Verbs are indicative of the Bhāvanā, and the Apūrvā proceeds from this*].

The Bhāshya here raises the question—' *What is a* ' *Bhāva* ' *and what are* ' *Bhāva-çabdas ?* ' " This question emanates from one who holds that in a sentence, the predominant factor in the denotation of such verbs as 'sacrifices' and the like, is that which is signified by the affixes in them; and that inasmuch as the conjugational affixes denote the Agent, the Verb cannot but be accepted as denoting either the *sacrifice as qualified by the agent,* or conversely, *the agent as qualified by the sacrifice.* Though a single question would also imply the other, yet, as without having quoted the words '*yajana,*' &c., the Bhāshya has quoted the words '*yajati,*' &c., as denoting the *Bhāva,*—it is clear that it is something superphysical that is meant by the word '*Bhāvaçabda;*' and as such none of the two questions is redundant.

To the questions thus put forward in the Bhāshya, the upholder of the *Siddhānta* theory replies by interpreting the word '*Bhāva*' as *Bhū + ṇic + ac = Bhāvanā,* and then by explaining the denotation of the verb to be purely concomitant with such *Bhāvanā,* and denying the fact of the verb denoting the Agent; and it is with all this in view that he quotes the verbs '*Yajati,*' &c.

The opponent however thinks that the denotation in question does not belong to anything besides the root '*Bhu*' with the causal affix, and that the verbal affix can have nothing to do with the *Bhāvanā;* specially as this latter is expressed by an altogether different root; he further thinks that though there may be other roots that might denote the *Bhāvanā*, yet there are no affixes denotative of it; and that as a matter of fact, even the roots, denoting as they do the sacrifice, &c., are not capable of denoting the *Bhāvanā;* with all this in view, the opponent has urged the argument: "*The words* '*yāga,*' '*homa,*' &c."

To these arguments we make the following reply: All verbs always clearly signify the *Bhāvanā* as interspersed with the *sacrifice, &c.*; and as such they are held to be '*bhāvarthāh.*' In the case of any word all that is not cognisable by means of any other word is held to be the meaning of that word; and as a matter of fact, wherever a verb is found, it is found to signify the meaning of the root, mixed up with the *Bhāvanā;* and it is for this reason, that the verb is called '*bhāvārtha.*' Words signifying Substances and Properties are always known to be apart from the *Bhāvanā;* and as such the question does not refer to them. And on this point, we have the following

PŪRVAPAKSHA (C).

"All the words signifying substances and properties, and denoting "well-known entities, are well capable of being taken as expressing "Instrumentality, &c.; and hence it is through this that they come to be "related to the Result. As a rule, the result, being a thing yet to be "accomplished, stands in need of the Means or Instrument which is an "already accomplished entity, and not in that of another Result. Thus "then, the substances signified by Nouns being well-established entities, "are capable of supplying this need of the Result, which need cannot be "supplied by the Verb, which itself is something yet to be accomplished. "For these reasons, the Result must be admitted to follow from the Sub- "stance, &c., (signified by Nouns) (and not from Verbs)."

SIDDHANTA (C).

The reply to the above is given in

***Sūtra* (1): All verbs are indicative of *Bhāvanās,* and the accomplishment of the *Apūrva* proceeds from these; because this particular fact is laid down.**

That is to say, the verbs that denote the *Bhāvanā* bring about the cognition of the accomplishment of the *Apūrva;* because the particular fact—that 'one should accomplish heaven by means of the sacrifice'—is laid down by these.

To explain further, it is a relationship with the main result that serves as the means of the cognition of the *Apūrva;* and then all relationship is preceded by a certain want (on the part of the members related); this want is found to emanate from words signifying *Bhāva* (action), and from those signifying Substance or Property; and for this reason the *Bhāvanā* of the *Apūrva* is recognised from the verbal conjugational affixes; and in this that which is signified by the verbal root is cognised, through proximity, to be the Instrument in the fulfilment of the main Result. Consequently we come to the conclusion that it is by means of the signification of the verbal root, recognised as the Instrument in the fulfilment of the final Result, that leads, through the apparent inconsistency (of the fulfilment of the Result at a time other than that of the performance of the Action), to an idea of the appearance of an *Apūrva.*

A question is here raised: "How is it that, in the case of the word "'*yajēta,*' the root '*yaji*' ('sacrifice') is set aside, and the *Bhāvanā* is said "to be signified by the Affix alone,—the meaning of the Injunctive affix "being laid down as = '*Bhāvayēt*' (one should accomplish)? (1) For, as "a matter of fact, the affixes, Injunctive and the like, would, by themselves, "signify mere *Injunction;* which part of the Affix then can denote that "which is expressed by the root *Bhū* with the causative Affix (*i.e.*, *Bhāvi*)? "Specially as the root '*yaji*' itself cannot signify the meaning of another "root ('*Bhū*') having, as it has, all its potentiality taken up in the "denotation of its own specific meaning. (2) Then again, as a matter of "fact, we find that whenever one object is expressed by a synonymous "word other than the one previously used, the words are never used to- "gether in speaking of this same object. For instance, when one says "'bring the *pika* (cuckoo),' if the person addressed fail to comprehend the "word '*pīka,*' he says 'bring the *kokila,*' and not 'bring the *pika kokila.*' "So, in the same manner, in the case in question, if the Injunctive Affix "be synonymous with the word '*karoti*' or '*bhāvayati,*' then in speaking "of the particular fact, we should use only these latter, and not the In- "junctive affix also. (That is to say, the Injunctive affix being synony- "mous with '*bhāvayati,*' we could not in this connection use the term "'*bhāvayēt*'): specially as, at the particular time it is not quite differenti- "ated which factor of the word signifies the Action. In the case in ques- "tion, however, we find you speaking of '*kuryāt,*' and '*bhāvayēt,*' where you "use the Injunctive affix together with the aforesaid roots. Thus then, "that which is signified by the affix in '*yajēta*' is exactly the same that "is signified by the affix in '*bhāvayēt;*' and as such if you explain the "meaning of the Injunctive in '*yajēta,*' by the word '*bhāvayēt,*' the addi- "tion of the root '*bhāvi*' is most improperly redundant. And consequently "your interpretation is wholly un-Vedic."

To this we make the following reply: In all cases, it is a general rule that when the Verbal conjugational affix donotes the action of an agent, who is a fully accomplished entity, then the sense of '*karoti*' (*accomplishes*) is recognised as co-extensive (with the meaning of the Verb). There are certain roots, added to which, a conjugational affix signifies only that action of the agent which ends in his acquiring his own existence,—*e.g.*, 'is,' 'exists,' and the like. In the case of other roots, when the agent is an already accomplished entity, the action signfied is that which brings about the existence of something else,—*e.g.*, 'sacrifices.' 'gives,' 'cooks,' and the like. And the word '*vyāpāra*' ('action') signifies only a particular substance,—endowed with peculiar potencies, moved in its pristine character, having a mixed nature, having an existence in the past and in the future,— as moved from its former position and not reached the next. And in the case of some Verbs it is the agent himself that is cognised as being in this position; while in that of others, where the Agent is a well-established entity, it is something else. Hence in a case where the Agent himself happens to be in the said unsettled position, he stands in need of something else, for the fulfilment of his own existence; and as such not functioning towards the accomplishment of any other substance, he cannot be spoken of as '*karoti*.' When, however, the Agent is a well-established entity, and functions towards the fulfilment of something else, then he is spoken of as '*karoti*' ('does'). Thus it is that when one asks '*kiṅ karoti*' ('what does he do?'), the reply given is '*pathati*' ('reads'), which latter combines within itself the generic ('*karoti*') as well as the specific action ('*pathati*') [since the word '*pathati*' = '*pātham karoti*']; whereas in reply to the same question, there can be no such reply as—'*bhavati*' (*exists*).

Thus then, it is clear that all conjugational affixes that signify the actions of Agents that are well established entities, have the the sense of '*karoti*' (*accomplishes*). And as such there must be *something to be accomplished;* because unless there is *something to be accomplished* the word '*karoti*' is never used; and it is the nominative of the verb 'to be' (*bhavati*) that becomes the objective of '*karoti*.' That is to say, the verb '*karoti*' being transitive, unless there is *something to be accomplished*, the sense of the verb is not complete. It is a well-recognised fact that all nouns, in whichever case, are nominatives of certain intervening minor actions; and then it is that, with reference to the Principal Action, they come to be recognised as the Objective, Dative, &c. And thus in the case of each individual Principal Action, there is a multiplicity of actions dependent upon the capabilities of the objects concerned. And according to this rule, we come to the conclusion that the nominative of the action '*to be*' is the objective of the action '*karoti*.'

For instance, that which *can never be*, as well as that which *always exists*, can never be *accomplished*,—*e.g.*, 'sky-flowers' and '*Ākāça*' respectively. That is to say, it is that whose *being* has commenced, or whose *being* is possible, that can be brought about by something else, and as such be spoken of as '*being accomplished*.' For certainly, no one is ever found to be accomplishing either the sky-flower or Ākāça. Though in certain cases—such as '*pādaṅ kuru*'—we find the verb to '*accomplish*' (*kuru*) used with reference to an already established entity—the foot,— yet what is meant here to be accomplished is not the *feet* themselves, but certain other processes in connection with them.

Though the root '*kṛ*' has many meanings, yet in all of them is a common element—that of the bringing about of something not before existent (and as such there is nothing incongruous in the general assertion that the word '*karoti*' cannot be used unless there is something to be accomplished). Or, it may be that it is only when the root signifies 'bringing about' (or accomplishing) that there can be a co-ordination of its meaning with the sense of the particular conjugational affix; and hence it is the object actually brought about that becomes the objective of the Verb.

Thus then, we have got at the true character of the action 'to be.' And it now follows that that which is the Nominative of the 'accomplishing' (*karoti*) is the Instigator of the action 'to be;' while the nominative of the action 'to be' becomes the Instigated of the former person. That is to say, on account of the peculiar character of the potentiality of the two roots '*Karoti*' and '*Bhavati*,' the relation between them is such that the former signifies the action of the Instigator, while the latter does that of the Instigated; exactly as there is between the roots '*pac*' (to cook) and '*viklidi*' (to become softened). (1) And in certain cases it happens that it is only the action of the Instigator himself that is directly expressed, the action (of *becoming ready*) of the Instigated (*kaṭa*) being implied, either by the peculiar potentiality of the declared objective (*kaṭam*), or by the aforesaid action of the *Instigator*,—*e.g.*, in '*kaṭam karoti*' (prepares the mat), '*odanam pacati*' (cooks the rice); (2) while in some cases, it is only the action of the Instigated that is directly expressed, that of the Instigator being indirectly implied;—*e.g.*, '*ghaṭo bhavati*' (the jar becomes ready), '*viklidyanti tanḍulāh*' (the rice is becoming softened); (3) in some cases the distinct actions of both are mentioned together,—*e.g.*, '*kaṭam karoti dēvadattah*' (Dēvadatta prepares the mat); (4) and in some cases, the action of the Instigator is made subservient to that of the Instigated, which latter alone is directly mentioned,—'*kriyatē kaṭo dēvadattēna*' (the mat is prepared by Dēvadatta), '*kriyatē kaṭah svayamēva*' (the mat is being prepared by itself); (5) there are certain instances in which that which is mentioned is the Action of the Instigator only, to which is made subservient the action of the Instigated, which latter is mentioned by a part of the same word; and in this case we find that the words '*karoti*' and '*pacati*' in their pure forms are incapable of giving the sense just mentioned; while the roots '*bhū*' and '*viklidi*' signify only the actions of the Instigated; and hence these too do not give the necessary meaning; and consequently the only way of rightly expressing the particular meaning is the use of the Causal forms '*bhāvayati*' and '*viklēdayati*,' where the function of the Causal may be taken to be either direct denotation or indirect implication. [*i.e.*, the word '*viklēdayati*,' though apparently mentioning the action of the Instigator, Ḍēvadatta only, clearly contains the elements of the actions of both; for the meaning of the assertion '*taṇḍulam viklēdayati*' is divisible into the two sentences '*Dēvadattah pacati*' (the action of the Instigator) and '*taṇḍulā viklidyantē*' the action of the Instigated]. As has been declared elsewhere: "Causal verbs are used in connection with the actions of the Instigator, though they always indicate the actions of the Instigated."

And further, because the roots '*bhū*' and '*viklidi*,' &c., are incapable of giving this sense, without the causal affix,—that is no reason why other roots '*karoti*' '*pacati*,' &c., should be equally incapable; or conversely, because these latter are capable of giving this particular sense,—that is no reason why all the roots should be so capable. Because the natural potentialities of objects cannot be questioned; and it is for this reason that roots and affixes signify many meanings.

Thus then, we find that, through the sense of '*karoti*,' all conjugational affixes have the sense of '*bhāvayati*.'

It is for this reason that persons knowing the true nature of *Bhāvanā*, explain it as the action of the person instigating, or bringing into existence that object which is the nominative of the Action 'to be.'

It has been urged above that—"Injunctive affixes do not signify anything other than Injunctions." But this is not correct; because what the Injunctive affixes do is to signify the *Verbal Bhāvanā*; as for the *Actual* (Material) *Bhāvanā*, this is expressed by all conjugational affixes.

That is to say, when we comprehend the *Bhāvanā*, in the shape of the action of a person, to be signified by the word '*karoti*,' as following from all conjugational affixes,—we also comprehend such specialities of the *Bhāvanā* as Injunction, Prohibition, Past, Future, Present, &c.,—all of which are signified by particular words other than conjugational affixes in general; and hence it is that in the case of all conjugational affixes the sense of '*karoti*' is comprehended as the general factor. For instance, we have such uses as—'What *is he doing*?' 'He is cooking.' 'What *did he do*?' 'He cooked.' 'What *will he do*?' 'He will cook.' 'What *should he do*?' 'He should cook.' 'What *should he not do*?' 'He *should not cook*.' And in all these we find that in the Actual *Bhāvanā*, there is an element of the peculiar functioning of the Injunctive affixes, &c., whereby they serve to instigate the person to activity or otherwise; and this function is something apart from the former *Bhāvanā*, which consists of the denotative property of words; and it is this that is called (Verbal) '*Bhāvanā*' or '*Vidhi.*' We have dealt with this in detail under the *Adhikaraṇa* treating of the *Arthavāda*.

It has been urged that—" in explaining '*yajēta*' by '*yāgēna bhāvayēt*,' there is an infringement of the laws governing the use of synonymous words (see above)."

To this we make the following reply: (1) Inasmuch as the mere root is not capable of being used,—(2) with a view to the expression of the Number, &c., of the agent,—and (3) for the sake of protecting the original form,—we make use of the affix (Injunctive) (in '*bhāvayēt*.') That is to say, if the mere roots '*kṛ*' or '*bhāvi*' were capable of being used, then we could not make use of the affix; as it would be like using together the words '*pika*' and '*kokila*;' but, as a matter of fact, a root by itself is never used; for such a use would be wholly incorrect. Thus then, it being absolutely necessary to make use of some one affix (when speaking of the meaning of a Verb), it is only natural that we should hit upon that very affix of which we are explaining the meaning; as in that case, the second mention of the affix could be taken as descriptive of the former, and helping the root in the usage; and any other affix is not used, because such another affix would signify something over and above what is signified by the original word.

Objection: " But the affixes *ik* and *stip* have been laid down as to be " used in connection with a root where one has to speak of the root as " such; and hence we could make use of such forms as '*bhāvih*' or '*bhāva-* " *yatih*,' '*kṛtih*' or '*karotih*.' "

This cannot be; because when these two affixes are joined to roots, all that the resulting word signifies is the *verbal form* only; and as such, having nothing to do with its signification, any such form could not be used in explaining the meaning of the conjugational affix (in '*yajēta*.')

Though there are certain cases where people do make use of roots with these affixes (*ik* and *stip*), even in speaking of what is signified by the root, —*f.i.*, '*yajih*' and '*yajatih*,' &c.,— yet in all these cases, the words used directly denote the verbal form only; and it is only indirectly that they indicate the meaning. In the case in question, however, we have no reason to have recourse to indirect Indication; and as such we cannot use a word that is not itself directly significant.

And again if we explained the Injunctive affix in '*yajēta*' by the word '*bhāvayatih*' or '*karotih*,' we would be holding that the roots '*kṛ*' and '*bhū*' are directly signified by the conjugational affix in question; which is far from desirable. For these reasons, in order to speak of the root with a view to its meaning, we cannot but use the roots '*kṛ*' and '*bhū*' together with a conjugational affix.

And again, if *Bhāvanā* were the only meaning of the Affix, and if the roots '*kṛ*' and '*bhavati*' were capable of expressing all that is denoted by the Affix,—then there might be some question as to using the roots '*bhū*,' &c., alone. As a matter of fact, however, none of these two contingencies is possible, and hence even though the roots serve to point out the *Bhāvanā*, yet the affix has to be used, in order to point out the number, &c., of the nominative (of '*yajēta*').

Thus then, the fact is that when we explain '*yajēta*' as '*yāgēna bhāvayēt*,' the denotation, by the Injunctive affix in the word '*bhāvayēt*' of the *Bhāvanā* itself must be taken as being descriptive of the same *Bhāvanā* that is already expressed (in '*yajēta*') [the chief use of this affix lying in the denoting of the number, &c., of the agent]; otherwise we would fall into a double mistake: (1) that *Bhāvanā* is the sole meaning of the Affix, and (2) that the roots '*kṛ*' and '*bhū*' themselves are denotative of the number, &c., of the agent also.

Further, the *Bhāvanā* that is expressed by the conjugational affixes is always in a form that shows it in the process of accomplishment. And if we made use of any other affix (than the Injunctive, in '*bhāvayēt*'), then the roots '*kṛ*' and '*bhū*' (as accompanied by some other affixes) would signify the *Bhāvanā* in the shape of an accomplished entity like a substance; and as such it would not be the same kind of *Bhāvanā* that is expressed by the conjugational affix. Hence it is absolutely necessary to make use of the particular affix.

Again, the *Bhāvanā* being comprehended in the presence of both the root and the affix, it is never exactly ascertained by which of these two it is exclusively signified. If it could be ascertained absolutely that the *Bhāvanā* is signified by the affix, then there could be an objection as to the mention of affixes with the roots '*kṛ*' and '*bhū*' being a useless repetition. But, as a matter of fact, it is not so; inasmuch as it is when both the affix and the root are present that the *Bhāvanā* is cognised. It is because of the impossibility of either the affix or the root being used apart from the other, that we can never rightly ascertain as to which of the two signifies the *Bhāvanā*; all that we can say is that it is signified (1) either by the Affix *as accompanied by the root*,—or (2) by the root as aided by the affix; or (3) by both together. Nor is there any particular reason for assuming any particular expressive potentiality in any one of the two; because the only ground for such assumption would be the Apparent Inconsistency (of the signification of the *Bhāvanā*), and this would apply equally to both (the

Affix and the root). As a matter of fact, there is no particular purpose served by ascertaining absolutely by which of the two the *Bhāvanā* is expressed.

The following objection might be urged: "Inasmuch as we do not find the *Bhāvanā* expressed by the roots ending in the *kṛt* affixes, we can safely assert that it is signified by the conjugational *affixes*, (and not by the roots)."

This is not right; because we find that no *Bhāvanā* is expressed by the conjugational affixes in '*bhavati*,' '*asti*,' &c. Nor is it an absolute fact that it is not expressed by roots ending in *kṛt* affixes, because even when these latter are used, we do comprehend a certain portion of the *Bhāvanā*.

For instance, in the case of *kṛtya* affixes, we meet with such words as '*bhōktavyam*,' '*yashtavyam*,' and the like; and the Bhāvanā that is signified by these is only slightly inferior to that which is signified by conjugational affixes. And here too, in the case of the Passive *kṛtya* affixes as in '*brāhmaṇō na hantavyah*' inasmuch as it is a substance—*Brāhmaṇa*—that is the predominant factor in the sentence,—the *Bhāvanā* denoted is much inferior to that which is signified by the *Bhāva-Kṛtya* affix (in '*Yashṭavyam*'); and the reason is that in the case of the latter no prodominance belongs to the action of an Instigator, the meaning of the root itself being the most predominant factor; whereas in the other case '*brāhmaṇo na hantavyah*,'—the verb signifies the action of the Instigated as along with that of the Instigator.

The same explanation holds respecting the conjugational affixes used in the sense of the Active and the Passive; because in the case of these also, the position of the action of the Instigator remains a subordinate one. And hence the case of the *kṛt* affixes cannot be said to be the same as that of the conjugational affixes.

So also in the case of Indeclinable *Kṛt* affixes, though these have the sense of the *Bhāva* (Active), yet the cognition of the *Bhāvanā*, cognised by itself, is slightly inferior to the foregoing. For instance—'*abhikrāman juhoti*' etc., etc.,—in all of which the *Bhāvanā* that is cognised is one that is dependent upon another *Bhāvanā*. So also in the case of such words as '*pakvah*,' '*pakvavān*' and the like, the cognition that is directly perceptible is that of a substance subservient to a *Bhāvanā* in its fully accomplished form; so too in the case of the words '*pācaka*' and the like.

Thus then, we find that in all cases, (of *Kṛt* affixes), there is always a need of a certain relationship between the Noun and the Verb (and this could not be without a *Bhāvanā*); for if there were no *Bhāvanā*, there would be no need of any such relation, exactly as there is none in the case of the compounds of root-words and words with nominal affixes. And the name Kāraka' (relation between noun and verb) is not applicable unless there is an action in the case; nor is there any action, which does not bring about something that did not exist before. Hence it is proved that the sense of '*karoti*' and *bhāvayati*' is present (in the case of *kṛt* affixes also).

And even without the fact of the *Bhāvanā* being shown in the process of accomplishment, we can show that the necessary co-ordination is present. For instance,—'What should be done?' 'Cooking should be done (*paktavyam*)' (where we have a co-ordination between the *cooking, pāka*, —and the affix *tavya*—'should'). '*Kathaṅkāram juhoti?*' '*Abhikrāmaṃ juhoti*,' and so on. In the case of the conjugational affixes also, there is no other ground for the *Bhāvanā*, but the co-ordination (of the affix) with the root '*kṛ*.'

Thus then we find that even roots do not entirely leave off the *Bhāvanā*, as has been well said (in *Bhatti-kāvya*—'Just as the root *kṛ* employs all the roots in their various meanings, so, &c., &c.' (?)

It is not the form, but the predominant character, of the *Bhāvanā*, that can be said to be directly signified, or indirectly implied, by the conjugational affixes, exclusively.

Objection: "In that case as soon as the word '*yāgēna*' has been mentioned, the full meaning of the root '*yaji*' becomes withdrawn from the word '*yajēta*,' and the *Bhāvanā* having thus been signified by the root-meaning, there can be no reason for the use of another word *bhāvayēt*."

This argument does not touch our position; because, as a matter of fact, the root ('*yaji*') has a twofold meaning; and in pointing out the two phases of the meaning separately, all that we do by mentioning the word '*yāgēna*' is to point out, separately, the peculiar *Instrumentality* of the sacrifice, which is a specific form of the signification of the root, the generic form consisting of the *Bhāvanā*, in order to point out which we make use of another word '*bhāvayēt*.'

Or, it may be that there are certain facts—f.i., (1) Instrumentality and (2) the number of the Agent—that are signified separately by the root and the affix (respectively); whereas the *Bhāvanā* being quite compatible with both of them, we can hold it to be denoted by both (root and affix) together. And it is for this reason that we find both the *Sūtra* and the *Bhāshya* speaking of all '*Karmaçabdāh*' (*complete* verbs) as being '*bhāvārthāh*' (signifying the *Bhāvanā*), where there is a distinct mention of coextensiveness (between whole *verb-roots and affixes* combined—and the signifying of the *Bhāvanā*).

In the *Mīmānsā-Çāstra*, however, the *Bhāvanā* is always held to be signified by the affix.

The sense of this theory may be thus briefly explained: (1) The sense of the Affix is always expressed by the Root and the Affix taken together; and as the *Bhāvanā* is the most important factor in this joint signification, it is held to be signified by the affix. That is to say, though there is no other ground for differentiating exactly, by which of the two the *Bhāvanā* is denoted, yet, inasmuch as it is a well-established fact that greater importance is always attached to the denotation of the affix, —and in the case in question, the *Bhāvanā* is the most important factor,—we naturally conclude that this *Bhāvanā* must be denoted by the affix.

(2) The Root and the Affix are always found to appear in a definite order of sequence; and as a matter of fact, we find that it is only when the Affix is heard to be pronounced, that we have an idea of the *Bhāvanā*; and this too leads us to the conclusion that the *Bhāvanā* is denoted by the affix. Because the invariable concomitance of any two objects is not only such that one cannot exist in the absence of the other, but also of a kind which we find in the present case, where we find that it is only when a particular word—the Affix f.i.—is pronounced that there is a denotation of the *Bhāvanā*; and as such, in accordance with the rule that when one object is always seen to appear when another appears, there is always an invariable concomitance between the two,—we must admit that the *Bhāvanā* is denoted by the Affix.

It has been argued above that—"in the case of such verbs as '*asti*,' and the like, we find the Affix giving up the denotation of the *Bhāvanā* (and as such there can be no concomitance between the two)." But this objection is equally applicable to all the theories; for instance, even if the *Bhāvanā* be held to be denoted by the Root, or the Root and the Affix conjointly, then too, the case of the verbs '*asti*,' &c., would be incompatible with the theories. Hence the fact is that, whenever the *Bhāvanā* is cognised, it is always expressed by the Affix, while in a case where it is not cognised, there is no occasion for any consideration as to by what it is expressed. And we have already shown under the *Tadbhūtadhikaraṇa* (of the *Tarkapāda*) that any stray contrary instance cannot vitiate a general rule.

Or, we may show that the case of the verbs *asti*, &c., does not afford instances contrary to our general rule with regard to the denotation of the *Bhāvanā*. Because even in the case of the words '*asti*,' &c., there is always a part of the Nominative agent that is yet to be accomplished; and hence there is always present a *Bhāvanā* (*accomplishing*) of this unaccomplished portion; but the *Bhāvanā*, in this case, is not distinctly cognised, because it does not appear (as it does in other cases) in a relation of subserviency to anything apart from the Agent himself. That is to say, in the case of the words '*asti*,' &c., though there is no functioning of the nominative agent perceptible, on account of the Agent himself being still unaccomplished, and of there being nothing besides the Agent to be accomplished, yet it is on account of the inherent potentiality of the Affix itself that we recognise the element of *Bhāvanā*. And (1) as for the *object* of the *Bhāvanā*, we have the Agent himself, there being no other object capable of being spoken of, on account of the unaccomplished character of the Agent; (2) for the *Instrument* of the *Bhāvanā*, we have the act of *being* (*bhavana*); and (3) as for the *Procedure*, we have the method of the bringing about, one after another, of the various parts of himself. And thus we find that all the three factors of the *Bhāvanā* are supplied in one way or the other, by the *act of being* itself, specially as the case admits of no other action. Thus then, of the Agent himself, there are certain parts that are still being called into existence, *i.e.*, being accomplished, while there are others that have already been accomplished, which serve as the Nominative agents. And the *act of being*, which exists in common in those that have been accomplished, as well as in those that are being accomplished, is spoken of as the *Bhāvanā*.

The same arguments apply to the case of such words as '*jāyatē*,' '*nishpadyatē*,' '*siddhyati*' and the like.

As for the word '*asti*' (*is*) it expresses a condition of things just following that which is expressed by '*bhavati*' (*becomes*) synonymous with '*takes birth*,' and as such accomplishes the *present being* of the self; and hence it is that it takes one of the conjugational affixes. And in this case also, the differentiation of the functioning of the *Actor* and the *acted upon* is to be made as before, with reference to the common character of *being* that extends over the various parts of the Agent, while differing from another in the point of time of their individual accomplishment. However, though there is such a *Bhāvanā*, yet there can be no Injunction or Prohibition with regard to such *Bhāvanās*; for the simple reason that they refer to the Agent, who is always a fully accomplished intelligent subject.

The following argument is possible: "We do often come across Injunctions of such *being*, &c. For instance, '*Rtvijā bhavitavyam*,' '*Rathantaram bhavati*,' '*Adhvaryuh syāt*,' '*Ukthyāni syuh*,' *&c.*"

The reply to this is that it is true that we meet with such Injunctions; but in these cases the word '*bhavati*' is not used in its ordinary sense; for instance, the meaning of '*Ṛtvijā bhavitavyam*' is that *one should accomplish the Ṛtvik-hood, necessary for the performance of the sacrifice, by means of such other actions as purchase, appointment and the like.* So also in the case of the sentence '*Rathantaram bhavati*,' though the direct meaning of the text is with reference to the *being* (or acquiring existence) *of the Rathantara*, yet, inasmuch as the *Rathantara* is an inanimate thing, no such *being* is possible; and hence what the Injunction means is that *one should accomplish the Rathantara*—a distinct case of *Bhāvanā.*

Whenever we have such sentences as 'one should *become* this or that' (*bhavēt*),—the root '*bhū*' having the sense of *stays* (*tishthati*),—there is always a possibility of *something to be accomplished*, the sense of the Injunction being that *one should accomplish something by staying.*

For these reasons, we conclude that the true character of *Bhāvanā* belongs to the action of the agent that *becomes*, only when the verb used signifies the Past, Present or the Future,—and not when it is in the Injunctive, &c.

In the expression of the *Past*, &c., also, when the complete action is signified by the verbal root itself, and there is no differentiation based upon the difference in the time of the appearance of the different portions of the Agent, then, in that case, the incongruity being patent, the signification of the verb must be taken as restricted to the denotation of the root only, and not extending to the *Bhāvanā*,—the Number, &c., of the Nominative being taken to be signified by the verbal affix. And we have already shown that any stray instance to the contrary cannot vitiate our general rule with regard to the *Bhāvanā.*

It has also been urged that we find the verbal root signifying the *Bhāvanā*, even in the case of the *Kṛt* affixes (as in '*pakvah*,' &c.).

True it is that the *denotation of the root* always accompanies the Bhāvanā; but for the very reason of the *Bhāvanā* being *indirectly implied* by these *denotations of the roots*, it can also be said that the *Bhāvanā* is not *directly expressed* by the root. That is to say, in the case of all words ending in *Kṛt* affixes, the character of the *Bhāvanā* is cognised as the secondary element, being indirectly implied by the nouns signified by the verbal root,—which latter therefore cannot be said to directly denote the *Bhāvanā*. Just as in the case of verbal affixes, inasmuch as *action* is the predominant element in the denotation of these, the Noun is always cognised as the secondary factor connected with the denotation of the verbal root; and hence the *Nominative* and the *Accusative* are not held to be directly expressed (by the verbal affix); in the same manner, in the case of the *Kṛt* affixes, the denotation of the Nominative, &c., not being otherwise possible, these would indirectly imply the *Bhāvanā*, which, for this very reason, cannot be said to be directly denoted by the word. And it is only with reference to this implied *Bhāvanā*, that we have such sentences as '*Kiṅ karōti?*' '*Pākam*'—where the last word is spoken of as co-ordinate with the word '*karoti*,' exactly as the word '*Dēvadattah*' is used along with the word '*pacati*.' And the relationship of the *Noun* too is possible only with reference to the indirectly implied *Bhāvanā*. Or, this relationship may be taken as with the denotation of the root (and not with the *Bhāvanā*), because of the fact of the nouns serving the purpose of accomplishing the denotation of the verbal roots, which are always subservient to the *Bhāvanā;* and the denotation of the root too stands in need of these Nouns (as serving the purpose of accomplishing the denotation of the root); and the *Bhāvanā* too refers only to such Nouns; hence there is no incongruity in the relationship in question.

In the case of the *Kṛtya* affixes (*tavya*, &c.), also, inasmuch as they denote the '*praisha*,' *urging*,—even though there be no direct denotation of the *Bhāvanā*,—the full signification of the word is not attained, until we have obtained a *Bhāvanā* fully equipped with all its three factors. Because all these words serve to urge the person to a performance of his functions; and the form of this function is the *Bhāvanā* endowed with the three factors. That is to say, apart from his own function, a man cannot perform anything else; and the *Praishas* serve to make him perform these. Hence if these words did not, in some way or other, refer to the function (of the man), they could not urge him to its performance; and thus too, in this case also, it is found that there is an indirect implication of the *Bhāvanā* (which is the name given to the functioning of the agent). As for the *Praishas* or Directions, contained in the *Brāhmaṇas*, all these have the character of *Vidhi*, Injunction, since what they lay down is not got at by any other means; and hence, in these cases, the *Kṛtya* affixes cannot but be accepted as having the Injunctive signification, even though this signification is not laid down by Pāṇini.

The only difference, however, between Injunction and Direction (*Vidhi* and *Praisha*) is that when the object is otherwise remembered, the *urging* (to it) is called '*Praisha*' *Direction;* while when the same *urging* is to that which is not otherwise got at, it becomes '*Vidhi*' *Injunction.*

Thus it is clear that the *Bhāvanā* is signified by the Affixes.

Objection: "If *Bhāvanā* be held to be a functioning of the *Instigator*, "then the character of the *Bhāvanā* will have to be admitted in such "actions as the laying of the vessel upon the fire, &c., (in the case of *cooking*), "and those of the mental determination, &c., (in the case of sacrifice),—these "being the actions of the Instigating Agent. And as it is these actions "that are signified by verbal roots, you cannot but admit the *Bhāvanā* "to be denoted by the root."

Reply: This does not affect our position; because though it is a fact that the *Bhāvanā* is never cognised, entirely apart from the signification of the verbal root, yet the *Bhāvanā* proper that is cognised in a general form (covering over many particular actions), is something entirely different. That is to say, in all the particular actions spoken of above,—*viz.* laying the vessel upon the fire, &c.,—we always perceive a common generic action, in the shape of '*karoti*,' 'does.' The action of *being softened*, *laying on the fire*, &c., that are spoken of by the words '*pacati*,' 'cooks, &c., are such as inhere in the object and in the Nominative Agent. And among all these actions, the mere action of *cessation from inactivity*, the mere *moving* towards the performance of an action, is what is meant by the word '*Bhāvanā*'; while all the particular actions, that go to lend colour to the mere *activity*, and which inhere in the object as well as in the Agent, become related to it, either in the shape of the *Instrument* or in that of the *Process*.

Objection: "But in that case, *Bhāvanā* comes to be nothing more "than a generic denotation of the verbal root."

Reply: True; the *Bhāvanā* does appear in a generic form; but it is only in the shape of *something to be accomplished*, and not in the particular forms of the *sacrifice*, &c. Because the generic idea that accompanies the *sacrifice* is in the form of the *Instrument*, which is entirely different from the *Bhāvanā*, which is *something to be accomplished*. With reference to each person, the *Bhāvanā* has its own peculiar generic and specific forms. And the *sacrifice*, &c., appear as Instruments in the *Bhāvanā*; and all that the signification of the verbal root does is to supply the elements wanting in this instrument of the *Bhāvanā*; it is this generic denotation of the Root that is expressed by the word '*karmaçabda*' 'Verb'; and inasmuch as the *sacrifice, &c.*, serve to qualify the *Bhāvanā*, they are known as the *peculiarities of the Bhāvanā*, and not as the *Bhāvanā* itself.

In scientific works, however, the words '*kriyāçabda*' and '*karmaçabda*' are used, sometimes with reference to the denotation of the verbal root, and sometimes with reference to the *Bhāvanā*, while at times, through proximity, with reference to both; in any case they are never used to express the particular forms of any of these. Because the *Bhāvanā* or the signification of the verbal affix, that is cognised in the case of a conjugational affix, is never expressed, in the same form, by any other word. That is to say, the word '*Bhāvanā*' signifies something that is a substantial objective reality, in an accomplished form, as qualified by a particular Gender and Number; and this is not what is signified by the conjugational affix (the Injunctive f.i.), whose denotation is entirely free from any element of Gender or Number. Similarly too, with the denotation of the verbal Root. For instance, the words '*karoti*,' 'does,' and '*bhāvayati*' 'accomplishes,' signify something entirely different from that which is expressed by the conjugational affix; since that which is signified by '*karoti*' and '*bhāvayati*' is the *Bhāvanā* that has *doing* and *accomplishing* for its Instrument; and as this is not the form of the *Bhāvanā* that is signified in the case of the word '*yajēta*,' the two ('*karoti*' and the Injunctive affix in '*yajeta*') cannot be said to be synonymous. And the sentence '*yāgēna bhāvayēt* should be explained, without taking into consideration the *Bhāvanā* that appears to be signified by the affix in the word '*bhāvayēt*.' Consequently the sentence in question cannot be quoted in support of the theory that '*bhāvayati*' or '*karoti*' is synonymous with the Injunctive affix in '*yajēta*;' because the use of the sentence can be explained as based upon a certain degree of close proximity between the two and not upon an absolute identity of meaning. Thus we conclude that the *Bhāvanā* cannot be expressed by any other word.

As soon as the *Bhāvanā* has been cognised, first of all there arises a desire to know what the *object* of the *Bhāvanā* is; because the *object* is the most important factor in it, and also because the object does not stand in need of the desire for any other factor. And in every *Bhāvanā* that is endowed with an Injunction, this Injunctiveness, even if previously cognised, is not accepted, until the *Bhāvanā*, as equipped with all its three factors, is perceived to be capable of being put into action. And before the Injunctive character asserts itself, we must always recognise the fact that the *Bhāvanā* should be fully equipped with all the elements that make it capable of being put into action. Any person that would do an act intelligently, is never found to be engaging in any action, unless he is fully cognisant of a certain desirable result that would follow from it. This desirable result too is never sought for anywhere else besides the object to be accomplished (by the *Bhāvanā*); because there is nothing more important than such a result, that could be the object to be accomplished.

Thus then, if in any *Bhāvanā*, the object to be accomplished were something different from that which is desirable to the agent, then no Agent would be found to be engaging in any activity towards the fulfilment of such an object; and as such the very *promptive* potency of the Injunctive affix would become thwarted. Hence it is that, though the denotation of the Root (*yaj*), as related to the Injunctive through the fact of being expressed by a part of the same word as the Injunctive, comes forward to supply the factor of the object of the *Bhāvanā*,—yet, on account of its inherent incapability (due to its not being something desirable by the Agent), it is set aside. (1) Because mere proximity is not the sole ground of any relationship,—the most important grounds being those of *Capability*, *Mutual Want*, &c., as we shall speak of later on. (2) Because all that the word '*yajēta*' directly denotes is the mere relationship between the denotation of the root '*yaj*' and the *Bhāvanā* (signified by the Injunctive affix); and it expresses nothing with regard to the former entering into any of the three elements of the latter. That is to say, the potency of the word having ceased with the denotation of the Relationship, the matter, as to the entering of anything into the three elements of the *Bhāvanā*, should be decided on the sole ground of *capability*. And inasmuch as the denotation of the Root is not found to be capable of being related as the Object, —on account of this factor being supplied by the Injunctive character, which, being expressed by the same Affix, is by far the most proximate (to the *Bhāvanā*),— we must conclude that it must be related in the shape of another factor (that of the *Instrument*). (3) The Affix can never serve the purpose of prompting towards the Object itself, inasmuch as the Agent always knows what is desirable for him, (and it is only in the matter of the particular *means*, &c., that he needs a prompting). That is to say, it is only in cases where the activity of the Agent is dependent upon Scriptural Injunctions, that we seek for Proximity or Non-proximity (as pointing out the various elements of the *Bhāvanā*). The *Object* to be accomplished, however, in the shape of Heaven, Cattle, Offspring, Landed property, &c., are such as are already known as desirable, without any Scriptural Instructions to the effect. Hence as soon as there arises a desire to know what is the object of the *Bhāvanā*, we at once recognise, even before we come across any scriptural text, that it is a certain Object desired by the Agent; and all that remains to be known is the particular Object so desired; but this particular object too is not in the shape of *something to be accomplished*, but only as the object of the particular *Bhāvanā* in question. Hence it is that the element in question is supplied by Heaven, &c., which, though at a distance from the word, is yet found to be the most capable of the said relationship. As for the relationship of the denotation of the Root, any acceptance of this as the *Object*, would be accepting something not required in the case at all; and as such the very potency of the Injunction being thwarted, there would be an inevitable contradiction of the *Çruti*. (4) Further, that alone,—which has been recognised as the nominative agent of the action of *being*, either in the same or another sentence, —can have the character of the *Object* (of the *Bhāvanā*); and, as a matter of fact, in the case in question, the denotations of the Root, &c., are not cognised as having any connection with the action of *being;* while Heaven, &c., found in connection with the word 'desiring,' are actually perceived to be connected with the action of *being*. Because the desire in the mind of the man is in the form 'May Heaven *be* mine,'—where Heaven is distinctly cognised as the nominative of *being;* and it is for this reason that it is accepted to supply a desideratum, something to be brought about, of the *Bhāvanā*.

The object of the *Bhāvanā* having been thus ascertained, there arises a desire to know its Instrument—by what Means it is to be accomplished. And it is always the '*yāga*,' 'Sacrifice' (denoted by the root '*yaji*' in '*yajēta*') that is recognised as the Instrument; (1) because the action of the Agent depending upon the scriptural Instruction, we cannot but seek after what is pointed out by Proximity, &c., as appearing in the text in question (and the root is always the most proximate to the Affix); (2) because Capability or Incapability too can not be recognised by any other means of right notion, save the text itself; (3) because it is only the 'sacrifice,' the recognition whereof as the Instrument is not incompatible with the tenor of the Injunction; (4) because there is no ground for rejecting the denotation of the root (*yaji*), that presents itself, as the Instrument, through its close Proximity to the Injunctive Affix; and (5) because, as a matter of fact, no *Bhāvanā* of a particular result is possible without the agency of that which is denoted by a verbal root. Though the 'Sacrifice' itself is not an accomplished fact, yet, it can accomplish the Result, after it has itself been accomplished by means of its own particular Instrument. And it is a fact of nature that everything in the world is, at one time, in an inaccomplished shape, and at another time, in a fully accomplished state. The accomplishment too (of the sacrifice) is of no particular use, prior to the action of the Scriptural Injunction; because the only use that the accomplishment of the Instrument has is at the time of the fulfilment of its particular result. And inasmuch as the Instrumentality (of sacrifice) is actually found to be extending over all the three periods of time, there is nothing very incongruous in speaking of the sacrifice (even while unaccomplished) as the Instrument (of the *Bhāvanā*).

For these reasons, the Instrumentality must be admitted to belong to the *sacrifice*, &c. But inasmuch as the Result appears at a time very remote from that of the performance of the sacrifice, the Instrumentality of this latter could not be possible, except through the intervening agency of the *Apūrva;* it is for this reason that the words denoting actions are said to bring about the recognition of the *Apūrva.* And thus the meaning of the *Sūtra* might be this: *Those* 'Karma-çabdas'—*words denotative of actions—which are* 'bhāvārtha,'—*which serve the purpose of accomplishing the Bhāvanā—such as the roots 'yaji' and the like—lead us to the cognition of the agency of the Apūrva.*

Objection: "(1) In accordance with the rule above laid down in connection with the relationship of the Object and the Instrument, it would "seem that the *Bhāvanā* could be signified by only such conjugational "affixes as appear in connection with *transitive* Verbs; that is to say, the "factor of the *object* being supplied only by such entities as are the *most* "*desired* (which is the definition of the *Objective*), no intransitive verb "could ever have anything to do with such an object. (2) Or, all the "Verbs would become transitive (if we admit the relationship of all verbs "with such objects.) (3) Or, lastly, it must be admitted that there is "no *Bhāvanā* signified in the case of *intransitive* verbs."

This, however, does not effect our position; because the objective of the denotation of the root, as found in the case of Transitive Verbs, is something entirely different from that which is referred to by the denotation of the Affix. For instance, in the case of such transitive Verbs as '*odanam pacati*' 'cooks the rice,' '*grāmam gacchati*,' 'goes home,'—the objective of the root-meaning is entirely different from that of the *Bhāvanā*. Though it often happens that the objective of the root-meaning itself becomes also the objective of the *Bhāvanā*,—the meaning of the sentence being '*pākēna odanam bhavayati*,' 'accomplishes the rice by means of cooking;'—yet it is often that the *Bhāvanā*, as accompanied by the root-meaning together with its own particular objective, has an independent objective of its own,—the meaning of the sentences in this case being—'*odanapākēna grāmagamanēna vā svārtham bhāvayati*,' 'one seeks to fulfil his desired end by means of the cooking of the rice, or by going to his home.' Thus then, the Objective of the *Bhāvanā* is found to be recognised, after the root-meaning, only as something to be *acquired* (and to be accomplished); and as such though it happens to be covered over by the meaning of another root ('*Kāma*,' desiring), yet it is always recognised as the objective of the *Bhāvanā*; and this peculiar relationship of the *Bhāvanā* and its objective is, in many cases, mentioned by the word '*Kāma*' (to desire). For instance, even in the case of intransitive verbs—such as the verbs '*Āsa*,' to sit, and '*Çi*' to lie down,—we have such sentences as '*sukhakāma āsīta*,' 'one *desiring comfort* should sit down,' and '*Svāsthyakāmo Çayīta*,' 'one *desiring health* should lie down.' And though these two roots are intransitive ones, yet there is always a factor of '*karoti*' 'does,' or 'accomplishes,' signified by the particular Affix; and it is of this '*karoti*' (transitive) that *Comfort*, &c., are cognised to be the objective. And this '*karoti*' being always transitive, even in the case of the conjugational affixes appearing in connection with Intransitive Verbs, there is always a certain co-extensiveness between the signification of the particular root and that of the word '*karoti*;' as we actually find, the questions—'*Kiṅ-karoti*,' 'what is he doing?'—answered by '*āstē*, 'he is sitting,' '*cētē*,' 'he is lying down;' and thus even in the case of these roots we find the *Bhāvanā* having a definite objective (though the roots are intransitive). As a matter of fact, even in the case of the transitive verb '*yaji*,' *to sacrifice*, though the real object is the *Deity* to whom the sacrifice is offered, yet the objective of the *Bhāvanā* is something entirely different, in the shape of *Offspring*, *Heaven*, *Cattle*, and the like. Thus then, in the case of Transitive, as well as in that of Intransitive Verbs, we have such sentences as '*āsanēna bhāvayēt sukham*,' 'one should seek to accomplish his pleasure by *sitting* down.'

Question: "What then would be the difference between Transitive and Intransitive Verbs."

Reply: In a case where the root-meaning is *always directly* concerned with a certain objective, the root is Transitive; whereas in a case where the connection with an objective is only indirect, through the medium of the *Bhāvanā*, the root is Intransitive. For instance, in the case of the root *to sit, to lie down*, the objective is not always definitely cognised; and as such they are spoken of as *Intransitive;* whereas the roots *to cook*, &c.; are always accompanied by an objective, which is directly connected with it, through the actions of *Softening*, &c.; and as such these are spoken of as *Transitive*. But this does not make any difference between the two kinds of roots, when referring to a *Bhāvanā*.

The *Bhāvanā* then having its two factors—of the Objective and the Instrument—duly supplied, there arises a desire to learn the *process* of this Instrumentality; as without a certain process of action no real Instrumentality is possible. And then, Sense-Perception, &c., not being found to be capable of helping the *Bhāvanā* in any way, a cognition of the Process depends entirely upon the Scripture; and as such for a due cognition of this, we must take our stand upon Proximity, &c. (of the Verbs occurring in the Scriptural Injunction); and when this is not possible, the Process is pointed out by some other means;—either (1)directly by scriptural Injunctions, or (2) indirectly by the particular Implications of the generic Injunction, (3) or by the Apparent Inconsistency of an entirely transcendental help (required in the case).

Thus, being duly equipped with all its three factors, the *Bhāvanā* becomes capable of being accomplished; and as such it becomes the object of an Injunction. And because the *Bhāvanā* is enjoined, it is on account of the Apparent Inconsistency of this, that we have the Injunctions of sacrifice, &c., (as forming the factors of the said *Bhāvanā*). And thus the *Sūtra* becomes duly established.

Says the *Bhāshya* :—"*There are certain Karmaçabdas, &c.*," And though the proper words to be cited as examples were '*yāga*,' '*yajana*,' &c., yet the Bhāshya has cited the words '*Çyēna*,' &c., which are accomplished as such only through their co-extensiveness with the aforesaid words; and the words '*Çyēna*,' &c., are easily recognisable as *Karmaçabdas*, because of their denoting certain actions occurring after the Injunction of such instruments as those of the '*yāga*,' *sacrifice*, &c.; and thus these are dependent upon something else, it being absolutely impossible for an independent word to be spoken of as '*bhāvaçabda*' (and as such there is nothing incongruous or tautological in the sentence '*bhāvarthāh karmaçabdāh*'). Specially as the '*yāga*,' 'sacrifice,' &c., by themselves, are capable of being inferred to be '*bhāvārtha*.'

There are certain 'bhāvārtha' words that are not 'Karmaçabdas.' And in this connection the proper examples to cite were '*bhāvayēt kuryāt*,' &c.; but the *Bhāshya* cites the words '*bhūti*,' which signify the action of that which is *prompted;* and as such they are not capable of being cited as instances of '*bhāvartha*,' as explained above. And though one of the words cited by the Bhāshya could, by taking it in the causal sense, be spoken of as '*bhāvārtha*,' yet the other two are not capable of such constructions; though these latter also can have their denotation split up into two parts—one part being the action of the Prompter and another that of the Prompted; and with reference to the latter, they can be spoken of as '*bhāvārtha;*' and it is for this reason that the Bhāshya has cited them. Or, it may be that, in accordance with the interpretation in the following *Sūtra*, the purpose of the *Bhāvanā* may be taken as served by only a partial signification (only that of the action of *being*); and hence even though the words in question do not signify the whole of the *Bhāvanā*, yet they can be spoken of as '*bhāvārtha*.'

Question: "Why should not these ('*bhavartha words*') be spoken " of as *Karmaçabdas*, when all verb-roots are called *Karmaçabdas?*"

Answer: An undefined generic action (that of *being*) being incapable of being performed, such words cannot be spoken of as *Karmaçabdas.* And hence it is that it is only such verbal roots, as denote particular actions, that are recognised as *Karmaçabdas;* and hence the question does not affect our position.

If the *words* '*Cyēna*,' '*Citrā*,' &c., (names of sacrifices) were *directly* related to the particular results (mentioned in the sentence '*Çyēnēnābhiçaran yajēta*,' &c.), then the *Sacrifice* itself would not have any instrumental agency in the accomplishment of the results; and then the words '*Çyēna*,' &c., could not be taken as Names; because it is only because of the co-ordination of the Instrumental *Sacrifice* with the *words* '*Çyēnēna*,' &c., that these latter are taken as *names;* and then these words would have to be taken as laying down *materials* for the sacrifices (which has been shown above to be absolutely untenable). It is for this reason that the *Bhāshya* has said—'*When we have the present Adhikaraṇa*, etc., etc.' (That is to say, when, according to the present *Adhikaraṇa*, the *Sacrifice* is taken as the Instrument of the *Bhāvanā*, then the '*Çyēna*' cannot but be taken as a mere Name of the sacrifice).

It may be asked why the fact of the sacrifice being the Instrument of the *Bhāvanā* was not ascertained on the previous occasion. But the reason was that the particular fact has no connection with the subject-matter of the former *Adhyāya*, which treats only of the means of knowing *Dharma.* Then there is the question — why should not the fact of 'Cyēna' &c., being names of sacrifices have been left to be treated of on the present occasion? But the reason of this is that this fact has no connection with the *Marks of Difference* (among Actions), which forms the subject-matter of the present *Adhyāya.* Therefore the treatment of the two facts must be accepted in their present order of sequence.

Says the *Bhāshya* — '*Na caishāmarthinā, &c.*'; and this refers to the word mentioning the Result; *i.e.*, the mention of the Result has no direct concern with the word '*Citrayā.*'

Says the *Bhāshya* :— '*Vivibhaktikatvāt;*' and this may mean — (1) *because of the disappearance of the Conjugational affix that signifies the peculiar relationship*; or (2) *because of the presence of the particular Declensional affix which signifies an accomplished entity.* For these two reasons, the words '*Citrā,*' &c., that denote certain substances, can have no connection with the particular results mentioned; as has been declared — 'The relationship of the means and the object always rests in the *Bhāvanā*; and hence the said relationship could never be accomplished without an affix denoting the *Bhāvanā.*'

Sūtra (2): Objection :—"But *Bhāva* forms the meaning of all words."

"We cannot admit of the fact of the *Apūrva* being expressed by the "Affix, or by the Root by itself directly; and as for expressing it in-"directly, this can be equally done by the Noun also.

"That is to say, if it were held that the *Apūrva* can be expressible only "by that which denotes the *Bhāvanā*, or by the root alone by itself, "independently of the Affix, then, the theory that it is expressed by Nouns "would have been untenable. As a matter of fact, however, just as the "root, expressed by the Affix is capable of denoting the instrumentality (of "the *Apūrva*), indirectly through the agency of the *Bhāvanā*, so also is the "Noun; and as such there is no difference in the two theories."

Sūtra (3): Reply: Such words, on the utterance whereof the forms of the objects denoted are directly cognised, are Nouns; and as such these do not stand in need of anything else, on account of their being self-sufficient in regard to their denotation.

It has been already shown above that when the *Apūrva* is expressed by any one factor of the sentence, all else becomes subsidiary to it; and we are now going to show the difference in the very characters of the different words themselves.

For instance, we cannot admit of a distinct *Dharma* being manifested with each word of a sentence; because that would necessitate the admission of many transcendental agencies; and we have yet to show that the Noun can have no direct relationship with the result of the sacrifice. That is to say, when the particular transcendental agency is held to be accomplished by any one word of the sentence, all else is very rightly taken as accomplishing certain visible results and thereby becoming subsidiary to the former; and this theory appears to be the simplest under the circumstances. If, however, for the sake of making the latter subsidiary to the former, we have got to assume other transcendental results to follow from these, then it would be very much simpler to hold all the words to be equally related to the Result; nor will this entail the trouble of assuming diverse relationships in the sentence.

Now then, if the Noun be held to be directly related to the Result, we would have to call, to the aid of the former, the signification of the Root. This signification of the root, however, being self-sufficient, could not bring any visible help to the denotation of the Noun which is an accomplished entity; nor does this latter stand in any need of such visible help; because the denotation of the noun is recognised as a fully accomplished entity, at the very time of its being uttered; and because that of which it is said to stand in need (*viz.*, the *Sacrifice* as signified by the Root) is yet to be accomplished.

The word "*prayoga*" in the *Sūtra*, means *that with regard to which the word is used*, i.e., the object denoted by it; and it is through this that there is a recognition of the accomplished form of the denotation of the word.

The form of the Action is said to be *perishable*, only with a view to point to the fact of that form not having yet appeared; specially as even when the action has been accomplished, inasmuch as it is extremely transitory in its character, it always stands in need of repeated accomplishments.

Tēbhyah parākāṅkshā.—This may be explained (1) as that these Nouns do not stand in need of anything else that would serve as their primary—in this case it being necessary to supply the words '*na vidyatē;*' or (2) the need for anything else is far away from these.

"How"? The reply is '*bhūtatvāt*'—that is to say, because of these being accomplished entities; this has been added only with a view to show the real character of things; which serves as a reason for the view held by the *Sūtra*.

***Sūtra* (4): Such words, on whose utterance the objects denoted are not found to exist, are Verbs; hence it is by means of these that the *Apūrva* is cognised; because of the object being dependent.**

It is always the denotation of the root, as contained in the Verb, that is cognised as *something to be accomplished;* and when this is held to be connected directly with the Result, the Noun must be taken as serving only a visible purpose.

That is to say, from its very character, the denotation of the Root is cognised as *something to be accomplished*, which latter is distinctly specified by such roots as form parts of particular verbs. Hence when such a denotation of the Root is laid down as the means to a Distinct Result, inasmuch as the former itself is something yet *to be accomplished*, it stands in need of an Instrument; and what the Noun does is to lay down either the accessories of the *sacrifice* (denoted by the Root), or to appear only as the *Name* of a particular sacrifice; or do both; and thereby it becomes subsidiary to the denotation of the Root.

Objection: "If you hold it to appear as the Name, then, inasmuch "as the word that appears as the Noun would also be something to be "accomplished, this too would be equal in all respects to the denotation "of the Root."

Reply: Not so: (1) Because if the Name be held to be directly connected with the Result, it would only be taken as an Accessory; and as such an accomplished entity (and this would strike at its very character of the Name). And (2) because though the denotation of the root has the character of *something to be accomplished*, yet when it happens to be expressed by a Noun, it is always cognised as an accomplished entity, exactly like any ordinary substance.

That is to say, though the denotation of the Root is in the form of *something to be accomplished*, yet whenever it happens to be mentioned by a Noun, it is always accompanied by distinct notions of Gender and Number, and as such a fully accomplished entity. And it is a recognised fact that the syntactical needs of words depend upon the particular verbal expression, and not upon the real state of things described; hence it must be admitted that such a need belongs to the Root, and not to the Noun.

"*Because of the object being dependent,*"—this serves to point out the difference between the Noun and the Verb, as based upon the degrees of proximity to the words. In connection with the *Bhāvanā*,—which has the character of a particular activity of the person concerned—this person requires a certain relationship of the denotation of the Root; and as there is no reason for setting aside this fact, there is no need of the mention of the Noun; and this is a sufficient ground of difference.

ADHIKARAṆA (2).

[*The Existence of Apūrva.*]

The above discussion, as to the means of the comprehension of the *Apūrva*, has presupposed the existence of the *Apūrva* itself; but inasmuch as its existence is not generally accepted, the next *sūtra* is introduced with a view to establish the existence of the *Apūrva*.

Sūtra (5): There is an *Apūrva*; because of the Injunction.

Inasmuch as sacrifices have been laid down for the purpose of certain definite results, to follow after the lapse of a long time,—such deferred fruition of the Action would not be possible, unless there was an intervening agency of the *Apūrva*. That is to say, the Apparent Inconsistency of the relationship of sacrifices and such results as the attainment of Heaven, &c., laid down in the Veda,—points to the fact that the existence of the *Apūrva* also is laid down in the Veda itself; and as such it is quite authoritative.

Some people—notably the author of the *Vṛtti* on the *Sūtras*—thinking themselves to be exceptionally clever, seek to disprove the *Apūrva* in the following manner. And this serves as the

PŪRVAPAKSHA (1) of the *Adhikaraṇa*.

"Being not amenable to either of the first five means of right notion, the *Apūrva* must be admitted to be amenable to the sixth—Negation. That is to say, the first five means of right notion—Sense-perception and the rest—serve the purpose of giving ideas of certain things; consequently an object which is not amenable to any of these, cannot but be accepted to be non-existent, being amenable to the sixth means of right notion—Negation. And, as a matter of fact, none of the former five are found to be applicable to the *Apūrva*; and hence, being totally foreign (*A-pūrva*) to the means of right notion, it is a non-entity, and as such the name '*Apūrva*' is quite proper for it.

"(1) The *Apūrva* is not cognised by means of Sense-perception, because not being of the nature of the objects of Sense,—Colour, &c.,—it cannot be cognised by means of the eye, &c.

"(2) Nor is it cognisable by means of Inference; because it has never been found to be actually concomitant with any characteristic mark (that could serve as the middle term of the Inferential Syllogism); as a matter of fact, no relationship—either general or particular—has ever been cognised, with regard to the *Apūrva*; and we have also shown above that Inference is never able to prove the mere *existence* of objects.

"(3) We do not know of any word or sentence denotative of the *Apūrva*; and hence it cannot be held to be an object of verbal cognition. And as for its cognition being based upon the Veda, this could be possible, only if it were expressed by either a Word or a Sentence. And as a matter of fact, there is no word that is directly expressive of the *Apūrva*. As for the word *Apūrva* itself, it only expresses the true state (non-existent) of any such thing; and as such denies its existence totally. And as a rule, words cannot apply to a thing not cognised by any other means of cognition; as it has already been shown that the Word itself is not an independent means of notion. And as for the Sentence, it cannot serve as the means of cognising the *Apūrva*; for the simple reason that the sentence is totally incapable of expressing any such thing as an *Apūrva*; because what is expressed by a sentence is either the identity or difference, or some sort of relationship between any two or more objects; while as a matter of fact, there are no such objects, of which the *Apūrva* could be either the identity or difference or any other relationship. Though for the cognition of difference among objects, the *Sūtra* lays down such means as *Different Words*, &c., and *Direct Assertion*, &c.,—yet these also are applicable only to the differentiation or usage of such objects as have a natural existence of their own; and they cannot serve to point out the existence of anything; and as such they cannot serve as the means of cognising the *Apūrva*. And as for Indirect Implication (*Atidēça*), this cannot apply to anything that has not been cognised by means of Direct Assertion. And further, the whole of the Veda treating of mere Injunctions and Prohibitions, it is never found to point out the existence of objects; and hence there can be no scriptural authority for the *Apūrva*.

"(4) That which has never been seen, and hence anything similar to which has never been seen, can never form the object of Analogy. In fact, being never perceived, the *Apūrva* could be held to be analogous only to non-entities, like the hare's horns, which also are never perceived.

"(5) Even Apparent Inconsistency does not show that there actually "is any such thing as *Apūrva*; because the relationship of the Sacrifice "and its Result is capable of other explanations.

"That is to say, (*a*) as for the Apparent Inconsistency of something "actually seen, this can be shown to be as irrelevant here as in the case "of the proving of the existence of *Dharma*. That is, as a proof of the "existence of *Dharma*, people bring forward the fact of there being dis-"crepancies in the conditions of different people; but this discrepancy is "otherwise explicable,—being held to be due to the nature of the "individuals concerned; in the same manner, the relationship of the Sacri-"fice with its results being otherwise explicable, it cannot point to any "such thing as the *Apūrva*. (*b*) As for the Apparent Inconsistency of "something that has been directly asserted, this applies only to such cases "where the Inconsistency is perceptible. In the present case, however, "we have to deal with something that is assumed; and certainly any "such thing cannot be said to be *inconsistent* with something else. For "instance, when it is said that the material to be offered should be cut out by "the *Sruva*, it is distinctly perceptible that such materials as *Meat, Cake* "and the like are incapable of being cut by it; and as the general direc-"tion is applicable to these latter also, the direction is interpreted as that it "is only the *cutting out of liquids*, or semi-liquids, that is to be done by the "*Sruva*. And this assumed interpretation is not inconsistent with anything; "because it does not entail the rejection of something directly laid down and "the assumption of something not so laid down. As for the *Apūrva*, it "can never be conceived of as the means to a result; and as such it can-"not be urged that from among various means to the Result, all others "being inapplicable to the case in question, it is the *Apūrva* alone that "can be accepted as the *means*, by the Law of *Pariçēsha* (Alternatives).

"And further, if the mere fact of the inapplicability of other means "were to serve as the sole ground for the application of the said Law of "Alternatives, why cannot we assume the Horns of the Hare to be the "means in question? That is to say, the mere fact of the absence of any "other cause, cannot justify the assumption of *Apūrva* being the neces-"sary means; because the reason would be equally applicable to the "agency of the 'hare's horns' as well.

"And, further, if the *Apūrva* be held to be something brought about "by the Sacrifice, then that would mean a rejection of the Heaven, which "is the directly asserted objective of the Sacrifice, and the assumption "of a thing not so asserted. And secondly, if the *Apūrva* be held to be "the means to the particular Result, that would mean the rejection of the "Sacrifice, which is the directly asserted means to the Result, and the "assumption of something not so declared. And there is no third "character that could be attributed to the *Apūrva.* Consequently, on "the strength of the Scripture, it must be held that the Result follows "directly from the Sacrifice.

"If it be asked—how can the Sacrifice, being itself immediately "destroyed, bring about the result?—all that we have to say, in reply, "is that, when such an effectiveness is mentioned in the Scriptures, why "should it bother your head? For certainly, what is your authority for "holding that the long-standing (*Apūrva*, left by the Sacrifice) brings "about the Result? If it be a law that it is only long-standing causes "that can bring about any effects, then why should it not be held that the "Results are brought about by the *Ākāça*, and such eternal things? If it be "urged that, 'we assume the Result to be brought about by the *Apūrva*, "simply because that alone is capable of a continuous existence other "than what is possible for that (Sacrifice) which is laid down as the "'means'—then, it would be far more reasonable to assume the Result "to follow from the *Ākāça*, &c.; but in this latter case, inasmuch as "the existence of these is universally recognised, you would have to as-"sume only their agency in the bringing about of the Result; where-"as in the case of the *Apūrva*, you have got to assume everything, "beginning from its very existence, without any authority whatever.

"If you mean to say that, 'the Result must be brought about by "some such agency as has some degree of permanence, and *is connected* "*with the Sacrifice* (which cannot be said of *Ākāça*, &c.)',—even then, "(1) it would be very much simpler to assume the Result to be brought "about by the Soul of the Sacrificer, which is connected with the Sac-"rifice, and is permanent. That is to say, the Sacrifice itself being tran-"sitory, if the Result brought about by something connected with it "can be spoken of as brought about by the Sacrifice,—then certainly "it is very much simpler to assume that it is brought about by the soul "of the person who has performed the Sacrifice. (2) Or, the *destruction* "of the Sacrifice could bring about the Result (all Destruction being per-"manent); and the assumption of this agency would not require any "great effort on our part, inasmuch as it is correlative to the Sacrifice which "is directly laid down in the Veda. That is to say, the Sacrifice itself "being transitory, what we have to admit is that the Action itself is "destroyed; but on account of the truthfulness of the Scripture, its "Result is sure to follow at some other time. And it is a rule that that which "leads to the cognition of something else is the means to this latter; and "in the case in question, we find that it is the *destruction* of the action "that gives us an idea of the occurrence of the Result at some other "time; and hence this Destruction must be admitted to be the means to "the Result.

"It may be urged that a non-entity is never held to be an effective "agent. But in reply to this, we ask—where have you come across that "effective agency of the *Apūrva*, that you accept it in the present case? "And when it becomes absolutely necessary to renounce the ordinarily "acknowledged character of the Means,—and we come to consider whether "we should assume the agency of the *Apūrva* or that of *Negation*,—it "cannot but strike us that the assumption of the agency of *Negation* "which is accomplished in itself, is far more reasonable than, and cannot "be rightly given up in favour of, that of the agency of the *Apūrva*, "which itself has got to be assumed.

"And further, if the words of the Veda itself could express the fact "of the Result following at some other time, then alone could we, on the "strength of that, assume the intervening agency of something else. "That is to say, the Vedic Injunction is found to serve the purpose of "pointing out the relation between a certain Action and a Result; and no "mention is found therein of any other time; and hence from the nature "of Actions in general, we would naturally assume the result of the Ac-"tion enjoined to follow immediately after it; why then should we, in "the first place, assume the result to occur at some other time, and then, "secondly, assume the intervening agency of the *Apūrva*?

"Here it may be urged that—'at the time that the Action is per-"formed, the Result is not found to appear immediately after it; and we "are forced to the conclusion that the Result must follow at some other "time, and that the *Apūrva* is the agent that intervenes between the perfor-"mance of the Action and the appearance of the Result.'

"But this is not correct; it is only *after* he has ascertained the pure "meaning of of the Scriptural Injunction that a person engages in the per-"formance of the Action enjoined; and after the Action has been performed, "he does not trouble himself with the meaning of the said Injunction. "That is to say, none that is ignorant of Vedic Injunctions is entitled to "the performance of any Sacrifice; and hence prior to the performance "of the Sacrifice, it is absolutely necessary for the performer to have "a full comprehension of all that is implied in the Injunctions. And "as a matter of fact, at the time of this comprehension, there is not "the least idea of the fact of the Result of the Action not appearing at "the time of its performance. And that which, at the time of the com-"prehension of the Scriptural Injunction, has not been cognised as con-"tained in the Injunction—how can it be possible that it is always cog-"nised subsequently?

"Then again, inasmuch in the case of all men, we find the Result "not appearing immediately after the Action—we can attribute this fact "to some deficiency in the performer himself; and as such there is no

"Inconsistency in the non-appearance of the Result, that could justify "the assumption of the *Apūrva*. That is to say, we actually find a certain "deficiency (in the performer or in the performance of the Action), which "supplies the necessary explanation of the fact of the Result not appearing "immediately after the Action is performed; and hence there can be no "ground for assuming an *Apūrva*, for the sake of the appearance of the "Result at some other time. Because the authority of Apparent Inconsis-"tency being equally applicable to both assumptions, it is more reason-"able by far to assume some such deficiency, even when any such be not "perceptible, than to assume an altogether unprecedented agency of the "*Apūrva*.

"Nor can the *Apūrva* be assumed with a view to the appearance of "Results during future lives. Because Heaven and Hell consisting of only "Pleasure and Pain, respectively, these two are actually experienced by the "person during this very life, immediately after the performance of actions. "That is to say, there are no Heaven and Hell either in the shape ex-"tremes of Pleasure and Pain, or in the shape of certain well-defined "localities,—so that these could not be experienced during the present life; "specially as if these were transcendental, we could not have any longing for "or aversion to them; and as for the ordinary pleasures and pains, these "appear immediately after the performance of the Action; and so there is "no difference in the case of such results, that could justify an assumption "of the *Apūrva*.

"Further, in the case of Prohibitions, the declaration of the Scripture "is not found to bring about an *Apūrva*; and hence any *Apūrva* proceeding "from an infringement of the Prohibitions could not have the authority "of the Scriptures. That is to say, in the case of the sentence—'the "Brāhmaṇa should not be killed,' what is declared by the Scripture is "that one should *desist* from such killing; and such *desisting* cannot bring "about any result at any other time; and as such this does not stand in "need of the assumption of an *Apūrva*. Of the killing of the Brāhmaṇa, "however, the result is the fall into Hell; and if this Result could be "made the ground for assuming an *Apūrva* to be produced by such *killing*, "inasmuch as the *killing* is not enjoined in the Veda, the *Apūrva* in ques-"tion would be brought about by an ordinary (non-Vedic) action; and as "such it could not be said to rest upon the authority of the Veda. And "even if such an *Apūrva* were assumed, being itself without any action, "it could not be capable of carrying the body of the person to any other "place, at some other time; and thus too it would be absolutely useless.

"Nor is it possible for the *Apūrva* to have any substratum; because "the substratum of the action itself is the sacrificial Cake, and such other "things appertaining to the sacrifice; and all these are destroyed with "the Action; and nothing apart from such substrata of the Action could "serve as the substratum of the connected *Apūrva*.

"The same arguments apply also to the rejection of the *Subsidiary* "*Apūrvas*. And further, if the Subsidiary *Apūrvas* be held to lead to the "Principal *Apūrva* at a distance, then the subsidiaries not being directly "related to the Principal Action, they could not serve any useful purpose. "That is to say, even if we assume a subsidiary *Apūrva*, this could not be "of any use, unless related to the Principal Action. Nor is it possible for "it to fall in with either the Principal Action itself or its *Apūrva*, because "of the immaterial character of these.

"As for the particular result that is said to accrue to the substance— "Corn, for instance—through its being washed;—even this ends with "that result; and as such not moving any further, it could not in any "way help the Principal *Apūrva* in bringing about the main Result of the "Principal Action.

"If the Subsidiary *Apūrvas* were held to inhere in the soul of the "sacrificer, then, in that case they would become included in a purpose "desired by the agent; and as such it would lose its character of being "subsidiary to the Action.

"And further, inasmuch as all subsidiary actions are mentioned "simultaneously by a single sentence, all the subsidiary *Apūrvas* would ac-"cord their help simultaneously; but no such simultaneous action is pos-"sible unless they are related to one another; as a matter of fact, however, "there is no ground for any such relationship. The same argnments apply "to the simultaneous action of the Principal *Apūrvas* towards the comple-"tion of the Result. Therefore we conclude that on account of the mere "fact of its being performed, the Principal Action produces the Result in "the Man, and the subsidiary Actions bring about their results in the "Principal Action.

"Nor again is it possible for the *Apūrva* to be either *produced* or *mani-*"*fested*.

"Because it could not be *produced* all at once, by a number of actions "that appear one after the other; and being devoid of constituent parts "it could not be believed to be produced in any sequential order. And "hence it can never be said to be *produced*.

"Nor can it be *manifested*; because a manifestation is possible only "through some sort of an effect produced upon the sense-organs, or the "objects of sense, or both of these; whereas we do not find any such effect "to be produced by Sacrifice, &c. That is to say, all manifestations are "brought about by means of the effect produced upon one of the afore-"said three (the sense, the object, or both); and hence in the case in "question, it becomes necessary to assume another such effect (*Saṅskāra*).

"Then again, for the sake of this last, we have to assume another *Saṅs-* "*kāra*; and hence this theory cannot be said to have any authority. If the "*Apūrva* were perceived after the performance of the Action, then we "could speak of its being *manifested* (because it is only that which exists "that can be manifested),—and that too, if there were some authoritative "means of cognising its existence. As a matter of fact, however, none of "these two contingencies exist. Consequently, we conclude that there is "no such thing as *Apūrva*, and that the present *Sūtra* does not treat of "any such thing; hence the said interpretation of the *Sūtra* cannot be "accepted as correct."

To all this, we make the following reply:

SIDDHANTA.

The peculiar kind of *Apūrva* that you have reared up in your own imagination, to have a tangible body, is nothing to us, and as such a refutation of that need not trouble us at all. For the simple reason that the *Apūrva* that we hold is not what you have refuted, but we mean by it a certain *capability* in the Principal Action or in the Agent, which did not exist prior to the performance of the action, and which is duly based upon the authority of the Scriptures. Before the Principal or the Subsidiary actions are performed, men are incapable of reaching Heaven, and the Principal Sacrifices are incapable of bringing about their results. And it must be admitted that both these incapabilities—one in the agent and another in the Principal Action—are set aside by the duly performed Principal and Subsidiary sacrifices, which then produce a certain capability in them. Because unless the said capability be produced the Actions remain as good as unperformed. And it is this capability, in the Agent or in the Principal Sacrifice, that is called, in our philosophy, the '*Apūrva.*'

You have urged that the *Apūrva* is not cognisable by any of the recognised means of right notion, Sense-perception and the rest. This is true; inasmuch as the only means of cognising the *Apurvā* is the Apparent Inconsistency of something mentioned in the Veda; and hence your argument does not quite affect our position. Specially because we also hold only such Apparent Inconsistency to be the means of knowing the *Apūrva;* and inasmuch as this Apparent Inconsistency forms a part of Verbal Testimony, our sole authority for the *Apūrva* is the Scripture itself.

That is to say, there are certain Vedic passages which declare that attainment of Heaven proceeds from the sacrifice, and that the subsidiary sacrifices, the *Prayāja* and the rest, impart a help to the Principal Sacrifice; and on account of such passages it must be admitted that these actions, whether destroyed or not, have a certain potency for bringing about the results mentioned in the said passages; specially as no effects can be produced by an entity that is devoid of all potency.

Now then, we must admit the said potency to belong to the Sacrifices, after they have been performed. Because all actions being transitory, it is not possible for even a single action to exert a simultaneous influence upon the Result; how then can this be possible in the case of many actions? That is to say, when the action is taken in hand, inasmuch as it is made up of many momentary parts, it is incapable of applying al at once to any Result, and this becomes all the more impossible when the Actions—such as the *Darça-Pūrṇamāsa*, etc.—are made up of many supplementary Actions. For instance, at the time that the *Darça* is performed, there is no *Pūrṇamāsa;* and by the time that the *Pūrṇamāsa* is performed, the *Darça* has long ceased to exist; and so also in the case of a single sacrifice, at the time that the *Āgnēya* is performed, the *Agnīshomīya* and the *Upāñçu* sacrifices do not exist; and when any one of these exist, the other two do not; and thus no simultaneity is possible. Consequently if the *Darça-Pūrṇamāsa*, or any part of it, were to be destroyed, without leaving behind any capability in the Agent, then they would be in the same position as that which they had before their performance; and as such any subsequent action not having any concomitance, either directly or through some potency left behind, with the foregoing actions, such performance of the latter Principal Action would in no way differ from this same Action, when performed alone by itself, without the foregoing subsidiaries (as at the time of the bringing about of the final result it would have, in both cases, to depend solely upon itself); and hence there would not appear the Result, which is laid down as following from the Principal Action as accompanied by the Subsidiary Actions; because neither the *Darça* by itself, nor any other Action, has been laid down as the means of that Result.

Even those who declare that the Result must always follow immediately after the Action, will have to admit that the Result should appear at the end of *all* the Actions concerned; and consequently, according to them, Action performed last being the immediate precursor of the Result would be the only means to the Result, all the others having been long destroyed. If however all the Actions leave behind them certain capabilities, called '*Apūrvas*,' then there being no use of the actual presence of the Actions themselves, even when their physical forms have ceased to exist, the functioning of the Result would have a simultaneity based upon such capabilities; specially as it is only such simultaneity that is found to be the basis of all usage. For instance, all objects are found to act their parts, in all ordinary usage, only by means of their capabilities; and hence the usage can be accomplished by means of the capabilities, even if the physical form of the action exist at some other time and place. Even in the case of ordinary actions of the world, when the Results of such actions are found to appear at some other time, the said capability must exist; but this capability is not called '*Apūrva*.' That is to say, even in the ordinary world there are many such Actions as, Farming, Eating butter, and Study &c., the Results of which are found to appear at some future time; and inasmuch as these actions themselves cannot continue to exist till the appearance of the result, we must admit the Result to be brought about by certain potencies left behind them, which continue to exist all along. But inasmuch as these actions do not appertain to the Veda, these capabilities are not called '*Apūrvas*.'

Thus then, before the action is performed, at the very time that the Vedic Injunction of the Action has been heard, we at once recognise the Result therein mentioned to be capable of being brought about by the due performance of many Subsidiary and Principal Actions; and having a firm faith in the veracity of the Veda, we at once come to the conclusion that all the various Subsidiary and Principal Actions must continue to have some sort of an existence, up to the time of the actual appearance of the Result; and inasmuch as we find the physical forms of these actions to be destroyed as soon as they are performed, we conclude that they can have no existence, except in the shape of some sort of a capability left behind.

It has been urged that the assumption of the *Apūrva* entails the rejection of that which is directly mentioned in the Veda, and the assumption of something not so mentioned. But such is not the case; because as a matter of fact, (1) either the Result may be said to be brought about by the Sacrifice itself, through the said Capability, or (2) the Result itself may be said to have been produced, immediately after the action, in the shape of a certain subtile potency.

(1) If the Result were brought about by something totally unconnected with the Sacrifice, then the said objection would apply to us. As a matter of fact, however, that which is brought about by the potency left behind in the Agent by the Sacrifice, is brought about by the Sacrifice itself; specially as all Causes in the world, in the bringing about of their particular results, stand in need of certain intermediate actions. (2) Or conversely, all effects, in the shape of the Curd, &c., when appearing from their causes, as Milk, &c., do not all at once appear in the thickened form (of the curd); in fact, in the interval (between the milk and the fully-developed curd) the milk undergoes, at every step, various subtile modifications. In the same manner, a result, like Heaven, undergoes several intervening modifications, in the shape of the *Apūrva*, which is in the

shape of a *sprout* (that would blossom forth into the fully-developed Heaven). And hence, in the appearance of this sprout-like *Apūrva*, the Heaven itself becomes produced; and in this case, all the time that intervenes between the determination to perform the sacrifice and the experiencing of the last iota of the Result, is counted as the *Present.* It has also been declared elsewhere: 'When one says one should cook the food by means of fuel, the action of *burning* is understood; and as soon as the sprout has sprung up, it is taken for granted that the tree has grown.'

It has been urged above that before the Action has been actually performed, there can be no idea of any such thing as the *Apūrva.* But this is not true; because all Means, either Vedic or of the ordinary world, are known to be transitory; and then unless there is some idea of the permanence of some sort of a potency left behind by the Means, how could such a Means be enjoined in the Veda? That is to say, unless we actually recognise the fact that the potency left behind by the Means, which itself is past and gone, subsists till the final accomplishment of the Result,—there is no possibility of a transitory Action being enjoined; and hence it is proved that the idea of the possibility of such a potency exists before the Action is performed.

Nor can the Result be said to be brought about by the souls of the persons that have performed the sacrifice; because, in accordance with your theory, there is no difference made in the soul, either by the performance or the non-performance of the sacrifice. If the sacrifice were to disappear without leaving any trace behind, then, being as good as not performed, what would be the difference between the soul of the person that has performed the sacrifice and that of one who has not performed it? Because the character of the *soul* exists equally in both; and the character of the *sacrifice* too belongs equally to that which is performed and has disappeared, and to that which is not performed. And as for the character of the *performer* (of the sacrifice), it does not persist in the soul of the person who is at some other time devoid of the action, and occupies an altogether different position. Nor can it be urged that the potency of the *Performer* subsists; because the sacrifice being performed even before the appearance of this *potency* (which appears only after the action has been performed), it cannot be said to be any such cause of the Action as functions by its very presence. And further, if the Man (his soul) were the means of the Result,—then the means of all Results, pleasant and as well as unpleasant, being one and the same, all the Results would always be of one and the same kind. And again, the character of *having performed sacrifices* would inhere equally in one who has performed many sacrifices and one who has performed only one; and then there would be no difference in the results accruing to these two persons. And this argument would strike against all those that perform many sacrifices; specially because the verb not signifying the performing agent, how could it be cognised that such and such a person has the character of having performed *many* sacrifices. For one who accepts the production of *Apūrva*, there is a distinct *Apūrva* for each action performed, and as such there would be no incongruity in the multiplicity and multifariousness of Results.

And further, among the subsidiaries also, if the soul of the performer alone were the sole means to the end, then inasmuch as the traces left by the subsidiaries, as performed along with one Principal Sacrifice, would subsist in the soul of the performer at all times, there would be no performance of the same subsidiaries, along with another sacrifice (in which two they are laid down as to be performed separately). That is to say, according to your theory, all the subsidiary sacrifices, the *Prayāja* and the rest, being transient, there could be no proximity of the Result with the physical forms of these, and consequently, the help that the subsidiaries would accord to the Principal, must be done by the Performer; and this help of the Principal too, in the absence of an *Apūrva*, must accord its help to the soul of the Performer himself; thus then, one who has performed the subsidiary *Prayāja*, &c., in connection with the Principal Sacrifice, would remain ever-endued with the aid accorded by these subsidiaries; and hence—without performing these along with another sacrifice, which is laid down as to be performed exactly in the same way as the former Principal Sacrifice,—he would attain its Result all the same; and so there could be no performance over again of these subsidiaries; and in that case there could be no room for such injunctions as that—'during the *Prayājas* one should offer the *krshnala* (a material laid down as the substitute of the ordinary materials offered at the sacrifice in connection with one Principal Sacrifice). It might be urged that—" the times of the performance of the two sets of sacrifices being different, the one performance of the subsidiaries could not obviate the necessity of performing them over again." But the reply to this will be given under the *Sūtra* '*Arthasyāvikrtatvāt*' where it will be shown that the aid accorded by the performance of the subsidiaries being held to be in the shape of the soul of the Performer, this aid would remain exactly the same, whether the object aided be near at hand or at a distance; and that thus it would make no difference, even if the Principal Sacrifice to be performed were not quite proximate to the subsidiaries.

The above objections apply also to the theory that the Result proceeds from the Destruction of the Action. Because one who holds the Result to follow from such Destruction could have no difference among the Destructions of good and evil actions, or between those of one or many actions, or among various kinds of negation itself—*viz.*: Prior Negation,

Posterior Negation, &c. ; because all of these equally are *non-entities* ; and as such there could be no diversity or multifariousness of results. For instance, one who has been cured of one disease, as well as one who has been cured of many,—in the case of both of these men, the fact of *being cured* is just the same.

If the Destruction of each particular action be held to be distinct, then it becomes an *entity;* and as we know of no such entity, it is only the entity in the shape of the *Apūrva* that would be called by the name of 'Destruction.'

And further, the Results are not mentioned as following from the Destruction of Actions ; and specially as this Destruction is nothing more than the contradictory of the sacrifice, a result that would follow from it could not be said to follow from the sacrifice. That is to say, all that the Veda says is that—'one desiring Heaven *should perform sacrifices,*' and not that *he should procure a negation of sacrifices.* And hence, the sentence being actually found to rest upon the causal relationship between two *entities,* if one were to assume it to deal with such relationship between non-entities, he would be striking at the very authority of the Veda itself. Because that which proceeds from the Destruction of the Action cannot be said to be (causally) connected with the Action itself ; because of the two (Action and its Destruction) being contradictory to one another; for instance, the burning caused by the *heat* of fire cannot be said to be connected with cold. Or, it may be that, just as when the Result is laid down as following *from the sacrifice,* you assumed it to follow *from its destruction,* so in the same manner though the result laid down is *Heaven,* yet it may be assumed to be the *Negation of Heaven!* It may be urged that the said objection applies equally to the *Apūrva* theory also. But then, it is not so ; because it is only a *capability* brought about by the Action, and as such, it is not quite different from it. As we have already shown that that which is brought about by the *Apūrva* is brought about by the sacrifice itself, and that in the production of the *Apūrva,* the result itself is produced.

Even in ordinary experience we never find any negation to have a causal action ; even if any such may be shown, there too, we can always attribute the effect to some other *entity.* In the case in question, however, we perceive no other active entity save the *Apūrva.*

It has been urged above that in ordinary experience the *Apūrva* too has never been perceived to have a causal action. But this is not correct ; because in all cases we find the causal efficiency belonging to some sort of a Potency or Capability in general ; and the *Apūrva* is nothing more than a particular sort of Potency.

Another argument that has been brought forward is that—" the

Injunction does not speak of any Result following at any other time; and the only theory that is in keeping with the scriptural Injunction is that the Result follows immediately after the action has been performed; and hence it is only such immediate sequence of the result that can be said to be enjoined;" but in refutation of this we have already brought forward the fact that the Actions being many and all transitory, no immediate sequence to the Action is ever possible.

As for Heaven and Hell also, these represent the very extremest degrees of Pleasure and Pain respectively; and as such are capable of being experienced only at some other place and time, and could never be experienced immediately after the performance of actions,—as we shall show in the beginning of the Sixth Adhyāya.

Even such ordinary worldly results—as children, &c.—having the nature of appearing gradually, do not appear immediately after the performance of the action; and people do not ever think of obtaining the Result immediately after the action. As for such results as the acquisition of landed property in a village, such acquisition by itself does not constitute all the Result, which lies chiefly in the use to which the property is brought; and this takes some time, and could not be fulfilled without certain intervening causes. Inasmuch as such objects as landed property, &c., have their full fruition in the use to which they are brought, which requires a certain amount of time, such fruition would be impossible immediately after the Action; hence in the course of this time, whenever the activity of the cause would cease, the Result would be finished and done with all at once; consequently it is absolutely necessary that there should be some sort of a causal agency subsisting till the accomplishment of the last iota of the Result.

And this fact being duly ascertained before the performance of the Action, it cannot be rightly urged that the Apparent Inconsistency of the fruition of the Result would be equally explicable on the ground of certain deficiencies in the character of the Performer, detected after the performance of the sacrifice has been found to be not immediately followed by the Result.

It has been urged that there is no scriptural *Apūrva* in the case of Prohibitions. But just as in the case a Scriptural Injunction, an *Apūrva* follows from the Act enjoined, so, in the same manner, in the case of Prohibitions, an *Apūrva* must follow from that which is prohibited. That is to say, just as it is only certain ordinary objects of the world—such as certain materials, &c.—that becoming Vedic, after the particular Injunction of the Veda has been laid down which connects them with a definite result, are found to bring about certain transcendental *Apūrvas*, only amenable to the Veda;—in the same manner, though such prohibited actions as the killing of a Brāhmaṇa, are not ordinarily recognised as leading to a fall into Hell, yet when the particular prohibition (of such killing) has been met with, it naturally leads to the assumption of its bringing about an *Apūrva* capable of leading the person into Hell; and this *Apūrva* too is as Vedic in its character as the former *Apūrvas.*

Even though the *Apūrva* is devoid of any such apparent actions as motion and the like, yet by a mere connection with the performer, it becomes capable of such actions as leading him to other places, &c.; and as such the absence of any apparent activity cannot be urged against it with any effect. And it is the soul of the performer himself that serves as the substrate of the *Apūrva;* hence the said action also rests in this soul itself; as we have already shown, under the chapter on 'Soul,' that of all Actions the active agent is the Soul. That is to say, it has been shown that of all such actions as the cutting out of the Cake, and offering it, &c., it is the Soul that is the active agent, through its specific action of *determination*, &c. And thus we conclude that as the said actions go on disappearing, one after the other, they leave behind them, in the Soul certain *potencies* capable of bringing about the experience Heaven, &c.

It may be asked—'How can the potency of that which has been destroyed subsist?' But to this we make the following reply: If the potencies of actions were held to lie within themselves, then on the destruction of these, they could not subsist; but when they inhere in the soul of the performer, there is no reason why they should not subsist.

Question: "But how can the potency of one thing inhere in another?"

Answer: (1) There is no absolute difference between the Action and the Soul of the Performer. (2) And as a matter of fact, when looking for a potency, inasmuch as its assumption rests upon its effects, we must always accept it to lie in a substrate where it might be of the greatest use,—be this substrate the Action itself or something else. That is to say, when we find that a destruction of the Action makes entirely useless any potency that inheres in that Action,—and that it is absolutely necessary to postulate such a potency,—then, just as its peculiar form, so its substrate too, must be assumed to be such as would make it of the greatest use.

And thus it is that the subsidiary *Apūrvas*, resting in the Soul, become related to the Principal *Apūrvas*, through the fact of both of them inhering in the same Soul; and hence, when proceeding to help (in the accomplishment of the Result), they do it from a distance, on account of there being left no place in the substrate (by the Principal *Apūrvas*) for any direct functioning (of the subsidiary *Apūrvas*).

It has been urged above that, if the *Apūrva* inhere in the Soul, then it becomes only an end in itself desirable by men. But this does not affect our position; because one thing becomes subservient to another, only when its sole use lies in the serving of some purpose of this latter, and not merely when it rests in this; for instance, though the Red Dye is carried by the camel (and as such rests upon its back), yet it serves the purposes of the king (for whom it is carried). Nor can it be urged that there can be no relationship of the container and the contained in the case of an immaterial thing (like the *Apūrva*). Because such relationship is as feasible as the presence of Pleasure, &c., in the Soul (which is immaterial).

As for the effects produced in the corns by the action of washing, &c., this subsists till the action of the cutting of the cake into two parts extend over the whole series of such actions as the setting aside up of the several conditions of the corn—as the Rice, &c.; and inasmuch as the Principal Action also inheres, to a certain degree, in the corn, the aforesaid effect rests aside, only after it has helped in the accomplishment of the Principal *Apūrva*. And it is for these reasons that, like the actions that help from a distance, the actions of washing, &c., are not accepted as helping in the fulfilment of the Principal Action, as a whole.

And just as the connection between the Subsidiary and the Principal *Apūrvas* rests upon the fact of their inhering in the same Soul, so also the same may be said with regard to the connection among the subsidiary *Apūrvas* themselves on the one hand, and among the Principal *Apūrvas* on the other. And thus it is that the simultaneous activity of all these becomes possible.

Question: "How is it that the Principal *Apūrvas*, appearing as "they do one after another, are helped all at once, by the subsidiary "*Apūrvas*, which also appear one after the other, some before and some "after the Principal *Apūrvas*?"

To this some people make the following reply: The Principal Action lying among the Subsidiaries, brings about its *Apūrva*, by means of the *Apūrvas* left by the subsidiaries gone before it, as also by those coming after it,—these latter also having been already moved into activity, by the force of the fixed procedure of the Action as a whole. But being, like the *Atīthyā* and the *Varhi* offerings, common to many, the said subsidiary *Apūrvas* do not become fully utilised in helping in the fulfilment of a single Principal *Apūrva*.

Question: "But how can any help be given by those *Apūrvas* that are themselves yet to come?"

Reply: This help is presupposed on account of the relationship being known to be absolutely certain; just as when the action of *eating* is close at hand, the cups, &c., are washed beforehand.

Question: "If it be such that while the subsidiary *Apūrvas* are yet

" to come, the Principal *Apūrvas* are accomplished, then in that case, there " would be no need of actually performing the subsidiary sacrifices (as " their purposes will have been fulfilled prior to their performance)."

Reply: But wherefore should they not be performed, when the matter is such that though the Principal *Apūrva* is accomplished by the prospective help of the *Apūrvas* of the subsidiary Actions to be performed, yet it does not bear its final fruit, until these actions have been actually performed?

Others, however, offer the following reply to the above question: Each subsidiary Action brings about its own *Apūrva* independently of all other subsidiaries; similarly the Principal Action also—*f.i.*, the *Āgnēya*—brings about its own peculiar *Apūrva*, by the mere help of certain old-standing *Apūrvas*, inhering in the soul of the performer, independently of the *Apūrvas* of all its own subsidiaries—which it has not yet been equipped with,—and independently also of any other Principal Action, which has not yet appeared. Thus, then, in the case of the *Darça-Pūrṇamāsa* sacrifice, taken as a whole, when the *Apūrvas* of the *Darça* together with all its subsidiary *Apūrvas* have been accomplished, then what the *Apūrvas* of all the subsidiaries (of the *Darça-Pūrṇamāsa*) do is to bring all at once to the Principal Sacrifice, a help, in the shape of an *Apūrva*, which appertains equally to all the correlated Subsidiaries and Principals, and which is assumed on the strength of the Injunctive passage implying such simultaneity, specially as after the final feeding of the Brāhmaṇas in connection with the *Darça* has been finished, the very same actions are not laid down as to be performed over again. And then through that the various Principal *Apūrvas* also joining together bring about another *Apūrva*, in the shape of the capability of bringing about a single joint Result,—and thereby become fully accomplished. And this joint *Apūrva* continues unmolested till the last iota of the final Result has been attained.

Question: " When as a matter of fact the Result is found to appear " at the proper time, without any impediments, then, is it absolutely " necessary to assume an *Apūrva?*"

Reply: Certainly; because it has been shown above that without an *Apūrva* the fruition of the complete Result is not possible.

Question: " How is it that each subsidiary *Apūrva* does not, by " itself, help in the Principal *Apūrva*, and each of the Principal *Apūrvas* " does not, independently by itself, fructify into the final Result?"

Reply: True; but this does not affect our position; because in the case in question all that Apparent Inconsistency justifies is the assumption of a single *Apūrva;* and then for the fulfilment of this *Apūrva*, we can postulate a number of other *Apūrvas*. That is to say, inasmuch as with regard to the main Result all the Principal Actions are mentioned simultaneously, and so are also the Subsidiary Actions with regard to the Principal ones,—all the necessary requirements of the said relationships being fulfilled by the assumption of a single *Apūrva*, we conclude that there is no authority for assuming any other *Apūrva*. And then it is that finding that it is impossible for this *Apūrva* to be brought about, all at once, by means of a number of actions that are performed one after the other, we come to assume the existence of an *Apūrva* for each of these Actions. And it is a rule, in all cases, that a large number of unseen agencies may always be assumed, when all of them are justified by some authority; while even the hundredth part of an unseen agency should not be assumed, if there is no authority for it.

Here, some people urge the following objection: "If the subsidiary "*Apūrvas* brought forth on the day of the *Paurṇamāsī* subsist till the day "of the *Amāvāsyā*, then all the purposes of the person being fulfilled on "both occasions, he would not perform the subsidiary sacrifices over "again (for the *Darça*); and in that case he would directly infringe "the Vedic declaration that there are *thirteen* libations at the *Darça* "sacrifice."

To this, some people make the following reply: There would always be a repetition of the subsidiaries; because the *Darça* and the *Paurṇamāsa* sacrifices, each *with all its accessories*, being performed at different times, the admixture of these two should necessarily be helped by all the subsidiaries performed twice over. Or, we can offer the following explanation: The Instrumental case-ending in the word '*darçapaurṇamāsābhyām*' distinctly sgnifies the fact that it is only when the *Paurṇamāsī* is equipped with all its subsidiaries that it can, with the help of the fully-equipped *Darça*, accomplish its purpose; and consequently, in accordance with the aforesaid reasoning, we conclude that the three Principal *Apūrvas* of the *Paurṇamāsī*, aided by its subsidiary *Apūrvas*, brings forth one *Apūrva* and ends there; while the one *Apūrva* thus brought about, preceded by such another *Apūrva* of the *Darça*, brings forth another final *Apūrva*. Thus then, the subsidiaries performed in connection with the *Paurṇamāsī* having disappeared (after having helped in the bringing about of the *Apūrva* proper of the *Paurṇamāsī*), there can be no reason for neglecting the performance of those subsidiaries in connection with the *Darça*. And thus there is nothing objectionable in the said repetition.

The same course of reasoning might be adopted in meeting the objections with regard to the impossibility of the *Apūrva* being either produced or manifested. It has also been declared that: "Just as in a frequent repetition of the Veda, the impression made upon the mind is always gradual, being as it is, in the form of the various parts of the sentences, (one by one); so also would be the case with the appearance of the *Apūrva.*" Nor is it an absolute rule that there can be no parts of an immaterial object. Because the aforesaid Apparent Inconsistency would also justify the conclusion that the immaterial *Apūrva* is cognised in the form of extremely minute parts. Even though, the production of an absolute non-entity being impossible, the *Apūrva* be held to have an eternal existence and only to be manifested (by the sacrifice),—yet inasmuch as it is held to be brought about by sacrifices, distinctly for each person, we must accept its manifestation to be in the form of turning the person towards the accomplishment of the Result,—such manifestation being entirely different from any functioning of words, &c. And as a matter of fact the manifestation of things is not always in one and the same form; consequently the manifestation of the *Apūrva* would be in the shape of its being brought out of the soul wherein it has all along been lying latent. Or, it may be that by its very nature, the Soul of man is ever capable of obtaining all things; and such acquisition being barred by certain impediments, it is these latter that are removed by means of Sacrifices (and in this removal of the obstacle lies the manifestation of the *Apūrva*).

Thus then, we conclude that the *Apūrva* does exist; and the *Sūtra* too cannot be taken in any other sense, that would be of any use in the present context; and hence we take the meaning of the *Sūtra* to be that *the Injunction of the Action is the Injunction (authority) of the Apūrva.*

[Says the Bhashya—*If it be urged that 'on the authority of the mention of the Result we could hold that the Action (sacrifice) itself has not been entirely destroyed'*] The view here tentatively brought foward emanates from one who finds the assumption of the *Apūrva* to be utterly groundless, and hence prefers the comparatively reasonable theory of the non-destruction of the Action.

I. [In reply to this theory, the Bhāshya says—*we do not perceive any shape of the Action;* and against this it is urged that] "This assertion "is not quite correct; because Action has been distinctly mentioned as "perceptible by the Senses, under *Sūtra* 'Rūpaçabdāvibhāgācca [?]."

II. "Again [the Bhashya has said—*That which carries its substrate to another place is known as an Action;* and against this it is urged that] "the subject-matter of the discourse is *Sacrifice*, which is not of the "nature of *Motion;* and yet the Bhāshya cites a definition that applies "only to such actions as are of the nature of Motion; and this cannot but "be rejected as irrelevant."

To the above, we make the following replies:

I. What is meant by the assertion that no shape of Action is perceived is that we are not cognisant of any such form of Actions as would enable them to function at a future time; and as for the impermanent forms of Actions that are perceived, these can be of no use in the bringing about of the final Result. That is to say, though a shape of the Action is perceived, yet, inasmuch as this does not continue for any length of time, it can be of no use in the bringing about of the Result; and as such it is as good as "not perceived" and is spoken of as such.

II. Though the subject treated of is the *Sacrifice*, yet the Bhāshya has cited an instance of an Action of the nature of *Motion*, because, even in the Sacrifice, we have such actions in the shape of the throwing of the materials (into the fire). That is to say, the mere determination to offer, on the part of the Agent does not accomplish the Result, because the Result is laid down as following from the Action taken as a complete whole, as made up of all its accessories and appurtenances of procedure; and, as a matter of fact, we find that in the body of the Sacrifices, there are such actions as the cutting up of the Cake, the throwing into the fire of the Material, the holding and collecting of the various utensils, &c.; and inasmuch as all these actions consist of Conjunctions and Disjunctions, if they have to last for any length of time, they must have substrates of their own. And it is such a substrate that we do not find; nor is any manifested outward shape perceived. As for the actions of Determination also, inasmuch as one Determination is always shrouded over by another Determination, even this cannot have any lasting existence.

As for this continuance too, this could be only either as inhering (A) in the Soul, or (B) in the materials offered.

[A]. As for the Soul, no motion can inhere in it; because being omnipresent, there is no place from which it would be away, or to which it would go; and hence it can have no motion. As for the question—how can the Soul be omnipresent?—the only reply is that it is so, because we perceive its functioning everywhere. That is to say, the notion of 'I' (which is all the notion that we have of the Soul) always points to the mere existence of the Soul, which is of the nature of pure Consciousness; and does not in any way qualify it with any specifications of Time or Place. Consequently, that the existence whereof is not specified by time and place, being held to be eternal and omnipresent,—the Soul cannot but be accepted as omnipresent. Thus then we find that the expression 'the perception of its functioning everywhere' only points to this unspecified idea of 'I.' Or it may be taken as referring to the experiencing of Pleasure, Pain, &c.; because wherever the Soul goes, it is never without an experience of these. And we have already shown under the section on 'Ātmā' (in the *Tarkapāda—Çlokavārtika*) that these experiences do not belong to the Body. Hence if the Soul were not omnipresent, then there would be an experiencing of pleasure, &c., only in such cases where the Body would be in contact with a Place occupied by the Soul.

The upholder of the theory that the Soul is wholly encased within the Body, urges the following: "*The perception of its functioning every-" where is a sure sign of the Soul having come from one place to another*; and "as such firstly, the reason that you bring forward in support of its "ominpresence proves to be contrary to your conclusion. That is to say, "if the functioning of the Soul were actually perceived at all places, at "one and the same time, then alone could such perception point to its "omnipresence; as a matter of fact, however, the said functioning is "perceived in different places one after the other; and as such the nature "of the Soul comes to be similar to that of the Body. That is to say, if "we could ever perceive a functioning of the Soul, apart from the Body,— "or if we could find the pleasure, &c., of one Soul appearing in another "body,—then alone could we accept the Soul to be omnipresent. As it is "however, the functioning of the Soul is found only in that Body which "it occupies; and as such wherever this Body goes, there, one after the "other, we come across the said experiences; and hence these function- "ings of the Soul together with the Body becomes (in its extension) "exactly like those of the Body itself. Otherwise the Body would also "be held to be omnipresent. Thus then movement from one place to "another, being found in the soul also, it comes to be as active and "mobile as the Body itself. *Secondly*, the argument brought forward "may be discarded as leading to an uncertainty: inasmuch as it can "prove two contradictory conclusions. For instance, it has been declared "that the Soul is mixed up with the Body, because it is always in contact "with it; *and because, it is only in such and such places that the function* "*of the Soul is perceived.*"

It is in reply to these objections that the Bhāshya has said: *There is nothing incongruous in denying such mobility of the Soul.*

In the aforesaid *objection*-passage, some people read '*na tu* tadēva, &c.;" and in that case, we can take this passage as denying the argument that could be brought forward by the opponent,—namely, that the perception of its functioning everywhere would point to the Soul's moving from one place to the other; and then the next sentence gives the grounds for this denial.

Objection: "How can the fact of there being nothing incogruous in "denying the movement of the Soul be any reply to the above arguments? "Because the mere absence of incongruity cannot establish any theory; "specially as such absence of incongruity is equally applicable to the con- "trary theory; as it is equally open to the opponent to say that there is "nothing incongruous in admitting of the motion of the Soul."

To this, we make the following reply: The absence of incongruity being found to be applicable to both theories, the assertion of the Bhāshya, that "there is nothing incongurous, &c.," clearly shows that it means that there is an incongruity in the contrary theory. That is to say, the sense of the reply is that if we deny the motion of the Soul, there is nothing incongruous, while if we accept its motion, there are many incongruities.

We proceed to show these incongruities. (1) The Soul being itself immaterial, it can never be mixed up with material elements; and being untouched by these elements, it cannot be taken from one place to another. That is to say, even in the case of extremely subtile particles of matter,—such as the light emanating from the Sun or the Moon,—we find that they are not mixed up with grosser materials, like lumps of Earth, &c., or are carried about along with these; how then can such mixture or movement be postulated with regard to the Soul, which is in its very nature purely immaterial, or a mere series of *Ideas* (as held by the Bauddha)? Though the *Jaina* declares that "the Souls in the state of bondage being never found apart from the Body, they can be held to be material,"—yet such an assertion would involve a vicious circle;—namely that the fact of the Soul being material would depend upon the fact of its being mixed up with the Body, while this latter fact would depend upon the material nature of the Soul. Consequently, drawing our conclusion from the case of the liberated Souls, we can declare that in its very nature the Soul is immaterial; and as such it can have no materiality, based upon the fact of its contact with a material body. Thus then, the Soul being something different from the Body, and not in material contact with it,—it cannot, on account of this absence of contact, be carried along with it; and hence when the Body would be moving from one place to another, the Soul (if an entity limited in space) would be left behind, exactly like the portion of space vacated by the moving Body; specially as the Soul cannot be wafted along either by Air or by Earth, &c., and as such it is absolutely incapable of being carried about, either by itself or by anything else. As for such objects as Flame and the like, inasmuch as these are tangible, they are capable of being carried about by air-currents, or along with lighted torches, &c., and as such these can move from place to place. On the other hand, if the Body were to move about by itself, it would be inanimate; when, however, the Soul is omnipresent, wherever the Body goes, it is always endowed with the Soul; and hence it is only right that the Body should always be followed by intelligence. Exactly as, when one point of space has been vacated by the Body, another point of space is at once afforded to it; and this is possible, only on account of the omnipresent character of space.

(2) And further, in case the Soul be denied to be omnipresent, while occupying the Body, the Soul could be either extremely small as an atom, or of the size of the Body; but none of these is possible. And we have already shown (in the *Tarkapāda—Çlokavārtika*) that the Soul is not a mere *series of Ideas*. And the Soul being eternal, and located within the Body,—if it were extremely small, then it could not extend over the whole Body; and in that case, it would be absolutely impossible for us to have any experiences of pleasure or pain, throughout the Body. That is to say, if the Soul is extremely small, then it would be possible to have experiences of pleasure and pain of only that part of the Body, where the Soul would be located; and hence it would not be possible, at one and the same time, to have an experience of pain in the head and in the foot. If it be urged that, "being extremely mobile, the Soul would swiftly move from one part of the Body to the other, and would thereby make such varied experiences possible,"—then, all that we can say is that there are no grounds for believing in such mobility of the Soul; specially as we are not cognisant of any difference in the point of time of the pain in the head and that in the foot; and further, if the Soul would be constantly moving, there would be no point of time at which we could afford to have any sensation, and hence there would be no sensation in any part of the Body. Consequently we cannot but reject the offered explanation. And again, the various limbs of the Body are strengthened, and do not wither away, simply because of their being pervaded over by the Soul; because at death we find that they wither away quickly. Hence, if the Soul were something very small, that point of the Body, wherefrom it would be absent, would be liable to instant decay.

On the other hand, if the Soul were to be assumed to be of the exact size of the Body, as held by the Jaina, then too it would be necessary to make many gratuitous assumptions.

For instance, we would have to make the following assumptions:—(1) that the Soul has many parts; (2) that these parts are innumerable; (3) that without any other agency, there is a conglomeration of these parts; (4) that even though partite, the Soul is eternal; (5) that the Soul is capable of the very extremes of expansion and contraction; (6) that the Soul has a motion from one body to another, on death; (7) that there is a point of time intervening between its departure from one body and the occupation of another; and (8) that there is some cause for such motion of the Soul.

All the above assumptions—the existence of the Soul's parts, &c.—are such as are not at all amenable to Sense-perception, &c.; and as such they could at best be only the creations of one's imagination, &c.; and as such they should be rejected, in the same manner as we have rejected (under the chapter on *Words*) the assumption of parts of words. Then again, when the Soul is only as large as the Body, we can never assume its parts to be innumerable or endless; and in the absence of any fluidity in these parts, it is not possible for them to conglomerate together in one compact whole; and unless they conglomerate thus, they can have no power of bringing into existence a single living being. And further (even if such conglomerations were possible), all Conjunction always ending in Disjunction, the living Soul would be, exactly like a jar, amenable to occasional destruction. And when one part of the part has been cut off, there is no ground for assuming that the particles of the Soul, that were contained in that limb, escape from it when severed from the Body, and spread themselves over the rest of the Body. And as for the temporary mobility perceived in the severed limb, this is due to the momentum imparted by the severing stroke to the air enclosed within it, and not to the presence in it of any Soul-particles. Because in that case, there could be no ground for believing in any expansion or contraction of these particles. As for the light emanating from the lamp, its expansion or contraction is held to be possible, because we actually perceive such contraction and expansion. Though in reality, there is no contraction of the light of the lamp; because even when the lamp is covered up by an opaque vessel, all the light outside the cover is destroyed; because the flame is capable of emitting a circle of light round itself, only when it is uncovered, and not when it is covered up. The same arguments hold respecting the expansion of such lights; the fact being that the apparent expansion of light is due to the appearance of new particles of light, added to one another, and not to the expansion of the former particles themselves. It is only in the case of such things as are tangible (and solid) that one cannot take the place occupied by another; and hence, when a number of such things appear, they form a gradually expanding series, which gives an idea of *expansion*. The particles of Soul however are immaterial; and as such there being nothing impossible in all of them occupying the same point in space, they would ever remain in the condition of an atom (howsoever much their number might increase). How too, is it possible for the particles of the same Soul to expand or contract within the limits of the Body of an elephant or an insect (which the Soul inhabits during different lives on the Earth)? And further, this theory would necessitate many such groundless assumptions—as that at death the Soul-particles move into an intermediate body,—that such an intervening body exists, that though existing this body is not perceived, on account of certain obstacles (in the way of such perception)—and that this intervening body throws the Soul into the next body born into the world (after some time).

For these reasons we must accept the Soul to be omnipresent.

As for the declaration in the Upanishads that the Soul is of the size of a grain of corn, &c., &c.,—it is only meant to show the extreme subtility of the Soul, which has been elsewhere declared to be omnipresent. As for the assertion in the *Mahābhārata* (*Vana-parva* Adh. 296—16763) that "*Yama* extracted the thumb-sized man from the body,"—this is only a flight of poetry, meant to show up the clear practices of the Death-god, forming, as it does, a part of the eulogy bestowed upon the woman wholly devoted to her husband; and this passage is to be taken as an *Arthavāda*, exactly like that which speaks of Prajāpati having cut out his own fat. And we actually find the same Vyāsa speaking, in many places in the *Bhagavadgītā*, of the omnipresent character of the Soul.

Objection: "If the Soul be omnipresent, a single Soul would belong to all bodies."

Reply: It is not so; because we actually find the bodies to be many, and each body to be endowed with distinct experiences of its own. If it were not so, all purposes of the world being fulfilled by a single body, there would be no use of a number of bodies. Nor can it urged that for the same Soul, the existence of many bodies could be held to be as useful, as different bodies during different lives; because in this latter case, another body is brought into existence for the sole purpose of enabling the Soul to experience the particular pleasure, pain, &c., consequent upon his deeds in the previous life; while if a single Soul occupied all the bodies in the world, at one and the same time, each individual being would be experiencing the pleasure, &c., of all the beings in the world; and, as the one Soul would always carry on the functions of seeing, &c., by means of the organs present in any one body, there would be no likelihood of any persons being blind or deaf, &c.; nor could there be any difference in the actions laid down in the Veda, for men of different castes; because the same Soul inhabiting all bodies, the same person would belong to all castes.

None of these absurdities appear, if Souls are held to be many; and even though all these Souls are omnipresent, there would be nothing incongruous in their simultaneous existence; inasmuch as being immaterial, none of them would stand in the way of another. And it is on account of this indivisibility of souls, and also on account of all Souls being of the nature of pure Consciousness, that the Upanishads speak of all Souls as *one*.

Question: "How is it that, the Souls being many (and omnipresent), "and all of them being related to all bodies, the pleasure or pain of one "being is not experienced by another?"

To this question, some people make the following reply: Even when the Soul is held to be nothing more than the Body, just as the pleasure, &c.,

of the Soul encased in the body of the child in the womb are not experienced by the mother,—so, the same would be the case with the case in question. That is to say, even one who holds the Soul to be of the same size as the Body, would be open to the above objection; inasmuch as the Soul of the mother inhabits the same body that is also inhabited by the Soul of the child in her womb, the pleasure, &c., of the child would be experienced by the mother. And the explanation that would be brought forward in this case would also apply to the case in question.

The above reply might hold good, if some reasons were brought forward; as it is, however, the mere fact of the amenability of the contrary theory to the same objection, cannot be counted as a reason in support of one's own theory; because a third party could effectively bring forward the said objection against both of these theorists. And further, the Soul being a modification of the organ of touch, and the position of the Soul in the space within the Body not being accepted as that of something apart from it, there is no contact of the Soul of the mother with the child's body; and as such the said objection would not apply in this case.

For these reasons, the above question should be answered in the following manner: The absurdity urged in the question would apply to our theory, only if mere spatial contact were held to be the sole ground of the experiencing of pleasure, &c.; as a matter of fact, however, we have an experience of only such pleasures, &c., as are *capable of being experienced;* and as such there is no room for the said absurdity. That is to say, if, in the Soul's experiencing of pleasure, &c., the sole cause were held to be the mere co-existence in space, then we would be open to the said objection; as a matter of fact, however, as in the case of the eye, &c., so in the case in question also, the cause of experience is held to lie in the *capability* of the Soul. Consequently just as even though the colour of an object is existent in space with its touch, yet it is not perceived by the sense of Touch,—so in the case in question also, one Soul does not experience the pleasure and pain brought about by the *Dharma* or *Adharma* of another Soul. Thus then, the relationship between the experiencer and the experienced being that of ownership,—as explained under the chapter on *Ātmā*—our theory is not open to the said objection.

Thus then, the Soul being omnipresent, it must be admitted that it can have no mobility (and as such the Actions cannot inhere in it).

[B] Nor could the Action inhere in the materials (such as the pieces of the Cake)—because, says the Bhāshya, *such materials are always destroyed.* Nor can this destruction be denied; because we actually find that the cake that has been offered into the fire has become transformed into ashes. Nor can it be urged that at that time there are certain obstacles in the perception of the materials, in their own forms; for the simple reason that there are no such obstacles. Even if such obstacles were assumed on account of the apparent inconsistency of the non-perception,—then too, we would have to assume many more groundless and absurd imperceptible things than the single *Apūrva*. For instance, we would have to assume—(1) the continuation of the material in its undestroyed form; (2) that it is not perceived (even though existing); (3) the existence of obstacles to such perception; (4) that there are obstacles to the perception of the obstacles, and so on and on *ad infinitum*; (5) the continuation of the action which is momentary; and (6) the reason for the non-perception of this action. And certainly an assumption of the *Apūrva* would be a very much simpler process than this.

These would be the arguments against the assumption of the continuation of the Action, independent of any substrate.

If however it be held that the action is contained in the Soul itself, bringing about certain definite conjunctions and disjunctions,—this also would involve the contradiction of a directly perceptible fact, and the assumption of one not perceptible.

And hence we conclude that it is by far the most reasonable process to assume the agency of the *Apūrva*.

The purpose served by the main *Adhikaraṇa* may be thus summed up:

(1) If the Result were directly connected with the material, &c., the mention of the particular materials too would, like the Action itself, have transcendental results; which would make it absolutely impossible for any other material being substituted for the principal material (in case something happened to it in course of the action). In case, however, the Result is directly related to the Action, the use of the material is a visible one, lying in the mere accomplishment of the Action; and as such its place could very well be taken by a substitute, which is known to be capable of serving the same *visible* purpose. Thus then, if the principal material of the sacrifice becomes spoilt, the following would be what our opponent will have to do, in order to save himself from the sin proceeding from the non-completion of a sacrifice that has been begun: He will have to finish the action by any material that he could obtain; and it would not be necessary for him to try to obtain a material similar to the original material; because (in the case of a transcendental result) the result would not follow even from a similar material (as it would also be other than the one which is laid down as leading to the particular result); and as for the Action, all other materials (similar or dissimilar to the original) being equally unprescribed, it would be equally completed by means of all

these materials. Nor can these materials be spoken of as *substitutes* of the orginal material; because they are not similar to it, and because they serve an entirely different purpose; because the original material was being employed towards the fulfilment of a particular transcendental result, while the material now taken up is used either with a view to ward off the sin accruing from the non-completion of the sacrifice, or to complete an action which is being performed for the sake of a minor result.

(2) Another use of this Adhikaraṇa lies in connection with the ascertaining of the Names of Sacrifices; and we have already explained this under '*Nāmadhēya*' (Adh. I, Pāda IV).

ADHIKARAṆA (3).

[*Division of Actions into Primary and Subsidiary.*]

***Sūtra* (6): Actions are of two kinds—the *Primary* and the *Subsidiary*.**

It would seem from the above that there is always an *Apūrva* in connection with each distinct Verb; consequently the Author now proceeds to differentiate the Subsidiary from the Primary Actions (which latter alone are followed by an *Apūrva*).

But on this point we have the following—

PŪRVAPAKSHA.

"All verbs having the common character of a verb, inasmuch as the "potency of the objective, proceeding from the object to be accomplished, "is always brought about by fully accomplished objects, the actions de-"noted by all verbs are equally Primary. That is to say, so long as a "definite purpose can be assumed, it is only right that every action, being "expressed by a verb, should be accepted as serving a distinctly useful "purpose, and as such, being Primary, and the means of bringing about "an *Apūrva*. Consequently, like the verb '*yajati*' (offers a sacrifice), the "meaning of the verbs (*avahanti*), and the like also have so many distinctly "useful purposes served by the *Corn*, &c. That is to say, just as the *sacrific-"ing* is accomplished by the materials offered; so is the *threshing* accom-"plished by the *corn* that is threshed. And as such the *threshing* must "bring about an *Apūrva*."

To the above, we make the following reply:—

SIDDHANTA.

In the matter of the relationship subsisting between the Noun and the Verb, that action alone of which we do not perceive any distinct purpose, can be accepted as leading to a transcendental result; which cannot be in the case of any other action; and such a supposition would be absolutely

groundless. That is to say, in all cases where a certain Action is related to a certain material, inasmuch as no Action can be accomplished without a certain material, the Material, being in the first instance found to bring about the Action, is at once taken as serving the distinctly visible purpose of accomplishing the Action. Subsequently, however, in certain cases, the Action turns upon itself, and imparts an aid to the material itself (as in the case of *Threshing* which serves to purify the corn); while in other cases, the Action rests within itself, its sole purpose lying in its own fulfilment (as in the case of *sacrificing*). And in this latter case, there naturally arises in us a desire to know what the use of the Action would be; and as no visible purpose is found to be served, we can always assume a transcendental one (in the shape of the *Apūrva*). In that case, however, where the Action is found to have its sole purpose in the fulfilment of a visible purpose—such as the preparation of Rice for instance,—we can have no business to assume any transcendental purpose; and the Injunction of the Action having been justified by a visible purpose, the Action is not recognised as bringing about any transcendental result.

ADHIKARAṆA (4).

[*The Definition of Primary Action.*]

***Sūtra* (7): Those that do not seek to make a material, are Primary Actions; because the material is a secondary factor.**

Those actions which do not seek to make up, or prepare, a material either in its material from, or in that of a certain property of it,—such actions, for instance, as the *Prayājas*—these being the principal factors, with regard to their appurtenances,—they serve the purpose of bringing about transcendental results.

ADHIKARAṆA (5).

[*The Definition of Subsidiary Actions.*]

***Sūtra* (8): Those that are meant to make a material are recognised as Subsidiary; because with regard to these, the material is the dominant factor.**

Those Actions, however, that either *produce* a material, *e.g.*, the Fire by the *Laying*, or *accomplish* or *prepare it*, *e.g.*, the *preparing* of the Priest by *appointment*, or *purify* it, *e.g.*, the purifying of the corn by the *threshing*, or the preparing of the rice by *grinding*—are all Subsidiary ones; because they are always subservient to the preparation of the material.

Objection: "When, as a matter of fact, we find that, whether the "Action be one that leads to transcendental results, or one that brings "about only visible ones, it is performed equally well, what is the use of "differentiating them into the Primary and the Subsidiary?"

Reply: Without the aforesaid differentiation, we would have the following anomalies: In accordance with the theory of the *Pūrvapaksha* (of Adhi. 4), even where the material to be offered is the rice of the *Priyañgu*, the *threshing*, which would be necessary for the preparation of the *Priyañgu*, would come to be applied to the *Vrīhi* corn; because according to that theory the *threshing* also is a Primary Action; and as such the material mentioned along with it (*viz:* the *Vṛīhi*) could not set aside the Subsidiary material; just as in the case of the Butter in connection with the Prayājas; and consequently the *threshing* could not be removed from the *Vrīhi*. Whereas in accordance with the *Siddhānta*, the Subsidiary materials would be set aside; because the material that is of use in the Primary Action, is affected by the preparatory actions also; and hence the *Priyañgu* corn to be used at the sacrifice, would certainly have to undergo all the processess of threshing, washing, &c.

Objection: "Even in accordance with the *Pūrvapaksha* theory, if the "primary *threshing* were applied to the *Vrīhi*, it would serve no useful "purpose in connection with the main sacrifice in hand; and hence in a "case where the material to be offered is the *Priyañgu* rice, the *threshing* "could not be applied to the *Vrīhi* corn, which is not taken up by the "Principal Action."

Reply: It is not so; because according to the *Pūrvapaksha*, the relationship of the *Vrihi*, as mentioned in the Scriptural Injunction, with the Sacrifice and the Threshing, is equal; nor do we find, in the *Vrihi*, any such mark of uselessness, as is found in the case of the *Vājina*. That is to say, we have two equally authoritative Injunctions—(1) "One should offer the *Vrīhi* corn in sacrifice," and (2) "One threshes the Vrīhi corn;" and we do not perceive any reason for making any such distinction, as that this action (offering) is useful, while that other (threshing) is useless; nor is the *threshing* such an action as can be accomplished in the wake of another action, as we find in the case of the *Vājina*, which is the water of the milk left behind after the curdled masses have been removed; nor is it one whose requirements are all fulfilled by an agency whose chief function lies elsewhere,—as we find in the case of the *Padakarma* (rites in connection with the seventh footstep of the Cow given in exchange for the Soma), where the requirements are all fulfilled by the one-year-old *Cow* given as the price of the *Soma*, and no new cow has to be got; nor has the *threshing* the character of a part of a material, as we find in the case of the *Uttarrārdha* (second half of the Cake); nor lastly, has the *threshing* the character of the action of indicating any other purpose,—as we find in the case of the covering up of the chaffs by the cup in which the Cake is to be cooked; consequently the action of *threshing* cannot but be regarded as *useful*. Nor, according to this theory, is it absolutely necessary that the *Vrīhi* corn should be threshed for the purposes of a sacrifice; because the serving of some useful purpose is equally present in an ordinary action of the word also. Nor, in the present instance, is there any authority for taking up the original action; because the Context does not serve to make any such distinction. Nor could a differentiation be made on the ground of the fact of that person alone being entitled to the *threshing* who is entitled to the performance of the *Darçā-Pūrṇamāsa:* because of the reasons propounded under *Sūtra* IX—i—19. When the *threshing* is taken as a *purificatory* action, then, in that case, no purification being needed for the corns employed for ordinary worldly purposes, the original action (of the sacrifice) would, with great difficulty, be got at, by means of the Specification, in the shape of the capability of bringing about the *Apūrva*. And in case the *threshing* be also accepted as a Primary Action, and as such serving the purposes of the sacrifice from a distance (transcendentally), then there would be no uselessness attaching to it, even if it were performed by the ordinary *Vrīhi* corn; and as such, on the strength of direct Scriptural Injunction, it would be equally right to take up any *Vrīhi* corn. Specially because in that case the *Threshing* would be a pure *Dharma*; and as such it would have to be done but once,—exactly like the threshing of the *Sarvaushadhi* (a mixture of certain medicinal herbs, &c.),— and not to be continued until the preparation of the Rice; and as for the *Vrīhis* to be employed in the Rice to be offered at the sacrifice, these could be done into rice even by the other processes—such as that of tearing the husks, &c. (the prescribed *threshing* being an independent *Dharma* by itself, and having nothing to do with the subordinate purpose of the preparation of the Rice). And on account of the peculiarties of the context, the *threshing* would also come to form part of such sacrifices as the *Sānnāyya* and the *Upāñçu*, &c., as also in the various modifications of these (because it would have only a transcendental effect, and as such there would be nothing incongruous in its employment in all these actions).

And it is with a view to these anomalies that the above distinction has to be made.

ADHIKARAṆA (6).

[*The character of the Primary does not belong to such actions as the cleaning of the Sruva, &c.*]

***Sutra* (9): "In the case of all *Dharmas*, every Action would "be the Primary, because of the non-fulfilment (of anything visible) "—exactly as in the case of the *Pryāja*."**

The Bhāshya has cited the cleanings of the *Sruk*, the *Paridhi*, the *Agni* and the *Puroḍāça*,—because each of these is differently related to the Principal Action. The sense of the *Adhikaraṇa* is that even when the aid imparted by a substance to the Primary Actions is from a distance,—inasmuch as it is connected with a certain Action, the Substance cannot attain the position of the Primary.

But, on the strength of the aforesaid definition of Primary Actions (in *Sūtra* 7), we have the following

PŪRVAPAKSHA.

"The action that is accomplished by the substance itself is not found "to impart any aid to the Action; and consequently such actions as "*Cleaning*, &c., cannot but be regarded as Primary Actions."

SIDDHĀNTA.

***Sūtra* (10): But on account of the similarity of declaration, they would be similar to others (Subsidiary Actions).**

The differentia of the Subsidiary action is not that it should seek to make a substance;—because it is distinctly shown in Adh. III that subserviency or subsidiary character does not consist in the imparting of a certain aid to the Primary, but in the fact of a certain action being for *the sake of another*; and we shall show later on that this latter kind of subserviency is based upon the authority of Direct Assertion, &c.,

and it does not depend upon the imparting of any perceptible aid (to the Primary).

Question: "Why then should the *Sūtra* have brought forward the "fact of the action *seeking to make a material?*"

Reply: The actions of *threshing*, &c., have been cited only with a view to show that there is no *Apūrva* in the case of those Actions, which have been proved to have the character of the *Çēsha* (*i.e.*, being for the sake of other Actions) and which are found to serve distinctly visible purposes. That is to say, in a case where the Subsidiary character depends upon the fact of the action seeking to make a substance, we should not recognise any distinct *Apūrva*.

The *Pūrvapakshī*, however, runs away with the idea that this is the sole definition of the Subsidiary Action; and hence not finding it applicable to such actions as the said *Cleaning*, &c., he has concluded that these are Primary Actions.

But the sense of the *Siddhānta* is that it is only when the fact of one Action being for the sake of another has been ascertained by means of Direct Assertion, &c., that we can find it actually serving a visible purpose, or—in the absence of any such visible purpose—we can assume a transcendental result to follow from it. Thus then, the fact of the action of *threshing*, &c., being subservient to another Action, having been indicated by the Accusative case-ending (in "*Vrīhīn*") by means of its signification of the predominance of the material, denoting, as it does, that which is the most desired (to be accomplished),—the action of *threshing* is found to serve a visible purpose; and thus it has all its requirements fulfilled. Though such is not the case with the aforesaid *Cleaning*, &c., which, for this very reason, are held to serve transcendental purposes yet that does not in any way deprive them of the character of *Çēsha*, or subserviency, which has been previously ascertained by means of Direct Assertion, &c.

Sūtra (11): Objection: "But there is an injunction of the material"—if this be urged,—

The opponent urges: "Though, by negative and positive concom-"tance, the subservient character (*Çēshatva*) is found to depend upon the "aid imparted,—yet the character of the Accusative case-ending is such "that it can never be concomitant with Predominance or Primary "character.

"That is to say, only that is accepted as the proper means of right "notion, which is universal in its application; in the matter of Predomi-"nance, however, the Accusative ending has a doubtful application;

"because it is found along with even such materials, as are distinctly "laid down as subsidiaries—*e.g.*, the ending in '*Saktūn*' in the sentence "'*Saktūn juhōti*;' and similarly we find the Predominance of the *Ājya*, "even when it is not accompained by the Accusative ending—*e.g.*, in the "sentence '*prayājaçēshēṇa ājyēna haviṅshyabhighārayati.*' Consequently "we conclude that in the case of the sentence '*Vrīhīnavahanti*,' though "both characters are possible, yet, we conclude that the material (*Vrīhi*) "has the primary character, because of the fact of its imparting a "distinct aid, and because of the Accusative ending. We find no such "aid, in the case of the actions of Cleaning, &c.; therefore in the case of "these also (*i.e.* in the sentence '*Sruvam sammārshti*'), the Accusative "ending must be taken as only laying down the material (and having "nothing to do with its predominance)."

***Sūtra* (12): Then the Reply is: It is not so; because it (the Action) is for the sake of that (material); just as in ordinary life; specially as that (Action) is subservient.**

Let the question of usage rest awhile; because the usage of words being mere *usage* is always set aside by the more authoritative *Smṛti* (Rules of Grammar); because the manner of expressing one's thoughts is multifarious; while the Rule is ever one and definite.

That is to say, if the usage were always of one uniform kind, then there would be no necessity of collecting and preserving the *Smṛti* Rules. As it is, however, usage is so confused that it can hardly be found in a definite form; and hence it is that right usage is preserved by means of *Smṛti* Rules. And these Rules distinctly lay down that the Accusative ending denotes predominance;—*Vide* Pāṇini's *Sūtras* II—iii—2 and I—iv—49; and it is in accordance with these rules that we have such sentences as '*ghatam karoti*' (in ordinary parlance) and '*Vrihīnavahanti*' (in the Veda).

The Bhāshya next proceeds to cite such instances met with in ordinary parlance, as appear to be against the said rules: (1) '*Taṇḍulān ōdanam paca*,' (2) '*Valvajān çikhanḍakān kuru*,' (3) '*Taṇḍulānādāya juhudhi.*' In all these cases it seems clear that the accusatives in '*taṇḍulān*' and '*valvajān*' have been used in the place of the Instrumentals '*taṇḍulaih*' and '*valvajaih*'; and as such in these cases the Accusative cannot but have the sense of the Instrumental (which latter always indicates subservience).

We proceed to explain these apparent anomalies. In all matters relating to cooking, the Rice, &c., have a twofold form (the Primary and the Subsidiary); and it is in consideration of the Primary form that we have the Accusative ending (in '*tandulān*,' &c.). That is to say, when the Rice is spoken of as the means of accomplishing *something else*, in the shape of the *cooked rice*, or the straw as that of bringing about something else in the shape of the *bundle*,—then alone are these to be used with the Instrumental ending; when, however, (1) the Rice is spoken of as *itself* being modified into the form of the cooked rice, in order to be capable of being eaten,—(2) or the straw itself being changed into the bundle, with a view to keep it soft,—or (3) after the rice has been found to be laid down in the Veda as an accessory in the *Agnihotra* sacrifice, when it so happens that the wife of the sacrificer has prepared some exceptionally fine rice, then, either with a view to show off her own excellent work, or with a view to the special result (strength) that is said to follow if the Rice is offered at the sacrifice, she addressing the sacrificer might say, 'Sir, make an offering of *rice* to-day',—in all these cases the words come to take the Accusative ending. And it is a well-known fact, that in ordinary parlance people always seek to speak of the same thing in many ways. And it often happens that even that which is admittedly the subordinate element is often spoken of as the predominant factor, and *vice versa*; at times it is spoken of as both, and at times as neither the one nor the other. Nor is there any authority for holding that the idea that is desired to be conveyed must be accepted as directly expressed by the words used. Because for the purpose of meeting the wishes of the speaker we have at our command such indirect means of expression, as Indication and the like; and hence no abandoning of the original meanings of words is justifiable. Consequently we conclude that the Accusative really expresses *predominance* only.

Question: "How is it then that in the sentence '*Saktūn juhoti*,' "the Accusative is found to denote subservience?"

Reply: In that case also, the Accusative by itself expresses *predominance* only; but this being found to be incompatible with the rest of the sentence, we accept it to indicate its correlative, *subserviency*. That is to say, by its own natural potency, the accusative always expresses the *objective*, in the character of the predominant; but this natural meaning is found, in the sentence in question, to be incompatible with something more authoritative; and as such it cannot be admitted then, finding that the character of the '*Kāraka*' or case-relation is also indicated by the Accusative, as its invariable concomitant, we accept this indicated meaning of the Accusative, as not incompatible with the rest of the sentence; which thus comes to mean that *the Saktu has something to do with the accomplishment of the Homa*. But such generic agency not being of much use, we naturally seek for a specific function of the *Saktu*; and thus come to the conclusion that it must be taken as the *Instrument*;

specially in accordance with the law that 'that which is an accomplished entity is laid down for the sake of that which is yet to be accomplished'—as propounded in *Sūtra* VI—i—1.

Question: "But in what way do you find the predominance of the "*Saktu* incompatible with the rest of the sentence?"

Reply: Only that substance is held to be an object of purification or preparation, which has already been utilised or is to be utilised; as for the *Saktu*, it is never going to be used (after the Homa); nor has it ever been utilised before. That is to say, that substance which is found to have been utilised in some way, or which is to be utilised at some future time, is capable of any process of purification; and as such it attains a predominance with reference to the Action. And when the substance concerned is such as has never been utilised, not is going to be utilised, any purification of that would be absolutely useless; and hence any injunction of such preparation would be wholly purposeless. The *Saktu* in question is such that it is never used before the Homa, nor can it be used after it, having been turned into ashes; specially as there is no Injunction as to any such ashes of *Saktu* being used. Under the circumstance, the only alternatives that we have are—(1) that the whole sentence is absolutely useless, or (2) that the Accusative is to be taken in its indirect sense. And the authority of the Veda having been an established fact, there can be no hesitation in accepting the second alternative. It is a common fact that the direct meaning of a word is always set aside as mistaken, whenever it is faced by such exceptional circumstances (of incompatibility). And the acceptance of the indirect meaning of a word is always due to the necessity of avoiding the uselessness of the sentence; otherwise if there were no such uselessness, it would be always possible to accept the original direct signification of the word. It is for these reasons that we accept the sentence in question to be an Injunction of a *Homa* with the *Saktu* as the necessary material.—such an Injunction being in keeping with the Context in which it occurs.

The Bhāshya puts the question: "The *Saktu* being mentioned in the "context, it would naturally follow that it is of some distinct use in the "sacrifice." And the sense of this is that the *Saktu* offered in the *Homa* would be distinctly useful, inasmuch as it helps the *Jyotishtoma* sacrifice, in whose context the said sentence occurs.

The Siddhānti (in the Bhāshya) makes a dodge, and retorts—'Who says it is not so?'—his meaning being that the said usefulness belongs to the *Saktu as the material offered in the Homa.* In all cases, we find that for all substances, there is no other use save the accomplishment of the *Action* connected with the sentence (in which the name of that substance occurs); because they have no connection with the procedure of the action. That is to say, the *Homa*, being of the nature of an *Action*, stands in need of *something to be accomplished by it;* and consequently along with the principal procedure, it is taken as forming the *process* of action helping in the said accomplishment. This, however, cannot be said of the Substance. Nor can the Substance alone justify the assumption of anything transcendental; because all transcendental results are brought about by Actions alone.

Even in a case where a substance itself is laid down as leading to a particular result,—*e.g.*, in the Injunction 'one should sacrifice with the milking vessel for one who desires cattle,'—no *Apūrva* would be possible, except through the agency of some other *Action*, though having a different end. Under the circumstances, how can any such assertion be made with reference to the *Saktu*, which is not found to be enjoined with regard to any particular result?

Nor is there any authority for making such an assumption. As for the Accusative in '*Saktūn*,' this cannot serve as an authority for any such assumption; because what the Accusative does is to directly express the predominance of the *Saktu;* and as such it would point to the fact of the *Homa* being for the sake of the *Saktu*, and not to that of a certain *Apūrva* following from the *Saktu*. Thus then, through the help of the Accusative the *Homa* would be for the sake of the *Saktu*.

How could the *Homa* be pervaded over by the *Saktu?* Because it could not serve any other purpose,—no such other use being mentioned. Thus then, it is only when the *Homa* has been performed that the *Saktu* becomes related to the *Homa;* and hence before the purpose has been served, the Accusative has had its end; hence even in the case of the useless *Saktu*, the Accusative becomes justified, in consideration of its predominance. And thus the meaning of the sentence having been accomplished, the *Saktu* could not be of any subsequent use, either to the Person or to the Sacrifice; and having recognised this fact, we could either assume a transcendental result, on the strength of the sentence in question, or accept the notion of predominance (as expressed by the Accusative) to be a misconception. (And hence the only reasonable course left is to take the Accusative in its indirect sense of the Instrumental). It is in consideration of these facts that the Bhāshya has said—*the sentence cannot justify any assumption of the transcendental* (Apūrva). It is far more reasonable to reject the notion of predominance (expressed by the Accusative); and hence we cannot but accept the indication of the Instrumental. It is in consideration of this fact that the author of the Mahabhāshya has declared: 'The Accusative is used in place of the Instrumental.'

Thus then, we find that there is a diversity between the *Homa* and the aforesaid *Cleaning*. Because the *Saktu* having no other purpose to serve, it is taken to be for the sake of the *Homa;* while such substances as the *Cake* and the like, inasmuch as they are subservient to something else, are capable of such purificatory actions as their being circled round by fire.

When the true meaning of the scripture has been got at, it is only when we do not find any visible use, that we assume a transcendental result. And even in ordinary life, we find certain purificatory rites being kept up by usage with the sole purpose of something transcendental; for instance, when a man returns from a journey, fire, salt, &c., are moved round his head, with a view to the pacifying of all evil influences impending over him. Nor can the fact of such rites bringing about something transcendental be denied; because the performance of these is based upon the authority of well-established usage.

Thus then, we find that even those that lead to something transcendental have a subordinate character, because of the uniformity of assertion.

Objection: "Such being the case, in all cases the predominance of the "substance would depend upon the fact of its serving a useful purpose; "and hence it is not right to say—'on account of the uniformity of "assertion.' Or else, it should be shown how, independently of any "useful purposes served, predominance is denoted solely by the Accusa-"tive or, how the subordinate character is denoted solely by the "Instrumental."

Reply: As for an instance of predominance expressed solely by the Accusative, we have it in the case of the sentence '*Aindryā gārhapatyamupatishṭhatē*,' where the indirect implication of the name '*Aindrī*' shows that the *mantra* in question is addressed to Indra; and then on account of its being mentioned along with the '*gārhapatya*.' If this '*gārhapatya*' be taken only as the means of worshipping Indra, then the Accusative ending in it would be absolutely out of place; and hence it is only on the strength of the Accusative ending that we admit the *Gārhapatya* to be the predominant factor in the sentence. Similarly, as for an instance of the subservient character being expressed solely by the Instrumental, we have it in the case of the sentence—'*Sūktavākēna prastaram*' where though both the *Sūktavāka* and the *prastara* are equally useful, yet on account of the Instrumental ending, the former is taken as subservient to the latter.

Thus then, the comparative predominance or subserviency being expressed by the case-endings themselves, all that *uselessness* does is to form an exception to the former general rule; and the usefulness or uselessness of any object can never be taken as the sole ground of differentiating the said predominance or subservience.

The purposes of the present *Adhikaraṇa* that are enumerated in the Bhāshya are not quite acceptible (in the way therein put forward) for the following reasons :—

(1) In the sentence '*Çamīmayyah scrucah*' the fact of *being made of Çamī wood* has been laid down with reference to all *Sruks.* But according to the *Pūrvapaksha*, as also according to the *Siddhānta*, that qualification is recognised as applying to the Primary as also to the subsidiary sacrifices. As for the *Priyaṅgu* corn, the original Injunction distinctly lays it down as for the sole purpose of the Primary sacrifice; and as such it is only proper that it is not employed in the subsidiaries. As for the qualification of *being made up of Çamī wood*, on the other hand, it has been laid down simply with reference to the *Sruk;* and hence in accordance with the rule laid down in *Sūtra* III—vii—2, on account of the superior authority of Syntactical Connection, the said qualification is recognised as applying both to the Primary and the Subsidiary, and not to the Primary alone, as shown by the Context (which is a much weaker authority). Nor do we find any qualifying clause, which would point out the *Sruk* as the one that is employed in the Primary Sacrifice; and even if there were such a clause, as it would only be a qualifying adjunct of the subject of the sentence, no significance could be attached to it. Therefore in accordance with the *Pūrvapaksha* also, it is clear that the *Sruk of Çamī wood* appertains to all Primary Sacrifices, as also to all the *Cleaning*, &c., that help the Sacrifice from a distance (transcendentally); and as such there would be no chance of there being any *cleaning* of the *Sruk* made up of many woods. It might be urged that—'in accordance with *Sūtra* III—viii—35, all the peculiar features of the Subsidiary sacrifices being subservient to the Primary Sacrifice, the *Sruk of Çamī*, in the case in question, cannot be said to be for the sake of both the Primary and the Subsidiary.' But this is scarcely correct; because in a case where we recognise the relationship of an object with the Primary, as mentioned by a Sentence, there alone could such an assertion be possible; as a matter fact, however, no such thing is recognised in the case in question. For instance, in the case of the sentence '*yajnātharvaṇam vai kāmyā ishṭayah, tā upaṅçu kartavyāh,*' we find the qualification '*upāṅçu*' connected only with the Primary Sacrifices mentioned by the word '*kāmyāh*;' and as such it cannot be taken as enjoined with reference to the subsidiary, as we shall explain later on; but in the case in question, we have no such distinct relationship with the Primary; and this makes all the difference.

Objection: "It may be that the *fact of the Sruk* being of *Çamī* is for "use in the Primary, though it is enjoined by implication, also in the "subsidiary sacrifices not yet fully mentioned."

Reply: This cannot be; because we shall show (in the chapter on *Atidēça*) that the subsidiaries renouncing that which is enjoined in close proximity to themselves, become connected with their Primaries; because they stand in need of such aids as have been fully accomplished (along with the Primaries). That is to say, an Injunction of many things (by a single sentence) being unallowable, in the sentence in question, the *Sruk* must be taken as simply mentioned with reference to the fact of the *Sruk* being of *Çamī* wood (which alone is enjoined). Consequently, even though the *Sruk* might be enjoined in connection with the subsidiaries, yet such an Injunction would stand in need of the fact of the employment of the *Sruk of Çamī* at the Subsidiaries being got at by Implication (from its employment at the Primaries). And the time that is taken in this latter implication of the *Sruk* of the Primary is exactly the same that is taken by the direct Injunction of the *Sruk* of the subsidiaries; and as such there is no difference between the two processes.

And further, if the fact of the *Sruk* being made of *Çamī* wood applied to the Primaries alone, then even in the *Vāruṇapraghāsa* sacrifice, which is a subsidiary, we would have the employment of the *Sruk* used at the Primary sacrifices of the *Prayāja*, &c. And the means by which we could avoid these *Prayāja Sruks* are the same by which the *Sruks for cleaning* are avoided. But this is not quite desirable; as there is no reason for such avoidance. Even though there may be some cause for the relationship of a certain Primary, yet, in accordance with the Rule laid down in connection with the '*Saumikavēdidakshiṇā*,' the element required would be got at indirectly (by concomitance itself); and as such no collecting of the Primary Class would be proper.

(2) Then again, the shape of the *Paridhi* vessel is pointed out by the use to which it is put; and hence there could be no *cleaning* of that *Paridhi* which would not serve that purpose. That is to say, *Paridhi* is the name of that substance which is used in the keeping intact of the fire; just as '*Juhū*' is the name of an implement used in the *Homa*. Then, in accordance with the *Sūtra* IV—i—26, we could speak of the *Cleaning* being useless. And then, on having heard of the *Paridhi* being made of the *Bāṇavat*, if we were to clean the *Palāça* wood before it has been made into the *Paridhi*, we would only be cleaning that which is not *Paridhi*. If the *Palāça* be made into the *Paridhi* (before being cleaned), then the keeping of the Fire having been done, it could not serve any useful purpose in the Primary Sacrifice. Nor do we ever find a mixture of two things that serve the same purpose (the *Palāça* and the *Bāṇavat* in the present case). Therefore

there would be no need for making another *Paridhi*.

(3) As for the *Avabhṛtha*, inasmuch as this is a new action, it ends wholly in what is directly mentioned in the Veda; and as the whole of this action, together with all its accessories, is laid down as to be performed in water, what could be that *Cleaning*, in which we would have to make use of Fire, and hence have to burn it?

Thus then, none of the above three can be accepted as the uses of the present *Adhikaraṇa*.

There is only one example which has been rightly cited. In the case of the sentence '*mānsantu savāniyānām*' in accordance with the *Siddhānta*, *the character of being made up of tārasa (meat)*, not being related to all *Cakes*, and thus being '*asavanīya*,' it would not be connected with that *Cake* which has been purified by being carried round the fire. And the word '*Savanīya*' is never used with reference to the subsidiary of the '*Savanīya*;' because it deals with that alone which is related to the *Savanīya*. As for the subsidiary of the *Savanīya*, inasmuch as this serves no useful purpose in the *Savana*, it is impossible to have any cake in it made up of the *Vrīhi* corn; specially as the sentence '*Vrīhibiryajēta*' distinctly shows that the Vrīhi corn is to be employed in the Cake used at the Primary Sacrifice. And thus, it is not quite certain which is the material, of which that Cake is to be made, which is purified by being taken round the Fire. And herein lies the use of the present *Adhikaraṇa*.

But even this is not quite correct. Because in that case in accordance with the maxim of the '*Kānsabhojī*' the conditions of the scriptural Injunction (that 'the Cake is circled round the fire') would be fulfilled by the circling of the Meat-Cake; and consequently there would always be a likelihood of the performance of an Action like what is described in the *Siddhānta*.

Thus then, the *corn-cake* having been taken up, in some way or other, for the Primary Sacrifice, it must be held that the *circling round fire* is a means of accomplishing that Cake; especially as such is the inclination of the scripture. But even in that case, such an action being useless, in accordance with the maxim of the 'one-year-old cow,' there would be a total disappearance of that action. And hence it is in the avoidance of this disappearance that lies the use of the present *Adhikaraṇa*.

Or, it might be in the fact of there being no definite material for the Cake; nor does the maxim of the '*Kānsabhojī*' apply to the case; because the mere flesh does not represent the Cake. It it be asked, 'how this comes about in the *Savanīya* Cake?' we reply that in that case it is not the *Cake* that is desired; what is enjoined by the sentence is the *flesh* itself, independently of any Cake in the place of the Cake; exactly a in the case of such corns as the *Dhānā*. Because in no way is it possible to make such corns out of the flesh. Consequently, it must be admitted that in accordance with the maxim of the '*Priyaṅgu*,' it is only in the Primary Sacrifice that the Cake is to be made up of the flesh. As for the *circling round fire*, this applies to the Cake only; and as for the material of this Cake, it may be uncertain, or it may be the *Vrīhi* or the *Yava*, as is shown by the conditions of the Primary Sacrifice.

As a matter of fact, however, the real uses of the *Adhikaraṇa* are the following: (1) In the Primary Sacrifice, there being *many* auxiliaries to the *Cleaning of the Sruk*, we conclude that the number of such auxiliaries must be *three* only, in accordance with the maxim of the '*Kapiñjala*' (XI—i—38-45); and hence even when there is a multiplication of vessels, —as in the case of the '*Paçucāturmāsya*', only *three Sruks* would have to be cleaned, in accordance with the theory of the *Pūrvapaksha*. In accordance with the *Siddhānta*, on the other hand, all the *Sruks* have to be cleaned; because of the necessity of repeating the purifiactory process with each substance. (2) And again, in accordance with the maxim of the 'Paçu' (IV—i—11-16), significance attaching to the number 'one,' only one *Paridhi* would have to be cleaned, according to the *Pūrvapaksha*; while according to the *Siddhānta*, all the *Paridhis* would have to be cleaned; and there would be some distinction made in a case where there is a multiplication of *Paridhis*. (3) And similarly, the *circling round fire*, believed (according to the *Pūrvapaksha*) to appertain to one Cake, comes (according to the *Siddhānta*), to apply to all the Cakes. (4) Similarly, according to the law '*Vishayē laukikam syāt*,' in the case of the sentence '*agnimupasamādhāya stuvate*,' the *cleaning* would pertain to the *ordinary* fire, according to the *Pūrvapaksha*; while according to the *Siddhānta*, any cleaning of ordinary fire being absolutely useless, the Cleaning laid down must appertain only to such *sacrificial* fires, as the '*Ahavanīya*' and the like.

That is to say, if the hymn in question consist of a *Mantra*, the object described in which does not exist at the time, then this object would carry away the Hymn from its present context, and as such, there would be a setting aside of that which is directly laid down. For instance, in a case where we have an Injunction laying down the use of a particular hymn on a particular occasion, if the Injunction happen to contain the name of a Deity—as in the case of a Hymn addressed to Indra being laid down as to be sung in connection with the "*Māhēndragraha*" sacrifice,—the Injunction would depend upon the Deity therein mentioned; and hence in a case where that particular Deity (Indra) does not exist, (as in the case of the *Māhēndra* sacrifice),—the particular Hymn will have to be carried away from the *Māhēndra* sacrifice to another sacrifice where Indra might exist. And this would be a direct contradiction of what is authorised by the Order and Position of the Hymn, &c. The particular sequential Order that would be contradicted in the present instance is that in which the *mantra* is laid down as to be recited in the subsequent hymns; while the Position contradicted would be—either the mention of the Hymn by the Injunction of the *Rathantara*, or the particular Context in which they occur.

***Sūtra* (15): *Objection:* "But (in the instance cited) the word (that appears to make the Deity something quite different) would be only a qualificatory one,—exactly like the word 'barren' (in the expression 'Ajāvashā')."**

"The above objection does not apply to the case in question. Because "a carrying away of the *Mantra* could be possible only if it mentioned "something entirely different; in the case in question however, the "Hymn in question belongs to the same Deity that is referred to by the "name 'Māhēndra'; because the words 'Indra' and 'Mahēndra' are "non-different. That is to say the Indra, that is hymned by the "Hymns in question, is the same that is sacrificed to in the *Māhēndra* "sacrifice; and as such the object referred to being actually present, "wherefore should there be any necessity of carrying it away from "its Context? Nor is it absolutely necessary for the *Mantra* to make "mention of every minute detail of the object connected with the sacrifice; "because it is always found to mention something more or less than that, "in accordance with its own expression or capability (and as such it does not "matter if the Injunction of the Hymn speaks of *Indra* only, without the "qualification 'Mahā'). Consequently, the Hymn should be taken as "pointing to Indra *as apart from any attributes*, because much significance "does not attach to the attributes, as the attributes are pointed out "by the context itself;—all this being exactly similar to the pointing out "of materials apart from qualifications. Nor does the Deity consist of the "word alone—as we shall show under chapters IX and X. [And hence "Indra cannot be taken as different from Mahēndra, simply on the ground "of difference between the words.]

"Thus then, it must be admitted that that which is mentioned by the "word 'Indra' is the same that is mentioned by the word 'Mahēndra'; "specially as there is no reason for assuming the two to be distinct. "Consequently, there being no ground for the charge of the improper "carrying away of the Hymns, these must be admitted to be the subser-"vient accessories (of the Deity").

***Sūtra* (16): Reply: Not so; because it forms part of the scriptures.**

It has been urged above that the Hymns pointing to Indra, as apart from all qualifications, there is no need for any carrying away. But this is not so; because the carrying away of the hymns is by no means avoidable.

For, if there were sufficient grounds for holding the identity of Indra and Mahēndra, then alone would it not be necessary to carry away the Hymns; as a matter of fact, however, there is a distinct difference between the two.

To explain—In the case of the word '*Mahēndra*' some people, seeking, to establish its identity with the word 'Indra,' explain it etymologically thus: '*Mahān*' + '*Indrah*' = *Mahēndrah* (the Great Indra), and then *Mahēndro dēvatā asya*'—'Māhēndra' (That sacrifice of which the Great Indra is the presiding Deity). And in that case what the word 'Māhēndra' would signify would be *that of which the preceding Deity is Indra as endowed with the attribute of greatness.* But such a connotation is not possible; because the signification of a word taken as one complete whole is always more authoritative than that which is sanctioned by its etymological constructions; and hence the word 'Mahēndra' more directly denotes a distinct Deity in the shape of Mahēndra, than it does the 'Great Indra.'

Then again, if the word 'Mahēndra' is broken up etymologically (as shown above), there is a distinct syntactical split; and if, in order to avoid this split, the etymological explanation is not resorted to, then the word 'Mahēndra' distinctly denotes something entirely different from Indra.

Says the Bhāshya, *the nominal affix in "Māhēndra" would not be possible if the word 'Indra' stood in the need of a mention of greatness;* and what is meant by this is that it is not possible for us to take the word in its etymological sense. And the chief reason for this is that in the due functioning of a compound, as also in that of the Nominal Affix, *capability* is always laid down as the necessary qualification. In case we have recourse to the etymology of the word the said qualification becomes impossible to get at, in both cases.

That is to say, in the two *sūtras* '*samarthah padavidhih*' (Pāṇini II—i—i) and '*samarthānām prathamādvā*' (*Ibid* IV—i—82), it is distinctly laid down that '*sāmarthya*' or *capability* is the necessary qualification in the functioning of both the Compound and the Nominal Affix. Consequently, in the absence of this *capability*, no functioning of any of these is possible.

I. For instance, if the Compound and the Affix were simultaneously explained—that is to say, if the word '*Māhēndra*' were explained as '*Mahān Indro devatā asya*,' then there would be no *capability* in either of these. Because, if the chief stress were laid upon 'greatness' as being needed (by the word 'Indra'), then this last word could not have any relationship with the Nominal Affix; and, on the other hand, if the factor chiefly needed were the Affix itself, then there could be no connection with *greatness.*

This 'capability' is explained by some to be in the shape of (1) '*ēkārthībhāva*'—the Identity of purpose, the fact of conjointly forming a single entity,—and by others as (2) '*vyapēkshā*'—*i.e.*, Relationship based upon mutual requirements. And neither of these two is applicable to that which stands in need of something else.

(1) That is to say, when one factor is independent of everything else—save the other factor in question,—then alone can there be any identity of purpose between these two. In a case, however, where one factor is distracted by other agencies, no such identity of purpose is possible. As a matter of fact, it is only when two objects are not distracted on many sides, that they can rightly be said to be dependent on one another, which is not possible when they are so distracted; because in a case of such distraction, our perceptive faculties fail to function rightly. That object, which is pointed out conjointly by the two parts of a word as equipped with the two characteristics, is always the same that is pointed to by each of these parts independently by itself. When, however, there happens to be a dependence upon others, there is always a doubt in the matter, and the whole does not point to any one definite end. Thus then, in the case in question, there is no possibility of a *capability* in the shape of *identity of purpose.*

(2) As for the *capability* in the form of *Vyapēkshā* (Relationship based upon mutual requirements)—the word '*Vyapēkshā*' itself distinctly points to the *absence of Apēkshā* (dependence on others); and as such there can be no room for it, in a case where the object depends upon other factors; and hence any such *capability* is not possible in the case in question.

That is to say, that which *depends* upon others can never be spoken of as '*Vyapēksha*' (free from dependence).

Thus then, there being no chance for the *capability* of any of the two kinds, it becomes absolutely impossible for either the Compound or the Nominal affix to function in the matter. These are the discrepancies in the case of the word 'Māhēndra' being all at once explained as '*Mahān Indraḥ dēvatā asya.*'

II. If, however, the functionings of the Compound and the Affix be explained separately, one after the other, then, inasmuch as the words will have to be often times repeated, there would be a split of the sentence; because in that case, after we have expounded the Compound, it will be necessary for us to give utterance again to the two words 'Mahat' and 'Indra.' It is with a view to this that the Bhāshya has declared—*The word 'Indra' when taken up by the functioning of the Affix cannot be connected with 'greatness.'* The sense of this is that when the word 'Indra' would be taken with the Affix it would be broadened (changed into 'Aindra'); and as for 'greatness', inasmuch as it is always connected with a distinct substance, it could have nothing to do with the word 'Indra,' which, as already forming part of the word '*Aindra*,' occupies only a secondary position. That is to say, in that case we would have the form 'Māhaindra,' the qualification 'great' having nothing to do with Indra, because that which occupies a secondary position, and as such has its own denotation suppressed, cannot be connected with any other qualifications.

The declaration of the Bhāshya—*when taken up by the functioning of the Compound*, &c., &c.—refers to the 'split of the sentence' mentioned above.

Thus then, having explained the improbability of any gradual functioning, the Bhāshya again brings forward the theory of simultaneous functioning, but only with a view to point out other discrepancies in the theory.

In accordance with the maxim propounded in the *Sūtra* I—iv—8, there would be another syntactical split consequent upon the fact of the word 'Indra' being the predominant factor with reference to 'greatness,' while it occupies a subordinate position with reference to the Nominal Affix.

And there would be yet another syntactical split, on account of the Injunction having to serve the double purpose of pointing out *greatness* as the qualification of Indra, and that of declaring Indra to be the Deity of the sacrifice. For instance, what the Injunctive affix will have to do would be to point out—(1) that Indra is qualified by 'greatness' and (2) that 'Indra' is related to the material offered at the sacrifice; and this would lead to an inevitable syntactical split.

For these reasons, the word 'Māhēndra' cannot be explained as that Indra is the deity of the sacrifice, and that Indra is qualified by *greatness.* What is possible is that the word be taken as one independent whole, independently of the component parts; as in that case alone could the Nominal Affix be rightly explained. And thus it is established that Mahēndra is a deity other than Indra.

Nor can it be urged that Indra himself came to be called 'Mahēndra,' the 'Great Indra,' after he had performed the grand feat of killing *Vṛttra*, because in that case the Veda, in which the word 'Mahēndra' occurs, would have a beginning in time. Consequently the mention of the killing of *Vṛttra* must be taken as only eulogising 'Mahēndra,' which is a name eternal and complete in itself.

***Sūtra* (17). Also because of names.**

That is to say, Indra must be distinct from Mahēndra, because of the difference in their names. Thus alone could there be any restriction with regard to the *Mantras* in question; as otherwise there would be an option; and as such in one case, the *mantra* would be set aside from its legitimate purpose. And if there were no difference between Indra and Mahēndra, the only purpose that the mention of two distinct *Mantras* could serve would be to bring about a transcendental result, which is not allowable in the case.

Therefore, just as the Sun, &c., are different from Indra, so also is Mahēndra; and as such it would be absolutely necessary to carry away the Hymn elsewhere (as shewn above).

(Thus ends the exposition of the *Adhikaraṇa* in accordance with the Bhāshya).

The Vārtika, however, takes exception to the above, and brings forward the following arguments against it:—

If we have recourse to the above explanation, and if the Nominal Affix were regarded as possible only in case the word were taken as one complete whole, then in that case, the same would be the case with such words as '*Āgnīshomīyā*' and the like; and the word '*Agnīshomīya*' could not be taken as pointing to the two deities Agni and Soma; and as such no action could have two presiding deities (which would set at nought all the rules of *atidēça*, &c., laid down below). That is to say, just as in the case of the word 'Māhēndra,' neither a gradual nor a simultaneous functioning of the Compound and the Affix is possible, on account of the word 'Indra' standing in need of 'greatness' and the Affix,—so, in the same manner, 'Soma' standing in need of 'Agni,' there could be no Affix (in the word '*Agnīshomīya*'); and when it would stand in need of the Affix, there could be no compounding with 'Agni.' So also, if there be a gradual functioning—one after the other—of the Compound and the Affix, a repeated utterance would be necessary; and this would lead to a syntactical split; because, as shown above in the case of the word 'Māhēndra,' when the word would be taken up by one functioning, it could not be taken up by another; and as before, there would be a diversity in the character of the word 'Soma,' which would be the predominant factor in one case, and the subordinate element in another; and so also the Injunctive Affix would have to refer to more than one object. Thus, in short, all the objections that have been shown above, as applying to the case of the word '*Māhēndra*,' would apply to the case of the word '*Agnīshomīya*' also; and hence this word also will have to be taken as one whole in itself; and consequently there would never be any case of any sacrifice having two presiding deities.

But it is by no means possible for words like these to be spoken of as conventional *wholes* by themselves, because everywhere in the scriptures, the particular actions are laid down as having two presiding deities.

For instance—(1) in course of the consideration of the texts dealing with the 'quartering' of the '*āgnēya*' cake, the '*Indrapīta*' and the '*Pūshāprapishta*,' we shall explain how the words 'āgnēya,' &c., which point to *Agni alone* as the deity, are incapable of including the '*Aindrāgna*,' the '*Agnīshomīya*,' &c., which point to Agni, &c., as the deities, only in the company of some other deity. (That is to say, the *Aindrāgna* cake cannot be treated in the way that is prescribed for the '*Agnēya*' cake; for if the word '*Āgnēya*' were to refer to the '*Aindrāgna*' also, then, inasmuch as the word '*Agni*' would be dependent upon '*Indra*,' there could be no nominal Affix in the word '*Agnēya*.') If these words were conventional wholes, what would be dependent upon what? (2) So too we shall show later on that the *Aindrapaushna* is held to be subsidiary to the *Agnīshomīya*, &c., on the sole ground of both of them having two presiding Deities (and this would not be possible if the words did not signify the presence of two Deities). (3) Similarly in the case of the sentence '*Mēdhapatibhyām mēdham*,' we shall show how two significations are accepted, as explained under *Sūtra* IX—iii—35. And again, (4) it will be shown under the '*Manotādhīkarana*' (X—iv—42) that in the case where Agni and Soma are the deities, Agni alone is not a deity, though both are intimately related to the Action. (5) It is not quite reasonable for us to deny such etymological changes in the compound '*Agni + Soma*' as are due solely to the fact of its forming a duality of deities—such changes, *f.i.*, as the lengthening of the '*ī*' and the change of 'sa' into 'sha' (as according to Pāṇini VI—iii—37, and VIII—iii—82, respectively). If no authority be attached to grammatical rules, then the rule laying down the addition of affixes, denotative of Agni, &c., being the deity, would also be unauthoritative, and as such Agni, Soma, &c., would cease to be known as deities. If, however, this latter fact is admitted, then on exactly the same grounds, it would be necessary to admit the duality of the deities also. And as such the word cannot be taken as a complete whole in itself independently of its component parts.

For the same reasons, it is not right to assert that the *Dvandva*-Compound in '*Agnīshomīya*' could be explained as compounded, only for the sake of accentuation, &c., and having no other significance, as we have in the case of the words '*Açvakarṇa*' (the name of a plant) and the like. Because a grammatical rule can be said to be for the mere sake of certain modifications of accentuation, &c., and to have no other significance, only in a case where the senses conveyed by the word be, in some way or other, not in keeping with a well-recognised fact of ordinary perception.

In the case of the words '*Mahat*' ānd '*Indra*,' it is certainly necessary to assume a distinct significance for each (because we do not find any disagreement from a perceived fact); and inasmuch as these words signify, one the *qualification* and the other the *qualified*, we come to the conclusion that one word qualifies the other. And as soon as these words are pronounced together, we are at once led, by our previously-acquired notion of their relationship, to the joint cognition of the one as qualified by the other; and there is nothing to set aside this joint cognition. Nor is there any reasonable ground for assuming, for the compound, any significance, apart from those of the component words. Then again, it is only when the whole word by itself has been duly established as complete in itself, independently of the component words, that the denotation of this word, as such a whole, would set aside that which is provided by the component words (in case of course the two happen to be mutually contradictory). But no such word could be taken to be a duly established entity by itself, until we actually found it used as such, apart from having anything to do with the signification of its component parts.

And further, we find a great difficulty in believing in the existence of Indra; and it would entail a much greater difficulty to assume the existence of another and an altogether distinct deity in the shape of Mahēndra.

As a matter of fact, we find that even in the case of a perceptible object, there can be no reasonable ground for assuming a multiplicity of denotative potencies for a word; and it would be very much more unreasonable to make any such assumption in a case where the very object—*Mahēndra* f.i.—has got to be assumed. We accept the existence of an object in the shape of Indra, simply on the ground that, otherwise, the use in the Veda of the word 'Indra' would not be explicable. And thus if the use of the word '*Mahēndra*' too were equally inexplicable, then alone we could have any ground for assuming the existence of an object in the shape of Mahēndra. As a matter of fact however, the use of the word 'Mahēndra' is quite explicable, as based upon the well-recognised denotations of the two words '*Mahat*' and '*Indra*'; and hence the word is found to convey an idea of the same *Indra* as qualified by '*greatness*'; and as such there is no ground for assuming the existence of any other object. And hence it is proved that Mahēndra is none other than *Indra qualified by greatness.*

Further, when we expound the fuctioning of the Compound first and then explain that of the Affix, there is no incapability pertaining to anything; because at the actual time of the functioning of the compound, or that of the Affix,—there is nothing else that the factor stands in need of. Nor is there any syntactical split due to repeated utterance; because all that we do, by the repeated utterance, in expounding the compound, is to give expression to the many meanings that are expressed by the word pronounced but once. The word '*Māhēndra*' has a double functioning in the shape of the Compound and in that of the Affix; each of these functionings represents a distinct sentence; and it is the meanings of these two sentences that we give distinct expression to by the expounding of the Compound and the explanation of the bearing of the Affix. And as for the repetition that we have recourse to, in the re-expounding, it is not that of any Vedic sentence; because there is no such Vedic sentence as "*Mahānçcāsāvindraçca, Mahēndro dēvatā asya it Māhēndrah.*" Nor is it the Vedic word itself that is so disjoined; because all disjunction being brought about by human agency, the word ceases to be Vedic altogether. The fact is that in the Veda, the word '*Māhēndrah*' occurs in its own complete form; and it is only the meaning of this word that is explained by means of the aforesaid disjoinings and etymological explanations &c., proceeding from human sources.

As a matter of fact, words are endowed with various potencies, bringing about as they do, the cognitions of one or many meanings. And the meaning of a word is explained, sometimes by means of another word, and sometimes by means of a sentence, and that too being one or many, consisting of two or more words. For instance, the meaning of the word '*Pika*' is explained by '*Kokila*'; '*Aupagava*' is explained as 'the son of Upagu,' or as 'one who was produced by Upagu from out of his wife.' The verb '*pacati*' (*Parasmaīpada*—Present Tense, Third Person, Singular) is explained as 'the action of cooking, affecting another person, as being accomplished at the present time, by the agent who is one—the action extending over many moments.' And certainly, in these explanations, there is no syntactical split. Nor is the explanation found to refer to any portion that is not denoted by the word explained. In the same manner, when the meaning of the word '*Mahēndra*' happens to be explained by persons cognisant of the various significations of words, who employ one or more words of their own, without touching the Vedic text itself—where is there a symtactical split? For our own sentence, even if uttered a hundred times, would not vitiate the Vedic sentence. And when the meaning of the Veda is explained, the word itself does not become human. And when a certain fact is being spoken of by a man, it is necessary that it should be spoken of in a certain order of sequence, and that too in accordance with the due sequence of the roots and affixes —*f.i.* '*Mahāṇçcāsāvindrah, &c.*'; and certainly, in this there is no dependence upon other factors.

Then again, even in the case of one factor depending upon another factor, there is every ground for there being a Compound, provided the former be the predominant factor; consequently if the word '*Indra*' were dependent upon the Nominal Affix, it could be very well compounded, because of the fact of its being the predominant factor, with regard to 'greatness.'

Thus then, even though, in case of the simultaneous functionings (of the Compound and the Affix), there is nothing incongruous in the fact of the factors being dependent upon other factors, yet the functioning in question is gradual. Because the word '*Indra*,' though dependent upon the Affix, is yet compounded on account of its predominant character; and when dependent upon *greatness* it becomes subordinate, and hence the functioning of the Affix has to come in later on. That is to say, in a case where the predominant factor is dependent upon something else, the functioning must be one of this kind; and hence it is the compounding that comes in first. If, however, after the compounding has been done, the functioning be held to come in its wake, of its own accord,—then the result would be that *Indra* by itself would be connected with the Affix; and on the other hand, the same pure Indra would come to be compounded; and as such we would have, for the deity in question, Indra alone, without any qualifications; and as such the mention of the qualification 'great' would become absolutely useless. Nor is it possible to assert that, as in the case of the 'red one-year-old cow,' so in that of 'Indra' and 'Mahat' also, the two coalesce in the denotation of the Affix, and as such serve to limit one another. Because where there is no Action in question, there can be no such simultaneous coalescence. Nor is it possible for that which is not an Action to draw within itself any qualifications. Even if it could so draw them in, it would come to denote the fact of '*Mahat*' and '*Indra*' denoting two deities. And then, the words '*Mahat*' and '*Indra*' being more than one, when not compounded, there would be no possibility of the Affix that we do actually find in it, because this affix is laid down as coming in only when the Deity in question is *one* (and hence the word '*Mahēndra*' would be possible only in case *Mahēndra* were one deity, and not if the word 'Mahēndra' contained the names of two distinct deities). And again, if the words '*Mahat*' and '*Indra*' were two distinct Nouns, with independent declensional affixes, then there could be no such noun as '*Mahēndra*,' and hence no chance for the affix in question; and if there are no such Nouns ending in declensional affixes, then they could not form a compound.

For these reasons, simultaneous functioning is not possible; and hence through the aforesaid gradual functioning, we conclude that the object signified by the Compound itself is the deity. And consequently *Mahēndra* is none other than *Indra qualified by greatness.*

Thus then, we find that for reasons above explained, the *Pūrvapaksha* position appears to be quite reasonable; and hence we must have recourse to another line of argument with a view to its effectual refutation.

And this we are going to do now, in expounding what we shall call—

SIDDHANTA (B).

As a matter of fact, the Deity enters into the sacrifice, not in its material form, but in the verbal (*i.e.*, in the form in which it happens to be mentioned in the scriptural Injunction); consequently, inasmuch as it is by the word '*Mahēndra*' that the Deity is mentioned, we cannot but accept *Mahēndra* as the Deity. Even if the meanings of the two words '*Indra*' and '*Mahēndra*' be identical,—the deity in the particular sacrifice in question must be that which is spoken of by the word '*Mahēndra*' in accordance with the law laid down under *Sūtra*: '*Vidhiçabdasya mantratvē, &c.*,' (X–iv–23)— and none other. And hence the character of the deity could not belong even to those mentioned by such names as '*Vṛhadindra*,' &c.,— words that are more akin to 'Mahēndra' than 'Indra,'— to say nothing of such other words as '*Indra*' and the like.

When we find a certain Deity in a certain form laid down in connection with a certain sacrifice,—even though the Deity be the object denoted, and not the merely Verbal form, yet, if we find the slightest difference from it in another otherwise expressed, we cannot admit this to be the Deity of that sacrifice.

That is to say, the character of the Deity is such as is not cognisable by the ordinary means of cognition, Sense-perception and the like; and hence the only means of knowing it is afforded by Vedic Injunction alone; hence we can be assured of the fact of the sacrifice having been performed in due accordance with the Injunction in the Veda, only when we actually find that the Deity invoked has been exactly the same as is therein laid down. If however, the slightest difference is made in that,—the functioning of the Injunction having ceased with the laying down of the real Deity, &c.—, we will have to look for another authority for this slightly different Deity; but as a matter of fact, there is no such authority; and as such the invocation of that Deity cannot but be unauthoritative. This will be explained later on, where it is shown that 'Agni is the Deity of the *Ashtākapāla,* and not of the Ājya' (because with regard to the latter Agni is not laid down as the Deity). In accordance with this rule (1) when the Injunction has spoken of Indra as the Deity, the deific character cannot be attributed to Agni,—(2) when Indra is laid down as the Deity of *Soma*, He cannot be the Deity of the Cake,—(3) when Indra is laid down as the Deity of the *pounded* Soma, He cannot be the Deity of the creeper itself,—(4) when pure Indra is laid down as the deity, we cannot have him as qualified by some attributes;—so in the same manner, when we find the Injunction laying down the qualified 'Great-Indra' (Mahēndra) as the Deity, we cannot invoke *Indra* alone.

Another reason for this is that, inasmuch as in the Injunction in question, the Deity is *predicated* of something else, due significance must be attached to its qualifications and adjuncts: specially as no such significance could be attached to them, only in case the Deity were that with regard to which something else was predicated. That is to say, if in the matter of the relationship expressed by the nominal affix (in "*Māhēndra*"), the Deity were that with regard to which it was predicated, then we could not attach any importance to the mention of its attributes. If, however, the Deity were not predicated, it would not have the character of the Deity, and hence we cannot but admit it to be predicated. And as such, due significance must be attached to its qualifications; and hence the removal of the qualification would do away with the very character of the Deity. For instance, in such sentences as—'the white-clothed person should be fed,' 'the red-turbaned priests pass along,' 'the person with the stick repeated the *Praisha Mantras*,'—if we take away the qualification, what is left behind ceases to form a material part of the Sacrifice. If however, the qualifications were such as having something else predicated of them—*f.i.*, "bring in those that have white clothing"—the men could very reasonably be brought even without the white clothing (which they might lay aside before coming in). Hence, in the case in question, even if the Deity were to enter into the sacrifice, in its material form, we could not accept it as without its qualification; as a matter of fact, however, we find that it helps the sacrifice, in its verbal form,—and consequently anything else, that would be mentioned by a word apart from the Injunction, could not be recognised as the prescribed Deity.

70

And further, when the Deity is mentioned by means of a compound, it would not be open to the fault of the Injunction referring to more than one thing. Hence the Deity that would belong to the '*Māhēndra-graha*' could never be mentioned by the word '*Indra*.' That which is mentioned by this latter word can never be the Deity of that sacrifice; and as such in the case of an injunction of this sacrifice, any mention of that Deity would be absolutely useless.

Thus then we find that the sense of *Sūtra* 16 comes to be that the cognition of the Deity depends upon actual verbal expression; and the fact of a certain word expressing the Deity comes to be accepted only if it is found that such expression is in keeping with the character of the Nominal Affix. Hence we conclude that there is a distinct difference between the deities Indra and Mahēndra.

Question: "But how do you reconcile the Bhāshya with the above explanation?"

Reply: It is as follows: What the *Pūrvapakshī* urges is that there is no necessity of carrying aside the Hymn in question. And for one who holds that the *mantra* mentioning 'Indra' need not be removed from the '*Māhēndra*' sacrifice, — inasmuch as it would be absolutely useless to have expressed a Deity that is not needed in the Action, it must be desirable to admit that simply *Indra* is the Deity pointed out. But no such admission can be made by his mere wish; nor is there any other authority for its acceptance; because the only authoritative means of knowing the Deity, in the present case, is the Nominal Affix that we meet with in the passage laying down the '*Māhēndra*' sacrifice; and this occurs in the "*Māhēndra*" only. If this Nominal Affix were rent apart from the compound, and explained along with the word "*Indra*" only, then, in that case, the mention of the Deity would be in keeping with the direct denotation of the *Mantra*.

It is this position of the opponent that the Bhāshya takes for granted, and hence it speaks of the word "*Indra*" as withdrawn from the word '*Māhēndra*,' in the passage: "*that Indra is the Deity is cognised by the presence of the Affix;*" while, as a matter of fact, inasmuch as the word "*Indra*" stands in need of "greatness," so long as the compounding is not done, the word '*Indra*' remains the subordinate factor, and as such incapable of any contact with the Nominal Affix.

Says the Bhāshya: "*When depending on contact with the nominal affix, &c., &c.*" And the sense of this is that, though the compounding is quite possible when the principal factor is dependent upon something else, there is room for the nominal affix when it is in the pure condition of the Noun; but at the time that the affix appears, there being no declensional ending, no compounding would be possible. Thus then, the rule laid down by Patanjali — that "compounding is possible also when the factor dependent upon something else happens to be the predominant one" — applies to those cases in which a Noun with a declensional ending, standing apart, stands in need of another word which is capable of being connected with it,—as for instance '*Rājpurushah çobhanah.*'

If there were a need of the Nominal Affix, before the compounding was done, then we would have to admit the appearance of the affix along with a sentence (in the form of '*Mahān Indrah*'). On the other hand, if the affix were attached to the word '*Indra*' only, then the qualification (*greatness*) would fail to enter into it.

As for the gradual functioning (one after the other) of the Compound and the Affix, you do not admit of it. If the affix were attached in the first instance—*i.e.*, before the coming in of the word '*Mahat*'—then, we would be open to the two objections urged above (Text, p. 397)—*viz*: (1) the *greatness* would apply to the material of the sacrifice, and not to the Deity, which would become the subordinate factor; and (2) the final shape of the word would be '*Mahaindra*' and not '*Māhēndra!*'

The *mere* word '*Indra*,' when functioning along with the Compound, could not be related to the nominal Affix. (This is what the Bhāshya means). For these reasons, it will have to be admitted that in the single word, the relationship (between '*Indra*' and '*Mahat*' and the Affix) comes in all at once. And then, in accordance with the *Sūtra* I—iv—8, we would as before be open to the objection of the diversity in the character of Indra (it being the predominant factor in relation to 'greatness' while subordinate in relation to the affix).

Says the *Bhāshya*: *It is clear that* Mahēndra *is something totally distinct from Indra.* And the sense of this is that, prior to the compounding, the Injunction is one of more than one object, *i.e.*, *greatness and Indra* this would also be got at from the words of the complete compound itself, and this would lead to a syntactical split, which is avoided by having recourse to compounding.

Therefore, says the Bhāshya, *the deity in question is not* (*mere*) *Indra unqualified by greatness*, (but the qualified Indra). This would be the sense of the Bhāshya, if we read it as '*amahattvaviçishṭah*;' if, however, we read '*mahattvaviçishṭah*,' the meaning would be that the deity is not that which is mentioned by the mere word '*Indra*,' but that which is spoken of by that word qualified by '*Mahat*;' specially because the affix in question would be possible only if the noun were in the form of a compound.

Says the Bhāshya—*Not by the relationship of the component parts*; and this should not be taken as absolutely denying the etymological meaning of the word; all that it means is that the affix does not appear by means of the relationship of the component parts, because it is absolutely impossible for any such part to be withdrawn from the compound (for the propose of being attached to the affix).

Says the Bhāshya—*Therefore it must be a distinct deity.* That is to say, even though the object Indra is one only, yet the two are spoken of as distinct deities, on account of the difference between the unqualified ("*Indra*") and the qualified ("*Mahēndra*"). For instance, we find the same man to be an *uncle* and a *preceptor;* and he is spoken of differently, according as the particular requirements of the time may refer to the one or the other phase of his character.

As for the Vedic sentence "it was after Indra had killed Vṛttra that he came to be called *Mahēndra*"—the Pūrvapakshī thinks that (even in the case of the '*Māhēndragraha*') mere *Indra* having been previously recognised as the Deity, what the qualification 'great' does is to subsequenty eulogise the character of the previously recognised Deity, and it does not enter into the deific character itself. The reply to this is clear in the Bhāshya itself.

Mahēndra thus being known as a deity, distinct (from Indra), it is mere groping in the dark, to make such bold assertions as that—'the word *Mahēndra* points to mere Indra as the deity,' 'the mere word *Indra* points to the qualified Mahēndra as the deity,' 'even though the Injunction distinctly mentions the qualified Mahēndra, yet the character of the deity belongs to mere Indra,' 'though the word used be '*Indra*' only, yet the deific character belongs to the qualified 'Mahēndra,' and so forth. None of these assertions are reasonable.

Consequently it must be admitted that the Hymns in question will have to be carried away to that place where there is a complete harmony between the Injunction and the *Mantra* (i e., a place where *Indra* would be the Deity),—if we were to accept the Hymn to be subservient to the Deity (*i.e.*, if we take the *Mantra* as pointing to the Deity), as held by the Pūrvapaksha. Whereas in accordance with our theory, the Hymn is a principal action by itself, leading to a distinct transcendental result; and as such capable of being taken along with any and every deity; as in all cases it would, by means of its own specific transcendental result, help in the completion of the sacrifice; (and there would, in this case, be no need of carrying away the Hymn).

Sūtra (18): The mention of the qualification too would be absolutely useless.

Whether the qualification be eternal or transient (*i.e.*, natural or caused), if it be taken only as eulogising Indra, and not as entering into his deific character, then its mention (in the sentence *Māhēndrgraha*, &c.') would be absolutely useless. Because the only purpose for which a deity is spoken of or enjoined is to show how the particular Action could be performed with reference to Him. And whether the qualification be laid down or not, when the performance of the Action would be quite possible with regard to mere Indra, there would be no use of laying down the qualification.

And further, the qualification not being included (in the Deity itself), it could only be mentioned after the Injunction of the Deity; or it would have to be mentioned as describing the Deity. But for you neither could be possible; because of the 'qualified Indra' not having been mentioned anywhere else. That is to say, the relationship of mere Indra with the particular '*graha*' (the *Māhēndra*) is not laid down anywhere; and hence it could not be possible for the qualification to be laid down solely with a view to the description of Indra contained therein; on the other hand, we have never found any such Deity as 'Great Indra' laid down; and as such it is not possible for 'greatness' to be spoken of as serving the purpose of pointing out a particular Deity. And thus the mention in the passage in question, of the word 'Māhēndra,' being such as is not found elsewhere, we must admit it to be the Injunction of a distinct Deity.

***Sūtra* (19): So also with regard to the Yājyā and the Purōruc.**

The difference of names in these also is to be explained in the same way as that in the foregoing Mantra. That is to say, it is only in accordance with the aforesaid explanation that we could explain the separate mention of the *Yājyā and the Puronuvākyā.*

***Sūtra* (20): In the case of the 'barren goat,' we perceive the object as actually existing.**

[It has been urged above in *Sutra* 15, that the object laid down as the 'barren goat' is subsequently spoken of as 'goat' only, and hence the qualification 'barren,' and also 'great,' must be taken as qualifying the object, and not as having any independent significance.] But the fact is that such objects as the 'barren goat' and the like, help the sacrifice, by their material forms; and as such all their specifications being directly perceptible, when it is found that the purpose is equally served by the use of a generic form 'goat' only, the *Mantra* does not attach much importance to the actual words ("barren goat") employed in the foregoing Injunction.

***Sūtra* (21): Objection: "There may be (a carrying away of the Hymn in question) to an action wherever mere Indra might be the Deity; and as a distinctly useful purpose would be served by it (there can be nothing objectionable in it)."**

The *Sūtra* may be interpreted in two ways: I. "The Pūrvapaksha "could be rightly renounced only if it were found to be opposed to a "strong authority. As a matter of fact, however, it is not so; because "the authority of *Liṅga* (Indicative Power) of the words of a Hymn "is certainly much stronger than that of Order or Context, &c.; and hence "we cannot very well give up the *Pūrvapaksha* theory."

II. "The word 'Indra' being a part of the word 'Mahēndra' could "be taken as signifying the sense of the latter compound; as by so doing "we reconcile the otherwise contradictory bearings of the *Liṅga* and the "*Krama*; just as we have in the case of the word 'Agni' as occurring in "the *Manotā* (Vide X—iv—42). That is to say, it would not be neces-"sary to remove the Hymn, as on account of close proximity, we could "accept the part 'Indra' to indicate the whole 'Mahēndra'; specially "as in so doing we avoid the contradiction between *Liṅga* and *Krama*, "and also the necessity of having to assume a transcendental result (for "the Hymn). For instance, in the case of the *Agnīshomīya*, though we "find the word 'Agni' alone in the *Manotā Mantra*, yet finding, from con-"text, that it forms part of a compound ('*Agnīshoma*'), we accept it "as indicating *Soma* also, and as such affording the sense of the whole "compound.

"Consequently there is nothing incompatible, even if we do not "remove the Hymn from its place."

Sūtra (22): Reply: This could not be the case with those (Mantras) that are directly laid down.

As a matter of fact we find that in many places we do not find the same meaning in all the *Mantras* that are laid down in that connection, when these latter are removed from that context. For instance, in the case of the sentence '*yāmyāh çaṅsanti*' and the like,—inasmuch as Yama is not the Deity of the other *Grahas*, if the Mantras laid down in that context were to be removed from there, they could not point to him. And as in that case the very injunction of these would be useless, it would be necessary to admit the fact of their leading to transcendental results. And this may be said of all similar cases (as the one in question). And hence we cannot accept the Hymn to be merely subservient to the Deity.

Sūtra (23): Objection: "But we actually perceive it."

(This *Sutra* proceeds to show that the removing of the *Mantra* would not make any Injunction useless).

"Though *Yama*, &c., are not the Deities of the *grahas*, yet they could "be indicated by the Mantras, as being of use in other actions. For "instance—(1) the *Mandūka Hymn* is used in the *Agni*, as it is therein "laid down that the Fire is be drawn in with the *Mandūka sūkta*; (2) "the *Akshasūkta* is employed in the *Rājasūya*, as therein it is laid down "that the gambling is done with the dice (*aksha*) ; (3) the *Mūshikāsūkta* "is employed in the *Ekādaçinī*, as in this the sentence '*ākhustē*, &c., "having described the connection of a certain place, this makes the "Hymn one eulogising that place. As for the '*Kushumbhaka*' and other "hymns, if we do not find any particular use of these, we can accept them "as having their use in those cases where the general term *Mantra* is "used in the Injunction (and no particular *Mantra* is specified); as for "instance, we find that *all Mantras* are laid down as to be employed in "the *Vācastoma*. So too in the case of the *Āçvina* sacrifice, it is laid "down that in case the sun should rise before the sacrifice is finished, *all* "Ṛk verses should be recited (as an expiatory rite). In cases like these, "however, inasmuch as we find that the Mantras laid down do not "mention any object that appears in the sacrifice in its material form, "we have to accept the fact of their leading to transcendental results. "But because a transcendental result is admitted in one case, that is "no reason, why we should reject a visible purpose, even when it is pre- "sent, and always assume a transcendental one. For instance, because "the reciting of the *Vaīshnavī* verse is found to serve only a transcen- "dental purpose it does not follow that only transcendental results fol- "low also from that of the *Yājyā* and the like, which are found to serve "distinctly visible purposes."

***Sūtra* (24): Reply: Because of the fact of the direct mention (of the Genitive, &c.), the words 'stauti' and 'çaṅsati' appearing in the context, would have to be taken as having their use in bringing about distinct transcendental results (Apūrvas).**

It has been urged that like the word 'Agni' in the *Manotā*, the word 'Indra' would indicate the sense of the compound, 'Mahēndra.' But this is not correct, because there being nothing incompatible in the directly expressed meaning of the word 'Indra,' there is no reason why it should give up its direct denotation, (and take to indirect Indication)? And then again, as it would always be possible, by some sort of an indirect indication, to find a visible result for all that is held to be leading to transcendental results,—this process of interpretation is by no means allowable.

Then it has been urged that there would be nothing wrong, even if the Hymn were removed from its place. But it is not so; because Direct Assertion, as defined by Proximity, distinctly points to the fact of the Hymn in question forming a part and parcel of the collection of Hymns with which it is mentioned. And as for the functioning of *Liṅga*, it can have no injunctive potency, until the recognition of a general relationship (between the *Mantra* and the Deity).

That is to say, if the case were such that it was absolutely definitely ascertained that the Hymn serves a visible purpose,—in that case alone could the Direct Assertion, defined by Proximity, be set aside. When, however, the case is such that it is only after the Hymn has been employed that its use is sought after, and the commencement of the action does not depend upon the use.—then the Hymn having been employed in accordance with the authority of Order and Proximity, it does not matter whether we assume a visible or an invisible result. As for the Hymn, when removed from its place, we do not find any reason for employing it in any other place. As for *Linga*, all that it could do by its power of pointing to the Deity, would be to point out the *form* of the Deity (and not its relationship with any action); and in that case it would become absolutely useless. *Linga* can have nothing to do with regard to the expression of any relationship between the Deity and the Action. As a matter of fact, *Linga* is found to have an actually enjoining force, only when the general relationship of the Deity with the Action has been defined by some *Mantra* or other,—and then there arising the question as to how the Deity would help the Action, what the *Linga* does is to point out the character of the Deity, thereby showing forth in what way that Deity is capable of helping the Action. In the case in question, however, we do not find any ground for such general relationship. Consequently if the Hymns are removed from these places, they cannot but become useless; and hence it is only right to accept the fact of their bringing about transcendental results.

And further the various case-endings that we come across—*viz.*, the Locative in '*Kavatishu stuvati*,' the Genitive in '*Indrasya vīryāni*' and the Accusative 'in *praugam çaṅsati*'—as also the words "*Stauti*', *Çansati*' and the like, would have their direct meaning (only according to our theory); according to you, they will have to be taken as signifying something else. That is to say, the action of denoting the qualification and the qualified resting in the letters of a word, thus alone could the presence of the Locative be explained. If, on the other hand, the *Kavatī* were taken as serving the purpose of pointing out the Deity, then the word would have to appear with the Instrumental ending.

Nor can it be rightly urged that, "even if we accept it to be an Eulogy, the *Kavati* remains a *means* and as such amenable to the Instrumental ending",—because in our case the *Kavati*-hymn has the character of the *substrate*, as also that of the *means*; and hence it is quite optional in what way it is to be spoken of. As for the pointing out or manifestation of the Deity, all such manifestation in the first instance must reside in (have for its substrate) the Self of the person; and subsequent to the comprehension of the character of the Action, the manifestation of the Deity (as the Result) resides in the Deity; while as for the *Kavati*, it must always remain the Instrument or means (of that manifestation); and this makes a great difference between the two theories.

Then again, the injunction or *Bhāvanā* of eulogy—in the words '*Stauti*', '*Çaṅsati*'—is cognised as extending over a definite period of time; and in this Injunction, the denotation of the Root serves as the *means*; while all the other nouns, with the several endings, come to be related, only inasmuch as they help in the fulfilment of the Root. Thus then, when the *mantras* serve the purpose of accomplishing the Hymns, then, inasmuch as they accomplish something that is desired, they serve a purpose laid down in the Scriptures, and as such come to have a distinctly useful end. When they do the manifestation of the Deity, on the other hand, they do something that is not laid down in the Scriptures; and as such are found not to serve any apparent purpose. Hence it is more reasonable by far to have the Hymns serving distinctly useful purposes.

Further, for us, the genitive (in '*Indraysa vīryāṇi*' etc.,') directly expresses the subordinate character of the Deity; and that which is subordinate cannot be the predominant factor; hence it being impossible for the Deity to be the predominant factor, the *mantras* could not be taken as subservient to them; and consequently predominance must be attributed to the Hymn. If in the case in question, predominance belonged to the Deity, then being expressible by a noun only, the word mentioning it would be found with the nominative ending, which could not express anything else,— as we find in the sentence '*agnirmūrdhā*, &c., &c.' In the case in question, however, even that which we find having the nominative ending is actually found,—on account of the fact of the homogeneity of the sentence as preceded by the capability of the words used,—to be for the purpose of expressing the connection of the qualification; as for instance,—'*Indro yāto jangamasyāvasitasya rājā.*' And as there is no use of the qualifications, these cannot be accepted as the predominant factor; and hence the only reasonable course open to us is to accept the word expressive of the Deity to be subservient to the Hymn (which latter cannot be taken as subserviently pointing out the Deity).

There should be a stop in the Bhāshya after the word '*Satyam*' (as otherwise the word could not be construed in anyway).

Thus then according to the laws of *Arthavāda*, inasmuch as all other words (save those with nominative endings) would become useless,—even though, in the first instance, it is possible for the word expressing the

ADHIKARAṆA (7).

Treating of the Primary character of the Stuti *and the* Çastra *Hymns.*

(*Mahēndrādhikaraṇa*).

***Sūtra* (13): "The *Stuti* and the *Castra* are subservient, exactly like the *Yājyā* mantras,—because they distinctly signify the Deity."**

The case of the *Stuti* and the *Çastra* has been introduced, as an exception to the general definition laid down in *Sūtra* II—i—8. By the word "*Stuti*" is meant a *hymn;* and the "*Çastra*" also is a hymn which is made up of *mantras* that cannot be sung. A Hymn is that which describes the relationship subsisting between an object and its properties; and as such, in the first instance, it is accomplished by such objects and properties; specially as in the absence of these the Hymn would be mere words, and as such not capable of being called a "Hymn." Of these two again, inasmuch as the properties described do not form part of the Action to be performed, they serve no useful purpose with regard to the Action; and as such they are taken absolutely as serving the purpose of completing the Hymn itself. Then the question arises—The Hymn thus accomplished, does it serve the purpose of bringing about an idea of the object hymned, and as such, is subservient to this latter? or, is it something independently by itself, leading to a certain transcendental result? On this point we have the following

PŪRVAPAKSHA.

"Inasmuch as we actually find the Hymns perceptibly bringing "about a rememberance of (of the Deity) that serves to accomplish the "sacrifice, we cannot but admit them to be subservient to such Deities."

SIDDHĀNTA.

***Sūtra* (14): But in that case, the mention of the name of the Deity would have to be carried away by its meaning; because such mention is always subservient to the meaning.**

The *Sūtra* points out the fact of the *Pūrvapaksha* being contrary to other authoritative evidences.

Deity to be the predominant factor, yet the only rightful course is to take it along with the sentence, only as subsidiary to the Eulogy.

And thus the words '*Stauti* and '*Çaṅsati*' cannot in any way be taken as serving the purpose of the indirect indication (of the Deity); and as such predominance must be attached to the Eulogistic Hymn only.

Sūtra (25): Because of the distinctness implied by the word.

We find it declared in the Veda that "the Agnishtoma is accompanied by *twelve* Hymns"; and here the mention of the number 'twelve' shows that each hymn is distinct by itself. If it were not so, and if all the hymns equally served the purpose of pointing out the Deity, there could be no mention of the number 'twelve.' If, on the other hand, the manifestation of the Deity by all the Hymns be not accepted to be identical, a distinct Deity would come to be pointed by each verse, and by each word, and thus being innumerable, they could not be spoken of as 'twelve'.

The opponent might urge—"The same argument applies to the case "of Hymns also; if all the Hymns be considered identical, then there is "only one Hymn; if they are distinct, then each verse would constitute "a hymn; and there is no third alternative, which would be in keeping "with the mention of 'twelve.' If again, the collection of a definite "number of verses be taken as one Hymn, in accordance with the musi- "cal *hiatus* perceptible in certain definite places,—then we can have the "same definition with regard to the manifestation of the Deity also."

To this we make the following reply: Inasmuch as all actions have their end in certain definite results, they are counted in accordance with the number of results; and hence in the case in question, inasmuch as we find twelve distinct transcendental results (*Apūrvas*) appearing, we conclude the number of the Hymns to be *twelve* also. On the other hand, if the *mantras* were to serve the purpose ot pointing out Deities, then, inasmuch as such pointing out would be done by each verse and each word,—and as there would be no means of ascertaining the end of the Action (of pointing out),—there would be no ground for mentioning the definite number 'twelve.' When, however, the *mantras* are taken to serve the purpose of bringing about certain transcendental results, such results being cognisable solely by means of Scriptures, there would be no ground for holding the appearance of that result prior to the appearance of the *hiatus* (that is taken as the closing sign of one Hymn); and the result would be found to be accomplished only by means of the collection of a certain number of verses; and the final accomplishment of this result being taken as the mark of the end of a particular Action (of Hymning), —the number 'twelve' of the results would naturally determine the number of Hymns also to be *twelve.* There is no ground for assuming the appearance of such a transcendental result, either from each verse, o from all the Hymns taken together. Whereas in the case of *manifestation* (of Deity), we actually perceive the word and the Deity.

Sūtra **(26): The mention would be absolutely useless.**

In the case of such sentences '*āgnēyā grahā bhavanti*' and then again, '*āgneyīshu stuvanti*'; inasmuch of Vedic verses are incapable of being assumed or tampered with, the former sentence being enough for the purposes of pointing out the fact of the '*Āgnēyi*'-*mantras* being the means of hymning Agni, there would be absolutely no use for the second sentence. That is to say, if the word *Āgnēyi* only served the purpose of pointing out the fact of *Agni* being the Deity, then the employing of these Hymns would be enjoined by the first sentence itself; and hence there would be no use for the second sentence. As a matter of fact, however, the second sentence should be taken as serving the purpose of pointing out the Hymn as an independent Action.

Sūtra **(27): Because we distinctly find the meanings of the two to be different.**

All relationship being based upon a certain difference between the objects related,—inasmuch as we find the two sorts of Hymns '*Stotra*' and the '*Çastra*' mentioned as related to each other, these two must be taken as distinct from each other, which could not be, if both equally served the purpose of pointing out the Deity.

Objection: "Both the Stotra and the Çastra being equally *stuti* " the above argument would apply to the case of that also. As for the " fact of the two being two different individuals, those grounds of difference " could be urged in favour of the Pūrvapaksha also."

The reply to this would be in the shape of the arguments brought forward above in connection with the mention of the number *twelve.* That is to say, the transcendental results following from the *Stotra* and the *Çastra* being totally distinct, it is on the ground of this difference in the results that the Actions themselves are held to be different; and on this difference would be based the mention of their relationship. While as for the manifestation of the Deity, there is no such difference either in the action of manifestation or in its results.

Sūtra **(28): The mention too is accompanied by the Accusative.**

I. Such mention as '*pra-ugam çansati,*' inasmuch as the *Pra-uga-*

Hymn is spoken of by means of the Accusative, this would be another argument in favour of the view that the *Hymn* is a *principal* by itself. The principal Action is always such as is *desired* for its own sake (and as such accompanied by the Accusative ending)—e. g., '*agnihotram juhoti*,' '*āghāramāghārayati*.' This could not be the case with the subsidiary Actions, which are wholly subordinated to others, and as such not *desired* in themselves.

II. The *Sūtra* may be explained in another way: The very mention of the two names '*Stotra*' and '*Çastra*' is meant to point to the fact of these being *principal* Actions; otherwise the word used should have been *prakāçana* (manifestation) only; or there would be no name at all, as in the case of the words '*avahanti*' and the like.

Sūtra (29): Because of the fulfilment of the result.

The particular desirable results that are asked for in the *Mantra* would be possible, only if the Hymn were a principal action by itself; because requests are always preferred to one who occupies the predominant position. According to you, on the other hand, the Results would be asked for from the Deity, which you hold to be the predominant factor, as in the case of ordinary sacrifices; because so long as the Master (Principal factor—Deity) exists, no one would think of preferring his request to the servant (the Subsidiary-Hymn which serves the purpose of manifesting the Deity).

ADHIKARAṆA (8).

[TREATING (A) OF THE NON-INJUNCTIVENESS OF MANTRAS, AND (B) OF *Denotation* AS THE THIRD FUNCTION OF VERBS.]

***Sūtra* (30): The *Vidhi* and the *Mantra* serve the same purpose, inasmuch as they contain the same words.**

In accordance with the Bhāshya, the *Adhikaraṇa* is explained as follows: Taking for example certain *Mantras*, there arises a question as to whether or not the injunctive words occurring in them serve the purpose of enjoining, as do those occurring in the *Brāhmaṇa* passages. And on this, the position of the *Pūrvapaksha* is that, inasmuch as the words in the *Mantra* are the same as those in the Brāhmaṇa, there is no reason why the former should not have injunctive potency. And this is met by the *Siddhānta*, which holds that, inasmuch as it is a *Mantra*, and has its subject already laid down in other passages, it cannot have any injunctive potency; hence all that the *Mantra* does at the time of the performance of the sacrifice is to recall to the mind that which has been previously laid down in the *Brāhmaṇa* passage. That is to say, the action *Goyāga*, for instance, spoken of in the *Mantra* is not different from the same action mentioned in the *Brāhmaṇa*, because it is actually recognised as the same; nor does the *Mantra* lay down any accessories of the action (with regard to which it might be taken to have an injunctive potency); nor, lastly, can it be taken as containing an eulogy of something enjoined in another sentence; because the *Mantra* is an independent sentence altogether, and as such cannot be taken along with any other sentence.

In contradistinction to serving the purpose of recalling to the mind that which has been laid down elsewhere, all that the *Mantra* could be taken as, would be an Injunction or an *Arthavāda*. As matter of fact, however, none of these is possible. In the first place, the form of the Action, that would form the object of injunction, is already known as laid down elsewhere; as for its accessories, in the shape of the Material, the Result and the Occasion, none of these is mentioned in the *Mantra*, which therefore cannot be taken as laying down these. Secondly, when the injunction in the case occurs in another (Brāhmaṇa) passage, which has all its needs already fulfilled, it is not possible for the *Mantra* to be taken as an

Arthavāda to that Injunction. This we have already explained under the *Adhikaraṇa* on *Mantras* (Adhyāya I). For these reasons, *Mantras* should be taken only as recalling what has already been enjoined elsewhere.

Against the above explanation of the *Adhikaraṇa* we bring forward the following objections :—

(1) What reason is there by which the injunctive potency of the verb is suppressed simply by the fact of its occurring in the Mantra, and is enlivened by appearing in the Brāhmaṇa? We actually find verbs in *Mantras* serving the purposes of injunction, e.g., "*Vasantāya Kapinjalānalabhatē*; and conversely there are, sometimes, verbs occurring in the Brāhmaṇa, not having the injunctive potency :—e.g., "*Yasyobhayam havirārtimārchēt, &c.*" Therefore there can be no such absolute rule as has been shown in the above *Siddhānta.*

(2) Further, if the *Mantra* be taken as supplementary to the Brāhmaṇa, simply on the ground of the action having been enjoined in the latter,—why could not we take the Brāhmaṇa injunction itself as simply recalling the action previously enjoined by the *Mantra?* That is to say, there is no special reason whereby it could be ascertained whether the *Mantra*, having its injunctive potency suppressed by the fact of the Action having been enjoined by the Brāhmaṇa, should serve the purpose recalling the action thus enjoined, or *vice versa.* Thus then, we conclude that, inasmuch as neither the *Mantra* nor the *Brāhmaṇa* is capable of being taken as supplementary, specially as there is no feature in either that could point it out as distinctly supplementary, both are equally injunctive. And as for the repetition of the same Injunction—as occuring in the *Mantra* and in the *Brāhmaṇa*—we can take the two as two distinct actions. As for the fact of the one being recognised to be the same as the other, we shall explain this under the "*Abhyāsādhikaraṇa*" (VI—ii—23, &c.). Therefore the non-injunctive character of *Mantras* cannot be taken as established in the above manner.

Some people assert that, inasmuch as the *Mantras* are laid down by the Brāhmaṇas, as *instrumental* in the performance of sacrifices,—exactly as the *corn, &c.*, are,—they cannot have any injunctive potency, just as the corn, &c., have none.

But these people also have only been led astray by a misleading semblance between the two cases. Because the mere fact of the *Mantra* being laid down in the Brāhmaṇa as to be employed in the sacrifice cannot do away with its injunctive potency. Therefore the *Mantras* would serve the injunctive purpose, and also, on account of their being laid down in the

Brāhmaṇa, serve to recall that which has been enjoined by the Brāhmaṇa. Because there is no authoritative law which lays down that that which has been laid down as to be employed cannot serve the purposes of an Injunction; specially if it happens to be naturally endowed with the injunctive potency. If, however, the presence of this potency in the Mantra be denied absolutely,—then it would be altogether needless to bring forward the fact of its having been laid down as to be employed, for the purpose of denying that potency (because much reasoning is not required in denying what is impossible). Nor is there any self-contradiction in the fact of the *Mantra* performing both the functions. For instance, even the Brāhmaṇa, though in itself injunctive, could serve the purpose of recalling something enjoined elsewhere; this we shall explain under the *Sūtra* V—i—16.

And further, in the case of those *Mantras* that are not laid down in any Brāhmaṇa passage, as to be employed in a sacrifice, your argument being inapplicable, there would be no ground for denying the injunctive potency of these. Hence even this argument of yours does not help in the matter.

—o—

As a matter of fact, however, there is no necessity of bringing in the *Mantras*, especially in the present Adhikaraṇa, as they have no particular connection with the present context. Hence we explain the *Adhikaraṇa* otherwise, as follows:—

Verbs have been declared, in the preceding *Adhikaraṇa*, to be of two kinds only—the Primary and the Subsidiary. And the question now started is as to whether these are the only two methods of the functioning of Verbs, or there is yet another method. And the position of the *Pūrvapaksha* is that there is no third method.

In reply to this Pūrvapaksha, we have the following

SIDDHANTA.

Sūtra (31): But, because of the power of usage, the Mantra would express mere denotation.

There is a third method—that of *denotation*. Just consider the following: Those verbs, that have their injunctive potency destroyed by the presence of such words as 'yat' and the like (words which make that which they precede, an *Uddēçya*, and which therefore can never be the *Vidheyā* or object of Injunction), must, in all cases, serve the purpose of simple Denotation. That is to say, whether the verb occurs in the *Mantra* or in the *Brāhmaṇa*, when its injunctive potency happens to be set aside by the presence of another word, then, in that case, the verb must be admitted to be denotative.

Examples: (1) In '*na tā naçanti, &c.,*' the Injunctive having become suppressed by the word '*yat,*' becomes supplementary. (2) In '*ahe budhniya mantram mē gopāya,*' the suppression is by the Vocative ending. (3) In '*dāmi gṛhṇāmi,*' it is done by the First Person ending. (4) In '*yadi somamapaharēyuh,*' it is done by the word '*yadi.*'

The fact is that such instances occur *mostly* in *Mantras;* and that is the reason why the Bhāshya has mentioned the *Mantras* only; specially as it is a common idea that *Mantras* are not injunctive. In *Brāhmaṇas,* on the other hand, there are many Injunctive affixes, and that is why the Brāhmana is commonly known to be injunctive. And it is only a very few instances where the Brāhmaṇas are not injunctive; that is the reason why no *Brāhmaṇa* passage has been cited as an instance.

In the matter of the *Brāhmaṇa* or the *Mantra* being injunctive or not, there is no other reason save that which has been explained above (*viz.,* the presence or absence of such words as '*yat*' and the like); and the presence or absence of the injunctive potency is not determined by the fact of the sentence being a *Mantra* or a *Brāhmaṇa.*

But we do perceive the following point of difference (between the *Mantra* and the *Brāhmaṇa*): In the case of the *Brāhmaṇa,* the injunctive potency of the verb occurring in it having been suppressed (by the above causes), this Verb comes to be recognised as serving the purpose of pointing out something which affords the occasion for another action; and the mere verbal form of the *Brāhmaṇa* is not capable of being employed in the sacrifice. In the case of the *Mantra,* on the other hand, as soon as we learn its form—such as *dāmi*' '*gṛhṇāmi, &c.* . . . '*agnīn vihara,* &c., &c.,'—we at once realise that even the verbal form can serve the purpose of recalling certain actions; and hence we come to the conclusion that the words of the *Mantras* are to be used in the sacrifice. Because in the performance of Actions, it is necessary that there should be a recalling (or remembering) of certain things; and inasmuch as this recalling cannot be done by any means other than *Mantras* (*vide Mantrādhikaraṇa* Adh. I), we find it only accomplished by such *Mantras* as have no other function. That is to say, at the time of the performance of a sacrifice, nothing can be duly performed, unless it is duly remembered, and thus the *recalling* of certain things being absolutely necessary, it would stand in need of a fit means of its accomplishment; and as such it would begin to take up such means as either the recalling of the words of the injunctive *Brāhmaṇa* passage, or the recalling of what has been performed in the preceding moment, or the remembering of the Kalpasūtra bearing on the point, or the recalling of the very sentence which gave the first idea of that action, or a certain witnessing priest chiefly employed for that purpose. Consequently when, at such a time, it is found that there are certain *Mantras* mentioned in the context, which have no other purpose to serve,—and which are taken along with the injunctive sentence, with a vague general notion that something might be done by them,—and it is realised that these *Mantras* are just the sort of sentences that are required for the purposes of *reminding*,—we come to infer, on the strength of *Liṅga* and Context, a *Çruti* passage laying down the employing of these *Mantras*; and then these come to serve the purpose of simple *Denotation*. And it is also ascertained that it is only when we perform the action as recalled by these *Mantras* that the proper desirable results follow.

Now we have to explain the Bhāshya in accordance with the above interpretation of the *Adhikaraṇa*. The assertion of the *Bhāshya*—"*Na, asakṛdapyuccāraṇē tatparyāt*"—does not refer to the fact of the Action having been already enjoined elsewhere. What it means is that on account of the presence of the word "yat," the verb in the *Mantra* distinctly says that the *Mantra* speaks of something laid down elsewhere. If the Verb, with the words 'yat,' &c., be uttered even a hundred times, it can never, by itself, give rise to any idea of an *Apūrva*; and it is on account of this fact that we have the idea of the action being laid down elsewhere.

ADHIKARAṆA (9).

Explanation of the name 'Mantra.'

***Sūtra* (32): The name 'Mantra' applies to those of which the purpose is Denotation.**

As shown above, there is no significance attaching to the special citing of *Mantras* in the preceding *Adhikaraṇa:* it is only by the way that the *Sūtra* brings in a definition of what is meant by the word '*Mantra*,' as it occurs in the previous *Sūtra*. And as it is introduced only by the way, there is no necessity why this *Adhikaraṇa* should have preceded the last one (as mentioned in the Bāshya). Specially as the last Adhikaraṇa could have been discussed, without any reference to *Mantras*, basing the discussion upon any ordinary sentence. As for the Author of the Bhāshya, he has laid stress upon the order of the *Adhikaraṇas*, simply because he attached importance to the use of the word '*Mantra*' in the last *Sūtra*.

The sense of the *Sūtra* is that the name '*Mantra*' applies to those that serve the purpose of *denoting* or *recalling*,—the compound '*taccodaka*' being explained as a *Bahuvrīhri*. The Bhāshya mentions the Genitive form, with a view simply to the verbal explanation.

This definition has been given here, for the sake of its terseness, specially because it is thus that it is spoken of among teachers and students and other experienced people, and also because it applies to almost all *Mantras*.

The Bhāshya (p. 125) says that a definition has been given, because it is not possible always to teach by the system of *pṛshtākota*. And the sense of this is, that without a definition, the teacher would have to undergo the trouble of pointing out each and every *Mantra* to his student, and this would be as painful a process as the curvings of the back undergone at the time when many things round one's self have to be pointed out to the standers-by.

On this point we have the following verses: Even the great Sages, can never come to the end of all individual objects that have to be defined; and it is only by means of a definition that the learned get to the end of such individuals. The Vṛtti has given the following specific definitions of different kinds of *Mantras:* (1) Ending in 'asi'; (2) ending in '*tvām*'; (3) making a request; (4) praise; (5) number;

(6) useless talk; (7) complaint; (8) direction; (9) searching; (10) question; (11) answer to some question; (12) distant relationship; (13) employment; and (14) capability.

As an example of (6) we have '*akshī tē Indra pingalē dulerivā*'—'*duli*' =Tortoise. Of (12) we have '*pratipunātu çabdamecchidrēṇa pavitrēṇa*. By 'capability' (14) is meant the power of expression. In '*yē mān dugdhavantasta ēva nirākṛtavantaḥ*,' we have the *complaint* (7) of the cow. In '*Amutaḥ somamāhara*,' occurring in the story of Garuḍa, we have the direction (8) of Vinatā to her son Garuḍa. In '*Vēda karnavatīm sūrmim*'—where '*sūrmi*'-pole—we have an instance of question (10). (For the example of others *vide Bhāshya*, p. 126.)

ADHIKARAṆA (10).

Explanation of the word 'Brāhmaṇa.'

Sūtra (33): The name 'Brāhmaṇa' is applied to the rest.

The Bhāshya says: *Since the definition of Brāhmaṇa could be inferred from that of the Mantra—as all that is not Mantra is Brāhmaṇa—therefore it is not necessary to give a definition of Brāhmaṇa.* And at first sight the sense of the Bhāshya appears to be that under the circumstances, it was not necessary to introduce the *Sūtra.* But as a matter of fact, inasmuch as we find the word 'rest' in the *Sūtra,* which does not give any independent definition of the *Brāhmaṇa,* it is clear that the above passage of the Bhāshya is only an amplification of the *Sūtra.*

Question: "What, then, was the use of bringing in this *Sūtra?*"

Answer: There would have been no use of introducing it, if it were known to all men that the Veda consists only of *Brāhmaṇas* and *Mantras.* As a matter of fact however, there are many people who are ignorant of this fact; and since such people are liable to entertain the notion that there may be a third kind of Vedic sentence, therefore it is absolutely necessary to state clearly that all that is not *Mantra,* in the Veda, is *Brāhmaṇa.*

The different kinds of the Brāhmaṇa are enumerated in the Bhāshya: '*Parakṛti* (1) is the description of something done previously by a single person; *Purākalpa*' (2) that of something done by many people; '*Vyavadhāraṇa-kalpanā* (3) is that in which a fact that appears on the face of a sentence, is assumed to be otherwise on account of the peculiarities of the preceding and following contexts,—*e.g.*, we meet with the passage '*Yo'çwam, pratigṛihṇīyāt vāruṇāstam pratīgṛhnāti,*' and as it is the passage means that one who accepts the gift of a horse is seized by the disease of 'Varuna'; but on looking more closely at the context, we find that what is actually meant is that the disease seizes him who gives away the horse; and hence the word '*pratigṛhṇīyāt*' is changed into '*pratigrāhayati.*'

The Bhāshya uses the word '*Vidhilakshaṇam*'; and in this the word '*Vidhi*'-*Brāhmaṇa.*

ADHIKARAṆA (11).

[*Treating of the fact of the Character of Mantra not belonging to the modifications in it.*]

Sūtra **(34): The character of Mantras does not belong to that which is not actually mentioned in the Veda, as it is only with reference to the sentences actually mentioned in the Veda that we have the above distinction.**

The *Mantra* '*Agnayē jushtam nirvapāmi*'—which is laid down as one to be employed in connection with the offering to Agni—is modified into '*Sūryāya*,' &c., when the offering is made to Sūrya; and here we have an instance of modification ('*Ūha*'). And when the presiding Ṛshis of the family of the sacrifices are recounted, we have what is called the '*Pravara*.' And when the Sacrificer, and his son, etc., are named, we have what is called '*Nāmadhēya*,'—*e. g.*, in the *Subrahmaṇyā*, the declaration is made that "it is Devadatta who is offering the sacrifice."

PŪRVAPAKSHA. [A]

"And inasmuch as all these are covered by the aforesaid definition of *Mantra*, and as they appear within the body of the *Mantra*, we must admit them to be actual *Mantras*."

SIDDHANTA. [A]

And the reply to the above is that in all that is found in the Veda, only those are *Mantras* that have actually been spoken of as such by the learned authorities; and mere *denotativeness* (of something connected with the sacrifice) is not a specific characteristic of *Mantras*.

Another question in connection with this is:—"When only one word in a *Mantra* is modified, does the whole *Mantra* lose its Mantric character, or it is only the modified word that does so?"

And on this we have the following

PŪRVAPAKSHA. [B]

"The whole *Mantra* ceases to be a *Mantra*, because the name "'Mantra' is applied to a certain conglomeration of vowels and consonants "arranged in a definite order: and hence as soon as the slightest change "is made in this, the name ceases to apply to it. That is to say, when "in a *Mantra* the slightest part is changed from that which has been "known to be its form, it ceases to be recognised as that 'Mantra.' "If it be held that the character of 'Mantra' would reside even in a "part (namely that which has not been modified), then all words, even "in ordinary parlance, would become *Mantras*, inasmuch as all of them "form parts of certain *Mantras*. Consequently the modification of even "the slightest letter having set aside the character of the *Mantra*, "it ceases to be amenable to all processes attendant upon a *Mantra*. "And then just as in the case of a modified *Mantra*, any mistake, whether "in the modified or in the unmodified part, would not make the "sacrificer liable to an expiatory rite, so also there would not apply "to such a *Mantra* any of those expressions that are laid down with reference "to the *Mantra* or the *Veda*; and hence even when a single word, or "part of a word, happens to be modified, all the specific Vedic "processes (of grammar, accent, &c.) cease to apply to the *Mantra*; and "then what has to be used is the word of ordinary parlance."

To this we make the following reply:—

SIDDHANTA. [B]

It is only the modified portion that ceases to be *Mantra*; because the generic form of the *Mantra* having been ascertained to exist in a certain sentence, that generic character does not entirely disappear by a mere excess or diminution in a certain part of it. For instance, when a swelling appears on the neck of the cow, or when its horns have disappeared, it does not entirely cease to be a 'cow'; and the reason of this is that there are other parts of its body that are enough to show that it belongs to the class 'Cow'; and we find that so long as even a part of the original body remains, the whole body is recognised as the same. In the same manner, it is a fact of ordinary perception that the character of a *Mantra* manifested by the presence of a number of vowels and consonants arranged in a definite order, does not entirely disappear on the slightest modification made in it.

For instance, there are many cases where the change of a letter or its deletion, or some modification in the accent, is actually laid down in the Scriptures; and certainly when these changes happen to be made in a *Mantra*, it does not *cease* to be a *Mantra*; *e.g.*—(1) we have the direction in the Veda '*Airam kṛtvodygēyam*' (the *Mantra* should be recited after the word 'girā' has been changed into 'irā'); (2) though a certain *Mantra* has three accents, at the time of the reading up of the Veda, yet it is laid down as to be recited in a single accent, at the time of the performance of sacrifices; and in neither of these two cases, do people cease to think of the *Mantras* (thus modified) as *Mantras.*

It might be urged that in the cases cited, the Mantric character is not denied, because of the modifications having been made in accordance with directions contained in the Veda.

But this explanation is scarcely satisfactory, because all that the Vedic direction does is to lay down that the Mantra is to be used in a particular way, and it does not declare that the Mantric character does not cease thereby. Nor is it necessary that all that is laid down as to be employed has the character of the *Mantra;* for we find that Corns are laid down as to be employed in sacrifices; and certainly Mantric character does not belong to these Corns; and thus it comes to this, that the said Vedic directions lay down the use of non-Mantric sentences. But the sentences cannot be said to be non-Mantric; as they are actually recognised as *Mantras.* Consequently it must be admitted that the non-Mantric character belongs to the modified word '*irā*' and the rest, and not to the whole sentence. But as a matter of fact, even of the modified words like those just cited, we cannot totally deny the Mantric character; because when we have looked into the whole of the Veda, from the very beginning, we come to the conclusion that in certain cases, the *Mantra* contains the word '*girā*,' while in others it contains '*irā*' (this latter when we recall the direction '*Airam kṛtvā*, &c.) and that in certain cases, the *Mantra* has three accents, while in others it has only one.

Objection: "If such be the case, then all modifications would have "the character of *Mantras;* because even in the case of the modifica-"tions that are made in the subsidiary sacrifices in accordance with the "Primary ones, when we have looked over the direction that 'the Subsi-"diary is to be performed as the Primary'—we could have the idea "(authorised by the said direction) that 'in the Primary the *Mantra* "should contain the word '*Agni*' and in the Subsidiary it should contain "the word '*Sūrya*.'"

Reply: The two cases are not identical; because in a case where the change is in due accordance with an express direction of the Veda, the Mantric character is admitted; in case, however, of the changes being assumed, on the sole strength of reasoning, the Mantric character can never be admitted. That is to say, on looking into the Vedic direction we come to the following conclusion: in that case the *Mantra* is of this form and in the other case of that form. On the other hand, words like 'Sūrya' are introduced in place of the words like 'Agni,' simply on the strength of the exigencies of circumstances and reasoning; and certainly no Mantric character can be ascertained by mere reasoning, and this makes a deal of difference between the two cases.

Objection: "Inasmuch as we find *Atidēça* (transference of words) "to be a process authorised by the Veda, we must admit all modification "&c., to be so authorised; or otherwise they would be wholly without "authority. For certainly, it is not a fact to be determined by Sense-"perception that a relation of subserviency subsists between any two "actions. Therefore there can be no difference between the change of "'*Agni*' into '*Sūrya*' and that of '*Girā*' into '*Irā*.'"

Reply: It is true that modification too is authorised by the Veda; in fact it is for this reason that the Sūtra denies the Mantric character *in all that is not actually mentioned in the Veda.* Of the Veda certain portions are directly perceived, while others are only inferred. And it is only that which is directly perceived that is said to be '*Āmnāta*' ('*Actually* Mentioned'). And, as a matter of fact, we do not find any direct mention of the change of '*Agni*' into '*Sūrya*,' as we do that of changing '*Girā*' into '*Irā*.'

Objection: "But we find the Vedic injunction '*Sauryam carum* "*nirvapēt*'; and inasmuch as the Deity is always mentioned in the "text of the Veda, the said injunction would serve to lay down the use "of the word '*Sūrya*.'"

Reply: The injunction you speak of does not lay down the putting in of the word '*Sūrya*' into the *Mantra;* as all that it does is to point out that at the time that the offering is being poured out, the name of 'Sūrya' should be pronounced as '*Suryāya Svāhā*,' and not that it should be introduced into the body of the *Mantra*, which could be done only by '*Atidēça*' (Transference). And inasmuch as all sentences laying down such 'Transference' are inferred by reasonings, they cannot be said to be 'directly mentioned in the Veda.' And consequently, the use of the word 'Sūrya' being found to be laid down by sentences not directly mentioned in the Veda, no Mantric character can belong to it.

Objection: "If such be the case, then, inasmuch as the Recounting "of the Pravara, and the Naming of the Sacrificer, are directly laid down, "they would have to be accepted as *Mantras*."

Reply: This would certainly be the case if the actual verbal forms of such Recounting, &c., were mentioned in the Veda. As a matter of fact, however, we find that the said Recounting, &c., are done in accordance with the sense of a general injunction,—*e.g.*, "The Pravara-Ṛshis should be recounted,"— and not in a form literally mentioned in the Veda; and as such they are not included among *Mantras*.

Objection: "If such be the case, then in a case where the Vedic "injunction mentions only a pronoun, if the sacrificer pronounces another "name in its place, the character of the *Mantra* would not belong to it."

Some people admit that it would be so. But the fact is that there being an endless number of individuals, and these too not all existing at one and the same time, it is absolutely impossible for all of them to be directly mentioned in the Veda; the only way in which the pronouncing of the sacrificer's name, &c., could be laid down, is by means of a Pronoun (which refers equally to all nouns); and it is clear in this case that the Pronoun has been put in simply because the place could not be left blank; and hence that the *Mantra* actually contains the word (the name) that is being brought in (in place of the Pronoun). Otherwise, the Pronouns not being capable of being used, in case they did not serve the purpose of mentioning the particular names (to be subsequently brought in), the place in the *Mantra* now occupied by the Pronoun would be left blank and the form of the *Mantra* would be deficient in that part, and the use of the Pronoun would be absolutely useless. And the injunction of these being in the generic form, like those of the *Recounting of the Pravara*, &c., we assume the use of words in the places left blank. And thus we find that such words are actually 'directly mentioned'; and as such they could very well be endowed with the properties of the *Mantra*. The specific names of the *Pravara*, &c., on the other hand have not the slightest trace of themselves at the time of the actual reciting of the *Mantra*; because the Brāhmaṇa passage dealing with them, do not make any mention of the specific forms of these names; and as such, we could not attribute to them the Mantric character, even on the basis of the fact of the newly-introduced names being explanatory to the *Brāhmaṇa*. Consequently, in the case of the Subsidiary Sacrifices, there being a chance of the whole *Mantra* being employed, in accordance with the denotation of the Mantra itself, as also the injunctions of certain Ṛshis, certain other words are thrown into it, on account of the absence of certain conditions of the original Primary sacrifice, and the presence of new ones; and it is only these words that are of the character of ordinary parlance, and not of that of the *Mantra*; the rest, however, is just as it was originally laid down, and is actually recognised as a *Mantra* required by the Sacrifice; and consequently this latter cannot be absolved from the processes of accentuation, &c., consequent upon Vedic character; nor would a mistake in this be free from the expiatory rites.

ADHIKARAṆA (12).

Definition of Ṛk.

Sūtra (35): **Among the Mantras, the name 'Ṛk' is given to those wherein there is a division into metrical feet, in accordance with the limitations of the meaning.**

Though the definition of these various classes of *Mantras* has got no direct connection with the subject-matter of the *Adhyāya*, yet the *Sūtras* treat of them, because a consideration of these is connected with *Mantras*, a consideration whereof was introduced in connection with the question as to their primary or secondary character.

Inasmuch as the meaning of words is cognisable through the usage of old experienced people, even though the definition has been given by the *Sūtra*, yet the Bhāshya speaks of the teaching of trustworthy persons as the very root of all verbal denotation.

In the case of the *Ṛk* '*Agnih pūrhvēbhhih &c.*,' there is no verb in the first foot, and as such, there being no sense completed within it, the division into feet in this case is in accordance with the metre and not the meaning.

Objection: "In the case of the *Ṛk* '*Agnimīlē &c.*,' also, inasmuch "as the whole *Ṛk* contains the expression of a single sense, the sense "is not completed in each foot, and consequently in this case also the "division into feet cannot be said to be based upon the sense."

Reply: Why cannot it be said to be so? In the first foot of the *Ṛk* we actually find the completion of a single sense. And as for the incompleteness of the sense of the other two feet, as a matter of fact, those two also are not incomplete; as the sense of them also is completed by the supplying of the verb '*ilē*.' Hence it is rightly said that in this case the foot-division is in accordance with the meaning. The *Bhāshya* does not mean that in this case the foot-division does not depend upon the exigencies of metre. And hence there can be nothing against the fact of these *Mantras* having the character of the '*Ṛk*.'

ADHIKARAṆA (13).

Definition of Sāma.

Sūtra (36): The name 'Sāma' is given to songs.

"Among Mantras"—'*tēshām*'—has to be supplied to this *Sūtra* from the previous *Sūtra*. In this case also the Bhāshya brings in the authority of the teachings of trustworthy persons, in the same manner as in the last *Sūtra*. The mention of the instances 'Curd is sour,' &c., should have been made in the preceding *Sūtra*; but the Bhāshya did not do so; because it did not attach much importance to it. Or, it may be that the examples have been cited here, with a view to show that, 'just as, even though there are many attributes in the *Curd* and in the *Sugar*, yet the words 'sour' and 'sweet' only express the peculiar tastes of the curd and the sugar respectively, so in the same manner, the word 'Sāma' expresses only the 'capability of being sung.'

Objection: "In the case of the curd and the sugar, inasmuch as "their taste is perceptible by the senses, any teaching of trustworthy "persons on this point can be merely descriptive, and as such can have "no special authority."

Reply: This does not touch our position; because the mention of '*iti*' in the Bhāshya distinctly points to the fact of the example being one of direct sense-perception; and the sense is that just as the idea that 'curd is sour,' or 'sugar is sweet,' is authoritative (true), so also is the teaching of trustworthy persons.

The 'capability of being sung' being a qualification, its cognition would precede that of the '*Mantra*'; and hence the denotability of '*Sung Mantra*' should be explained as being similar to that of the 'Class.' That is to say, just as in the case of the word 'go,' the word is found to denote an object (the cow) as qualified by one portion ('*Gōtva*') (of the cow),—and consequently the qualification is held to be denotable by the word,—so in the case of the word 'Sāma' also, as it is found to denote the '*Sung Mantra*' as qualified by the 'capability of being sung,' this last qualification forms the denotation of the word 'Sāma.'

ADHIKARAṆA (14).

Definition of 'Yajush.'

***Sūtra* (37): To the rest, the name 'Yajush' is given.**

This Sūtra is to be interpreted in the same manner as *Sūtra* 33.

ADHIKARAṆA (15).

Nigadas included in 'Yajush.'

PŪRVAPAKSHA.

Sūtra **(38): "The Nigada must be taken as the fourth "because of its peculiar qualification."**

Sūtra **(39): "Also, because of being named differently."**

The word '*vā*' serves the purpose of taking exception to the sweeping assertion made in the last *Sūtra*.

"*Nigada* would be the name of a fourth kind of *Mantras*; because of "its qualification being other than those of the preceding three. When "we have such an injunction as that 'The *Nigada* should be uttered "loudly,' if the *Nigada* were the same as '*Yajush*,' then, by being "uttered loudly, it would lose the characteristic of the '*Yajush*' (which is "laid down as to be uttered *quietly*); and hence with a view to avoid this "incongruity, we must hold the *Nigada* to be something other than the "*Yajush*. If again the said Injunction be held to be only descriptive, even "that is not possible unless there is a distinct difference between the "'*Yajush*' and the '*Nigada*.'"

SIDDHĀNTA.

Sūtra **(40): They must be regarded as *Yajush*, because they have the same form as that.**

(1) In the passage "*Ahē budhniya mantram mē gōpāya, &c. &c.*," we find the number of the kinds of Mantras distinctly mentioned as '*three*' only; and we find that in the Veda, the word '*Nigada*' is used as identical with 'Mantra'; (2) it is quite possible for the *Nigada* to have its peculiar qualification, and to be named differently, even without renouncing the character of '*Yajush*'; and (3) the aforesaid definition of '*Yajush*' is found to be quite applicable to it; for these three reasons, the *Nigadas* must be regarded as '*Yajush*.'

Sūtra **(41): It is on account of (the fact of the Nigada) being employed in indicating (to others) that the peculiar qualification of the Nigada is mentioned.**

The direction that the *Nigada* is to be uttered loudly, is based upon the exigencies of circumstances and reasoning; and as such being merely descriptive, the *loudness* is not spoken of as being *enjoined.* The sense of the *Sūtra* is that the *loudness* of the *Nigada* is mentioned simply because, if uttered slowly, it would not serve the purpose (of indicating to others) for which it is uttered.

***Sūtra* (42): Also because a distinct purpose is served (by such indicating to other people).**

There is a distinct purpose served by the addressing, to other people, of such sentences as '*Agnīd vihara,*' &c.: unless this were addressed to other people, the action of 'walking' round the fire by the *Agnīdhra* priest would not be accomplished; and there would be no use of addressing, unless it were done loudly enough for others to hear; it is for this reason that the particular qualification 'loudness' is mentioned. It is in this way too that the etymology of the word 'Nigada' becomes explained. As for the 'quiet utterance,' though it is directly enjoined by the Veda (as belonging to all Yajush), yet as such utterance would hamper our purpose, it could not rightly form part of the Action; and hence we take that injunction to refer to the *Yajush other than the Nigadas.*

***Sūtra* (43): The different naming is simply for the purpose of expressing the particular qualification.**

That is to say, the difference in name is to be explained as being similar to the assertion 'Feed the Brāhmaṇas with curd, and the Parivrājakas with milk'; where the *Parivrājakas* also are Brāhmaṇas, but with a particular qualification. So in the case in question also, the *Nigadas* are *Yajush,* but with this qualification, that they are to be uttered loudly.

***Sūtra* (44): Objection: "The name 'Nigada' would apply to all."**

That is to say, if the word '*Nigada*' be explained as 'that which is recited *loudly* ('gadyatē'), then all *Mantras* would become *Nigadas* (because the Ṛk and the Sāma Mantras also are recited *loudly*); and hence the name cannot be said to be for the purpose of expressing a particular property.

***Sūtra* (45): Reply: Not so, because of their being distinctly named as 'Ṛk.'**

There can be no such incongruity as mentioned above; because we find Vedic texts laying down in certain cases the use of the Ṛk, after having denounced the *Nigada* (as for instance, in the sentence '*Ayājyā vai nigadāh*'). And if both Ṛk and Nigada were the same, then these texts would enjoin the same thing that they had denounced; and this is an impossibility. Nor is there any incongruity in the signification of the root 'gada'; because what it does is to denote a particular property of sentences *that have the character of the Yajush* (and as such it could not apply to the *Ṛk* and the *Sāma*).

ADHIKARAṆA (16).

Definition of 'One-Sentence.'

***Sūtra* (46) : So long as there is mention of the same object, the sentence must be regarded as a *Yajush*, and as *one sentence ;* specially when it is such that if it be broken up, the divided portions become deficient (in certain necessary elements).**

Some people interpret this *Sūtra* as affording a definition of 'Sentence.' And there too, they declare as follows :—

"Though it is possible for the definition to belong to Vedic as well "as to ordinary sentences, yet inasmuch as the reasons propounded are "known more easily as belonging to ordinary sentences, we must take "it to be a definition of such sentences, and not of Vedic ones. Because "in ordinary parlance we find that a sentence is used with regard to "the object that has been cognised by other means of knowledge; and "it is only in such cases that we can ascertain the singleness of that "object; and as such it is in such cases that we can easily recognise the "fact of the sentence being one."

"That is to say, in the case of the sentences of ordinary parlance, "we find that the singleness of the meaning expressed by them, as well "as the meaning itself is cognised by other means of knowledge ; and hence "on the strength of this well-recognised fact, it is possible for us to "recognise the singleness of sentences. In the case of Vedic Sentences, "on the other hand, the meaning expressed not being amenable to any "other means of knowledge, its singleness cannot be ascertained prior "to the utterance of the sentence itself ; because until the object has been "recognised, there can be no idea of its singleness ; and thus the definition in "question not applying to these, its Apparent Inconsistency would lead us "to a converse definition with regard to Vedic Sentences—*viz.*, that *the* "*singleness of the meaning is due to the singleness* of the sentence. That "is to say, just as the object—Sentence—denotes another object, in the "shape of the Meaning, so the property—Singleness—of the sentence "would denote the property—Singleness—of the meaning. It has also "been declared elsewhere : 'Inasmuch as the meaning of the Vedic "Sentence is always cognisable by means of the sentence, the functioning "of the meaning of the Veda is always in keeping with the sentence ; "and hence, as without the sentence there would be no meaning, the "(Vedic) Sentence cannot be said to be controlled by the meaning ?"

Against the above interpretation of the *Sūtra*, we urge the following arguments: (1) When Jaimini is engaged only in the explanation of the Veda, by what connection would he lay down the definition of an ordinary sentence? (2) As for a definition of the Vedic sentence also, what connection could it have with the chapter dealing with *Differences* (among Actions). (3) Why should not he have mentioned this definition in the chapter (first) dealing with the *Means of Knowing* (*Dharma*)? (4) There was no use of mentioning the word 'one'; because the definition required would have been complete by merely mentioning that "so long as one sense lasts, it is a sentence. (5) How is it that in the course of dealing with *Mantras*, the *Sūtra* proceeds to lay down something wholly unconnected with it? (6) We find the Bhāshya expressly supplementing the *Sūtra* with the qualification "*among the yajush that are found to be read in close contiguity*"; and this supplementing being quite reasonable, we see no reason why it should have been passed over in favour of another interpretation. (7) And further, if the *Sūtra* went about laying down a definition of the *singleness of a sentence*, having left off the treatment of *Differences* among *Mantras*, where—either in the *Mantra*, in the *Brāhamana*, or *in ordinary parlance*—could such a definition be of any use?

As for the *Ṛk* and the *Sāma*, the limit of these is well defined by the capability of each being used in connection with sacrifices; and as such in the case of these, no useful purpose could be served by a definition either of Sentence or of its singleness. So in the case of the *Brāhmaṇa*, the passages laying down the *Agnihotra*, etc., having effectually led the persons concerned to the accomplishment of the particular *Bhāvanā*, as endowed with the three factors of the Result, the Means and the Process,—where would there be any use for a due knowledge of the character of the sentence or its singleness?

It might be urged that the use of such knowledge would lie in the avoiding of syntactical splits. But even this use is not possible; because a syntactical split is nothing more than the incapability (of the sentence to have two distinct predicates)—on the ground of such double predicability necessitating the repetition of certain words, etc.; and this incapability is always ascertained independently of all knowledge of the singleness or multiplicity of the sentence. That is to say, the repetition of a word, or of a part of a word, or of a number of words—or the cutting up of the word itself—is known to be an anomaly, by people, independently of any knowledge of the singleness or multiplicity of the sentence. And in the case of the breaking up of the word there are yet other anomalies, *viz.*, the necessity of rejecting the perceptible connection (between the members of the sentence and that word), and also that of assuming various unheard of potentialities (of the words concerned). While in the case of the repetition of the word, etc., as such repeated words would not have the character of the Veda, they could not be equally authoritative.

For these reasons we conclude that no useful purpose is served by a definition of the *Singleness of a Sentence* (in the matter of Vedic sentences).

In the case of the sentences of ordinary parlance also, inasmuch as all usage is actually found to be carried on, independently of any definition, any such would be of no use at all.

And further, if the singleness of the sentence were to be ascertained by the singleness of the meaning expressed by it,—then, inasmuch as the only purpose served by the sentence is to bring about the cognition of its meaning, after this meaning, and also its singleness, has been duly cognised—what would be the use of a subsequent cognition of the singleness of the sentence itself? As for the speakers, their sole purpose is to express a certain fact to other persons, and for their own sake, they have no need of any such definition. While as for those hearing him, when the sentence addressed to them treats of something wholly unknown to them, for them, there is not much difference between such a sentence and a Vedic one; while if it treat of something already known to him, then it is a mere repeated description, and as such no importance is to be attached to it. So in any case, even an ordinary sentence does not stand in need of such definition.

Then again, (if the *Sūtra* be taken as embodying a definition of the ordinary sentence), wherefore should it not have laid down one of Vedic sentences also? It cannot be urged that the definition of these also has been implied through Apparent Inconsistency. Because the proper process would have been to directly lay down the definition of Vedic sentences, and then to imply, by Apparent Inconsistency, that of ordinary sentences. As a matter of fact, however, no such Inconsistency is possible in the case in question; because it is not such that a knowledge of the said definition of ordinary sentence is not possible without a (implied) definition of the Vedic sentence.

Further, it is not yet established that what you point out as the definition of Vedic sentences (as implied by Apparent Inconsistency), really applies to such sentences; because what the definition does is to bring forward the fact of the singleness of the meaning being based upon that of the Sentence. Then again, inasmuch as it is quite possible to believe the original definition in the *Sūtra* itself to pertain to Vedic sentences (and not to ordinary sentences),—or that the definition of Vedic sentences may be something entirely different,—there is no inevitable Inconsistency in the matter. Nor can the definition be said to have the character of *Parisankhyā* (that is to say, it cannot be said that the definition, while applying to ordinary sentences, also serves to preclude Vedic sentences as having the contrary character), because there is no mention made of the relationship of the general and particular. That is to say, if it were so that the general definition had been mentioned, and then that definition were subsequently pointed out as applying only to ordinary sentences, then alone could it be concluded, through *Parisaṅkhyā*, that the definition in question does not apply to Vedic sentences. But the definition in question cannot be said to be a particular one; because in that case there would be many irregularities. On the other hand, we can, quite reasonably, lay down the contrary proposition that—'Because of the *multiplicity* of the meaning, the sentence is one, specially when it is such that on being separated, there remains nothing wanting in it'; or that 'Because of the singleness of the meaning the sentences are many.' Consequently none of the above positions is rightly tenable.

Further, how can the singleness of the sentence be ascertained independently of the meaning? for certainly any such singleness of the sentence is not cognisable in the mere verbal form of the sentence. That is to say, it is always the singleness of the meaning that is ascertained from the singleness of the sentence; and hence it must be admitted that the singleness of the sentence is always independent of the singleness of the meaning; and we do not perceive any limit of the sentence—be it made up of a hundred or a thousand letters. For when a certain number of letters not having their meanings known, are found to exist in one as well as in many sentences, we never come across a cognition of any limit of the sentence.

For these reasons it must be concluded that those words, on hearing which we are clearly cognisant of a single meaning, must be taken as forming a 'single sentence.' And it is only this definition that is not found incompatible with the character of any sentence—either ordinary, or of the *Mantra* and *Brāhmana*.

It has been urged above that, "prior to the cognition of the sentence, there is no idea either of its meaning, or of its singleness."

And to this we make the following reply: The meaning of the sentence is always signified by the meanings of words as known in the ordinary world; and hence it cannot be said to be brought about by means of the singleness of the sentence. That is to say, if the sentence had an independent denotation of its own, like the word, then, somehow or other, it might have been possible for us to hold the meaning of the sentence to depend upon the singleness or multiplicity of that sentence. As a matter of fact, however, we find that the meanings of words having been expressed by each word, independently of one another, it is solely from the connection among these word-meanings, that there follows the cognition of the meaning of the sentence (made up of those words), independently of any functioning of the words (towards this latter cognition); and it is from this that it is concluded that so many words form a single sentence; and towards this result we find nothing that is contributed either by the sentence or its singleness. And in this explanation there is nothing that is incongruous.

Now then, that which forms the meaning of the sentence (in the Veda) is the *Bhāvanā*, qualified by its accessories; and differences in the *Bhāvanā* are always found to be cognised by such means as the presence of another word, and so forth (*vide* next *Pāda*). That is to say, in the case of a collection of words, where we do not find any other *Bhāvanā* expressed by such agencies as the presence of another word and so forth, we conclude that the sentence is one only; and thus its multiplicity would always depend upon the denotation of other *Bhāvanās*. Consequently, inasmuch as both of these—singleness and multiplicity—are recognised by other means, the singleness of the sentence cannot be any reason for the singleness of the meaning.

In view of the above argument, then, we should explain the *Sūtra* exactly in accordance with the *Bhāshya*.

In the *Adhyāya* dealing with Differences, the special subject introduced being the *Mantras*, the different forms of these, in the shape of the Ṛk, the Yajush and the Sāma have been described; and then there naturally arising a desire for enquiring further into the subdivisions of these, each distinct Ṛk or Sāma being definitely known, each by itself, to the traditional generations of students, any definition of these is not attempted. The *Yajush*, however, are found in the text, mixed with one another, and as such one *Yajush* could not be distinguished from another without a sort of a definition; consequently it is such a definition that the *Sūtra* proceeds to give. Nor can it be urged that each *Yajush* could be distinguished by means of the directions (contained in the Brāhmaṇas) which always mention the opening word of each *Yajush*. Because the Brāhmaṇas do not contain directions with regard to all *Yajush*; nor is the rule that—'the beginning of the second *Yajush* means the end of the first'—found in the Veda; it is only a rule that the author of the *Sūtras* themselves have made with reference to directions contained in the *Brāhmaṇas*.

Thus then the *Bhāshya* explains the first part of the *Sūtra* as—'*that collection of words which is employed as one whole, in a sacrifice, is one Yajush*'; and it will be evident that this explanation is based upon the etymological formation of the word '*Yajush*' (which has its source in the root '*yaj*'= to sacrifice). As a matter of fact, we find that in the case of all

Mantras, there is always in the first instance, cognised a direction—in the form 'this *Mantra* is to be employed at sacrifices'—inferred from the context (in which the *Mantra* occurs). It is after this that,—it being realised that the *Mantra* cannot, directly by itself, be utilised in the sacrifice,—we conclude that it helps in the completion of the sacrifice by the pointing out of its auxiliaries (in the shape of the Deity, etc.). It is for this reason that it has been said (in the *Bhāshya*) that that collection of words which serves to recall the auxiliaries of a sacrifice is one *Yajush*, and it is also known as a *sentence* (*Vākya*), because it has to be *spoken out* (pronounced or recited). A '*Vākya*' (sentence) is that which can be spoken out (*uchyatē*); and only that can be spoken out (at the performance of sacrifices) which is capable of serving its function,—nothing more or less than that; and it is by means of that much alone that the sacrifice is accomplished. Then arises the question as to the character of the *Yajush;* and this is answered by the second part of the *Sūtra*—'*It is that which expresses a single fact, and has its parts depending upon one another.*' If only so much were a *Yajush*, then anything over and above this must be taken as another sentence, and as such spoken of as a distinct *Yajush*. Thus, in all cases, be it from the beginning or from the end, only such words are accepted as a *Yajush*, as are capable of expressing a single fact, leaving aside all that is not so capable,—all those of the latter sort forming distinct *Yajush* by themselves.

Says the Bhāshya—*Inasmuch a sentence is known to be one on account of the aforesaid reason, we conclude that a collection of words expressing a single fact forms one sentence.* The sense of this is that the definition of a single sentence being explained as above, through that, we also get at the definition of the distinctness of *Yajush*, as also that of the distinctness of sentences.

The *Bhāshya* puts the question—*What is the example?* This question emanates from one who takes the word '*artha*' (in the *Sūtra*) to mean '*signification*' and thereby considers it impossible for the *Sūtra* to contain the two definitions (of the distinctness of *Yajush* and of the distinctness of sentences). And the sense of the question may be thus explained: "It is the word that would have a single signification (*artha*); "but it has not its parts depending upon one another; and the collection "of. words (sentence), which has its part dependent upon one another, "has not a single signification. That is to say, it is possible for the word "to have a single denotation in the shape of the Class; but it is not "such that when its component letters, roots or affixes are separated, there "is any element wanting in it; because in that condition the word is "absolutely without any power of signifying anything." As for the collec- "tion of words, on the other hand,—its part, *i.e.*, the words themselves, "stand in need of one another, on being separated; but they do not afford "a single meaning; because each word has a distinct signification of "its own, and the collation of these is not known to have any meaning "apart from that of the component words. And hence there being nothing "that could form the right object of the definition, it cannot be a definition "at all (in the sense that is attached to it by the *Bhāshya*)."

In reply to the above question, the *Bhāsya* has cited the *Mantra* '*Dēvsya twā*,' etc., and the reply is based mainly upon the fact of the word '*artha*' being taken in the sense of '*purpose*' (and not in that of 'signification').

The opponent says in the *Bhāshya*: "*The word 'pada' here has only one meaning*"; and in this he further explains what he means,—the sense of it being this: "When apart from the signification of the word "there is no signification of the sentence, as one impartite whole, then "Distinction and Connection, as signified by the sentence, would only be "the properties of the significations of the component words themselves, "they being recognised as belonging to them, on account of extreme "proximity."

With a view to all this it has been said in the *Bhāshya*: *Even then the signification would not be one only;* because by "Distinction" is meant the mutual differentiation or specification among the words; and this cannot be one, as it is different with each word. In accordance with the theory that words signify *Individuals*, all individual cows being spoken of by the word "Cow," all that the qualifying words 'white,' etc., can be said to do is to distinguish them from the *black;* and they cannot serve the purpose of signifying the connection (of *whiteness* with the individual *cow*); and as for the connection of this qualification, this being included in the signification of the word, it cannot form the meaning of the sentence; and hence what is cognised is only the distinctness (of the objects signified by the words), in which the said *connection* enters as a secondary element. And just as the distinctness belongs to the word 'cow' because of the word 'white' differentiating it from the 'black,' etc.,—so in the same manner the distinctness belongs to the word 'white' as differentiated by the word 'Cow' from the 'Horse,' etc. And thus the objects to be differentiated from (or set aside) being many, there is no authority for declaring the singleness (of the Connection or Distinctness). If recourse be had to "Distinctness' *in general*, then this *class* 'Distinctness' being always one, all sentences would become synonymous. If again, the meaning of the sentence be said to consist of the meanings of the component words, as accompanied by the said distinctness, then the 'Multiplicity' becomes an established fact.

So also (in the case of the theory that the meanings of the component words consists in their *Connection*), this Connection among the denotations of the words is only a mutual attachment among them; and as this differs in each couple, no *singleness* could be cognised. Even in accordance with the theory that the denotation of the word consists of the *Class*,—the classes 'Whiteness' and 'Cow' as denoted in their respective forms, would, on account of proximity, exert a mutual attachment; and as this would constitute the meaning of the sentence, the distinctness whereof would be indirectly established. This connection too—either in the shape of *whiteness* in the class "cow," or in that of the 'cow' in 'whiteness'—would be found to reside completely in each individual (cow); and as such it could not but be *many*. Though in the case of a sentence containing only two words, it might be possible for the *connection* to be the same in regard to both words,—yet in the case of sentences containing many words, there would be various places where each set of two words would come into contact; and the connection thus being found in so many different places, it could not but be *many*.

And further, the meanings of words being self-important, both Distinctness and Connection are only their properties; and as such they would always differ with the difference in the objects of which they are properties; and hence they could never be *one*. That is to say, so long as we do not admit of a *singleness* or *unity of purpose* among certain words, the significations of these being all self-sufficient, could never bring about any unity; and as such each of them would bear with itself independently the said *distinctness* and *connection*. And for this reason also they would be *many*.

Though for us, who hold the "Class" to form the denotation of a word, we do not hold the said *Distinctness* to form the signification of a sentence (such signification being held only by the upholders of *Apoha*—the Bauddhas),—yet, inasmuch as the *Purvāpakshi* had brought up that also as an alternative, there is nothing incongruous in our accepting it for the sake of argument. And as for the explanation of the *Siddhānta* itself, this is very rightly done by taking the word "*artha*" (in the *Sūtra*) in the sense of "purpose" (and in this it is not necessary for us to accept the *Apoha* or any other theory contrary to our tenets).

Thus then, it is also possible to declare that it is only the object denoted by a single word that is the principal factor, and it is only as the qualification of that object that everything else is mentioned; and as such on account of the Distinctness and the Connection of that object there can be only one Distinctness or Connection. And thus, as being in intimate relationship with the action, the *Mantra* being found to serve a distinctly visible purpose in connection with the action, the function of the whole collection of words forming the *Mantra* lies in the pointing out of the action of *Nirvāpa*, as qualified by the denotation of the words '*Savitri*' and the rest; and as such the example is found to be quite apt.

The opponent, however, not realising the fact of the *Nirvāpa* being the predominant factor, is made to ask, in the *Bhāshya*—"*Nanvatra devasya, etc.*" And in reply to this the author says that such would have been the case only if the word *Nirvapāmi* were construed in one place and also in another; because such double construction would be possible only when the *Nirvāpa* would be the secondary factor. But, as a matter of fact, we find that this cannot but be the predominant factor, as it serves a distinctly useful purpose; while as for *Savitṛ, etc.*, inasmuch as these do not form part of the action, they are only subservient to the action of *Nirvāpa*; and hence all the words have one and the same *purpose* (namely that which is served by the *Nirvāpa*).

Another objection has been raised in the Bhāshya: "*Wherefore should the Sūtra have laid down both the conditions?*" The sense of this question is this: (A) "In a case where a number of words together "serve a single purpose, it naturally follows that, when separated, they "would be wanting in certain elements (because each by itself could not "serve that purpose); and as such it is not necessary to mention the second "condition separately; (B) conversely each of the words separately "could not be wanting in a certain element, unless they were so placed "that they all conjointly served one and the same purpose; because it "is always possible for each of them by itself to serve distinct pur- "poses; and hence the first condition being already implied in the "second, there is no need for mentioning both."

In reply to this objection, the Bhāshya proceeds to cite counter-instances. (A) In this connection it is shown that the single purpose of pointing out the division of the *Cake* is served by the words independently of one another. (That is to say, if we left off the second condition, then "*bhago vām vibhajatu aryamā vām vibhajatu*" would become one *Mantra*, which, as a matter of fact, it is not; and this is avoided by the mention of the second condition, because each sentence *bhago vām vibhajatu*, when separated from the other, is not found to be wanting in any element).

Though the objection as to the multiplicity of the *Cake-division* has already been answered before, yet it has been brought forward again, with a view to show that there being no qualification collectively mentioned, as the word '*vibhajatu*' is repeated, there is no fault of the aforesaid *anushaṅga*' (*i.e.*, there is no necessity of carrying the same '*vibhajatu*' from one place to another).

The reply to this objection is that we shall show later on how, even when there are distinct independent accessories mentioned (as for instance, *Bhaga* and *Aryamā* in the case in question), the action is not more than one. And we have already set aside all chance of the predominance of the Accessory; and hence any specifications due to the accessory, not forming an integral part of the action, cannot be regarded as significant; and hence both the sentences—'*bhago vām vibhajatu*' and '*aryamā vām vibhajatu*'—must be taken as only expressing the 'Division' in general; and as such both being found to serve the same purpose (they would come to be taken as forming a single *yajush*, if we left off the second condition in the *Sūtra*).

(B). In the case of the sentence '*varhirdēvasadanam dāmi tasmin sīda*'—if we leave off the first condition, then, even though the latter sentence '*tasmin sīda*' is dependent upon the former, yet, the purposes served by the two being distinct, they are taken as two distinct sentences (which would not be possible if the *serving of a single purpose* were not laid down as a necessary condition).

For these reasons it must be admitted that the two conditions together form the required definition.

ADHĪKARAṆA (17).

Conditions of the Diversity of Sentences.

***Sūtra* (47): When the sentences are equally independent of one another, then they are "distinct."**

PŪRVAPAKSHA.

"In the case of those sentences, the fact of whose intimate relation-"ship with the action is not perceptible, and the use whereof is laid down "only by direct directions (in the Brāhmaṇa), in the absence of any "indication of such use by the words of the sentence itself,—we must "accept all that extends in the text up to the point where the next "(well-known) *Mantra* begins, to form a single *Mantra*. Because the "direction of its use being wholly verbal, it would be necessary to assume "an imperceptible result (as following from such use); and on this score "it is the assumption of the least possible Imperceptible Result that can be "permissible; and when a single purpose being thus assumed for the "whole, if they would be separated, they would be found wanting in some "element (and as such both the conditions of the previous *Sūtra* being "fulfilled, the sentence must be regarded as one). That is to say, "inasmuch as there is no authority for making unnecessary assumptions "of many imperceptible results, we are led to assume a single result "as following from all the sentences in question; and hence each part of "the sentence being incapable of bringing about that result, we have the "condition that when separated the sentences become deficient; and "as such the sentence must be regarded as one (in accordance with "the two conditions laid down in the foregoing *Sūtra*).

"The following questions might here be brought forward: '(1) In "accordance with this theory, how do you account for such distinct "directions (contained in the Brāhmaṇa) as—'*he should cut the branch of* "*the tree with the Mantra ishe tvā*,' '*and should wash it* with *ūrje tvā*' "(which distinctly lay down each part of the sentence as a separate "*Mantra*)? And (2) how do you account for the plural number in "*klṛptīḥ* in the direction *klṛptīrvācayati* where we find each *hope* (*klṛpti*) "mentioned distinctly as *āyurme kalpatām, prāṇo me kalpatām*; if all of "these *hopes* were taken as forming a single sentence, why should there "be the plural number in *klṛptīḥ*?'

"To the above question we make the following reply: (1) It is "quite possible for a single *Mantra* to be spoken of by means of several " words (contained in it), and (2) we have *klṛiptīh* in the plural, " because the word '*kalpatām*' is often repeated.

"That is to say—(1) a *Mantra* can be pointed out by pronouncing " any word therein contained—be that word in the beginning, in the " middle, or in the end; and there is nothing incompatible in this; " hence in the case in question, so long as the direction will continue, " the whole *Mantra* will have to be pronounced with each distinct action " because any mere part of the *Mantra* is wholly useless;—(2) and inas- " much as we find the word '*kalpatām*' repeated frequently, there is " nothing incompatible in the plurality of the *klṛiptīh*."

SIDDHANTA.

To all this we make the following reply: The above view cannot be maintained; any idea of the employment and the purpose of the *Mantra* is possible only after its verbal form has been duly recognised; and hence first of all it becomes necessary for us to ascertain the verbal form of the *Mantra* itself, before we proceed to examine whether all its constituent parts are distinct *Mantras*, or they collectively form a single *Mantra*.

For the present we shall leave aside the ordinary argument in favour of our position—such, for instance, as the presence of distinct purposes, or the presence of distinct directions for each part. As a matter of fact, the form of the *Mantra* cannot be said to be ascertained *after* its purpose or use has been ascertained. Because the form of the *Mantra* is always found to be definitely ascertained directly from the Vedic text itself, independently of all use or purpose, etc.; and the employment or the Purpose of the *Mantra* is always accepted in accordance with its singleness or multiplicity as cognised at the time that the text of the *Mantra* is ascertained. We have already shown above that there is nothing wrong in assuming many imperceptible factors, or results, provided that we have sufficient authority for such assumption. And, as a matter of fact, we find that at the time that the text of the *Mantra* (*Ishe tvā, etc.*) is ascertained, we have no idea either of the fact of its various portions being dependent upon one another, or of all of them serving a single purpose. And for this reason there being nothing against the conclusion that each part is distinct by itself, even subsequently we do not find any ground for taking them as one only. Nor is it possible for us rightly to assume a mutual interdependence among the several parts, when no such dependence has been actually perceived. And though, even in the absence of this dependence, it would be possible for the several parts to serve a single common purpose, yet as one of the two chief conditions (of syntactical unity) would be wanting, the whole *Mantra* cannot be taken as a single sentence. And hence it is all the more impossible for it to be taken as one when we find that the text of each part being different, there is a different use laid down for each; and the uses of these being different,—even though they may bring about imperceptible results,—the purposes served by the various parts cannot but be distinct.

Our opponent also will have to admit that there must be a distinct purpose with each direction. The only difference then between us is that while you hold all these results to follow from the whole *Mantra*, according to us each of them follows from each distinct part of the *Mantra*. Nor, in our case, is it necessary to assume any imperceptible results as following from each part of the *Mantra*, as each of them actually serves a distinctly useful purpose laid down in the *Brāhmaṇa*.

(1) And for the sake of the due fulfilment of these purposes it becomes incumbent on us even to supply whatever words—as '*chinadmi*' and the like—might be wanting in the *Mantra* as it stands, to duly accomplish the purpose; for instance the cutting of the branch, mentioned in the *Brāhmaṇa*.

(2) Or it may be that—as in the case of the Brāhmaṇa direction—that 'the Māhendra hymn is represented in the rumbling of the chariot,' even though the *rumbling* is not significant of any meaning, yet, at the peculiar time, by the mere remembrance of the Brāhmaṇa-direction in question, people recognise the *rumbling* as the actual singing of the hymn,—so, in the same manner, on account of the Brāhmaṇa-directions in connection with the Māntra '*Ishe tvā*,' *etc.*, the various parts thereof—'*ishe tvā*,' '*urjē tvā*,' *etc.*—would bring about the idea of *cutting*, *etc.* (and in this case it would not be necessary to supply the word '*chinadmi*').

Both of these processes (1) and (2) are equally authoritative; and hence the authors of the Kalpasūtras have recourse to one or the other in different places.

Thus then in any case, we must come to the following conclusion Inasmuch as it is absolutely impossible to make use of a senten wanting in a necessary factor, and as it is not right to make use of non significant words, we must have recourse to the supplying, from without, of the wanting word. Or, inasmuch as the *Mantra* should be used exactly as it is found in the Veda, we must convince ourselves of the fact of the words of the *Mantra*, as they actually stand, bringing about the idea of all that is necessary. The acceptance of the one or the other alternative is optional in the performance of the sacrifice.

And hence we find that the various parts of the *Mantra* in question must be taken as distinct sentences, also on account of the difference in the distinct perceptible purposes served by each of them.

Further, each part of the *Mantra* being found to have a distinct function of its own, as pointed out by the Brāhmaṇa-directions, each of them by itself must *help in the sacrifice;* and this alone constituting the etymological meaning of the word '*yajush*' (*ijyatē anēna*), each part must be admitted to be a distinct *yajush* by itself.

In the same manner, in the case of the sentences—'*āyuryajnena kalpatām,*' '*prāṇo yajnena kalpatām,*' *etc.,*—though the same purpose is served by all the sentences, yet they cannot be taken as a single sentence; because each is distinctly perceived in its own form, independently of the others. As a matter of fact, however, they do not even serve the same purpose, because the '*kalpanā*' (*preservation*) of '*āyu*' is distinctly different from that of '*prāṇa*' and the rest. Nor can it be urged that, "as in the case of the sentence *açvinorbāhubyām nirvapāmi pushṇo hastābhyām,* the *nirvāpa* is accepted to be the same in both cases; so in the case in question also the 'preservation' would be the same in all"; because we find the word '*klṛiptīh*' in the plural number, in the Mantric Injunction. Then again, in this case, the '*kalpanas*' not forming an integral part of the sacrifice, much significance cannot be attached to them; and the only purpose of the *Mantras* lies in its recitation; and in the *Mantra* we actually find mentioned many '*kalpanas*'; and as the difference of *kalpanas* is not possible without a difference in their significations, we regard the significations, that are subservient to the letters of the word, to be *many.*

The *Bhāshya* has said that the mention of particular *kalpanas* has a distinctly perceptible purpose; and this is with reference to the accomplishing of many *Mantras.*

The *Bhāshya* speaks of an objection: "*The kalpana spoken of in "each case may be taken in the sense of kalpana in general, as in the case of "the Cake-division with reference to the sentences Bhago vām vibhajatu* "and *Aryamā vām vibhajatu.*" And the citing of a fresh instance is based upon the fact that the case of the *kalpanas* is different from that of *Nirvāpa,* in that this latter is mentioned only once (whereas the *kalpana* and the *vihbāga* are repeated). The sense of this is that, just as though frequently repeated the 'Division' ('*Vibhaga*') is not accepted to be many, even though the Instrumentality thereof (in the shape of Bhaga and Aryamā, etc.) is diverse,—so, in the same manner, in the case in question there would be no diversity *of kalpanas.*

The reply to this is: *It is not so;* because in the case in question no useful purpose is served by taking '*kalpatām*' in the sense of *kalpana in general.*

Or '*yathā vibhāgē*' may be construed with the Reply, the sense thereof being that 'as in the case of the Division, so here also, etc., etc.'

Objection: "As a matter of fact, there is a diversity in the case "of the *Division*; and as such it was not right to put this instance in the "mouth of the objector."

Reply: In that case we will explain the citing of that instance to be, not for the purpose of pointing out unity, but only with a view to identifying the case in question with that of the instance, and thereby making the former open to alternative processes; just as we have in the case of the Vibbāga (where there is an option between the agency of Bhaga and that of Aryamā). The sense of the objection thus comes to be that "we have an option in the case of *vibhāga*,—why then cannot we have the same in the case in question also?"

The reply to this is that this cannot be; because there is an option only in that case where the subject is the same in both alternatives. In the case in question, however, we do not find anything to show that the significations of all '*kalpanas*' are the same (in the shape of *kalpana in general*); and hence we cannot take them all as synonymous, as in the case of '*vibhāga*'; specially as we find that each sentence expresses a hope for *āyu*' (longevity) and the rest, as qualified by '*klṛipti*' (preservation). In the case of '*vibhāga*' inasmuch as no important purpose is served by the accessories (in the shape of Bhaga, etc.), the *action* of *vibhāga* (Division) in general itself comes to be the predominant factor; and as such it is this action alone that is indicated by the *Mantra* (and the matter of the instrumentality is left optional). In the case in question, on the other hand, what are hoped for are a 'long life' (*āyu*) and the rest; and as such it is these that are the predominant factors; and it is as qualification of these that we have the mention of '*kalpana*' (preservation); and it is not the *kalpana* as qualified by 'long life,' etc., that is indicated by the *Mantra*; because no useful purpose would be served by this indication. Even if this Action (*Kalpana*) were the predominant factor, then, too, there being a clear difference between *āyu*, *prāṇa*, *etc.*, the action (preservation of these) also could not but be many. And in support of the theory of diversity, we have the fact of each of them serving a distinct perceptible purpose.

Or, it may be that the word '*klṛipti*' in the injunction '*klṛpitīr vācayati*' does not refer to the *Mantra* ('*Āyuryajnena kalpatām*,' *etc.*); what it does is to denote the multiplicity of the *action* (of *kalpana*); because all words depend upon the objects they signify. Consequently, firstly, because the plural number distinctly denotes a diversity of Actions, and secondly, because a distinct diversity is accepted as based upon the diversity of the qualifications ("*Āyu*," *etc.*),—the *Mantra* (*Āyuryajnēna kalpatām, etc.*) in question comes to be taken as referring to *Kalpana as qualified by Āyu, etc.*; and in this manner they come to fulfil what is laid down in the Brāhmaṇa-direction ('*klṛiptīrvācayati*'); thereby coming to serve distinctly perceptible purposes, each part must be taken as having a distinct purpose of its own.

Objection: "In that case, how is it that the *Brāhmaṇa* uses the "word '*vācayati*'? because the object of this Verb must be a *word* (while "the word '*klṛipti*' has been explained as 'something qualified by *Áyu*,' "which could not be the object of '*vācayati*,' *etc.*, which means 'makes "to pronounce')?"

Reply: This is no incongruity at all; because the word is used in both senses. That is to say, just as people use the word '*vācayati*' with reference to a person uttering a *word*, so, in the same manner, when a person is found to speak of a certain *object* by means of a certain word, then with regard to the person who *makes him speak of it*, we use the word '*vācayati*' (=*makes to speak*). Hence the sense of the injunction *klṛiptīr vācayati* comes to be that when the sacrificer proceeds to pronounce the word expressive of the action of *Klṛiptī* (or *Kalpana*), then the *Adhvaryu* priest *makes him pronounce it* ('*vācayati*'). And inasmuch as the *Mantras* ('*Āyuryajnena kālpatam*' and the rest) indicate so many distinct *Kalpanas*, it is only when each of them is accepted as a distinct *Mantra* by itself that it is found to serve a perceptible purpose and hence in such cases the sentences must be admitted to be distinct.

ADHIKĀRAṆA (18).

[*Definition of Anushaṅga.*]

***Sūtra* (48) : Anushaṅga is the means of completing the Sentence ; because it is such as is equally applicable (to it).**

In connection with the *Jyotishṭoma*, three *Homas* are laid down (*viz.*, the *Āgneyī*, the *Saumī* and the *Vaishṇavī*) ; and it is laid down—by the sentence '*agnimanikam*,' *etc.*, that in the beginning of each of these the *Agneyī Homa* has to be offered. And the three *Mantras* enjoined for the *Agneyī*, accompanying the first of these, the *Brāhmaṇa* lays down in its complete form—*e.g.* (1) '*Yāte agnē ayāçayā tanūrvarshishṭhā*, ... *swāhā*' ; and those for the other two are mentioned only in their incomplete forms—such as (2) '*Yātē agnē rayāçaya*' and (3) '*Yātē agnē harācaya*.'

In the case of these two, inasmuch as the subject is introduced by the word '*yā*' (*that which*), which is in the feminine gender, the sentences cannot be complete without some word denotative of a feminine object. And no use can be made of an incomplete sentence ; consequently, with a view to avoid this inconsistency, it becomes necessary to supply a part of the sentence that would supply the missing factor. Because in the Veda, not even a single incomplete sentence is found to be used ; consequently in cases where the sentence met with happens to be incomplete, the factor necessary for its completion must be sought out from somewhere else.

Nor, too, is actual sensuous Perception the only means of cognising Vedic *Mantras ;* because they can be cognised by means of Inference and the other means of knowledge just as well as by means of Sense-perception. Hence it is only when all the five means of knowledge have ailed, that a certain sentence can be relegated to the sixth one of Negation (*i.e.*, actually denied). In the case in question we should not rest idle ; no sooner we find Sense-perception not affording us the requisite knowledge of the completing factor, if we also find Inference and the rest all equally inoperative, then alone we should conclude the *Mantra* to be made up of that incomplete sentence alone. If, however, any one of these means of cognition supplies the knowledge of the missing factor, then the *Mantra* is to be taken as made up of the sentence thus completed, which, before the addition of this factor, was wanting. Thus then, it is by Apparent Inconsistency that we are led to the general conclusion that *there is a missing factor.* And thus there being no room for the functioning of Negation, the incomplete sentence is wholly incapable of being used.

Thus then, there arises the question as to whether this missing factor is to be supplied out of the Veda, or out of certain sentences of ordinary parlance,—in the former case the missing factor being found in the preceding *Mantra*, in the shape of '*tanūrvarshishṭhā*,' *etc.*

PŪRVAPAKSHA.

"It is to be supplied out of sentences of ordinary parlance. Because "a part of the Vedic sentence, being naturally bound up with this "sentence, cannot go to any other place; sentences of ordinary parlance, "on the other hand, can be used anywhere and for any purpose that one "likes. That is to say, just as such Vedic objects as the '*Āhavanīya*' "fire and the like never turn aside from their purposes as definitely "laid down in the Veda, so, in the same manner, a part of a Vedic "sentence is bound hard and fast to that sentence of which it actually "forms part in the text; and as such it cannot be used anywhere else. "A part of the ordinary sentence, on the other hand, is not so bound "up; and as such it can be used anywhere one likes; and as such there "would be nothing incongruous in its being taken up for the purpose "of the supplying of the missing part of any sentence. Consequently, "it is only a part of the ordinary sentence that can be brought in to "complete two *Mantras* in question.

"On the ground, however, of the Vedic sentence being found ready "to hand, and as such its use being much easier, while the ordinary "sentence has to be composed,—if someone were to supply the missing "part out of a Vedic sentence, taking it only as an ordinary sentence, "then nothing can be said against it. All that we mean is that "any such sentence, separated from its proper place, should not be "considered as *Vedic.* For instance, when during the reading of such "works as the *Mahābhārata* and the like, if we come across certain "Vedic sentences, we read them as ordinary sentences, and not with the "restrictions of pronunciation, etc., attendant upon the Vedic sentence.

"And further, if,—on the ground of the sentence '*yāte rajāçayā*' "being as closely proximate to the sentence '*tanūrvarsishṭhā*' *etc.*, as the "first sentence '*yātē ayāçayā*'—the '*tanūrvarsishṭhā*,' *etc.*, should be "taken along with '*yātē rajāçayā*,'—then in that case the *Mantra* should "be pronounced exactly as it would be found in the text (*i.e.*, it should "be read as '*tanūrvarshishṭhā* . . . . *svāhā yāte rajāçayā*'), which "would be absurd. For this reason, too, the missing factor cannot be "supplied out of the Vedic sentence."

SIDDHĀNTĀ.

To the above we make the following reply: It is only when the Veda has ceased to function towards a certain end, that there can be an occasion for the functioning of ordinary sentences; and the functioning of the Veda can be believed to have ceased, only after all effort and attempt to find it out has totally failed.

That is to say, a Vedic sentence can be completed only by supplying the missing part from out of a Vedic sentence, and not from out of an ordinary sentence; because the Veda is the only means of knowing *Dharma*. If, however, the most diligent search on our part fails to show us a Vedic sentence duly functioning towards the required end, then alone can the Veda allow of the completing of its sentence by the help of ordinary sentences. And this search proceeds from what is most proximate (to the incomplete sentence) to one remote from it.

For instance, a meaning that is not found in the root is looked for in the affix; that which is not found in the whole word is looked for in another word (of the same sentence); that which is not found in the same sentence is looked for in another sentence (of the same context); if again it is not found in any such sentence, it is looked for in another context altogether.

That is to say, when a certain fact as expressed by the root or the affix is found to be wanting in a certain factor, then if another meaning capable of supplying the missing link is found in the same (root or affix), then it is all well and good. If it is not found in the same root or affix, then, without being idle, we must look for it in the affix or the root (respectively). If, however, it is not found in any of these, then it should be looked for in the word preceding or following it immediately. If it is not found in the immediately proximate word, then it is looked for in another word, a step or two removed from the original word. If it is not found in the same sentence, then in the same manner as in the case of the word, it should be sought after in other sentences in the same context. If not found even there, then it should be looked for in other contexts, in the order that they may present themselves. If, however, it is not found anywhere in the Veda, then alone can we reasonably seek for it in the sentences of ordinary parlance. When not found even in these, then we must conclude it to be non-existent; and then accepting our notion of incompleteness to be a mistaken one, we must accept the *Mantra* to be complete, just as it is.

In all cases, when we do not find the missing factor in a sentence close to the incomplete sentence, then we can bring it in from one removed from it. But in case one happens to be found much nearer, the bringing in of a remote sentence is as unauthoritative as if it were non-Vedic.

Hence in the case in question, the missing factors of the two sentences—'*yā tē rajāçayā*' and '*yā tē haraçayā*'—not being found either in any one word contained in the sentence, or in the sentence itself, we conclude that this missing factor must be found in another sentence. And just the same factor that is wanted in these sentences is found in another sentence, which immediately precedes the one incomplete sentence, and is only one step removed from the other—(that is to say, the sentence '*yā tē agnē ayaçayā tanūh*,' *etc.* Though this factor ('*tanurvarsishthā*,' *etc.*) having got all that is necessary for it in the first *Mantra*, does not stand in need of the subsequent *Mantras*, yet inasmuch those two *Mantras* are incomplete without that factor, and not finding anything else mentioned in closer proximity to themselves, they lead the person concerned to the following conclusion: 'Though it was not possible for this missing factor to be read but once, and then in close proximity to all the three *Mantras*, and as it is not actually repeated over and over again, on account of its being got at by other means,—yet it is such that it is distinctly indicated by our purpose or need also,—and as such, people should not be led away, by attaching undue significance to the fact of proximity, to connect it with one (the first) *Mantra* only.'

Though it is true that the factor, '*tanūh*,' *etc.*, actually precedes the *Mantra*, '*Yā tē rajāçayā*,' yet it can be supplied only in that place of this *Mantra* where it is actually wanted to complete the sentence. Because that sentence appears in the place that it does, only with view to point out that it forms part of the next sentence also; and a due consideration of its capabilities and its position in the second *Mantra* is regulated in accordance with that in the previous *Mantra*. The sentence being actually mentioned only once, it is absolutely impossible for it to be mentioned in that part of the subsequent sentences where it is required; and hence it is mentioned in its due sequential order in connection with one *Mantra* only; and as for the other two, its indication is just enough to show that it forms part of these also. Thus then, being duly comprehended to be so, (1) because it is naturally incapable of occupying any other position; (2) because the incomplete sentences themselves do not want it in any other place; and (3) because in the case of the first *Mantra* it has been found to be capable of occupying a position at the end of the sentence; therefore even in the case of the other two *Mantras* it is only at the end that it is added.

The author of the Bhāshya, however, holds that inasmuch as the factor in question is read between the first and second *Mantras*, it is not expressed to which of these two it is more intimately connected; and hence to both of them it must be taken as equally proximately related; and then he raises a doubt as to its connection with the third *Mantra*, from which it is one step further removed; and in order to meet this difficulty of intervention what the Bhāshya does is to take the second and the third *Mantras* together as forming a single composite whole, which removes the difficulty due to the intervention of the second *Mantra*, between the missing sentence and the third *Mantra;* but then there arises the difficulty that in that case the missing factor would complete the composite whole (formed by the two *Mantras*), and not both of them separately; and this is met by the declaration that, inasmuch as the composite whole is incapable of being employed (at a sacrifice), the missing factor must be connected with each part of it; and hence it is concluded that both parts being equally predominant, and both being equally incapable of being otherwise completed, the whole of the missing factor is to be connected with each of them.

Having arrived at this conclusion, however, the Bhāshya proceeds to offer another explanation: '*Ap ca sākaṅkshasya sannidhau, etc.*,'—the sense of this being that when the missing factor will have been introduced in the second *Mantra*, it would immediately come to precede the third *Mantra* also, and thus there would be no intervention.

Some people hold that the Bhāshya has mentioned the two explanations as equally correct, and as such optional.

But others declare, that not satisfied with the former explanation the *Bhāshya* has offered the second. The reason for the said dissatisfac-is as follows:—

The two sentences have never been composed by any person as a single composite whole; and if they were so, we do not see any reason why they should have been again composed separately. That is to say, any two sentences can be taken as one composite whole, (1) either when they serve the same purpose, or (2) when they contain the same words. In the case in question, however, we find none of these two conditions present. It may be urged that they actually have the same purpose in the shape of being completed by the same sentence. But one who brings forward this argument would evince, on his part, a grand conception of the functions of *Mantras!* The *being completed by a sentence* would only constitute a *want* on their part,—how could it be an *action or purpose* of theirs? And as the sentence supplied is only a missing factor, on the sole strength of this, it is not proper to speak of the two *Mantras* as forming one composite whole. And when you also subsequently come to acknowledge its relationship with each *Mantra* separately, we do not see how you can make a single composite whole of the two *Mantras.* The assertion that they become a composite whole, and then each of them becomes connected with the missing factor, would be as unbridled as the freaks and tricks of a single (and favourite) son of the king. And further, in that case, because the missing factor precedes the composite whole, it would have to be added in the beginning. Nor can it be rightly urged that there is no difference between the relative positions of the *Mantras* with regard to the missing factor. Because there is a distinct difference of locality which makes a difference in the relative position of the *Mantras*; for instance, we find that the missing sentence is actually found, in the first *Mantra*, in the same place that it is required; while it is not so in the other two *Mantras*.

For these reasons the only explanation that is reasonabie is the following:—

Ākankshā (Want), *Sannidhāna* (Proximity) and *Yogyatā* (Capability),—these three conjointly constitute the ground of relationship, and not mere *immediate sequence*. That which, being one, is yet mentioned as related to many things, must be in closer proximity with only one of these; and it is not this *proximity* alone that is accepted as being the only ground of relationship. Because even in this case, the relationship is based upon all the aforesaid three grounds (and not upon mere immediate sequence). What the Proximity does is to give rise to a mistaken notion (as to relationship), on account of its bringing about an idea of its own substrate. And this mistaken notion ceases when some other related object is pointed out, conjointly, by *Want*, *Proximity* and *Capability*. Just as the idea of *Bhāvanā* being denoted by the verbal root ceases on account of the capability of the *Bhāvanā* to take up the accessories that can never belong to the meaning of the verbal root.

The conclusion arrived at in that case is this: (1) The missing factor being mentioned for the sake of all incomplete sentences (in question); (2) it being impossible for it to be mentioned in the immediate sequence of all of them; and (3) the sentence being one only—it is found in close proximity to one of them. Consequently mere *immediate sequence* can be no ground of relationship.

By the word '*sannidhi*' (in the Bhāshya) is meant the *moving about in the mind*; and this is possible when there is immediate sequence as well as when there is an intervention. In fact the intervention of a word that is related to the factor to be related is only a sort of immediate sequence. Because that which is related to the first would (when thus related) be in immediate precedence of the second also; and when appearing in the second, it would come to have an immediate proximity to the third also. That is to say, the missing factor required by the *Mantra* '*Yā tē rajāçayā*' not being found in the passages following it, is looked for in the preceding passage, and is therein found, in the form of '*tanūrvarshisṭhā*' *etc*; and when attached to this second *Mantra*, it becomes immediately proximate to the third *Mantra* '*Yā tē harāçayā*,' and thus becomes related to this last also. And beyond this, no other *Mantra* being mentioned, the factor in question rests there.

Thus then, in all cases, the wants of a sentence, extending both backward and forward, takes its stand upon one and thereby becomes closely proximate to another sentence; and it goes on taking in all that is required, until it fails to find something capable of being related to it, and comes across something altogether incapable of it. And then having taken in all that it has extended over, its operation comes to an end.

Though on account of the *Mantras* being pronounced one after the other, we come to cognise a *proximity* and *remoteness* (in the case of the *Mantras* '*yā tē rajāçayā*,' and '*yā tē harāçayā*'),—yet the Veda being eternal, whether the sentences be proximate or removed, their mutual requirement and relationship are always simultaneous (because though pronounced one after the other, all words of the Veda are equally eternal, and there is no real precedence or sequence in the case of Vedic words); and hence the mere fact of a sentence appearing subsequently does not make any difference in its authoritative character.

Thus then, the relationship of words in a sentence, and that of sentences in the context, remain intact, so long as all the intervention that there is, is only by such words as (1) are themselves wanting (in a certain element), (2) are capable of the same relationship, and (3) are capable of making the other sentence also equally proximate (to the factor of relationship).

Says the *Bhāshya*: *Avyavadhānē viccehēdē'pi*;—and the sense of this is that when there is no intervention, even though there is no proximity, the factor becomes related, so long as the intervention of a sentence at a distance is not by means of a word which is contrary to such relationship.

For these reasons *Anushaṅga* is a '*samāpti*'—*i.e.*, the means of completing a sentence (*samāpyate anēna iti samāptiḥ* = *that which completes*).

SUPPLEMENTARY ADHIKARAṆA TO ADHI (18).

Question: The above discussion applies to those cases where a sentence itself is wanting in an essential part. There are cases, however, where the sentences are complete in themselves, and it is only a certain part of the sentence that is found to be standing in need of sentences to which it could be attached; as for instance we have a series of complete sentences—'*Citpatistvā punāta,*' '*Vākpatistva punātu,*' '*Devastvā savitā punātu*'; and at the end of these we find the words '*acchidrēṇa pavitreṇa.*' And in this case how would this last be construed?

On this we have the following

PŪRVAPAKSHA.

"The concluding words would have become fully satisfied by being "construed with the sentence that immediately precedes them; because "all the other sentences being complete in themselves, there would be "no reason for admitting of an *Anushanga.*"

SIDDHANTA.

To the above we make the following reply: If the words formed part of the whole of that *sentence* which precedes them immediately, then it could be as asserted above. But as it is, they are found to be related only to the *verb* '*punātu*'; and as such they cannot but be construed with all the three sentences (as all of them contain that same verb). That is to say, independently of any immediate sequence, the words in question become related to the verb '*punātu*'; and as this verb is the same in all the three sentences, the meaning of this verb too must be the same in all. Nor can the difference of nominatives—*Citpati*, *Savitr*, *etc.*—make any difference in that meaning as connected with *Citpati* or *Vākpati* or *Savitri* or *Deva.* Nor is the action concerned (*i.e.*, of *purifying*) subservient to the instrumentality (of *acchidra pavitra*) whereby it would rest satisfied with its single contact with such instrumentality. Thus then the *instrument* (*acchidreṇa pavitreṇa*) being subsidiary to the action (Verb: '*punātu*'), the words denoting the instrument will have to be used as often as the verb would be used, just as the fuel is used so long as there is *cooking.*

The following argument might be urged here: "Though the action of *purifying* is one, yet, that which should be connected with the instrument, is the Action which is qualified by that nominative, in connection with whom the relationship of the Instrument is found to be mentioned directly. For instance, (1) in the *Jyotishṭoma* sacrifice, the *cooking in milk* is found to be spoken of in connection with that Agent who is connected with the *Maitrāvaruṇagraha* (and not the other *grahas* mentioned along with it); and hence the said *cooking* is not found to go beyond that which is qualified by the *Maitrāvaruṇagraha*; and (2) the nominative '*Citpati*' is joined to one '*punātu*' only and not to all the three. (In the same manner, the '*acchidrēṇa pavitrēṇa*' would be joined to that *punātu* only which has for its Nominative '*Savitṛ*' and not all the three)."

To the above we make the following reply: The restricted application of the aforesaid 'cooking' is due to the fact of each *graha* giving rise to a distinct *Apūrva* (Result); and in the case of the second instance cited, the nominative '*Citpati*' is not construed with all the three '*punātu*,' simply because of the distinct mention of other nominatives (in the shape of *Vākpati and Savitṛ*'). That is to say, inasmuch as the repetition of the *grahas*, such as those of the *Aindra*, *Vāyāva*, *Maitrāvaruṇa*, *&c.*, serve to bring about transcendental results, the difference among these results restricts the applicability of the 'cooking.' In the case in question there is no such restrictive agency. Because, as for the Instrument, it is used up in serving the purposes of the Action; and hence by means of the expression of the Instrument, it is the same action that comes to be expressed over and over again. And the *action* being the same in all the three cases, it stands, in each case, in need of a mention of the Instrument. Though the mention of the nominative '*Vākpati*' sets aside the nominative character of '*Citpati*,' as both have exactly the same action of *purifying* yet, in no case do we find any other Instrument that could take the position of the '*acchidra pavitra*' and oust it out of the sentence. Nor is the Instrument due to the Nominative; and as such, a difference in the Nominative could not necessarily make a difference in the Instrument; because all cases of nouns being taken up by the verb, they have no relations amongst themselves.

Objection: "In that case the instrument in question would have "to be construed with the word '*punātu*' in whichsoever *Mantra* it might "be found."

That does not touch our position: Just as in the case of the *Darçapūrṇamāsa* sacrifice certain purificatory rites are laid down in connection with the grass therein used (and they are not applied to the grasses used in all sacrifices), so in the case in question also, the particular instrumentality mentioned would not belong to any and every '*punātu*'; all that it would mean would be that the instrumentality of the *acchidra pavitra* belongs only to that action of the word '*punātu*,' which is meant in this particular context. And as a matter of fact, we actually perceive that this action is the same in all the three *Mantras* in question, and not in any other *Mantra*; because in other *Mantras*, the action denoted by the word '*punātu*' is the purification of other materials (and not the one meant to be purified by means of the three *Mantras* under consideration).

Objection: "In that case, all the three having the same action, the "*Mantras* would become optional alternatives."

Reply: True it would be so; but in the absence of an Injunction distinctly laying down the *number* 'three' with the regard to the *Mantras* to be used,—how do we know that all the three *Mantras* are to be employed conjointly (that is to say, there is nothing incongruous to the three *Mantras* being used alternately). All the three '*punātu*' continuing in the mind, when the words '*acchidrēna pavitreṇa*' are pronounced, the requisite proximity of these latter with each '*punātū*' becomes quite possible in the case of the three *Mantras* under consideration; and this could not be said with regard to any other *Mantras*.

Thus then, we conclude that though the word '*punātu*' occurs in all the three *Mantras*, yet being (in all cases) taken up by the instrumentality expressed by the words '*acchidrēṇa pavitrēṇa*' it is always as qualified by that instrumentality that the Verb '*punātu*' comes to be wanted (in all the three *Mantras*).

That is to say, the words '*acchidrēṇa pavitrēṇa*' occurring at the end of all the repeated *Mantras*, and having no other refuge, they take their refuge in the word '*punātu*'; then the Verb comes to be in the form '*punātu acchidrēṇa pavitrēṇa*'; and as the word '*punātu*' in the sentence immediately preceding these words is the same as that in the other two *Mantras*, at the time that the connection of the action '*punātu*' with the instrumentality of '*acchidrēṇa pavitrēṇa*' is expressed, (and as such the Verb is taken up by that instrumentality), the other words of the sentence standing in need of an action, they admit of *an action as together with the said instrumentality*; and hence we must admit of the *Anushaṅga* of the words in question in all the three *Mantras*.

When through this *Anushaṅga* the words '*acchidrēṇa pavitreṇa*' should be repeated with each sentence, if people pronounce the *Mantras* as they are, leaving the relation of the instrumentality to be understood, it must be regarded as due to mere idleness. And as we have shown above that the missing factor may be found either in the preceding or in the following sentences, the assertion of some people—that it is to be taken from a preceding sentence only—should be taken only as showing how the *Anushaṅga* works in a generality of cases (and it does not preclude the possibility, in special cases, of its being taken from the following sentences also).

ADHIKARAṆA (19).

[*Treating of the absence of Anushaṅga in cases of interruption.*]

***Sūtra* (49) : There is no Anushaṇga where there is an intervention (of unconnected words).**

This *Adhikaraṇa* is brought in simply by way of a counter-instance to the functioning of mere *Proximity* (in the matter of the *Anushaṅga*). As it is found that where the intervention is by words not connected with the factor to be brought in, we do not accept an *Anushaṅga* in view of the incongruity involved.

For instance, in the case of the sentences (1) '*Santē vāyurvātēna gacchatām,*' (2) '*Sanjayatrairangāni,*' and (3) '*Sanyajnapatirāçishā,*'— though the missing factor '*gacchatām*' is admitted as forming part of the *first Mantra*, it is found to be incapable of being taken along with the *second*, because of the *plural* number of the noun '*angāni*' (which would take the verb '*gacchantām*' and not '*gacchatām*'); and thus the factor in question not being equally construable with all the *Mantras* in question, it cannot be taken along with the *third Mantra*, though the nominative in this—'*yajnapatih*'—is in the singular and as such quite compatible with the singular of '*gacchatām.*' [It is on account of the intervention, of the unconnected second *Mantra*, between (1) and (3), that this verb '*gacchatām*' is not taken with (3)].

And thus the missing factor of (2) and (3) not being found in the Veda, we are forced to admit one out of ordinary parlance; and hence in both of these we supply the necessary word from without. And though the words '*gacchantām*' (in the second *Mantra*) and '*gacchatām*' (in the third) are not actually pronounced, yet their existence must be admitted; as otherwise the signification of the sentence would remain incomplete (for want of a Verb).

Thus then in the case in question there is no *Anushaṅga.*

The use of this discussion lies in the fact that, if certain words formed an *Anushaṅga*, they would form a *Mantra*; and as such any mistakes, etc., in the pronunciation of these would have to be accompanied by expiatory rites; whereas if the words supplied are out of ordinary sentences, they do not constitute a *Mantra*, and hence any mistakes in pronunciation, etc., are not so serious as to entail an expiatory rite.

To this end it has been declared that—(1) that which is directly mentioned in the Veda, and (2) that which is brought in by means of an *Anushaṅga*, are counted as having the character of *Mantras*, whereas all sentences of ordinary parlance, being similar to assumed sentences, can never be recognised to have the character of *Mantras*.

Thus ends the First Pāda of Adhyāya II.

ADHYAYA II.

PĀDA II.

ADHIKARAṆA (1).

[*Treating of Difference in the Apūrvas of Subsidiary sacrifices.*]

Sūtra **(1): When there is a different word, there is a different karma, because of its being specially qualified.**

In the foregoing introductory chapter we have dealt with all matters connected, directly and indirectly, with the subject under consideration; and now we are going to take up the subject-matter of the *Adhyāya* in the shape of the difference among actions on the ground of the difference among words, etc. etc.

And first of all we take up the differences caused by the difference of expressions, because it is this difference that points out most clearly the difference among actions. In connection with this we should have cited the examples of all verbal forms connected with one or many verbal affixes—such as '*yajati,*' '*dadāti,*' '*juhoti,*' '*nirvapati,*' *etc.* The Bhāshya has cited only three—'*yajati,*' '*dadāti*' and '*juhoti,*' because, inasmuch as all these denote the *giving away* of something, their significations are all akin, and as such they naturally appear to have identical meanings.

And on this point, inasmuch as there are *three* kinds of *Pūrvapaksha* introduced in the Bhāshya, it seems as if the doubt on the point in question should also have been expressed in three ways.

These are:—(1) Do the three *Bhāvanās*—denoted by the three words (*yajati,* &c.)—bring about a single *Apūrva,* or three distinct *Apūrvas?* (2) Do the three denotations of the three roots qualify a single *Bhāvanā,* or three distinct *Bhāvanās?* (3) Do the three roots denote a single object or three distinct objects?

The Bhāshya uses the word '*kārya*' equally with regard to the *Apūrva,* the *Bhāvanā* and the *object denoted by the roots,* because each of these is equally helped by something else; inasmuch as (*a*) the *Bhāvanā* serves to *produce* the *Apūrva,* (*b*) the *denotation of the root* qualifies the *Bhāvanā,* and (*c*) the root expresses the *denotation of the root*; and as such these latter three are spoken of as 'helps' to the former three respectively.

The ground of doubt is this: We find that things exert their causal efficiency in two ways, *viz.*, *singly* and *collectively*; and, consequently, whenever we find certain objects acting, there naturally arises a doubt as to the character of the object themselves.

As a matter of fact, however, there is only *one doubt* in connection with this subject: In the case of the three verbs, is there only one *Bhāvāna* as qualified by the denotations of the three roots, or is there a distinct *Bhāvanā* for the denotation of each root? What the word '*kārma*' (in the *Sutrā*) denotes is the *Bhāvanā* as qualified by the denotation of the root. And it is the *Bhāvanā* that would be differentiated by means of different words, etc. As for the *Apūrva*, inasmuch as it is not directly expressed by the words in question, and as it follows in the wake of the action itself, it cannot form a subject of separate treatment. Though the "*unity* of three root-meanings" spoken of in the Bhāshya is not possible in the case of all root-meanings, yet it might be mentioned, somehow or other, in connection with the roots '*yaji*,' *etc.*, in question; but in the case of these, though it may be possible, yet much stress should not be laid upon this unity. Thus then the root-meanings being really different, there seems to be yet another ground for doubt in the mind of the *Pūrvapakshi*, *viz.*, Is the *Bhāvanā* mentioned as subservient to the root-meaning, and as such does it end with each Root-meaning? or are Root-meanings subservient to the *Bhāvanā*, and as such they conjointly serve to qualify it?

On this we have the following

PŪRVAPAKSHA (A).

"It is *conjointly* that the Root-meanings qualify the *Bhāvanā*. "Inasmuch as the Bhāshya often uses the word '*samudāya*' ('combin-"ation')—as in the sentences, '*samudāyaçcikīrshitah*,' '*samudāyādēkam-" apūrvam*,' '*na cāçabdah samudāyah*,' *etc.*—and as it speaks of the *Apūr-" va* as one only, it seems clear that the idea desired to be conveyed "was that *a single Apūrva follows from all the three Bhāvanās.* And in "support of this idea the Bhāshya brings forward the following arguments: "In the first instance, that which is not seen is concluded to be *non est*; "and also so long as (in the absence of the unseen factor) there appears "no incompatibility in what is actually seen (with what is spoken of), "it is concluded that the unseen does not exist; it is only when there "is a contradiction between the *seen* and the *spoken*, that we can rightly "assume the existence of the *unseen*; and hence, when the contradiction "is removed by the assumption of only one such unseen factor, there "need be no assumption of many such factors. It is with a view to this "that it has been declared: 'When there is a contradiction, then alone "can an unseen factor be assumed, whereby the *seen* or the *heard* would "become supported.' And under the circumstances if there were no "difference—on the ground of simplicity—between the assumption of one "and that of many factors, then we might go on assuming many factors; "but, as a matter of fact, we do perceive such a difference; hence it must "be admitted that a single unseen '*Apūrva*' follows from the combination "of the three *Bhāvanās*." [Thus is Purvapaksha A.]

This statement of the *Pūrvapaksha*, however, is open to the following objection: 'What is that word that has laid down the *Combination of Bhavanās*, wherefrom the single *Apūrva* would follow?' And in view of this objection the Bhāshya states the *Pūrvapaksha* somewhat differently as follows:—

PŪRVAPAKSHA (B).

Says the *Bhāshya*: "*Atha vā yajētētyētasya purvo bhāgo, etc.* And "the sense of this is that *the words denote a single Bhāvanā as qualified "by the denotations of the three roots.* In support of this we have the "following arguments: Inasmuch as (in all verbs) it is the denotation "of the Affix (which is the *Bhāvanā*) that is the predominant factor, "it cannot, as such, be different with each Root; inasmuch as the Root-"meanings are spoken of as subservient to that denotation of the Affix, "they must be taken as collectively (qualifying it). That is to say, "if, in the case of verbs, the Root-meanings formed the predominant "factors, then alone would the *Bhāvanā* be subservient to them, and "as such would be different with each Root-meaning; as a matter of "fact, however, in all verbs, predominance belongs to the *Bhāvanā*; "and specially as the Root and the Affix are both parts of the denotation "of the Affix (*i.e.*, the *Bhāvanā*), it must be admitted that the *Sacrifice* "(denoted by the root '*yaj*' in '*yajati*'), the *gift* (denoted by the root "'*dā*' in the word '*dadāti*'), and the *libation* (denoted by the root "'*hū*' in '*juhoti*'), all conjointly qualify a single *Bhāvanā*; just as in the "case of the sentence '*Aruṇayā piṅgākshyā ēkahāyanyā gavā somam krīṇāti*,' "all the adjectives mentioned conjointly qualify the *cow*. Then (as to "why, if the *Bhāvanā* meant is only one, there are three distinct "affixes, along with the three words '*yajati*,' *etc.*), though it is not "possible for the principal object to be repeated with each of its "subsidiaries (qualifications), yet, inasmuch as it is absolutely impossible "for the Root by itself or the Affix by itself to be used in a sentence, it "becomes necessary for us to repeat the Affix with each root, at least "with a view to making the use of the root possible (as without an affix "the root could not be used, and a use of the root s necessary, as "pointing out the qualifications of the *Bhāvanā*). If we met with the "affix alone, as we do with '*Kriṇāti*' (in the sentence before quoted), "then, though pronounced but once, it would become connected with "all the roots, just as the verb '*kriṇāti*' becomes connected with all "the adjectives, '*aruṇayā*' and the rest. But as the Affix by itself "could never form a word, no such can ever be met with; and it has "to be repeated. And we have often met with instances where there are "repetitions for the sake of the connection of different qualifications, *e.g.*, "'*āyuryajnēna kalpatām*' and '*prāṇo yajnena kalpatām*'; and again '*Dadhnā* "*juhoti*' and '*payasā juhoti*';—'*Aindravāyavam gṛhṇāti*' and '*maitrāvaru-* "*ṇam gṛhṇāti*,' and so forth. We even find a repetition of the same action, "for instance, the '*Jyotishṭoma*' is performed many times over, with a "view to connect it with the various Deities laid down in connection "with it.

"Thus then, inasmuch as all the verbs concerned serve the single "purpose (of denoting the *Bhāvanā*), all of them—'*yajāti*,' '*dadāti*,' "and '*juhoti*'—must be taken as forming a single sentence; and thus the "Action being one, the resultant *Apūrva* must be one only."

It is only this second statement of the *Pūrvapaksha* that is the correct one; and not the former one, which was based upon a combination of all the *Bhāvanās*. Because (1) when the *Bhāvanās* are distinct, their results, the *Apūrvas*, must necessarily be many; and (2) because the *Bhāvanās* could not be taken as forming a single collective whole, unless they be expressed by a single word.

That is to say, (1) if the *Pūrvapakshi* admits the *Bhāvanās* to be distinct, then, inasmuch as this distinctness could not be possible without their resultant *Apūrvas* also being distinct, he would have to admit these latter also to be distinct and many; and then what useful purpose could be served by the statement of the Pūrvapaksha? (2) And we can admit of a collective whole being formed of many individuals, only under two conditions, *viz.*: (*a*) when we find that many are spoken of, subsequently, by a single name; *e.g.*, having laid down three sacrifices, the Veda concludes with 'one who performs this *Paurṇamāsī* sacrifice, etc.,' where we find the single name '*Paurṇamāsi*' applied to the previously enjoined *three* sacrifices; and (*b*) when many actions are found to conjointly lead to a single result; *e.g.*, 'one should offer the *Rājasūya* if he desires the Kingdom of Heaven,' where the name '*Rājasūya*' is given to a number of sacrifices, which together lead to the specified result. In the case in question, however, we find none of these two conditions; and as such we cannot admit of a single collective whole being made up of the three *Bhāvanās*.

Objection: "But we do meet with the sentence '*jyotishṭomēna*,' etc.

"from which it is clear that a single composite whole is formed by the "'*yajati*,' etc."

Reply: But it is not so; because the word '*Jyotishṭoma*' identifies itself only with the root '*yaji*' (to sacrifice); and as such it would point to the sacrifices only.

For these reasons the former representation of the *Pūrvapaksha* is not tenable.

We have therefore to interpret the portion of the Bhāshya that appears to be a statement of the previous *Pūrvapaksha*, in the following manner:—

The *Pūrvapaksha* comes to be this: "The Action laid down by the "three sentences is one only, but variously coloured, like the rainbow, "by the denotations of the three roots; and in support of this the "following arguments have been brought forward: If we accept this "conclusion then it is necessary to make but a slight assumption of "the unseen factor. If the actions are held to be different, then it "would be necessary to assume many unseen factors, for which there "could not be the least justification. For these reasons 'a single composite "is meant to be expressed,'—by which it is meant that there are many "parts of a single Action. Therefore we must conclude that in the word "'*yajēta*,' the first part '*yaji*' signifies the *sacrifice*, and the second part "signifies the *Bhāvanā*, and so forth. Some people seem to think that the "expression '*atha vā*' in the Bhāshya is a mistaken reading. But it could "be very well explained in the following manner: The *Bhāshya* has brought "forward two sets of arguments in favour of the *Pūrvapaksha*; having "explained the first of these, in the shape of the advantage of assuming "less of the unseen than what is necessary in the other theory, it is only "right that it should introduce the second by '*atha vā*' ('*or, secondly*'). "That is to say, the sense of the Bhāshya comes to be this: It is not "necessary for us to point out the disadvantage, in the other theory, of "having to assume much more of the unseen element; as it is by means "of the words themselves that we shall prove the Bhāvanā to be one only. "And it proceeds to do this by showing that though the first parts of the "verbs differ from one another, yet inasmuch as all of them have "the same affix, their denotations are identical. This is what is meant "by the sentence (in the *Bhāshya*): '*tathā dadātīti pūrvo dadātyartham* "*uttarastamēva bhāvayēditi*.' The latter portion of this seems at first "sight to mean that *the second part shows that the object of the Bhāvanā* "*is the Root-meaning*; but this is not what is meant; because it has been "shown that in all cases that which is denoted by the Root can never "be the object of the *Bhāvanā;* and also because any such assertion "could never be of any use to the *Pūrvapakshi*. In the same manner "it cannot be said that the Root-meaning is *described* by the second "part of the verb. Therefore we must construe the sentence as follows: "In the word '*dadāti*,' the first part (the root '*dā*') signifies *to give;* "and the second part (the affix) serves to describe that—*Bhāvanā*—which "has been previously denoted by the affix in '*yajēta*,'—the only purpose "of this descriptive reiteration by '*dadāti*,' of the previously denoted *Bhāvanā* being the connecting of the said *Bhāvanā* with the denotation of a "root other than the former ('*yaji*'). The same may be said with regard "to the word '*juhoti*' also. That such is the sense of the *Bhāshya* "is also shown by the fact that in connection with the word '*yajēta*,' "the *Bhāshya* does not make use of the word '*anuvadati*' (describes), "the only reason whereof being that in this case there is no *Bhāvanā*, "previously expressed, that could be *described* (by the affix in '*yajēta*'). "If the *Bhāshya* had meant the denotation of the Root to be the object "of the *Bhāvanā*, then this would apply to the first verb, as well as to the "other two (and thus there could be no difference in the way of "explaining the signification of the three verbs); and the Bhāshya could "not have left off the first verb ('*yajēta*') and made the declaration "(of the root denotation being the object of the *Bhāvanā*) with regard "to the last two only. Consequently we must take the Bhāshya only as "pointing to the *singleness* of the *Bhāvanā*. Thus then, there is a single "*Bhāvanā*, and a single *Action*, in the case in question.

"The *Bhāshya* passage—'*Yadvā yajatiçabdena vihitam*,' etc.,—must "be taken as pointing out the fact of the meaning of all the three roots "in question being the same, because in all three we have the common "factor of *giving up one's possession.* Even if, for purposes of taking the "verbs '*dadāti*' and '*juhoti*' as merely descriptive of '*yajēta*,' we have "to have recourse to indirect indication (by those two words),—then "too, this would be far more reasonable than the assumption of many "unseen factors, which would be necessary, in case we took the three words "as expressing three distinct actions. Specially as in descriptions, the "process of indirect indication is not objectionable, because the purpose "of the 'description' is to lay down a particular accessory. For instance, in the case of the sentence ('*ātreyāya hiraṇyam dadāti*'), the "first sentence lays down the *action of giving*, the *gold* as the object to "be given, and *Ātreya* as the person to whom it is to be given; and what "the following sentence does is simply to lay down the '*Dākshiṇā*' as the "object to be given away. It might be urged that '*Dakshiṇā*' being "the name (of a sacrifice) it could not be taken only as laying down "an accessory detail (the object to be given away). But the reply to "this is that the word can be taken as a *name*, only if we accept the "sentence, in which it occurs, to be an injunction of a certain action.

"As a matter of fact, however, we hold it to be only 'descriptive' of what "has gone before; and hence, as otherwise the sentence would become "absolutely meaningless, we must admit it to be the injunction of an "accessory detail. Thus, then, it must be admitted that it is with reference to the denotations of the verbs '*yajati*,' '*dadāti*,' and '*juhoti*,' that "the Bhāshya has declared '*ēkam kāryam*,' which only means that the "signification of the roots is one only; and hence, in accordance with "the maxim that 'anything besides a certain object must be for its sake,' "we conclude that the roots imply a single *Apūrva* and the verbs denote "different actions."

SIDDHANTA.

To all that has been urged above, we make the following reply:—

Whenever there is a difference in the denotations of the Roots, we must conclude that the *Bhāvanā* also is distinct in each case. And when a *Bhāvanā* has once appeared as qualified by the denotation of one Root, it is not possible for the same *Bhāvanā* to be subsequently qualified by others as well.

That is to say, though the word denoting the *Bhāvanā* is one only, and its denotation—the *Bhāvanā*—forms the predominant factor, yet whenever there is a difference in the qualifying Root-denotation, the *Bhāvanā* must be admitted to be distinct also. Nor is it possible for three Root-denotations to fall in within a single *Bhāvanā*. Nor can they form a single composite whole, because all them equally have the same purpose of expressing the instrumental factor (of the *Bhāvanā*); and also because each of them is expressed by a different word, quite independently of another. Nor is it possible for a single Root-denotation to include within itself three Root-denotations; and it is not possible for three Roots, independent of one another, to be laid down, in a single word, for the sake of any Affix; because in the matter of the adapting of affixes Pānini uses the word '*dhātōh*' (III-i-91), where great significance attaches to the singular number (and this shows that in one word one root can be adapted to only one affix). Nor is it possible for the three verbs to form a single sentence; as they do not serve the same purpose, they do not appear incomplete on being separated (and as such they do not fulfill the conditions of syntactial unity); and it is not possible to make a single sentence out of them, by assuming a single *Apūrva* (as following from them); because such an assumption has been negatived under *Sūtra* II-i-47, and also because the difference or non-difference among Actions is not dependent upon a difference or non-difference among *Apūrvas*; as a matter of fact it is quite to the contrary (*i.e.*, the difference or non-difference of *Apūrvas* depending upon that of Actions).

And further, if it were possible for the *Bhāvanā by itself* to be expressed by any word, then alone could it be possible for it to be referred to by the other verbs, and to be referred to and simultaneously qualified by the denotations of the three roots, *viz.*, the *Sacrifice*, the *Gift*, and the *Libation*, like what we find to be the case when a single *cow* is qualified by many adjectives 'red,' etc., occurring in the same sentence, or when the action of *Homa* is qualified by many materials 'Dadhi' and the rest, mentioned in many sentences. As a matter of fact, however, we never find the *Bhāvanā* by itself to be even expressed (by the Affix) apart (from the Root); and hence we must conclude that in the case in question, the *Bhāvanā* must be brought about either by one, or by all, of the verbs ('*dadāti*,' etc.). Then, if it be held to be brought about by all of them, then, inasmuch as there could be no bringing about of that which would have been once brought about by one (word—'*dadati*'), we could not but admit each of these verbs to express different actions. If, on the other hand, the *Bhāvanā* were held to be brought about by only one of the three verbs,—then, there being no reason in favour of any particular word, it could not be ascertained by which one of them it is brought about; and it would be taken as brought about by *any one of the three;* and under the circumstances, it could not be qualified by any root other than that which occurs in the word denoting it. And further the *Bhāvanā*, having primarily appeared in connection with one root-denotation, this denotation, as based upon Direct Denotation, would be the most authoritative of all, and as such it would never admit of any optional alternative qualifications in the shape of the denotations of other Roots. And then, these other Roots having been set aside from that *Bhāvanā*, they must come to qualify distinct *Bhāvanās* of their own, signified by the words in which they themselves occur. Thus then we find that in the case of each of these *Bhāvanās*, the qualification by means of the Root-denotation mentioned in the same word as the *Bhāvanā* would be such as is inborn (or natural) to them, and based upon direct denotation (of the word); whereas a qualification by the denotations of other roots could, at best, be something extrinsic, and would be based upon the exigencies of syntax and the context (and as such the former would be by far the most authoritative process). For instance, if the word '*dadāti*' would attend upon the *Bhāvanā* bound up with the word '*yajati*,' then as the *Bhāvanā* would not be mentioned in the same sentence) as the word '*dadāti*' itself) and as it would be following in the wake of an altogether different word ('*yajati*'), it could get at that *Bhāvanā* only through the peculiarities of the context or the syntax. And so also with the other words '*yājati*,' and the rest.

Question: "When the *Bhāvanā* would be mentioned by the word "'*dadāti*,' it would be directly recognised as the same (as that which "was previously expressed by the word '*yajati*'); and as such it is not "right to assert that the relationship of the word '*dadāti*' with that "*Bhāvana* would depend upon the syntax and the context."

Answer: Who is there among the upholders of the theory of the Actions being different, that does not accept a *generic* unity (*i.e.*, as a *class* we all regard 'Bhāvanā' to be one only; just as the class 'cow' is one, though it is the *individual* cows and the *individual* Bhāvanās that are different and many).

Question: "But in the case in question, there is no ground for "holding a multiplicity of *Individual Bhāvanās.*"

Answer: How do you say that there is no ground, when, as a matter of fact, we actually find that the *Bhāvanā* is distinctly recognised as different with each word, on account of the presence of different Roots?

Question: "Just as in the case of words, we hold their apparent "difference to be due to attendant accessories, and not real, so in the "same manner, the apparent difference in *Bhāvanās* also may not be "real (but only due to accessories)."

Answer: It is not so; because even in the case of words, there is no one who does not accept, to be real, the differences of 'ga' and the other letters; in the same manner, in the case in question also, the difference among the *Bhāvanās* having been established by the difference among the Root-denotations, '*Sacrifice*,' etc., we come to think of all *Bhāvanās* as one under the *class* '*Performance*'; just as we think of all words as one under the *class* '*Çabdatva*.' Then again, in the case of the word, we have such agencies as those of sound and the like, which, being distinct from the Word itself, make unreal any such distinctions of words as into the 'Short,' etc.; whereas in the case in question, the *sacrifice*, etc. (which are signified by a part of the same word as the *Bhāvanā*) are neither removed nor totally distinct from the *Bhāvanā* itself; and as such the distinctions based upon those (*sacrifice*, etc.) cannot be said to be unreal.

For these reasons the actions expressed by the three verbs must be held to be different. In support of this we have the following: When a piece of rock-crystal has been spoken of as *red*, the mention of 'black' could not but be taken as referring to another piece of crystal; in the same manner, when one word has spoken of the *Bhāvanā* as connected with one Root-denotation, the mention of other Roots could not but be taken as referring to other *Bhāvanās*.

Further, with regard to the denotation of the Root and the Affix, there is always a definite order,—based upon grammatical rules as also upon actual usage,—in which they appear; and hence when the comprehender will have been taken up by the denotation of the Root which appears first, the Affix coming in after this, it could not but signify its object as connected (with the denotation of the Ṛoot). It is for this reason that we never come across the pure denotation of the Affix by itself. It has also been declared that 'the terminations, Accusative, etc. appearing from out of nouns, always show that *the denotation of the noun is* their *qualifier.*'

Says the Bhāshya: '*Prayogavākyaçeshabhāvēna hi samudāyasya sattāsambandhah*' (the collective whole is believed to exist only on account of the supposed Directive Sentence that recapitulates all the subsidiaries as belonging to a single Primary). The sense of this is this: The opponent has based his declaration of the *Bhāvanā* being qualified by the three Root-denotations collectively, on the sole ground of the assumption of a single *Apūrva.* And it is a well-known fact that an *Apūrva* is assumed only with a view to rationalise the connection between a certain Action and a certain remote Result; and it is also known that it is only when the sentences laying down the subsidiaries are all taken along with a single supposed Directive Injunction, that they become connected with the particular result with which, by themselves, they have no connection at all. And what the supposed Directive Injunction does is to take in only those Actions whose particular forms have been duly ascertained; and thus when once the distinct form of each of the Actions has been ascertained, they come to be recognised as distinct from one another; and then it is not possible for them to be unified into one composite whole.

Nor again, in the case of the words '*dadāti*' and '*juhoti*' do we find them forming part of any supposed Directive Injunction, because the only such injunction that we have is '*yajeta svargakāmah*'; and this mentions the '*yāga*' (*sacrifice*) only. Nor can the word '*yāga*' be said to indirectly indicate the '*Dāna*' and the '*Homa,*' because that would entail the word '*yāga*' renouncing its own signification; for if the word '*yāga*' were to signify the 'sacrificing' and *at the same time* indicate the 'giving,' then we would have the absurdity of Direct Denotation appearing simultaneously with Indirect Indication. For these reasons there can be no reasonable assumption of any *combination.*

Thus, then, the fact of the roots being different making the words themselves different, it is cognised that the *Bhāvanā* is qualified (by the Root-Denotation). And this cognition is not found to be sublated by any other cognition. Nor again can the denotations of all the three Roots be said to be identical, because while '*yāga*' means the mere *giving up of one's own ownership*, '*Homa*' means this *giving up plus* the action of *pouring into fire*; and '*Dāna*' means the *creation of the ownership of another person* over and above the *giving up* of one's own. Nor can it be held that '*Dāna*' and '*Homa*' indicate the mere *giving up of one's own ownership*; because the *Direct* Significations of the words are quite compatible with the sentences in which they occur (and as such there can be no ground for having recourse to *Indirect Indication*).

Nobody knows of any such material as the '*Dakshiṇāni*,' and hence on account of the word occurring along with '*juhoti*' (which denotes the action of *Libation*), we must accept it to be the name of an Action. And then, with a view to avoid the sentence becoming absolutely meaningless, we accept the *Homa* to be enjoined by the word '*juhoti*.'

In the case of '*dadāti*,' if it were taken as laying down a material with reference to the '*yāga*,' then, inasmuch as it would be necessary for the sentence containing that word to express the relationship of the *giving* with the *given*,—the *gold* and the person *Atrēya* (as the recipient),—there would result a syntactical split; and hence in this case the difference of the action of '*Dāna*' from that of '*Yāga*' would be based upon the difference of the *accessory materials*, and not on that of mere *difference in words* (which is what is meant to be exemplified here); and hence we should cite as example another '*dadāti*' (*i.e.*, other than the one occurring in the sentence cited in the Bhāshya),—which would have either only one accessory material, or none at all.

ADHIKARAṆA (2)

[*Treating of the difference in the Apūrvas of the Samit and other sacrifices.*]

***Sūtra* (2): The repetition of the same word also (is a means of differentiation); because if there were no such specification, the repetition would be useless.**

After the *Adhikaraṇa* treating of the differentiation of actions by means of *different words*, what comes in the mind foremost is the idea that 'there can be no such differentiation when the same word is repeated'; and hence it is that the *Bhāshya* now introduces the *Adhikaraṇa* with this *Pūrvapaksha*.

Having quoted the sentences—'*samidho yajati*,' '*tanūnapātam yajati*,' etc.,—what the *Bhāshya* does is to leave aside the words '*samidhah*' and '*tanunapātam*,' etc., and then to put forward the question: "The word '*yajati*' is found to be mentioned five times; and does it all express a single action, or do the five express five distinct actions?"

This way of putting the question, however, is objected to by some people, as follows: "The words '*samit*,' etc., could be taken either as "*names* of actions, or as expressing *accessories* of actions; and as these "two facts would duly differentiate the actions laid down by the sen- "tences in question, the mere repetition of the '*yajati*' would have nothing "to do with that differentiation. There are six means available for the "differentiation of actions; and each of these should be shown distinctly "as functioning in due accordance with the special capability of each; "consequently in the case in question, so long as we have not set aside "the capability of the *Accessory* and the *Name* to differentiate actions, "it is not possible for the *Repetition* to have any influence in the matter, "which rightly lies within the jurisdiction of others. And hence, we "should cite another example. As a matter of fact, however, no such "example is possible, because, in the whole Veda, a verb is never used alone "by itself; and whenever a noun happens to be used, it must be either "as a *Name* or as an *Accessory*; and so there would be nothing in the "way of differentiation left to be done by the Verb. For instance, "in the case of all such sentences as '*aindravāyavam gṛhṇāti*' and "the like, we find that the Actions mentioned in them differ from one "another, on account of the fact of each of those Actions being intimately "connected with a distinct Accessory of its own. And in the case of "such sentences as '*bhinnē juhoti*,' '*skannē juhoti*,' and the like, as "each of the Actions is mentioned in connection with a distinct *occasion*, "they are regarded as different from one another, as shown under *Sūtra* "II—iii—25: And in this case, as each '*juhoti*' serves the purpose of connecting the action of *Homa* with each particular *occasion*, it cannot be said "to be useless; and as such, it cannot be the means of differentiating the "Actions concerned. Some people quote, as an example (of the differentiation by Repetition), the sentences '*Pancaçāradīyēshu tān paryagnikṛtān, tān paryagnikṛtān*,' etc., but they lose sight of the fact that the "repetition in this case is merely descriptive of the same Primary Action "(and as such no differentiation is possible); nor do we find in these "sentences the word '*yajati*,' a repetition of which would express a "difference among the Actions. And hence we conclude that no example "of differentiation by Repetition is available."

We base our reply to the above side-objection to the *Bhāshya*, on the very sentences that have been quoted by the Bhāshya. As a rule, whenever a Noun appears in connection with a Verb, it is almost always subservient to this latter; and hence it is the Verb, as the predominant factor, to which belongs the capability of expressing the difference or non-difference (of Actions). That is to say, those nouns that express an object of predication are subservient to the Verb, and as such, always following in its wake, they stand in need of the functioning of the Verb. Hence when the Verb has entered into the Primary Action, the noun also becomes either a name of the same Action, or mentions an Accessory for it; and if the Verb points to an *Apūrva*, then the noun also belongs to that *Apūrva;* and thus the difference or non-difference of Actions having been duly recognised (by means of the Verb), the words 'Samit' and the rest, coming in subsequently, become useless and indifferent (as regards the pointing out of the said difference or non-difference); and it is for this reason that we leave aside these words, and take into consideration the Verb only.

Question: "In that case, (1) the *Name*, and (2) the *Accessory* would "never be the means of the differentiation of Actions."

Answer: Certainly they would serve the purposes of this differentiation, in cases where the Verb does not operate (towards it); the examples of such cases, to be cited later on, are (1) '*athaisha jyotih, etc.*' and (2) '*vājibhyo vājinam, etc.*' [in (1) the differentiation being due to the *name* and in (2) to the *accessories*]. In the latter sentence we do not find any verb; and in the former, though we do find a verb, yet, inasmuch as it is possible for it to become related to the Primary Action by way of serving to point out the connection of the particular Result with the particular Accessory,—the differentiation required will have been done by the *names* '*jyotih, etc.*,' which have a prior operation. Even in a case where the force of the verb makes its connection with the Primary Action impossible, there is laid down an Accessory not otherwise possible; and in this case too the differentiation is done by the Accessory; as it will be shown (in the Adhikaraṇa dealing with the Accessory as the means of differentiation), by the Bhāshya after accepting the facts brought forward by the opponent—'*this connection of the Deity and the Sacrifice being enjoined etc., etc., etc.*' (the sense of which is that the sacrifice having been enjoined in a previous sentence, what the repetition of the same does is to point out its connection with an Accessory, in the shape of the Deity). But a differentiation by the Accessory is possible, only when the Verb is found to have lost its differentiative potency; and hence it is only right that first of all we should consider the Verb (as the means of differentiation).

The Bhāshya puts forward the question in the form—'*kimekamapūrvam?*';—and this implies the question of the difference or non-difference of the Actions; or it may be taken as "does the word '*yajati*,' repeated five times, lay down one Action and one '*Apūrva*,' or five Actions and five *Apūrvas?*"

And on this question, we have the following

PŪRVAPAKSHA.

"They indicate only *one* Apūrva; because, as shown in the previous "*Adhikaraṇa*, though the signification of the affix be the same, yet a "difference in the Roots serves to differentiate the Actions; when, however, "the Root also is the same, what would be there to point out the Actions "to be different?

"Further, on the utterance of the first sentence—'*samidho yajati*'—"an idea of the Action '*yāga*' presents itself to the mind; and hence when "the same Verb is pronounced again, the Action denoted by this is at "once recognised as the same that had previously come to the mind; and "as such the repetition does not point out any difference in the Action.

"That is to say, when the word '*yajati*' has been once directly "heard, if it happens to be pronounced again, it is at once recognised "as the same word that had been previously heard, and no difference is "perceived between the two words; so also in the case of its denotation "(which being comprehended once is always recognised to be the same, "whenever that word is uttered). And in the case in question, all that the "second '*yajati*', though directly heard, does is to express over again that "same Action of *yāga* which has already been cognised (by means of the "first '*yajati*'); and though, as such, it becomes redundant, yet it "cannot make the two '*yajati*'s' distinct words; and in the same manner, a "repetition of the word, even though becoming otherwise superfluous, "could not make the meaning of one '*yajati*' different from that of the "other. For certainly '*superfluousness*' (like Inconsistency) is not a "*means of right knowledge.* Only that which the Veda lays down "should be accepted as the authoritative means of knowledge, by people "taking their stand upon the authority of the Veda. And in the case "in question, we find that the Veda, in using the same word '*yajati*,' "distinctly points to a non-difference between the Actions; and hence "he who would hold them to be different, would be going against the "authority of the Veda itself. And as a matter of fact, there is "nothing wrong in the admitting of the superfluousness of certain words, "if such superfluousness happen to be necessitated by a higher authority.

"But we have the following ways of avoiding the said superfluousness:—

"(1) The word '*yajati*' as repeated in the second and the following "sentences, being touched by the supposed Directive Injunction dealing "with the Primary Action together with all its subsidiaries, could be "taken as not affording any meaning, but only as laid down for the sole "purpose of being *verbally* repeated. (And in this way there would be "no repeated mention of the Action of '*yāga*').

"(2) The repetition may be taken as only serving to emphasise the "same fact. We actually find that in ordinary parlance, people go on "repeating certain words (by way of emphasising)—even more than "twice—until the idea meant to be conveyed by them is fully comprehended by the person to whom the words are addressed. So also, in the "scriptures, we find, in course of the story of '*Pancendra*,' that the old "spinster asks for a husband *five times.* And though in the case of this "story, the person to whom the request was preferred was a Deity "(Indra) capable of playing pranks (whereby he gave the spinster "*five* husbands, taking her repeated requests as distinct demands),— "yet, in the case in question, we have no such playful person to deal "with; and hence we cannot take the five repetitions of the word '*yajati*' "as denoting *five* distinct sacrifices.

"(3) The Injunction of the Action being accepted to reside in all "the five utterances of the word '*yajati*,' the Action enjoined comes to "be one only; just as though we find the injunction of the '*Jyotishṭoma*' "in many Vedic Rescensions, yet we accept the '*Jyotisṭoma*' itself to be "one sacrifice only. Thus then, as when many words have the same meaning, they come to be taken as optional alternatives, so we conclude that it "is the same *sacrifice* that is enjoined, at one time, by the sentence '*samidho* "*yajati*,' and at another by the sentence '*tanūnapātam yajati*.' And "(in the case of optional alternatives, there can be no superfluousness "in the matter, which could lead us to take them as expressing distinct "*Actions;* because) when we find the *Vrīhi* and the *Yava* serving the "same purpose, we do not accept one of them to be useless, and as such "serving an altogether different purpose.

"(4) The subsequent sentences may be taken as laying down distinct "Deities—'Tanūnapāt' and the rest—for the sacrifice; and thus too, "the repetition would not be useless. If the second '*yajati*' enjoined "an Action, then alone could the word '*tanūnapāt*' be taken as the *Name* "of the Action; as a matter of fact, however, the second '*yajati*' only "refers to the same *sacrifice* that has been expressed by the first '*yajati*'; "and as such the word '*tanūnapāt*' cannot be a *Name*; it must be taken "as laying down an *Accessory* (Deity) for the same sacrifice. And thus "too, the repetitions cannot be taken as pointing out different actions.

"And further, as a matter of fact, the same word or object, "even when appearing in places far apart, is always recognised "as the same; and in this case it cannot be said that they are different; "just as when a man returns home after a long absence, and recognises "his people to be the same as those he left behind him, they are not "taken to be other than these. And when such is the case when they "occur in distant places, how could it be otherwise in the case in question "when the two sentences occurring close together, the impressions pro-"duced by them are still present in the mind while the second is uttered.

"If there were a distinct meaning each time that the word were "pronounced, then the denotation of each word would consist of *ever-"changing individuals* (and not of an *eternal class*, as held by the *Mīmānsaka*).

"And further, in the case of the sentences in question there is no "such thing as the *class* 'Sacrifice' as apart from the Individual Sacri-"fices, just as there is no class '*gatva*' apart from the individual "letter '*ga*'); and thus the word '*yāga*' being restricted to an individual "*Sacrifice*, how could there be a different action (expressed by the word "'*yajati*' in the second sentence for instance)? That is to say, "even though with a view to justify the repetition of the word, the "sacrifice might be performed five times over, yet the Action would be "one and one only; as we find that, though the *Jyotishṭoma* is performed "thrice, yet it is admitted to be a single Action (though in the case of this "latter we have a distinct Injunction of its being performed thrice). "In the case in question, however, we have no such ground for repeating "the performance; because all that the repetition of the word '*yajati*,' "with '*tanūnapāt*,' etc., does is to lay down alternative Deities in con-"nection with the same Sacrifice.

"For these reasons, we conclude that in the case in question, the "Sacrifice pointed out is one and one only."

SIDDHĀNTA.

To the above, we make the following reply:—

The repetition of the same word would also be so:—*i.e.*, exactly like different words, that also would be a means of differentiating Actions.

Because, by its direct denotative potency, the Verb, in the first instance, lays down the Action; and it is only when this potency has been forestalled by another—*i.e.*, when the Action has been already mentioned by another word—, that it requires that Action to be referred to along with itself.

If the mere fact of the '*sacrifice*' continuing in the mind of the person (at the time that the second '*yajati*' is pronounced) were the sole cause of this latter '*yajati*' referring to the 'sacrifice' denoted by the former '*yajati*,' then alone would it fail to give us an idea of a different Action. As a matter of fact, however, the mere fact of such continuance in the mind is not sufficient cause for making the second '*yajati*' a secondary reference (to what has gone before); the fact is that it is only the particular form of such reference (*Anūvāda*) that is shown by the idea born of the context; and the *generic* fact that there is an *Anuvāda* is shown by the sentence itself.

That is to say, when the Injunctive potency of the Injunctive Affix, is removed from the denotation of the Root, then, in that case, there being no potency for more than one Injunction, we look for a mere secondary reference to the denotation of the Root; and this want is supplied by the aforesaid continuance (in the mind, of the idea of the previously-expressed Action). And the removal of the Injunctive potency from the Root-meaning is due to the fact of the Injunctive potency having taken up another object for Injunction (and to the said continuance); as for instance in the case of such supplementary sentences as—'*Vrīhibhiryajeta*,' '*dadhnā juhoti*' (the verbs '*yajeta*' and '*juhoti*' are repeated only for the purpose of laying down other materials for the '*sacrifice*' and the '*Homa*' which have been laid down in the preceding sentences, and which are only referred to by the verbs in these supplementary sentences). In all these cases, where many objects are mentioned in various sentences,—inasmuch as it is not possible to have a multiplicity of Injunctive potencies,—we naturally conclude that there is only one object of the Injunction, which one should be referred to by all the subsequent verbs; and when looking for that one particular object, we come to the conclusion, that it must be that which keeps continuing in the mind. And hence it is that in the case of the sentence '*dadhnā juhoti*,' as it is only the *dadhi* that has not been mentioned before, we take the Verb ('*juhoti*') as only referring to a previously-expressed *Homa*, with reference to which the sentence lays down a fresh material in the shape of the *dadhi*. When, however, there are not many objects meant to be enjoined, then, in the case of that sentence we do not look for anything that would be referred to by the subsequent verbs. And hence, so long as the sentence itself does not give us any general idea of the presence of such secondary reference, what useful purpose could be served by the said 'continuance,' which depends upon a due fulfilment of the general idea of the presence of an *anuvāda*, and which is the sole ground for admitting of a particular form of reference (*Anuvāda*)? Thus then the definition of '*Anuvāda*' is, not that 'that which has been previously laid down, is referred to subsequently,' but that 'that (1) with regard to which there is an idea that it ought to be referred to, and (2) which happens to have been previously laid down, is that which is referred to; and there can be no such Reference, when neither of these two conditions is absent—*i.e.*, neither by the mere desire for reference, nor by the mere fact of its having been previously laid down. Consequently then, though there is a desire for *Reference*, yet, inasmuch as the object is not one that has been laid down before, we cannot but admit it to be an Injunction of an Action with certain qualifications; and conversely, even though the object may be known to be such as has been previously laid down, inasmuch as there is no desire for a secondary Reference, we cannot but admit the Injunction to refer to a different Action altogether, notwithstanding the fact of the Root as well as the Affix being actually recognised to be the same (as in the case of '*yajati*').

It has been urged above that the proximity of the previously-mentioned *sacrifice* being very strong, even if the word '*yajati*' were to be pronounced a hundred times, the idea of that *sacrifice* would not disappear. But all such disappearance would appear quite possible if the opponent only knew the comparative strength or weakness of the various means of knowledge. For instance, it is by *Direct Signification* that we recognise the Actions to be different, while it is by means of *Proximity* that they are cognised as identical; and hence for those who are cognisant of the fact of Direct Signification of the word being more authoritative of the two, how could the Actions appear to be one and the same? When the Injunctive word ('*yajati*') has not its injunctive potency thrown aside from its legtimate object, then it is taken up with the meaning of the Root and the *Bhāvanā* (signified by the Affix); and it is with regard to these that that word gives birth to an Injunction, which has for its object something not otherwise got at; and as such it tramples under its foot the idea of the *sacrifice* (mentioned by the second '*yajati*') having been already laid down (by the former '*yajati*'); and thereby leads us to the conclusion that the object of this Injunction is such another Action as is quite capable of being enjoined by it. And hence if this Injunction should follow the Direct Word, it points to a distinct Action; while if it should follow *Proximity*, then the Actions are identical.

If, however, the Injunctive Word is taken up elsewhere—for instance, the laying down of the material, etc.,—then in such a case, we admit of the Actions being identical, as pointed out by Proximity; because in this case such an assumption is not contrary to any higher authority.

Consequently, it must be admitted that the idea of all the various Actions being identical is a mistaken one,—due to the fact of all these '*sacrifices*' imparting the same aid to the Primary Sacrifice, and as such being spoken of as 'sacrifice' in general. There is no ground for recognising each individual 'sacrifice' to be the same as the one mentioned before. That which is actually recognised as *one* in reality, there is no difference of opinion as regards the unity of that. For instance, in the different kinds of sacrifices—the '*Paçu*,' the '*Soma*' and the '*Ishṭi*'—the generic character of 'sacrifice' is one and the same, and it is only with reference to specific Individuals that we think of any difference among them.

Objection: "In the case in question, it is the direct *mention* of the "same word '*yajati*' which distinctly points to the identity of the "Actions; and as such it cannot be said that the idea of oneness is "based upon *Proximity*, and not upon *Direct Word*."

Reply: It is not so; because all that the *Direct mention* of the word '*yajati*' does is to give rise to the simple idea that what it speaks of is 'a sacrifice'; and it has nothing to do with any idea as to whether it is the same as the one mentioned before or different from it. That is to say, the second '*yajati*' does not mean that the 'sacrifice' denoted by it is the same as that denoted by the previous '*yajati*'; and thus the denotation of the word being actually silent on this point (of difference or non-difference), people, not cognisant of the fact of the notion of identity being due to *Proximity*, are led to the mistaken conclusion that the recognition of sameness is based upon *Direct Word*.

Objection: "Inasmuch as the word does not denote the Individual "(according to the *Mimāṅsaka*), it is only the single '*class*' 'sacrifice' "that would be denoted by the word '*yajati*,' whenever it may be used; "and as this *class* is always one and the same, the sameness in question "must be admitted to be denoted by *Direct Word*."

Reply: It is because the Individual is not denoted by the word, that the *Direct Word* points out the Actions to be distinct. For instance, what are laid down are the Individuals (sacrifices) as qualified by the *Class* ('Sacrifice') and hence in the case of all Injunctions, all consideration of difference or non-difference should be with regard to the Individuals.

That is to say, the generic entity, that forms the real denotation of the word (‘*yajati*’ for instance), being incapable of being performed, it cannot form the object of an Injunction; and hence in all cases it is the Individuals that form the objects of Injunctions. Hence it must be admitted that the sentence ‘*Samidho yajati*’ lays down one specific individual sacrifice, and ‘*Tanūnapātam yajati*’ lays down another. And in the case in question we have the Injunctions of five such distinct individual sacrifices.

It has been suggested above that “just as there is no difference “between the letter ‘*ga*’ and the ‘*gatwa*’ so, in the same manner, there “may be no difference between the individual *sacrifice* and the *class* “‘sacrifice.’”

True, there is no difference; but it is only after we actually conclude from the very form of the Action that it is one only, that we can be sure of there being no difference; prior to such conclusion, we are absolutely certain of a difference. For example, in the case of the letter ‘*ga*,’ when we found it to form a member of the classes of ‘Letter,’ ‘Sound’ and ‘Property,’—we concluded that the differences perceived in the various tones of the letter ‘*ga*’ itself, must be due to the specific properties of *quickness, etc.*, which belong, not to the letter itself, but to the organ of its utterance; and hence (there not being distinctin dividual ‘*ga*,’ we did not admit of any such generic entity as ‘*gatwa*’ (the *class* ‘*ga*’); in the same manner, when we find that all the sacrifices—down to the ‘*Samit*’—form members of such classes as ‘Entity,’ ‘Action,’ and ‘Sacrifice,’ we conclude that each of these sacrifices does not become distinct, by the mere fact of the time, place or agent of its performance being different; because these differences are not in the sacrifice itself; and as such are exactly in the same position as the properties of ‘quickness’ etc., in the case of the letter ‘*ga*.’ That is to say, the ‘*Samit* sacrifice’ performed on the *Paurṇamāsi* day is nothing distinct from the same sacrifice performed on the *Amāvāsyā* day; so also a difference in the performer, or in the places of performance, does not make the Action different.

But as a matter of fact, it is not that we admit of an actual difference only in cases where the difference is cognised by direct sense-perception; because on this point there is no difference between the authority of Sense-perception and that of the *Word* (Vedic). Hence we must admit of a difference among Actions, only in so far as is shown by the six means (enumerated in the present *Pāda*)—such as ‘Different words’ and the like. Because in the case of the sacrifices—‘*Ishṭi*,’ ‘*Paçu*,’ ‘*Soma*’ ‘*Ēkāha*,’ ‘*Ahīna*’ and ‘*Satra*’—the idea of difference among them that we have is never actually found either to be due to any extraneous properties or circumstances, or to be other than correct. Hence when the individual '*Ishṭi*' etc. are always found to be the objects of Injunctions, the words giving expression to them naturally become regarded as different; and it is from these individuals that the Results follow; though all of them belong to the single *class* 'Sacrifice,' and there are no sub-classes (as '*Ishṭitva*' and the like).

Objection: "But such sub-classes as '*Ēkāhatwa*' and the like are "admitted."

Reply: Not so; because the fact of many sacrifices being all called '*Ekāha*,' and recognised as such, is only due to the fact of all of them being performed in a definite period of time (one day) [and not to the fact of their belonging to any such class as '*Ēkāhatwa*']; just as the word '*Daṇḍī*' (with stick) applies to many persons (not on account of all of them belonging to any such class as '*daṇḍitva*,' but only on account of all of them happening to hold sticks). That is to say, certain sacrifices are called '*Ēkāha*,' because they are finished in a *single day*; those that take from two to eleven days are called '*āhīna*'; those finished in twelve days are spoken of as both; while those extending from twelve days to a thousand *days* ('*samvatsara*' in this case has been explained as 'day') are called '*Satra*'; those in which the offering is of food-grains are called '*Ishṭi*'; those in which animals are offered are '*Paçu*'; and those in which the material offered consists of vegetables (leaves, plants, creepers, etc.) are '*Soma.*'

If, however, you insist on assuming sub-classes, that does not touch our position at all adversely. Thus, too, even if there happen to be such classes as '*Jyotishṭomatwa*' etc., and if each performance of the sacrifice ('Jyotishṭoma' for instance) becomes a distinct sacrifice by itself,— then too our position remains unsullied. So also, conversely, if all sacrifices be taken as one only, on the ground of all of them only consisting of *the offering of certain materials to certain Deities*,—then too, inasmuch as the performance of each would be distinct from that of the other, there would be no hindrance to their ordinary performance, etc.

Objection: "In that case, the repeated performances of the *Samit* "sacrifice would not be distinct Actions; just as the repeated performances "of certain actions during the performance of the *Jyotishṭoma* are not "recognised as so many distinct actions."

Reply: In all cases, the differentiation of *Dharmas* is based upon the difference in the *Apūrvas* brought about by them, (and as a rule, a distinct *Apūrva* always follows from an Action each time that it is repeated). And it is on account of the following reason that in the case of the repeated performance of the '*Samit*' sacrifice, we have an idea of each of them being a distinct Action, whereas in the case of the *Jyotishṭoma* we take the difference to lie only in the repeated performances (and not in the Action). In the former case we have an Injunction of the Action or performances of all the sacrifices distinct from one another; while in the latter case, the various repeated performances are all included in the single name '*Jyotishṭoma*'; and hence though the character of 'sacrifice' belongs to each repeated performance, yet the character of '*Jyotishṭoma*' does not belong to it; and thus it is that we come to look upon each repeated performance as a part of the one sacrifice '*Jyotishṭoma*'; but such is not the case in the repeated performances of the '*Samit*,' because in this case we do not have any composite whole made up of these performances (as we have in the case of the *Jyotishṭoma*). And thus the conditions of the two are not identical.

What is the special purpose of all this differentiation, we shall show later on under *Sūtras* ii—17-20.

Says the Bhāshya: *Hence the sacrifice has got to be repeated*; and this assertion is in accordance with the view that the name '*Prayāja* belongs to all the five sacrifices (expressed by the word '*yajati*' repeated five times), just as the name '*Jyotishṭoma*' belongs to the repeated performance of certain Actions. Or it may be taken as referring to the fact that though the individual 'Sacrifices' are distinct, yet, inasmuch as the word '*yajati*' in all cases denotes the *class* 'sacrifice' (to which the individual sacrifices belong), we must take the performance of the five sacrifices to be the repetition of that of the single class 'Sacrifice.'

An objection is raised in the Bhāshya: "*It has been said that it is* "*incapable of enjoining another object;* and the sense of this is that the "injunctive potency of the second '*yajati*' having been taken up in "laying down *Tanūnapāt* as the Deity, there is no incompatibility of this "Injunction with that of the previous '*yajati*,' an idea of which is "still present in the mind."

But in accordance with the rule laid down the *Sūtra* I—iv—4, the words '*Samit*' etc. come to be recognised as *names* of sacrifices, on account of their relationship with the Deities pointed out by the words of those *Mantras* which contain those words ('*Samit*' etc.), and which come to be employed in the Samit and other sacrifices, in the same order in which they are found in the text (that is to say, the first *Mantra* is employed in the *Samit* sacrifice; the second in the *Tanūnapāt*, and so forth; and the words of these *Mantras* distinctly point out the Deities of each of these sacrifices); and hence, the Deity being already once pointed out, it cannot form the object of another Injunction by the sentence '*Tanūnapātam yajati*'; and as such the injunctive potency of the sentence would be thrown aside from its legitimate object.

This is what the *Bhāshya* should have said in reply to the opponent. What it actually does, however, is to grant his contention, and then crush him on his own ground. The sense of the *Bhāshya* is this: You accept the first '*yajati*' to be the Injunction of a 'Sacrifice' on the ground of this latter not being laid down before; but this is scarcely correct; because the 'Sacrifice' has already been enjoined in the sentence '*Darçapūrṇamāsābhyām yajeta*'; and as such the first '*yajati*' also can be taken only as merely *referring* to the 'sacrifice' laid down before (just as you take the second '*yajati*' as referring to the 'sacrifice' laid down by the previous '*yajati*'). And then all the '*yajati*,' being mere *references* to the previously enjoined 'Sacrifice,' what the words 'Samit' and the rest can do is to lay down either the *material* to be offered or the *Deity* to whom the offering is to be made; (in connection with the 'Sacrifice' laid down by the sentence '*Darçapūrṇamāsābhyām yajeta*'; but we find that both of these accessories of that sacrifice have already been laid down in the sentence '*Āgneyo'shṭākapālo*' (where *Agni* is mentioned as the *Deity* and the *cake* as the *material*)— a sentence which is found directly connected with the original Injunction itself; and hence if it were to have these accessories pointed out by the sentences '*samidho yajati*' etc., this would be directly contrary to the former mention of the accessories (as the former sentence has not been found to mention the '*Samit*,' etc., as either the Deity or the Material). Then, inasmuch as (according to you) it is absolutely necessary to make the sentence '*samidho yajati*' lay down the relationship of the Deity (*Samit*) with a certain sacrifice,—and this is impossible without another *sacrifice* (being mentioned by another '*yajati*'; because the '*yajāti*' in the same sentence you have taken as *referring* to another sacrifice); and hence, too, you have to admit the *sacrifice* denoted by one '*yajati*' to be different from that denoted by another '*yajati*',—even when you take the sentences as Injunctions of Accessories. Thus then, inasmuch as it would be impossible for each succeeding sentence to lay down the Accessory for the sacrifice laid down in the preceding sentence, all the *sacrifices* must be taken as different from one another. And as such all your trouble over the taking of the sentences as Injunctions of Accessories becomes wholly lost. As a matter of fact, however, no such Injunction of Accessories is possible in the case in question; because the *material* to be offered can never be spoken of by a word like '*samidhah*' (Accusative Plural)—as we have explained under *Sūtras* II—i—11-12; specially as the verb '*yajati*' can have no connection with a *material* which is mentioned by a word with an *Accusative* ending (as an Instrumental ending is what would be necessary in that case); nor can it be an Injunction of the Deity; as we shall show later on, under the *Sūtra* IX—i—9.

Thus then, we conclude that the sentences under consideration must be the injunctions of distinct Actions.

ADHIKARAṆA (3).

[*Treating of the Relation of Subserviency between the Āghāras and the Āgnēya, etc.*].

***Sūtra* 3: The context refers to the Paurṇamāsī (as the *principal*), specially as none of the details are mentioned (of other sacrifices).**

The Bhāshya has quoted all the Injunctions of the Sacrifices, in connection with the '*Darça-Purṇamāsa*'; and then the question started by it is as to whether all the sacrifices enjoined are distinct primaries, or it is only some of these that are so.

An objection is raised against this statement of the question of the Adhikaraṇa: "The consideration of the question of primaries and "subsidiaries forms the subject of the fourth *Adhyāya*; by what "connection, then, has it been introduced in this *Adhyāya*, which deals "wholly with the Differences of Actions? That is to say, after having "dealt (in the foregoing *Adhikaraṇa*) with the differentiation of Actions "by means of *Repetition*, it was necessary to consider the differentiation by "means of *Number*; and yet how is it that having taken no notice of that, "the *Bhāshya* starts a question which is of no use in the subject-matter of "the present *Adhyāya?*"

To this some people make the following reply: "The question started "by the Bhāshya forms a declared subject of the *Adhyāya*; because at "the very outset of the *Adhyāya*, the Bhāshya on Sutra II—i—1 has de- "clared—'*after that the Primaries and the Subsidiaries will be taken into "consideration.*'

"But this is scarcely correct; because in that place (*i.e.*, the Vārtika "on II—i—1) we have rejected that interpretation of the Bhāshya, which "we have explained in a different manner; we have shown there that it is "for the purpose of showing the difference among *Apūrvas* treated of in "Adhyāya III, that the question of Primaries and Subsidiaries was "introduced in the Bhāshya on II—i—1. The question of the relation of "subserviency between Actions, however, can in no way be connected "with the subject of the present Adhyāya. Specially as we shall devote "a great deal of time and trouble for establishing such relations among "Actions—under *Sūtras* IV—iv—29-33. And the bearing of this *Adhikaraṇa* being quite clear, it cannot be explained in any other way. Consequently the question of the relation of subserviency between Actions "need not have been considered here. Nor can any of the questions—'whether the sentences *ya ēvam vidvān amāvāsyāyām yajati* and *ya ēvam vidvān paurṇamasyām yajati* conjointly refer to the Primary sacrifices, or "they are the Injunctions of two independent Actions, and the other "sentences are all Injunctions of Accessories'—have any connection with "the *Adhikaraṇa* in the way that it has been suggested by the *Bhāshya*. "And if it is these questions that are to be chiefly considered in the "*Adhikaraṇa*, then there would be no use in introducing the question of "Relative Subserviency. And further, it has been shown above that "Difference of Words and Repetition are capable of pointing out Differences among Actions; how is it, then, that these have been brought in "by the Bhāshya, as establishing the equal importance of all Actions? "To utilise the means of establishing *Difference* in establishing *equal importance* is certainly a very queer process of argumentation. Nor, in "the very body of the two *Adhikaraṇas*, do we find the conclusions and "the Premises stated apart from one another; and as such we cannot "bring in the Premises of the one to the proving of another conclusion."

In view of the above objections we must justify the *Bhāshya* in the following manner: The present *Adhikaraṇa* had to be introduced as dealing with the exceptions to the conclusion arrived at in the foregoing *Adhikaraṇa*; and hence from among all the sentences quoted, we must take only *two* as the basis of this *Adhikaraṇa*; viz., '*ya evam amāvāsyāyām yajati*' and '*ya ēvam paurṇamāsyām yajati.*' And then the question comes to be this: *Do these two 'yajati's lay down two entirely independent Actions,—or being qualified by the words 'amāvāsyā' and 'paurṇamāsi,' which denote actions connected with the times expressed by these, the two 'yajati's only refer to the six primary Actions (the 'Āgneya' and the rest that go to form the 'Darça-Purṇamāsa' sacrifice)?*

Then again, the difference of the *Āgnēya* and the other five Primary sacrifices from one another being established by the difference in their *Accessories*, that between the subsidiary *Prayājas* themselves being established by *Repetition*, and that of the subsidiary *Āghāras* by means of the difference of *words*,—the Bhāshya has brought in the two declarations of 'equal importance' and 'relative subserviency' only; such is the real upshot of the real *Pūrvapaksha* and the *Siddhānta* of the *Adhikarana*. (That is to say, if the '*yajati*'s lay down independent Actions—as held by the *Pūrvapaksha*—, then all the various sacrifices—

the *Āgnēyā*, etc., as well as the *Prayājas*, etc.,—would be of equal importance; while if the two '*yajati*'s be taken only as referring to the previous six primary sacrifices—the *Āgnēya* etc.,—then these alone would be the Primary sacrifices; as on account of their being *referred* to by the two sentences, and as being related to the enjoined times of the *Amāvasyā* and the *Purṇimā*, these two words would be taken as the names of these six sacrifices, which alone would, therefore, come to be connected with the Result; and in that case the *Prayājas*, etc., would all become subsidiary to it). And these questions of 'equal importance' and 'relative subserviency' have not been introduced as forming integral parts of the *Adhikaraṇa* itself; and so these two are not to be taken as embodying the *Pūrvapaksha* and the *Siddhānta*, respectively.

Thus then, the three stages in the position taken up by the *Pūrvapaksha* come to be these: (1) "The two '*yajati*'s are independent injunctions; (2) the actions enjoined by them are distinct from any previously enjoined; and (3) the *Prayājas* and the *Āgharās* are all *primary* actions of equal predominance"; and in these three stages the one that follows is the direct outcome of that which precedes it; and thus all three are inseparably linked up with one another. In the same manner, the three stages in the *Siddhānta* are these: (1) The two '*yajati*'s only *refer* to the sacrifices mentioned before; (2) the Actions expressed by them are not different from the previously mentioned (*Āgnēya*, etc.); and (3) The *Āghāras* and the *Prayājas* are subsidiary to the *Āgnēya* and the rest. And in each of these trios, each member is so inseparably connected with the others, that if one of them happens to be established as true, the others necessarily follow as its corollaries. And hence the *Bhāshya*, thinking that the desired purpose would be served by establishing any one of the three positions, has brought in the third and the last, because it is the final outcome of the preceding two, and as such necessarily leads up to them. And though the difference or non-difference (of the sacrifices expressed by the two '*yajati*'s from those previously laid down) would be implied by the truth or otherwise of the *Siddhānta* as put by the *Bhāshya*, yet, towards the end of the *Adhikaraṇa*, in summing up the whole discussion, the *Bhāshya* mentions the 'Difference or Non-difference,' simply with a view to make it clear to the student (that this follows from the conclusion arrived at in the *Adhikaraṇa*).

Objection: "How is it that having neglected the subject of Difference "and Non-difference, in the beginning, the *Bhāshya* has thought it fit to "bring it in again, through the question of *equal importance* or *relative* "*subserviency*"?

Some people reply to this that it is only a method of exposition peculiar to the Teacher; for instance, in the foregoing *Adhikaraṇa* also, he spoke of the *Difference of Apūrvas* (and through that, of the Difference of *Actions*).

Or it may be that the 'perception of the indicative feature'—in the shape of the fact of the *Prayājas* occurring among the subsidiary sacrifices—that will be spoken of in the eighth *sūtra* below, is not capable of directly precluding all chance of the sacrifices being different (from the previous sacrifices)—(because all that the said feature indicates is that the *Prayāja*, etc., are not primary actions, and not that they are different actions altogether); and as such all that the said feature would do would be to set aside the 'Equal Importance' of all the sacrifices concerned; and when this is set aside, there would follow the setting aside of the fact of the two '*yajēta*'s being distinct Injunctions by themselves, inasmuch as this latter has been shown to be the invariable concomitant of the theory of 'Equal Importance'; and thus we find that the question of 'Equal Importance' has been brought in only with a view to utilising the fact urged in the *sutras*, which would be absolutely inoperative, if the question were only with regard to the difference of actions.

On this question then, there are two kinds of *Pūrvapaksha*: "(A) "The *Āgnēya*, etc., being all of equal importance, the two '*yajati*'s mentioned along with the words '*Paurṇamāsi*' and *Amāvāsyā*, are distinct "Injunctions, and as such lay down sacrifices other than the *Āgnēya* and "the rest, etc." (B) The two sentences—'*ya ēvam vidvān paurṇamāysañ* "*yajati*' and '*amāvāsyām yajati*'—are the only injunctions of sacrifices, "all the other sentences quoted being only the injunctions of accessories "of these two sacrifices."

PŪRVAPAKSHA (A).

First of all we take up that *Pūrvapaksha* which holds the two 'sacrifices' (enjoined by the two '*yajati*'s to be distinct from the *Āgnēya*, etc. "Inasmuch all the sacrifices in question are mentioned by *different words* "and also by *repetitions of words*, they must be all of equal importance. "Though these two reasons—Difference of words and Repetition—are not "connected directly with the fact of 'Equal Importance,' yet they are "taken along with this, through the difference in actions (that these "would indicate), which is also implied in the assertion of 'Equal "Importance' (as shown above). That is to say, the sacrifices denoted by "the two '*yajēta*'s are shown to be different from those of the Actions "(mentioned along with the *Dārça-Pūrṇamāsa*) that are not *yāga* (but "*Homa*, etc.), by the *difference in words*; while they are shown to be "different from the *yāgas*, by the *repetition* of the word '*yajate*'; and "hence they must all be taken as of equal importance. (That is to "say, when each '*yajēṭa*' mentions a distinct sacrifice, all the sacrifices "mentioned in the passages quoted become independent of one another, "and as such all equally are *primary* sacrifices).

"Nor could any special purpose be served by taking the two "*yajati*'s in question as mere references to the previously enjoined "sacrifices (because the only purpose that is found to be served by such "references is the pointing out of fresh accessories); and as a matter "of fact we do not find any accessories in the shape of materials etc. "mentioned in the two sentences in question; and as such we cannot "make the injunctive potency of these '*yajēta*'s give up the function "of laying down the actions themselves.

"Nor do we know of any such names—as '*Paurṇamāsya*' or '*Amā-*"*vāsyā*'—as belonging to any particular sacrifice.

"Though we find the verb '*yajatē*' in the Present Tense, yet we "can take it as injunctive, by accepting it either as a *Prayogavacana* (Direc-"tive Injunction), or *Arthavāda* (Eulogistic word), or as in the '*Lēt*' Mood "(which has the injunctive signification though the form of the Present "Tense),—just as we have in the case of the sentence '*Samidho yajati*' "(where the word '*yajati*,' though in the Present Tense, is admitted "to have an Injunctive meaning).

"And though we find the sentences introduced by the word '*yat*',— "in '*ya evam*, etc.'—(which always precludes the injunctive character)—, "yet we can not very well deny its injunctive potency; because on "this point too it is exactly like the sentence '*yadāgneyo shṭākapālo*, "*etc.*,' which has been accepted as an injunction.

"Nor can it be urged that 'the two *yajēta*'s, though having the injunc-"tive force, are yet not the injunctions of independent actions, but "are only the alternative injunctions of the same sacrifices as those pre-"viously enjoined, just as we admit of the Injunctions of the same "*Jyotishṭoma* sacrifice met with in the various Vedas being only "alternative injunctions of the same sacrifice.' Because in the latter "case, the different Vedic texts are meant for different persons, and "as such the different injunctions of the same sacrifice would not be "useless. In the case in question, however, there is no such difference "in the character of the persons addressed, and as such the repeated "mention of the word '*yajātē*' can serve no other useful purpose, save "the laying down of distinct *sacrifices*; specially as they can not be taken "as eulogising any other injunction, because they are not capable of "being taken along with any such other Injunction.

"It may be asked—what are the *Materials* and the *Deities* of the two "sacrifices laid down by these two '*yajate*'s? And to this we make the "following reply:—The butter kept in the *Dhruvā* vessel is the material "common to all sacrifices; and the Deities would be that which would "be indicated by the words of the *Mantras* recited at their performance; "and thus, these two sacrifices being found to have their details fully "supplied, they must be taken as enjoined distinctly by themselves.

"That is to say, we have the Vedic declaration that 'the butter kept "in the *Dhruvā* is used at all sacrifices,' and hence just as we take this "butter as the material of the '*Upānçu*' sacrifice, so could we also do "with regard to the two sacrifices in question. And as for the Deity, we "find that in connection with *Ājyabhāgas* there are four *Anuvākyā* verses "mentioned in the same order as the *Ājyabhāgas*; two of these addressed "to *Agni*, and two to *Soma*. And in accordance with the authority of Syn- "tactical Connection, which is always stronger than that of Order, the said "verses are separated from the *Ājyabhāgas* and joined on to the two sacri- "fices in question; and the Syntactical Connection that would authorise "such transference would be of the text—'*Vārtraghnī paurṇamāsyām* "*anūcyētē, vṛdhanvatī amāvāsyāyām*'—because there are no other actions, "save the two sacrifices in question, that could be spoken of as '*Paurṇa-* "*māsī*' and '*Amāvāsyā*' (and '*Vārtraghnī*' and '*Vṛdhanvatī*' are the names "of the two pairs of the said *Anuvākyā verses*). It may be argued that the "sentence quoted only lays down the times at which the verses have to be "recited, and they do not refer these verses to any actions. But, we ask, "—what would be the use of laying down the connection of the verses with "any particular time? Nor can the fact of the words '*Paurṇamāsyām*' and "'*Amāvāsyāyām*' having the locative ending be urged against us; because "we actually find many instances where sacrifices mentioned by words with "locative endings are accepted as primary;—*e.g.* '*yēna kārmaṇertsēt tatra* "*jayām juhuyāt*,' where the principal action is that which is referred to by "'*tatra*.' Thus then the two '*Ānuvākyās*—the *Vārtraghni* and the *Vṛdhan-* "*vatī*—being found to serve the same purpose, they come to be taken "as optional alternatives. And then again (as the *Anuvākyā verses* "are recited before the performance of the sacrifice, and as such could "not serve the purpose of indicating the Deity) it becomes necessary to "assume the corresponding *Yājyā verses* (which are recited during the "performance, and as such are capable of indicating the Deity.) Or it "may be that the two *Anuvākyās* being simultaneously enjoined, they "may be taken (and used) conjointly; and thence we are led to the "conclusion that the sacrifice has two Deities connected with it; and con- "sequently it becomes necessary for us to assume two *Yājyās* correspond- "ing to each pair of *Anuvākyās* (which *Yājyās* would indicate the two "Deities). Or we might assume a single *Yājyā* with reference to the "single (joint) Deity *Agni-Soma*. Or again, we might take one of the two "'*Vārtraghni*' *verses*, and also one of the two *Vṛdhanvatī verses*, as the "required *Yājyā* in each case. And thus we find that in whatever way "we might get at the *Yājyā*, the apparent inconsistency of the declaration—in the Vedic text '*Vārtraghni paurṇamāsyām* etc.,'—of the relationship between the *Mantra* and the *Sacrifice*, leads us to conclude that in "the two sacrifices, *Agni* and *Soma* are the Deities concerned. Then as "for the *Ājyabhāgas*, from which the *Mantras* (indicative of the Deity) "have been separated, their Deities are already mentioned by a sentence in "the form of the *Purākalpa Arthavāda*—'*Yasyaikasyaīcīt dēvatayai* "*havirnirvapannājyasyaiva nau purastādyajan.*' Then as far the *Mantras* "in connection with the *Ājayabhāgas*, the *Yājyās* have already been laid "down (and these have not been separated from them), and the *Anuvākyā* "*Mantras* (that have been removed elsewhere) also would come in, in "accordance with the direction: '*dāçatayībhyah kartavyah*'; and thus there "is nothing incongruous in the way that we have dealt with the subject.

"And thus even when the sacrifices enjoined by the two *Yajati*'s "in question are distinct from the *Agnēya* etc., they are found to have "distinct forms of their own; and hence they must be admitted to be "distinct actions; and as such, there being nothing to show that the "results follow from the six primaries *Agneyā* and the rest only, (because "the only sentence that had been accepted as showing this was '*Ya evam* "etc., which, however, has been shown to be the Injunction of a distinct "sacrifice altogether), the character of the primary belongs equally "to all the sacrifices mentioned in the various sentences quoted (*i.e.*, "to the *Prayāja* etc., the *Āghāra* etc., as well as to the *Āgnēya* etc.).

PŪRVAPAKSHA (B).

"We admit that the sacrifices are distinct; but we can not admit "of the fact of the character of the Primary belonging equally to all. "Because the names '*Amāvāsyā*' or '*Darça*' and '*Paurṇamāsī*' would "apply only to some of the sacrifices, and not to all; and the result is "spoken of as following from those that are qualified by these names; "and as such there can be no equality in the character of all the sacrifices. "That is to say, the words '*Darça*' and '*Paurṇamāsa*' denote sacrifices "with a qualification (that of being named by these words); and as from "the sentence—'*Darçapaurṇamāsābhyām svargakāmo yajēta*'—it is clear "that it is only from such qualified sacrifices that the particular result "could follow, we must take these alone as the primary sacrifices; and all "other sacrifices mentioned along with them (and without any distinct results of their own) must be accepted as the subsidiaries of these two."[1]

---

1 It may be noted that this second *Pūrvapaksha* is at variance with the *Siddhānta* only as regards the difference of the sacrifices mentioned by the two '*Yajeta*'s from the primary sacrifices of the *Darçā-Purṇamāsa*.

The upholder of *Pūrvapaksha* (A) objects to the *Pūrvapaksha* (B) on the following grounds:

"That which is itself well known serves to qualify or specify that "which is less known; and hence in the case of the sentence—'*Darça-"purṇamāsābhyām swargakāmo yajeta*'—the signification of the names "'*Darça*' and '*Pūrṇamāsa*' must be ascertained with reference to that "of the root '*Yāji.*' That is to say, in all cases, where we have the "Injunction of an action with a name, these two being recognised to be "co-extensive, it is sometimes the particular signification of the root '*yaji*' "(*sacrifice*) which is defined or specified by the *name*; while at other "times it is the *sacrifice* that defines or specifies the *name.* And between "these two, that which happens to be the better known of the two, turns the "other to its own purposes. For instance, (1) in the case of the sentence "'*Jyotishṭomēna yajēta*' we find that the name '*Jyotishṭoma*' is better "known from beforehand,—on account of its being related to the three "*stoma* songs, called '*Jyotih*'—; and hence this *name* serves to restrict "the signification of the root '*Yaji*' in this case to the *Somayāga*, "after having alienated it from the *Dīkshaṇīyā* etc.; and (2) in the case "of the sentence '*Rājasūyena yajēta*,' the name '*Rājasūya*,' not having its "signification pointing to any relationship with sacrifices, is taken up by "the root '*yaji*,' whose signification has been well known from the previ-"ously mentioned primary sacrifice.

"Thus then, in the case in question, we find that the significations of "the two nouns (*Darça* and *Purṇamāsa*), of the compound (*Darçapūrṇa-"māsābhyām*), and of the dual number (in this compound), are not known "beforehand (as in any way connected with the performance of sacrifices); "and hence the root '*Yaji*' cannot be taken as having its signification "referring to (or) defined by that name. On the other hand, the root "'*Yaji*' is applicable to all sacrifices; and as such, through the mention "of the particular result (*Svarga*), it comes, in the case in question, to be "applied to the sacrifices mentioned in the context under consideration; "and as such it would apply the word '*Darçapūrṇamāsa*' to its own "object (*viz.*, all the sacrifices—primaries as well as subsidiaries—that "happen to be mentioned in the context).

"For these reasons, we conclude that in the word '*Darçapūrṇa-"māsābhyām*' no significance is to be attached to either the component "words, or to the compound, or to the dual number—because the "word is only a particular combination of letters, simply pointing out "the instrument, or means, in connection with all the sacrifices mentioned; "exactly as in the case of the word '*Rājasūya.*' And as for the dual "number, we can explain it, in accordance with the rule '*Supām supo "bhavanti*,' as having been used in the place of the plural, or in that "of the singular—this singularity being based upon the fact of all the "sacrifices being taken as one complete whole.

"*Objection:* 'How can the word '*Darçapūrṇamāsābhyām*' be said "to have its signification not well known, when, as a matter of fact, we "find that, from among the sacrifices mentioned in the context, there are "some (the *Āgneya* etc.) which are laid down in connection with the points "of time (*Amāvāsyā* and *Pūrṇamāsī*) signified by the words '*Darça*' "and '*Pūrṇamāsa*'; while there are others (the *Ājyabhāga* etc.) which are "spoken of in the dual number; and certainly the signification of the "word '*Darçapūrṇamāsābhyām*' is well-known to be applicable to these "sacrifices. That is to say, a word renounces all its own meaning, and "waits upon the signification of other words, when even a certain portion "of it is found to be unknown; in the case in question, however, we "actually find that certain sacrifices—*Āgnēya* etc.—are connected with "the time '*Amāvāsyā*' and '*Pūrṇamāsī*' (signified by the words "'*Darça*' and '*Pūrṇamāsā*'), while others—the *Ājyabhāga* etc.—are "connected with the dual number (which we find in the word "'*darçapūrṇamasābhyām*'); and under the circumstances, it is not proper "to speak of the signification of the word '*Darçapūrṇamāsābhyām*' "(being unknown as applicable to any sacrifices) and as such to be "renounced.'

"To the above, we make the following reply:—It is the *Base and* "*Affix* (*i.e.*, the compound '*Darçapūrṇamāsa*' and the dual termination) "taken as a joint whole, that can specify or qualify the root '*Yajati*'; in "the case of the *Agnēya* etc., on the one hand, and the *Ājyabhāga* etc., on "the other, each of these is devoid of any connection with one part "of the word. That is to say, though in the '*Āgnēya*' etc., we find a "connection with the times denoted by the words '*Darça*' and '*Pūrṇa-*"*māsa*,' and as such the signification of the Base (*Darçapūrṇamāsa*) "would reside in them,—yet, inasmuch as these sacrifices are many, "the signification of the dual termination (in '*Darçapūrṇamāsābhyām*') "cannot apply to them; and as such the word '*Darçapūrṇamāsābhyām*' "as a whole is incapable of applying to the *Āgnēya* etc. And also, "though we find *duality* in the *Ājyabhāga* etc., yet the Base (*Darçaparṇa-*"*māsā*) is absolutely inapplicable to these; and so the word as a whole "cannot apply to these either. Nor is the co-extensiveness (of the *sacrifice* "and the '*Darçapūrṇamāsābhyām*') clearly mainfested either by the "meaning, or the context, or the use of different words; and as such "it is not possible for the name '*Darçapūrṇamāsābhyām*' to be taken as "referring to the sacrifices,—either on the ground of the similarity "of certain letters (in accordance with the law of the corruption of names "by which a slight difference in certain letters does not completely "alter the name), or by taking the word '*Darçapūrṇamāsābhyām*' in "its secondary signification as indirectly indicating the sacrifice.

"*Question:*—'Why can not we take the sentences (*Ya enam vidvān* "*amāvāsyāyām yajate* and *ya evam paurṇamasayām.* etc.) as laying down "these two independent sacrifices for the accomplishment of the result? "For, even in accordance with the *Siddhāntā* theory, these two words (*yajatē*) "will be said to lay down these two as composite actions (made up of the "six primary sacrifices) towards the fulfilment of the particular result. It "might be urged that the expression *Darçapurṇamāsā* being different "from the expression *Āmavāsyapaurṇamasa*, the actions referred to in "the sentence mentioning *Svarga* as the result could not be recog- "nised to be the same as those mentioned by the two '*Yajate*'s in the "sentences in question. But this objection is equally applicable to all "parties. For instance, for the upholder of the *Pūrvapaksha* also, what "are meant to bring about the result are the two composite sacrifices "named *Paurṇamāsya* and *Amāvāsyā*; and certainly these are not recog- "nised to be the same as those in the sentence *Darçapūrṇamāsabhyām* "*svargakāmo yajēta.* If it be urged that in this case, though the names "are not the same, yet, the names would be applicable to the composites "because of their being performed at the points of *time* expressed by the "words,—then, the relationship of the *time* is equally present in my "case also; the meaning of the sentences being that *one should perform* "(*yajēta*) the *Paurṇamāsa* on the *Paurṇamāsī* day, and the *Amāvāsyā* "on the *Amavāsyā* day.'

"*Answer:*—This cannot be; because this relationship of the *time* "being common to these two sacrifices, as also to the six sacrifices "*Āgneya* and the rest, we do not see any reason why the result should "be attributed to these two only. That is to say, when all the eight "are equally connected with the particular time, there is no reason for "attributing the result to the two only.

"It might be urged that from among these eight the result might "be attributed to *any* two sacrifices.

"But this would be most improper; because without any particular "reason, such attributing of the result to any two sacrifices would be a "most unauthorised procedure; and secondly, the relative subserviency "of these eight would become a matter of option; and this leading to a "great anomaly, could never be allowed. That is to say, unless we find "a special reason for doing so, as long as we find the relationship of the "specified time equally present in all the eight sacrifices, those two that "would be chosen out as leading directly to the result, would make "all the other six subsidiary to them; and inasmuch as these six have all "the marks of primary actions, there would be a very great anomaly.

"It might be urged that the said importance being a matter of option, "it could, by turns, be attributed to all the pairs concerned; but in that "case, there would be another anomaly, *viz.*, the same sacrifice would "at one time be the primary, and at the other subsidiary; and further, "from among those having the characters of both the primary and "the subsidiary (as it is only that which is subsidiary in the *Āgnēya* "that is said to be capable of being introduced into its corresponding "*Prayāja*), a certain sacrifice would, in its subsidiary character, be liable "to be introduced in the corresponding *Prayājas* of the *Āgnēya* etc.; while "the same would, in its character of the primary, be incapable of "being so introduced; and thus there would be an eternal doubt as to "what should be really introduced into the *Prayājas*. And further, as "a matter of fact, all numbers subsist in the objects numbered, only through "a certain secondary property; in the case in question, however, either "in the two independent sacrifices (meant to be enjoined by the sentences "in question), or in the *Āgnēya* etc., we do not find in any part of these "any such *sub-class* or secondary property, whereby we could recognise "their *duality*. Specially as whichsoever of them would be taken up, "its *duality* would be directly set aside by the *plurality* of other sacrifices "and also by the *singleness* of that sacrifice itself. And thus we do not "find the dual number applicable to any of the sacrifices in question.

"In accordance with the *Siddhānta*, on the other hand, the two words "(*Darça* and *Pūrṇamāsa*) express *two* composite sacrifices; and as such "there being a distinct dissimilarity from the theory in which all the sacri-"fices are not taken as forming any composites, we find the requisite "sub-property (in the form of the *compositeness*), and as such the "connection *of duality* becomes possible; and through this there would "be a relationship with the specified *time* also; and thereby in a way, the "application of the nouns '*Darça*' and '*Pūrṇamāsa*' also becomes "possible; and thus in this case it becomes possible for the word '*Darça-pūrṇamāsābhyām*' to be taken as qualifying the sacrifice. In accor-"dance with the *Pūrvapaksha*, however, this is not possible; because, "inasmuch as it does not admit of any composite sacrifices, the number *two* "can not in any way be applicable (and hence it could never admit of the "result to follow from any *two* sacrifices); and hence the result must be "attributed to each and every one of the sacrifices mentioned in the context.

"The following question might be put to us: 'Why cannot we have "all the eight sacrifices, as qualified by the duality of the times *Amāvāsyā* "and *Pūrṇamasī*, as enjoined by the sentences in question (in this case "the *duality* pertaining to the points of time and not to the sacrifices)? "Just as in accordance with the *Siddhānta*, we have the six primary "sacrifices enjoined with regard to the *duality* of the two composites.'

"To this the reply that we make is that such hazy processes can not "set aside the verb from each and every one of the sacrifices mentioned; "because it actually rests upon every one of these. And then, too, the "*time* being something entirely diffierent from the *sacrifice*, the number "belonging to the former can in no case appertain to the latter. In "the *Siddhānta*, the case is different; as according to that, there is "no absolute difference between the component parts (sacrifices) and "the two composite wholes (to which latter the number belongs); and "as such there is nothing incompatible in connecting the number of the "whole with the component parts.

"Thus then, we conclude that, in accordance with the *Pūrvapaksha*, "as the application of the names *Darça* and *Paurṇamāsa* depends upon "the signification of the root '*Yaji*,' all the sacrifices in question must, "be admitted to be equally primary."

SIDDHĀNTA.

To the above, the *Sūtra* makes the following reply: "*Prakaraṇa*"—that which is performed—would be the substratum of the words connected with '*Paurṇamāsya*' and '*Amāvāsyā*'; or the context would help these two words; and consequently we must accept that alone to be enjoined which is denoted by these.

That is to say, in all cases, we find that the Injunctive word prompts us to certain specific sacrifices; and in case the sentences '*ya ēvam* etc.' are taken as enjoining independent sacrifices, as they do not make any mention of the material or the deity related to these sacrifices, people would never be found to take up the performance of such unspecified sacrifices.

That is to say, the words '*yajate*' in these sentences, or the words '*Amāvāsyā*' and '*Pūrṇamāsa*,' do not denote *sacrifice in general*; nor do you (who hold the sentences to lay down two independent sacrifices) admit of these words pointing to all the sacrifices in question. Then all that you can do is to make them lay down two independent sacrifices. But in that case, inasmuch as the details (material deity &c.) of these sacrifices are not mentioned, no one would be found to perform them; and hence the sentence would become wholly futile. If, however, they are taken as referring to the sacrifices mentioned in the context, then, the materials and the deities of all these sacrifices, as also the particular points of time at which they have to be performed, being found to be duly mentioned, the full form of the sacrifices becomes known; and as such the sentence becomes utilised (in pointing out the time at which they should be performed).

It has been argued above that the Material and the Deity of the four sacrifices are also clearly cognisable. But though it is true that the common material, *Dhrauva*, might be taken as the material to be employed, yet inasmuch as there is no mention of a Deity, the sacrifice remains as indistinct as ever.

Nor is it possible for the Deity to be indicated by the words of the *Mantras* employed; because the *Mantras* in question are distinctly pointed out, by the *Order* in which they occur, to belong to the *Ājayabhāgas.* Nor is it possible for this *Order* to be set aside by the *Sentence;* because in the case in question there is no direct antagonism between these two; because when it is possible for the sentence '*Vārtraghnī Amāvāsyāyām* etc.'—to be taken in such a way as to be quite in keeping with the indication of the Order, then we cannot but renounce, as untenable, any other theories that might entail a contradiction between the two. In the sentence '*Vartraghnī amāvāsyāyām* etc.'—if the words '*Paurṇamāsī*' and '*Amāvāsyā*' denoted Actions, then the antagonism (between the Order and Sentence) could not be removed: (because in that case the Sentence would refer the *Mantras* to those Actions, while the Order refers them to the *Ājyabhāga*). As a matter of fact, however, these words only denote *time*; and as such there is no antagonism between the two. And when there is a common ground for both the Sentence and the Order, it is incumbent on us to lend support to that theory which reconciles them. And further, at the very outset, the words '*Amāvāsyā*' and '*Paurṇamāsī*' denote particular points of time; and it is only subsquently (if the denotation of the time be found to be incompatible with the rest of the sentence) that they can indicate the Actions, through their connection with those times; and hence by priority (and because there is nothing incompatible in it) we admit the words to be denotative of time. Because if the commonly recognised signification of time (by these words) were not compatible with the sentence, then alone could we reject it and take the words to be indicative of Actions. Then again, we find that the Locative termination (in the words '*Amāvāsyāyām*' and '*Paurṇamāsyām*') is more compatible with the signification of time (than with that of Action); because Time is always known as the *Adhīkaraṇa* (Substratum, Container) of Actions; and as it is not possible for Actions to be such an *Adhiharaṇa*, the Locative ending, in that case, could hardly be explained in any way. It has been argued above that no purpose is served by such connecting of the *Mantra* with any particular time. But if *tādarthya (being for the sake of)* were the only relation possible, and if it were this relation that were asserted by us (as between the *Mantra* and the Time), then the said objection would be all right; but, as a matter of fact, the case is this: The *Mantra* appearing (by the particular Order in which the

Mantras are mentioned) to have been laid down as for the sake of the *Ājyabhāgas*, it remains doubtful as to which *Mantra* is to be employed in which particular *Ājyabhāga*; and hence what the mention of the words '*āmāvāsyāyām*' and '*paurṇamāsyām*' (in the sentence '*Vārtraghnī*' etc.) does is to point out that the *Mantra* known as the '*Vārtraghnī*' is to be used in the *Ājyabhāga* performed at one time (the *Amāvāsyā*), and that called '*Vṛidhanvatī*' in that performed at another (the *Paurṇamāsī*).

And further, according to our theory, inasmuch as the *Ājyabhāgas* are already known to have a particular Deity, the Injunction (of time) is found to serve a visible purpose (that of pointing out the time). In your case, on the other hand, it becomes necessary to make many gratuitous assumptions. That is to say, in all cases, the relationship of things is ascertained by means of their mutual requirements; hence the *Ājyabhāgas*, that have their Deity already known, standing in need of *Mantras* capable of pointing out that Deity, would at once take up such *Mantras*, and it would not require any very great effort on our part to connect the two. In your case, on the other hand, the sacrifices denoted (by the sentences in question) being altogether new, their Deities are not known; and as such they do not stand in any immediate need of *Mantras* (indicative of those Deities); hence it becomes necessary for you to make the following assumptions: (1) you will have to assume the *Mantra*, and its *duality*, thereby making the single Injunction have many meanings; (2) you will have to assume the existence of many Deities indicated by those *Mantras*, while it is not necessary for a single sacrifice (which is held to be enjoined by the sentence in question) to have more than one Deity or more than one *Anuvākyā*; (3) there is an assumption of a *Yājyā* verse (not found in the Veda) (4) as also fresh *Puronuvākyās*, not mentioned in the Veda, for the *Ājayabhāgas*. It has been declared above that "one of the two *Vārtraghnīs*, as also one of the two '*Vṛidhanvatīs*' would be the *Yājyā*, while the other is the *Anuvākyā*. But this is scarcely possible, as the taking of any of these as *Yājyā* would be contrary to the fact of their being named '*Anuvākyā*.'

Further, since you admit the potency of pointing out the factors to be employed in the particular sacrifice, to the Sentence, and to the *Mantra*,—and since the Sentence ('*Vārtraghnī amāvasyāyām, etc.*' does not speak of the *instrumentality* of the *Mantras* (*Vārtraghnī* and *Vṛīdhanvatī*) in the sacrifice, it becomes necessary for us to assume the recitation of these *Mantras* to have certain *invisible* results—just as we have in the case of the recitation of the '*Vaishṇavī*' verses; and as such the *Mantras* could not be taken as serving the *visible* purpose of pointing out the Deity; specially as the *Mantra* is not required at all by that which has to be pointed out. And under the circumstances, instead of assuming a

Deity to be indicated by the *Mantra*, it would be far better to assume the *Mantras* to exert an indirect influence towards the accomplishment of the Action. On the other hand, the *Ājyabhāgas* being two, and they also being recognised as having two Deities (*Agni* and *Soma*),—the *Mantras* indicative of those Deities are actually required by them (for the purpose of lending authority to their cognition); and these *Mantras*, being pointed out as to be used at the sacrifice, by the indications of the *Mantras* themselves, as also by the order in which they happen to be mentioned,—they come to serve a distinct visible purpose. And thus, the *Mantra* and its duality etc., all having been pointed out, what remains to be done by the sentence ('*Vārtraghnī, etc.*') is to lay down distinct restrictions with regard to the time at which the various *Mantras* are to be used; and this process is certainly much simpler than that involving the above-mentioned endless assumptions.

Nor, in this case, does the said sentence become altogether useless; because the aforesaid restriction with regard to time cannot be accomplished by mere Proximity (and hence the use of the sentence lies in this restriction).

For these reasons there can be no Injunction of the Deity, through the sentences brought forward; because these have been shown to have no connection with the matter. And hence the sacrifice held to be enjoined by the sentence '*Ya evam, etc.*', not having its details of material and Deity clearly mentioned, it cannot be taken as one different from those previously laid down.

Question: "What would be the use of making the sen-"tence '*Ya evam, etc.*' a mere *reference* to the other sacrifices—*Āgneya* "and the rest? Because an Injunction that fails to enjoin anything "expressed by a word, by its part, or by a sentence, can never be of any "use in matters relating to *Dharma*, (and hence as in the case of *Reference*, "the sentence in question would not contain any of these injunctions, it "could not be of any use in regard to *Dharma*).

Answer: Just as the sentences laying down the various sacrifices (*Āgnēya* and the rest) form parts of the Joint Direction ('*Darçapūrṇamāsābhyām svargakāmo yajēta*'), so also do the two sentences in question ('*Ya evam, etc.*'); because it is these latter alone that render the Dual number (in '*Darçapūrṇāmāsābhyām*') compatible with the whole thing. That is to say, *firstly*, it is only when the two sentences in question have spoken of the Primary sacrifices as *two composite wholes*, that the Dual number in '*Darçapūrṇamāsābhyām*' becomes possible; and herein lies a distinct use of the two sentences; and there is no such rule as that it is only an Injunctive Sentence that can be of use; specially as we find many non-Injunctive sentences (such as the *Arthavāda*) serving useful purposes, in association with Injunctions;—*secondly*, the mention of the various sacrifices—*Āgnēya* and the rest—extending over many sentences, they can never be spoken of as 'two,' except by the two sentences in question ('*ya evam*, etc.'). And it is with a view to this fact that the *Bhāshya* has mentioned, as the *Siddhānta*, the fact of there being a Relation of subserviency among the sacrifices, which necessarily follows from what we have explained above. Otherwise, it would have been impossible to bring forward the theory of the two sentences in question merely *referring* to the previous sacrifices, until the *chance of uselessness* urged in the second *sūtra* (in favour of the repetition of the same verb denoting distinct Actions, to which the case of the sentences considered in the present *Adhikaraṇa* is meant to be an exception) has been removed by showing the distinctly useful character of the *reference* (by the two sentences in question to the previous sacrifices).

Thus then, it must be admitted that there is a distinctly useful purpose served by taking the whole sentence as merely *referring* to the previous sacrifices; and there is no incongruity in this theory.

Question: "How is it possible to speak of many distinct sacrifices "as one or two composite wholes?"

Answer: It is quite possible; just as many trees located in one place are spoken as a single composite 'forest,' so though the sacrifices are many and distinct, yet inasmuch as they are all performed at the same time, they can very well be spoken of as a composite whole. That is to say, when we see many trees in a place, we have an idea of a composite whole, and we come to think of them all as 'a forest'; in the same manner, when we find many sacrifices performed on a single day, it is only natural that we should come to think of them as a single composite whole; and it is only on account of the singleness of this composite whole that we have the singular number in '*paurṇamāsīm*.'

Though, as a matter of fact, the words '*Paurṇamāsī*' and '*Amāvāsyā*' really denote the component sacrifices, yet they take the singular ending, on account of the singleness of the composite whole indicated by these sacrifices; and these words are not the names of the composite wholes themselves. Because it is only on account of the co-extensiveness (of the 'sacrifice' as signified by '*yajēta*' with the name '*Darça*' and '*Purṇamāsa*,' mentioned in '*Darçapūrṇamāsābhyām*'), that we take these words to be the *names of sacrifices*; and certainly the character of *sacrifice* belongs to the individual sacrifices '*Āgnēya*' and the rest, and not to the composite whole made up by these. That is to say, in the sentence '*paurṇamāsīm yajati*' (or in '*darçapūrṇamāsābhyām yajēta*'), inasmuch as the *sacrifice* denoted by the root '*yaji*' is found to be co-extensive with the name '*paurṇamāsī*,' we conclude that '*Paurṇamāsī*' is the name of a *sacrifice*; and the character of *sacrifice* does not belong to any composite whole made up by the *Āgnēya*, etc., but to the individual *Āgnēya*, etc., themselves; and hence just as the root '*yaji*' (sacrifice) is applicable to each one of these sacrifices, so also is the name in question. Nor is it possible for the *whole composite* to appear at one and the same time, because at the time that the *Āgnēya*, etc., are performed, they are performed independently of one another; and hence at that time there does not appear any idea of their forming a composite whole. And hence even in consideration of the time of actual performance, we can say that the name belongs to each individual sacrifice.

And further, if the two words were the names of the composite wholes, independently of the component sacrifices, then the Directive sentence—'*Darçapūrṇamāsābhyām svargakāmo yajēta*'—would also lay down the composite wholes towards the fulfilment of the particular result; and in that case, the component sacrifices not being the means of bringing about that result, there would be a single *Apūrva* proceeding from the composite whole itself; and thus there being no individual *Apūrva* with each individual sacrifice, there would be absolutely no use of performing (or laying down) so many distinct sacrifices. And further, the actions laid down in connection with the various sacrifices, all tending towards a single *Apūrva*, there would be no restriction as to which action should be performed in the course of which particular sacrifice; nor would each of the sacrifices be connected with any specific method of performance; and consequently, there would be no use for the consideration (in subsequent *Adhyāyas*) of the questions as to the repetition of the Actions performed in course of the *Āgnēya* in another sacrifice; and further the '*Saurya*,' for instance, being a form of the '*Āgnēya*,' there would not be any *method of performance* applicable to it; as there being no such method applicable to the *Āgnēya* only, the only method that would be available would be that of all the three Primaries (*Āgnēya* and the rest); and as the '*Saurya*' is not a form of these three, any such method could not be applicable to it; nor again could we have such declarations as—'The Paurṇamāsī has only *one* cake,' 'the *Amāvāsyā* is without the *sānnāyya*,' and so forth; because the number of cakes would be the total of all that are employed in all the sacrifices that go to form the composite whole, and that number could not be applied to the lesser numbers—'one,' etc.,—because the number would be exactly like the number 'thousand,' which is not applicable to any part of itself.

We meet with such declarations as—'because of the composite whole not being enjoined,' and 'because the composite whole is an accessory,' and so forth;—we must conclude that such words as those in question signify the component parts (and not the whole); as otherwise, being denoted by the word, it would be the composite whole that would be enjoined; and as such, being directly connected with the result, that would be the Predominant Action (and as such both the above declarations would be false).

For these reasons, it must be concluded that the words '*Paurṇamāsī*' and '*Amāvāsyā*' denote the individual sacrifices as qualified by the two composite wholes. And, though, these sacrifices being many, the name would have to take a Plural ending,—yet the singular number is due to the indication (of the single composite whole by the individual sacrifices); and it is with a view to this that the *Bhāshya* has declared—*samudāyaçabdatayāvakalpayishyate* (*It would be taken as indicating the composite whole*). So again, the *Bhāshya* declares—*bhavati hi bahūnāmēkavacanāntaḥ samudāyāpēkshaḥ* (*the singular ending in the case of many things is possible, as referring to the composite whole*); where the *Bhāshya* also has spoken of only an '*apekshā*'—indirect influence—of the *composite whole*, and it does not speak of this latter as being actually signified by the word. The words 'crowd,' 'forest' and the like can be taken as similar instances, only when these also are taken as signifying the component individuals as qualified by the composite whole; if, however, they signify the composite whole, then they can serve as instances only so far as the singular ending based upon the singleness of the composite whole is concerned.

From the above it also follows that the words '*Darça*' and '*Pūrṇamāsa*' are synonymous with '*Amāvāsyā*' and '*Pūrṇamāsī*' respectively (because only under the above conditions could we have the dual ending in '*darçapūrṇamāsābhyām*').

Thus then we find that *the reference* to the composite whole (formed by the sacrifices), by the two sentences in question, has its use in making possible the two singular endings (in '*paurṇamasīm*' and '*amāvāsyām*'), as based upon the fact of these two names indicating two composite wholes; and this will be explained later on, under *sūtra* IV-IV—34. And the words '*Darça*' and '*Pūrṇamāsa*' also following the duality of the composite wholes, come to refer to the same (*i.e.*, to the *Āmāvāsyā* and the *Paurṇamāsī*); specially as there is much similarity between the words '*paurnamāsī*' and '*pūrṇamāsī*'; and on account of the word '*darça*' appearing along with '*pūrṇamāsa*' (while '*Amāvāsyā*' appears with '*Paurṇamāsī*'), the word '*darça*' also comes to be synonymous with '*amāvāsyā*'. Or it may be by the figurative method of 'contrary expression' that it would be easier to get at the comprehension of the *Amāvāsyā* by means of the word '*Darça*'—just as the *blind* is spoken of derisively as 'one having eyes'; because it will be declared later on that "because the moon is *not seen* on the *Amāvasyā*, therefore, the *Amāvāsyā* is (derisively or figuratively) spoken of as '*darça*'." So also at the close of the '*Anvārambhaṇīyā*' sentence, it will be shown that the words '*darça*, and '*amāvāsyā*' are synonymous.

Thus then, the Result being found to follow from only those sacrifices that go to form the *composite wholes*, all the sacrifices other than these must be taken as subsidiary to them (the former ones, the *Agnēya* and the rest, being taken as the Primary Sacrifices; and as such they are not all of 'equal importance').

Question: "When all this has been fully dealt with in the present "*Adhikaraṇa*, there is no use for introducing the same discussion in the "Fourth *Adhyāya*."

Answer: There is nothing very wrong in this: Because it is only when the conclusion in the present *Adhikaraṇa* has been arrived at, that the possiblity of the root '*yaji*' pointing to all the sacrifices mentioned in the context gives rise to the corresponding Adhikaraṇa in Adhyāya IV, and the *Siddhānta* too of that *Adhikaraṇa* would be arrived at only by the help of the present *Adhikaraṇa*; otherwise the *Pūrvapaksha* would have to be admitted as the *Siddhānta*; hence the *Adhikaraṇa* introduced in the fourth *Adhyāya* is only by way of a deduction from the present one.

There is yet another useful purpose served by the Reference (*Anuvāda*) in question. It is by means of that alone that we get at the direction—'The *Amāvāsyā* is to be performed on the *Amāvāsyā* day and the *Paurṇamāsa* on the *Paurṇamāsa* day,' which lays down the time for the performance of the two sacrifices in question.

Against this, the following objection might be urged: "Even this "direction is absolutely useless, because the time for the performance is "duly pointed out by the sentence which originally enjoined the sacrifice—"*viz*: the sentence '*yadāgnēyo*' *shṭākāpālo amāvāsyāyām paurṇamāsyāncā*-"*cyuto bhavatī*."

To this we make the following reply: In the sentence that we have found, we find the *time* forming part of the *means* (of accomplishing the Result); whereas in the original Injunctive Sentence, we find it, very differently from this, connected with various sacrifices independent of one another.

That is to say, in the original Injunctive Sentence, we find the *Time* mentioned in such a way that it is connected with the Primary sacrifices —*Āgnēya*, etc.,—independent of one another, and wholly devoid of their subsidiaries. In the sentence that we have brought forward, on the other hand, the *Time* is mentioned by words with the Instrumental termination; and hence it forms part of the *Means* (of the accomplishment of the particular result); and the instrumentality of these has been cognised as belonging to the Primary Sacrifices together with their subsidiaries, as connected with one another, in accordance with the Directive Sentence ('*Darçapūrṇamāsābhyām svargakāmo yajēta*'); and hence any further mention of the Instrumentality of these would not be necessary; specially as they are laid down only with reference to the particular Time. And inasmuch as what is meant to be so connected with Time is the Trio of Primaries, together with the subsidiaries, and connected with one another, one of these trios being connected with the *Paurṇamāsī*, and another with the *Amāvāsyā* day. And the relationship of the sacrifices is such that the moment that one of the trio having been begun is being completed,—at that very moment, the other two are also taken up; and thus each trio comes to be performed as forming a single action. If they were to be performed in accordance with the time laid down in the original injunctive sentence, then each of the three would come to be performed by itself, separately from the subsidiaries. And thus there is a distinct difference between the two ways of taking the sentences.

Objection: "In that case, as the result would be brought about by "the two trios with all their subsidiaries, there would as great a necessity "for the two Trios being performed together, as there is of the performance "of the subsidiaries along with the trio of Primaries; and hence just as "the subsidiaries of one trio are recognised as to be performed at the "time of its performance, so also would the one trio—the *Pūrṇamāsī*—"have to be performed together with the *Amāvāsyā* (on the *Amāvāsyā* "day), and *vice versa*; and hence both of these would come to be performed "on both days. Nor would such performance be contrary to the restric-"tion of time in the original injunctive sentence, because the *Paurṇa*-"*māsa* would be performed on the *Paurṇamāsi* day (and also on the "*Amāvāsyā*). For if one performs the *Amāvāsyā* on the *Paurṇamāsī* day, "it does not follow that it can never be performed on the *Amāvāsyā* day; "so also with the *Paurṇamāsa.* Nor does the original Injunctive sentence "prohibit the performance of the sacrifices on days other than those "mentioned therein; because all that the sentence does is to lay down "the performance of the sacrifice on that particular day."

To the above we make the following reply: That sacrifice of which the specific time is not known, and of which the specific form does not disappear (in the absence of such knowledge of its time),—if the time of such a sacrifice is said to depend upon something else, there is nothing wrong in this.

That is to say, the *Amāvāsyā* sacrifice, having its time duly mentioned in the original Injunction, does not look out for another time, in the shape of the *Paurṇamāsī* day, which it would get at, by means of its association with the *Paurṇamāsī* sacrifice; and similarly the *Paurṇamāsī* sacrifice would not look for the *Amāvāsyā* day; and under the circumstances, if these two trios (the *Paurṇamāsa* and the *Amāvāsyā*) were performed at any other times, such performance would not be in keeping with the correct forms of these sacrifices as laid down in the original Injunctions; and as such they would altogether cease to be the '*Darça*' and the '*Paurṇamāsa*' (as not performed on these days). As for the subsidiaries, however, any particular time for the performance of these is not mentioned; and as such they look forward to the mention of such a time; and consequently, there being no chance of an incompatibility with the time mentioned in the original Injunction, there is no impediment in the way of their being connected with the time that is indicated by their peculiar associations.

On this point we have the following objection: "The subsidiaries "always being performed at the time that their respective primaries are "performed, we would have a clear idea of their time, even without such "a sentence (as that '*amāvāsyāyām amāvasyāyayā*, etc.), and hence this "sentence cannot be admitted to have anything to do with the pointing "out of the time of the subsidiaries."

To this objection we make the following reply: That the time for the subsidiaries is the same as that of the Primaries is not declared by any *mantras*; on the other hand, it is this very sentence (that you have objected to) that forms the basis of that assertion.

Objection: "Those (subsidiaries) that are far removed (in point "of time) cannot in any way help the Primary."

Reply: Whence have you got such a law that it is only when a certain thing is in close proximity with another, that it can afford any help? For it is only in accordance with the declarations in the scriptures that we ascertain whether or not one Action will help another. Hence until we have met with a declaration to the effect that it is only proximate objects that can render any help, there can be no authority for asserting that that which is remote cannot help.

Objection: "The performance of the Primary *together with* the "subsidiaries is pointed by a sentence other than what you bring forward. "For instance, we have the sentence—'*ya ishṭyā paçunā somēna yajēta sa* "*amāvāsyayā paurṇamāsyā yajēta*,'—where the word 'Ishṭi' has the "Instrumental ending; and being laid down with reference to the *time* "of the performance of itself together with all its Component Sacrifices "and subsidiaries, the required mention of the time is got at by that "means."

Reply: True, it is got; but the desired performance is not accomplished. Because the word '*ishṭi*' refers either to the whole collection of sacrifices (Primaries and Subsidiaries) or to each of them singly; and it never refers to any 'trio of sacrifices'; consequently, a performance based upon that word would be altogether different. That is to say, it is ascertained that the word '*ishṭi*' does not refer to any '*trio*'; and thus the word applying to each *sacrifice* (as '*ishṭi*' is etymologically equivalent to 'sacrifice,' '*yajña*'), it would follow, from the sentence you have brought forward, that each one of the sacrifices, singly, would be performed on one *Amāvāsyā* or on one *Pūrṇamāsī* day. (That is to say, one sacrifice would be performed on one *Amāvāsyā* and another on another *Amāvāsyā*); and as such a proper performance of the sacrifices will not be accomplished. It might be urged that—"the word '*ishṭi*' might be applied, by a particular convention, to all the sacrifices *Āgnēya* and the rest, and the word would thus be as applicable to each 'trio' as it is to the *Soma*." But thus too, inasmuch as the Directive sentence —'*darçapūrṇamāsābhyām svargakāmo yajēta*'—is one only, both the composite sacrifices the '*Darça*' as well as the '*Paurṇamāsa*' would be performed either on the *Amāvāsyā* or on the *Pūrṇamāsi* day; and in this there would be a contradiction of the restriction of time laid down in the original Injunction. It might be urged that, "in deference to the original Injunction (and also to the signification of the sentence we have brought forward), we can accept the two points of time as two alternatives." But then also, just as in accordance with the original Injunction, each Primary Sacrifice would be performed alone by itself upon a distinct *Amāvāsyā* day,—so also, inasmuch as the Subsidiaries are not differentiated as to some of them belonging to the '*Amāvāsyā*' while others belong to the *Paurṇamāsa,* the performance of all of these Subsidiaries would be done in any one place only. And hence, the sentence that you have brought forward cannot serve the same purpose that is served by the sentences '*Amāvāsyām amāvāsyayā, etc.*'; and as such it can be of no use with regard to the Primary Sacrifices; hence all that it could do would be to connect the particular time with the other modifications of the Primary Sacrifices.

Objection: "The performance of all the sacrifices, together, as one "action, could very well be brought about by the sentence—'*samē darça*-"*pūrṇamāsābhyām yajēta*'; because inasmuch as no significance could be "attached to the *place* (denoted by the word '*same*' = on level ground), all "that the sentence does is to show that all the sacrifices (the Primary "along with its subsidiaries) have to be performed together. (Because "the sentence speaks of '*darçapūrṇamāsa*' as the *means*; and they could be "mentioned as the means only when accompanied by all their Subsidiaries, "as urged above by the *Siddhānti* himself)."

Reply: All that the sentence quoted does is to point out that the fact of the ground being *level* (*sama*) applies equally to all the Sacrifices; and hence the sense of the sentence would only be that in all the sacrifices one should have a single *level* platform, and not *many* platforms. That is to say, even when the sacrifices are performed separately, as they are not performed in different places, the mention of a *place* applies commonly to all of them. It might be argued that, "the *common application* that the sentence would imply being that on account of the peculiar relationship between the *Davça* and the *Pūrṇamāsa*, one of them becomes connected with the level platform at the same time that the other does." But in that case, inasmuch as all the six primary sacrifices are mentioned simultaneously, it would be necessary to perform them simultaneously also; and this would be incompatible with the restriction of time laid down in the original Injunction. If, however, they were to be performed in accordance with the original Injunction, then it would be necessary to bring about an association of all these sacrifices,—each of which would be connected with the prescribed time,—with reference to the 'level platform'; and as such the whole performance would end with the performance of the six Primary Sacrifices only; and as for the Subsidiaries, they would have to be performed, as not restricted by the time specified for the Primaries (because the original Injunction does not prescribe the time for the Subsidiaries); and as such they would come to be performed between the performances of two Primaries (*i.e.*, between the two *Amāvāsyās* on which the two Primaries would be performed). And further, as it is only right for the Subsidiary to be repeated with each Primary, each Primary with its Subsidiary would be completed by itself (and there would be no composite sacrifice).

It might be argued that, "we should connect all the sacrifices with the *level platform* simultaneously, only leaving off that margin of time which would be contrary to the prescription of the time in the original Injunction." But in that case, both the 'trios' being performed on one *Amāvāsyā*, or on one *Paurṇamāsī* day, the Subsidiaries would be performed in proximity to any one of them only. Or again, it would also be possible for the Subsidiaries to be performed on any day during the fortnight (between the *Amāvāsyā* and the *Pūrṇamāsī*). Because in a way the whole of this fortnight would be the time for the performance of the Primary; because all that can be meant by the Injunction that the Subsidiaries should be performed at the same time as the Primary is that they should not overstep the time-limit of the Primary, and not that they should be performed close upon it; because this latter would not be possible. And thus then, even the sentence that you bring forward would not accomplish the desired performance.

The above arguments also apply to the case of the sentence '*darçapūrṇamāsābhyām svargakāmo yajēta*' (*i.e.*, even this sentence cannot serve the purpose of. pointing out the time); because like the *place* (mentioned by '*samē*' in the sentence brought forward by the opponent), the *Result* also cannot form the object of a sentence; and hence what this sentence would lead to would be the performance of all the Primary Sacrifices—connected with one another and accompanied by all their Subsidiaries—at one and the same time, and thus, too, the desired method of their performance would not be achieved; and a single result would be brought about by Sacrifices performed at different times.

It might be argued that—"the sentence may be taken as directly "laying down that at the time of the actual appearance of the result, we "should perform, simultaneously, all the Primary Sacrifices, together with "all their Subsidiaries, which would show *how*, and *by means of what*, the "appearing Result could be brought about; and as such there would be "no difference of time in the performance of the sacrifices."

But in that case, too, we would have an anomaly in the shape of the simultaneous performance of two composite sacrifices. Or, on the other hand, in consideration of the original Injunction, each of the sacrifices would come, as shown above, to be performed on distinct *Amāvāsyā* days. Nor is the time of the actual appearance of the result perceptible to us; as that time also is specified only by the time of the actual procedure of the sacrifice. Thus then, in consideration of the time prescribed in the original Injunction, we would conclude that the time of the appearance of the Result would be that time which is taken up by the actual performance of the Primary and its Subsidiaries; and that the said simultaneity would be only so far as that time is concerned; and thence the completion of all the Primaries with their Subsidiaries would rest either in the six Primaries—the three *Paurṇamāsas* and the three *Āmāvāsyas*, or in the two composites (*Darça* and *Paurṇamāsa*) only. And then the Subsidiaries would come to be performed, either along with any one of the two Composite Sacrifices, or on any day during the fortnight, as shown above.

For these reasons we conclude that even this sentence—'*Darçapūrṇamāsabhyām svargakāmo yajeta*'—cannot bring about the performance of each '*trio*,' together with its Subsidiaries, at the proper time; and this must be got at by means of other sentences,—such as the one we have pointed out above, *viz*: "*amāvāsyāyām amāvasyayā*, etc.," which thus comes to serve the distinctly useful purpose of pointing out the time for the performance of each of the two '*trios*,' etc., etc.

Objection: "In that case, the mention of time in the original Injunction would be superfluous."

Reply : Why should it be superfluous ? Just look for a moment upon what follows : If the original Injunction did not mention the connection of the sacrifices with a particular time, then there would be no ground for taking the sentences '*ya evām* etc.' as *references* to the two composite sacrifices ; that is to say, the words '*Paurṇamāsya*' and '*Amāvasyā*' in the sentences '*ya evām* etc.'—are held to refer to sacrifices connected with the times expressed by these words. And unless we had a mention of the time in the original Injunction, we could never know which sacrifices are referred to by these words. And this being unknown, as the sacrifices denoted by '*yajatē*,' in the sentences '*ya evām* etc.', would not be specified by the words '*Darça*' and '*Pūrṇamāsa*' as comprehended in their true signification, the sentences '*ya evām* etc.' would have taken in all the sacrifices mentioned in the context ; and as such all these equally would be *Primaries.* Consequently, it becomes necessary that the sacrifices should have been previously connected with particular points of time. It is on account of this being absolutely necessary that even though the sentence '*ājyasya ma nau upānçū paurṇamāsyām* etc.' forms part of a '*Purākalpa Arthavāda*' (and as such is not a pure injunction), yet it has been quoted by the *Bhāshya* as the original *Injunction* of the *Upānçu* sacrifice, (which is the one next to the *Āgnēya*), simply because the sentence contains the word '*paurṇamāsyām*, and as such connects the *Upānçu* sacrifice with a particular point of time (which is not done by the sentence which is the real original Injunction of the *Upānçū*).

Sūtra* (4) : *Also because we find a peculiarity* (in the shape of the appearance of the subsidiary *Prayāja* in the modifications of the Primaries) ; (we cannot hold all to be equally Primaries); because *they* (the Prayājas) *could not appear in them* (the modifications) *if all were equal.

If the sacrifices mentioned by the sentences '*ya evām* etc.' were distinct from all others, then the Āghāra and the other Subsidiaries would all equally be Primaries ; and hence, in accordance with the *sūtra* VIII. i, 20, the subsidiary *Prayājas* etc., also, like the *Agnēya* and the other Primaries, would enter into the instrutmental factor (in the bringing about of the principal result) ; and as such they would no longer be able to supply the want of the *method* in the *Bhāvanā* (bringing about) of the modifications of the Primary, which has its Instrument or Means already laid down ; and as such these modifications would no longer take into themselves these *Prayājas* etc. ; they are actually found to be taken up by these modifications ; as otherwise we could not have a text enjoining '*Kṛshṇala*' as the material to be used at the *Prayāja, when performed in connection with the modifications.*

Consequently in order to establish the fact of the *Prayāja* etc. being subsidiary to the *Agnēya* and the rest, we must take the two sentences in question as *referring* to the previously mentioned Sacrifices.

***Sūtra* (5) : *Objection : " The sentences ('yadāgneya " etc.') lay down accessories, because of the direct men- " tion* (of the root ' yaji ' in the other sentences)."**

" If we accept distinct sacrifices to be laid down by the sentences " '*ya evam* etc.', then we have the following advantages : (1) The singular " number in the word ' *paurṇamāsīm* ' becomes quite explicable with refer- " ence to the noun itself, without having recourse to any indirect indication, " by the word, of the composite of sacrifices. (2) If we accept these " sentences as Injunctions, we have a further advantage, *viz* : the root '*yaji*' " is found to be directly mentioned, and it is not necessary to infer it " from the mention of the Deity (as you have got to do in the case of " holding the Injunction to lie in the sentence '*yadāgneya* etc.'). (3) In " your case the sacrifices enjoined by these inferred '*yājis*' being more than " one, their *Apūrvas* would also be more than one ; and thus in compari- " son with the process of taking the sentences as referring to the before- " mentioned sacrifices, that of taking them as independent Injunctions is far " more advantageous. As for the appearing of the *Prayājas* in the modifi- " cations (urged in the preceding *Sūtras*), it can be explained, either by " qualifying the injunction of *Kṛshṇala* in the performance of the " *Prayājas* in the modifications, by adding the condition ' in such cases " where there are sentences that must be taken as *anuvāda*',—or by taking it " as laying down a material for the *Prayāja* occurring in the Primary it- " self."

" It is with reference to all this that the opponent says (in the *Bhsāhya*): " These two alone are the Injunctions of Sacrifices ; all other are mere " injunctions of the accessories."

The opponent next proceeds to meet the objection that these two Sacrifices have no details, Materials or Deities, mentioned : " The words " '*Amāvāsya*' and '*Paurṇamāsī*,' occurring in the sentences '*yadāgney-* " *o'shṭākapālo* etc.', refer to the sacrifices enjoined by the sentences '*ya evam* " etc.' ; and as those sentences—'*yadāgneya* etc.'—distinctly lay down the " Deities, etc., we have the Deities of our two sacrifices mentioned " directly by the Vedic sentences themselves."

Sūtra* (6) : *Reply : But they are Injunctions ; as otherwise many accessories would be declared simul-

taneously; because if they appeared after the sacrifices had been enjoined, then their such appearance could be only for the sake of the accessories; and as such we would have to admit of an injunctive word with each accessory.

The sentences '*yadāgneya* etc.' cannot be taken as laying down the accessories of the sacrifices enjoined by the sentences '*ya evam* etc.' Because it is a well-recognised rule that when the Action is one that has been already enjoined (by a previous sentence), we cannot lay down more than one accessory with regard to it; as it is only when the Action has not been otherwise enjoined that even a number of accessories could be laid down by a single effort (of that Injunction).

That is to say, in all original Injunctions of Actions, the Injunctive Affix proceeds to enjoin only the *Bhāvanā*, because it is only this factor that is not got at by other means. And so long as this *Bhāvanā* is not fully equipped with all its factors, by means of the Denotation of the Root, and the other factors in the sentence (denoting the various auxiliaries of the sacrifice), it cannot be brought to action; and hence until all this has been fully laid down, the Injunction is not complete. And when it so happens that by the apparent inconsistency of the generic character of the auxiliaries that are recognised as constituting the factors of the *Bhāvanā*,—this inconsistency leads us to look for a specification of the said auxiliaries,—then it is that the *Bhāvanā* comes to be specified by those specifications which are implied by the Instrumental case-endings found in the same sentence, and which also are on the look-out for the *Bhāvanā* (as the object to be specified). And in the case of each word, the *Class*, *Gender* and *Number*, that belong to an object,—all these come to be recognised, by means of the direct signification of the particular case-ending, as auxiliaries to the *Bhāvanā*; because all these (*Class*, etc.), on account of being expressed by the same word, have among themselves the relation of the qualification and the qualified, and are not recognised as belonging to, or depending upon, one another (and as such must be concluded to form part of something else; and that is the *Bhāvanā*). And thus it is that all words, near the *Bhāvanā*, or removed from it, fall in with the *Bhāvanā*, notwithstanding their remoteness or proximity,—in the way that we have explained under the *Adhikaraṇa* on *Anushaṅga* in the foregoing *Pāda* of this *Adhyāya*. And it is only then that, having got hold of a *Bhāvanā* fully endowed with all its qualifications, the Injunction becomes complete.

And as in all such cases the Injunction lays down the *qualified Bhāvanā* by a single effort, it does not entail any such anomaly as the assumption of various potencies in the Injunction. Because it is only when the *direct functionings* of words are multiplied that it becomes very complicated ; and when the words end in expressing a single fact, then there is nothing incompatible in the *indirect implication* of many things. That is to say, the direct Injunction having been once utilised in the laying down of the qualified *Bhāvanā*,—if it were taken again to *directly* function towards the laying down of something else, then it would be necessary to repeat the Injunctive word over again ; and this being incompatible with the Veda, would not be warrantable ; when, however, the Injunctive word has ceased its functioning with once having laid down the *Bhāvanā*, then, on account of the apparent inconsistency of its own signification, it would give birth to (*i.e.*, indirectly imply) other Injunctive words expressive of such qualifications (as would be necessary for removing the said inconsistency) ; and in this the original Injunctive word would not have to give up its one form as appearing in the Vedic text ; although it would serve all the purposes that would be served by various repetitions of itself.

And though in this manner the Injunction of the qualification would appear *after* the original Injunction of the *Bhāvanā* itself, yet, in accordance with the law laid down under the *Adhikaraṇa* on '*Ākṛti*' (in the first *Pāda* of the first *Adhyāya*), the qualifications themselves will have appeared before that. That is to say, though, as a matter of fact, the Apparent Inconsistency due to the fact of the *Bhāvanā* being qualified, appearing subsequently, leads to an idea of the Injunction of the qualification, long after that of the original Injunction (of the *Bhāvanā*),—yet, in accordance with the rule arrived at in the *Adhikaraṇa* on '*Ākṛti*,' as it is impossible for the *Bhāvanā* to be *qualified*, in the absence of the qualifications themselves, it must be admitted that these must have been full-fledged entities from before ; as it is through these alone that any idea of the *Bhāvanā* being *qualified* could be brought about.

All these Injunctions (of qualifications), pointed out by the apparent inconsistency of a perceptible fact, operate either simultaneously or one after the other. And thus we find that if we admit a sentence to be the Injunction of a fresh *Bhāvanā*, then it becomes an easy matter to get at the Injunctions of its accessories, by the help of the original Injunction of the *qualified Bhāvanā*, which is capable of giving birth to various Injunctions.

On the other hand, however (if the sentence be taken as only referring to a *Bhāvanā* previously enjoined by another sentence), this is not possible. Because, as a rule, it is only when the Primary is carried to a place, that it draws with itself all its accessories ; while if it is one of the accessories that is carried, it does not carry with itself another Accessory, because these two are not so intimately connected. That is to say, when the *Bhāvanā* is such as has been got at from another sentence, then the Injunctive word in the sentence in question cannot enjoin that *Bhāvanā* over again—as a repeated injunction of the *Bhāvanā* would be as useless as the powdering of that which has already been powdered; and then, not performing its injunctive function, it does not become the means of giving birth to various Injunctions with regard to things connected with that *Bhāvanā*; as it is only when the Injunctive word *enjoins* the qualified *Bhāvanā* that it makes possible the assumption of such Injunctions; and this is not possible in the case in question; hence the Injunctive Affix is found to be such as has its direct expressive potency quite inoperative (towards the injunction of the *Bhāvanā*); and hence, in accordance with the rule laid down under the *sūtra* '*ānarthakyāt tadangeshu*,' that Injunctive Affix comes down from the *Bhāvanā* and directs itself towards the auxiliaries connected with it. And then those qualifications of Class, Gender and Number, which qualify the auxiliary expressed by a single word, serve to point out that auxiliary,—exactly in the way that we have explained in the case of the Injunction of a qualified *Bhāvanā*: and as such these qualifications are all enjoined; and hence, in the case of a single word, even though the *Bhāvanā* has been enjoined by another sentence, it is possible to have the Injunction of many things (in connection with it). When, however, there is a combination of many auxiliaries mentioned by many words (as in the case of the sentences '*agnēyoshṭākapālaḥ* etc.'),—then, in that case, there being no sort of relationship among these auxiliaries themselves, the words expressing them also remain unconnected (with one onother); and hence when the Injunction betakes itself to one of them, it has nothing to do with any other; and when it would betake to this latter, it could not have anything to do with another, and so on; because of all of them being wholly unconnected with one another. For these reasons it is not possible, in this case, to have the one implied by the other, as we had in the case of the Injunction applying to the *Bhāvanā*.

Thus then in this case, the original Injunction not giving birth to other Injunctions, the former, being one only, would be wholly taken up in the laying down of one auxiliary; and then the declaration that it lays down another also, would not be possible, unless we meant to repeat the original Injunction; this would entail the anomaly of all these repeated Injunctions being of human origin (and as such having no authority). This is what is meant by the second half of the *sūtra*, which means that if the sentence were taken as laying down an action that has been already previously enjoined, as such laying down could only be for the purpose of mentioning the accessory, the Injunctive word would have to be repeated for the sake of the Injunction of each one of the accessories.

The Bhāshya says:—'*parasparasambandhe cāsati* etc.' (when there is no mutual connection etc.); and this is meant to show that when there is no such connection, there is no apparent inconsistency that could serve as the ground for having an injunction of the qualified *Bhāvanā*.

Even in everyday life, we find that when the chief man—the king, for instance, is carried to a place, he always carries with himself all his invariable attendants; whereas when one of these attendants goes to a place, no other attendant moves a single step; for the carrying of each attendant, it becomes necessary to make a fresh effort; and it is absolutely impossible to move all the attendants by a single effort; hence it is impossible for many accessories to be taken up by a single Injunction.

It is this fact that the *Bhāshya* proceeds to explain in detail: The sentence '*āgnēyoshṭākapalaḥ* etc.' cannot be taken as laying down the *ashṭākapāla* with reference to the *Paurṇamāsi* sacrifice (held to be enjoined by the sentence '*ya ēvam* etc.'); because the mention of the form of the *Āshṭākapāla* has still got to be made; and as such mention could be got at with very great difficulty, how could the sentence serve the purpose of laying down any other object? This is what is meant by the assertion (in the *Bhāshya*) that '*there being no relationship of the word* bhavati, *there is no connection (of the sacrifice) with āgnēya*' [that is to say, in the sentence '*ashṭākapālo bhāvati*' the word '*bhāvati*' denotes the *existence* of the *asṭākapāla*, and as such the *Paurṇāmasi* is connected, by means of this sentence, with the *asṭākapāla*, and not with the *Āgnēya*, because this latter is in no way connected with the '*bhavati*']. If, however, the sentence be taken as laying down the *Āgnēya* with reference to the *Paurnāmāsī* sacrifice, then too, we have the same difficulty of having a mention of the actual form of the *Āgnēya*; and as this difficulty in both cases is exactly similar, the *Bhāshya* has not noticed it in connection with this second alternative, and has only pointed out the fact of the sacrifice, in this case, not having connection with the *ashṭākapāla*. Even when we take the sentence as meaning that 'the *Āgnēya* qualified by the *Paurṇamāsi* sacrifice is *ashṭākapāla*,' or that 'the *ashṭākapāla* qualified by that sacrifice is *Āgnēya*,'—in any case we are faced by the following difficulties: (1) the mention of the origin of that *Āgnēya* or *Āshṭākapāla* which is described; (2) the difficulty of connecting them with the *Paurṇamāsi* sacrifice; (3) the mention of the origin of that (*Āgnēya* or *Ashṭākapāla*) which is enjoined (with reference to another); and (4) the difficulty of connecting the *Āgnēya* and the *Ashṭākapāla* with each other; and thus the whole thing would become too complicated. If the word '*paurṇamāsī*' be taken with both of them at one and the same time, then, in the first place, it would be necessary for us to have origins for both; and secondly, we would have to assume a mutual relationship among them. Nor can the two be said to qualify (or restrict) each other—as is done by the various qualifications mentioned in the sentence '*aruṇayā pingākshyā ekahāyanyā gavā soman krīṇāti*';

because that would entail the anomaly of having a qualified Injunction. Consequently, it must be admitted that it is the *Paurṇamasī*, as unaffected by the *Āsṭākapāla*, that is connected with the *Āgnēya*, or that it is the *Paurṇamāsī*, as unaffected by the *Āgnēya*, that is connected with the *Āsṭākapāla*; and as such there can be no connection between the *Āgneya* and the *Āshṭākapāla*.

With a view to meet this difficulty if one were to take the sentence at the very outset, as laying down the material (*Ashṭākapāla*) and the Deity (*Āgni* mentioned in the word '*Āgnēya*') of the *Paurṇamāsī* sacrifice, then he would have to face the following difficulties : (1) the mention of the actual forms of these two (*Āgnēya* and *Ashṭākapāla*), (2) the injunction of one in regard to another, (3) the connecting of these two with one another, when both are enjoined at one and the same time; (4) and then over and above all these, the connecting of these two with the *Paurṇamāsī* sacrifice (which is held to be enjoined by another sentence—'*Ya ēvam* etc.')

And then, for the purpose of meeting these difficulties, it becomes necessary to take the sentence '*yadāgneyaḥ* etc.' as only laying down the connection of the *Āshṭākapāla* in connection with the sacrifice, with reference to the Deity mentioned in some other sentence : this is what is meant by the *Bhāshya*, "*kena cit āgnēyaḥ sankalpitaḥ*"; some people take this sentence as meaning that "if one were to bring in the *Āgnēya* that had been given away by another performer"; but this does not appear correct, because such *bringing* would be tantamount to stealing, in the midst of his performance, the material prepared by another person. Therefore, we must take the word '*sankalpitaḥ*' as containing a double causative affix,—the meaning of the sentence thus being "if we take *Āgnēya* as laid down in another passage,—for instance, the one that contains the word '*rukkāmaḥ*' (desiring a bright complexion, etc.).

In reply to this argument it is said that in that case, the word *Āgnēya* (as understood from that other sentence) being taken as simply mentioned (in the sentence '*yadāgneyaḥ* etc.') for the purpose of establishing the connection of the *Ashṭākapala* (with the Paurṇamāsī sacrifice), then it is not known what is the Deity in the *Paurṇamasī* sacrifice; and if it be held that the *Āgnēya* is laid down with reference to the *Ashṭākapāla as qualified by the Paurṇamāsī*, then there is a syntactical split : and in this way we can go on showing the endless syntatical splits consequent upon all the various constructions that could, in accordance with the opponent's theory, be put upon the sentence—the constructions that have been shown under the *Adhikaraṇa* on *Ākṛti* in Pāda i. of Adhyāya I.

Thus then in the sentence '*Āgnēya* etc.' we must have the injunction of the connection of a material and a Deity; but this connection is not possible with regard to any sacrifice that may have been previously enjoined by other sentences; and hence, in accordance with the *sūtra* '*guṇaççāpūrva-sambandhaḥ*' we must admit a distinct sacrifice to be actually enjoined by this sentence ('*yadāgneyaḥ* etc.') ; and then we have the same '*rūpavacana* (non-mention of the form)' that was urged in the third *sūtra ;* and as such the sentence '*ya ēvam* etc.' must be taken as only referring to the sacrifices enjoined by the sentence '*yadāgnēyaḥ*, etc.' And by this we are forced to have recourse to indirect indication, etc., for the purpose of explaining the singular ending (in '*Paurṇamāsīm*').

And further, the sentence '*yadāgneyaḥ* etc.' cannot be complete until it lays down an action not laid down by any other sentence; and so long as its own full signification is not complete, it cannot require the aid of another sentence. That is to say, that '*the Āshṭākapāla becomes*' is not a functioning by the human agent ; nor is it possible for a sentence to lay down only the functioning of a cake ; because such functioning would not have the character of any particular *Bhāvanā*. And thus it being necessary to assume a particular functioning of the human agent, we naturally fall upon the assumption of the *sacrifice.* And though when a functioning (that of the cake) is actually perceptible, it is not quite right to assume an inferred one,—yet, in the case in question, the sentence being not incomplete, and (as such not standing in need of another sentence) the mere fact of the root '*yaji*' (signifying the *sacrifice*) being found in the sentence containing the words '*amāvāsyā*' and '*paurṇāmāsī*' (*i.e.*, the sentence '*ya ēvām* etc.'), which is not in close proximity to the sentence in question, cannot preclude the aforesaid inferential assumption. And when the 'sacrifice' has been inferred, the sentences '*ya ēvam* etc.' are found to have the exact form of mere description (or reference) ; and for this reason they are actually admitted to be as such.

And further, because in the sentence '*yadāgneyo* etc.' the word '*yat*' is co-extensive with (refers to) the *Action* (of *being*, of the cake), while the '*yat*' in the sentence '*ya ēvam* etc.' refers to the agent,—and as it is the latter kind of '*yat*,' and not of the former, that precludes the injunctive function—the mere presence of the word '*yat*' in the former sentence cannot be in the way of its being taken as an Injunction. On this, we have the following declaration:—"When connected with the verb, the word '*yat*' does not disable the Injunction; when, however, it is connected with the Agent, then it distinctly points to the fact of the sentence being a mere reference to something that has been enjoined in a previous sentence."

Sūtra (7): *The mention of these also is like that.*

If the *Amāvāsyā* were a single sacrifice, then the two materials—the *Sānnāyya* (Curd and Butter) and the *Oshadhi* (Herbs)—would be optional alternatives; and then, why should there be any mention of the preparation of one of these before the other, (as it would be necessary to employ and prepare only one of the two alternative materials)?

When there are various sacrifices, then the *Sānnāyya* and the *Oshadhi* come to be taken as both forming the materials to be offered in various sacrifices, and as such all the various materials having to be prepared for the *Amāvāsyā* sacrifice, it becomes quite relevant to speak of the preparation of one of these before the other,—which would be entirely irrelevant in any other case.

And further, in accordance with the *Pūrvapaksha*, over and above the three sacrifices, there would be a fourth (in the shape of that enjoined by the sentence '*ya ēvam* etc.'); and as such the passage quoted in the Bhāshya would refer to them as '*uttarāṇi*' (in the plural), and not as '*uttarē*' (in the Dual) (which refers to the two composite sacrifices, the *Darça* and the *Paurṇamāsa*).

Sūtra* (8) : *Also because we find* (in the Veda) *indicative words.

If the sentences '*ya ēvam* etc.' enjoined two distinct sacrifices, then the number of sacrifices would be more, and if they enjoined accessories, the number would be less than 'thirteen' and 'fourteen,' which are the numbers that are mentioned in connection with the Libations in the *Darça* and the *Paurṇamāsa.* Because these numbers could be possible only if in the *Paurṇamāsa* there were three, and in the *Darça* two, primary libations (and this would not be the case if the sentences '*ya ēvam* etc.' are taken either as the Injunctions of independent sacrifices, or as the Injunctions of Accessories).

For these reasons we conclude that the sentences '*ya ēvam* etc.' merely refer to the two previously mentioned composite sacrifices. To this effect, we have the following declaration: "(1) Because the enjoined sacrifice has no form (material, etc.), (2) because the words of the sentence directly denote the sacrifices mentioned in the context, and (3) because it is only in these latter sacrifices that we find distinct forms and details,—we must admit the sentences '*ya ēvam* etc.' to be mere references to the two composite sacrifices laid down in the preceding sentence."

ADHĪKARAṆA (4).

[*Treating of the First Exception to the foregoing Adhikaraṇa.*]

PŪRVAPAKSHA.

***Sūtra* (9) : "*The case of the upānçu would* be like the *Paurṇamāsī*."**

The following three *Adhikaraṇas* treat of the exceptions to the general rule arrived at in the foregoing *Adhikaraṇa*.

[There is one sentence :—'*jāmi vā etadyajnasya kriyatē yadancau purodāçau, upānçuyājamantarā yajati*,' and then we have a set of sentences—'*vishṇurupānçu yashṭavyo'jāmitvāya, prajapātirupānçu yashṭavayo'jāmitvāya, agnīshomāvupançu yashtavyāvajāmitvāya*'; and on these there arises the following question : does the expression '*upānçuyājam*' in the first sentence only serve to speak of (refer to) the whole batch of sacrifices mentioned in the latter set of sentences ? or does it serve to lay down an independent sacrifice by itself ? And on this question, we have the *pūrvapaksha* embodied in the *sūtra* ; and in support thereof we have the following arguments.]

"To the sentence '*upānçuyājam etc.*' apply all the conclusions arrived " at in the foregoing *Adhikaraṇa*."

"Because, inasmuch as the sacrifices laid down in the latter set of " sentences have their accessories in the shape of the respective deities duly " mentioned, while that which is mentioned in the first sentence has no " such accessory mentioned, we cannot but conclude that this latter " sacrifice depends upon the former sacrifices.

"That is to say, in the three sentences, we have the affix *tavya* with " the verb ; and as such they have the character of absolute Injunction, " and hence, if we were to assume these sentences to enjoin independent " sacrifices, then we would render ourselves open to all the aforesaid objec- " tions of the details of these being unknown, and also of the neccessity of " having to assume many unseen factors."

"And further, we find each of the latter three sentences mentioning the " removal of the evil effects of the *jāmi* (a technical flaw in the perform "ance of a sacrifice, explained below); and it is with regard to this flaw of "the *jāmi* that the first sentence mentions the *upānçū* sacrifice. That is to "say, looking at the whole section, from the first sentence to the last, "we find that the mention of '*jāmi*' (in the first sentence) and the "'*removal of jāmi*' (mentioned in the last three) form one subject; and "from this it is clear that it is the last three sentences that contain the real "Injunctions, whereas in the first sentence we do not find any distinct "*Arthavāda* or Injunction (by which it could be taken as containing the "Injunction of a sacrifice). Then again, the special purpose served by the "first sentence *referring* to the whole set of the three sacrifices (laid down "in the latter sentences), is that it is only thus that any one of the three "sacrifices (laid down by the three sentences) can be taken as a sacrifice in-"dependent of the other two; it is only by making the first sentence (which "mentions a definite point of time, in the shape of the interrim between "the offerings of two *cakes*) supplementary to the last three sentences, that "all the three sacrifices becoming connected with that particular time,—"each of them comes to be taken as an independent primary sacrifice.

"The Bhāshya has represented the opposer of the *Pūrvapaksha* as "bringing forward the objection that the first sentence might be taken as "laying down a sacrifice with the *upānçū* as its accessory (and as such the "sacrifice laid down by it cannot be said to be without a definite accessory). "And some people take exception to this sentence of the *Bhāshya*, on the "ground that the *Deity* and the *Material to be offered* being the only two "accessories of a sacrifice, one '*upānçū*' cannot rightly be spoken of as such "an 'accessory.' But this is not a very effective objection; because any-"thing that characterises or specifies a sacrifice (distinguishes it from other "sacrifices) is its *accessory*; and there is no doubt that the '*upānçu*'-*ness* "(*i.e.* the quietness with which the *Mantras* are recited) serves to dis-"tinguish a sacrifice: and as such it can very well be spoken as an "'*accessory.*'"

"The *Pūrvapakshin* meets this objection by declaring that *such a word* "*as* upānçūyāja *cannot very well*, etc. And the sense of this is that "if the word '*upānçayāja*' be etymologically explained in a way that "would point out *upānçu* as the distinguishing feature of the sacrifice, "*i.e.*, if the compound be explained as *upānçū ijyate yah sa*—then "the resultant word would be '*upānçūyāga*' and not '*upānçūyāja*,' "in accordance with Paṇini's *sūtra* VII—iii—52. While on the other hand, "if the word '*upānçūyāja*' be taken as the name (of the whole set of three "sacrifices, and not as laying down the accessory of an independent "sacrifice), inasmuch as no etymological explanation of a *name* is "necessary, there would be no room for the grammatical anomaly—the "word being taken as a complete whole by itself."

"The opponent brings forward another objection—*nānvēvam sati* etc. "And the sense of this is that even when the word is taken as a *Name*, then "in accordance with the *sūtra* I—iv—4, the applicability of that name "(*upānçūyāja*) to the set of three sacrifices would depend solely upon the "presence in each of these three sacrifices, of the feature of *upānçu-ness*,— "which presence is laid down by the sentence '*vishṇurupānçū yashṭavyaḥ*' "etc.: and then the etymological explanation and the consequent anomaly "cannot be avoided."

"The Purvapakshin replies to this objection by declaring that it is not "necessary for us to take the word '*upānçuyāja*' as referring to the set of "three sacrifices, as this reference can be made by the word '*yajati*' in the "same sentence (and all that we mean is that the first sentence only "refers to the three sacrifices). Then, too, it is only in the case of an "Injunction that it is necessary for each word to fit in with the particular "sacrifice; while in the case of the Name, the applicability of this word is "made to rest upon the fact of the root '*yaji*' only referring to the set "of three sacrifices; and thus there being even a slight ground of "similarity, there would be nothing incongruous in the applicability of the "Name (and hence it is not necessary to have recourse to an etymological "explanation; and hence there will be no occasion for the grammatical "anomaly)."

SIDDHĀNTA.

Sūtra* (10): *But it is an Injunction, because of there being no other sacrifice mentioned in the context.

The sentence '*upānçūyājam yajati*' is the Injunction of an independent sacrifice; and it is not a mere reference to the set of three sacrifices mentioned in the three sentences. (1) Because there being no other sacrifices mentioned in the context, the sentence cannot be taken as a mere *reference*; and (2) because no sacrifice is actually enjoined by the sentences '*vishṇuḥ* etc.'

In the case of the sentence mentioning the *Vaiçvānara* sacrifice, we find that from beginning to end the text treats of '*twelve* cakes,' and hence the mention of the numbers '*eight*' and the rest come to be taken as forming part of the 'twelve'; and as such the sentences mentioning these smaller numbers are not taken as separate Injunctions of those numbers. In the same manner in the case in question, we find that the Injunction is introduced by the words '*jāmi vā ētat*' which describe a certain flaw in the sacrifice; and it is clear that such mention of the flaw must have some bearing on—and be needed by—a certain enjoined sacrifice; consequently it appears that the sentences '*vishṇuḥ* etc.' speaking of the removal of that flaw serve the purpose of eulogising that enjoined sacrifice. When it so happens that between the offering of two cakes there is no other action to be performed, then we have what is called the flaw of '*jāmi*'; and hence the mention of the 'removal of *jāmi*' must be taken as eulogising that action which would be laid down as to be performed between the two offerings; and from this it follows that in the case in question, what has to be eulogised is the sacrifice *Upānçu*, which is distinctly laid down as to be performed "in the *interrim*"; while in the sentences '*vishṇuḥ* etc.' we find described the 'removing of the '*jāmi*' which is the eulogy required by the aforesaid *Upānçu* sacrifice; and consequently we disregard the injunctive character of these sentences, because their injunctiveness is nowhere found to be required; and hence all of them come to be taken as mere eulogistic sentences. Specially as we do not find the "interrim" mentioned as the time, in the sentences '*vishṇuḥ* etc.'; and as such the '*jāmi*,' with a mention of which the context was introduced, not having any direct connection with these sentences, these cannot be taken as embodying the Injunctions of any actions for the removal of that '*jāmi*'; and hence too the "removing of *jāmi*" mentioned in these sentences cannot be taken as eulogising these latter Injunctions. On the other hand, that action, which is mentioned directly in connection with the time "interrim," is distinctly found to be the object of Injunction by the sentence that begins with the mention of '*jāmi*'; and then on this ground, the other sentences come to have their use in eulogising that Action; under the circumstances, it is scarcely right to accept an Injunction that would entail the assumption of many imperceptible elements.

And further, in the case of the sentences '*vishṇuḥ* etc.', these being taken as connecting the sacrifices with Vishnu etc., the 'sacrifice' would be *indirectly* implied as subordinate to that connection; and so long as a directly-expressed sacrifice is available (in the sentence '*upānçum* etc.') it is not right to accept an indirectly implied sacrifice to be enjoined.

That is to say, the affix '*tavya*' in '*yashṭavyaḥ*' is in the passive, and as such the predominant factor in the sentence is '*vishṇu*' to whom the 'sacrifice' is subordinate (the sentence meaning etymologically that *Vishṇu is the objective of the sacrifice*); and the performability of the sacrifice could be only inferred indirectly from the sentence,—the factor of the 'sacrifice' being extracted out of the word "*yashṭavyaḥ*"; and this would be scarcely proper; because we have a direct Injunction of the Sacrifice in the sentence '*antarā yajati*'. Even though it were possible for the sentence '*vishṇuḥ*' to be taken apart from the sentence '*antarā yajati*', yet all that they could do would be to lay down the Deities for that sacrifice which is laid down as to be performed " in the interrim " (in the sentence '*antarā*, etc.') ; and they could not lay down distinct Actions.

As a matter of fact, it is not possible even for the Deity to be laid down by such sentences. Because the word '*yashṭavyaḥ*' in these does not signify either the *Deity* or *that to which something is given*; because all that they actually signify is a *material* subordinate (belonging) to the sacrifice; consequently what we have to do is to take the potency of the *objective* as the predominant element; and as such what the word would signify would be what is signified by the Accusative case-ending; and certainly that does not establish the character of the Deity. Because the root '*yaji*' meaning 'to give away,' its actual objective is *that which is given away*; and hence the only possible explanation would be that the Deity approached by the object given away, comes subsequently to be indirectly connected with the Sacrifice. But in this way, the words come to have two objectives; and hence, in accordance with the *sūtra* '*samaptiḥ çabdārthaḥ*,' [II—iv—23] what happens is that the objective, in the shape of the thing given away, is set aside, and another, in the shape of the Deity worshipped, becomes manifested; and the verb thereby coming to be recognised to have only one objective (in the shape of the Deity worshipped), it is only after its Dative potency has been wholly suppressed, that the Deity could be spoken of as the objective, as in the sentence '*vishṇum yajati*' (in the Active voice) or '*vishṇuryashṭavyaḥ*' (in the Passive). And certainly in this we do not find any denotation of the Deity; all that we find is that the character of Deity (of Vishṇu) is indirectly indicated by the apparent inconsistency of its objective character.

Objection: "The root '*yaji*' signifying the *worshipping of a Deity*, "the word signifying the objective of that root would be synonymous with "the word 'Deity'; and hence it is scarcely correct to say that in the "sentences quoted the *Deity* is only *indirectly indicated*."

Reply: As a matter of fact, the root '*yaji*' does not directly signify *the worshipping of a Deity*; because if that were the case, then *Hymning* also, which is a kind of *worship*, would come to be denoted by the root '*yaji*'; but we shall show later on that when there is a Hymning of the Deity, that Deity cannot be said to be thereby worshipped, in the way that the guest is worshipped. That is to say, at the time that one is hymning a Deity, even if he be engaged in actual worship, it is not said '*sa yajatē*.' And inasmuch as, in this case of Hymning, the actual form of the sacrificial Deity (namely that of being one to whom an offering is made) is not present in the Deity hymned, that Deity does not attain the character of an object of *worship*, like the Guest. And further, that the root '*yaji*' does not signify *worship*, we shall show later on, in Adhyāya IX. Even when the root '*yaii*' is taken to mean '*giving*', the Deity to whom the gift is made cannot be said to have the character of the *objective;* as for instance, the Teacher who is worshipped by means of gifts is not found to have the character of the objective.

Objection : "In that case, the word mentioning the Deity would "always have the Dative ending (and then how would you explain the pres- "ence of other case-endings in words actually mentioning the Deity) ?"

Reply: The *sampradānatva* (the principal element in the Dative) of the Deity is never of the same precise type as that of the Teacher; because the Deity is not the actual *receiver of the gift* (not having a body, etc.). And further, we do, in certain cases, find the Dative ending with words mentioning the Deity, for instance, '*yādābhyam grihītvā somaya yajate* etc.' But, in all cases, the Deity has got neither the precise character of the *sampradāna* (receiver of the gift), nor that of the particular *objective* ; nor by itself could it be either the *receiver of the gift* or the *objective,* with reference to the root '*yaji*' (sacrifice). Then the character of one of these two is attributed to it, simply because, while being actually found to help in the accomplishment of the Action—and thereby having the character of the '*kāraka*' (Instrument)—there is no seventh case that could fit it exactly. Nor by itself, in the form that is signified by the word expressive of the Deity, does the Deity become related to the denotation of the root '*yaji.*' Under the circumstances, even though the actual *receiving of the offering* is not present in the case, yet by the mere fact of the offering being made with regard to it, we assume the presence of the complex conditions of the Dative; and hence speak of the Deity in the Dative; and at times, the *character of being reached*, that belongs to one with regard to whom the offering is made, is assumed in the case of the *offering;* and as such the Deity is, sometimes, spoken of as the *objective* of the whole root '*yaji.*'

Thus then, (1) in a case where we find an Injunction wherein the Deity is mentioned in the Dative Case, for instance, '*somāya yajatē*,' we must explain it as meaning that 'the offering should be made to that Deity, as if creating its right of ownership in the object offered';—(2) when we meet with an Injunction in which the Deity is mentioned as the *objective* (for instance, *vishnuryashṭavyaḥ*), its meaning is that it is the Deity reference to whom should be made for making the offering. It is for this reason that in a case where the only action of the Offerer lies in referring to (or thinking of) the Deity, and there is no actual *offering* made, we find the direction '*hotaryaja*' (where all that the *Hotri* priest does is to think of the Deity to whom the offering has been made).

Thus we find that both of these—the Dative and the Objective character —apply to the Deity only indirectly. And of these two again, we find that the character of the *Dative* is more closely related to the Deity (than that of the Objective), because it is the Dative alone that is an invariable concomitant of the action of *giving*, though its complete applicability has been found to be open to objection; while as for the *Objective*, we find that it is present also in actions other than *giving*, and as such not being a necessary concomitant of the action of *giving*, it is not so closely related to the Deity. Hence it is concluded that the character of the *Objective* of the root '*yaji*' is not fully applicable to the word 'Deity', just as the character of the Deity too is not found to be wholly applicable in the case in question. Because, as a rule, the Deity is always mentioned either by the use of the word 'Deity' itself, or by the use of a word with a nominal affix which signifies the Deity; and never by means of any of the case-endings. For instance, when laying down the appearance of the Nominal affixes signifying the Deity, the words that Pāṇini employs are not in the forms '*idamagnayē*' (with the *Objective* ending) or '*tēna krītam*' (in the *Instrumental*);—that is to say, in all the rules laying down the use of Nominal affixes, we find that its use is laid down by means of words with those very case-endings, which themselves are capable of signifying the same meaning that is meant to be expressed by the Nominal affix laid down; for instance, we have such rules as (1) '*tad vahati*' (with the Objective), (2) '*tena kṛtam*' (with the Instrumental), (3) '*tasmai hitam*' (with the Dative), (4) '*tata āgataḥ*' (with the Ablative), (5) *tasyāpatyam* (with the Possessive-Genitive), and (6) '*tatra bhavaḥ*' (with the Locative);—in the case of the *Deity*, however, we find that the appearance of the Nominal affix expressive of the Deity, is laid down by such words as '*sa'sya devatā*,' and not as '*tasyai idam*' (with the Dative) or '*tāmanēna*' (with the Objective). And hence we conclude that the Deity is not denotable by any other means save by the actual mention of the word 'Deity' itself, or by the Nominal affixes specially laid down as expressing the Deity.

Thus then, it must be admitted that the sentence '*Vishṇurupānçu yashṭavyaḥ*' does not serve the purpose of pointing out a Deity. And consequently, in taking this sentence as an independent Injunction, we would have to get at the requisite *Bhāvanā* only by undertaking all the trouble of assuming a Deity. And certainly in comparison with all these assumptions, it is more reasonable by far to take the sentence as a mere *Arthavāda* (of the sacrifice laid down in '*antarā yajati*').

On the other hand, in the case of the sentence '*antarā yajati*'—though it might be argued that it is an injunction of the *time* (of the sacrifice) as the "interrim",—and as such it cannot be taken as laying down the sacrifice itself,—yet, as there is no other way of taking it, we take the sentence to be an Injunction of the *sacrifice as qualified by the particular time*; specially as we find that this sentence cannot be taken otherwise, not even as an *Arthavāda* like the other sentences ('*vishṇuḥ* etc.).'

Objection: "But we have shown above that the sentence '*antarā*, etc. " has its use in speaking of the three sacrifices (to Vishṇu, etc.) as one "composite whole".

Reply: How the sentence cannot serve this purpose we shall show later on, when explaining the *sūtra* '*anyārthadarçanāt*' [II—iii—29]. And further, in this sentence we find that inasmuch as the '*interrim*' is a point of time, it cannot form the predicate of a sentence; and as such (the 'interrim' not being an object of Injunction), we admit the *Action* to be the object of the Injunction contained in the sentence; and then too, as we find that the *sacrifice* in question, that could be connected with the *time*, is not laid down (in any other sentence), we have also to admit the sentence ('*antarā*, etc.') to be the *original* Injunction of the *sacrifice* also. That is to say, in the sentence in question, we find that a distinct self-sufficient *Bhāvanā*, with all its accessories, is laid down with reference to a point of time (the "*interrim*") which, by itself, could be the predicate of the sentence; and we do not find any such *Bhāvanā* denoted by the sentences '*vishṇuryashṭavyaḥ*, etc.'; and hence there is nothing incongruous in accepting the former sentence as the *original* Injunction (of that *Bhāvanā*).

Even if the sentences '*vishṇuḥ*, etc.' could be taken as injunctions of sacrifices, the particular sacrifice laid down by the sentence '*antarā*, etc.' must be an entirely distinct one; and this sentence could not be taken as merely referring to these sacrifices. It is with a view to this that the *Bhāshya* has declared—*karmāntarasya vācakaḥ syāt*. As there is nothing incompatible in the Deity being an object of Injunction, the sentences '*vishṇuḥ*, etc.' could be taken as laying down *deities* for the sacrifice (enjoined by the former sentence); and thus too we find that it is these sentences ('*vishṇuḥ*, etc.') that serve the purpose of *referring* to a previously enjoined sacrifice (for the purpose of laying down its Deities), and not the former sentence itself.

Even if these sentences are taken as Injunctions of Sacrifices, though there is an original sacrifice (in the shape of that enjoined by the sentence '*antarā*, etc.'), yet there are no such original sacrifices as have Vishṇu, etc., for their Deities;—this is what the word '*aprakṛtatvāt*' in the *sūtra* means.

Or the *Bhāshya*—'*karmāntarasya vācakaḥ syāt*'—may be explained in the following manner: the sentence '*antarā*, etc.' would denote only that sacrifice which is enjoined as distinct from the *Āgnēya* and the rest. Consequently on account of the time "interrim" not being capable of forming the predicate, it must be admitted that the sentence is the absolute Injunction of a sacrifice; and as such the other sentences must be mere *Arthavādas*. And as for the Injunctive affix (in *antarā yajāti*), it would be functioning more closely when laying down the denotation of the root with reference to something else (in the shape of the particular point of time).

Says the *Bhāshya—sa tu vidhīyatē upānçuyagasambandhaḥ*; and the sense of this is that the word *upançuyājam* lays down an accessory detail of the sacrifice (*viz.*, that the sacrifice is to be performed with *mantras* quietly recited).

Against this view it has been argued that "the word '*upançu-yājam*' "cannot be taken in that sense, as in that case the form of the word would "become '*upançuyāgam.*'"

And in reply to this we urge that this objection applies equally to the opponent also; because in the case of all words, what is desired first of all is the cognition of the relationship between the word and the meaning it denotes; and it is only after this cognition that we come to ascertain that meaning to have the character of an *Injunction* or that of a mere *Reference.* That is to say, when the fact of a certain meaning being denoted by a certain word has been duly ascertained, it is only then that the object thus denoted comes to be taken either as *Injunction* or as the *enjoined*, as the *referred* to or as the *reference*; in all these cases, however, the relationship of the word to its meaning continues to be the common factor, and as this relationship always remains constant, whatever its character might be (and it is only on this latter point that we differ), the excellences or defects in that relationship would be equally applicable to both of us; and hence any such defect should not have been urged against any one of us only.

On this point, it might be argued that—"as a matter of fact we find "that a descriptive reference is made even by such words as are not "directly expressive of the object described; but no injunction is ever "found to be brought about by means of non-expressive words; and as such "the objection is not equally applicable to both of us."

To this we reply that in our case also, the sacrifice being enjoined by the word '*yajati*,' the word '*yāja*' could be taken as referring to it; and the *upānçutva* mentioned along with '*yāja*', being taken as connected with the aforesaid Injunction, there would be no incongruousness at all.

Nor could the word '*upānçuyāja*' be taken as the name of a sacrifice according to the *sūtra* I—iv—4; because '*upānçu-tva*' has not been enjoined by any other text. For instance, it cannot be taken as enjoined by the sentences '*vishṇuḥ*, etc.'; because these have been shown to be mere *Arthavādas*; nor by the sentence '*upānçu paurṇamāsyām*'; because this sentence is wholly taken up by the laying down of the *time* (*paurṇamāsi*), and it is not capable of further injunctions. Therefore, we must admit it to be enjoined by the word '*upānçu*' occurring in the original Injunction itself ('*antarā*, etc.'); this will be pointed out in the next *sūtra* also.

As for the removal of the flaw of '*jāmi*,' this is known to be possible in various ways—for instance, (1) by means of a material, (2) by accentuation, or (3) by means of a Deity. And hence in the case in question, when it is found that a '*jāmi*' has occurred, we find that for making it up some sort of a sacrifice—whether to Vishṇu, or to Prajāpatī or to Agnīshoma, or to some other Deity—is enjoined; and then no definite Deity being recognised, as the one to whom the requisite sacrifice has to be offered, the Veda, meaning to show the fact of the Deities of the sacrifice being various, mentions *Vishṇuḥ* and some other well-known Deities; and hence though in the sentences in question Vishṇu etc. are not the only Deities to whom the sacrifice has to be offered, yet the mention of these, though only by way of eulogising (the sacrifice through these well-known Deities), may, somehow or other, be taken as laying down the accessory (Deities) of the sacrifice.

The Bhāshya represents another party declaring that—'*these sacrifices (to Vishṇu &c.) are enjoined in the texts of other rescensions of the Veda.*' But no such texts are cited; and if any weight could be attached to such vague assertions, then there would be nothing that would want a corroborative proof; and further, we find that in Adhyāya X, *sūtra* 49, the question of the Deity has been raised, and answered in *sūtra* 52, by showing that the Deity is one that is indicated by the words of the *mantra* employed; and all these discussions would be futile if we had any such texts as declared by the opponent. And as a matter of fact, that the opponent himself had doubts on the point of there being such a text is clearly shown by his own half-hearted declaration—"*even if they be not laid down by such a text, etc.*"

Then the opponent has declared (in the *Bhāṣhya*) that—"the property of '*upānçu*' having been laid down, some action is performed in honour of Prajāpati, during the sacrifice." But this too is scarcely correct; because that would upset the syntactical order of the word; as we have no such sentence as that 'that which is *upānçu* belongs to Prajāpati',—the sentence that we have is in the form 'that which belongs to Prajāpati is *upānçu*.' Therefore the mere property of '*upānçu*' cannot point to the fact of *belonging to Prajāpati*.

Then again, the *Bhāshya* itself declares that *we actually cite the text enjoining Agni and Soma as the Deities.* And against this assertion, the following objections have been raised: "The sentence cited in the Bhāshya "cannot serve the purpose of laying down the Deity, because it is neither "the Dative ending, nor the Deific-nominal affix, nor the words of a *mantra* "(which three are the only means of mentioning the Deity). (2) Be-"cause Agni and Soma made a certain declaration, what would that "matter to the sacrificer, who would remain in the dark as to that declara-"tion pointing to him the Deity to be sacrificed to? (3) The sentence "being a distinct injunction of the *time* (*Pūrṇamāsī*), it cannot serve the "further injunctive purpose of laying down the Deity; and if it be taken "as the Injunction of the Deity, it would have to renounce its injunctive-"ness with regard to the *time*; and then the sacrifice could not be referred "to by the word '*Paurṇamāsī*'; and not being expressible by the "word '*Paurṇamāsī*' (and thereby having no connection with the "sentence '*darçapūrṇamāsabhyām*, etc.') it would cease to be a primary, "and become a subsidiary sacrifice. The author of the *sūtra* also, in "Adhyāya X, has brought forward the sentence cited as an Injunction of "time, with the sole aim of showing that the '*Amāvāsyā*' is not an "*Upānçuyāja*."

In answer to these objections we have the following arguments: It has been found that the Deity is indicated by the words of the *mantra*. In the order of the *upānçuyāja*, we find mentioned the *mantras* dedicated to Vishṇu, Prajāpati and Agnīshoma, as also the pairs of *Yājyas* and *Puronuvākyās*; and as all of them serve the purpose (of pointing out the Deity for the *Upānçuyāja*), they come to be taken as optional alternatives; and consequently, the choice of a Deity also becomes optional. And it is that section of the Veda where these *mantras* appear which has been spoken of as the '*mantra*'-section of another Rescension of the Vedic text. In fact, even in the '*Ādhvaryava*' section we find the mention of the *Yājyās* and the *Anuvākyās*, in the shape of the *Hautra*; and the mention of 'another Rescension' may be with reference to this fact (of the *Hautra* appearing in the *Ādhvaryava*). And the mention of the qualification '*upānçu*' too is for the purpose of showing this fact of the *mantra* belonging to another Rescension (*viz*: that of the *Yajush*; as it is the *Yajush* that is recited quietly). Otherwise if another Deity (that of the *Ṛk* for instance) were to be brought into the *Upānçuyāja*, then it would have to renounce its own characteristic of *loudness* (belonging to the Ṛk) and to take up the foreign characteristic of *quietness* (belonging to the *Yajush*); and this would entail a great incongruity. It would be very incongruous again if we assume another Deity in place of *Agnīshoma*. In the case of *Vishṇu* and *Prajāpati*, however, we find that their properties are quite close to them, and hence there is no incongruity in this case (that is to say there is no incongruity if we assume another Deity in place of Vishṇu, etc.; and hence though the objection applies to the *Pūrvapaksha*, it does not apply to our case).

The declaration of the *Bhāshyā*—'*tātha'gnīshomayostu*, etc.'—means that no injunction of the Deity being possible, the Deity is accepted according to circumstances; and hence in the sentence laying down *Pūrṇamāsī* as the time, a reference to *Agnīshoma* strengthens the introduction of the Deity (without which the said Reference would be wholly inconsistent).

Sūtra (11) : *Because of the mention of the Property.*

That action (is enjoined by the sentence '*antarā*, etc.') in connection with which we find the property of '*upānçu*' mentioned in the sentence '*upānçu paurṇamāsyām yajan*', which serves the purpose of laying down the time (*Paurṇamāsī*) for the sacrifice. But this sentence is not the original injunction of the said property; because the sentence not embodying an injunction of a sacrifice, the said injunction of the property would involve the injunction of many things (which is highly objectionable). And for this reason we must take the sentence '*upānçu paurṇamāsyām*, etc.' as only describing that which has been enjoined by the sentence '*antarā* etc.'

Sūtra (12): *Because of the mention of the 'Prāye.'*

We find the sentence '*hṛdayamupānçuyājah*', which eulogises the *Upānçu* sacrifice *as if it were* (*prāya*) the principal limb (heart) of the Sacrificial Person; and thus clearly shows that it is a Primary (and not Secondary) sacrifice.

Question: "But how does the *pūrvapaksha* make the *Upānçu* a sub-"sidiary sacrifice?"

Answer: The *Upānçu* being (according to the *pūrvapaksha*) taken as referring only to the three sacrifices to Vishṇu, etc., as one composite whole, it is the *Agnīshomīya* sacrifice alone that would come to be enjoined as to be performed on the *Paurṇamāsī*; that is to say, in that case, the mention of '*Pūrṇamāsa*' would point out, as leading to the particular result, only that one sacrifice—connected with the particular time—and having Agnīshoma for its Deity—which is mentioned by the sentence '*tāvavrūtāmagnīshomau*, etc.' And inasmuch as the sacrifices to *Vishṇu* and *Prajāpati* are subsidiary to that sacrifice, the whole sentence declaring the primary character of the *Upānçu* sacrifice (*viz.*: '*hṛdayamupānçuyājaḥ*') becomes incompatible and incongruous.

Objection: "In your case also, there being the anomaly of various "optional alternative Deities, the character of the Primary would belong "to the sacrifice only when *Agnīshoma* would be the Deity sacrificed to; "and hence, even according to you, the mention of the everlasting "Primary character of the *Upānçu* is not altogether compatible."

Reply: This does not touch our position; because we do not find the sentence '*tāvavrūtām*, etc.' enjoining any connection between the *time* (*Paurṇamāsī*) and the *deity* (Agnīshoma); and as for the Action itself, which is meant to be indicated by the *time* and *deity*,—it is found to exist in other places also (for instance, in the sacrifices to *Vishṇu*, etc.).

That is to say, if the sentence were to lay down the connection of

Paurṇamāsi with the deity *Agnīshoma* alone, then such connection would not be present in the case of Vishṇu or Prajāpati being the deity. What, however, the sentence actually does is to mention the connection of the *time* with the *Action* qualified by the deity *Agnīshoma.* And in every case we find that when the qualification is absent, the qualified object becomes cognised by itself, as we shall show under the *sūtra*—'*anapāyaçca kālasya lakshaṇam hī puroḍāçau.*'

Nor is it possible for the same Action to be the primary at one time, and subsidiary at another. Such double character would be possible only if there were many *Upānçu*-sacrifices; but this multiplicity of the *Upānçu* is not possible; in view of the singleness of the *Upānçu* sacrifice, we must admit, as an Injunction, only the sentence '*upānçuyājamantarā yajati*' (and not the sentences '*vishnurupānçu yashṭavyaḥ*, etc.').

ADHIKARANA (5).

[*Treating of the independent character of the Āghāra*, etc.]

***Sūtra* (13): "*The words* '*Āghāram*' *and* '*Agnihotram*' (are mere references) *because they are without accessory details.*"**

[This *adhikaraṇa* is based upon two sets of passages. (1) We have the sentences '*ūrdhvamāghārayati*,' '*santatamāgharayati*,' and '*ṛjumāghārayati*,' followed by '*āghāramāghārayatī*'; and (2) we have the sentences '*dadhnā juhoti*,' and '*payasā juhoti*, etc.', followed by '*agnīhotram juhoti*'. And the question is as to whether the two sentences '*āghāramāghārayati*' and '*agnihotram juhoti*' lay down actions totally distinct from those mentioned in the preceding sentences, or they only refer to those same actions? And the position taken up by the *Pūrvapaksha* is that the sentence '*āghāramāgharayati*' only refers collectively to the set of actions mentioned by the sentences '*ūrdhvam*, etc.'; and so also with the sentence '*agnihotram juhoti*'. Nor can this Adhikaraṇa be said to have been included in the foregoing one; because] The '*āghāra*' and the '*homa*' that present themselves to the mind, on the utterance of the sentence '*ūrdhvamāghārayati*' and '*payasā juhoti*', are exactly as they are pointed out by these sentences; nor in this case is there a suppression of the *Bhāvanās* of the '*yāga*' and the '*homa*' by the supervening character of the material; as we have in the case of the sentence '*vishṇurupānçu yashṭavyaḥ*.' And further, in the case in question the various sentences cannot be taken together as forming a single sentence (as in the previous *Adhikaraṇa*); nor does any of the two parties admit of the fact of the sentences being mere eulogistic ones; and hence the Injunction would be an absolute one, of the Action, just as (in the previous case) you hold it to be that of the Accessory.

That is to say, we do not, as in the case of the sentences '*upānçu*, etc.', admit the fact of all the sentences in question forming a single sentence; nor do they serve the purposes of glorification; and hence according to both parties, the sentences come to be accepted as Injunctions; and the only question that arises is as to whether the Injunction is one of the Accessory only, or that of the Action as accompanied by that Accessory? And on this we have the following—

PŪRVAPAKSHA.

"The Injunction is one of the Action. Because the Injunctiveness, "being mentioned by the Affix, can never belong to the Noun. It may be "urged that the Injunction of the Noun would follow from the *Bhāvanā*; "but in that case, it would be the *Bhāvanā* that would be enjoined first.

"That is to say, the Injunctive character does not rest with the "words '*dadhi*' and the rest; and being expressed by the Affix, that "character could not be related to the Curd, etc., except by means of "the *Bhāvanā* and the *Root-meaning*. For we have no such sentence as "'*dadhṇā-yāt*' (the '*yāt*' being the injunctive affix only, apart from the "Verbal Root); the sentence that we have is '*dadhnā kuryāt*' where the "relationship of the *dadhi* with the *affix* is through the root '*kṛ*.' Thus "then, the performability of the *dadhi*, etc., being due solely to the *Bhāvanā* "and the *Root-meaning*,—how is it that these letters are denied to be the "objects of Injunction? For, certainly, without the injunction of these, we "can never point out any injunction of the Accessory. Because no sooner "do we proceed to show such an Injunction than the Injunction of the "*Bhāvanā* and the *Root-meaning* presents itself forcibly. Consequently we "must admit that what is enjoined is either the *Homa* or the *Bhāvanā as* "*qualified by the dadhi*, etc.

"And then, each of these *Bhāvanās*, being duly recognised as having "distinct accessory details of its own, the very fact of their following one "after the other, points to the fact of their forming a single collective "whole; and it follows that it is this collective whole that is referred to "by the sentence '*agnihotram juhoti*.' And the use of this reference lies "in the unification of the Injunctions of the *Means* and the *Result* of these "sacrifices. And thus *dadhi* and the other materials, each belonging to a "distinct Action by itself, we are saved the undue necessity of taking them "as optional alternatives.

"In the same manner, in the case of the sentences '*ūrdhvamāghāra-* "*yati*, etc. etc.',—though we do not find the material or the Deity of these "mentioned, yet, in accordance with the rule laid down in connection with "'*upānçu*', qualifications of '*ūrdhva*, etc.' may be taken as specifying "differentias; and through these those Actions being taken as having "their accessories mentioned, it is only the action mentioned by the "sentence '*āghāramāghārayati*' that remains without a mention of its "accessory details; and as such, being wholly incapable of attracting men "towards itself, it has to be taken as a mere reference to the pre- "viously mentioned sacrifices. And in this case too, the use of such "reference lies in the unification (of the three sacrifices) which is necessary "for the purpose of the employing in them of the *mantra* '*iḍa ūrdhvo* "*adhvara*, etc.'; and the connection of the single Deity mentioned in the "sentences '*tasyāghāramāghārya*, etc.'

Sūtra (14): "*Also because of the application of the "names ('āghāra' and 'agnihotra').*"

" And further, names are employed only with a view to pointing out "a certain definite peculiarity; and in the case in question we do not "perceive what these peculiarities are (that are pointed out by the names "'*aghāra*' and '*agnihotra*' unless we take them as referring to the fore-"going sacrifices). If the name '*agnihotra*' were taken only as pointing to "*Homa in general*, then, inasmuch this is already known, it would not be "any new Action (mentioned by the word). And as already known, there "is nothing in it that has to be known; and as such no injunction of that "would be possible.

"Then again, *Actions*, not having the character of Nouns, could never "be connected with the Accusative ending (*i.e.*, if the word '*agnihotra*' "lays down an Action, it could not take the Accusative ending). As for "the *collective whole* (formed by the various actions), this can very "well serve as the objective, because such a whole is actually *brought* "*about* by the constituent actions.

"That is to say, the presence of the Accusative in the words "'*āghāram*' and '*agnihotram*' would be possible only for a Noun that "would be *wanted* by the Verb; and certainly the actions of '*homa*' and "'*āghāra*' could never *want* to get at themselves; because such self-activity "would be incompatible. As for the collective whole (of Actions), how-"ever, inasmuch as it is mentioned apart from the constituent actions, by "means of another word, it can very well be spoken of as *something to be* "*accomplished*; just as in the case of the sentence '*odanpākam pacati*' the "particular kind of cooking is *wanted* by the generic cooking mentioned by "the Verb; and as such it is spoken of in the Accusative.

"*Objection*: "The *whole* having no existence apart from the parts, it "can never have the character of *something to be accomplished*; and as "such, even in this case, the Accusative ending is not proper".

"*Reply*: Not so; because the *whole* is something that is actually "*brought about* by a conglomeration of the constituent Actions. It is only "from the constituent parts taken together that the *whole* cannot be held to "be different; from each of them individually, however, there is no doubt "that the *whole* is totally distinct; and it being impossible for the *whole* "to be accomplished without the individual constituents, there is nothing "incongruous in the Accusative character of the former.

"*Objection*: "All such words (as '*agnihotra*') have been on a former "occasion shown to be expressive of the constituent actions; and hence "the undue self-activity of these constituents remains as incongruous "as before."

"*Reply*: This does not affect our position; because even though the "noun may directly denote the parts, it could be taken as indirectly in-"dicating the *whole*; and as such, like its *singleness*, the accusative "character also of the *whole* could very well be perceived. Nor is it "possible, as in the case of the *cooking*, for the same action to be expressed "by the Verb and also by the Accusative, through its two-fold character "of the *general* and the *particular*; because in the case in question, we do "not have the *general* and the *particular* actually mentioned.

"The above arguments could be applied, on behalf of the *siddhānta*, "to the case of the sentence '*paurṇamāsīm*, etc.'; and hence also it "follows that like the word '*paurṇamāsī*' '*agnihotram*' also should be "taken as a mere reference to the foregoing sacrifices.

Sūtra (15): "*Because of its not being* Prakṛta (related to the Context)."

"*Objection*: 'Under *sūtra* II—ii—5, the view was stated that the "Action would obtain its accessories from the other sentences, which "are Injunctions of accessories only; and in the same manner, in the "case in question, the sentence '*agnihotram juhoti*' may be taken as the "originative injunction of an Action, which would have its accessories as "mentioned by the sentences '*taṇḍulair juhoti*', '*dadhnā juhoti*, etc.'

"*Reply*: This cannot be; because in the case cited the doubt as to "the particular words being mere references rested upon the words "'*paurṇamāsya*' and '*amāvāsyā*' occurring in the sentences themselves; "in the case in question, on the other hand, we do not find the word "'*agnihotra*' in the sentences '*taṇḍulair juhoti*, etc.'; the word '*juhoti*' "that we do find in these is common to all *Homas*; and as such cannot be "taken as pointing to the injunction of the *Agnihotra* alone.

"*Objection*: 'The particular *Homa* would be indicated by the *Pra-*"*karaṇa*. (Context, or mutual want).'

"*Reply*: Not so; *because of there being no prakaraṇa*. That is to say, "in the originative sentence ('*agnihotram juhoti*') we do not find any "'*prakaraṇa*' of Actions; because it is only after the action has been "connected with a particular result, that there arises a *prakaraṇa* (or "desire) of knowing how that Result is to be brought about by means of "that Action; and as such the *Prakaraṇa* could only proceed from the "assumed sentence that would sum up all the three factors of the *Bhāvanā* "in connection with the Action in question.

"The following may be urged against us; 'The *Agnihotra* would be "connected with its Deity and *Material*, when it would appear in the "assumed sentence you speak of (and thus it would be an Action by "itself).'

"In reply to this it is urged that an Action that has its accessory "details unknown, could never be enjoined with reference to a definite "result; and hence it is only such actions as have their details fully "known that can be mentioned in the aforesaid assumed sentence, (and "these Actions are the various actions mentioned by the different '*juhoti*'s).

"*Objection*: 'We have such sentences as *tasyāghāramāghārya*, etc., "*iḍa ūrdhvo*, etc., *āghāram*, etc.,—which are found to point out the "*material* and the *mantric* Deity; and as such the mere mention of the "name (*Āghāra*) would point out its accessory details.'

"*Reply*: Not so; because the word '*āghāra*,' apart from the denota-"tion of its verbal Root, cannot serve the purposes of a specification. A "name expresses a peculiarity only in that case where the *name* has "been applied with a distinct reference to a certain peculiarity. In the "case in question, however, we have in close proximity such sentences as "'*ūrdhvamāghārayati*', where the literal denotation of the verb is found to "be quite perceptible; and as such even in the sentence '*āghāramāghāra-yati*,' the word '*āghāram*' cannot be taken in any other sense, save the "literal one of *pouring*; and as such it cannot be taken as pointing to "any particular *pouring*.

"*Objection*: 'The particular *pouring* would be got at from the *Pra-karaṇa*.'

"In reply to this, we have the present *sūtra*, which means that the "*āghāra* is not the '*prakrta*'; because it occurs in a context dealing with "the *Darça-paurṇamāsa*: and certainly the *Prakaraṇa* of one Action can "have no application in the case of another.

"*Objection*: 'The particular action could be pointed out by means of "proximity.'

"In reply to this also we have this same *sūtra*,—the sense being that "what you say is not possible, because it is only the superior authority of "Syntactical Connection that can establish a relationship with something "not occurring in the same context. And thus there is an agreement be-"tween *Syntactical Connection* and *Context*, when the originative sentences "themselves are admitted to have within themselves the mention of the "material and the Deity. It is only when even a slight detail of the "Action is mentioned, that the character of the Action being thereby duly "ascertained, other details come to be connected with it, in some way or "another. And in the cases in question, we find that in regard to each "of the actions, we have such details as '*ūrdhva*,' etc., and '*taṇḍula*', etc.; "whereas we have not the slightest details mentioned in the two "sentences '*āgharamāghārayati*' and '*agnihotram juhoti.*' Consequently "these two sentences cannot but be taken as merely referring to the "former Actions."

SIDDHĀNTA.

Sūtra (16): ***They are injunctions*** **(of independent Actions);** ***because the words distinctly express something to be performed; and the repetition of the same words is for the purpose of laying down the accessory details.***

The Bhāshya speaks of the sentences being the *Injunctions* of *other* actions; though what is meant is that they are Injunctions of Actions; hence this assertion of the *Bhāshya* should be taken as shown above (on p. 486 of the *text*, *Translation*, p. 674).

It is clearly perceived that the words '*āghārayati*' (in '*āghāramāghārayati*') and *juhoti*' (in '*agnihotram juhoti*'), not having their Injunctive potency taken up by any other word, cannot but distinctly express the injunction of definite actions. Nor can it be urged that the actions of '*Āghāra*' and '*Homa*' are already enjoined by the sentences '*ūrdhvam*, etc.' and '*dadhnā*,' etc.; because the Injunctive potency of these sentences is taken up by the laying down of the accessories in the shape of '*ūrdhva*' and '*dadhi*', which are not laid down by any other sentence; and as such we cannot very well discard the idea of these sentences merely referring (by the words '*āgharāyati*' and '*juhoti*') to the actions of *Āghāra* and *Homa* (enjoined by the two former sentences).

Nor is the law of 'Qualified Injunction' (*sūtra* I—iv—9) applicable to these sentences, because of the saving clause '*if they are not enjoined by another sentence.*' It is this that is meant to be shown by the Bhāshya:—*In the case of the sentences* '*ūrdhvam, etc.*' *the injunction of the action of the Āghāra and Homa could not be indirectly indicated by the expressed relationship of the* '*dadhi*' *and* '*ūrdhva*'; *because so long as we have direct injunctions of these actions (in the sentences* '*āghāram, etc.*' *and* '*agnihotram, etc.*'), *they cannot be taken as indirectly indicated, etc.* And the sense of this is that so long as we have direct Injunctions, we cannot have them as indirectly indicated by any relationships; or that so long as we have an Injunction of a member of relationship, the other sentences may be taken as laying down accessories, and as such we cannot accept *mere relationship.* Consequently it is not possible for the actions of *Āghāra* and *Homa* to be indicated by the injunctions of relationships, independently of the two sentences ('*āghāram*, etc.' and '*agnihotram*, etc.'); and as such on the mere strength of any such indication, these latter sentences cannot be taken as mere *references* to previously enjoined actions.

It may be argued that—"no Injunction could ever give up the *Bhāvanā* and the Root-meaning, and betake itself to the *Dadhi* (as held by you)". This is quite true; but we do not dissociate the Injunction from the *Bhāvanā* altogether; what we mean is that the accessory—*dadhi*—is touched by the Injunction as pertaining to the *Bhāvanā*; specially as the case-ending (in '*dadhnā*') serves to throw that accessory into the *Bhāvanā*.

Thus then, the upshot of all this is that, whenever we come across an Injunction of a qualified Action, what we have to consider, in the first instance, is what factor of the object of Injunction is such as has been laid down elsewhere, and what is not so; and when this has been duly discriminated, the Injunction comes to be taken as pertaining wholly to that factor which has not been laid down elsewhere; in the case of the sentence '*dadhnā juhoti*', as the object of injunction is the action of *Homā as qualified by Dadhi*, when we find that the *Homa* has already been laid down by the sentence '*agnihotram juhoti*', we conclude the Injunction in question to pertain to the *Dadhi* only, and the *Bhāvanā* and the *Root-meaning* (denoted in '*dadhnā juhoti*') are said to be mere references to those enjoined elsewhere; and it is never said that from the very beginning the sentence '*dadhnā juhoti*' enjoins only the accessory with reference to the previously enjoined *Bhāvanā* and *Root-meaning.*

Thus then, it is this subsequent restriction of the Injunction with a view to explain which, to people of dull intellects, our Author has laid down a sort of a rule which is not very accurate; and some people have been led to regard this to be the actual view of the author himself: and as such with a view to lead people astray, just as they themselves have been led astray, these people laid down the following eight methods of the Direct Injunction (of Actions), where the one that follows is held to be weaker in its authority than the preceding one: (1) the injunction of the Root-meaning; (2) the injunction of the qualified Root-meaning; (3) the injunction of the Root-meaning with reference to something else; (4) the injunction of the qualified Root-meaning with reference to something else; (5) the injunction of something else with reference to the Root-meaning; (6) the injunction of the Relationship of the Root-meaning with the other two; (7) the injunction of the Relationship of the Affix as qualified by the Root-meaning with the other two; and (8) the injunction of the Relationship of the other two, apart from the Root-meaning.

Now then, as an instance of (1), people cite the sentence '*agnihotram juhoti*'. But this is scarcely correct; because it is never the case that the Injunction renounces the *Bhāvanā* and betakes itself to the Root-meaning; nor does a man ever engage himself with anything other than the *Bhāvanā*; because it is the *Bhāvanā* wherein is centred the activity of the agent; while the Root-meaning often rests in the Action only; as for instance, the *offering* (which is the meaning of the Root in '*juhoti*') rests in the *partition of the cake* (offered); and certainly the action of one can never be performed by another; consequently it must be admitted that the meaning of the Root '*hū*' as qualified by the *dadhi*, etc., is enjoined only as specifying the particular *Bhāvanā* (and not independently by itself). And it has been already explained under *sūtra* II—i—1 that the Root-meaning is never enjoined as *something to be accomplished* (but only as an Instrument); and when it is not an Instrument (but something to be accomplished), it does not stand in need of another object to be accomplished; and as such it could not be enjoined, by any other sentence, with reference to any definite Result.

As an instance of (2), they quote '*somēna yajēta*'; but here also, in accordance with the method laid down under I—i—25, the Root-meaning and the various objects spoken of in the sentence, bearing no definite relationship among themselves, just like the 'redness,' 'one year old', etc. in the sentence '*aruṇayā*, etc.,' come to help one another only after they have been connected with the *Bhāvanā*; as we shall show further on, in the beginning of Adhyāyas VII and IX; and as such there can be no Injunction of the qualified Root-meaning. And if the '*yāga*' (the Root-meaning), having the character of the Instrument towards the *Bhāvanā*, were to be an objective to the material offered, then we would have the anomaly pointed out under *sūtra* I—iv—8; and hence there can be no Injunction of the qualified Root-meaning.

As an example of (3) they quote '*vrīhīn prokshati*'; but in this case we are cognisant of no such relationship, as '*prokshaṇēna vrīhīn*'; (because both are *kārakas* and as such cannot be related) and hence both of these being related to the sense of '*karoti*' (the sense of the sentences being '*prokshaṇeña vrīhīn kuryāt*), it is not the meaning of the Root ('*proksha*') that is enjoined with reference to the *vrihi*. If its Injunction be spoken of as referring to the *Bhāvanā*, then such injunction of the *Bhāvanā* being present in all cases (there would be no difference in the various methods of Injunction): consequently the present method of Injunction could not be any weaker, (the ground of its having a qualified object; and as such there is no reason why it should be given the third place.

As an instance of (4) they cite '*daçāpavītreṇa graham sammārshṭi*'; but the arguments urged against the last two apply to this also; and hence it is not right to accept the Injunction of the qualified Root-meaning with reference to something else.

As an instance of (5) they quote '*dadhnā juhoti*'; but in this case also the words do not signify that *the person does the dadhi in the Homa* ('*dadhi homē karoti*'); because the Homa is neither expressed by the word, as a *place*; nor is it so, in the actual state of things; nor is the *dadhi something to be done*, because it has always the character of the Instrument. This method of Injunction is more authoritative than the two methods of qualified Injunction; because so long as the Injunction of one only is possible (as in the present instance), it is not right for it to appertain to many; and as for the anomaly of the Injunction pertaining to something removed from it, this is common to both parties; and as such cannot be brought forward against any one party only; and the remote object is admitted only because of the impossibility of a more proximate object; and where both (the Remote and the Proximate) are accepted, the anomaly of the simultaneous acceptance of two contradictory objects, as also of the simultaneous possibility and impossibility of the same, would be admitted, only because there is no way out of it; and in cases other than these, it would not be any more complicated than the Injunction of the qualified Root-meaning; and as such this should have been placed in the fifth place. In fact it should have been mentioned either immediately after the Injunction of the pure Root-meaning, or after that of the Root-meaning with regard to something else.

As an instance of (6), they quote '*prākāçau adhvaryavē dadāti*,' where, it is held, the relationship of the *Prākāça* with the *Adhvaryu* is enjoined with reference to the meaning of the verb '*dadāti*'. But this is scarcely correct; because such an interpretation bespeaks a sad want of a due understanding of the syntax of the sentence; as in all sentences that which is introduced by the word '*yat*' is the subject, and that which is mentioned by the word '*tat*' is the Predicate. Consequently, in the sentence in question, if it were meant to enjoin the relationship of the *Prākāça* and the *Adhvaryu*, in *that which is given* ('*yat dadāti*'), then inasmuch as this latter clause would refer to all '*givings*', the sentence would come to mean that all sacrificial gifts are to be transformed into the *Prākāça*; and as for the capability of enjoining more than one thing (*i.e.*, the *Adhvaryu* and the *Prākāça*), it has not been denied in the case of the action being an enjoined one. Whenever a relation is enjoined, it always implies the members related; in the case of the injunction of the Root-meaning, however, there is no relative member to be laid down; for otherwise the Relative would be subordinate to the Relationship, and not to the Action.

Here it may be argued that—"the affix accompanied by the Root-meaning, while laying down the Relationship, would lay it down with reference to the Root-meaning." If this be meant, then the next two (7 and 8) methods of Injunction would be included in this; and it would be useless to speak of them separately. Either in the sentence '*vāyavyam çvetamālabhēta*' (cited as an instance of 7) or in '*dadhnēndriyakāmasya juhuyāt*' (cited as an instance of 8), the Affix accompanied by the Root-meaning does not lay down the Relationship; as a matter of fact, the root '*ālabha*,' being uttered only as a mark of the Primary Sacrifice in question, does not in any way help, by its colouring, in the injunction of the Relationship between the material (*çveta*) and the Deity (*Vāyu*); nor can this relationship be accomplished by means of the root '*ālabha*'; because the Deity and the Material appertain to the *sacrifice* (and not to the *ālambhana*, touching *killing*). If, in the accomplishment of the relationship, the Root did anything besides the bringing about of the utterance of the affix, then, in the case of the injunction of the Relationship between the *Dadhi* and the *sense-organs*, why should the *Homa* have been left out? Or again, why should the *Homa* be taken only as pointed out by the context? Therefore we conclude that there can be no injunction of the relationship of something else, with reference to the Root-meaning. And as shown above, we should deny the fact of the Root-meaning being a place, and also that of the *kāraka* (or thing) being something to be *done*. And it has already been explained that prior to the connection of the *Bhāvanā*, there is no injunction of even the Relationship, with reference to the Root-meaning.

Thus then, we cannot take the sentence as laying down the Relationship with reference to all *givings*. If the *giving* be taken *as qualified by the Adhvaryu*, or the *Adhvaryu* be taken *as qualified by the giving*, even then, as these would be a qualified reference, there would be a syntactical split. If the reference be to the *Adhvaryu* alone, then, though the *giving* would certainly be implied by the Dative ending (in '*adhvaryavē*'), yet, inasmuch as the peculiar relationship between the *object given* and the *person receiving the gift* would not be possible without the verb '*dadāti*', we would have to assume the latter; just as the verb '*yajāti*' has to be assumed from the relationship of a certain material with a Deity; and hence there can be no form of the sentence, wherein there could be a relationship of the other two, with reference to the Root-meaning. As a matter of fact in the case in question, the *giving* and the *Adhvaryu* being such as have been laid down elsewhere, what the sentence in question does is to lay down only the two *Prākāças*; and in this case the injunction of the Relationship is implied; and hence it is not right to bring this forward as a distinct method of Injunction. This will be further explained under the '*Jāghanyādhikaraṇa*' (*sūtras* III—iii—20-22), where it is shown that where out of two things, any one is such as has not been previously laid down, it is this latter that is enjoined with reference to the former (which has been enjoined elsewhere), and their Relationship is implied;—while in a case where both are such as have been laid down elsewhere, or where none of them is so, we have the injunction of the Relationship only.

In all these three (the sixth, the seventh and the eighth) cases, the fact of the Relationship being implied by the Affix is common; and as such there can be no difference in the strength or weakness of their authority. Nor is it possible for us ever to be faced by a contradiction of these three methods, when all of them happen to apply to the same cases—where a knowledge of their comparative strength or weakness could be of use to us; and hence the mention of these in a definite order does not serve any useful purpose.

Thus then, in all cases, we must, in accordance with the present *Adhikaraṇa*, admit the injunction to be of the qualified *Bhāvanā*; and whatever else may be found to be mentioned in the *Bhāshya*, it must be taken only as a means of making clear, to the dull intellect, what is not easily intelligible to it in the strictly accurate form.

The mention of 'proximity' and 'remoteness' is with reference to the fact of the objects spoken of being the qualifications of the *Bhāvanā*, wherein the injunction all along rests.

Question: "How could the *Bhāvanā* be enjoined when it is already laid down by another sentence?"

Answer: The *Bhāvanā qualified* (as it is in the sentence in question) has never been laid down before; and hence it would be in the qualified form that the *Bhāvanā* would be enjoined; and what it really comes to is that the Injunction is for the sake of the qualification, as we shall explain later on.

Objection: "In that case, the injunctive word not functioning over the "qualifications, if it were to lay them down through the *Bhāvanā*, then, even "in the case of the injunction of an action that has already been laid down, "it could lay down many qualifications, in the same manner as it does in "the case of an action never laid down before; and as such a case would "not be amenable to the law that 'when an action has been enjoined, what-"ever is mentioned is for its sake, and hence particular qualifications would "be mentioned for particular actions.'"

Reply: This does not affect our position; because even though the injunctiveness appertains to the *Bhāvanā*, there is always a distinction made as to whether it is for the sake of that *Bhāvanā* only (or for that of something else); and it is only when there are many qualifications that there occurs a split of the sentence. That is to say, in a case where the Injunctiveness pertaining to the *Bhāvanā* is taken as being for the sake of the *Bhāvanā* itself, the injunction of the qualification comes to be implied by it; and in this case we do not perceive any syntactical split. When, however, the Injunnctivness is ascertained to be for the sake of the qualification of the *Bhāvanā*, then, inasmuch as this would entail the removal, to a distance, of the *Bhāvanā*, which naturally has had a proximate position, —there being a contact of many qualifications, the injunction could be of that qualification alone, for whose sake it would have been ascertained to be, and not of any other, even though this latter may be located in the same place,—just as the eye does not pertain to *touch*, etc.; and thus there would be the necessity of splitting up the sentence into various sentences. And we have already shown that even though the Injunctiveness, in all cases, extends over the same place, yet, in point of fact, it is actually moving from one place to the other, and resting itself upon one object after the other. And thus we do not find any incongruity in this.

As for the objection that in the case of the injunctions of the *Abhyuditeshṭi* and the *Prākāça*, there would be the anomaly of the Injunction serving various purposes,—this is applicable to all parties; and as to how it does not apply to us, we shall show under the sections treating of those subjects.

—o—

[The *Vārtika* now proceeds to deal with certain *questions* and *answers* set forth in the *Bhāshya*.]

—o—

(The author has declared that the sentences '*dadhnā juhoti* etc.' serve the purpose of laying down the qualification of the *Bhāvanā* of *Homa*, and on this the objector puts the question).

"*The qualifying word might very well qualify the object denoted by it; "but as a matter of fact, we do not, in the case in question, perceive any "functioning of the qualification.* And the sense of this is that so long as the "qualification is not directly laid down, the Agent could not engage him-"self in it; and as such even if he would perform the particular "sacrifice, without taking any notice of that qulification, he would feel "that he had done his work."

In reply to this objection, the Author puts the question—*What would happen then?* And this question refers to the fact of the Injunction being in the form of a sentence. The author proceeds to make his point clear by adding—*even though the qualification would be inoperative, the meaning of the word would be duly ascertained.* This latter sentence of the Bhāshya may also be taken as emanating from the objector, who is cogitating over the matter in his own mind.

It is with a view to this that we have the next Question and Answer.

Question: "*What would be the use of the proximity of the word denoting "the qualification* (when the Qualification will have been expressed by the "Injunction)?"

(And the answer to this is that *it may be taken as useless*).

Question: "*How can a word of the Veda be useless?* This question "refers to *sūtra* I—ii—8."

Answer: *When there is actually no use, what else could we say?* And the inner purport of this is that it is the objector who makes the word useless, by denying all functioning of the qualification. According to our theory, it serves a distinctly useful purpose; and as such it cannot be said to be useless.

Objection: "*In that case the injunction of the qualification would rest* "*upon the authority of syntax*,—that is to say even though the Injunction, "pertaining to the qualified *Bhāvanā* is a direct one, yet, in the way you "put it, it would come to rest upon the authority of the *syntax*."

Answer: *So long as we have a certain fact expressed by direct Assertion, we do not have recourse to the implications of the syntax*;—that is to say, we may have that (*i.e.*, *Bhāvanā*) itself as the object of the Injunction, through which the Qualifications come to be enjoined.

Objection: "*True, it is so; but when that Bhāvanā is not meant to be* "*enjoined, then we could have the Qualification as the object of the Injunction.* "In support of this the transference of the Injunctive potency will be "dealt with under the *sūtra* '*na cedanyena çishtāḥ*' (I—iv—9)."

Answer: *Why should it not be meant to be enjoined?* This question is put with a touch of pity for the opponent; or it may be taken as an assertion of the Author himself.

The *Bhāshya* concludes—*Thus it is proved that the repetition of* '*dadhnā juhoti*' *is for the purpose of laying down the qualifying materials.* The sense of this is that, '*because of its proximity*'—*i.e.*, because of the fact of the qualification having entered into the *Bhāvanā*, it becomes an object of Injunction; or that because of the proximity of Qualification, there is a transference of the Injunctive Potency; or that because of the proximity of the Injunction (by another sentence) of the *Bhāvanā* and the *Root-meaning* (of '*juhoti*'), the Injunction (in the sentence in question) is that of the Qualification, specially as there is no incompatibility between Direct Assertion and Syntax.

Says the *Bhāshyā*—*The utterance of* 'juhoti' (in the sentences '*dadhnā juhoti*', *etc.*) *is with a view to referring to the previously enjoined Homa, for the purpose of connecting it with the materials* (dadhi, etc.). Though the mention of the word '*juhoti*' was quite clear, yet the Author has explained it only with a view to show that by that he refers to all verbs under similar circumstances (for instance, '*āghārayati*' and the rest).

Question: "*If the word* '*juhoti*' *only serves to refer to the Homa, by* "*what word is the qualifying material enjoined?*"

Answer: *You should not run away with the idea that I declare it to be enjoined by the word* '*dadhi*'. This bearing of the sentence is to be explained in the manner shown under the *Adhikaraṇa* on '*Vajapēya*' (I—iv—6-8). The answer is that in the word '*juhoti*' (in '*dadhnā juhoti*') the affix serves the purposes of enjoining (the qualifying material), and it is only the Root that serves to refer to a previous *Homa*, (and thus there is no difficulty about the said Injunction).

Question: "*If the words are injunctive, when the object in question has "already been laid down, why should they be pronounced again?* That is to say, "when the *Bhāvanā* has already been previously enjoined, how can there "be another Injunction (of the same)?"

Answer: *The words are pronounced again for the purpose of laying down what is expressed by the whole sentence* ('*dadhnā juhoti*'). Inasmuch as the material *dadhi* is expressed by the single word '*dadhi*' it cannot be said to be expressed by the sentence; and hence what the answer means is that what is enjoined is the *Bhāvanā as qualified by dadhi* (as it is this that is actually expressed by the sentence in question).

Thus then we conclude that the sentences '*agnihotram juhoti*' *and* '*āghāramāghārayati*' *are the injunctions of Actions.* This should be explained in the same way as we have pointed out above (*text*, p. 486, *translation*, p. 674) with regard to the '*upānçu*'.

[We now proceed to meet the arguments brought forward by the *Pūrvapaksha*].

(1) As for the names '*Agnihotra*' and '*Āghāra*', they can be explained as serving the purpose of pointing out the peculiarity indicated by the verbs '*juhoti*' and '*āghārayati*'; and in the present instance, they serve to distinguish the two actions in question from all other actions (of *Homa* and *Āghāra*), on the ground of these two being enjoined.

(2) As for the absence of the accessory details (as urged under *sūtra* 15), we find that the Material and the Deity are distinctly pointed out by the context. Nor can it be urged that there being no *method* mentioned in the injunctive sentence (there would be no *context*); because no such *method* would be looked for until the relationship with the Result had been established.

(3) Nor is it impossible for us to have the Injunction of the Result with regard to an Action of which the Material and the Deity have not been laid down. Because the Result might very well be laid down with regard to the *Homa* only, of which the Material and the Deity might be mentioned later on; and there would be no incongruity in this.

(4) As a matter of fact, in similar cases, we do admit of reference to previously enjoined actions. But the acceptance of this Reference always depends upon the fact of the action referred to being one that has been already enjoined (or mentioned); and as such it always stands in need of recognising the Action as the same as that which has been previously enjoined.

(5) The mere fact of the *Āghāra* being mentioned in another *Prakaraṇa* does not do away with all the intervening *Prakaraṇas* of the *Āghāra*.

Because even in the case of the *Āghāra* (as laid down by the sentence '*āghāramāghārayati*'), the conjugational affix always raises in us a desire to know the *Object*, the *Instrument* and the *Method* of the Action; and hence it is quite possible for the Material and the Deity to be indicated by the *Prakaraṇa* (as the said desire could be fulfilled only by an indication of these).

Then again, your theory would necessitate the assumption of many unseen factors. Because you make each of the sentences—'*dadhnā juhoti*, etc.' and '*ūrdhvamāghārayati*, etc.'—lay down an independent Action; and we do not find any deity laid down either for the *Homa* of *Dadhi*, or for the *ūrdhva āghāra*, etc; and in the case of the sentence '*ūrdhvamāghārayati*' the material too is not mentioned; and inasmuch you hold each of them to be the injunction of an independent action, they could not be taken as laying down the *materials*, etc., for one another.

For these reasons it must be as we have put it.

(6) It has been argued above that in the sentence '*agnihotram juhoti*,' if the first word were to express an action, then, inasmuch as an Action could never be the objective, the accusative ending (in '*agnihotram*') would be wholly inexplicable. In reply to this we urge that an Action can be the objective of such verbs as '*saṅkalpa*' (determination) and the like; and as such the accusative ending in '*agnihotram*' could be explained as with reference to the 'determination' implied by the word '*juhoti*'; and as such there is nothing incongruous in the accusative ending in '*agnihotram*'.

Objection: "In connection with *Agnihotra*, we find the sentences—
"'*yadagnaye ca prajāpatayē ca sāyam juhoti*', and '*yatsuryāya ca prajāpatayē*
"*ca prātaḥ*'; and inasmuch as these distinctly lay down more than one
"Accessory (Deity) for the Action, it becomes open to the arguments
"brought forward under *sūtra* II—ii—6. In fact some people actually
"admit this as an inevitable fact. And it is only thus that we have a dis-
"tinction between the *Agnihotra* offered in the morning and that offered
"in the evening,—a distinction which is clearly pointed out by the
"injunction that 'the offering in the evening should not be precisely the
"same as that offered in the morning.' Nor, in this case, as in the case of
"the using of the various vessels at the *Jyotishṭoma*, can the evening
"*Agnihotra* be taken as a part of the morning one; because each of these
"is found to be complete by itself. It is thus alone that it becomes
"possible for the whole procedure of the morning offering to be repeated
"wholly in the evening offering, exactly as in the case of the '*Darça-*
"*Pūrṇamāsa*.' Otherwise the single performance of the procedure in the
"morning would have sufficed for the evening offering also, in accordance
"with the law laid down under X—iii—1-12. Nor is there any useful

"purpose served by making the two *Agnihotras* one and the same. Hence "we conclude that the sentence '*agnihotram juhoti*' is a *reference* to the two "offerings collectively (though it may not be one to the *Homas* laid down "by the sentences '*dadhnā juhoti*, etc.')"

To this we make the following reply:

We do not find any useful purpose served by such reference to the two offerings collectively; and as for their unification in the sentence laying down their performance, we could get hold of one, exactly as we do in the case of the '*Rājasūya*.' That is to say, the reference to a number of actions collectively is always based upon the fact of their unification expressed in words that speak of them collectively; and in the same manner, we could also in the case in question have a *reference* to the two *Agnihotra offerings* necessitated by such unification, in the sentence '*agnihotram juhuyāt svargakāmaḥ*' (and the necessary reference having been accomplished by this sentence, there is no use of having them referred to again by the sentence '*agnihotram juhoti*'). And just as in the case of a *Rājasūya*, all necessary reference is accomplished by the single sentence '*rājasūyēna svārājyakāmo yajēta*', and no other sentence is wanted for the reference,—so would it also be in the case of the *Agnihotra*.

Objection: "In that case, inasmuch as the name '*Agnihotra*' would "apply to all *Homas*, the Result, Heaven, mentioned in the sentence '*agniho-"tram juhuyāt svargakāmaḥ*' would pertain to all these *Homas*; and con-"sequently even those *Homas* that are offered into Fires other than those "used at the *Agnihotra* would become endowed with the character of "a Primary Sacrifice."

Reply: But by what means would this primary character of such *Homas* be set aside by the mere fact of the word '*agnihotram*' serving the only purpose of a collective reference to the *Homas* (mentioned in the sentences '*dadhnā juhoti*, etc.'? In the case of the sacrifices called by the names '*Paurṇamāsya*' and '*Amāvasyā*', we find that the requisite differentiation is made by the Fires specified by these names; and there is no such means of differentiation in the case in question.

Question: "The name '*Agnihotra*' may be taken as '*that wherein the offering is made to Agni*'; and this would serve as a differentiating characteristic."

Answer: That will not do; because even those *Homas* that are offered into other Fires have the same Agni for their Deity. And further, this interpretation would land you in another difficulty: namely, that the morning libations of the *Agnihotra* being offered (to *Sūrya* and *Prajāpati*, and not to *Agni*) would cease to be directly called '*Agnihotra*', and as such would become a mere auxiliary to the *Agnihotra*.

Thus then, we find that whether we take the word '*Agnihotram*' as a mere reference to the other *Homas* or not, it does not make any difference with regard to the objection urged above (as to the primary character of all *Homas*). As a matter of fact, if the *Homas* offered into other Fires be different from the *Agnihotra*, or if in all Fires (that of the *Agnihotra* as also the other fires) the same action (of offering) be repeated,—in any case, all that the word '*agnihotra*' would express would be (1) a proximity (to the action laid down by the originative Injunction), (2) the presence of Fire, and (3) the character of *Homa*; and hence all the *Homas* that would fulfill these three conditions would be related to the particular Result, and would all equally have the primary character.

Thus it is that, according to certain *Vaidikas*, the word '*Agnihotra*' is applied to all these *Homas*; for we find that having laid down four libations each in the *Gārhapatya* and the *Anvāhāryapacanīya* Fires, and two in the *Āhavanīya* Fire, they sum up all these in the sentence 'one who knowing this performs *this fully equipped grand Agnihotra*, etc., etc.'

For these reasons, the sentence '*agnihotram juhoti*', having no other useful purpose to serve, must be taken as the true Injunction of the Action (of *Agnihotra*). And thus alone would it be possible for us to take the sentences laying down the libations into the *Gārhapatya*, etc., as pointing out the accessories (in the shape of the various Fires) of the *Agnihotra*, just like the sentences '*dadhnā juhoti*, etc.'; and thereby we would have done away with all grounds for taking those libations as Actions different from the *Agnihotra*; because in all these libations we recognise the same original action of the *Agnihotra*.

Question: "Inasmuch as all these Fires appertain to the same Action, "why should not they be taken as optional alternatives, just like the "materials *dadhi*, *taṇḍula*, etc.?"

To this some people make the following reply: "They are not so "taken, in consideration of certain transcendental uses; that is to say, "inasmuch as the libation could be poured on the bare ground, with-"out any particular receptacle, in the shape of a duly sanctified Fire, the "specification of the Fire must be taken as with a view to certain tran-"scendental results; and as many such results could be possible, the *Homa* "is repeated in each of the Fires (and not in one only)."

We do not accept this explanation; because if such be the case, then there would be nothing to preclude the presence of the *Āhavanīya* Fire at the libation that is laid down to be offered at the place where the cow with which the *Soma* has been purchased puts its seventh step (because in this case also a transcendental result could be possible). It may be argued that in this latter case *Homa* is mentioned only once, and hence the Fire is precluded from the 'seventh step Libation'; because its presence would necessitate an unwarranted repetition of the *Homa*; but then the same could be said of the case in question also (because in this also the number of libations is specified). Hence the explanation given does not save us from having to take the various Fires as optional alternatives.

Therefore the only ground that we have for taking all these *Homas* into the various Fires as collectively forming the '*Agnihotra*' lies in the sentence 'the fully equipped grand *Agnihotra*, etc.,' and also in the law laid down under *sūtra* XII—iii—30.

Otherwise, if the transcendental result were the only ground, the particular *Apūrva*, or transcendental result, would follow from the Fires only when these would be made the receptacles of the offerings; and as the place of the receptacle would be occupied by one Fire, there could be no room for any other. That is to say, though the presence of the Fire may be for the sake of certain transcendental results, yet, on account of the Locative ending (in the word expressive of the Fires), such results could be accomplished by the Fire being made the receptacle of the offering; and then, as the receptacle is a visible thing, so long as the place would be occupied by one Fire, there would be no room for another; and hence in this case the various Fires cannot but be taken as optional alternatives.

Question: "Why cannot the various *Homas* be taken as different actions, on the ground of the differences in the number of libations, just as we have in the case of the sentence '*tisra āhutirjuhoti*'?"

Answer: This cannot be; because it is after the complete action of the *Agnihotra* has been duly laid down by the originative Injunction ('*agnihotram juhoti*') and comprehended as such,—that the other sentences laying down the number of libations into the various Fires come up as subsequent corollaries to the original Injunction. It is only when the number appears in the originative Injunction that it serves to differentiate the Action referred to—as in the case of the sentence '*tisraḥ*, etc.' In the case in question, however, the number appears after the Action has been fully comprehended; and as such it can only be made up by so many repetitions of the same action,—as in the case of the 'eleven prayājas'; and it cannot serve the purpose of making the Actions themselves radically different. Hence we conclude that in all the various Fires, the same action of the *Agnihotra* is repeated a certain number of times.

It has been urged above that—"the sentence '*yadagnayē*, etc.', and '*yatsuryāya*, etc.', serving many purposes, form independent injunctions of Actions."

In reply to this we urge that the times (morning and evening) of the Libations having been already enjoined by the sentences '*sāyam juhoti*' and '*prātarjuhoti*', all that the sentences in question do is to refer to the same *times* with the sole view of pointing out the Deities to whom the several Libations are to be offered.

Objection: "In that case, as these sentences would refer to the "Libations as qualified by the particular times, there would be a syntac- "tical split."

Reply: Not so; because the Action (Libation) being pointed out by the Context, what the sentences do is to lay down the Deities *with reference to the time only*; and as the *time* cannot by itself be related to the Deities, we connect the Deities with the *time as affected by the Action pointed out by the Context* (and hence there is no actual reference to the Action qualified by the Time, that would bring about the split). Or, the mention of the time (in the sentences '*yadagnayē*, etc.') may be taken as serving the purpose of indirectly recalling the original *Homa*, which is wanted by the peculiar character of the *receiver of a gift* in which the Deities enjoined are represented in the sentences (where the words expressing them have the Dative ending), (as without an offering of the Homa, this character of the Deities would not be possible); and certainly when the *Homa* is only *indirectly* indicated, it cannot lead to any split in the sentence; nor does the time 'evening' indicate a performance at any other time; hence we conclude the sentences to mean only that 'of the evening Libation Agni and Prajāpati, and of the morning one Sūrya and Prajāpati, would be the deities,' (and they do not lay down independent Actions).

Objection: "Thus too, inasmuch as each of these sentences would "lay down two deities, there would certainly be a syntactical split in "them (because that would necessitate a double functioning of the same "injunctive sentence)."

Reply: Not so: Some people offer the following explanation: '*Because* "*the words expressing the two Deities have the same case-ending*; it is "only when there is a diversity of case-endings that there is a difference "in the functioning of the Injunctive sentence; so long as the case-ending "remains the same, even if there be a thousand objects to be laid down, "they are all amenable to a single syntactical operation.'

But against this explanation, we urge the following: When a single case-ending happens to be connected with many words, it cannot be enjoined except by the Injunctive Affix being repeated over and over again (and this would entail different Injunctive operations). That is to say, the case is signified by the termination; and where there is a single termination, as in the case of *Agnīshoma*, there is a single operation of the Injunctive affix; in a case, however, where a single case happens to be mentioned by many words, each having a distinct termination with itself, —as in the case of the sentence in question '*agnayē ca prajāpatayē ca*',— inasmuch as it is not possible for the Affix to take up both at one and the same time, it must be admitted that Agni and Prajāpati are taken up by the Affix, separately, one after the other (the sentence being construed as '*agnayē juhoti, prajāpatayē juhoti*'. As a rule, the case-ending employs the Affix (Injunctive) for the purpose of taking up the object denoted by the noun; and hence when the case-ending is pronounced more than once, it cannot but employ the Affix more than once; and thus there is a repetition of the Affix (which brings about the syntactical split urged by the opponent).

Thus then, the explanation given above not meeting the objection, we offer the following: Both the sentences in question lay down Prajāpati alone; because *Agni* and *Surya*, as deities of the *Agnihotra*, are pointed out by the very *mantras* laid down by the sentences as to be employed at the morning and evening offerings (*viz.*, '*suryo jyotiḥ*, etc.' and '*agnirjyotiḥ*, etc.'). And the Deities having been laid down by these *mantras*, they are mentioned again in the sentences in question, which lay down *Prajāpati* as the Deity, only by way of an eulogy (*i.e.*, 'an offering to *Agnī* and *Sūrya* is as good as that to *Prajāpatī*'). Though the Bhāshya has cited these sentences under *sūtra* I—iv—4, as laying down the four Deities of the *Agnihotra*, yet the quotation must be taken only as showing that the sentences also serve to recall the Deities pointed out by the *mantras;* because it is thus alone that we are saved from a needless repetition of the Injunctions contained in the *mantras.* Otherwise in the meeting of the arguments brought forward under *sūtra* I—ii—31, we would have to undergo the trouble of taking the sentence '*yadagnayē*, etc.' either as the Injunction of an accessory detail, or as a *Parisaṅkhyā*, or as an *Arthavāda*. For these reasons, we conclude that in the case in question there is no syntactical split.

It has been argued above that—"we do not conceive of the morning "and evening libations as the parts of any single action (and hence they "must be taken as distinct actions)."

But the non-recognition of these as such parts is due to the fact of all the accessory details of the one being repeated *in toto* in the other; just as in the case of the *Dākshāyaṇa* sacrifice (though as a matter of fact they together form a single action spreading over the two times).

Objection: "In that case, all the accessory actions of the morning "and evening libations being exactly the same, they would be identical, "and as such they would be optional alternatives; and the *Agnihotra* "would be performed either in the morning alone, or in the evening alone, "and not at both times."

Reply: It is not so; because the *Agnihotra* has been laid down as to be performed 'throughout one's life'; and when one has offered the evening libation, if he lives till the morning, it behoves him to offer the morning libation also, because all the conditions present in the preceding evening, present themselves again.

Objection: "True; it may be in this manner; but the difficulty is "that, inasmuch as the same operation is to be performed both in "the morning and in the evening, when the evening operation is being "performed, if during that performance something untoward happens to "the sacrificer, then he must, somehow or other, perform the morning "one also; because thus alone could he be saved from the sin of leaving "incomplete an action that had been begun. When, however,—like the "performance of the *Jyotishṭoma* in the spring,—the evening operation is "duly finished, then there is no necessity of performing the morning "one. And further, an action that is done with a definite result in view, "must be performed, by one desiring that result, as fully equipped with "all its accessories; and on this score too, it would be a matter of option "whether the Action is performed in the morning or in the evening. In "accordance with the theory that the same action is repeated at the two "times, it becomes necessary for the performer to complete all the "accessories, at both times. In any case, how can we escape from the "fact of the two libations being optional alternatives?"

Reply: We do not take them as alternatives because of the fact of the two libations being distinctly mentioned in the Veda as together constituting a single Action; for instance, having begun with '*pravargyo vā eshaḥ*' the Veda goes on to say '*sa vai sāyam ca prātaçca jūhoti*, etc.' Even when the two Libations are taken as distinct Actions, the fact of their being taken together would be based upon the word '*ca*' in the sentence. Nor would such conjunction of the two necessitate their performance in close proximity with each other; because the text quoted does not lay down a conjunction of the times of their performance; and hence there is no incongruity in the matter. That is to say, the times being laid down in the sentences, all that the text quoted does is to point out the fact of the two Actions together going to form a single Action; and hence there is no syntactical split. Therefore we conclude that it is the same action that is repeated at both times (and it is these two repetitions that are conjointly called '*Agnihotra*').

It has been urged above that "these two libations being subsidiaries "(to the *Agnihotra*), they could not be performed separately by them-"selves."

But this does not affect our case; because when the Action is laid down with reference to a time, then alone does it require a full connection with all its subsidiaries; hence when the Evening Libation appears as the Primary Sacrifice, then the subsidiaries that aid in its performance are those that are possible at that time, and none else;

because of the non-affinity of these (to the Evening Libation); similarly also with the Morning Libation; and hence there is a repetition of the subsidiaries (as it happens that the same subsidiaries are possible at both times).

It has been urged that "there is no useful purpose served by the theory of the present Siddhānta."

In reply to this we point out that in connection with the '*Kuṇḍapāyināmayana*,' we find the sentence '*māsamagnihotram juhoti*'; and as this sentence apparently lays down a single Action, we naturally look out for only one method of procedure; and hence what we would take up are the accessories either of the Evening Libation alone or of the Morning Libation alone; and as such we would perform but once every day during the month, the Action with a single set of accessories (this would be the case if the evening Libation were an action totally different from the morning one). When, however, the two libations are the same (being repetitions of the same act) the *Agnihotra* that we would perform in connection with the *Kuṇḍapāyināmayana* would be exactly the original one (*i.e.*, it would be performed both morning and evening, not only once).

ADHIKARAṆA (6).

[*Treating of the fact of the 'Paçu' and the 'Sŏma' being independent Actions.*]

Sūtra (17): Because of the connection with certain materials the words 'paçu, etc.' and 'soma, etc.' contain injunctions; as in the context the mention of the mere material would be useless—specially because the words do not serve the purpose of laying down accessory materials.

[(1) We have a sentence '*paçumālabhēta*'; and in continuation of this we have the sentences '*hṛdayasyāgre*' *vadyati, atha jihvāyā atha vakshasaḥ.*' (2) Then again we have the sentence '*somēna yajēta,*' and in its continuation, the sentences '*aindravāyavam gṛhṇāti, maitrāvaruṇam gṛhṇāti,* etc.' And the question that arises is this: Is '*ālabhēta*' a mere *reference* to the actions laid down by '*avadyati*'? and is '*yajēta*' a mere reference to those laid down by '*gṛhṇāti*'? or do they lay down independent actions by themselves?]

The case of '*paçu*' is mentioned first, because it is the more difficult to be explained. As a matter of fact, in the sentence '*paçum, etc.*', there are two words that are suspected of being mere references to a number of actions taken collectively; these words are '*paçu*', and the root '*yaji*' (to *sacrifice*) which (though not actually present in the sentence) is implied by the relationship of the *paçu* with the deity *Agnīshoma*; because the sentence ('*agnīshomīyam paçumālabheta*') in its complete form would be in the form of '*agnīshomīyēna paçunā yajēta*' whereof one part is directly mentioned, while another is only inferred (from the relationship mentioned in it). Thus then, the form of the question too becomes this: Is the word '*paçu*' a mere reference to the '*hṛdaya,* etc.', and the word '*yaji*' to the sacrifices implied by the word '*avadyati*'? or do they lay down an independent '*yāga*' and *paçu* (as its material), the other sentences only serving to point out their accessory details?

In the same manner, the question with reference to the other set of sentences is this: Is the word '*yājēta*' a mere reference to the sacrifice implied by the relationship of the material and the Deity, as mentioned in the sentences '*aindravāyavam*, etc.', and the word '*soma*' to the *juice* used at those sacrifices? or the sentence '*somēna yajēta*' lays down an independent action together with the material to be used in it?

The *Bhāshya* has said: *Kimavadyatigṛhṇātibhyām coditānām karmaṇām*, etc. But, inasmuch as the actions of '*avadyati*' and '*gṛhṇāti*' are not synonymous with 'sacrifice', we must take the *Bhāshya* as referring to those actions that are inferred from the relationship of the actions of '*avadyati*' and '*gṛhṇāti*,' and which are laid down by means of the conjugational affixes in these two verbs. And as a matter of fact, the word '*ālabhēta*' also serves the purpose of indicating the *sacrifice* that is implied by the action of '*ālabhati*' (*killing*).

Or, it may be that no mention is made by the *Bhāshya* of the fact of the action of '*avadyati*' indicating the *sacrifice* at all; what then is meant to be the question is as to whether the word '*ālabhati*' ('=killing') is a mere *reference* to the '*killing*' implied by the action of '*āvadyati*' (=cutting);—and the fact of each of these *pieces cut* being related to a definite deity leads to the inference of so many *sacrifices*,—or the '*killing*' mentioned by '*ālabhēta*' leads to the inference of a single *sacrifice* of the Paçu? In the same manner, in the case of the other sentence, does the 'sacrifice' (indicated by the word '*gṛhṇāti*') consist in the mere 'holding' ('*grahaṇa*') of the material? In this manner the words of the *Bhāshya*, embodying the question, could be taken literally.

On this question, then, we have the following:—

PŪRVAPAKSHA.

"The words in question are mere references to a number of actions "taken collectively.

"Because, as in the case of the sentences '*yadāgneyoshṭakapālaḥ*, etc." "the real end of the sentence is not served until the 'sacrifice' has been "inferred (because the Cake cannot be spoken of as '*āgneya*' until it has "been *offered in sacrifice* to the Deity *Agni*),—so also, in the case of the "sentences '*aindravāyam*, etc.', their full signification would not be "accomplished until they implied a 'sacrifice' (at which the *Soma* would "be offered to Indra-Vāyu, when alone it could be spoken of as "'*aindravāyavam*'). That is to say, the relationship of the Deity and the "material mentioned in the word '*aindravāyavam*' cannot be complete "until a 'sacrifice' has been implied; and so long as the sentence itself is "not complete, it cannot stand in need of any other sentence (in the shape "of '*somēna yajēta*', for which, according to the *Siddhānta*, it would lay "down an accessory detail); and as such the sacrifice mentioned by the "sentence '*somēna yajēta*' could not yet come in as the 'sacrifice' sought "after; nor, on the other hand, would it be possible for the sentences "'*aindravāyam*, etc.' to lay down the Deities for the sacrifice laid down by "the sentence '*somēna yajēta*', which, having no Deity mentioned, is "wanting in an accessory detail. When, however, the sentences '*aindravāyavam*, etc.' have implied a 'sacrifice', then, inasmuch as one 'sacrifice' "cannot serve as the accessory detail of another sacrifice, we are forced to "admit that that spoken of in the sentence '*somēna yajēta*' is a mere "reference to those sacrifices that have been laid down in the context (by "the sentences '*aindravāyavam gṛhṇāti*, etc.').

"As for the anomaly of having to accept a qualified Injunction, this is "found in your theory also; because, according to you also, what is enjoined "is the *sacrifice at which Soma is the material offered.* In fact you have to "admit a qualified injunction in the case of the *Agnīshomījya* as well as in "the case of the *Aindravāyava* sentences; whereas we have to admit it "only in the latter; and this makes a vast difference between our "positions.

"Further, the kind of Action that you will seek to have enjoined (by "the sentence '*somēna yajēta*') can never form the object of an Injunction, as we have shown above, in connection with the *Agnihotra*, where "it has been pointed out that the injunctive potency pertains directly to "the directly-mentioned *material* (*soma*); and as such the sentence could "not serve the purpose of enjoining the *sacrifice*; and as such we cannot but "admit the '*yaji*' (in '*yajēta*') to be a mere reference to certain previously mentioned sacrifices; what, then, the sentence does, in connection "with the said sacrifices, is to specify the material (*soma*), which had been "generally implied by the verb '*gṛhṇāti*.' Or, it may be that the *Soma-juice* "being mentioned by certain auxiliary sentences in the same context—such, "for instance, as '*somam krīṇāti*', '*somamabhishuṇoti*,' '*somampāvayati*,' "etc.',—it is with reference to this *juice*, that we have the Injunctions in "the word '*gṛhṇāti*'; and thus then, *Soma* cannot be the object of Injunc-"tion (in the sentence '*somēna yajēta*'); and consequently, inasmuch as "the word '*soma*' has the Instrumental-ending it becomes co-extensive (or "synonymous) with the 'sacrifice' which is the material Instrument (in "the accomplishment of the result); hence in accordance with *sūtra* "I—iv—4, the word '*soma*' becomes the *name* of the sacrifice (the mean-"ing of the sentence thus being that 'one should offer the sacrifice called "*Soma*').

"*Objection*: 'We have already got a name for this sacrifice—'*Jyotish-*"*ṭoma*'; what then would be the use of another name?'

"*Reply*: What harm is there if we have another name? Very often "we find people speaking of one sacrifice by two names.

"The useful purpose served by such reference to a number of sacrifices, "as we hold, is that it is only when all these sacrifices are referred to "collectively as one, that they could be spoken of in the singular number, in the final sentence that sums up their performability (*viz.*, the "sentence '*jyotishṭomena svargakāmo yajēta*'). Hence we conclude that "the sentence in question is a mere reference to previous sacrifices.

"*Objection*: 'What you say may apply to the case of the sentence "*somēna yajēta*, because the sentences *aindravāyavam*, etc., express a "relationship between the *material* and the Deities; in the case of the "sentence *paçumālabheta*, however, we find that in the sentences *hṛdayasyāgre'vadyati*, etc., we have the mere verb *avadyati*,—exactly as in the "sentence *vatsamālabheta*, which is connected with the material only, in the "shape of the *hṛdaya*, etc., without any connection with any deity; and as "such how could such a verb as *avadyati* lay down a *sacrifice?* And how "then could the mention of the word '*paçu*' be a mere reference to the "*hṛdaya*, etc.?'

"*Reply*: Just as in the case of the mention of '*paçu*' (animal) in general, "the *mantra* leads us to believe that the *goat* is meant,—so, in the same "manner, the mention of the limbs *hṛdaya*, etc., points to that animal "itself, as the source (or material cause) of those limbs. That is to say, "the *hṛdaya*, etc., stand in need of a source from which they would "come forth; and the *mantra* having pointed to the *goat*, it is the "'*paçutva*' of this goat that is referred to by the word '*paçu*' (in the "sentence '*paçumalabheta*'); and the Deity of the actions mentioned in "these sentences ('*hṛdasyāgre'vadyati*, etc.') being laid down by the "sentence '*agnīshomīyam paçumālabhēta*,' there would be nothing in "the way of those sentences laying down the *sacrifice.*

"Or, it may be that, in accordance with the law '*sānnāyyam vā* "*tatprabhavatvāt*', the '*avadyati*' (of the sentences '*hṛdayasya*, etc.') "may be taken as a part of the '*avadyati*' in connection with "the *Sānnāyya*; and this latter is wellknown as serving the pur- "pose of preparing (or purifying) the material for the *Darça-* "*Pūrṇamāsa* sacrifice; and hence it is only when the *hṛdaya*, etc., "are the materials used at the *Darça-Pūrṇamāsā*, that they become "connectable with the verb '*avadyati*'; consequently, just as, when we "meet with the sentence laying down the *pounding* of the *Putīkā* "(as a substitute for *Soma*), we conclude that it must be connected "with some *sacrifice*—even when no such connection is directly mentioned; "because otherwise, there would be no use of the said '*pounding*';—so, in "the same manner, in the case in question, there being no use for the "'*avadyati*', unless it implied a *sacrifice*, we conclude that there must be a "*sacrifice* connected with it; and it is these sacrifices, inferred in connection

" with each of the limbs (*hṛdaya*, *grīvā*, etc.) mentioned, that are referred " to by the word '*ālabhēta*'. And as the necessity of such inference of " sacrifices is equally present in your theory also, it cannot be brought " forward as a special weakness in our theory.

" Further, if there were, as you hold, a single *Soma-sacrifice* (for " which the sentences '*āindravāyavam*, etc.' would lay down accessory " details), then, inasmuch as 'Indra,' 'Vayu,' and the rest would all " serve the same purpose of the Deity at that sacrifice, they would " become optional alternatives; and as such they should not have " been mentioned in a definite order, one after the other; nor should " they have been subsequently mentioned collectively. That is " to say, just as in the matter of the making of the sacrificial " post, when we have many kinds of wood mentioned,—though all serve " the same purpose of a tethering post for the animal,—in the shape " of the *Palāça*, the *Khadira*, etc., we take them as optional alternatives, " —so, in the same manner, in the case in question we must regard the " various Deities as optional alternatives. In our theory, on the other " hand, each of the Deities belonging to a distinct sacrifice, and all the " Deities and sacrifices serving to bring about transcendental results, it is " only natural that all of them should be laid down by a single word " ('*jyotishṭoma*') with regard to the Result (attainment of Heaven); and " as such there is nothing incongruous (in their being mentioned " collectively, or in a definite order of sequence). (And as all the sacri- " fices are laid down collectively with reference to the result, they have " all to be performed, and they cannot be taken as optional alterna- " tives).

" Though in the case of the '*Paçu*' also, we find that the various " '*avadyati*'s' are mentioned in a definite order, one after the other— " '*hṛdayasyāgre'vadyati, atha jihvāyāḥ, atha vakshasaḥ*'; and then again " we find them mentioned collectively, in the sentence '*ēkādaça vai paçora- " vadānāni*'; yet this has not been mentioned above (along with the " *soma*); because even in a single sacrifice, the eleven *pieces* could be offered " one after the other (and as such each '*avadyati*' would not necessarily " mean a distinct sacrifice). Specially as even if the *hṛdaya* and the other " limbs had not been mentioned collectively, there could have been no " offering of the *whole animal*, as mentioned in the original Injunction; in " any case a *cutting* out of the various limbs would be a necessity, because " there is an established law that only those parts of the body should be " offered in sacrifice which are not thrown aside according to other texts " (for instance, the *blood*, is always to be thrown aside). In the case " of the *Soma*, however, even the original Injunction does not lay down " the *whole Soma* (*i.e.*, all the *Soma* in the world); and hence this alone

89

"has been mentioned in connection with the sequential mention of the "various '*grḥṇāti*'s.

"For these reasons, we conclude that the sentences in question must "be taken as mere references to previous sacrifices."

SIDDHANTA.

To the above we make the following reply:

It is only when the sacrifice mentioned in a sentence is actually recognised to be the same as those mentioned before, that we take it to be a mere reference to these; in the cases in question, however, we do not find this to be the case.

That is to say, if in the case in question we recognised the sacrifice to be exactly the same in all its details as those mentioned before,—as we do in the case of the *Paurṇamāsa* sacrifice,—then we could take the sentence as a mere reference. If again, the sentence were held to be a reference to the root '*yaji*' alone, then we could conclude it to be a reference bereft of the qualifications. In the cases in question, however, we find that the sacrifices mentioned before are (1) those that have the '*hṛdaya*, etc.,' and (2) those having the *Juice*, for the material to be offered; while the sacrifices mentioned by the sentences in question have, for their materials, the *Paçu* and the *Soma* respectively; and thus these latter not being recognised to be the same as the former ones, we cannot take these sentences to be mere references to the former sacrifices.

It might here be argued that—"inasmuch as the modifications are "generally spoken of as the original substance, we could take the words "'*paçu*' and '*soma*' as indirectly referring to their respective modifications, "the limbs '*hṛdaya*, etc.' and the *juice*."

But this cannot be; because without sufficient reason we cannot have recourse to such indirect indication. It is only when we find a word spoken of as co-extensive or synonymous with another word that has an altogether different signification, (as in the sentence '*agnirmāṇavakaḥ*'),—or when the direct meaning of the word is found to be incompatible with the rest of the sentence,—that we can have recourse to the secondary indirect significations of words. In the case in question, we have none of these two conditions; because there is nothing incompatible in the fact of the sentences in question laying down distinct sacrifices, at which the *Animal* and the *Soma*—which are directly expressed by the words used, '*paçu*' and '*soma*'—would be the respective materials offered; nor is there any incongruity in the fact of these words not finding a place in the midst of the former sentences. Consequently, even though the verbs '*avadyati*' and '*gr̥hṇāti*' be taken as laying down certain sacrifices, these must be totally different from those laid down by the sentences in question.

Question: "Why cannot we take the sentences in question as laying "down the *Paçu* and the *Soma* only as the material origin of the materials "laid down for the sacrifices laid down by the other sentences?"

In answer, the Bhāshya has said—*çrutyā hi rasa aindravāyavaḥ*: According to the *Pūrvapakshīn*, who denies the sentence '*paçum*, etc.' to be the originative Injunction of an Action, it must be taken only as laying down the Deity (*Agni-Soma*) for the previous sacrifices; and as such the other accessory, in the shape of the material *paçu*, not being capable of being enjoined by the same sentence (because the sacrifice having been laid down by the sentences '*hr̥dayasya*, etc.', the subsequent sentence '*paçum*, etc.' could not lay down more than one accessory; on account of the law '*prāptē karmaṇi nānēko vidhatum çkyate guṇaḥ*'); and for this reason, in answering the above objection, the Bhāshya mentions the case of *Soma* only; the sense of the Bhāshya is that the injunction of the *Soma plant* (as the material for the previously-mentioned sacrifices) could only be by means of Syntactical Connection (*Vākya*), while that of the *juice* is by means of Direct Assertion (in the sentence '*aindravāyavam*, etc.'); and thus when the former would be pitted against this latter, it could have no connection at all with the sacrifice in question (because of the admittedly superior authority of Direct Assertion over Syntactical Connection).

Question: "The Injunctions of the *Aindravāyava*, etc., not mentioning "any particular material, how can the *juice* be said to have been laid "down by Direct Assertion? As a matter of fact, it is indicated only by "the *Context*; and as the Context is always weaker in authority than "Syntactical Connection, the *Soma-plant* which is laid down by this latter "must be admitted to be more authoritative than the *juice*."

Reply: The connection with some sort of a material is *directly mentioned* by means of the Deific Affixes (in '*Aindravāyavam*', etc.); and what the Context does is only to specify that material. We shall show below, under *sūtra* 23, that the Direct signification of the nominal Affix having connected, with the Deity, a particular material that is pointed out by the indications of Syntactical Connection, Context, etc., there arises a question as to what this particular material is, and then it is only this pointing out of the particular material that is done by Syntactical Connection, etc.; and it is not these latter that lay down the connection with the Deity.

And further, we find that the *juice* is laid down by the originative Injunction itself, whereas the *Soma-plant* is got at from another sentence; and as such the plant cannot but be less authoritative, for one who is seeking after the previously mentioned sacrifice only.

And thus, even on the ground of the difference in materials, there would be a difference between the sacrifices laid down by the former sentences, and that enjoined by the sentence in question.

These arguments, however, can be successfully met by the opponent who will argue as follows :

" In the case of the '*ashṭākapāla*' cake, etc., though we find that these " cakes are directly laid down as the materials, yet we accept the *Corn* (*Vrīhi*) " as the material, though this is pointed out only by Syntactical Connec- " tion ; and in the same manner we could accept the *Soma* as the enjoined " material. It is only when there is a contradiction between two things " that the stronger sets aside the weaker ; and this is not the case when " the two things are quite compatible with one another. In the case in " question we find that the *Soma* is quite compatible with the *juice*, " because this latter stands in need of something from which it could be " extracted, and the *Soma-plant* comes in as fulfilling this requirement. " For instance, in the case of the sentence '*āgnēyo'shṭākapālaḥ*, etc.', though " we find that the '*ashṭākapāla*' is directly laid down by the sentence, yet " when the *Vrīhi* and the *Yava* come to be laid down as the materials, there " is no contradiction ; for these *corns* are actually required as the material " out of which the *ashṭākapāla* cake would be made ; and certainly, in taking " up the *Vrīhi* one does not give up the making of the *Ashṭākapāla* ; and " hence in this case the action with reference to which *Vrīhi* is laid down as " the material is not recognised as any other than that for which the '*Ashṭa-* " *kapāla*' has been laid down. Exactly in the same manner, in the case in " question, in taking up the *Soma-plant*, one does not give up the *juice* ; " and hence there being no incompatibility between the two, inasmuch as " the '*Soma*' mentioned in the sentence in question can very well be taken " as the material for the sacrifices laid down by the other sentences, the " sentence in question cannot be taken as laying down a distinct Action, " merely on the ground of a difference in the materials mentioned. And " further, the argument applies equally to the *Siddhānta* also ; becsuse the " *Siddhānta* also does not hold that the *unpounded Soma-plant* is to be offered " at the sacrifice ; and hence just as for you the *Plant* would only be the " source of the *Juice*, so also would it be for the *Pūrvapakshin*. As a matter " of fact, it is your own theory that would be the more incongruous of the " two. For in your case, if the Plant, as mentioned in the originative In- " junction, were to be the sole means of accomplishing the sacrifice, then it " would never do to turn it into *Juice*, in accordance with other sentences. " In our case, inasmuch as the *juice* would not be possible without its origin " (in the shape of the *Plant*), our sentence would always be on the look- " out for the mention of this source ; and hence even if such source happens " to be mentioned by another sentence, there is nothing incongruous in our " having recourse to it. In your case, on the other hand, inasmuch as the "original *Plant* itself is quite capable of being offered bodily by itself, it "does not stand in need of any mention of its modifications; and as such "any connection of these would be wholly incompatible; consequently, we "could not accept any such connection as laid down by other sentences."

In view of these arguments, based as they are on the firm ground of such examples as the aforesaid injunction of *Vrīhi*, etc., which completely shut our mouth, it is best for us not to start the question of the Injunction of Materials, and to confine ourselves solely to the refutation of the view of the sentences in question being mere references to previously mentioned sacrifices. In the case of the '*Paçu*', however, as the animal as a whole is not capable of being bodily offered at a sacrifice, the above arguments of the opponent would not apply; and hence for this case alone, the argument of the Injunction of different materials would be a good one for the *Siddhānta*. But in the case of '*Soma*', it becomes necessary for us to refute the opponent's arguments based upon the Injunction of the *Vrīhi*; and for this purpose we have the next *sūtra*.

Or, we may take it thus—that having refuted the former *Siddhānta* arguments (by means of the arguments based upon the Injunction of *Vrīhi*), the true conclusion is arrived at by means of the arguments embodied in the following *sūtra*.

Or, lastly, we can take the present *sūtra* as embodying the *Pūrvapaksha*, and the next *sūtra*,—in which the '*ca*' may be taken in the sense of '*tu*' (which is a sign of the *Siddānta-sūtra*)—as putting forth the *Siddhānta*.

It may be asked how the present *sūtra* can be taken as expressing the *Pūrvapaksha*. This we proceed to explain as follows:

The question being,—do the sentences '*hṛdayasya*, etc.' and '*aindravāyavam*, etc.' serve the purpose of laying down accessory details, like the *Dadhi*, etc.; and the subsequent sentences ('*paçum*, etc.' and '*somēna*, etc.') are the originative Injunctions of the sacrifices concerned?—or do the former sentences themselves serve as the Injunctions of sacrifices?—we have the following

PŪRVAPAKSHA.

"The sentences '*hṛdayasya*, etc.' or '*aindravāyavam*, etc.' do not "serve the purpose of laying down accessory details, like the sentences "'*dadhnā juhoti*' and the rest; in fact these themselves are original In-"junctions. Why? *Because of the mention of materials,—i.e.*, because of "the mention of such materials as *hṛdaya*, etc., these sentences are the

"Injunctions of the *Paçu* and the *Soma.* As otherwise, through the Con-"text, the connection of *Hṛdaya*, etc., would become subsidiary to the "sacrifice; while as a matter of fact, it is not possible for this connection "to serve as its accessory; because that would be contrary to the '*paçu*' "and the '*soma-plant*' laid down in the original Injunctive sentences. "Or, in accordance with a previous law, the '*Paçu*' and the '*Somā*' "having been obtained from other sentences, the mention of the con-"nection of materials, in the present context, would, in your theory, "be wholly useless. In my theory, on the other hand, the word '*Soma*' "(in '*somēna yajēta*') is the name of the sacrifice, and the sentence "'*agnīshomīyam paçum*, etc.' serves the purpose of laying down the Deity "*Agnī-Soma*; and thus none of these two sentences making mention of "any material, the mention of materials in the other sentences is not at "all superfluous. Consequently we conclude that the real Injunctions of "the sacrifices are contained in the sentences '*hṛdayasya*, etc.' and "*aindravāyavam*, etc.' (and the sentences '*agnīshomīyam paçum*, etc.' and "'*somēna yajēta*' are mere references to these sacrifices taken collectively,—"the former serving the purpose of pointing out the Deity for the offer-"ings of the pieces, and the latter supplying the name of the sacrifices "taken collectively)."

SIDDHĀNTA.

***Sūtra (18)*: *But as* (laying down) *purificatory rites they cannot be injunctive* (of independent Actions).**

The sentences in question cannot be taken as mere references to previous sacrifices, *because of these latter not being the sacrifices treated of by the context,*—an argument that has already been explained on a previous occasion, in *sūtra* II—ii—10.

Question: "But how is it that these are not the sacrifices treated of "by the Context?"

Answer: Because the words '*avadyati*' and '*gṛhṇāti*' are not injunctive of sacrifices; as what they do is only to lay down certain purificatory or preparatory rites; because they are actually found to end with them: as when a sentence is actually found to have its sole ending in the pointing out of such rites, there is no ground for assuming a sacrifice to be indirectly indicated.

Because such a sacrifice, if it could be assumed, could only be assumed in the following manner: 'when a substance is taken up with reference to a certain deity, unless it is connected with some sacrifice, it does not become dedicated to that Deity'. But in this no sooner do we proceed to assume a *sacrifice*, on account of the said apparent Inconsistency (of the fact of the substance having been taken up for a particular Deity), than we are faced by a direct mention of the 'sacrifice' in a sentence close by (*viz*: '*somēna yajēta*'), which at once makes possible all the relationships between the substances and Deities in question; and as such, it completely shuts the door of any authority for assuming another sacrifice; and when no such sacrifice would be mentioned by the sentences ('*gṛhṇāti*, etc.'), to an aggregate of what would the sentence in question be a reference?

(1) It has been urged above—that "as in the case of the sentence "'*agneyo'shṭākapālo*, etc.', until the sentence ('*gṛhṇāti*, etc.') has actually "indicated a sacrifice, it cannot stand in need of any other sentence (for "instance, '*somēna yajēta*" which would supply the necessary element "of the 'sacrifice')."

To this we make the following reply: In all cases a sentence is completed by means of a direction for the activity of a human agent; and so long as this direction is not got at, the sentence remains incomplete; while when that direction has been got at, it is complete, and can very well be taken along with other sentences. For instance, in the sentence '*āgnēyo'shṭākapālo bhavati*,' we do not perceive any other action of the human agent than the *sacrifice*; and hence until this sacrifice has been duly indicated the sentence remains incomplete. In the case in question, however, the sentence '*aindravāyavam gṛhṇāti*' serves to direct the human agent to *take up* (the vessel containing the juice, etc.), and thus, even without the indication of a *sacrifice*, it has got a distinct object for its injunctiveness, and as such is quite complete in itself; and that the sentence stands in need of something else is quite another matter (having nothing to do with the completeness of the sentence); because in all cases, even when the sentence is complete in itself, it does not, by that fact, give up all its need for other factors; nor does the fact of its being in such need make the sentence incomplete; and as we recognise the fact that this need is supplied by another sentence, there can be nothing incongruous in the fact of a complete sentence bing related to another sentence. Consequently when we proceed to assume a *sacrifice* in connection with each of the sentences ('*aindravāyavam gṛhṇāti*,' etc.), the '*sacrifice*' mentioned by the sentence '*somena yajeta*' at once presents itself (and thus puts a stop to the said assumption); and there is nothing incongruous in this.

In the case of the sentence '*āgneyo . . . . bhavati*,' the action of '*being*' does not belong to the human agent; and as such until the 'sacrifice' is assumed there is no object, either enjoined or prohibited, and hence the sentence being incomplete, and as such having no capability of requiring the aid of any other sentence. the '*sacrifice*' (necessary for the completing of the sentence) has got to be inferred; consequently no 'sacrifice' that is mentioned in any other sentence, comes to be related to it; and herein lies the great difference between the two sentences '*āgneyo*, etc.' and '*aindrāvāyavam*, etc.'

(2) Another objection urged above is that the '*paçu*' and the '*soma*' "being laid down in the originative injunction, it cannot be proper for us "to modify them (into *juice* and the *limbs*, respectively, as laid down by "the various '*gr̥hṇati's*' and '*avadyati's*')."

The following is the reply to this objection: It is only when the two substances concerned are wholly different from one another, that there can be any comparison between their respective authoritative character; in the case in question, however, through the *juice* and the various *limbs* also, it is only the *soma* and the *animal* that form part of the sacrifices concerned. If the sentences wholly renounced the *Soma* and the *Animal* laid down in the originative injunction, and laid down other substances wholly different from them, then alone could there be a contradiction (between the substances enjoined by the two sentences).; as it is, however (what the subsequent sentences lay down is that), the sacrifice is accomplished by means of the *Animal* itself, through its various *limbs*, as also by means of the *Soma*, through its *juice*; and certainly there can be no contradiction in the presence of (different) methods of procedure. For the *Animal* and the *Soma*, being laid down as the means of performing the sacrifices, stand in need of the method of that performance; and it is this method that is supplied by the mention of the fact that the animal has to be cut up into its several limbs and then offered in sacrifice, and the *Soma* has to be pounded into *juice* before it is offered; and thus the mention of the '*hr̥daya*,' etc., and the '*juice*' only serves to help the original mention of the substance, and there is no chance of contradiction.

(3) Another objection is that—"the *Soma* having been mentioned, as "the substance to be offered, by other sentences in the same context, such "as '*somam krīṇāti*,' etc., the further mention of the same substance "'*soma*' (by the sentence '*somenā yajeta*') is wholly superfluous."

In reply to this, we have the *Sūtra* itself; the sense being that those sentences—'*Somam krīṇāti*,' etc., do not serve the purpose of enjoining either the *Soma* or the *Animal*; as all that they do is to speak of the method of *preparing* these. That is to say, the substance (*Soma*), as laid down by the sentence '*somenā yajeta*', having been recognised as tending, in some way or other, to accomplish the sacrifice, what the sentences, '*somam krīṇāti*,' etc., do is to lay down that the sacrifice is to be performed by means only of such *Soma* as has been purchased in a certain manner, and prepared into the form of *Juice* by *pounding*, etc.

(4) Nor are the words of the *mantras* capable, as urged in the

Pūrvapaksha (*text*, p. 507), of pointing out the *goat*, which has not yet been laid down; what those words do is to set at rest the uncertainty with regard to the character of the '*paçu*' as laid down by the sentence '*paçunā yajeta.*' Nor does the verb '*avadyati*' necessarily imply 'sacrifice'; and even without the 'sacrifice' the verb would mention the mere 'cutting,' which would, by itself, be of use, either in connection with the Veda, or in ordinary life. On the other hand, the peculiar relationship between the Substance and the Deity, as expressed by the word '*aindravāyavam*,' would not be possible without a 'sacrifice'; and as such there is a great difference (between the *inference* or implication of the 'sacrifice' by the sentence '*aindravāyavam*,' etc., and that by '*hṛdayasyāvadyati*,' etc.

(5) The '*avadyati*' of the *Sānnāyya* is not laid down in connection with the Primary Sacrifice of the Context under consideration; because it is only indirectly implied; and as such the qualifications and accessories of that '*avadyati*' could not be transferred to the '*avadyati*' in question. Nor is the *fact of being for the sake of the sacrificial substance* the *method* of the '*avadānā*' (*cutting*); and thus too, the said fact could not be transferred (as it is only the *method* that can be thus transferred). Nor in such cases, can we have any operation of the *Sāmānyatodṛshṭa* Inference (towards the inference of the 'sacrifice'). As for the *pounding of the Putīkā*, and the *eating of the Phalacamasa*, it is by means of Syntactical Connection and Context that they are cognized as helping in the completion of the sacrifice; and consequently the case of the *pounding of the Putīkā* is not identical with that of '*avadyati*' in the matter of the implication of the 'sacrifice.' In the case of the sentences dealing with '*Soma*' also—('*Somenā yajeta, aindravāyavam*, etc., etc., etc.'), the qualified Injunction (of the *sacrifice by means of the Soma*) being *directly mentioned*, there is no room for any *implied sacrifice;* and as such the case of these too is different (from that of the '*pounding of the Putīkā*').

(6) In the case of the sentences '*aindravāyavam*, etc.,' even if they are secondary sentences laying down accessory materials, there is no syntactical split, as in the case of the sentence '*āgneyo'shṭākapālo, etc.*'

Because, though as mentioning more than one deity (*Indra* and *Vāyu*), the sentence has more than one object of Injunction, yet, on account of there being another action (in the shape of the '*grahaṇa*'), there is every possibility of the Injunction being that of a qualified object. That is to say, the sentence can very well be taken as an Injunction of the *Bhāvanā of the 'grahaṇa' qualified by the deities Indra, Vāyu and the rest.* Or, it may be that the '*grahaṇa*' being necessarily implied, the sentence serves the purpose of laying down a single joint Deity (Indra-Vāyu) mentioned by means of the *Dwandwa* compound; and thus there would be no

90

incongruity in the case. And as the connection of these with the Primary Sacrifice (*Jyotishṭoma*) is pointed out by the Context, there would be no incongruity, even if the sentence in question were taken as a secondary sentence (laying down accessory details).

Thus then, the actions (mentioned in the sentences '*aindravāyavam* etc.') having the character of mere *Preparatory Actions*, they stand in need of the mention of a '*sacrifice*' somewhere else; and as such there would be nothing incongruous in the fact of such a 'sacrifice' being laid down by another sentence ('*somēna yajēta*, etc.').

And our way of taking the sentences has the following advantage: (1) The singular number in '*jyotishṭomēna*' becomes capable of being taken directly (and not figuratively, as necessitated by the *Pūrvapaksha*, which makes it refer to *many* sacrifices); (2) we are saved the useless trouble of accepting the word '*soma*' (in '*somēna yajeta*') as a second name for the *Jyotishṭoma*; (3) nor is it necessary for us to accept the apparently useless fact of the sentence in question being a reference to all the other sentences, as in the case of the *Purvāpaksha* in connection with the *Āghārāgnihotra*.

For these reasons we conclude that the sentences in question are injunctions of the *Animal* and the *Soma* sacrifices.

***Sūtra* (19): Because of difference, there is a repetition of the Action; as the substances are distinct, it would be useless (to mention another connection); hence there is a difference (in the '*grahana*'); specially as it is subservient to the substance.**

[*Sūtra* (20) *is not specially dealt with by the Vartika; it is thus*: **The preparatory action does not differ, because the substance being for the sake of something else, it has a subordinate position.]**

[*Sūtra* (19) embodies the reply to the objection urged in the text on p. 509, beginning with the words '*çakyaparihārantwidam*.']

As the opponent has not urged the objection based upon the fact of the '*avadyati*'s' being mentioned in a definite order, etc., etc., with reference to the 'Paçu,' we lay aside this sentence for the present, to be dealt with under *Sūtra* X—vii—1 *et seq*., where we shall deal with the question as to whether the offering should be cut out from the whole animal, or from each of its limbs, or from only one limb, or only from those enumerated, namely, the *Heart* and the rest.

What concerns us now is the meeting of the objection with reference to the '*Soma*' (as it is with reference to this alone that the objection has been levelled against us). And to that we make the following reply:—

If the Deities of the sacrifice were separately mentioned directly by the sentences, then alone could they be taken as optional alternatives;

as a matter of fact, however, we find that all of them are mentioned as being connected with the sacrifice simultaneously. In a case where the sentence mentions a relationship independently of everything else, there alone could all the deities, serving the same purpose of accomplishing the sacrifice, be taken collectively.

That is to say, if we had such direct injunctions as '*aindravāyavena yajēta*' or '*Indravāyubhyām yāgam nirvartayēt*', then, inasmuch as the Deities would be pointed out as serving the same purpose, by sentences independently of one another, they would come to be taken as optional alternatives. As a matter of fact, however, in the case in question, we find that they are mentioned as in connection with '*grahaṇa,*' and become connected with the 'sacrifice' only indirectly by means of *Context* (and not directly by the Sentence). And as for the *Context*, it does not operate variously (or separately); and as such it could not connect, with the 'sacrifice,' each individual Deity independently by itself; consequently, what actually happens is that all the various '*grahaṇas*' having been simultaneously taken as constituting the *method* (of the sacrifice), the Deities mentioned in connection with these (*grahaṇas*) not having their ends duly fulfilled by that (*grahaṇa*) alone, all of them at once, being required by the 'sacrifice' dealt with in the Context, become simultaneously connected with it; (and as such there is nothing wrong in their being mentioned collectively).

As a rule, too, we accept a number of things to be optional alternatives when they are mentioned as employed for the same purpose, independently of one another; and the reason for this is that in such cases, the individual capability of each of these, by itself, is distinctly expressed by the sentence; and hence if they were to depend upon one another, this individual capability would be destroyed; and hence they are all accepted to be optional alternatives. In the case in question, however, the capability of accomplishing the *Jyotishṭoma* is not found to belong singly to each one of the deities mentioned—Indra, Vāyu, etc.; because we have no direct declaration of such capability. Though each one of them has the capability of accomplishing a sacrifice in general, yet, the particular sacrifice, in the shape of the *Jyotishṭoma*, can be accomplished only in the way laid down in the scriptural text; and hence each of the deities mentioned does not serve the same purpose. On the other hand, we find the two kinds of corns, the *Vrīhi* and the *Yava*, serving the same purpose; and hence they are taken as optional alternatives; specially because each of them is laid down as independent of the other, by independent sentences, as to be employed in the sacrifice.

Objection: "We find that we have actually a *sentence* '*aindravāyavam* "*gṛhṇāti*' laying down the deities Indra and Vāyu; and hence the

" sentence that follows '*maitrāvaruṇam gṛhṇāti*' is distinctly recognised " as capable of pointing out a deity, independently of the preceding " sentence."

Reply: It is true that with reference to the '*grahaṇa*,' the deities are laid down independently of one another; but in that case, all of them do not serve the same purpose; because being only a purificatory or preparatory action, the '*grahaṇas*' can have only transcendental results; and thus varying in each case, and not serving the same end, the various deities mentioned cannot be taken as optional alternatives.

Question: " But how do you conclude them to have only transcen- " dental results ? "

Answer: When a certain thing, having been mentioned in connection with the Primary Action, happens to be directly mentioned in connection with the Preparatory Action, then in that case, such a thing serves a visible purpose; and so also when, as a matter of fact, the Preparatory Action cannot actually be accomplished without that thing. That is to say, (1) if the deities having been previously connected with the 'sacrifice' (in the sentence '*somēna yajeta*') were again directly mentioned with reference to the *grahaṇas*,—as they are mentioned in connection with the *nirvapa* and the *āvāhana*; or (2) if without these Deities, the '*grahaṇa*' could not be accomplished;—then the mention of the Deities in connection with the '*grahaṇas*' would be for the purpose of a visible end, in the shape of recalling to the mind the Deities in connection with the coming sacrifice. In the case in question, however, we find that the Deities Indra, Vāyu, and the rest have not been previously mentioned in connection with the *Jyotishṭoma*; nor is it that without those Deities, the '*grahaṇas*' could not be accomplished; and consequently, under the circumstances, when we find the '*grahaṇa*' mentioned along with a certain Deity, this cannot but be taken as fulfilling an imperceptible transcendental result.

Objection: " When we have come to know that these deities belong " to the sacrifice, then, even without a previous mention of these (in con- " nection with the primary sacrifice), we could take all of them as serving " the same visible purpose of recalling the Deities in connection with that " sacrifice."

Reply: It is not so; because as a rule, it is at the time of the actual Injunction that the purpose served by the factors enjoined is sought after; and hence it is with reference to that time that we should ascertain whether the purpose served is a visible or an invisible one. That is to say, it is at the time of the operation of the sentence '*aindravāyavam gṛhṇāti*' that we have a want to know what purpose is served by it; and though at that time, we do, somehow or other, come to ascertain, through the Context, the connection of the 'sacrifice' with 'the *grahaṇa*,' which embodies the *method* (of that sacrifice), yet, inasmuch as the Deities themselves are connected with something (*i.e.*, the '*grahaṇa*') other than the sacrifice, and as they themselves have not the form of actions, they are not pointed out, by the Context, as serving the purpose of accomplishing the sacrifice; and consequently, the use (of these Deities) in connection with the '*grahaṇa*' must be taken as something independent of any connection with the 'sacrifice'; and such a use cannot but be invisible (or transcendental). And this transcendental purpose having been ascertained at the time of the operation of the Injunction in question, if at the time of the actual performance of the Action therein laid down, a certain visible result is found to come about, how could the previously ascertained transcendental result be set aside by that? Nor could any such visible result (appearing by the way) control the operation of the Injunction in question. And thus the connection of the deity, mentioned in each of the sentences in question, cannot but fulfil certain transcendental purposes; and as such all the deities in question must be taken as all conjointly (helping the accomplishment of the sacrifice through the said transcendental results).

And unless the '*grahaṇa*' is not repeated (with each deity), the separately mentioned deities can not be connected with the '*grahaṇa*' in accordance with the law that 'that which is done in connection with the *Samit* is not done in connection with the *Tanūnapāta*'; and hence there must be a '*grahaṇa*' (holding) of the *Soma*, with reference to each deity.

Thus, then, the *Sūtrā* must be taken as follows: '*tadbhēdāt,*'—*i.e.*, on account of the connection of the deity being different in each case,—'*there must be a repetition of the action*' *of grahaṇa*; because '*on account, of the distinctness of the substance*', that is to be prepared or purified by means of the *grahaṇa* in connection with the said deities, if any other connection were mentioned, '*it would be wholly useless*'; as it would not be performed; and hence '*there is a difference*' of the *grahaṇa*, '*because it is subservient to the substance*' to be purified (by that *grahaṇa*).

Inasmuch as these '*grahaṇas*' in connection with the various deities are mentioned in a section dealing with sacrifices, it follows that, without a '*sacrifice,*' they cannot prepare the substance '*Soma*' for the sake of any deity; and this leads us to the conclusion that there must be a certain sacrifice, that would establish the relationship of the substances with the deities in question. On the other hand, we find that the 'sacrifice' (laid down in the sentence '*somēna yajeta*') has no deity laid down (by the original Injunction); nor is the requisite deity pointed out either by Direct Declaration, or by Indirect Indication by the words of the text, or by those of any sentence; and as for the *Context*, it can have nothing to do in connection with that (*i.e.*, the Deity) which is not an Action; and hence the Context comes to point out the fact of the '*grahaṇas*' being performed (in connection with the sacrifice in question). These '*grahaṇas*' too, not being laid down *separately* (by the Context, which never operates separately), and serving to accomplish only invisible (transcendental) results, come to be taken all at once (simultaneously); and through these '*grahaṇas*' we come to take the deities (mentioned in connection with them) also collectively.

Objection: "We find that even when certain things are pointed out "by the Context, if they are found to serve the same purpose, they are "taken as optional alternatives; as for instance, the *mantras* employed at "the dividing of the sacrificial cake."

Reply: It is true that they are so taken; but in that case it is not the Context alone that operates towards the pointing out of them; because the fact of each of the said *mantras* being connected with each *Division* being pointed out by the Direct Declaration inferred from the indications of the words of the *mantras*, all that the Context does, in this case, is to point out that it is at the Division of the Cake *in connection with the Darça-Pūrṇamāsa sacrifices* that the *mantras* have to be employed; because of their being of no use at other divisions. Hence even if the *Darça* and the *Pūrṇamāsa* were to take up all the *mantras* collectively, those sacrifices would have no capability of taking them up, independently of the intervening agency of the Division (of the Cake); and this agency is found to be connected with many alternatives, and not in a collective form. In the case in question, however, the conditions are totally different; because in this case, the intervening agency is that of the '*grahaṇas*,' and it is with reference to these that the deities are found to be mentioned collectively; and hence even though the collection, or aggregate, of the deities may be capable of being taken up with each '*grahaṇa*' separately, yet inasmuch as it is through the agency of the '*grahaṇas*' that the *deities* can be taken up, what could it do in this case (but point to the performance of the collective performance of the '*grahaṇas*' also)?

Objection: "As a matter of fact, we find that each of the '*grahaṇas*' has got the capability of helping the Primary Action, by means "of the bringing up of the substance (*Soma*), and also by pointing out "the requisite deity; and thus the case of these *grahaṇas* being identical "with that of the aforesaid *mantras*, they must be taken as optional "alternatives."

Reply: Such could have been the case, if the sacrifices in question had been previously cognised as having many deities (connected with them); as then alone could the various bringings up of the substance be taken as being for the sake of those various deities. As a matter of fact, however, we find that in the case in question, no such sacrifice with various deities has been previously cognised; and hence the mention of the various presentations of the substance must be taken as serving only an imperceptible (or transcendental) purpose.

These presentations of the substance, too, must differ from one another, on account of the difference among their qualifications (the deities); as with a single presentation of the substance, it is not possible for many deities to be taken, either singly or collectively. Because as for their being taken collectively (simultaneously), this is precluded by the sentences (*'aindravāyayam gṛhṇātī,' 'maitrāvaruṇam gṛhṇāti'* etc.) which speak of them as appearing one after the other; and (even if such simultaneous taking of many deities with a single material were attempted) we would have an *aggregate* (of deities), which would not have the character of a sacrificial deity at all, as we have no authority for asserting any such character with reference to an aggregate of Indra, Vāyu and the rest; specially because we find each of them mentioned separately by means of nominal affixes with each word. Nor is it possible for all of them to be taken separately (in connection with the same presentation of the substance); because the substance is always laid down with reference to the deity; and it is not possible for a single substance to be laid down (by a single sentence) with reference to more than one deity. If the substance could be referred to the deities, either prior to, or after, the '*grahaṇa*,' then that would be doing something not enjoined by the texts. And further, a substance is always referred to a deity in such terms as 'this belongs to such and such a deity'; and hence if the same substance were to be referred to another deity, the former offering would certainly be done away with. That is to say, a certain *Soma juice* having been set aside with the expressed idea that 'this is to be offered to Indra and Vāyu,' it is as good as already offered; and as such the sacrificer no longer having any control over it, how could he speak of the same juice as to be offered to 'Mitra and Varuṇa?' For if an offering once made to a deity, were to be made again to another deity, it would have to be snatched away from the former deity. Or, in view of the previous determination (to offer the substance to one Deity), the subsequent determination (to offer it to another) could never be taken as true; and in any case, such an action would mean a most unworthy procedure, and not the fulfilling of the Vedic Injunction.

For these reasons, we conclude that the '*grahaṇa*' must be distinct, with each of the deities in question.

Further, even without the actual '*grahaṇa*' of the substance, it would be quite possible for us to refer it to a certain deity, no matter in what place the substance may be; and as such the injunction of the '*grahaṇas*' could only be with regard to certain transcendental results. That is to say a '*sacrifice*' consists of the action of *giving away of one's ownership in favour of a Deity;* and this giving away of one's ownership or possession over the *Soma* would be quite possible, in whatever condition the *Soma* may be, either in the state of being clarified (without putting it into separate vessels), or in any condition after it has been purchased; and hence the injunction of the various rites, purificatory and preparatory, of the *Soma* must be taken as with a view to certain transcendental results. In a case where the substance laid down is the *Cake*, or some such thing, such preparatory actions as the *threshing* and *shifting*, etc., of the corn, are found to have a visible result in the shape of the preparation of the Cake (as without those actions, the Cake would not be made). In the case in question, however, we have no such Injunction as that the offering must be made out of the Soma *kept in the sacrificial cup*, etc.; because all that the Injunction lays down is the *Soma-plant*; and consequently the '*grahaṇas*,' or *holdings*, of the Soma in the various vessels, though serving to bring about distinct transcendental results, must be taken as collectively (helping by these results the accomplishment of the sacrifice).

Then again, in the same Context, we find the sentence '*daça mushṭīrmimītē*,' which serves to lay down the measure of the quantity of *Soma* to be employed; and hence we conclude that this sentence qualifies the Injunction '*somena yajēta*,' which comes to mean that 'the sacrifice is to be by means of *ten handfuls of Soma*.' And then this definite quantity of *Soma* having been pounded with a fixed quantity of water, could not be kept in small cups, unless it were 'held' (in the hand) each time that it would be kept in a cup; and as such these 'holdings' ('*grahaṇas*') must be many and distinct (as there are many cups to be filled with the *Soma juice*); and it is by means of the *Soma* thus held in the various cups, that the sacrifice is to be performed. And as, unless the sacrifice is repeated over and over again, all that has been just said (with reference to the offering of the *Soma juice* in the various cups dedicated to various deities) is not possible,—the *sacrifice* comes to be repeated, for the sake of a definite purpose.

In view of these facts, we can also take the *Sūtra* (19) as follows: '*tadbhēdāt*,'—*i.e.*, because of the diversity of the prepared *Soma*—'*there is a repetition of the action*' of Sacrifice; '*because of the separateness of the material*' accepted;—if all of them were not offered up, the whole '*would be useless*'; and hence even though in the original Injunction, the 'sacrifice' has been mentioned but once, yet '*there is a diversity*' of its performance, because of the fact of the originally enjoined '*substance being subservient*' to the various conditions mentioned in other sentences.

The substance, too, must be offered in the same way as it has been held in the various cups; as, if the whole thing were to be mixed up again, the previous holding into separate cups would become wholly useless; and the deities, to whom the cup-fuls have been previously dedicated, would not become connected with (possessed of) their specified shares; nor is it possible for all the deities to be referred to at the time of the (single) offering; hence it is not possible for people, afraid of repetition, to mix up all the juice and make a single offering of it; specially as even if this were done, it would lead to a confusion of the shares (previously specified). And when the shares have been once separately specified, it becomes necessary for the other party to clear up the said confusion, unless of course he has a scriptural text distinctly laying down such confusion. Thus then, it being necessary to make the offering as previously determined, it is only when all the deities (and the *grahaṇas*) are taken collectively, that the following sentence—*daçaitānadhwaryuh prātahsavane gṛhṇāti, āçwino daçamo gṛhṇāti, tam tṛtīyam juhoti*, etc., etc. (laying down the definite order and the summing up of the various '*grahanas*')—becomes explicable.

Thus then we conclude that the whole forms a single action (of the Jyotishṭoma).

The use of the present *Adhikaraṇa* lies in the fact that, according to the *Pūrvapaksha*, among the sacrifices subsidiary to the Soma sacrifice (the *Jyotishṭoma*), we would have the performance of the details with regard to one *cup*, and that, too, only once; whereas, according to the *Siddhānta*, the whole thing has to be done exactly as in the Primary Sacrifice (the *Jyotishṭoma*).

ADHIKARANA (7).

[*The Differentiation of Actions by means of Number.*]

Sūtra **(21): Because of the fact of its inhering in separateness, Number would serve to differentiate the Actions.**

The treatment of the three exceptions to the Law relating to the Repetition of Words has been finished, and we now proceed to show how Actions are differentiated (or distinguished) by means of Number.

In this connection we should cite such sentences as '*tisra āhutīrjuhoti*' '*dwādaça dwādaçāni juhoti,*' which are laid down as co-extensive with the actions enjoined by previous originative Injunctions, and which are accompanied by definite numbers.

And on this, we have the following :—

PŪRVAPAKSHA (A).

"Inasmuch as the word '*juhoti*' is mentioned but once, the action laid down is one only; and as for the *Number* ('three' etc.) it could be made up by frequent repetitions of the same Action."

SIDDHANTA (A).

To the above we make the following reply: In the case in question the Number is mentioned in connection with the *Homa*, while it is being enjoined, and not *after* it has been enjoined, as in the case of the sentence '*ēkādaçaprayājān*'; and without an idea of '*separateness*' the Number does not attain its true character. Nor can the Number be said to be made up by a repetition of the same Action; because it is only when there is no other way of explaining the *number*, that it is held to be made up by Repetitions, as in the case of the *Prayājas*, the *Upasadas* and the like, which have had their own limits previously specified. In the case in question, however, inasmuch as no other Number of the Action has been previously specified, the Number (three) must be taken as pointing out the separate character of the Actions themselves. And hence as the Number is found to inhere in the separateness of the actions themselves, we cannot accept it as referring to the separateness due to the mere repetitions of the same action; as we shall show later on, under the *sūtra* '*āgamādvā'bhyāsasyāçrūtatwāt*' (X—v—16).

Objection: "Inasmuch as in the first instance, a single *Homa* has "been expressed by the word '*juhoti*,' it is clear that the Number "'three' is to be made up by repetitions of the same *Homa*."

Reply: Not so; the action denoted by the word '*juhoti*' having no material reality (*i.e.*, being incapable of being connected with any Gender, Number, etc.), the number ('one') cannot apply to it; as for the Number (singular) that is denoted by the affix in the word '*juhoti*,' it applies to its Nominative, and not either to the *Bhāvanā* or to the *Root-meaning*. Consequently when the word '*juhoti*' would proceed to indicate a *single* Homa indirectly by means of the fact of its (the word '*juhoti*') being mentioned only once, we would be stopped, at the very outset, by the number 'three' mentioned *directly* in the sentence, and would be led to accept the *Homa* as qualified by this latter Number, and the action (*Homa*) would come to have so many distinct forms. And hence the three *Homas* must be taken as distinct actions.

—o—

Though the above was the proper representation of the *Adhikaraṇa*, yet the *Bhāshya* has expounded it in connection with the sentence '*saptadaça prājāpatyān*, etc.', because he means that he will establish the fact of the Number pertaining to the *material* also serving to distinguish the Actions—a fact that is very difficult to prove.

The ground of doubt in connection with this sentence may be thus explained. In the word '*prājāpatyān*', is the compound '*ekaçesha Dwandwa*' to be taken as being formed after the appearance of the Nominal Affix (in '*prājāpatyān*')?—or is the Affix to be taken as appearing after the compound has been formed? That is to say, if the word were explained as "*ēsha ca, ēsha ca, ēsha ca, iti*, '*ētē*' (the *Ekaçesha* compound)—*Prājapatiḥ ēshām dēvatā iti* '*Prājāpatyaḥ*' ('*Prajapati*' + the deific *Affix*), *tān*",—then the word would denote the relationship of a single substance mentioned by the Pronoun '*esha*,' with a single Deity (Prajāpati); and in that case the action referred to would be *one* only. If, however, the word be explained as "*Prajāpatiḥ devāta asya iti* '*Prājāpatyaḥ*' ('*Prajapati*' + the Affix),—*Prājāpatyaçca Prājāpatyaçca Prājāpatyāçca iti* '*Prājāpatyāh*' (*the Ekaçesha* compound), *tān*,—then the word would clearly point out *seventeen* distinct connections of the deity; and each of these connections implying a 'sacrifice,' the Actions referred to could not but be seventeen distinct ones.

In connection with this doubt, we have the following :—

PŪRVAPAKSHA (B).

" The Action referred to is *one* only, because in the word '*Prājāpatyān*' we find the *plurality* distinctly belonging to that which is denoted " by the Affix; and as the *Ekaçēsha* compound is due to that *plurality*, the " compounding could not be of the basic noun. That is to say, one who " explains the words as '*Prājāpatyaçca Prājāpatyaçca, etc.*,' takes the compound as belonging to the basic noun as well as to the Affix; but the only " ground for this lies in the Apparent Inconsistency of the plurality in " '*Prājāpatyān*'; but as a matter of fact, we find that the *Plurality* is " not found in the basic noun; and as such, this latter cannot be compounded into an '*Ēkaçesha*'; nor is it such that the *Plurality* cannot be " referred to the denotation of the Affix, without there being an *Ēkaçēsha* " of the basic Noun; because this Plurality is distinctly expressed, at the " time that the formation of the word '*Prājāpatyān*' is explained, by the " Pronoun '*ēshām*.' Thus then, we conclude that the Deity '*Prajāpati*,' " mentioned but once, is connected with many materials.

" Further, when only a little assumption is found to serve our purpose, it would never do to assume a number of actions, not directly " mentioned, and their *Apūrvas*. That is to say, even if we were to " accept the latter of the two explanations of the word '*Prājāpatyān*,' we " could not rest with the mere fact of having the compound formed *after* " the application of the Affix; as it would be necessary for us to assume a " number of unseen and unheard-of Actions and their *Apūrvas*; and that " we cannot assume any number of these at our will has already been " shown in the *Çabdāntarādhikaraṇa* (in the beginning of the present " *Pāda*), where we have shown that we can assume, by means of Apparent Inconsistency, only that much of the unseen and unheard of, without which the connection of the mentioned Deity with the enjoined " material remains inexplicable; as the said Apparent Inconsistency does " not warrant any more of the unseen and unheard of. It would, however, " be necessary for you to assume from one to seventeen Actions and as " many *Apūrvas*. But as the assumption of the very first of these would " complete all the Primaries (as in the case of the *Prayājas*),—*i.e.*, as the " determination to offer the first animal to Prajāpati would apply equally " to all the other animals, whose case is not found to be different from that " of the first,—the performance of that single offering will have connected " all the rest with the *sacrifice*; and as such, we could not carry on the " assumption any further.

" Then again, the difference of one thing cannot bring about the " difference of another; for certainly because of there being distinct

" pieces, in the shape of the Heart, etc., it does not follow that there are " different Actions also. That is to say, if the diversity of the materials " were to make a diversity among Actions, then there would also be a diver- " sity of Actions on account of the diversity of the pieces of the animal's " body. As a matter of fact, however, no such diversity is possible, as " we shall show later on, under *Sūtra* VI—iii—12; where it is shown that " the whole animal having been laid down as the means of accomplishing " the Primary sacrifice (of the *Agnishṭoma*), and the Animal having to be " given away also as a whole, the fact that the sacrifice is to be accom- " plished by means of the Animal, only as being the source from which " the eleven pieces would be obtained, is got at from other sentences; and " as such the 'cutting of the pieces' becomes a qualification of the " *Animal*, and not that of the *Sacrifice*. In the case in question also, all " the seventeen animals being known as the means of accomplishing the " sacrifice, the implied direction would apply the *process* of one animal " (of its being cut into eleven pieces) to all the seventeen animals; and " as such there would be nothing very incongruous in the fact of a single " sacrifice taking up (utilising) all the seventeen groups of 'eleven pieces " each. And for these reasons we conclude that the Action referred to is " one only."

SIDDHĀNTA.

To the above, we make the following reply:—

If there were only one Action, there would be a single Injunction (in the form of 'the Subsidiary Sacrifices are to be performed in the same way as the Primary'); and thereby the material to be employed being pointed out as a single 'eleven-piece' group (as the Primary makes use of only one such group), there would be no use for all the seventeen animals. That is to say, the sentence in question does not rest with the declaration '*Prājāpatyān paçūn*,' as there is yet another part of the sentence to be supplied, *viz.* '*prakṛtivat*.' And if there be a single Action, it is the '*Savanīya*,' that is, the *Primary* in question; and as at that the sacrifice is performed by means of a single 'eleven-piece' group, it follows that in the action in question there should be only one such group; and as this *group*, too, in the case of the Primary Sacrifice, is supplied by a *single* animal—which is mentioned by a word wherein the singular number is meant to be significant,—it would be the same in the action in question also. And thus the action having been accomplished by means of a single animal, none of the other sixteen animals would become connected with Prajāpati; and thereby we would be neglecting the Plurality expressed in the same word ('*Prājāpatyān*'), as also the number 'seventeen' mentioned in the same sentence. When, on the other hand, the idea accepted is that there are 'seventeen' sacrifices, then the said

Injunction '*prakṛtivat*, etc.,' coming in for each of the sacrifices, would point to as many 'eleven-piece' groups; and for the sake of obtaining these groups, we could have as many animals, even if they were not actually laid down as 'seventeen'; and there can be no doubt on the point when the Number is distinctly laid down.

Objection: "It does not appear quite proper to reject the directly "perceptible *singleness* of the sacrifice, and assume its *plurality* on the "ground of an implied injunction ('*prakṛtivat*, etc.'). For whether the "sacrifice is one or many is ascertained at the time that the sacrifice is "enjoined; and it is on this Direct Injunction that an Implied or *Extended* "Direction (*Atidēça*) is based; and it is never the case that the Direct "Injunction is based upon the Extended Direction. That is to say, it is "at the time that the Action is originally laid down, that we ascertain the "fact of its being one only or many; and in all cases the original mention "of the Action is by means of a Direct Injunction, and not by an Implied "Direction. For, until the Action has actually appeared (as enjoined), "there is no question as to its *method*; and until the *method* has ap-"peared (and is found to be wanting in certain factors) there is no Extended "Direction. Consequently as the Extended Direction ('*prakṛtivat*, etc.') "is found to appear long after the unity or diversity of Actions has been "ascertained, no such Extended Direction can rightly be taken as leading "us to accept a diversity of Actions."

To the above we make the following reply: It has been shown above that whenever there is a doubt, it is always set at rest either by means of 'supplementary sentence' (*Sūtra* I—iv—29) or by means of Indirect Implications (I—iv—30); and in the case in question we find that we have both these means available for ascertaining the doubtful point. That is to say, in the case in question, it is not by means of the Extended Direction alone that we come to accept the Diversity of Actions; in fact it is by means of the Direct Injunction contained in the word '*prājāpatyān*' itself. As this Injunction had, at the first instance, been cognised only in the form of the material, the Deity and the 'Sacrifice', it had nothing definite to say with regard to the measure (or number) of that sacrifice, because of the doubt (in regard to the word '*prājāpatyān*') attaching to the precedence and sequence of the Nominal Affix and the *ekaçesha* compound, as pointed out above (see above, p. 723); and this doubt is removed by the said number being ascertained (1) by means of the 'supplementary sentence' in the shape of the aforesaid Extended Direction, and (2) also by means of the capability of the word itself to imply that number. Though it is true that the Extended Direction appears afterwards, yet, as in the case in question, from the very beginning, the presence of that Direction is known to be as sure as anything else; and hence the

Direct Injunction also comes to be taken in a sense that would not be incompatible with that Direction. Consequently, even though the interpretation of the sentence in question is begun with explaining the word '*prājāpatyān*' as '*Prajāpatirdēvatā eshām, tān*,'—yet inasmuch as this interpretation is subsequently found to be incompatible with what follows (in the Extended Direction), the interpreter, if an intelligent person, does not fail to conclude that he had committed a mistake, at the very outset, in explaining the said word. There is no such rule as that the Extended Direction must always be in keeping with the idea taken up by us in the beginning. Nor is the Extended Direction capable of referring the seventeen 'eleven-piece' groups—not mentioned in connection with the Primary '*Savanīya*'—to a single Action; nor again can a single animal be the source from which all the seventeen 'eleven-piece' groups should be obtained; nor is there any doubt on this point, that would be removed by means of the Direct Injunction (in the sentence in question). Nor is there an absolute contradiction between the Extended Direction and the Direct Injunction, because the full bearing of this latter is still doubtful; and hence there would be nothing to set aside the employing of a single 'eleven-piece' group at one sacrifice.

The fact, too, of the Action referred to being one only is not directly enjoined. And in all cases, it is an accepted law that so long as there can be a compatibility (between the Direct Injunction and the Extended Direction) we cannot take them as contradictory to each other; and in the case in question, we find that the two can be made compatible with each other by taking the Actions to be many. And hence the construction of the word in question must be taken as—"*Prajāpatirdevatā asya, iti* '*Prājāpatyaḥ*,'" and the *ekaçēsha* would imply the mention of the *seventeen Prājāpatyas*. And thus, the connections between the Deity and the Material being diverse,—just as in the case of the '*Āgnēya*,' the '*Agnīshomīya*,' etc.,—the 'sacrifices' referred to cannot but be accepted as many and diverse.

It has been urged above that—"the *cutting into eleven pieces* being a "property of the animal, it would be different with each of the seventeen "animals, even when the Action is accepted to be one only."

But this is not quite correct; because in the case in question, the Implied Direction does not refer to the *Method* of the Material; because the want of a *Method* always arises with reference to an Action; and as such it stands in need of the properties and qualifications of the Action (and not that of the Material). That is to say, the desire for the method is in the form—'In what way is the result to be accomplished *by the sacrifice of the Prājāpatya animal*'?—and not as 'how' *by the animal*?' In the Primary *Savanīya* sacrifice also, we find that the property of *being accomplished by means of the 'eleven-piece' group obtained from a single animal* belongs to the *sacrifice*, and not to the *animal*, as the mention of a property of the Animal would be useless; because if the property belonged to the Animal, then all that the property would do would be to purify the animal; and there would be no use of such a purification, as the animal will have been destroyed (before the offering is made). As for the sacrifice, there is a distinct purpose served by its accomplishment, as also by the accomplishment of its *Apūrva*; and hence the *cutting of the eleven pieces*, etc., could all very well be taken as the *method* by which the sacrifice and its *Apūrva* would be accomplished. Thus then, a single sacrifice cannot take up more than one 'eleven-piece' group; and when no more than one such group would be used, more than one animal too could not be taken up. Though some people might think that 'the fact of the source of the pieces being one only is set aside by the mention of the number *seventeen*, and hence we can take the single group of eleven-pieces out of more than one animal,'—yet, even then, only *eleven* animals would be necessary (for the cutting out of the eleven pieces), and not *seventeen*.

The Bhāshya represents the opponent as declaring that—"*in a single sacrifice, we could make an offering of the seventeen eleven-piece groups*." And the sense of this assertion is this: "Fearing the necessity of having to assume an unseen factor, we take the word '*paçu*' as indicating the 'Piece-Group' through its proximity to the Sacrifice, and the number 'seventeen' may be taken as specifying that Group."

But this cannot be; because in the case in question we find no ground for the said Indication. So long as there is no incongruity (in the Direct Signification) we cannot rightly have recourse to Indication. And then what the sense of the sentence comes to be, according to you, is this: '*Seventeen* animals should be taken up, and a *single* sacrifice should be accomplished by means of a *single* eleven-piece group obtained from a *single* animal'; certainly such a performance would never be possible!

If it be urged that the Number mentioned in one place could be taken elsewhere,—then too, it would come to be taken along with the sacrifice, on account of the greater proximity of this with the *Apūrva* (and thus we would have *seventeen* sacrifices, and not *one*). And we have already explained above that we cannot rightly set aside any part of the Injunctive sentence, unless we find it to be actually incompatible.

As for the necessity of assuming an unseen factor, so long as there is sufficient authority and ground for such an assumption, there can be nothing wrong in it.

The Bhāshya brings forward another theory, in the sentence—"*yadi çṛṅgābhiprāyā varṇābhiprāyā rūpābhiprāyā vā abhavishyan.*" This has been brought in as a solvent for the sentence that lays down the *whole* animal as the offering; and the sense of the sentence is that—" from among " various animals that may have either seventeen horns, or seventeen " colours, or seventeen shapes, one is to be made the *Prājāpatya*."

In reply to this it is said in the Bhāshya: ***But the animals are subsequently laid down clearly as* '*black, hornless*,'** (and hence the 'seventeen-coloured' or the 'seventeen-horned' ones could not be meant). **And hence we conclude that there are *seventeen sacrifices*.**

The use of the *Adhikaraṇa* is this: Though the *Pūrvapakshi* does not wish it, yet, in accordance with his theory, only one animal would be the means of accomplishing the sacrifice, and the other sixteen would be taken up only for the purpose of making up its enjoined number ('*seventeen*'); and hence the Pieces would have to be cut out of that one animal; consequently if there would be anything amiss in this cutting out, it would be necessary, not to take up another animal for the cutting out of the pieces only, but also another batch of sixteen for the purpose of making up the enjoined number with reference to this newly-brought animal. Or again, when the purification of the first batch of sixteen would be only half done, if even one becomes amiss,—with reference to that, then and there, it would be necessary to repeat all of them over again (while according to the *Siddhānta*, each animal being used in a distinct sacrifice, if there was anything amiss with one, that one alone would have to be replaced, and not all).

Objection: " In the case of the contiguous (or joint) performance of " many sacrifices, we find that if there is anything wrong with the " performance of any one of them, then, in accordance with the law laid " down under the *Sūtra* VI—v—56, while the other sacrifices have yet to " be performed, what is performed over again is only that one sacrifice, " and not all of them; and the same rule might very well hold in the case " in question, where we have a combined or joint material."

Reply: This is not possible; because in the case in question, we find that the capability of accomplishing the sacrifice in question inheres in seventeen of the same object, *i.e.*, the seventeen animals taken as a single object; and as such, like the number, it appertains to all of them taken collectively; consequently the purificatory rites—*upākaraṇa* and the rest—of these should be performed as such a whole; consequently, when even a single animal out of these would die during the purification, there would be a destruction of the exact Material for accomplishing the sacrifice; and hence, even though the other animals be quite intact, the purificatory rites of the material *as a whole* would have gone wrong; and as such these rites would have to be done all over again. But even when a fresh

92

animal would be brought in, the rites would appertain to that animal only, as forming the Material for the sacrifice; and as the exact character of the Material would not be attained by that *one* animal unless it be accompanied by the other sixteen animals,—it would be necessary to bring in a fresh batch of *seventeen* animals, each time that there may be the slightest mistake during the performance.

In accordance with the *Siddhānta*, on the other hand, each of the animals has the character of the Material, independently of the others; and what is done is only the performance of the sacrifices together; and hence in this case if there is anything wrong with regard to one animal, it is that one alone that has to be replaced.

Objection: " If what you say is true, then, according to the *Pūrvapak-* " *sha*, in the case of the Injunction '*Stotraçastrēshu tāncaturbhirādattē*,' " if there happens to be something wrong in the reciting of one *Mantra*, " all the *Mantras* would have to be repeated."

Reply: Not so; in that case each *Mantra* forms a distinct means by itself, and what the Injunction does is only to mention them collectively. As a matter of fact, in all that the *Mantras* do, with regard to the making up of the Hymns, etc., they have each a distinct capability of supplying a distinct want (in the shape of the pointing out of the requisite Deity, *e.g.*); as otherwise all of them would form a single sentence (according to the *Sūtra* II—i—46). Thus then the fact is that each *Mantra* having fulfilled its own specific function, the effects of all these functionings combine to bring about another effect (in the shape of a transcendental potency, etc.), and the character of aiding the sacrifice does not belong to the *Mantras taken collectively*. In the case of the seventeen Animals, however, it is found to belong to them taken collectively as a single whole.

Objection: " The effects of the *Mantras*, then, acting conjointly, if " there were anything wrong with one, all of them would have to be " repeated."

Reply: Not so; because when there would be nothing wrong in the cause (the *Mantra*), there could be none in its effect. Specially as the action of man appertains to the *Means* (of accomplishing a certain action), all performances should be regulated by mistakes in these *Means* (and not by those in the effects).

ADHIKARAṆA (8).

[The Differentiation of Actions by Names.]

***Sūtra* (22): Name also (serves to distinguish Actions); because of its occurring in the originative Injunction.**

The Differentiation of Actions by means of Accessories and Context, bristling with many discussions, is postponed for a future occasion; and we proceed to consider the case of Name.

[In connection with the sentence '*athaisha jyotiḥ, atha viçvajyotiḥ, atha sarvajyotiḥ,*' there arises the following doubt—Do these names only serve to refer to the *Jyotishṭoma*, for the purpose of laying down 'a thousand' as the sacrificial gift in connection with it? or do they lay down other Actions at which that is the sacrificial gift? And on this we have the following]—

PŪRVAPAKSHA.

"Inasmuch as the words '*atha*' and '*ēsha*' stand in need of something that has gone before, and as the rejection of the original subject and the taking up of another is a faulty process,—it follows that the various names apply to the single sacrifice '*Jyotishṭoma*,' for which, as in the case of the *Dākshāyaṇa* sacrifice, another detail (in the shape of the gift of 'a thousand') is laid down. And when we already have a sentence ('*Jyotishṭomēna svargakāmo yajēta*') that lays down the connection between the Material and the Result, if we accept the words in question to be the names of the same Action, we are saved the necessity of assuming (1) another Action, (2) an *Apūrva* in keeping with that Action, and (3) wholly unheard of methods for the accomplishment of that *Apūrva*, etc., etc.; and there would be the further advantage that as the mention of the gift of 'a thousand' could be taken as laying down a method of procedure with regard to the *Jyotishṭoma*, we would not have to set aside this sacrifice (which forms the original subject of the Context). If the sentences in question were to be the Injunctions of other Actions, there would be no use for the word '*atha*,' which refers to something gone before; for one sacrifice does not stand in need of another; nor does any significance attach to any order of "sequence among the sacrifices, (that are independent of one another) " as we shall show later on. And hence the word '*atha*' cannot be taken " as signifying this order of sequence.

"Nor does the *Name* express a *Bhāvanā*; nor is the *Root-meaning* " found to be mixed up with the Name, in the sentences in question, as " is the case with the root '*yaji*' (which is often mixed up with names of " sacrifices); and as such there could be no idea of difference among the " Root-meanings. Nor again is the Name an *injunctive word*, whereby it " could urge people to other actions (than the *Jyotishṭoma*); and " so long as the human agent is not urged into activity, even if a " difference could be cognised, we could attach no significance to it, " exactly as we do with regard to the singular number in '*graham*' " (in the sentence '*graham sammārshti*'). The injunctive word (in the " sentence '*ētēna sahasradakshiṇēna yajeta*') that we have in connection " with these sentences, is taken up by the mention of the accessory detail " (in the shape of the sacrificial gift of 'a thousand'); and as such it " cannot pertain to the form of any Action. If the Injunctive word were " not thus set aside, then too, the difference of the two 'sacrifices' would " be based upon the repetition of the word '*yajētā*,' and not upon the " Names.

"The mention of a Result also does not give rise to the idea of dif- " ference among Actions, in accordance with the *Sūtra* II—iii—26. Or, it " may be that inasmuch as the 'gift of a thousand' rests upon the " previously mentioned *Jyotishṭoma*, the particular result mentioned in " connection with this gift may be taken as following from the employ- " ment of this accessory 'gift' in connection with the same *Jyotishṭoma*; " just as the employing of different accessories (at the same sacrifice), " such as '*dadhi*,' and 'milking vessel,' is laid down, with a view " to particular results, (in the shape of the obtaining of an *organ of sense* " and *Cattle* respectively). And thus, too, the Action referred to cannot " be a new one.

"In the case of the words '*Jyotiḥ*,' etc., there is a further peculi- " arity: they form part of the name '*Jyotishṭoma*'; and as such they " cannot fail to give an idea of the *Jyotishṭoma*. Specially as we find the " *Jyotishṭoma* actually spoken of as '*Jyotiḥ*,' in the sentence '*vasantē* " *vasantē Jyotishā*,' etc.

"For these reasons, we conclude that, inasmuch as in the case in " question, we find none of the abovementioned grounds of diversity,— " *viz.*, Difference of words, Repetition of the same word, Number, the " mention of an Accessory incompatible with the original Action, and a " Difference of Context—the Actions referred to cannot be any other than " the original *Jyotishṭoma*."

SIDDHĀNTA.

To the above we make the following reply: When no word expressive of the Action has been used, the *name* that happens to be mentioned first cannot but give rise to the idea of something new. That is to say, in a case where the Action has been already laid down by means of a previously pronounced Verb, before the Name comes to be mentioned, the unity or diversity of the Actions concerned having, in this case, already been ascertained elsewhere by means of the verb, the subsequently appearing Name would not distinguish the Actions. In the case in question, however, we find that the *name* is mentioned in connection with an Action that has yet to be laid down (by the subsequent sentence '*ētēna sahasradakshiṇēna yajēta*'); and as such, like the Number, it must be expressive of *Separateness*. Because in all cases, it is most improper to use one word in more than one sense, or to express one thing by more than one word; and hence whenever we come across a new *thing*, we look for a new *name;* and *vice versa*, whenever we find a new *name* we look for a new *thing*. When, however, we directly perceive both of these to be the same that has been known before, then this perception sets aside the weaker authority of the aforesaid character of the *Name*. But so long as there is no such recognition of identity, there is nothing to set aside the idea of difference naturally afforded by the difference of *Names*.

For instance, in the case in question, we find that entirely different from the previously mentioned *Jyotishṭoma*, there is, later on, a new name '*atha gauḥ*'; and as this latter has apparently no connection with what has gone before, it cannot bring about any idea thereof; and hence it gives rise to the notion of something else coloured by itself (*i.e.*, the name '*gauḥ*'). And then we proceed to look out, in what follows as well as in what has gone before, for that thing of which this is the name; and we find that all the '*yajatis*' that have gone before refer to, and have been absorbed by, the *Jyotishṭoma;* and as such cannot refer to anything else, or have any other *name*; but as for the '*yajati*' that comes afterwards (in the sentence '*ētēna sahasradakshiṇēna yajēta*') though, on account of the mention of the Result, the Injunctive potency is taken up by the laying down of something else (*i.e.*, the accessory gift of 'a thousand'), and as such the Injunction itself does not serve to distinguish the Action,—yet, inasmuch as, according to *Sūtra* II—i—49, on account of the intervention of an unconnected word '*gauḥ*' (between the passages dealing with the *Jyotishṭoma* and the sentence '*athaisha jyotiḥ*, etc.'), the word '*gauḥ*' does not very well fit into what has gone before; and hence the idea of what has gone before not presenting itself at the time that the sentence '*atha gauḥ*' appears, the continuance of the previous Context is broken off, and the mind naturally seeks for something else; and the subsequent '*yajēta*' presenting itself to this expectant mind, and being incapable of referring to the *Jyotishṭoma* sacrifice, which is already possessed by another name,—and turns itself to an object other than the taking up of that the continuation of which has been broken off. Consequently then, the subsequent '*yaji*' being separated from the previous Context, by the river of the name ('*gauh*'), cannot go over to it; nor does the previous context go over to it; and hence *perforce* it goes over to another object.

Thus, then, the word '*atha*,' not being able to be taken as signifying either a reference to what has gone before, or immediate sequence, is taken as serving the purpose of introducing another Action. The word '*esha*' also, being expressive of that which is perceptibly near it, is as applicable to what has gone before as to what appears subsequently; because both are equally perceptibly proximate to it; and hence the signification of this word does not affect the discussion.

As for the rejection of the previously mentioned and the acceptance of that which has not been mentioned, as it has to be accepted on the strength of the Direct Mention of the Name, there is nothing wrong in it.

Says the *Bhāshya*: *Nāsāmimāḥ punaḥçrutayaḥ* (*these are not mere repetitions of those*); and the sense of this is that as the Names in question have been used for the very first time, there can be no question of their being mere repetitions. That is to say, they are not mentioned with reference to a previously enjoined Action.

And further (according to you), the whole of the sentence '*athaisha*, etc.' would become redundant; as even without these, the accessories, in the shape of the 'gift of a thousand,' etc., could very well be laid down.

Then, too, in accordance with the view that the names refer to the same Action as the previous one, inasmuch as the gift of 'twelve-hundred' has already been laid down in connection with the *Jyotishṭoma*, the mention of 'a thousand,' with reference to the same, would lead to these two gifts being taken as optional alternatives, as both would serve the same purpose; and this is not quite allowable. When, however, the Actions are different, there is no such anomaly.

Nor can it be urged that the mention of the latter accessory has its end in connection with a new Result; as the substratum of the accessory (the *Jyotishṭoma*) being hopelessly rent asunder by the intervention of the Name, there is no idea of that substrate at the time that the latter Accessory is laid down.

And further the relationship of the Name, the Accessory and the

Result with the 'sacrifice' mentioned subsequently, is based upon Syntactical Connection; while that with the previous *Jyotishṭoma* would be based upon Context (which is weaker than the former); and for this reason also the Actions must be regarded as different.

Nor are the words '*Jyotiḥ*' etc. in the case in question (necessarily) the parts of the word '*Jyotishṭoma*'; because the name '*Rathantara*' (of one kind of *Sāma*) is not recognised as a part of the name '*Kaṇvarathantara*' (another kind of *Sāma*). As for the sentence '*vasantē vasantē Jyotīshā yajēta*,' we take the word as indirectly indicating the *Jyotishṭoma* (and not directly expressing it), because of this fact being pointed out by other means of right notion. In the case in question, however, we do not find any such other means, whereby the word '*Jyotiḥ*' could be taken as referring to the '*Jyotishṭoma.*' As for the use of the word '*Jyotiḥ*' with reference to the *Trivit*, etc., in the sentence '*ētāni jyotinshi*, etc.,' such use must be taken in a secondary sense, allowable in this sentence alone, on account of the fact of the two being spoken of (in the sentence) as co-extensive; and as such this sense could not be accepted in all cases. For instance, though in the case of the sentence '*sinho māṇavakaḥ*,' the word '*sinha*' is taken as referring to the Boy (*Māṇavaka*), only in its secondary sense of Brave, etc., yet when the word '*sinha*' is used in another sentence, *e.g.*, '*Sinhamālabhētā*,' it is not taken in the same secondary sense (but in its direct sense of the *Lion*).

Thus then, we conclude that in consideration of the direct signification of the words '*Jyotiḥ*,' etc., these names must be taken as differentiating the Actions referred to by them from what has been mentioned before.

ADHIKARAṆA (9).

[*Differentiation of Actions through their Deities.*]

***Sūtra* (23): An accessory also (serves to differentiate Actions), when it is a new one, and incapable of being connected with the foregoing (action); because both the sentences are equally (independent of each other).**

Before dealing with the differentiating of Actions by Context, we proceed to consider the Diversity and Unity of Actions based upon their Accessories.

In connection with the *Cāturmāsya* sacrifices, with reference to the *Vaiçvadeva Parva*, we find the sentence '*vaiçvadevyāmikshā*,' which serves to lay down the *sacrifice* implied by the connection between the Material and the Deity herein mentioned; and following on this we find the sentence '*vājibhyo vājinam*.' And on this point there arises the following doubt: Does this second sentence lay down an accessory Material for the sacrifice laid down by the former sentence, or does it serve to lay down a distinct sacrifice implied by the particular connection of the Material and the Deity mentioned in itself?

Though there was a third alternative also possible, namely, that both the Material and the Deity mentioned in the second sentence are laid down with reference to the previous sacrifice, yet this has not been put forth; because it has been shown in the *Adhikaraṇa* dealing with the *Paurṇamāsī* sacrifice, that it is not possible for many accessories to be laid down in connection with an Action that has been already enjoined by a previous sentence.

Thus, then, the question comes to be this: Is the material *vājina* connected, in the previously laid down sacrifice, with the Deity (*Viçvēdevas*) of that sacrifice, or is it connected with another Deity (*Vāji*), another sacrifice and another *Apūrva*?

On this, we have the following:—

PŪRVAPAKSHA.

"The second sentence serves to lay down the material *Vājina* with "regard to the previous sacrifice.

"Because of the word '*Vāji*' being taken as *one who has vāja or Food,* "and the Food meant being the *āmikshā* that has been laid down in the "immediately preceding sentence ('*Vaiçvadevyāmikshā*'), it is the "*Viçvedēvas* themselves that are denoted by the word '*Vājibhyaḥ*'; and "the action too referred to in this second sentence being the same as that "laid down in the former sentence, what this second sentence does is to "lay down a new Material, in the shape of the *Vājina*.

"That is to say, we do not know of any such deities as the 'Vājis'; "and no unknown meaning of words can serve to complete the meaning "of a sentence; but as a rule, whenever the meaning of a word as a "whole is unknown, what we do is to accept the meaning that is afforded "by its constituent parts; and in the case in question we find that in the "first sentence, the *Viçvedevas* are represented as '*Vāji*' because of "their having the *Āmikshā* (which is a Food, '*Vāja*'); and then these "same Deities being understood, in the second sentence, to be connected "with the material '*Vājina*,' they cannot be set aside from this connec- "tion (because there is no other known meaning of the word '*Vāji*' as "a whole). These Deities (the *Viçvedēvas*) are already impressed with "the connection of the sacrifice previously implied by the first sentence; "consequently, when, with a view to establishing their relationship with "the material *Vājina*, we come to assume a 'sacrifice,' we find that "there is no reason why we should set aside the *sacrifice* that is pointed "out by the word '*vāji*' (which is synonymous with *Viçvēdevās*, and as "such points to the sacrifice implied in the former sentence); and while "we have that sacrifice, there arises no further Inconsistency with "regard to anything else; and hence we conclude that in the second "sentence we have the same *sacrifice*, the same *Apūrva* and the same "*Deity* as those in the previous sacrifice; and as such there is no reason "for assuming any other sacrifice.

"For these reasons we conclude that in view of the two sentences in "question, the two Materials, *Āmikshā* and *Vājina*, must be taken as "pertaining to the same sacrifice, to be employed in it either as optional "alternatives, or both jointly.

"Though it is true that the *Āmikshā* is laid down in the same "sentence that lays down the sacrifice (and as such this being the more "authoritative of the two materials, they cannot both be taken either as "alternatives or conjointly),—yet what the sentence could do would be "to extract the 'sacrifice' from the previous sentence, and then lay down "a fresh Material (*Vājina*) for it (and in this way both the Materials "would be equally authoritative). Though, as a matter of fact, the "'sacrifice' is implied by the connection of the Deity and the Material, "and it is not mentioned directly as extracted (from the previous sen-

93

"tence), yet there is always an idea of the *sacrifice* being something that "is implied as apart from the Material, etc.; on account of its having "the character of an *Action.* Or it may be that what is implied in the "second sentence is the word '*yāga*' (from the previous sentence); and "this does not disappear even when the *Āmikshā* (of the previous "sentence) has ceased to exist (in the second); and the word '*vāji*' "(in '*vājibhyaḥ*') too is put in only for the purpose of indicating the "sacrifice implied by it (as synonymous with '*Viçvedēvas*' of the pre-"vious sentence). Nor is the connection between the '*Vāji*' and the "'*Vājina*' understood to be independent of that sacrifice; because "there can be no mutual relationship between the two nouns them-"selves.

"For these reasons we conclude that the action mentioned in the "second sentence is not different from that laid down in the first."

SIDDHĀNTA.

To the above, we make the following reply:—

Inasmuch as the sacrifice laid down by the first sentence has already a Material mentioned for it, another Material (mentioned in the second sentence) cannot possibly belong to it; and hence the mention of such a material, for the sake of establishing its relevancy, could not but indicate another Action.

The meaning of the *Sūtra* thus comes to be this: Inasmuch as the '*Guṇa*' (material) *is new* and *incapable* of being connected with the previous Action, it gives rise to the idea of a distinct Action; specially as the two sentences are equal, *i.e.*, independent of each other. That is to say, each of the two connections between Deity and Material (that the two sentences speak of), not allowing the presence of the other, as incompatible with itself, lays down a distinct Action.

Objection: "It is true that when the subsequently mentioned acces-"sory is found to be inapplicable to the previously mentioned Action, it "indicates another Action. But in the case in question, why cannot the "accessory, '*Vājina*,' be connected with the previously mentioned *sacri-"fice* or its *Deity?*"

Reply: The only reason for this non-connection lies in the fact of that Action having its material already laid down as something else.

"But why cannot both the materials be used jointly?"

Because when a number of things are found to serve the same purpose, they are always taken as optional alternatives, as we shall show under the *Sūtra* XII–iii—10.

"Then they may be taken as optional alternatives."

But that is not possible; because the two are not equally strong in the authority of their applicability to the same sacrifice.

We proceed to show this inequality: The connection of the *Viçvedevas* and the Action mentioned in the first sentence, with the *Āmikshā*, is one that is *directly mentioned* by the word ('*Vaiçvadēvī*'); while that of those with the '*Vājina*' is indicated by the sentence ('*vājibhyo vājinam*'). And in all cases, there are three methods of mentioning the Deity: (1) By means of the deific nominal affix, (2) by the Dative case-ending, and (3) by means of the words of the *Mantra* used; and among these that which precedes is always more authoritative than that which follows.

Objection: "The *mantra* being non-injunctive, it is only natural that "it should be weaker in authority than Direct Assertion; but why "should there be a difference of strength between the Nominal Affix "and the Dative case-ending?"

Reply: It is by Direct Assertion that the connection of the Deity is mentioned by means of the Nominal Affix; whereas in the case of the Dative ending, that connection is expressed by the syntactical connection between the two words lying in close proximity to each other.

For instance, in the case in question, in the case of the word '*vaiçvadevi*,' the presence of the Deity (*Viçvedēvas*) is expressed by the Direct Denotation of the word; while in the case of the Dative ending (in '*Vājibhyaḥ*') it is implied indirectly by the proximity (and syntactical connection) of the two words in the sentence '*vājibhyo vājinam*' (and certainly Direct Denotation is always stronger than Indirect Implication by syntactical connection).

Objection: "In the case of the sentence '*vāiçvadevyāmikshā*' also "the connection between the Deity *Viçvedēvas* and the material '*Āmikshā*' is expressed by the proximity of the two words in the sentence; "and thus in both cases the fact of the connection being implied by "syntactical connection is equally present. If it be urged that the "character of the Deity is mentioned directly by the word '*vāiçvadevī*,' "while it is only the connection of the material '*āmikshā*' that is "implied by the syntactical connection,—then this is also found to be the "case in the other sentence, where the character of the Deity being "mentioned directly by the dative ending (in '*vājibhyaḥ*') it is only "the connection of the material *Vājina* that is implied by syntactical "connection. If again it be urged that the connection also with *material in general* having been mentioned by the Nominal Affix, what "syntactical connection does is only to specify that material,—then, this "too would be found to be the case with the other sentence as well. "Because the single word '*vājibhyaḥ*' directly denotes the character of

" the *receiver of the offering* ; and as this character would not be possible " without an *object to be offered,* some such object in general would be " indicated by the said Direct Denotation itself; and all that the " proximity of the word '*Vājina*' would do would be to specify that object. " And further, granted that the Direct Denotation of the Nominal " Affix mentions the connection with some *material in general*; even then, " inasmuch as the '*Vājina*' also is included in the 'object in general,' there " would be nothing incongruous in taking this latter also as the specified " material for the same sacrifice (as held by us); the only incompati- " bility would be between the two particular materials, the *Āmikshā* and " the '*Vājina*'; and both of these being equally indicated by syntactical " connection, there would be no difference between the authoritative charac- " ter of these. And as such they must be taken as optional alternatives."

Reply : The Nominal Affix does not denote the Deity of the material in general; what it does is to express the Deity of the particular material mentioned by the word '*asya*' (which is present in the expression '*sa'sya dēvatā,*' which expresses the presence of the Nominal Affix).

For instance, in the case in question, the Nominal Affix in the word '*Vaiçvadevī*' being explained as '*viçvēdevā devatā asyāḥ*', the pronoun '*asyāḥ*' expresses, not the material in general, but the particular material in close proximity with itself; specially as it is only a particular object, and not the indefinite generic class 'object', that is capable of being utilised. Consequently that the object expressed by the basic noun ('*Viçvedevāḥ*') is name of the Deity of the particular material pointed out by other means. is the direct denotation of the Nominal Affix in '*Vaiçvadēvī.*' Thus then, the idea of the particular material, as bearing in itself the particular relationship, and as being subservient to the Deity, is brought about directly by the word with the Nominal Affix, independently of every other word; and we proceed to look out for the particular material whose Deity has been mentioned by means of the Nominal Affix; and then it is that this is pointed out by means of the word '*āmikshā.*' And thus as the connection (between the Material and the Deity) has been mentioned before the appearance of the qualified idea, there is in this case no need of an Indirect Indication. Though as a matter of fact, in the case of all words, the basic noun and the affix have independent significations of their own that follow closely upon each other, and it is as between these two that the Relationship in question is cognised,—yet, in the case of the word in question ('*Vaiçvadevī*'), as the relationship (of the Material with the Deity) appears in the same word (as the members related), it has a distinctly stronger authority than that which is indicated by means of the proximity of two words ('*vājibhyo vājinam*'); and it is for this reason that it is spoken of as 'directly denoted by the word.'

Thus then, in the sentence '*vaiçvadevyāmikshā*' there are two relationships: (1) the Relationship of the Material with the Deity, and (2) the Relationship of the qualifier and the qualified; and of these the former is directly mentioned by the word, while the latter is indicated by Syntactical Connection.

For this reason, the qualification of the word '*āmikshā*' by the word '*vaiçvadevī*' is not through the meaning of these words; as it is in the case of the expression '*nīlotpalam*'; what the fact is, is that the Nominal Affix itself directly denotes the *Āmīkshā* together with the Deity (*Viçvedevāḥ*); and the particular material referred to (by the pronoun '*asyāḥ*' in the expounding of the Nominal Affix) is indicated by the proximity of the word '*āmikshā*.'

That is to say, in the case in question, it is not that the word with the Nominal Affix denoting one object, and the word '*āmikshā*' denoting another, the qualification of one of these by the other applies subsequently; because this relationship is expressed, at the very outset, by the word with the Nominal Affix; but what actually happens is that the word with the Nominal Affix having the capability of expressing that which cannot be utilised (that is, the *Material in general*), it stands in need of the proper particular object for itself; and then what the additional word (*āmikshā*) does is to present to it this particular object; and thus, as a matter of fact, through the proximity of the word '*āmikshā*,' the word '*vaiçvadēvī*' itself denotes the material '*āmikshā*.' Nor does the word '*āmikshā*' in that case come to be a mere reference to the '*āmikshā*' denoted by the word '*vaiçvadēvī*'; because without that word, the word with the Nominal Affix is not cognised as having that (*Āmikshā*) for its object. Nor does the *Āmikshā* become the meaning of the sentence; because that which is denoted by the word with the Nominal Affix is not known to have a separate existence. As a matter of fact, we have a *sentence*, only when there are at least two independent denotations of words. Thus then, all that the word '*āmikshā*' does is to bring forward that which is denoted by the word with the Nominal Affix; and as such it does not remove to a further distance (and thereby render weaker) the direct denotation of the Nominal Affix

It is with a view to all this that we have the following declaration: 'It is by the Direct Denotation of the pronoun '*asyāḥ*' that the meaning of the second word ('*āmikshā*') is denoted; and as that is expressed by the Nominal Affix, all the three (the Pronoun, the Affix and the *Āmikshā*) become denoted by the single word (with the Nominal Affix '*Vaiçvadēvī*')." Thus then, what is denoted by the word '*vaiçvadevī*' is that '*that which is the Āmikshā is to become connected with the Deity Viçvedevāḥ*.' And hence in this case, the co-ordination is between the words, and not between their denotations.

In the case of the sentence '*Vājibhyo vājinam*' on the other hand, the case is wholly different.

Because, *firstly*, in the sentence '*vājibhyo vājinam*,' the material to be offered is not denoted either by the noun '*vājin*', or by the Dative affix (in the word '*vājibhyaḥ*'); nor do any of these express the connection of that Material with the Deity; and hence we cannot cognise these by any other means save the syntactical connection (of the two words). That is to say, in the word '*vājibhyaḥ*,' either the basic noun, or the affix, or both of them together, express either the material in general, or a particular Material, or the connection of some Material with the Deity; all that the word denotes is that *the object signified by the noun is the recipient*; and certainly there is no idea of the relationship of the *material* included in the word; and hence it has to be cognised by means of the syntactical connection, based upon the proximity of the word '*vājinam*.'

And secondly, in the case of the word '*vaiçvadēvī*', we find that the signification of the Pronoun '*asyāḥ*' is included in the Nominal Affix; but in the case of the word *vājibhyaḥ*' the Dative is not laid down in the sense of 'that *of which* the object signified by the basic noun is the receiver of the gift.' That is to say, in the case of the former, we find that the Nominal Affix has been laid down by grammarians in the sense of 'that *of which* the object signified by the basic word is the Deity'; while the Dative has not been laid down in the sense that 'that which is signified by the basic noun is the receiver *of that* (a certain gift)'; and as such in the case of a word with the Dative ending, there can be no indication of the meaning of the Pronoun '*asya*'; and as a matter of fact, what such a word actually expresses is the mere character of the *Recipient;* and hence, it is only on account of the inconsistency of the mention of a 'recipient,' without the 'object to be received,' that the word with the Dative can give rise to a desire on our part for some such thing; and certainly this does not make this thing to be directly expressed by that word; as, in that case, all that is signified by the sentence would become the denotation of that word. All that the said *desire* (raised by the Dative) does is to bring about the requisite relationship when the other word is uttered; for if there were no such desire raised by the first word, even the second word could not bring about the said relationship.

Thus, then, though the Dative Affix directly denotes the deific character (of *Vājin*), yet its relationship with the Material (*vājina*) is indicated by syntactical connection alone. Our contention is with regard to this relationship (of the Material and the Deity); and there is no doubt that the relationship of the Material *vājina* (with the Deity *Vājin*) (as indicated by syntactical connection) is very much weaker in authority (than that of the *Amikshā* with the *Viçvedevas*, because this latter is mentioned directly by the Nominal Affix in the word '*vaiçvadevī*.'

Further, it is a well-recognised fact that that which is *expressed directly* by the word is more nearly related to it than that which is *indicated* by syntactical connection, this latter being very much remoter than the former; and hence we proceed to show how, what you hold to be the sense of the sentence '*vājibhyaḥ*, etc.' is far remote (from the direct signification of the words). (1) For instance, in the case in question, the relationship of the *āmikshā* (with the *Viçvedēvas*) being in close proximity to the word, is recognised as being *expressed directly* by the word; while the relationship of the *vājina* with the *Viçvedevas* being far removed, is recognised as *indicated* by syntactical connection. Though the Nominal Affix (in '*Vaiçvadēvī*') does not express the fact of the *Viçvedēvas* being the Deity of the particular Material (*āmikshā*), yet it does express the fact of their being the Deity of some Material in general; while the word with the Dative ending does not express anything with regard to any material, either general or particular; and this makes a great difference between the two cases. It has been argued above that the material in general expressed by the Nominal Affix in '*Vaiçvadēvī*' could also pertain to the *vājina* (which would thus come to have the *Viçvedēvas* for its Deity). But this is scarcely correct; because in the word '*vaiçvadēvī*' we find a feminine ending, which, though appearing in connection with the generic term, yet distinctly points to the fact that the material meant must be that which is mentioned by a word in the feminine gender that may be found in close proximity with the former word; and none of these conditions (which are fulfilled by the *āmikshā*) are found to be fulfilled by the *vājina*, as it is neither mentioned by a word in the feminine gender, nor is it in close proximity with the word '*vaiçvadēvī*'; and as such this latter is not accepted as the material in connection with the Viçvedēvas.

(2) The relationship of the *vājina* with the *Vājins* is not mentioned in the form '*vājibhyo vājinam kuryāt*'; and hence for the mention of that relationship, we must supply some word expressive of 'giving' and the like. As for the word '*kuryāt*' (denoting performability), this has got to be supplied even in the sentence dealing with the *āmikshā*, either from above, or out of the final sentence laying down the actual performance of the Action in question; and as such the question of the expression of this performablity has not been urged against the opponent. In the sentence '*vājibhyo vājinam*,' however, the said relationship is wholly uncognisable, until the root '*dā*' (=to give) is supplied from above; though in the expression '*vaiçvadēvyāmikshā*' (we have the relationship directly expressed by the Nominal Affix, which leaves nothing that could have to

be supplied from above). And the reason for this is that in all sentences, there are only two ways in which the relationship of nouns is expressed; *viz.*, either by the mention of *co-extensiveness*, or by *the word in the genitive case;* and in the sentence '*vājibhyaḥ*' etc., we do not find either co-extensiveness or the genitive word; and as for the case-ending in '*vājibhyaḥ*,' it cannot (being a case-ending) be related to any word other than the verb; and we do not find any verb mentioned; hence it becomes necessary to supply the verb from above; this is one ground for the aforesaid remoteness. And the other lies in the extremely complicated nature of the connection among the three words ('*vājibhyaḥ*,' '*vājinam*' and '*dadyāt*').

It may be argued that—"in the case of the sentence '*vaiçvadēvī*' etc., also there is an equal necessity for *supplying the verb* 'sacrifice.'" But the two cases are not parallel, because in the case of this latter sentence, the 'sacrifice' is inferred after the relationship of the *āmikshā* with the *Viçvēdevas* has been fully cognised; and the cognition of the relationship does not depend upon the verb 'to sacrifice.' For you, on the other hand, the mere fact of bringing about the ownership of another person (which is implied by the Dative ending) being impossible (without the mention of the 'sacrifice'), the 'sacrifice,' would be necessary for the bringing about of a cogent relationship among the factors expressed (by the word); and hence, from the very beginning, it would be necessary to assume the verb 'to give,' for the sake of the establishment of the syntactical connection between the word denoting the Material and that denoting the Deity.

It is only when this verb 'to give' has been supplied, that the nouns, previously disjointed, become joined in a common bond of relationship; and thus both these words, having the same purpose, come to restrict each other; and this process is very complicated. In the case of the sentence '*Vaiçvadēvyāmikshā*' on the other hand, there are no such complications, and the process is very much simpler.

(3) Though the *Vājin* and the *vājina* are directly related to each other, yet (none of their terminations being such as to express a co-extensiveness between them), there is a distinct remoteness between them. In the case of the sentence '*Vaiçvadēvyāmikshā*' on the other hand, there is a distinct co-extensiveness (expressed by the common Nominative ending); and hence we have a proximity between them; as we shall explain, later on, how 'the words having the same endings are more capable than those with different endings.'

(4) Further, all that the Dative in '*vājibhyaḥ*' could do would be to denote the fact of the *Vājins* being *Recipients*; and it is only by a far-fetched process that the *Vājins* can be indicated as the Deities related to the

vājina. Because the Dative is not, like the particular Nominal Affix, laid down by grammarians as denoting the Deity; as all that it is said to express is the character of the *Recipient*; and certainly the 'Recipient' is not the same as the 'Deity'; for in the sentence 'he gives the gold to Ātrēya,' Ātreya cannot be taken as a Deity. If the Deity were the (same as the) Recipient, then there would be no difference between *giving* and *sacrificing*. Then again, that object which operates towards the accepting of a gift, is called the 'Recipient'; while we do not find the Deity operating towards any such accepting; therefore all that we can have the Dative do is to indirectly indicate the Deity as *one with reference to whom the gift would be made*, which is something that comes before the *Recipient*; or, it may be taken as indicating the ownership that follows after the possession of another person (the Recipient) has been brought about; because the character of the Deity is known to be identical with such ownership. Even if the character of the Deity be held to be that of the Recipient in the shape of one not denying the gift, this would entail the indication of a character not compatible with the general character (of the Deity); and this would be a very far-fetched and complicated process.

(5) There is yet another cause of *remoteness*, in the shape of the doubtful nature of the word '*vājibhyaḥ*,' which can be taken both in the Dative and the Ablative; whereas in the case of the Nominal Affix, there being no such doubt, the intellect has not got to be over-strained. That is to say, when we come across the word '*vājibhyaḥ*,' until we have set aside (on certain grounds) its ablative character, and decided to take it as the Dative, the mind is in the tossing state of uncertainty. The opponent argues that—"the signification of the Nominal Affix (in '*vaiçvadevī*') is also doubtful, inasmuch as there are many meanings of that Affix, in the shape of the Patronymic and the rest." But this argument is not quite relevant, or on the same lines as ours; because what we have urged was the *verbal* doubt (in connection with the word '*vājibhyaḥ*'); while you have brought forward a doubt with regard to the *meaning*; for in all cases, whatever the meaning, the word "*vaiçvadēvi*" can not lose its character of ending in a *Nominal Affix*; and as for the meaning, we settle upon its denoting a *Deity*, because we find none of the other significations of the Affix compatible with the sentence. For you, on the other hand, even when (after a long cogitation) the word '*vājibhyaḥ*' has come to be ascertained to be in the Dative, inasmuch as there are many meanings of the Dative, there always remains a doubt as to whether the Dative in question is an *Upapada-vibhakti* or a *Kāraka-vibhakti*; and thus also the latter being accompanied by a double doubt, this is certainly more far-fetched than the former. Specially as the doubt with regard

to the meaning, being common to both of us, cannot be urged against any one of us only; while as for the doubt with regard to the *word* itself, it occurs in your case only, and not in mine, and as such can very well be brought forward against you.

(6) Then again, the *āmikshā* is related to the sacrifice (to the Viçvedevas), which is pointed out (as implied) in the same sentence where it is itself mentioned; whereas the *vājina* is, according to you, related to the sacrifice (the same as the above) which is pointed out in another sentence. And there can be doubt as to the greater authoritativeness of that material which is mentioned in the same sentence along with the *sacrifice* at which it is employed.

(7) Nor is it possible for the second sentence to draw out the 'sacrifice' only from the former sentence, and then to lay down another material (the *vājina*) in connection with it; because the impropriety of this has been shown under the *Adhikaraṇas* dealing with '*Citrā*' and '*Vaiçvadēva*' (*Pāda* IV, *Adhyāya* I).

(8) Then again, in accordance with the rule laid down under the *Adhikaraṇa* on '*Vaiçvadēva*,' the sentence mentioning the *vājina* would stand in need of the further help of the *Context*. Because the relationship of the Deity and the Material (spoken of in the sentence '*vājibhyo vājinam*') only stands in need of *some sort of a sacrifice*; and that this *sacrifice* is the same as that at which the previously mentioned *āmikshā* has been employed, could only be ascertained by means of the Context. That is to say, the *vājina*, not being capable of being related to the Deity '*Vājins*' without a 'sacrifice,' stands in need of some sort of this latter; and then the conclusion, that the *vājina* also is a part of (*i e.*, is to be employed at) the same sacrifice as that at which the *āmikshā* is used, can be got at by means of the Context alone. Thus, then, even though it be by Syntactical Connection alone that the *Viçvedēvas* are pointed out as the Deity for the offering of the *āmikshā*, yet we find that the *āmikshā* is mentioned independently of anything else; and inasmuch as the *vājina* could be taken as forming part of the same sacrifice, by means of a Syntactical Connection that depends (for such signification) upon the Context,—the employing of the *āmikshā* is found to be distinctly more authoritative than that of the *vājina*; and this makes a great difference between the two theories. If then, the *vājina* be connected with a sacrifice, independently of the Context, there being no other known sacrifice cognised along with it, we would come to conclude that it belongs to an independent sacrifice by itself; but in this, the *vājina* being separated from the *Vaiçvadēva* sacrifice, you would be landing upon the *Siddhānta* standpoint. And we have already explained above, in connection with the word '*āgneya*,' that in the case of all such

sentences as do not directly mention the action of the human agent, until some sort of a 'sacrifice' has been inferred in connection with them, they do not stand in need of the help of any other sentence. (And in the case of the sentence '*Vājibhyo vājinam*' when the *sacrifice* has been inferred, or implied, within itself by the relationship between the *Vājins* and the *vājina*, this relationship becomes duly established; and as such the sentence could have no need of any other sentence of the Context such as '*Vaiçvadēvyāmikshā*'; and consequently there would be nothing to show that the sacrifice spoken of in this latter sentence is the same at which the aforesaid '*vājina*' would be employed.)

(9) In the case of the sentence '*vaiçvadēvī*,' *etc*., the '*Viçvedēvas*' as connected with the *āmikshā* are expressed by means of the fully recognised signification of the word '*viçvedēva*' *as a whole* (contained in the word '*vaiçvadēvī*'); while with the *vājina* (mentioned in the other sentence) they could be connected only by means of the far-fetched signification of the broken-up constituent parts of the word '*vājibhyaḥ*.' That is to say, the Viçvedevas could be spoken of as '*vājins*' only by taking this latter word in the sense afforded by its component parts. And as such a signification of the word could be got at by joining together the sense afforded by the two parts of the word (*vāja* + *in*); and this would be exactly like the meaning of a sentence which is got at by joining together the meanings of its constituent words; and as such it could not but be very much weaker in authority than the well-recognised meaning of a word *as a whole*, which is always obtained by a mere mention of the word; and for this reason too the connection of the *Vājina* with the *Vaiçvadēva* sacrifice is very much weaker than that of the *āmikshā*.

(10) The word '*vājin*' as a whole is actually found to have such well-known significations as the 'horse' and the like; and hence to take it as signifying the *Viçvedēvas* would entail much needless trouble. Because, as for the character of the Deity, it must always be taken in precisely the same form as that mentioned by the word, no attention being paid to the capability or incapability of that which is so mentioned; and that character does not depend upon the generic *class* '*Dēvatātva*'; and hence too the word '*vājin*' could not (by the mere generic character of '*Dēvatātva*') be taken as referring to the *Viçvedēvas*. Thus then the word '*vājibhyaḥ*' would directly denote the fact of the *Horses* being the Deity; and hence to take it as referring to the *Viçvedēvas* would necessitate, without sufficient cause, the taking of that word in the much less authoritative sense afforded by its constituent parts; and this makes another great difference between the two theories.

(11) Even when the word '*vājin*' is taken in the sense afforded by

its constituent parts, as that sense would equally refer to all the Deities that may be connected with the offering of the *Cake* (because the *Cake* is a *food*, '*vāja*,' just like the *āmikshā*); and hence to restrict the word to the *Viçvedēvas* alone would entail a further effort. For instance, all the deities, Agni and the rest, would come to be pointed out by the word '*vājin*,' on account of their being connected with such 'foods' as the Cake and the like; and hence your theory would, at the very outset, necessitate the gratuitous assumption that the word 'food,' '*vāja*' (in the word '*vājin*'), refers to the *āmikshā*, and not to the Cake, etc.; and then again, there would be another assumption that, though the word '*vāja*' refers to *āmikshā in general*, yet it points to that particular *āmikshā* which is offered at the *Vaiçvadēva* sacrifice, and that as such the word '*vājin*' indicates those (*i.e.*, the *Viçvedēvas*) to whom that particular *āmikshā* is offered. Thus then it comes to this: Though the word '*vājin*' directly by itself refers to many other Deities, yet, by means of the Context, it is restricted to the particular Deity (the *Viçvedēvas*). And we see no ground for this recourse to the Context; because the Deity is always mentioned only as an accessory detail; and as such if it were spoken of as something to be *purified or prepared* like the '*vrīhi*' in the sentence '*Vrīhīn prokshati*,' then somehow or other, on account of the fact of such purification helping the *Apūrva* of the sacrifice, there could be established a connection with the Deity mentioned in the same Context; [that is to say, in that case, as the purification of the Deity spoken of in the second sentence could only be the cause of a certain transcendental result, the sentence could be taken along with the Deity of a certain previously mentioned sacrifice]. In the case in question, however, we do not find the Deity mentioned as something to be *purified;* because even without its having the form of such purification, the action mentioned is found to serve a distinct purpose. Even if the sentence could be taken as mentioning a *purification*, this latter could only be in the form of the *utilising* of the *vājina*, and it would have nothing to do with purifying the Deity. For even if the sentence were to refer to the Deity mentioned in the same Context, there would be no certainty as to which one Deity is meant, as there are many Deities, Agni and the rest, that are mentioned in the Context. It may be argued that—"inasmuch as all the Deities would be included in '*Viçvedēvas*' (which word means *all deities*) it is the *Viçvedēvas* alone that we take as referred to by the sentence in question." But this is scarcely right; because there is no authority for the *collecting of all deities.* If it be urged that—"all are included, on account of the direct mention of the Plural number (in '*vājibhyaḥ*),"—we deny this; because the Plural number may rest with *three* only. It might be argued that there is no reason why the number should be limited to *three* only. But we have such a reason, as shown under the *Sūtra* '*mukhyañcāpūrvacodanāt lokavat*' (XII—ii—23). Therefore there is no ground for taking the *Viçvedēvas* (as referred to by the word '*vājibhyaḥ*').

(12) It is only when the Deity stands in need of some fact for making its mention explicable, that it becomes connected with a Material; and in the sentence in question, inasmuch as, in accordance with your theory, the Deity mentioned by the word '*vājibhyaḥ*' has its Material already supplied (in the shape of the '*vāja*'),—and as such it is actually cognised as having all its wants duly supplied *by the same word*,—it cannot be taken along with any other Material (in the shape of the *vājina*, whose connection would be based upon *syntactical connection*). And as such there is a deal of difference between the authoritativeness of the two theories.

(13) And further, it is always by means of Direct Assertion that the Deity becomes connected with its sacrifice; and in the case in question we find that the *direct* mention of the *Viçvedēvas* by the word '*Vājin*' is hardly possible. If in connection with the offering of the *vājina* also, the *Viçvedēvas* themselves be accepted as the Deity, then, in all places where the sacrifices are recapitulated, it would be necessary to pronounce the word '*Viçvedēva.*' But in the case in question we find that this word is not mentioned in the sentence that serves as the Injunction of the *Vājina* offering (*i.e.*, the sentence '*vājibhyo vājinam*,' which uses the word '*vājīn*' and not '*Viçvēdēva*'); and as such a *direct mention* of the *Viçvedēvas* in this connection is hard to be got at; as the only way it could be got at would be in the following manner: (1) the word '*vājin*' has a literal signification; (2) as the sentence in which that occurs does not mention the sacrificial detail (in the shape of the Deity), the word indicates (indirectly) the word '*Viçvedēva*'; and (3) then this latter word comes to be laid down as the one which is to be uttered at the time of the offering of the *Vājina*. This would be a highly complicated process. Then, too, if the denotation of the word '*vājin*' were to indicate a *word*, this latter could be in the forms '*sarvē-dēvāḥ*,' '*nisçēshā-dēvatāḥ*,' and so forth, all of which are synonymous; and as such it would be extremely difficult to get at the precise form '*Viçvēdēva*.' And when some other word ('*sarvē-dēvāḥ*') is pronounced, it cannot point to the fact of the particular Deity of the *Viçvedēvas* being the Deities concerned; as we shall show later on, in Adhyāya X, that the Deity of an Action is always recognised precisely in the same form as it is mentioned in the Injunction (X—iv—23). In the sentence '*vājibhyaḥ*,' etc., we find that the human agent is urged to the offering of the material to the Deity mentioned by the particular word '*vājin*'; and as such, at the time of the actual offering, the Deity should be mentioned by pronouncing the precise word

'*vājin*' (and not any of its synonyms). Thus then, even if it be granted that the same Deity of the *Viçvedēvas* is mentioned by means of the word '*vājin*' (in connection with the offering of the *vājina*), and by the word '*Viçvēdēva*' (in connection with that of the *āmikshā*)—yet, in accordance with the law laid down above in connection with the words 'Indra' and 'Mahēndra' (*vide Sūtras* II—i—15-16),—inasmuch as the Deities in question are mentioned by two distinct words,—they must be regarded as wholly distinct; and consequently the second sentence must be taken as mentioning a quite different relationship of Deity and Material; and then, inasmuch as it is not allowable for many accessories (in the shape of the Material '*vājina*' and the Deity '*Vājin*') to be laid down in regard to a sacrifice that has been previously enjoined (*i.e.*, the *Vaiçvedēva* sacrifice), we come to the conclusion that in the case in question the mention of the accessory ('*vājinam*') serves to distinguish this latter Action from that which is laid down by the former sentence.

***Sūtra* (24): When, however, the word mentioning the previous Action is not accompanied by the mention of any Accessory (the mention of an accessory in another sentence does not make it the injunction of another Action).**

This *Sūtra* mentions a counter-instance to the foregoing. The sense of it is that when a certain Action has not got any definite Accessory laid down by its original Injunction, if another sentence is found mentioning an Accessory, this latter sentence can be taken as laying down the Accessory for the same sacrifice that has been laid down by the previous sentence; and hence in such cases, the mention of the Accessory does not serve to distinguish the Action (from the previous one).

ADHIKARAṆA (10).

[*Sūtra* 24 has been taken by the *Bhāshya* as forming a distinct Adhikaraṇa—the tenth—by itself. Its sense is explained as that when no other material is mentioned in the second sentence, the Actions spoken of in the two sentences must be accepted as being one and the same.]

ADHIKARAṆA (11).

(*The mention of certain materials—dadhi, etc.—is with a view to distinct results.*)

***Sūtra* (25): "Because of the mention of a distinct Result, " there would be a distinct Action (laid down by the sentence); " specially as the Result is always connected with a definite " Action."**

In continuation of the sentence '*agnihotram juhoti*,' we find the sentence '*dadhnēndriyakāmasya juhuyāt*'; and this gives rise to the following doubt: Does this second sentence lay down an Action different from that laid down by the former sentence? or does it only serve to mention a distinct result as following from the offering of a particular material at that same sacrifice?

Two conclusions have been previously arrived at: (1) If the original Injunction of the Action contain the mention of no accessory, the accessory mentioned in a subsequent passage pertains to the Action laid down by that injunction; (2) if the original Injunction contain the mention of an accessory, there being no possibility of the connection of more than one enjoined accessory, the mention of another accessory pertains to another Action. In the case in question, we find that the sentence laying down the original Action—'*agnihotram juhoti*'—does not mention an accessory; and the other sentence cited mentions more than one accessory (*viz.*, the Material '*dadhi*' and the Result '*acquiring of sense-efficiency*'); and there arises a doubt as to the likelihood or otherwise of these latter appertaining to the former Action.

For the purpose of settling this doubt, we have got to settle at first the question as to whether the Result mentioned in the second sentence follows from the *Homa*, or from the particular Material *Dadhi*.

Question: "How is it that the Bhāshya has totally neglected the " sentence '*godohanēna paçukāmasya praṇayet*,' which had been cited in " connection with the present Adhikaraṇa by the author of the " *Vṛtti?*"

Reply: The only reason is that the sentence in question is of no use in showing whether the two Actions are identical or different. If the question at issue were as to whether the particular Action serves simply to help the completion of the sacrifice, or it accomplishes something that is desirable for the agent, then, in that case, there would be a difference between the case of the sentence cited by us and that cited by the Vṛtti; as however at present we are dealing with the question of the diversity or identity of Actions, it is necessary that the sentence cited should be one that would help in a satisfactory conclusion being arrived at, in connection with the question at issue. The "bringing in" (*praṇayana*), spoken of in the sentence cited by the *Vṛtti*, being of the nature of carrying a certain thing from one place to another, is not affected one way or the other by the diversity or identity of the Actions concerned; as whether the Result follows from the 'milking vessel,' or from the 'bringing in by means of that vessel,' in any case, the performance of the main Action would be exactly the same. In the case of the sentence cited by us, on the other hand, if the Result followed from the material (*Dadhi*), then *Dadhi* would be the material that should be offered in the morning and evening Libations (of the *Agnihotra*); whereas if it followed from the *Homa*, then this *Homa* of the *Dadhi*, having no fixed time for its performance, would be wholly different from the Agnihotra-Homas, the time for which is fixed; and thus having the character of an independent Action by itself, like the *Darvi-homa*, it would be performed only once, and independently (of the *Agnihotra*); and thus in this case a great difference is made in the case by the Action being different.

Objection: "Even if the Result followed from the *Homa*, in accordance "with the law '*Sannidhau tvavibhāgāt*' (II—iii—26), the Action laid down "would be the same, just as the actions laid down in the sentences "'*yāvajjivamagnihotram juhuyāt*' and '*agnihotram juhuyāt svargakāmaḥ*' "are the same as the original *Agnihotra*."

Reply: It is not so; because as a rule, if the Action subsequently mentioned be recognised as not being different from the one mentioned previously, then the Actions are taken to be the same; otherwise they are concluded to be different. When an Action is laid down with reference to a certain Result, and in connection with a certain occasion, etc, it could not be connected with these latter, unless it had been previously enjoined; and hence it proceeds indirectly to acquire the character of the originative Injunction. Thus, then, if in the sentence mentioning the Result, the original form of the previous Action put forward by the more authoritative proximity of the mental image partake of the form of that Action, then, in that case, on account of the incompatibility of the independent originative potency (of the sentence mentioning the Result), it is concluded, on the strength of recognition, that the Action mentioned in this sentence is the same as that mentioned in the previous sentence. If, however, we happen to perceive the slightest difference in the subsequent Action from the one previously mentioned, then there is no idea of the two being the same; and hence, in this case, the subsequent sentence becomes an originative Injunction by itself, and not having its injunctive potency set aside by another Injunction capable of laying down exactly the same Action; though apparently pointing to something else (*i.e.*, the material *dadhi*), yet as this something is mentioned with reference to that (*i.e.*, the Result) which by itself cannot be taken up for performance, it serves to distinguish this Action from the one previously laid down.

Thus it is that in the case of the sentence '*dadhnēndriyakāmasya juhuyāt*,' inasmuch as the Action of the *Homa qualified by Dadhi* is mentioned with reference to the acquirement of *sense-efficiency*, the idea, brought about by the sentence, of the said qualified *Homa*, is not set aside by another sentence putting forth the origination of that same Action. Because the *Homa* mentioned in the previous sentence ('*Agnihotram juhuyāt*') is pure and simple, while that which is mentioned in the sentence in question is qualified by the *Dadhi*; and as such this latter is cognised as different from the former. That is to say, the Action originally laid down in the sentence '*agnihotram juhoti*' is *Homa* pure and simple, while that in the sentence is one qualified by *Dadhi*, and hence we do not have, in this case, the "non-difference" spoken of above as the only ground for identity; and consequently the Action is concluded to be different from the previous one.

Objection: "The Homa qualified by Dadhi is also found to be previously laid down by the sentence '*dadhnā juhoti*' (found in connection with the *Agnihotra*); (and as such the sentence '*dadhnēndriyakāmasya juhuyāt*' cannot be taken as laying down an Action never mentioned before)."

Reply: Not so; because the sentence '*dadhnā juhoti*' is not the originative Injunction of any Action; because the Action, for which this sentence lays down an accessory material, has been originally laid down by the sentence '*agnihotram juhoti*' where it is not qualified by the *Dadhi*; while the sentence wherein it is qualified by *Dadhi* (*i.e.*, in the sentence '*dadhnā juhoti*') is not its originative Injunction, as has been fully established under the *Sūtra* "*tatsannidhērguṇārthena punaḥçrutiḥ*" (II-ii-16). When the originative potency of the sentence mentioning the Result is set aside by another originative Injunction, then alone is the possibility of the Action mentioned by the former being different from that which is laid down by the latter set aside by the said originative Injunction; and this can never be done by a sentence which (like the sentence '*dadhnā juhoti*') only lays down an accessory detail (for the previously mentioned sacrifice); because such a sentence never serves as an originative Injunction. And the sentences in the Context that lay down such accessory details as the Material, the Result and the Occasion, etc., are all related to the originative Injunction of the Context, and not among themselves. Because all these accessory details stand in need of the original mention of an Action ; and because this original mention is found in close proximity to those sentences ; while as for the details themselves, inasmuch as they are not related to one another, they would be removed from one another (by the originative Injunction). That is to say, inasmuch as an Action not originally laid down cannot be connected with any accessory details, all these details stand in need of the original Injunction of the Action ; and there is no ground for any mutual relationship among the Details themselves. As for the originative Injunction, inasmuch as it pervades through all the sentences laying down the accessories in connection with the Action enjoined by that Injunction, it is not interrupted by any foreign factor, in its relationship with each one of the details. As for the Accessory details on the other hand, inasmuch as they are '*parārtha*' (for the sake of *something else*, vide *Sūtra* III--i—22), they are not related to one another ; and consequently when they happen to be interrupted by even a single unconnected element, none of them can be taken along with another. And for this reason, the sentence '*dadhnā juhoti*' does not present itself in connection with the sentence '*dadhnēndriyakāmasya juhuyāt.*' This will be further explained under the *Adhikaraṇa* "*ēkasya tūbhayatvē sanyogapṛthaktvam*" (IV—iii—5).

The following might be urged here: "The same originative "Injunction ('*agnihotram juhoti*') as qualified by the *Dadhi* mentioned "in another sentence ('*Dadhnā juhoti*'), might present itself in connec-"tion with the sentence '*Dadhnēndriyakāmasya juhuyāt,*' and set aside "the idea of the diversity of Actions."

But this would be scarcely possible ; as, in that case, just as that Action (*Agnihotra*) is qualified by the *Dadhi* mentioned by another sentence, so in the same manner is it also qualified by many such materials as '*taṇḍula,*' '*payaḥ*' and the like, also mentioned by other sentences ('*taṇḍulairjuhoti,*' *payāsa juhoti*, etc.) occurring in the same Context ; and hence the Action could not be of one form (if in the Injunction itself any signification were attached to the mention of accessories in other sentences). That is to say, in the originative Injunction ('*Agnihotram juhoti*') the Action is found to be pure and simple ; and hence this cannot be recognised as the same (as that mentioned in the sentence '*dadhnēndriyakāmasya juhuyāt*'). If it be held that the original Injunction is taken as qualified by the sentences laying down the accessory details, occurring in the same Context (*f.i.*, the sentences '*dadhnā juhoti*' etc.),—then, too, inasmuch as, in that case, the Action would be cognised as qualified, not by a single material, *Dadhi*, but by many such materials, as the *taṇḍula* and the rest, the Action mentioned by the sentence '*dadhnēndriyakāmasya juhuyāt*' cannot be recognised as the same as that mentioned by the sentence '*agnihotram juhoti*' qualified by that subsidiary sentence alone which mentions the *dadhi* (*i.e.*, '*dadhnā juhoti*').

Objection: "Inasmuch as the sentence '*dadhnēndriyakāmasya* "*juhuyāt*' requires the mention of the *dadhi* alone, even though there "may be many such materials as the *taṇḍula* and the rest, in connection "with the original Action of the *Agnihotra*, yet they are rejected as "being not required, and as such as good as non-existing; and conse-"quently the *dadhi* alone of the previous Action is taken up when the "same Action comes to be mentioned by the sentence in question."

Reply: In that case, it will come to this, that the sentence '*dadhnā juhoti*' would be the originative Injunction (connected with the sentence '*dadhnēndriyakāmasya juhuyāt*,' which thus would have no connection with the sentence '*agnihotrām juhoti*'); and this contingency we have already rejected above.

Further, in connection with the *Agnihotra*, *dadhi* is only one of ten alternative materials; while in the case of the sacrifice performed for acquiring sense-efficiency, it is the only one material to be employed. In the original *Agnihotra*, if all the ten materials, *dadhi* and the rest, were offered conjointly, then it might be admitted that the same variegated Action has been mentioned in the sentence in question, though only by the mention of only one constituent of its mixed material. As a matter of fact, however, the *dadhi* and the rest are optional alternatives; and hence the chance of any one of them being employed in the *Agnihotra* is as one to ten. Consequently even if the sentence in question were to refer back to the sentence '*dadhnā juhoti*,' this latter sentence would point only to the *dadhi* that is one among the ten alternatives. But the *dadhi* spoken of in connection with the acquiring of sense-efficiency is the only one all-important material; and as such the Actions cannot be recognised as identical (because the Action mentioned in the sentence in question has for its material the *all-important* Dadhi, while that mentioned in the previous sentence has '*dadhi*' as only an alternative material).

Nor can the sentence in question be construed as '*yad dadhnā juhoti tad indriyakāmasya*'; because this would make the Result the object of the Injunction, which is absurd. The real construction of the sentence is this: 'when one desires sense-efficiency he should offer the *Homa of dadhi* and *dadhi alone*'; and there is no doubt that no such *Homa* has been laid down anywhere else.

Objection: "The form of the *Homa* alone would be recognised as "the same; and this recognition would establish the identity of the two "Actions. As for the non-recognition of the sameness of the materials, "that cannot be a ground for making the Actions different from one "another. Hence it must be admitted that what the sentence in question "does is to mention the same Action as the previous *Agnihotra*, with the "additional mention of an accessory (*Dadhi*)."

Reply: It is not so; because we have already shown above that with reference to an Action previously laid down, more than one accessory detail can never be laid down; and in accordance with what you say, the sentence in question would come to lay down more than the relationship (*viz.*, that of the Material '*dadhi*' and the Result 'sense-efficiency'). And hence the sentence in question laying down the relationship of the *dadhi* and the *Homa*, and then again that of the *Homa* and the Result, there would be a syntactical split. And for this reason you must accept the sentence to be a qualified Injunction. And thus it must be admitted that this mentions a distinct Action (as such a qualified Action has never been found to have been laid down by any other sentence).

Just as when the Action laid down being the *Homa* alone pure and simple, there is an indirect implication of that which employs various indefinite materials,—and then the special mention of the *dadhi* restricts the Injunction to one substance only,—so in the same manner, though the *Homa* mentioned by the sentence '*dadhnēndriyakāmasya*, etc.' may be assumed as employing ten alternative materials, laid down by ten injunctive sentences independent of one another, yet the mention of '*dadhnā*' serves to specify the one material *dadhi* to be particularly employed, setting aside the *taṇḍula* and the rest. But as this specification of the Action with the single material is not mentioned by any other sentence except the one in question ('*dadhnēndriyakāmasya*, etc.'), the particular result ('sense-efficiency') cannot but be taken as following from the *Homa* itself; and as such the *Homa* mentioned by the sentence in question must be wholly different from that laid down by the previous sentence ('*agnihotram juhoti*').

—o—

Thus then there being every reason for a doubt in connection with the sentences in question, we proceed at first to deal with the following

PŪRVAPAKSHA.

"Though in the case in question, the previous sentence ('*agnihotram* "*juhoti*'), mentioning the Action, does not make any mention of the "material, yet the sentence in question ('*dadhnēndriyakāmasya juhuyāt*') "lays down a distinct Action; because this latter contains, *i.e.*, distinctly

" mentions, a Result ('sense-efficiency'); and it is only from an Action " that a Result can follow.

" The whole of the *Bhāvārthādhikaraṇa* (II—i—1-4) serves as the " present *Pūrvapaksha.* Because the conclusion therein arrived at was " that it is only *Verbs*, and not Nouns or Adjectives (laying down the " material or other accessory details), that are connected with the word " speaking of the Result; and hence inasmuch as the Result is always " connected with an Action, when there is a distinct Result mentioned, " the sentence in question must be taken as laying down a distinct Action, " and not as only pointing out another material (*dadhi*) for the previ- " ously-mentioned Action (*Agnihotra*).

" Because the *Material* having been already mentioned once, the same " cannot be enjoined over again; and if you hold the sentence to lay " down a material that has not been already laid down, then the men- " tion of the Result would be altogether superfluous (as no Result can " ever follow from the material, *dadhi*). That is to say, in a case where " the word speaking of the Action does not speak of a Material, we can " take another sentence as laying down that material, only if either " that material does not happen to have been laid down already by " a previous sentence, or if the sentence in question is not found " capable of asserting anything more than what has already been men- " tioned. In the case in question, however, we find none of these condi- " tions present; as the material. *dadhi*, has been previously laid down " by another sentence ('*dadhnā juhoti*'); and the sentence in question " mentions a Result ('sense-efficiency') over and above what has been " spoken of before. It is with a view to all this that the *Bhāshya* has " summed up the *Pūrvapaksha* in the words: *we find a distinct result " mentioned in the sentence in question, and a (distinct) Result can, rightly " speaking, follow from a (distinct) Action only.*

[The *Vārtika* now proceeds to explain the words of the *Pūrvapaksha Bhāshya.*]

In the *Bhāshya* here we meet with the words *kin dṛshṭam hi karmaṇaḥ phalam.* This sentence appears to be capable of a double interpretation: (1) The subsequent sentence '*nēti brūmaḥ, no hyetaddrishtēnānēna siddhyati*' embodying a sort of a disavowal of the *Pūrvapaksha*, and as such affording a glimpse of the final *Siddhānta*, the question ends with '*kim*'; the meaning being '*how (is it that rightly speaking the Result follows from an Action)?*'—and the reply to this is *dṛshṭam hi karmaṇaḥ phalam—because we actually see the Result following* from *the Action.* And then we have the retort, '*nēti brūmaḥ*, etc.' And in this way various questionings and answerings go on up to the sentence '*tasmānnaivanjātīyakeshvētad bhavati*' (*Bhāshya*, p. 159, l. 20).

In accordance with this interpretation, the sole question—'How is it that rightly speaking the Result follows from the Action?'—would emanate from the *Siddhāntin*. And as this appears to be wholly unconnected (or irrelevant) immediately after the *Pūrvapakshin* has summed up his own declarations, we must interpret the sentence in the following manner:—

(2) The *Pūrvapakshin* having declared '*tacca karmaṇo nyāyyam*,' the *Siddhāntin*, with a view to avoid the meaninglessness of the word '*dadhi*' in the sentence in question, finds the conclusion arrived at under the *Bhāvārthādhikaraṇa* (II—i—1) to be incapable of applying to the case in question; and thereby finding the sentence in question wholly incapable of expressing (the connection between the previous *Homa* and the Result, 'sense-efficiency'), he puts the question: 'Do you conclude that the particular Result mentioned follows from the *Homa*, on the basis of an Inference from the similar case of *Field-cultivation*, where the Result is actually found to follow from the Action?' Though as a matter of fact, *Dharma* has been declared to be cognisable by means of Vedic Injunctions alone,—and it has been shown that Inference and the other means of knowledge do not appertain to such matters,—yet the operation of these means of knowledge has not been denied with regard to the consideration of the bearings of the Vedic texts; and as such there could be nothing objectionable in the introducing of an Inference, in connection with the consideration of the meaning of the Vedic sentence in question.

In reply to the above question of the *Siddhāntin*, the *Pūrvapakshin* having his mind imbued with the *Bhāvārthādhikaraṇa* retorts thus: "Do not you taunt me with having been forced to bring forward an "Inference, by the fact of the incapability of the words themselves, of "directly expressing what is held by us; because, as a matter of fact, "when we have words directly supporting our view, it is not an Inference "that we put forward in the sentence '*dṛshṭam hi karmaṇo nyāyyam*.' "Specially as such an Inference from similar cases does not support "our standpoint; as such an Inference is beset with many such fallacies as "'*asiddha*' (the *probans* being unknown or not universally accepted), "'*Anaikāntika*' (doubtful character of the Premises), '*viruddha*' (premises "proving the contrary conclusion), and so forth.

"For instance, if the inferential argument put forward be in the "form—'the *Homa* brings the result, *as it is actually seen to bring about "the Result*,'—then, inasmuch as the premises (bringing forward of the

" Result) form part of the conclusion, it is wholly incapable of rightly leading to the said conclusion. If again, the premises were in the " form—'because the actions of Field-cultivation and the like are found to " bring about Results,'—then in that case the premises would not speak " of the *Probans* as having any connection with the Minor Term (*Homa*) " [and as such the conclusion would not be a legitimate one].

" If it be urged that—'even though the *Probans* is not connected " with the Minor Term, yet we could deduce the conclusion, simply " because we wish it to follow from the premises,'—then, in that case, " the premises could, equally legitimately, be taken as leading to the conclusion that the Result follows from the Material (*Dadhi*).

" It might be urged that—'we could deduce our conclusion from a " similarity with well-known cases (such as those of Field-cultivation and " the like), which similarity is found to exist between the Actions of " *Cultivation* and *Homa*, in the fact of both being *actions*, and not between " the *Cultivation* and the *Material*; because this latter is not an *Action*.' " But there is certainly some sort of a similarity between *Cultivation* " and the *Material* also; and if you deny this similarity, in the case in " question, simply because of the nearer similarities of other things " (with *Cultivation*),—then, inasmuch as there are things which have a " much closer similarity with *Cultivation*, than the *Homa* has, we could, " on this very ground, set aside this similarity also; this is what is meant " by the *Bhāshya*—the *Homa is also dissimilar*;—that is to say, because it " differs from *Cultivation* in its *Means*, *Form* and *Result*. The sentence " of the Bhāshya—'*atha kincit sādṛçyam gṛhyatē taddravyasyāpi sadanityam*'—shows what we have just explained; that is to say, the *Material* also has some sort of a similarity with *Cultivation*, in that both are " ephemeral, are connected with substances and are effects.

" It might be argued that—'there are other things more similar to " the *Cultivation* than the *Material*; and as *similarity* is always comparatively relative, when we are looking for something very similar, that " which is only slightly similar is as good as *not similar* at all; and hence " when we are looking out for the common character of *Action* as inhering in the *Cultivation* and in *Homa*, the similarity of the transient " character, etc., of the *Material* becomes far removed; and as such it is " taken as *dissimilar*.'

" But in that case, inasmuch as we find many other Actions, such as " *Eating* and the like, which have a still closer similarity with *Cultivation* (than the *Homa*), as these Actions (like *Cultivation*) bring about " visible results (which the *Homa* does not do);—in view of this " much closer similarity between *Eating and Cultivation*, that between " *Cultivation* and the *Homa* may be rejected as being as good as non-

" existent. And as such, this similarity could not serve as the means of " getting at the desired conclusion.

" This has also been declared elsewhere, in the following words: " We do not find any *absolute* similarity between *Cultivation* and the " *Homa;* and as for the presence of a *slight* similarity, this is found in " the *Material* also; and as such the fact cannot be ascertained (on the " sole ground of similarity).

" The *Bhāshya* has said—*na caitat siddham*. The sense of this is " that, by the mere citing of an analogous instance, or by the inference of " mere similarity, it is not right to conclude all the properties of one " thing to belong to another, until we have actually found an invariable " concomitance between the two factors. As otherwise, all things in the " world would become one and the same (as there is some sort of a simi- " larity among all things). And the Bhāshya has already said (under " *Sūtra* I—i—2) that, because Dēvadatta is black, it does not necessarily " follow that Yajñadatta is also black. For though the *Gavaya* is *similar* " to the *Cow*, yet we do not find the *presence of the Dewlap*, etc., in the " former; and though the subsidiary sacrifices are laid down as to be " *similar* to the Primary, there are certain elements of the latter—such " as the Result and the like—that are not found to be present in the " former.

" Says the *Bhāshya—When a certain thing has been found to be a cause,* " *in connection with an already known object,*—*i.e.*, with that which is cited " as the *Instance* in connection with the Inference,—*if the same thing* " *happens to be cognised as the cause, in connection with the subject of the* " *Inference, then, in that case, such a thing proves the conclusion.*

" Some people take this declaration of the *Bhāshya* to mean that in " all cases of Inference, it is only the Cause that can rightly point to the " effect (and *vice versa*). But this interpretation of the *Bhāshya* is not " correct; because we actually find such properties as '*kṛtakatva*' (that " of being a product) leading to the conclusion of '*anityatva*' (imper- " manence), in which case there is no relation of cause and effect. And " even between the cause and the effect, the cause does not serve the " purpose of pointing out a particular effect, in the same way as the effect " points to the cause; because there are many effects of a single cause; " and as such there is always a chance of mistake in the former case. " Therefore it must be admitted that what the *Bhāshya* means is that, " in all cases of Inference, when a certain characteristic has been found " to be present in (*i.e.*, concomitant with) a well-known object, and as " such to indicate the existence of this latter, then such a characteristic " (serving as the *Probans* of the Inference) comes to be recognised as " serving the purposes of indicating (the existence of the subject of the

"Inference). This has been fully explained under the *Hētvadhikaraṇa.* (I, ii, 26—30.)

"This is what is made clearer by the Bhāshya in the sentence—*It* "*should be duly considered whether the similarity even though existing, does,* "*or does not, lead to the desired conclusion.* And if on this examination, "it is found that the *similarity* is such a cause, and as such points to the "desired effect, then the form of the argument would be—'In the "sentence, *dadhnēndriyakāmasya,* etc., that which is the *Action* brings "about the Result, because it is an Action, like Cultivation,' or that "'the Result mentioned is to be brought by an *Action,* because it is a "Result, like the growing of corns.'

"The Bhāshya puts forth another syllogism—*that which is an Action* "*has a distinct Result,* etc. And this serves to present a counter-argument "that makes the efficiency of the previous arguments doubtful. As the "*Bhāshya* proceeds to explain that there are cases where, even after the "Action of Substances—that of the *threads* for instance—has ceased, we "find certain distinct results in the shape of another substance—the *cloth* "—following (not from the *Action* but) from the *conjunction* of those "substances (the threads). The mention of the *cessation* of Action is "meant to show that Results are brought about even apart from "Actions.

"It might be argued that—'It may happen that in some cases the "Result may be brought about by means of Actions.' And in reply to "this the Bhāshya has indicated a counter-argument,—that in the "sentence '*dadhnēndriyakāmasya,* etc.' the *Dadhi* brings about the Result "because it is a substance, like the aforesaid threads; or that *sense-*"*efficiency* is brought about by substances, because it is a Result (or "effect), like the aforesaid *Cloth.*

"Says the *Bhāshya*—*the Cultivation is not found to bring forth an im-*"*perceptible Result.* This shows the contradictory character of the "inferential argument in question. The sense is that it may be that your "premiss based upon similarity ('because *Homa* is an action like *Cultiva-*"*tion*') proves the fact of the Action bringing about the Result, or that "of the Result being brought about by the Action; but it would also "prove the fact of the *Homa* bringing about a visible result, or a result "in some such form as the *growth of the corn* and the like (and certainly "this would be far from desirable, even for you).

"Thus, then, inasmuch as we have all these discrepancies cropping "up, if we accept the aforesaid causal relation, it does not follow that "because a certain thing is seen in one case, it must be present in "another place also.

"At this point of the discussion, the *Siddhāntin* might retort—

" ' When you yourself have set aside the inference that the Result follows " the Action, how is it that you hold to the position that *rightly speaking*, " *the Result follows from the Homa?* '

" [This retort, as put in the *Bhāshya*, may be taken as extending as " far as '*iti*'.

" But we have the following rejoinder ready: That the Result fol- " lows from the *Homa* is cognised directly from the words themselves (of " the sentence in question); as has already been shown in detail under " the *Bhāvārthadhikaraṇa* (II—i—1). *Therefore we conclude that the only* " *rightful conclusion is that the Result follows from the Homa.*

" The Bhāshya adds—*and it is not right to say that the Result follows* " *from the Material Dadhi;* and the purpose of this apparently useless " repetition of a fact already implied in the previous sentence is simply " to show that the two theories are not equally authoritative; as the " previous sentence might leave an impression that both might be right- " ful conclusions.

" *And further, the Dadhi is not capable of doing both* (*i.e.*, the accom- " plishing of the *Homa* and the bringing about of *sense-efficiency*). " Because the *Dadhi* has no instrumentality of its own (towards the bring- " ing about of the Result), apart from an Action; and as such, it could " not, by itself, be connected with any Result. Consequently then (if " the *Dadhi* had such an instrumentality) it would be necessary to dis- " tinctly lay it down as accomplishing both (the *Homa* and the Result); " but no such laying down is possible.

" It might be urged that a double purpose could be served by the " *Dadhi* (without two distinct Injunctions); just as we find that the act of " washing the blanket with the feet serves the double purpose of wash- " ing the blanket and cleansing the feet; this argument may be taken as " urged, either with a view to show the fact of the connection of an " Action being only something by the way (and very immaterial), or to " set aside the fact of the incapability of substances (to bring about " double results); because the opponent's assertion that *the Dadhi is not* " *capable of doing both*—is found to distinctly speak of the *incapability* " *of a substance, Dadhi*).

" The *reply* to this is that we do not mean to say that a single " substance cannot serve two purposes. That is to say, we do not mean " to deny the capability of Substances; all that we mean is that even " though the Substance (*Dadhi*) were capable (of serving two purposes), " it could not be utilised as such, in performance, unless it had been dis- " tinctly enjoined (as to be so utilised); and consequently, it would " become necessary for you to take the sentence in question as laying " down the *Dadhi*, both for the fulfilment of the *Homa* and for the accom-

"plishment of the Result—'sense-efficiency.' But this would not be "possible, as such a procedure would entail a syntactical split.

"Then again, in all cases, we find that it is only when the factor (of "the root-meaning), which is more proximate (to the Injunctive word), "is not capable of being taken as the object of Injunction, that we accept "the remoter factor (of the material) to be its object. In the case in ques-"tion, we find that the connection of the *Dadhi* with the *Homa* is very "much more proximate than that of the *Dadhi* with the Result; and as "such if both these connections were laid down simultaneously, we would "have to accept, at one and the same time. both the probable and the "improbable. And hence when it becomes necessary to give up one of "the two, there remains no chance for your theory (because that would "mean the acceptance of the Remoter, and the rejection of the Nearer, "factor); and hence, on account of close proximity, we come to connect "the *Dadhi* with the *Homa*, and the *Homa* with the Result.

"And thus, the Action (mentioned in the sentence *dadhnēndriya-"kāmasya juhuyāt*) being found to be connected with the Action (of "*Homa*), the sentence in question cannot but be taken as laying down a "distinct Action."

—o—

SIDDHĀNTA.

***Sūtra* (26): The two sentences not being exactly similar, the second sentence should be taken as laying down an accessory for the previously-mentioned Action.**

The sentence in question is not similar to those with reference to which it has been concluded, under the *Bhāvārthādhikaraṇa* (II—i—1), that the Result follows from that which is expressed by the Root. Because so long as the potency of the Injunctive has not been removed from that which is expressed by the verbal root, whatever Result is mentioned is taken as pertaining to that Root-meaning; when, however, the potency of the Injunctive is transferred to the Accessory, if a Result happens to be mentioned, then, inasmuch as this mention of the Result would be touched by the Injunction of the Accessory, it is along with that necessory that the Result comes to be taken.

That is to say, the Injunctiveness, in reality residing in the *Bhāvanā*, is transferred from one to the other factor, according as that factor comes to be recognised as helping that *Bhāvanā*. And at the time that the Injunctiveness, as transferred to the Root-meaning, gets at the *Bhāvanā* with a particular result,—it is the Root-meaning that is made the Instrument (of its accomplishment); and everything else becomes subservient to that Root-meaning. This (fact of the Injunctiveness pertaining to the Root-meaning) is found to be the case, in connection with the sentence '*agnihotram juhuyāt svargakāmaḥ*', where the name ('*Agnihotra*') is incapable of wresting, for itself, the operation of the Injunctive. On the other hand, in the case of the sentence in question ('*dadhnēndriyakāmasya juhuyāt*'), the word '*dadhi*' has got none of the various characteristics of a *Nāmadhēya* (Name of a Sacrifice) (as detailed in the Fourth *Pāda* of the First *Adhyāya*); and hence it must be taken as something enjoined; and as such it wrests to itself the Injunctive operation that had been pointing to the Root-meaning. Thus then, the *Bhāvanā* in question, affected by its contact with the *Dadhi*, comes to stand in need of a *reference* (to a previous Action) by means of the Root-meaning in the sentence; and consequently, when we find a Result mentioned, we at once conclude this Result to be something to be brought about by the instrumentality of the *Dadhi*, and not by that of the *Homa* (expressed by the Root-meaning of '*juhuyāt*'); specially because those that are not enjoined can never be accepted to have the character of the Instrument; and when we have accepted a certain other thing to be the object of the Injunction, we can never take the sentence as laying down that from which the Injunctive operation has been wrested, as we have already shewn above (under *Sūtra* II—ii—16). Just as on account of the Injunctive operation being wrested by the *Dadhi* we deny the fact of the sentence enjoining the *Homa*, so, in the same manner, on account of the presence of the word mentioning the Result, we cannot take the sentence as enjoining the *dadhi with reference to the Homa* (because of the chance of syntactical split, etc., etc.); hence what we hold is that the sentence enjoins the *Dadhi with reference to the Bhāvanā*; and as such, it must be admitted that the Result follows from the *Dadhi*.

Question (*Bhāshya*): "*In the sentence in question, which is the word* "*that denotes the exertion of a personal agent?* The sense of this question " is that the words '*dadhi*' (denoting the material) and '*indriyakāmasya*' " (denoting the Result) not serving the purpose of expressing the *Bhāvanā*, " they cannot directly form the objects of the Injunction; and as such " we would look out for a verbal affix (that would express the *Bhāvanā* " or the personal exertion, and afford the object of the Injunction); and " then, in accordance with the *Sūtra* II—i—4, it becomes impossible to " entirely reject the Root-meaning (because the presence of the affix " would be impossible without a verbal root); and consequently, the " Result must be admitted to follow from that Root-meaning."

The *reply* given to this is by a single word '*juhuyāt*'; that is to say, the word expressing human exertion is '*juhuyāt*,' wherein the *Siddhānti* separates the Affix from the Root, the former serving the purpose of expressing the object of Injunction, while the latter serves only as a reference (to a previously mentioned Action).

Objection:—" *But the word 'juhuyāt' directly denotes something connected with Homa, while it would be by means of the indirect method of syntactical connection that it would indicate the connection of Dadhi.* " This passage of the *Bhāshya* serves to clear up the position of the " opponent. As *human exertion* too is said to consist of the *Bhāvanā* as " connected with the Injunction (the word '*juhuyāt*' cannot be said to be " expressive of that exertion)."

The *reply* to this is that though, in accordance with the conclusion arrived at under the *Bhāvārthādhikaraṇa*, what you say has been found to be the case, on account of the stronger authority of Direct Assertion, in regard to other sentences,—yet, in the case in question, *those who would admit your theory would be all the more contradicting Direct Assertion.* Because in your theory, (1) you would have to admit many objects of Injunction, while it is quite possible for very little to be its object; (2) it would be necessary to have recourse to Possessive Indication; (3) or else, there would be a total rejection of the word ('*dadhi*').

That is to say, (1) in all cases, it is a well-established law that when it is possible for a smaller number of things to form the object of an Injunction, it always rejects a larger number. *Secondly*, according to you, the *Homa* being the instrument in the accomplishment of the *Bhāvanā* of the Result, the meaning of the sentence would be '*bhāvayēt indriyam homēna*'; and thus the *Homa* would come on an equal footing with *Dadhi*, which is distinctly mentioned as the instrument (by the word '*dadhnā*'); and thus both the *Homa* and *Dadhi* having the same instrumental character, no direct relationship between them would be possible; and as such it would be absolutely necessary for us to have recourse to Possessive Indication, taking the word '*dadhnā*' as = '*dadhimatā*',—the sentence thus coming to mean '*dadhimatā homēna indriyam bhāvayēt*';—and there is absolutely no ground for this Possessive Indication. *Thirdly*, inasmuch as the word '*dadhi*' fulfils none of the conditions of a *Nāmadhēya*, it cannot be taken as one; and thus the word '*dadhi*', falling from the position of a *Nāmadhēya* as well as from that of the *Instrument*, becomes altogether useless; consequently for the sake of the property of a word, in the shape of its *proximity* (whereby the root signifying the *Homa* is taken as the object laid down by the Injunctive affix, appearing in the same word),—you come to reject the word ('*dadhi*') itself; and certainly this entails a greater contradiction of Direct Assertion than that involved in our theory. If, however, the sentence be taken as laying down the *Dadhi* as the Instrument in the accomplishment of the *Bhāvanā* of the Result, then there is no rejection of any word (or its property).

It is argued—"*That way of taking the sentence would set aside the "word 'juhoti.'*"

The reply to this is that in any case *it would be absolutely necessary to use the word 'juhūyat'*, (and as such the root '*juhoti*' would not be rejected). Because there could be no connection between the *Dadhi* and *sense-efficiency*, unless there was an affix expressing the *Bhāvanā*; and no affix could be present, except along with a verbal root.

That is to say, it is absolutely necessary to pronounce the Affix, for the purpose of laying down the *Bhāvanā* qualified by *Dadhi* and *Sense-efficiency*; and as the affix can never be pronounced by itself, and as it is absolutely impossible for an affix to be present apart from a verbal root, it must always be used in the wake of a root; and thus when it comes to the using of some such root or other, the particular root that comes to be admitted is that which expresses the *Homa*, inasmuch as this is pointed out by the Context. And as for the relationship of this *Homa* with *Dadhi*, it would only be in the form of the relationship between the *basis and the based* (*container and the contained*),—which relationship also would only be referred to in the sentence in question, as it has already been previously mentioned in the sentence '*dadhnā juhoti*'.

In the case of the sentence '*graham sammārshṭi*', it has been shown that the *case-ending* (in *graham*) does not serve the only purpose of expressing the singular number; as the only purpose served by such an ending is the mere fact of the word being an active noun; but whenever it is uttered, is has to be uttered along with a certain *number* which is its invariable concomitant; and thus even though no real significance is meant to be attached to this *number*, yet the word signifies it all the same. In the same manner, in the case in question, even though the Root may be used only for the sake of making possible the use of the Affix, yet, on account of the powerful character of the relationship (between the Root and the Affix), it could not but signify its own meaning, even though no real significance might be meant to be attached to it. Hence (in order to meet the objection that our theory would mean the rejection of the Root as useless) we must insist upon the fact that the signification of its own meaning is not the only purpose that can be served by the Root.

Objection: "*Nanu ucyamāne'pi, etc.* That is to say, even though "pronounced only for the purpose of making the presence of the Affix "possible, yet the Root must express its own meaning also; and there "is no reason why no significance should be attached to it—as to the "*singleness of the vessel* in the sentence above cited; consequently, inas-"much as it is absolutely impossible to express mere '*karoti*' (a generic "verb, simply affording room for the presence of the affix), what you say "is most unreasonable."

Reply: That does not touch our position; because even when there is a connection between the *Dadhi* and the *Homa,* the sense of '*karoti*' is not absent (*i.e.*, it is present along with the '*Homa*'); and our purpose is served by that much also of its presence (*i.e.*, the utterance of the Root ceases to be useless even if it expresses only that much); specially as the peculiarity attaching to the '*karoti*' (by its connection or combination with '*Homa*') does not militate against any of our theories; as that peculiarity might serve to specify the *Bhāvanā* in a manner other than that of the *Instrument.*

Objection: "*In that case, there is the same discrepancy;* that is to say, "when the '*Homa*' is not set aside (but is admitted to the present), "then it would make itself obvious as the *Instrument.*"

The *reply* given by the *Siddhānti* is that it is the frequent repetition of the word '*juhuyāt*' in the context, in many other sentences ('*agnihotram juhuyāt*', '*dadhnā juhuyāt*', and so forth), that leads you to believe, wrongly, that *Homa is the Instrument.* Because when we come to look into the matter closely, we find that in the case in question, though, on account of the proximity (of the Root-meaning with the Injunctive Affix), the *Homa* might appear to have the character of the *Objective* (of the *Bhāvanā*), yet being (on account of its not being something in itself desirable for the agent) found to be incapable of that character, it is removed from that position; and in the same manner, in consideration of the presence of the word '*dadhi*' (which has the Instrumental ending, and is not capable of being taken as anything else), the '*Homa*' could not but be denied the character of the Instrument also; and just as in the former case the *Homa* is cognized only as qualifying the *Bhāvanā*, through another *element* of it, so, in the case in question also, it would qualify it by serving as the *basis* or substratum for the (operation of the) material '*dadhi*'. *It is with reference to this that the author of the Vṛtti has declared—'The Result would be brought about by the material as based upon the Homa.'*

Question: "Is this relationship of the *basis and the based* (held "to exist between the *Dadhi* and the *Homa*) something distinct, or non-"different, from the three factors of the *Bhāvanā, viz.*: the *Objective*, the "*Instrument*, and the Method of *Procedure?*"

To this some people make the following reply: 'It is wholly distinct 'from those; because just as in other cases, the *Bhāvanā* is cognised as 'standing in need of the said three factors, so, in the case in question, the '*Bhāvanā*, being qualified by a distinct material, stands in need of the 'fourth factor. That is to say, in a case where the *Bhāvanā* enjoined is 'one in which the Root-meaning serves as the *Instrument*, all its require-'ments are supplied by the three factors; in such cases, however, where a 'certain material is distinctly laid down as the Instrument,—so that it is 'only in the character of the Instrument, and not in that of a disinterested 'onlooker, that the said material could help to accomplish the Result,—'inasmuch as it could not have the real character of the *Instrument* until 'it helped to bring about that which is expressed by the Root, there 'naturally arises a fourth need for the *Bhāvanā*, as to the exact character 'of this something expressed by the Root, by bringing about which the 'Instrumental Material would accomplish the Result. And that some-'thing expressed by the Root which would be the object brought about 'by it is spoken of as the *basis* or *substrate* of the *Material*, as it is by the 'help of that that the true Instrumental character of this latter is attain-'ed.' Thus then, the sentence in question itself being wholly given to the 'mention of the relationship between the *Material* and the *Result*, and 'being itself incapable of affording the required basis, on account of the 'chance of a syntactical split,—we are led by the Context to the conclusion 'that the *Agnihotra Homa* is the *basis* required (for the operation of *Dadhi*). 'And being thus got at, the *Homa* is only *referred* to by the Root (in *juhu-'yāt*), which is used for the purpose of making the presence of the Affix 'possible, and which as such, forms a necessary feature of the Injunction; 'just as in the case of the use of the word *ālabhēta*, we accept the fact of its 'being a reference to a previously mentioned action of *ālambhana* (*i.e.*, in 'the case in question, we accept the Root to serve the purpose of referring 'to the previous *Homa*); and hence, in accordance with the law—that *when 'the Apūrva follows from a single cause, everything else is subservient to that 'cause*—, we come to take the Root-meaning as helping that which is 'expressed by the noun (*Dadhi*).'

But, as a matter of fact, we can very reasonably deny the fact of there being any need of a fourth factor, in the case in question. Because all that we find is that it is only the need for the *Instrumental* factor that has been extended a little further; that is to say, by means of the Root-meaning the *Bhāvanā* is accomplished more quickly than is done by means of the *Material*—inasmuch as the *Instrumental* character of this latter is accomplished only after the connection of the *Action* (expressed by the Root) has been established. (And thus all that is done in the case in question is that that functioning of the Instrument is removed one step); and consequently there are only *three factors* needed by the *Bhāvanā*.

Thus then, the *Material* being taken as having its *Instrumentality* accomplished through the *Homa*, and as leading to a distinct Result, there arises a question as to the *Method* to be employed; and this is answered by the Method of Procedure employed in connection with the previously mentioned *Agnihotra*. It is this what is meant by the *Bhāshya*—*anayā'gnihotrētikartavyatayā*—which only serves to point out the said fact,

—after the conclusion of the present *Adhikaraṇa* itself has been arrived at,—which really forms the subject of the '*Sansthādhikaraṇa*' (*Sūtras* III, vi, 41—47).

Some people take this sentence of the *Bhāshya* to mean that *the Agnihotra itself is the required method.* But this is not correct; because the *Method* is something wholly distinct from the *Instrument*, and the *Homa* (constituting the *Agnihotra*) has been shown to be non-different from the *Instrumental factor* (of the *Bhāvanā*). Consequently we conclude that what is meant by the expression '*agnihotrētikartavyatā*' is the aggregate of such actions as the preparing of the Fire, and so forth (that are performed during the *Agnihotra*).

Objection: "*How is this?* That is to say, how is it that that which "is not signified by the Root (*i.e.*, the *Dadhi*) is connected with the "*Method*?"

Reply: Phalasādhanasya dadhnaḥ. That is to say, just as in your case, it is only on account of its being the Instrument (in the accomplishment of the Result) that the *Homa* (expressed by the Root) comes to be helped by the *Method*,—so, in our case also, it is on account of the very same reason (that of being the means of accomplishing the Result) that the *Dadhi* becomes connected with (and helped by) the said *Method*.

There are two other arguments brought forward by the *Bhāshya*:—(1) *because of the proximity of this Method* (of the Agnihotra), and (2) *because we find the denotation of the root 'juhoti' present as a feature of the Injunction.* But none of these arguments appear to be quite proper; because as for the former, it entails an acceptance of '*samānavidhānatva*' (the fact of the *equality of Injunction*), which is distinctly denied under the *Sansthādhikaraṇa* (III, vi, 41—47); while as for the latter, inasmuch it only brings forward the law of *Atideça*, it is wholly irrelevant. And further, if the requisite relationship is accomplished by mere *proximity*, what would be the use of the presence of the said feature of Injunction? And conversely, if the presence of this feature were the reason for the relationship, there could be absolutely no use for the mention of 'proximity'; because that reason would apply equally to one that is at a distance (and not in proximity).

In view of these objections we must explain the said expressions of the *Bhāshya* as follows:—(1) *Because the said Method is made closely proximate* by means of the particular *Homa*, which is found to be most helped by that Method; and (2) *because we find the Root-meaning of 'juhoti' which is a feature of the Injunction*, and which affords a ground for *Atideça*.

And because the Root-meaning of '*juhoti*,' appearing through the Context only, as a feature of the Injunction, is only *referred* to (in the sentence in question),—therefore the Affix (in '*juhuyāt*') cannot be taken as enjoining either the appearance of that Action (of *Homa*), or the Result as following from it.

Question: "*By what has the Homa been previously mentioned, to which " Homa the 'juhuyāt' in question would be a reference?*"

Answer: *You do not certainly mean to say that there is no other sentence laying down the Homa.*

Some people explain this last sentence of the *Bhāshya* differently, as meaning that it is not the case that apart from the 'sense-efficiency' brought about by '*Dadhi*' there are no results, in the shape of Heaven and the like, following from the *Homa* of the *Agnihotra*; because such a result, in the shape of *Heaven* at least, is mentioned in the very sentence that lays down the *Agnihotra* itself ('*agnihotram juhuyāt svargakāmaḥ*').

But inasmuch as this interpretation would represent the *Bhāshya* as saying something wholly unconnected with the question put forward, and as such being wholly irrelevant,—we must accept the former explanation as being the more reasonable.

Thus then, we conclude that the Action mentioned in the sentence in question is not different from the previous *Agnihotra*; all that the sentence does is to declare that if *Dadhi* is employed at the Action, 'sense-efficiency' is the result that follows,—by the help of *Homa* (which serves to make possible the use of the *Dadhi*). Or, the sentence may be taken as declaring that the Result follows, neither from the *Dadhi* nor from the *Homa*, but from the connection of the *Dadhi* and the *Homa*,—and the words '*dadhi*' and '*homa*' only serve the purpose of expressing that connection;—(1) because for reasons already given, the word '*dadhi*' cannot be said to have been wrongly inserted; and (2) because the Result could not follow from the *Dadhi* alone by itself.

In this case, however, in accordance with a rule explained above, the sentence that has previously mentioned the relationship of the *Homa* and the *Dadhi* (*viz.*, the sentence '*dadhnā juhoti*') not being capable of being taken along with the sentence in question ('*dadhnēndriyakāmasya juhuyāt*'),—the said relationship of the *Dadhi* and the *Homa* cannot be taken as accomplished (for this latter sentence); and hence this relationship not being capable of being taken as pointed out by the Context, we must conclude that it is the sentence in question itself that establishes that relationship; and then lays down the Injunction of that relationship, in reference to the particular Result; and thus the sentence containing the Injunction of more than one thing, there is a distinct syntactical split.

For these reasons we conclude that the former interpretation—that the result follows from Dadhi—is the only correct one. The final summing up (in the *Bhāsaya*) also is in keeping with that interpretation: it being in the form—*therefore we conclude that the result follows from the Dadhi as connected with the homa.* And hence the sentence '*atha vā, etc.*' must be taken only as pointing another possible alternative.

Some people, however, declare as follows: 'It is one and the same 'view—*that the result follows from the Dadhi*—that is put forward from 'beginning to end, with all the arguments in its favour (and there is no 'mention of any alternative); and hence the proper reading of the *Bhās-'hya* is—*dadhiçabdasya vivakshitatvāt*, and the words *atha vā* afford a 'wrong reading'.

But this assertion—that the alternative explanation is not possible and that the reading is wrong—can be refuted in the following manner: As soon as we construe the sentence in question as that 'for one desiring sense-efficiency, the result should be accomplished by means of Dadhi', we at once become cognisant of the fact that the Result follows from the *Dadhi* as the Instrumental means; and this instrumental character, not being otherwise possible, points to its connection with some sort of an action; and as the relationship of the agent and the Action is always in the form of a *potency*, the said connection is included in the Instrumental ending; and then, inasmuch as that which is denoted by the affix is the principal factor in the sentence, what the sentence comes to do finally is that it lays down, for the sake of the Result, the connection of that of which what is expressed by the basic noun ('*dadhi*') is the subordinate element. And when that connection has been laid down, then. as before, the Context serves to point to a particular Action, in the shape of the *Homa*. And, then, in accordance with the law regulating the relationship of the Material and the Deity, the connection of the Result with the relationship of the Action and the Agent having been brought about, there arises a question as to the character of the particular Agent of Action; and hence, for the purpose of establishing the relationship of the Qualification and the Qualifed (between the *Dadhi* and the *Homa*), the *Homa* is brought up by the Context. And hence it is that the *Bhāshya* speaks of *the connection between the Dadhi and the Homa being laid down for the sake of the Result.*

Thus then, the reading '*atha vā*' is found to be quite correct; though the conclusion and the final summing up are those of the former interpretation. Or even these might be taken as those of the latter interpretation; as in that case also, inasmuch as what is mentioned is the *Dadhi as connected*, this connection is that of which the *Dadhi* is the subordinate element; and as such there would be no incongruousness in this.

Objection: "In the case of the sentence in question (if it be taken as "laying down the Result as following from the Material), the Injunction "would involve the functioning of two words—'*dadhnā*' and '*indriyakā-*"*masya*'; and this would give rise to a syntactical split".

Reply: This is no argument against us; because the mere fact of a sentence expressing various relationships does not bring about a syntactical split; it is only when the potency of the Injunction itself is manifold, that we have that split; and as a matter of fact, we have no such manifold potency of the Injunction in the case in question. That is to say, it is quite possible for many things to be connected together by means of a single sentence; and in this fact alone, there is no split of the sentence. Because it has been distinctly pointed out that it is only the multifariousness of the Injunction itself that brings about a syntactical split. There is no such multifariousness in the case in question; because the Result is not an object of Injunction. The construction of the sentence thus comes to be this: *the accomplishment of sense-efficiency* (this being a mere *reference* and not an Injunction) *is to be brought about by means of Dadhi*. As a rule, when a person desires something, he exerts himself to its attainment; and hence for the acquiring of such a desirable thing as *sense-efficiency*, the person would exert himself naturally (without any Injunction from outside); and hence what the Injunctive affix in question does is to lay down the *Bhāvanā with its Instrumental factor*, with *reference* to the same *Bhāvanā as endowed with the objective factor* (*i.e.*, the Result); and thus the object of Injunction being one only in the shape of the Instrument (as the Result is only *referred* to),—there is no syntactical split.

Consequently, we conclude that for the sake of making the word '*dadhi*' serve a useful purpose, the sentence must be taken as laying down the Result as following from the Material *Dadhi*, and not as laying down a distinct Action.

ADHIKARANA (12).

[The *Vāravantīya, etc.*, are distinct Actions.]

***Sūtra* (27):—When the sentences are similar (the Results) would be connected with distinct Actions.**

We now proceed to deal with an exception to the foregoing *Adhikaraṇa.*

The subject of the *Adhikaraṇa* is thus shown: (1) we have the sentence—'*trivṛdagnishṭudagnishṭomaḥ, tasya vāyavyāsu ēkavinçamagnishṭomasāma kṛtvā brahmavarcasakāmō yajēta*'; and then in continuation of this *Agnishṭut* sacrifice, we have the sentence '*vāravantiyamagnishṭomasāma kāryam,*' which lays down an accessory (in the shape of the *vāravantīya*); and then we come to the sentence, (2) '*etasyaiva rēvatīshu vāravantiyamagnishṭomasāma kṛtvā paçukāmō hyētēna yajēta*'. [The difference between the bearing of the two sentences being that when the *Vāravantiya* is sung in connection with the *Vāyavya* verses then the result is in the shape of 'Brahmic glory', while when the same is sung in connection with the *Rēvati* verses, the Result is in the shape of 'Cattle.']

Here too, we have, as before, the following doubt:—Does this last sentence enjoin an *independent* action, distinct from that laid down in the previous sentence, as qualifed by a distinct material (in the shape of the Vāravantiya *in connection with the Rēvati verses*)? Or, does it only serve to lay down this distinct material only, with reference to the same Action, just as in the case of the sentence dealt with in the foregoing *Adhikaraṇa?*

And on this, we have the following

PURVAPAKSHA.

"In view of the reasons detailed, and the conclusion arrived at, in the "foregoing *Adhikaraṇa*, it must be admitted that the sentence in question "serves only to lay down the Result as following from a particular accessory (in connection with the previously mentioned action). Because, as "a matter of fact, we find that the Injunctive potency of the sentence is "taken up by the connection between the *Rēvatī* and the *Vāravantīya*: "and then we find a Result mentioned along with this Injunction; "consequently we cannot take the sentence as laying down the *Sacrifice* (as "that would entail a dual functioning of the Injunction, thereby leading "to syntactical split). And as for the connection between the *Rēvatī* "and the *Vāravantīya*, this would be brought about, without a repetition "of the Injunctive affix, by the word '*kṛtvā*' which is mentioned dis-"tinctly by itself (and as such this would not involve the said syntac-"tical split).

"That is to say, it might be argued that—'inasmuch as the sen-"tence involves the Injunction of the appearance of the connection "between *Rēvatī* and the *Vāravantīya*, and then an Injunction also of that "Connection with reference to the Result, there would be a repetition of "the Injunctive affix, which would give rise to a syntactical split'. But "this reasoning would be scarcely valid; because the Vedic sentence itself "enjoins only the Result,—the fact being that the said connection having "been established by the clause '*rēvatīshu vāravantīyam kṛtvā*', what "the Injunctive affix following after the root '*yaji*' (in '*yajēta*') does "is to lay down only the relationship (causal) of that Connection with the "particular result. And thus there is no chance of the anomaly result-"ing from a repetition of the Injunctive affix.

"Then too, inasmuch as the '*Rēvatī* verses' are spoken of as the "substrate or basis (of the *Sāma*), they are distinctly subordinate in "their character; and hence it is the *Vāravantīya sāma* which, on account "of its predominant character, comes to be enjoined with reference to "the Result.

"That is to say, in the sentence in question, on account of the "mention of an Accessory, the potency of the Injunctive, being removed "from that which is expressed by the Verbal root ('*yaji*'), serves to lay "down that accessory, for the sake of the particular result; and as such "it is found to lay down that which has not been cognised as subservient "to anything else. As for the *Rēvatī verses*, inasmuch as they are "spoken of in the Locative, they are subservient to the *Vāravantīya sāma*; "and as such not standing in need of any other purpose, they could not "be connected with the Result; while the *Vāravantīya*, having the *Rēvatī* "verses for its subordinate accompaniment, is cognised as the predominant "factor, on account of its being mentioned in the Accusative; and as such "it becomes connected, in the manner of the Root-meaning, with the "*Bhāvanā* denoted by the verb '*kṛtvā*'; and thus being on the look-out "for a purpose, it becomes connected with the Result.

"Or, in this case also, we can reject both the *Rēvatī* and the *Vāravan-"tīya*, and hold the Result to follow only from the Connection of these two.

"Thus then, we distinctly recognise the following facts in connec-"tion with the sentence in question: (1) that at the time of its utterance, "the idea of the previously mentioned 'sacrifice' is still present in the "mind; (2) that the word '*ētat*' (in '*ētasya*') distinctly points to "that which has been spoken of before; (3) that the genitive (in '*etasya*'), "appearing after that '*etat*' which is co-extensive with (refers to) the "'sacrifice', signifies the relationship of the *Basis and the Based*, pointed "out by the Context, between that sacrifice and the Accessory as leading "to the Result; (4) that the word '*ēva*' serves to preclude any other "basis or substrate for that Accessory, because no such other substrate is "possible; (5) that the *Vāravantīya* qualified by the connection of the "*Agnishṭomasāma* is already laid down by the previous sentence. And "all these facts distinctly point to the conclusion that the Action ('sacri- "fice') mentioned in the sentence in question is none other than that laid "down in the previous sentence; and as such, inasmuch as that same "Action is referred to in the sentence in question, the Injunctive affix in this "sentence will not be put to the trouble of laying down the Action, over and "above the Accessory).

"While if the sentence be taken as laying down a distinct Action, "as in that case nothing will have been previously laid down, the "Injunctive affix would have to enjoin all that is necessary.

"And as a matter of fact, no such injunction of all things is possible; "because the Injunctive, by its very nature, is always endowed with a "single potency; and when its purpose is fulfilled by the Injunction of "even a little thing, it can never enjoin any more than that.

"Thus then, we find that the word '*kṛtvā*' establishes the connection "between the *Rēvatī* and the *Vāravantīya*, while the Injunctive affix lays "down only the relationship of that Connection with the particular result. "And as such, there being no necessity of accepting a manifold potency of "the Injunctive, there can be no doubt as to the superiority of the theory "that the sentence in question serves only to lay down an Accessory "(with reference to a previously mentioned Action).

"As all the references enumerated above are included in and based "upon the reference of the 'sacrifice', it is only this last that has been "spoken of in the Bhāshya, and all the rest have been left to be inferred. "For these reasons we conclude that the sentence in question does not "lay down a distinct Action."

SIDDHĀNTA.

To the above we make the following reply: **When there is an Accessory which accepts the previously mentioned Action as its substratum, then alone is it so that we do not perceive any difference between the Actions** (mentioned in the two sentences); and the reason is that in such a case, what the latter sentence does is only to *refer* to the previous Action for the sake of its connection with the new Accessory.

That is to say, we find the sentence in question, '*etasyaiva rēvatīshu, etc.*', containing the mention of 'sacrifice' directly by means of the root '*yaji*'; under the circumstances, if the exact sort of 'sacrifice' that is herein mentioned had been previously mentioned in another sentence, then alone could we conclude that the one mentioned in the sentence in question is not a distinct sacrifice. As for instance, in the case of the sentence '*dadhnēndriyakāmasaya, etc.*', we find that the sentence directly lays down only the relationship with the particular Result; and then the Context helps to supply the other substrate of the relationship,—in the shape of *Homa*; and in this case we admit the mention of '*Homa*' in the sentence to be a mere reference to a previously mentioned '*Homa*'; and another reason for this is that the *Dadhi* by itself also is capable of directly accomplishing the *Homa.* In the case in question, on the other hand, we find that the *Vāravantīya qualified by the Revatī verses* is not, by itself, capable of directly accomplishing the Sacrifice; because it is neither a Deity nor a Material (which two alone are capable of directly accomplishing the Sacrifice); because the Sacrifice requires, for its accomplishment, no other helping factors, except those of the Deity, the Material, and the Performer; and hence it is never accomplished directly by means of a *Sāma* (*Vāravantīya* and the like).

Thus then, though, through the peculiar character of the Context, the 'Sacrifice' (previously mentioned) is present in the mind, yet it does not become cognised as the substrate of the said *Sāma*, because of its inherent incapability of having that character; and hence that '*Sacrifice*' cannot be accepted as *referred* to by the sentence in question ("*Rēvatīshu, etc.*"); specially as we have no grounds for believing that the 'sacrifice' herein mentioned is the same as the one previously mentioned. As for the *Hymning*, that forms a part of the previous 'sacrifice', and which, being accomplished by means of the *Vāravantīya Sāma*, is capable of being taken as its substrate,—it is not pointed out by the Context; because the presence of *Hymning* in the previous 'sacrifice', the '*Agnishṭut*', is only based upon an indirect implication.

It is with reference to this, that it has been declared that—though the *Sāma* is inherently capable of accomplishing the *Hymning*, yet as no such *Hymning* is pointed out by the Context, it cannot be taken as the substrate of the *Sāma* in question.

The following argument might be brought forward by the other party: "The *Sāma* could base itself upon the *Sacrifice*, in that very "capacity whereby it would help the performance of the sacrifice; and "conversely the '*Sacrifice*' also would become the substrate of the *Sāma*, "in whatever capacity it would be able to act as a true substrate; such "cognition being based upon the general rule whereby the meanings of all "verbs are ascertained in accordance with the capacities of things. And "then (even though the *Sāma* may not be able to help directly in the "performance of the sacrifice itself, yet) in accordance with the *Sūtra* "III—i—18, it would be quite capable of directly accomplishing the "*Hymning* which forms an integral part of the '*Agnishṭut*' sacrifice; and "as such, there would be no incongruity in the said relationship of the "*Basis* and the *Based* (between the *Sāma* and the '*Sacrifice*'), which "would be due to an integral part of the latter, in the shape of the "Hymning."

Reply : That is not possible; because we have already shown that that alone can be taken as the subsidiary part of a sacrifice which has been actually laid down as such a part; that, on the other hand, which appears distinctly as independent by itself, can never become a subsidiary part.

That is to say, in the case of the sentence '*Saptadaçāratnirvājapēyasya yūpaḥ*' (the sacrificial post at the *Vājapēya* is to be seventeen cubits in length), we find that the 'seventeen-cubit-length' is distinctly laid down as a subsidiary detail; and then, inasmuch as it is not found to be capable of being directly connected with the *Vājapēya* sacrifice, we conclude that it should help in the performance of this sacrifice in whatever way it can; and consequently it comes to be taken as a qualification of the *sacrificial post* which forms an integral factor in the performance. If, in the case in question also, the *Vāravantīya* had been laid down as a subsidiary detail of the sacrifice,—then alone, being found incapable of directly serving the Sacrifice, would it come to be taken as helping the *Hymning*, which forms an integral part of the sacrifice.—As a matter of fact, however, we find that the *Vāravantīya*, being laid down in regard to a particular result, stands in need of a substrate, or basis, in the shape of an *Action*; and under the circumstances, if it could find any Action, already previously mentioned, that could form its substrate, then it would directly connect itself with that Action; when, however, it finds no such Action already mentioned, then the sentence in question distinctly points to something else (a fresh *Action* hitherto not mentioned) as the requisite basis. Nor would the *Vāravantīya* become wholly useless, by not being connected with any previously mentioned Action; as it will have its use in the new Action that would be laid down by the sentence in question.

And further, inasmuch as the action of *Hymning* is wholly different from that of *Sacrifice*,—by accomplishing the former, the *Vāravantīya* cannot be said to have accomplished the latter. And hence, even if the *Sāma* helped in the *Hymning*, it would remain as unconnected with the *Sacrifice*, as if it had been mentioned and performed in connection with another *sacrifice* altogether. In the case of the sentence '*saptadaçā-*

ratnirvājapēyasya yūpaḥ,' on the other hand, we find that the Genitive in '*vājapeyasya*' signifies mere *relationship in general*; and as such, there is, in this case, nothing incongruous in the relationship subsisting indirectly, in the subsidiary details. And as such there can be no similarity between the sentence '*saptadaça, etc.*' and the sentence in question.

Even though it be possible for the *Sacrifice* to form the substrate (of the Sāma), indirectly, through the *Hymning*,—yet, in that case the *Sāma* would come to be connected with all kinds of *Hymns*; and as such the specification, in the sentence in question, of the Hymn as the '*Agnishṭoma Sāma*' would be wholly meaningless. For if the Hymn called the '*Agnishṭoma Sāma*' be taken as the required substrate indicated by the sentence itself, then there would be a syntactical split (the sentence laying down the fact of the *Vāravantīya* being based on the *Agnishṭoma Sāma*, and also that of its bringing about the particular Result). Then again, if the sentence be taken as indicating a general relationship (of the *Vāravantīya*) with the *Agnishṭoma Sāma*,—this general relationship being specified by the expression '*ētasyaiva*',—then too there is a syntactical split; and the pronoun '*ētasya*' indicating the relationship of that which has gone before, this would make the *Vāravantīya* connected with all the *Hymns* of the previous sacrifice; and then its specification as *Agnishṭoma Sāma*' would also entail a syntactical split. And lastly, in view of the great complications arising from making the *Vāravantīya* connected (at one and the same time) with the *Revatī Ṛk*, as well as with the *Agnishṭoma Sāma*,—they remain as before.

Objection: "When the *Agnishṭut* sacrifice is obtained as the required "substrate, all the rest that is required would be obtained from the previ-"ous Injunction; and as for the *Vāravantīya*, when it would rest upon a "sacrifice, it would not exist in any place except that wherein it is found "to help the Sacrifice; and the Sacrifice too would not seek for the *Vāra-"vantīya* in any other *Hymn* (save that which forms part of itself). And "as there is no reason for rejecting the *Vāravantīya that is connected with "the Agnishṭoma Sāma of the Sacrifice previously mentioned in the Context*, "there can be no question as to a connection with any other Hymn or "Sacrifice."

Reply: It is not so; we could have all this only if the sentence in question—'*Rēvatīshu, etc.*'—stood in need of the previous sentence laying down the *Vāravantīya* in connection with the *Agnishṭoma Sāma*; as a matter of fact, however, we find that there is no such need; because we have already shown above that there is no mutual relationship between sentences laying down such things as the Accessory and the like.

Then again, the relationship of the Sacrifice with the *Vāravantiya* that is mentioned in the sentence in question, is wholly different from the previous relationship (because in the previous case the *Vāravantīya* was in connection with the *Vāyavyā* verses, whereas in the sentence in question, it is in connection with the *Rēvatī* verses); and as such it could never attain to the position assumed by the previous relationship. Specially as in the previous sentence, the *Vāravantīya*, forming a part of the Action itself, is recognised as connected with the *Agnishṭoma Sāma* of that (*Agnishṭut*) sacrifice; while in the case in question, we find it mentioned as being something in itself desirable by man (as is indicated by the distinct mention of the word '*kṛtvā*'); and as such the Veda could not relegate this latter to the same position as the previous one. And as for any assumptions based upon the *Sāmānyatodṛshṭa* Inference, we have already shown above that such things as we are dealing with are not amenable to Inference.

To the same effect, we have the following declaration: That *Sāma*—which is laid down as independently, by its own form, bringing about the Result,—stands in need of the text of the Veda only, for the propose of its appearance.

That is to say, if the *Vāravantīya Sāma* had originally appeared, first of all, at the *Agnishṭut* sacrifice, then we could not but take it as appertaining to that sacrifice, even if such connection were not mentioned. As a matter of fact, however, we find that in the case in question, the *Sāma* depends, for its appearance, on the Vedic text only; and it is as taken directly from the Veda that it is laid down for the sake of a definite result. And consequently the *Agnishṭut* sacrifice and the *Agnishṭoma Sāma* connected with that sacrifice do not in any way differ from other Sacrifices and Hymns,—in the matter of their being connected with the *Vāravantīya Sāma* mentioned in the sentence in question. (That is to say, the *Sāma* is as unconnected with the *Agnishṭut* sacrifice as with any other of the previously mentioned sacrifices, etc., etc.).

If the sentence in question had laid down a certain purification of the *Vāravantīya*, then we could, somehow or other, identify it with that which had been previously mentioned (in connection with the *Agnishṭut* sacrifice),—as we do in the case of the sentence '*vrīhīn prokshati*' which lays down a purification of the corn. But, as a matter of fact, the sentence in question does not lay down any such purification. Consequently we conclude that the *Vāravantīya* of the sentence in question has no connection with the *Agnishṭoma Sāma* of the previous sacrifice.

Objection: "Though the *Vāravantīya* serves to fulfil an end desired "by the human agent, yet, so long as it does not help to bring about the "completion of the sacrifice, it cannot fulfil that end either; and thus the "accomplishment of the *sacrifice* also being indirectly indicated, the said

" *Sāma* attains the position that had been previously found for it (at that " sacrifice), just as though the *Curd* and the *Milk* help in the performance " of the sacrifice, yet they become connected with the details of the " *Praṇītā* vessel."

Reply: Such is the case only when the details are mentioned as qualifications. In the case in question, however, the *Agnishṭoma Sāma* is not a qualification of the *Vāravantīya*. It could be such a qualification, only if the sentence in question actually referred to its context—which latter fact has still to be established (by the *Pūrvapakshin*). If, in some way or other, a certain relationship of the *Vāravantīya* with the *Agnishṭoma Sāma* were cognised, then there would be nothing to interfere with the application of the details of the latter to the former, like those of the *Praṇītā* to the *Curd* and *Milk*.

Thus then, even this last argument of the *Pūrvapakshin* does not affect the reasoning of the *Siddhānta*; and hence it is only by taking the sentence as laying down an independent Action that we can avoid a syntactical split (and make the sentence a single whole).

Because in that case, even when all the elements of the latter sentence are such as have not been previously mentioned, all of them are capable of being laid down by the process of "qualified Injunction"; while there can be no difficulty as to such an Injunction, when, as a matter of fact, many of the details spoken of in the sentence in question are such as form part of the details of the previously mentioned *Agnishṭut* sacrifice, and are applied to that mentioned in the sentence in question, only by indirect implication.

For instance, (1) the word '*ētat*' (in '*ētasya*') would refer, by indication, to the details of the previous sacrifice, specially as such indirect indication is not faulty in the case of a *Reference* or *Description* (as it is in that of an Injunction). Or the pronoun might directly denote the Action to be immediately mentioned; as the pronoun '*ēsha*' does in the case of the sentence '*athaisha jyotiḥ, etc.*';—(2) as for the *Vāravantīya*, it appears in the previous sentence as helping in the performance of the sacrifice; and as such, in that form, it would become referred to in the sentence in question, as appertaining thereto by indirect implication;—(3) and the operation of the Injunctive also would be very much simplified by making it enjoin only the *sacrifice* as qualified by the peculiar relationship of the *Rēvatī* and the *Vāravantīya* as pointed out by the word '*kṛtvā*'.

Objection: "Inasmuch as what would be enjoined in this case are— " (1) the relationship of the *Agnishṭoma Sāma* with the *Rēvatī* and the " *Vāravantīya*, as well as (2) the sacrifice,—the case in question would be " a great deal different from other cases of "qualified Injunction" (as in all " these cases, the object of Injunction is the *sacrifice* only). Because "the qualifications of two distinct Actions cannot be amenable to the "same (injunctive) effort, when an Injunction has served to lay down one "Action, we should have recourse to another Injunction for the purpose "of laying down another Action. That is to say, those properties and quali- "fications that belong to a single Action are all implied by that Action "when it is enjoined, and as such, they do not necessitate any diversity in "the operation of the Injunctive word; while, on the other hand, when the "qualification belongs to an Action other than the one that is enjoined, "it is not implied by the enjoined Action, because it is not in any "way related to this latter,—and as such, for the sake of such qualifica- "tions, it would be absolutely necessary to repeat the operation of the "Injunctive; and this would certainly involve a syntactical split."

Reply: The latter *Bhāvanā* (which is signified in the word '*yajēta*') takes in, as its subject, only that which is denoted by the word '*kṛtvā*'; and that (*Bhāvanā*) too which is denoted by this latter word would take in only that qualification which belongs to its own specific object. Then, when the new sacrifice (mentioned in the sentence in question) has taken up the *Ṛk* (*Rēvatī*) and the *Sāma* (*Vāravantīya*), the position assigned to the *Rēvatī* would be in accordance with the *Sāma* that has its position already ascertained.

That is to say, while the denotation of the word '*kṛtvā*,'—after having established the relationship between the *Rēvatī* and the *Vāravantīya*—is waiting on the look-out for the second *Bhāvanā* [that denoted by the word '*yajeta*'], it becomes taken up, as specified by its qualification (in the shape of the said connection between the *Vāravantīya* as based upon the *Rēvatī* verses), by the '*Sacrifice*' (mentioned by the root '*yaji*' in '*yajēta*'). And consequently what the 'sacrifice' implies is its own qualification (and not that of any other Action). That, however, which is denoted by the word '*kṛtvā*'—*i.e., accomplishing* or *bringing about*—is not directly connected with the said relationship (of the *Ṛk* and the *Sāma*); and as such, inasmuch as that relationship comes to have a subordinate character, it is relegated to the subsidiaries of the sacrifice; and consequently, in accordance with the *Vāravantīya*, which has its position already known by indirect implication, the *Rēvatī* verses also come to be referred to the same (*Vāravantīya*). Thus then, though the sentence in question does not lay down the *Agnishṭoma Sāma*, yet the qualification of the '*Sacrifice*' extends to that *Sāma*, and as such there is no incongruity in this.

For the above reasons, it is clear that, in your theory, there is no relationship between the sacrifice in question and *Vāravantīya.* Because it is only when the qualifications or accessories have not themselves the character of *Actions* that they betake themselves to an Action; as for the *Vāravantīya*, inasmuch as it is *sung* (and as such forms an action in itself), what can it have to do with another Action (the Sacrifice, for instance)?

That is to say, in the case of such accessories as the *Dadhi*, the *Milking vessel* and the like, we find that, without an Action, their very character of "Instrument" cannot be attained; and as such they stand in need of some such Action. As for the *Vāravantīya*, however, inasmuch as it is denotable by the root '*gāyati*', it is an action in itself; and as such, even without any other Action, it is capable by itself, just like the *sacrifice*, of accomplishing the desired result; and thus not standing in need of another Action, it would not be connected with any such, it would, when sung by itself on the basis of the *Rēvatī* verses, bring about its result, independently of the performance of any such sacrifice as the *Agnishṭut*. And in that case, the words—'*ētasya*', '*agnishṭoma-sāma*', '*kṛtvā*' and '*yajēta*'—would all become wholly unconnected (and irrelevant) with the previous sacrifice (the *Agnishṭut*).

Consequently we must conclude that the Result (mentioned in the sentence in question) follows from the *Sacrifice*; and this *sacrifice*, being spoken of as qualified by properties wholly at variance with those of the previously mentioned *Agnishṭut*, is wholly distinct from that sacrifice.

The Bhāshya explains the *Sūtra* as—*Samēshu ēvañjātīyakēshu bhinnavākyēshu karmayuktam phalam bhavet.* In this the word '*samēshu*' expresses, either the fact of the (previous) sacrifice (the *Agnishṭut*) and the (latter) accessory (*Vāravantīya*) not standing to each other in the relationship of the *Basis and the Based*, because of the inherent incapability of the two,—or that of the *Vāravantīya*, which is an Action by itself, being wholly independent of any other Action. The expression '*bhinnavākyēshu*' means that though in the case of both theories—*i.e.*, whether the sentence in question be taken as mentioning a particular result following from the employment of a certain accessory in connection with the action mentioned in the previous sentence, or as laying down an altogether distinct Action,—the meaning of the second sentence would be different from that of the former, and as such the sentences would be distinct;—yet the distinctness of the two sentences would be better justified by both of them laying down two distinct Actions; because otherwise, there would remain a certain semblance of the two sentences forming a single compound sentence (which would not be quite justifiable in face of the distinctness of their significations).

Says the *Bhāshya*—*nahyētasya revatyaḥ santi, etc.* It is just possible that some people might construe the sentence in question as that—'*ētasya yā rēvatyaḥ, tāsu vāravantīyam kṛtvā*'; but, though, in this case, in view of the Context, the reference to the *former qualified Sacrifice* would not involve a syntactical split, yet, inasmuch as the fact of bringing about (or employing) the *Rēvatī* verses themselves has not been previously laid down, any *reference* to this (as is inevitable in the said construction) cannot be quite allowable. And hence the sentence will have to be construed as—(1) '*tatra rēvatyaḥ prayoktavyāḥ*, (2) *tāsu ca vāravantīyam, etc.*'; and this would involve a syntactical split, and make the word '*ētasya*' wholly redundant.

The following argument might be brought forward: "For the sake "of the word '*etasya*', we could take the sentence as follows—(1) the "Injunctive part: '*ētasya revatyaḥ kartavyāḥ, tāsu ca Vāravantīyam,* "*tacca phalāya*', and (2) the *reference* part; the word '*yojeta*' being taken "as merely referring to the previously mentioned *Agnishṭut* sacrifice."

But thus too, the sentence is made to lay down three distinct facts; and as such syntactical split becomes inevitable; and further, as for the *Agnishṭoma Sāma*, we cannot speak of its connection as being either enjoined or only referred to (in the sentence in question). If this connection were enjoined, then inasmuch as the mere presence of the *Agnishṭoma Sāma* has been pointed out by the previous Injunction, the word '*etasya*' would be absolutely useless; and such an Injunction would also involve a syntactical split. This is one way of taking the said text of the *Bhāshya*.

Some people, however, take the word '*ētat*' in the sense that is pointed out by its position,—namely, that of qualifying the *Rēvatī*. And in that case, the construction of the sentence in question would be like this: '*ētasya yā Revatyaḥ tāsu vāravantīyam Agnishṭoma sāma kṛtvā.*' But in this case also, inasmuch as there is no specification of the *saçrifice* (at which all this is to done),—as the word '*ētasya*' is wholly taken up in qualifying the *Rēvatī*, we do not take it with '*Agnishṭoma*', as '*etasyā agnishṭoma*'; specially as even if such a relationship between the two words were meant to be expressed, there would be a syntactical split.

Though the question—"*how do you yourself avoid the syntactical split?*"—should have been put by the opponent, after all the possible constructions of the sentence in question, in accordance with the *Pūrvapaksha*, had been refuted,—yet the *Pūrvapakshin* reasons thus in his mind: 'When we have so thoroughly refuted the position of the *Siddhāntin*, all these *syntactical splits* that he has brought forward are mere magical illusions in the void (of his own intellect); and so I will just put him the question,—*how do you yourself avoid the said syntactical split?*'

The *Siddhānti* replies by putting forward the following construction: '*Revatīshu ṛkshu vāravantīyam sāma kṛtvā paçukāmo yajéta*'; and the sense of the reply is that when the sentence in question is taken as laying down a new Action, it is quite possible for this Action to be laid down in a qualified form (in the way shown in the construction put forward); and as such the sentence having a single predicate, there would be no syntactical split involved.

Question: "*Nanu arthabhedaḥ: yāgaçcaivam hyapūrvaḥ kartavyaḥ*, "*Revatīshu vāravantīyam apurvam*'. That is to say, inasmuch as the "sentence would involve two *Bhāvanās* mentioned in the sentence—*viz.*, the one mentioned by the word '*kṛtvā*' and another by the word '*yajēta*', "there could not but be a split in the syntax."

Answer: Not so; because what we mean is that the sentence lays down only one principal *Bhāvanā* (that signified by '*yajeta*') as qualified by another secondary *Bhāvanā* (signified by '*kṛtvā*').

Objection: "The relationship of the *Revatī* and the *Vāravantīya* could "not be enjoined; because as there could be no injunction of a qualification "of qualifications (*i.e.*, of the *connection* which is a qualification of the *bring-* "*ing about*, denoted by the root in '*kṛtvā*', which again, according to "you, is the qualification of the '*yāga*');—any such connection could not "be enjoined by means of the Injunctive Affix (*Liṅ.*); and as for the affix "'*ktvā*' (in '*kṛtvā*'), it has not been mentioned by Pāṇini, as having "the function of the Injunctive. Hence, though the *Bhāvanā* may be "*spoken of* as connected, yet, inasmuch as the activity of the human "agent should depend upon an *Injunction*, he would take that *Bhā-* "*vanā* to be as good as non-existent. Thus then, both the *Revatī* and the "*Vāravantīya* being qualifications of the *Bhāvanā* of the 'sacrifice' only, "they could not be employed outside the sacrifice itself; and as there is "no ground for either of the two restricting the employment of the other "(that is whether the *Revatī* restrict the *Vāravantīya* or *vice versâ* is not "ascertainable), both of them would come to refer to one and the same "*stotra* (Hymn); and then there being no such rule as that both of them "should be employed in one and the same place, there would be many other "*Sāmas*—the *Gāyatrī*, and the rest—that could be based upon the *Revatī* "verses (there being no rule restricting the *Revatī* verses as the basis of "the *Vāravantīya Sāma* only); and conversely the *Vāravantīya Sāma* also "would come to be based upon other verses—such as the *Gāyatrī*, the "*Bṛhatī* and the like. And under the circumstances, the idea brought "about by the expression '*Revatīshu Vāravatīyam*' would become abso- "lutely useless. Hence it must be concluded that the sentence seems to "lay down the *Revatī* verses, in reference to the *Vāravantīya*, which has "had its position duly ascertained (in connection with the previous "*Āgnishṭut* sacrifice)."

Reply: The above argument does not affect our position; because though the word '*kṛtvā*' does not *directly* express an Injunction, yet in such cases as the one in question, it is taken as pointing to an Injunction all the same. That is to say, whenever we meet with a sentence like '*idam kṛtvā idam kuryāt*' (*having done this*, one should do that),—if the action denoted by the verb with the '*ktvā*' affix is one that has been previously mentioned elsewhere, then its mention in this sentence is simply in the shape of a motive *cause* or occasion (for the performance of the second action); when, however, that action is not one that has been previously mentioned, then it is a *means* or instrument of the accomplishment of the second Action; because that Action, which is distinctly laid down as to be performed *after the accomplishment of a previous Action* (that which is mentioned by the word ending in '*ktvā*'), can never be performed, unless that previous Action has been performed; and as such the performance of the Action being found to be absolutely necessary, it is admitted to be as good as directly *enjoined*. Thus, in the case in question, the relationship of the *Revatī* and the *Vāravantīya* (mentioned by the word '*kṛtvā*') is such as has never been mentioned prior to the Injunction contained in the sentence in question; and as such it cannot be taken as a mere motive cause for the 'sacrifice'; and hence it cannot but be accepted as *something to be actually performed or accomplished.*

Objection: "If the said *connection* comes to be *something to be accomplished*, how is it that it becomes related to the second *Bhāvanā*, which "also is something to be accomplished?"

In reply, the *Bhāshya* says: *dvavētāvarthau kṛtvētyēsha çabdaḥ çaknoti vaditum, abhinirvṛttim pūrvakālatāñca* (the word '*kṛtvā*' is capable of signifying both *accomplishment* and *sequence*) [and as signifying *sequence* it is only natural that it should point to something that would be performed *afterwards*]. As to how a single word can have two significations, the *Bhāshya* says—*we find this to be the case in certain instances,*—as, for instance, in '*çoṇamānaya*' (bring the *çoṇa*),—where though the '*bringing*' has been previously cognised by other means, yet, the word '*çoṇa*', though used in the sense of the 'red horse', and as such taking the place of the two words 'red' and 'horse', does not entail a syntactical split (and the only reason for this is that the single word signifies both *redness* and the *horse*). In the same manner, in the case in question, the affix '*ktvā*' would signify *accomplishment* as well as *sequence.*

[It has been argued above—*Text*, page 563—that the Injunction of the qualification of a qualification is not possible; but this does not affect the case in question; as] the qualification of a qualification can not be enjoined only in that case where that qualification, forming part of the *Material*, is not recognised as part of the Action itself. That is to say, we shall show under *Sūtra* IV—i—ii that it is only the qualification of the sacrificial material that is not touched by the Injunction. As for the connection between the *Rēvatī* and the *Vāravantīya,* it serves as a necessary qualification of the action of "*accomplishment*" (denoted by the root '*kṛ*' in '*kṛtvā*'); because mere "*accomplishment*" being a generic term, unless it were qualified, it could not be recognised as *something to be brought about.*

Thus then, in accordance with the declaration "*mṛshyāmahē havishā viçeshaṇam*" it must be admitted that the '*accomplishment*' (denoted by '*kṛ*' in '*kṛtvā*'), which serves to qualify the Bhāvanā expressed in connection with the root '*yāji*' (in '*yajēta*'), is itself qualified by the connection between the *Rēvatī* and the *Vāravantīya.* Thus it is, too, that certain Materials and Deities, qualifying the *Prayājas* that are qualifications of an Action (the *Darça-Pūrṇamāsa*), come to be laid down as to be utilised in those sacrifices.

For these reasons, we conclude that the sentence in question serves to specify the *Ṛk* (Rēvati) and the *Sāma* (Vāravantīya) in connection with the *Bhāvanā* (expressed in '*yajēta*'), which is qualified by a certain relationship (of that *Ṛk* and that *Sāma*) that has been duly *accomplished* (as expressed by the word '*kṛtvā*'). And in this case, the word '*kṛtvā*' should be taken as denoting the particular order of sequence in which the various factors of the sacrifice are to be thought of (or determined upon), and not as denoting actual performance; because the *Sāma* is not employed before the Sacrifice itself (and if the word '*kṛtvā*' expressed actual performance, then the *sāma* would have to be used before the sacrifice, as indicated by the *sequence* expressed by that word); and hence we do not take the sentence to mean that *we should perform the sacrifice after the Vāravantīya Sāma has been sung in connection with the Rēvatī verses*; all it does denote is that we should *think* of the *singing of that Sāma* as *to be performed,* and then proceed with the actual performance of the sacrifice.

Objection: "*Thus too, there are many objects of the Injunction—the " Rēvatī verses, the Vāravantīya, the relationship of these, the Sacrifice,* and "*the desire for cattle.* That is to say, the Injunction being assumed in " connection with each object that happens to be mentioned in the sen- " tence, there come to be many objects for it; and that leads to a syntactical " split."

Reply: This does not affect us; because we have already explained that the multiplicity of objects spoken of does not bring about the multiplicity of the object of the Injunction.

If, however, what you mean is the multiplicity of those that are enjoined as fulfilling some useful purposes,—then, we offer you the following reply: Even though many such useful objects may be mentioned, yet there is only one that forms the object of the Injunction; and this one object, in the case in question, is the *qualified Bhāvanā* connected with the 'sacrifice'.

Objection: "The *Rēvatī* verses also are found to be enjoined in the sentence in question (over and above the said *Bhāvanā*). Your reply "would be all right, if the said multiplicity of objects depended only "upon that which is directly mentioned; in the case in question, however, "we find that all of the objects—*Rēvatī*, etc.—are distinctly enjoined as "useful; and as such there can be no doubt as to the said multiplicity."

Reply: All that happens to be predicated is not spoken of as '*artha* (meaning or object of the Injunction); that alone is spoken of as the 'object' which is connected with the principal Injunction; and there can be no doubt that there is only one such object in the sentence in question. This is what is meant by the *Bhāshya—nahyatrānēkasya proyojanatvēnābhiprētasyānēkam padam vidhāyakam.* That is to say, inasmuch as all other minor actions spoken of in the sentence form part of the principal action of the *Sacrifice*, their cognition cannot be complete until that of the *Bhāvanā* of 'Sacrifice'; and when this *qualified Bhāvanā* has been enjoined, there remains nothing more to be looked for.

Thus then, we conclude that the real object of the sentence being one only, there is no syntactical split; while we have shown the many splits that are consequent upon the taking of the sentence as the Injunction of an accessory detail for the previous *Agnishṭut sacrifice.*

The Bhāshya brings forward another argument of the opponent: "*Athocyēta Revatyādisarvaviçeshaṇaviçishṭo yāga ētasyāgnishṭutō vidhīyatē.*" This argument has been brought forward with the sole purpose of justifying the use of the word '*ētasya.*' Though this argument admits of the Action mentioned by the sentence in question being distinct from the previous *Agnishṭut*, yet, inasmuch it makes the sentence lay down the Result as connected with the Action,—yet it is opposed to our own view; and hence we shall refute it. The argument may be thus explained: "The "text in question may be construed thus—*Rēvatīshu Vārvantīyam agnishṭoma sāma kṛtvā ētasyāṅgēna yajēta* (Having sung the Vāravantīya in "the Rēvati verses, one should perform this sacrifice, as subsidiary to the "previous *Agnishṭut*). The advantages attendant upon this construction "would be two-fold: (1) there would be no reason for rejecting that "which is pointed out by the Context, and (2), the use of the word "'*ētasya*' would be justified as pointing to that (*Agnishṭut*) which is "in close proximity with itself, in the Context."

To this argument, we make the following reply: The above construction is not possible; because that would make the word '*paçukāmaḥ*' wholly irrelevant; and if you do not reject it as such, its inclusion would involve a syntactical split; as a single Action cannot, at one and the same time, be laid down as forming part of another sacrifice (*the Agnishṭut*) and also as accomplishing a certain result (Cattle).

Objection: "*Athaivamucyēta* '*Revatīshu kṛtena vāravantīyena paçukāmo yajēta.*'"

Though this view has been already dealt with, yet it is brought forward again by the *Bhāshya*, with a view to show another discrepancy in it. Or it may be that, in all cases where an Injunction mentions the fulfilment of a desirable end by means of certain accessories, people performing sacrifices have two distinct notions:—(1) some people, like the *Mīmāmsakas*, believe the Result to follow from the Accessory, (2) while others believe that the Accessory only helps in the Sacrifice, and it is the Sacrifice thus aided that brings about the particular result. And it is in accordance with this latter view that the above objection has been put forward.

The construction of the texts, in accordance with the above argument of the opponents, would be as follows:—"'Desiring Brahmic glory, we "should always perform the Agnishṭut; but if we desire the acquisition "of cattle, then we should perform the same sacrifice as qualified by the "*Rēvatī* verses (and the Vāravantīya sung in connection with them).' In "this case, we find that the Injunctive affix (in the '*Yajeta*' of the sentence "in question) would serve to enjoin what is in close proximity with it "(*viz.*, the *Agnishṭut* sacrifice); but being taken up by something else "(*i.e.*, the qualification), it would not lay down the original appearance of "that Action; and as for the qualified character of the sacrifice, this "would be based upon the Injunction. That is to say, inasmuch as the "affix would enjoin the sacrifice with reference to the Result, it would not "have to be removed from its legitimate sphere; and as not pointing to the "appearance of any Action, it could not lay down any such appearance; "then as for the Injunction of many things,—just as in the case of the "sentence laying down the original appearance of a distinct Action, "such Injunction of many things is said to be for the purpose of the said "Injunction of the Action; so, too, would it be in the case of the sentence "being the Injunction of the Result; as in this case also what is actually "enjoined is the Action itself, with reference to the particular result. It is "with a view to all this that we have said—'*atha Rēvatishu kṛtena* "*Vāravantīyēna paçukāmo yajēta.*' As for the Instrumental ending in '*Vār-* "*vantīyēna*,' it actually denotes Instrumentality, inasmuch as the *Vāra-* "*vantīya* is an Instrument that helps, through the *Stotra*, the performance "of the sacrifice. Or it may be taken as denoting a characteristic,—the "sense of the sentence being that 'one desiring cattle should perform the "*Agnishṭut* sacrifice as characterised by the *Vāravantīya*, etc."

To the above, the *Bhāshya* makes the following reply: *naivam çakyam, ṛgantarapragānāt viçeshahānāt vaiguṇyam.* That is to say, if the Action meant in the sentence in question be the same as the previous *Agnishṭut* sacrifice, then, inasmuch as the previous sentence has laid down the

Agnishṭoma sāma, in connection with that sacrifice, as based upon the *Vāyavyā* verses,—if in accordance with the sentence in question, the same *sāma* were to be sung as based upon the *Revatī* verses, that would cause a flaw in the sacrifice, as being deprived of the previously mentioned basis of the *sāma*, in the shape of the *Vāyavyā* verses.

Objection: "When you yourself were faced by the argument that—"'many other *sāmas* also come to be sung in connection with the Revatī "verses'—you urged in defence the argument that—'the word *kṛtvā* "serves to lay down the fully accomplished relationship of the *Revatī* and "the *Vāravantīya* for the sake of the sacrifice, for the word is quite capable "of signifying two meanings etc., etc., etc., etc.' (And so we too could "bring forward the same argument in support of our view.)"

The *Siddhānti*, however, thinks that an Injunction of many things is possible only in the case of the sentence laying down a new Action, and not in any other case; with this in view, he makes the following reply: What we say is possible in our case, *because there is a direct declaration to the effect*; while, in your case, as there is no such direct declaration, it would be impossible to obtain the *Revatī* verses by merely getting hold of the *Vāravantīya*; and as such, the said argument cannot help you.

The opponent retorts—"*Then we too may have a direct declaration*—"*such as* '*paçukamo Rēvatīshu vāravantīyamabhinirvartayet tato yajeta*';—"that is to say, the Injunction would be that of a qualified Action with "reference to a particular result; or that the word '*kṛtvā*' being the "required Injunctive word, the '*yajeta*' *may be a mere reference to the* "*previously mentioned Agnishṭut sacrifice*; and the sense of this is that "even though the Injunction lays down the accessory with reference to the "*Result*, there is nothing in the sentence that lays down the original "appearance of the sacrifice."

In reply to this, the *Siddhānti* proceeds to show his own desirable conclusion that he draws from the Apparent Inconsistency of the said 'Injunction of many things:' If any such declaration as you bring forward becomes an established fact, then the fact of the sentence in question laying down a distinct Action, and not the mere accessory of the previous *Agnishṭut*, becomes fully established.

Objection: "*Nanu tato yajēta iti yāgānuvādāt yāgēnāsyāngaprayo*-"*janasambandho bhavishyati.* [*In that case, the word* '*yajēta*' *referring* "*to the previous sacrifice, what is laid down in the sentence in question would* "*be taken as related to the Agnishṭut as its subsidiary.*]"

In this the opponent only reiterates (in the *Bhāshya*) his former argument, not admitting the defeat meant by the Siddhānti to be inflicted by the bringing forward of the 'direct declaration.' He is met by the assertion (in the *Bhāshya*), *This is not possible, etc.* The sense of this argument of the *Siddhānti* is that if the *Vāravantīya qualified by the Revatī verses* be taken as laid down (by the sentence in question) with reference to the sacrifice (the Agnishṭut),—then, in that case, it would be necessary (for the sentence in question) to make a reference to that sacrifice; and hence as it would be merely referred to in the sentence, it could not be related either to the accessory or to the Result mentioned in the sentence; and as such the reference itself would be wholly superfluous; if, on the other hand, it be related to any or both of them, there would be a syntactical split. If again the sentence be taken as laying down a sacrifice as qualified by certain accessories,—then, inasmuch as there would be no reason for recognising this sacrifice to be the same as the *Agnishṭut*, it could not but be admitted to be a distinct Action by itself. Nor could the sentence be construed as '*yat paçukāmo yajēta*, etc.'—the reference being to the *Result*; this would not be possible, because as the particular result herein mentioned is not mentioned previously in the context, there could be no reference to it.

This argument also sets aside the view that the sacrifice (*Agnishṭut*) is the motive cause of the Injunction of the *Vāravantīya*.

Thus then, inasmuch as there would be no very strong ground for connecting the *Vāravantīya* with the *Revatī* verses (and not with the other verses), the rejection of the particular *Vāyavyā* verses previously mentioned would make a deficiency in the sacrifice.

Objection: "*Atha yāgasambandho'nuvādaḥ, prakaraṇēna caṅgāta.* "That is to say, the result following from the Accessory, what the sen- "tence does is to refer to the fact, pointed out by the context, of that "being subsidiary to the sacrifice."

It might be argued, against the *Bhāshya* bringing forward this objection, that there is no difference between this objection and that brought forward with regard to the particular relationship of the *Basis and the Based*, that has been already refuted (see *Text*, page 558).

But there is a distinct difference between the two cases. On the former occasion, we have refuted the application, to the case in question, of the law laid down under *Sūtra* III—i—18; that is to say, that application could be possible only on the recognition of the said subsidiary character, and hence the relationship of the *Agnishṭoma-sāma* would become very easy.

To the above objection, the *Bhāshya* makes the following reply: *The Syntax is always more authoritative than the Context.* The said relationship of the *Basis and the Based* could be accepted only when it is found to be possible, as being in keeping with the connection of the particular result; but we have already shown that no such connection is possible; while the relationship of the *Primary and Subsidiary* (or *Whole and Part*) could be possible only by being included in the Procedure of the Sacrifice; as a matter of fact, however, it is not so included, as we shall show under *Sūtra* III—iii—11, where it is mentioned that *that which is not connected*, etc., etc., *becomes included in the Procedure*,—while we find the sentence in question connected with a particular Result.

Thus then, there being no incongruity, the sentence in question must be taken as laying down a distinct Action qualified by a particular Accessory and a definite Result.

The following argument might here be brought forward: "Even "though the sentence may lay down a distinct Action, the Result would "follow from the Accessory as helped by that Action."

This is refuted by the well-recognised fact of the Result following from the sacrifice, as is distinctly indicated by the proximity of the Injunctive affix (with the root '*yaji*'), as has been shown under the *Bhāvārthādhikaraṇa* (II—i—1), wherein the two alternatives (as to the result following from the Accessory or the Action) have been duly considered. Consequently the sentence in question must be taken as forming the injunction of an independent Action.

Objection: "The qualified sacrifice being the object enjoined, how "could the *Agnishṭoma-sāma*, which is an Action other than that sacrifice, "be connected with the particular qualification (in the shape of the "*Vāravantīya* as sung in connection with the *Revatī* verses)?"

Reply: It is by direct assertion. As shown before, the assertion meant here is the one whose existence is cognized by means of indirect implication, in the form—'the connection of the *Revatī* and the *Vāravantīya* is to be wrought out of the *Agnishṭoma-sāma*.' Though as a matter of fact, there exists no such particular *sāma* named '*Agnishṭoma*,' out of which the *Vāravantīya* might be wrought out,—yet what is meant is that it is to be wrought out of the *Yajñāyajñīya-sāma*, which is mentioned in the context. Or, the expression 'out of the *Agnishṭoma-sāma*' might mean that the *Vāravantīya* would exist in the midst of the effects of the *Stotra* (the *Agnishṭoma*), as serving the purpose of accomplishing it.

For these reasons we conclude that in the case of similar sentences, the Result would be connected with the Action.

ADHIKARAṆA (13)

[A single result follows from the *Saubhara* and the *Nidhana.*]

Sūtra **(28): "Because of the mention of human effort in "connection with the Saubhara, there must be a distinct desirable "result connected with the Nidhana."**

From among the *Ukthya* Hymns, the *Saubhara* is the *Brahmasāma* that has been laid down in connection with the *Jyotishṭoma* ; in connection with this we have the sentences '*Yadi Rathantaram,*' etc., which serve to lay down certain motive causes ; and then later on, we meet with the sentence—(1) '*Yō vṛshṭikāmo yo'nnādyakāmō yaḥ svargakāmaḥ sa saubharēṇa stuvīta*',—which mentions the three results in connection with the *Saubhara* which is a necessary accompaniment of the *Jyotishṭoma* sacrifice, in accordance with the rule that all such desirable results are connected with the necessary accompaniment, because this is equally present in all cases ; and it will be shown later on, under *Sūtra* IV—iii—5, that such an accompaniment can be only that which helps the sacrifice and fulfils a desirable end of the human agent ; and under *Sūtra* IV—iii—26, that the several results mentioned follow from the said necessary accompaniment, alternatively. Then again, with reference to the aforesaid *Saubhara*, we have the following sentence—(2) '*Hīshiti vṛshṭikāmāya nidhanam kuryāt, ūrgityannādyakāmāya, ūṅ iti svargakāmāya.*' ['*Nidhanam*' is the concluding part of the *sāma.*]

In connection with these two sets of texts, we proceed to consider the following question: Does the *Saubhara* (mentioned in the former sentence) bring about its result by itself, independently of the *Nidhanas*, '*hīsh*' and the rest (mentioned in sentence (2)), which bring about separate results of their own (apart from that of the *Saubhara*),—or these '*hīsh,*' etc., have been laid down as the various instruments which, when employed in connection with the same aforesaid *Saubhara*, help it in bringing about the said results ?

Though this question has nothing to do with the difference or non-difference of Actions, yet it has been introduced here as in a way connected with the subject. Or, it may be that, like the difference and non-difference of Actions, the difference and non-difference of the resultant *Apūrva* also forms the subject-matter of the *Adhyāya.*

Specially as the question herein introduced affects the actual performance of the Action also: for instance, at the time that the *Saubhara* has been commenced by one who wants *Rain* (1), would the other two *Nidhanas* (*ūrg* and *ūṅ*) be used at the time (along with the *Saubhara*), with a desire for the other two results (*Food* and *Heaven*), and a distinction be made between the two desires for *Rain* also,—if the three results mentioned in the latter passage as following from the three *Nidhanas* were different from those very results mentioned in the former passage as following from the *Saubhara* itself; (2) or the latter sentence only serves to specify the particular *Nidhanas* for the same *Saubhara* (as leading to the three particular results), and hence at the time that one has commenced the *Saubhara* for the sake of *rain*, he should make use of the "*Hīsh*" *Nidhana* only, the *Rain* mentioned (in the second sentence along with this *Nidhana*) being the same (as that mentioned previously along with the *Saubhara*);—and similarly with the *Saubhara*, when performed for the sake of Food or Heaven.

As to the origin of this *Doubt*, some people explain it as lying in the two peculiar constructions that the *Bhāshya* has put upon the sentence in question; and accordingly the question becomes reduced to a verbal one, *viz*: "Are the words '*hīsh*,' etc., connected directly with the words '*desire for rain*, etc.,' or with the word '*Nidhana*' only?" Though the word '*Nidhana*' is not mentioned along with '*ūrg*' and '*ūṅ*,' yet there is always a desire on our part to learn what these are; and through *proximity* they come to be recognised as '*Nidhanas*.'

On the above question, we have the following

PŪRVAPAKSHA (A).

"The '*hīsh*' and the rest mentioned in the latter sentence bring "about distinct results of their own,—(1) because they are laid down "over again, (2) because the distinct mention of the result in the latter "sentence could be justified only if these results were distinct; and (3) "because this interpretation makes possible the acquisition of many "more desirable results.

"That is to say,—(1) If the results mentioned in the latter sentence "were the same as those that followed from the *Saubhara* itself, then "their repetition (in the latter sentence) would be wholly useless; be-"cause in that case, there would be nothing that would be laid down by "the sentence in question; because the '*hīsh*' and the rest are already "known, from other Vedic texts, as the *Nidhanas* of the *Saubhara* (and the "only other object spoken of in the sentence is the result, and this you "take to be the same as that previously mentioned; and so the sentence "would have nothing new to say). Nor can it be urged that the "sentence in question would serve the purpose of restricting the *Nidhanas* "because these being directly laid down (in other Vedic texts) as the "*Nidhanas* to be employed, they can not rightly be set aside on the "strength of any such implied restrictions. As a matter of fact, in all "cases, restriction, as serving the sole purpose of setting aside something, "is highly objectionable. But when all other objects are indirectly im-"plied, then it is possible for the one that is directly laid down to set "aside those; in the case in question, however, the use of the '*hīsh*' and "the rest is not implied indirectly; and hence the injunction of any one "of them cannot set aside the rest. Because we find that they are all "directly laid down by the text that lays down the *Saubhara*; and under "the circumstances, it is scarcely right to take any one of them as set-"ting aside the rest, on the mere ground of a repetition actuated by an "Injunction; specially when this latter admits of another explanation. "In accordance with our theory, however, the use of '*hīsh*' and the rest "having the capability of bringing about distinct results of their own, "would be more desirable, for the agent, than those that have been men-"tioned as forming part of the *Saubhara* and thereby helping in the "accomplishment of the sacrifice; and on the ground of this greater "desirability the former would very rightly set aside all the latter.

"(2) The sentence in question would serve a useful purpose, only "if it laid down the relationship (causal) between the 'Rain,' etc., and "the '*hish*,' etc., which is not laid down in any other sentence. And "this would also save us from the anomaly of taking the word '*Vṛshṭi-*"*kāmaḥ*' as a mere qualification of the *Saubhara*, in a sentence which "would be taken as serving to restrict the *Nidhanas*,—while it is quite "capable of being taken directly by itself (as mentioning the result "following from the *Nidhanas*).

"(3) In the *Veda*, which consists of Injunctions, we always want a "lot of desirable results, because that makes it easier for the Injunctions "to urge the human agents to action.

"For these reasons we conclude that the results following from the "*Nidhanas* are distinct from those mentioned as following from the "*Saubhara* itself."

SIDDHANTA.

***Sūtra* (29): Inasmuch as those mentioned in the sentence in question are exactly the same as those mentioned before, the mention of the Results would refer to the Saubhara; and the repetition would serve the purpose of restricting the Nidhanas.**

To the above *Pūrvapaksha* we make the following reply—

SIDDHĀNTA (A).

The '*hīsh*' cannot be connected with the Result, because that would make the mention of the *nidhana* wholly redundant; while if the *nidhana* be taken as connected with the *Saubhara*, the Result could be taken as qualifying the *Saubhara*.

That is to say, if we were to take the sentence as—'one should bring about rain by means of the *hīsh*, and by that as a *nidhana* of the *Saubhara*'—, there would be a syntactical split; for if the '*hīsh*' were not connected with the *Saubhara*, then the sentence would be wholly redundant. In accordance with our theory, there is nothing without some use; and out of the things spoken of in the sentence in question, the *Saubhara*, as bringing about Rain, etc., mentioned in another sentence, has already been laid down elsewhere, as also the Results themselves; and hence all that the sentence has got to lay down is the relationship between the '*hīsh*,' etc., and the *Saubhara*; and as such there is no syntactical split.

Nor is the sentence altogether useless, as it serves the purpose of restricting the particular *nidhanas*. Even apart from any consideration of the one being more desirable, there is, in the case in question, a distinct setting aside of the one by the other, on the ground of one being more generic in its character than the other; as for instance, the word '*Saubhara*' applying to all parts of that *sāma*, it is only by indirect indication that all its *nidhanas* (*hīsh*, etc.) could be mentioned by the sentence speaking of the '*Saubhara*'; while the sentence in question mentions the particular *nidhanas* directly; and as such this latter is more authoritative than the former (and as such this would very well restrict the use of the *nidhanas* implied in the former sentence). And just as that which is implied is set aside by that which is directly mentioned, so is also that which is indirectly indicated. Or, the sentence in question does not set aside any thing of the *song* mentioned by the word "*Saubhara*"; because all that it does is to lay down certain letters '*hīsh*' for instance; and as such it would set aside certain other letters only (and not the *song* itself). If the sentence had laid down the part of some other song, then the part of the *Saubhara* would be set aside by that; as a matter of fact, however, the restriction of the *nidhana* only serves to preclude certain letters of the *stobha* (the *sāma*). And as such there is no anomaly of the preclusion of that which has been directly laid down.

For these reasons, we conclude that the repetition of the Results in the sentence in question serves to restrict the *nidhanas*.

There is something to be said against the above interpretation of the *Adhikaraṇa*; and this we proceed to show as follows:—

As for the form of the *Doubt* itself, there can be no such doubt; because the construction of the sentence in question is wholly different from that on which the abovementioned Doubt has been based; because (in the sentence '*hīshiti vṛshṭikāmāya nidhanam*'), '*hīsh*' cannot be taken along with '*nidhanam*,' because of the intervention, between them, of the word '*vṛshṭikāmāya*,' as it would be very undesirable to take the sentence as '*hīsh is the nidhana*, etc.' (This is the case of the above representation of *Pūrvapaksha*.)

So also in the case of the above representation of the *Siddhānta*, if the sentence be taken as laying down the '*hīsh*' with reference to the '*nidhana*' as qualified by '*desire for rain*,'—then, inasmuch as it would contain a reference to a *qualified* object, there would be a distinct syntactical split. If it be taken as laying down the *hīsh* with reference to the *nidhana* only (not qualified by '*desire for rain*'), then the mention of the Result would be wholly useless. Because the connection with all *nidhanas* has already been laid down by the mere mention of the '*Saubhara*'; and hence no useful purpose would be served by the sentence laying down such a connection only. If again, the sentence be taken as—'*vṛshṭikāmāya yat saubharam tasya yannīdhanam tatra hīsh padamprayuñjīta*' (one should use the word '*hīsh*' in the *nidhana* of that *Saubhara* which is sung for the sake of Rain),—then, inasmuch as this would involve various predications, there would be a syntactical split. Though 'desire for rain,' '*Saubhara*' and its '*nidhanas*' have all been mentioned before, yet, inasmuch as there are many other *nidhanas* present in the *Saubhara*, it is necessary to make an attempt to preclude these; and thereby the sentence would come to serve more purposes than one; and that would entail a syntactical split.

Then again, the *Siddhānta*, as represented above, has not quite effectually refuted the *Pūrvapaksha*; as the fact of the *hīsh*, etc., being *nidhanas* is mentioned by the Veda itself.

For the above reasons, we must explain the *Adhikarava* as follows:—

The *hīsh* being taken with the word '*vṛshṭikāmāya*,' there arises a doubt as to whether the sentence points to its connection with the Result or with the Means. That is to say, the sentence being taken as '*hīshiti vṛshṭikāmāya*,' there arises a doubt as to whether the *hīsh* is related directly to the Result, or to a particular *Means* (in the shape of the *Saubhara*) as qualified by that Result?

In fact, it is this construction of the sentence that has been shown in the *Bhāshya*, by means of the sentences—*hīshīti nidhanamiti, ētat phalam bhavatīti*. The sentence—*vṛshṭikāmāyēti saubharaviçēshaṇam* (*Bhāshya*) —means that the *Saubhara* not being mentioned by name in the sentence in question, it is only by means of indirect indication that it could be qualified by the Result therein mentioned. The assertion—*na hīshā sambandhāt*—means that the *hīsh* has no connection with the form of the result.

And then, inasmuch as the position of the *Pūrvapaksha* based upon the repetition of the Injunction would be established otherwise, through the force of the collective Injunction relating to the sacrifice in question, we proceed to put forward the following position of the

PŪRVAPAKSHA (B).

"If every one of the *nidhanas* were restricted with reference to the "*Saubhara* as engaged in fulfilling its own function,—then, inasmuch "as the Injunction of the *hīsh* and the rest would be established by the "very fact of these being brought forward by the collective Injunction of "the sacrifice in question, there would be no use of another Injunction of "them (in the sentence in question). No such collective Injunction, how-"ever, is capable of expressing the independent relationship of the *hīsh* "with the particular Result; and as such, in giving expression to this rela-"tionship, the sentence would be serving a distinctly useful purpose.

"And further, the word '*vṛshṭikāmāya*' having directly mentioned "the human agent concerned,—it is only natural that when this agent "comes to look for the means of accomplishing that Result, this want is "supplied by the mention of '*hīsh*', etc. Otherwise (if the result be-"longed to the *Saubhara*, then) this *Saubhara* could be mentioned as the "*means* sought after, only through indirect Indication, based upon the "fact of its occurring in the same context and being capable of bringing "about the Result in question. And certainly there can be no ground for "having recourse to such an indirect Indication (so long as the want is "found to be supplied by means of direct Assertion).

"This representation of the *Pūrvapaksha* appears to have been intended "by the *Bhāshya*, as is shown by the sentence—*tathāçrutilakshaṇā vishayē* "*ca.*"

SIDDHANTA (B).

The *Siddhānta*, in that case, would be represented as follows:—

The previous sentence having spoken of a certain Result as following from the *Saubhara as a whole*, what the sentence in question does is to restrict the particular *nidhanas* of the *Saubhara* with reference to each one of the results mentioned (and thus the mention of the results in the previous latter sentence is a reference to the very same results mentioned in the sentence).

That is to say, inasmuch as the results mentioned in the sentence in question are distinctly recognised as being the same as those mentioned previously in connection with the *Saubhara* as a whole,—we can never believe them to be distinct results (following from the particular *Nidhanas*).

To the question—"Why then should there be a repetition?"—the answer is—*Nidhanārthā punaḥçrutiḥ* (the repetition is for the purpose of restricting the *Nidhanas*).

Question: "Why should not the *Hīsh*, etc., be taken as connected with "the Results mentioned in the same sentence with themselves?"

Answer: Just as in the previous *Adhikaraṇa* (II—ii—27) the *Vāravatīya* was found not to obtain its desired substrate in the '*Sacrifice*,'—so, in the case in question also, the *Hīsh*, etc., do not obtain their proper receptacle in the Results. That is to say, if we take the sentence as meaning that 'one should accomplish the particular result by means of the *Hīsh*,'—we are at once led to look for the *substrate*, resting upon which the *Hīsh* would accomplish that Result. And then, the '*Saubhara*,' that happens to be mentioned in the Context, cannot be cognised as the required substrate; because it is *the whole sāma* that is expressed by the word '*saubhara*'; and certainly the whole *sāma* cannot be accomplished by means of the '*Hīsh*,' in the same manner as the *Homa* is accomplished by means of the *Dadhi*; because the *Dadhi* is capable of extending over the whole of the *Homa*, while the '*Hīsh*' cannot extend over the whole of the *Saubhara*; which is made up of many letters; and so long as the '*Hīsh*' does not accomplish the *Saubhara*, there cannot be any such relationship between them as that of the *Basis and the Based*. What the '*Hīsh*' can accomplish, by pervading over it, is the *Nidhana*; but that does not form the subject of the Context; and as such, it could not be the required *substrate* (of the '*Hīsh*'), except on the authority of the syntax (of the sentence in question). And thus, the sentence itself serving the purpose of pointing out the relationship (of the '*Hīsh*') with the result as its substrate,—there would be a distinct syntactical split.

So also, if we take the sentence as laying down the relationship of the '*Hīsh* with reference to every one of the *Nidhanas*, then, that would set aside the Context, and make the '*Hīsh*' connected with all the *Sāmas*; and then it would be necessary, somehow or other, to specify the *Sāma* as the '*Saubhara*'; and this would require a deal of mental effort.

Then again, even though the '*Hīsh*' could be the means of accomplishing the *Saubhara*, through one of its parts,—yet inasmuch as the *Saubhara* consists of many parts, it is not quite clear where the '*Hīsh*' is to be put in. That is to say, as a matter of fact, the accomplishment of the *Nidhana*, which is a part of the *Saubhara*, does not accomplish the *Saubhara* itself that forms the subject of the Context; because the part is not known as the *Saubhara*; and we have already shown above that the *Saubhara* would be taken as the substrate of the '*Hīsh*', in whatever way it could be found to be capable of being such a substrate. But even if we grant the fact of its being the substrate,—inasmuch as the *Saubhara* is made up of many such parts as the '*Prastāva*' and the like, it is not quite known in which part the '*Hīsh*' is to be inserted; specially as it cannot be said to be inserted in the *Prastāva*, in accordance with the law laid down under *Sūtra* XII—ii—23; because in that case it could not be referred to as '*Nidhana*' (which is the concluding part of the *Sāma*).

The following argument might be brought forward: "In the case of "the *Ukthyas* (Hymns) laid down for the sake of certain results, we find "that they have their substrate in the *Jyotishṭoma*, which is pointed out by "the Context, and over the whole of which they do not extend; and though "it has many constituent parts, yet the said Hymns are, in accordance "with another text, always placed at the end; and in the same manner, "in the case in question also, the '*Hīsh*' and the rest, laid down for the "sake of certain results, would have the *Saubhara* for their substrate; and "therein their position would be fixed by the Veda itself as the end of the "*Sāma*; and it would be this their character of '*Nidhana*' that would be "referred to in the sentence in question."

To this we make the following reply: What you say is not possible; because in the case of the Hymns, inasmuch as they could not be employed at any other place, their position was fixed; as for the '*Hīsh*' on the other hand, it is capable of occupying many positions; and hence it is not quite surely indicated at which place it should be inserted. That is to say, as for the *Hymns*, inasmuch as they are never found in any other place, and are something superphysical, it is only right that they are never inserted in the midst of the sacrifice; as a matter of fact, we have never found them occupying any other place; and so long as their position is not ascertained, their true form cannot be ascertained, nor can they be connected with any result; and if they existed anywhere else, they could not be spoken of as '*Ukthya*,' which is a name applied in accordance with the form (of the *Sāma*); and as for the particular position that is pointed out by another sentence, it is not found to help the sacrifice in any way; and as such that position comes to be taken along with the mention of the particular Results; and hence it comes to be recognized as helping in the accomplishment of those results. In the case in question, however, the natural position of the '*Hīsh*' pointed out by the Veda has been mentioned by the Injunction of the *Saubhara* as helping the sacrifice and also as helping the accomplishment of a desirable result for the human agent; and in the sentence in question, inasmuch as the '*Hīsh*' is laid down independently by itself, with regard to the particular result, there is nothing to show whether it (the '*Hīsh*') is to be used in ordinary parlance, or in a Vedic sentence, or in another *Sāma*, or in another part of the *Sāma*, or in that part of the *Sāma* which occurs in the Context. If the '*Hīsh*' were recognised as laid down in connection with that (part of the *Saubhara*) which forms the subject of the Context, then, inasmuch as the place of this part is already known, there would be no doubt as to the exact position of the '*Hīsh.*'

Objection: "As the word is one and the same, the word '*Hīsh*' that "would be used in the case in question would be the same as that employed in ordinary parlance; and as such to whatsoever the '*Hīsh*' may "be cognised as pertaining, it would always occupy the same position."

Reply: This cannot be; because, even though the word be one only, it has a diversity of potencies, as with reference to the purpose served by it; and hence the position that the word occupies at one time, could not be the same at another time, when the purpose served by it would be wholly different. That is to say, the mere fact of the word being one does not lead to the conclusion that the position in which it has been found to be effective, in one place, would be its position in all cases; for certainly the position occupied by Devadatta while taking his food is not the same as that occupied by him when fighting; as the particular position that a thing would occupy depends upon the purpose to be served, and not upon the form of the thing itself; and the form remains always the same, whatever the position may be. Consequently, when the purposes to be served are different, a single thing comes to occupy different positions. So, in the case in question, the position of the '*Hīsh*', as helping the accomplishment of the *Saubhara*, cannot be believed to be the same as that occupied by it while accomplishing a desirable result for the human agent.

Objection: "As a matter of fact the *Hīsh*, in both cases, serves to "accomplish the desirable result of a human agent; and it is only by the "way that it helps also in the accomplishment of the *Saubhara* (and thus "the purpose remaining the same, there would be no difference in the "position)."

Reply: It is not so; because before the particular position of the '*Hīsh*' has been duly ascertained, the *Saubhara* cannot be laid down as accomplished by it; and then, what you say would involve a mutual interdependence: the position of the *Hīsh* being ascertained by the fact of its helping in the accomplishment of the *Saubhara*, and this latter fact being based upon that position of the *Hīsh*.

Objection: "Just as in the *Abhyuditēshṭi*, even though the *madhyama-*"*taṇḍula*, etc., are mentioned, yet the *taṇḍula* that is used is the same "that has been mentioned in the Context,—so, in the case in question "also, the *Hīsh*, etc., would be taken as those referring to that (*Saubhara*) "which is mentioned in the Context."

Reply: What you say is quite proper in the case of the *Abhyuditēshṭi*; *firstly*, because we find the *taṇḍula* that is mentioned above to be referred to by the sentences mentioning the connection of Deities, which supply the element wanting in the sentence containing the word '*Vibhājati*,' which distinctly points to that which has been mentioned in the Context; and *secondly*, because the *division of the Madhyama*, etc., which are mentioned by means of the word '*Yat*', does not give rise to any idea apart from that of the *taṇḍula* mentioned in the Context; and hence no other *taṇḍula* is taken up. In the case in question, however, we find none of these reasons applying to the case of *Hīsh*, etc., and hence there is nothing to set aside the idea obtained through the ordinary method of comprehension.

Thus then, inasmuch as the meaning of the sentence cannot be as the *Pūrvapakshi* explains, we offer another explanation.

When, look howsoever much we do, we do not find any relationship of the Result directly mentioned (in the sentence in question), then, in order to save the Direct Denotation of the sentence from being rejected, we take it as referring to the means of accomplishing the mentioned results, which have been previously spoken of in the Context; and hence the meaning of the sentence comes to be this: 'The word *hīsh* is subsidiary to the means of accomplishing the Rain, etc., that have been mentioned in the Context.' The word '*vṛshṭikāma*' in this sentence pointing to that '*vrstikāma*' which has been mentioned before, comes to indicate only the *Saubhara*, as the means of accomplishing itself, and nothing else; nor is it cognised as indicating the means of the accomplishment of any other result. And even though the '*Hīsh*,' etc., may have been already laid down (as part of the *Saubhara*), yet the sentence in question would serve the distinctly useful purpose of restricting the *Nidhanas*, as has already been explained above (under *Siddhānta*, A). And these, '*hīsh*,' etc., would be restricted by the sentence in question, exactly in the same form as that in which they are implied by the *Saubhara*; and (this form being that of the *Nidhana*), their character of *Nidhana*, becoming accomplished even without the actual mention of the word '*nidhana*,' it is this character that is merely *referred* to in the sentence in question (thus there being no occasion for any syntactical split). This is what is shown in the *Bhāshya* — *vṛshṭikāmāya saubharamastyeva*, etc., etc.

This *Adhikaraṇa* embodies the exception to two of the foregoing *Adhikaraṇas*, *viz.*, that the result follows from the Accessory (II—ii—26), and that it follows from the Action and not from the Accessory (II—ii—27). Because what is herein shown is that the sentence in question does not lay down the Result, but only indicates the '*Hīsh*,' etc., as part of the *Saubhara* leading to the aforesaid results.

The *syntactical split* that had been urged against us, would have been possible, if we admitted of a relationship of the *Nidhana* (with the *Hīsh*, etc.) or if we took the *Nidhana* as directly qualifying the *Saubhara*. As a matter of fact, however, we do none of these; as we hold the relationship to exist between the *Hīsh* and the word '*vrshṭikāma*'; and the fact of the *Nidhana* being the qualification of *Saubhara*, we deduce from the Context; and certainly the peculiarities deduced from the Context do not cause a syntactical split. And hence the anomaly of syntactical split does not quite apply to us.

[SUPPLEMENTARY ADHIKARAṆA.]

There is yet another point to be considered, in this connection: (1) Does the sentence in question serve to restrict the *Hīsh*, etc., with reference to the means of accomplishing Rain, etc., in the shape of the *Saubhara*, in whatever Rescension of the Veda the *Sāma* may be found to appear? or is the *Saubhara* to be employed for one desiring rain, in that form in which it appears in that Rescension wherein it is found with the *Hīsh* as its *Nidhana*? Similarly with the other two *Nidhanas*—*Ūrg* and *Ūṅ*.

And on this point we have the following

PŪRVAPAKSHA.

"As all the *Saubharas* appearing in the thousand Rescensions of the "*Sāmavēda* are recognised as optional alternatives, what the sentence in "question does is merely to restrict the *Hīsh*, etc., with regard to the *Desire* "*for Rain, etc.*, (the *Saubhara* being of any Rescension of the *Sāmaveda*)."

SIDDHĀNTA.

To the above we make the following reply: As a general rule, the song to be employed for the sake of Rain, etc., must be of that particular Rescension in which that song appears with those particular *Nidhanas*.

Because in order that the form of the song may not be utterly destroyed, one song is never connected with the parts of another song; and hence what is recognised as the alternative to be employed is the *whole of the song* (together with its *Nidhana* and other parts); and as such all its restrictions should always follow the way in which it appears in the Veda.

That is to say, the form of a *Sāma* is ascertained wholly from the

Veda; and hence even the very slightest difference made in its text makes it wholly unrecognisable as the same. Consequently if the *Nidhana* of one Rescension were to be employed in the song of another Rescension, the song itself would become wholly changed. Nor are any modifications of the song allowable, except in cases where we have a direct Vedic declaration of such modification,—as in the case of the word '*girā*' being changed into '*airam*'; and also because of the possibility of the contradiction being avoided by taking up the *song* of the same Rescension, there would be nothing to warrant the modification; as in all cases we admit of the modification, only on the ground of the original form being impossible to be used. In the case in question, however, we have a distinct *song* (wherein the *Nidhana* is quite compatible); and hence it is with regard to this song of the *Saubhara* with the Nidhanas '*Hīsh*,' etc., that it appearing doubtful as to which of the *Nidhanas* is to be employed, the sentence in question serves to restrict the use of each Nidhana. And as the many alternatives conceived of are all in the form of the whole *Sāma* (*Saubhara*, as with the one or the other *Nidhana*), and not in that of its parts, there can be no room for the *Nidhana* peculiar to other Rescensions. And the sentence in question restricting the part (*Nidhana*), the whole of the *Sāma* becomes restricted thereby (as the restriction of the part cannot be possible without the whole being affected at the same time); just as when the Pupil is enjoined to eat out of a *Kānsya* vessel, and that too of the food left by his Teacher, it becomes necessary for the Teacher also to eat in a vessel of the same metal (as otherwise the Pupil could not eat of the food left by him in the *Kānsya* vessel).

The sentence in question is capable of yet another interpretation. The sentence lays down the mere relationship between the *Saubhara* and the *Hīsh*, both of which have been mentioned previously,—the construction of the sentence being: '*yat vṛshṭikāmāya saubharam, yacca hīshityevam nidhanam, tadēkatra sampādanīyam.*'

Thus then, we conclude that the sentence serves to restrict the use of the whole *Saubhara-sāma* (with reference to the various results).

THUS ENDS THE SECOND PĀDA OF ADHĀYA II.

ADHYAYA II.

PĀDA III.

ADHIKARAṆA (1).

[*The Grahāgratā is subsidiary to the Jyotishṭoma.*]

***Sūtra (1)*: "The Accessory, being in connection with the "Sacrifice, would bring about a distinct Action, because the con- "nection is in its entirety."**

In connection with the *Jyotishṭoma*, from among the various alternative *Sāmas*, the *Bṛhadrathantara* has been laid down as the means of accomplishing the particular Hymn (*Pṛshṭha*) ; and then we find the sentence—'*Yadi Rathantarasāmā somaḥ syāt aindravāyavāgrān grahān gṛhṇiyāt, yadi Bṛhatsāmā çukrāgrān*' ('If the *Soma* is connected with the *Rathantara sāma*, precedence should be given to the holding of the vessels dedicated to Indra and Vāyu, etc., etc., etc.').

And in connection with these two sentences, there arises the following *question* with regard to the Action with its Accessory, that is mentioned in the latter sentence: Is it an action distinct from the *Jyotishṭoma*, or is it the same *Jyotishṭoma* mentioned over again, for the purpose of pointing out the reason for the precedence of the various vessels at the same sacrifice, as characterised by the *Rathantara Sāma ?*

For the sake of this question, we have got to consider the following question— Is the *Rathantara* related to the sacrifice in its entirety (*i.e.*, is the *Rathantara* the only *Sāma* to be used at it) ? or is it related by mere existence (*i.e.*, the *Rathantara* is one of the many used in the sacrifice) ?

And this leads us to yet another question—Is the *Rathantara* accepted as qualified by the *Sacrifice*, or the *Sacrifice* as qualified by the *Rathantara* ?

Objection: "Inasmuch as the presence of the word '*yadi*' distinctly "points out the *Rathantara* as a conditional motive, and as that forms "the subject of the proposition, there could be no relation of the quali- "fication (between the *Sacrifice* and the *Rathantara*)."

Reply: The *Rathantara* could be taken as a conditional motive, only if it had been mentioned elsewhere, in the form that it is cognised as having in the case in question. When, however, such a *Rathantara* has not been mentioned elsewhere, we must admit its injunction by means of the sentence in question. And then, if the *Jyotishṭoma* were always of the same character as that which is mentioned in the sentence in question, as having the conditional character, then, in that case, the mention of it in the sentence in question could be taken as serving the purpose of laying down an accessory detail for the same *Jyotishṭoma*; if, on the other hand, the *Jyotishṭoma* is not of that character, then it would be necessary to impose upon it that character, and then make it serve as the condition. That, without whose relationship the conditional character does not appear, becomes the qualifier of the Condition also; as it will be declared under the *Ārtyadhikaraṇa* (VI—iv—22, 23) that 'we can allow of a qualification by the material offered' (Bhā., p. 683). And thus there would be no anomaly in the form of the reference being made to a qualified object (as the reference would be to the object only).

The conclusion that would suggest itself at the first sight, in connection with the above questions, would be as follows: The action mentioned in the sentence in question is none other than the *Jyotishṭoma* itself—(1) because the presence of the *Rathantara Sāma*, as also that of the *Bṛhat Sāma*, is mentioned by another sentence; (2) because the word '*yadi*' distinctly points to the conditional character, which depends upon the previous mention of that which is laid down as the condition; (3) because the particular precedence of the vessel is included in the collective sentence laying down the whole procedure of the Action collectively; (4) because the Accessory mentioned in the sentence is not set aside by any other Accessory mentioned more authoritatively elsewhere; specially so, in accordance with the *Sūtra* II—ii—16.

In opposition to this position of the *Siddhānta*, we proceed to put forward the *Pūrvapaksha* as embodied in the *sūtra*:—

PŪRVAPAKSHA.

"The Action mentioned in the sentence in question is a distinct Action "because a compound is possible, only when the words compounded have "a certain capability; and this capability is held to exist in the qualifying "*Sāma*; and the qualification serves to differentiate the object qualified; "while in the *Jyotishṭoma*, we do not find the *Rathantara* differentiating "the sacrifice (by precluding all other *Sāmas*).

"It has been explained above, under *Sūtra* II—ii—23, that it is only "when the Accessory mentioned is wholly unconnected with the pre-"viously mentioned action, that it serves to differentiate the Action "mentioned in the sentence from that mentioned before. In the case in "question, however, we find that the existence of the object expressed by the "*Bahuvrīhi* compound—'*Rathantarasāmā*'—is pointed out, by the word "'*yadi*', as the condition (for the precedence of the vessel); and the charac- "ter of the condition is not found to belong to the *existence of the mere* "*Rathantara*; as that has only a subordinate position in the compound "(being only a qualification of that which is expressed by the compound). "Specially as in the sentence, we do not recognise the *Rathantara* to be "qualified by the *Sacrifice*,—we could not very well take the existence of "the *Rathantara* as the condition. Nor is it possible for the *Sāma* (*Rathan-* "*tara*) to be differentiated by the *Sacrifice*; because that (*Sāma*) exists "elsewhere also. It could have been so differentiated, if the *Rathantara* "was the *Sāma* peculiar to the *Sacrifice* in question alone; but as a matter "of fact, this is not so.

"Therefore we must take the compound as expressing the fact of "the *Rathantara being the only Sāma connected with the particular sacrifice*; "and inasmuch as we do not find either the *Jyotishṭoma*, or any other "sacrifice, connected with that *Sāma* only, the presence of the mere "*Rathantara* could not be the condition of any such sacrifice.

"Thus then, having to renounce all notion of *condition*, we find the "word '*Rathantarasāmā*' to be inexplicable; and from this apparent "inconsistency of the word, we come to take it as laying down an alto- "gether distinct Action, at which the *Rathantara* would be the only "*Sāmā* employed. Specially as that distinct Action is quite capable of "being performed. And the mere existence of the *Rathantara* can- "not be a qualification; as it does not extend over the whole of the "sacrifice; and not being a qualification, it cannot have the capability, "(of being compounded); and without the capability, there can be no "compound; but as a matter of fact, we find the *Samāsa* actually present "in the case in question; consequently the Action mentioned in the sen- "tence is not recognised as being the same as the one mentioned before.

"*Question:* 'Wherefore should we not take the *Jyotishṭoma* itself, as "having, in one alternative case, the *Rathantara Sāma* only?'

"*Answer:* It cannot be taken in this way; because such an assump- "tion would be a direct contradiction of the Injunction of other *Sāmas* "mentioned in connection with the *Hymns* directly laid down with "regard to the *Jyotishṭoma*. The *Rathantara sāma*, though mentioned "as connected with the Sacrifice, is found to be of no use in the "performance of the Sacrifice itself; and hence, in accordance with the "*Sūtra* III—i—18, comes to be *indirectly* taken along with the *Hymns* "(sung at the Sacrifice); while the *Gāyatrā* and the other *Sāmas* are laid "down *directly* in connection with those *Hymns*; and as such the presence "of these latter is more authoritative than that of the *Rathantara* "(whose presence is only implied indirectly). When, however, the sentence "is taken as laying down a distinct Sacrifice, it would directly lay down "the *Rathantara* as related to that Sacrifice; and as such in this case the "*Rathantara* would be more authoritative than the other *Sāmas*, which are "all mentioned along with the original Injunction; and so in this case "there is nothing incongruous in the mention of the *Rathantara*.

"Thus too, the word '*Rathantarasāmā*' being taken as referring to "something distinct from that which is denoted by the words ('*Rathan*-"*tara*' and '*sāma*') themselves,—the presence of the *Bahuvrīhi* compound "would become justified; as the predominant factor in that compound "is always something apart (from that denoted by the component "words). Otherwise (*i.e.*, if the *Rathantara* be taken as the qualification "of the previous sacrifice) the compound in question would have to be "taken as pertaining to the subordinate element (as the qualifying ad-"junct always occupies the subordinate position in a *Bahuvrīhi* com-"pound; just as in the case of the compound '*lohitoshṇīshāḥ*' (in the "sentence '*lohitoshṇīshā ṛtvijaḥ pracaranti*,' where all the other factors "being found to have been previously mentioned, the sentence is taken "as laying down only the *redness* of the turban).

"If again, the word '*Rathantarasāmā*' be construed along with "the sentence that lays down the Precedence of the particular vessels, "— then, there would be two diverse Injunctions, that of the "*Rathantara* and that of the Precedence; and hence they could be accom-"plished through the Injunction of an altogether fresh *Bhāvanā* (of a "distinct Sacrifice). The expression '*somaḥ syāt*,' through the extreme "proximity of the two words, would directly point to the fact of the "*Soma* being something to be brought about; while the accomplishment "of the fact of the Sacrifice having the *Rathantara sāma*, could, at best, be "assumed only indirectly. And in accordance with our view, all that the "word '*somaḥ*' would do would be to point out that the new *Sacrifice* "(laid down in the sentence in question) is only a modification of the "*Jyotishṭoma*; specially as the word '*somaḥ*' distinctly points to the pri-"mary original of the Sacrifice in question.

"Hence we conclude that the sentence in question is the Injunction "of a distinct Action.

"This is what is shown in the *Bhāshya*, by means of the sentence— "'*yadi Rathantarasāmētyasya ko'rthaḥ, etc., etc., etc.*'

"As for the particular precedence of the vessels, it would apper-"tain to the other Action (laid down by the sentence), either by means of "*syntactical connection*, or by *the sub-context*. Though the intervening "component sentences have no authority, in the face of the whole taken as "one compound-complex sentence, yet no useful purpose being found to "be served by that complete sentence as a whole, no significance can be "attached to it; and as such the having recourse to the intervening component sentences could not adversely affect the Injunctive potency in "question.

"With a view to the fact of completing a certain factor (*viz.*, that "which forms the denotation of the *Bahuvrīhi* compound) by supplying "its deficiencies being more reasonable than its rejection, the Bhāshya "adds—*atha vā yadi icchēta, etc.* (if one desires, etc.); because, the "element of *Desire* is always implied by the fact of the Action being "something to be performed, the supplying of this element in the sen-"tence in question must be accepted as authoritative, and not a mere "gratuitous assumption.

"In consideration of the fact, that in comparison with this supply-"ing from without (of the element of *Desire*), it would be far simpler to "accept the indirect function of the word itself as taken with another "word removed from it by certain steps, as this would entail only the "disregarding of the property (proximity) of words (and leave the words "intact),—the Bhāshya takes up another position, by citing the instance "of such sentences as '*yadi çālim bhunjīta tatra dadhyupasincēta*' "(that is to say, just as this sentence is accepted as laying down the "eating of *Çāli*, so, the sentence in question may be taken as laying "down the fact of the *Soma-sacrifice having the Rathantara for its* "*Sāma*.

"The opponent, however, retorts by putting forward the fact of the "corroborating Instance itself not being duly established—'*How does the* "*eating of Çāli come to be laid down by that sentence?*'

"The answer is that the said laying down would be got at by invert-"ing the order of the sentence, which really means that—'if one wants "to mix curd with his food, *he should eat Çāli*'; that is to say, the '*Liṅ*' "(Injunctive) affix in '*upansincēta*' is taken as having the force of the "*Desiderative*, in accordance with Pāṇini's *sūtra*—'*kāmapravedanē*, etc.' "(III—iii—153).

"And in accordance with this construction, the meaning of the sen-"tence in question comes to be this: 'If one wishes to accord precedence "to the vessels dedicated to Indra and Vāyu, *he should perform the sacrifice* "*at which Rathantara is the Sāma employed.*' And thus the real Injunctive-"ness comes to belong to the two words '*Somaḥ syāt*,' apart from the "conditional '*if*' ('*yadi*'). And though in this case the word '*gṛhṇīyāt*' 'is deprived of its direct injunctiveness, yet, being taken as serving the "purpose of denoting '*desire*,' it would, in reality, come to serve the pur-"pose of the Injunctive also; inasmuch *as one always does what he desires.*

"Or, it may be that the Injunctive (in '*gṛhṇīyāt*') lays down the *prece-* " *dence* of the particular vessel, as desired by the agent.

"The *Bhāshya* puts forward yet another explanation, in consideration " of the fact that the following explanation does not require any such " indirect and remote constructions as necessitated by the foregoing " explanation. The explanation is put forward by the *Bhāshya*, in the " sentence—*The Injunctive affix denotes the causal relationship*, in accord- " ance with the laws of Pāṇini. That is to say, (1) the Injunctive in " '*Somaḥ syāt*' denotes the *Cause*, while that in '*gṛhṇīyāt*' denotes pure " Injunction itself; and the sense of the sentence, in that case, comes to " be this:—*One should hold the vessel with due precedence of those* " *dedicated to Indra and Vāyu, as caused by that Soma-sacrifice which em-* " *ploys the Rathantara sāma*; and as this latter Sacrifice could not serve the " purposes of the Cause, until it is itself duly accomplished, the injunc- " tion of its performability also comes to be implied in the sentence;—(2) " or, the Injunctive in '*gṛhṇīyāt*' may be taken as denoting the *effect* (that " which is caused), that in '*syāt*' being taken as denoting the Injunction; " though in this case, the *Soma-sacrifice* would not be directly mentioned " as the *Cause*, yet its causal character would be implied by its proximity " with the *effect* (as mentioned in '*gṛhṇīyāt*'), and the meaning of " the sentence would thus come to be that—*one should perform the* " *sacrifice, as being the cause of the according of a particular precedence to* " *the vessels dedicated to Indra and Vāyu*.

"The various alternative theories here put forward are summed up " in the following verse:

"(1) *The rejection of the conditional 'yadi'*; (2) *the supplying of the* " *element of 'Desire'*; (3) *the inverting of the construction of the two parts* " *of the sentence*; and (4) *the taking of the Injunctive Affix as denoting the* " *causal relationship*.

"As every one of these theories will be of use in the *Siddhānta* of the " next Adhikaraṇa (dealing with *Avēshṭi*), they have been explained " here in detail.

"Then again, it is a general rule that the *Cause* itself must be a duly " established entity before it serves to bring about the effect; and in the " case in question, we find that *the presence of the Rathantara* is not quite as " well established as the existence of the *Sacrifice* itself. That is to say, " the precedence of the holding of the vessels occurs in connection with " the Morning Libation, while the *Rathantara sāma* is sung at the Midday " Libation; and so inasmuch as this *Sāma* itself would not be a duly " accomplished entity *in the morning*, it could not be the cause or condi- " tion of the said *precedence*; because in this case the word 'condition,' " '*nimitta*,' is equivalent to 'cause.' For us, on the other hand (who hold "the sentence to lay down a distinct sacrifice), there is no need of any "such 'condition' or cause; or even if we require such a cause, the *sacrifice* itself would serve as the cause or 'condition' required; and the *sacrifice* will be an established entity from the very beginning (and so there "would be nothing incongruous in its serving as the 'condition' of a "certain detail in connection with the Morning Libation).

"Lastly, inasmuch as the *Jagat-sāma* does not appear in the *Jyotishṭoma*—as will be shown under *Sūtra* X-v-58,—the *Soma-sacrifice*, mentioned in the sentence as having this *sāma*, cannot but be admitted to "be wholly distinct from the *Jyotishṭoma*; and, consequently, the case of "the Soma-sacrifices with the other *Sāmas* (*Rathantara* and the rest) being "exactly similar to that of the one with the *Jagat-sāma*, we cannot but "admit those also to be wholly distinct from the *Jyotishṭoma*.

"And hence we conclude that the whole of the sentence in question "lays down a distinct Sacrifice."

SIDDHANTA.

***Sūtra* (2).—The same Action having diverse characteristics, these could be mentioned for a certain purpose,—the Action being one only, on account of the sentence (in question) being subsidiary (to the previous sentence).**

On account of the reasons shown briefly at the opening of the present *Adhikaraṇa*, we conclude that the sentence in question merely lays down accessory details for the previously mentioned *Jyotishṭoma*, and does not put forward a distinct sacrifice. (1) Because it is the same sacrifice of the *Jyotishṭoma* that is mentioned with its several characteristic *Sāmas*, with a view to serve the purpose of showing the cause or condition of the precedence to be accorded to one or the other of the vessels; and inasmuch as the sentence in question is subsidiary to the foregoing sentence, it cannot give rise to any notion of a distinct sacrifice; and hence the *Sacrifice* in question is believed to be one and one only. (2) Or, because of the fact of the *Rathantara*, etc., being laid down in the sentence in question, it is concluded that it is the *Jyotishṭoma* sacrifice that is laid down as having these *Sāmas*, mentioned in sentences that are subsidiary to the original Injunction of the *Jyotishṭoma*; and, consequently, the Action mentioned in the sentence in question is none other than the *Jyotishṭoma*, which, therefore, is the only one sacrifice spoken of in the two sentences.

Objection: "Inasmuch as the *Rathantara sāma* does not serve to "differentiate the sacrifice in question, and as a qualification it stands in "need of other *Sāmas*, the compound '*Rathantara-sāmā*' is altogether "impossible."

Reply: That which applies to a thing only partially is also found to be accepted as qualifying it by its mere *existence* (and not by differentiating it from others); and in the case in question, that is held to be the condition which appears as the *qualified* at the time that the compound is broken up (*i.e.*, the compound is broken up as '*yatsambandhi Rathantara-sāma saḥ*,' the qualified in this case is the *Soma sacrifice*, and there is nothing objectionable in the fact of this sacrifice forming the *condition*).

That is to say, if it were such that one *Rathantara* existed in the *Jyotishṭoma* always, and that always in the company of another *sāma*, then it might not have served to differentiate it; as a matter of fact, however, we find the *Jyotishṭoma* being performed even without the *Rathantara*; and hence the *presence of Rathantara* can very well serve the purposes of a qualification differentiating this performance of the *Jyotishṭoma* from that in which the *Rathantara* is not used. If there be no notion of a 'qualification' without the intensifying word '*ēva*' (*i.e.*, if unless the qualification spoken of be specified as the *only one* possible, it be not cognised as a *qualification*), then too, we could explain the conditional clause as '*yadi Rathantara-sāma astyēva.*' And inasmuch as the *Bahuvrīhi* contains within itself the force of the Possessive affix, which latter includes the factor of *existence*, the assumption of the intensifying '*ēva*' would not be wholly unfounded. Or, the word '*ēva*' might be inserted after '*sāma*,' the clause being explained as '*yadi Rathantaram sāmaivāsya bhavati*'; and in this case the force of the word '*ēva*' may be explained in the following manner: Though the *Rathantara* is always *sāma*, yet when it is not employed in a certain sacrifice, then, so far as that sacrifice is concerned, not helping it in the manner of a *sāma*, it is as good as *not-sāma*; while when the *Rathantara* does exist in a *sacrifice*, then it is spoken of as '*sāma*'; for the character of '*sāma*' meant in the clause in question must be taken as depending upon its presence, or otherwise, *in the sacrifice*; otherwise, if the mere form of the *Rathantara*, independently by itself, were meant, then the use of the word '*sāma*' again (in the word '*Rathantara-sāmā*) would be a useless repetition.

Nor, so far as the *Jyotishṭoma* is concerned, is the *Rathantara* dependent upon other *sāmas*; and as such there would be nothing incongruous in the compound in question. Because such dependence is found in cases where many *sāmas* are mentioned by means of a single *Dvandva* compound as appertaining to a single Hymn. In a case (like the present), however, where each *sāma* is mentioned separately, as accomplishing a distinct Hymn, the instrumentality of each towards such accomplishment is wholly independent ; and there is no harm done to this instrumentality (by such independence).

Or, it may be that, inasmuch as the word '*sāma*' is a mere repetition, it is to be taken as indicating the Hymṇ accomplished by means of the *sāma* ; and hence the compound indicates the *Stotra* (Hymn) that is brought about by the *Rathantara* (and as such there is no dependence upon other Hymns).

Or again, it may be that, inasmuch as the *Bṛhat* and the *Rathantara* are spoken of in the same sub-Context, and are endowed with secondary functions, they are opposed to each other ; and as such, vying with each other,—inasmuch as both have the same character of being references to the existing state of things,—they serve the purpose, independently of all other *Sāmas*, of precluding each other (from being employed at the *Joyotishṭoma*), and thereby attaining to the character of a *qualification.* And in this way there is nothing incongruous in taking the *Sacrifice qualified by the Rathantara* as the condition (of the particular precedence of certain vessels).

Or, lastly, we can admit the *Rathantara itself, as qualified by the Sacrifice*, to be the condition laid down.

Objection : " But as a matter of fact, the Rathantara is not cognised " as being qualified by the sacrifice."

Reply : True, it is not so recognised ; but when, as you hold, the *sacrifice* is not cognised as qualified by the Rathantara, because of the fact of this latter not extending over the whole of the sacrifice,—then, on expounding the compound (in '*Rathantarasāmā*') as '*Rathantaramasya sāma*', we find the relationship of the Qualified and the Qualification reversed; and certainly there could be nothing wrong in the cognition of this relationship ; and thus inasmuch as in the expounding, the '*sacrifice*' would have the genitive ending, it would be cognised as the qualification (as in '*Rājñaḥ purushaḥ*', the Rājā is the qualifying factor). And this would be the sense desired to be conveyed, because of the impossibility of the *sacrifice* having the character of the *Qualified*, as pointed out by the compound at first sight.

Though, as a matter of fact, the *Rathantara* is present, in its natural form, in other sacrifices also, yet the mere fact of its presence in the *Jyotishṭoma* would be enough to point it out as its qualification. Because, as a rule, for one thing to be recognised, in a sentence, as the qualification of another, all that is necessary is that, *in that particular sentence* it should be mentioned as a property peculiar to that object,—and not that it should always belong to that object alone ; for if it were so, then, 'blue' could not be cognised as qualifying the 'lotus,' or 'possessed by Devadatta' as qualifying the " Cow " ; as throughout the world, the *Cow* is not the object *possessed by Devadatta* ; and so too the property 'blue' does not belong to the *lotus alone*; so that, according to you, these two could not be spoken of as *qualifications.*

On the other hand, if the recognition of one thing as the qualification of another depended upon the fact of its really belonging to that *object* alone, then such a relationship would never be sought to be expressed in words; for certainly there is no use of mentioning such a qualification as that 'the Fire is hot'. Therefore all that we should accept as the means of such recognition is the fact of the property being mentioned, *in that sentence*, as belonging to that object alone.

This condition we find fulfilled in the case in question; because in the sentence in question what is meant to be spoken of as the condition of the particular *precedence* is the *Rathantara as belonging to the Jyotishṭoma only.* And, under the circumstances, there is no ground for rejecting the foremost cognised conditional character of the *Rathantara*, and attributing it to something else.

Thus we find that in any case, there is nothing incongruous in the fact of the said *Rathantara* being the condition; and, consequently, we cannot accept any of the four alternatives—'Rejection of the word *yadi*', etc.—propounded by the *Pūrvapakshin.* (See above, p. 810.)

As for the assertion that the Injunctive Affix denotes *either* the presence of Desire or the causal relation,—none of these two denotations could be cognised until the aforesaid conditional character has been duly comprehended; and so long as the cognition of this latter is possible, it is not right to accept any other denotation that has not been cognised.

As a matter of fact, we find, even in ordinary experience, the conditional character belonging to objects, present, past and future; and as such the fact of the *Rathantara* being sung at midday, while the vessels are held in the morning, cannot be effectively urged against the said conditional character of the *Rathantara.* Then again, that which is known in the morning as sure to come is as good as *present*; and in the case in question we find that at the time that the performance of the *Jyotishṭoma* is just beginning, it is already well known that the *Rathantara* would be sung at midday; because, as a rule, all doubtful details are fully settled before the performance is actually begun; and so all the priests, as well as the sacrificer himself, must be fully aware of the fact of a certain thing to be done in course of the performance, before they actually proceed with the performance itself; specially as it is only by such previous settling of all doubtful details that people become accustomed to, and experts in, the performance of sacrifices.

Then again, as a matter of fact, the *Condition* helps the *Conditioned*, not by it ctual material presence, but simply by being fully known; and hence even though the *Rathantara* may not have been actually sung in the morning, yet, inasmuch as it has been determined upon (in the very act of determining the performance of the sacrifice), and is fully known as such, it could very well serve as the *condition* (for the particular order of precedence in the holding of the vessels in the morning). And when it is the *sacrifice*, as qualified by the *Rathantara*, even though existing in only one part of it, that is the condition of the *precedence*—then, inasmuch as the *sacrifice* is present in the morning also, there would be no incongruity in this.

Nor is the use of the Injunctive Affix regulated by connection with any point of time; and as such it could not be taken as indicating the conditional character of a thing existing at any definite point of time; because the affix in '*syāt*' is quite capable of affording the meaning that—'if the sacrifice *be*, or *has been*, or *will be*, connected with the Rathantara *Sāma*, etc.'; and it is only by the indirect implication of the sentence that the *Rathantara*, in the case in question, is *to be*.

As for the last argument (of the *Pūrvapaksha*), based upon the similarity of the *Rathantara*, etc., with the *Jagat-sāma* (which is not present at the *Jyotishṭoma*)—it is not quite proper; (1) because in such superphysical matters, an inference from similar instances can have no authority; and (2) because the case of the *Jagat-sāma* is not quite similar to those of the *Rathantara* and the rest; the former being as incapable of being included in the *Jyotishṭoma*, as the injunction of the *First day of the month as qualified by duality and plurality*. And further, even in the case of the *Jagat-sāma*, the action is not wholly different from the *Jyotishṭoma*; because all that it does is to represent the condition attaching to the *Vishuvat* sacrifice mentioned elsewhere.

For these reasons we conclude that the sentences in question only serve the purpose of laying down certain conditions of *precedence* [and do not lay down distinct actions].

ADHIKARANA (2).

[*The Avēshṭi is a distinct Sacrifice.*]

***Sūtra* (3).—Because of the mention of the Avēshṭi being connected with the mention of the Sacrifice, it must be accepted as pointing chiefly to a Sacrifice (and not to an Accessory).**

In the same context with the sentence '*Rājā rājasūyēna svārājyakāmo yajēta*', we find the sentence—I. '*āgneyo'shṭākapālo-hiraṇyandakshiṇā*' and so forth, which serve to lay down, by mentioning the relationship of certain substances with particular deities, the sacrifice known as 'Avēshṭi'; and then, subsequently, we come across the following sentence: II. '*Yadi Brāhmaṇo yajēta Bārhaspatyam madhyē nidhāyāhutimāhutim hutvā hutvā'bhighārayēt, yadi Rājanya Aindram, yadi Vaiçyo Vaiçvadēvam.*'

With regard to this last sentence, there arises a doubt, as before; and it is this: A. Does it serve to lay down the *inserting of the Bārhaspatya*, etc., as due to (conditioned by) the connection of the Avēshṭi—as forming part of the *Rajasūya*—with the various castes,—a connection that has already been laid down in the previous sentence? Or, does it lay down a distinct performance (of the Avēshṭi), in connection with the *Brāhmaṇa*, etc., not mentioned before?

This leads us to the further question: *viz.*: B. Are all the three castes entitled to the performance of the Rājasūya, or the Kshatriya only? [As if the latter, then the connection of the three castes with the Avēshṭi of the *Rājasūya* cannot be said to have been previously mentioned.]

C. And this last question would lead us to the consideration of the word '*Rājā*', which is the word that specifies the Agent entitled to the performance of the *Rājasūya*; and in connection with the word "*Rājā*", we shall have to consider the question as to whether it signifies the '*Kshatriya*', or 'one who *performs the functions of a king.*'

Objection: "Inasmuch as we find another sentence—'*ētayā annādyakāmam yājayēt*'—which is wholly distinct from that which lays down "the performance of the *Rājasūya* with its subsidiaries, and which lays "down the *Avēshṭi*, as not connected with any particular caste,—it is clear "that the connection of the three castes is already mentioned; and hence "there could be no doubt as to the sentences in question mentioning the "connection of the castes only by way of pointing out the conditions for "the inserting of the *Bārhaspatya* and the rest."

Reply: It is not so; because we find that the *Avēshṭi* is already recognised (through the sentence '*Rājā Rajasuyēna*, etc.') as one to be performed by the *Kshattriya*,—and that the other sentence also ('*ētayā annādyakāmam*, etc.') does not lay it down as to be performed by Agents other than the *Kshattriya*; consequently, we find no ground for the performance of the *Avēshṭi* apart from the *Rājasūya*; as such it comes to be taken as forming a part of the *Rājasūya* itself; so we conclude, in accordance with the law laid down in the *Sūtra* IV—iii—5, that the 'Kingdom of Heaven' ('*svārājya*') (mentioned in the former sentence) is the result common to the *Rājasūya* and the *Aveshṭi*; while the 'food' ('*annādya*', mentioned in the sentence quoted by the objector) is the result peculiar to the *Avēshṭi* itself. And even if the *Aveshṭi* be performed apart from the *Rājasūya*, it would be performed by the Kshatriya only, when desiring the particular result of obtaining *Food*; and as such there would be no connection with the other two castes. As for instance, the Action of *studying the Veda* and the *laying of Sacrificial Fire* being known as to be performed by the three higher castes only,—even though the sacrifices depending upon these two Actions may be found connected with any and every agent that may be desirous of obtaining the results following from those sacrifices, yet they come to be finally recognised as to be performed only by the *non-Çūdra* castes; and as in the case of the *Rājasūya* itself, even though all men may be equally desirous of the 'Kingdom of Heaven', yet on account of the Action being specified for the *Rājā* only, it is the *Rājā* alone who could be the acquirer of that result (by the performance of the *Rājasūya*).

Thus then there are only two alternative theories to be considered: (1) The *Avēshṭi* (as connected with the three castes) is laid down in the sentence laying down the *Rājasūya*, and (2) it is laid down by the latter sentences.

And on this question we have the following

PŪRVAPAKSHA.

"In view of the conclusion arrived at in the foregoing *Adhikaraṇa*, "it must be admitted that the latter sentences only serve to lay down the "conditions for the particular *insertions*.

"And to the performance of *Rājasūya*, all the three castes are entitled, "as shown by the word '*Rājā*', which signifies 'one who performs the "functions of a king.' Because all through the world, it is only one "performing the kingly functions that is spoken of as '*Rājā*.' And it is "thus alone that the text in question can have an extended application.

"That is to say, when it is possible for the word '*Rājā*' to be taken "both ways (*i.e.*, as signifying the *Kshattriya*, and as signifying 'one who "performs the kingly functions'), it is far more advisable to accept the sig-"nification of all the three castes; because this interpretation alone "would be compatible with the mention (in the subsequent sentences) "of the conditions ('*yadi Brāhmaṇaḥ*, etc.'), and with the Context, etc.; "and also because this interpretation would not curtail the scope of the "declaration of all the three castes being entitled to the performance of "the *Rājasūya*.

"For these reasons it must be admitted that persons of all the three "castes, performing the functions of a king, are "*Rājās*; and these func-"tions are well known to consist in the *protection of the people* and the "*removal, from among them, of all troublous factors.*

"The Bhāshya speaks of the word '*Rājā*' being used in the above "sense by the *people of Āryāvarta* (North India); and this is meant to "show the authoritative character of the signification, in accordance with "the *Sūtra* I—iii—9.

"*Objection*: 'The *Bhāshya*, by declaring that *trustworthy people use* "*the word Rājya in the sense of kingly functions*, admits the independence "of the word *Rājā*, which forms the base of the word *Rājya*. (That is to "say, the said declaration makes the signification of the word *Rājya* de-"pendent upon that of the word *Rājā*, which is the word appearing in the "text in question; and hence what the declaration does is to seek to ex-"plain the word—*Rājya*—not in the text—by the help of that—*Rājā*—"which occurs in the text; and consequently the word *Rājā* being inde-"pendent, it could not be explained as *Rājyakartā*). Because the word "*Udamēgha* is not comprehended by being explained as related (as father) "to *Audamēghi*; in fact it is the word *Audamēghi* that is comprehended by "the help of *Udamēgha*, which itself is independent. (And so the word "*Rājā* cannot be rightly comprehended by the help of the word *Rājya*).'

"*Reply*: Though the people of old comprehended the word '*Rājā*' "by itself, and deduced from that the meaning of the word '*Rājya*',—"yet for us, people of the present day, it is quite the other way.

"That is to say, when the direction '*Gāmānaya*' is used, the person "using it and the person comprehending it, understand it as—'*yo gauḥ* "*sa ānētavyaḥ*'; (that which is the *ox* is to be brought), and yet the "third person standing by, who is ignorant of the meaning of the "word '*gām*', but knows that of the word '*ānaya*', takes the direction to "mean that '*ya ānēshyatē sa gauḥ*' (that which will be brought is the "*ox*),—just as the '*sacrificial post*' is recognised as such only when the "sacrificial animal is tethered to it. In the same manner, though such an-"cient writers as *Pāṇini* and *Manu* have declared—'*yo Rājā tēna janapa-"darakshaṇam kartavyam, yacça Rājā tasya karma Rājyam*' ('He who is "the king has for his duty the protection of the people, and he who is the "*Rājā*, his function is *Rājya*'),—yet we, who are not quite sure of the "signification of the word '*Rājā*' though quite sure of that of the word "'*Rājya*', comprehend the said declaration of *Manu*, etc., in the follow-"ing way: 'Inasmuch as the Smṛtis have made the above declaration, "we must conclude that they understood the word *Rājā* as signifying "*something capable of doing Rājya* (*i.e.*, performing the functions of the "king),—just as the word '*yūpa*' is applied to something to which the "sacrificial animal can be tethered.

"This '*Rājya*'—kingly function—is found to be performed by people "of all the four castes; and hence all of these are *Rājās*. But inasmuch "as, in accordance with other laws and regulations, the word '*Rājā*' is "found to have its ends fulfilled among the three higher castes only, "the *Çudra* becomes naturally precluded by the fact of his being devoid "of Vedic study, etc. There is, however, no such ground of precluding "any other caste; and hence we conclude that all the three higher "castes are entitled to the performance of the *Rājasūya*.

"*Objection*: 'As a matter of fact, the kingly functions have been "specially laid down for the *Kshattriya*; and hence it is only by an unlaw-"ful assumption of others' functions that the *Brāhmana* and the *Vaiçya* "perform those functions; and as such these latter cannot be rightly "called *Rājās*.'

"*Reply*: This argument does not touch our position; because by "the mere fact of having performed the kingly functions, these two castes "also acquire the title of '*Rājā*'; and this (performing of the kingly func-"tions) is all that is required by the *Rājasūya-Injunction*. As to whether "these functions are performed lawfully or unlawfully, that is a question "affecting the character of the performing agents, and as such cannot "have anything to do with the sacrifice (*Rājasūya*).

"*Objection* (in the *Bhāshya*): '*We find the word Rājā applied even to* "*such Kshattriyas as do not perform the kingly functions of protecting the* "*people, etc.*'

"This argument has been brought forward here as forming the "basis of the *Siddhānta*; and hence we proceed to refute it; but before "doing that we must find out what it means. It means simply this: 'It "has been said above, in connection with the words *varhiḥ*. *ājyam* and "the like, that when even a single part of the word has been found to sig-"nify the *Class*, we cannot assume any other signification for it (and so in "the case in question also, when, even in the case of a single person, the "word *Rājā* has been found to signify the *Kshattriya-class,* we cannot very "well assume any other meaning for it).'

"The reply to this is that in the case of the word '*Rājā*', we find the "literal signification (that afforded by its constituent parts) to be more "reasonable than any other (that is dependent upon mere popular con-"vention). This is what is meant by the *Bhāshya*, when it says—*praka-"raṇavaçāt, yadiçabdasamabhivyāhārācca.*

"Then, concludes the Bhāshya—*na karmāntaram vidhāyishyatē.* "This means that the sentence would not lay down the *performance* of the "*Avēshṭi* apart from that of the *Rājasūya* : (the word '*karmāntaram*' being "taken indirectly in the sense of *prayogāntaram*); or it may mean that—if we "admit of the same construction as that shown above, in the case of the "sentence '*yadi çālim bhunjīta dadhyupasincet*', then the same sentence "could not serve to lay down both the connection of the *Brāhmaṇa*, as "well as the insertion of the *Bārhaspatya* ; and in this case the word '*kar-"māntaram*' of the Bhāshya would be taken directly in the sense of 'another "*Action*', and not indirectly as in the former case.

"The above reply to the objection has been given by admitting both "significations of the word (*i.e.*, that accepted by the people of the Andhra "country, who use the word '*Rājā*' in the sense of *Kshattriya*, as well as that "accepted by those of *Āryāvarta*, who apply the word to the *performer "of kingly functions*). But we now proceed to show that there is no reason-"able ground for applying the word 'Rājā' to a person devoid of kingly "functions.

"It will be readily admitted that that which is accepted by *all men* "must set aside that which is not accepted by all of them (and there can "be no doubt that all men apply the word '*rājā*' to real *kings*, while it is "only the Āndhra people that apply it also to one without the functions "of a king, simply if he happens to be a *Kshattriya*).

"Another argument brought forward in the Bhāshya is—*That which "is admitted by people without contradiction is more authoritative than that "which is decried, though accepted.* But this is the same argument as the "former, only expressed differently, for '*decrying*' and '*non-decrying*' are "nothing apart from '*non-acceptance*' and '*acceptance*' respectively. Or, "it may be that the former argument brought forward merely the existence, "or otherwise, of the acceptance of the significations; while the latter "speaks of their contradiction or non-contradiction. And as there is a "clear difference between *Ignorance* and *Mistaken Knowledge*, the two argu-"ments cannot be said to be mere repetitions of each other. Says the "Bhāshya—*āryāvartanivāsinām .... mlecchēbbyaḥ samīcīnatara ācāro bhava-"ti*; and here the mention of '*āryāvartanivāsinām*' only serves to show, "as before, the greater authoritativeness of the one signification, in "accordance with the *Sūtra* I—iii—9; while the clause '*samīcīnatara* "*ācāro bhavati*' refers to the *usage of the word.*

"For the above reasons, we conclude that the sentence in question "serves to mention the *Brāhmaṇa,* etc., already mentioned in the former "sentence as conditioning the insertion of the *Bārhaspatya,* etc. Specially "because, there can be no doubt as to the sentence '*yadi rājanya aindram*' "mentioning the *Rājanya* (Kshattriya), already mentioned in the previous "sentence (for there can be no doubt as to the *Kshattriya* being spoken of "by means of the word '*Rājā*'), simply as conditioning the insertion of "the Aindra; and then the cases of the other two sentences—'*yadi Brāh*"*manaḥ,*' etc., and '*yadi Vaiçyaḥ,* etc.'—being exactly similar, the same "must be admitted with regard to these also."

SIDDHANTA.

To the above we make the following reply:—

The sentence in question serves to lay down the connection of the Brāhmaṇa, etc., with the Sacrifice; because such connection has not been mentioned before,—the mere performing of kingly functions not sufficing to make one known as '*Rājā.*'

That is to say, the word '*Rājā*' denotes the *Kshattriya,* and cannot be taken in its literal sense. Because the literal meaning might consist either in the *performing of the kingly functions,* or, according to the signification of the root '*rāj,*' in *Brightness* or *Effulgence*; and both of these are impossible; because we find the word having a well-known meaning apart from the *literal*; and even though this meaning may be known in one part of the country only, yet it will always set aside the applicability of the *literal* meaning; and then too, there is no one definite literal meaning that is recognised as universally applicable; as on the one hand, the word '*Rājā*' is not found to be applied to such *bright* things as Fire and the like; nor, on the other, to such representatives of the king as are not duly *anointed,* though *performing* quite well *the kingly functions* of protecting the people, and the like.

Objection: "As for the Representative of the king, inasmuch as he "performs those functions by being appointed to it by another person, "the word '*Rājā*' is not applied to him; just as the word 'sacrificer' "('*yajamāna*') is not applied to the sacrificial Priests."

Reply: This is not right; because we actually find the word '*Rājā,*' in many cases, applied to the Rulers over smaller subsidiary estates, to which they have been anointed by the all-powerful Emperor, to whom they are subordinate.

Question: "Then, inasmuch as the word is found to be applied to "those that have been *anointed* to the functions of a king, it may be "taken as expressing that 'anointment' (and not the '*Kshattriya*' "caste)."

Answer: That would not be possible; because, the *Anointment* also is declared by the knowers of Law to belong to the *Kshattriya* only, just like the word '*Rājā*'; and hence that too could not belong to a *non-Kshattriya*.

The word could be recognised as expressing *Anointment*, if this formed the independent and absolute cause of the application of the word (*i.e.*, if the word were applied to anyone and everyone whom we would *anoint*); while, as a matter of fact, we find this *Anointment* restricted, by all Smṛti laws, to the *Kshattriya only*; and as such it is only at the time of its Injunction (by the sentence '*Rājānam abhishincēta*') that it becomes connected with the word '*Rājā*',—just as the '*chopping*' becomes connected with the word 'grass.'

It is for this very reason that the word '*Rājā*' is not taken as signifying, like a compound word, both of these—the '*Kshattriya*' caste and 'Anointment'—conjointly (*i.e.*, the word is not accepted in the sense of the 'anointed Kshattriya'). Specially because the word could be so taken, only if it were always actually found to be applied to the *Kshattriya* and the *Anointment* conjointly, and never to the *Kshattriya* caste alone,—or if the 'Anointment' were laid for other castes also. As a matter of fact, however, we find that the word is applied, in the very Injunction '*Rājānamabhishincēta*', to the person to be purified by *Anointment*, long before the Anointment has actually taken place.

Hence we conclude that the word '*Rājā*' is generally accepted as denoting the caste '*Kshattriya*.'

Nor can it be urged that—"the Injunction '*Rājānamabhishincēta*' serves to point out a name to be applied in the future (its meaning being that *one should anoint that person who would, after that Anointment, be known as* '*Rājā*')." Because a *name* is always found to be used as already pertaining to the object named; and it is only when such application has been found to be impossible that, in certain cases, we admit of a *name* being based upon future applicability. In the case in question, however, we find that one signification (the *caste Kshattriya*) is an established entity already; and so we cannot rightly assume another signification (in the shape of the *anointment*), as the use of the word is found to be quite possible even without such an assumption.

And even if the word be taken as signifying 'Anointment,' people knowing the Law do not apply it to a *non-Kshattriya*; while as for one who would so apply it, disregarding the Law on the point, such unlawful application could not be recognised as the basis of the word's signification;

just as if a *Çūdra* happen to *lay* the *Fire*, that Fire does not come to be recognised as the '*Āhavanīya*' ('sacrificial') Fire.

And further, the Word, its Meaning, and the Relation between them,—all three, being eternal, pertain to the natural state of things existing; and as such they do not base themselves upon impermanent causes, gratuitously assumed by us for the occasion. For instance, in the case in question, the word '*Rājā*' being eternal, its signification too must be one that is permanent, because there can be no real relationship between the Permanent and the Impermanent. This permanence is cognised as depending either upon the nature of things or upon an expressed Vedic Injunction. Then, as for the *Anointment*, it is not found to be permanently inherent in any person, like his *caste*; and hence its permanence will have to be accepted as based on an Injunction; but as a matter of fact, we do not find any Injunction laying down the applicability of the word '*Rāja*' to a *non-Kshattriya*; and hence, after all, we come to the conclusion that it is the *caste* '*Kshattriya*' only that is the invariable signification of the word '*Rāja*'; and hence that alone must be accepted as denoted by it.

The above argument also serves to preclude the possibility of the signification of the word '*Rājā*' being based upon the *performing of kingly functions*; because those *functions* also are found to be connected with the *Kshattriya caste*, only *after* they have been laid down as pertaining to the *Rājā*,—just like the said *Anointment*. And, as a matter of fact, we have found the word '*Rājā*' applied to one who has neither been *anointed*, nor *performs the functions of the king*,—and *not* to such persons as have been *anointed* and *perform those functions*, but are *not Kshattriyas* (this latter usage is met with among the *Draviḍas*).

Hence too we conclude that persons of all the *three castes* cannot be called '*Rājā*.'

Further, all grammarians explain the word "Rājanya" as '*Rājñaḥ apatyam*,' deriving it from the basic noun '*Rājan*'; and yet the word '*Rājanya*' has no other meaning but the *Kshattriya caste*. If the word '*Rājā*' were applicable to all the three castes, then the off-spring of the other two castes would also be spoken of as '*Rājanya*.' Because the word '*Rājanya*' is applied by universal convention to the *Kshattriya*; while if all the three castes were '*Rājās*', will you please explain to me why the word '*Rājanya*' should not be applied to the off-spring of the other castes?

Objection: "If the word '*Rājanya*' denotes the *Kshattriya* only, what "would be the use of the patronymic affix? Because the word '*kshattriya*,' "denoting the *caste*, is equally applicable to the Father and the Son; and "hence in all cases the *Rājanya* should always be spoken of as '*Rājā*.' "That is to say, just as the *offspring of the crow* is called the 'crow,' so "the *offspring of the Rājā* would be 'Rājā.'"

Reply: This does not quite affect our position; because though as a matter of fact the word '*Rājanya*' is synonymous with '*Rājā*,' yet it is only by way of showing its grammatical formation that it is explained as '*Rājñaḥ apatyam*'; and the said explanation is possible only when both refer to the same caste, as the offspring always belongs to the same caste as the Father.

Objection: "The word '*Rājanya*' would denote the *Kshattriya* caste, "on account of the *sūtra* 'when the patronymic is affixed to '*Rājan*' it de- "notes the class' (*Vārtika on Pāṇini Sūtra* IV—i—137), and not on account "of the word being explained as '*Rājñaḥ apatyam*'; and consequently the "denotation of the word '*Rājanya*' could not affect that of the word "'*Rājā*.'"

Reply: It is not so; because inasmuch as the Vārtika you quote does not mention any particular *class*, it might be taken as referring to the comprehensive class 'Man'; and so, according to this Vārtika, the word '*Rājanya*' would come to denote that *class* 'Man' (and not the '*Kshattriya*').

Objection: "As a matter of fact, we find the teachers of Law and "Sacrifices laying down different duties for the *Rājā* and the *Rājanya*, "which shows clearly that the word '*Rājā*' is different from '*Rājanya*.'"

Reply: True, we meet with such differentiated duties; but that is in accordance with the maxim of the '*Brāhmaṇaparivrājaka*'; that is to say, the word '*Rājā*' refers to the particular Rājanya who has undergone anointment (just as the word '*Parivrājaka*' is applied to the particular Brāhmaṇa who has gone through the rites of Renunciation).

It has been argued that—"the word '*Rājā*' being found to be cap- "able of having both significations, *i.e.*, the *Kshattriya caste*, and the *perfor- "mer of kingly functions*,—it is the latter that comes to be accepted, in the "present instance, as being more in keeping with the Context, etc." And it is this argument that we now proceed to refute, as follows:

Both the words—'*Rājā*' and '*Rājya*'—could not have their significations wholly independent of the other; because the fact is that when one of them has its signification fixed by convention, that of the other follows from it.

To explain this further: when the word '*Rājā*' has been known, by convention, as signifying the *Kshattriya* caste, then the signification of the word '*Rājya*'—explained as 'the function of the Rājā'—comes to be based upon that of the word '*Rājā*'; and so long as this is possible, it is not right to assume an independent denotative potency for this latter word. As even without such an independent denotative potency, there would be nothing incompatible in the usage of the people of *Āryāvarta* (who apply the word '*Rājya*' to the 'kingly functions of protecting the people' and the like). If, conversely, it be held that—"the word '*Rājya*' itself has its signification of the *function of protecting the people* fixed by convention, before that of the word '*Rājā*' is known,"—then too, the word '*Rājā*' would, as based on the word '*Rājya*', come to be applied to the *performer* of that function; and it would not be necessary to assume any independent denotative potency in the word '*Rājā*'; and as such there would be nothing incongruous in the usage of the *Draviḍas*, who apply the word '*Rājā*' to the *Kshattriyas*, who are capable of the said functions of *protection*, etc. Though the particular usage is peculiar to the *Draviḍas*, yet the *Bhāshya* attributes it to the *Āndhras*, because these also, like the *Draviḍas*, inhabit the southern part of India.

For the above reasons, we conclude that the words '*Rājā*' and '*Rājanya*' cannot be regarded as both having their meanings fixed by convention, independently of each other, or as both having only such sense as is afforded by their constituent parts.

And when it comes to the acceptance of one of the two words having its independent signification fixed by convention, it is distinctly more reasonable that it should be accepted with regard to the word '*Rājā*'; because, as a rule, whenever there is a doubt caused by a disagreement between usages, a satisfactory conclusion is always arrived at by the help of the stronger authority of a properly compiled *Smṛti*.

That is to say, Manu and other writers of *Smṛti* declare that the function of *protecting the people*, etc., which is expressed by the word '*Rājya*,' belongs to the *Kshattriya*; Pāṇini and others also expound the word '*Rājya*' as '*the function of the Rājā*,'—wherein, they hold (vide *Pāṇini, Sūtra* V—i—124), that to the word '*Rājā*,' which has its signification independently fixed by convention, the affix '*shyañ*' is added (to make the word '*Rājya*'). Other grammarians explain the grammatical formation of this word ('*Rājya*') as with the affix '*yak*,' which is an affix particularly laid down for the word '*Rājā*' which appears to be mentioned in the *group* of words beginning with '*patyantapurohita*' (*Pāṇini, Sutra* I—v—128); and it is thus alone that we could have the presence of an accentuation that is peculiar to the affix '*yak*,' and that of the *udātta* accentuation in the beginning of the word. For these reasons, we must take the *Bhāshya* on the point as declaring that it is the formation of the word '*Rājya*' that should be evolved out of the word '*Rājā*,' and not that of the latter from the former. For if the formation of the word '*Rājā*' were evolved out of the word '*Rājya*,' then there should be certain definite grammatical rules laying down either the elision of the letter '*ya*' (in '*Rājya*'), or the modification of the word '*Rājya*' into '*Rājā*.'

For these reasons, the construction must be explained as '*Rajñaḥ karma Rājyam*' (the function of the *Rājā* is '*Rājya*'), and not as '*Rājyasya kartā Rāja*' (the performer of the kingly functions is '*Rāja*')

Nor can the latter explanation be accepted on the mere ground of the apparent inconsistency (of the use of the word among the people of *Āryāvarta*) ; because such usage of the word '*Rājā*' is known in another part of the country. And even if the Apparent Inconsistency were rightly brought forward, the aforesaid *Smṛtis* of Manu and others would distinctly point to the fact of the functions of protecting the people, etc., belonging to the *Kshattriya* ; and as such it would be the *Kshattriya* that would come to be known as '*Rājā.*'

Then again, as a matter of fact, we find that the whole of the word '*Rājā*' is present in the word '*Rājya*'; and hence it is only right that the latter should be held to have its denotation governed by that of its constituent part ('*Rājā*') ; which, however, cannot be said of the word '*Rājā*' wherein we do not find the whole word '*Rājya*' entering into its constitution.

Objection: "True; in this way the word '*Rājya*' does come to have "its denotation fixed by that of its constituent part '*Rājā.*' But in that "case, the word '*Rājā*' could never be applied to a *non-Kshattriya* who may "perform the functions of the king ; and hence it cannot be denied that "there would be an incompatibility of the usage common among the people "of *Āryāvarta*; as the said explanation of the word '*Rājā*' would at once "mark down as incongruous such uses of the word as '*na Çūdra-rājyē* "*nivasēt*' (one should not live in a country where a *Çudra is the* "*rājā*)."

Reply: *Yogāt lokaḥ prayuṅkte* : that is to say, the word '*Rājya*' is explained as formed by its connection with the '*Rājā*,' and then the presence of the *Rājya* (kingly functions) in the *Brāhmaṇa*, etc., makes the word '*Rājā*' indirectly applicable to these latter castes also.

Question: "In that case, you admit the fact of the word '*Rājā*' "being taken as formed by its connection with '*Rājya*' (kingly func-"tions)."

Answer: That does not touch our position ; because we hold the word '*Rājā*' to be only *indirectly* (or figuratively) applicable to the *Brāhmaṇa*, etc. It would be only if we made the word *directly* applicable to these, that the *Adhikaraṇa* would be wholly reversed. While as for the indirect application, inasmuch as it is always set aside by the direct application, even if it were admitted, it could not set aside the *Siddhānta*. Hence it must be admitted that the word '*Rājā*' is applied to the *Brāhmaṇa*, etc., only in consideration of the fact of these latter being the proxy of the *Kshattriya*, in the performance of his legitimate functions (of protecting the people).

This is what is meant by the *Bhāshya* when it says—*na tvēvam smaranti Rājyāyogāt Rājēti*; which must be taken to mean that *usage* being much less authoritative than *Smṛti* (*vide* Adh. I, Pāda iii), the said usage must be explained as being figurative or indirect.

It has been urged above that—"as the word '*Audamegha*' gives us an idea of its basic noun '*Udamegha*,' so the word '*Rājyā*' could afford an idea of its basic word '*Rājā*.'" But this Indirect Inference is set aside by the Direct Perception of the usage common among the *Draviḍas*.

If the *performer of kingly functions* were to be spoken of as '*Rājā*,' then, in that case, it would be necessary for us to *infer* the existence, *firstly*, of the said relationship of Action and its Performer, and, *secondly*, of certain grammatical rules definitely laying down the presence of that relationship in the case in question. And certainly very much more authoritative than any such *inferred* grammatical rule, is the already existing rule that lays down the formation of the word '*Rājya*' as '*Rājñaḥ karma*' (the functions of the *Rājā*).

The opponent argues thus: "*Yō yō rājyam karoti, etc., etc.* "That is to say, the relationship of the *Denoter* and the *Denoted* is always "ascertained by invariable concomitance or non-concomitance; and "there is no doubt that the word '*Rājā*' is always concomitant with "the presence of the *performance of kingly functions* (and as such the "word '*Rājā*' is taken as denoting *the performer of kingly functions*); "while the word '*Rājya*' is not found to be always concomitant with "the *functions of the Rājā* (and as such this latter word cannot be taken "as denoting these functions). Then as for the grammatical rules brought "forward above, all that such rules do is to differentiate between the "correctly-formed and the incorrectly-formed words; and as such, they "can have nothing to do with the case in question; because both the "words '*Rājā*' and '*Rājya*' are equally correctly formed; and hence the "bringing forward of grammatical rules is altogether improper."

To the above we make the following reply: It is true that such is the common usage, and the grammatical rules have nothing to do as to what word has its denotations governed by the presence of which other word; though it is so, yet, it is by the explanation of the correct or the incorrect formation of words that the fact of certain words governing the denotation of other words is pointed out; as for instance, in the case in question, the formation of the word '*Rājya*' being explained as '*Rājñaḥ karma*' (king's functions), it is clearly pointed out (by this formation of the word) that the denotation of the word is fixed by that of the word '*Rājā*.'

Thus then, the greater authoritativeness of the grammatical *smṛtis* distinctly points to the fact that it is the word '*Rājā*' (and not '*Rājya*') that has an independent denotation of its own (*fixed solely by convention*). And as for the particular usage that you have brought forward in support of your contention, we find that it is not observed among the *Draviḍas.* According to us, on the other hand, no special importance is attached to usage; and as such the fact of our theory not being in keeping with the usage of *Āryāvarta* does not in any way tarnish it. But, as a matter of fact, even in *Āryāvarta* we do find the presence of *kingly functions* whenever the word '*Rājā*' is used; and thus there can be nothing incongruons in our theory; as all that it does is to explain what is used, and leave off the explanation of the fact of the word not being used (by the people of *Āryāvarta*) with reference to those *Kshattriyas* that are devoid of kingly functions.

And further, in all cases, a *qualification* is such as is peculiar to the object in question; and hence the word '*Rājya*' refers only to such functions as belong to the '*Rājā*' alone, and not to such other actions as *thinking* and the rest. That is to say, *protection of the people* is the distinctive function of the King; and hence it is this that is spoken of as '*Rājya*'; and as for such actions as those of *thinking, winking* and the like, inasmuch as these are found to exist in kings as well as in other men, they do not serve to distinguish the king, and as such, are not spoken of as '*Rājya*.'

Thus then, even though the fact of the word '*Rājā*' denoting the *Kshattriya* may not be countenanced by the usage of *all men*, yet, in accordance with the *Sūtra* I—iii—9, we cannot but admit it (to be more authoritative and acceptable). And it has been shown above, under *Sūtra* I—iii—10, that in matters of merely *verbal* usage, which pertains to ordinary perceptible things, a certain authoritativeness attaches also to the inhabitants of countries lying on the frontiers of *Āryāvarta.*

Thus then, the *Rājasūya* sacrifice being concluded as being for the *Kshattriya* only, the sentences in question must be taken as laying down the *Brāhmaṇa*, etc., as performers of the *Avēshṭi* (which is an Action distinct from the *Rājasūya*).

And hence the particular Result—obtaining of *Food* (mentioned in the sentence '*ētayā annādyakāmam, etc.*')—would follow from the performance of the *Avēshṭi*, apart from the *Rājasūya.* Because the performance of the *Avēshṭi* in the midst of the *Rājasūya* will have been completed by the obtaining of the *Kingdom of Heaven* (the specific Result of the *Rājasūya*); while its performance apart from that would be in need of the mention of a Result for itself (as that of the *Rājasūya* can no longer appertain to it); and consequently the Result (Food) subsequently mentioned would naturally attach itself to this latter performance.

Objection: "The *obtaining of food* must be accepted as the Result "following from the *Avēshṭi* in all cases; because it is mentioned directly "in connection with this Sacrifice,—in the sentence '*ētayā annādyakā-*

"*mam*, etc.'; while the Result spoken of in connection with the *Rājasūya* "could apply to the *Avēshṭi* only *indirectly*; and there can be no doubt "that what is mentioned *directly* would set aside that which is only "indirectly pointed out."

Reply: It is not so; because there is no contradiction between the two Results. That is to say, if the two Results were found to be mutually incompatible, then it would be necessary to admit the fact of one setting aside the other; as the accepting of both would necessitate the assumption, either of the fact of the two as optional alternatives, or of the repetition of the Action in question (for the bringing about of the two results) [and such assumptions have been often shown to be extremely objectionable]. When, however, the two Results are capable of being reconciled by means of the limiting of their scope, there is no need of any such objectionable assumptions. As a matter of fact, there is nothing incompatible in the fact of a single Action of the *Avēshṭi* bringing about many results; because distinct results might very well follow from its distinct performances. As for *Repetition*, it will be shown later on, that it is objectionable only when the Results are spoken of as following conjointly (from the same Action). Specially in the case of the *Avēshṭi*, a repetition is inevitable, as it has been laid down in connection with the *Brāhmaṇa*, etc., on the one hand, while, on the other, it is also included in the *Rājasūya* (which cannot be performed by the *Brāhmaṇa*).

If the sentence '*ētayā annādyakāmam*, etc.,' were the originative Injunction of the *Avēshṭi*, then it could reject the applicability to the *Avēshṭi* of the subsequent *Rājasūya*-Injunction. As a matter of fact, however, we find that both these sentences—'*ētayā*, etc.' and the *Rājasūya* Injunction—mention results in connection with the Action of the *Avēshṭi*, which is originatively laid down in the sentence '*āgnēyóshṭākapālo*, etc.'; and as they do not mention the two results as appearing at one and the same time, we do not perceive any difference between the authoritative character of the two sentences (and hence the one cannot set aside the other); because just as the *Rājasūya*-Injunction is found to mention a result in reference to the Actions mentioned in close proximity to something else, so also is the sentence '*ētayā*, etc.'; specially as neither of them makes mention of the '*Avēshṭi*' by name. Because the word '*Rājasūya*' is not a generic name (applying to many sacrifices), like the word '*Paurṇamāsī*'; as what it denotes is *the Avēshṭi as a part of the sacrifice as accompanied by the complete group of sacrifices mentioned in connection with it* (while the word '*Paurṇamāsi*' applies to each of the sacrifices composing it; and hence the word '*Rājasūyena*' cannot be taken as denoting the *Avēshṭi*). And so, on this ground too, none of the two is found to be weaker than the other. The only difference between the two is that while the one (*Rājasūya*-Injunction) mentions many sacrifices, the other ('*ētayā*, etc.') mentions only a few; and certainly this does not make any very great difference (in the authoritativeness of the two sentences).

"*Objection:* Inasmuch as the pronoun '*ētayā*' points directly "to the *Avēshṭi* mentioned in the Context, there is a distinct difference "between this and the *Rājasūya* Injunction which refers to it only "indirectly."

Reply: This would have been quite true, if the pronoun '*etat*' (in '*ētayā*') were connected with the Result, or if it pointed to something, *to be spoken of*, as we find in the case of the sentence '*atha ēsha jyotiḥ*.' As a matter of fact, however, we find that even in the sentence '*ētayā*, etc.,' it is on account of the proximity of the root '*yaji*' to the Injunctive Affix (in '*yājayēta*') that the Result—food—is mentioned in connection with the *Avēshṭi*, which is indicated by that root ('*yajī*'); and this indication of the *Avēshṭi* is found to be done also by the root '*yaji*' occurring in the *Rājasūya*-Injunction; and so even this does not make any difference in the authoritative character of the two Results. Then again, even though the pronoun '*etayā*' refers to the *Avēshṭi* laid down in the Context, yet it could not refer precisely to the *Avēshṭi*, without the help of the sentence '*āgnēyoshṭākapalaḥ*, etc.'; and with the help of this sentence, the *Rājasūya*-Injunction also would refer to the *Avēshṭi* equally well; and thus also, both must be admitted to be equally authoritative.

Objection: "There is a distinct difference between the two, on "the ground that the sentence '*ētayā*, etc.', occurs in the particular sub-"context (of the *Avēshṭi*), while the *Rājasūya* Injunction ~~is a~~ general "statement (and as such takes in the *Avēshṭi* also, among many other "sacrifices that go to form the *Rājasūya*)."

Reply: But this is just the same as what we have pointed out before—*viz.*, that the only difference lies in the fact of the one referring to many more sacrifices than the other; but at the time of the actual referring to the *Avēshṭi* in particular, both are equally authoritative.

Further, if there were an absolute non-difference between the *Avēshṭi of the Rājasūya*, and the *Avēshṭi performed by the Brāhmaṇa*, etc. (which latter is the one referred to by the sentence '*ētayā*, etc.')—then what you say might have been all right (*i.e.*, then alone could the mention of the two Results be said to be incompatible). As it is, however, we have just shown that the two *Avēshṭis* are wholly distinct. And thus the very fields of the two results—*Kingdom of Heaven* and *acquiring of Food*—being distinct, there is no contradiction between them.

But though the two *Avēshṭis* may be different, yet, the mention of only such details as the *inserting of the Bārhaspatya*, etc., distinctly indicates that the origin of this *Avēshṭi* also is the same *Avēshṭi* that has been previously mentioned in the Context.

Then as for the "*Rājasūya*" (spoken of in the sentence '*yadi rājanyaḥ*, etc.'),—inasmuch as his activity also (towards the performing of this distinct *Avēshṭi*) would be equally possible, specially as the word mentioning the result of the distinct Avēshṭi (*i.e.*, '*Food*') is equally connected with the sentence '*yadi rājanyaḥ*, etc.',—by him also, this *Avēshṭi* would be performed, either as a distinct sacrifice by itself, or as a repetition (of the *Avēshṭi* that he may have performed along with the *Rājasūya*).

And for the Rājanya also, the mention of the *inserting of the Aindra in the middle* would be possible, only if the *Avēshṭi* were performed by him, independently by itself, *as a single sacrifice* made up of the various minor offerings of the Cake to Agni, to Indra, to Bṛhaspati, etc. (as thus alone could the Aindra—offering to Indra—be offered as the middle offering); whereas when the *Avēshṭi* is performed in course of the *Rājasūya*, inasmuch as the sacrificial gifts (of each of the offerings that go to form the *Avēshṭi*) are different (from each other, as also from that of the *Rājasūya*), each of these offerings (*Ishṭis*) to Agni, Indra, etc., would be performed independently by itself; and as such (all of them not constituting a single performance), the mention of putting any one of these '*in the middle*' would be wholly irrelevant (as there being no single performance made up of these performances of the several *Ishṭis*, of what would this be the '*middle*'?).

For these reasons, it must be admitted that the sentences in question serve to lay down the connection of the *Brāhmaṇa*, etc., not mentioned before.

ADHIKARAṆA (3).

[*The Ādhāna is an object of Injunction.*]

***Sūtra* (4): The laying of fire forms an object of Injunction, because it does not form an integral part of all sacrifices.**

In connection with the sentence '*vasantē Brāhmaṇo'gnīnādadhīta,*' there is a doubt, as in the previous instance, as to whether the *ādhāna* (Laying of Fire) has been previously mentioned elsewhere, or not. If it be found, in some way or other, to have been mentioned, then even in the absence of the conditional 'if', the sentence would be taken as laying down the condition (for the particular season to be chosen); and in that case, the construction of the sentence in question being,—"*yad Brāhmaṇa ādadhīta tad vasantē*"—the '*vasanta*' and the '*Brāhmaṇa*' would come to restrict one another (*i.e.*, the Spring would be the time for the *Brāhmaṇa*, and the *Brāhmaṇa* would be the performer in the *Spring time*). While, on the other hand, if the *Laying of Fire* be not found to have been previously mentioned, then the sentence in question would become the Injunction of the *Laying as performed by the Brāhmaṇa at the time of the Spring*; and the following would be the advantages of this latter interpretation:—(1) In the three sentences—(*a*) '*vasantē Brāhmaṇo'gnīnādadhīta,* (*b*) *grīshmē Rājanyaḥ,* (*c*) *çaradi Vaiçyaḥ*',—inasmuch as the *Laying* mentioned in the first sentence would be wholly taken up by the accessories (*Brāhmaṇa* and *Vasanta*) mentioned in the same sentence, the Accessories mentioned in the other two sentences would point to distinct actions (of *Laying*); and as such there would be *three* Layings of Fire; (2) the presence of the *Ātmanepada* affix in '*ādadhīta*' would point to the necessity of the sacrificer himself laying his own Fire; (3) the *Çūdra* would become precluded (from sacrifices, as only the three Layings of Fire are laid down, and without the laying of Fire, no sacrifice could be performed). If, on the other hand, the sentences be taken, not as Injunctions of the *Laying*, but as simply laying down conditions, then we would have the reverse of all these three advantages.

What is said in regard to the sentences in question would also apply to such other passages as—'*vasantē Brāhmaṇamupanayīta grīshmē Rājanyam, çaradi vaiçyam*'; as the condition of these sentences is exactly like that of those dealt with in this *Adhikaraṇa*.

The Adhikaraṇa may be briefly summed up thus:—

THE PŪRVAPAKSHA.

"*The Laying of Fire* having been implied by an Injunction of *a sacri-"fice in general* (as '*svargakāmo yayēta*'), or laid down by a general Injunc-"tion (such as '*Ya evamvidvānagnīnādhattē, etc.*'),—its mention over again "in the sentences in question must be taken as mentioning the various "castes as conditions for the particular times of the *Laying*.

"That is to say, in the first instance the first argument in our favour "is that, inasmuch as the Injunctions of such actions as the *Agnihotra* "and the like would not be possible without the sacrificial Fire made "ready by the proper method of *Laying* it, this *Laying* of the Fire must be "taken as implied by those very Injunctions; and hence the mention, in "the sentences in question, of the same *Laying* must be taken as serv-"ing the purpose of laying down the *Brāhmaṇa*, etc., by way of specifying "certain conditions. If, however, it be argued, that, on account of these "Injunctions having other direct objects of Injunction, they cannot "rightly serve the purpose of indirectly implying any such action as the "said *Laying*,—then, in that case, we would bring forward another "independent Injunction of the *Laying* itself,—in the shape of the sen-"tence '*ya ēvamvidvān āgnīnādhattē*, etc.,'—an Injunction which is "wholly distinct from the previous Injunction, which has its injunctive "potency taken up by the laying down of the Accessory details. And "thus then, the *Laying of Fire* having been already laid down in this In-"junction, the sentences in question could not be taken as enjoining the "same *Laying of Fire*."

SIDDHANTA.

The argument of the *Siddhānta* may be thus summed up: So long as we have a direct Injunction, we cannot very well admit of an implied or inferred one; and hence either the mention of the purpose to be served, or that of the existing state of things, can never serve as Injunctions.

That is to say, the mere mention of the *purpose* to be served by the *Laying of Fire* (in the shape of the accomplishment of the sacrificial, *Āhavanīya*, Fire for the Agnihotra, etc.) cannot be taken as necessarily pointing to the injunction of the said *Laying*; as the necessary Fire could be obtained by merely begging it of another Agnihotra-performer, specially as in the case of the injunction of the *Laying* of Fire being implied by those of *Agnihotra*, etc., there is no *Ātmanēpada* restricting the Fire to that which is prepared by the sacrificer himself. When, however, the necessary Injunction is found to be directly asserted (by a Vedic text), there is no Inconsistency which could lead us to assume an unheard-of text (as containing the required injunction),—the only ground for assuming such texts being some sort of an Apparent Inconsistency. Then, as for the mention of the existing state of things,—in the sentence '*yā ēvamvidvānagnīnādhattē*, etc.',—so long as we find a direct Injunction of the *Laying of Fire*, in the shape of the sentences in question—'*vāsantē Brāhmaṇo'gnīnādadhīta*,' etc., etc.—any mere description of the existing state of things can never acquire an Injunctive potency (to the same effect); specially as this latter has got to serve a distinct purpose of laying down all such details as the fetching of the water, etc., mentioned in the original direct Injunction.

For these reasons, it must be admitted that the sentences in question serve to lay down the hitherto unmentioned *Laying of Fire* as performed by the *Brāhmaṇa*, etc.

[We now proceed to explain the words of the Bhāshya putting forth the aforseaid Pūrvapaksha and Siddhānta.]

THE PŪRVAPAKSHA-BHĀSHYA.

"*The sentences in question serve to mention the Brāhmaṇa, etc., as conditions for the previously mentioned Laying of Fire.* '*Why so?*' *Because the words are similar to conditional phrases.*

"*Question:* '*On what is the similarity based?* That is to say, when there are no such conditional words as '*yadi*' and the like, how can the sentence be said to be similar to conditional clauses?'

"*Answer: The ground of similarity is the utterance of the words Brāhmaṇa, etc., along with the words Vasanta, etc.* That is to say, the injunctive potency of the sentence having been used up in laying down the relationship between other words (*i.e., Brāhmaṇa, etc.*, and *Vasanta, etc.*), the sentence could not serve to enjoin the *Laying of Fire*, and as such it could only be taken as laying down certain conditions—(in the shape of the said relationship between the *Brāhmaṇa* and *Vasanta*).

"*Objection:* '*But we find the word Brāhmaṇa uttered, in the sentence, along with the verb* TO LAY *also.* That is to say, the sentence could be taken as laying down the *Laying* of Fire as qualified by *Vasanta*.'

"*Reply: As a matter of fact, however, the relationship of the Brāhmaṇa with the Laying of the Fire is not unknown.* That is to say, inasmuch as the relationship between the *Brāhmaṇa* and the *Laying of Fire* is already known, it could not form the object of any fresh Injunction.

"*Question:* '*Being mentioned by what is this relationship known?*'

"*Answer: It has been mentioned by the texts speaking of certain desirable results to be obtained.* The stray reply is given with a view that as the position is not capable of being shaken, there is no need yet of bringing forward the strongest authority available in the shape of the text "('*ya evam, etc.*'), that directly lays down the *Laying of Fire.* (And this is "kept in store for future emergencies.)

"*Objector*: '*What are the texts speaking of desirable results in the "matter of such an Injunction?*'

"*Reply: The texts laying down the results following from the Agniho-"tra, etc., are such texts.* Though what the objector meant was an angry "denial of the capability of such texts to lay down the *Laying of Fire*, yet "the reply that is given is with the view that the objector is ignorant of "the forms of the texts themselves.

"*Question*: 'How can these texts, that are actually found to lay "down something else, be said to enjoin the *Laying of Fire*?'

"In reply to this, the *Bhāshya* brings forward an Apparent Incon-"sistency: In accordance with the *Sūtra* VII—iii—28, we find that the "actions mentioned in these texts include within themselves the sacrificial "Fire also; and inasmuch as the sacrificial Fire could not be brought "about by any other means save that of *Laying*, the Injunction of the "Action naturally includes that of the *Laying of Fire* also.

"*Then again, if the sentence were taken as laying down the relationship "of the Brāhmaṇa with both the Vasanta and the Laying of Fire, then there "would be a syntactical split.* That is to say, we can admit of the injunc-"tion of a qualified object, only when all other ways of Injunction are "found to be impossible; in the case in question, however, we find that "the simple method of Injunction is quite possible; and as such we can-"not admit of a qualified Injunction."

THE SIDDHĀNTA-BHĀSHYA.

To the above arguments we make the following reply: As in the previous *Adhikaraṇa*, so here also, the sentences in question serve to lay down the *Laying of Fire. Because such Laying is not subsidiary to the actions.* That is to say, if the *Laying of Fire* were subsidiary to the Actions, then there could be a question as to whether it is implied by these or not. As a matter of fact, however, we find that, in accordance with law laid down under *Sūtra* VII—iii—29, the Actions end with the inclusion of the *Āhavanīya* and other sacrificial Fires; and there is no reason to show that the *Laying of Fire* is a subsidiary part of them.

Though in *Sūtra* III—vi—15, the *Laying of Fire* is spoken of as helping *all actions*, yet, this will be explained as merely referring to the fact of the *Laying* helping the *Fire*, which helps to accomplish all Actions.

"*Question*: '*But what, if it be so* (*i.e.*, even if the *Laying* be not a "part of the Actions, how does that affect the present question)? The "sense of this is that even the Action could also imply, through

"Apparent Inconsistency, the subsidiary (*Laying*) of its own subsidiary "(*Fire*)."

"The reply to this is that what is done by Apparent Inconsistency is that "the *texts, laying down the fulfilment of certain desirable ends by means of cer- "tain actions, indicate the Fires, and not the Laying of these.* (Because it is "possible for the Fire to be obtained by asking for it from another *Agni- "hotri*, therefore there is no Apparent Inconsistency in the Fire that would "necessarily point to the *Laying*.)

"*Question: 'But Laying is the means of having the sacrificial Fires.* "We take the mere material form of the object, only in cases where that "object is capable of being brought about by the ordinary ways of the "world,—as for instance, in the case of such objects as a piece of Cloth, "a Cart, and the like; the sacrificial Fires, however, are not capable of "being brought by means such worldly ways; and hence it is absolutely "necessary for the means of their accomplishment to be mentioned or "implied in the Veda itself; and as there is no such means save the *Lay- "ing*, this also is implied by the *Fires* (*i.e.*, by the Apparent Inconsistency "of the Fires, which would not be possible without the *Laying*)."

Answer: It is not so, because of there being no such absolutely invariable connection. That is to say, *Laying* is not the only means of obtaining the Fires, which could be obtained by many such means as *begging, pur-chase*, and so forth. And all these methods would supply the only defi-ciency of the sacrificial Fires that is felt in the texts speaking of certain desirable results; and hence there is no absolutely certain indication of the *Laying* (by the Fires or by the Actions); and as such there is room for the Restrictive Injunctions of the Laying of Fire (as by means of the sentences in question).

The following argument might here be urged: "The Fires, obtained "by such means as *begging* and the like, could not have the character of "'*sacrificial* fires'; because this character depends upon the fact of the "Fire having undergone certain purificatory rites."

Reply: Though it is true that, in the first instance, the three sacri-ficial Fires (the *Dakshiṇāgni*, the *Gārhapatya* and the *Āhavanīya*) are pro-duced by means of *Laying*,—yet, when they have been once thus duly prepared (by one person), there would be nothing to deter another person from subsequently obtaining those Fires by the means of *begging*, etc., just as we find in the case of the Corn. That is to say, in the case of the Corn, we find that though it is not possible for the Corn to be originally produced by any other means save that of *agriculture*, yet it is not necessary for all men to obtain it by the same means; as it could be very well obtained even by purchase, etc. (after it has been once produced by the farmer by means of agriculture). In the same manner, in the beginning one man would produce the sacrificial Fires by the orthodox method of *Laying*; and then other people would obtain it from him by the other means of *begging*, etc. Just as we find the potter making jar after jar, and selling it and giving it away,—so in the same manner, any one person would go on producing the Fires by the orthodox method, and then selling them or giving them away to other persons. Thus then, as the *Laying of the Fire* would have been laid down by such texts as '*Agnihotram juhuyāt svargakāmaḥ*,' in one case (of the first man who would produce the Fires by the orthodox method), while in other cases (of other people), it would not have been laid down by those texts. And as such there is distinct room for the laying down of the *Laying of Fire* (at least for the sake of those persons who could not obtain it by other means). Though we shall show later on that even in the other case, it was not possible for the Laying to have been laid down by those other texts.

If, on the other hand, the sentence in question be taken as the direct Injunction of *Laying*, then it at once sets aside the possibility of all other means of obtaining the Fire; specially as, in that case, the *Ātmanēpada* affix in '*ādadhita*' distinctly shows that the result of the *Laying* would accrue to him alone who actually does the *Laying*; consequently the accomplishment of the Sacrificial Fires, which is the result of the *Laying*, would not belong to one who does not himself perform the *Laying*; for whom the Fire, even if obtained from one who has duly laid it, would be as *non-sacrificial* as ever. While if the Injunction of the *Laying* be taken to be implied in the texts speaking of certain results as following from the *Agnihotra*, etc.,—then, inasmuch as such an inferred Injunctive sentence would contain neither the *Parasmaipada* nor the *Ātmanēpada* affix, the result of the *Laying* would accrue equally to one who has and who has not performed it; and hence, there would be nothing to set aside the emyloying of the other means—begging, etc.—of obtaining the Sacrificial Fires. And hence it would be absolutely necessary for the *Laying* to be directly enjoined.

And further, so long as we have direct declarations of the Laying of Fire,—in the shape of the sentences in question,—no other texts can be taken to merely imply such an Injunction. That is to say, such texts cannot be accepted as enjoining the *Laying* even for the first person who could seek to prepare the Sacrificial Fire. It has been explained above that all Restrictive Injunctions serve to lay down something not mentioned before; because so long as there is a direct Injunction, there can be no assumption of an implied one. And as a matter of fact, we have direct Declarations of the *Laying of Fire*; and hence it is not possible for any to be merely indirectly assumed or inferred. If there were no such direct declarations, then, in that case, inasmuch as without a properly laid Fire, the performance of the *Agnihotra* and the rest would be impossible, the Injunction of these sacrifices would become meaningless; and hence in that case these Injunctions would, for their own sake, imply the Injunction of the due *Laying* of Fire. But when we have such direct declarations, there can be no assumption of these; as it is not right to assume that which is not mentioned in the Veda; specially when it is so that the other texts also, that speak of certain results following from certain sacrifices, lay down actions that are to be performed only by those for whom the sentences in question lay down the *Laying of Fire*.

With a view to set aside all the arguments that have been hurled against him, the *Pūrvapakshi* retorts: "There is a direct Injunction of "*Laying*, other than the sentences in question, the existence whereof "makes these latter merely denotative of certain conditions;—and that "Injunction we have in the sentence '*ya ēvam vidvānagnīnādhattē, etc.*'"

The reply to this is that *this text that you have brought forward only serves the purpose of laying down the preparatory details of the Laying.*

The opponent thinks that the preparatory details are laid down elsewhere in the Context by means of a sentence which is distinct from the sentence '*ya ēvam, etc.*'; and with this in view he replies by saying—"The sentence that I have brought forward is the one that serves as the "originative Injunction of *Laying*; because this sentence, speaking as it "does of the *Laying of Fire*, cannot be taken as serving the same purpose "as the sentences speaking of the *fetching of water* and the other prepara-"tory details."

Reply: The difference in the purposes served by the two sentences—'*ya ēvam vidvān, etc.*' and that mentioning the *Fetching of Water, etc.*—would have syntactically separated them, only if the former actually laid down the *Laying of Fire*. This *Laying*, however, we find to be laid down in the sentence '*Brāhmaṇo vasantē, etc.*'; and as such the mention of it again in the sentence '*ya evam, etc.*' is only for the purpose of laying down the preparatory details.

Question: "But how is it ascertained which of the two sentences—"'*vasantē, etc.*' and '*ya ēvam, etc.*'—is the real originative Injunction of "the *Laying*?"

Answer: In the sentence '*vasantē, etc.*', we find the Injunction *directly expressed* (by the word '*ādadhīta*'), while in the case of the other sentence —'*ya ēvam, etc.*'—it would be got at, very indirectly, from out of the *Arthavāda* therein contained—'*ya ēvam . . . . sapatnam bhrātṛvyam avārtim sahatē.*'

That is to say, if both sentences were equally injunctive (of *Laying*), then the object of both being the same, there could have been some rivalry between them, as to which one should be accepted as the true

Injunction. As it is, however, one sentence—'*vasantē, etc.*'—is injunctive, while the other—'*ya ēvam, etc.*'—is only eulogistic. And certainly a mere eulogistic sentence cannot set aside the Injunctiveness of the sentence '*vasantē, etc.*,' because an eulogy is a helper (and not an obstructor) of Injunctions. If, on the other hand, the sentence '*ya ēvam. etc.*' had the character of the Injunction, then, inasmuch as the enjoining of what has already been enjoined once would be most improbable, our theory might have been thwarted. As a matter of fact, however, the case is that the *Laying* having been enjoined by means of the Injunctive affix (in '*ādadhīta*'), the other sentence—'*ya ēvam, etc.*'—speaks of it only for the purpose of eulogising the preparatory details connected with it; and as such it can have no injunctive character. Then again, the injunction of the Root-meaning ('*dhā*' in '*ādadhīta*') by means of the Injunctive affix, occurring in the same word, is got at by *direct denotation*; while it is only indirectly, through syntactical connection, that an eulogistic sentence could point to such an Injunction, which, in this case, can, at best, be only an assumed or inferred one; and certainly an indirectly assumed Injunction has its injunctiveness very much farther removed than that of one expressed directly.

Objection: "*That 'the Brāhmaṇa should lay the fire' is also a sentence.* That is to say, in this sentence also, it is only by *syntactical connection* that the Injunction (contained in the word '*ādadhīta*' is connected with the *Brāhmaṇa*, etc."

Reply: So long as the *Laying* itself is directly enjoined (by the Injunctive affix in '*ādadhīta*'), it does not matter whether all the rest—the connection of the *Brāhmaṇa*—is implied by syntactical connection. In the case of the other sentence, on the other hand, there is no eulogy expressed in the same word (that speaks of the *Laying*—'*ādhattē*'); and it is got at only when that word is joined on to the words '*sapatnam bhrātṛvyamavartim sahatē*'; and thus in this case, the *Laying* too is connected with the eulogy, only by means of syntactical connection.

In the case of the sentence '*vasantē, etc.*,' we can avoid the syntactical split, by taking it as the injunction of *the Laying of Fire as qualified by a particular performer and a particular time.* And thus there can be no doubt as to the injunctiveness of the sentences in question.

ADHIKARAṆA (4).

[*The Dākshāyaṇa, etc., are accessories.*]

Sūtra **(5): "The Dākshāyaṇa, etc., are enjoined as distinct "actions; (1) because of the particular names attached to "them."**

[In connection with *Darça-Pūrṇamāsa*, we find the sentence, '*Dākshāyaṇa-yajñēna yajēta prajākāmaḥ, sākamprasthāpyēna yajēta paçukāmaḥ, sankramayāgēna yajēta annādyakāmaḥ.*' And in connection with this there arises a doubt as to whether these sentences simply lay down certain accessories for the *Darça-Pūrṇamāsa* as bringing about certain definite results, or they lay down distinct sacrifices, independent of the *Darça-Pūrṇamāsa.*]

PŪRVAPAKSHA.

"In connection with the sentence '*dadhnēndriyakāmasya juhuyāt,*' "it has been shown above (II—ii—25, 26) that this sentence lays down "a certain result following from a certain accessory of the same sacrifice. "And this is quite proper; because in that case the *Dadhi* is not mentioned "as co-extensive with the *Homa*; and as such it could not be taken as "a name of the *Homa*, that would, on account of this name, be taken as "different from the previous *Homa*. In the case in question, on the other "hand, we find that the name '*Dākshāyaṇa*' is mentioned as co-extensive "(identical) with the *Sacrifice*, and has not been applied to the pre-"vious sacrifice (the *Darça-Pūrṇamāsa*); consequently, in this case, there "can be nothing incongruous in the fact of the word '*Dākshāyaṇa*' pointing "to a distinct *sacrifice*, qualified by that name. Nor is there any such "substance as '*Dākshāyaṇa*' known to exist, as we do find those like "the *Dadhi*. Consequently, on account of the reasons shown under II—i "—1, we conclude that, inasmuch as the sentence lays down a *sacrifice* "with reference to a definite result, that sacrifice is wholly distinct from "the previous *Darça-Pūrṇamāsa*."

Sūtra **(6): "(2) Because the Injunction of the Action does not "pertain to the Accessory."**

"That is to say, the Injunctive potency of the sentence in ques-"tion has not been removed away from the Action, so that it could "go over to the Accessory."

***Sūtra* (7): "(3) Because the sentence is quite complete with the mention of the Result."**

"Inasmuch as the Result can never form the object of Injunction, the sentence cannot be said to lay down the Result with "reference to the Sacrifice,—in the same way as the Corn is taken as laid "down, in the sentence '*vrīhibhiryajēta*'; and as such the sentence "must be taken as enjoining an Action (as no third object of Injunction "is possible in the sentence); and (inasmuch as no Action that has already "been enjoined once could form the object of another Injunction) "it must be admitted that the Action herein enjoined is distinct "from all—*Darça-Pūrṇamāsa, etc.*—that have been enjoined before."

SIDDHĀNTA.

***Sūtra* (8): It is a modification (of the previous sacrifice), because of the Context.**

Even though the sentence be the injunction of Action, yet, that Action cannot be any other than the one laid down before,—for reasons shown under *Sūtra* II—iii—26; specially as the sentence is found to bring about an idea of the (causal) relationship between an Accessory (*Dākshāyaṇa*) and a Result (acquiring of children);—just as in the case of the sentence '*dadhnēndriyakāmasya, etc.*,' it must be admitted that the sacrifice referred to is the same that has been laid down before.

It has been argued that there is no Accessory known as '*Dākshāyaṇa*.' But this is scarcely true; because the fact of there being such an accessory is pointed out by the Context itself—just as are many other accessories, like the *Ukthya* and the rest; that is to say, we find in the Context that after the sentence in question has laid down the *Dākshāyaṇa* as an Accessory, there is another sentence that points out the actual form of that Accessory.

And just as in the case of *Dadhi*, so here also, the *Dākshāyaṇa* is not to be taken as co-extensive or identical with the *Sacrifice*.

And further, even if the *Dākshāyaṇa*, etc., be taken as co-extensive with '*sacrifice*,' then too, on account of their proximity to the *Dadhi*, etc., these sacrifices would be recognised as mere modifications (of the *Darça-Pūrṇamāsa*). Consequently, even in this case, what the sentence would do would be to lay down the Result following from a modification of the *Darça-Pūrṇamāsa*, and not from any other sacrifice wholly distinct from it.

In this way, an utter disruption of the Context would also be avoided.

Though there will be a rupture of the Context in connection with the *Dākshāyaṇa* to this extent, that that which is mentioned as leading to a definite Result (*e.g.*, the *Dākshāyaṇa*) cannot be taken as part of the procedure,—yet inasmuch as the *Darça-Pūrṇamāsa* would form the substrate of the *Dākshāyaṇa*, the mention of the *Darça-Pūrṇamāsa* could very well be connected with subsequent sentences (under consideration), and thus help them (in their denotation).

Sūtra (9): **Also because we find Vedic texts indicative (of non-difference).**

[We have the sentence—'*Trinçatam varshāṇi Darça-pūrṇamāsabhyām yajēta; yadi Dākshāyaṇayājī syāt atho api pancadaçaiva varshāṇi yajēta; atra hi ēva sā sampadyatē; dvē hi paurṇamāsyau yajēta dvē amāvāsyē, ātra hi ēva khalu sā sampad bhavati.*' ('One should perform the *Darça-Pūrṇamāsa* for thirty years; but if the sacrificer happens to be a performer of the *Dākshāyaṇa*, he could finish it in fifteen years .... as in this sacrifice two *Paurṇamāsīs* and two *Darças* are performed; and hence the requisite number of these latter would be completed by the *Dākshāyaṇa* being performed for fifteen years only.']

This completion of the 'thirty years' and the '*Darça-Pūrnamāsa*' (by the performance of the *Dākshāyaṇa*) distinctly indicates the non-difference of the *Dākshāyaṇa* from the *Darça-Pūrṇamāsa*. For the thirty-year course of the *Darça-Pūrṇamāsa* could not be made up by the performance of an altogether different sacrifice (while the text distinctly lays down the fact of the thirty-year course being made up by the fifteen-year course of the *Dākshāyaṇa*). Nor could there be a gratuitous rejection of the thirty-year limit, whereby the fifteen-year course would be due to a different sacrifice (that is to say, the mere performance of an altogether different sacrifice could not justify a rejection of the original thirty-year limit). Nor can it be urged that the course of the *Darça-Pūrṇamāsa* itself is reduced to one of '*fifteen years*' by reason of the performer being a performer of another sacrifice in the shape of the *Dākshāyaṇa*. Because if this latter were wholly distinct from the former, there would be no relationship between the two (whereby the performance of one could reduce the course of another). And also because in that case, there would be no justification for the explanatory sentence '*dvē hi paurṇamāsyau dvē amāvāsyē*' (which lays down the fact of two of each of these being performed in the *Dākshāyaṇa*, instead of only one, as in the case of the ordinary *Darça-Pūrṇamāsa*, as the reason for the thirty-year limit being reduced to one of fifteen only).

Sūtra (10): The name ('*Dākshāyaṇa*') is due to the peculiarity of the Accessory.

(This *Sūtra* meets the *Pūrvapaksha* argument of *Sūtra 6*).

The *Name* serves the purpose of distinguishing an Action from others, only when it occurs in the originative Injunction of that Action, and is not recognized to have a connection with any previous Action. In the case in question, however, we find that the name '*Dākshāyaṇa*' is not connected with any originative Injunction; specially as in this case we do not find the sentence introduced by any word expressing the beginning of a new action,—as we do in the sentence '*atha esha jyotiḥ, etc.*' And then, inasmuch as the Name is quite capable of being explained as mentioning an Accessory of the previous Sacrifice, it cannot serve the purpose of distinguishing the Action. That the word '*Dākshāyaṇa*' denotes a mere repetition of the previous sacrifice of the *Darça-Pūrṇamāsa* is shown by the sense afforded by the components of the word itself, as also by the above-quoted text (that there are two *Darças* and two *Paurṇamāsas*, in the *Dākshāyaṇa*). Hence we conclude, from the Context, that the Result mentioned in the sentence in question follows from the *Dākshāyaṇa* as based upon the *Darça-Pūrṇamāsa*. The word '*Daksha*' means 'the Sacrificer who is expert and very quick at the performance of the sacrifice (of thirty years, in only half the time)'; the Priests appointed by such a sacrificer are '*dāksha*' (appointed by the clever sacrificer); and the '*ayana*' (performance) of these priests is the '*Dākshāyaṇa*' (and thus we find that the constituent parts of the word also point to the same fact that is mentioned in the text quoted above).

The name '*Sākamprasthīya*' also means that the substance referred to by this word is *offered* ('*prasthīyatē*') *along with* ('*sākam*') the smaller vessels, before the cutting up of the *Sānnāyya* cake; and thus this name also is found to belong to a material only, in connection with the previous sacrifice; and hence in this case also, there is nothing to oppose the recognition, in the sentences in question, of the Action that has been mentioned before.

Sūtra (11): There is nothing peculiar in the completion (of the sentence with the mere mention of the result).

[This meets *Sūtra 7.*]

Though the sentence does not enjoin the Result in reference to the Action, yet, inasmuch as it does not speak of any connection between the Action and the Result, the Action herein mentioned cannot be different from the previous sacrifice. Just as the fact of the Result following from the Action has been established under *Sūtra* II—i—1 *et seq.*—so, exactly in the same manner, has it also been shown, under *Sūtra* II—ii—26, that there are certain sentences that serve the sole purpose of establishing the relationship between a Result and a certain Accessory of the previous sacrifice. And hence there being a doubt as to which of these two previous conclusions should be applied to the case in question, the presence of certain other words (such as those cited under *Sūtra* 9) distinctly point to the conclusion that in the present case, the Result is mentioned as following from the Accessory (of the previous sacrifice) and not from any distinct sacrifice.

ADHIKARAṆA (5).

[*Actions mentioned along with Substances and Deities are distinct sacrifices.*]

***Sūtra* (12): "It is a mere preparatory rite, as not occurring "in the Context (of any particular sacrifice); specially as "there is no word denoting an Action."**

Without reference to any particular sacrifice, we find the sentence—'*Vāyavyam çvetamālabhēta bhūtikāmaḥ,*' '*sauryam carum nirvapēt brahmavarchasakāmaḥ.*' And in connection with this there arise the following questions:—I. Inasmuch as, as a general rule, all sentences, not appearing in reference to any particular sacrifice, are taken as serving some purpose of the Action mentioned in the Context,—does the sentence simply lay down the accessories 'Çveta' and 'Caru' respectively of the 'Touching' and 'Preparing,' that form part of the *Darça-Pūrṇamāsa* sacrifice, which is the action mentioned in the Context? or does it lay down two independent and distinct Actions? II. (If the Actions mentioned are distinct and independent), are these actions only those that are mentioned by the actual words of the sentence? or is it these actions as accompanying the 'sacrifice' that are meant?

The fact of the sentence in question not occurring in reference to any particular Action has been specially pointed out, in the Bhāshya, with a view, (1) to show that there is sufficient ground for doubt, (2) that the present *Adhikaraṇa* is not a mere repetition of what has been dealt with before, and also with a view to afford some sort of a ground for the (3) *Pūrvapaksha* and (4) its Refutation.

(1) If the 'Touching' and the 'Preparing' had been mentioned in reference to a previously mentioned sacrifice, then the idea of that sacrifice would be present when we came across the sentences in question; and as such there could never be any question of the sentence laying down a distinct sacrifice. While when they do not appear in reference to any such sacrifice, inasmuch as the accessories of *Çvēta, etc.*, are quite capable of forming the objects of Injunction, it might be that these might be taken as enjoined with reference to the 'Touching' and the 'Preparing' spoken of at a distance (in the sentence laying down the *Darça-Pūrṇamāsa*);

or it might be that no idea of that previous sacrifice being present in the mind at the time, the sentence may be taken as laying down a distinct Action; and thus the matter would be doubtful.

(2) The sentence in question would, at first sight, appear as laying down an Action connected with the 'sacrifice,' and hence as having been already dealt with under *Sūtra* II—ii—17. But as the sentence in question does not appear with reference to any sacrifice, and hence there is no sacrifice, in this case, which could be referred to by it,—secondly, as the accessories of '*Çvēta*,' etc., are quite capable of being laid down by themselves with reference to the Action connected with the substances mentioned in that sentence itself,—the injunction of an action connected with the 'sacrifice' could, in the case in question, scarcely be got at; and hence it becomes necessary to take up its consideration on the present occasion.

(3) It is only when the sentence does not refer to any previous action that the *Pūrvapaksha* could have the slightest semblance of plausibility; because, no other 'Touching' and 'Preparing' being found in the same Context with the sentence in question, it could not but be taken as laying down certain accessories with reference to the original 'Touching' and 'Preparing' (of the *Darça-Pūrṇamāsa*).

(4) The Refutation of this *Pūrvapaksha* also would be possible only when the sentence in question is known as not occurring in reference to any previous sacrifice. Because then alone could it be argued that, inasmuch as the sentence does not occur in any particular Context, it could have no distinguishing feature whereby it could pertain to the original 'Touching' and 'Preparing'; specially as the connection of these is actually found to be materially impossible; and as such these original 'Touching' and 'Preparing' could never be mentioned in the sentence in question.

The 'Touching' and the 'Preparing' have been spoken of in the Bhāshya as '*guṇavidhi*,' because they form the objects of the *guṇavidhi*.

On the above questions, we have, at first, the following

PŪRVAPAKSHA A.

"Just as in the case of the *Dākshāyaṇa* it has been found (in "the foregoing *Adhikaraṇa*) that, the sentence mentioning the connection "of the Accessory, and thus there being no word injunctive of any Action, "the sentence could not be taken as laying down a distinct Action, "—so would it also be in the case in question. This similarity "between the two cases is what is implied by the word '*ca*' in the "*Sūtra*.

"The *Sūtra* mentions the word '*aprakaraṇē*' with a view to "point out the exact object, with regard to which the sentence in "question would lay down the Accessories. Or it may mean that, "though there is this difference between the sentence in question "and that dealt with in the previous Adhikaraṇa, that the present one "does not appear in the Context of any particular Action,—yet inasmuch "as the connection of the original action (*Darça-Pūrṇamāsa*) is not "obstructed by the presence of the Injunction, in the sentence, of "any other Action, the sentence must be taken as mentioning the "original actions of 'Touching' and 'Preparing', only with a view to lay "down certain accessories in connection with them. Hence the sentence "'*Çvētamalabhēta*' must be taken as enjoining that the *Cart-pole* at "the *Darça-Pūrṇamāsa should be touched* after it has been made "*white*; and similarly the sentence '*carum nirvapēt*' should be "taken as enjoining that the 'preparing' (or holding), at the same "*Darça-Pūrṇamāsa*, is to be of the *Caru* (boiled rice), or that it is "to be measured by the *Rice*.

"Then, as for the mention of the results of 'prosperity' and "'Brahmic glory' spoken of in the sentence as following from 'Touching' "and 'Preparing', it would be a mere reference to the same results "following from the *Darça-Pūrṇamāsa*, which is specially spoken of "as accomplishing *all* desirable results.

"Then as for the word '*Vāyavyam*,' that too could be taken as "only referring to the *cart-pole* of the *Darça-Pūrṇamāsa*; because "the pole is made of the *wood* of a certain tree, and *Vāyu* is the presiding "Deity of all trees. And as for the word '*Saurya*,' that would be "a reference to the *Āgnēya* cake of the *Darça-Pūrṇamāsa*, because "both *Agni* and *Sūrya* are the deities of Light.

"For these reasons we conclude that the sentences serve to lay "down accessories for the Actions mentioned in connection with the "*Darça-Pūrṇamāsa*."

***Sūtra* (13): "Mere 'Touching' and 'Preparing' are the distinct "actions laid down by the sentences; because all Actions "are based upon Direct Vedic Declarations."**

[In reply to the above *Pūrvapaksha* we have the following arguments, which, however, embody another Theory not acceptable to us, and which is refuted in the next *Sūtra*. Hence this is treated as a distinct *Pūrvapaksha*.]

PURVAPAKSHA B.

"If 'Touching' and 'Preparing' were wholly incapable of "having the character of the *enjoined*, then alone could the sentences in "question be taken as laying down mere Accessories. As a matter of "fact, however, it is those Actions themselves that are meant to be enjoined "by the sentence.

"For the present we lay aside the word '*Vāyavya*,' and proceed "to refute the aforesaid arguments, on the basis of the word express-"ing the result.

"If the '*White*' and the 'Rice' be taken as laid down with refer-"ence to previous 'Touching' and 'Preparing,' then the mention of "the Results (Prosperity and Brahmic glory) would be wholly meaning-"less. For even if the mention of these were mere references to the "'all results' following from the *Darça-Pūrṇamāsa*, then too the parti-"cular results of 'Prosperity' and 'Brahmic glory' would be only "two among the many alternative results; and as such the mention "of these as if they were the only results would not be quite compatible. "If again, these Results be taken as mentioned by way of qualifica-"tions, then there would be a syntactical split. If then the sentences "be taken as laying down the relationship between the Accessory and the "Result, then, inasmuch as the original 'Touching,' etc., of the "*Darça-Pūrṇamāsa* would not be capable of serving as the substrate "of this relationship, the sentence itself would also have to lay down "the connection of the necessary substrate; and this would entail a "syntactical split.

"Whereas there is no objection to the view that the sentence "lays down the *Touching* as qualified by '*white*';—it is with a view to "this that the *Sūtra* says—*because actions are based upon Direct Vedic* "*Declarations.* That is to say, in the case in question, it is the Action that, "being the object of Injunction, is based upon the authority of that "Declaration; and hence the Injunction of the mere Property of "'*white*' would not have the authority of the Veda.

"Or, the *Sūtra* may be taken as follows: The action meant to "be laid down *is just what is distinctly mentioned*, and not as accompanied "by '*Sacrifice*'; *because the only basis for Actions is Direct Declaration*; "that is to say, the element of '*Sacrifice*' not being mentioned in the text, "it could not well be accepted as enjoined by it. Nor is that "element so very necessary that without it nothing can be accomplished; "as it is quite possible for the 'Touching' and the 'Preparing' to bring "about the Results, and thus serve as the Principal Actions. Specially as "there is no ground for believing that the Action that has once been known "as subsidiary to another, can never appear as a Principal Action, "even when it is actually spoken of as such; because the Principal or "subsidiary character of an Action depends upon the Veda; and "there is nothing inherent in the Actions themselves that would mark "them out as the one or the other.

"As for the word '*Vāyavyam*' (which might be urged as pointing "to the fact of the 'white object' being *offered to the Deity Vāyu*, which "offering would constitute a *sacrifice*), it could be explained away, as being "a mere reference, on the ground that all substances are capable of "being, in some way or other, related to certain deities (even without "their being actually *offered* to them). Or, the sentence might be "taken to mean that—'when one has set aside a certain object for "the sake of *Vāyu*, if we happen to *touch* it, it would bring prosperity "to us.' And as the sentence embodies a qualified Injunction, "there would not be any very great trouble in taking the sentences "thus. Or, the sentences might mean that the desirable results are ob-"tained as soon as the white object is touched for the sake of Vāyu, "or when the boiled rice is prepared for the sake of the Sun. And cer-"tainly it is not in a *sacrifice* alone that anything can be done for "the sake of certain Deities. Because there is no incompatibility "in something being done for the sake of a certain Deity, whenever "that happens to be enjoined for being done as such (even if it be not a "sacrifice). Therefore all that the sentence in question means, in "accordance with the expressed Injunction, is that 'something "white should be touched for the sake of *Vāyu*.'

"Having shown that there is a syntactical split, if the sentence "be taken as laying down an Accessory, and then, the connection of "the Result,—the Bhāshya now grants, for the sake of argument, the "rejection or neglect of the word expressing the result; and then "it proceeds to show anomalies in the above *Purvapaksha*: *Atha vā* "*yo'sau vidhāyakaḥ çabdaḥ*, etc. The sense of this is that, though it will "be said later on that the sentences that do not appear in connection "with any particular Action serve the purpose of mentioning some-"thing for the original Action of the Context,—yet, this declaration is not "one that has an absolute verbal authority; as it is only based upon "the fact of these factors mentioned in the sentences being otherwise in-"capable of serving any useful purpose, apart from the original action. In "the case in question, however, we find that the existence of 'Touching' "and 'Preparing' elsewhere (*i.e.*, apart from the original action) is not "wholly impossible,—because they are met with even in ordinary worldly "experience. Then if the 'Touching' were meant to be specified in the "sentence in question with the sole purpose of precluding the 'touching' "of the ordinary world,—then, there being no other specifying word, the "specification would have to be done by the Injunctive affix itself; and "hence all that the word '*ālabhēta*' could mean would be '*that touching which has been laid down as something to be done*'; and the potency of the "Injunctive having been wholly spent up in this, any further injunction "of the Accessory would be absolutely impossible. Nor can the "single injunctive word '*ālabhēta*' serve the twofold purpose of indicat-"ing the former '*Touching*', and laying down the accessory '*white.*' "If again the word '*ālabhēta*' be taken as referring only to the *Root-meaning* (the *Touching* previously mentioned), then as the mere '*Touch-ing*' would exist in the ordinary world also, the accessory would come "to be enjoined for such ordinary *Touching* also; and as such Injunction "of the accessory for the ordinary *Touching* would not bring about any "results, the word would become meaningless. But this mere meaning-"lessness, without the action of any Context, etc., cannot lead us to accept "only the Verdic 'Touching' and 'Preparing' as to be meant by the "sentences in question.

"And hence, there being no ground for connecting the sentences with "any original Action mentioned before, they must be taken as laying "down a distinct '*Touching*' and '*Preparing*.'"

SIDDHANTA.

***Sūtra* (14): But the 'sacrifice' is laid down; because of the mention of the enjoyer of the Substance and the Result, which are related to some sort of an Action.**

Just as the presence of the word speaking of the Result has been urged as setting aside the former *Pūrvapaksha* that the sentences lays down an Accessory,—so, in the same manner the latter Pūrvapaksha also, which holds mere 'Touching' to be the object enjoined, can be refuted by means of the words expressing the Deities ('*Vāyavyam*' and '*Sauryam*').

Inasmuch as, as a matter of fact, the Injunction in question depends upon each of the words contained in the sentence, it must be taken, in the case in question, as pertaining to the relationship of the substance, the Deity and the word ('*vāyavyam*') expressing that relationship. And as the relationship would not be possible without the action of '*sacrifice*,' it naturally implies such an Action; specially as no other action is capable of bringing about that relationship. For if we were to *touch* the subtsance, without offering it to the Deity *Vāyu*, it would not be '*vāyavya.*' Nor can the sentence be taken to mean that we should touch only that particular substance which is ordinarily known as '*vāyarya*' (dedicated to Vayu); because such dedication to a Deity can be brought about only by *performance*. Hence the sentence could not but be taken as meaning that 'the white substance should be offered to Vāyu'; and from this we conclude that the sentence is the Injunction of a 'sacrifice' (in the shape of offering). Because the 'Injunction of Sacrifice' will be defined later on as '*yajaticodanā dravyadēvatakriyām samudāyē krīyārthatvāt*' (IV—ii—27).

And thus the 'touching' and 'preparing' mentioned in the sentences in question would be mere 'references' to the same Actions mentioned in the original Injunction (in connection with the *Darça-Pūrṇamāsa*).

Though the Pūrvapakshi has brought forward the objection of the highly complicated character of the theory of the sentence being a qualified Injunction,—yet as it must have been carelessly brought forward, and that too against an assumed adversary, we take no notice of it here (because we do not hold to that theory; what we hold is that the Injunction is of the *Sacrifice* only, there being mere references to *Touching* and *Preparing*).

Sūtra (15): Also because we find texts indicating the same conclusion.

We have the text—'*Saumāraudran carun nirvapēt. . . . pariçritē yajēta*'; and in this as soon as the word '*saumāraudram*' (which speaks of the connection of the Caru with the Deities *Soma* and *Rudra*) has been uttered, though there is no word expressing 'sacrifice,'—yet, inasmuch as the sentence '*pariçritē yajēta*,' which lays down the proper *cooking of the rice*, refers to a previous *Sacrifice* by the word '*yajēta*,'—we always recognize the sentence as laying down a certain action connected with 'sacrifice.' In fact, in the case of the sentence '*agnīshomīyam paçumālabhēta*,' it is only by the above reason that the presence of 'sacrifice' is admitted.

In the previous *Adhikaraṇa* we considered the question as to whether the sentence is an Injunction or a mere reference to a previous Action; while what we have considered in the present *Adhikaraṇa* is the question as to,—the Injunctive character having been established,—what sort of an Action (either mere *Touching or Sacrifice*) is enjoined by it. And as such there is no mere useless repetition.

ADHIKARAṆA (6).

[*The Touching of the Calf, etc., is a mere purificatory rite.*]

***Sūtra* (16): In a doubtful case, the correct conclusion is arrived at by a perception of similarity.**

Some people declare that—'whatever is mentioned in glosses and commentaries is present in the *Sūtra*; as it is the *Sūtra* that is the source of all meanings; everything is contained in *the Sūtra*.'

And against these people the following is urged: A reason never establishes its conclusion until the form of this effect has been duly shown. And, as a matter of fact, we find the *Sūtra* mentioning only the reason,—'*prāyadarçanāt*.' Nor is the meaning of the *Sūtra* or the *Context*, etc., capable of showing what special instance is meant to be dealt with, or what the question and conclusion are? Thus then the *Sūtra* being altogether unintelligible, it devolves upon the commentators to try and remove this deficiency of the *Sūtra*. Specially as the supplying of words, from outside, into the *Sūtra*, has been prohibited, only with reference to such *Sūtras* as are quite explicable without it; and all that is meant by that prohibition is that, inasmuch as the sole motive of the author of the *Sūtra* is to train the intellect of the pupil, only that much of extraneous matter should be assumed, without which the *Sūtra* would be inexplicable, and all sorts of matter are not to be saddled on to it.

And hence inasmuch as the subject, etc., of the *Adhikaraṇa* have not been mentioned in the *Sūtra*, the author of the *Vṛtti* shows what they are. This is how people explain the *Bhāshya*, when it proceeds to draw upon the gloss of Upavarsha.

In connection with the present *Sūtra*, Upavarsha has cited the sentence '*vatsamālabhēta*,' found in the *Agnihotra* section, in connection with the *milking of the cow*. And he has shown that, with regard to this sentence also, we have a threefold doubt: (1) Does the sentence lay down the *calf* with the reference to the 'Touching' originally mentioned in the Context? (2) Or, does it lay down mere '*Touching*'? (3) Or does it lay down a '*Sacrifice*'?

As to the first alternative, it has been left out, because, there being no specification in the sentence, there is nothing in it to point to the

'Touching' previously mentioned in the Context;—as shown in the foregoing *Adhikaraṇa*.

And inasmuch as the conclusion arrived at in the foregoing *Adhikaraṇa* points to the fact of the sentence under consideration here also being the Injunction of a *Sacrifice*, the Bhāshya proceeds to explain the present Adhikaraṇa as an exception to the foregoing one.

Though, as a matter of fact, on account of the sentence dealt with here being a counter-instance of the foregoing *Siddhānta* argument based upon the connection of the *Enjoyer*, the *Pūrvapaksha* of the present *Adhikaraṇa* has almost wholly been represented (in the shape of the *Siddhānta* of the foregoing *Adhikaraṇa*); yet the *Bhāshya* proceeds to present it afresh; because of the peculiar character of the intellect of certain persons; as there are some people, so imbued with the idea of the Logician, that they think of interpreting the Veda also by means of Inferences from similarity; and these persons would never grasp the fact of the *Pūrvapaksha* having been refuted, unless it has been duly set forth previously.

Some people accept the word '*ālabhēta*' as synonymous with '*sacrifice*,' on the strength of the foregoing *Adhikaraṇa*; while others take it as merely implying the 'sacrifice'; and it is both these views that they bring forward in connection with the sentence in question also. And we have in connection with this a twofold

PŪRVAPAKSHA:—

namely: "(1) The sentence in question lays down a distinct sacrifice,— "(2) it lays down the *calf* in connection with the sacrifice that has been "laid down previously."

THE SIDDHĀNTA

view is that in the case of the sentence dealt with in the foregoing *Adhikaraṇa*, we accepted the injunction of the 'sacrifice,' on the sole ground of the relationship between the substance and the Deity therein mentioned (by the word '*vāyavyam*'),—and not, either on the strength of a newly-discovered expressive potency of the word '*ālabhēta*,' or on that of a fallacious Inference (of the implication of 'sacrifice' by the word '*ālabhēta*'). In the case in question, however, as we have no word expressive of the said relationship (of Deity and Substance), we must take the word '*ālabhēta*' in its simple direct signification. Thus would the similarity of the present '*touching*' with the purificatory secondary actions of *cow-milking* and the like be explained; as the 'Touching' also would be a mere secondary rite; and this 'touching of the calf' at the particular time of milking the cow, would serve a visible purpose of making the cow yield more milk.

Sūtra (17): Also because of the possibility of the connection with the particular Arthavāda.

Close upon the sentence in question we have the sentence '*vatsanikāntā hi paçavaḥ*' ('Animals love their young ones dearly'); and this could be taken as an *Arthavāda* showing a reason for the previous Injunction, only when the preceding sentence '*vatsamālabhēta*' is taken as enjoining the 'touching' by way of fondling it for the purpose of making the cow yield more milk [the two sentences together meaning that 'one should touch (fondle) the calf, with a view to the cow yielding more milk, *because animals love their young dearly*'].

If, on the other hand, the word '*ālabhēta*' meant 'touching for the purpose of killing' (by way of offering to a Deity), the mention of the fact of the young being dearly loved by animals would be wholly irrelevant; for in that case the purport of the two sentences would be this: 'Because the calf is loved by its mother, therefore it should be touched for being killed'—certainly not a very relevant proposition! In the other case (*i.e.*, when '*ālabhēta*' means *touching by way of fondling*) it would be quite natural to expect that, inasmuch as the cow is fond of the calf, if we fondle the calf, or the calf fondles us, the cow would be moved to yield more milk, the flow of which would be accelerated by the sight of her calf being fondled.

Thus also, it must be admitted that the sentence in question lays down mere '*Touching*' as a secondary action calculated to serve a useful purpose.

ADHIKARAṆA (7).

[*The Naivāra Caru is for the purposes of Ādhāna.*]

***Sūtra* (18): As connected with the word mentioning an Action, it must be taken as being for the sake of that Action; specially as such is the direct signification of the words of the text.**

The Adhikaraṇa before last having dealt with the significations of the words '*ālabhēta*' and '*nirvapēt*' as contained in the sentences '*çvetamālabhēta*' and '*sauryañcarunnirvapēt*,'—the last *Adhikaraṇa* has dealt with the counter-instance of the first part of that Adhikaraṇa; and the present *Adhikaraṇa* proceeds to deal with the counter-instance of the second portion dealing with the 'Preparing' in connection with the *boiled rice*. Nor is the case of this exactly similar to that dealt with in the foregoing *Adhikaraṇa*; as in this we have a further ground of doubt, in the shape of the mention of a Deity (Bṛhaspati).

[In connection with '*Agni*,' we meet with the sentence '*naivāraçcarurbhavati*,' and then '*yadēnam carumupadadhāti*'; and here arises the question as to whether the *boiled rice* is laid down for the purpose of the sacrifice (the sense of the texts being that 'having *sacrificed* out of the rice, the remnant is to be *kept* aside), or that it is laid down for the sole purpose of being *kept* aside.]

And on this question, we have the following

PŪRVAPAKSHA.

"The character of a subsidiary to Sacrifices is inherent in all "such substances as *boiled rice, cake* and the like; and hence in all cases, "it is necessary to give up one's ownership of these substances (in favour "of someone else). Consequently, what the word '*upadadhāti*' in the "sentence '*carum upadadhāti*' means is that there is to be a '*pratipatti*' "(keeping aside, throwing away) of the *Caru*; and as no such '*pratipatti*' "of a thing would be possible until it had been already utilised, we are "led to look out for that at which the boiled rice could have been utilised; "and the foremost of all, that which presents itself as being most capable "of affording an occasion for the said utilisation of the Rice, is the "'Sacrifice'; and hence we are led to accept the fact of the *Caru* "being of use at the *sacrifice*. Subsequently too, we meet with the "sentence '*Bṛhaspateretadannam yannivārā, etc.*', which distinctly mentions Bṛhaspati as the Deity of the *Rice*; and under the circumstances, if "the connection between the *Rice* and that Deity were not duly established "by means of a sacrifice, the mention of the Deity would be absolutely "meaningless. Therefore we must take the sentences in question to mean "that—'after having performed the sacrifice of the *Bārhaspatyacaru*, "which forms a part of the *Āgnēya* sacrifice, we should desist, for a "time, from proceeding with the other sacrifices connected with the "*Āgnēya*, and *keep aside* the Rice (that has been offered to Bṛhaspati).'"

SIDDHĀNTA.

To the above we make the following reply: There is nothing inherent in the *Rice* that would always make it employed at sacrifices; in fact the use to which such things are to be put is ascertained by means of the authoritative directions that may be found with regard to them. As soon as the appearance of the *Rice* has been mentioned, we naturally seek for the use to which it could be put; and we are met by the sentence '*yadēnam carum upadadhāti*,' which directly lays down the fact of the *Rice* helping towards the preparation of the altar for the reception of the Fire to be used at the sacrifice. And the Rice thus having its use clearly defined, it could not have any connection with another Action, even if such an action were directly mentioned; and hence it is all the more impossible for it to have anything to do with an Action that is not even mentioned (but only indirectly implied). Nor can the *keeping* spoken of be said to have the character of the *Pratipatti*; because we do not know of any use to which it could be put prior to the *keeping*.

Further, even in the case of an action which is performed with regard to an independent purpose, the *Rice* has a certain predominance over the *keeping*; and hence as unless the Rice is purified by the said *keeping*, it cannot help in the preparation of the altar,—there is nothing incompatible in the presence of the Accusative ending (in '*Carum*').

Then again, inasmuch as there are only three ways of the direct mention of the connection of a Deity [*viz.*, (1) the Nominal Deific affix, (2) the Dative ending, (3) the Indicative words contained in the *mantras*],—the connection of the *Nīvāra Rice* with the Deity Bṛhaspati mentioned in the *Arthavāda* could, at best, be only an implied (or inferred) one; as that *Arthavāda* is devoid of all the three means of directly mentioning the Deity.

That is to say, the Deity Bṛhaspati, being mentioned in connection with the *Nīvara* (in the *Arthavāda* passage), could be connected with the *Rice*, only by a highly complicated process. For instance, (1) first of all, 'Bṛhaspati,' though mentioned in the supplementary *Arthavāda*, would have to be taken as the Deity in reference to the Injunction, which, however, does not stand in need of any such connection of Deity;—then (2), the deific character of Bṛhaspati would have to be assumed, even in the absence of any of the three indicators of Deity—the Nominal Affix and the rest;—and (3) lastly, there would be the necessity of having to assume the fact of the 'sacrifice' being implied by the sentence '*naivāraçcarurbhavati*.'

For these reasons, it is far more reasonable to take the *Caru* (Rice) as serving the purpose of being *kept aside*.

Some people bring forward the supplementary sentence '*Bārhaspatyo bhavati*,' as containing the word '*Bārhaspatyaḥ*,' which is co-extensive with '*caruḥ*,' and which serves to point out, by means of the nominal affix, the Deity connected with the *Caru* (Rice). But for these people also, it would be necessary to take the Injunction, in the very first instance, as pointing to the fact of the *Caru* being for the purpose of being *kept*; and then as there would be no deficiency felt in the Injunction, for want of a Deity, it would not be possible for the sentence to lay down any Deity. Consequently, the present tense in the sentence '*Bārhaspatyo bhavati*' would indicate that the *character of being related to Bṛhaspati*, that is attributed to the *Caru* (in the sentence '*Bṛhaspatervā etadannam yannīvārāḥ*') by way of eulogising it, is the same that we perceive as belonging to it, at the present time; and thus the meaning of the sentence '*Bṛhaspatervā, etc.*' comes to be the same as that of the sentence '*Bārhaspatyo bhavati*' (though this latter occurs in the *Taittiriya* Text, while the former in the *Mādhyandinīya*).

For these reasons we conclude that the sentence in question lays down, not a *sacrifice*, but that alone which it distinctly mentions—*viz.*, the *keeping aside* of the Caru.

ADHIKARAṆA (8).

[The *Tvāshṭra Pātnīvata* is subservient to the *Paryagnikaraṇa.*]

***Sūtra* (19): Inasmuch as the Pātnīvata is recognised as the previous one, the sentence in question must be taken as serving the purpose of precluding (the subsequent subsidiaries).**

In connection with what has gone before, we proceed to consider whether the word '*utsṛjati*' signifies the *sacrifice* or not.

The sacrifice having been laid down in the sentence, '*Tvāshṭram pātnīvatamālabhatē*,' we find another sentence—'*Paryagnikṛtam pātnīvatamutsṛjanti.*' And in connection with this latter sentence, there is a doubt as to whether it lays down an Accessory (to the sacrifice laid down in the former sentence), or a distinct Action,—the doubt being due to the twofold construction of which the sentence is capable. And on this, we have the following

PŪRVAPAKSHA.

"The sentence lays down a distinct Action; because the Injunctive "potency of the sentence pertains, as in the case of the sentence '*vāyavyam çvētamālabhēta*,' to the relationship between the substance and the "Deity.

"And further, inasmuch as the sentence in question does not contain "any mention of *Tvashṭā*, the action mentioned therein cannot be recognised "as the same as that mentioned in the previous sentence (in which the word "*Tvāshṭra* forms an important factor); and (if the action mentioned in "the two sentences be taken as the same on the ground of both sentences "laying down the '*pātnīvata*'), then, on account of the sentence in "question containing the mention of '*paryagnikaraṇa*' also, there would "be a syntactical split (if it laid down the *Pātnīvata* also).

"That is to say, if in the sentence in question, both the words "('*paryagnikṛtam*' and '*pātnīvatam*') were mentioned as mere qualifica-"tions, as the two words ('*tvāshṭra*' and '*pātnīvatam*') are in the pre-"vious sentence,—then the action mentioned in the sentence in question "could be recognized as the same as that mentioned in the previous "sentence. As a matter of fact, however, in the case in question, "we have not even the slightest touch of such a recognition,—as we have "that of '*Mahēndra*' in the *Indrapragātha*; and hence even on account of "the action mentioned in the second sentence being connected with "a distinct Deity (Agni), it cannot but be taken as distinct from that "mentioned before (which is connected with *Tvashṭā* as its Deity).

"If again, the sentence be taken as laying down the '*giving away*' "('*utsṛjati*') with reference to the *Pātnīvata*, then, inasmuch as it is "also found to mention the qualification of '*paryagnikṛtam*,' there would "be a syntactical split; and it would be in an indirect way that the "'giving away' would be connected (with the *paryagnikaraṇa*). And "further, as the '*giving away*' of the *Pātnīvata* has already been men-"tioned in the previous originative Injunction, its repetition in the sentence "in question would be useless (if the Actions were the same). Nor is any "useful purpose served, in the present instance, by the injunction of the "*Paryagnikaraṇa* (in connection with the action in question); because its "existence in that Action is already indicated by its presence in the "original Primary of that Action. Nor can we accept the sentence as "containing an alternative injunction of the Action having *Pātnīvata* for "its Deity; as the position of the Deity is already occupied by *Tvashṭā* "mentioned in the originative Injunction.

"Nor can the difference of the two Actions be asserted on the mere "ground of the repetition of the *Paryagnikaraṇa*, whose helpfulness in the "original Action has been duly ascertained,—as in the case of the *Gṛha-*"*mēdhīya*. Because the sentence in question mentions the *Paryagnikaraṇa* "merely as a subordinate factor. Nor can the word '*Paryagnikaraṇa*' "be taken as denoting the subsidiary procedure ending with the *Paryagni-*"*karaṇa*; and as such the mere mention of the '*Paryagnikṛtam*' "could not serve to separate the part of the procedure ending with the "*Paryagnikaraṇa*, from the subsidiary actions that come after it. Nor "again is the word '*Paryagnikṛtam*' expressive of *time*; and hence the "sentence could not be taken to mean that the *giving away* is to be done "*at the time of the Paryagnikaraṇa*. And there is no ground for taking the "word '*Paryagnikṛtam*' as indirectly indicative of the *time*; specially "when the direct signification of the word makes the sentence quite "compatible and explicable.

"Then again, all the subsidiaries of the sacrifice being equally laid "down as to be performed along with it,—and the performance of none of "these being prohibited by any other sentence,—when the time of the "*Paryagnikaraṇa* comes, all the subsidiaries would come to be performed; "and it could not be definitely known which one of the many subsidiaries "is to be performed at that time; because if all of them were to be "performed at that time, the prescribed time would be transgressed;

"while if attention were paid to the observance of the time (by the "performance of any one of the subsidiaries), that would mean the neglect "of the other subsidiaries (consequently the sentence cannot be taken as "laying down the *time* of the *Paryagnikaraṇa*, for the performance of the "sacrifice mentioned in the previous sentence).

"The same arguments also serve to set aside the view that the "sentence lays down the particular state of the 'giving away'; because "the previous Injunction itself has laid down that the *Pātnīvata* is to be "given away when in the state of the *Paryagni* (and so this could not be "enjoined over again in the sentence in question). If it be urged that "the sentence serves to preclude the condition subsequent to the *Paryagni-"karaṇa*, then that would entail the three anomalies (of *rejecting the "enjoined*, *accepting that which is not enjoined* and so forth, which have "been shown to attach to all Preclusive Injunctions).

"Thus then, we find that in the sentence in question, there is nothing "that could be laid down with reference to the previous sacrifice; and as "such we conclude that it lays down a distinct Action, connected with the "Deity (*Agni*) and the material (*Pātnīvata*),—having for its original "either the sacrifice mentioned in the previous sentence (which has the "same Deity and Accessory), or the Agnīshomīya sacrifice."

SIDDHANTA.

To the above, we make the following reply: Inasmuch as the sacrifice mentioned in the sentence in question is actually recognized as the same as the one mentioned in the previous sentence, we cannot perceive any other sacrifice in it; and what the sentence in question does is to lay down, with regard to the same sacrifice, all the subsidiary procedure ending with the *Paryagnikaraṇa*.

The word '*Pātnīvata*' in the sentence in question can very well denote the previous sacrifice, even though it is accompanied by two qualifications,—just like the word '*agni*' in connection with the *Manotā* sacrifice. And the words '*paryagnikṛtamutsṛjati*' also are cognised, on account of the Context, as laying down an accessory for that same sacrifice.

Objection: "But we have shown above that none of the various "ways of the injunction of accessory is possible in the sentence in "question."

Reply: True; all the rest have been rejected as impossible; but you have not refuted the theory that the accessory laid down is the Subsidiary Procedure ending with the *Paryagnikaraṇa*.

Though the word '*Paryagnikṛtam*' itself does not, like the word "*iḍānta*', directly express *that which ends in that* (*Paryagnikaraṇa*), yet it is quite capable of implying it; especially as one cannot be spoken of as *having finished the Paryagnikaraṇa*, until all that precedes it has also been done. Consequently the mention of the '*Paryagnikaraṇa*' alone also implies all that precedes it.

And then, the sentence laying down the performance of the *Tvāsṭra* is found to stand in need of the mention of the method of procedure to be employed in regard to it; and inasmuch as it would have no reason for going beyond the group of subsidiaries ending with the *Paryagnikaraṇa* (the capability of whose usefulness has been perceived),—it would not stand in need of *all subsidiaries* of the original *Agnīshomīya*. And thus, it having been duly ascertained that, the subsidiaries connected with the *Tvāshṭra* sacrifice ending with the *Paryagnikaraṇa*,—and the mere form of this sacrifice having been mentioned in the previous sentence,—what the sentence does is simply to preclude (or separate) the presence of the subsidiaries subsequent to the *Paryagnikaraṇa*, from the *Tvāshṭra* sacrifice. And hence it is this *separation* (or *preclusion*) that is spoken of in the *Sūtra* as the effect of the sentence; hence the *Sūtra*—'*pūrvatvādavacchēdaḥ*'.

In this way we would be saved from all the trouble of inferring a distinct sacrifice, a distinct *Apūrva*, etc., etc.

Nor is it that the '*giving away*' has been made connected with the word '*Paryagni*,' which removes it from its natural precincts. Because the object of Injunction being the '*giving away*' as qualified by the subsidiaries ending with *Paryagnikaraṇa*,—though the form of the 'giving away' has been already mentioned, yet what the sentence does is to lay down the subsidiaries ending with *Paryagnikaraṇa*, with reference to that 'giving away' which has been previously mentioned; and as such there is no removal of any factor from its natural precincts; and hence in one way it is the 'giving away' itself that has been spoken of as the object of Injunction.

In accordance with your theory, on the other hand, the Root (in *utsṛjati*') would come to denote something wholly distinct from itself, just as in the case of the sentence '*dadhnēndriyakāmasya juhuyāt*' (as you would have to take '*utsṛjati*' as laying down something different from 'giving away', its rightful denotation). And for this reason also, we should accept the action mentioned in the sentence in question to be the same as that mentioned in the previous sentence.

Then again, inasmuch as the Context also favours the view taken of the subsidiaries ending with *Paryagnikaraṇa*, no significance can be attached to the mention of the '*Pātnīvata*'; as this last word serves as a mere reference to (description of) what already exists; and this explanation meets the objection urged above, as to our theory necessitating the acceptance of the mention of only a portion of the reference to a qualified object.

For these reasons, we conclude that the sentence in question serves to lay down an Accessory with reference to an Action previously mentioned.

ADHIKARAṆA (9).

[*Adābhya*, etc., are the names of *Grahas.*]

***Sūtra* 20: When the name appears by itself without any mention of the sacrificial material, it would be subservient to the Action.**

[In no particular connection we find the sentences, '*ēsha vai havishā haviryajatē yo'dābhyam gṛhītvā somāya yajatē,*' and '*parā vā ētasyāyuḥ prana ēti yonçum gṛhṇāti*'.]

And with regard to the holding of the *Adābhya* and the *Ançu*, there is a threefold doubt, just as in the case of the *ālambha* (Touching). And just as in that case, so here also, after having set aside the two other alternative theories, we have the following

PŪRVAPAKSHA.

"The sentences in question enjoin *two sacrifices.* The arguments in "support of this view are as follows: It has been shown above (under "'*Nāmadhēya*') that the name of a sacrifice serves to distinguish it even "from that sacrifice which may have been originally mentioned in the "Context; and hence it will distinguish actions all the more easily from "those that are not mentioned in the same Context, with regard to which "there can be no idea of identity.

"In the case in question we find that the names '*adābhya*' and "'*Ançu*' are not known to belong to any sacrifice mentioned in the "Context; and hence the sentence cannot be taken as laying down a mere "repetition of the same. Consequently we conclude that the sentence "lays down the *Ēkāha* sacrifice which forms part of the *Jyotishṭoma*— "this conclusion being pointed out by the similarity of the injunction of "'*holding*.' Nor is the case in question similar to that of the 'touching "of the calf'; (1) because in the first of the two sentences in question, "we find the direct mention of the 'sacrifice,' and in the second, we have "a specific name, which serves to distinguish the Action so named from "all other Actions; and (2) because the presence of the injunction of "'holding' in the sentences transfers, to the actions herein mentioned, "all the details of the *Jyotishṭoma*; and as such these actions become "fully equipped with all the necessary factors of the Material and the

"Deity, etc. (which is not found in the case of the sentence '*vatsama*-"*labhēta*').

"And for these reasons, we conclude that the sentences lay down "distinct sacrifices."

SIDDHĀNTA.

To the above we make the following reply :—

In the case of sentences where we have only the *Name* and the *holding* mentioned (as in the case in question), the chances of the mention of a *sacrifice* are very much less than in the case of the sentence '*vatsamālabhēta*'; because the former is devoid even of the mention of a Material.

That is to say, we find that, in the sentences in question, the mention of the Deity is a long way off; and even the object that would form the objective of the mentioned 'holding' is not mentioned. Because the substance cannot be pointed out except by a *class* or by a *property*. And so long as it has not been ascertained that the actions mentioned in the sentences are sacrifices, there can be no idea as to the sacrifices being similar to the *Jyotishṭoma;* and as such '*Soma*' (the material offered at the *Jyotishṭoma*) could not be recognized as the material to be *held*. And as for the verb '*gṛhṇāti*,' also, there is no reason to believe that it is always concomitant with the *Jyotishṭoma*; because all that it expresses is mere *holding* (and this action is present in all sacrifices).

Nor are the names in question—'*Adābhya*' and '*Ançu*'—the names of any sacrifices, whereby they could serve to distinguish these sacrifices. Because these words have been accepted as names, simply on the ground of their co-extensiveness with 'holding'; and as for the difference of 'holding' from the previous sacrifices, we also admit it; but it does not follow from this that the sentence lays down a distinct *Sacrifice*.

As a matter of fact, we have proved, under *Sūtra* II—ii—18, that even when such sentences are accompanied by the mention of Deities and Materials, they cannot be taken as laying down *sacrifices*. While in the case in question, we do not find even this (mention of the Deity and the Material). As for the *sacrifice* that is mentioned by the word '*yajēta*' in the sentence speaking of the *Adābhya*, it cannot, in the present instance, be taken as enjoined by the Injunctive affix (in '*yajēta*'), which has its injunctive potency transferred elsewhere (to the Accessory),—as shown under the *Pūrvapaksha* of the *Sūtra* II—ii—27. Therefore the sentence (speaking of Adābhya) must be taken as laying down the 'holding' with reference to a certain sacrifice (laid down before).

Question : "But how do you connect the Ançu with a sacrifice (as "the sentence speaking of it does not contain the word '*yajati*')?"

In reply to this some people assert that its connection with a sacrifice is established by means of the *Jyotishṭoma*, with which it has the similarity of the presence of 'holding.' As a matter of fact, however, we find that both the sentences in question occur again in connection with *Jyotishṭoma*, in the *Taittiriya* Rescension of the Text. And this repetition of the sentences having no other use, would serve the purpose of pointing out the fact of the *Ançu* and the *Adābhya* being employed in certain Actions. And just as in the case of the sentence '*saptadaça sāmīdhēnīḥ*, etc.,' the mention of the 'seventeen' not occurring in any particular context, it is utilized by being taken along with the *Sāmidhēnī*, and its use is pointed out by the sentences in the same Context;—so also would it be in the case in question.

Hence we conclude that the only reasonable position to take up, in regard to the sentences in question, is that which is expressed in the *Sūtra* II—iii—12,—*viz.*, that they lay down secondary preparatory rites.

is established by means of the Apūrva, with which it has the similarity of the purpose of 'holding.' As a matter of fact however, we find that the sentence in question occur again in connection with [illegible], in the [illegible] of the [illegible]. And this repetition of the sentence, having no other use, would serve the purpose of pointing out the fact of the Āpya and the [illegible] being employed in certain [illegible]. And just as in the case of the sentence '[illegible]', etc., the mention of the '[illegible]' not occurring in any particular context, is utilised by being taken along with the [illegible], and its use is pointed out by the sentences in the same context,—so also would it be in the case in question.

Hence we conclude that the only reasonable position to take up, in regard to the sentence in question, is that which is expressed in the Sūtra II—iii—12,—viz., that they lay down secondary preparatory rites.